BUSINE$S &
PLEAS▽RE™

BY PETER FINKBEINER | ZELLMANN

W0007510

BUSINESS & PLEASURE PUBLISHING
MUNICH · PARIS · NEW YORK

Publisher

Jürgen C. Mahnert-Lueg

CIP-Kurztitelaufnahme der Deutschen Bibliothek

Finkbeiner-Zellmann, Peter:
Business & [and] pleasure: the internat. businessman's guide; making the most of one night in 100 important market places, Europe / by Peter Finkbeiner-Zellmann. – München; Paris; New York: Business-and-Pleasure-Verlags-GmbH, 1986
ISBN 3–925 414–01–0
NE: HST

ISBN 3–925 414–01–0

Art Direction: Oanh Pham Phu, Munich
Production: Reinhard Fischer, Munich
Colour reproduction: La Cromolito, Milan, Italy
Printed in West Germany by Mohndruck Graphische Betriebe GmbH, Gütersloh

The champagne glass trademark

and the pending trademark application

**BUSINE$S &
PLEAS� RE**

are trademarks of
BUSINESS & PLEASURE Verlags GmbH, Munich

Business travel may not necessarily mean a luxurious ride to a beautiful place where lovable gentlemen receive you in style and bow to your wishes, before they take you to civilized establishments for sophisticated fun.

The majority of agreements, bargains and compromises are not reached over Châteaubriand and Château Lafite at the Ritz (be it in London, Paris or Madrid), and every visit to an industrial fair is not quite the same as an outing to Las Vegas, alas. Sober calculations, time and weather, reservation struggles for cruise, cot and conference room, loneliness of the long-distance dealer – let alone problems with language, habits and taboos – determine business travel more frequently than one likes.

We have tried to encompass the Continent with ration and style in mind, limiting the information on each city to the bare necessities and the best stops. If you want to know *everything* about Bologna, Berne or Birmingham – move there. (But who would want to indulge in all the pleasures of Mannheim when he comes from Athens or Amsterdam for ONE NIGHT?)

Wherever you go, on whatever business – there's no business like BUSINESS & PLEASURE.

The Author

Contents

Germany (West)

Greece

Hungary

Iceland

Ireland

Italy

Contents

Contents

Assistant Author
Jane Michael-Rushmer

Acknowledgements
Prinzessin Ehrengard von Preußen
Ulrike von Sobbe

Editiorial Office
BUSINESS & PLEASURE VERLAG
Reitmorstrasse 51
8000 München 22
West Germany
Telephone: (89) 29 21 59 / 29 98 87
Telex: 521 20 17 bupl d

Office Manager
Gisela Albus

All information without liability

The individually selected establishments have been chosen for their quality and standing within the city and have been allocated to the categories of BUSINESS or PLEASURE because of an emphasis towards one or the other. (Needless to say, this is a personal recommendation rather than a categorical restriction).
To facilitate quick–reference choice, the categories are distinguished by the following colours:

Business-character
Lunch, Dinner

Pleasure-character
Lunch, Dinner

Meeting Points, Cafés, Bars,
Nightclubs, Shopping,
Art & Antiques

The City

›Vienna, Vienna, only you . . .‹ is not exclusively the national anthem of the ›dream-city's‹ chauvinistic natives, but more than represents the yearning, the opinion and the goal-line of most globetrotters. Of course, there is Salzburg for festivals and maybe Innsbruck as a ski-lift terminus in winter, but Graz is remembered rather as the half-way house between Vienna and Venice. How shortsighted the far-travelling can be. If you want to experience the best of Austria, the splendid Alpine landscape descending to the mild climate waking the presentiment of the Mediterranean Sea, the nostalgic grandeur of the imperial past mixed with the energetic reality of Styria's capital and Austria's second-largest city, the quaint alleys winding through the motley collection of historic houses and spa gardens and the optimistically good-humoured people with their irresistible self-deprecating charm – then you have to come to Graz. The city, like Budapest, was a former weekend refuge for Vienna's imperial society, and a visit here is like a journey in time back to the sleepy illusions of Hapsburg grandeur. The colours of its highly styled architectural landscape are almost shy, and the variety of forms here in the Old City – the largest and best preserved in any German speaking country – is something one must gradually discover for oneself. And yet, despite its romanticism, Graz still manages to maintain itself as one of Austria's most productive industrial centres. The vagaries of international politics have denied the city its former access to the Adriatic and provided it with ›dead‹ borders to Hungary and Yugoslavia, virtually putting an end to its rôle as a trading centre. Important here are middle-sized companies – some 10,000 of them – which provide the country with everything from machines, steel and heating systems to paper, cardboard, textiles and beer, and provide the world with important research results in medicine and the production of combustion engines. A relaxing change from the heavy baroque atmosphere of Vienna and the tourism of Salzburg and Innsbruck, Graz is Austria in its purest form where natural beauty, human warm-heartedness and understated sincerity find a worthy stage.

Founded: first mentioned in 1128.

Far-reaching events: 12th century – fortress built near original fishing village; 1379–1619 – Graz the residence of a branch of the Hapsburg family; 16th century – fortification of the town to withstand threats from Turks; 1564 – Graz the capital of Austria under emperor Frederick III; 1586 – foundation of university; 1797–1809 – Napoleon occupies the town on three occasions; 19th century – the Industrial Revolution; 1944 – Graz heavily bombed, but reconstructed after the Second World War.

Population: 300,000; 2nd largest city in Austria.

Postal code: A-8000 **Telephone code:** 361

Climate: continental with strong Mediterranean influences; warm, pleasant summers; relatively mild winters; much fog in the autumn; precipitation evenly divided throughout the year.

Best time to visit: May to October.

Calendar of events: *Styriarte Graz* (Jul) – music festival in the Old City; *World Championships in Bodybuilding* (27–28 Sep, 1986); *TRIGON* (Oct) – tristate biennial festival; ›*Steyrishe Herbst*‹ (Oct) – autumn cultural festival, widely acclaimed in Europe; *Christmas Market* (Nov/Dec).

Fairs and exhibitions: *MARKETING IMPULSE CONGRESS* (Mar); *AUSTRIAN IRON FAIR FOR HEAVY INDUSTRY* (Apr); *GRAZ SOUTH-EAST FAIR* (1st weekend in May & Oct); *HOLIDAY AND RECREATION FAIR* (May); *TECHNOVA* (May) – international technical trade fair; *EUROPEAN DATA PROCESSING CONGRESS* (May); *COMPUTER SOFTWARE CONFERENCE* (May); *UN CONFERENCE ON NATURAL RESOURCES* (May); *INTERNATIONAL ASTRONAUTICAL FEDERATION MEETING* (Oct); *BÜRODATA* (Nov) – office information; *MEDICAL TRADE FAIR* and *CONGRESS FOR GENERAL MEDICINE* (Nov).

Best views of the city: from the terrace of the *Schlossberg*.

Historical and modern sights: *Hauptplatz* – main square with fine buildings and a lively market; *Schlossberg* – the city's main landmark, a citadel with gardens and the original bell clock-tower; *Arsenal* – weapons and suits of armour for distribution to volunteers, recalling Graz' earlier strategic importance; *Cathedral* (1432–68) – Baroque high altar; *Johanneum* – the earliest provincial museum in Austria (stained glass, altarpieces); *Maria-Hilf Kirche* – 17th-century pilgrimage church dedicated to the patron saint of Graz; *Mausoleum* – Emperor Ferdinand II's Baroque resting-place.

Special attractions: *Eggersberg Castle* – 17th century (8 km/5 miles); *Katerloch* caves – stalactites and an underground lake (80 km/50 miles); *Theatercafé* – piano bar meeting place of the international jet-set when in Graz.

Important companies with headquarters in the city: *Steweag; Steyrische Ferngas* (fuel); *Humanic-Schuh; Steyrische Brauindustrie* (beer); *Daimler-Puch; Graz-Köflacher Eisenbahn und Bergbaugesellschaft* (mining); *Simmerling-Graz-Pauker; Dynafil; Andritz AG; Arland Papier* (paper); *Ed. Ast & Co Bau* (construction); *Vianora Kunstharz* (synthetic resin).

Airport: Graz-Thalerhof, GRZ; Tel.: 29 55 08; 12 km/7 miles.

The Headquarters

STEIRERHOF

12 Jakominiplatz
A–8010 Graz
Telephone: 76 3 50
Telex: 311 282 steiho
General Manager: Dr. I. Eger
Affiliation/Reservation System: Dial Austria
Number of rooms: 90 (14 suites)
Price range: ÖS 1,200–2,500
Credit cards: AE, DC
Location: city centre
Built: 1780 (recently renovated)
Style: historic townhouse
Hotel amenities: car park, terrace, sauna, solarium
Main hall porter: Harald Mitterhammer
Room amenities: colour tv, minibar/refrigerator (pets allowed)
Bathroom amenities: bidet, bathrobe, hairdrier
Room service: 6.00/a.m.–24.00/12 p.m.
Laundry/dry cleaning: same day, weekend service
Conference rooms: secretarial services, ballroom

Bar: ›Steirerhof‹: (19.00/7.00 p.m. – 2.00/a.m.) Helene Lammer and Uschi (barkeepers), pianist, modern style décor
Restaurants: ›Steirerhof‹: (11.30/a.m.–15.00/3 p.m. and 19.00/7 p.m.–24.00/12 p.m.) H. Hofmann (maître), Peter Zach (chef de cuisine), international and Austrian cuisine, open-air dining; ›Steirerhof-Stuben‹: (11.30/a.m.–15.00/3 p.m. and 18.00/6 p.m.–24.00/12 p.m.) H. Hofer (maître), Peter Zach (chef de cuisine), international and Austrian cuisine, rustic-elegant style, open-air dining; ›Bierstüberl‹: (9.00/a.m.–24.00/12 p.m.), H. Wimmer (maître), Peter Zach (chef de cuisine), Austrian and local cuisine, open-air dining;
Private dining rooms: three

By comparison with the ornate Baroque palaces or picturesque converted castles which house some of the other leading auberges in the land, the unadorned exterior of the Steirerhof is almost self-effacing in its modesty. First impressions can be misleading, however; the foremost hotel in Graz can compete with the best in terms of standard, efficiency and Austrian charm. The dignified eighteenth-century building provides bed and board comfortable enough for the crowned heads, elected statesmen and fêted celebrities from the Old World and the New who visit the town for the architecture, the nostalgia, and the music festival – even Queen Elizabeth II and Giscard d'Estaing. That the public and private rooms are furnished in varying but harmonious styles, from the Louis-something fauteuils in the bedrooms to the rustic chairs in the dining room, only confirms its understated but highly personal note. The staff are friendly and the warmth of the Styrian welcome ensures a happy atmosphere for even a serious conference.

The Hideaway

SCHLOSS PICHLARN

28 Gatschen
A–8952 Irdning (180 km/110 miles)
Telephone: (36 82) 28 41
Telex: 38 190 hopich
Owning Company: Haack & Partner KG
General Manager: Wolfgang Fischl
Closed: 1st Nov–18th Dec
Number of rooms: 72 (5 suites)
Price range: ÖS 1250–1600 (single)
          ÖS 1100–2500 (double)
          ÖS 1700–2200 (suite)
Credit cards: AE, DC, Visa
Location: 180 km/110 miles from Graz
Built: 1547 (renovated: 1969–1972)
Style: castle; antique-style décor
Hotel amenities: garage, house limousine service, library/gaming room, grand piano, beauty salon, sauna bath, solarium, massage, hairstylist, newsstand, boutique, tobacconist, florist, house doctor
Room amenities: air conditioning, colour tv (remote control)
Bathroom amenities: bidet, bathrobe, hairdrier
Room service: 24 hours
Laundry/dry cleaning: same day (weekend service)
Conference rooms: 2 (up to 200 persons), overhead projector, flip chart, secretarial services, ballroom
Sports: golf, table-tennis, riding, indoor tennis court
Sports (nearby): hunting, fishing, shooting, riding, 18-hole golf course
Tagesbar: (10.00 a.m.–14.00/2.00 p.m.); pianist, antique style décor
Restaurant ›Golfstüberl‹: (7.00/a.m.–10.00/a.m.; 12.00/a.m.–14.00/2.00 p.m. and 19.00/7.00 p.m.–21.00/9.00 p.m.); Bertram Zisser, Karl Wallner (maîtres), Heinz Kahnhäuser (chef de cuisine), pianist, orchestra, open-air dining

Lying in the picturesque Enns valley amidst the awe-inspiring mountains and pine forests of Styria, an unhurried half-day's drive from Graz, stands the fairytale fortress of Schloss Pichlarn, one of the few castle hotels which has successfully assimilated the requisite accessoires of twentieth-century leisure and luxury without losing its patina of antiquity. The whitewashed and turreted building is the favoured retreat of skiing, hunting, shooting, fishing and golfing industrialists who arrive by Mercedes or private plane to step back into a more gracious world where the peaceful majesty of the surroundings provides a fitting background for sporting activities or undisturbed rêveries. To the elegant antique furnishings have been added a thermal swimming pool, an indoor tennis court and a sauna which, with the excellent cuisine and exemplary service, guarantee that you will live like a latter-day prince during your stay at Schloss Pichlarn.

13

Lunch

STEIRERHOF
12 Jakominiplatz
Telephone: 7 63 50
Affiliations: Chaîne des Rôtisseurs
Owner/Manager: Hotel Steirerhof Graz
G.m.b.H.
Closed: never
Open: 11.30/a.m.–15.30/3.30 p.m. and
19.00/7 p.m.–24.00/12 p.m.
Cuisine: international, local and modern
Austrian
Chef de cuisine: Peter Zach
Specialities: Styrian menu; game pâté
with Cumberland sauce; lamb chop with
courgettes, olive rice and tomato; hot
puddings and cakes
Location: in the Hotel Steirerhof
Setting: three dining rooms furnished in
contrasting styles, from international
modern elegance to rustic comfort
Amenities: hotel; banqueting hall
(240–400 persons); bar; pianist; open-air
dining in garden; partial air condition-
ing; car park
Atmosphere: cosmopolitan, civilized and
stylish
Clientèle: when in Graz ... local aristocracy and Haute Bourgeoisie mix with visiting luminaries, politicians and artists
Dress: nothing too outlandish or outrageous
Service: friendly and welcoming
Reservations: advisable
Price range: moderate to rather expensive
Credit cards: AE, DC

Lunch

MILCHMARIANDL
31 Richard-Wagner-Strasse
Telephone: 3 44 00
Owner/Manager: Fritz Just
Closed: Sunday
Open: 11.30/a.m.–15.00/3 p.m. and
18.00/6 p.m.–23.00/11 p.m.
Cuisine: international and local
Chef de cuisine: Peter Lendl
Specialities: escalope with leaf spinach
and prunes; cream of asparagus soup;
médaillons of veal with mushroom sauce
and croquette potatoes; potato noodles
with poppy seeds and sugar; a glass of
sparkling wine on your patron saint's day
(Namenstag)
Location: near the university
Setting: elegantized rustic dining room
Amenities: open-air dining in delightful
garden
Atmosphere: steeped in local colour
Clientèle: heterogeneous mixture of local
officials, academics, students and businessmen
Dress: as you like it, as long as they like
you

Service: efficiently charming
Reservations: necessary
Price range: good value for money
Credit cards: AE, DC, Euro, Visa

Dinner

STERNWIRT (›Pichlmaier‹)
9 Petersbergenerstrasse
Telephone: 4 15 97
Owner/Manager/Chef de cuisine: Karl
Pichlmaier
Closed: Sunday; public holidays
Open: 11.00/a.m.–22.00/10 p.m.
Cuisine: Austrian and international
Specialities: breast of Barbary duckling
in Pinot noir cream; salmon and sole with
asparagus tips in white wine sauce; breast
of guinea-fowl in Veltliner sauce; Bavarian cream with strawberry sauce and
fruits; walnut ice cream with chocolate
sauce
Location: in the suburb of St. Peter; 10
minutes' drive from the centre of Graz
Setting: small dining room in neo-rustic
style with appropriate paraphernalia;
open fireplace; porcelain stove
Amenities: private dining rooms (10–50
persons); open-air dining in garden; air
conditioning; car park
Atmosphere: understated, yet cordial
Clientèle: conservative; predominantly
middle-aged
Dress: informal
Service: fast and professional
Reservations: necessary
Price range: moderately expensive
Credit cards: AE, DC

Lunch

HOFKELLER
8 Hofgasse
Telephone: 70 24 39
Owner/Manager: the Schögler family
Closed: Sunday
Open: 11.00/a.m.–14.00/2.00 p.m. and
18.00/6.00 p.m.–24.00/12.00 p.m.
Cuisine: nouvelle (highly individual)
Chef de cuisine: Josef Schögler
Specialities: duck's liver on artichokes;
fillet of rabbit with thyme sauce; salmon
steak with vermouth sauce; mousse au
chocolat; orange and dates on grenadine
Location: by the castle (Burg) and the
park (Stadtpark)
Setting: attractively renovated old build-
ing; small gourmet restaurant with pret-
tily laid tables; fine china and glass
Amenities: small bar for apéritifs; car
park in the vicinity
Atmosphere: festive but not forbidding
Clientèle: connoisseurs from Bad Aussee
to Zell am Ziller

Dress: elegant
Service: unobtrusively knowledgeable; directed by Andrea Schögler
Reservations: essential (pets permitted)
Price range: philanthropic
Credit cards: AE, DC, Euro, Visa

Dinner

HIRSCHENWIRT
115 Rupertistrasse, Hohenrain
Telephone: 4 46 00
Owner/Manager: Ingrid and Siegfried Hasenhütl
Closed: Sunday; Monday
Open: 11.00/a.m.–22.00/10.00 p.m.
Cuisine: traditional Austrian
Chef de cuisine: Ingrid Hasenhütl
Specialities: roast chicken (Backhendl); escalope of veal (Wiener Schnitzel); cream of cucumber soup; roast kidneys; ›oyster‹ mushrooms in cream sauce; doughnuts ›Hirschenwirt‹; apricot strudel (Marillenstrudel)
Location: on the outskirts of town (Lustbühel)
Setting: typical Styrian auberge with unpretentious décor and a beautiful garden for outdoor dining in summer
Amenities: car park
Atmosphere: cheerfully uncomplicated
Clientèle: a large contingent of resident habitués plus discriminating visitors anxious to sample the delights of traditional local food in attractively unpretentious surroundings
Dress: mostly rather casual but not careless
Service: fast and friendly
Reservations: essential
Price range: medium

Café

GLOCKENSPIEL
4 Glockenspielplatz
Telephone: 8 02 91
Owner/Manager: Hans-Jörg Slavnitsch
Closed: Sunday
Open: 8.00/a.m.–20.00/8 p.m.
Location: in the city centre
Setting: designed by a well-known Graz architect; chic but comfortable modern décor with dark wood, mirrors and glass
Amenities: excellent coffee, sandwiches and Austrian traditional hot puddings (Mehlspeisen)
Atmosphere: an attractive mixture of twentieth-century flair and nineteenth-century coffee-house charm
Clientèle: Graz' In-Crowd; friends of former discothèque owner Hans-Jörg Slavnitsch hoping to catch up on the latest society gossip
Service: smiling and helpful

Bar

MAHE
3 Trauttmansdorffgasse
Telephone: 70 07 22
Owner/Manager: Carlo and Manzi
Closed: Mondays
Open: 21.00/9 p.m.–3.00/a.m., weekend till 4.00/a.m.
Location: in the old part of the town, the so-called ›Bermuda Triangle‹
Setting: light blue walls and upholstery, modern style
Amenities: air conditioning; parking nearby
Atmosphere: cheerfully extrovert
Clientèle: heterogeneous; youthful habitués; businessmen; the after-dinner crowd
Service: very good
Reservations: not necessary
Credit cards: AE, DC, EC, Visa

Bar

MR. BOJANGLES
15 Gleisdorfergasse
Telephone: 7 88 61
Owner/Manager: Helmut Schilling
Closed: Monday
Open: café: 12.00/a.m.–4.00/a.m.; disco: 18.00/6 p.m.–4.00/a.m.
Location: central
Setting: combination of café and discothèque; café all in red, with mirrored walls; discothèque with two glass dance floors lit from underneath by means of a light synthesizer
Amenities: what more can you want
Atmosphere: exclusive, stylish and elegant – but inevitably rather loud at times
Clientèle: rather young (or young at heart) businessmen and students mingle with eccentric disco-freaks
Dress: individualistic but not too extreme
Service: amazingly efficient
Reservations: not necessary
Credit cards: AE, DC, Euro, Visa

Shopping

EVERYTHING UNDER ONE ROOF
Kastner & Oehler   6 Sackstrasse

FOR HIM
Knilli   9–11 Joanneumring

FOR HER
Schwarz   3 Herrengasse

BEAUTY & HAIR
Friseur Dietmer   3 Enge Gasse

JEWELLERY
Schullin   3 Herrengasse

LOCAL SPECIALITIES
Prokopp (women's fashion)
2 Herrengasse
Mothwurf (costumes)
6 Herrengasse
Jim & Jenny (children's fashion)
23 Schmiedgasse
Pelzhaus Mangold (furs)
4 Stubenberggasse
Jos. A. Kienreich (books)
6 Sackstrasse
Glasgravur Haiden (gifts, glass)
1 Enge Gasse
Breineder-Gibiser (baggage & travel accessories) 3 Am Eisernen Tor
Geigenbauer Hiebler (violin maker)
8 Bindergasse
Laufke (food and beverages)
Elisabethstrasse
Ferdinand Haller (confiserie)
23 Herrengasse

THE BEST OF ART
Bleich-Rossi   (contemporary art)
2 Wegenergasse, Tel. 37 77 44
Droschl, Maximilian   (modern art)
1 Bischofsplatz, Tel. 8 18 57
Steeb, Wolfgang (antiques 18th/19th century) 3 Leonhardstrasse, Tel. 3 45 93

The City

The 800-year-old Tyrolean capital on the north-south axis of Central Europe's seasonal migration has retained much of its Gothic-Baroque fairytale image, and despite the Brenner Pass Motorway and the Europa Bridge allowing for speedy transit, it remains a popular stop-over camp for Italy-bound travellers from the north. The historical town centre has become an open-air museum without succumbing to the vices of commercial tourism, and while offering all the amenities of an Alpine resort, Innsbruck maintains its rustic charm and down-to-earth Tyrolean spirit as well as providing for more than just hospitality-and-souvenirs-related business. The second-largest city in the entire European Alpine chain (after Grenoble) is still one of the more important trading posts in this part of the world, being active also in the manufacturing industries, such as construction materials and textiles. Having hosted the Winter Olympics twice (1964 and 1976 – once more than Grenoble), Innsbruck has received international attention leading to more interest in business as well. First and foremost, however, is the concentration on visitors to the city, for the unspoilt landscape and for winter sports on the surrounding ski-slopes between the super-runs of Hafelekar and Patscherkofel up to fashionable Seefeld. Hiking, mountain climbing and golf are magnetizing more guests in summer than the city can accommodate, but the ones who have ever spent some time here will admit that the hospitality is overwhelming. Affection for foreigners is less professional than in Switzerland, and the Tyrolean joviality less pungent than in neighbouring Bavaria, but with their quiet natural dignity and a humour-tinged belief in God, the recovery of South Tyrol and the inevitability of an adequate seasonal fall of snow, business in Innsbruck is likely to be pleasurable and no-one will feel encouraged to take flight with a sad rendition of Emperor Maximilian's favourite nostalgic folk song: ›Innsbruck, I must thee leave.‹

Founded: in the 1st century, as a Roman settlement; Innsbruck – ›the bridge over the Inn‹.

Far-reaching events: 1180 – the Counts of Andechs build a new settlement and call it ›Insprukke‹; 1239 – incorporation; 1240 – Innsbruck capital of Tyrol and imperial residence under Emperor Maximilian I (1490–1519); centre of arts and music in the 16th century under Ferdinand II; Maria Theresia takes up residence in the Hofburg in the 18th century; railways give the city new importance in the 19th century, the Olympics in the 20th.

Population: 120,000; capital of the state of Tyrol.

Postal code: A–6020   **Telephone code:** 5222

Climate: the winters are cold, the summers warm; the ›Föhn‹ – the Alpine wind which brings blue skies and headaches – often occurs unexpectedly.

Best time to visit: June–October for warmth, September and October for mountain climbing, January–March for skiing.

Calendar of events: *Music and Dance of the Nations* (Jul) – music festival incorporating one week of Japanese music and dance; *Ambras Castle Concerts* (Jul/Aug) – changing international chamber orchestras perform classical works in the castle; *Festival of Early Music* (Aug/Sep); *Christkindlmarkt* (Dec) – Christmas Fair, magical booths in an alpine setting.

Fairs and exhibitions: *SPRING FAIR* (Apr) – house and garden exhibition; *INNSBRUCK AUTUMN FAIR* (Sep) – tourism and alpine agriculture; *ANTIQUE FAIR* (Sep); *TKS* (Oct) – Tyrolean handicrafts and souvenirs exhibition; *SENIOR AKTUELL* (Nov) – everything for the older generation; *OFFICE FAIR* (Dec).

Best views of the city: from the *Belfry*, beside the old Town Hall; from the *Hungerburg* or *Sonnenburgerhof* castles on the road to Brenner.

Historical and modern sights: *Maria-Theresienstrasse* – 17th-century houses and an Alpine panorama; *Hofkirche* (16th century) – Franciscan church erected to house the tomb of Emperor Maximilian I – his remains are elsewhere, but his mausoleum is most impressive; *Hofburg* – Maria Theresia turned this former residential palace into a Baroque monument; *Goldenes Dachl* – (15th century), Innsbruck's main landmark; *Helblinghaus* – once Gothic, magnificent building given a rococo face-lift in the 18th century; the *Silver Chapel* (16th century); *Hungerburg* – former fortress overlooking the city; the 15th century *City Tower* (Belfry) – once a prison, next to the *Town Hall*; the *Olympic Village* – where the games were held; the *Congress Hall* – the transparent centre for international conventions.

Special attractions: the *Tyrol Museum of Popular Arts* – Tyrolean dress, customs and pleasures; the *Ferdinandeum Tyrol Museum* – dedicated to the fine arts in Tyrol; the *Bergisch Museum* – devoted to the heroic feats of Tyrolean freedom fighter Andreas Hofer; the *Alpine Zoo* – a unique collection of all the animals that live in the Alps.

Important companies with headquarters in the city: *Adambräu* (brewery); *Bank für Tirol und Vorarlberg* (banking); *Landes-Hypothekenbank Tirol* (banking); *Kurt Schwarzkopf – Kematen* (cosmetics); *Seidensticker Wäschefabrik* (clothing); *Wagner'sche Buchdruckerei* (printing); *Bauunternehmung Innerebner & Mayer* (construction); *Verlagsanstalt Tyrolia* (books); *Tyrolean Airways* (air taxis); *Tiroler Loden* (loden fashions); *Swarovski* – Wattens (crystal).

Airport: Innsbruck-Kranebitten, INN; Tel.: 2333; 4 km/2 miles.

The Headquarters

EUROPA TYROL

2 Südtiroler Platz
A–6020 Innsbruck
Telephone: 3 55 71
Telex: 53 424 europ (from 1 Jan 87 on: 533 424)
Owning Company: Imperial Hotels Austria AG
General Manager: Wolfgang Bracke
Affiliation/Reservation Systems: Steigenberger Reservation Service; Distinguished Hotels, New York; Business consultants Japan, Tokyo
Number of rooms: 128 (3 suites)
Price range: ÖS 890–4,800
Credit cards: AE, DC, EC, Visa, MC, Access, JCB
Location: city centre
Built: 1951 (renovated 1984–1985)
Style: Tyrolean and Biedermeier style
Hotel amenities: garage, hairdresser, newsstand, tobacconist, house doctor
Main hall porter: Herbert Mair
Room amenities: radio, colour tv, minibar/refrigerator (pets allowed)
Bathroom amenities: bidet, bathrobe, hairdrier

Room service: 24 hours
Conference rooms: 5 (up to 230 persons)
Florianibar: (11.00/a.m.–1.00/a.m.) Karl Greissing (barman)
Restaurant: ›Philippine Welser‹ (11.30/a.m.–14.30/2.30 p.m. and 18.30/6.30 p.m.–23.30/11.30 p.m.), Franz Rieder (chef de cuisine), traditional and creative cuisine
Private dining rooms: two

In many cities around the globe you are spoilt for choice when looking for the best, most beautiful and convenient hotel in town – in Innsbruck you have none: the Europa Tyrol incorporates all three characteristics and stands out among the innumerable Alpine inns like a Ritz amongst youth hostels. Across from the station – an advantage here, with no disturbance of peace thanks to all the sound-proofing – and around the corner from every other place of interest in this capital of Tyrol and skiing, the Imperial Hotels Austria (Imperial and Bristol in Vienna, Goldener Hirsch in Salzburg) has firmly established an outpost of the highest renommé, intelligently blending the local traits of warmth and hospitality with the international standard of professionalism and service. The charm prevails in the interior of the halls and bedchambers – partly modern, partly with the eiderdowned-chalet allurement – and a touch of grandeur exudes from the Baroque banquet room. All the important meetings, conferences, conventions and galas are held here, all the important people coming on an official mission reside here, and everybody of importance and standing – for industry, trade or the slopes around – tries to stay here. A reason in itself is the Philippine Welser restaurant, where restrained nouvelle cuisine meets Austrian gluttony à la hauteur.

The Hideaway

SCHLOSSHOTEL IGLS

2 Viller Steig
A–6080 Igls (5 km/3 miles)
Telephone: (5222) 77217
Telex: 53314 spohot
(from 1 Jan 87 on: 533314)
Owner: Fred and Annedore Beck
Affiliation/Reservation System: Relais et
Châteaux
Closed: April and November
Number of rooms: 19 (4 suites)
Price range: ÖS 1,500–1,600
Location: 5 km/3 miles from city centre, 8
km/5 miles from airport
Built: 1900
Style: castle mansion; elegant antique décor

Hotel amenities: garage, valet parking,
house limousine service, sauna, massage,
newsstand, florist, tobacconist, indoor
swimming pool
Main hall porter: Traudl Gellner
Room amenities: air conditioning, colour
tv (remote control) (pets allowed)
Bathroom amenities: bidet, bathrobe,
hairdrier, telephone
Room service: 24 hours
Laundry/dry cleaning: same day (weekend service)
Conference rooms: 1 (up to 12 persons)
Sports (nearby): Alpine and cross-coun-
try skiing, curling, golf, tennis
Bar: ›Am Kamin‹ (11.00/a.m.–
24.00/12.00 p.m.), elegant style décor
Restaurants: ›Schlosshotel‹ and ›Blauer
Salon‹ (12.00/a.m.–15.00/3.00 p.m. and
18.00/6.00 p.m.–21.00/9.00 p.m.); H.
Mehrlen (maître), F. Hofer (chef de cui-
sine), international and Austrian cuisine,
open-air dining

*Since the town of Innsbruck, its picture
postcard prettiness heightened by the dramatic backdrop of the Alps, fulfils so perfectly the visitor's expectations of a Tyrolean wonderland, it is singularly appropriate that no long journey is necessary to
reach a hideaway where even the micro-
metropolis' gentle hubbub seems far away.
Schlosshotel Igls, in a stone-walled garden
perched on a plateau high above the Inn
valley, is a whitewashed turn-of-the-century Disneyland castle-cum-manor house
with arched windows, turrets and bays. Its
conversion into a luxury auberge with a private-house atmosphere has been a labour
of love by Fred and Annedore Beck, who
also own the nearby Sporthotel. They have
lavished on it their collection of antiques
and heirlooms, creating a gay-nostalgic
ambience as immortally Austrian as a
Strauss waltz. In winter a cheery open fire
burns in the wood-panelled lounge, and the
bedrooms – individually decorated in
styles ranging from the Biedermeier to the
Viennese – all have porcelain tiled stoves.
But Schlosshotel Igls is perfect for a summer weekend too, when the après-ski Gemütlichkeit gives way to the peaceful contemplation of the splendours of an Alpine
sunset.*

19

Lunch

KAPELLER
96 Philippine-Nelser-Strasse
Telephone: 43106
Owner/Manager: Ferdinand Happ
Closed: Sunday; public holidays;
January
Open: 11.30/a.m.–14.00/2 p.m. and
18.00/6 p.m.–22.00/10 p.m.
Cuisine: modern, with a regional accent
Chef de cuisine: Rudolf Prader
Specialities: chicken livers with lentil sa-
lad; brains with Parmesan cheese; milk
lamb cutlets with spring salad; monkfish
(Seeteufel) with basil cream sauce and
home-made spinach noodles; apple cake
(Apfelküchle) with apple ice-cream and
Riesling sabayon; figs in port wine with
walnut ice-cream and raspberry sauce
Location: 1 km (3/4 mile) from town cen-
tre; on outskirts of town, near motorway
Setting: quiet situation; wood-panelled
dining-rooms with carved figures, pewter
and decorative farm paraphernalia
Amenities: private dining room (20 per-
sons); open-air dining on terrace; car
park
Atmosphere: comfortable and welcom-
ing; authentic local colour
Clientèle: mostly businessmen at lunch-
time; in the evening, Innsbruck In-
Crowd, local habitués and a fair sprin-
kling of tourists
Dress: within reason
Service: expert and friendly
Reservations: advisable (pets allowed)
Price range: medium – high
Credit cards: AE, DC, Euro, Access, Mas-
ter Charge

Dinner

BELLE EPOQUE
7 Zeughausstrasse
Telephone: 28361
Owner/Manager: Friedrich Wolf
Closed: Sunday
Open: 18.30/6.30 p.m.–1.00/a.m.
Cuisine: French and international
Chef de cuisine: Friedrich Wolf
Specialities: spinach flan; garlic soup
with croûtons; raw salmon with salmon
roe and green pepper sauce; angler fish
steak in lobster sauce; escalope of salmon
in sorrel sauce; calves' sweetbreads in
morel mushroom cream sauce; poppy
seed parfait with plums in rum
Location: 10 minutes' walk from the town
centre
Setting: large picture windows with view
of the garden; Belle Epoque décor; neutral colour scheme, mirrors and potted
palms
Amenities: hotel; bar; open-air dining in
romantic paved garden in summer; nightclub

Atmosphere: turn-of-the-century eleg-
ance with a hint of nostalgia
Clientèle: comfortable mixture of local
habitués, artists, politicians and econ-
omists
Dress: casually elegant to elegantly ca-
sual
Service: excellent
Reservations: requested (pets allowed)
Price range: moderate
Credit cards: AE, DC, Euro, Visa

Lunch

SCHWARZER ADLER
2 Kaiserjägerstrasse
Telephone: 27109/32486
Affiliations: Bund Österreichischer Gast-
lichkeit
Owner/Manager: the Ultsch Family
Closed: January 8th–22nd
Open: 12.00/a.m.–14.00/2 p.m. and
18.00/6 p.m.–22.30/10.30 p.m.
Cuisine: local (modern) and international, plus Austrian reform cooking and
traditional Viennese (in the ›KuK‹ restaurant)
Chefs de cuisine: Werner Ultsch and
Bruno Plotecher
Specialities: traditional beef dishes; fillet
of beef ›Romantik‹ in butter pastry; garlic soup; carp dumplings; courgettes with
natural rice; stuffed buckwheat pancakes
(gefüllte Buchweizenpalatschinken); apple strudel
Location: in the Hotel Schwarzer Adler;
near the theatre and the Palace Garden
(Hofgarten)
Setting: historic auberge in a 17th-cen-
tury building; various dining rooms and
cellar furnished in different styles from
the Imperial to the Tyrolean rustic
Amenities: hotel; private dining room;
bar; car park
Atmosphere: from the festive (cellar) to
the gemütlich (ground floor)
Clientèle: fairly heterogeneous; local pol-
iticians, hommes de lettres and health-
food fans en passant
Dress: no special requirements
Service: knowledgeable and helpful; su-
pervised by Harald Ultsch
Reservations: advisable
Price range: medium
Credit cards: AE, DC, Euro, Visa, Master
Card

Dinner

›SIR RICHARD‹
162 Innsbruckerstrasse
Seefeld/Tyrol (21 km/16 miles)
Telephone: (5212) 2093
Owner/Manager: Richard and Hermine
Rass
Closed: May; November
Open: 11.30/a.m.–14.30/2.30 p.m. and
18.00/6 p.m.–22.00/10 p.m. (opening

hours vary from above outside the tourist season)
Cuisine: ›au goût du marché‹
Chef de cuisine: Hermine Rass
Specialities: potato soup with chanterelles (Kartoffelsuppe mit Eierschwammerln); loin of beef with chive cream and Swiss-style fried potatoes (Rösti); Veltliner sabayon with fresh cherries
Location: in Seefeld/Tyrol; 21 km (16 miles) north-west of Innsbruck along road 313 (route E6)
Setting: at the entrance to the village, opposite the lake; dining room decorated in English style; elegantly-laid tables
Atmosphere: comfortably chic
Clientèle: distinguished; discriminating; winter sports enthusiasts and gourmets en passant
Dress: après-affaires to après-ski
Service: friendly
Reservations: advisable (no dogs)
Price range: fairly expensive, even by Seefeld standards
Credit cards: AE, DC, Visa

Café

CENTRAL
5 Gilmstrasse
Telephone: 2 48 66
Owner/Manager: Franz Griesser
Closed: never
Open: 7.00/a.m.–22.15/10.15 p.m.
Location: in the Hotel Central (on the second floor)
Specialities: Sachertorte (chocolate cake); fruit tarts
Setting: large, high room with stucco ceiling, pillars, marble tables and appropriate accessoires
Amenities: the now rarely-offered glass of water with your coffee; large selection of Austrian and international newspapers and periodicals for customers' use
Atmosphere: a living monument to the good old days, Viennese style
Clientèle: local intelligentsia, as well as shopkeepers, shopgirls, housewives and pensioners
Service: courteous and welcoming

Bar

DIE KANNE
Seefeld/Tyrol (21 km/16 miles)
Telephone: (52 12) 26 21
Owner/Manager: the Seyrling Family/ Sigi Seyrling
Closed: never
Open: 17.00/5 p.m.–3.00/a.m.
Location: in the Hotel Klosterbräu

Setting: stylish and sporting lounge/nightclub in a 500-year-old former monastery, now a luxurious hotel; thé dansant at 17.00/5 p.m.; cabaret and dancing to live orchestra at night
Amenities: hotel; restaurant; bistro with open-air dining; private dining rooms (5–200 persons); bar; swimming pool; sports facilities; garage; valet parking service
Atmosphere: quietly genteel to sophisticated and lively après ski, depending on the time of day and the season of the year
Clientèle: princes, presidents, premiers and prominenti; jet set tycoons and stars of stage and screen
Dress: designer chic
Service: very courteous and personal
Reservations: advisable
Price range: appropriately expensive
Credit cards: AE, DC, Euro

Nightclub

LADY–O
2 Bruneckerstrasse
Telephone: 2 64 32
Owner/Manager: Dieter Sterr
Closed: never
Open: 20.00/8 p.m.–4.00/a.m.
Location: opposite the Post Office; by the railway station
Setting: nostalgic; elegant
Amenities: band (periodically); air conditioning; non-stop shows-from 22.00/10 p.m. to 4 a.m.
Atmosphere: stylish; civilized
Clientèle: Innsbruck's Haute Bourgeoisie; youngish and on-the-way-up to middle-aged, successful and definitely not moribund
Dress: disco elegance
Service: professional
Reservations: not necessary
Price range: expensive
Credit cards: all major

Shopping

EVERYTHING UNDER ONE ROOF
Kaufhaus Tyrol
33–35 Maria-Theresien-Strasse

FOR HIM
Einwaller 1 Pfarrgasse

FOR HER
Zelger-Damenmoden
Maria-Theresien-Strasse

BEAUTY & HAIR
Griesser
7 Meraner Strasse & Holiday Inn

JEWELLERY
Schmuckatelier Carré (Margit Kölblinger)
3 Sparkassenplatz
Josef Kölblinger 9 Meraner Strasse

LOCAL SPECIALITIES
Resi Hammerer (women's fashion)
1 Meraner Strasse
Herren-Zelger (men's fashion)
Anichstrasse
Meraner Strasse
Haidegger (children's fashion)
18 Wilhelm-Greil-Strasse &
9 Meraner Strasse
Schwammenhoefer, Franz (local leather fashion)
1 Burggraben
Pelzhaus Bloder (furs)
3 Herzog-Friedrich-Strasse
Tyrolia (books)
15 Maria-Theresien-Strasse
Tiroler Heimatwerk (gifts)
2–4 Meraner Strasse
Kristall und Porzellan vorm. Tollinger (porcelain).
Wilhelm-Greil-Strasse
Leder Lechle (baggage & travel accessories)
29 Burggraben & Marktgraben
Arthur Graf-Haus der Wohnkultur (interior decorating)
15 Wilhelm-Greil-Strasse
Hoertnagel (food and beverages)
4–6 Burggraben
Parfumerie Elisabeth (perfumery)
Maria-Theresien-Strasse
Trachten Lanz (local fashion, costumes)
15 Wilhelm-Greil-Strasse
Erika (candles)
Ursulinen-Passage

THE BEST OF ART
Annasäule (contemporary art)
7 A Adamgasse, Tel. 3 57 85
Krinzinger (contemporary art)
8 Adolf-Pichler-Platz, Tel. 3 21 31
Antiquitäten-Galerie St. Rochus (antiques)
55 Maria-Theresien-Straße
Tel. 2 04 29/33 89 63

The City

›The most beautiful city in Europe‹, according to 19th-century philosopher-scientist-globe-trotter Alexander von Humboldt and myriads of pilgrims to the world's finest and foremost festival town, where ›the hills are alive with the sound of music‹, echoing the grand operas and symphony concerts at the Festival Hall, the musical dramas and singspiels at the Winter Riding School, the choirs, recitals and chamber music at the cathedral, the castles and palaces where ›the speech of angels‹ is worshipped as in no other city on earth. Genius-idol and favourite son Wolfgang Amadeus Mozart is honoured before all – and everywhere around town, from shop-window decoration to confiserie creations –, but with almost every day of the year a festival day and the world's music élite queuing to take the stage, none of the composers between Bach and Britten gets a raw deal in Salzburg. All the star performers assemble here for world acclaim – Pavarotti, Pollini & Co., wunderkinder galore. The ›other‹ favourite son, maestrissimo Herbert von Karajan, is the ›Salt-Fortress‹ châtelain: his majestic baton directs not only the stars and orchestras but the Upper Crust from every continent to ›his‹ city as well. Of lesser importance but on an equally high level are the theatre productions by the most famous directors, from Peter Hall to Ingmar Bergman to Claus Peymann. The framework for this oasis of the ideal world is uniquely splendid – Baroque in abundance with elements of all the ›Belles Epoques‹ dotted about the two banks of the River Salzach, interlaced with picturesque alleys and mews adorned by gingerbread houses, towered by wooded hills and dramatically shaped rocks, surrounded by a ›Pastorale‹ landscape. Few cities are so well-built, well-learned and well-behaved, none of that size so worldly at the same time. Business plays a minor role here, and whatever there is, it will be conducted adagio.

Founded: 696 – by Bishop Saint Rupert; Salzburg – ›salt fortress‹.

Far-reaching events: 8th century – Salzburg becomes an archbishopric; 13th century – the bishops-in-residence are granted the title of Princes of the Holy Roman Empire; 17th century – Italian architects give the city its Baroque face; 1756 – birth of Mozart; 1802 – secularization; 1809 – Salzburg ceded to Bavaria, returned to Austria in 1815; 1922 – Salzburg Festival held for the first time.

Population: 140,000; capital of Salzburg province.

Postal code: A-5020   **Telephone code:** 6 62

Climate: clear – Alpine – fickle – warm winds bring sudden changes – too much rain.

Best time to visit: all the year round – for architecture, setting, atmosphere and music.

Calendar of events: *Mozart Week* (late January) – musical tribute to the city's favourite son; *Music Festivals* at Easter and Whitsuntide – Herbert von Karajan's private mecca; *Salzburg Festival* (end of July to end of August) – initiated by Hugo von Hofmannsthal, Richard Strauss and Max Reinhardt in 1922 – music, theatre, ballet; *Hellbrunn Festival* – concerts at Hellbrunn Palace; *Mozarteum Foundation Concerts; Castle Concerts* (from May until October in Mirabell Palace) – in fact, almost limitless cultural events here all summer, every summer; *Salzburg Culture Days* (October) – opera, concerts and folklore to close the summer season.

Fairs and exhibitions: *JASPOWA* (Mar) – hunting and sports weapons; *GATEHA* (Sep) – household and garden technologies; *FASHION – MADE IN AUSTRIA* (Sep) – traditional Austrian folk dress and knitwear; *ÖSFA* (Sep) – sporting goods exhibition; *SOUVENIR FAIR* (Sep); *AUSTRO BÜRO* (Oct) – information and organization technology; *AUSTRIAN FURNITURE FAIR* (Oct).

Best views of the city: from the *Monks Hill;* from the *Hohensalzburg* fortress.

Historical and modern sights: *Cathedral* (1614–1628) – the most outstanding example of early Baroque architecture north of the Alps; *Hohensalzburg* – one of the few fully preserved fortresses in Central Europe, dating back to the 11th century; *St. Peter's* – Benedictine monastery, founded by St. Rupert in the 7th century, rebuilt and drastically changed in the 17th and 19th centuries; *St. Peter's Churchyard* – picturesque little cemetery where the relatives of many famous people lie buried, including Mozart's sister and Haydn's brother; *Residenz,* built in 1120, renovated 1600–1619 to match the imperial tastes of the times; *Residenz Gallery* – fine collection of 16th to 19th century European painting; *Mirabell Palace* (1606 – rebuilt in the early 18th century) with Baroque staircase and sculpture-filled gardens; *Hellbrunn Palace* (17th century) – in the grounds of the zoo.

Special attractions: *Getreidegasse* – a typical street of Old Salzburg; Mozart was born at number 9; *Grosses Festspielhaus* – the modern theatre with excellent acoustics and a timeless exterior; *House of Nature* – an impressive collection of animals, some still living; the observation terrace of *Cafe Winkler; Salzkammergut* lake district, especially Mondsee, St.-Wolfgang, Bad Ischl.

Important companies with headquarters in the city: *Mannesmann Demag* (machinery); *Austria Puma; Dassler* (sports articles); *Kässbohrer Austria* (trucks, buses); *Induplan Chemie* (chemicals); *Mirabella Küchen* (kitchens); *Oberascher Maschinenfabrik* (machinery); *Porsche Design, Stieglbrauerei* (breweries); *Tauernautobahn, Tauernkraftwerke* (energy); *Teekanne* (teas); *Universal Versand, Franz Welz Transporte; Blizzard* – Mittersill/Salzburg Province (skis); *Atomic* – Altenmarkt/Salzburg Province (skis).

Airport: Salzburg, SZG; Tel.: 85 12 04; 5 km/3 miles; Austrian Airlines, Tel.: 63 34 20

The Headquarters

GOLDENER HIRSCH

37 Getreidegasse
A–5020 Salzburg
Telephone: 84 85 11
Telex: 632967 hirsh
Owning Company: Imperial Hotels Austria AG
General Manager: Graf Johannes Walderdorff
Affiliation/Reservation Systems: Steigenberger Reservation Service, Hotel Reservation Service
Number of rooms: 56 (7 suites)
Price range: ÖS 1,400–2,400
Credit cards: AE, DC, EC, JCB, Visa
Location: city centre
Built: 1407 (renovated 1984)
Style: antique
Hotel amenities: garage, valet parking, house limousine service, newsstand, boutique, house doctor
Main hall porter: Peter Drazdik
Room amenities: colour tv, mini-bar/refrigerator, radio
Bathroom amenities: separate shower cabin, bidet, bathrobe, hairdrier, telephone
Room service: 7.00/a.m.–24.00/12 p.m.
Conference rooms: 2 (up to 150 persons)
Bar: (10.00/a.m.–24.00/12.00 p.m.) Kurt Bayer (barman), antique décor
Restaurant: ›Goldener Hirsch‹ (11.30/a.m.–14.30/2.30 p.m. and 19.00/7.00 p.m.–24.00/12.00 p.m.) Karl Lettner (maître), Herbert Pöcklhofer (chef de cuisine), Austrian and international cuisine, antique décor; ›S'Herzl‹ (10.00/a.m.–24.00/12.00 p.m.), Austrian cuisine
Private dining rooms: three

For more than four centuries the ›Golden Stag‹ has triumphantly asserted its supremacy as Mozart-Town's mini-castle in the very heart of it. Right on the quaint shopping promenade Getreidegasse, across from the musical wunderkind's birthplace and a few bars away from the Festival Hall, the cathedral and the animated coffee-houses, international aristocracy, local dignitaries, la jeunesse platinée and the worshippers of Karajan & Co. need not fear stumbling over Sound-of Music-caravans. The Goldener Hirsch is directed by Count Walderdorff like a fort for the fortunate, Lords Shawcross and Weidenfeld, Gunter Sachs and Gabriele Henkel, goddess Ann Getty and figurehead Eliette von K. passing through daily during the seasonal festivals even though they all have their own castles in the vicinity. When you can't get a ticket through Salzburg's Saint Peter, concierge Peter Drazdik, come at least for a drink at Kurt Bayer's bar where the world passes by. If you manage to get a room, you will be in heaven – pretty, picturesque, cute, doll's house luxury Trapp-family style.

The Hideaway

SCHLOSS FUSCHL

A–5322 Hof bei Salzburg
(18 km/11 miles)
Telephone: (62 29) 25 30
Telex: 633 454 shlof
Owning Company: Max Grundig Stiftung
General Manager: Uwe Zeilerbauer
Affiliation/Reservation Systems: The
Leading Hotels of the World, Relais et
Châteaux
Closed: February 2nd–24th
Number of rooms: 86 (21 suites)
Price range: ÖS 2,000–4,000
Credit cards: all major
Location: 18 km/11 miles from Salzburg
Built: 15th century
Style: castle and local style buildings
Hotel amenities: garage, valet parking,
house limousine service, indoor swim-
ming pool, sauna, solarium, massage,
florist, newsstand, tobacconist, whirl-
pool, private beach (pets allowed)
Main hall porter: Eva Schramml

Room amenities: colour tv, mini-bar
Bathroom amenities: separate shower,
bidet (in some rooms), bathrobe
Room service: 7.00/a.m.–22.00/10 p.m.
Conference rooms: 4 (up to 200 persons)
Sports (nearby): golf, tennis, sailing,
windsurfing, fishing, hunting, swimming
Bar: (12.00/a.m. to closing time) Gidi
(barman), antique décor, open fireplace
Restaurants: ›Wintergarten‹ (12.15/p.m.–
14.00/2.00 p.m. and 19.00/7.00 p.m.–
21.30/9.30 p.m.) H. Seifner (maître), H.
Fleischhacker (chef de cuisine);
›Salon‹ as Wintergarten
Private dining rooms: three

*The erstwhile hunting-lodge of the prince-
bishops of Salzburg stands amidst the
mountains of the Salzkammergut Lake
District on a small promontory jutting out
into the Lake Fuschl. With one of the loveliest locations in the world Schloss Fuschl
became, under the more secular and benevolent suzerainty of German electronics
magnate Dr. Max Grundig, the favoured
retreat for the Festival In-Crowd and celebrities in search of seclusion. Manager
Uwe Zeilerbauer and his staff keep up the
tradition of discreet hospitality, offering –
as well as the pleasure of the chase favoured by the lords spiritual and the high
and mighty who were their guests – such à
la mode sports as golf and windsurfing, in
an ambience which radiates the charm of
centuries without sacrificing modern comfort. A romantic dîner à deux at dusk in the
winter-garden or on the terrace overlooking the lake is a multi-sensory aesthetic experience, the memory of which will linger
long after the last rays of sunlight have left
the mountain peaks. Listed amongst the
Top Twenty Summer Resorts by the prestigious IN World Guide, Schloss Fuschl is
undoubtedly a nonpareil amongst châteaux relais in Europe.*

Lunch

GOLDENER HIRSCH
37 Getreidegasse
Telephone: 84 85 11
Owner/Manager: Graf Johannes Walderdorff
Maître: Karl Lettner
Open: 11.30/a.m.–14.30/2.30 p.m. and 19.00/7 p.m.–24.00/12 p.m.
Cuisine: Austrian and international
Chef de cuisine: Herbert Pöcklhofer
Specialities: mousse of smoked trout; crayfish soufflé; roast goose liver; boiled beef (Tafelspitz) with chive sauce; apple strudel
Location: in the Hotel Goldener Hirsch; on a busy shopping street, near the Mozart House and the Festival Hall (Festspielhaus)
Setting: building dating from 1407; elegant dining room furnished with valuable antiques
Amenities: hotel; private dining rooms (180 persons); car park (garage); bar
Atmosphere: as essential a stop over as the castle and Mozart's birthplace; the only place to be after a festival performance
Clientèle: the rich; the famous; the noble; the distinguished; beautiful people and jet-setters – mostly old friends and acquaintances of director Graf Walderdorff
Dress: suitably sophisticated, elegant and expensive
Service: particularly friendly; clad in local loden
Reservations: advisable to essential (well in advance) for Festival evenings
Price range: appropriately expensive
Credit cards: AE, DC, Euro, Visa, JCB

Dinner

KuK RESTAURANT
2 Waagplatz
Telephone: 84 21 56
Owner/Managers: the Koller brothers
Open: 11.30/a.m.–14.00/2 p.m. and 18.00/6 p.m.–22.30/10.30 p.m.
Cuisine: innovative and traditional Austrian
Chef de cuisine: Johann Kögl
Specialities: shellfish; according to season and market availability – ›lamb week‹; ›game week‹; ›fish week‹; ›asparagus week‹
Location: near the cathedral (Dom) and the ›Glockenspiel‹; pedestrian area
Setting: traditional burgher-building – vaulted cellar; various dining rooms; Austrian rustic style with wooden tables, original paintings, fine linen and fresh flowers

Amenities: private dining room (up to 70 persons); terrace (no reservations; restricted menu)
Atmosphere: gemütlich
Clientèle: eat-and-run tourists jostle with local top-brass and visiting luminaries from the worlds of art, music and politics
Dress: jeans and camera to cashmere and pearls
Service: friendly and efficient; supervised by Helmut Postingl
Reservations: advisable (pets permitted)
Price range: rather expensive
Credit cards: AE, DC, Euro, Visa

Lunch

FRIESACHER
Anif, Salzburger Land (6 km/4 miles)
Telephone: (62 46) 20 75
Owner/Manager: the Friesacher family
Closed: Wednesday
Open: 11.30/a.m.–14.30/2.30 p.m. and 18.00/6 p.m.–21.30/9.30 p.m.
Cuisine: Austrian
Specialities: much of the food home-produced; semolina dumpling soup (Griessnockerlsuppe); boiled beef with horseradish and parsley potatoes (Tellerfleisch mit Kren und Petersilerdäpfel); curd cheese strudel (Topfenstrudel); pancakes (Palatschinken)
Location: in Anif; 6 km (4 miles) from Salzburg along the road to Berchtesgaden
Setting: a local-style country inn; dining room furnished in the country farmhouse idiom; unpretentiously welcoming; fresh flowers on the tables
Amenities: open-air dining on terrace in summer
Atmosphere: Austrian folklore, yet original and appealing
Clientèle: Salzburg citizens en fête and en famille; the Bavarian weekend crowd en masse on Sundays – and a sprinkling of travellers en passant
Dress: Sunday casual to Sunday best
Service: friendly waitresses in dirndls
Reservations: essential (pets permitted)
Price range: average
Credit cards: DC

Lunch

CASTELLO
1 Wredeplatz, Mondsee (25 km/16 miles)
Telephone: (62 32) 23 88
Owner/Manager/Chef de cuisine: Countess Micheline Almeida
Closed: October 1st – April 30th
Cuisine: Austrian and international
Specialities: soups; lobster; beef; fresh fish from the lake; salads; calorie-conscious sweets

Location: at Mondsee, 25 km (16 miles) east of Salzburg along A1 motorway
Setting: a castle in a picturesque lake and mountain environment; small dining room; pretty, flowery décor
Amenities: private club for elegant parties (50 persons)
Atmosphere: that of a French château relais; leisurely and chic
Clientèle: prominent visitors to Salzburg before, during and after the Festival
Dress: Laroche and Lanvin to Denkstein and Ennsmann
Service: attentive; under the watchful eye of maître d'hôtel Herr Fritz
Reservations: advisable (no dogs)
Price range: on the expensive side
Credit cards: not accepted

Dinner

PLOMBERG-ESCHLBÖCK
41 St. Lorenz, Mondsee (30 km/19 miles)
Telephone: (62 32) 29 12–0/31 66–0/35 72–0
Affiliations: Chaîne des Rôtisseurs
Owner/Manager/Chef de cuisine: Karl Eschlböck
Closed: January
Open: 12.00/a.m.–14.00/2 p.m. and 19.00/7 p.m.–22.00/10 p.m.
Cuisine: Nouvelle, with a strong Austrian accent
Specialities: calves' liver on tomato foam; ris de veau aux écrevisses; crabs in their own juice with vegetables; ragoût of woodland mushrooms (Steinpilzragout); tripe au gratin; lamb on creamed onions and lentil purée; mousse au chocolat
Location: at Plomberg, Mondsee, in the Salzkammergut Lake District – 30 km (19 miles) east of Salzburg along A1 motorway
Setting: 300-year-old Alpine chalet-style building; built originally as a coaching inn where the horses would be changed before tackling the mountain pass; inherited by Karl Eschlböck from his parents; dining rooms in various styles, from Jugendstil to Alpine rustic; oriental rugs and an abundance of light wood
Amenities: hotel; bar; open-air dining on two terraces (one overlooking the lake and the other in the sun); private bathing beach; sports facilities; car park; garage
Atmosphere: fashionable, yet unpretentious
Clientèle: followers of Karl Eschlböck's culinary career since his days at the ›Sacher‹ in Vienna; Salzburg's summer season glitterati, from Stavros Niarchos to Paul Getty Junior
Dress: according to season and circumstances
Service: charming; directed by the wife of the patron, Monika Eschlböck

Reservations: advisable to essential (dogs permitted)
Price range: fairly expensive
Credit cards: AE, DC, Euro, Visa

Bistro

DAIMLER'S BEISL
17 Giselakai
Telephone: 7 43 12
Owner/Manager: Heidemarie and Richard Braschl
Closed: lunchtime
Open: 18.00/6 p.m.–12.30/p.m.
Cuisine: French and local unpretentious
Chef de cuisine: Richard Braschl
Specialities: garlic cream sauce; lamb chop with leaf spinach, leeks and courgettes; cream of mushroom soup; charcoal-grilled meat; salad buffet
Location: below the Kapuzinerberg; directly on the Salzach
Setting: 15th-century building; comfortable wine bar on the ground floor; elegantized bistro-restaurant on the first floor (window seats afford a view of the old city and the castle)
Amenities: bar
Atmosphere: légère but refined
Clientèle: bons vivants; teenage trendies, artists, sculptors and men of letters
Dress: casual but not careless
Service: friendly and familiar
Reservations: essential (no dogs)
Price range: medium
Credit cards: AE

Café

TOMASELLI
9 Alter Markt
Telephone: 84 44 88
Owner/Manager: Karl Tomaselli
Closed: two weeks in February
Open: 7.00/a.m.–21.00/9 p.m.
Specialities: pâtisserie; Austrian sweets
Location: in the old part of town (Altstadt)
Setting: archetypal coffeehouse patronised by the Haute Bourgeoisie; marble tables; closely-packed wooden armchairs; chandeliers, pictures and wood panelling
Amenities: open-air dining on terrace
Atmosphere: the place where everyone goes; as much a part of the Salzburg scene as Mozart and the mountains
Clientèle: a heterogeneous collection including the local ›In‹ crowd, media-men, tourists – and the occasional casual passer-by
Service: Salzburg-moody

27

Bar

GOLDENER HIRSCH BAR
37 Getreidegasse
Telephone: 84 85 11
Owner/Manager: Graf Johannes Walder-dorff
Barman: Kurt Bayer
Closed: never
Open: 10.00/a.m.–24.00/12 p.m.
Location: in the Hotel Goldener Hirsch
Setting: comfortably furnished with valuable antiques
Amenities: hotel; restaurant (Austrian and international cuisine); car park (garage)
Atmosphere: that of an elegant but cosy pub transported into a ›Sound of Music‹ setting
Clientèle: Salzburg's perennial and seasonal social élite, for a pre-prandial sherry or a post-performance cognac
Service: under the experienced direction of chief barman Kurt Bayer
Reservations: advisable
Credit cards: AE, DC, Euro, Visa, JCB

Nightclub

HALF MOON
4 Anton-Neuymayer-Platz
Telephone: 84 16 70
Owner/Manager: Helmut Lumpi
Closed: never
Open: 22.00/10 p.m.–4.00/a.m.
Location: opposite the Mönchsberg casino
Setting: four rooms in cellar vaults with natural stone pillars; blue ceiling; black walls; modern lighting effects; contemporary pictures
Amenities: discothèque; three bars; private members' lounge with cocktail bar, backgammon, periodicals and glass doors to reduce the noise level to that conducive to normal conversation
Atmosphere: from loud to very loud; determined by the guests
Clientèle: jeunesse salée; the few festivaliers who are able to hear Mozart at eight and Motown at eleven, including celebrities from the worlds of economics, sport and the arts – from Jimmy Hartwig to Niki Lauda and Mathias Gruber
Dress: designer sweater to tweed jacket
Service: well-schooled; good teamwork
Reservations: advisable
Credit cards: AE, DC, Euro, Visa, Master Card

Shopping

EVERYTHING UNDER ONE ROOF
Forum 11 Südtiroler Platz
FOR HIM
Dantendorfer 33 Getreidegasse
FOR HER
Resmann ›R‹ (Couture) 6 Rudolfskai
BEAUTY & HAIR
Bundy & Bundy 11 Judengasse
JEWELLERY
Kuebeck Theatergasse

LOCAL SPECIALITIES
Lady Bass (women's fashion)
4 Getreidegasse
Resmann ›R‹ (men's fashion)
5 Dreifaltigkeitsgasse
Leder-Schaller (leather fashion)
6 Judengasse
Pelzatelier Wilk (furs) 2 Münzgasse
Alpenverlag (books)
2 Rudolfskai
Heimatwerk (gifts)
Residenzplatz
Delarue (baggage & travel accessories)
18 Schwarzstrasse
Pfanzelter (interior decorating)
3 Judengasse
Stranz & Scio (food and beverages)
9 Getreidegasse
Lanz (costumes)
4 Schwarzstrasse
Dschulnigg (armoury)
8 Griesgasse

THE BEST OF ART
Academia GmbH (20th-century paintings/sculptures) Residenz, Tel. 84 51 85
Ropac, Thaddäus J. (contemporary art) 40/1 Kaigasse, Tel. 2 77 31
Salis (20th-century paintings) 13 Goldgasse, Tel. 84 54 34
Wlz (20th-century paintings) 16 Sigmund-Haffner-Gasse, Tel. 84 17 71
Sailer KG. (carpets) 5 A.-Neumayr-Platz, Tel. 4 64 83
Stollnberger, Johann (19th/20th-century antiques) 5 Goldgasse, Tel. 4 14 96

The City

Nowhere in the world does the Baroque splendour of Europe's imperial past live on quite so convincingly as it does in Vienna. From the intellectual coffee-houses to the lavish galas, from the eternally critical carping of the Viennese to their indiscriminate adoration of its glorious history, Vienna is a nostalgic city of tradition with a lively interest in the future. One of the leading centres of Europe's cultural avant-garde (from the Viennese School to Vienna's own Wizard of Oz – André Heller), Vienna is also the commercial hub of Austria, with every major international company being represented in one way or another, and an important turntable of international relations between North and South and East and West. The Vienna Woods are still there, the Danube is still beautiful – and blue again – and here in the city where the Hapsburgs taught the world the meaning of elegance, where Mozart und Beethoven and all the Strausses composed the music to move the soul and Sigmund Freud discovered sex, life goes on as a constant search for new illusions.

Founded: ca. 400 B.C. by Celts; Wien (German) – named after the Roman settlement Vindobona.

Far-reaching events: 1st century – the Romans erect the fortress Vindobona; 5th century – the Huns invade; 12th century – Vienna becomes the residential city of the ruling Babenberg family; 1282 – the Hapsburgs come to power and stay there for 600 years; 1365 – foundation of the oldest German-speaking university; 1529 and 1683 – Turkish invasions – the Battle of the Kahlenberg saves Christianity in Europe and makes Vienna one of the world capitals; 18th century – Maria Theresia and Josef II turn Vienna into a Baroque wonderland which becomes the home of Haydn, Mozart, Beethoven and Schubert; 1805 and 1809 – Napoleon and the French invade the city; 1814–15 – Congress of Vienna reshapes Europe after Napoleon's downfall; 1848–1916 – Emperor Franz Josef transforms Vienna into the capital of Europe; 1939–45 – heavy bombing in World War II; 1945 – entry of the Red Army; the city is divided into four zones by the allies; 1955 – Vienna is reunited, Austria declares its neutrality and the capital becomes the stage for international peace talks between Khrushchev and Kennedy, and Brezhnev and Carter.

Population: 1.5 million; capital and largest city of Austria.

Postal code: A-1010   **Telephone code:** 222

Climate: mild, neither extremely hot in summer nor bitterly cold in winter; there is always a slight breeze, the ›Wiener Lüfterl‹.

Calendar of events: *Fasching* (Jan–Mar) – the carnival celebrations, galas, balls, concerts and parades; *Opera Ball* (Feb–Mar); *Viennale Film Festival* (Mar); *Vienna Spring Marathon* (Mar); *Stadtfest* (Apr) – dancing in the streets and squares of the inner city; *Vienna Festival* (May/Jun) – music indoors and out, exhibitions, theatre, one of Europe's best festivals; *Musical Summer* (Aug/Sep) – concerts everywhere; *Schubert Days* (Nov)

Fairs and exhibitions: *VIENNA RECREATION FAIR* (Feb) – tourism, camping, boating, flying and tennis; *VIENNA SPRING FAIR* (Mar) – for household goods, music, gardening, agriculture, cooking, machines and tools; *SPIEL* (Apr) – Austrian toy fair; *IFABO* (May) – international trade fair for office organization; *VINOVA* (Jun) – international wine fair; *JUWELIA* (Sep) – jewelry and watches trade fair; *AGRARIA* (Sep) – agricultural exhibition; *HIT* (Sep) – annual fair for home entertainment, electronics and household technology; *VIENNA AUTUMN FAIR* (Sep) – for construction, agriculture, musical instruments, cooking, machines, tools, furs and winter articles; *IE* (Oct) – international trade for industrial electronics.

Historical sights: *Hofburg* – the imperial palace, with royal apartments, the Imperial Treasury and museums; *Albertina* – gallery with one of the world's best collections of graphic art; *Belvedere* – two late Baroque palaces now housing the *Austrian Gallery of 19th and 20th Century Art,* the *Museum of Medieval Art* and the *Museum of Baroque Art;* the *Karlskirche* and the *Stephansdom* – the most interesting churches; *Schloss Schönbrunn* – the ultimate Baroque palace; *Post Office Savings Bank* – a ›Jugendstil‹ gem; *Capuchins' Crypt* – macabre tombs of the Hapsburgs; *Museum of Fine Arts.*

Modern sights: the *church by Fritz Wotruba;* Hans Holbein's architecturally extraordinary *boutique décors;* the *Subway designs* of the gruppe 4; *Vienna International Centre.*

Special attractions: *Viennese coffee-houses; Heurigen* – taverns selling new wine (in Grinzing) with live music and inimitably Viennese atmosphere; *Spanish Riding School; Vienna Boys' Choir;* a horse-drawn *fiacre ride; Vienna Woods; Prater* – a Viennese Disneyland; *Burgtheater* – Vienna's Old Vic; an evening at the *Opera; Mayerling* – where a lovers' suicide changed the course of history.

Important companies with headquarters in the city: *Kreditanstalt* (banking); *Länderbank* (banking); *Österreichische Industrie Verwaltung* (industrial administration); *Konsum Österreich* (trading); *Bundesländerversicherung* (insurance); *Montana* (chemical products); *Austria Tabak* (tobacco); *Österreichische Mineralöl Verwaltung* (oil); *Mobil Austria; Shell Austria; Austria Metall* (aluminium); *Austrian Airlines; Siemens Austria* (electrical equipment, electronics), *Vereinigte Edelstahlwerke* (stainless steel); *Grundig Austria* (entertainment electronics); *Philips Austria* (entertainment electronics); *Unilever Austria* (food products)

Airport: Wien-Schwechat, VIE; Tel.: 77 70 29 50; 20 km/13 miles.

The Headquarters

IMPERIAL

16 Kärntnerring
A–1015 Vienna
Telephone: 65 17 65
Telex: 112630 imhota
Owning Company: Imperial Hotels Austria AG
General Manager: Georg W. Engelhardt
Affiliation/Reservation System: The Leading Hotels of the World
Number of rooms: 165 (17 suites)
Price range: ÖS 1,700–17,000
Credit cards: AE, DC, EC, Visa, JTB
Location: city centre
Built: 1873 (recently renovated)
Style: Viennese neo-Renaissance
Hotel amenities: house limousine service, hairstylist (pets allowed)
Main hall porter: Erich Benesch
Room amenities: colour tv, mini-bar
Bathroom amenities: bidet, telephone
Room service: 6.00/a.m.–24.00/12 p.m.
Laundry/dry cleaning: 7.00/a.m.–17.00/5.00 p.m.
Conference rooms: 4 (up to 120 persons)
Bar: ›Maria-Theresia‹ (11.00/a.m.–1.00/a.m.) Walter Bergmann (barman)
Restaurants: ›Zur Majestät‹ (12.00/a.m.–15.00/3 p.m. and 19.00/7 p.m.–24.00/12 p.m.) Leo Ebinger (maître), Werner Pusswald (chef de cuisine)
›Café Imperial‹ (7.00/a.m.–24.00/12 p.m.) Herbert Zeiler (maître), J. Schwaiger (chef de cuisine), open-air dining

›The most beautiful hotel we have ever stayed in‹, according to Queen Elizabeth II – and her fellow-monarchs from Belgium, Denmark, Holland, Jordan, Saudi Arabia, Spain and Sweden didn't contradict her when they occupied the Royal Suites here. Nixon loved the Imperial as much as his interlocutor Khrushchev, his go-between Kissinger and his successor Carter and to Kurt Waldheim, Doctor Kreisky and Professor Fuchs it is home around the corner from home. (The only ones missing are Emperor Franz Josef on the balcony, Johann Strauss fiddling in the Café and Sigmund Freud talking to Stefan Zweig in the restaurant.) The reasons for this high esteem and deep affection for the Imperial around the world are manifold: the former ducal palace (built in 1873) has retained all splendour, architecturally, in décor and service and plays host to the world of any colour and taste with such – Viennese – perfection that you shiver at the mere thought of having to stay at the Hilton, Intercontinental or Marriott here. The ambiance is formal and light at the same time, the concierges are personalities of yester-year, the cuisine is gourmetland and the charm of materials, accessoires and servants are only found on the stage these days. Court Marshal Georg Engelhardt leaves the palatial air intact, while secretly changing and rearranging the framework to make it even better; to keep it ›the finest hotel in the world.‹

The Hideaway

PALAIS SCHWARZENBERG

9 Schwarzenbergplatz
A–1030 Vienna
Telephone: 78 45 15
Telex: 136 124 hps v
Owner: Prince Karl J. Schwarzenberg
General Manager: Werner Breitenecker
Affiliation/Reservation Systems: Relais et Châteaux, Preferred Hotels Worldwide, Swiss International Hotels
Number of rooms: 38 (6 suites)
Price range: ÖS 3,000–9,000
Credit cards: all major
Location: city centre
Built: 1727 (renovated 1983)
Style: Baroque grandeur
Hotel amenities: valet parking, house limousine service, car rental, newspapers, outdoor swimming pool, tobacconist, florist, ballroom (pets allowed)
Room amenities: colour tv
Bathroom amenities: bidet, bathrobe
Room service: 24 hours
Laundry/dry cleaning: same day
Conference rooms: 6 (up to 250 persons)
Sports: tennis courts, golf course nearby
Bar: ›Palais‹ (11.00/a.m. till last client leaves) Baroque architecture
Restaurant: ›Schwarzenberg‹ (12.00/a.m.–15.00/3.00 p.m. and 18.00/6.00 p.m.–24.00/12.00 p.m.) Gottfried Pecher (maître), Benny Poppe (chef de cuisine), French and Austrian cooking
Private dining rooms: 2 (up to 200 persons)
Marble hall: luxury banqueting, receptions, music recitals, lectures

Tempora mutantur – but here, at least, with more flair and charm than on the other side of the Ringstrasse. Palais Schwarzenberg epitomizes Viennese pomp and circumstance at its most gloriously nostalgic; the right wing of the palace, built in 1727 by the twin nonpareils of Austrian Baroque, Lukas von Hildebrand and Johann Bernhard Fischer, has been open since the war to members of the public who appreciate beauty, dignity and a soupçon of fantasy. Werner Breitenecker and his staff avoid with consummate skill any sense of functionality which might detract from the ambience that a prince could take for granted in his own castle. French Empire-style bronzes, Old Masters, stucco ceilings and marble floors blend beautifully with the exquisitely co-ordinated doll's house décor in the attic rooms with their sloping ceilings; all are merely details within a harmonious framework which attracts the crème de la crème from around the world. Chef de cuisine Benny Poppe delights them with nouvelle cuisine specialities and Viennese dishes alike, and the noble view across the park from the glassed-in terrace restaurant helps them to forget for a while that the days of imperial splendour are past and that the hubbub of the city is just down the road.

Lunch

KORSO BEI DER OPER
Hotel Bristol
2 Mahlertstrasse
Telephone: 5 15 16–5 46
Owner/Manager: Georg Engelhardt
Closed: Saturday lunchtime
Open: 12.00/a.m.–15.00/3 p.m. (last orders 14.30/2.30 p.m.) and 19.00/7 p.m.–2.00/a.m. (last orders 23.30/11.30 p.m.)
Cuisine: nouvelle (›au goût du marché‹) and Viennese
Chef de cuisine: Reinhard Gerer (ex-Mattes and Tantris)
Specialities: freshwater crabs on broccoli salad; lamb's kidneys with courgettes; Wachau wine soup with croûtons; médaillons of turbot in chive and basil sauce; glazed saddle of veal with wild mushroom sauce and spinach; cream strudel (Milchrahmstrudel); ›Premieren-Menü‹ (appropriate to the opera in question); gourmet menu; family lunch on Sundays
Location: in the Hotel Bristol; opposite the Opera (Oper)
Setting: turn-of-the-century pomp and circumstance; walnut paravents, gilt-framed mirrors, red carpet, gold-framed old oils; crystal chandeliers
Amenities: hotel; private dining room (20 persons); bar; pianist with old-world repertoire; car park (garage)
Atmosphere: the chicest restaurant in Vienna, reflecting the nostalgic glamour of the Korso, Vienna's Rotten Row in the 1900 s
Clientèle: aristocracy, royalty, Haute Société; opera stars, producers and audience
Dress: designer dirndl at lunch to the occasional designer dinner jacket after the opera
Service: excellent team-work
Reservations: advisable (no dogs)
Price range: understandably high
Credit cards: AE, DC, Euro, Visa

Dinner

STEIRERECK
2 Rasumofskygasse
Telephone: 73 31 68/73 51 68
Owner/Managers: Heinz and Margarete Reitbauer
Closed: Saturday; Sunday; public holidays
Open: 12.00/a.m.–24.00/12 p.m.
Cuisine: Franco-Italo-Austrian cuisine sophistiquée
Chef de cuisine: Heinz Reitbauer
Specialities: beef in aspic with pickled tongue; terrine of calves' offal, sage and wild mushrooms; char ravioli in crab butter; breast of wild duck in juniper sauce

with cranberries; dumplings of curd cheese (Topfen) and mascarpone in elderberry sauce; white peaches in yoghurt sauce
Location: between the Central Station and the Prater; near the Rotunda Bridge (Rotundenbrücke)
Setting: recently renovated; luxurious almost to the point of pomposity (but not quite)
Amenities: bar; open-air dining on terrace; car park; air conditioning
Atmosphere: country-castle charm
Clientèle: popular rendezvous for the after-theatre crowd; diplomats, industrialists and families en fête
Dress: fairly conservative
Service: welcoming and a little ceremonious
Reservations: advisable (no pets)
Price range: fairly aristocratic
Credit cards: AE

Dinner

KÖNIG VON UNGARN
10 Schulerstrasse
Telephone: 52 65 20
Owner/Manager: Pedro Masana
Closed: never
Open: 12.00/a.m.–15.00/3 p.m. and 18.00/6 p.m.–22.30/10.30 p.m.
Cuisine: Viennese and international
Specialities: Viennese boiled beef (Tafelspitz) with vegetables; saddle of veal with dill sauce; médaillons of venison
Location: in the Hotel ›König von Ungarn‹
Setting: in a 16th-century building; vaulted ceiling with marble columns; classic-style décor with period furniture; crystal chandeliers; elegant table-settings
Amenities: hotel; private dining room; two bars; car parking in the vicinity
Atmosphere: understatedly harmonious; welcoming but stylish
Clientèle: well-informed, well-heeled, well-dressed, well-travelled and (sometimes) well-known
Dress: rather conventional
Service: knowledeable and professional
Reservations: advisable (no pets)
Price range: on the expensive side
Credit cards: DC, Visa

Lunch

PALAIS SCHWARZENBERG
9 Schwarzenbergplatz
Telephone: 78 45 15
Owner/Manager: Werner Breitenecker
Maître: Philipp Reichenberger
Closed: never
Open: 12.00/a.m.–14.30/2.30 p.m. and 18.00/6 p.m.–23.00/11 p.m.

Cuisine: traditional Austrian and classic French
Chef de cuisine: Benny Poppe
Specialities: boiled beef (Tafelspitz); sole with goose liver; goose liver goulash; pâtisserie
Location: in the Hotel Palais Schwarzenberg
Setting: three dining rooms; different colour schemes; classically elegant décor with baronial to bourgeois accessoires; the most beautiful terrace in Vienna (open-air dining in summer overlooking the gardens)
Amenities: hotel; private dining rooms (2–30 persons); pianist; car park
Atmosphere: intimate; nostalgic; as if time had stood still during the heyday of the Hapsburg monarchy
Clientèle: visiting dignitaries with a predilection for the finer things in life, plus a sprinkling of discriminating locals
Dress: appropriately stylish
Service: suave perfectionism
Reservations: essential
Price range: aristocratic
Credit cards: all major

Dinner

MATTES
8 Schönlaterngasse
Telephone: 52 62 75
Owner/Manager/Chef de cuisine: Rudolf Schmolz
Closed: Sunday; August
Open: 18.30/6.30 p.m.–24.00/12 p.m.
Cuisine: nouvelle with a Viennese accent
Specialities: fish and shellfish; fillet of whitefish (Egli); saddle of lamb; game and poultry; nougat parfait
Location: a psalm away from the cathedral (Stephansdom)
Setting: understated luxury; sophisticated and elegant
Amenities: air conditioning
Atmosphere: harmonious and exclusive
Clientèle: prelates, presidents and professors; company directors, successful actors and producers
Dress: tends towards the conservative
Service: unobtrusive
Reservations: essential (no dogs)
Price range: inevitably expensive
Credit cards: AE, DC, Euro, Visa

Dinner

ZU DEN DREI HUSAREN
4 Weihburggasse
Telephone: 52 11 92
Owner/Managers: Uwe Kohl and Ewald Plachutta
Closed: Sunday (Dec–Mar and Jul–Aug); five weeks holiday end of July – end of August
Open: 18.00/6 p.m.–dawn

Cuisine: Viennese and light inventive
Chef de cuisine: Ewald Plachutta
Specialities: goose liver on mushroom noodles with mange-tout; cream of asparagus soup with basil; home-made lobster soup with puff pastry; sauté of lamb with stuffed courgettes and potato médaillons; calf's heart with cream; offal with dumpling (Salonbeuscherl mit Serviettenknödel); Husarenpfannkuchen; Schmankerlparfait with cherries; mousse of white and dark chocolate with praliné sauce
Location: near St. Stephen's Cathedral (Stephansdom) and Kärntnerstrasse
Setting: the epitome of Viennese tradition and culture; antique furniture, original oil paintings, tapestries and valuable carpets; candlelight, fresh flowers, soft music – timeless elegance and comfort
Amenities: private dining rooms (50 persons); bar; air conditioning; pianist
Atmosphere: perfect for any occasion, from pompous feasts to quiet séparée dinners
Clientèle: local gourmets frequently outnumbered by visiting celebrities from the Kings of Sweden and Nepal to Richard Nixon
Dress: jacket and tie
Service: appropriately multilingual
Reservations: essential (no dogs)
Price range: excusably high
Credit cards: AE, DC, Euro, Visa

Dinner

OSWALD & KALB
14 Bäckerstrasse
Telephone: 52 69 92
Owner/Manager: Daimler, Milovic and Tesan GmbH
Closed: lunchtime every day
Open: 18.00/6 p.m.–1.00/a.m.
Cuisine: unpretentious
Chef de cuisine: Maridi Oswald
Specialities: traditional Styrian and old Viennese dishes; daily changing menu; beef salad; herb soup with cream; roast pork; home-made vanilla ice-cream with strawberries
Location: a psalm away from the cathedral (Stephansdom)
Setting: vaulted ceiling; rustic décor; wooden tables with white table-linen
Amenities: bar
Atmosphere: lively and casual
Clientèle: youthful; approachable and self-assured; media-men, journalists and politicians
Dress: come-as-you-please
Reservations: essential (no pets)
Price range: moderate
Credit cards: not accepted

Bistro

DO & CO (Karvansaray)
3 Akademiestrasse
Telephone: 52 64 74
Owner/Manager: Attila Dogudan
Closed: Sunday
Open: 9.30/a.m.–18.30/6.30 p.m.
Cuisine: international sophisticated
Chef de cuisine: Herbert Danzer
Specialities: fillets of sole with mushrooms; oysters (Sep–May); fillet of pork en croûte de chanterelles; salade de fruits de mer; Caribbean fruits with rum and strawberry sorbet
Location: a few waltz steps away from the Vienna State Opera
Setting: small tables; mahogany and brass predominate; 12 metre long delicatessen counter
Amenities: food store; catering service; outdoor dining on small terrace; lobster and Turkish speciality restaurants in same building
Atmosphere: casual, informal and chic – with a touch of snob appeal
Clientèle: popular and fashionable rendezvous for lunch for the successful and smart – advertising agents, entrepreneurs, sales managers and lawyers
Dress: from designer jeans to dark suit
Service: efficient and friendly, even at busy times
Reservations: essential – or get there early (dogs allowed)
Price range: rather expensive
Credit cards: not accepted

Night Bar

CARIN'S CLUB
8 Annagasse
Telephone: 52 19 75
Owner/Manager: Carin Lackner
Closed: Sunday
Open: 17.00/5 p.m.–2.00/a.m.
Location: central – vis-à-vis ›Take Five‹
Setting: small; lower salon with oval bar; first-floor lounge with tables; nostalgic décor – rose colours, candles, palm trees and mirrors
Amenities: orchestra (private parties only); air conditioning; snacks (sandwiches)
Atmosphere: romantic, chic; up and down
Clientèle: ambassadors; actors; politicians; Vienna's intellectual and showy Upper Crust, leavened by international celebrities from Falco and Julio Iglesias to Placido Domingo and Roberto Franco
Dress: légère
Service: under the cheerful guidance of Tunisian barman Joseph
Reservations: not necessary
Price range: reasonable (private membership cards entitle holder to 50% discount on drinks)

Meeting Point

REISS CHAMPAGNERTREFF
1 Marco d'Avianogasse
Telephone: 5 12 71 98
Owner/Manager: Michael Satke
Closed: never
Open: 11.00/a.m.–3.00/a.m.
Location: at the New Market (Neuer Markt); two bars away from the Opera and two beats from Kärntnerstrasse
Setting: successful avant-garde; U-shaped bar counter plus a few tables by the window
Amenities: buffet (12.00/a.m.–15.00/3 p.m. and 22.00/10 p.m.–1.00 a.m.); snacks (lobster soup, toast with snails or caviar; oysters in season); air conditioning
Atmosphere: chic; sophisticated
Clientèle: youngish, dynamic and on the way up, plus quite a few who have already made it – Niki Lauda, Udo Jürgens and local prominenti from the world of business and politics
Dress: self-consciously eye-catching – from way-out to way-in
Service: friendly and efficient
Credit cards: DC

Café

DEMEL
14 Kohlmarkt
Telephone: 66 17 17
Closed: never
Open: 9.00/a.m.–19.00/7 p.m.; (Sunday and public holidays) 10.00/a.m.–19.00/7 p.m.
Specialities: Sacher Torte (a slight variation on the so-called original one); confectionery
Location: behind the Hofburg
Setting: Austria's imperial court confectioners; fin-de-siècle flair at its most grandiose
Amenities: private dining rooms; buffet at lunchtime
Atmosphere: the most typically Viennese of the colourful palette of historic coffeehouses which the capital offers
Clientèle: characteristically heterogeneous
Service: matronly waitresses in black dresses who still address the customer in the third person (›Will the well-born lady take her coffee with milk, cream, whipped cream or rum?‹)

Bar

CONTE
3 Kärntner-Ring
Telephone: 52 02 42
Owner/Manager: Frau Allaschmar
Closed: Sunday; public holidays
Open: 15.00/3 p.m.–4.00/a.m.
Location: next to the Hotel Bristol and the Opera (Oper)
Setting: subdued lighting and live music
Amenities: bar; snacks and light meals; air conditioning
Atmosphere: a credit to its élite location on the Kärtnerring
Clientèle: very cosmopolitan; very select
Dress: suit and tie de rigueur
Service: waitresses with a Parisian air
Reservations: advisable

Nightclub

EDEN-BAR
2 Liliengasse
Telephone: 5 12 74 50
Owner/Manager: Heinz W. Schimanko
Closed: never
Open: 22.00/10 p.m.–4.00/a.m.
Location: city centre; a champagne cork's trajectory from the cathedral (Stephansdom)
Setting: 19th-century imperial grandeur; large room with small balcony; bandstand; dance-floor surrounded by tables and private boxes; semicircular bar
Amenities: the best live nightclub music in Vienna
Atmosphere: a Viennese institution; gay and elegant, with a hint of nostalgia
Clientèle: men of fashion mingle with aristocrats, artists and the affluent after-dinner crowd
Dress: evening dress
Service: dexterous
Reservations: advisable
Price range: on the expensive side
Credit cards: AE, DC, Euro, Visa, Carte Blanche

Amenities: discothèque; bar; snacks and steaks; air conditioning
Atmosphere: free-and-easy
Clientèle: heterogeneous collection of young, not-so-young and young-at-heart noctambules
Dress: anything goes
Service: anxious-to-please
Reservations: essential at weekends (pets permitted)
Price range: average
Credit cards: AE, DC

Heuriger

ZIMMERMANN
5 Armbrustergasse
Telephone: 37 22 11
Owner/Manager: Martin Zimmermann
Closed: lunchtime every day; Sunday; July 17th – September 4th; December 22nd – January 21st
Open: 11.30/a.m.–23.30/11.30 p.m.
Cuisine: Austrian
Specialities: new white wine (Heuriger) with buffet displaying snacks and typical local dishes; ham noodles (Schinkenfleckerl); spinach or broccoli au gratin; minced beef; roast loin of pork; curd cheese strudel (Topfenstrudel)
Location: north of city centre; in Grinzing
Setting: picture-postcard inn with trailing vines; blossoming oleander barrels and a riot of red geraniums; well-scrubbed wooden tables and well-worn wooden benches
Amenities: private dining rooms; open-air dining in inner courtyard
Atmosphere: typical Viennese Heuriger tavern
Clientèle: fairly exalted; those accustomed to treading the corridors of power and those aspiring to join them
Dress: designer casual to designer dirndl
Service: discreet
Reservations: essential (no dogs)
Price range: expense-account
Credit cards: Euro

Nightclub

TAKE FIVE
3a Annagasse
Telephone: 52 32 76
Owner/Manager: Nikolaus Czernin
Closed: Sunday; Monday
Open: 22.00/10 p.m.–4.00/a.m.
Location: in a side-street off the Kärnterstrasse; two bars away from the Opera (Oper)
Setting: one main room with a few séparées; comfortable décor

Shopping

EVERYTHING UNDER ONE ROOF
Kaufhaus Steffl   19 Kärntnerstrasse

FOR HIM
Braun   14 Graben

BEAUTY & HAIR
Intercoiffeur Ossig
4 Stephansplatz/Singerstrasse

JEWELLERY
Koechert   15 Neuer Markt

LOCAL SPECIALITIES
Fuernkranz (women's fashion)
39 Kärntnerstrasse
House of Gentlemen (men's fashion)
12 Kohlmarkt
Pomme d'Api (children's fashion)
10 Kruger Strasse
Pelz Liska (furs)
8 Kärntnerstrasse
Prachner (books)
30 Kärntnerstrasse
Lobmeyr (gifts)
26 Kärntnerstrasse
Augarten (porcelain)
3–4 Stock im Eisen Platz
Schulz, Franz (baggage & travel accessories)
Führichgasse
Wiener Handwerk (interior decorating)
1 Franziskaner Platz
Wild (food and beverages)
10 Neumarkt
Lanz Trachten (national costumes)
3 Kärntnerstrasse
Hammerer, Resi (country look)
Kärntnerstrasse

THE BEST OF ART
Ariadne   (contemporary art)
6 Bäckerstrasse, Tel. 52 94 79
Curtze, Heike   (contemporary art)
15/14 Seilerstätte, Tel. 52 93 75
Hilger, E.   (modern art/prints)
5 Dorotheergasse, Tel. 52 53 15
Insam, Grita   (contemporary art)
6 Köllner Hofgasse, Tel. 52 53 30
Galerie Krinzinger (contemporary art)
16 Seilerstätte, Tel. 5 13 30 06
Nächst St. Stephan   (contemporary art)
1/II Grünangergasse, Tel. 52 12 66
Ulysses   (contemporary art)
21 Opernring, Tel. 57 12 26
Würthle   (20th-century paintings)
9 Weihburggasse, Tel. 52 23 12
Bednarczyk   (17th-19th-century works
of art, furniture, old master paintings),
12 Dorotheergasse, Tel. 52 44 45/52 71 26
Demmer, M. u. H.   (jewellery)
1 Göttweihergasse, Tel. 52 07 39
Galerie bei der Albertina   (art nouveau,
art déco)
1 Lobkowitzplatz, Tel. 53 14 16
Kovacek, Peter   (glass)
2 Stallburggasse, Tel. 52 83 58
Siedler, Georg Wilhelm   (16th–19th century antiques)
3 Kohlmarkt, Tel. 52 17 41
Zacke   (oriental art)
15 Schulerstrasse, Tel. 52 22 23
Dorotheum   (auctioneers)
11 Dorotheergasse, Tel. 5 28 56 50

The City

For the art-loving pleasure traveller the countenance of this most Flemish of cities – where even the opera is sung in translation – is a shimmering blend of warm colours and vivid chromatics overlaid with translucent shadows and luminous reflections. Antwerp – the home of Peter Paul Rubens, of Jacob Jordaens, Anthony van Dyck and the other disciples of the North European Baroque school, of Frans Hals, Pieter Brueghel and Hieronymus Bosch – is a town where the glorious past is constantly on view in the Renaissance-gabled houses and the neo-classical mansions tucked away in the winding alleyways, in the magnificent Gothic cathedral (the biggest in Belgium), or in the magnificent town-houses which border the tree-lined avenues and the medieval squares. Architecture and paintings reflect Antwerp's position as the largest city in the world in the sixteenth century, and as the richest in the seventeenth, its prosperity resting on its weaving trade and its location as a commercial centre and trading crossroads between France and the Netherlands, between Germany and the Belgian coast. Yet vying with this forum of museums and monuments is the bustling reality of the present – the city on the River Scheldt is the fourth most important port in the world after Rotterdam, New York and London, thanks to the Albert canal and the deep water river channel. As such it is the seat of heavy industries – zinc, copper and lead smelting, car manufacturing and chemicals, but it is also – more glamourously – the world capital for trade in uncut diamonds. The large Jewish community controls the buying and selling, the cutting and polishing, of the most precious of gemstones in the square mile surrounding the Pelikaanstraat. Antwerp is a city which harmonizes the illustrious remnants of the past and the concrete actuality of today as in a Flemish painting – a stylized Belgian trademark, a place where trade marks success.

Founded: 7th century; Antwerpen (Flemish)/Anvers (French) – ›the detached hand‹.

Far-reaching events: 837 – invaded by Normans; 1312 – the town receives its charter; 1460 – the world's first stock exchange founded here; 16th century – the largest city in the world; 17th century – the richest city in the world, enriched by the art of Peter Paul Rubens; 1516 – sacked by the Spanish; 1648 – Treaty of Westphalia closes the Scheldt to navigation, causing the decline of Antwerp as a port; 19th century – Napoleon re-opens the Scheldt to navigation and Antwerp's modern period of expansion begins; occupied by German troops and heavily damaged during World War II.

Population: 650,000 (metropolitan area); second largest city in Belgium.

Postal code: B-2000 to 2050 (according to district)   **Telephone code:** 3

Climate: continental and cloudy; proximity to the sea has a clearing influence.

Best time to visit: May to September.

Calendar of events: *Flanders Festival* (Aug–Oct) – Europe's musical élite in concerts, opera, ballet and jazz sessions; *Biennial Sculpture Festival* (in uneven years) – in the open-air museum of Middelheim Park.

Fairs and exhibitions: *BOUW & PREFAB SALON* (Jan) – building and prefabrication show; *HOLIDAY AND SPRING SHOW* (Jan/Feb); *JE HUIS . . . EN THUIS* (Feb) – home decoration show; *BUROTIKA* (Mar) – office equipment and computer industry fair; *ANTWERPS MEUBELSALON* (Mar) – building show; *HORECANT* (Apr) – enterprises fair; *INTERNATIONAL TRADE FAIR* (May); *ISOLATIE & ENERGIE-SPARING* (Sep) – insulation and energy conservation; *JEDIFA* (Sep) – diamonds and jewelry; *BENELUX ROBOT AUTOMATION* (Oct); *VLOEREN, WANDEN, HAARDEN* (Nov) – floors, walls and fireplaces; *KEUKEN EN SANICOMFORT* (Nov) – kitchens and bathrooms; *INTERNATIONAL FOOD AND DOMESTIC COMFORT FAIR* (Dec).

Best view of the city: from the tower of the *Notre-Dame Cathedral.*

Historical and modern sights: *Notre-Dame Cathedral* (1352–1520) – the largest Gothic church in Belgium, with important works by Rubens; *Grote Markt* – Antwerp's forum, with Gothic *Town Hall* and 16th and 17th-century patrician houses; *St. Carolus Borromeuskerk* – Baroque church with a fine façade; *Rubenshuis* – home of the artist between 1610 and 1640; *Plantin-Moretus Museum* – exhibition of books and printing; *Mayer van den Bergh Museum* – paintings and objets d'art; *Steen Maritime Museum* – in a 9th-century fortress; *Koninglijk Museum voor Schone Kunst* – art collection with an incomparable collection of works by Rubens, Van Dyck, Cranach and other masters; *Handelsburs* – the world's first stock exchange.

Special attractions: *Antwerp Diamond Centre* – the largest in the world ; the *Windmill* on the left bank is a lovely reminiscence of energy before OPEC; the *Harbour* can be toured by car or in a Flandria ship; the open-air museum *Middelheim*, with an important collection of sculptures by Rodin, Henry Moore etc; the *coffee-houses* in the town centre – a warm, old-world atmosphere; *Zoo* – one of the best in Europe.

Important companies with headquarters in the city: *BASF* (chemicals); *Bell Telephone* (telecommunications); *Metallurgie Hoboken Overpelt* (metals); *Siemens* (electronics); *Agfa-Gevaert* (photographic systems); *Tecnomatic* (robots); *Bayer* (chemicals); *Esso; General Motors Continental; Ebes; Belgian Petroleum; Petrochim; J. G. A. O.; Cargill; Mercantile-Beliard; Degussa Antwerp; SIBP; Interescant.*

Airport: Antwerp-Deurne, ANR; Tel.: 30 58 10; 3 km/2 miles.

The Headquarters

SWITEL

2 Copernicus-laan
B–2018 Antwerp
Telephone: 23 16 7 80
Telex: 33 965 eurant
Telefax: (03) 2 33 02 90
General Manager: Pierre Vogt
Affiliation/Reservation System: Golden Tulip, Horis, Utell
Number of rooms: 350 (9 suites)
Price range: BF 2,600–18,500
Credit cards: all major
Location: central
Built: 1974
Style: modern de luxe
Hotel amenities: valet parking, limousine service, car rental, fitness centre, massage, indoor swimming pool, sauna, solarium, Turkish bath, whirl-pool, 2 outdoor tennis courts, health club, grand piano, secretarial services, newsstand, tobacconist
Room amenities: colour tv, video, minibar, Reuter 24-hour news on tv (pets allowed)
Bathroom amenities: bidet, bathrobe, hairdrier
Room service: 24 hours
Laundry/dry cleaning: same day
Conference rooms: 7 (up to 600 persons), all audio-visual equipment, closed circuit tv in ballroom
Golden Gate Bar: (opens 11.00/a.m.), Patrick (barman)
Restaurant: ›De Beukelaer‹ (6.00/a.m. to 23.00/11.00 p.m.) rustic décor, M. Moncef (chef de cuisine), M. Robert (maître), French and regional cuisine

Spoiled globe-trotters, used to the Ritzes, Grands and Palaces of the world, may not fall in love at first sight with the former Eurotel, but then Genevois Pierre Vogt does not want to compete with the house of Rubens and is not expecting many scattered roamers from the Marbella-Monte-Carlo-Mykonos trail, either. Antwerp is all business, with two sacred pastimes – les beaux-arts and la bonne cuisine. Of the former you can have a taste when you stay in the spectacular Salvador Dalí Suite, complete with gilt jacuzzi, designer chairs, ikebana décor and a wide-angle view over the city; the latter is one of the Switel's fortes – in the restaurant as much as in the truly 24-hour room service and in their banqueting department. A sparkle away from the diamond business centre and around the corner from the Central Station and the zoo, the location is perfect – and so is the Switel altogether. The welcome by the English voiturier is as much a joy as the glittering foyer, the fast check-in, the comfortable rooms, the multi-lingual service throughout, swimming pool, sauna, fitness centre, tennis courts and the exceptional cuisine in the De Beukelaer *restaurant. Swiss tradition of inn-keeping transplanted into this perfectly kept and serviced house more than justifies this modern establishment's byname – The Leading Hotel of Antwerp.*

The Hideaway

DE ROSIER

21–23 Rosier
B–2000 Antwerp
Telephone: 2 25 01 40
Telex: 33 697 rosant
Owner/General Managers: Bob Claes, Theo Bonné, Walter de Bie
Number of rooms: 15 (3 suites)
Price range: BF 5,000–25,000
Credit cards: AE, DC, EC
Location: city centre
Built: 1627
Style: Empire/Regency/manor house style
Hotel amenities: car rental desk, sauna, solarium, grand piano, indoor swimming pool
Room amenities: mini-bar (pets welcome)
Bathroom amenities: bathrobe
Room service: suites only
Laundry/dry cleaning: 24 hours
Conference rooms: 3 (up to 60 persons)
Bars: for residents only
Restaurant: ›De Rosier‹ (12.00/a.m.–14.30/2.30 p.m. and 19.00/7.00 p.m.–21.30/9.30 p.m.) Marc Rigout (chef de cuisine), French cuisine, open-air dining in summer
Private dining rooms: three

The narrow street in the heart of the oldest part of Antwerp gives no hint to the unsuspecting visitor of the unanticipated treasure-house in store behind the dignified seventeenth-century façade. One of the patrician town-houses reflecting the city's mercantile prosperity at that time, De Rosier – a Top Twenty Charm Hotel according to the famous IN World Guide – is a hideaway which exudes an air of rural enchantment in marked contrast to its urban setting. Behind the fine front door begins a world of studied beauty, boudoir elegance and finesse. Observant newcomers who noticed the antique shop next door will evince no surprise at finding this city manoir furnished in similar style, each item, impeccably chosen and strategically placed, a period piece worthy of a Sotheby's auction. The fifteen bedrooms are all different – named, not numbered – and portray a gamut of moods and styles for every taste and every season. Regency and Empire predominate, with an abundance of burnished mahogany and an elegance of form offset by pretty fabrics, Flemish paintings and oriental rugs. The entrance-hall is almost classic in its marble-floored austerity and the winter-garden restaurant brings the freshness of perpetual spring to the grayest December day. The Roman-style indoor swimming pool and Florentine walled garden evoke nostalgic yearnings for summer days in sunnier climes. The Three Musketeers of Antwerp's hôtellerie have created in De Rosier a private universe in which the aesthetic harmony of a Van Dyck portrait is allied to a profound sentiment of spiritual well-being.

Lunch

DE LEPELEER
8–10 Lange Sint-Annastraat
Telephone: 2 34 22 25
Owner/Manager: Antwerp Entertainment/Marleen Sels
Closed: Sunday; Saturday lunchtime; two weeks in August; between Christmas and New Year
Open: 12.00/a.m.–14.00/2 p.m. and 19.00/7 p.m.–22.00/10 p.m.
Cuisine: French (nouvelle)
Chef de cuisine: Van Elen
Specialities: fish; game in season
Location: central
Setting: 16th-century house in cobbled alley; beamed ceiling, open staircase, unrendered brickwork and quarry-tiled floor; open fireplace; copper and pewter accessoires; Delft pottery and contrasting modern paintings; lace tablecloths
Amenities: lounge area with leather armchairs; open-air dining on terrace
Atmosphere: restful and relaxing
Clientèle: descendants of the Flemish weavers who once lived in this part of the city; businessmen and the occasional tourist en passant
Dress: fairly sober
Service: friendly and efficient
Reservations: advisable (dogs allowed)
Price range: fairly expensive
Credit cards: AE, DC, Euro, Visa, Master Charge

Lunch

LA RADE
8 E. van Dyckkai
Telephone: 2 33 49 63/2 33 37 37
Owner/Manager: Gaston Laugs
Closed: Sunday
Open: 12.00/a.m.–14.30/2.30 p.m. and 18.00/6 p.m.–21.30/9.30 p.m.
Cuisine: French
Chef de cuisine: Patrick Masquillier
Specialities: calves' sweetbreads and kidneys with wild mushrooms and beer; grilled turbot with Dijonnaise sauce; lamb with vegetables in season
Location: not far from the main market-square (Grote Markt); overlooking the River Scheldt
Setting: nobleman's town house (1883); freemasons' lodge; spacious Jugendstil dining room with potted palms and period accessoires; Venetian-style mosaic ceilings
Amenities: private salon for 12 persons, with view of the river Schelde
Atmosphere: soothing, with a hint of nostalgia
Clientèle: businessmen and bankers with a penchant for the romantic
Dress: as you wish
Service: helpful and attentive; under the direction of the proprietor's son, Eric Laugs
Reservations: advisable (pets allowed)
Price range: medium
Credit cards: AE, DC, Euro, Visa

Dinner

PETRUS
1 Kelderstraat
Telephone: 2 25 27 34
Owner/Manager: Jean Jacques de Busscher and Josy Peeters
Closed: never
Open: 12.00/a.m.–14.30/2.30 p.m. and 19.00/7. p.m.–22.00/10 p.m.
Cuisine: French (nouvelle)
Chef de cuisine: Jean Jacques de Busscher
Specialities: turbot with celery; poularde with spices; crêpe soufflée with fruits according to season
Location: city centre
Setting: small dining room; modern in the classic idiom
Amenities: air conditioning
Atmosphere: businesslike
Clientèle: cross-section of men of commerce, journalists, men-in-the-street and the occasional foreign visitor
Dress: no special requirements
Service: efficient – supervised by the patron, Josy Peeters
Reservations: advisable (no dogs)
Price range: moderate
Credit cards: AE, DC, Euro, Visa

Dinner

THE FOUQUETS
17 de Keyserlei
Telephone: 2 32 62 09
Owner/Manager: Bruno de Hassella/Jerry Frateur
Closed: never
Open: 12.00/a.m.–14.00/2 p.m.; 19.00/7 p.m.–23.00/11 p.m.
Cuisine: French (nouvelle)
Chef de cuisine: Dirk Strengs
Specialities: ›Le Cardinal du Mer au four‹ (Lobster from the oven) ›Mignon de boeuf au trois garnitures‹ (Mignon with three different sauces)
Location: near central station
Setting: 1930s décor, reminiscent of the ›Cotton Club‹; lots of marble, heavy curtains, mirrors on the walls
Amenities: 2 restaurants: downstairs ›Taverne‹ for apéritif and snacks, upstairs restaurant
Atmosphere: cosy, chic
Clientèle: predominantly local habitués
Dress: fairly casual downstairs; rather formal for dinner in the restaurant
Service: always efficient
Reservations: obligatory, preferably well in advance for the weekend (pets prohibited)

Price range: rather expensive
Credit cards: all major

Lunch

KASTEEL LINDENBOS
139 Boomsesteenweg
Aartselaar (12 km/8 miles)
Telephone: 8 88 09 65/8 88 34 22
Affiliations: Aux Etapes du Bon Goût;
Club des Gastronomes; Chaîne des Rô-
tisseurs; Ordre Coteaux de Champagne
Owner/Manager: Hugo Mettens
Closed: Monday; August
Open: 12.00/a.m.–15.00/3 p.m. and
18.30/6.30 p.m.–22.00/10 p.m.
Cuisine: ›inventive‹
Chef de cuisine: Claude Kessedjian
Specialities: fricassée of lobster and
shrimps with ›coral‹ butter and wild rice;
sautéed fillet of beef and grilled duck's
liver with Pomerol and shallots
Location: 12 km (8 miles) south of Antwerp; 20 km (13 miles) north of Brussels
Setting: castle situated in parkland;
Flemish–style interior with beamed ceiling, chandeliers and a predominance of
browns and beiges
Amenities: private dining room (80 per-
sons); open-air apéritifs and coffee on
terrace by lake with fountain; pianist; orchestra and dîner dansant (Saturday
evenings); air conditioning; car park
Atmosphere: manorial
Clientèle: bons vivants from Antwerp
(plus a few from Brussels); Haute Bourgeoisie en fête and en famille; business-
men or government officials
Dress: tends towards the conservative
Service: comme il faut
Reservations: advisable (pets prohibited)
Price range: fairly expensive
Credit cards: AE, DC

Dinner

SIR ANTHONY VAN DIJCK
16 Oude Koornmarkt (Vlaaikensgang)
Telephone: 2 31 61 70
Owner/Manager/Chef de cuisine: Marc
Paesbrugghe
Closed: Saturday; Sunday; one week at
Easter; first three weeks in August; between Christmas and New Year
Open: 12.00/a.m.–14.00/2 p.m. and
19.00/7 p.m.–21.30/9.30 p.m.
Cuisine: French
Specialities: frequently changing menu;
salad of Norway lobster and goose liver
sautéed in hazelnut oil; crayfish, sorrel
and asparagus in puff pastry; suprême de
turbot au champagne; gratin de fraises
with coconut ice-cream
Location: in the shadow of the cathedral
Setting: 17th-century Flemish renaissance; museum-style interior with period
furnishings and exquisite accessoires;
classical background music

Amenities: private dining rooms (8–30
persons)
Atmosphere: luxurious, refined ambience
created by a connoisseur with a fine eye
for culinary and artistic detail
Clientèle: local savants-vivre and discri-
minating visitors
Dress: lounge suit
Service: excellent
Reservations: advisable (pets prohibited)
Price range: predictably high
Credit cards: AE, DC, Euro

Café

DEN ENGEL
3 Grote Markt
Telephone: 2 32 08 80
Owner/Manager: Gustav Liysen
Closed: never
Open: 9.00/a.m.–5.00/a.m.
Specialities: dark and delectable ›De Ko-
ninck‹ (›The King‹) beer
Location: on the market place (Grote
Markt)
Setting: historic building; very unpreten-
tious décor
Amenities: ›Barrel‹ game (De Tun) in
which brass cylinders are tossed at the 12
holes in a board
Atmosphere: lively; a famous and popu-
lar old haunt; frequently packed
Clientèle: local devotees from all walks
of life, plus strangers from all the corners
of the earth
Service: with a smile

Bar

KULMINATOR
Vleminckveld
Telephone: 2 32 45 38
Owner/Manager: Dirk van Dyck
Closed: Sunday; public holidays
Open: 11.00/a.m.–24.00/12 p.m. (Saturday from 17.00/5 p.m.; Monday from
20.15/8.15 p.m.)
Specialities: 250 varieties of beer, all
served at the proper temperature and in
the correct glasses
Location: near the Police Tower
Setting: a typical Flemish pub with a
summer garden for fine-weather drinking
at the back
Amenities: snacks
Atmosphere: great fun for those who wish
to try out a variety of brews – particularly
the Berlin speciality after which the pub
is named, which is served extremely cold
in a receptacle smaller than a cognac
glass
Clientèle: aficionados of the malt and the
hops
Service: knowledgeable
Reservations: not necessary
Credit cards: not accepted

Shopping

EVERYTHING UNDER ONE ROOF
INNO　80–82 Meir

FOR HIM
Bracksim　1 Meirbrug

FOR HER
Louis Fèraud　2 Huidevetterstraat

BEAUTY & HAIR
Hair Studio Women　90 Frankrijklei
Harlow　26 Meir

JEWELLERY
Diamond Land　179 Venneborg Laan

LOCAL SPECIALITIES
Mr. en Mevr. Evens-Verloo
(tobacco)
158 A Amerikalei
Leonard (women's fashion)
31/32 Konigin Astrid Laan
My Lord (men's fashion)
20 Meir
Dujardin (children's fashion)
39–41 Huidevetterstraat
Benoît (leather fashion and furs)
19 Americalei
Standard (books)
55–59 Huidevetterstraat
Het Present (gifts and porcelain)
Schrijnwerkerstraat
Delvaux (baggage & travel accessories)
Leopoldstraat
Delrey (confiserie)
5 Appelmannsstraat

THE BEST OF ART
›121‹　(contemporary art)
121 Mechelsesteenweg, Tel. 2 18 68 73

Capital of Belgium, residence of the Royal Family, melting pot of the rivalling Walloons and Flemings and conference table of Europe, Brussels is – despite its quaint Old-World ambiance centering around the Grand' Place – one of the continent's most cosmopolitan communities. A mere eight miles from the plain of Waterloo, the Headquarters of NATO is now a city where four-star generals regularly sit down to dinner at three-star restaurants. The Belgians themselves refer to their capital as ›Petit Paris‹ and the sophisticated international population does lend the city's old-world ambience an undeniable air of urbanity. Here, the cultural élite comes to honour Maurice Béjart's Ballet of the 20th Century while conspicuous consumers go shopping in narrow cobblestone streets for the traditional specialities for which Belgium is known – lace, pewter, guns and chocolate. In addition to being one of the main arenas of international politics, Brussels is also one of Europe's most important industrial centres, the hub of the country's extensive iron, steel, chemical, textile and sugar industries. Brussels is indeed a ›fine built city‹ – Victor Hugo considered the ›Grand-Place‹ the most beautiful in the world – and life is as pleasant here as in medieval Bruges and in industrial Liège put together – with a touch of Paris.

Founded: 977; as a fortification by the Count of Lorraine; Bruxelles (French)/Brussel (Flemish) – ›the house in the swamp‹.

Far-reaching events: first inhabited by the Romans, then the Franks (7th century); a centre of the wool trade in the 13th century; 1384 – Brussels becomes the seat of the dukes of Burgundy; era of prosperity marked by artistic achievements (Brussels tapestries); 1516 – coronation of Charles V; 16th century – involvement in religious wars (1568 – execution of Count of Egmont) – Spanish rule; 1714 – Austrian rule; 1795 – French rule; 1815–30 – union of Holland and Belgium under the House of Orange – the Hague and Brussels joint capitals; 1830–1 – Belgium an independent monarchy, Brussels the capital; 1948–60 Benelux Union with the Netherlands and Luxembourg.

Population: 1 million; capital and largest city of Belgium.

Postal code: B-1000 to 1200 (according to district)   **Telephone code:** 2

Climate: much more pleasant all year round than most continental parts of Europe under the mild influence of the North Sea

Best time to visit: May to October, though tourist traffic is heavy from June to August.

Calendar of events: *Queen Elisabeth Music Competition* (May) for violin and piano, every two years (1986 – piano); *Avant Garde Theatre Festival* (spring, biennial – uneven years); ›*Ommegang*‹ (1st Thursday in Jul) – huge parade of the city's representatives in medieval costumes, at the ›Grand' Place‹; *Flanders Festival* (end of Aug–Oct) – international orchestras and conductors on the platform in Brussels; *Meyboom* – (Aug 9) – setting up the Maypole, in August for some reason; *Brueghel Festival* (Sep 9) – re-enactments of the famous paintings in full costume.

Fairs and exhibitions: *LEATHER GOODS FAIR* (Jan); *AQUA-EXPO* – water technology; *BATIBOUW* (Feb) – construction industry; *EUROBA* (Mar) – for bakers, chocolatiers and confectioners; *INTERNATIONAL TRADE FAIR* (Mar); *INVEST-EXPO* (Mar) – investment opportunities; *SPORT EQUIPMENT FAIR* (Mar); *AUTOTECHNICA* (Apr) – automobile accessories; *INTERNATIONAL FURNITURE FAIR* (Nov); *EUREKA* (Nov/Dec) – industrial innovations; *HORESCA* (Nov) – hotels.

Best views of the city: from the city hall at the Grand-Place; from the Atomium at the exhibition centre.

Historical sights: *Grand-Place* – Italian Baroque Landmark of the city; *Maison du Roi* – museum of the history of Brussels in a reconstructed house; *Town Hall* – pure Gothic; *Mannekin Pis* – landmark statue, à poil despite the collection of 341 costumes in the Maison du Roi; *Fine Arts Museum* – Rubens, Brueghel, Van Dyck, Franz Hals and other Flemish masters; *St. Michael's Cathedral* (13th–17th centuries); *Royal Museums of Art and History* – Belgian decorative arts, classical antiquity and Egyptian collection; *Notre-Dame-de-la-Chapelle* (13th–15th centuries) – Brabantine style church; *Museum of Musical Instruments; Palace of Justice* (19th century).

Modern sights: *European Communities* (1963–69) – star-shaped seat of the EC; *Atomium* – a molecule of steel enlarged 165 billion times; pleasant place for a stroll and a view of the *Exhibition Centre*, where the 1958 World Fair and the 1975 ›Brussels International Trade Mart‹ took place.

Special attractions: *Place du Grand-Sablon* – patrician townhouses, antique shops and a market at the weekend; *bars* in the area around the Grand-Place; the *Forest of Soignes*; *Waterloo* – the battlefield where Wellington and Blucher put an end to Napoleon's ambitions in 1815.

Important companies with headquarters in the city: *Sabena* (national airline); *ACEC* (motors and telecommunications); *Sobermap Borghans* (electricity); *Chapeaux* (urban planning and water purification); *Côte d'Or* (sweets); *Laine d'Aoust* (yarn); *Sabca* (aeroplane construction); *Solvay* (chemical products); *IBM Belgium; Petrofina* (oil); *UCB* (chemicals); *Lurgi-Benelux* (engineering); *Fourcray* (alcoholic beverages); *Pfizer* (pharmaceuticals).

Airport: Brussels – National, BRU; Tel.: 7 51 80 80; 15 km/10 miles.

The Headquarters

HYATT REGENCY

250 Rue Royale
B–1210 Brussels
Telephone: 2 19 46 40
Telex: 61 871 hyatt
Owning Company: Hyatt International
General Manager: Alfred Hurst
Affiliation/Reservation System: Hyatt Hotels
Number of rooms: 315 (14 suites)
Price range: BF 5,260 (single)
BF 7,810 (double)
BF 9,360–BF 28,215 (suite)
Credit cards: all major
Location: central
Built: 1976 (recently renovated)
Style: modern
Hotel amenities: garage, valet parking, limousine service, car rental, ballroom, shopping gallery, ›Regency Club‹
Main hall porter: Andrea Tasselli
Room amenities: air conditioning, colour tv (pets welcome)
Bathroom amenities: bathrobe and hairdrier in Regency Club rooms and suites
Room service: 24 hours
Laundry/dry cleaning: same day, weekend service
Conference rooms: 12 (for up to 510 persons), all facilities
Bars: ›Hugo's Bar‹ (11.00/a.m.–23.00/11.00 p.m.) Mario Orro and Sergio Pezzoli (barmen), live piano music on Fridays and Saturdays, snacks
Restaurant: ›Hugo's Restaurant‹ (7.30/a.m.–10.30/a.m., 12.00/a.m.–14.30/2.30 p.m. and 19.30/7.30 p.m.–22.30/10.30 p.m.) nouvelle cuisine, Michel Addons (chef de cuisine)
Private dining rooms: banqueting facilities for up to 800 persons

Among the ›chains‹ (hotel corporations giving their names and image as well as their management to individual establishments all over the world) Hyatt certainly stands out like a dépendance of Sotheby's on the flea market. The concept is luxury, service and efficiency, with visual elements and culinary individuality adapted to the city itself. Overlooking both the Botanic Gardens and the adjacent Jacqes Brel Cultural Centre, within walking distance of the old city and many international institutions, this regal Regency is no exception to Hyatt's philosophy. Lively bar off the lobby, elegant Hugo's restaurant one of the alternatives to the starred temples of gargantuan joys, and countless comfort in the suites above. New World amenities reign in Old World tastefulness, and Christian Le Prince sees to it that American presidents feel as pleased as diplomats, businessmen and incognito travellers from the corners of the globe.

The Hideaway

AMIGO

1–3 Rue de l'Amigo
B-1210 Brussels
Telephone: 5 11 59 10
Telex: 21 618 amigho
Owning company: Société Hôtelière Saint-Michel
General Manager: Pierre Bouchard
Affiliation/Reservation Systems: Utell, Koma Hotel Rep.
Number of rooms: 183 (11 suites)
Price range: BF 3,550–4,700 (single)
BF 4,200–5,150 (double)
BF 7,550–16,500 (suite)
Credit cards: Access, AE, DC, EC, MC, Visa
Location: city centre, behind the Grand' Place
Built: 1958
Style: traditional (Louis XV, Louis XVI)
Hotel amenities: garage, valet parking, house limousine service, car rental desk
Main hall porter: Jos Joosten
Room amenities: air conditioning, colour tv (pets welcome)
Bathroom amenities: bathrobe and hairdrier, bidet (some)
Room service: 24 hours
Laundry/dry cleaning: same day
Conference rooms: 5 (up to 180 persons), all facilities
Bars: ›Bar Amigo‹ (11.30/a.m.–23.00/11 p.m.), Spanish Tavern
Restaurants: ›Restaurant Modern‹ (12/a.m.–14.30/2.30 p.m. and 19.00/7.00 p.m.–21.30/9.30 p.m.) international and classic cuisine

The Amigo is a well-designed post-war hotel on enviable ground immediately behind the Gothic Town Hall on Brussels' Grand-Place. It shares all the charm of the area but, thanks to its ›back-street‹ location and excellent sound-proofing, provides a haven of tranquillity from the noise and bustle of the capital. The intérieur is reminiscent of an elegant country house, with chandeliers, silk-lined walls, oak panelling, velvet upholstery and Spanish colonial furniture. The suites on the sixth floor have gabled terraces overlooking the city. The public rooms, with their attractive pillars and nooks, provide an ideal setting for a quiet drink, a business chat or a small reunion, as well as the most sought-after platform for festivities in style, from place to service to cuisine. The concierge will be your best ›amigo‹ during your stay – you can almost forget about a secretary when you do ›business‹ with him. There are many fine hotels in the countryside around Brussels but none can match the combined advantages of location, style, individuality and intimacy all put together.

Lunch

LA MAISON DU CYGNE
9 Grand-Place
Telephone: 5 11 82 44/5 11 40 86
Owner/Manager: Théo Bogaerts
Closed: Saturday lunchtime; Sunday; one week in mid-August; one week at Christmas
Open: 12.00/a.m.–15.30/3.30 p.m and 19.15/7.15 p.m.–24.00/12 p.m.
Cuisine: grande tradition and nouvelle
Chef de cuisine: François van Gasbecq
Specialities: casserole of lobster and turbot with asparagus; fish with garlic; saddle of lamb; game; warm quail salad; scallops with lobster coral; pheasant à la brabançonne
Location: on the main square of Brussels (Grand'Place)
Setting: in a beautiful historic building with a little statue of Everard t'Serclaes set in its façade; according to the legend, those who rub his arm and make three wishes are assured of good fortune; lift to dining room upstairs; panelled walls, sumptuous banquettes, open fireplace and a huge rôtisserie-grill at one end; room dividers lending a feeling of intimacy
Amenities: private dining room (up to 70 persons); car park (attended) in the Rue Duquesnoy
Atmosphere: redolent of the history of the self-declared ›Petit Paris‹ – luxurious, hospitable and with a hint of romance
Clientèle: visiting premiers, presidents, princes and four-star generals, plus the local dignitaries wishing to impress them
Dress: rather conservative (pin-stripes allowed; medals optional)
Service: discreet, sincere and unaffected
Reservations: strongly recommended
Price range: inevitably expensive
Credit cards: AE, DC, Euro, Visa

Lunch

L'ECAILLER DU PALAIS ROYAL
18 Rue Bodenbroek
Telephone: 5 12 87 51/5 11 99 50
Manager: René Falke
Closed: Sunday; public holidays; August
Open: 12.00/a.m.–14.30/2.30 p.m. and 19.00/7 p.m.–22.30/10.30 p.m.
Cuisine: French
Chef de cuisine: Basso Attilio
Specialities: the best seafood in town; ›Solettes de Zeebrugge Meunière‹; suprême of turbot with green aniseed and aubergines; outstanding selection of French wines and champagnes; exquisite desserts; chocolate cake with coriander cream
Location: central, in the ›Grand-Sablon‹ district

Setting: classical décor, very stylish, elegant and comfortable first class restaurant
Atmosphere: a gourmet's paradise, with total concentration on cuisine, wines and impeccable presentation of the two
Clientèle: industrialists, lawyers and ladies of High Society; well-to-do foreigners mingle with distinguished burghers of Brussels
Dress: fairly conservative and elegant
Service: helpful
Reservations: advisable
Price range: rather expensive
Credit cards: AE, DC, EC, Visa

Lunch

DE BIJGAARDEN PVBA
20 Van Beverenstraat, Groot-Bijgaarden
Telephone: 4 66 44 85/4 66 26 75
Affiliations: Aux Etapes du Bon Goût
Owner/Manager: W. Vermeulen
Closed: Saturday lunchtime; Sunday; one week at Easter; three weeks in August/September
Open: 12.00/a.m.–14.45/2.45 p.m. and 19.00/7 p.m.–21.45/9.45 p.m.
Cuisine: French
Chef de cuisine: Olivier Schlissinger
Specialities: marinated salmon with dill; oven-roast turbot with mustard-seed sabayon; saddle of lamb spiked with truffles; caramelized pear with gratin d'amandes
Location: at Groot-Bijgaarden, 7 km (4 miles) west of Brussels (exit no. 11 on ring road)
Setting: small dining room; elegantized rustic luxury; dominated by long buffet table in centre
Amenities: private dining room (26 persons); car park
Atmosphere: refined
Clientèle: Brussels Haute Bourgeoisie en fête, plus a selction of visiting academics, industrialists and epicures
Dress: rather elegant
Service: impeccable
Reservations: advisable
Price range: grande maison
Credit cards: AE, DC, Euro, Visa

Dinner

LA CRAVACHE D'OR
10 Place A. Leemans
Telephone: 5 38 66 76
Owner/Manager: Madame Maillan
Open: 12.00/a.m.–14.30/2.30 p.m. and 19.30/7.30 p.m.–21.45/9.45 p.m.
Cuisine: nouvelle and classic
Chef de cuisine: Luigi Cicciriello
Specialities: ducks' liver with carrots and honey; wolf-fish in a vinegar sauce with

truffles and basil; la truffe à la croque au sel

Location: in one of Brussels' more elegant areas, close to the Avenue Louise
Setting: stylish; furnished in classic style
Amenities: private dining rooms
Atmosphere: sophisticated intimacy, relaxed and refined
Clientèle: admirers of Luigi Cicciriello's cuisine, businessmen, lovers and a gourmet bishop or two
Dress: pin-striped suits allowed
Service: impeccable; supervised by Robert Benhaddou
Reservations: essential
Price range: medium high
Credit cards: all major

Dinner

COMME CHEZ SOI
23 Place Rouppe
Telephone: 5 12 29 21/5 12 36 74
Affiliations: Traditions et Qualité
Owner/Manager/Chef de cuisine: Pierre Wynants
Closed: Sunday; Monday; between Christmas and New Year; July
Open: 12.00/a.m.–14.00/2 p.m. and 19.00/7 p.m.–22.00/10 p.m.
Cuisine: original and innovative
Specialities: les mousses Wynants (eel, salmon, chicken liver, woodcock, ham); fillets of sole with Riesling mousseline sauce and grey shrimps; suprême of steamed sea-perch; sauté of calves' sweetbreads with truffles and wild mushrooms; breast of duckling with apples; caramelized pears in puff pastry; hot soufflé tart with fruit purée
Location: in the heart of the city
Setting: behind an old-fashioned greentiled façade; small, rather narrow dining room reminiscent of a 1920s bistro; mahogany and green glass screens; glass door between kitchen and dining room; framed photographs
Amenities: private dining room (20 persons); air conditioning
Atmosphere: sublime culinary perfection in an ambience of discreet and modest bourgeois comfort, reflecting the personality of Pierre Wynants – one of the great chefs of our time who prefers the kitchen to the limelight
Clientèle: connoisseurs of fine food, following in the footsteps of Winston Churchill; local habitués to Bocuse, Girardet, Vergé and Chapel on their weekend off
Dress: fairly conventional
Service: disarmingly authoritative and attentive; directed by the wife of the patron, Maria-Therese Wynants
Reservations: absolutely essential – preferably well in advance
Price range: medium
Credit cards: AE, DC

Lunch

ROMEYER
109 Groenendaalsesteenweg
Hoeilaart (11 km/7 miles)
Telephone: 6 57 05 81/6 57 10 16
Telex: 20 385 AMCB
Affiliations: Traditions et Qualité; Relais et Châteaux (Relais Gourmand); Union Internationale des Clefs d'Or
Owner/Manager/Chef de cuisine: Pierre Romeyer
Closed: Sunday evening; Monday (except public holidays); February; August
Open: 12.00/a.m.–14.30/2.30 p.m. and 19.00/7 p.m.–21.30/9.30 p.m.
Cuisine: French (classic and nouvelle)
Specialities: oysters in champagne; truite au bleu à ma façon; sole farcie Romeyer; stuffed shrimps à la Nantua; calves' sweetbreads Brillat Savarin; duckling au Chambertin; steak Châteaubriand with truffles; saddle of rabbit with rhubarb sauce or raisins; symphonie de desserts
Location: at Hoeilaart, 11 km (7 miles) south-east of Brussels
Setting: in the Forest of Soignes; park (floodlit at night) with lake, fountain and swans; spacious elegant rustic dining room – exposed beams, leather-upholstered chairs and benches – with picture windows overlooking garden
Amenities: private dining room (60 persons); bar; car park
Atmosphere: relaxing; luxuriously away-from-it-all
Clientèle: expense-account gourmets; culinary journalists; resident aristocracy and well-heeled visitors
Dress: tenue de ville
Service: as elegant as the setting
Reservations: advisable (dogs allowed)
Price range: appropriately high
Credit cards: AE, DC, Euro, Visa

Lunch

BARBIZON
95 Welriekendedreef, Jezus-Eik
Overijse (13 km/8 miles)
Telephone: 6 57 04 62/6 57 14 29
Affiliations: Relais et Châteaux (Relais Gourmand)
Owner/Managers: Alain and Myriam Deluc
Closed: Tuesday; Wednesday; February; three weeks during July/August
Open: 12.00/a.m.–14.30/2.30 p.m. and 19.00/7. p.m.–21.45/9.45 p.m.
Cuisine: ›au goût du marché‹
Chef de cuisine: Alain Deluc
Specialities: jowl of salmon with green peppercorns, sauce grelette; homard en chemise (the shirt is meant to be eaten too); tartare of wolf-fish and salmon with hazelnut oil; sauté of duck with ginger and turnips; calves' sweetbreads with celery hearts and truffles

Location: at Jezus-Eik, 13 km (8 miles) south-east of Brussels
Setting: whitewashed timbered Normandy-style villa in well-cared-for garden on the edge of the forest of Saignes; elegant rustic dining room with timbered ceiling and unrendered brick walls; décor in dark brown, pink and beige; fine china and glass
Amenities: private dining room (40 persons); outdoor dining in garden and on terrace; car park
Atmosphere: a luxuriously civilized fête champêtre
Clientèle: Brussels savants-vivre plus large numbers of Germans, Americans and other rich foreigners
Dress: no special requirements
Service: welcoming, smiling and efficient
Reservations: advisable (pets permitted)
Price range: appropriately high
Credit cards: AE, DC, Euro, Visa

Dinner

HOSTELLERIE BELLEMOLEN
9 Bellemolenstraat
Essene (15 km/9 miles)
Telephone: (53) 66 62 38
Owner/Manager: Pierre van Ransbeeck
Closed: Sunday evening; Monday; July; between Christmas and New Year
Open: 12.00/a.m.–14.30/2.30 p.m. and 19.00/7 p.m.–21.30/9.30 p.m.
Cuisine: French
Chef de cuisine: Henri van Ransbeeck
Specialities: according to season; hop sprouts' menu in spring, game menus in the autumn; turbot with baby vegetables and cress sauce; lamb with hop sprouts and gratin dauphinois; saddle of rabbit with three sorts of mustard; suprême of pheasant with green cabbage and celery purée; crêpe soufflée with raspberry juice
Location: at Essene; 15 km/9 miles west of Brussels
Setting: 12th-century water-mill, lovingly restored by the present owner; two dining rooms and lounge-bar area with a wealth of old beams; sloping ceilings; open fireplace; wrought iron light-fittings; tapestries, velvet upholstery; period accessoires
Amenities: hotel; bar; air conditioning; attended car park
Atmosphere: seductively nostalgic; one of the most beautiful places to eat – and sleep – on the Continent
Clientèle: le Tout Bruxelles from the worlds of politics and the arts, plus romantically-inclined businessmen tired of the Belgian capital
Dress: designer elegant to Dior original
Service: irreproachable
Reservations: advisable (no dogs)
Price range: fairly expensive
Credit cards: AE, DC, Euro

Dinner

LE PARC SAVOY
3 Rue Emile Claus
Telephone: 6 40 15 22
Owner/Manager: Alain van der Hove
Closed: Sunday; Saturday lunch time
Open: 12.00/a.m.–14.30/2.30 p.m and 19.00/7 p.m.–22.00/10 p.m.
Cuisine: classic
Chef de cuisine: Willy Roesens
Specialities: fish pâté with tomato sauce; minced steamed scallops with butter; suprême du turbot with tomatoes and vegetable mousse; bitter chocolate ice-cream with sauce anglaise
Location: 2 km (1 mile) from city centre
Setting: London-look awning and shrubs outside; light, airy (picture windows and white walls); mixture of classic and Art Déco; original paintings
Amenities: bar (with pianist); car parking service at lunchtime and for functions (car park 5 minutes' walk away); private dining room (30 persons) with separate entrance
Atmosphere: reminiscent of a London club; soothing and sophisticated, but without the corpses in leather armchairs hidden behind the ›Times‹
Clientèle: post-office and pre-dinner drinks crowd earlier on; serious diners give way to hungry after-theatre set in search of an elegant snack as the evening wears on
Dress: from Lanvin casual to lounge-suit to the occasional dinner-jacket
Service: young, enthusiastic and well-trained
Reservations: advisable (pets prohibited)
Price range: fairly expensive
Credit cards: AE, DC, Euro, Visa

Dinner

VILLA LORRAINE
75 Avenue du Vivier d'Oie
Uccle (8 km/5 miles)
Telephone: 3 74 31 63/3 74 25 87
Owner/Manager: Madame Marcel Kreusch/Henri van Ranst
Closed: Sunday; first three weeks in July
Open: 12.00/a.m.–14.30/2.30 p.m. and 17.30/5.30 p.m.–21.45/9.45 p.m. (last orders)
Cuisine: French
Chef de cuisine: Freddy van de Casserie
Specialities: oysters in champagne; grilled Norway lobster; duckling with preserved figs; casserole of calves' sweetbreads
Location: at Uccle; 8 km (5 miles) south of city centre
Setting: converted farmhouse in the Bois de la Cambre; pretty décor; lush carpeting and gilt lumières; glassed-in veranda overlooking garden

Amenities: private dining room (36 persons); open-air dining on terrace; bar; attended car park
Atmosphere: that of an elegant country house whose owner understands the art of gracious living
Clientèle: distinguished; discriminating; self-confident; successful
Dress: jacket and tie for dinner; more casual for lunch
Service: impeccable; warm and welcoming; directed for the past 20 years by Henry van Ranst
Reservations: recommended (dogs on leads only)
Price range: justifiably expensive
Credit cards: AE, DC, Euro, Visa

Café

LE VIEUX SAINT-MARTIN
38 Place du Grand-Sablon
Telephone: 5 12 64 76
Owner/Manager: Philippe Niels
Closed: never
Open: 9.00/a.m.–24.00/12 p.m.
Location: central
Setting: small tavern-restaurant with ultra-modern décor; leather upholstery
Amenities: private dining room (120 persons); terrace (apéritifs only); air conditioning; car park
Atmosphere: confidential to intimate, depending on your companion
Clientèle: jet-set lawyers, Common Market ministers and globe-trotting tourists – plus the occasional ordinary man-in-the-street
Service: to perfection

Meeting Point

LA CHALOUPE D'OR
24 Grand-Place
Telephone: 5 11 41 61/5 11 29 32
Owner/Manager: Jacques Achedigian
Closed: never
Open: 9.00/a.m.–2.00/a.m.
Specialities: Scotch Campbell (beer!) from a pewter mug
Location: on the main square (Grand'Place)
Setting: three large rooms on three floors; elegantized rustic décor
Amenities: terrace; air conditioning; car park
Atmosphere: an historic moment at any hour of the day
Clientèle: tired tourists; thirsty men-in-the-street; casual passers-by and local habitués
Service: fast but never furious
Reservations: essential, preferably well in advance (!)

Bar

L'EQUIPE
40 Rue de Livourne
Telephone: 5 38 31 84
Owner/Manager: SODIRES (Société anonyme)
Open: 22.00/10 p.m. to dawn
Location: near the Place Stéphanie; a few Gucci steps from the city's most important hotels
Setting: in a former patrician townhouse; private bar with winter garden and small lounge
Amenities: air conditioning; car park (Hotel Ramada) next door
Atmosphere: an ideal place to unwind
Clientèle: as popular with the early-evening cocktails crowd as with the local night owls
Service: proficient
Reservations: advisable
Credit cards: AE, DC, Euro, Visa

Bar

L'INTERDIT
45 Rue de Livourne
Telephone: 5 38 18 71
Owner/Manager: Gérard Debailleul
Closed: Saturday; Sunday
Open: 17.00/5 p.m. – 3.00/a.m. (at least)
Location: near the Place Stéphanie
Setting: bar-café; rustic décor; leather banquettes; small dance floor with strategically-placed mirrors; old cannon (purely decorative!)
Amenities: air conditioning; soft music, often in rather nostalgic vein
Atmosphere: well on the way to becoming an institution; confidential to intimate, depending on your mood (or your companion's)
Clientèle: Brussels' crème de la crème; Beau Monde, top brass, businessmen and a few ordinary mortals
Dress: jacket and tie de rigueur
Service: hospitable; efficiently supervised by Henriette D'hondt
Reservations: not necessary
Credit cards: AE, DC, Visa

Nightclub

CROCODILE
5 Rue Duquesnoy
Telephone: 5 11 42 15/Telex: 62 905 Roywit
Owner/Manager: Walter Jakobitsch
Closed: Sunday; two days at Christmas
Open: 22.00/10 p.m. to dawn
Location: in the basement of the Hôtel Royal Windsor
Setting: tropical-style décor; dark green leather upholstery and potted palms

Amenities: bar; discothèque; special shows at the weekend (sometimes a flamenco band); air conditioning; car park
Atmosphere: decorously intimate, with a hint of exoticism
Clientèle: heterogeneous; hommes d'affaires, university lecturers, students and secretaries plus lovers of any age, nationality and sex
Dress: relatively conventional to positively eye-catching
Service: efficiently enthusiastic
Reservations: recommended

Nightclub

SAINT LOUIS
35 Rue Defacgz
Telephone: 5 38 35 07
Affiliations: Club of Clubs
Owner/Manager: Jacques Dupont
Closed: never
Open: 21.00/9 p.m.–4.00/a.m.
Location: near the Avenue Louise, one of Brussels' most fashionable thoroughfares
Setting: tiny; intimate; elegant
Amenities: bar; discothèque
Atmosphere: refined; exclusive
Clientèle: well-mannered, well-heeled and well-travelled; ambassadors, international barristers and celebrities from Claude Brasseur to Jackie Ickx
Dress: jacket de rigueur
Service: irreproachable
Reservations: obligatory

Shopping

EVERYTHING UNDER ONE ROOF
Innovation   Rue Neuve

FOR HIM
Degand   415 Avenue Louise

FOR HER
Nathan   158 Avenue Louise

BEAUTY & HAIR
Roger   88 Avenue Louise

JEWELLERY
Wolfers   82 Avenue Louise

LOCAL SPECIALITIES
Davidoff (tobacco)
8–10 Rue Lebeau
Mies, Louis (women's fashion)
261 Avenue Louise
de Vlaminck (men's fashion)
56 Boulevard de Waterloo
Dujardin (children's fashion)
8–10 Avenue Louise
Loewe (leather fashion)
6 Place Louise
Eduard (furs)
Port Louise
Librairie de Rome (books)
50 Avenue Louise
Chaban (gifts)
Boulevard de Waterloo
Mills (porcelain)
20 Place Stephanie
Delvaux (baggage & travel accessories)
Toison d'Or
Chandoir (interior decorating)
56 Rue de Ailes
Bernard (food and beverages)
93 Rue de Namur
Lui et Elle (perfumery)
Avenue de la Toison d'Or
Manufacture Belge de Dentelles (lace)
6–8 Galerie de la Reine
Meert, Nina (lingerie)
5 Rue Florence

THE BEST OF ART
Baronian, Albert   (contemporary art)
8 Villa Hermosa (Condenberg),
Tel. 5 12 09 78
Brachot, Isy   (contemporary art)
62a Avenue Louise,
Tel. 5 11 05 25/5 11 79 04
Guimiot, Philippe   (modern art)
138 Avenue Louise, Tel. 6 40 69 48

In the shadow of cosmopolitan Brussels, glittering Antwerp and glorified Bruges, this industrial and industrious city in the East End of Belgium is unjustifiably neglected by travellers sans portefeuille. Religious headquarters for over 1000 years, capital of coal and iron since medieval times and armoury of many countries for centuries, Liège is not only at the crossroads of commerce and stop-over for the natural beauty of the Ourthe Valley and the Ardennes Mountains, but a centre of culture in its own right, documenting its past in attractive architecture, impressive treasures of art and noteworthy theatrical and musical life. Even the cuisine is of astonishing hauteur and the local gourmandises rightly praised. Georges Simenon may have left his home town for Paris to follow in the footsteps of Commissaire Maigret, and César Franck for the same destination to reach the musical zenith, but there is a distinctly French note in the ambiance of the city, despite its proximity to Germany. Located at the confluence of the Meuse and the Ourthe Rivers, overlooked by cliffs of slate, Liège is the cultural centre of French-speaking Belgium, where galleries and gourmet restaurants amiably mix with stand-up bars serving Genever in the shadow of aristocratic palaces. Classically laid out park grounds offer a green contrast to the slate roofs of the low buildings, while the faint smell of roses and the strains of the street musicians fill the air, providing a romantic accompaniment to the view of the patrician houses, the silhouettes of ruins, the quay and the charmingly antiquated dance halls. As the home of Europe's third largest inland harbour, Liège is a transportation hub, whose industries justify its reputation as a ›city of fire.‹ On the right bank of the Meuse rise the smokestacks of the city's all-important iron, steel, machinery, textiles and armaments factories, all of which contribute to making Liège one of the continent's more important industrial centres.

Founded: 705, by Bishop Lambert of Maastricht; Liège (French)/Luik (Flemish).

Far-reaching events: 717 – a bishopric; 980 – an imperial principality; 10th-12th century – Liège expands territorially and earns itself the nickname ›Athens of the North‹; 14th–15th centuries – religious wars; 1468 – Liège razed to the ground by Charles the Bold; 1477 – Liège independent, and the struggle for power between the mining and armament manufacturers' guilds and the prince-bishops begins; church rule ends with the French Revolution; 1815 – Liège becomes part of the Kingdom of the Netherlands; 1831 – unification of the Kingdom of Belgium; considerable damage in World War II.

Population: 420,000 (metropolitan area); capital of Liège province and fourth largest city in Belgium.

Postal code: B-4000 **Telephone code:** 41

Climate: continental, with ocean influences keeping it relatively mild, summer and winter.

Best time to visit: end of April to mid-October; early autumn is the prettiest time.

Calendar of events: *St. Pholien Folklore Festival* (4th Sunday in Jun); *Folk Festival* (15 Aug) – in the Ourthe-Meuse Quarter; *Nights of September* (4th Sunday in Sep) – a Walloon (Belgian French) music festival; *Living Nativity* (25 Dec) – Christmas plays.

Fairs and exhibitions: *VERT* – tourism, camping and caravan fair (Feb); *INTERNATIONAL COLLOQUIUM OF CHEMICAL INDUSTRIES* (Mar); *INTERNATIONAL FAIR* (Sep).

Best views of the city: from the Citadel; from the park above the Minorite courtyard.

Historical and modern sights: *St. Bartholemew's Church* (10th century) – former collegiate church in typical Meuse region style, with a neo-classical portal and a famous bronze font; *Montagne de Bueren* – 373 stairs lead directly to the *Citadel; Palace of the Prince-Bishops* – the largest non-state Gothic building in the world, with 60 variously decorated halls and beautifully ornamented inner courtyards; *Town Hall* (18th century) – classicistic construction on the Market Square, at the centre of which can be seen the 13th century *Perron Columns*, symbols of Liège's fighting spirit of old; *Curtius Museum* – an imposing Renaissance building now housing the archeological and artisans' museum collections; *Cathedral* (13th century) – museum and an impressive display of church treasures; *St. Denis' Church* – with a Gothic choir and magnificent altar; the *Weapons Museum* – one of the largest collections of firearms in the world; *Folklore Museum* – Walloon life and customs; the *Conference Centre* – very modern, with sculptures illuminated at night.

Special attractions: *La Batte* – an open-air market which has been taking place every Sunday from 9 a.m. to 1 p.m. since the 16th century, on the magnificently romantic Quai de la Goff; the *Marionette Theatre* – well-known among aficionados around the world; the *Planetarium*.

Important companies with headquarters in the city: *Air Liquide Belge* (gas); *Confort & Chaleur* (plumbers' appliances); *Cop & Portier* (building); *Derwa* (meat); *Dumont-Wautier* (limestone quarrying); *Hauterat & Watteyne* (bulk coal and oil); *Imperial Hournal* (printing); *Jubilé* (cigars); *La Meuse S.A.* (newspaper); *Legia Labo* (pharmaceuticals; *Lhoist e Leons* (lime); *Somef* (removals).

Airport: Liège-Bierset, LGG; 8 km/5 miles; Sabena, Liège, Tel.: 23 58 35, 33 85 82 or 23 24 30.

The Headquarters

RAMADA

100 Boulevard de la Sauvenière
B–4000 Liège
Telephone: 22 49 10
Telex: 41 896 ramaho
General Manager: J. C. Robinet
Affiliation/Reservation System: Ramada International
Number of rooms: 105 (5 suites)
Price range: BF 2,600–5,000
Credit cards: AE, DC, MC, Visa
Location: central, 10 km/6 miles from airport
Built: 1973 (recently renovated)
Style: modern
Hotel amenities: garage, valet parking, house limousine service, car rental desk, travel agent, ballroom, grand piano, non-smoker areas, hairstylist, drugstore, newsstand, florist
Room amenities: air conditioning, colour tv, video, mini-bar (pets welcome)
Bathroom amenities: bathrobe; hairdrier
Room service: 6.00/a.m.–24.00/12 p.m
Laundry/dry cleaning: same day
Conference rooms: 5 (up to 500 persons)
Bar: ›Cercle de la Sauvenière‹ (11.00/a.m.–2.00/a.m.), Michel Pauquet (barman)
Restaurant: ›Rôtisserie de la Sauvenière‹ (11.00/a.m.–24.00/12.00 p.m.), R. Gielen (chef de cuisine), nouvelle cuisine, pianist
Private dining rooms: for 10–24 persons

Half-way between the medieval church of St. Martin, perched high on a hilltop, and the picturesque old houses clustered round the former citadel of the prince-bishops stands the unadorned low-rise concrete edifice which houses the Liège dépendance of the American Ramada group. Twentieth-century functionalism has replaced Gothic flights of fancy to produce a modern hotel which is comfortable enough for the textile manufacturers and steel executives who come to do business in the ›city of fire‹. Vaguely transatlantic no-fuss décor in the reception areas is replaced in the bedrooms by co-ordinated soft furnishings in warm but neutral tones. The ambiance of the restaurant, by contrast, is typically Liégeoise. The wooden beams and pillars create a feeling of rustic intimacy in spite of the size; red table-linen, nouvelle cuisine, friendly service, live piano-music and a pleasantly informal atmosphere make the Rôtisserie de la Sauvenière as popular amongst the locals as is the bar, which in summer moves outside to become a boulevard café à la française. The Ramada is, in fact, a well-run hotel combining streamlined efficiency and genuine local colour.

The Hideaway

LA COMMANDERIE

28 Rue Joseph-Pierco
B–4155 Villiers-Le-Temple
(20 km/13 miles)
Telephone: (85) 51 17 01
Telex: 42 220 eurofr
Owner: The Lorneau family
Affiliation/Reservation System: Relais et
Châteaux
Closed: January 4th–end of February
Number of rooms: 14 (2 suites)
Price range: BF 1,700 (single)
            BF 1,750–3,000 (double)
            BF 3,000 (suite)
Credit cards: AE, EC, Visa
Location: 20 km/13 miles from Liège city
centre, 80 km/50 miles from Brussels air-
port
Built: 1257

Style: country manor house with antique
style décor
Hotel amenities: valet parking, outdoor
swimming pool
Room amenities: colour tv (pets allowed)
Bathroom amenities: bidet, bathrobe
Room service: breakfast only
Laundry/dry cleaning: 24 hours
Conference rooms: 2 (up to 300 persons)
Sports (nearby): tennis, golf, riding, fish-
ing
Restaurant: ›La Commanderie‹ (12.00/
a.m.–15.00/3 p.m. and 19.00/7.00 p.m.–
21.30/9.30 p.m.), French cuisine

*Hidden away in a tiny hamlet amongst the
gorse-covered hills of the Ardennes, a leisurely half hour's drive downstream of
Liège, is one of the most romantically historic relais in Europe. Seven hundred years
ago the Commanderie was the headquarters of a chapter of the Knights Templar,
whose aim it was to convert the heathen.
The former fortress has been lovingly converted by the Lorneau family, whose ancestors have lived in the historic village on
Charlemagne's Highway for more than
three hundred years, into a temple of
beauty and authenticity with a hint of mystery which again attracts pilgrims from far
and wide. The medieval trappings have
been faithfully preserved; the ancient stone
walls, the high pitched roof with exposed
beams and supporting joists; the flagged
floors, the minstrels' gallery and the open
fireplaces. To these have been added period furnishings and antique museum-
pieces, creating an ambience of aesthetic
harmony enhanced by the natural beauty
of the surrounding gardens. Jean-Claude
Lorneau, son of the mentor of this tranquil
retreat, serves scallops in puff pastry with
cress purée and calf's sweetbreads with
chervil fit for a banquet in the best courtly
tradition, whilst the tradition hospitalière
in this haven of peace and plenty seems to
belong to the realm of the fairy tale.*

Lunch

ILE DE MEUSE
2 Esplanade de l'Europe (Palais des Congrès)
Telephone: 43 15 52
Owner/Manager: Service de Restauration du Palais des Congrès
Closed: Sunday evening
Open: 12.00/a.m.–15.30/3.30 p.m. and 18.30/6.30 p.m.–22.00/10 p.m.
Cuisine: French
Chef de cuisine: Joseph Boschi
Specialities: frequently changing menu according to season; chicken legs in brown beer; pear ›fine bouche‹
Location: central; in the Palais des Congrès
Setting: dining room with classic-style décor directly overlooking the River Meuse
Amenities: private dining rooms (25–1000 persons); open air dining on terrace; bar; air conditioning; car park
Atmosphere: understated elegance
Clientèle: characteristic mélange of local hommes d'affaires, hommes de politique, hommes de lettres et hommes de loisir
Dress: as you like it
Service: good-natured and rapid; directed by maître d'hôtel Raymond Hardy
Reservations: advisable
Price range: fairly expensive
Credit cards: AE, DC, Euro, Visa

Lunch

L'ECAILLER DU PERRON
(›Les Ouhès‹)
21 Place du Marché
Telephone: 23 32 25
Owner/Manager: Louise Cordonnier
Closed: Sunday; Saturday for lunch; July 15th to 31st
Open: 11.00/a.m.–22.00/10 p.m.
Cuisine: French
Chef de cuisine: Alex Sulon
Specialities: médaillons of crayfish; magret de canard aux pleurotes
Location: central; on the famous Place du Marché
Setting: an antique ›brasserie‹; classic décor
Atmosphere: comfortable elegance, secluded and peaceful
Clientèle: managers, lawyers, members of the liberal professions and distinguished tourists with a gourmet's palate
Dress: rather conservative
Service: professional, friendly and helpful
Reservations: essential
Price range: medium high
Credit cards: AE, DC, EC, Visa

Dinner

LA GRASSE POULE
18 Rue de la Poule
Telephone: 22 37 19
Owner/Manager: Joseph Ledent
Closed: Sunday; Wednesday evening; July
Open: 12.00/a.m.–13.30/1.30 p.m. and 19.00/7 p.m.–21.00/9 p.m.
Cuisine: French
Chef de cuisine: Joseph Ledent
Specialities: escargots à la forestière; salad with fillet of smoked duckling; rabbit's head with cauliflower
Location: next to the Place du Marché
Setting: small but very comfortable restaurant with classic décor
Atmosphere: intimate, refined, welcoming
Clientèle: businessmen, doctors, lawyers and industrialists
Dress: rather elegant
Service: impeccable
Reservations: essential
Price range: average
Credit cards: not accepted

Lunch

LE CHENE-MADAME
70 Avenue de la Chevauchée (Bois de Rognac)
Neuville-en-Condroz (18 km/11 miles)
Telephone: 71 41 27
Owner/Manager: Marcel Tilkin
Closed: Sunday evening; Monday; August; December 23rd–January 5th; one week at Easter
Open: 12.00/a.m.–14.00/2 p.m. and 19.00/7 p.m.–21.00/9 p.m.
Cuisine: traditional and nouvelle ›au goût du marché‹
Chef de cuisine: Marie-Louise and Philippe Tilkin
Specialities: mousse of chicken livers; salmon and asparagus with sauce mousseline; calves' kidneys à la liégeoise with juniper berries; lobster fricassée; scallops in steamed seaweed with white sauce and caviar
Location: 18 km/11 miles south-west of Liège on the road to Marche
Setting: modern country house on the edge of the forest; comfortable salon for apéritifs with open fireplace and cavernous armchairs; recently-renovated dining room in warm shades of brown and gold
Amenities: bar; air conditioning; attended car park
Atmosphere: very Belgian; ceremonious, festive and yet a warm-hearted and welcoming family-run restaurant
Clientèle: large faithful following of local pillars of society; middle-aged, well-to-do and rather conservative – plus

growing numbers of visitors from further afield attracted by Marie-Louise Tilkin's culinary reputation
Dress: conventional
Service: leisurely, knowledgeable and professional advice from Marcel Tilkin, aided by son Jean-Luc and head waiter Guy Sullon (who speaks fluent German)
Reservations: recommended
Price range: fairly – but justifiably – expensive
Credit cards: AE, DC

Lunch

LA RIPAILLE
12 rue la Goffe
Telephone: 22 16 56
Owner/Manager: Robert Paulus
Closed: Sunday; Monday for lunch
Open: for lunch and dinner, till 22.00/10 p.m.
Cuisine: highly individual, local and French cuisine
Specialities: fried black pudding with onions and grapes; calves' kidneys à la liégeoise; rabbit with prunes in cream sauce; salade liégeoise
Location: close to city centre
Setting: typical bistro-like restaurant; nostalgic décor
Atmosphere: relaxed, cheerful and with a sense of humour
Clientèle: businessmen en fête and en famille, lovers of any age, sex and nationality and a sprinkling of interesting foreigners
Dress: as you like it
Service: anxious-to-please; helpful
Reservations: essential
Price range: medium

Dinner

LE DOMAINE DU CHATEAU DE FRAINEUX
4 Rue de la Chapelle
Nandrin (26 km/11 miles)
Telephone: (085) 51 14 37
Owner/Manager: Madame J. Pieteur
Closed: Tuesday evening; Wednesday; January; February
Open: 12.00/a.m.–14.00/2 p.m. and 19.00/7 p.m.–21.00/9 p.m.
Cuisine: French
Chef de cuisine: Claude Noaillon
Specialities: fricassée of lobster with cucumbers; ballotines de foie gras au jus de truffes; saddle of lamb with spring vegetables; pigeon de Bresse with sweet garlic and Burgundy; baked figs and peaches with cinnamon and vanilla ice-cream

Location: at Fraineux; 2 km/1 mile west of Nandrin – 26 km/16 miles south-west of Liège
Setting: historic seventeenth-century manor-house; extensive park, lake and chapel; two pretty dining rooms decorated in local Renaissance style; attractively-laid tables
Amenities: hotel (6 bedrooms); private dining room (50 persons); car park
Atmosphere: beguilingly tranquil and refreshing, with a hint of romance
Clientèle: businessmen tired of Liège; local Haute Bourgeoisie en fête and en famille – and gourmet birds of passage
Dress: Sunday casual to Sunday best
Service: exemplary
Reservations: advisable; pets permitted
Price range: fairly expensive
Credit cards: AE, DC, Euro, Visa

Dinner

AU VIEUX LIEGE (›Maison Havart‹)
41 Quai de la Goffre
Telephone: 23 77 48
Owner/Manager: Renzo d'Inverno
Closed: Sunday; Wednesday evening; public holidays; August
Open: 12.00/a.m.–15.00/3 p.m. and 18.30/6.30 p.m.–22.00/10 p.m.
Cuisine: French
Chef de cuisine: Jean Jaques Cornet
Specialities: shrimps and lobster in aspic with smoked salmon; Challans duckling with limes; game (in season); fillets of sole ›Vieux Liège‹; médaillons of lamb stuffed with foie gras in Marsala sauce; iced sabayon; pistachio ice-cream with raisins macerated in Sauternes
Location: city centre; on the river Meuse, near the Pont des Arches
Setting: 16th-century listed building; lower storeys timber-framed; upper storeys slate-covered with mullioned windows; elegantized rustic dining rooms with unrendered brick walls, floral curtains, antique furniture, domestic bric-à-brac and white napery
Amenities: private dining rooms (up to 70 persons); air conditioning
Atmosphere: a living museum of Walloon language and culture; pleasantly homelike and welcoming
Clientèle: local Liégeois and curious travellers in almost equal numbers – plus periodic visitations by presidents, premiers and monarchs seeking a suitable setting to impress visiting dignitaries
Dress: fairly casual to rather formal
Service: smiling and friendly
Reservations: advisable (pets permitted)
Price range: moderately expensive
Credit cards: AE, DC, Euro, Visa

Meeting Point

CLUB PRIVE ›LE MUST‹
145 Boulevard de la Sauvenière
Telephone: 22 04 82
Owner/Manager: Vinciane Quoidbach
Closed: Tuesday
Open: 22.30/10.30 p.m.–6.00/a.m.
Location: central
Setting: marble floor; mirrored walls; marble columns; quiet lounge; luxurious bar; dance hall
Amenities: discothèque; with-it dancing at the weekend; American bar during the week; air conditioning
Atmosphere: congenial and vaguely club-like in the lounge; companionable in the bar; chic and lively on the dance-floor
Clientèle: Liège's Younger Set for the dancing; middle-aged (but not moribund) senior managers and members of the liberal professions for a relaxing cocktail in the lounge
Dress: bon chic, bon genre; no T-shirts or track suits
Service: efficient
Reservations: advisable (pets permitted)
Credit cards: AE

Shopping

EVERYTHING UNDER ONE ROOF
Bon Marché, Au   Place de la République Française

FOR HIM
Gray   8 Rue de l'Université

FOR HER
Féraud, Louis   112 Rue de la Cathédrale

BEAUTY & HAIR
Delboves intercoiffeur   27 Vinâve d'île

JEWELLERY
Matelot   12 Place de la Cathédrale

LOCAL SPECIALITIES
M. et Mme. Carlo-Troussart (tobacco)
161 Rue Haute Wez
Deman, Ancien Maison (women's fashion)
21 Vinâve d'île
Duck (men's fashion)
46 Galeries Cathédrale
Ptilapin (children's fashion)
Passage Lemonnier
Irina, peaussier (leather fashion)
9 Rue des Dominicains
Nihon, Nestor & Fils (furs)
13 Rue de l'Université
Librairie Liègoise des Arts (books)
38 Galeries Cathédrale
Sélection-contemporain (gifts)
21 Passage Lemonnier
Tilquin (porcelain)
94 Rue de la Cathédrale
Borsut, le Maroquinier
(baggage & travel accessories)
8 Place de la Cathédrale
Destexhe Deprez (interior decorating)
Place de la Cathédrale
Jean-Marie & Fils (food and beverages)
8 Rue Lulay
Dans un Jardin (perfumery)
Centre Commercial Opéra, Place de la République Française
Verlane, Juliette (shoes)
29 Vinâve d'île
Fil à fil (chemisier)
18 Vinâve d'île
Lutetia (lingerie)
36 Galeries Cathédrale

With a name that would conjure up visions of the Spanish queen before almost everybody ›behind‹ the Iron Curtain would think of the 5000-year-old capital of Bulgaria, Sofia is not only one of the lesser known metropolises of Europe but also one of the most neglected. True, the city is better known for its Soviet-satellite bondage according to the individualistic interpretation of ›Life's a Party‹ rather than for its coat-of-arms motto ›Ever growing, never old‹, and no-one would search for lust and luxury here, but for the newcomer to Bulgaria's showcase the wide streets, mammoth squares and monumental marble edifices render a certain grandeur à la socialiste, and the tree-lined avenues and the 500 parks make it one of the world's greenest cities. Traces of the Thracians are found in the immense gold treasures, but Greek, Roman, Byzantine, Turkish and Russian vestiges are dwarfed by the functional architecture employed after the war to rebuild the majority of the city. Enthroned on a plateau embraced by the Vitosha mountain range, Sofia is a queen among cities in Eastern Europe. Only half an hour away from some of the continent's most picturesque peaks, the city's surroundings offer the visitor a wonderland for wanderers and a winter paradise for skiers. But politics and economics are the only game in town, with congresses, conventions and symposia taking place continuously in the prestigious pomp-Palace of National Culture. The major industries not only have their headquarters in the capital, but much of the fabrication is done in the city itself – heavy industry, textiles, tobacco, leather, electronics, cars, chemistry, foodstuffs, chemical and pharmaceutical goods. After hours, Sofia presents itself as the arena for culture – two opera houses, theatres, concerts and folklore on stage or alfresco distract somewhat from the everyday business. Visiting churches and museums will have to make up for Western pastimes, but as with all Second-World countries human relations are the most rewarding pastimes in Sofia as well.

Founded: capital of the Roman province of Dacia, with traces of a settlement going back to 5,000 B.C.

Far-reaching events: 1st century A. D. – the Romans colonize and fortify the town; 4th century – Constantine the Great rules the city; 5th century – Goths and Huns perpetually at war over Sofia; 6th century – Emperor Justinian has the city rebuilt following the plundering by Attila and his Huns; 1018 – Sofia goes Byzantine; 1329 – the city passes to the kingdom of Bulgaria; 1382 – five centuries of Ottoman rule in Sofia begin; 1878 – the Russians liberate the city and Sofia becomes the capital of the principality of Bulgaria; 1946 – Bulgaria becomes a People's Republic, retaining Sofia as its capital.

Population: 1 million, capital and largest city of Bulgaria.

Postal code: BG-Sofia   **Telephone code:** 2

Climate: continental with Mediterranean influences.

Best time to visit: May to July; September; for winter sports November to April.

Calendar of events: *Koleduvane Festival and Survakane Festival* (Nov and Jan) – a daringly long carnival season cum New Year's celebration; *New Bulgarian Music* (Feb) – a festival for Bulgarian composers; *National Choir Festival* (May); *International Sofia Music Weeks* (May/Jun) – the biggest musical event in Bulgaria; *Sofia Philharmonic Orchestra* – season from September to June; *Bulgarian Jazz and Contemporary Music Show* (Nov) – just what the name says.

Fairs and exhibitions: *GREAT INTERNATIONAL BOOK FAIR* (May).

Best views of the city: from various points in the nearby Balkan Mountains; from the top of the television tower; from the top floor restaurants of the hotels ›Sofia,‹ ›Moskva,‹ and ›Vitosha-New-Otani.‹

Historical sights: *Sveti Georgi* (4th century) – a round church from Roman times, once a bath-house, with magnificent frescoes; *Sveta Sofia* (6th century) – early Christian basilica; *Alexander Newski Memorial Church* – Neo-Byzantine with 12 gilded cupolas, seating for 5000 and a unique collection of Bulgarian icons; *Sveta Petka Samardshijska* (14th century) – another church, medieval with layered frescoes; the *Bujuk Mosque* (15th century) – the golden treasures of Valtshitrau; *Banja-Baschi Mosque* (16th century) – with a richly ornamented prayer hall, a beautiful example of Turkish-Islamic architecture; *National Art Gallery* in the former royal palace – modern Bulgarian artists and foreign masters.

Modern sights: *National Culture Palace Ljudmila Shivkova* – a new glass and steel construction with excellent facilities including a convention hall for 4700 delegates, a press centre for 1200 journalists, restaurants, cafés, a post office and shops.

Special attractions: *Freedom Park* – 58 acres of avenues, rose gardens, an observatorium, stadium and tennis courts; *folklore concerts*; *puppet theatre*.

Important companies with headquarters in the city: *Agromachinaimpex* (agricultural machinery); *Bulgarcoop* (co-operative association); *Bulgarkonserv* (jams and preserves); *Bulgartabac* (cigarettes); *Elektroimpex* (electrical products); *Filmbulgaria* (films); *Intransmasch* (machinery); *Intercommerce* (trade); *Machinoexport* (machinery); *Mineralimpex* (mineral products); *Pharmachim* (chemicals and pharmaceuticals).

Airport: Sofia, SOF, 9 km/6 miles; Tel.: 7 12 01 or 72 07 58; Balkan Air, Tel.: 8 84 93 or 88 44 33.

The Headquarters

VITOSHA NEW OTANI

100 Anton Ivanov Boulevard
BG–Sofia
Telephone: 62 41 51
Telex: 22 797
Owning Company: Balkantourist
General Manager: C. Christov
Affiliation/Reservation System: Inter-hotel Chain
Number of rooms: 454 (14 suites)
Price range: $ 56 (single)
  $ 74 (double)
Credit cards: AE, DC, BA, Visa, EC, Access, MC
Location: 3 km/2 miles from city centre, 10 km/6 miles from airport
Built: 1979
Style: modern
Hotel amenities: garage, valet parking, house limousine service, grand piano, health club, beauty salon, sauna/solarium, massage, hairstylist, newsstand, boutique, tobacconist, florist, babysitting, swimming pool
Room amenities: air conditioning, colour tv, mini-bar/refrigerator
Bathroom amenities: separate shower cabin, bidet, bathrobe, hairdrier, phone
Room service: 24 hours
Laundry/dry cleaning: same day, weekend service
Conference rooms: 7 (for up to 1000 persons), simultaneous translation into 5 languages, sonorization, radio-microphones, overhead and film projectors, secretarial services, ballroom
Bars: ›Convention‹ (16.00/4.00 p.m.–22.00/10.00 a.m.) modern style; ›Hotel Cocktail Sport Interclub‹ as Convention Bar
Restaurants: ›Vitosha‹ (12.00/a.m.–15.30/3.30 p.m. and 19.00/7 p.m.–23.30/11.30 p.m.) European and Bulgarian dishes, Oriental dishes, Vitosha style, orchestra, open-air dining; ›Lozenets‹ (19.00/7 p.m.–23.30/11.30 p.m.) Lozenets-Bulgarian cuisine, Lozenets-Bulgarian national restaurant, orchestra, open-air dining; ›Sakura‹ (12.00/a.m.–15.30/3.30 p.m. and 19.00/7 p.m.–23.30/11.30 p.m.) Sakura-Japanese restaurant, orchestra, open-air dining; ›Moussala‹ (12.00/a.m.–15.30/3.30 p.m. and 19.00/7 p.m.–23,30/11.30 p.m.) European and Bulgarian national dishes, Oriental dishes, Moussala-modern style, orchestra, open-air dining, panorama view
Ambassador Nightclub: (22.00/10.00 p.m.–4.00/a.m.) orchestra, variety programme

If native son Christo were to wrap the New Otani in pink satin it would certainly be declared a work of art. Unwrapped – it represents the ultimate in hôtellerie in this People's Republic. Thanks to the entrepreneurial Japanese, East and West can meet here for business – and nothing else.

Lunch

SOFIA RESTAURANT
3 Narodno Sobranie Square
Telephone: 87 88 21
Affiliations: Interhotels
Owner/Manager: Balkantourist
Open: 12.00/a.m.–15.00/3 p.m. and
19.00/7 p.m.–23.30/11.30 p.m.
Cuisine: Bulgarian and European
Location: in the heart of the city
Setting: two restaurants (Main and Panorama) – one large with modern décor and the smaller Mehana Restaurant, decorated in national style
Amenities: open-air dining on terrace of Panorama Restaurant; pianist; orchestra; bar; nightclub
Atmosphere: comfortable, if a little impersonal
Clientèle: local luminaries; Muscovites on holiday; a sprinkling of visitors from Vladivostock and places west
Dress: correspondingly
Service: helpful
Reservations: advisable
Price range: fairly expensive
Credit cards: AE, DC, Euro, Visa, Bankamericard, Access, Mastercard, Carte Blanche

Dinner

RUBIN
1 Lenin Square
Telephone: 87 47 04
Affiliations: Interhotels
Owner/Manager: Balkantourist
Open: 12.00/a.m.–24.00/12 p.m.
Cuisine: national and European
Location: central
Setting: comfortable medium-sized restaurant (by Sofian standards) furnished in the modern idiom
Amenities: terrace
Atmosphere: characteristic Balkantourist ambience
Clientèle: local hommes d'affaires mingle with businessmen from Belgrade to East Berlin
Dress: tends towards the conservative
Service: friendly
Reservations: advisable
Price range: moderately expensive
Credit cards: AE, DC, Euro, Visa, Bankamericard, Access, Master Card, Carte Blanche

Lunch

PARK HOTEL MOSKVA
25 Nezabravka Street
Telephone: 7 12 61
Affiliations: Interhotels
Owner/Manager: Balkantourist
Open: 6.30/a.m.–10.30/a.m.; 12.00/a.m.–15.00/3 p.m. and 18.00/6 p.m.–23.00/11 p.m.
Cuisine: European, Bulgarian and Slavonic
Location: 3 km (2 miles) from city centre; in the Park Hotel; in the Park of Liberty, one of Sofia's largest public gardens
Setting: modern; large and rather impersonal, but quite comfortable
Amenities: Winter Garden (12.00/a.m.–23.00/11 p.m.); Russian Restaurant (19.00/7 p.m.–23.00/11 p.m.); Mehana Restaurant (19.00/7 p.m.–23.00/11 p.m.); Panorama Restaurant (19.30/7.30 p.m.–2.00/a.m.); nightclub
Atmosphere: Interhotels charm
Clientèle: families en fête; government officials; civil servants and the occasional overseas visitor
Dress: conservative to national costume
Service: apt to be on the slow side, especially at busy times
Reservations: advisable
Price range: de luxe category
Credit cards: AE, DC, Euro, Visa, Bankamericard, Access, Mastercard, Carte Blanche

Dinner

VODEMICHARSKI MEHANI
Dragalevtsi Residential Area
(5 km/3 miles)
Telephone: 67 10 01
Affiliations: TK Balkantourist, Sofia
Owner/Manager: Balkantourist
Open: 11.30/a.m.–23.00/11 p.m.
Cuisine: European and Bulgarian
Location: 5 km (3 miles) from city centre; in the Dragalevtsi Residential Area in the foothills of the Vitosha Mountains
Setting: Bulgarian national style
Amenities: open-air dining on terrace; folklore programme
Atmosphere: worth the drive – especially on a summer evening; colourful live entertainment in traditional Bulgarian style
Clientèle: popular venue for family excursions, or for businessmen hoping to impress visiting industrialists
Dress: Sunday casual to Sunday best
Service: efficient
Reservations: advisable
Price range: relatively expensive
Credit cards: AE, DC, Euro, Visa, Bankamericard, Access, Master Card, Carte Blanche

Bar

SOFIA BAR
3 Narodno Sobranie Square
Telephone: 87 88 21
Affiliations: Interhotels
Owner/Manager: Balkantourist

Closed: never
Open: 8.00/a.m.–0.30/12.30 a.m.
Location: in the same building as the Sofia Restaurant
Setting: modern; relatively small
Amenities: restaurant and nightclub in same building
Atmosphere: favourite venue for post-breakfast or pre-dinner drinks
Clientèle: manufacturers, committee members – and the occasional thirsty tourist
Dress: grey flannel prevails
Service: friendly
Reservations: advisable
Credit cards: AE, DC, Euro, Visa, Bankamericard, Access, Mastercard, Carte Blanche

Bar

SOFIA NIGHTCLUB
3 Narodno Sobranie Square
Telephone: 87 88 21
Affiliations: Interhotels
Owner/Manager: Balkantourist
Closed: never
Open: 23.00/11 p.m.–4.00/a.m.
Location: in the same building as the Sofia restaurant
Setting: modern
Amenities: restaurant; bar; orchestra; variety programme
Atmosphere: Sofia-chic
Clientèle: the young; the not-so-young; those hoping to regain their lost youth
Dress: GUM to Gucci
Service: reliable
Reservations: advisable
Credit cards: AE, DC, Euro, Visa, Bankamericard, Access, Master Card, Carte Blanche

Nightclub

PARK HOTEL MOSKVA
25 Nezabravska Street
Telephone: 7 12 61
Affiliations: Interhotels
Owner/Manager: Balkantourist
Closed: never
Open: 22.00/10 p.m.–4.00/a.m.
Location: in the Park Hotel Moskva
Setting: modern
Amenities: hotel and restaurants in the same building; orchestra; variety programme
Atmosphere: fairly quiet to moderately loud
Clientèle: rendezvous for Sofia's night owls

Dress: high-fashion; low-fashion; no-fashion
Service: good
Reservations: advisable
Credit cards: AE, DC, Euro, Visa, Bankamericard, Access, Master Card, Carte Blanche

Nightclub

PARK HOTEL MOSKVA BARS
25 Nezabravska Street
Telephone: 7 12 61
Affiliations: Interhotels
Owner/Manager: Balkantourist
Closed: never
Open: 8.00/a.m.–23.00/11 p.m.
Location: in the Park Hotel Moskva
Setting: two bars; modern furnishing and accessoires
Amenities: hotel; restaurants and nightclub in the same building
Atmosphere: popular and informal rendezvous for the local In-Crowd, for pre-lunch or post-office drinks
Clientèle: cross-section of men from the media, men from the ministries and visiting students of Sofia night-life
Dress: unobtrusive to eye-catching
Service: reliable
Reservations: advisable
Credit cards: AE, DC, Euro, Visa, Bankamericard, Access, Mastercard, Carte Blanche

Shopping

EVERYTHING UNDER ONE ROOF
Zar 8 Kajolan

JEWELLERY
Mineralsouvenier 10 Boulevard Ruski

LOCAL SPECIALITIES
2 Boulevard Ruski (leather fashion)
4 Slavjanska (leather fashion)
5 Kajolan (furs)
133 Rakovski (furs)

THE BEST OF ART
Aho ›Hemus‹ (modern art)
7 Lewski, Tel. 44 31 48

The City

To discover the riches of the ›Golden City‹ ›you have to change your life‹, according to one of the ›Mother of all Cities‹ favourite sons, melancholic poet Rainer Maria Rilke. Melancholy has always been in the air of this 1000-year old capital of Bohemia, the Holy Roman Empire, of the sciences and culture, of revolutions and repressions and of the state of Czechoslovakia since 1918. In the music of Bedřich Smetana, and Antón Dvořák, the writings of Franz Kafka and Franz Werfel, and in the acts of Jan Hus and Jan Palach this trait so characteristic of Prague shines through as in the citizens of today. Even if you don't change your life for the exploration of this ›diamond in the world's stone crown‹, your life will be enriched by the beauty, dignity and melancholic warm-heartedness of the city where the Big Brother and his sycophants cannot erase the glorious past, so tangible here that one can almost grasp it. No matter where one looks there are innumerable buildings which have either played some momentous role in history or are so imposing that one feels they ought to have done so. Of the many cities which have, at one time or another, been called the most beautiful in Europe, few can match the Czechoslovakian capital for uniqueness and individuality. The lighthouse of that deep, dark and mysterious part of Europe known as Bohemia, Prague is an architectural treasure chest, a maze of Baroque, rococo, Renaissance and Art Nouveau masterpieces dominated by the hauntingly Gothic spires of the Cathedral of St. Vitus. And yet, despite its seeming imponderability, it is a city teeming with vitality and spontaneity, as if the irregular angularity of the buildings had inspired the people with a special instinct for diversity. Settled on both banks of the Vltava River, Prague is an important port city and industrial centre, producing automobiles, machinery and a large range of other industrial goods. As the country's capital, it is not only the seat of government, but also the most important cultural and intellectual centre, worthy to fertilize the world again after the next ›Spring in Prague‹.

Founded: 9th century; Praha – ›a threshold‹.

Far-reaching events: 973 – founding of the bishopric Prague; 1234 – building of the city walls, around what is now referred to as the ›Old City‹; 1346 – residence of emperors of the Holy Roman Empire; 1348 – founding of university, the first in Central Europe; 1526 – Bohemia under Hapsburg rule; 1618 – the Thirty Years War begins as a result of the Defenestration of Prague; the city also figures prominently in the War of the Austrian Succession (1740–48), the Seven Years War (1756–63) and the Revolutions of 1848; 1918 – capital of new Czechoslovak republic; 1939–45 – German occupation; 1968 – Prague Spring – liberalization under Dubcek crushed by Soviet invasion.

Population: 1.2 million; capital and largest city of Czechoslovakia.

Postal code: CSSR-Praha **Telephone code:** 2

Climate: cold and dry in winter; sunny summers.

Calendar of events: ›Prague Spring‹ (May) – music festival.

Fairs and exhibitions: PRAGOTHERM (November) – international exhibition of heating, air conditioning, ventilation and cooling; INTER-KAMERA (Mar) – international audio-visual exhibition.

Historical and modern sights: Cathedral of St. Vitus (1344) – one of Europe's most famed and most remarkable Gothic cathedrals, on the Hradčany, the Bohemian Acropolis; Royal Palace (1493–1502) – where the Thirty Years War was hatched; Church of Loreto (1734) – with a famed ›Glockenspiel‹ and crown jewels including a monstrance containing 6666 diamonds; Palais Kinsky – Prague's most beautiful rococo building, now housing the graphics collection of the National Gallery; Lustschloss Belvedere – the most beautiful Renaissance palace north of the Alps, with a collection of Bohemian glass; Tyl Theatre (1783) – where Mozart's ›Don Giovanni‹ was given its première; St. Jacob's (1232) – monastery and church founded by Wenceslas I, King of Bohemia; Klementinum (1653–1722) – Prague's second largest building complex, housing the university library; Representation House of the City of Prague (1906–11) – excellent example of ›Prague Secession‹ architecture; Karl Bridge (1357) – Prague's world famous landmark bridge; St. Maria de Victoria (1636–44) – the city's oldest Baroque church; Church of St. Peter and Paul (1887) – in the heroes' cemetery can be found the graves of Dvořák and Smetana; Old New Synagogue (1275) – the oldest synagogue in Europe; Pincas Synagogue (12th century) – now a memorial for Czech Jews who died in Nazi concentration camps; Hradčany Square – site of the Palace of the Archbishop, the Sternberg Palace (now the National Gallery).

Special attractions: Mala Strana – narrow streets and old patrician houses; a nightly walk through the gas-lit mews and alleys of the old city; Lanterna Magica; Wenceslas Square – where the action is, with a monument to St. Wenceslas; the scene of the big demonstrations in 1968.

Important companies with headquarters in the city: Centrotex (textiles); Cekoslovenska Keramika (ceramics); Ferromet (metallurgical products); Chemapol (chemicals); Intergeo (geological exploring); Investa (leather products); Koospol (food); KOVO (electronics); Ligna (paper); Merkuria (consumer goods); Metalimex (metallurgical products); Motokov (cars); Omnipol (aeroplanes); Pragoinvest (machines); Strojexport (industrial projects); Technopol (machines); ZSE (electrotechnics).

Airport: Prague-Ruzyné, PRG; Tel.: 36 78 27; 17 km/10 miles.

The Headquarters

EUROPA

29 Vàclavskè Nàmesti
CSSR–Prague 1
Telephone: 26 27 49/26 39 05
Owning Company: Restaurace a jidelny v Praze
Number of rooms: 82 (3 suites)
Price range: Kcs 400/approx. US$ 40 (double),
Kcs 800–1,100/approx. US$ 80 to US$ 110 (suite)
Credit cards: AE, DC
Location: central
Built: 1905 (renovated 1924)
Style: Art Nouveau
Hotel amenities: valet parking, souvenir shop
Room amenities: colour tv (some rooms) (pets allowed)
Bathroom amenities: all rooms with private bathroom facilities
Room service: 6.00/a.m. to 2.00/a.m.
Laundry/dry cleaning: same day
Conference rooms: 2 (35 and 20 persons)
Bar: ›American Bar‹ (18.00/6.00 p.m. to 2.00/a.m.); Art Nouveau décor
Restaurants: ›Francouzska Restaurace‹ (11.00/a.m.–15.00/3.00 p.m. and 18.00/6.00 p.m.–22.30/10.30 p.m.) French-style restaurant, traditional Bohemian cuisine and quality Moravian wines, open-air café; ›Plzenska Restaurace‹ (11.30/a.m.–15.00/3.00 p.m. and 18.00/6.00 p.m.–22.30/10.30 p.m.) as ›Francouzska-Restaurace‹
Private dining rooms: two

Thanks to its location on historic Wenceslas Square, the Europa has been witness to many of the crucial events in Czechoslovakia's history since it was built in 1905. The monument to the beloved thirteenth-century King of Bohemia immortalized in the traditional Christmas carol has always been a focal point within the capital; in fact the demonstrations in 1968 took place before the very portals of this fine hotel. Nowadays this strategic location near the commercial centre of the old city and the National Museum, makes the hotel suitable for industrialists and tourists alike: both are attracted by the pleasant décor behind the elegant Art Nouveau façade. Franz Kafka frequented the galleried and chandeliered café with its marble-topped tables, which nostalgically recalls the last years of the Hapsburg empire. The glass-domed restaurant, on the other hand, provides a setting festive enough for today's managers celebrating fought-over contracts. Friendly, multilingual staff, comfortable surroundings and Bohemian spontaneity combined with cosmopolitan savoir-faire make the Europa the first choice for businessmen in Prague.

Dinner

U LABUTÍ (›The Swans‹)
11 Hradčanské náměstí
Telephone: 53 94 76
Owner/Manager: Karel Tomek
Closed: lunchtime; Sunday
Open: 19.00/7 p.m.–1.00/a.m.
Cuisine: Bohemian and international
Chef de cuisine: Oldřich Stránský
Specialities: turtle, crab or asparagus soup; goose liver with ham; goose liver gratiné; Bohemian dishes; haunch of venison with madeira sauce; pheasant; fillet steak ›Old Prague‹; fruits with ice cream; fruits flambés
Location: 200 metres (1/8 mile) from Prague Castle
Setting: 250 years old; surrounded by some of the most distinguished buildings in the city; two small dining rooms – the ›Club‹, with Baroque décor, and the ›Stable‹, decorated as a mediaeval banqueting hall; both with antique furniture and old paintings
Amenities: snack bar (10.00/a.m.–19.00/7 p.m.); outdoor dining on terrace in summer (11.00/a.m.–19.00/7 p.m.) – both with restricted menus; air conditioning
Atmosphere: nostalgic, with a hint of past splendours
Clientèle: those seeking to recapture the Good Old Days
Dress: evening dress recommended
Service: impeccable
Reservations: essential (pets prohibited)
Price range: rather high
Credit cards: AE, DC, Euro, Visa

Dinner

U MECENÁŠE
10 Malostranské náměsté
Telephone: 55 38 81
Affiliations: Restaurace a jídelny v Praze 1
Closed: lunchtime; Saturday
Open: 17.00/5 p.m.–1.00/a.m.
Cuisine: international
Chef de cuisine: Rudolf Slanina
Specialities: moussaka oriental; steaks in various guises
Location: opposite the church of St. Nicholas
Setting: under a shady pergola; Renaissance-style building; a tavern since 1604; two vaulted dining rooms with fine antique furniture and period accessoires – weapons, domestic paraphernalia and Gothic scrolls
Atmosphere: medieval taproom ambiance in the front room; an aristocratic tea-party in the rear chamber
Clientèle: Prague's public executioners in the 17th century have been replaced by a more comfortable mixture of businessmen, media-men and artists

Dress: informal casual (no jeans, Bermuda shorts or tracksuits)
Service: friendly and helpful
Reservations: essential
Price range: moderately expensive
Credit cards: AE, DC, Euro, Visa

Dinner

U MALÍŘŮ (›The Painters‹)
Malá Strana, 11 Maltézské námésti
Telephone: 52 18 83
Affiliations: Restaurace a jídelny Praha 1
Owner/Manager: Stanislav Fiala
Closed: lunchtime; Sunday
Open: 17.00/5 p.m.–1.00/a.m.
Cuisine: Bohemian and international
Chef de cuisine: Jiří Janeček
Specialities: Mikulov mixed dish; Moravian calves' liver; steaks; pancakes
Location: in Prague's ancient Lesser Town, not far from the Charles Bridge
Setting: a tavern since 1581; two rooms with vaulted ceilings, painted walls and antique furnishings
Amenities: what you would expect of a restaurant of this calibre
Atmosphere: leisured; relaxed and redolent of history
Clientèle: traditional meeting-place for the liberal professions and artists from near and far – plus a fair sprinkling of tourists
Dress: informal
Service: alert and adroit
Reservations: essential
Price range: medium expensive
Credit cards: not accepted

Dinner

LOBKOVICKA VINARNA
(›Lobkovic Wine Tavern‹)
17 Vlašská
Telephone: 53 01 85
Affiliations: Restaurace a jídelny v Praze 1
Owner/Manager: Jiří Dvořok
Closed: lunchtime; Christmas Eve; New Year's Eve
Open: 17.00/5 p.m.–1.00/a.m.
Cuisine: Bohemian and international
Chef de cuisine: Vrastislav Chadraba
Specialities: pork steak ›Strahov‹; steak ›Count Lobkowitz‹; roast goose liver; steamed trout
Location: 3 km (2 miles) from city centre; in the historic quarter of Prague
Setting: 18th-century tavern, recently renovated; interior appropriately furnished with period furniture and accessories
Amenities: pleasant light background music
Atmosphere: restful; intimate

Clientèle: local bigwigs; visiting delegations
Dress: evening dress recommended
Service: attentive
Reservations: essential
Price range: moderately expensive
Credit cards: not accepted

Café

EUROPA
29 Václavské námĕsti
Telephone: 26 27 49/26 39 05
Owner/Manager: Restaurace a jídelny v Jiri Dvořák
Closed: never
Open: 7.00/a.m.–23.30/11.30 p.m.
Location: in the Hotel Europa
Setting: virtually the entire ground floor of the hotel; an Art Nouveau gem – décor, furnishings and accessoires all in period; marble, chandeliers, small round tables and a gallery where chess is still played
Amenities: hotel; two restaurants; bar; open-air dining on café terrace; valet car parking service
Atmosphere: a Prague legend; evocative of the last years of the Austro-Hungarian empire
Clientèle: a pot-pourri of artists, mediamen, journalists, academics and housewives – post-shopping, pre-conference or just imbibing a bit of nostalgia with their cup of coffee
Service: solicitous and friendly

Bar

EUROPA BAR
29 Václavské námĕstí 29
Telephone: 26 27 49/26 39 05
Owner/Manager: Restaurace a jídelny v Praze 1/Jiri Dvořák
Closed: never
Open: 18.00/6 p.m.–2.00/a.m.
Location: in the Hotel Europa
Setting: Art Nouveau at its zenith; liana and snake-line contours; period accessoires
Amenities: hotel; two restaurants; snacks available in bar; valet parking service
Atmosphere: a nostalgic evocation of the heyday of bar-and-café society
Clientèle: favourite after-hours rendez-vous for locals and visitors alike
Service: old-fashioned charm
Reservations: advisable
Credit cards: AE, DC

Nightclub

VARIETE PRAGA
30 Vodičkova ulice
Telephone: 24 40 18
Owner/Manager: Restaurace a jídelny v Praze 1
Closed: Monday
Open: 19.30/7.30 p.m.–2.00/a.m.
Location: in Nové Mĕsto, near Wenceslas Square
Setting: manège-like circular dance-floor surrounded by tables on two levels – the ›stalls‹ and the ›circle‹; stage at one end
Amenities: two-hour variety and floor show (programme changes regularly); mixture of circus and nightclub variety acts, with dancing in the intervals to a live orchestra; quick meals and snacks available as well as drinks
Atmosphere: the only nightclub of its kind in Prague; a Czech kaleidoscope
Clientèle: cheerful; uncomplicated; outgoing; enthusiastic
Dress: elegant
Service: efficient
Reservations: advisable
Price range: moderately expensive
Credit cards: not accepted

Shopping

EVERYTHING UNDER ONE ROOF
Kotva, Praha 1, 8 Nam. Republiky

FOR HIM
Adam, 8 Nam. prikope

FOR HER
Dum mody, Praha 1, 58 Vaclavske Nam.

BEAUTY & HAIR
Salon Vlasta, Praha 1, 8 Nam. mustku

JEWELLERY
Klenoty, 28 Vaclavske Nam.

LOCAL SPECIALITIES
Prior-Detsky dum (children's fashion)
15 Nam. prikope
Dum kozesin (furs)
14 Zelezna
Dum potravin (food and beverages)
59 Vaclavske namesti

THE BEST OF ART
Art Centrum   (modern art),
16 Nerudova, Tel. 53 34 67

The City

Not only in the twinkling eyes of Danny Kaye, alias story-teller Hans Christian Andersen, is it ›Wonderful, Wonderful Copenhagen‹, but also to millions of visitors who fall in love at first sight with this royal residence on the isle of Zealand, closer to the Vikings' saga of the goddess Gefion than to the democratic reality of Queen Margrethe. The worldly metropolis – the largest in Scandinavia – with the global perspective of an important harbour and the picture-postcard quaintness of an ›antique‹ town, is a place for all seasons and sentiments (without the melancholy and pessimism of Søren Kierkegaard). The good-natured sincerity, polite manners and charming modesty enchant the sober businessman, the cultural tourist and the social globe-trotter equally, and no-one can escape the physical beauty – Baroque castles, modern churches, colourful water-front houses and open-air-museum parks –, the casual ambiance – the closest you can come to a Sicilian alfresco lifestyle north of Munich with street theatres and happenings à la routine – and the quality of life which reflects in more ways than just the materialistic one. Tasteful rather than elegant, robustly healthy rather than drolly sophisticated, Copenhagen is full of attractions, entertainment and joy – from museal landmarks by the dozen to Nyhavn frivolities à l'extrème (or rather clean fun in Europe's jazz capital), from going wild on the world's longest shopping boulevard, Strøget, to going crazy in the summer-carnival Tivoli Gardens. There is definitely nothing rotten in the state of Denmark's capital.

Founded: ca. 1045, as a little fishing village named ›Havn‹; København – ›Købmanden's harbour‹.

Far-reaching events: 1167 – fortress built by Bishop Absalon, around which the town grew up; 1369 – the Hanseatic League destroys the settlement; 1416 – King Erik takes up residence, the city prospers and quickly becomes a major Baltic port; 1443 – Copenhagen capital of Denmark; 16th and 17th century – prosperity and expansion and a Swedish invasion; damage to the city by fire in 1728 and 1795 and British bombs in 1807; 1940–1945 – German occupation.

Population: 1.5 million (metropolitan area); capital of Denmark.

Postal code: DK-1000 to 2450 **Telephone code:** 1 (inner city), 2 (outer districts).

Climate: relatively mild, by Scandinavian standards, thanks to the warm sea winds.

Calendar of events: *Dronningens Fødselsdag* (16 Apr) – the Queen celebrates her birthday; *Tivoli Season* (1 May to the 2nd weekend in Sep) – soloists and orchestras from around the world play in the Tivoli Gardens; *Wonderful Copenhagen Marathon* (mid-May) – jogging Scandinavian style; *Sjaelland rundt* (last two weekends in Jun) – a sailing regatta surrounds the city; *Midsummer Eve* (23 Jun) – bonfires and fireworks to celebrate the year's longest day; *Jazz Festival* (1st week in Jul); *Tattoo* (end of Aug) – the royal guard on parade in front of the Rosenborg-Slot; *Copenhagen Summer Festival* (Jul & Aug) – music and dancing in the streets.

Fairs and exhibitions: *INTERNATIONAL TRADE FAIR* (Jan); *MIKRODATA* (Jan/Feb); *FORMLAND* (Feb) – giftware, handicrafts and applied art; *INTERNATIONAL BOAT SHOW* (Feb); *FUTURE FASHION SCANDINAVIA* (Feb/Mar & Aug); *REJS* (Mar) – travel and tourism; *SCAN FAIR* (Mar) – hardware, glass and chinaware; *SCANDEFA* (Apr) – dentistry; *SCANDINAVIAN FURNITURE FAIR* (May); *WORLD FISHING* (Jun); *TEXPO* (Aug) – home and household textiles; *WORLD CONTRACT MEETING* (Sep); *KONTOR & DATA* (Oct) – business and data; *AUTOMATIK* (Oct) – industrial automation; *INDUSTRITRANSPORT* (Nov) – road transport, internal materials, handling and storage systems; *INTERTOOL* (Nov) – machine tools and tools; *INDUSTRIROBOT* (Nov) – industrial robots and robot technology; *KEM-TEK* (Nov) – plant and equipment for the chemical processing industries.

Best views of the city: from the top of the SAS Scandinavia Hotel; from the *Round, Zoo* or *Town Hall Towers.*

Historical and modern sights: *Radhus* (1892–1905) – the town hall, with a noteworthy astronomical clock; *Christiansborg Slot* (1167) – the remains of the first castle in Copenhagen was the foundation of the current seat of the Danish Parliament, erected from 1907 to 1928; *Børsen* – the old stock exchange, one of Christian IV's projects to embellish the city; the 17th-century *Holmens Church* and the *Vor Frelsers Church* (of Our Saviour), with an outdoor staircase; *Amalienborg* – rococo residence of the royal family, where the guard changes colourfully at noon, whenever the Queen is at home.

Special attractions: *Tivoli Gardens* – Copenhagen's Central Park, opened in 1843; concerts, fireworks and 86,817 coloured lights (May–Sept); the *Louisiana* open-air sculpture museum (40 km/25 miles).

Important companies with headquarters in the city: *Christiani & Lielsen* (construction/engineering); *De Danske Zukkerfabrikker* (sugar); *De Forenede Bryggerie* (brewery; Carlsberg and Tuborg); *DFDS A/A* (transport, shipping, travel); *F. L. Smidth & Co.* (construction; building materials); *Gutenberghus Gruppen* (printing); *ISS Securitas* (security systems); *Lauritzen Konzernen* (shipping, cargo, energy); *Monberg & Thorsen* (systems engineering); *Store Nodeske Telegraf Selskab* (telecommunications); *Superfos (chemicals); Tulip* (foods).

Airport: Copenhagen-Kastrup, CPH; Tel.: 54 17 01, 10 km/6 miles.

The Headquarters

ANGLETERRE

34 Kongens Nytorv
DK–1050 Copenhagen
Telephone: 12 00 95
Telex: 15 877/16 643/16 744 angho dk
Owning Company: Profundo AB
Managing Director: Per Kjellström
Affiliation/Reservation Systems: The Leading Hotels of the World, Utell International
Number of rooms: 139 (17 suites)
Price range: DKr 1,025–1,650
Credit cards: all major
Location: city centre
Built: 1755 (renovated 1984/85)
Style: from Empire and Louis XVI to modern
Hotel amenities: valet parking, hairstylist
Main hall porter: John Jensen
Room amenities: colour tv, video, mini-bar/refrigerator, radio
Bathroom amenities: bathrobe, hairdrier, telephone, scales
Room service: 7.00/a.m.–24.00/12 p.m.
Conference rooms: 8 (up to 350 persons)
Bar: ›Angleterre‹ (11.00/a.m.–13.00/1.00 p.m.) Jens Thornbeek (barman), library style décor
Restaurant: ›Reine Pédauque‹ (19.00/7.00 p.m.–23.30/11.30 p.m.) Ole Grønvang (chef de cuisine), French cuisine, pianist

The English have enriched life with so many worldly pleasures, being the mentors of the Grand Tour, Côte d'Azur and St. Moritz fashion, cognac, port and sherry culture, competitive adventure and the dine-and-dance tradition, that in reverence to the stamp on this international life-style, many Grand Hôtels around the continent – from the Grande-Bretagne in Athens to the Inghilterra in Rome to the Victoria-Jungfrau in Interlaken – named the most noble auberges after this ›scepter'd isle‹. The noblest of them all in the Kingdom of Denmark serves two masters, sporting the United Kingdom's name in French. Copenhagen's regal residence for over 200 years recently received a new shine by the new company putting it on top of Scandinavian grand hotels and amongst the stately palaces of Europe's capitals. The location is splendid – with the city's Bond Street, Strøget, starting here – the Old World charm floods the club-like foyer and the bordering Palm Court, and the boulevard terrace bar-café-restaurant serves as the quick-lunch stop and meeting point par excellence. The famous and acclaimed La Reine Pédauque restaurant rates as one of the gourmet temples and the piano bar one of the liveliest corners in gay Copenhagen. The rooms also have regained their one-time splendour, having been furnished with beautiful objets de confort artistiques, some antique, always comfortable, and given warm und light colour schemes and harmonious lighting that would even have put a melancholic pessimist like favourite-son Sören Kierkegaard into euphoria.

The Hideaway

KONG FREDERIK

23–27 Vester Voldgade
DK 1552 Copenhagen V
Telephone: 1–12 59 02
Telex: 19 702 kings
Owning Companies: Profundo A.B./Carl-Erik Bjoerkegren/Philipsson Invest A.B.
General Manager: Per Kjellström
Affiliation/Reservation System: Utell International
Number of rooms: 127 (4 suites)
Price range: DKr 695–3,500
Credit cards: all major
Location: Town Hall Square; 10 km/6 miles from airport
Built: around 1900
Style: classic, old English style
Hotel amenities: valet parking
Room amenities: colour tv, video, mini-bar, radio
Bathroom amenities: separate shower cabinet, bidet, telephone (some rooms), hairdrier
Room service: 7.00/a.m.–24.00/12 p.m.
Laundry/dry cleaning: same day
Conference rooms: 4 (up to 60 persons)
Bars: ›Queen's Pub‹ (11.00/a.m.–1.00/a.m.)
Restaurants: ›Queen's Grill‹ (7.00/a.m.–1.00/a.m.) international cuisine
Private dining rooms: three

This royal retreat's location is so central, that once you step outside its beflagged gate, you are borne along, nolens volens, by the maelstrom of good-humoured gaiety which characterizes Copenhagen. Behind the arched and balconied turn-of-the-century façade just off the Radhusplads, however, all is tranquillity, unhurried stylishness and the timeless good taste for which this country is rightly famous. If you are arriving off-season or at night only the bright smiles or the shiny accessoires will flicker in the cloistered calm: once inside this wood-panelled foyer you will imagine yourself in a private club despite the one-hundred-odd rooms and suites. Rare paintings, etchings and antiques adorn the halls and couloirs, fine materials and warm colours contribute to the aristocratic air and comfortable bedchambers are inviting enough to pass rainy days inside indulging in the fairy-tales of Hans Christian Andersen or in the culinary poetry of the regally talented chef. In fact, the Queen's Grill is fit for any king, the local one as well as all his fellow monarchs. No wonder it is one of the favourite gourmet stops in town as well as one of the most beautiful restaurants in the land. The Queen's Pub, on the other hand, is a meeting point for quick lunches of daily specials – fish variations galore – and the inner-court terrace the refuge from the bustle in the warm season. Of singular beauty is the terrace view from the top-floor suites over the Old Town, putting you into the mood of ›sur les toits de Copenhagen‹.

Lunch

BELLE TERRASSE
3 Vesterbrogade, Tivoli Gardens
Telephone 12 11 36
Owner/Manager: Jan Kurt Christensen
Closed: mid-September–May 1st
Open: 11.00/a.m.–24.00/12 p.m.
Cuisine: French and international
Chef de cuisine: Finn Lytie
Specialities: fillet of sole with truffled goose liver sauce; fillet of veal with shellfish; roast fillet of beef with chive sauce
Location: Tivoli Gardens
Setting: overlooking the Tivoli lake and the Town Hall; attractive ›Gay Nineties‹ décor
Amenities: bar; open-air dining on terrace; pianist and bass player; air conditioning
Atmosphere: luxurious; agreeably reminiscent of Marienbad
Clientèle: as popular with the Danish Ministry of Foreign Affairs as with the tourists and overseas visitors themselves – famous past guests like Eisenhower and Kennedy, not forgetting Marlene Dietrich and John Lennon
Dress: formal (jacket and tie)
Service: courteous and correct
Reservations: essential (pets prohibited)
Price range: moderately expensive
Credit cards: AE, DC, Euro, Visa, Access, Master Charge, Carte Blanche

Dinner

DIVAN II
3 Vesterbrogade, Tivoli Gardens
Telephone: 12 51 51
Affiliations: Chaîne des Rôtisseurs
Owner/Manager: Kurt J. Vøttrup
Closed: mid-September to May
Open: 11.30/a.m.–15.00/3 p.m. and 17.30/5.30 p.m.–23.30/11.30 p.m.
Cuisine: French and international
Chef de cuisine: Jens Andersen
Specialities: fresh fish and game in season
Location: in the Tivoli Gardens
Setting: French summer pavilion; flowers in abundance (roses on every table); handpainted Royal Copenhagen porcelain, tapestry-upholstered chairs and primrose-yellow table-linen; dominant Art Nouveau porcelain flower trough in the shape of a dusky African beauty with a basket of flowers on her head
Atmosphere: luxurious, yet delightfully bright, welcoming and refreshing
Clientele: the Who's Who of distinguished visitors to Copenhagen; from Queen Elizabeth II to ex-President Carter
Dress: casually elegant
Service: sometimes rather less inspiring than the surroundings
Reservations: essential
Price range: expensive
Credit cards: AE, DC, Euro, Master Charge, Carte Blanche

Dinner

FISKEHUSET
34 Gammel Strand
Telephone: 14 79 16/14 76 30
Owner/Manager: Grethe Nielsen, Leif Andreassen and Arne Larsen
Closed: Sunday
Open: 11.30/a.m.–21.30/9.30 p.m.
Cuisine: international; seafood
Specialities: fresh fish; shellfish; a few meat dishes
Location: a lobster quadrille from the Thorvaldsen Museum
Setting: Copenhagen's oldest fish restaurant; pre-war drawing room décor; painted wooden panelling, period accessoires in restrained colours
Atmosphere: old-fashioned; unpretentious; but not without charm
Clientèle: Copenhagen's In-Crowd, international financiers and off-duty diplomats
Dress: bound to be brighter than the surroundings
Service: knowledgeable
Reservations: advisable to essential
Price range: fairly expensive
Credit cards: AE, DC, Euro, Visa, Access, Master Card, JBC, Dankort

Lunch

SØLLERØD KRO
35 Søllerødvej
Holte-Søllerød (20 km/12 miles)
Telephone: 80 25 05
Affiliations: Traditions et Qualité; Relais et Châteaux (Relais Gourmand)
Owner/Manager: Jørgen Tønnesen
Closed: Christmas Eve (December 24th)
Open: 12.00/a.m.–22.00/10 p.m.
Cuisine: Danish and international
Chef de cuisine: Michel Michaud
Specialities: langoustine ravioli with herbs; turbot with fricassée of artichokes; breast of pigeon with juniper; fillet of lamb baked in a salt crust; cold chocolate dessert with coffee cream
Location: at Holte-Søllerød; 20 km (12 miles) north-west of Copenhagen; motorway E4 (exit Søllerød) – direction Holte
Setting: in an historic model village; near the church, the castle and the forest; traditional inn (1677) with thatched roof; whitewashed walls; interior wood-panelled, with antique accessoires and old paintings
Amenities: private dining rooms (12–90 persons); lounge area; outdoor dining in courtyard; flower-filled garden

Atmosphere: country-château atmosphere – perfect for a summer lunch
Clientèle: twentieth-century man in search of tranquillity; exotic birds of all descriptions; cognoscenti from Paris and New York
Dress: designer jeans to Eistrup and Bang
Service: overwhelmingly hospitable
Reservations: essential (no pets)
Price range: inevitably high
Credit cards: AE, DC, Euro, Visa

Dinner

KONG HANS KAELDER
6 Vingardsstraede
Telephone: 11 68 68
Affiliations: Relais et Châteaux (Relais Gourmand)
Owner/Manager: Sven Grønlykke and Klaus Rifbjerg
Closed: Sunday lunch (in summer); July
Open: 12.00/a.m.–14.00/2 p.m. and 18.00/6 p.m.–22.00/10 p.m.
Cuisine: French and international
Chef de cuisine: Michel Michaud
Specialities: gourmet salads; soufflés; turbot; duck
Location: a bar away from the Royal Theatre
Setting: ›the most beautiful restaurant in the city‹
Amenities: the King's Wine Cellar (dating back to 16th century)
Atmosphere: harmonious, romantic
Clientèle: francophile gourmets; expense-account aesthetes; theatre buffs; drama critics
Dress: elegant to informal
Service: solicitous and well-informed
Reservations: advisable
Price range: medium to high
Credit cards: AE, DC, Visa

Dinner

Sct. GERTRUDS KLOSTER
32 Hauser Plads
Telephone: 14 66 30
Owner/Manager: Eddie Møller
Closed: lunchtime; Christmas; Easter
Open: 17.00/5 p.m.–2.00/a.m.
Cuisine: international
Chef de cuisine: Even Nielsen
Specialities: Lobster Thermidor; roast saddle of venison with glazed Pigeon apples, braised salad, pommes Château and cranberry sauce with cream; desserts
Location: central
Setting: 700-year-old former hospice for wayfarers and journeymen; a labyrinth of candle-lit brick vaults; spiral staircases; book-lined lounge areas, ecclesiastical works of art and a wealth of oak beams, panelling and furniture enhanced by a profusion of fresh flowers

Amenities: private dining rooms (10–70 persons); bar; séparées; air conditioning
Atmosphere: intimate; nostalgic; seigneurial in medieval style
Clientèle: twentieth-century descendants of the travellers who once sought refreshment here; popular with Copenhagen's Haute Bourgeoisie with cause for celebration
Dress: no special restrictions or requirements
Service: professional and welcoming
Reservations: advisable
Price range: fairly expensive
Credit cards: AE, DC, Euro, Visa, JCB, Master Card

Meeting Point

COPENHAGEN CORNER
18 H.C. Andersens Boulevard
Telephone: 14 45 45
Owner/Manager: Urban Paulsson
Closed: never
Open: 11.30/a.m.–24.00/12 p.m. (last orders 23.30/11.30 p.m.)
Cuisine: international
Specialities: according to season and market availability
Location: on the corner of Town Hall Square (Rådhus-Pladsen)
Setting: spacious modern bistro in a luxurious winter garden; small tables and tan-upholstered banquettes amidst a riot of foliage; green carpet
Amenities: private dining rooms (8–40 persons), underground car park
Atmosphere: a cross between an exotic tropical garden and a Victorian conservatory; perpetual summer even on a grey Nordic winter's day
Clientèle: bankers, brokers, businessmen and Town Hall boffins at lunchtime give way to a younger, more extrovert, more pleasure-seeking set at night
Dress: casual to formal
Service: attentive and observant
Reservations: advisable
Price range: moderately expensive
Credit cards: DC, Euro, Visa, Access, Master Card, JBC, Dankort

Meeting Point

AMAGERTORV
8 Amagertorv
Telephone: 13 71 01
Owner/Manager: Jørn Due
Closed: Sunday
Open: (Monday–Friday) 10.00/a.m.–17.00/5 p.m.
(Saturday) 10.00/a.m.–13.00/1 p.m.
Location: near Højbro Plads
Setting: in the same building as the shop and showrooms of Royal Copenhagen Porcelain – one of the city's most beauti-

ful renaissance-style edifices; neutral décor; small round tables and rattan chairs
Amenities: restaurant serving lunches as well as a café offering the usual calorie-laden treats
Atmosphere: bustling and popular meeting-place for all and sundry
Clientèle: ladies lunching their best girl friends after a shopping expedition; artists, media men and the occasional casual passer-by
Service: friendly waitresses in blue-and-white aprons

Bar

WONDER BAR
69 Studiestraede
Telephone: 11 17 66
Owner/Manager: Erik Lauritsen
Closed: never
Open: 21.00/9 p.m.–5.00/a.m.
Location: two and a half bars from the Town Hall Square (Radhusplads)
Setting: classic modern décor; dark ceiling and walls with spotlights illuminating pictures and sculptures of the female form as seen by artists of different periods; red carpet and comfortable chairs and banquettes
Amenities: dancing every night of the week
Atmosphere: exclusive, sophisticated and relaxing
Clientèle: industrialists, export managers, advertising executives and journalists
Service: attractive and friendly hostesses
Reservations: advisable
Credit cards: AE, DC, Euro, Visa, Access, Master Card, JBC

Nightclub

TORDENSKJOLD
19 Kongens Nytorv
Telephone: 12 03 04
Owner/Manager: Mr. Finn
Closed: never
Open: 22.00/10 p.m.–5.00/a.m.
Location: a quickstep away from the Headquarters
Setting: old paintings, comfortable niches, long bar and small dance-floor
Amenities: discothèque
Atmosphere: primus inter pares among the semi-private discos in town (arrange entry through the hotel)
Clientèle: middle-aged, successful, well-dressed
Dress: elegant to eccentric
Service: very good
Reservations: advisable
Credit cards: AE, DC, Euro, Visa

Shopping

EVERYTHING UNDER ONE ROOF
Illum   52 Østergade

FOR HIM
Brd. Andersen   7–9 Østergade

FOR HER
Bee Cee   24 Østergade

BEAUTY & HAIR
Gunn Britt   4 Skovbogade

JEWELLERY
Georg Jensen   40 Østergade

LOCAL SPECIALITIES
W. Ø. Larsen (tobacco)
9 Amagertorv
Vagn (women's fashion)
13 Østergade
Lord Nielsson (men's fashion)
39 Vimmelskaftet
Créatix Jeunesse (children's fashion)
32 Grønnegade
A. C. Bang (leather fashion)
27 Østergade
Birger Christensen (furs)
38 Østergade
Gads Boghandel (books)
32 Vimmelskaftet
Bee Cee Ting + Sager (gifts)
16 Grønnegade
Kgl. Porcelainfabrik (porcelain)
6 Amagertorv
Lysberg Hansen (baggage & travel accessories)
3 Bredgade
Lysberg Hansen (interior decorating)
3 Bredgade
Oste Hjørnet (food and beverages)
56 Store Kongesgade
Parfumeur Français (perfumery)
1 Grønningen
Billing Sko (shoes)
53 Østergade

THE BEST OF ART
ASBAEK   (contemporary art)
8–10 Ny Adelgade, Tel. 15 40 04
Birch, Borge   (contemporary art)
25 Admiralgade, Tel. 13 16 16

The City

1812 marked two historic events: the fall of Napoleon as the world crusader in Russia and the rise of Helsinki as the capital of the Grand Duchy of Finland, if under Russian rule. Neighbouring Big Brother is just watching, nowadays, while this neutral metropolis is looking westward and absorbing all the trends from Stockholm, Hamburg and London without abandoning its very own lifestyle close to nature even in the heart of commerce, traffic and rush. ›The appearance of the town is entirely modern, in some respects suggesting America rather than Europe. Many granite buildings erected since 1900 show a praiseworthy attempt at originality of style‹ expressed the grandfather of guides, Baedeker, in the era of Expressionism. The description still holds for the modernity in the realistic Eighties, with Finnish touches having marked parts of America rather than Helsinki showing signs of Chicago, physically. Carl Ludwig Engel's imposing neo-classical structures blend with masterpieces of fascinating simplicity by internationally acclaimed maestri Eero Saarinen and Alvar Aalto. The city is so generously laid out that hundreds of parks find room within, and with the water around, innumerable islands at the doorstep and thousands of lakes in the hinterland, the functional, pleasantly cool and partly avant-garde agglomeration of buildings will hardly render a feeling of uniform sobriety. The pulsating harbour, the colourful markets and the artful design, the lively streetside cafés, life on the water and even the action at night – not only in mid-summer – will moderate all prejudices about the Daughter of the Baltic's neutrality also showing in her sons and sins. The northernmost capital in mainland Europe is adorned with southern streaks, hospitable warmth and punctiliousness in business. And though the import of lumber, paper, furniture, furs or glass may be the chief aim of most, don't miss the natural splendour to which Helsinki is so close and that only favourite son Jean Sibelius could describe.

Founded: 1550 by the Swedish king Gustavus I.; Helsinki (Finnish)/Helsingfors (Swedish).

Far-reaching events: 1640 – the original settlement is moved further south, to the sea; 1808 – fire devastates the city; 1812 – the rebuilt city becomes the capital of the Grand Duchy of Finland, under Russian sovereignty; 1828 – founding of the university, which develops as a centre for Finnish nationalist activity against Russian domination; 1863 – Finnish and Swedish declared the official languages; 1917 – Finland granted independence in the wake of Russia's October Revolution; 1939–44 – Finland occupied by Nazi troops; 1952 – Summer Olympic Games held here; 1975 – ›Helsinki Accords‹ signed in closing the ›Conference for Security and Co-operation in Europe‹.

Population: 710,000 (metropolitan area); Finland's capital and largest city.

Postal code: SF–00100   **Telephone code:** 0

Climate: cold winters; relatively warm summers, with the Gulf Stream countering the effect of the northerly latitude.

Best time to visit: June and July.

Calendar of events: *Vappu Night* (3 Apr) – a carnival-like celebration of spring; *Midsummer Night* (21–22 Jun) – the longest day of the year is longer here than in most places and well worth celebrating; *Rowing Regattas* – all summer long; *Helsinki Seajazz* (Aug) – jazz on the nearby island Snomerlinna; *Helsinki Festival* (Aug/Sep) – theatre, classical concerts, folklore, ballet and cultural events; *Great Fish Market* (Oct).

Fairs and exhibitions: *FINNISH FASHION FAIR* (Jan and Aug); *INTERNATIONAL FUR AUCTION* (Jan–Feb–Mar, Dec); *FORMA* (Feb and Sep) – *GIFTWARE TRADE FAIR; INTERNATIONAL BOAT SHOW* (Feb); *ELKOM* (Mar) – professional electronics fair; *FINNISH BOOT AND SHOE FAIR* (Mar and Sep); *EUCEPA* (May) – environmental protection in the '90s; *FINNTEC* (Nov) – technical fair; *FINNCONSUM* (Dec) – consumer goods.

Best view of the city: from the dome of the cathedral.

Historical sights: *Presidential Palace* – former hotel for Russian czars; *Uspenski Cathedral* (1868) – crowned by a golden onion-shaped dome, the most beautiful Greek Orthodox temple in Finland; *Seurasaari* – a museum island with old farmhouses; burgher houses and other architectural gems from the past; *Ateneum* – art museum (Finnish painting and sculpture); *Parliament Building* (1931); *City House* – neo-classical with the noteworthy *Havis Amanda Fountain.*

Modern sights: *Esplanade* – window-shopping for Finnish fashions in the city's luxury street; *Church of the Rock* – built on solid black granite; *Finlandia* – congress and concert hall, a symphony in white marble by architect Alvar Aalto.

Important companies with headquarters in the city: *A. Ahlström* (wood and paper processing machines); *Eka-yhtymä* (foodstuffs, clothes); *Enso Gutzeit* (wood and paper processing machines); *Hankkija-yhtymä* (agricultural machinery and chemicals); *Karl Fazer* (sweets, chocolates); *Kemira* (chemicals); *Kesko* (foodstuffs, clothes); *Kone* (engineering); *Kymi-Strömberg* (wood and paper processing machines); *Nokia* (electronics, cables, tyres); *Outokumpu* (metals, mining); *Perusyhtymä* (consulting, engineering); *SOK* (consumer goods, cafés, shops); *Tambella* (mechanical engineering, paper, cellulose); *Valio* (dairy products); *Valmet* (machinery, docks); *Wärtsilä* (docks).

Airport: Helsinki-Vantaa, HEL; Tel.: 8 29 21; 20 km/14 miles.

The Headquarters

INTER-CONTINENTAL

46 Mannerheimintie
SF–00260 Helsinki
Telephone: 44 13 31
Telex: 122 159 incon
Telefax: 408 670
Owning Company: Nordic-Hotel Oy
General Manager: Olof C. Jurva
Affiliation/Reservation System: Inter-
Continental Hotels
Number of rooms: 555 (12 suites)
Price range: FMk 590–1,600
Credit cards: AE, DC, CB, GM, Visa
Location: within walking distance of Hel-
sinki's business centre
Built: 1971 (recently renovated)
Style: modern
Hotel amenities: parking, beauty parlour,
shopping gallery, hairdresser, car rental
desk, Finnair check-in service
Room amenities: air conditioning, colour
tv, radio, non-smoking rooms, rooms for
allergy-sensitive guests (pets allowed)
Bathroom amenities: hairdrier, telephone
Room service: 24 hours
Conference rooms: for up to 800 guests
Sports: indoor swimming pool, sauna,
massage
Bars: ›Baltic‹ (13.00/1.00 p.m.–
1.00/a.m.) cocktail lounge; ›Ambassador‹ cocktail bar adjoining the rooftop
restaurant
Restaurants: ›Brasserie‹ (7.00/a.m.–
24.00/12.00 p.m.), Finnish and international cuisine; ›Ambassador‹ (19.30/7.30
p.m.–3.00/a.m.) international and local
specialities, rooftop (9th floor)

*It's not to be confused with the subtle articu-
lations of an edifice à la Eero Saarinen
or Alvar Aalto, but the functional concrete
façade is certainly not unworthy of the
White City of the North. With its 550
rooms this northernmost European link in
the famous world-encircling Inter-Continental chain offers the same standards of
quality, comfort and service as its sister establishments in San Francisco or Sydney,
and would even be big enough to house all
the delegates to the Helsinki Conference.
Practicality is the raison d'être behind the
extensive modern building, conveniently
situated near the commercial centre and
the main tourist attractions of the Finnish
capital. However, both public and private
rooms are decorated in a welcoming manner which combines Nordic design with
classic Anglo-Saxon urbanity. Visiting executives can conduct preliminary discussions in the club-like cocktail bar and celebrate a signed contract against the panoramic view in the elegantly festive* Ambassador *roof-top restaurant before a session
in the sauna, as de rigueur for visitors to
the country as for the Finns themselves.
And when it's time to go home, the city-centre air terminal is, in fact, in the same complex as the Inter-Continental.*

The Hideaway

HAIKKO MANOR

SF–06400 Porvoo (6 km/4 miles)
Telephone: (915)15 31 33
Telex: 1734 hahot
Owning Company: Wuoristo-Concern
Managing Director: Veikko Vuoristo
Affiliation/Reservation System: Best
Western, Finlandia Hotels
Number of rooms: 180 (5 suites)
Price range: FMk 445–1,200
Credit cards: AE, DC, EC, Visa
Location: Gulf of Finland, 6 km/4 miles
from Helsinki; 49 km/31 miles from air-
port (Vantaa)
Built: 1913 (renovated 1966)
Style: antique and contemporary
Hotel amenities: valet parking; piano;
health club; sauna, solarium; newsstand
Room amenities: air conditioning, colour
tv (pets allowed)
Room service: 7.00/a.m.–24.00/12 p.m.
Conference room: 12 (up to 440 persons),
secretarial services, ballroom
Sports: tennis, curling, indoor swimming
pool, keep-fit-hall, gymnasium
Sports (nearby): windsurfing, croquet,
skiing, golf, yacht club
Old Bar: (12.00/a.m.–2.00/a.m.)
Restaurants: ›Banquet Hall‹ (7.00/a.m.–
1.00/a.m.; 7.30/a.m.–12.00/p.m. on Sun-
days); Pauli Kuosmanen (maître), Juha
Niemiö (chef de cuisine), international
and Finnish cuisine, antique style décor,
orchestra, open-air dining; ›Baroque
Hall‹, ›Yellow Salon‹ (as Banquet Hall)
Nightclub: ›Temptation‹ (23.00/11.00
p.m.–2.00/a.m. Tuesday–Saturday)
Private dining rooms: three

*During the almost perpetual daylight of
midsummer, but also in winter, Haikko
Manor provides a perfect setting for a
weekend break out of town. The innumerable lakes and desolate plains of the Finnish countryside, so hauntingly evoked by
the music of Sibelius, are in themselves a
compelling reason for escaping from Helsinki; Haikko Manor offers the visitor with
limited time available a hint of the mysterious fascination of this largely untouched
land. The white classical-style building
stands in its own grounds on the Gulf of
Finland, a short drive from the capital;
there's a private beach for sun-worshippers,
hardy bathing enthusiasts or keen windsur-
fers, whilst sports facilities on terra firma
include tennis and croquet on the lawns in
front of the pillared and porticoed façade.
The intérieur is furnished in a mixture of
contemporary and antique styles – the latter particularly in evidence in the spacious
dining room with its huge semicircular bay
window. The staff are friendly, the menu
offers a choice between local and international specialities, and for insomniac
guests who prefer to take their exercise after dark there is a nightclub for dancing the
night away – not to the music of Sibelius,
but to the sounds of the Eighties.*

Lunch

SVENSKA KLUBBEN
6 Maurinkatu
Telephone: 62 87 06/63 28 96
Owner/Managers: Rivoli-Company/
Ragni Rissanen
Closed: Sunday; July
Open: 11.00/a.m.–1.00/a.m.
Cuisine: Finnish traditional
Chef de cuisine: Hannu Lehtinen
Specialities: lobster; smoked roast elk; juniper-smoked salmon; roast mallard; fish and game buffet (Monday 19.00/7 p.m.–24.00/12 p.m.); home-made petits-fours
Location: fairly central
Setting: elegant period setting; gilt-framed pictures, candlesticks; oriental carpets; attractively-ruched curtains; carefully-chosen accessoires
Amenities: groups of up to 130 persons catered for; pianist
Atmosphere: harmonious; classic; refined
Clientèle: bankers; businessmen; local dignitaries; lawyers
Dress: rather conservative (pin-stripes allowed)
Service: professional
Reservations: recommended
Price range: very high
Credit cards: all major

Lunch

SAVOY
14 Eteläesplanadi
Telephone: 17 65 71
Affiliations: Relais et Châteaux (Relais Gourmand)
Owner/Manager: Arctia Ltd
Closed: Saturday; Sunday; in July evenings and week-ends
Open: 11.30/a.m.–1.00/a.m.
Cuisine: international and Finnish
Chef de cuisine: Karl-Johann Sudell
Specialities: traditional local dishes; nouvelle cuisine menu; mutton and beef stew with anchovy, herrings and onion; charcoal-roasted Finnish whitefish; reindeer steak with cream and cognac sauce
Location: central, 300 metres from the market place
Setting: designed by Alvar Aalto; timelessly elegant classic dining room on the top floor of an office building; fine view of the city through picture windows; well-spaced round tables; fine glassware and china; candle-lit at night
Amenities: private dining room (100 persons)
Atmosphere: Finnish food at its best in sophisticated surroundings; the only Relais Gourmand in the country
Clientèle: resident epicures; managing

directors and top industrialists; Helsinki's Haute Societé with and without cause for celebration, from President Koivisto downwards
Service: expert and friendly
Reservations: recommended (no dogs)
Price range: rather expensive
Credit cards: AE, DC, Euro, Visa, Access, Master Card

Dinner

KARL KÖNIG
4 Mikonkatu
Telephone: 63 85 03/17 12 71
Affiliations: Chaîne des Rôtisseurs; Dégustateurs Mondial
Owner/Manager: Jalle Lundström
Closed: Saturday; Sunday; July
Open: 11.00/a.m.–24.00/12 p.m.
Cuisine: classic Scandinavian, with a French accent
Chef de cuisine: Keijo Markkanen
Specialities: cold smoked salmon; smoked reindeer meat; Russian bortsch soup; morel mushroom soup; suprême of ptarmigan with blackcurrant jelly; menu in five languages
Location: on Helsinki's main boulevard
Setting: in the vaults of a bank; attractive traditional Nordic décor; oak; wrought iron; Belle Epoque details; silver cutlery and platers; white damask tablecloths
Amenities: groups of up to 60 persons can be catered for
Atmosphere: established in 1892; an essential stopover for lovers of fine food
Clientèle: Helsinki's Haute Bourgeoisie; expense-account gourmets; diplomats; visiting delegations; a sprinkling of celebrities since Finland's best-known composer, Sibelius
Dress: elegant
Service: knowledgeable; helpful advice during menu-planning
Reservations: essential (no dogs)
Price range: rather expensive
Credit cards: AE, DC, Euro, Visa, Access, Master Card

Lunch

HAVIS AMANDA
23 Unioninkatu
Telephone: 66 68 82
Owner/Manager: Vilhelm Noschis
Closed: Saturday; Sunday
Open: 11.00/a.m.–1.00/a.m.
Cuisine: seafood
Chef de cuisine: Erkki-Matti Ritola
Specialities: sea trout; whitefish; Baltic herring; crayfish (in season); marinated Baltic herring cocktail; deep-fried vendace; shrimp bisque; braised turbot in sour cream; menu illustrated in Finnish, Swedish and English

Location: by the market place
Setting: fish restaurant in an historic building; named after the statue of a young girl on a nearby boulevard
Amenities: groups of up to 100 persons can be catered for; one private dining room (16 persons)
Atmosphere: the best seafood restaurant in Finland
Clientèle: fairly cosmopolitan; fish gourmets; discriminating, self-confident and intelligent
Dress: fairly elegant to fairly casual
Service: welcoming and attentive
Reservations: recommended
Price range: on the expensive side
Credit cards: AE, DC, Visa, Access, Master Card

Dinner

BELLEVUE
3 Rahapajankatu
Telephone: 17 95 60
Owner/Manager: Ragni Rissanen
Closed: Saturday lunchtime; Sunday
Open: 11.00/a.m.–13.00/1 p.m. and 18.00/6 p.m.–1.00/a.m.
Cuisine: Russian
Chef de cuisine: Seija Virtanen
Specialities: salted cucumber, soured cream and honey; blinis with fish roe; ham in yeast dough; Turkestan-style saddle of mutton with saffron rice; fillet steak à la Novgorod; chicken Kiev; Armenian kisses' dessert (very sweet!)
Location: in the harbour district of Skatudden; not far from the palace of the president
Setting: in the shadow of an onion-towered Russian Orthodox church set on a hillside; at the entrance to a cul-de-sac; rather unprepossessing exterior; two small, narrow dining-rooms
Amenities: car park
Atmosphere: candlelight
Clientèle: cross-section of homesick Muscovites, men from the media, journalists and artists
Dress: casual to formal
Service: good
Reservations: advisable
Price range: moderately expensive
Credit cards: AE, DC, Euro, Visa, Access, Master Card

Café

FAZER
3 Kluuvikatu
Telephone: 66 65 97
Owner/Manager: Peter Fazer
Closed: Sunday (in summer)
Open: (winter) Monday–Friday 8.30/a.m.–21.30/9.30 p.m., Saturday 8.30/a.m.–18.00/6 p.m.

Sunday 12.00/a.m.–19.00/7 p.m.
(summer) Monday–Friday 8.30/a.m.–19.00/7 p.m., Saturday 8.30/a.m.–16.00/4 p.m.
Specialities: the best cakes in town
Location: central; near the railway station
Setting: established in 1897; typical Finnish coffee-house – main branch of a chain of cafés of the same name; affiliated to Finland's largest music firm
Amenities: baker's shop and confiserie; bistro-style lunch menu
Atmosphere: nostalgic evocation of the heyday of café society
Clientèle: heterogeneous; shopgirls, shopkeepers, suburban ladies and senior citizens
Service: solicitous

Bar

ADLON
14 Fabianinkatu
Telephone: 66 46 11/66 60 72
Owner/Manager: Jarl Lundströn
Closed: Sunday; July
Open: (Monday) 11.30/a.m.–17.00/5 p.m. (Tuesday–Friday) 11.30/a.m.–2.00/a.m. (Saturday) 19.00/7 p.m.–2.00/a.m.
Location: in the Stock Exchange complex
Setting: behind an imposing façade; interior dominated by dark red velvet furniture
Amenities: restaurant; occasional dances in the stock exchange courtyard; air conditioning
Atmosphere: favourite meeting-place for exchange of news, views, hot tips and takeover bids
Clientèle: brokers, bankers and businessman and entrepreneurs
Dress: formal to elegant (no jeans)
Service: discreetly courteous
Reservations: advisable for dining
Credit cards: all major

Nightclub

GROOVY
4 Ruoholahdenkatu
Telephone: 69 45 118
Owner/Manager: Mr. Kan̕darauyndado
Closed: Saturday lunchtime; Sunday
Open: (Monday–Friday) 11.00/a.m.–1.00/a.m.
(Saturday) 18.00/6 p.m.–1.00/a.m.
Location: central
Setting: bar with live jazz groups performing six evenings a week, including local and international celebrities
Amenities: lunch menu
Atmosphere: Helsinki's best jazz club; cosmopolitan; swinging to moody; a place where aficionados are sure to find fellow fans

Clientèle: heterogeneous; students to stockbrokers; Upper Crust to bohémiens
Dress: casual
Service: with a smile
Reservations: advisable
Price range: medium
Credit cards: AE, Euro, Visa

Shopping

EVERYTHING UNDER ONE ROOF
Stockmann   52 Aleksanderinkatu

FOR HIM
Kuusinen   46–48 Aleksanderinkatu

FOR HER
Kuusinen   46–48 Aleksanderinkatu

BEAUTY & HAIR
Leporento Beautysystems
23 Kalevankatu

JEWELLERY
A Tillander   48 Aleksanderinkatu

LOCAL SPECIALITIES
Nicole Oy (women's fashion)
3 Keskuskatu
Morris (men's fashion)
7 Pohjoisesplanadi
Bunukka (children's fashion)
44 Kasarmikatu
Boutique Kari Lepistoe (men's leather fashion) 8 Arkandiankatu
Pentik, (women's leather fashion)
25 A Pohjoisesplanadi
Boutique Tarja Niskanen (furs)
30 Unioninkatu
Boutique Furi YX (furs)
22 Etelesplanadi
Akateeminen Kirjakauppa (books)
1 Keskuskatu
Navara (baggage & travel accessories)
3 Keskuskatu
Artek (interior decorating)
3 Keskuskatu
Kalevala Koru (jewellery, local specialities)
25 Unioninkatu
Aarikka (gifts, woodwork)
25 Pojoisesplanadi

THE BEST OF ART
ARTEK   (modern art)
25 B Pohjoisesplanadi, Tel. 66 99 89
Taide Art Oy   (modern art)
5 Bulevardi Tel. 64 05 67

The City

Bordeaux is not simply a French title found on the labels of some of the world's best wines. It's also the name of the fifth largest city in France, ›a cross between Versailles and Antwerp‹, according to Victor Hugo. An élitarian city in the world's most élitarian country, Bordeaux is one of the most classically beautiful cities in Europe. Its regal boulevards, formal squares and magnificently façaded buildings with their elegant wrought iron ornamentation seem to have been designed for providing a proper setting for properly enjoying the fine bouquet of its vintage wines. Over 3500 vintners ply their trade in and around Bordeaux, producing some four hundred million litres of the city's main product each year. But the city which Henry James described as being ›dedicated to the worship of Bacchus in the most discreet form,‹ does more than just grow, taste and sell its own wines. It's a city which provides prima facie evidence that originality of political thought is not a prerogative of the citizens of the capital; philosopher-bel-es-prit Montesquieu was president of the parliament here, and the same mood of challenge which permeates ›L'Esprit des Lois‹ has produced, in the twentieth century, the political works of critic-playwright Jean Anouilh and the engagement of Jacques Chaban-Delmas. The seat of over 30 consulates has developed into an important international convention centre in recent years, hand in hand with its rapidly rising industrial production. Located on the Garonne River, Bordeaux is an important port city with a thriving shipbuilding industry, increasingly productive oil refineries and blossoming aviation, aerospace and armament industries. The local oysters and truffles aren't bad, either. A French city par excellence, it's hard to be bored in Bordeaux.

Founded: 1st century B.C., by the Romans; Bordeaux – from Burdigala, Latin name for the capital of the Bituriges.

Far-reaching events: an episcopal see in 315, and shortly thereafter an archiepiscopal see; Vandals, Goths, Franks and Saracens wage war over in the next centuries; 1154–1452 – English rule and much prosperity; 18th century – Bordeaux's beautiful centre is built, as the city enjoys the benefits of French colonialism; centre of Girondin movement during the French Revolution; temporary seat of the French government in 1870, 1914 and 1940.

Population: 750,000 (metropolitan area); capital of Gironde department.

Postal code: F-33000   **Telephone code:** 56 (incorporated in number since 1986)

Climate: mild and temperate, due to the influence of the Atlantic Ocean; precipitation rarely exorbitant; lots of sun; pleasantly warm summers; winters cool but not really cold.

Best time to visit: April to October.

Calendar of events: ›Musical May‹ (May) – Bordeaux's big music festival; *International Jazz Festival* (Aug); *Sigma Meeting* (Nov) – contemporary art festival.

Fairs and exhibitions: *ANTIQUES FAIR* (Feb); *INTERNATIONAL FAIR* (May); *VINEXPO* (Jun) – wine fair; *VINITECH* (Jun) – trade fair for the wine industry; *OYSTER FESTIVAL* (Aug) – in the oyster beds of Arcachon; *SRIBA* (Oct) – word processing, office equipment and automation exhibition; *RADIO, TELEVISION, ELECTROACOUSTIC AND AUDIOVISUAL SHOW* (Oct); *BATIBOIS* (Oct) – international exhibition for the use of wood in construction; *CONFOREXPO* (Nov) – interior decorating and furniture exhibition; *RACING CARS AND RACING MOTORBIKE EXHIBITION* (Nov).

Best views of the city: from the bell tower of the *Church of St Michael.*

Historical and modern sights: *Palais Gallien* (3rd century) – the ruins of a Roman amphitheatre for 15,000 spectators; *St. Andrew's Cathedral* (13th–14th century) – Gothic with a free-standing bell tower; *Church of St. Seurin* – with a modern façade and a 12th-century crypt; *Church of St. Michael* (16th century) – late Gothic with a Renaissance altar; the *Grand-Théâtre* – the most beautiful 18th-century theatre in France, with its neo-classical Corinthian façade; *Hôtel de Ville* (18th century) the former archbishops' palace – a very imposing city hall; *Pont de Pierre* (1822) – 17-arched bridge built by Napoleon; the *Museum of Decorative Arts*; the *Esplanade des Quinconces* – notable monument to the Girondists, one of the few groups that kept their heads in the French Revolution; *Quartier du Lac* – a modern part of town with man-made parks and lakes for water sports, along with the architecturally daring *Aquitaine Bridge*; the *Mériadeck* quarter – a modern complex of offices, hotels, restaurants and elegant shopping; *Place Gambetta* – one of the loveliest squares in the town.

Special attractions: a boat trip around the *harbour*; the *Rothschild vineyards* in Pauillac, 40 km (24 miles) north of town; the *oyster beds* of Arcachon; the national park of *Les Landes.*

Important companies with headquarters in the city: *Bichots* (wine); *La Cellulose du Pin* (paper); *Ford France* (vehicles); *IBM France* (computers); *Laboratoire Labaz; SAVIC Export* (shoes); *SEP* (Société Européenne de Propulsion); *SNPE* (Société Nationale des Poudres et Explosives); *Total* (oil refinery).

Airport: Bordeaux-Mérignac, BOD; Tel.: 56 34 81 84, 10 km/6 miles; Air France, Bordeaux, Tel.: 56 93 81 22.

The Hideaway

**GRAND HOTEL
ET CAFE DE BORDEAUX**

2–5 Place de la Comédie
F–33000 Bordeaux
Telephone: 56 90 93 44
Telex: 541 658 ot bordo
Owning Company: Sphère Group
General Manager: François Broine
Affiliation/Reservation System: Resinter
Number of rooms: 93 (3 suites)
Price range: FF 300 (single)
　　　　　　　 FF 410 (double)
　　　　　　　 FF 750 (suite)
Credit cards: AE, DC, Visa, EC, CB
Location: city centre, on the famous Place
de la Comédie
Built: 1780 (modernized 1979)
Style: classical
Hotel amenities: parking next to hotel,
hairdresser, boutique
Room amenities: air conditioning, colour
tv, mini-bar (pets allowed)
Bathroom amenities: bathrobe
Room service: 7.00/a.m.–23.00/11 p.m.
Laundry/dry cleaning: next day
Conference rooms: 6 (up to 120 persons),
all modern conference facilities
Bars: ›Café de Bordeaux‹ (7.00/a.m. to
1.00/a.m.) elegant décor and live piano
music

*It is somehow fitting that the leading hotel
in this most classically beautiful of European cities should be housed in an eighteenth-century building of nobly harmonious proportions. The setting is appropriate,
too – on the bustling and central Place de
la Comédie, opposite the Corinthian façade of the Municipal Theatre. Recent
renovations, however, have transformed
the intérieur into a predominantly contemporary haven of comfort and good taste;
leather armchairs in the lounge, subdued
lighting in the bar and luxurious grands lits
in the bedrooms, plants. in profusion and
smiling service everywhere. Plus, lest the visitor should harbour feelings of regret at
the disappearance of past splendours, a
magnificent Napoléon II reception hall
with frescoed ceiling, gilt, mirrors and glittering chandeliers. The eponymous café is
a favourite meeting-place for Le Tout Bordeaux, who gather over coffee under the
graceful arched ceiling of the salon in winter or on the lively boulevard terrace during
fine weather.*

The Hideaway

LA RESERVE

74 Avenue du Bourgailh (10 km/6 miles)
F–33600 Pessac Alouette
Telephone: 56 07 13 28
Telex: 560 585 resflou
Owner: Claudine and Roland Flourens
General Manager: Claudine Flourens
Affiliation/Reservation System: Relais et Châteaux
Closed: mid-Nov – mid-March
Number of rooms: 22 (1 suite)
Price range: FF 200 (single)
FF 550 (double)
FF 700 (suite)
Credit cards: AE, CB, EC, Visa
Location: 10 km/6 miles from city centre, 5 km/3 miles from Bordeaux airport, Rocade freeway exit 13
Built: 1965 (recently renovated)
Style: modern
Hotel amenities: car park, car rental desk, music room, billiard room, terrace, private gardens (pets welcome)
Room amenities: many rooms with private terrace, air conditioning, colour tv
Bathroom amenities: hairdrier, bathrobe
Room service: 6.00/a.m. to 11.00/a.m.
Laundry/dry cleaning: on request
Conference rooms: for up to 80 persons
Sports: tennis
Restaurant: ›La Réserve‹ (12.00/a.m.–14.00/2.00 p.m. and 19.30/7.30 p.m.–22.15/10.15 p.m.) nouvelle and regionale, Pierre Bugat (chef de cuisine)
Private dining rooms: on request

If you travel by helicopter you can reach ›La Réserve‹ in a matter of minutes. It takes marginally longer by car, of course, but your first sight of this enchanting relais de campagne nestling amongst the trees of its own private park, surrounded by acres of the vineyards which produce the world-famous claret, will convince you that you are about to enter another domain. Whilst the house itself is basically modern – almost American – in style, the welcome from Claudine and Roland Flourens recalls the house-parties of yesteryear. The absence of a noisy nightclub is seen as a distinct advantage by the guests, who come from both sides of the Atlantic to stroll in the gardens or fit in a game of tennis before sampling the delights of Pierre Bugat's innovative cuisine on the pretty terrace or in the attractive dining room. With hunting, golfing and fishing in the vicinity and the beaches of the Atlantic coast only an hour away, in future you're bound to want to reserve a room at La Réserve for all your trips to claret country – for which La Réserve can organise châteaux visits.

Lunch

CLAVEL
44 Rue Charles Domercq
Telephone: 56 92 91 52
Owner/Manager/Chef de cuisine: Francis Garcia
Closed: Sunday; Monday; February 10th–24th; three weeks in July
Open: 12.30/p.m.–14.00/2 p.m. and 20.00/8 p.m.–21.30/9.30 p.m.
Cuisine: ›au goût du marché‹ and regional (Gascon)
Specialities: lobster gazpacho; rabbit or hare à la royale; truffle flan; chicken with morel mushrooms stuffed with foie gras; selection of desserts ›Rêve d'Enfant‹ (›Childhood Dream‹)
Location: near the St. Jean railway station (Gare St. Jean)
Setting: small dining room; contemporary décor in black and rose; attractive lighting
Amenities: private dining room (20 persons); pianist; air conditioning; car park (fee-paying); bistro (round the corner; open until 23.00/11 p.m.)
Atmosphere: intimate and harmonious
Clientèle: hommes d'affaires; hommes de lettres; hommes de politique
Dress: no special restrictions or requirements
Service: alert and spontaneous; directed by Géraldine Garcia
Reservations: advisable (pets prohibited)
Price range: fairly expensive
Credit cards: AE, DC, Visa

Lunch

LA CHAMADE
20 Rue des Piliers de Tutelle
Telephone: 56 48 13 74
Owner/Manager/Chef de cuisine: Michel Carrère (ex-Saint James)
Closed: never
Open: 12.00/a.m.–14.00/2 p.m. and 20.00/8 p.m.–22.00/10 p.m.
Cuisine: ›au goût du marché‹
Specialities: aiguillettes de canard aux raisins à l'armagnac; escalope of turbot with shrimps; ice-creams with fruits in season
Location: an apéritif away from the theatre
Setting: 18th-century vaulted cellars in light-coloured stone; contemporary décor
Amenities: private dining room (40 persons); air conditioning
Atmosphere: exquisitely comfortable and refined – perfect for business by day and pleasure by night
Clientèle: industrialists, wine exporters and academics during and out of working hours

Dress: come-as-you-please
Service: exemplary; directed by the wife of the patron
Reservations: advisable
Price range: medium
Credit cards: AE

Dinner

CHRISTIAN CLEMENT (Dubern)
42 Allée de Tourny
Telephone: 56 48 03 44
Owner/Manager/Chef de cuisine: Christian Clément
Closed: Saturday lunchtime; Sunday; public holidays
Open: 12.00/a.m.–14.15/2.15 p.m. and 20.00/8 p.m.–22.15/10.15 p.m.
Cuisine: local and nouvelle
Specialities: wild salmon with cucumbers; duck with honey and lime; fricassée of frogs in chervil aspic; ragoût fin d'écrevisses; calves' liver and kidneys (›nobles‹) forestière
Location: central; on one of Bordeaux' main boulevards
Setting: historic building housing a succession of salons on the first floor decorated in Louis XVI style
Amenities: private dining room (25 persons); rustic-style bistro on ground floor (with open-air dining in summer); piano bar in cellar; air conditioning; attended car park (fee-paying)
Atmosphere: elegant but not overpowering
Clientèle: businessmen at work and at leisure; a sprinkling of visiting celebrities
Dress: what you will (as long as they will like you)
Service: distinguished but not disdainful
Reservations: advisable (pets permitted)
Price range: rather expensive
Credit cards: AE, DC, Euro, Carte Bleue

Dinner

JEAN RAMET
7/8 Place Jean-Jaurès
Telephone: 56 44 12 51
Owner/Manager/Chef de cuisine: Jean Ramet
Closed: one week in January; two weeks at Easter; two weeks in August
Open: 12.15/p.m.–14.00/2 p.m. and 20.00/8 p.m.–22.00/10 p.m.
Cuisine: ›au goût du marché‹
Specialities: according to season; ragoût of scallops with fresh noodles; escalope of duck liver with caramel; roast duckling with limes; game; sautéed lambs' sweetbreads with lemon cream sauce; chocolate honey ice-cream; crêpes soufflées with praliné sauce

Location: between the theatre (Grand Théâtre) and the River Garonne
Setting: small dining room with subtle modern classic décor in fresh pastel tones
Amenities: air conditioning
Atmosphere: soothing and relaxing
Clientèle: Town Hall officials, expense-account gourmets and disciples of Jean Ramet's cuisine of ex-Troisgros and Guérard renown
Dress: casually elegant
Service: friendly and welcoming
Reservations: advisable to essential
Price range: fairly expensive
Credit cards: Carte Bleue

Lunch

SAINT-JAMES
3 Place Camille-Hosteins
Bouliac (9 km/6 miles)
Telephone: 56 20 52 19
Affiliations: Relais et Châteaux (Relais Gourmand)
Owner/Manager/Chef de cuisine: Jean-Marie Amat
Open: 12.00/p.m.–14.00/2 p.m. and 20.00/8 p.m.–22.00/10 p.m.
Cuisine: nouvelle
Specialities: flap mushroom ravioli; fillets of eel with new onions; civet de canard; terrine of aubergines with cumin; Norway lobster with oyster ravioli; Peking duck à la bordelaise; roast pigeon with saffron; chicken with fresh coriander and garlic
Location: at Bouliac; 9 km (6 miles) south-east of Bordeaux along the D10
Setting: a white villa perched on a hillside overlooking the river Garonne; dining room reminiscent of a modern art gallery; high beamed ceiling; rather stark ivory-coloured walls with an excellent collection of oil paintings and watercolours; draped pillars with antique vases
Amenities: private dining room (20 persons); open-air dining on terrace shaded by mature trees with a view of the garden sloping down towards the river
Atmosphere: highly individualistic and inventive; a reflection of the uncompromisingly original character of the proprietor-chef, Jean-Marie Amat
Clientèle: intelligent, self-confident
Dress: as you like it
Service: efficient but rather reserved
Reservations: necessary (no dogs)
Credit cards: AE, DC, Visa

Dinner

LE CHAPON FIN
5 Rue Montesquieu
Telephone: 56 44 76 01
Owner/Manager: Christian Cormouis
Closed: (summer) Saturday; (winter) Monday; Sunday; August

Cuisine: regional cuisine
Chef de cuisine: Jean Ramet (ex-Troisgros and Guérard)
Specialities: ray with vegetables and orange; fried black pudding with red cabbage; calf's head; poached egg à la greque; suprême de volaille with cucumber; plain chocolate fondant gâteau
Location: central
Setting: worth a visit for its own sake; recently-renovated turn-of-the-century rock-garden; columns and ornate capitals, luxuriant greenery and two waterfalls; red and green colour scheme
Amenities: air conditioning
Atmosphere: a nostalgic evocation of the frivolous grandeur of days gone by
Clientèle: Bordeaux's Top Ten and curious tourists following in the footsteps of the erstwhile illustrious company who once graced the town's most famous restaurant – the exiled Alphonse VIII of Spain, Sarah Bernhardt and Georges Mandel
Dress: informal
Reservations: advisable
Price range: medium
Credit cards: Visa, Carte Bleue

Café

CAFE DE BORDEAUX
Place de la Comédie
Telephone: 56 90 93 44
Owner/Manager: Société du Grand Hotel et Café de Bordeaux
Open: 7.00/a.m.–24.00/12 p.m.
Location: opposite the Grand Théâtre in the centre of town
Setting: English pub-style décor
Amenities: boulevard terrace on the ›Place de la Comédie‹; car park in the vicinity
Atmosphere: bon chic, bon genre
Clientèle: local dignitaries; visiting luminaries, from the mayor of Bordeaux to international opera stars
Service: courteous and welcoming

Meeting Point

NO. 5
5 Allée de Tourny
Telephone: 56 52 29 40
Owner/Manager: Sarl Cinq
Closed: Sunday evening
Open: 18.00/6 p.m.–2.00/a.m.
Location: a curtain call from the Grand Théâtre
Setting: piano bar; salmon-pink walls; modern décor with Parker Knoll furniture
Amenities: restaurant; terrace for al fresco drinks in summer; air conditioning; car park

Atmosphere: a good place to see and to be seen in; sophisticated, chic and frequently rather crowded
Clientèle: young, self-assured and on-the-way-up
Service: welcoming and well-trained
Reservations: advisable for restaurant
Credit cards: Carte Bleue

Bar

L'ORCHIDEE NOIRE
2 Place Pey
Telephone: 56 44 40 04
Owner/Manager: Jacky Vignal
Closed: Sunday
Open: 18.30/6 p.m.–2.00/a.m.
Location: a gin fizz from the Town Hall (L'Hôtel de Ville); a champagne cork's trajectory from the cathedral
Setting: cocktail bar with claret-coloured moquette walls; comfortable armchairs and an interesting collection of paintings to survey until your companion arrives
Amenities: air conditioning; car parking in the vicinity
Atmosphere: confidential or intimate, depending on your mood
Clientele: local habitués; visiting managers; international lawyers; restaurateurs
Service: punctilious and professional
Dress: nothing too outrageous or outlandish
Reservations: not necessary
Credit cards: not accepted

Shopping

EVERYTHING UNDER ONE ROOF
La Fayette　　Rue Sainte-Cathérine

FOR HIM
Rainbow　　30 Allée de Tourny

FOR HER
Claudia Benetton
47 Cours de l'Intendance

BEAUTY & HAIR
Antonio　　Centre de Mériadeck

LOCAL SPECIALITIES
Tabac la Régence (tobacco)
10 Cours du 30 Juillet
Mod (women's fashion)
1 Place de la Comédie
Francesco Smalto (men's fashion)
6 Rue Voltaire
Bout Chou (children's fashion)
Centre de Mériadeck
Tartine et Chocolat (children's fashion)
1 Rue Franklin
Molat (books)
15 Rue Vital Carles
Bradley's Book Shop (books)
32 Place Gambetta
Maison Ecompagne (gifts)
9 Rue Franklin
Vinothèque de Bordeaux (food and beverages)
8 Rue du 30 Juillet
Parfumerie de l'Opéra (perfumery)
10 Allée de Tourny

THE BEST OF ART
Image Nouvelles　 (modern art)
15 Rue Maubec, Tel. 56 96 76 55
Zographia　 (contemporary art)
62 Rue Boric, Tel. 56 44 45 82

›And all the little oysters stood and waited in a row‹ – Brest is the land of milk and honey for gourmets who prefer crustacés and crêpes. The capital of Bretagne is also the capital of Bélons, fruits de mer and cidre. Business in Brest also means les plaisirs de la table. In fact, if you arrive during the evening, screenwriter-novelist Alain Robbe-Grillet's home town may remind you of the year before last in Marienbad, since locals and visitors alike are feasting on coquilles St.-Jacques or lobster à l'armoricaine rather than imitating the Régine's routine. Daylight, however, reveals Brest to be a bustling modern port. Gone are the narrow streets and the seventeenth-century defences built under Richelieu and Colbert, the German submarines and the bunkers – replaced by broad, straight boulevards and no-fuss architecture, which seem appropriate to a city harbouring the most important French maritime base with a naval academy. Commercially, the port is thriving too – there are deep-water anchorages for supertankers as well as dock facilities for smaller vessels. In view of the town's ideal location on the headland, where the English Channel meets the Atlantic Ocean, but protected from the violence of the prevailing gales by its own bay, this development was a foregone conclusion in times past and is still the city's raison d'être today. Brest is not a great tourist centre per se, but instead of heading for Paris as soon as business is over, it can provide a convenient base for excursions by private yacht or for an exploration of the mysterious and myth-laden Brittany peninsula. Its Celtic heritage is all-pervasive, the sagas – and even the place-names – betraying the British origins of the fifth-century settlers who brought with them the Arthurian legends, Tristan and Isolde and the Druidic megaliths and menhirs which dot the countryside. It may lack the exotic undertones of Marseilles, the dolce-vita of Cannes, or the sophisticated veneer of Deauville, but France's most westerly stopover before the open sea is a city whose inhabitants, according to an old proverb, are born with sea-water in their veins – which ensures here, as in more illustrious watering-holes, a soupçon of Attic salt to enliven any encounter.
Founded: ca. 20, B. C., as a Roman military colony.
Far-reaching events: 13th century – hotly contested by France and England the Hundred Years War; 1631 – Cardinal Richelieu sheds his grace on Brest and turns it into a major port city; 1694 – site of the defeat of the English-Dutch navy, by the French; 1793 – site of the defeat of the French navy, by the English; heavy damage in the First World War, near to complete destruction in the Second World War; 1975 – oil-drilling in the Mer d'Iroise opens up a new future for the port of Brest.
Population: 170,000; capital of Finistère department.
Postal code: F–29200   **Telephone code:** 98 (incorporated in number since 1986)
Climate: mild winters and pleasantly warm summers (average temperature in August 20° C/68° F); a fair amount of rain.
Calendar of events: *International Bagpipe Festival* (Oct).
Fairs and exhibitions: *JOURNÉES VERTES* (Jun) – agricultural fair; *FOIRE ST. MICHEL* (Sep) – antiques fair.
Historical and modern sights: the *Château* (17th century) – built by Louis XIV, now home of the Naval Museum and the Prefecture of the Sea; *La Motte-Tanguy Tower* (16th century), with the *Old Brest Museum;* the *Recouvrance Bridge* – Europe's largest lift bridge, capable of rising 29 m in 2 minutes and 28 seconds; *Palace of Justice* – with Courbier's great Statue of Law and Justice; *St. Luke's Church* (19th century) – very square; *Church of St. Louis* (20th century) – with high vertical ribs of concrete; *City Museum* – with a collection of Flemish, Italian and Dutch masters from the 17th to the 20th centuries; the modern *Palais de la Culture* cum monument, in the Avenue Georges-Clemenceau; *Church of Ste. Thérèse du Landais* (1960) – round and black, with magnificent stained-glass windows and a bell tower in the new Quilverzan section of town.
Special attractions: *Rue de Siam* – the main street, with cinemas, elegant shopping and typical Breton bistros; view of the harbour; *Atlantic cruises and excursions* can be booked at Cameret, Les Tas de Pois, Ile de Sein.
Important companies with headquarters in the city: *Gelagri Bretagne-Landerneau* (vegetables); *Promogros* (fruit); *Société Silva* Export (poultry and preserves); *Tafra Hypermoquettes* (carpets).
Airport: Brest-Guipavas, BES; Tel.: 98 84 61 49, 11 km/6 miles.

The Headquarters

SOFITEL OCEANIA

82 Rue de Siam
F–29200 Brest
Telephone: 98 80 66 66
Telex: 940951 oceania
General Manager: Philippe Minchin
Affiliation/Reservation System: Resinter, Sofitel
Number of rooms: 82 (9 suites)
Price range: FF 298–FF 398 (single)
            FF 338–FF 448 (double)
            suite on request
Credit cards: AE, DC, EC, Visa
Location: city centre, close to the railway station and the harbour area
Built: 1980
Style: modern
Hotel amenities: valet parking, car rental desk, hotel shop
Room amenities: colour tv, mini-bar (in some rooms), radio (pets allowed)
Room service: 6.00/a.m.–22.00/10 p.m.
Laundry/dry cleaning: same day
Conference rooms: 5 (up to 200 persons), all modern conference facilities
Bars: ›Drakkar‹ (12.00/a.m.–1.00 a.m.)
Restaurant: ›Oceania‹ (12.00/a.m.–14.00/2.00 p.m. and 19.30/7.30 p.m.–22.00/10 p.m.) French nouvelle cuisine, seafood specialities
Nightclubs: ›Nautilus‹ (22.30/10.30 p.m.–4.00/a.m.), discothèque

Strategically situated on one of Brest's principal boulevards, opposite the Post Office and just a few steps from the Place de la Liberté, the Oceania is the obvious choice for the endless stream of shipping executives and export managers who come to do business in the town. A dépendance of the well-known French Sofitel group, the Oceania offers the same standard of practical comfort as its sister hotels which stretch from North America to West Africa and the South Seas. The square modern grey building with its terraced roof section dominates the busy Rue de Siam, but thanks to efficient soundproofing guests can work, relax and sleep in peace. The reception area is cheerfully welcoming, with light wood fittings and bright green and white upholstery. This friendly atmosphere is continued in the restaurant, where the warm neutral tones provide a restfully informal atmosphere for the fine nouvelle cuisine menu, where specialities naturally include the day's catch fresh from the Atlantic.

Lunch

LES VOYAGEURS
15 Avenue Georges-Clemenceau
Telephone: 98 80 25 73
Owner/Manager: Auguste Lombard
Closed: Sunday evening; Monday; July
15th–August 6th
Open: 12.15/p.m.–14.00/2 p.m. and
19.15/7.15 p.m.–20.30/8.30 p.m.
Cuisine: classic, with a hint of nouvelle
Chef de cuisine: André Chaumeau
Specialities: oysters; shellfish; skate with
capers; calves' sweetbreads with Norway
lobster; scallops with leek fondue; Brest
fish soup; almond pear tart
Location: in the Hôtel des Voyageurs
Setting: first-floor hotel restaurant; com-
fortable modern décor
Amenities: hotel; private dining room
(120 persons); brasserie-restaurant; air
conditioning
Atmosphere: understated; stylish; wel-
coming and relaxing
Clientèle: favourite haunt of local top
businessmen, for intimate dîners à deux
or confidential déjeuners d'affaires
Dress: designer casual to dark suit
Service: distinguished and attentive
Reservations: advisable
Price range: moderately expensive
Credit cards: AE, DC, Euro, Visa

Dinner

FRERE JACQUES
15 bis Rue Lyon
Telephone: 98 44 38 65
Owner/Manager/Chef de cuisine: Jacques
Peron
Closed: Saturday lunch; Sunday; July
28th–August 11th
Open: 12.00/a.m.–13.30/1.30 p.m. and
19.30/7.30 p.m.–21.30/9.30 p.m.
Cuisine: nouvelle, with a local accent
Specialities: ›Demoiselles de Loctudy‹;
angler fish with leek cream sauce;
mousse of salmon and Norway lobster;
ragoût of lambs' sweetbreads and
tongues with truffle juice; crab bisque;
poire chaude en feuilleté
Location: central
Setting: behind a rather unprepossessing
façade; an elegantized bistro restaurant
with well-spaced, prettily-laid small
round tables and lovely flower arrangements; attractive lighting and comfortable chairs
Amenities: private dining room (25 persons)
Atmosphere: the most prestigious restaurant in Brest; intimate and refined
Clientèle: Finistère's most discriminating
food fans; admirals, bankers, chargés
d'affaires and local admirers of ›Frère
Jacques‹ cuisine

Dress: ›correcte‹
Service: charmingly smiling welcome by
Madame Peron
Reservations: preferred
Price range: relatively modest
Credit cards: Euro

Lunch

LE POULBOT
26 rue d'Aiguillon
Telephone: 98 44 19 08
Owner/Manager/Chef de cuisine: Jean-
Pierre Martin
Closed: Saturday lunchtime; Sunday;
August 20th–September 8th
Open: 12.00/p.m.–22.00/10 p.m.
Cuisine: local and inventive
Specialities: salad of calves' sweetbreads
and foie gras; pigeon with mussels and
saffron; grilled sea-perch with beurre
blanc; calf's liver with morello cherries;
strawberries from Plougastel
Location: central; on Place Wilson
Setting: attractive little bistro overloo-
king the trees and shrubs of one of Brest's
most attractive squares; understated dé-
cor
Amenities: air conditioning; car park
Atmosphere: very French; lively; alert;
one of total concentration on the food
Clientèle: popular meeting-place for all
and sundry; media-men, local politicians,
journalists and businessmen – plus a
sprinkling of casual passers-by
Dress: within reason, anything goes
Service: Gallic charm
Reservations: medium
Price range: medium
Credit cards: AE, DC, Carte Bleue

Dinner

AUBERGE DU KRUGUEL
7 rue de la Mairie
Lampant-Plouarzel (22 km/14 miles)
Telephone: 98 84 01 66
Owner/Manager: Christian Cabon
Closed: Sunday evening; Wednesday;
Thursday lunchtime; two weeks in Sep-
tember; three weeks in February
Open: 12.00/a.m.–13.30/1.30 p.m. and
19.15/7.15 p.m.–21.15/9.15 p.m.
Cuisine: nouvelle
Chef de cuisine: Gabriel Quesnel
Specialities: Charolais beef with three
sorts of mustard; crab with artichokes;
fresh salmon au gros sel; stuffed saddle
of lamb en croûte; duck; warm duck's
liver with raspberry vinegar; langoustines
with julienne of vegetables; desserts
Location: at Lampant-Plouarzel, 22 km
(14 miles) from Brest
Setting: a former lawyer's house set in
parkland in a sleepy Breton village; stone
walls, wooden beams and old-fashioned
bourgeois décor

Amenities: private dining room (25 persons); terrace (coffee only); car park
Atmosphere: delightfully nineteenth-century; comfortable, comforting and light years away from the pressures of modern life
Clientèle: Brest bankers seeking a respite from the rigours of the board-room; over-stressed industrialists seeking a respite from the twentieth century
Dress: as you like it
Service: excellent
Reservations: recommended (no dogs)
Price range: fairly expensive
Credit cards: Euro

Café

VESPUCCI
Port de Plaisance
Telephone: 98 42 10 88
Owner/Manager: Crêperie des Plaisanciers/Danièle Bella
Closed: Wednesday
Open: 9.00/a.m.–1.00/a.m.
Location: by the yachting harbour; on one of the main roads into town
Setting: a miniature oasis right by the sea; palm-tree potted plants and a stove for less than tropically-warm days
Amenities: restaurant; pizzeria; bar; large open terrace; car park in the immediate vicinity
Atmosphere: vaguely Italian; warm and friendly
Clientèle: heterogeneous; singers; actors; writers; local habitués and a sprinkling of foreign visitors
Service: fast but never furious
Reservations: advisable (in winter) to essential (in summer)
Credit cards: AE, DC, Euro, Visa, Carte Bleue

Bar

LE WINDSOR
8 rue Pasteur
Telephone: 98 44 71 28
Owner/Manager: André Laot
Closed: never
Open: 15.00/3 p.m.–2.00/a.m.
Location: central; in a small street running parallel to the Rue de Siam, one of Brest's main thoroughfares
Setting: feudal-style bar; high ceilings and a suit of armour or two
Amenities: open-air garden terrace; sale of ice-cream as well as drinks and cocktails
Atmosphere: calm and collected
Clientèle: sales managers, advertising executives and members of the liberal professions
Service: relaxed and friendly; supervised by the proprietor, André Laot

Reservations: not necessary (pets permitted, subject to approval by the patron's Great Dane)
Credit cards: not accepted

Nightclub

NAUTILUS
Sofitel Oceania
82 rue de Siam
Telephone: 98 80 66 66
Owner/Manager: Philippe Minchin
Closed: never
Open: 22.30/10.30 p.m.–4.00/a.m.
Location: in the Hotel Sofitel Oceania
Setting: discothèque – nightclub; modern and functional décor, with a degree of elegance and flair
Amenities: hotel; restaurant; private dining rooms (10–200 persons); bar; valet parking service
Atmosphere: very popular and lively; fairly loud to fortissimo at times
Clientèle: favourite haunt of local night owls and insomniac visitors to the town
Dress: disco elegance
Service: attentive
Reservations: advisable
Credit cards: AE, DC, Euro, Visa

Shopping

FOR HIM
Ema Homme 124 rue Jean-Jaurès

FOR HER
Infinitif 31 rue Jean-Jaurès

BEAUTY & HAIR
Quentric, Yves 1 Avenue Clémenceau

JEWELLERY
Pronost, Pierre 106, rue Jean-Jaurès

LOCAL SPECIALITIES
Rosemay (fashion for her)
3 rue Etienne-Dolet
Bodenes Confection (fashion for him and her) 34 rue de Siam
Degriff'Mome (children's fashion)
119 rue Jean-Jaurès
Roux, Le (books)
1 rue Saint-Martin
Civette, La (gifts)
27 rue de Lyon
Prax (porcelain) 30 rue Traverse
Travailleuse, A La (shoes)
119 rue Jean-Jaurès
Flore (flowers) 11 rue Jean-Jaurès

›Decent men don't go to Cannes‹. Even if Henry James didn't, just about anybody who is anybody, thinks he's anybody or wants to be anybody in the beautifully peopled and deeply tanned world of modern High Society, does. Cannes is the icing on the cake that calls itself the Côte d'Azur, living proof of Solomon's wisdom, ›Vanity of vanities, all is vanity.‹ European royalty, American magnates and lovers of luxury from around the world, and their hangers-on, have been swarming to Cannes since the middle of the last century, making it one of the best places in the world for not getting away from it all. In the course of time they have filled the city with château replicas, voluptuous villas and palatial playgrounds so overwhelming that ›one could place the Pyramids, the Taj Mahal and Grant's Tomb in the centre of it and they would scarcely be noticed.‹ The main industry here is pleasure, but there is another side to Cannes. Far from the madding crowds of La Croisette and the Rue d'Antibes, surrounded by deep forests of mimosa trees in the glens of the old city, the easy ambiance of Mediterranean ease still pervades. Here the myriad tiny perfume distilleries and the kitchens of the picturesque houses of the locals fill the air with the scents of Provence, reminding the visitor what it is that made the region so popular in the first place. Aside from the perfume, cosmetic, silk and metal industries, Cannes has also recently added aircraft construction to its repertoire, and the city is slowly developing into one of the Côte's main convention centres, lending its beautiful framework, its perfect weather and its modern facilities. But the main business here is catering to its pleasure-seeking visitors, from the Hollywood mobs who descend each year for the film festival to the rest of its year-round admirers who have made Cannes one of the world's leading resorts, summer and winter.

Founded: uncertain; the site of a Roman monastery in the 2nd century B.C.; Cannes – ›reeds‹.

Far-reaching events: 50 B.C. – Caesar takes the Côte, and Cannae is a Roman trading post, later a fishing port, strongly fortified against pirates; 14th century – Cannes belongs to the County of Provence; 1481 – the County of Provence belongs to the Kingdom of France; 1834 – British Lord Brougham goes into quarantine at Cannes, an unknown and unimportant fishing village – within a few years it develops into a major resort for the European aristocracy; ca 1950 – tourism takes over.

Population: 220,000 (metropolitan area).

Postal code: F–06400 **Telephone code:** 93 (incorporated in number since 1986)

Climate: typical Mediterranean; hot, humid summers, pleasant, mild winters; rainy from December to February; in spring the ›Mistral,‹ a strong, cold wind sometimes pays a visit or two; other than that the sun shines 300 days a year.

Best time to visit: any time of the year; March to June and September to November are particularly pleasant.

Calendar of events: *MIDEM* (Jan) – international record and music publications festival; *International Amateur Film Festival* (Feb); *Church Hymn Festival* (Apr); *International Cabaret and Coffeehouse Theatre Festival* (Jun); *International Advertising Film Festival;* *Blues Festival* (Aug); *International Puppet Festival* (Dec).

Fairs and exhibitions: *INTERNATIONAL FILM FESTIVAL* (May) – celebrated and much-sung, with a huge film convention; *INTERNATIONAL BOAT WEEK* (Sep); *IDCOM* (Oct) – video and communications exhibition.

Best views of the city: from the *Observatorium;* from the *Suquet Tower.*

Historical and modern sights: the *Old Port,* with yachts, promenades and a flower market; *Notre Dame de l'Espérance* (15th century) – a Gothic church here where one would least expect it, with a pretty statue of St. Anne; the *Castre Museum* – in the former castle of the Abbots of Lérins; *Municipal Museum* – in the 16th-century village castle; *Suquet Church* – with a 22m high watchtower, built to provide warning against Saracen raids; *Parc François André* – tropical plants and the *piscine* filled with the girls that make Cannes what it is today; the ultra-modern *Festival and Congress Palace* – less unanimously approved than the girls.

Special attractions: *La Croisette* – Europe's most spectacular, exhibitionist and self-adoring promenade; at the end is the old, traditional *petanque* or *boule* area; horse racing in July and August at the *Cagnes-Sur-Mer racetrack;* the two *Casinos;* the 18-hole golf course in *Mougins;* boat trips to the islands of Lérins.

Important companies with headquarters in the city: *Balitrand* (construction materials); *Chantier Naval de L'Esterel* (docks); *CLBI* (railway equipment)

Airport: (International) – Nice-Côte d'Azur, NCE; Tel.: 93 83 03 56 or 93 72 30 30; VIP lounge, Tel.: 21 30 30, 25 km/15 miles; (national) – Cannes, CEQ; Air France Cannes, Tel.: 93 83 91 00.

The Headquarters

MARTINEZ

73 La Croisette
F–06400 Cannes
Telephone: 93 68 91 91
Telex: 470 708 matiz
Owning Company: Hotels Concorde
General Manager: Richard Duvauchelle
Affiliation/Reservation Systems: The
Leading Hotels of the World, Centrale
Reservations Paris/Supranational Center
Number of rooms: 420 (15 suites)
Price range: FF 415–2,000
Credit cards: all major
Location: city centre
Built: 1929 (renovated 1983/84/85)
Style: Art Déco
Hotel amenities: valet parking, beauty
salon, boutique, swimming pool
Main hall porters: V. Caisson, M. Venturini
Room service: 24 hours
Laundry/dry cleaning: same day
Conference rooms: 8 (up 600 persons)
Bar: ›L'Amiral‹
Restaurants: ›L'Orangeraie‹ (12.00/a.m–
15.00/3.00 p.m and 19.00/7.00 p.m–
22.00/10.00 p.m) M. Bouillet (directeur
des restaurants), Christian Willer (chef de
cuisine), classic cuisine, orchestra, classic
style décor, open-air dining; ›La Palme
d'Or‹ (12.00/a.m.–19.00/7 p.m. Jan–Jun;
19.00/7 p.m.–24.00 Jun–Sep), records,
Art Déco style; ›De la Plage‹ (as above)

*A palace among palaces along the most
fashionable stretch of beach-front, a stopover for stars and a residence for demanding international executives as well as a dépendance for yacht captains and assorted
globe-trotters, Le Martinez is back on top
as the ivory tower on the Côte d'Azur after
a restoring rejuvenation under the Concorde management of Richard Duvauchelle. Art Déco splendour throughout the
elegant halls and salons and tasteful comfort in every room allure the guests as much
as the location, the view, the air and the
glamour. In the centre of La Croisette –
the aorta of the world's vanity fair in season, between the Palais des Festivals, Port
Canto harbour and Palm Beach casino –
the hotel is itself the nucleus of action in
every respect. For business there is simply
no other hotel as fit and equipped as this
one – conference rooms for over 600 persons – and for pleasure accompanying the
former, it stands out for its seven new private tennis courts, heated swimming pool,
private sandy beach, the most sumptuous
lunch buffet on its own private beach across
from the hotel and the grandest cuisine in
its new* Palme d'Or *restaurant above the
terrace. The* Amiral *bar and* L'Orangeraie
*restaurant complete the glittering kaleido-
scope of entertaining attractions which
make Le Martinez the most prominent palace of them all.*

The Hideaway

HOTEL DU CAP – EDEN ROC

Boulevard J. F. Kennedy
F-06602 Cap D'Antibes (10 km/6 miles)
Telephone: 93 61 39 01
Telex: 470 763 hocap
Owner: EUFRA Holding
General Manager: Jean-Claude Irondelle
Affiliation/Reservation System: The Leading Hotels of the World
Closed: November–March
Number of rooms: 94 (8 suites)
Price range: FF 1,100–2,150
Credit cards: not accepted
Location: 5 km/3 miles from Antibes; 18 km/12 miles from Nice airport
Built: 1865 (renovated 1975–1985)
Style: Second Empire
Hotel amenities: valet parking, limousine service, newsstand, florist, swimming pool, tennis courts
Room amenities: air conditioning, tv on request
Bathroom amenities: separate shower cabin, bidet, bathrobe, hairdrier
Room service: 24 hours
Laundry/dry cleaning: same day (weekend service)
Conference rooms: 2 (up to 200 persons)
Bar/Cocktail Lounge: ›Eden-Roc‹ (8.00/a.m.–2.00/a.m.) Jacques and François (barmen), classic style décor
Restaurant: ›Eden-Roc‹ (see Restaurants)

It's a resort, an estate, a castle, a club, a home-away-from-home (what a home it must be) – in any case, it's a backdrop for paradise and a daydream-come-true for bel-esprits, disciples of La Belle Epoque and Le Beau Monde. Jean-Claude Irondelle chooses his guests in the manner of the doorman at New York's Palladium: not too many stars, not too many aristocrats, not too many millionaires. Still, the world meets at the Cap as if it were the summer Lourdes of the Happy Few. La grande entrée through the iron gate leads you on a wide gravelled pathway to the white mansion where marble floors end in high-ceilinged suites adorned with antiques and luxurious accoutrements seducing the clientèle to spend more time inside than planned. The ex-Villa Soleil could have been under the tutelage of Louis XIV not only because of its name, but for the beauty and splendour of its setting, architecture, intérieur and gardens and for the Eden-Roc pavilion on the rocky promontory overlooking the most beautiful bay of the Côte d'Azur. Walks through the 25 acres of luxuriant flora, tennis under pine trees, lazy lounging around the pool with refreshing champagne cocktails served on silver trays to your mattress (or swallow dives into the sea), sunsets on the terrace and grande cuisine in the restaurant where every dinner becomes an operettic gala – life at the Cap belongs amongst the last grandiose joys in this world.

Lunch

LA PALME D'OR
Hôtel Martinez
73 La Croisette
Telephone: 92 98 30 18/93 68 91 91
Owner/Manager: Hôtels Concorde/ Richard Duvauchelle
Closed: (Monday/Tuesday) lunchtime; (July/August) lunchtime every day; mid-November – mid-December; (1987) February 1st – March 15th
Open: 12.30/p.m.–14.30/2.30 p.m. and 19.30/7.30 p.m.–22.30/10.30 p.m.
Cuisine: cuisine gastronomique française
Chef de cuisine: Christian Willer
Specialities: fish according to market availability, with sauce of fresh olives; terrine of sole with almonds; tartelettes friandes d'agneau à la provençale
Location: in the Hôtel Martinez
Setting: Art-Déco style dining room, reminiscent of the 1930s; open-air dining on terrace overlooking the bay of Cannes
Amenities: hotel; two further restaurants; bar
Atmosphere: Vanitý Fair
Clientèle: mostly more glittering and glamourous than elsewhere, even in Cannes
Dress: Mic Mac to Lanvin prevails
Service: in keeping with the ambiance
Reservations: advisable to essential
Price range: inevitably expensive
Credit cards: all major

Dinner

LE MOULIN DE MOUGINS
Notre Dame de Vie
Mougins (8 km/5 miles)
Telephone: 93 75 78 24/Telex: 9 70 732 F
Affiliations: Traditions et Qualité
Owner/Managers: Roger and Denise Vergé
Closed: Monday; Thursday lunchtime; mid-February – end of March; mid-November – December 23rd
Open: 12.00/a.m.–14.00/2 p.m. and 20.00/8 p.m. – 22.30/10.30 p.m.
Cuisine: nouvelle – classique – régionale
Chef de cuisine: Roger Vergé
Specialities: escalope of salmon on truffled scrambled eggs; fillets of red mullet in fig leaves; lobster in Sauternes; suprême de pigeon à l'ail et aux endives; aiguillettes de canard au sang; roast rabbit with sorrel; langouste au poivre rose
Location: 8 km (5 miles) from Cannes; 1 km (½ mile) from motorway A8 (exit Cannes, direction Grasse – Mougins) on left-hand side
Setting: lovingly restored 16th-century Provençal oil mill on the outskirts of Mougins, surrounded by olive and pine trees; three dining rooms; white walls; subdued shades of olive and beige; antique domestic accessoires and original oil-paintings; candles, fine crystal and old-fashioned china
Amenities: guest wing (6 bedrooms); bar; open-air dining on shady terrace; car park; bistro ›L'Amandier de Mougins‹ in village
Atmosphere: a gastronomic idyll in a perfect setting
Clientèle: religious gourmets; Upper Crust pilgrims to this temple of culinary excellence
Dress: nothing too outrageous
Service: very attentive and friendly
Reservations: essential
Price range: excusably expensive
Credit cards: AE, DC, Visa

Lunch

EDEN – ROC
Hôtel du Cap
Boulevard J. F. Kennedy
Cap d'Antibes (10 km/6 miles)
Telephone 93 61 39 01
Owner/Manager: J. C. Irondelle
Closed: November to April
Open: 13.00/1 p.m.–15.00/3 p.m. and 20.00/8 p.m.–22.00/10 p.m.
Cuisine: French (traditional and nouvelle)
Chef de cuisine: M. Poitu
Specialities: Mediterranean sea-bass in basil sauce; scallops on tarragon-flavoured pancake with parsley butter and asparagus tips
Location: 10 km (6 miles) from Cannes
Setting: Oregon pinewood panelling; trompe-l'oeil paintings on ceilings; view of Mediterranean sea
Amenities: bar; large terrace overlooking sea
Atmosphere: leisurely but distinguished; yacht club, golf club
Clientèle: beautiful, rich and famous people; jet-set and industrial and shipping magnates on holiday
Dress: elegantly informal for lunch; formally elegant for dinner
Service: efficient
Reservations: advisable
Price range: expensive
Credit cards: not accepted

Dinner

L'OASIS
Rue Jean-Honoré-Carle
La Napoule (8 km/5 miles)
Telephone: 93 49 95 52/Telex: 4 61 389 F
Affiliations: Traditions et Qualité
Owner/Manager/Chef de cuisine: Louis Outhier

Closed: Monday evening; Tuesday; November 5th – December 15th
Open: 12.30/p.m.–14.00/2 p.m. and 20.00/8 p.m.–21.30/9.30 p.m.
Cuisine: classic and nouvelle, with occasional Thai undertones
Specialities: skewered langoustines with Bélon oysters; truffle surprise; mille-feuille de saumon with chervil; crayfish with Thai herbs; home-made rye bread with smoked salmon; wild asparagus and morel mushrooms in a cream sauce; lamb with ginger and green mango.
Location: 8 km (5 miles) west of Cannes
Setting: luxurious and elegantly-furnished dining room supplemented by a shady patio under the baldachin of a gigantic tree and a flowered terrace
Amenities: private dining room (20 persons); air conditioning
Atmosphere: the most glittering gourmet stop for all who concentrate not on luxury alone, but also on ›raffinement‹
Clientèle: disciples of Louis Outhier's genial cuisine, from Bangkok (where he supervises the food at the Oriental Hotel) to Baltimore
Dress: jacket and tie
Service: charmingly led by the wife of the patron and his daughter Françoise
Reservations: advisable (pets permitted)
Price range: irrelevant
Credit cards: not accepted

Dinner

LA FERME DE MOUGINS
10 Avenue Saint-Basile
Mougins (8 km/5 miles)
Telephone: 93 90 03 74
Owner/Manager: Henri Sauvanet
Closed: mid-November – mid-December; February 15th – March 15th
Open: (summer) 12.00/a.m.–14.00/2 p.m. and 20.00/8 p.m.–22.30/10.30 p.m. (winter) 12.00/a.m.–13.30/1.30 p.m. and 19.30/7.30 p.m.–21.30/9.30 p.m.
Cuisine: cuisine légère
Chef de cuisine: Patrick Henriroux
Specialities: according to season and market availability
Location: at the foot of the village of Mougins, 8 km (5 miles) from Cannes
Setting: in an old Provençal farmhouse; rustic dining room with an open fireplace; shady garden terrace overlooking swimming pool for open-air dining in summer
Amenities: private dining room (30 persons); car park
Atmosphere: welcoming; intimate
Clientèle: discriminating
Dress: tenue correcte
Service: personal and professional
Reservations: essential
Price range: fairly expensive
Credit cards: AE, DC, Euro, Visa, Master Card

Meeting Point

LE FESTIVAL
52 La Croisette
Telephone: 93 38 04 81
Owner/Manager: Mr. Andréani
Closed: end of November – beginning of December
Open: 1.00/a.m.–23.00/11 p.m.
Location: on the promenade
Setting: typical seafront restaurant/bar with an attractive terrace
Amenities: lunch and dinner menus as well as drinks and snacks; air conditioning
Atmosphere: justifiably popular amongst all those who like to be at the centre of things; chic but not chichi
Clientèle: the Festival In-Crowd; film directors, aspiring actors, attractive actresses and backstage boys
Service: prompt and smiling
Reservations: advisable
Credit cards: AE, DC

Café

SCHIES
84 Rue d'Antibes
Telephone: 93 39 06 90
Owner/Manager: the Schies Brothers
Closed: never
Open: 8.30/a.m.–12.30/p.m. and 14.30/2.30 p.m.–19.00/7 p.m.
Location: central
Setting: typical Mediterranean café
Amenities: one of the best pâtissiers in town; excellent ice cream; cakes made to order for special occasions (4 days' notice required)
Atmosphere: genteel
Clientèle: a preponderance of charming elderly ladies succumbing to the delights of iced Kouglof (cherry parfait with currants) or Coupe Impériale (ice-cream with meringue and caramel) – but there is no lower limit for entry to this paradise for those with a sweet tooth
Service: very good

Bar

LE BLUE
48 la Croisette
Telephone: 93 39 03 04
Owner/Manager: Madame Brals
Closed: Tuesday (except July/August); June 27th – July 6th
Open: 8.00/a.m. – the last guest has gone
Location: next to the Palais Croisette
Setting: a de luxe snack bar with a comfortable glassed-in salon; vaguely like an ocean liner; in the former Palais des Festivals
Amenities: open-air dining on terrace;

light meals (plats du jour; cannelloni; desserts); air conditioning
Atmosphere: attractively busy and bustling; a good place to see and be seen
Clientèle: a firm favourite amongst the town's bankers and businessmen for quick working lunches; also popular amongst film producers, critics and stars during the Festival
Service: efficient
Reservations: advisable for restaurant
Credit cards: not accepted

Bar

LE BRUMMELS
3 boulevard de la République
Telephone: 93 39 07 03
Closed: Tuesday
Open: 22.00/10 p.m. – dawn
Location: north of town centre
Setting: small triangular bar
Amenities: live music (piano/singers/etc)
Atmosphere: one of the most appealing bars in Cannes
Clientèle: an engaging amalgam of Cannes hommes d'affaires and artists
Service: feminine charm
Reservations: advisable
Credit cards: AE, DC, Visa

Nightclub

STUDIO CIRCUS
48 Boulevard de la République
Telephone: 93 38 32 98
Owner/Manager: Paul Pacini
Open: 23.00/11 p.m. – dawn
Location: to the north of the town centre
Setting: large nightclub in a converted cinema – a fairyland of sumptuous lighting effects and stunning sound
Amenities: numerous shows with a variety of special effects; video animation
Atmosphere: an eclectically brilliant cocktail of multisensorial stimuli
Clientèle: includes a sprinkling of Rolls-Royce or yacht-owning moguls from Monte-Carlo, the Middle East and Mustique
Dress: elegant to casual
Service: excellent – under the supervision of nightclub king Paul Pacini; (Whisky a Gogo, Pygmalion, Régine …)
Price range: rather expensive

Nightclub

JACKPOT
Place Franklin-Roosevelt (Pointe de la Croisette)
Telephone: 93 43 91 12
Owner/Manager: Paul Ardisson
Closed: never

Open: 23.00/11 p.m.–3.00/a.m.
Location: in the Palm Beach Casino
Setting: somewhat reminiscent of the interior of a slot machine
Amenities: discothèque; live band; bar
Atmosphere: exclusive; expensive
Clientèle: preserve of chauffeured heirs (and heiresses) as well as their parents – who, however, do show a tendency to gravitate towards the casino and the bar
Dress: tie de rigueur
Service: amazingly efficacious
Reservations: recommended

Shopping

FOR HIM
Féraud, Louis   72 rue d'Antibes

FOR HER
St Laurent Rive Gauche
19 bis rue d'Antibes

BEAUTY & HAIR
Michel Didier
8 boulevard de la République

JEWELLERY
Debove   25 rue d'Antibes

LOCAL SPECIALITIES
d'Astree, Elisabeth (women's fashion)
69 rue d'Antibes
Durif (men's fashion/shirts)
29 Bis rue d'Antibes
Christine (children's fashion)
27 rue d'Antibes
Céline (leather fashion)
96 rue d'Antibes
Chevrier (furs)
2 rue d'Antibes
Caprice (gifts)
2 rue d'Antibes
Vog (glass)
61 rue d'Antibes
Céline (baggage & travel accessories)
96 rue d'Antibes
Pavillon St. Germain (interior decorating)
9 rue d'Antibes
Christofle, Pavillon (silver/porcelain)
109 rue d'Antibes
Bruno (chocolate)
50 rue d'Antibes
Bouteille, Parfumerie (perfumery)
59 rue d'Antibes
La Grande Maison de Blanc (lingerie)
49 rue d'Antibes
Primavera (flowers)
54 rue d'Antibes

THE BEST OF ART
Becker, Joachim
(contemporary art)
7 rue Bivouac Napoléon, Tel. 93 38 20 48
Herbage   (Fine Art)
17 rue des Etats-Unis, Tel. 93 39 19 15

The City

Every year the same dilemma of deciding where to go: Sylt, South Hampton, Punta del Este? Or Mykonos, Marbella, Monte-Carlo? (In any case, not St. Tropez, La Costa Brava or the Algarve.) The ones who frown upon their photograph in Vogue and ›W‹, the ones who love to have and to be, but not to show, are most likely to be found on the Normandy coast, in a little outgrown village, also known as the 21st arrondissement of Paris. ›Deauville does not need a Hollywood-style extravaganza to bring the rich and famous to its slate-grey shores. Ever since the town was founded in 1861 by the Duc de Morny, half-brother of Emperor Napoléon III, it has been a late-summer gathering place for Europe's affluent. In the peak month of August, when the population swells from 5,000 to 50,000, Deauville may boast more personal wealth per square foot than any other 880-acre piece of real estate in the world.‹ This is only one side of the golden coin of this North Sea resort, for the season in Deauville is year-round, if of lesser glamour in November and March, bien entendu. Congresses, conventions, incentive tours and seminars find here a platform of beauty, tranquillity, luxury and health, and all the amenities to go along as well as the distractions to regenerate the energy: the sea at your doorstep, the Casino in the centre of town, tennis, horses, and a handful of championship golf courses in the vicinity; lovely little hideaways for a tête-à-tête, grand hotels with equal service and a cultural programme worthy of Baden-Baden and Montecatini. Deauville must be blessed by God (who is probably French, anyway). Distinctly separated from its twin-sister town Trouville by the River Touques, the Norman spa for the BPs, PPs and VIPs is so well-behaved, however, that incidental travellers without money, title or a visa are as welcome as the Aga Khan, the Rothschilds or the Prince of Wales who used to cross the Channel for a polo tournament. No matter, what weather, Les Planches – two kilometres of fine sand dotted with restaurants, cafés and chic boutiques – are even fun for promenades when the rain soaks your cashmeres and the wind blows you right into one of the little wooden huts where the bouillabaisse is à la Marseillaise. The greatest shows take place in the Casino, with the most famous stars performing – and many stars in the audience-, sports events and many more pastimes adorn the calendar here. Lucien Barrière is the host of Deauville, his empire of institutions rivals that of the Société des Bains de Mer in southern Monte-Carlo – the Casino, the best hotels and restaurants, sports arenas et al. If you don't come for the races, for the select Yearling Sales or the American Film Festival, arrange your meetings here and spend, if possible, more than ›One Night In‹ Deauville.

Founded: 1860, by the Duke of Morny; previously a fishing village.

Far-reaching events: without any tradition, at the turn of the century, Deauville develops into a major health resort with a promenade along the harbour, a casino, sports facilities and an Olympic swimming pool; between World Wars I and II the fame of the Parisian jet-set suburb fades, only to develop new and fresh glamour after 1945.

Population: 5,500.

Postal code: F–14800   **Telephone code:** 31 (incorporated in number since 1986)

Climate: mild, Atlantic climate; constant westerly winds keep the summers warm, but not hot; mild winters with little rain.

Best time to visit: April until mid-October.

Calendar of events: *Côte Fleurie Rally* (mid-Feb); *Oldtimer-Rally* (Feb); *International Triathlon Contest* (Jun); *International Bridge Festival* (Aug); *American Film Festival* (mid-Sep); *Paris-Deauville Vintage Car Rally* (Oct).

Fairs and exhibitions: *INTERNATIONAL DOG SHOW* (Jul); *AUCTION OF THOROUGHBRED YEARLINGS* (Aug).

Best view of the city: from the hills of *Mont Canisy*.

Historical and modern sights: *Les Planches*, the 3 km (2 miles) coastal promenade with magnificent Art Nouveau façades and a modern shopping area; the gardens with weekend mansions and de luxe hotels along the *Boulevard Eugène Cornuché*; museum in the *Villa Montebello* (Trouville) with 19th and 20th-century paintings.

Special attractions: *New Golf Club* with 27 holes; *Sailing Club; Aerosports Club; Polo Contests* in August; *horse racing* at the *de la Touques* and *de Clairefontaine* race courses with Grand Prix participation; the famous heated sea-water swimming pool; the *Parc des Enclos* with an impressive variety of trees; the *Ecological Aquarium* in Trouville, one of the earliest in France.

Airport: Deauville-Saint Gatien, DOL; Tel.: 31 88 31 28; 7 km/4 miles.

The Headquarters

NORMANDY

38 Rue Jean Mermoz
F–14800 Deauville
Telephone: 31 88 09 21
Telex: 170617 normand
Owning Company: Chaîne Lucien Barrière
General Manager: Fred Welke
Affiliation/Reservation Systems: Barrière Hotels, JDL, SRS (Steigenberger Reservation Service), Utell
Number of rooms: 347 (36 suites)
Price range: FF 660–1,000
Credit cards: AE, DC, EC, MC, Access, Visa
Location: near the Casino
Built: 1913
Style: Norman and mock Tudor
Main hall porter: Gérard Feuillie
Room service: 24 hours
Laundry/dry cleaning: same day (weekend service)
Conference rooms: 12 (up to 210 persons)
Bar: ›Bar du Normandy‹ (see Bars)
Restaurant: ›Table du Normandy‹ Patrick Giller (maître), J. J. Baise (chef de cuisine)
Nightclub: ›New Brummell‹ (see Nightclubs)

What Sylt is to Hamburg, Porto Ercole to Rome, The Hamptons to New York and Punta del Este to Buenos Aires – that's Deauville to Paris – weekend retreat, holiday resort and simply the capital's social suburb for sand, sun and sea. Among the many auberges de renommé – and towering above Lucien Barrière's relais realm – the Normandy is the most brilliant lighthouse, outshining any other grand hotel along the northern coast of France – and rightfully figuring among the Top Twenty Summer Resorts in the World of the IN World Guide. Mock-Tudor palace architecture, luxuriant garden surroundings and stylishly decorative halls and lounges are regally Norman, but the intimacy of the terrace apartments and the warmth of the gabled rooms' intérieur radiate an atmosphere of total leisure, familiarity and cosiness. Only a few steps to the sea, the hotel is the turntable for water-sports, but also sports its own tennis club and can make every guest a temporary member of the golfing paradise nearby. Horses for romantic rides through the woods or rough stampedes on the polo grounds are self-understood here, and the next-door casinos – one for summer and one for winter – almost seem to belong to the premises. The Normandy has it all, and spa-specialist Fred Welke sees to the perfection of every detail, and pays particular attention to the niveau of the cuisine ranking among the most acclaimed up here. Lunch in the inner courtyard and dinner in the grand dining room belong to the most coveted pleasures in Deauville. The Normandy is, above all, the ideal arena for conference and conventions – especially during off-season and in winter – offering the framework, the facilities, the tranquillity and the backdrop.

The Hideaway

LE PETIT COQ AUX CHAMPS

La Pommeray Sud, near Campigny
F–27500 Pont-Audemer (35 km/22 miles)
Telephone: 32 41 04 19, 32 41 19 17
Owner: the Pommier family
General Manager: Patrick Pommier
Affiliation/Reservation System: Relais et
Châteaux
Number of rooms: 12 (1 suite)
Price range: 800–900 (single)
1,470–1,690 (double;
including one menu)
Credit cards: AE, EC, Visa, CB, MC
Location: south-east of Deauville
Built: 1810
Style: Norman cottage
Hotel amenities: valet parking, house limousine service, garage, car rental, hairstylist, florist, tobacconist, boutique, heated swimming pool
Room amenities: balcony, colour tv, video (dogs allowed)
Bathroom amenities: bathrobe, bidet, hairdrier, telephone
Room service: 12.00/a.m.–24.00/12 p.m.
Laundry/dry cleaning: same day
Conference rooms: for up to 60 persons
Sports (nearby): tennis
Bars: ›Cocktail-Champagne Bar‹ (open till 4.00/a.m.), ›Kathy‹ (12.00/a.m. – 24.00/12.00 p.m.)
Restaurant: ›Le Petit Coq au Champs‹ (12.00/a.m. – 14.00/2.00 p.m. and 19.30/7.30 p.m. – 21.30/9.30 p.m.) Patrick Pommier and Louis Francis Pommier (chefs de cuisine)
Private dining rooms: for up to 60 persons

Surrounded by the green fields and orchards of the gently undulating Normandy countryside south-east of Deauville stands one of the prettiest hideaway relais in northern France. In fact this picture-postcard idyll is actually two nineteenth-century thatched cottages set in a lovingly tended old-fashioned garden full of pinks, poppies and flowering shrubs. Maître cuisinier Louis-Francis Pommier and his wife Marie-Madeleine originally owned a ›Little Cock‹, which crowed in the Saint-Lazare district of Paris; since they moved to the country they have created an auberge de campagne of great charm which nevertheless manages to retain more than a soupçon of the flair of their former home. The lounges, basically contemporary in style, are full of comfortable rattan furniture, an open fireplace and luxuriant pot plants; the dining room, with pretty pink tablecloths and blue-and-white china, has a carved antique farmhouse dresser and domestic bric-à-brac; the bedrooms have pretty floral curtains and – as always – a view of the garden. Son Patrick Pommier produces a cuisine ›au goût du marché‹ which attracts a discriminating clientèle, some of whom even arrive by helicopter from much further afield than Deauville to enjoy the scenery, the setting and the warm hospitality at ›Le Petit Coq aux Champs‹.

Lunch

CHEZ CAMILLO
13 Rue Désiré-Le-Hoc
Telephone: 31 88 79 78
Owner/Manager/Chef de cuisine: José Camillo
Closed: Wednesday; February
Open: 12.00/a.m.–14.00/2 p.m. and 19.00/7 p.m.–22.00/10 p.m.
Cuisine: classic
Specialities: escalope of turbot ›Normande‹; grilled lobster with two sauces; lobster bisque; John Dory ›Nantaise‹; fillet steak au poivre; pigeon with cream of green peas; hot apple tart
Location: off the Avenue de la République; five minutes' walk from the railway station (la Gare)
Setting: small dining room; restrained décor in subdued tones
Amenities: winter garden; bar (for restaurant customers only); aquarium
Atmosphere: understated; dependable
Clientèle: conservative; comfortably-off; local habitués with a preference for old favourites rather than culinary innovations
Dress: no special requirements
Service: attentive
Reservations: advisable
Price range: moderately expensive
Credit cards: AE, DC, Euro, Carte Bleue

Dinner

LE DRAKKAR
77 Rue Eugène Colas
Telephone: 31 88 71 24
Owner/Manager: Philippe Ciavatta
Closed: Monday; Tuesday; January; February 1–15th
Open: 12.00/a.m.–16.00/4 p.m and 19.00/7 p.m–24.00/12 p.m.
Cuisine: traditional
Chef de cuisine: Thierry Lerat
Specialities: crayfish; fish with sauces; grilled turbot with herbs; fillets of John Dory à la Duglerée; fillets of sole ›Normande‹; brill with leeks
Location: central
Setting: luxury pub decorated with an abundance of wood and leather; collection of polo trophies and photos
Amenities: outdoor dining on terrace; pianist
Atmosphere: bon chic, bon genre
Clientèle: youngish and on the way up to middle-aged, successful and definitely not moribund
Dress: tenue correcte
Service: under the eagle eye of patron Philippe Ciavatta
Reservations: not necessary
Price range: medium expensive
Credit cards: AE, DC, Visa

Lunch

LE CIRO'S
Boulevard de la Mer
Telephone: 31 88 22 62
Owner/Manager: Chaîne Lucien Barrière
Closed: never
Open: 12.00/a.m.–14.30/2.30 p.m and 19.30/7.30 p.m.–21.30/9.30 p.m.
Cuisine: traditional, with a hint of nouvelle
Chef de cuisine: Christian Girault
Specialities: seafood; émincé of haddock with ginger; brill in cider with fresh pasta; pink lobster with vegetables; sole with small shellfish; estouffade de turbot et saumon frais aux fettucine; piccata de veau normande – or just a crab cocktail and a glass of white wine
Location: on the seafront
Setting: recently-decorated dining room; light, bright and white; impeccable; sober; comfortable
Amenities: outdoor dining on terrace with a panoramic view of la Plage
Atmosphere: the only place to see and be seen at lunchtime; a local monument
Clientèle: le Tout Deauville (that is, tout le monde); habitués with fame, fortune and flair, from Anthony Quinn to Roman Polanski
Dress: as you like it (as long as they will like you!)
Service: exemplary
Reservations: essential
Price range: rather expensive, even for Deauville
Credit cards: AE, DC, Euro, Visa

Dinner

AUGUSTO (›Le Roi du Homard‹)
27 Rue Désiré-Le-Hoc
Telephone: 31 88 34 49
Owner/Manager: Jean-Claude Lebreton
Closed: Monday and Tuesday (except from July 1st–September 15th); January 15th–March 15th
Open: 12.15/p.m.–14.15/2.15 p.m and 19.15/7.15 p.m.–23.00/11 p.m.
Cuisine: traditional, with a hint of nouvelle
Chef de cuisine: Louis Amiez
Specialities: seafood; lobster in various guises (of course); – lobster soup with truffles; lobster ›façon Augusto‹; lobster ›grande dégustation‹; hot oysters with vegetables; fish casserole; salmon en papillote with ginger; gratin of fresh and exotic fruits with mandarin sabayon
Location: near the Place de Morny
Setting: four rooms in varying styles; on the ground floor, one room decorated in nautical style; one with a tent-like ceiling of green pleated silk; carpets and wall-

paper in warm red tones; on the first floor, two salons – ›Le Normand‹ and ›Le Jardin‹

Amenities: private dining room (15 persons); bar; very soft music; open-air dining on terrace

Atmosphere: the oldest restaurant in Deauville; warm and welcoming; stylish, but with a hint of homeliness

Clientèle: a mostly glittering and glamourous procession of princes, politicians, polo players and personalities; from Woody Allen to the Rothschilds...

Dress: nothing too outrageous or outlandish

Service: under the charming supervision of Claudine Lebreton, with Jean-Claude Lebreton in the rôle of sommelier

Reservations: advisable (pets permitted)

Price range: fairly expensive

Credit cards: all major

Dinner

LA FERME SAINT-SIMEON
Rue Adolphe-Marais
Honfleur (20 km/13 miles)
Telephone: 31 89 23 61
Affiliations: Relais et Châteaux
Owner/Manager: the Boeler family/Roland Boeler
Closed: Wednesday (October 1st to March 31st); December 4th to February 4th
Open: 12.00/a.m.–14.00/2 p.m. and 20.00/8 p.m.–21.15/9.15 p.m.
Cuisine: classic
Chef de cuisine: Pierre Arnaud
Specialities: seafood; sole with chives; steamed sea-perch with beurre blanc; scrambled eggs with Norway lobster; panaché de veau; hot puff pastry apple tart
Location: at Honfleur; 20 km (13 miles) north-east of Deauville
Setting: 17th-century Norman farmhouse in a flower-filled garden with grey-and-white-tiled exterior and colourful windowboxes overlooking the peaceful estuary (petrochemical installations on the other bank notwithstanding); small exquisite dining room with period fireplace and terrace for open-air dining
Amenities: hotel; car park
Atmosphere: one of the most seductively enchanting spots on the Normandy coast
Clientèle: erstwhile haunt of Impressionist painters, notably Boudin and Monet; now the preserve of connoisseurs of the finer things of life
Dress: elegant
Service: friendly and helpful; supervised by the Boeler family
Reservations: advisable to essential
Price range: rather expensive (unless you're a millionaire)
Credit cards: not accepted

Dinner

LE PETIT COQ AUX CHAMPS
Campigny, Pont Audemer (35 km/22 miles)
Telephone: (32) 41 04 19/41 19 17
Affiliations: Relais et Châteaux; Maîtres Cuisiniers de France
Owner/Manager: the Pommier family
Closed: never
Open: 12.00/a.m.–14.00/2 p.m. and 19.30/7.30 p.m.–21.30/9.30 p.m.
Cuisine: local; classic; ›au goût du marché‹
Specialities: carpaccio of salmon with coriander; lamprey with leek fondue; scallops with endives; salmon with nettle cream; aiguillettes of Barbary duckling with cider and apples; mignons de veau with lime and lemon and carrots; dessert ›le petit coq‹ with apple pancake
Location: at Campigny, 35 km (22 miles) south of Deauville
Setting: thatched Norman country cottage in an old-fashioned garden; pretty light dining rooms with picture windows; floral curtains, pink table-linen, blue-and-white china, fine silver and glass; antique dresser, domestic bric-à-brac
Amenities: hotel; private dining rooms (12–60 persons); lounges with piano and open fireplace; open-air dining on terrace; swimming pool; car park; helicopter pad; sports facilities and tourist attractions in the vicinity
Atmosphere: an elegantized rustic idyll; a family-run establishment more like a luxurious weekend cottage than a hotel
Clientèle: celebrities in search of seclusion who know that they can rely on the discretion of the Pommier family; jaded jet-setters, Parisians and members of the liberal professions seeking a respite from the twentieth century without sacrificing material comforts
Dress: suitably soignée
Service: exceptionally warm and welcoming; supervised by Louis Francis Pommier
Reservations: advisable (dogs permitted)
Price range: fairly expensive
Credit cards: AE, Euro, Visa, CA, CB, Master Charge

Meeting Point

BAR DE LA MER
Boulevard de la Mer – Sur les Planches
Telephone: 31 88 27 51
Affiliations: Lucien Barrière group
Owner/Manager: Lucien Barrière
Closed: November 12th – Easter; Saturday and Sunday (Easter–November 11th); never
Open: 10.00/a.m.–19.00/7 p.m.
Cuisine: seafood; quick lunches
Chef de cuisine: Christian Girault
Specialities: salads; scrambled eggs with

smoked salmon; carpaccio with spices;
moules marinière
Location: opposite Ciro's
Setting: seafront restaurant with large ter-
race for open-air dining
Amenities: cocktail bar
Atmosphere: the Fouquet's of the Nor-
mandy coast; a perfect place for whiling
away the afternoon over a bottle of wine
and watching the world go by en route for
Ciro's or the beach
Clientèle: Parisian star-gazers, horse-
lovers, golfers and gamblers; those who
prefer to see rather than to be seen
Dress: come-as-you-please
Service: efficient but friendly
Reservations: not necessary
Price range: fairly expensive
Credit cards: AE, DC, Carte Bleue

Bar

DU NORMANDY
38 Rue Jean Mermoz
Telephone: 31 88 09 21
Owner/Manager: Chaîne Lucien Barri-
ère/Fred Welke
Closed: never
Open: 11.30/a.m.–2.00/a.m.
Location: in the Hotel Normandy
Setting: luxurious piano bar decorated in
rustic Norman style
Amenities: pianist; hotel; restaurant; pri-
vate dining rooms (15–210 persons);
nightclub; valet car parking service
Atmosphere: busy rendezvous for those
wishing to catch up on the latest eques-
trian gossip
Clientèle: the Who's Who of visitors to
Deauville – en route for or coming back
from the races, the Film Festival, the
beach or the restaurant
Service: professionally directed by chief
barman André Pallares
Reservations: advisable
Credit cards: AE, DC, Euro, Visa

Nightclub

NEW BRUMMELL
Rue Edmond Blanc
Telephone: 88 29 55
Affiliations: Lucien Barrière group
Owner/Manager: Lucien Barrière
Closed: January; February
Open: March–June and September–De-
cember: Friday and Saturday; July/Au-
gust: every day 23.00/11 p.m. onwards
Location: in the Casino
Setting: cellar nightclub
Amenities: casino; two restaurants
Atmosphere: chic discothèque ambiance

Clientèle: the post-dinner crowd; glitter-
ing, glamourous and ultra-exclusive
Dress: jacket and tie
Service: attentive
Reservations: advisable (pets prohibited)
Credit cards: AE, DC, Carte Bleue

Shopping

EVERYTHING UNDER ONE ROOF
Printemps, Au   104 Rue Eugène-Colas

FOR HIM
Lapidus, Ted   Rue Eugène-Colas

FOR HER
Boutique Manon   Place du Casino

BEAUTY & HAIR
Beaussier, R. et P.   Rue Eugène-Colas

JEWELLERY
Cartier   Rue Gontaut-Biron

LOCAL SPECIALITIES
Tabac Catelain (tobacco)
73 Rue Désiré-Le-Hoc
Helen Sports (women's fashion)
98 Rue Eugène-Colas
Maxime (men's fashion)
76 Rue Eugène-Colas
Jules et Julie (children's fashion)
Rue Eugène-Colas
Esterel, Jacques (leather fashion)
Place du Casino
Dior, Christian (furs)
Rue Gontaut-Biron
Maison de la Presse (Miss Boyer) (books)
88 Rue Eugène-Colas
Hermès (gifts)
Place du Casino
Sellier, Au (baggage & travel accessories)
72–74 Rue Désiré-Le-Hoc
Callac Marine (boat accessories)
45 Rue Victor Hugo
Cave Oliffe (food and beverages)
44 Rue Oliffe
Christel (perfumery)
44 Rue Désiré-Le-Hoc
Jacquot (shoes)
55 Rue Désiré-Le-Hoc

The City

A glamourous lunch at Bocuse, a ruinous shopping spree through the Rue du Rhône and a romantic dinner at the Villa Sassi to round off the day may be a fashionable routine in Grenoble – Lyons, Geneva and Turin are triangularly set around the capital of the French Alps and just an Alpine's dash away – but there is no need to seek out far-off shores when you stop over in this mountain-resort-cum-scientific-brains-trust of La Grande Nation. With a film-set panorama and avant-garde city planning, hard-working, profoundly thinking, restful, sportive Grenoble is one of the most attractive locations for business and pleasure tourism. You won't encounter a shortage of energy, either: the valley is the country's epicentre of hydro-power and atomic energy, and the climate is inspiring. The intellectual and artistic one, too. The 600-year old Grenoble University is world famous for natural sciences and engineering while the cultural institutions are home to the upcoming jeunese dorée of the Fine Arts. And yet, Grenoble is not all work – almost throughout the year you can ski in the neighbourhood, with the status slopes of Megève, Courchevel, Val d'Isère, et al. another Alpine's dash away. Having hosted the Winter Olympics in 1968, the Ice Stadium in the sculpture-dotted Parc Paul-Mistral attracts visitors for its architecture as much as for skating and other sports. The natural beauty, the high concentration of intellect and sports, the favourable position in this international triangle (with the Côte d'Azur also within easy reach) and the cosmopolitan spirit make Grenoble one of the blessed cities in central Europe. For her local literato, Henri Beyle – dit Stendahl, as well: ›Ce que j'aime de Grenoble, c'est qu'elle a la physionomie d'une ville et non d'un grand village.‹ Even today.

Founded: 379 A.D., by the Roman Emperor Gratianus on the site of a Celtic settlement; Grenoble (French) – from Gratianopolis, ›city of Gratianus‹.

Far-reaching events: 3rd–4th centuries – gradual Christianization of the Roman mountain village; 415 – Visigoth rule; 5th century – Grenoble ceded to the House of Burgundy; 534 – to the Franks; 12th century – residence of the Counts of Albon, who later call themselves ›Dauphins‹; 1339 – foundation of the university; 1349 – Grenoble passes to the French crown and the title ›Dauphin‹ is accorded to the crown prince; 18th century – a bastion of the Revolution; 1815 – Napoleon slept here, on his way to Paris, giving the Hôtel Napoléon its name; 1869 – the first hydro-electric power station in France is built; 1968 – Xth Winter Olympic Games held here, leading to a tourist and construction boom.

Population: 400,000 (metropolitan area); capital of the Isère department.

Postal code: F–38000   **Telephone code:** 76 (incorporated in number since 1986)

Climate: alpine; fickle.

Best time to visit: any time.

Calendar of events: *Festival of Film Shorts* (Jul); *World Assembly of Dauphinois Kinsmen* (Aug); *Six-Day Bicycle Race* (Nov).

Fairs and exhibitions: *SEA* (Jan/Feb) – European antiques fair; *HOLIDAY AND TRAVEL FAIR* (Mar); *SIG* (Mar) - international winter sports equipment trade show; *DOG SHOW* (Apr); *SPRING AND AUTUMN FAIRS* (May & Oct); *SAM* (Apr/May) – mountain and ski resort equipment; *SCALE MODEL AND MINIATURE SHOW* (Jun); *ALPEXPO* (Nov); *ARTISA* (Nov) – art, arts and crafts fair; *INTERNATIONAL MOTOR SHOW* (Dec).

Best views of the city: from the restaurant and observation platform of the *Fort de la Bastille*, reachable by cable-car; from the top of the *Perret Tower*, reachable by lift; from the *Croix de Chamrousse*, a plateau at 2260 m, reachable by climbing.

Historical sights: *Notre-Dame Cathedral* (12th century) – nicely decorated, with a lovely tabernacle; *St. Andrew's Church* (13th century) – last resting-place of French hero Bayard; the *Palace of Justice* (15th century) – a beautiful Gothic-Renaissance hybrid with magnificent wood carvings; the *Garden of the Dauphins* – rare plants in an Alpine setting; *St. Lawrence's Church* (6th century) – one of the country's earliest Christian edifices, with a Merovingian crypt; the *Cours Jean Jaurès* – a lavish boulevard constructed at the turn of the century; the *Museum* – with one of the best collections of 19th and 20th – century French art outside Paris; *Couvent de la Grande Chartreuse* (11th century) – beautiful monastery of St. Bruno, with a 15th-century chapel and 14th-century cloisters;

Modern sights: the *Town Hall* in the Parc Paul-Mistral; *Maison de la Culture*; *Congress Centre*.

Special attractions: the *Olympic Ice Stadium; parachuting; water skiing, thermal baths* and, of course, *skiing.*

Important companies with headquarters in the city: *Allibert* (construction plastics); *Becton Dickinson* (medical and surgical instruments); *La Dauphinoise* (household and kitchen articles); *EFCIS* (electronic components and switches); *IMI Pacific* (heating appliances); *Pascal* (construction); *Rosner* (hydraulic bearings); *SAMS* (wires and cables).

Airport: Grenoble-St. Geoirs, GWB; Tel.: 76 65 48 48; 45 km/28 miles; Air France, Tel.: 76 87 63 48.

The Headquarters

PARK HOTEL

10 Place Paul-Mistral
F–38027 Grenoble Cedex
Telephone: 76 87 29 11
Telex: 320 767 parkgnb
General Manager: Henri Ducret
Number of rooms: 59 (3 suites)
Price range: FF 450 (single)
FF 790 (double)
Credit cards: AE, DC, EC, Visa
Location: city centre, facing the famous
Parc Paul Mistral & Chaîne de Belle-
donne
Built: 1961 (recently renovated)
Style: modern
Hotel amenities: parking, wheelchair ac-
cessibility (pets allowed)
Room amenities: air conditioning, colour
tv, radio, mini-bar
Bathroom amenities: bathrobe, telephone
Room service: 6.30/a.m. to 24.00/12.00
p.m.
Laundry/dry cleaning: same day
Conference rooms: (up to 50 persons)
Bars: ›Taverne de Ripaille‹ (6.30/a.m.–
1.00/a.m.)
Restaurants: ›Taverne de Ripaille‹
(11.00/a.m.–24.00/12.00) Jean-Jacques
Gigaut (chef de cuisine)

*The Park Hotel, standing proudly by Gren-
oble's Parc Paul-Mistral against the dramatic Alpine panorama of the Chaîne de
Belledonne, is prima facie evidence of the
Isère capital's important rôle in the electro-
economy and the nouvelle vague tourism of
France. A well-equipped modern de luxe
hotel with more than its share of natural
beauty in its surroundings and technological inventiveness in its facilities (radio-con-
trolled staff can be summoned at the touch
of a button), the Park is small enough to
treat its guests as individuals (a feeling enhanced by the varied furnishing schemes in
the bedrooms) but large enough to host a
wide range of international conventions as
well as playing a leading part in the various
official events staged in Grenoble in recent
years – from the Winter Olympic Games in
1968 to the Davis Cup in 1983. With an
ambiance which blends savoir-faire with
joie-de-vivre, this attractive hotel is popular
amongst visiting scientists and professional
sportsmen alike.*

Lunch

POULARDE BRESSANE (›Piccinini‹)
12 Place Paul-Mistral
Telephone: 76 87 08 90
Owner/Manager/Chef de cuisine: Jean-Charles Piccinini
Closed: Saturday lunchtime, Sunday; July 15th–August 15th; last week in December
Open: 12.00/a.m.–14.00/2 p.m. and 19.00/7 p.m.–22.00/10 p.m.
Cuisine: classic, with a hint of nouvelle
Specialities: gâteau de foies blonds au coulis d'écrevisses; wolf-fish with paprika and ginger; poularde de Bresse en vessie with vegetables and sauce au foie gras; tarte aux pralines
Location: near Grenoble's largest public garden (Parc Paul-Mistral)
Setting: rather grandiose dining room with a view of the kitchen on the one side and (through the bay windows) on the other the Belledonne Massif
Amenities: private dining room (60 persons); air conditioning
Atmosphere: rather festive, although not formidably so
Clientèle: le Tout Grenoble; resident academics, Haute Bourgeoisie and visiting businessmen
Dress: casually elegant to elegantly casual
Service: anxious-to-please
Reservations: advisable
Price range: fairly expensive
Credit cards: AE, DC, Euro, Visa

Dinner

THIBAUD
25 Boulevard Agutte-Sembat
Telephone: 76 43 01 62
Owner/Manager/Chef de cuisine: Pierre-Alain Thibaud
Closed: Sunday; public holidays
Open: 12.00/a.m.–14.00/2 p.m. and 19.30/7.30 p.m.–21.00/9 p.m.
Cuisine: traditional and local
Specialities: artichokes with bone marrow; Royan ravioli; grilled wolf-fish with tarragon sauce; grives (thrushes) à l'étouffée; Chartreuse ice-cream; le gâteau des Prélats (a speciality from Pau)
Location: central; near St. Joseph's church
Setting: large, handsome dining room furnished in English style; attractive lighting
Amenities: private dining room (12 persons); air conditioning
Atmosphere: vaguely Anglo-Saxon (except for the cuisine!)
Clientèle: Grenoble en fête; industrialists, publishers and members of the liberal professions; prosperous and dependable

Dress: no restrictions or requirements
Service: delightfully courteous; supervised by the wife of the proprietor
Reservations: advisable
Price range: fairly expensive
Credit cards: AE, DC, Carte Bleue

Lunch

L'ESCALE
Place de la République
Varces (13 km/8 miles)
Telephone: 76 72 80 19
Affiliations: Relais et Châteaux
Owner/Manager/Chef de cuisine: René Brunet
Closed: Sunday evening; (October–May) Monday; (May–October) Tuesday; first three weeks in January; first week in May; November 20th–28th
Open: 12.15/p.m.–14.00/2 p.m. and 19.30/7.30 p.m.–21.15/9.15 p.m.
Cuisine: nouvelle
Specialities: fillets of home-smoked fish with avocado salad; Alpine snails à la niçoise; beef in puff pastry with truffle sauce; fillet of turbot with crayfish; an array of desserts so dazzling that one is tempted to try them all
Location: at Varces, 13 km (8 miles) south-west of Grenoble along the N75
Setting: on the outskirts of Grenoble; charming little inn in an immaculately-kept garden; dining room with modern décor; satinized linen walls; veranda
Amenities: hotel consisting of wooden chalets in a garden; private dining room (16 persons); open-air dining on terrace by the Alpine garden; car park
Atmosphere: an epicurean paradise in exquisite surroundings
Clientèle: expense-account connoisseurs of fine food and good living
Dress: as you like it (as long as they will like you!)
Service: very helpful and welcoming
Reservations: advisable
Price range: expensive, even by Paris standards
Credit cards: AE, EC

Dinner

CHAVANT
Route Napoléon par Eybens village, Bresson (8 km/5 miles)
Telephone: 76 25 15 14
Owner/Manager/Chef de cuisine: Jean-Pierre Chavant
Closed: Wednesday; between Christmas and New Year
Open: 12.30/p.m.–13.30/1.30 p.m. and 18.30/6.30 p.m.–21.30/9.30 p.m.
Cuisine: classique
Specialities: vegetables with minced duck

(effeuillé du jardin aux émincés de canard); lamb with garlic; langouste à la nage; quail ›Emile Chavant‹; marinated salmon; turbot with morel mushrooms
Location: at Bresson, 8 km (5 miles) south of Grenoble along the D5
Setting: recently-renovated dining room; rather grandiose décor with an abundance of cherry-wood furnishings; enchanting terrace in a shady, flower-filled garden full of birdsong and mountain air
Amenities: hotel; private dining rooms (25 persons); air conditioning; car park
Atmosphere: heaven on earth for lovers of good food, especially on a sunny summer's day
Clientèle: gourmet habitués; bankers, brokers and businessmen tired of Grenoble; distinguished visitors, delegates, doctors and dentists
Dress: what you will
Service: particularly charming; directed by the sister of the proprietor, Danièle Chavant
Reservations: advisable (no dogs in restaurant)
Price range: philanthropic
Credit cards: AE, Visa

Café

LE GRAND
2 place Victor-Hugo
Telephone: 76 46 37 27
Owner/Manager: Jacques Veal
Closed: Sunday
Open: 7.00/a.m.–1.00/a.m.
Location: central
Setting: characteristic café with classic décor and a boulevard terrace for outdoor dining
Amenities: home-made pâtisserie (!!)
Atmosphere: Parisian
Clientèle: heterogeneous collection of local citizens from 9 months to 99 years, plus a fair number of footsore visitors to the town
Service: fast and friendly
Price range: medium
Dress: elegant and correct
Reservations: not necessary (pets allowed)
Credit cards: not accepted

Bar

AU PARC
40 Avenue du Mal-Randon
Telephone: 76 43 37 98
Owner/Manager: Jacques Guillet
Closed: Sunday; August 15th–September 15th
Open: 7.00/a.m.–24.00/12 p.m.
Location: a short walk from the cathedral
Setting: small bistro; bright, cheerful; modern décor
Amenities: bar/bistro serving seafood of the highest quality and freshness delivered regularly from the Brittany coast; large selection of hors d'œuvres from buffet
Atmosphere: lively; chic but not chichi
Clientèle: young, confident and on-the-way up to middle-aged, successful and definitely not moribund
Dress: come-as-you-please
Service: pleasantly attentive
Reservations: advisable
Credit cards: Carte Bleue

Shopping

THE BEST OF ART
David, Jean Claude   (modern art)
Tel. 76 42 11 53

The City

Philippe Auguste sacks the city, Philippe Le Bon restores it in splendour; Louis XIV personally leads the occupation as does Prince Eugene some time later; the Austrian army has to abandon its storming the Vauban Citadel after the French Revolution, but Ruprecht of Bavaria takes the fortress again in the First World War, and one war later the famous generals Molinié and Juin have to cede it yet again to the Germans. Napoléon slept here and Charles André Joseph Marie de Gaulle was even born here, but with all the battles and resulting heroism Lille has hardly reached the fame and image of a little seaside village like Saint-Tropez. La Capitale du Nord, of the French province of Flanders, fourth largest city of La Grande Nation (incorporating Roubaix, Tourcoing and almost Mouscron behind the Belgian border as well) and economically as important as Numbers 2 and 3, Lille even has architectural highlights, Flemish Baroque, beautiful parks in the city and forests around, historic inns and the oldest stock exchange, but somehow it has not yet managed to appear on the pleasure traveller's trail as one of the status stations in the area, let alone in the country. The only business apart from business seems to be the university (France's second largest); at second sight, however, you will discover not only the attractions of this little-known city among foreigners and Frenchmen alike, but also the joie-de-vie of its inhabitants who apparently make up for hard work with a sense for pleasure. Haute cuisine is not the only pastime here; there is quite a nightlife to speak of, and festivities range from the local ›ducasses‹ in each quartier to the Grande Kermesse at Pentecost and the even grander Grande Braderie. The Lillois love to fête, and a visitor is as welcome here as he may be snobbed in the capital. And the morning after, they will return to the factories and offices to continue the city's tradition of textiles – cotton, linen, jute, jersey – and metallurgy – locomotives, agricultural machinery, household appliances. Breweries and distilleries serve business and pleasure alike, as does the exceptional production of chocolates and candies. And with a perfect infrastructure linking it to every major city in the country – being ideally located between Brussels and Paris – there is no reason any more not to storm the Queen of Citadels.

Founded: first mentioned 1066; Lille (French), from ›L'île‹ – ›the island‹.

Far-reaching events: 11th century – capital of the County of Flanders; 15th century – under the rule of the Dukes of Burgundy; end of the 15th century – Flanders under Austrian rule; 1667 – captured by Louis XIV after a siege; 1668 – Aachen Peace Treaty cedes Lille to France; 1708 – Duke of Marlborough takes Lille; 1713 – returned to France under the Peace of Utrecht; 1939–45 – heavy bombing damage.

Population: 1 million (metropolitan area).

Postal code: F–59800   **Telephone code:** 20 (incorporated in number since 1986)

Climate: fairly temperate.

Best time to visit: mid-April to October.

Calendar of events: *International Festival of Short Subject and Documentary Films* (March); *Grand Parade and City Festival* (mid-Jun); *Open-Air Classical Music Festival* (July/Aug) – in the Parc Vauban, near the citadel; *Grande Braderie* (1 & 2 Sept) – antiques and flea market; *Festival de Lille* (Oct) – international cultural festival with classical and modern music, dance, theatre and puppet shows.

Fairs and exhibitions: *LILLE INTERNATIONAL FAIR* (Apr); *TOBACCO FAIR* (May); *APPLICA* (May) – practical electronics and information systems.

Best views of the city: from the top of the bell tower of the *Hôtel de Ville.*

Historical and modern sights: the *Old Town;* old *Stock Exchange* – a typical example of 17th-century Flemish architecture; *Citadel* (17th century) – designed by Vauban, the most important and best preserved in France; *Church of St. Maurice* – with five naves and an ornate 14th–15th century tower; *Hospice Comtesse* (13th century), founded by Jeanne de Flandres; *Palais des Beaux Arts* – one of France's best provincial museums, with an excellent collection of impressionists and a wide range of French, Flemish and Spanish artists; *Church of St. André* (18th century) – Jesuit with a Baroque gallery; *Notre Dame de Réconciliation* (13th century) – the oldest church building in Lille; *Town Hall* (1933) – with sculptures of Lille's guardian giants at the foot of the bell tower; *Cathedral* (19th and 20th centuries) – unfinished – with a statue of the town's patron saint, Notre-Dame-de la Treille; the *Palace of Justice* (1968) – both modern and original, with a pyramid-shaped spectator gallery and some very beautiful tapestries.

Special attractions: *Charles-de-Gaulle-Museum* in his birthplace at Rue Princesse 9; the *Old Town* at night; a *concert* in the Parc Vauban on a summer evening.

Important companies with headquarters in the city: *Le Blan & Cie.* (natural yarns and threads); *Crédit Mutuel du Nord* (banking); *Crepelle & Cie.* (pumps); *Kestner* (chemical and pharmaceutical appliances); *La Mondiale* (life insurance); *Neu* (industrial clothing, machines and appliances); *Sergic* (engineering); *TV Flandres* (transports); *Voix du Nord* (newspaper).

Airport: Lille-Lesquin, LIL; Tel.: 20 95 92 00, 8 km/5 miles; Air France, Tel.: 20 57 80 00.

The Headquarters

ROYAL

2 Boulevard Carnot
F–59800 Lille
Telephone: 20 51 05 11
Telex: 820 575 royalil
General Manager: Alain et Marie-Louise Daveluy
Affiliation/Reservation System: Resinter
Number of rooms: 102
Price range: FF 248–320 (single)
FF 281–380 (double)
Credit cards: ACC, AE, DC, EC, MC, Visa
Location: central, close to the Opera
Built: 1913 (renovated in 1983)
Style: traditional Flemish architecture
Hotel amenities: air conditioning, car park, wheelchair accessibility
Room amenities: tv, radio, mini-bar
Room service: 6.30/a.m.–22.00/10 p.m.
Laundry/dry cleaning: same day
Conference rooms: for up to 60 guests
Bar: ›American bar‹ (16.00/4.00 p.m.–24.00/12.00 p.m.

In an industrial country, some of the most important cities just have to be surrounded by mines and smoke-stacks, blast-furnaces and chain-production companies. Bless Nice and Bordeaux for sea, sun and wine, but Lille has its singularly rough charm and a mix of two worlds in an attractive blend – and, in the midst of it, surrounded by the Grand' Place, the opera house and the stock exchange, lies its foremost residence, Le Royal. Once linked to the prestigious Concorde chain, it is now part of Ibis and perfectly managed by Alain and Marie-Louise Daveluy. Modern, functional and efficiently geared to the never-ending stream of managers and executives for the innumerable industries based in the area, the building which dates back to the beginning of the century displays pleasant notes of French and Flemish origin. The proximity to the Belgian border is also felt in the international clientèle who come here for stop-overs, meetings, conferences or just a draught beer in the gay bar which proves everyone wrong who thinks that joie-de-vivre is only felt in the capital, the wine country and the Côte d'Azur. Don't dread the fact that there is no restaurant in the house; with its central location Le Royal is only a truffle's throw away from starred gourmet pantheons, picturesque inns and lively pubs. Le Royal is all business and no-frills décor, light colours, practical interior and quick service. Top-brass guests of the leading companies are all put up here. Make this your headquarters when you have to go to Lille.

Lunch

LE PARIS
52 bis, Rue Esquermoise
Telephone: 20 55 29 41
Owner/Manager: Loïc Martin
Closed: Sunday evening; early August–early September
Open: 12.00/a.m.–14.00/2 p.m. and 19.30/7.30 p.m.–21.45/9.45 p.m.
Cuisine: nouvelle (›au goût du marché‹)
Chefs de cuisine: Loïc Martin and Gérard Chamoley
Specialities: fortnightly changing menu; pike and sorrel cream flan; breast of chicken with ginger; veal with Morello cherries; coquilles St. Jacques sauce Véronique; profiteroles with fresh peppermint and bitter chocolate; charlotte aux fraises with pistachio-flavoured crème anglaise
Location: central
Setting: townhouse dating back to 1792; dining room in reds and beiges; stained-glass windows; dominated by large modern Aubusson tapestry entitled ›Soleil d'hiver‹
Amenities: two private dining rooms (20–80 persons)
Atmosphere: comfortable and comforting
Clientèle: local devotees, plus a sprinkling of presidents and premiers, from Giscard d'Estaing to Richard von Weizsäcker
Dress: elegantly conservative to conservatively elegant
Service: knowledgeable and efficient
Reservations: advisable (pets permitted)
Price range: moderately expensive
Credit cards: AE, DC

Dinner

BRASSERIE DE LA PAIX
25 Place Ribour
Telephone: 20 54 70 41
Owner/Manager: Claude Malapelle
Closed: Sunday
Open: 12.00/a.m.–14.15/2.15 p.m. and 19.00/7 p.m.–24.00/12 p.m.
Cuisine: modern bourgeois
Chef de cuisine: Jean-Marie Lamy
Specialities: oysters; braised veal and carrots; sauerkraut with fish; Challans duckling; pear tart
Location: central
Setting: stylised turn-of-the-century brasserie; an abundance of wood; velvet banquettes; Desvres ceramics portraying a succession of scantily-clad ladies; attractive lighting
Amenities: outdoor dining on terrace
Atmosphere: bon chic, bon genre
Clientèle: mostly young, self-confident, gay and on-the-way-up
Dress: predominantly casual

Service: friendly
Reservations: essential
Price range: medium
Credit cards: AE, DC, Visa

Lunch

L'ARMORIAL
1055 Rue Nationale
Prémesques (9 km/5 miles)
Telephone: 20 08 84 24/20 08 84 16
Owner/Manager: François Lepelley
Closed: Wednesday; Friday and Sunday evening; January; two weeks in August
Open: 12.30/p.m.–14.00/2 p.m. and 19.30/7.30 p.m.–21.00/9 p.m.
Cuisine: classic with a light accent
Chef de cuisine: Philippe Lepelley
Specialities: fresh foie gras de canard; casserole of fish ›Argonautes‹; venison with cassis (in season); home-produced poultry with truffles, foie gras and vegetables from the garden; fillets of sole with chives; sumptuous desserts
Location: 9 km (5 miles) north-west of Lille
Setting: Flemish-style country château set amidst parkland; lawns; cows, hens; a lake with swans; inside, dining rooms of various sizes; open fire in winter
Amenities: private dining rooms (10–150 persons); car park; helicopter pad
Atmosphere: seductively seigneurial
Clientèle: businessmen during the week give way to the Lille Saturday lunch crowd en famille at weekends, with banquets for those with cause for celebration at any time
Dress: according to season and circumstances
Service: deferential without a trace of obsequiousness
Reservations: advisable (pets permitted)
Price range: aristocratic
Credit cards: AE, DC, Visa

Dinner

LE FLAMBARD
79 Rue d'Angleterre
Telephone: 20 51 00 06
Affiliations: Maître Cuisinier; membre titulaire de l'Académie Culinaire de France
Owner/Manager/Chef de cuisine: Robert Bardot
Closed: Sunday evening; Monday; August
Open: 12.15/a.m.–14.30/2.30 p.m. and 19.15/7.15 p.m.–21.30/9.30 p.m.
Cuisine: cuisine artistique sur base classique
Specialities: gilt-head bream (daurade) with leeks; roast turbot with tomato butter and anchovies; roast de goujons au pistou; duckling pot-au-feu; roast Pyrenean mountain lamb; roast pigeon with

peach and spices; nougat glacé au coulis de fraises; regularly-changing menu
Location: a psalm away from Notre-Dame de la Treille
Setting: ›monument historique‹ – 17th-century former patrician palais; recently renovated – three dining rooms with unrendered brick, exposed beams, blue ceilings and leather upholstery
Amenities: bar (wood panelling)
Atmosphere: chaude et intime, mais avec classe
Clientèle: local expense-account gourmets during or after business hours; varying proportions of foreign visitors from Fort-de-France to Fiji
Dress: from Chanel to Jean-Louis Scherrer
Service: welcoming
Reservations: advisable (dogs permitted)
Price range: justifiably expensive
Credit cards: AE, DC

Bar

QUEEN VICTORIA
Rue de Pas
Telephone: 20 54 51 28
Owner/Manager: Paul Aubursin
Open: 11.00/a.m.–2.00/a.m.
Location: opposite the ›Palais des Congrès‹
Setting: bar downstairs serving quick lunches as well as drinks; quiet lounge on the first floor
Amenities: restaurant (40 persons); brasserie (60 persons); open air dining in summer; air conditioning; car park in the ›Palais des Congrès‹
Atmosphere: from the animated and rather noisy (especially at lunchtime) in the main bar to the secluded and peaceful upstairs
Clientèle: advertising excutives, mediamen, journalists, politicians and civil servants
Service: superior
Reservations: advisable
Credit cards: AE, DC, EC, Visa, Carte Bleue

Nightclub

LA RENARDIERE
227 Boulevard Victor-Hugo
Telephone: 20 57 03 46
Owner/Manager: SA La Renardière/ Gaston Mercier-Chauve
Closed: Sunday
Open: from 22.00/10 p.m. to 5.00/a.m.
Location: close to the Town Hall (›Hôtel de Ville‹)
Setting: a comfortable and intimate nightclub with mahogany décor, little vaults for all sorts of private affairs, Chippendale tables

Amenities: restaurant (12.00/a.m.–15.00/3 p.m. and 21.00/9 p.m.–5.00/a.m.) offering classic French cuisine including excellent fresh seafood (chef Jean-Claude Decodin); no pets allowed
Atmosphere: from an elegant tango to a modern disco-waltz
Clientèle: local members of the liberal professions; visiting Brussels businessmen; international birds of passage
Dress: relaxed but elegant
Service: welcoming
Reservations: advisable
Price range: medium
Credit cards: AE, CB, DC, EC, MC

Shopping

EVERYTHING UNDER ONE ROOF
France Printemps 43/45 Rue Nationale

FOR HIM
Renaud 32–34 Rue Faidherbe

FOR HER
Lasserre 9 Rue Neuve

BEAUTY & HAIR
Tendence 53 Rue de l'Hôpital-Militaire

JEWELLERY
Lepage 71–73 Rue Nationale

LOCAL SPECIALITIES
Tyko, Madeleine (women's fashion)
10 Rue Neuve
Francesco Smalto (men's fashion)
36 Rue de Béthune
Lingot d'Or (gifts)
46–52 Grand'Place
Au Depart (baggage & travel accessories)
73 Rue Nationale
Parfumerie du Soleil d'Or (perfumery)
64–66 Grand'Place
Jourdan, Charles (shoes)
26 Rue Nationale
Yanka (confiserie)
75 Rue Nationale
Flora (flowers)
30 Rue du Sec Arembault

Bocuse, of course. Lourdes or Collonges-au-Mont-d'Or – that is the question. But not for gourmets. Lyons is the world capital of Haute Cuisine, nouvelle or vieille, personnalisée, sophistiquée or spontanée. And with Madame Point, Chapel, Blanc, Troisgros and Pic in the neighbourhood, the pilgrimage is an involved one. France's second city is Number One for lunch, dinner and alimentary orgies – but also for metallurgy, textiles, silks and synthetics, and competing in various other industries such as heavy goods vehicles, chemicals, pharmaceuticals, leather products, paper manufacturing, printing and, again, food. Lyons is also one of the oldest and historically most important cities through twenty centuries – Caesar's camp, Claudius' cradle, Louise Labé's and Madame de Sévigné's salon, Robespierre's battlefield of revenge, the Résistance's nest during the Second World War and the outset for creativity in the sciences as well as the arts – Ampère, Montgolfier, Jacquard revolutionized the world in their fields and conserved their city's shining image. The theatre in all its forms has a firm place in the life and hearts of Lyons' burghers – from Rabelaisian guignoleries to political cabaret – just like black magic, and if you are lucky enough to be granted a private audience by ›Napauléon‹ Bocuse, you may witness a special performance, being played your favourite songs on his antique orgue (for which he built a house), one of the largest and most amusing in the world. But Lyons, all too neglected as a place of cultural and pleasure tourism, known – and used – as a stop-over between Paris and the Côte d'Azur, has many sights worth a visit even when you are on a diet. The Old Town ›traboules‹ – a labyrinth of mystery, the river banks from spring to autumn and life on the Place Bellecour is a joyful experience by itself. And a glass of Beaujolais in hand in one of the bistro-bouchers, tasting some of the simple delicacies of one of the city's famous ›Mères‹ and dreaming about the next meal at one of the city's even more famous wunderkind-chefs, you will agree with Colette that ›a few days in Lyons are eternity‹. But a pleasant one.

Founded: 43 B.C. by the Romans; Lyon (French) – from Lugdunum (Latin) – ›hill of ravens‹.

Far-reaching events: 27 B.C. – Lugdunum the capital of the Roman province of Gaul; 197 A.D. – Septimus Severus massacres the local Christian community; 843 – the town is ceded to Lotharingia, then to Burgundy; 1032 – becomes part of the Holy Roman Empire; 1312 – Lyon passes to the French crown; 16th century – Lyons establishes itself as a centre for silk weaving; 18th century – industrialization of the silk industry; 1793 – Lyons resists the revolutionary reign of terror and the Jacobins order the city to be razed; 19th century – the city, rebuilt by Napoleon, is the scene of riots by protesting silk workers; 1940–44 – the city is the centre of the French resistance movement.

Population: 1.2 million (urban area), capital of the Rhône department; second largest city in France.

Postal code: F–69000   **Telephone code:** 7 (incorporated in number since 1986).

Climate: temperate, but with frequent mists.

Calendar of events: *Festival de Lyon* (early summer) – concerts, theatre, ballet with renowned participants; *Flea Market* (Jun); *Berlioz Festival* (Sep) – famous and not-so-famous works by Berlioz; *International Marionette Festival* (beginning of Sep); *Film Festival* (Sep) – rare films shown by the Lumière Institute; *Music Festival* (Nov) – in the Old City of Lyons; *Festival of Lights* (Dec 8).

Fairs and exhibitions: *INFORAR* (Mar) – information and office organization; *FOIRE INTERNATIONALE DE LYONS* (Apr) – consumer goods; *MEUROPAM* (Sep) – furniture; *MIDEST* (Oct, biennial) – international suppliers' market; *SECUREXPO* (Oct) – industrial safety and protection; *POLLUTEX* (Nov) – environmental protection; *EXPOTHERM* (Nov) – heating technology; *EUROBAT* (Nov) – building exhibition.

Historical sights: *Roman Amphitheatre* (15 B.C.) – the oldest in France, with *museum* of antiquities; *Saint-Martin d'Ainay* (1107) – Romanesque; the oldest church in the city; *Cathédrale St. Jean* (1180) – a classic example of early Gothic architecture; *Hôtel de Ville* (16th century) – pure Renaissance except for the 18th-century roof; *Loge du Change* – another fine reminder of the Renaissance; *Musée des Arts Décoratifs* – furniture, tapestries, porcelain and objets d'art; *Musée Historique du Tissu* – fabrics; *Place Bellecour* (1800) – one of the largest in France.

Special attractions: French ›*Punch and Judy*‹ *shows* – invented here by Laurent Mourguet; *Parc de la Tête d'Or* – the scent of a million roses; *Château Lumière* – the villa of the film pioneering brothers Lumière, with a spectacular museum; a walk through the *Old City* with its ›traboules‹, rabbit-warren passageways leading from house to house and lane to lane, or along the *quays* of the Rhône or the Saône; lunch at *Bocuse;* a *TGV* ride to Paris; *National Car Museum;* including pre-1918 models (at Rochetaillée).

Important companies with headquarters in the city: *Banque Veuve Morins-Pons* (banking); *Billon Frères* (knitwear); *Companie Nationale de Rhône* (heavy plant); *Crédit Lyonnais* (banking); *Gifrer Barbezat* (pharmaceuticals); *Institut Mérieux* (trimmings); *Lionel-Dupont* (metal grills and grids); *Renault Véhicules Industriels* (heavy goods vehicles); *Solyvente-Ventec* (air conditioning); *Somatrans* (transport).

Airport: Lyons-Satolas, LYS; Tel.: 78 71 92 21; 25 km/16 miles; Air France, Tel.: 78 42 79 00.

The Headquarters

SOFITEL LYON

20 Quai Gailleton
F–69288 Lyons Cedex 02
Telephone: 78 42 72 50
Telex: 330 225 sofilyo
Owning Company: Sofitel/Accor
General Manager: Werner Seiss
Affiliation/Reservation Systems: Sofitel Hotels, Resinter
Number of rooms: 200 (10 suites)
Price range: FF 720–2,180
Credit cards: Access, AE, DC, EC, MC, Visa
Location: central, on the banks of the Rhône
Built: 1969 (renovated recently)
Style: modern
Hotel amenities: car park, shopping gallery, hairdresser, florist
Room amenities: colour tv, video, minibar, wheelchair accessibility (no pets)
Bathroom amenities: bidet, bathrobe, telephone (some)
Room service: 6.00/a.m.–24.00/12 p.m.
Conference rooms: sixteen
Bars: ›Le Fregoli‹, piano bar, near the Wintergarden ›Le Melhor‹, American bar on the 8th floor
Restaurants: ›Les 3 Dômes‹ on the 8th floor (12.00/a.m.–14.30/2.30 p.m. and 19.30/7.30 p.m.–22.00/10 p.m.); Guy Girerd (chef de cuisine), classic cuisine
Private dining rooms: seven

Lyons is the capital of Grande Cuisine, Haute Cuisine, Nouvelle Cuisine and Cuisine Scientifique Sophistiquée. Despite the importance of textiles, chemicals and electronics, notwithstanding the second largest population in France and the central location at the crossroads of the country with the TGV terminal as another forte for futurism – all the interest, talk and yearning is cuisine. Small wonder, all hostelries concentrate on neutral efficiency and fast turnover business – except one: Le Sofitel. France's foremost hotel chain, expanding over the globe, is faithful to its tradition d'hospitalité along with all modern facilities, high standard and personal service – and even its own brand of grande cuisine without competing with the Bocuses and Chapels and their disciples. Favourable location on the banks of the Rhône, private driveway with voiturier and quick baggage handling, underground garage and spacious lobby for immediate check-in and quiet comfort in the midst of the city because most rooms give onto an inner court and side-streets. The main shopping promenade is around the corner, but the hotel boutiques are right off the public areas, and should you be refused a reservation at ›Napauléon‹ Bocuse – or even be tired of him – Les Trois Dômes on the penthouse floor will satisfy any gourmet and voyeur. Even the spoilt are satisfied here.

The Hideaway

CHATEAU DU BESSET

Saint Romain de Lerps
F–07130 Saint Pérey (115 km/72 miles)
Telephone: 75 58 52 22
Telex: 345 261 besset
Owner: Rosny Besset Gestion
General Manager: Dominique Couture
Affiliation/Reservation System: Relais et
Châteaux
Closed: Nov. to March
Number of rooms: 10 (4 suites)
Price range: FF 1,400–2,200
Credit cards: AE, EC, CB, Visa
Location: 15 km/9 miles from Valence;
19 km/12 miles from airport
Built: 15th century
Style: castle; antique interior
Hotel amenities: garage
Room amenities: colour tv (remote control), mini-bar/refrigerator (pets allowed)
Bathroom amenities: bidet, bathrobe, hairdrier, telephone, mini-bar
Room service: 7.00/a.m.–1.00/a.m.
Sports: boule; riding, tennis
Bar: (open all day long)
Restaurant: ›Tapisseries du XVIIème‹; Dominique Couture (maître), Laurent Malnuit (chef de cuisine), nouvelle and traditional cuisine, open-air dining
Private dining rooms: one (up to 20 persons)

Of all the myriad châteaux hotels scattered across la Belle France, the fifteenth-century fortress perched on a vantage point in the wooded hills of the Ardèche a few miles west of Valence is the most discreet, the most private and the most enchanting. This hideaway par excellence, an hour and a half south of Lyons along the Autoroute du Sud, was rebuilt stone by stone under the genial direction of maecenas Roger Gozlan. It lies today in a walled jardin français surrounded by tree-studded parkland, a gaunt red-roofed castle with two circular towers standing sentinel over the sunny terrace dotted with statues and gay yellow sunshades against a sylvan landscape à la Lorrain. The intérieur is a chef d'œuvre of ordre et beauté, luxe, calme et volupté à la Baudelaire. Each of the ten bedrooms is an antique-studded cameo, the result of meticulous research by Suzanne Gozlan, professor of archaeology at the Sorbonne, evoking the colours, patterns and styles of times past – the Grand Siècle, Louis XVI or Charles X. The bathrooms are a serenade of jacuzzis and modern gadgetry, the lounge a fugue between avant-garde fauteuils and Watteauesque paintings, and the tapestried dining room a symphony in which the rough-cast walls, the precious wall-hanging, the blue table-linen and the cuisine of Laurent Malnuit coalesce in a harmonious cadence of quintessential perfection. Nothing is permitted to disturb the genius loci; the swimming pool and tennis court are hidden away, the cars parked out of view; peace reigns supreme in an ambience in which everyday reality is transformed into a dream-like rêverie.

Lunch

**ROGER ROUCOU
(LA MERE GUY)**
35 Quai Jean-Jacques Rousseau, Lyon –
La Muletière
Telephone: 78 51 65 37/Telex: 3 10 24
Owner-Manager: Roger Roucou
Closed: Sunday evening; Monday; one
week in February; August
Open: 12.00/a.m.–14.00/2 p.m. and
19.00/7 p.m.–21.30/9.30 p.m.
Cuisine: classique
Chef de cuisine: Hubert Coupanec
Specialities: foie gras en brioche; soles
soufflées Escoffier; poularde de Bresse à
la crème et morilles; shrimps au gratin
Location: 2 km (1 mile) from city centre
Setting: oak panelling and hunting tapes-
tries; Louis XV accessoires; winter gar-
den
Amenities: private dining room (200 per-
sons); open-air dining on terrace (even-
ings only); air conditioning; car park
Atmosphere: refined and relaxing
Clientèle: silk manufacturers to stars of
stage and screen; local dignitaries and
holidaymakers in search of refreshment
en route from Calais to Cannes
Dress: no special requirements
Reservations: advisable (dogs allowed)
Price range: moderately high
Credit cards: AE, DC, Carte Bleue

Dinner

PAUL BOCUSE
Pont de Collonges,
Collonges-au-Mont-d'Or (9 km/5 miles)
Telephone: 78 22 01 40
Affiliations: Traditions et Qualité
Owner/Manager: Paul Bocuse
Closed: never
Open: 12.00/a.m.–13.30/1.30 p.m. and
19.00/7 p.m.–21.30/9.30 p.m.
Cuisine: Haute Cuisine
Chefs de cuisine: Paul Bocuse and Roger
Jaloux
Specialities: leek and potato soup; mullet
with coriander; poulet de Bresse à la
broche (the best in the world); truffle
soup; duckling with olives; foie gras avec
une salade d'haricots; glace au chocolat
amer
Location: at Collonges-au-Mont-d'Or,
9 km (5 miles) north of Lyons along the
N 51
Setting: on the river; whitewashed, rather
square building; baroque décor, reminiscent of the Elysée Palace; a perfect reflection of the many facets of the personality
of the patron – latest scion of a family of
restaurateurs in the Collonges area since
1765
Amenities: private dining rooms (20 persons); open-air dining on terrace; air
conditioning; car park

Atmosphere: a theatrical one-man show;
a gala for a gourmet; dominated by the
much-praised, universally-celebrated star
of the Lyons gastronomic empire with a
heart of gold
Clientèle: pilgrims from Paris to Peking;
devotees from Darwin to Detroit; gourmets from Gothenburg to Granada
Dress: formal (jacket and tie)
Service: a chef d'oeuvre of team-work,
charmingly supervised by Raymonde Bocuse
Reservations: advisable (no dogs)
Price range: of no import
Credit cards: AE, DC, Carte Bleue

Dinner

PIERRE ORSI
3 Place Kléber
Telephone: 78 89 57 68
Affiliations: Relais et Châteaux (Relais
Gourmand)
Owner/Manager/Chef de cuisine: Pierre
Orsi
Closed: Sunday; August
Open: 12.00/a.m.–14.30/2.30 p.m. and
20.00/8 p.m.–21.30/9.30 p.m.
Cuisine: classique (›au goût du jour‹)
Specialities: gilt-head bream (daurade)
and monkfish (lotte de mer) in basil;
feuilleté of lobster and wild mushrooms;
wolf-fish (loup de mer) in olive oil; ai-
guillettes de canard with wild rice;
mousse au chocolat amer; tarte paysanne
Location: central
Setting: vine-covered house; comfortable
dining room with co-ordinated colour
scheme in dusty pinks and lilac, from the
upholstery and the table linen to the
Laura Ashley dresses of the waitresses
Amenities: private dining room (10 persons); air conditioning
Atmosphere: ambiance parisienne
Clientèle: hommes d'affaires – hommes
de loisir; public figures and personalities
from Alain Delon and Charles Aznavour
to Raymond Barre
Dress: strictly jacket and tie
Service: feminine and charming
Reservations: advisable (pets permitted)
Price range: moderately high
Credit cards: AE, DC, Carte Bleue

Lunch

LE VIVARAIS
1 Place Gailleton
Telephone: 78 37 85 15
Owner/Manager: Pierre Gerbel
Closed: Saturday, Sunday; three weeks in
May/June
Open: 12.00/a.m.–14.00/2 p.m. and
19.15/7.15 p.m.–22.00/10 p.m.
Cuisine: local traditional
Chef de cuisine: Pierre Gerbel

Specialities: ray in black butter; entrecôte steak ›marchand devin‹; rice cake with preserved oranges; diplomat pudding with rum
Location: central, just opposite the University, close to the Sofitel
Setting: one of the classic bistros of Lyons; mirrors on wooden walls; renovated in 1981
Amenities: garage nearby; private salon (16 persons)
Atmosphere: Lyonnais charm
Clientèle: mostly habitués, cosmopolitan birds of passage, distinguished foreigners, distinguished Lyonnais, actors, writers
Dress: casual
Service: very efficient and experienced
Reservations: essential (preferably well in advance); pets welcomed
Price range: medium
Credit cards: not accepted

Lunch

NANDRON
26 Quai Jean Moulin
Telephone: 78 42 10 26
Affiliations: Relais et Châteaux (Relais Gourmand)
Owner/Manager/Chef de cuisine: Gérard Nandron
Closed: Friday evening; Saturday; end of July–end of August
Open: 12.00/a.m.–14.00/2 p.m. and 19.30/7.30 p.m.–22.00/10 p.m.
Cuisine: nouvelle – classique – régionale
Specialities: quenelles de brochet; escalope of tuna marinated in chervil; l'aiguillette de canard au feuilleté de champignons des bois; saddle of rabbit; calves' sweetbreads with limes and pickled onions; desserts: hot chocolate soufflé with peppermint ice-cream; crêpes flambées au Grand Marnier; warm crêpes à la lyonnaise with apples
Location: central; near the Pont Lafayette
Setting: first-floor dining room overlooking the Rhône; nooks and alcoves; wood panelling, mirrors and a profusion of flowers
Amenities: private dining room (30 persons); air conditioning; car park
Atmosphere: nostalgic Lyonnaise
Clientèle: raffinée – ›politique et spectacle‹; expense-account gourmets
Dress: no special requirements
Service: hospitable and charming
Reservations: advisable (pets permitted)
Price range: elevated
Credit cards: AE, DC, Euro, Carte Bleue

Dinner

LEON DE LYON
1 rue de Pléney
Telephone: 78 28 11 33
Owner/Manager/Chef de cuisine: Jean-Paul Lacombe
Closed: Sunday; Monday lunchtime; public holidays; December 22nd–January 8th
Open: 12.15/a.m.–14.00/2 p.m. and 19.30/7.30 p.m.–22.00/10 p.m.
Cuisine: local; ›au goût du marché‹
Specialities: mullet and fennel in aspic; lambs' brains and sweetbreads with chanterelles and chives in puff pastry; sauté of leg of mutton with young beans and braised purple artichokes; potato salad with fresh herbs and clarified butter; madeleines with honey; bitter chocolate mousse; oeufs à la neige
Location: not far from the Hôtel de Ville
Setting: historic building, made famous as a restaurant by the present patron's father, Paul Lacombe; small dining rooms furnished in provincial style; wood and leaded glass
Amenities: private dining room (20 persons); air conditioning
Atmosphere: a haven of la dolce vita à la lyonnaise
Clientèle: Haute Bourgeoisie to Bocuse on his day off
Dress: elegantly casual to casually elegant
Service: waiters in vintners' aprons charmingly directed by Gisèle Lacombe, the patron's mother
Reservations: advisable
Price range: moderately expensive
Credit cards: Carte Bleue

Dinner

LA TOUR ROSE
16 rue du Boeuf
Telephone: 78 32 59 90
Owner/Manager/Chef de cuisine: Philippe Chavent
Closed: Sunday; August 22nd–September 6th
Open: 19.00/7 p.m.–22.00/10 p.m.
Cuisine: nouvelle
Specialities: bisque of sea-urchins; potato and caviar salad; mullet with artichokes and curry sauce; roast Norway lobster with asparagus cream; pot au feu de pigeon aux truffes et foie gras; peppermint ice-cream
Location: on the ›other‹ side of the river; in the old town
Setting: Venetian-style Renaissance villa; two dining rooms; ground floor more attractive, with grey table linen and fine silver; china to match the various dishes
Amenities: private dining room (60 persons); bar; air conditioning

Atmosphere: festively luxurious – from the apéritif to the coffee
Clientèle: discerning expense-account gourmets; the local Top Ten; Lyons' social élite with cause for celebration
Dress: elegant
Service: grande classe
Reservations: definitely advisable
Price range: fairly expensive
Credit cards: AE, DC, Euro, Carte Bleue

Bar

PUB ECOSSAIS
(Eddie and Domino)
6 Quai Gailleton
Telephone: 78 37 20 29
Affiliations: local president of Association ›Barman de France‹; Féderation Nationale de l'Industrie des Hôteliers
Owner/Manager: Eddie McBrise
Closed: Sunday; public holidays
Open: 17.00/5 p.m.–5.00/a.m.
Specialities: whiskies (more than 200 brands aged 8–50 years); 350 different cocktails à la carte
Location: central
Setting: Scotish pub décor with engravings of bagpipes; piano and cool jazz background music
Amenities: air conditioning
Atmosphere: Caledonian; the oldest pub in Lyons (opened in 1960) and still the best
Clientèle: favourite rendezvous for exiled Scots and Sassenachs, with a sprinkling of Gallic infiltrators (other nationalities welcome too!)
Dress: kilt not obligatory
Service: under the genial direction of cocktail champion Eddie McBrise
Reservations: not necessary
Credit cards: Carte Bleue

Façonnable (fashion for him)
11 rue du Plâtre
Rodier (fashion for him and her)
78 rue du Président Edouard Herriot
Jacadi (children's fashion)
93 Boulevard des Belges
Armand (leather fashion)
86 Cours Vitton
Fourrures de la Madeleine (furs)
96 rue du Président Edouard Herriot
Flammarion (books)
19 Place Bellecour
Cambet (gifts)
10 rue de la Charité
Christofle (porcelain)
65 rue de la République
Sellerie Victor Hugo (baggage & travel accessories)
3 rue Victor Hugo
Bocuse et Bernachon (food and beverages) 49 rue de Sèze
Ambre (perfumery)
99 rue du Président Edouard Herriot
Jourdan (confiserie)
2 rue du Colonel Chambonnet

THE BEST OF ART
Bertin, J.L.J. (contemporary art)
10 rue Auguste Comte, Tel. 78 42 62 87
L'OEil Ecoute (modern art)
3 Quai Romain Rolland, Tel. 78 42 23 65
Nelson (modern art)
99 Cours Emile-Zola, Tel. 78 94 00 69
Verrière (contemporary art)
25 rue Auguste Comte, Tel. 78 42 40 37

Shopping

EVERYTHING UNDER ONE ROOF
Galeries Lafayette   Place des Cordeliers

FOR HIM
Royal House   23 Place Bellecour

FOR HER
Clémentine   18 rue Emile-Zola

BEAUTY & HAIR
Dessange   Place du Maréchal Lyautey

JEWELLERY
Korloff   12 rue de la République

LOCAL SPECIALITIES
Tabac le Khedive (tobacco)
71 rue de la République
Diva, La (fashion for her)
34 Quai Saint-Antoine

The City

Marseilles doesn't care about superlatives – second-largest port of Europe or not, second-biggest city of France or not, highest percentage of *filles de joie* per capita or not, best bouillabaisse in the world or not. France's southern capital doesn't care much about Paris, either, and La Canebière doesn't want to be compared to Les Champs-Elysées from here to eternity. 2500 years of turbulent history – from Caesar to the Crusaders, from the Nazis to the Pieds Noirs – a colourful cocktail of races and cultures – large colonies of Africans, Greeks, Italians, Jews – world importance in industrial production and trade – shipbuilding may be raison d'être, but foodstuffs, chemical and electrical products account for a fair share, too – and, due to its geographical position on the sea, flanked by the nearby Côte d'Azur and the Triangle Sacré of some of the country's most beautiful towns, Arles, Avignon and Aix-en-Provence – Marseilles is as independent an entity in France as Barcelona is in Spain. Glory and Death, the insignia of the Légion d'Honneur (which keeps its headquarters here, in Fort St. Nicolas), are as much part of life in Marseilles as the sun and storm. The roughness of its people is of a brittle charm, the hospitality is genuine and whoever gets into trouble here, falls most likely prey to his fantasy from having seen too many films of a doubtful genre. Action, sin and danger there are galore, but they are all clearly marked and taking place according to fixed rules. Marseilles has been the source of legends and thrillers for centuries – the Count of Monte-Cristo outshining even the French Connection – but the interest today is more directed towards business. No longer merely the ›Gateway to Africa and the Orient‹, Marseilles has become a gateway to the world, with a harbour for the year 2000 and an infrastructure unique in the Mediterranean. Apart from the effervescent chaos à l'orientale, the quaint nostalgia of a fisherman's wharf and the frivolous friction of sex à l'extrème, the arts have flourished here since Antonin Artaud's ›Theatre of Cruelty‹, with favourite-son Roland Petit bringing the opera to international fame and mime actor Marcel Maréchal's Théâtre La Criée in a one-time covered fish market following the pioneer path of Jean-Louis Barrault. With a special sense for business and politics (the city's eternal mayor, Gaston Deferre, owns the left-wing and the right-wing newspapers), with a spirit of freedom (it took a platoon from this city to propagate the national anthem, composed in Strasbourg) and the tolerance for human pleasures and extravaganzas (Fernandel was a native, too), Marseilles is one of the most bedazzling cities on the continent.

Founded: 600 B.C., by the Phœnicians; Marseille (French) – from Massalia (Latin)

Far-reaching events: 49 B.C. – Caesar annexes Marseilles in the course of his Gallic Wars; 481 – the Visigoths displace the Romans; 11th–14th century – Marseilles a commercial centre and transit port for Crusaders on their way to the Holy Land; 1252 – Charles I of Anjou takes the town by storm, literally; 1481 – Provence, including Marseilles, becomes part of Kingdom of France; 1720 – the city is decimated by the plague; 1789 – Marseilles espouses the revolutionary cause; 1869 – the opening of the Suez Canal, along with the conquest of Algeria, brings Marseilles untold importance and prosperity, slightly dampened in recent years by the loss of Algeria and occasional closings of the Suez canal, though oil imports have helped absorb such shocks.

Population: 910,000; capital of Bouches-du-Rhône department and third largest city in France.

Postal code: F–13000   **Telephone code:** 91 (incorporated in number since 1986)

Climate: Mediterranean, occasionally interrupted by the Mistral wind

Calendar of events: *Mediterranean Horse Show* (Jun); *International Folklore Festival* in the Château Gombert (Jul); *Pilgrimage to Notre-Dame-de-la-Garde* (15 Aug); *Cinema Festival* (Sep); *Santons Market* (last Sun in Nov–6 Jan) – clay and carved wood nativity figures on sale for Christmas.

Fairs and exhibitions: *PROMO-LOISIRS FAIR* (Apr); – hobbys and leisure; *SETSO* (May) – energy techniques and security; *INTERNATIONAL FAIR* (Sep); *ANTIQUES FAIR* (Oct); *PHIRAMA* (Oct) – industrial and technical equipment.

Historical and modern sights: the old Cathedral of *Le Major* (12th century) – Romanesque-Provençal; *St. Victor Basilica* (11th century) – with crypts and catacombs; the bell tower of the *Accoules* (12th century), one of France's oldest churches; *St. Jean* and *St. Nicolas* (15th and 17th centuries) – the two forts guarding the old harbour; *Maison Diamantée* (16th century) – home of the Museum of the Old City of Marseilles; *Notre Dame-de-la-Garde* – the city's landmark basilica, a former Roman-Byzantine fortress with a chapel added in the 19th century; *Château d'If* – an island cliff with 16th-century ruins of the castle where the Count of Monte-Cristo languished; *Grobet-Labadié Museum* – antique furnishings in a patrician palais; *Ceramics Museum;* the *Cité Radieuse*, designed by Le Corbusier – high rises with gardens on the top.

Special attractions: *La Canebière* – Marseilles' answer to the Champs-Élysées; the *Corniche Président John F. Kennedy* – coast road with a spectacular view of the islands.

Important companies with headquarters in the city: *Barry Roghano* (shipping and freight); *Berton et Sucard* (sanitary fittings); *Comex* (harbour and underwater construction); *Detkachinie* (construction plastics); *Frahuil* (oil); *Jullian* (agricultural products); *Rivoire et Carret* (pasta); *S. O. G. E. R. I. C.* (paints).

Airport: Marseille-Marignane, MRS; Tel.: 91 89 90 10; Air France, Tel.: 91 549 292; 27 km/16 miles.

The Headquarters

**SOFITEL
MARSEILLE VIEUX–PORT**

36 Boulevard Charles Livon
F–13007 Marseilles
Telephone: 91 52 90 19
Telex: 401 270 sofimar
Owning Company: ACCOR
General Manager: Jean-Louis Chadel
Affiliation/Reservation System: Sofitel
Number of rooms: 219 (3 suites)
Price range: FF 395–1,950
Credit cards: AE, CB, DC, EC
Location: next to the ›Palais du Pharo‹
Built: 1976
Style: modern
Hotel amenities: car park, valet parking, boutique, wheelchair accessibility; outdoor swimming pool, solarium
Room amenities: air conditioning, tv, mini-bar (pets welcome)
Room service: 6.30/a.m.–23.30/11.30 p.m.
Conference rooms: 14 (up to 600 persons)
Bars: ›Verandah Bar‹ (10.00/a.m.–1.00/a.m.); ›Astrolabe‹ (12.00/a.m.–14.00/2 p.m. and 18.00/6 p.m.–2.00/a.m.); Pascal Liefooghe (barman)
Restaurants: ›Les 3 Forts‹ (12.15/a.m.–14.00/2 p.m. and 20.00/8 p.m.–22.30/10.30 p.m.) nouvelle cuisine, Marc Bayon (chef de cuisine); ›Le Jardin‹ (12.00/a.m.–14.30/2.30 p.m. and 19.30/7.30 p.m.–23.00/11 p.m.), open-air dining

The Vieux-Port and the neighbouring Château du Pharo, the former residence of the Empress Eugénie set in a lovely park, have – thanks to their location – one thing in common; both afford a spectacular view of the entrance to the Old Harbour at Marseilles. In the case of this southerly link in the prestigious French Sofitel chain, the best vantage point is the Astrolabe *bar, which is a popular rendez-vous for those wishing to observe simultaneously the locals and the procession of yachts and small boats entering and leaving the historic port (larger vessels use the deep-water harbour constructed in the nineteenth century). Here, as elsewhere in the hotel, can be found the pleasant modern décor and efficient management which are characteristics of the group's establishments in France and overseas. In spite of the stiff competition from other temples of the culinary arts in the area, the gourmet restaurant* Les Trois Forts *serves Marc Bayon's nouvelle cuisine specialities – carpaccio of wolf-fish with cucumber, or sardines with home-made pasta – to a discriminating collection of visiting gourmets and local savants -vivre, against the endlessly fascinating panorama of the city, the sea and the ships. With the past in front and the hotel and the commercial areas right behind, the congenial surroundings and the unique harbour back-drop merely confirm the choice of the Vieux Port as the best headquarters for the many export managers and shipping executives who come to do business in Marseilles.*

OUSTAU DE BAUMANIÈRE

F–13520 Les Baux-de-Provence
(86 km/54 miles)
Telephone: 90 54 33 07
Telex: 420 203 bauma
Owner: Raymond Thuilier
General Manager: Jean-André Charial
Affiliation/Reservation Systems: Traditions et Qualité, Relais et Châteaux
Closed: 21 January–6 March
Number of rooms: 37 (11 suites)
Price range: FF 725–1,000
Credit cards: AE, DC, EC, MC, Visa
Location: on the Routes Nationales 7 and 113 between Arles and St Rémy, 80 km/48 miles from Marseilles airport
Style: former shepherd's cottage; elegantized rustic décor
Hotel amenities: garage, hotel shop, outdoor swimming pool, tennis courts
Room amenities: air conditioning, colour tv, mini-bar (pets welcome)
Bathroom amenities: bathrobe, hairdrier
Room service: 7.00/a.m.–24.00/12 p.m.
Laundry/dry cleaning: same day
Conference rooms: for up to 60 persons
Sports: riding
Bars: cocktail bar
Restaurants: ›L'Oustaù de Baumanière‹ (12.00/a.m.–15.00/3.00 p.m. and 19.30/7.30 p.m.–24.00/12.00 p.m.), Jean-André Charial (chef de cuisine), personal and inventive cuisine traditionelle, elegantized rustic style

The ghostly remains of medieval grandeur of Les-Baux-de-Provence lie just over an hour's drive from Marseilles. There, in an awe-inspiring location overlooking the Val d'Enfer, stands l'Oustaù de Baumanière, one of the most enchanting and enchanted hideaways in the world. Raymond Thuilier, genial doyen of this secret domain, has lovingly converted a former abandoned shepherd's shelter into a place of pilgrimage for aesthetes and sybarites from all the corners of the earth. They come to play tennis or golf, to ride or to relax by the pool in the sunshine, or to stroll through the ancient olive groves in the enigmatic light which inspired so many of Van Gogh's chefs d'œuvre. The relais de campagne offers them tapestried walls, canopied beds, open fireplaces and fine antiques, consummately blended with traditional Provençal fabrics and accessoires to produce a cadre of total intimacy, luxury and charm. Culinary pleasures take pride of place in the stone-walled vaulted dining room, where son-in-law Jean-André Charial's uniquely innovative blend of traditional and regional cuisine du marché delights élite epicures with dishes which have become classics in their own right – filets de rouget au vin rouge, or gigot d'agneau en croûte. Amongst the countless famous visitors to this auberge par excellence was writer Jean Cocteau, who noted in the visitors' book ›Poetry is in what you do and not in what you say . . .‹

Lunch

MAURICE BRUN
18 Quai Rive-Neuve
Telephone: 91 33 35 38
Owner/Manager: Frédéric-Maurice Brun
Closed: Sunday; Monday; public holidays
Open: 12.00/a.m.–21.00/9 p.m.
Cuisine: local
Chefs de cuisine: Frédéric et Danielle Brun
Specialities: Provençal specialities; hot and cold hors d'œuvres; grilled fish; artichokes à la barigoule; spit-roasted guinea-fowl; goat's milk cheese; local nougat and sweet meats
Location: by the old port
Setting: on the top floor of an old house; dining room reminiscent of a Provençal nobleman's residence with typical local accessoires and portraits of Daudet, Mistral and other local writers on the walls
Atmosphere: a unique Provençal pot-pourri, somewhat marred by the recent decision to allow smoking at table
Clientèle: favourite venue for export managers entertaining visiting delegations
Dress: what you will (within reason!)
Service: knowledgeable and professional
Reservations: essential
Price range: fairly expensive
Credit cards: DC

Dinner

MAX CAIZERGUES
11 Rue Gustave-Ricard
Telephone: 91 33 58 07
Owner/Manager: Max Caizergues (former cookery teacher at Osaka; ex-Oliver, Maxim's and Mère Guy)
Closed: Sunday; Saturday lunchtime; (May–September) Saturday all day; August
Open: 9.00/a.m.–14.30/2.30 p.m. and 19.00/7 p.m.–23.00/11 p.m.
Cuisine: nouvelle
Chef de cuisine: Yves Dellmotte
Specialities: regularly changing fish specialities; salmon; filet de daurade; lotte
Location: central
Setting: comfortable townhouse; recently-renovated dining room with salmon-pink fabric-covered walls; stylish accessoires
Amenities: air conditioning; car park (fee-paying)
Atmosphere: serious but not dull; reliable but not boring
Clientèle: very popular amongst top industrialists wishing to clinch a deal or celebrate a contract
Dress: correct
Service: courteous but not obsequious
Reservations: advisable (no dogs)
Price range: fairly expensive
Credit cards: AE, DC, Visa

Dinner

CALYPSO
3 rue des Catalans
Telephone: 91 52 64 00
Owner/Manager/Chef de cuisine: Antoine Visciano
Closed: Sunday; Monday; August
Open: 12.00/a.m.–14.00/2 p.m. and 19.30/7.30 p.m.–22.00/10 p.m.
Cuisine: seafood
Specialities: local fish soup (bouillabaisse) – with or without lobster (the latter is the classic version; the former more expensive); wolf-fish (loup de mer) flambé au fenouil (fennel)
Location: near the Parc du Pharo
Setting: on the seafront, with a view of limestone cliffs and the Château d'If (where the Count of Monte-Cristo languished)
Amenities: twin restaurant ›Chez Michel‹ across the road (same manager, same menu, same prices)
Atmosphere: easy-come, easy-go
Clientèle: fish gourmets determined to try the best that Marseilles has to offer
Dress: as you like it
Service: welcoming
Reservations: essential
Price range: rather expensive
Credit cards: Visa

Lunch

LE PETIT NICE
(Restaurant Passédat)
Corniche Kennedy, Anse de Maldormé
Telephone: 91 52 14 39
Telex: 4 01 565 Passédat
Affiliations: Relais et Châteaux
Owner/Manager: Jean-Paul Passédat
Closed: Monday: January
Open: 12.30/p.m.–14.00/2 p.m. and 20.15/8.15 p.m.–22.00/10 p.m.
Cuisine: Nouvelle and local
Chefs de cuisine: Jean-Paul and Gérald Passédat
Specialities: courgette flowers in vegetable verjuice; daurade royale aux aubergines confites; frogs and pigs' trotters with endive; monkfish with saffron and garlic; blinis caramelized with honey, with sour apples
Location: just south of the old port
Setting: view of the bay and the islands dominates the bright and luxurious dining room
Amenities: hotel; private dining rooms (25 persons); open-air dining on terrace by swimming pool (dinner only); air conditioning; car park
Atmosphere: luxurious and peaceful; a family-run restaurant/hotel founded by the present owner's father

Clientèle: Marseillais en fête and en famille mingle with visiting businessmen and tourists
Dress: elegant to léger
Service: exceptionally reliable and pleasant
Reservations: essential for groups; otherwise advisable (pets permitted in hotel only)
Price range: understandably expensive
Credit cards: AE, Carte Bleue, Visa (no cheques on foreign banks)

Dinner

AU TEMPS PERDU
27 Cours Julien
Telephone: 91 48 25 09
Owner/Manager: Daniel Barnard/Robert Sabadell
Closed: Monday
Open: 19.00/7 p.m.–1.00/a.m.
Cuisine: traditional
Chef de cuisine: Robert Sabadell
Specialities: pancakes (crêpes) with various fillings – seafood, artichokes, duck in orange sauce, Roquefort ….; charcoal-grilled double sirloin or T-bone steak
Location: near the Place J. Jaurès
Setting: Provençal rustic dining room with niches for added privacy and an abundance of old wood
Amenities: crêperie (ground floor)
Atmosphere: intimate; friendly
Clientèle: favourite post-opera rendez-vous for all ages; ministers; actors and the Younger Set
Dress: casual but not careless
Service: welcoming
Reservations: essential for restaurant; impossible for crêperie
Price range: relatively inexpensive
Credit cards: AE, Visa

Dinner

COUSIN-COUSINE
102 Cours Julien
Telephone: 91 48 14 50
Owner/Manager/Chef de cuisine: Jean-Luc Sellam
Closed: Sunday; Monday lunchtime; September
Open: 12.00/a.m.–22.30/10.30 p.m.
Cuisine: nouvelle
Specialities: charlotte of aubergines and asparagus with mint; feuilleté de langoustines et d'écrevisses aux deux pâtes fraîches

Location: a short walk from the Place Jean-Jaurès
Setting: recently renovated small snack-bar
Amenities: open-air dining on terrace; air conditioning; car park (fee paying)
Atmosphere: quiet and romantic
Clientèle: young; discriminating; self-confident; successful
Dress: as you like it, as long as they like you
Service: helpful and friendly
Reservations: advisable
Price range: medium
Credit cards: AE, DC, Carte Bleue

Meeting Point

LONDON CLUB
73 corniche Kennedy
Telephone: 91 42 52 64 64
Owner/Manager: Hubert Martias
Closed: never
Open: 22.00/10 p.m.–till dawn
Location: on the coast road (Corniche Kennedy)
Setting: two dimly-lit rooms with mock wooden logs and stuffed animals
Atmosphere: rather museum-like; an institution in Marseilles for more than twenty years
Clientèle: the town's Top Twenty – local judges, senior police officials, dentists and garage proprietors with their wives, their girl-friends, their receptionists or their secretaries
Dress: elegant to légère and casual to formal
Service: old-fashioned charm
Reservations: advisable
Credit cards: AE, DC, CB

Bar

L'ASTROLABE
Sofitel Marseille Vieux-Port
36 boulevard Charles-Livon
Telephone: 91 52 90 19
Owner/Manager: Jean-Louis Jhedel
Closed: never
Open: 12.00 a.m.–14.00/2 p.m. and 16.00/4 p.m.–20.00/8 p.m.
Location: in the Hôtel Sofitel ›Vieux Port‹
Setting: a glass tower overlooking the old harbour; sea-green lighting effects
Amenities: hotel; two restaurants; air conditioning; car park
Atmosphere: a window on the world; a good place to be seen as well as to see
Clientèle: polyglot and heterogeneous
Service: efficient
Reservations: advisable
Credit cards: AE, DC, Euro, Visa

Nightclub

LE ROLLS
76 corniche Kennedy
Telephone: 91 42 52 21 21
Owner/Manager: Roger Cornacchio/
Patrick Azoulay
Closed: Sunday; Monday
Open: 21.00/9 p.m. – dawn
Location: near the London Club
Setting: rather like a vast submarine
Amenities: discothèque; piano-bar; late-night restaurant serving osso buco, meat casseroles etc.
Atmosphere: fairly sedate
Clientèle: a preponderance of rather mature pillars of the local establishment
Service: impeccable – from the uniformed porter at the door who sizes up potential guests to the waiters who serve you if you pass muster
Reservations: advisable
Price range: medium – high
Credit cards: AE, DC, CB

Shopping

EVERYTHING UNDER ONE ROOF
Galeries Lafayette   Rue Saint-Ferréol

FOR HIM
Ley's   20 Rue Montgrand

FOR HER
Catherine   78 Rue Saint-Ferréol

BEAUTY & HAIR
Lorenzy-Palanca   31 Rue Saint-Ferréol

JEWELLERY
Pellegrin   19 Rue Davso

LOCAL SPECIALITIES
Tabac la Régence (tobacco)
Rue Saint-Ferréol
Christiane (children's fashion)
23 Rue Davso
Michel Robs (leather fashion)
86 Rue de Rome
Guiramand (furs) 119 Rue Paradis
Lafitte, Jeanne (books)
25 Cours Estienne d'Orves
Melchior (gifts)
61 Rue Saint-Ferréol
Le boffe (baggage & travel accessories)
14 Rue Grignan
Blanc (food and beverages)
21 Avenue du Prado

THE BEST OF ART
Arca   (contemporary art)
61 Cours Julien, Tel. 91 42 18 01
Athanor   (contemporary art)
2 rue Moustier, Tel. 91 77 83 56

The City

And if it were only for the Place Stanislas, one of the most beautiful and harmonious squares in the world (and one of the most romantic by night), Nancy would be worth a journey. Neglected by the latter-day disciples of the Grand Tour, between Strasbourg and Rheims, this regal capital of Lorraine presents itself in such unexpected grace that you tend to forget about the heavy industries around (coal, iron, metal, plastic, construction, chemicals, et al.) but are rather reminded of the ›industries de l'art‹, a.k.a. the Nancy School, the brainchild of local son Emile Gallé, the God of Glass. Named after Nancy's beloved sovereign in the 18th century, Stanislas Leszczynski, Place Stanislas, in its symmetrical and decorative elegance without comparison, is the centre of all action and transit, of romantic encounters and tarrying in reverence, of cafés and restaurants and the palatial residence of the Grand Hôtel de La Reine. The city is divided into two quarters – la Vieille Ville with all the art treasures of the great past and the Ville Neuve with all the offices for the profitable future. Along with Metz, but much more refined, Nancy is an important economic entity in France, with some of the most renowned technical and scientific institutes, the School of Forestry and Mining, and a spectrum of commerce ranging from instruments of precision to breweries, from furniture to fashion. (Even when you have to do business in Metz it is advisable to spend the night in nearby Nancy for its flair, auberge de renommé, the restaurants, the surroundings and Place Stanislas.) There are many more sights and points of interest for the itinerant homme d'affaires with a few hours to spare, architecturally, atmospherically and culinarily. (Some of the best restaurants in eastern France are found in this area.) According to an old local proverb, the funeral of a duke in Lorraine belongs to the three most magnificent ceremonies in Europe: this solemn rite may be outdated in our times, but one of the most spectacular moments anyone can experience when coming to this city is certainly the view and walk over Place Stanislas.

Founded: mid-11th century, as the fortress of an Alsatian duke.

Far-reaching events: 1153 – Nancy capital of the duchy of Lorraine; 1475 – captured by Charles the Bold; 1476 – recaptured by the Duke of Lorraine; 1670 – the French take Nancy after several short-lived occupations; 1735 – Louis XV installs his father-in-law, Stanislas Leszczynski, ex-king of Poland, as duke of Nancy – he makes the town one of France's architectural showpieces; 1766 – Nancy reverts to the French crown; 1871 – Lorraine and Alsace become German again; end of 19th century – Nancy becomes the centre of Art Nouveau (the School of Nancy).

Population: 275,000 (urban area); capital of Meurthe-et-Moselle department.

Postal code: F–54000 **Telephone code:** 8 (incorporated in number since 1986)

Climate: continental, rather wet; bring two umbrellas.

Best time to visit: April to October.

Calendar of events: *University Theatre Festival* (Apr); *World Theatre Festival* (May); *Folklore Festival* (last Saturday in Jun), in honour of St. Jean; *›Son et Lumière‹ Drama Festival* (15 Jul to 15 Sep), and singing; *Jazz Festival* (Oct); *St. Nicholas Christmas Festivities* (1st week of Dec).

Fairs and exhibitions: *INTERNATIONAL FORESTRY FAIR* (Apr); *ANTIQUES EXHIBITION* and *FLEA MARKET* (Apr); *NANCY INTERNATIONAL FAIR* (Jun); *EURODESIGN* (Sep) – European fair for industrial innovations; *BUROTERT* (Oct) – exhibition for office and information services.

Best views of the city: from Notre-Dame-de-Bon-Secours.

Historical and modern sights: *Place Stanislas* (18th century) – classical perfection, with a statue of mentor Stanislas Leszczynski, *wrought iron gates* by Jean Lamour, the *Town Hall*, the *Museum of Fine Arts* (European paintings from 14th–20th centuries) and a *Triumphal Arch* (Emmanuel Héré); *Ducal Palace; Couvent des Cordeliers*, (15th century) – with the tombs of the dukes and an octagonal chapel; *Central Cathedral* (18th century) – St. Gauzellin's 9th-century evangelistary on view; *Eglise Notre-Dame-de-Bon-Secours* (18th century) – with a notable altar and Stanislas' grave; *Musée Lorrain; School of Nancy Museum* – exhibits from the cradle of Art Nouveau.

Special attractions: a walk through the *Parc de la Pépinière* – statue by Rodin; *Zoological Museum* – tropical aquarium; the medieval town of *Liverdun*; the *Forêt de Haye; Place Stanislas* by night.

Important companies with headquarters in the city: *Berger Levrault* (printing); *Bové* (isolation); *L'Est Républicain* (newspaper); *Midest* (fairs and exhibitions); *Norden et Compagnie* (heavy metal construction, iron and steel); *Pont & Mousson* (pipes and conduits); *Solvay* (chemicals).

Airport: Nancy-Essey, ENC; Tel.: 83 21 56 90; 4 km/2 miles; Air France, Tel.: 83 35 05 03.

The Headquarters

GRAND HOTEL DE LA REINE

2 Place Stanislas
F–54000 Nancy
Telephone: 83 35 03 01
Telex: 96 03 67 grhotel
Owner: the Taittinger Family
General Manager: Yves Ziegler
Affiliation/Reservation Systems: The Leading Hotels of the World, Supranational Concorde, Relais et Châteaux
Number of rooms: 50 (5 suites)
Price range: FF 480–710 (single and double)
FF 710–1,600 (suite)
Credit cards: AE, DC, EC, JBC, Visa
Location: city centre, 5 km/3 miles from airport
Built: 1755 (renovated 1985)
Style: Louis XV
Hotel amenities: valet parking, house limousine service, grand piano, tobacconist, house doctor on call
Main hall porter: Lucien Becker
Room amenities: colour tv, mini-bar/refrigerator (pets allowed)
Bathroom amenities: separate shower cabin (in some rooms), bidet, bathrobe, hairdrier
Room service: 6.30/a.m.–23.00/11 p.m.
Conference rooms: 5 (up to 260 persons), board, video, screen, projector, secretarial services, ballroom
Sports: indoor and outdoor swimming pool
Bar: ›Le Stan‹ (10.00/a.m.–2.00/a.m.), Christian Otter (barman), English style
Restaurant: ›Le Stanislas‹ (12.00/a.m.–14.30/2.30 p.m. and 19.00/7.00 p.m.–22.30/10.30 p.m.) François Felix (maître), Yves Jury (chef de cuisine), French cuisine, classic style, Louis XV
Private dining rooms: five

Place de la Concorde or Piazza Navona, Trafalgar Square or Praça dos Tres Poderes – whichever may be the most striking of them all, La Place Stanislas certainly belongs amongst the most beautiful, graceful and harmonious architectural arenas in the world. And the ›Reine‹, one of the cornerstones contributing to that splendour, is worthy of its location by virtue of standard, service and esprit. One of the sparkling links in the golden chain of the Concorde-Lafayette group of the Taittinger dynasty, this former patrician pavilion from the 18th century has been completely renovated to provide modern comfort amidst Louis XV glory, from its symmetrical façade to its bestatued balustrade. Rooms with marble bath and marvellous view will be the rule, grande cuisine in private atmosphere already is. The bar is the meeting point of the reigning dignitaries from across the street and Paris alike, and not even a king would have bad dreams in his suite when he comes here, brushing off the memories of Marie-Antoinette who stayed here on her way to the Dauphin and the guillotine.

The Hideaway

LES VANNES ET SA RESIDENCE

6 Rue Porte-Haute
F–54460 Liverdun (18 km/11 miles)
Telephone: 83 24 46 01
Owner: Yvan Simunic
General Manager: Michel Simunic
Affiliation/Reservations System: Relais et Châteaux
Closed: February
Number of rooms: 11 (2 suites)
Price range: FF 195–FF 250 (single)
FF 200–FF 420 (double)
Credit cards: AE, DC, Visa
Location: 18 km/11 miles from Nancy, 20 km/13 miles from airport in the historic town of Liverdun
Built: 1930 (recently renovated)
Style: modern (antique interior)
Hotel amenities: valet parking, grand piano, library (no pets allowed)
Room service: breakfast
Laundry/dry cleaning: on request
Sports nearby: golf-course (2 km/1 mile from hotel) fishing, hunting
Restaurant: ›Restaurant les Vannes‹: Gérard Simunic (maître), classic French cuisine (closed: Monday; Tuesday lunchtime)

It seems that Les Beaux Arts de la Cuisine have not only produced phenomenal creations but also created a phenomenon in its own right – restaurant avec hôtel (as in ›garden with house‹). The priority is also emphasized in the name of this Moselle relais, where wanderers are much more likely to arrive in limousines for the extraordinary cuisine than for the pleasant bedchambers: ›Restaurant des Vannes et sa Résidence‹. However, the résidence is well worth the visit itself. Comfortable pavilions with solid and functional interior allow for a quiet stay and the anticipation of another gargantuan banquet at the Simunic family mansion. The site is picture-postcard pretty and historically exciting: a fortified village from the thirteenth century with drawbridge, chapel, arcaded houses, fountains and numerous traces of the medieval past. And yet, Liverdun was never as famous before the Croatien Viennese Yvan Simunic chose to open a restaurant here in 1945. It is not only the affluent business clientèle from nearby Nancy who come for lunch and dinner, or the heavy industry big shots from Metz, but all gourmets and ›grands légumes‹ from France and international managers and private bons vivants galore. The whole family is engaged in this epicurean affair, three sons are in the kitchen and in the salon. When you indulge in the soupe de grenouilles Stanislas, the mousseline de turbot aux écrevisses, the canard des Dombes au poivre vert or the puddings of son Daniel you are likely to forget about the romantic river flowing below.

Lunch

LE GASTROLATRE
39 Rue des Maréchaux
Telephone: 83 35 07 97
Owner/Manager/Chef de cuisine: Patrick Tanesy
Closed: Sunday; Monday; 1 week at New Year; 2 weeks at Easter; 1 week at Christmas
Open: 12.00/a.m.–14.00/2 p.m. and 19.30/7.30 p.m.–22.00/10 p.m.
Cuisine: nouvelle; ›au goût du marché‹
Specialities: cabbage stuffed with Norway lobster, lobster and oysters; mousse de foies blonds de canard; aiguillettes de rascasse (scorpion fish) with courgettes and red pepper sauce; noisettes d'agneau au curry; Bourbon mousse
Location: central; at the entrance to Nancy's Epicures' Lane – just off Place Carrière
Setting: Parisian bistrot of 1900; small dining room; chic; comfortably-spaced tables and flattering subdued lighting
Amenities: private dining room (8–16 persons), open-air dining on terrace; air conditioning; convenient car parks
Atmosphere: intimate; relaxed and relaxing
Clientèle: local devotees of the Tanesy culinary tradition, handed down from father to son since 1888; local industrialists, students of architectural history and footsore but well-heeled tourists
Dress: within reason
Service: smiling and welcoming; under the supervision of Josette Tanesy
Reservations: advisable (pets allowed)
Price range: moderately high
Credit cards: AE

Dinner

LE BISTROQUET
97 Route Nationale
Belleville (15 km/9 miles)
Telephone: 83 25 90 12
Owner/Managers: Jean and Marie France Ponsard
Closed: Saturday lunchtime; Sunday evening; Monday; August
Open: 12.00/a.m.–14.30/2.30 p.m. and 19.30/7.30 p.m.–22.00/10 p.m.
Cuisine: ›au goût du marché‹; original, inventive and very personal
Chef de cuisine: Marie France Ponsard
Specialities: foie gras de canard poêlé; minute de saumon with pink berries; Norway lobster ravioli; tureen of Bresse poultry with tarragon cream; suprême de turbot with champagne sabayon and fresh tagliatelle
Location: 15 km (9 miles) north of Nancy; 39 km (14 miles) south of Metz
Setting: large typical Lorraine-style house by the main road; dining room in nostalgic 1930s style; a cross between a bistro de luxe and a winter-garden; interesting accessoires and striking flower arrangements
Amenities: private dining rooms (10–25 persons); air conditioning; car park
Atmosphere: refreshing, cheerful and chic
Clientèle: businessmen tired of Metz; bankers tired of Nancy; off-duty doctors; lawyers and members of the local Lions'Club
Dress: tenue correcte
Service: under the knowledgeable and watchful eye of Jean Ponsard
Reservations: advisable
Price range: fairly expensive
Credit cards: AE, DC, Euro, Visa, Carte Bleue

Lunch

LE PRIEURE
3 Rue du Prieuré
Flavigny-sur-Moselle (16 km/10 miles)
Telephone: 83 26 70 45
Owner/Manager/Chef de cuisine: Joel Roy (ex-Chantecler in Nice and Toison d'Or in Nancy)
Closed: Wednesday; Sunday evening; public holidays (evening only); August 26th – September 4th; Autumn half-term holiday (All Saints'); school holidays in February
Open: 12.00/a.m.–14.00/2 p.m. and 19.30/7.30 p.m.–21.30/9.30 p.m.
Cuisine: nouvelle
Specialities: smoked pike-perch pancake; pike sausage; fillets of preserved mullet with lemon; salmon and rhubarb vol-au-vent with cider; hot mirabelle plum soufflé
Location: at Flavigny-sur-Moselle; 16 km (10 miles) north-east of Nancy along the N 74 and the N 57
Setting: recently-opened restaurant in a large old house in the suburbs of Nancy
Amenities: private dining room (20 persons)
Atmosphere: an epicurean experience which more than compensates for the slightly unprepossessing surroundings
Clientèle: young, discriminating and self-assured; admirers of Joel Roy's inventive and original cuisine from Nice to Nancy
Dress: elegant
Service: friendly and helpful; supervised by Joelle Roy
Reservations: advisable
Price range: moderately expensive
Credit cards: AE, DC, Visa

Dinner

LE CAPUCIN GOURMAND
31 Rue Gambetta
Telephone: 83 35 26 98
Owner/Manager/Chef de cuisine: Gérard Veissière

Closed: Sunday; Monday; August
Open: 12.00/a.m.–14.30/2.30 p.m. and 19.30/7.30 p.m.–22.00/10 p.m.
Cuisine: classic, with a contemporary accent
Specialities: local dishes; grilled scallops with anis; blanquette of lobster with saffron; foie gras d' oie grilled with hazelnut oil; John Dory in pistachio sauce; honey ice-cream with coffee and orange sauce; nougat glacé à la croquante
Location: half-way between the railway station and Place Stanislas
Setting: Nancy's oldest restaurant (established 1929); superb turn-of-the-century décor, tastefully renovated in fresh new colours in the modern style of the school of Nancy
Amenities: private dining room (26 persons); air conditioning; attended car park (10 Francs); catering service
Atmosphere: the gayest restaurant in town, with just a hint of late-1920's nostalgia
Clientèle: chic and cosmopolitan; royalty from Queen Elizabeth the Queen Mother to Prince Nabuhito of Japan; expense-account gourmets and hommes de lettres
Dress: tie de rigueur
Service: cheerful and anxious-to-please; charming welcome from Yolande Veissière
Reservations: advisable (pets permitted)
Price range: fairly expensive
Credit cards: AE, Carte Bleue

Bar

LE STAN
Grand Hôtel de la Reine
2 Place Stanislas
Telephone: 83 35 03 01
Owner/Manager: Jean Aubert
Closed: never
Open: 10.00/a.m.–2.00/a.m.
Location: in the Grand Hôtel de la Reine
Setting: in a beautiful nobleman's palais on the celebrated Place Stanislas; lounge bar recently renovated by Slavik; wood panelling, velvet upholstery and mirrors reflecting the light from the crystal chandeliers
Amenities: hotel; restaurant ›Le Stanislas‹; private dining rooms (5–260 persons); valet parking service
Atmosphere: confidential and vaguely club-like
Clientèle: Nancy's In-Crowd; visiting VIPs since Queen Marie-Antoinette; managing directors, financiers, solicitors and transatlantic tourists
Dress: fairly casual to fairly formal
Service: expertly directed by head barman Patrice Novack
Reservations: advisable
Credit cards: AE, DC, Euro, Visa, JBC

Café

GRAND CAFE FOY
1 Place Stanislas
Telephone: 83 32 15 97
Owner/Manager: Jacqueline Rollier
Closed: Wednesday
Open: 8.00/a.m.–2.00/a.m.
Location: a pebble's throw away from the Headquarters
Setting: old coffee house for about 140 persons
Amenities: restaurant on the first floor; in summer the ›Place Stanislas‹ represents the ›terrace‹; car park just around the corner
Atmosphere: bon chic–bon genre
Clientèle: as popular with Nancy's housewives after a shopping spree as with exhausted sightseers or businessmen between boardroom and conference hall
Service: efficient

Nightclub

LE SCALA DE NANCY
22 Rue Saint-Dizier
Telephone: 83 32 83 42
Owner/Manager: Maurice Molina
Closed: Tuesday
Open: 22.30/10.30 p.m. till dawn
Location: close to Place Stanislas
Setting: four differently styled dance floors on three different levels; typical disco-décor, lasers, lighting effects and the hottest tunes in town
Amenities: 3 bars (one on each floor); the lowest level can be converted into a private salon for up to 100 persons
Atmosphere: sparkling elegance
Clientèle: international executives mingle with birds of passage, a businessman or two and the most beautiful girls of Nancy
Dress: Italian elegance (no jeans or tennis shoes)
Service: supervised by Gérald Krein, efficient and friendly
Reservations: advisable (pets prohibited)
Price range: medium
Credit cards: AE, CB, DC

Shopping

EVERYTHING UNDER ONE ROOF
Printemps   2 Avenue Foch

FOR HIM
Anthony   Rue des Dominicains

FOR HER
Anastasia   4 Grande-Rue

BEAUTY & HAIR
Salon Christian   9 Rue des Carmes

JEWELLERY
Prevot-Seaourt   4 Rue Saint-Georges

LOCAL SPECIALITIES
Franck & Fils (women's fashion)
39 Rue Saint-Jean
Rue Saint-Jean (men & women's fashion)
6 Rue Saint-Jean
Blaisse Junior (children's fashion)
14 Rue des Dominicains
Tollet Fourrures (leather fashion)
1 Rue de Phalsbourg
Gil Fourrures (furs)
14 Rue des Dominicains
La Sorbonne, Librairie
Papeterie (books)
12 Rue Saint-Dizier
Ets Nouvelec (gifts)
77 Avenue de la Libération, Laxou
Aux Lions de Faience (porcelain)
19 Rue Raimond Poincaré
Au Cachet (baggage & travel
accessories)
26 Rue Saint-Jean
Au Vieux Gourmet (food and beverages)
26 Rue Saint-Georges
Chaussures Kayser (shoes)
28 Rue Raimond Poincaré &
59 Rue Saint-Dizier

THE BEST OF ART
Art Actuel   (contemporary art)
13 Grande-Rue, Nancy
Divergence   (contemporary art)
24 Rue Saint-Eucaire, Metz,
Tel. 83 74 00 52

The City

Few travellers to France will put the capital of Brittany on their itinerary unless business lures them to this Atlantic port city. Deauville and Saint-Tropez, Strasbourg and Bordeaux, Courchevel and Biarritz evoke preconceived ideas and illusions, and even Rheims, Lyons and Toulouse enjoy a greater interest than Nantes among visitors to the country. The ones, however, who don't follow the beaten path but rather the River Loire to its estuary, will be astonished and delighted to find a metropolis with a splendid setting and historical beauty, an intellectual centre as well as an industrial one, dotted with renowned churches and museums but also luxuriant parks, lovely relais and lively brasseries. Jules Verne, local son and voyager to the centre of the earth, around the world and to the stars in a balloon, revelled about his native land that ›along the Loire, one of the most wonderful rivers in the world, mirroring from sea to source a hundred marvellous cities and five hundred magnificent castles, life is that of a king even when you are born a peasant‹. And when you come as a tourist, with a bit of time before travelling on to La Baule for a chic repose by the sea or to Quiberon for a chic diet and cure, you will have a regal stay in the midst of this big city presenting itself in its Old Town quarter like a country village, with all the winding alleys, the tree-lined boulevards, the roofs of slate, the flower-bedecked balconies, the quaint shops and bistros. The Château and the Cathedral, the Museum of Natural History and the one of Jules Verne, the Quartier Graslin and the Place Maréchal-Foch are more than just mere signs of antiquity. The atmosphere is beguiling, even when it isn't the time for Nantes' famous carnival. Business, production as well as trade through the Nantes–St.Nazaire harbour, is the basis of the city's claim to fame today, of course, with machinery, foodstuffs, wood and leather goods only some of the branches located here, but altogether the Nantais belong to the most joyful people in the Grande Nation. And the most peaceful – despite their many forceful defences against aggressors – with native Nobel Peace Prize winner Aristide Briand as a prime example.

Founded: an early Gallic settlement; Nantes (French) – from Namnetes (the Gallic tribe).

Far-reaching events: 3rd–8th century – Nantes involved in the wars between the kings of France and the dukes of Brittany; 939 – Alain Barbe-Torte chases away invading pirates and rebuilds the ruined city; ca. 1200 – Duke Pierre de Dreux makes Nantes the capital of Brittany; 13th–14th century – Brittany successfully defends itself against England (John ›Lackland‹) and France (Louis XI); 1460 – founding of university; 1598 – Edict of Nantes confirming the rights of the Huguenots to practise their religion; 1685 – suspension of the Edict by Louis XIV; 18th century – Nantes prospers – slave trading and sugar refining; end of 18th century – the most important port in France; 1943 and 1945 – air raids damage much of the new city; post-1945 – reconstruction.

Population: 400,000 (urban area); 7th largest city in France.

Postal code: F–44000   **Telephone code:** 40 (included in number since 1986).

Climate: maritime.

Best time to visit: May to mid-November.

Calendar of events: *Fêtes de Mi-Carême* (mid-Mar) – Festival of the Fast of Lent; *International Festival of Arts and Popular Traditions* (Jul/Aug).

Fairs and exhibitions: *INTERNATIONAL GRAND FAIR* (Apr); *WINE FAIR* (Jul); *PECHE* (Sep) – trade fair for fishing and the fishing industry.

Best views of the city: from the bell tower of the *Eglise St.-Nicolas.*

Historical and modern sights: the *Church of Ste-Croix* (17th century) – surrounded by the timbered houses of the old town; the *Ducal Castle* (15th century) – Renaissance and late Gothic and an inner courtyard with the Gothic *Grand Logis*; the *Cathedral St.-Pierre* (15th–19th centuries) – 15th-century carvings on the inner façade, and the tomb of Francis II; the *Psalette* (16th century) – a former chapter-house with a picturesque little tower; the church in *Loroux-Bottereau* – some noteworthy 13th-century frescoes; the *Grand Théâtre*, with its neo-Greek-façade; the *Place Louis XIV* with well-preserved houses and monument to the king; *Musée des Beaux-Arts* – with works by Flemish, French and Italian masters, including Monet and Rubens; the *Passage Pommeraye* – late 19th-century shopping arcade with staircases, mirrors and plaster work; *Cité Radieuse* – residential area disigned by Le Corbusier based on his Marseilles model; *Museum of Natural History.*

Special attractions: *Jardin des Plantes* – magnolias, camellias, greenhouses and a monument to local son Jules Verne; tour of the *Harbour* in a motorboat; the *Grand Circus* during the summer season.

Important companies with headquarters in the city: *Compagnie des Produits de l'Quest* (rubber products); *Aux Forges de La Loire* (tools); *Sagatrans* (transport); *Valexy-Levallois-Perret* (pipes and conduits); *Vang Pharma* (text processing).

Airport: Nantes-Château-Bougon, NTE; Tel.: 40 75 80 00, 10 km/6 miles; Air France, Tel.: 40 47 12 33; VIP Lounge, Tel.: 40 75 80 00.

The Headquarters

SOFITEL

Rue Alexandre Millerand
F-44200 Nantes/Beaulieu
Telephone: 40 47 61 03
Telex: 710 990 sofinte
Owning Company: Accor Group
General Manager: Gerard Bouclet
Affiliation/Reservation System: Resinter
Number of rooms: 100 (2 suites)
Price range: FF 370–430 (single)
           FF 430–490 (double)
           FF 750 (suite)
Credit cards: AE, DC, CB, EC, MC, Access
Location: on the Loire river, 3 km/2 miles from city centre, 9 km/6 miles from airport
Built: 1975
Style: modern
Hotel amenities: car park, car rental desk, heated outdoor swimming pool, tennis court

Room amenities: sound-proofing, air conditioning, colour tv, video, mini-bar (pets welcome)
Room service: 6.30/a.m. to 24.00/12.00 p.m.
Laundry/dry cleaning: same day
Conference rooms: 3 (up to 120 persons), all modern conference facilities
Bar: ›La Montgolfière‹ (10.00/a.m.–24.00/12.00 p.m.), Jean-Yves Morinière (barman)
Restaurants: ›La Pêcherie‹ (12.00/a.m.–14.30/2.30 p.m. and 19.30/7.30 p.m.–22.30/10.30 p.m.), Jean-Yves Bernard (chef de cuisine), fish specialities, open-air dining; ›Café de Nantes‹: informal
Private dining rooms: for up to 80 persons

On the island of Beaulieu, right in the middle of Nantes' modern commercial and administrative centre, the Sofitel manages to combine convenience with a highly attractive location – the latter due in no small part to the view across the Loire as it gently meanders towards the sea. This is not the land of Chambord, Chenonceaux, and Chaumont but of hard facts, no-nonsense business with much of the pleasure stemming from the daily catch – best experienced at La Pêcherie. Therefore, the clientèle is mostly expense-account-visitors to the town, with a fair sprinkling of local businessmen who drop in en passant to enjoy the lively, informal atmosphere in the bar and the sole with morel mushrooms in the restaurant. The hotel is functional, the rooms are soundproofed, the swimming pool is heated and the winding alleyways and antique shops of town are only a short taxi ride away. The staff – another sign of Sofitel's individualistic philosophy – are exceptionally friendly, thereby ensuring that your stay in Nantes will be more pleasurable when staying at the Sofitel.

The Hideaway

LE DOMAINE D'ORVAULT

Chemin des Marais du Cens
F–44700 Orvault (7 km/4 miles)
Telephone: 40 76 84 02
Telex: 700 454 domdo
Owner: Jean-Yves Bernard
General Manager: Aline Bernard
Affiliation/Reservation System: Relais et Châteaux
Closed: February
Number of rooms: 29 (1 suite)
Price range: FF 260–490
Credit cards: AE, DC, Visa
Location: 7 km/4 miles from city centre, 18 km/11 miles from airport
Built: 1972
Style: elegant country manor
Hotel amenities: valet parking, grand piano boutique, tobacconist
Room amenities: colour tv, mini-bar/refrigerator (pets allowed)
Bathroom amenities: bidet
Room service: 7.00/a.m. to 24.00/12 p.m.
Laundry/dry cleaning: same day
Conference rooms: 2 (up to 30 persons)
Sports: tennis
Bar: (19.00/7.00 p.m.–24.00/12 p.m.)
Restaurant: ›Iden‹ (12.30/p.m.–14.00/2.00 p.m. and 19.30/7.30 p.m.–21.30/9.30 p.m.) Aline Bernard (maître), Jean-Yves Bernard (chef de cuisine), classic cuisine, pianist (Friday night), open-air dining
Private dining rooms: on request

For the shipping magnates contemplating a new liner or clothes designers planning a new line – and for everyone arriving at the estuary of the Loire, this small hotel, so near to the centre of Nantes, is the atmospheric terminus. The whitewashed modern villa stands in a leafy garden on the outskirts of town, looking for all the world like an oil baron's seaside retreat. The private-house ambiance is in evidence everywhere – from the well-appointed and comfortable bedrooms – each furnished individually and with good taste – to the lounge and dining room. The latter, in particular, typifies the cooperative tour de force by owner-managers Jean-Yves and Aline Bernard – he at the stove, she front of stage. The memory of the Challans duckling with oranges and limes or the local peaches in puff pastry with beurre nantais will linger long after you have left this most westerly stretch of the Loire. Aficionados of spectator sports may want to spend some time and money at the race track just down the road, whilst disciples of the mens sana in corpore sano philosophy will be happy about the tennis court on the premises in order to atone for the gargantuan dinners of Jean-Yves' specialities. Lovers of any age will revel in the unlimited possibilities for doing nothing more arduous than gently exploring the historic town itself or the subtle beauties of the surrounding countryside for which le Domaine d'Orvault is the ideal hideaway.

Lunch

LES MARAICHERS
21 Rue Fouré
Telephone: 40 47 06 51
Owner/Manager: Marie Pacreau
Closed: Sunday; Monday; August 4th –
September 4th
Open: 12.00/a.m–14.00/2 p.m. and
20.00/8 p.m.–22.30/10.30 p.m.
Cuisine: imaginative
Chef de cuisine: Yves Baneteau (ex-Boyer
at Reims)
Specialities: warm duck's liver in hazelnut oil; fricassée of lobster with cucumber; blanquette of salmon and oysters;
hot oysters with truffles and lemon; pigeon de Retz with turnip flan; profiteroles with coconut sorbet and hot strawberry sauce
Location: near the Champ de Mars
Setting: elegantized renovated bistro;
small dining room with whitewashed
walls enlivened by modern paintings including a remarkable still life by Rohner
Amenities: air conditioning; 2 private
dining rooms for up to 30 persones
Atmosphere: bright; alert; self-assured;
dominated by the personality of the legendary Marie Pacreau
Clientèle: appropriately young at heart,
self-confident, discerning and intelligent
Dress: informal
Service: Parisian; supervised by Serge
Pacreau
Reservations: advisable to essential
Price range: rather expensive
Credit cards: AE, DC, Euro Visa

Lunch

LA PECHERIE
Hôtel Sofitel
Rue A.-Millerand
Telephone: 40 47 61 03
Manager: Gérard Bouclet
Closed: never
Open: 12.00/a.m.–14.30/2.30 p.m. and
19.30/7.30 p.m.–22.30/10.30 p.m.
Cuisine: fishspecialities, cuisine française
Chef de cuisine: Jean-Yves Bernard
Specialities: seafood salad; gratin of lan-
goustines with courgettes; oysters in
champagne; terrine de foie gras
Location: in the Sofitel hotel, on Beaulieu
Island, five minutes from the centre and
the railway station with view of the Loire
river
Setting: modern, classic and very comfortable
Amenities: 2 private dining rooms (up to
180 persons); open air dining: in the garden; terrace; air conditioning; hotel with
outdoor, swimming pool and tennis facilities;
Atmosphere: soft background music; elegant; candlelight

Clientèle: business men from Nantes;
Pop singers and the local In-Crowd
Dress: casual
Service: very stylish; fast and always with
a smile
Reservations: advisable (pets permitted)
Price Range: medium
Credit cards: AE, DC, EC, CB

Dinner

LES MOLIÈRES
Place Graslin
Telephone: 40 73 20 53
Owner/Manager: Georges Hemon
Closed: never
Open: 9.00/a.m.–2.00/a.m.
Location: central, next to the theatre
Setting: nostalgic 1925 – style café; secret
mirrors; velvet upholstery
Amenities: air conditioning; 2 private
dining rooms (for 30–80 persons)
Atmosphere: very intimate; private charm
unique and individual hospitality
Clientèle: visiting businessmen mingle
with students, actors, writers and artists
from every corner of this world
Dress: stylish elegance
Service: efficient and anxious-to-please
Reservations: not necessary
Price range: medium high
Credit cards: not accepted

Lunch

CLEMENCE
La Chebuette
St-Julien de Concelles (18 km/11 miles)
Telephone: 40 54 10 18
Owner/Manager/Chef de cuisine: Gilbert
Charette
Closed: Sunday evening
Open: 12.15/p.m.–13.45/1.45 p.m. and
19.15/7.15 p.m.–21.45/9.45 p.m.
Cuisine: regional (bordelaise)
Specialities: fish; pike-perch (sandre)
and pike (brochet) with beurre blanc – in-
vented here (so the legend goes) by the
eponymous Clémence (Lefeuvre) at the
turn of the century; ham from the Ven-
dée; sauté of frogs' legs Provençal; ai-
guillettes de canard aux pêches
Location: at la Chebuette, 18 km (11
miles) east of Nantes along the D 75
Setting: on the river bank; a fisherman's
inn decorated in elegantized rustic style
Amenities: private dining room (30 persons); car park
Atmosphere: pleasantly home-like and relaxing
Clientèle: gourmet anglers; the Nantes
in-crowd wanting to get away from it all
at weekends
Dress: come-as-you please
Service: enthusiastic
Reservations: advisable
Price range: medium
Credit cards: AE, Visa

Dinner

DELPHIN
3 Promenade de Bellevue, Carquefou
Bellevue (9 km/6 miles)
Telephone: 40 49 04 13
Owner/Manager/Chef de cuisine: Joseph
Delphin
Closed: Sunday evening; Monday; August 12th – September 2nd; school
Christmas holidays
Open: 12.00/a.m.–14.30/2.30 p.m. and
19.00/7 p.m.–23.00/11 p.m.
Cuisine: classic and nouvelle
Specialities: lobster royale with hazelnut
cream; langoustines with chive cream;
turbot in Muscadet; ragoût of fresh salmon with fennel; surprise de pigeon aux
foies blonds; petit menu ›de ville‹
Location: 9 km (6 miles) east of Nantes
along the D 68 and D 337
Setting: pavilion overlooking the sandy
banks of the Loire; smart, slightly self-
conscious décor
Amenities: private dining room (22 persons); car park
Atmosphere: chic, but with a hint of underlying conservatism
Clientèle: Nantes' social élite; academics, art historians, architects and hommes
d'affaires
Dress: what you will – as long as they will
like what they see
Service: very attentive
Reservations: advisable to essential
Price range: fairly expensive
Credit cards: AE, DC, Euro, Visa

Dinner

MON REVE
Sur la Divatte
Basse-Goulaine (8 km/5 miles)
Telephone: 40 03 55 50
Owner/Manager/Chef de cuisine: Gérard
Ryngel
Closed: Sunday evening; (October–
March) Wednesday; three weeks in February
Open: 12.15/p.m.–14.00/2 p.m. and
19.30/7.30 p.m.–21.30/9.30 p.m.
Cuisine: local and imaginative
Specialities: frogs' legs ›au vin du pays‹;
viennoise de saumon with creamed cress;
angler fish with saffron and wild rice; eel
terrine ›au vert‹; veal chop with tarragon;
turbot with langoustines; cocktail de
fruits rouges au vin rouge pétillant; low-
calorie menu; children's menu
Location: at Basse-Goulaine; 8 km (5
miles) east of Nantes, on the D 751 (south
of the Loire)
Setting: on the banks of the Loire; villa
set in large landscaped garden with roses,
shrubs and fountains; pretty dining

rooms in warm pinks and browns; small-
paned windows; judicious use of mirrors; attractively-laid tables
Amenities: private dining rooms (4–45
persons); open-air dining on garden terrace; car park; takeaway service
Atmosphere: intimate; welcoming; that
of an elegant country house whose owner
understands the art of gracious living
Clientèle: predominantly expense-account gourmets at lunchtime; discriminating couples with a penchant for the romantic at night; local Haute Bourgeoisie
en fête and en famille at the weekend
Dress: from Sunday casual to Sunday
best
Service: exceptionally charming; supervised by Cécile Ryngel
Reservations: advisable (pets permitted)
Price range: fairly expensive
Credit cards: AE, DC, Visa, Carte Bleue

Bar

TIE BREAK
1 Rue des Petites Écuries
Telephone: 40 47 77 00
Owner/Manager: Claude Guilbert
Closed: Sunday
Open: 22.00/10 p.m.–3.30/a.m.
Location: in the pedestrian precinct;
close to the market, in the Bouffay district
Setting: piano bar with jazz and live music entertainment; ancient walls; modernised rustic interior décor in rouge et noir
Amenities: air conditioning, car park on
the ›Place du Bouffay‹
Atmosphere: something for everyone; relaxed but stylish
Clientèle: jazz connoisseurs
Dress: ›tenue correcte‹
Service: informal but very efficient
Reservations: impracticable (pets permitted)
Price range: medium
Credit cards: AE, EC, Visa, CB

Nightclub

LE CASTEL
13 Rue Mathlin Rodier
Telephone: 40 47 60 46
Owner/Manager: Bernard Giffard
Closed: Sundays
Open: 22.30/10.30 p.m.–4.00/a.m.
Location: close to the cathedral and the
château
Setting: nightclub in the ancient vaults of
the château; rustic décor
Amenities: bar; private room for up to 25
guests; air conditioning; car park (facing
the cathedral)

Atmosphere: relaxed and cheerful
Clientèle: local chiceria, international singers and sporting personalities from near and far
Dress: conservative elegance
Service: smiling efficiency
Reservations: not necessary (no pets)
Price range: medium
Credit cards: AE, Visa, CB

Shopping

EVERYTHING UNDER ONE ROOF
Galeries Lafayette
18–20 Rue du Calvaire

FOR HIM
Fer 7   2 Place Ladmirault

FOR HER
Ermeline   22 Rue Crébillon

BEAUTY & HAIR
David, Jacques   6 Rue Rubens

JEWELLERY
Daguzé   2 Rue Crébillon

LOCAL SPECIALITIES
Tabac le Havane (tobacco)
21 Rue Grebillon
Boutique, La (women's fashion)
18 Rue Crébillon/Passage de la Chatelaine
Saint-Troc (men's fashion)
4 Rue du Chapeau Rouge
Jacadi (children's fashion)
2 Rue Anizon/Place Ladmirault
Chaussavoine, C. (leather fashion)
2 Place Delorme
Talon, Jean Fourrures (furs)
Passage Pommeraye (upstairs)
Beaufreton, Librairie (books)
24 Passage Pommeraye
Gadget-Club – La carterie (gifts)
6 Bis Rue du Chapeau Rouge
Aubert, Armand (porcelain)
5 Rue Boileau
Doge, Le (baggage & travel accessories)
6 Rue Racine
Boutique Ecossaise, La (interior decorating)
8 Rue Boileau
Ty Coz (crêperie)
1 Bis, Rue Camille Berruyer/Place Delorme
Sabatier, Edith (perfumery/beauty)
18 Rue Crébillon
Gueudet (shoes)
10 Rue Crébillon

THE BEST OF ART
Convergence   (modern art)
18 Rue Jean-Jaurès, Tel. 40 73 49 71

›La Grande Dame of the Riviera – ›. . . where matrons draped in Paris fashion prolong the twilight of their passions, in the pursuit of romance; . . . where every golden coat of suntan has cost the gold of more than one man, who wasn't warned in advance . . .‹. Mabel Mercer's chanson echoes only the champagne essence of the other final stop of the Train Bleu. La Belle Epoque – despite its many traces along the majestic Boulevard des Anglais – is gone, and the era of pragmatism, tourism and trade is radiated by France's fourth largest city in the same beautiful light and légèreté that once assembled Gotha-gods, gigolos, gamblers and gangsters from all over the world. Nice is business in the most pleasureable atmosphere, with a mild climate, a southern charm and Italian undertones. With Monte-Carlo the operetta stage, Cannes the vanity fair and Saint-Tropez the psychedelic playground in season, Nice is the market-place for agricultural goods of the Mediterranean as well as an important link in the chain of industrial cities, producing electronics, textiles, cosmetics and photographic equipment. And still, Nice is the centre of tourism along the Côte, with grand hotels and camping grounds, two grandiose casinos and a mini-Disneyland, festivals, flower parades, pop concerts, jazz sessions, gourmet grails and fast-food stalls, High Society habitués and hordes of visitors on a low budget. Something for everyone. Plus the commercial harbour and the only international airport between Marseilles and Genoa. The old city has a touch of Naples, the Rue du Paradis the scent of the Faubourg Saint-Honoré, some parts allure the romantic and others attract the investor. If you come for business, you won't have to search for pleasure – it's in the air.

Founded: as a Greek colony – *Nikaia* in the 3rd century B. C.

Far-reaching events: 4th century A. D. – Nice becomes the seat of bishops; 12th century – a city-state; 1388 – the House of Savoy takes the County of Nice; 1793 – Napoléon adopts it; 1814 – the House of Savoy-Sardinia takes it back; 1860 – Giuseppe Garibaldi, a native of ›Nizza‹, is forced to surrender the city to France, as part of his plan for a united Italy; late 19th century – Nice develops into an élite resort city and industrial centre.

Population: 400,000; 4th largest city in France (capital of the Département Alpes-Maritimes).

Postal code: F–06000   **Telephone code:** 93 (incorporated in number since 1986)

Climate: typically Mediterranean, hot and humid summers, mild rainy winters (ca. 80 days of rain per year); the Mistral, a cold and strong mountain wind pays brief visits in spring and fall.

Best time to visit: any time of the year, particularly pleasant from February to June and from September to November.

Fairs and exhibitions: *GRAND INTERNATIONAL FAIR* (Mar); *INTERNATIONAL BOOK FAIR* (May); *SCAME* (Sep) – summer fashion fair; *MEDAX MEDITERRANEAN* (Oct) – medical trade fair; *OFNUX* (Nov) – international exhibition for doors, windows, locks and accessories.

Calendar of events: *Carnival* (Feb) – two weeks of celebrations rivalling those in Rio, with processions, battle of flowers and music in the streets; *Great Market of Nice* (May); *Jazz Festival* (Jul) – in the Roman arenas of Cimiez; *Religious Music Festival* (Jul); *International Folklore Festival* (Jul) – music and theatre; *Holiday on Ice* (Aug); *Italian Film Festival* (Dec); ›*Christmas Bathing*‹ (25 Dec) – in the Baie des Anges.

Best views of the city: from the observation platform of the *Château*; *Plateau St. Michel* and *Plateau Mont Chauve;* from the *citadel* on Mont Alban; from the *Plateau of Mont Baron.*

Historical and modern sights: the *Château* (1706) – the ruins of a grand castle with a park and cascades; *St. Jacques* (17th century) – Jesuit Baroque; *Miséricorde* (17th century) – with panelled altars in the Baroque chapel; the *Franciscan Monastery* in Cimiez; *Russian Orthodox Church* (18th century) – with intriguing iconostasis; *Opera House* – fin-de-siècle, with an Italian Baroque façade from the 17th century; *Palais Lascaris* – with a grand 17th-century façade and a museum of rare antique musical instruments; *Musée National Message Biblique Marc Chagall* – with the world's largest individual collection of Chagalls and rooms for concerts and exhibitions; *Palais des Congrès* – completed in 1984, furnished with the most modern equipment, used for conventions and with art galleries, a press centre and restaurants.

Special attractions: the *Promenade des Anglais* is the main street where the atmosphere of the Belle Epoque still lives on; the Hotel Négresco, with its lavish interiors and glass dome is a sight to behold; the *Perfume Museum* in nearby Grasse, the former world centre of perfume, with antique flacons and porcelain; the two *Casinos* offering baccarat and roulette; a *helicopter ride* from Nice airport to Monaco lasts seven minutes and offers a magnificent view of the entire Côte d'Azur.

Important companies with headquarters in the city: *Dow Chemical; Digital Equipment; C. N. R. S.* (data processing); *Télémécanique; Deltatex* (industrial plastics); *G3S Infodif* (telecommunications).

Airport: Nice-Côte d'Azur, NCE; Tel.: 93 83 03 56/93 72 30 30; Air France, Tel.: 93 83 91 00; 7 km/4 miles.

The Headquarters

NEGRESCO

37 Promenade des Anglais; B. P. 379
F–06007 Nice Cedex
Telephone: 93 88 39 51
Telex: 460040 negresco nice
Owner: the Augier Family
General Manager: Michel Palmer
Affiliation/Reservation Systems: The
Leading Hotels of the World, SRS (Steigenberger Reservation Service), Horis
(Swissair), Keytel (Spain)
Number of rooms: 150 (25 suites)
Price range: FF 1,100–1,800,
            from FF 2,800 (suites)
Credit cards: AE, DC, Visa, MC, EC, CB
Location: city centre, on sea front
Built: 1912 (Edouard Niermans)
Style: Belle Epoque
Hotel amenities: valet parking, grand piano in the hotel, newsstand, boutiques
Main hall porter: Jean Chodzko
Room amenities: air conditioning, colour
tv (some with remote control), video (in
some rooms), mini-bar/refrigerator (pets
allowed)
Bathroom amenities: separate shower
cabin, bidet, bathrobe, hairdrier, telephone (in some rooms)
Room service: 7.00/a.m.–24.00/12 p.m.
Conference rooms: 9 (up to 500 persons),
conference equipment and secretarial
services on request, ballroom
Bar: ›Relais Bar‹ (11.00/a.m.–
24.00/12.00 p.m.) Michel Krochmalnicky
(barman), English style, pianist
Restaurants: ›Le Chantecler‹
(12.30/p.m.–14.00/2.00 p.m. and
19.30/7.30 p.m.–22.00/10.00 p.m.) Jean
Max Haussy (maître), Jacques Maximin
(chef de cuisine), Louis XV provençal
style, wine list: Ch. Lafite Rothschild
1918, Ch. Petrus 1950, Ch. Latour 1959,
records (closed in November)
›La Rotonde‹ fashionable gastronomic
Brasserie-style restaurant
Private dining rooms: for up to 200 persons

*One of the lighthouses of luxury along the
glamourous Côte d'Azur since 1912, this
architectural wedding cake of La Belle
Epoque is ›Paradise Regained‹ after a
philanthropic and aesthetic restoration by
the owning Augier family. The marbled rotonde and the tapestried hallways have
been walked by all the Valentinos and Garbos of the glorious past and are visited
again by all the Delons and Deneuves of
the somewhat less pompous present. Yet,
Le Négresco is by no means an enclave of
stars – with Nice one of the country's foremost business cities, you will meet men
from Ohio and Osaka (and culinary aficionados for Le Chantecler's own star,
Jacques Maximin) behaving, though, as if
they came from Belgravia or Bal Harbour.
Individualistic décor à la folie, service par
excellence, and La Promenade des Anglais
à la porte.*

CHATEAU DU DOMAINE SAINT-MARTIN

Route de Coursegoules (2 km/1 mile)
F–06140 Vence
Telephone: 93 58 02 02
Telex: 470 282 smartin
Owner: the Genève Family
General Manager: Andrée Brunet
Affiliation/Reservation System: Relais et Châteaux
Closed: end of Nov – beginning of Mar
Number of rooms: 25 (10 suites)
Price range: FF 1,200–2,600
Credit cards: AE, DC, EC, Visa, CB
Location: 2 km/1 mile from city centre; 20 km/13 miles from airport
Built: 1936
Style: Louis XV and Louis XVI
Hotel amenities: garage, valet parking, tennis, outdoor swimming pool
Room amenities: colour tv (remote control), mini-bar/refrigerator (pets allowed)
Bathroom amenities: bidet, bathrobe, hairdrier
Room service: 7.30 a.m.–21.30/9.30 p.m.
Conference rooms: 2 (up to 15 persons); conference equipment and secretarial services upon request
Sports: tennis, bowling, table-tennis
Bar: ›Château du Domaine Saint Martin‹ Pierre Bressan (barman)
Restaurant: ›Château du Domaine Saint Martin‹ (12.00 p.m.–14.30/2.30 p.m. and 19.30/7.30 p.m.–21.30/9.30 p.m.), Mr. René Leroux (maître), Mr. Dominique Ferrière (chef de cuisine), nouvelle and classic cuisine, open-air dining, panoramic style
Private dining rooms: one

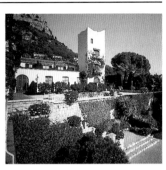

Away from the erotically bristling atmosphere of the Boulevards de la Côte and the perfume of diamonds, dollars and demi-monde, there is – only a mistral's blow away – a quieter side of the uniquely beautiful south of France, the rolling hills of Vence, full of olive trees, herbal air and the mysterious light of an impressionist painting. Many acres of this fairytale landscape surround one of the most breathtaking hideaways on this divine domaine where Andrée Brunet runs the owning family Genève's castle like a club for a selected few. Few the visitors are, for there are only a handful rooms and suites in this ex-commanderie, where luxurious amenities have been installed in an unobtrusive way, not to obstruct the twelfth-century fortress' character and charm. Overlooking the Blue Coast and the magic countryside at the same time, St. Martin offers itself to the rich romantic as well as to the aesthetical voyeur, to the creative introvert as well as to the tired locomotive. Flowers and antiques, grande cuisine and 19th-century wines, pool and tennis – and the service Somerset Maugham wouldn't want to live without up here.

Lunch

CHANTECLER
Hôtel Négresco
37 Promenade des Anglais
Telephone: 93 88 39 51
Owner/Manager: Famille Augier and Michel Palmer
Maître: Jean Max Haussy
Closed: November
Open: 12.30/p.m.–14.00/2 p.m. and 19.30/7.30 p.m.–22.00/10 p.m.
Cuisine: élaborée
Chef de cuisine: Jacques Maximin
Specialities: courgettes à la fleur et aux truffes; stuffed tomatoes with basil; lobster ravioli in shellfish bouillon; salmon in rock salt; red mullet and leek vinaigrette; homard au jus de truffe; white asparagus tips and foie gras in sauternes aspic; nougat glacé au coulis de framboises; gratin de fraises des bois; the best selection of chocolate cakes in the world (millefeuille au chocolat)
Location: in the Hôtel Négresco
Setting: a historic monument; one of the last grand palaces in the world – recently renovated; restaurant decorated in Louis XV Provençal style; with period rustic furnishing
Amenities: hotel; private dining rooms (20–200 persons); air conditioning; car parking service
Atmosphere: unapologetically luxurious
Clientèle: French aristocracy, German industrialists, Greek shipping magnates, Arab oil tycoons and Italian designers
Dress: from Mic Mac to Lanvin
Service: Niçois
Reservations: essential
Price range: who cares?
Credit cards: AE, DC, Euro, Carte Bleue

Lunch

LE BISTRO DE LA PROMENADE
7–9 Promenade des Anglais
Telephone: 93 81 63 48
Owner/Manager: Jean-Claude Rieu and Jacques Chiron
Closed: Sunday
Open: 12.00/a.m.–14.00/2 p.m. and 20.00/8 p.m.–22.30/10.30 p.m.
Cuisine: nouvelle
Chef de cuisine: Gérard Ferri
Specialities: soupe safranée en gelée aux trois poissons; suprême de canard with pickled turnips (navets); saddle of lamb in garlic cream with basil with potato pancake; sole with green noodles; mousseline of passion fruit; chocolate mousse gâteau
Location: on the seafront
Setting: small, luxurious brasserie-restaurant with an attractive terrace overlooking the beach and the Med; in the rear dining room an American bar with a pianist

Amenities: private dining room (20 persons); air conditioning
Atmosphere: fashionable and elegant, but not formidable
Clientèle: youthful; discriminating; intelligent; approachable
Dress: Gucci, Pucci and co.
Service: pleasantly attentive
Reservations: advisable
Price range: moderately expensive (by Nice standards, that is)
Credit cards: AE, DC, Visa

Dinner

LA POULARDE (›Chez Lucullus‹)
9 Rue Gustave-Deloye
Telephone: 93 85 22 90
Owner/Manager/Chef de cuisine: Marcel Normand
Closed: Wednesday; July 12th–August 18th
Open: 12.00/a.m.–22.00/10 p.m.
Cuisine: traditional
Specialities: suprême de sole ›Lucullus‹; calf's kidney flambé ›fine champagne‹; tournedos Rossini; grilled crayfish with herbs; trout with almonds
Location: a pleasant walk from the Place Massèna
Setting: a pre-war country tavern with a faint air of an oriental bazar; a wealth of wrought iron and other knick-knacks
Amenities: private dining room (25 persons); air conditioning
Atmosphere: charmingly anachronistic
Clientèle: conservative, comfortably-off, middle-aged epicures
Dress: formal
Service: particularly solicitous; supervised by M. Normand
Reservations: advisable
Price range: fairly expensive
Credit cards: AE, DC, Euro, Carte Bleue

Lunch

LA COLOMBE D'OR
Place du Général de Gaulle,
Saint-Paul-de-Vence (20 km/12 miles)
Telephone: 93 32 80 02
Owner/Manager: Michel Peyre
Closed: November; first half of December
Open: 12.00/a.m.–14.00/2 p.m. and 19.30/7.30 p.m.–22.30/10.30 p.m.
Cuisine: classic
Chef de cuisine: Serge Oblette
Specialities: hors d'œuvres; rabbit casserole; cream of chicken fricassée; grilled meats; pâtisserie
Location: at Saint-Paul-de-Vence, 20 km (12 miles) east of Nice
Setting: an auberge de campagne perched in the foothills of the Alps; pretty Provençal rustic dining room with a priceless collection of modern paintings by Miró, Rouault, Picasso, et al
Amenities: hotel; open-air dining on ter-

race overlooking Roman-style garden; air conditioning; car park
Atmosphere: sunny and welcoming, even on a wet day
Clientèle: discriminating globe-trotters still outnumber the Europe-at-the-gallop tourists by the beautiful swimming pool once beloved of the Côte d'Azur crème de la crème, from Simone Signoret to Yves Montand
Dress: couturier casual to patterned shirt and sneakers
Service: Grande Epoque
Reservations: recommended
Price range: fairly expensive
Credit cards: AE, DC, Euro, Visa

Dinner

LA CHAUMIERE
384 Boulevard de l'Observatoire (Les Quatre Chemins, Grande Corniche)
Telephone: 93 01 77 68
Owner/Manager: Nicole Cere-Pieri
Closed: lunchtime; Sunday; October 15th–January 15th
Open: 20.00/8 p.m.–22.00/10 p.m.
Cuisine: rustic
Chef de cuisine: Ferdinand Coppini
Specialities: charcoal-grilled meats; terrine ›maison‹; apple tart
Location: on the Grande Corniche, between Nice and Monaco
Setting: typical country auberge with pink rendered walls, shuttered windows and bay trees in tubs; dining room in traditional Provençal rustic style – brick fireplace, rush-seated chairs, red-and-white check tablecloths and herbs and onions drying from the ceiling beams
Amenities: open-air dining on covered terrace; car park
Atmosphere: unpretentious and homely, but with an indefinable air of chic emanating, no doubt, from the illustrious customers who dine here from time to time
Clientèle: European royalty and aristocracy; transatlantic stars of stage and screen, from Gregory Peck to Frank Sinatra – and the occasional ordinary mortal
Dress: casual
Service: welcoming and friendly
Reservations: advisable (pets permitted)
Price range: moderately expensive
Credit cards: AE, Visa

Dinner

ROTISSERIE DE SAINT-PANCRACE
Saint-Pancrace (8 km/5 miles)
Telephone: 93 84 43 69
Owner/Manager: Daniel Teillas
Closed: Monday; January 5th–February 5th
Open: 12.00/a.m.–22.00/10 p.m.
Cuisine: nouvelle
Chef de cuisine: Jean-Pierre Robert

Specialities: foie gras ravioli; game (in season); rosette of courgettes with fried scampi; cabbage stuffed with goose sausage; chicken breast with fresh pasta and foie gras; aiguillettes of angler-fish with sweet pepper sabayon; apple charlotte
Location: at Saint-Pancrace; 8 km (5 miles) north of Nice
Setting: a hunting-lodge perched nearly 1000 feet (300 m) above the valley of the river Var, with a panoramic view of the Alpine foothills behind Nice; light, bright dining room and shady garden terrace for open-air dining
Amenities: private dining room (50 persons); car park
Atmosphere: refined and refreshing for lunch; bewitchingly intimate at night
Clientèle: top executives tired of Nice; the suntan set seeking a change from sand and seashore; connoisseurs with a penchant for the romantic
Dress: casual to elegant
Service: under the capable guidance of Daniel Teillas, aided by Antoine Luciano, one of the best sommeliers on the Côte d'Azur.
Reservations: advisable
Price range: not too exorbitant
Credit cards: Visa

Café

LA PETITE MAISON ›FERRIER‹
3 Rue de l'Opéra
Telephone: 93 92 59 59
Owner/Manager: Marc Fischler
Closed: Saturday; Sunday; August
Open: 8.00/a.m.–20.00/8 p.m.
Location: near the Opera (l'Opéra) and the Town Hall (l'Hôtel de Ville)
Setting: nostalgic-elegant salon with lounge area (leather armchairs, marble-topped tables and magazines); dining tables with bentwood chairs; gilt mirrors, potted palms and a collection of Dali pictures on the wall
Amenities: restaurant (classic French cuisine with a hint of nouvelle); open-air dining on terrace; car park in the vicinity (Parking Saleya)
Atmosphere: classically charming
Clientèle: tout le monde; shopkeepers; shopgirls; well-heeled housewives; industrialists; journalists; artists; casual passers-by
Service: discreetly amiable

Bar

ALBERT'S
1 Rue Maurice-Jaubert
Telephone: 93 53 37 72
Owner/Manager: Claudine Malacarne
Closed: Sunday; public holidays; August
Open: 12.00/a.m.–15.30/3.30 p.m. and 18.00/6 p.m.–24.00/12 p.m.

Location: in the pedestrian precinct
Setting: comfortable English pub-style décor
Amenities: meals served (salad; veal Pojarski; sole meunière; chocolate charlotte)
Atmosphere: a popular haven of peace and tranquillity; an essential stopover for all those anxious to ›do‹ Nice
Clientèle: doctors, dentists, lawyers, bankers – leavened by the occasional glamourous bird of passage
Service: youthful, charming and feminine
Reservations: advisable for lunch
Credit cards: AE, DC, Carte Bleue

Bar

FELIX FAURE
12 Avenue Félix Faure
Telephone: 93 62 25 53
Open: 12.00/a.m.–1.00/a.m.
Location: near the Place Masséna
Setting: bar-brasserie
Amenities: light meals, seafood; pizzas; kebabs; excellent desserts
Atmosphere: très à la mode; sometimes so busy during the ›rush hour‹ that tourists may be stranded at the bar whilst regulars are shown to a table
Clientèle: lots of local habitués – advertising executives, media men, jeunesse dorée and Haute Bourgeoisie
Service: cordial and quick
Reservations: advisable!
Credit cards: AE, DC, CB

Nightclub

FINDLATTERS
6 Rue Lépante
Telephone: 93 85 09 54
Closed: Sunday; Monday
Open: 23.00/11 p.m.–2.00/a.m.
Location: city centre
Setting: summery décor; palm trees, chaises longues and blue sky; 1960s-style discothèque
Amenities: bar; discothèque; restaurant (reasonably-priced food until the wee small hours); excellent music (plans for live shows by local and international rock groups)
Atmosphere: everything your are likely to want from a nightclub – good food, a friend for a night or a lifetime, and fun
Clientèle: revellers; students; rock fans – amiable and approachable
Dress: preferably not jeans
Service: some of the nicest waitresses in Nice
Reservations: advisable
Price range: medium to high
Credit cards: not accepted

Nightclub

LA CAMARGUE
5 Place Charles-Félix (cours Saleya)
Telephone: 93 85 74 10
Owner/Manager: Roger Dalmas
Closed: Monday
Open: 23.00/11 p.m.–dawn
Setting: recently renovated; ultra-chic beige décor; a pot-pourri of ›in‹ music
Amenities: discothèque supervised by Nick, the only real disc-jockey in town
Atmosphere: the ›Temple of the Night‹ in Nice; select; sophisticated; superior
Clientèle: revellers; late risers; models, playboys and elegant Italians
Dress: everything but tennis shoes
Service: two seductively charming hostesses – Ketty and Ornella
Reservations: advisable
Price range: rather expensive
Credit cards: not accepted

Shopping

EVERYTHING UNDER ONE ROOF
Galeries Lafayette
6 Avenue Jean Médecin

FOR HIM
Riche Selection   5 Rue Paradis

FOR HER
Cacharel   1 Place Magenta

BEAUTY & HAIR
Tonia   8 Avenue de Verdun

LOCAL SPECIALITIES
Tabac Flamme et Fumée (tobacco)
16 Avenue Felix-Faure
Infinitif   (fashion for her)
24 Avenue Jean Médecin
Bonnucci, Claude (fashion for him)
10 Rue Masséna
Vogue (leather fashion)
13 Rue Masséna
Jama (furs)
3 Rue Paradis
Rudin (books)
12 Avenue Félix-Faure
Lancel (gifts)
24 Avenue Médecin
Pecha (porcelain)
3 Place Masséna
Vuitton (baggage & travel accessories)
2 Avenue de Suède
Contesse du Barry (food and beverages)
5 Rue Haléry
Auer (confiserie)
7 Rue Saint-François-de-Paul

THE BEST OF ART
Hervieu, P.   (modern art)
26 Rue Pastorelli, Tel. 93 80 02 10

The City

If you see the world as a pyramid, Paris is its peak. ›The City of Light‹, the ›Moveable Feast‹ belongs to the men – and women! – who make history, and to those who write it; to creators and performers; to the boffins, the bel-esprits and the Beau Monde, to the hedonists, the epicureans and the sybarites; to the ones who can buy everything and to those prepared to give it all up – including themselves. It's the most regal, elegant, stylish and exciting place on earth – and certainly worth more than a mass! It's the genesis for all the useless, tempting, luxurious – in short, pleasant things of life: lovely shapes, ravishing robes, tantalizing smells, seductive sounds and divine tastes. Paris is home to the Louvre, St. Germain, Montparnasse, Haute Couture, the Rothschilds, Cathérine Deneuve, Alain Delon, the ›right‹ Americans, the best restaurants, the most glamourous balls, Maxim's, the Ritz and millions of individualistic, pleasantly arrogant, totally fascinating people (to the rest of the world outside France). All business, all pleasure begins and ends here.

Founded: 52 B.C. as ›Lutetia‹ by the Romans; Paris – from the local Gallic tribe, the Parisii.

Far-reaching events: 486 – capital of the Merovingian empire under Clovis; 987 – capital of France; 1215 – foundation of University; 13th century – Paris the trading centre and largest city in the West; 1337–1453 – Paris suffers during the Hundred Years' War; 16th century – torn by the Wars of Religion; 17th century – Henri IV, Louis XIII and Le Roi Soleil make Paris the capital of the world during the Grand Siècle; 1789 – the arena of the Revolution; 19th century – Napoléon and his successors further embellish the city; 1871 – the Commune, following the Franco-Prussian War; Belle Epoque – Paris the glittering cultural centre of the world; 1878, 1889 – the World Exhibitions, marked by the construction of the Eiffel Tower; 1939–45 – Paris, by a miracle, escapes major damage; 1958–69 – the Gaullist era – France again the centre of the stage; 1968 – the Students' Revolution – the end of an epoch.

Population: 10 million (metropolitan area); capital and largest city of France.

Postal code: F-75000   **Telephone code:** 1

Climate: temperate

Best time to visit: every day of the year

Calendar of events: *International Tennis Championships* (May/Jun); *St. Germain Festival* – exhibitions, theatre, concerts, flea market; *Festival du Marais* (Jun/Jul); *French Open Tennis Championship* (mid-Jun); *Grand Steeplechase de Paris; Grand Prix de Paris* (Longchamp); *Prix de Diane, Prix du Jockey Club* (Jun); *Festival Estival* (Jul) – music; *Bastille Day* (14 Jul) – fireworks and dancing in the streets; *Tour de France* (Jul) – finishing line on the Champs Elysées; *Festival d'Automne* (Sep) – music, ballet, theatre; *Grand Prix de l'Eté* (Sep) – turf; *Grand Prix de l'Arc de Triomphe* (Oct) – at Longchamp; *Lancôme Golf Trophy* (Oct); *International Dance Festival* (Oct/Nov); *Bal de l'X* (Nov) – at the Opéra; *Prix Goncourt* (1st Tue in Dec) – literary award presentation.

Fairs and exhibitions *BOAT SHOW AND WATER SPORTS* (Jan); *LIGHTING AND LAMPS TRADE FAIR* (Jan); *FURNITURE TRADE FAIR* (Jan); *TOY FAIR* (Jan); *›ARTS MENAGERS‹* (Jan) – home economics; *SEHM* (Feb & Sep/Oct) – men's and boys' fashions; *SALON INTERNATIONAL DU PRET-A-PORTER FEMININ* (Feb & Sep); *SIF* (Mar) – furs; *SICOP-SPECIAL* (Apr/May) – office machinery; *TAPIS* (May/Jun) – rugs and floor coverings; *PARITEX* (May/Jun) – interior decorating; *INTERNATIONAL LEATHER WEEK* (Sep); *BIENNALE OF ANTIQUE DEALERS, JEWELLERS AND DECORATORS* (Sep); *SISELSPORT* (Sep) – sports and recreation: *SICOB* (Sep) – data processing, telecommunications, office organization; *EQUIP-HOTEL* (Oct/Nov) – hotel and catering equipment.

Historical and modern sights: *Notre-Dame de Paris* (1163) – great Gothic landmark cathedral; *Palais du Louvre* (1682) – erstwhile residence of kings, now the museum of museums; *Sainte Chapelle* (Palais de Justice) – stained glass symphony; *Pont Alexandre III* (1900) – the most distinguished shelter for clochards; *Place des Vosges* – Grand Siècle palaces, restored to former glory under André Malraux; *Les Invalides* – Napoléon's red marble tomb; *Panthéon* (1789) – tombs of Victor Hugo, Jean-Jacques Rousseau and Voltaire; the *Jardin du Luxembourg* and the *Tuileries* – flower power in formal style; *Père-Lachaise cemetery* – graves of le Tout Paris, from Georges Bizet to Sarah Bernhardt to Edith Piaf et al.; the *Rodin Museum; Le Musée Beaubourg* (Centre Pompidou) – the Old World's modern-art Parthenon.

Special attractions: Son et Lumière at *Versailles*; Paris at night – the *Ile Saint-Louis*, the *Rue de Rivoli*, the *Champs-Elysées*; a stroll through the *Marais*; *Fauchon* – a sybarite's labyrinth; *Galeries Lafayette* – a Belle Epoque Bloomingdale's; *Olympia* – when Aznavour, Bécaud et al. are performing; one night at the *Ritz*; a shopping spree on the *Foubourg St. Honoré*; a gala night at the *Opéra*; a sunny afternoon at *St.-Germain-des-Prés*, on the terrace of *Flore* or *Les Deux Magots*; a visit to an exhibition at the *Grand Palais* or the *Petit Palais*; a browse around the *Marché aux Puces*; a night at *l'Alcazar* and the *Crazy Horse Salon*.

Important companies with headquarters in the city: *the Who's Who of national and international companies.*

Airport: Charles-de-Gaulle, PAR-CDG; Tel.: 48 62 22 80; 30 km/20 miles; Orly, PAR-ORY; Tel.: 48 84 32 10; 16 km/10 miles, Air France, Tel.: 43 20 14 55.

The Headquarters

RITZ

15 Place Vendôme
F–75001 Paris
Telephone: 42 60 38 30
Telex: 670 112 ritzres 220 262 ritzmsg
Telefax: 42 60 23 71
General Manager: Frank J. Klein
Affiliation/Reservation System: The Leading Hotels of the World
Number of rooms: 188 (45 suites)
Price range: FF 1,955–2,415
Credit cards: AE, DC, Visa, CB
Location: city centre
Built: 1898
Style: Louis XV/XVI – original Ritz
Hotel amenities: underground car park, valet parking, limousine service (armoured cars available), beauty salon, newsstand, swimming pool, health club
Main hall porter: Gérard Avez
Room amenities: colour tv, radio, private telex available (pets allowed)
Bathroom amenities: shower cabin, bidet, bathrobe, telephone, jacuzzi and sauna in some suites
Room service: 24 hours
Conference rooms: 5 (up to 80 persons)
Bars: ›Hemingway‹ (available for private parties) Claude Decobert (barman); ›Vendôme‹ Michel Bigot (head barman), pianist; ›Espadon‹ pianist
Restaurant: ›Espadon‹ (12.00/a.m.–2.00/a.m.) Guy Legay (executive chef), Franco Gentileschi (maître), Georges Lepré (sommelier), classic cuisine, open-air dining, pianist

Mirror, mirror on the wall, who is . . . The Ritz, of course. Again. And the best. Forever. Thanks to the city of Paris: they declared it a national monument; thanks to proprietor Al Fayed: he honours history but flouts the laws of capitalism; thanks to Frank Klein: he runs the Ritz as if Coco Chanel were still living here, welcoming Joan Collins at the same time; thanks to César who made this dream come true. Imagine: Place Vendôme – Napoléon on a column, Cartier, Van Cleef, Boucheron et al. around; a Belle Epoque palace – pillared arches, marble stairs, crystal lustres, silk curtains, Persian carpets, golden stucco; a retinue of innumerable liveried servants – helping, holding, getting, offering; rooms to die in – everything in abundance, quality and taste, from the light switch to the bathrobe; a restaurant for the last supper – with haute cuisine, lord-like maîtres and Lords as guests; a bar for latter-day Hemingways and an atmosphere for devotees of Proust and Wilde: then you're in the Ritz. If you have no business in Paris, hate big cities, are indifferent to the French and reject conspicuous consumption and grand hotel haughtiness – The Ritz will change your anti-snobbism snobbism. Le roi est mort – vive le Ritz!

The Hideaway

PAVILLON HENRI IV

21 Rue Thiers
F–78100 Saint-Germain-En-Laye
(15 km/9 miles)
Telephone: 34 51 62 62
Telex: 695 822
Owner/Manager: Pierre Jammet
Affiliation/Reservation System: Robert F. Warner N.Y.
Number of rooms: 42 (3 suites)
Price range: FF 500–1,800
Credit cards: AE, DC, Visa
Location: 15 km/9 miles from city centre; 25 km/15 miles from airport
Built: 1830
Style: Louis XV and Louis XVI
Hotel amenities: garage, valet parking
Room amenities: colour tv (pets allowed)
Bathroom amenities: bidet, bathrobe, telephone
Room service: 24 hours
Laundry/dry cleaning: same day
Conference rooms: 7 (up to 300 persons), video, simultaneous translation equipment
Bar: (11.00/a.m.–2.00/a.m.)
Restaurants: ›Panoramique‹ (11.30/a.m.–22.30/11.30 p.m.), traditional cuisine, Louis XV, open-air dining; ›Historique‹ (11.30/a.m.–14.30/2.30 p.m.), traditional cuisine, Louis XV, open-air dining

Were it not for the unforgettable view of Paris across the Seine – on a clear day you can even see the white marble domes of the Sacré-Cœur – you could be forgiven for thinking that the City of Light was a million miles away. The Pavillon Henri IV is an oasis of tranquillity, elegance and gracious living only a short drive from the vibrant French capital. Set in a lovingly-renovated former royal palais, it proudly displays the room where Le Roi Soleil was born; furnishings and décor date from the reigns of his two successors, Louis XV and Louis XVI, with the addition of all the modern facilities and conveniences expected by today's discriminating guest. The two restaurants serve classic French cuisine of a very high standard, including fillet steak ›Henri IV‹ with sauce Béarnaise and pommes soufflées, both of which (according to the legend) were invented in the kitchens here. Dinners on the terrace – open-air in summer, glassed-in in winter – are as memorable as the discreetly charming service. It's not surprising that the Pavillon Henri IV is considered by connoisseurs to be the loveliest weekend hideaway in the Paris area. Pierre Jammet, the owner, who sold one of the world's palaces, Le Bristol, in order to retreat to – and refine – Le Pavillon, is rocking the Sun King's cradle back to Grand-Siècle splendour. Room by room, salon by salon and, literally, stone by stone he and his wife Heidi are retouching house and garden so that lovers of château-ambiance with the desire for push-button comfort are equally rewarded.

Lunch

LAURENT
41 Avenue Gabriel
Telephone: 4-2 25 00 39/4-7 23 79 18
Owner/Manager: Jimmy Goldsmith/Edmond Ehrlich
Closed: Saturday lunchtime; Sunday; public holidays
Open: 12.30/p.m.–14.00/2 p.m. and 19.30/7.30 p.m.–23.00/11 p.m.
Cuisine: French (classic)
Chef de cuisine: Marc Pralong
Specialities: Breton lobster salad (prepared at table); poached eggs with caviar; mignons de veau with morel mushrooms (morilles) and home-made spinach noodles; duck with truffles and asparagus; fondant de chocolat with preserved orange peel and coffee; les deux soufflés Laurent
Location: 8th arrondissement; near the Champs-Elysées
Setting: 19th-century villa on the site of a Louis XIV hunting-lodge; magnificent oval dining room with stucco ceiling, pillars and indirect lighting; colour scheme in gold and brown with well-spaced circular tables and picture windows overlooking gardens
Amenities: bar; private dining rooms (4–60 persons); open-air dining on terrace or in garden; pianist (evenings only)
Atmosphere: a cross between the Elysian Fields and the Garden of Eden
Clientèle: Parisian politicians; jet-set aristocrats; expense-account gourmets and millionaire aesthetes
Dress: appropriately enough – jacket and tie
Service: impeccable
Reservations: advisable (pet poodles to be left with mink coats in cloakroom)
Price range: medium to high
Credit cards: AE, DC

Dinner

LE JULES VERNE
2e étage de la Tour Eiffel
Telephone: 4-5 55 61 44
Owner/Manager: Pierre Ody
Closed: never
Open: 12.00 p.m.–14.30/2.30 p.m. and 19.30/7.30 p.m.–22.30/10.30 p.m.
Cuisine: French
Chef de cuisine: Louis Grondard
Specialities: menu depending on what the season has to offer
Location: on the Tour Eiffel
Setting: modern; elegant; gorgeous view on Paris
Amenities: air conditioning; private lift

Atmosphere: elegant
Clientèle: almost only French guests from Paris and province, some businesspeople in the evening
Dress: no jeans
Service: very efficient
Reservations: advisable (no pets allowed)
Price range: rather expensive
Credit cards: AE, Visa

Dinner

TAILLEVENT
15 Rue Lamennais
Telephone: 4-45 63 39 94
Affiliations: Traditions et Qualité
Owner/Manager: Jean Claude Vrinat
Closed: Saturday; Sunday; public holidays; one week in February; August
Open: 12 a.m.–14.30/2.30 p.m. and 19.00/7 p.m.–22.00/10 p.m.
Cuisine: French (nouvelle)
Chef de cuisine: Claude Deligne
Specialities: cannelloni with truffle juice; suprême de sea-perch in shellfish stock; aiguillettes of duckling with black olives; diplomate with Fougerolles morello cherries
Location: 8th arrondissement; a short walk from the Place de l'Etoile
Setting: Napoleon III's step-brother's town residence; the previous Paraguay Embassy; patrician palais with understatedly elegant dining room; wood panelling, crystal chandeliers and period accessories
Amenities: private dining rooms (up to 32 persons); air conditioning
Atmosphere: more like an aristocrat's home than a restaurant; intimate and very exclusive
Clientèle: top bankers, businessmen and politicians from Rockefeller to Chirac and Barre; film stars and show-business celebrities from Brigitte Bardot, Frank Sinatra and Omar Sharif to Catherine Deneuve and Alain Delon
Dress: tie de rigueur
Service: comme il faut
Reservations: absolutely essential – preferably well in advance (poodles and Pekinese allowed, but no Pyrenean mountain dogs or Dobermann Pinschers)
Price range: aristocratic
Credit cards: not accepted

Lunch

LE PRE CATELAN
Route de Suresnes
Bois de Boulogne
Telephone: 4-5 24 55 58
Affiliations: Traditions et Qualité
Owner/Manager: Colette Lenôtre
Closed: Sunday evening; Monday; two weeks in February

Open: 12.00/a.m.–14.00/2 p.m. and 19.30/7.30 p.m.–22.00/10 p.m.
Cuisine: classique et inventive
Chef de cuisine: Denis Bernal
Specialities: according to season; langoustines with coriander and lemon; mullet with spring onions and rock salt; turbot in lettuce; pigeon with foie gras de canard; calves' sweetbreads with avocado; aiguillettes de canard au calvados; game; fruit tarts; chocolates
Location: in the 16th arrondissement; in the Bois de Boulogne
Setting: Belle Epoque dining room designed by Caran d'Ache; winter-garden with French windows leading to a large terrace surrounded by chestnut trees and shaded by white Italian sun umbrellas
Amenities: private dining rooms (12–250 persons); open-air dining; car park
Atmosphere: comfortingly glamourous by the fireplace in the dining room on cold days; perpetual spring in the winter-garden; a bewitching fête champêtre à la parisienne on the terrace on a summer's day, when the flowers blossom and the birds sing
Clientèle: resident aristocracy; jeunesse dorée; rich, beautiful, successful and elegant people from all the corners of the earth
Dress: tie de rigueur
Service: capable and knowledgeable
Reservations: advisable (dogs permitted)
Price range: expensive
Credit cards: AE, DC, Visa

Dinner

LE GRAND VEFOUR
17 Rue du Beaujolais
Telephone: 4-2 96 56 27
Owner/Manager: Jean Taittinger/Gérard Mauger
Maître: Guy Courtois
Closed: Saturday; Sunday; August
Open: 12.30/p.m.–14.00/2 p.m. and 19.30/7.30 p.m.–22.00/10 p.m.
Cuisine: classic and nouvelle
Chef de cuisine: André Signoret
Specialities: sole Grand Véfour; escalope of salmon with beans; sea-perch with artichokes and truffles; émincé d'agneau; calves' kidneys with three sorts of mustard; eggs ›Louis Olivier‹; frogs' legs soufflé; poire ›Grand Véfour‹
Location: in the 1st arrondissement; near the Palais Royal
Setting: elegant 1760s café-restaurant; recently-renovated Directoire-decorated rooms in red, white and black lined with Venetian mirrors and paintings of Bacchus and friends at play
Amenities: private dining room (14 persons); air conditioning
Atmosphere: the lively gaiety of the old Parisian world of the arts, politics and history

Clientèle: a glittering procession of geniuses who have left their mark on world history or literature and their names on brass plaques in the dining room; from (reputedly) Napoleon and Josephine to George Sand, Victor Hugo, Colette and Jean Cocteau
Dress: lounge suit and tie
Service: in keeping with the ambiance and the food
Reservations: absolutely essential – at least two weeks in advance (no dogs)
Price range: decidedly expensive
Credit cards: AE, DC, Euro, Visa

Dinner

MICHEL ROSTANG
10 Rue Gustave Flaubert, 17ᵉ
Telephone: 4-7 63 40 77/Telex: 6 49 629
Owner/Manager/Chef de cuisine: Michel Rostang
Closed: Saturday; Sunday; August
Open: 12.00/a.m.–14.30/2.30 p.m. and 19.30/7.30 p.m.–22.30/10.30 p.m.
Cuisine: nouvelle
Specialities: oeufs de caille en coque d'oursins (October–March); fricassée de soles; warm salad of crayfish and artichokes with basil; morel mushrooms with asparagus; John Dory (St. Pierre) in sorrel sauce; canette de Bresse dans une sauce de sang; gâteau au chocolat
Location: 15 minutes' triumphal march from the Place de l'Etoile
Setting: modern; salmon-pink and beige lacquer; Art Nouveau vase in window
Amenities: private dining room (20 persons); car park; air conditioning
Atmosphere: second-generation grandeur
Clientèle: gourmet habitués; businessmen; a moderate sprinkling of foreign visitors from New Orleans to Osaka
Dress: designer casual to dark suit for lunch; dark suit to designer gowns for dinner
Service: grande classe (Marie-Claude Rostang)
Reservations: essential – preferably well in advance
Price range: rather expensive
Credit cards: Carte Bleue, Visa

Dinner

MAXIM'S
3 Rue Royale, 8ᵉ
Telephone: 4-2 65 27 94
Owner/Manager: Pierre Cardin/Jean Pierre Guevel
Closed: Sunday
Open: 12.30/pm.–14.00/2 p.m. and 19.30/7.30 p.m.–24.00/12 p.m.
Cuisine: classic

Chef de cuisine: Michel Menant
Specialities: maître d'hôtel's suggestions: smoked salmon; salad of lamb's lettuce, beetroot and celery; lobster; roast pheasant; scrambled eggs with shrimps; saddle of lamb with basil cream sauce; navarin d'agneau; Tarte Tatin; soufflé glacé aux fraises
Location: near the Place de la Concorde
Setting: Grande Salle with band for dinner; small room with potted plants for lunch; recently renovated Art Nouveau décor, with swirling mirrors, an abundance of mahogany, stained glass, brass and tortoiseshell
Amenities: private dining room (90 persons); air conditioning
Atmosphere: redolent of history; the erstwhile haunt of Edwardian rakes, Russian Grand Dukes, Polish princes and the great demi-mondaines
Clientèle: gourmet habitués; jeunesse dorée; the rich, the successful and the beautiful; gastronomic spies from Arcangel to Yokohama
Dress: Dior, Cardin, Cartier and co.; Friday evenings black tie and ball gown
Service: impeccable
Reservations: essential (no dogs)
Price range: formidably expensive
Credit cards: AE, DC, Carte Bleue

Dinner

LUCAS-CARTON
9 Place de la Madeleine
Telephone: 4-2 65 22 90
Affiliations: Relais et Châteaux (Relais Gourmand)
Owner/Manager/Chef de cuisine: Alain Senderens
Closed: Saturday, Sunday; public holidays; 3 weeks in August; 10 days at Christmas
Open: 12.30/p.m.–14.30/2.30 p.m. and 17.30/5.30 p.m.–22.30/10.30 p.m.
Cuisine: nouvelle
Specialities: according to season; foie gras de canard encased in apple and celery; scallop ravioli; crayfish médaillons with morel mushrooms; duckling ›Apicius‹ with honey (after an ancient Roman recipe); roast pigeon with peas and beans (the best in the world)
Location: 8th arrondissement; a champagne cork's trajectory from the Place de la Concorde
Setting: stunning Belle Epoque décor; exquisite woodwork, mirrored walls and redbrown velvet upholstery
Amenities: private dining room (45 persons); car park (attended) – 25, Place de la Madeleine
Atmosphere: festive; glittering; glamourous; the much-heralded and long-overdue renaissance of a Grande Dame amongst restaurants under the aegis of one of the geniuses of the culinary scene

Clientèle: the international In-Crowd; famous names and familiar faces; disciples of Alain Senderens' legendary cuisine from Edinburgh to Eugénie-les-Bains
Dress: elegant, exclusive and expensive
Service: charmingly and knowledgeably supervised by Eventhia Senderens
Reservations: absolutely essential – preferably well in advance
Price range: inevitably astronomic
Credit cards: AE, DC; Carte Bleue

Meeting Point

AUX DEUX MAGOTS
170 Boulevard Saint-Germain
Telephone: 4-15 48 55 25
Closed: August
Open: 8.00/a.m.–2.00/a.m.
Location: 6th arrondissement; a short stroll from Saint Germain des Prés Métro station
Setting: archetypal Left-Bank Parisian café, mirrored walls; mahogany-red banquettes and brass-edged tables
Amenities: boulevard terrace; entertainers ranging from sword-swallowers and fire-eaters to hurdy-gurdy men and aspiring folk-singers
Atmosphere: as perfect for breakfast or a quick cup of coffee as for a nightcap after an evening stroll through the Quartier Latin
Clientèle: academics, students and would-be philosophers (following in the footsteps of most of France's most distinguished hommes de lettres, from Alphonse Jarry to Jean-Paul Sartre) plus footsore foreigners in the tracks of Ernest Hemingway
Service: still dressed in black jackets and floor-length white aprons
Reservations: advisable
Credit cards: AE, DC, Visa

Café

CAFE DE LA PAIX
3 Place de l'Opéra
Telephone: 4-2 68 12 13/Telex: 8 612
Owner/Manager: Grand Metropolitan Ltd./Alain Meyrueis
Closed: August
Open: 12.00/a.m.–15.00/3 p.m. and 19.00/7 p.m.–24.00/12 p.m.
Location: 9th arrondissement; two-and-a-half bars away from the Opéra
Setting: recently-renovated 19th-century building (Monument Historique); from Napoléon III décor (restaurant) to gazebo chic (grill) to nostalgic Paris boulevard café; fine silver, glassware and china
Amenities: bar (Le Foyer Bar Opéra); two restaurants (Le Relais Capucines and Le Restaurant Opéra); air conditioning
Atmosphere: comfortable and elegant

Clientèle: the opera; tout le monde ›à la recherche du temps perdu‹
Service: Parisian
Reservations: advisable

Bar

FOUQUET'S
99 Champs-Elysées
Telephone: 4-47 23 70 60
Owner/Manager: Maurice Casanova
Closed: never
Open: 12.30/p.m.–15.00/3 p.m. and 19.30/7.30 p.m.–24.00/12 p.m.
Cuisine: grande cuisine française traditionnelle
Chef de cuisine: Pierre Ducroux
Specialities: salad of scallops and marinated salmon ›Fouquet's‹; scallops in honey ›Pierre Ducroux‹; aiguillettes de canard with limes; pineapple with pepper
Location: in the 8th arrondissement; halfway between the Rond Point des Champs-Elysées and the Place de l'Etoile
Setting: two dining rooms; Louis XVI décor restaurant on first floor; elegantized grill-brasserie with light woodwork on ground floor
Amenities: private dining room (60 persons); open-air dining on terrace overlooking the Champs-Elysées
Atmosphere: prestigious, chic and very Parisian
Clientèle: le Tout Paris of cinema and show-business
Dress: high-fashion; low-fashion; no-fashion
Service: efficient
Reservations: essential
Price range: rather expensive
Credit cards: AE, DC, Euro, Visa, Master Card, JCB

Bar

HARRY'S NEW YORK BAR
5 Rue Daunou
Telephone: 4-26 17 11 4
Owner/Manager: Andy MacElhone
Closed: never
Open: 10.30/a.m.–4.00/a.m.
Location: 5th arrondissement; half a Bizet aria away from the Opéra
Setting: pre-Prohibition New York; mahogany, copper and leather
Amenities: pianist and singer; air conditioning
Atmosphere: pure 1920's nostalgia
Clientèle: erstwhile haunt of famous Americans in Paris, from Scott Fitzgerald to Ernest Hemingway, from George Gershwin to General Eisenhower; other nationalities welcome too; packed
Dress: jacket and tie de rigueur
Service: ably organised by the son of the eponymous Harry
Reservations: not necessary
Credit cards: not accepted

Nightclub

LE LIDO
116 bis Avenue des Champs-Elysées
Telephone: 4-5 63 11 61
Owner/Manager: Christian Clérico
Closed: never
Open: 20.00/8 p.m.–2.00/a.m.
Location: 8th arrondissement; two-and-a-half pirouettes from the Place de l'Etoile
Setting: of secondary importance
Amenities: dîner dansant (20.00/8 p.m.) followed by revue (22.00/10 p.m. or 0.15/12.15 a.m.) with horses, dolphins, waterfalls, magicians, acrobats – and the amazing Bluebell Girls, as beautiful with their fantastic costumes as without (the original topless show – much ado about nothing at the time); air conditioning
Atmosphere: Panache – the most glittering, glamourous, amusing and spectacular ›spectacle‹ of its kind in the world
Clientèle: predominantly semi-serious students from Singapore to Seattle trying to solve the frivolous riddle of Paris nightlife
Dress: tie de rigueur
Service: unobtrusive by comparison
Reservations: advisable
Credit cards: AE, Visa

Nightclub

CLUB CASTEL
(Cercle Saint Germain des Prés et de Saint Sulpice) 15 Rue Princesse
Telephone: 4-3 26 90 22
Telex: 2 03 835 Casclub
Affiliations: private club; members of Club of Clubs accepted
Owner/Manager: Jean Castel
Closed: never
Open: 21.30/9.30 p.m.–dawn
Location: in the 6th arrondissement, in the heart of Saint Germain des Prés
Setting: in the cellar; Roaring Twenties décor; big enough to accommodate all the Beautiful People; très parisienne
Amenities: discothèque; three restaurants (lunch & dinner); air conditioning
Atmosphere: a bastion of non-conformity, and yet an essential element in the empyrean of Parisian nightlife
Clientèle: on the whole, more beautiful, younger and more intelligent than elsewhere
Dress: the more exotic, the better
Service: personally supervised by Jean Castel and his charming wife
Reservations: essential for dining; unnecessary for the discothèque
Credit cards: not accepted

Shopping

EVERYTHING UNDER ONE ROOF
Galeries Lafayette
40 Boulevard Haussmann, 9è

FOR HIM
Lanvin   22 Faubourg-Saint-Honoré, 8è

FOR HER
Balmain, Pierre   Haute Couture,
44 Rue François 1er, 8è

BEAUTY & HAIR
Carita   11 Faubourg-Saint-Honoré, 8è

JEWELLERY
van Cleef & Arpels
22 Place Vendôme, 1er

LOCAL SPECIALITIES
Boutique 22 (tobacco)
22 Avenue Victor-Hugo
Chanel (women's fashion)
31 Rue Cambon, 8è
Cardin, Pierre (men's fashion)
59 Faubourg-Saint-Honoré, 8è
Ted Lapidus (men and women's fashion)
6 Place Victor-Hugo, 16è
Baby-Dior (children's fashion)
28 Avenue Montaigne, 8è
Hermès (leather fashion)
24 Faubourg Saint-Honoré, 8è
Révillon (furs)
40–42 Rue de la Boétie, 8è
Brentano's (books)
37 Avenue de l'Opéra, 8è
Armorial (gifts)
98 Faubourg Saint-Honoré, 8è
Baccarat (porcelain)
30bis Rue des Paradis, 10è
Vuitton, Louis (baggage & travel accessories)
78bis Avenue Marceau, 8è
Besson, Gérard (interior decorating)
Avenue Marceau, 8è
Rouve (bathroom accessories)
15 Rue des Mezières, 6è
Fauchon (food and beverages)
26 Place de la Madeleine, 8è
Guerlain (perfumery)
68 Champs-Elysées, 8è
Céline (shoes)
24 Rue François – 1er, 8è

THE BEST OF ART
Artcurial   (modern art)
9 Av. Matignon, Tel. 2 99 16 03
Bama   (modern art)
40 Rue Quincampoix, Tel. 2 77 38 87
Bernard, Claude   (contemporary art)
9 Rue des Beaux-Arts, Tel. 3 26 97 07
Broutta, Michèle   (contemporary art)
31 Rue des Bergers, Tel. 5 77 93 71/93 79
Cadot, Farideh   (contemporary art)
77 Rue des Archives, Tel. 2 78 08 36
Durand-Dessert, Liliane & Michel
(contemporary art)
3 Rue des Haudriettes, Tel. 2 77 63 60
Fabre, Eric   (20th-century paintings)
6 Rue du Pont de Lodi, Tel. 3 25 42 63

Flinker, Karl   (modern art)
25 Rue de Tournon, Tel. 3 25 18 73
Gillespie/Laage/Salomon   (contemporary art)
57 Rue du Temple, Tel. 2 78 11 71
Lahumière   (20th-century prints)
88 Bd. de Courcelles, Tel. 7 63 03 95
Lambert, Yvon   (contemporary art)
5 Rue du Grenier Saint Lazare,
Tel. 2 71 09 33
Maeght, Adrien   (modern art)
42, 46 Rue du Bac, Tel. 5 48 45 15
Maeght, Lelong   (modern art)
13 Rue de Tehéran, Tel. 5 63 13 19
René, Denise   (contemporary art)
196 Blvd. St. Germain, Tel. 2 22 77 57
Seroussi, Natalie   (modern art)
34 Rue de Seine, Tel. 6 34 05 84
Stadler, Rodolphe   (modern art)
51 Rue de Seine, Tel. 3 26 91 10
Templon, Daniel   (modern art)
30 Rue Beaubourg, Tel. 2 72 14 10
Zabriskie   (photography)
37 Rue Quincampoix, Tel. 2 72 35 47
Le Louvre des Antiquaires (antiques, works of art, furniture, Old Master paintings)
2 Place du Palais Royal,
Tel. 2 97 27 10
Ader-Picard-Tajan   (auctioneers)
12 Rue Favart, Tel. 2 61 80 07

The City

The cathedral and the champagne, of course. (Not necessarily in that order, however.) Halfway between Brussels and Paris, the architecture of the one and the substance of the other are the reasons to come here for cultural pleasure. (Without these two, everybody would travel on to either capital – save the devotees of Boyer.) The fellow-citizens of Jean-Baptiste Colbert have well understood their and the Sun King's favourite's preachings (not at Notre-Dame), by concentrating – true to the philosophy of mercantilism – on the production of unique luxury goods for export, while protecting their home market at the same time. (Up to this day you won't find German Sekt or Italian Spumante on a wine list here.) But in many other branches Rheims has established a renommé as well – textiles (the local sheep – on the Champagne grass diet – produce an especially valuable wool), glass (many famous artists have created in the local workshops – such as Villon, Chagall, Braque, da Silva), even less glamourous industries like metal, chemistry and construction. But French Champagne – ›so good for your brain‹ is the raison d'être for the city's international image, and many of the world-renowned houses offer tours and tastes in their historic chalk caves: Pommery, Lanson, Heidsieck, Roederer, Laurent-Perrier, Krug, Veuve-Clicquot, René Lalou and Taittinger are only the more popular ones. (It has become fashionable to have special reserves made under your own label – like Bocuse.) Only Moët & Chandon – with their status bubbly Dom Pérignon – are headquartered in neighbouring Epernay. The centre of town is the stately Place Drouet d'Erlon, the hub of social activity, full of restaurants, bars, cafés and entertainment; yet, around the corner, La Cathédrale de Notre-Dame (outshining even its namesake in Paris) is a singular reason to come to Reims even as a prohibitionist.

Founded: by Gauls; Reims (French) – from the name of the tribe, the Remii.
Far-reaching events: 1st century B.C. – conquered by the Romans, who build the fortified town of Durocortorum; 17 A.D. – the capital of the province of Belgian Gaul; 4th century – Rheims an archiepiscopal see; 496 – Clovis I, king of the Franks, baptized here, founding the French Monarchy, and beginning the tradition of celebrating coronations in Rheims; 12th century – the town prospers as the wool trade flourishes; 1429 – coronation of Charles VII in the presence of Joan of Arc; 17th century – the legendary Dom Perignon changes the world's drinking habits; 1914–18 – city centre largely destroyed; 1945 – Germany signs unconditional surrender agreement in Rheims.
Population: 182,000.
Postal code: F-51100 **Telephone code:** 26 (incorporated in number since 1986)
Climate: hot summers and relatively cold winters; precipitation evenly spread throughout the year.
Best time to visit: May to mid-October, though July and August can be very hot.
Calendar of events: *Joan of Arc Festival* (May); *Rheims Jazz Festival* (Jun); *Summer of Culture in Rheims* (Jul–Aug) – concerts, plays and bubbling entertainment; *Fiction and Crime Film Festival* (Oct).
Fairs and exhibitions: *INTERNATIONAL PHOTO EXHIBITION* (Apr); *AUTUMN FAIR* with *AUTOMOBILE EXHIBITION* (Sep); *ANTIQUES FAIR* (Oct).
Best views of the city: from the *Montagne de Reims;* from the *Route du Champagne.*
Historical sights: *Cathédrale Notre-Dame* (13th century) – Gothic grace and splendour, restored after wartime damage – stained glass windows by Chagall; the former abbey-church *St. Remy,* (11th–12th century) – pilgrimage church; the *St. Jacques Church* (13th–16th century) – with modern abstract stained-glass windows; the Baroque *Town Hall* (17th century); *Palais du Tau* – royal residential palace, now a museum – statues, tapestries and the cathedral treasures; *Museum of St. Denis* – local art, statues, tapestries and French painting from 1600; *Porte Mars* – Roman triumphal arch in honour of Augustus.
Modern sights: *Church of St. Niçoise* (20th century), decorated with Lalique glass; *Fort de la Pompelle* – fortress now housing a war museum; *Foujita Chapel* – a Japanese artist, baptized at Rheims, painted the frescoes; *Maison de la Culture* (1970) – post-modern architecture, theatre, galleries, a library and a discothèque, on a number of levels.
Special attractions: sightseeing and tasting in the *Champagne Cellars;* a champagne dîner à deux at *Les Crayères* (Boyer); a shopping spree and night on the town in *Paris.*
Important companies with headquarters in the city: *Caisse Régionale de Crédit Agricole* (banking); *Gervais Danone* (dairy products); *Mumm* (wine); *Roederer* (champagne); *Nord-Est-Alimentation* (foodstuffs); *Piper-Heidsieck* (champagne); *Pommery* (wines); *Reims Aviation* (aviation); *Taittinger* (champagne); *Veuve Clicquot Ponsardin* (wine, champagne); *Verreries Mécaniques Champ* (glass packaging); *Usines et Fonderies Arthur Martin* (foundries).
Airport: Rheims-Champagne, RHE; Tel.: 26 07 18 85/26 07 03 60; Air France, Tel.: 26 47 17 84; 9 km/5 miles.

145

The Headquarters

BOYER LES CRAYERES

64 Boulevard Henry Vasnier
F–51100 Rheims (Champagne)
Telephone: 26 82 80 80
Telex: 830 959 boyer
Owner: Gérard and Elyane Boyer
Affiliation/Reservation Systems: Traditions et Qualité; Relais et Châteaux (Relais Gourmand)
Number of rooms: 16 (1 suite)
Price range: FF 850–1,500
Credit cards: AE, DC, Visa
Location: near the cathedral of St. Rémy
Built: 1900
Style: fin-de-siècle
Hotel amenities: car park, tennis court, private gardens, (pets welcome)
Room amenities: spacious, exquisitely furnished rooms, extremely comfortable
Bathroom amenities: bathrobe
Room service: till 23.00/11 p.m.
Laundry/dry cleaning: same day
Sports (nearby): 18 hole golf course (5 km/3 miles), fishing, hunting, swimming
Bar: English style
Restaurant: ›Restaurant Boyer‹, Gérard Boyer (chef de cuisine), classic and modern cuisine, Belle Epoque décor
Private dining rooms: one (up to 24 persons)

In 1980 M. Gardinier, proprietor of the renowned champagne firms Pommery and Lanson, decided to renovate the majestic but sadly dilapidated Château de Crayères and enabled Gérard and Elyane Boyer to transform it into one of the most elegantly luxurious relais in Europe. The palais, built in 1900 for Louise Pommery, stands in a private park à l'anglaise near the cathedral in Rheims, where Charles VII was crowned King of France in the presence of Joan of Arc. The metamorphosis from a semi-ruin into a glittering palace was completed in 1983, since when Les Crayères has been noted in the address-books of gourmets and savants-vivre from Paris and further afield as well as amongst local champagne manufacturers and industrialists. The building recalls an eighteenth-century nobleman's residence; sweeping driveway, semi-circular portico and be-statued balustrade in front; flights of stairs leading down from the terrace to the gardens behind. The hall provides a suitably dignified entrée, the panelled and tapestried dining room a suitably festive setting for Gérard Boyer's nightly star performance crowned by Michelin's highest accolade – lobster fricassée with morel mushrooms, pigeon à l'ail doux, ragoût fin of calf's kidneys and sweetbreads and a selection of more than one hundred different champagnes. The English-style bar in the former music room, the sixteen sumptuously-furnished bedrooms, priceless antiques everywhere and service par excellence combine to create a stylish oasis of considerable charm where l'art de vivre is still cultivated with dedication and finesse.

The Hideaway

HOSTELLERIE DU CHATEAU

F–02130 Fère-en-Tardenois
(46 km/29 miles)
Telephone: 23 82 21 13
Telex: 145 526 otelfer
Owner: Blot Family
General Manager: Gérard Blot
Affiliation/Reservation System: Relais et Châteaux
Number of rooms: 23 (8 suites)
Price range: FF 480–1,200
Credit cards: AE, EC, Visa
Location: Picardie-Champagne, 46 km/29 miles from Rheims, 110 km/70 miles from Paris airport
Built: 16th century
Style: Renaissance and Louis XV
Hotel amenities: parking, boutique, (small dogs allowed in the restaurant)
Room amenities: colour tv, mini-bar
Bathroom amenities: bathrobe, hairdrier, telephone
Room service: 7.30/a.m.–21.00/9 p.m.
Conference rooms: 2 (up to 30 persons)
Sports: mini-golf
Sports nearby: tennis
Bar: one
Restaurant: ›Hostellerie du Château‹ (12.30/a.m.–14.00/2 a.m. and 19.30/7.30 p.m.–21.00/9 p.m.), Patrick Michelon (chef de cuisine); Jean-Luc Koscioleck (chef pâtisserie) three salons with Louis XVe décor, nouvelle cuisine
Private dining rooms: for up to 30 persons

On a wooded eminence just outside the village of Fère-en-Tardenois stand the melancholy ruins of the eponymous château, a thirteenth-century fortress reached by a Renaissance bridge, largely demolished in the eighteenth century by Philippe Egalité to provide construction material for the Palais-Royal in Paris. The sixteenth-century hostelry which is one of the last true bastions of la vie de château in France is no humble inn, but a Renaissance-style edifice of noble proportions surrounded by a park with fine old trees. Gérard Blot, châtelain of this exquisite relais, aided by his wife Paulette, his sisters Gisèle and Janine, and his mother, continues the fine tradition of l'art d'hospitalité established by his father, who transformed this turreted and crenellated château into a haven of beauty and comfort. Fine antique furniture, pretty wallpaper, woodwork with the patina of centuries and period accessoires are juxtaposed with consummate skill to create an ambiance of luxury without a trace of pomposity, an appropriate setting for the innovative cuisine of Patrick Michelon, who serves warm seafood salad, paupiette de truffes and calf's kidneys with parsley followed by the mouth-watering desserts of chef pâtissier Jean-Luc Koscioleck. L'Hostellerie du Château is a hideaway par excellence for those who wish to savour the gracious way of life of a more unhurried era.

Lunch

LE FOCH
37 Boulevard Foch
Telephone: 26 47 48 22
Owner/Manager/Chef de cuisine: Patrick Gonzales (ex-La Flamiche at Roye)
Closed: Sunday evening; Tuesday; second half of July; second half of January
Open: 12.00/a.m.–14.00/2 p.m. and 19.00/7 p.m.–21.00/9 p.m.
Cuisine: nouvelle
Specialities: salmon in Bouzy; sole with tomato and fresh mint ›en papillote‹; fillet of duck with mangoes; warm salad of brill with spinach; mousse of glacé fruits
Location: on one of Rheims' most famous boulevards; near the station
Setting: turn-of-the-century townhouse; discreet Empire-style décor
Amenities: private dining room (10 persons); car park
Atmosphere: fashionably luxurious
Clientèle: Rheims' Haute Societé; distinguished, discriminating and self-assured
Dress: casually elegant
Service: rather shy but friendly and welcoming
Reservations: advisable
Price range: moderately expensive
Credit cards: AE, DC, Euro, Visa

Dinner

LE CHARDONNAY
184 Avenue d'Epernay
Telephone: 26 06 08 60
Owner/Manager: Dominique Giraudeau
Closed: Saturday lunchtime; Sunday; August 4th–September 2nd; December 22nd–January 15th
Open: 12.00/a.m.–16.00/4 p.m. and 19.30/7.30 p.m.–21.30/9.30 p.m.
Cuisine: modernised bourgeoise and local
Chef de cuisine: Dominique Giraudeau (ex-pupil of Gérard Boyer)
Specialities: pike-perch in Bouzy; sea-trout with sorbet; rib of beef in red wine; andouillettes (small sausages); lamb casserole (navarin) with vegetables
Location: on the outskirts of town: southwest of centre
Setting: bright, well-lit house with a view of the open country side
Amenities: car park
Atmosphere: comfortable, friendly
Clientèle: local habitués who remember ›le Chardonnay‹ as ›la Chaumière‹ directed by the renowned Boyers; plus growing numbers of gourmets, converted to Dominique Girardeau's simple but excellent cuisine
Dress: informal
Service: charming welcome
Price range: moderately expensive
Credit cards: AE, DC, Euro, Visa

Dinner

BOYER (Les Crayères)
64 Boulevard Henri-Vasnier
Telephone: 26 82 80 80
Affiliations: Traditions et Qualité; Relais et Châteaux (Relais Gourmand)
Owner/Managers: Gaston and Gérard Boyer
Closed: Monday; Tuesday lunchtime; December 22nd–January 15th
Cuisine: original and innovative
Chef de cuisine: Gérard Boyer
Specialities: according to season and market availability; fricassée of wild mushrooms; mussel soup with saffron and orange; sea bass with artichokes; roast pigeon with garlic and parsley; gratin of raspberries; nearly 100 different kinds of champagne
Location: a jet-propelled champagne cork's trajectory from the cathedral
Setting: a lovingly-renovated 18th century-style château in a lovely park; exquisitely harmonious dining room in warm shades of gold; wood panelling, period furnishings, potted palms and crisp white napery.
Amenities: hotel; private dining room (40 persons); open-air dining on terrace; air conditioning; car park; helicopter landing-pad
Atmosphere: a temple of culinary perfection in a bewitchingly beautiful setting
Clientèle: culinary aesthetes and connoisseurs of the finest things in live from all the corners of the earth
Dress: appropriately elegant
Service: in keeping with the cuisine and the ambience
Reservations: recommended
Price range: who cares?
Credit cards: AE, DC, Euro, Carte Bleue

Lunch

L'ASSIETTE CHAMPENOISE
Châlons-sur-Veole (10 km/6 miles)
Telephone: 26 03 14 94
Owner/Manager/Chef de cuisine: Jean-Pierre Lallement
Closed: Sunday evening; Wednesday; school holidays in February
Cuisine: imaginative and very original
Specialities: hot duck's liver; roast duckling in Bouzy; salad of langoustines with saffron; fillets of dab (limande) with mushrooms; marinated ray salmon with melon; rabbit with truffles and cabbage; peach sorbet
Location: at Châlons-sur Veole, 10 km (6 miles) west of Rheims
Setting: in a sleepy Champagne village; amidst woodland; picture-postcard country inn; two small dining rooms with wooden beams; elegantized rustic-style décor with antique furniture; view of flower-filled courtyard

Amenities: private dining room (25 persons); open-air dining; car park
Atmosphere: irresistibly charming; a gourmet's paradise in a chocolate-box rural idyll
Clientèle: admirers of Jean-Pierre Lallement's highly individual cuisine – plus a fair number of local dignitaries, doctors, dentists and delegates
Service: professional
Reservations: advisable (no dogs)
Price range: rather expensive
Credit cards: AE, DC, Visa

Dinner

LE FLORENCE
43 Boulevard Foch
Telephone: 26 47 12 70
Owner/Managers: Jean-Pierre and Denise Maillot
Closed: Monday; three weeks in August; school holiday in February; (November 1st–Easter) Sunday evening
Open: 12.00/a.m.–14.00/2 p.m. and 19.00/7 p.m.–21.30/9.30 p.m.
Cuisine: nouvelle
Chef de cuisine: Yves Mesean
Specialities: turbot braised in champagne; suprême de canard; grilled fillets of John Dory with purée of garden peas and onions; aiguillettes de canard aux herbes; hot caramelised pears in puff pastry
Location: near the railway station (1a gare)
Setting: attractive townhouse on a tree-lined boulevard; comfortable and luxurious Louis XV. décor
Amenities: private dining room (30 persons); car park
Atmosphere: refined and harmonious
Clientèle: champagne exporters, chief executives and accountants
Dress: rather conservative
Service: in the old tradition; supervised by Jean-Pierre and Denise Maillot.
Reservations: advisable
Price range: fairly expensive
Credit cards: AE, DC, Euro, Visa

Bar

LE PALAIS
14 Place Myron Herrick
Telephone: 26 47 52 54
Owner/Manager: Jean-Louis Vogt
Closed: Sunday
Open: 7.30/a.m.–20.30/8.30 p.m.
Location: close to the cathedral, in the heart of the city
Setting: a charming and typically French café with a hint of kitsch; collection of paintings by local artists
Atmosphere: informal, fashionable and very popular

Clientèle: favoured meeting point of students, judges, musicians, managers, writers and industrialists
Service: very French

Bar

ROYALTY
67 Place Drouet d'Erlon
Telephone: 26 88 52 88
Owner/Manager: Franck Belpalme
Closed: never
Open: 15.00/3 p.m.–3.00/a.m.
Location: in the very heart of the city
Setting: intimate cocktail bar; leather upholstery; dim lights; lithographs on the walls
Amenities: car park in the vicinity
Atmosphere: intimate and peaceful, yet warm and welcoming
Clientèle: rendezvous of local upper crust; cosmopolitan managers, industrialists and exotic birds of passage
Service: professional, welcoming and charming
Reservations: not necessary (pets permitted)
Credit cards: AE, EC, Visa

Nightclub

LE BRIGITH'S
7 Boulevard du Général Leclerc
Telephone: 26 47 22 71
Owner/Manager: Françoise Jacquet
Closed: never
Open: 22.00/10 p.m.–dawn
Location: close to the ›Place Drouet d'Erlon‹
Setting: a luxurious and comfortable nightclub; the ideal place to sit, gaze at each other and hold hands
Amenities: cocktail bar; air conditioning
Atmosphere: the most intimate and elegant nightclub in town
Clientèle: cosmopolitan jeunesse dorée of the Seventies mingle with international hommes d'affaires
Dress: elegantly casual to casually elegant
Service: excellent
Reservations: advisable, especially at the weekend (no pets)
Price range: medium
Credit cards: CB

Shopping

FOR HIM
Carnaby-Boutique Saint Germain
13 to 17 passage Talleyrand

FOR HER
Subé, Boutique   13 passage Subé

BEAUTY & HAIR
Mick   146 Rue de Vesle

JEWELLERY
Au Grand Cadran   12 passage Subé

LOCAL SPECIALITIES
Tabac la Régence (tobacco)
44 Place d'Erlon
Cannabis (fashion for her)
119 Rue Gambetta
Bleu blanc rose (children's fashion)
79 Rue de Vesle
Michaud (books)
9 Rue du Cadran Saint-Pierre
Lys d'Or (gifts)
2 Rue de l'Arbalète
La Porcelaine Blanche (porcelain)
20 Rue des Capucins
Colbach (baggage & travel accessories)
19 Rue de Talleyrand
Intérieur Actuel (interior decorating)
3 Place du Forum
Delices champenoises
(food and beverages)
2 Rue Rockefeller
Parfumerie du Cadran Saint-Pierre
(perfumery)
15 Rue du Cadran Saint-Pierre
Charles Jourdan (shoes)
16 Rue du Cadran St.-Pierre
La cave aux fromages (cheeses)
12 place du Forum

The City

The little brother in the trio of European capitals (next to Brussels and Luxembourg) has more charm than its elders combined, and more reasons to be the epicentre of European unity after being occupied and freed innumerable times in the course of history and wars – mostly between the two brotherly arch-rivals, France and Germany. The Chant de l'Armée du Rhin – the Marseillaise to the rest of the world – was composed here, and European diplomats like Goethe and Metternich went to the university which has lost none of its reputation since their days. Strasbourg has always been the intellectual and economic capital of Alsace and the east of France, and its position is growing stronger. Hard-working, but with a joyful lust for life's many pleasures, the historically fascinating and architecturally alluring city is one of the most rewarding tourist centres in central Europe. The unique Gothic cathedral may be of world importance, the museums, monuments and restored relics of the past centuries the main attraction for scholarly travellers, but raison d'être for most businessmen – European or not – is the fabulous cuisine and its equally attractive showrooms in and around the city. Goose liver at Le Crocodile, sauerkraut-choucroute at Maison Kammerzell, or Alsatian specialities à la Haute Cuisine at the gourmet temples in the hinterland belong to the pleasures of visiting ministers as much as of the burghers themselves. The scenery is Hansel-and-Gretel romanticism, the joviality legendary. The industries and the Rhine harbour keep the city and part of the country alive, but the Old Town, encircled by the River Ill, remains untouched and out of sight. Strasbourg, the symbol of peace and human qualities down to the lovably profane ones, is a worthy platform for all parties.

Founded: 16 A. D., as Argentorate; Strasbourg (French) – ›the town at the crossroads‹

Far-reaching events: 5th century – destroyed by the Huns; 496 – conquered by the Franks; 842 – the Oath of Strasbourg; 858 – passes to the Holy Roman Empire; 1262 – a free imperial city; 1434–47 – Gutenberg perfects his printing press in Strasbourg; 1681 – university founded and Strasbourg, one of the centres of the Reformation, becomes French again; 1792 – Rouget de Lisle composes the ›Marseillaise‹ at Strasbourg; 1871 – ceded to Germany following the Franco-Prussian War; 1919 – regained by France; 1940 – occupied by Germany; 1945 – returned to France; 1949 – seat of the European Council; 1958 – seat of the European Parliament.

Population: 410,000 (Greater Strasbourg); capital of the Bas-Rhin department (Alsace).

Postal code: F–67000 to 67200   **Telephone code:** 88 (incorporated in number since 1986).

Climate: mild and humid.

Best time to visit: May to October.

Calendar of events: *Annual Music Festival* (Jun); *Festival International de Musique* (Jun) – classical music; *Film Festival of Human Rights; Foire St. Jean* (Jun/Jul) – fair; *Festival de Danse* (Jul); *Spectacle son et lumière* (all summer long) – daily illumination of the cathedral at 21.00/9 p.m.; *Musica* (Sep) – contemporary music, performances in the city, on the Rhine and in the neighbourhood of Strasbourg.

Fairs and exhibitions: *FOIRE DE PRINTEMPS* (Apr) – national fair of consumer goods; *FOIRE EUROPÉENNE DE STRASBOURG* (Sep) – consumer goods.

Best views of the city: from the *Münster*, the cathedral.

Historical sights: *Cathedral* (11th–15th centuries) – Gothic splendour, with an astronomical clock and a Silbermann organ – the city's landmark; *Museum Notre-Dame* – local medieval and Renaissance art; *La Petite France* – timbered houses in the former tanners' district; *Les Ponts Couverts* – bulwarks, part of the town's defences in the Middle Ages; *St. Thomas Church* (9th–14th centuries) – early Gothic with a noteworthy Silbermann organ; *Old Customs House* (1358) – with a display of Impressionist and modern art; *Gasthof Rabenhof* (16th century) – historic inn with picturesque wood galleries; *Rohan Palace* (1742) – formerly a reception hall for cardinals, now a museum with collections of Italian paintings, ceramics and archaeological specimens; *Stag Apothecary* (1268) – the oldest chemist's shop in France, next to the cathedral; *Broglie Square* (18th century) – where the French national anthem, the Marseillaise, was sung for the first time in 1792; *Palais du Rhin* (1888) – palace built for Kaiser Wilhelm, very Berlin; *Place de la République* – with a moving monument to the fallen in the many wars Alsace-Lorraine has endured.

Modern sights: *Council of Europe Building* (1977) – meeting place for European institutions; *Palais des Congrès* – setting for meetings and conferences; *Peace Synagogue* – in the home of the European Parliament.

Special attractions: dinner at *Maison Kammerzell* (1467); an *organ recital* or *Son et Lumière* at the cathedral; the *folklore festival* at the Palais des Rohan or *jousting* on the Ill.

Important companies with headquarters in the city: *Banque Populaire; Clark Equipment* (heavy plant and building appliances); *Kronenbourg* (brewery); *Laminois de Strasbourg* (air conditioning, isolation materials, lead); *Lilly* (pharmaceuticals); *Peugeot* (vehicles); *Timken* (ball-bearings) – at Colmar.

Airport: Strasbourg-Entzheim, SXB; Tel.: 88 78 40 99; 13 km/8 miles; Air France: Tel.: 88 32 99 74.

The Headquarters

HILTON

Avenue Herrenschmidt
F–6700 Strasbourg
Telephone: 88 37 10 10
Telex: 890 363 hiltels
General Manager: Jean-Claude Noël
Affiliation/Reservation System: Hilton Reservation Service
Number of rooms: 247 (6 suites)
Price range: from FF 475 (single)
from FF 525 (double)
Credit cards: AE, DC, Visa, CB, Access, Interbank, EC
Location: 1 km/0.6 miles from city centre, 16 km/10 miles from airport
Style: modern (marble/glass/steel), glass roof and windows with interior garden
Hotel amenities: valet parking, house limousine service, health club, sauna bath with whirl-pools, solarium, massage, newsstand, drugstore, boutique, tobacconist, individual safe deposit, doctor
Main hall porter: Jean-Marie Lecot
Room amenities: air conditioning, colour tv, video, mini-bar/refrigerator, rooms for non-smokers, cassette player (pets allowed)

Bathroom amenities: bidet, bathrobe, hairdrier, specially equipped bathrooms for handicapped persons
Room service: 24 hours
Laundry/dry cleaning: same day (weekend service)
Conference rooms: 5 (up to 400 persons), secretarial services, ballroom
Sports: tennis
Pianobar: ›Bugatti‹: (11.30/a.m.–13.30/1.30 p.m. and 17.30/5.30 p.m.–1.30/a.m.) pianist, orchestra (Friday)
Restaurants: Bernard de Villèle (maître), Dominique Michou (chef de cuisine); ›La Maison du Bœuf‹: (12.00/a.m.–15.30/3.30 p.m. and 19.00/7 p.m.–23.30/11.30 p.m.); French cuisine; wood panelling and wall mirrors; open-air dining; ›Le Jardin‹: regional dishes, garden style, open-air dining

The many devotees of the American chain's firmly established world-wide reputation for quality, comfort and efficiency will find that the Strasbourg dépendance more than lives up to expectations. Since its opening in 1981 the steel-and-glass tower block has won universal acclaim for its enhancement of the architectural, social and culinary landscape in the cosmopolitan mini-metropolis. The view of the city may be better from the top of the cathedral spire, but after celebrating a signed contract at La Maison du Bœuf *you'll certainly feel on top of the world.*

The Hideaway

LA CHENEAUDIERE

F–67420 Colroy-La-Roche
(62 km/39 miles)
Telephone: 88 97 61 64
Telex: 870 438 chenau
Owner: Marcel and Arlette François
Affiliation/Reservation System: Relais et
Châteaux
Closed: Jan.–mid-March
Number of rooms: 23 (8 suites)
Price range: FF 520–1,080 (suites)
Credit cards: AE, DC, EC, CB
Location: at Colroy-la-Roche, 40 km/25
miles from Entzheim airport
Built: 1975
Style: local traditional
Hotel amenities: boutique, garage, tobac-
conist (no pets)
Room service: until 23.00/11 p.m.
Sports: tennis
Restaurant la Chenaudière: (12.00 a.m.–
14.00/2.00 p.m. and 19.00/7.00 p.m.–
22.00/10.00 p.m.), Jean Paul Bossée (chef
de cuisine), nouvelle cuisine
Private dining rooms: up to 25 persons

*Half hidden amidst the vast pine forests in
the foothills of the Vosges mountains, a leisurely hour's drive south-east of Strasbourg, lies a hideaway for unrepentant epicures. La Chenaudière is a traditional
chalet-style whitewashed Alsatian farmhouse relais with a long sloping tiled roof
and geranium-filled window-boxes along
the wooden balcony. Ex-lawyer Marcel
François and his wife Arlette had their
dream cottage in the country built a decade
ago, and have created in it a refined rural
paradise in which son-in-law Jean-Paul
Bossée, who served his culinary apprentice-
ship in such august establishments as the
Plaza-Athénée, Taillevent, Jamin and
more recently in Le Crocodile in Strasbourg, conjures up nouvelle cuisine specialities such as goose liver in puff pastry and
chicken breast and truffle ravioli for gourmets from both sides of the Rhine. The
oak-beamed dining room has a huge central open fireplace and the vaguely countri-
fied Louis XV-style décor together with the
large picture windows creates an impression of welcoming brightness and space.
The foyer, by contrast, with its fine panelled ceiling, curved reception desk and
oriental rug, is almost formal and resembles the reception area of a select London
club. The lounge is restfully Louis; the bedrooms are spacious and all have balconies
affording a view of the surrounding peaks.
A post-prandial eau-de-vie de mirabelles
from the home distillery, to the accompaniment of the glories of a mountain sunset, is
a superior alternative to a lively nightclub;
indeed, La Chenaudière is a luxurious refuge for those for whom a walk through the
woods or a quiet corner with someone's
hand to hold represent a welcome respite
from the surfeit of consumer-oriented pleasures of metropolitan life.*

Lunch

LE CROCODILE
10 Rue de l'Outre
Telephone: 88 32 13 02
Affiliations: Traditions et Qualité; Relais et Châteaux (Relais Gourmand)
Owner/Manager: Emile Jung
Closed: Sunday; Monday; 4 weeks July–August; between Christmas and New Year
Open: 12.00/a.m.–14.00/2. p.m. and 19.00/7 p.m.–22.00/10 p.m.
Cuisine: progressive and imaginative, with a local accent
Chef de cuisine: Claude Manne
Specialities: preserved quail Brillat Savarin; pike-perch stuffed with sauerkraut in juniper cream sauce; coquelet de Gilerlé with Riesling sauce and fresh pasta; pheasant en croûte with thyme lentils; cress flan with frogs; bitter chocolate cake and vanilla ice-cream
Location: just off the Place Kléber
Setting: two dining rooms; neutral fabric-covered walls; light wood; pot plants; dominated by large painting of the local populace en fête in 1875
Amenities: private dining rooms (10–40 persons); air conditioning
Atmosphere: refined simplicity
Clientèle: Strasbourg's social élite, plus visiting dignitaries, diplomats and distinguished persons
Dress: fairly casual for lunch to rather formal for dinner
Service: admirably observant
Reservations: advisable (no dogs)
Price range: philanthropic
Credit cards: AE, DC, Euro

Dinner

LA MAISON DU BOEUF
Hôtel Hilton
Avenue Herrenschmidt
Telephone: 88 37 10 10
Affiliations: Hilton Hotels
Manager: Bernard de Villèle
Closed: Saturday; February 11th–17th; three weeks in August
Open: 12.00/a.m.–14.30/2.30 p.m. and 19.00/7 p.m.–22.30/10.30 p.m.
Cuisine: nouvelle
Chef de cuisine: Dominique Michou
Specialities: seafood; John Dory with two vegetable flans and lime cream sauce; mousseline of mullet with leek purée; turbot with chive cream sauce; home-smoked fish; veal kidneys in claret; the eponymous beef, flown in fresh from the U.S.A.; steaks; roast beef ›au gros sel‹
Location: in the Hilton Hotel
Setting: ground-floor dining room; luxurious English club décor; blue velvet upholstery; dark woodwork; soft lighting; understated elegance

Amenities: hotel; private dining rooms (up to 300 persons); brasserie ›Le Jardin‹; open-air dining; air conditioning; car park
Atmosphere: vaguely Anglo-Saxon; discreet, sober but not severe
Clientèle: increasing numbers of Gallic and Germanic gourmets attracted by the originality of Dominique Michou's cuisine, plus conservative transatlantic visitors reassured by the familiarity of at least some of the items on the menu
Dress: tie de rigueur
Service: helpful and professional
Reservations: recommended (dogs permitted)
Price range: moderately expensive
Credit cards: AE, DC, Euro, Visa

Dinner

BUEREHIESEL (Chez Westermann)
4 Parc de l'Orangerie
Telephone: 88 61 62 24
Affiliations: Entente Nationale des Cuisiniers et Hôteliers de Métier; Association des Maîtres Cuisiniers de France; Relais et Châteaux (Relais Gourmand)
Owner/Manager/Chef de cuisine: Antoine Westermann
Closed: Tuesday evening; Wednesday; between Christmas and Epiphany; two weeks in February/March; two weeks in August
Open: 12.00/a.m.–14.30/2.30 p.m. and 19.00/7 p.m.–21.30/9.30 p.m.
Cuisine: ›au goût du marché‹; inventive and highly individual
Specialities: according to season; goose liver with salad of calves' sweetbreads and rabbit liver; mullet and Norway lobster with cabbage and honey vinegar; shellfish and chervil soup; rabbit and pickled endive salad; clear soup with frogs' legs and wild mushroom ravioli; escalope of sea-perch (bar) in red wine; sot-l'y laisse with parsley and truffles
Location: in the Orangerie Park (Parc de l'Orangerie)
Setting: 17th-century Alsatian farmhouse; wooden beams and parquet floors; small dining rooms; subdued lighting
Amenities: private dining room (40 persons); apéritifs and coffee served in the garden; one table on covered terrace; car park
Atmosphere: enchanting; intimate
Clientèle: distinguished and discriminating diplomats, connoisseurs and chief executives with a penchant for fine food in a romantic atmosphere
Dress: tends towards the conservative
Service: friendly and welcoming; personally supervised by Antoine Watermann and his charming wife Viviane
Reservations: advisable (pets permitted)
Price range: moderately expensive
Credit cards: AE, DC

Lunch

L'AUBERGE DE L'ILL
Rue de Collonges,
Ribeauvillé-Illhaeusern (60 km/38 miles)
Telephone: 89 71 83 23
Affiliations: Traditions et Qualité
Owner/Managers: Paul and Jean-Pierre Haeberlin
Closed: Monday evening (in winter all day); Tuesday; February; first week in July
Open: 12.00/a.m.–14.00/2 p.m. and 19.00/7 p.m.–21.00/9 p.m.
Cuisine: classique et inventive
Chefs de cuisine: Paul and Marc Haeberlin
Specialities: hors d'œuvre de l'Auberge; mullet and Norway lobster salad; mousseline de grenouilles; warm salad of cheek of pork and goose liver; fillet of lamb braised in a black pepper and herb crust; pigeonneau des Dombes in puff pastry with cabbage and truffles; venison and woodland mushrooms; strawberries with almond milk ice-cream; pêche Haeberlin
Location: 60 km (38 miles) south of Strasbourg; at Illhaeusern, between Sélestat and Colmar
Setting: on the banks of the river Ill; large dining room with patio doors to the garden; blend of classic and modern décor (Louis XV and Empire) in cream, with elegant upholstered chairs and fine china and glass
Amenities: private dining room (10 persons); apéritifs and coffee on terrace overlooking garden; air conditioning
Atmosphere: rural Utopia à l'alsacienne; an oasis of good humour and good living – emphatically worth the drive
Clientèle: diplomats and European MPs; businessmen tired of Strasbourg; gourmet refugees from Saarbrücken to Schaffhausen; visiting monarchs and heads of state
Dress: casual for lunch; more formal for dinner
Service: presided over by the affable, aimiable and attentive Jean-Pierre Haeberlin – assisted by Michel Scheer, Marco Baumann, Serge Dubs (ler Sommelier de France) and Philippe Moser
Reservations: essential (poodles, Pekinese and pointers on leashes only)
Price range: philanthropic
Credit cards: AE, DC

Dinner

MAISON KAMMERZELL
16 Place de la Cathédrale
Telephone: 88 32 42 14
Owner/Manager: Paul Schloesser
Closed: Wednesday
Open: 12.00/a.m.–14.00/2 p.m. and 19.00/7 p.m.–22.00/10 p.m.
Cuisine: local (ground floor) and nouvelle (upstairs)
Chef de cuisine: Daniel Girard
Specialities: duck's liver ›Kammerzell‹; gâteau de pigeonneau with pickled garlic; fillet of John Dory with endive fondue; sauerkraut (choucroute) with goose liver
Location: next to the cathedral
Setting: one of Strasbourg's most distinguished historic buildings, dating from 1465; leaded windows; attractively-furnished dining rooms of varying sizes
Amenities: private dining rooms (10–60 persons); open-air dining on terrace
Atmosphere: warm, lively and welcoming
Clientèle: local habitués; men from the media; artists, journalists, local congressmen and tourists
Dress: as you like it (as long as they will like you)
Service: efficiently directed by maître-sommelier Pascali Funaro
Reservations: advisable (pets permitted)
Price range: medium
Credit cards: AE, DC, Carte Bleue, Euro

Dinner

ZIMMER-SENGEL
8 Rue du Temple-Neuf
Telephone: 88 32 35 01
Owner/Manager/Chef de cuisine: Georges Sengel
Closed: Saturday; Sunday; August
Open: 11.30/a.m.–15.00/3 p.m. and 19.00/7 p.m.–22.00/10 p.m.
Cuisine: ›au goût du jour‹
Specialities: fish terrine with ginger; salmon marinated in herbs; foie gras with salad; sweetbreads with pea purée; sole and frogs' legs on cabbage; fruit sorbet
Location: central; between the cathedral and Place Kléber
Setting: from the outside, a typical old-fashioned shop-front; inside, a cross between an elegantized bistro and grandmother's dining room – subdued shades of brown, lace tablecloths, old pictures and wicker chairs
Amenities: private dining room (40 persons); open-air dining on terrace; air conditioning
Atmosphere: very French; lively, alert and attentive above all to the quality of the food – and yet nostalgically charming
Clientèle: discerning; intelligent; well-informed; well-travelled; globe-trotting reporters, writers and politicians
Dress: jeans to jacket and tie
Service: anxious-to-please
Reservations: advisable
Price range: moderately expensive
Credit cards: AE, DC, Visa

Meeting Point

LE PETIT MAXIM'S
29 Place Kléber
Telephone: 88 32 50 38
Owner/Manager: Albert Schmitt
Closed: never
Open: 12.00/a.m.–6.00/a.m.
Location: on Strasbourg's most famous square
Setting: bar/restaurant/café complex on three floors; rooms decorated principally in English style, with attractive niches for extra privacy; pianist
Amenities: restaurant serving full meals; bar and tearoom serving light meals, snacks and ice creams as well as cocktails and drinks; air conditioning; car park
Atmosphere: bon chic, bon genre
Clientèle: young, gay, approachable and with-it – plus the occasional local celebrity
Service: quick and smiling
Reservations: advisable
Credit cards: AE, DC, Euro, Carte Bleue, Master Card

Café

PATISSERIE CHRISTIAN
10 Rue Mercière
Telephone: 88 32 04 41
Owner/Manager: the Christian family
Closed: Sunday
Open: 8.00/a.m.–17.30/5.30 p.m.
Location: a hymn away from the cathedral
Setting: 15th-century house in the centre of town; salon with understated but elegant décor in shades of beige and brown; an abundance of natural wood and fabric-covered walls
Amenities: air conditioning
Atmosphere: a family-run establishment
Clientèle: the local In-Crowd mingles with footsore tourists

Bar

PIANO BAR BUGATTI
Hôtel Hilton
Avenue Herrenschmidt
Telephone: 88 37 10 10
Owner/Manager: Société d'Exploitation hôtelière du Palais/Jean-Claude Noël
Closed: never
Open: 11.30/a.m.–13.30/1.30 p.m. and 17.30/5.30 p.m.–1.30 a.m.
Location: in the Hilton Hotel
Setting: open bar with piano music by international musicians; orchestra on Friday evenings; retromobile style with designs and engravings of famous oldtimers by Ettore Bugatti, who lived and worked near Strasbourg
Amenities: hotel; restaurant; brasserie; open-air dining on terrace; air conditioning; car park
Atmosphere: modern; masculine; rather business-like
Clientèle: company chairmen; managing directors; financiers; accountants; visiting VIPs; President Reagan; local pressmen
Dress: rather conservative
Service: expert
Reservations: advisable
Credit cards: AE, DC, Euro, Visa, Carte Bleue, Carte Blanche, Access, Interbank

Shopping

EVERYTHING UNDER ONE ROOF
Printemps Grandes Galeries
1–5 Rue de la Haute Montée

FOR HIM
Lemnel Rue du Dôme

FOR HER
Caroll 25 Rue du Dôme

JEWELLERY
Streisguth 26 Rue de la Mésange

LOCAL SPECIALITIES
Tabac la Civette (tobacco)
21 Rue des Arcades
Petit Bateau Boutique (children's fashion)
24 Rue du 22 Novembre
Gangloff (books)
20 Place de la Cathédrale
Longchamp (gifts)
13 Rue du 22 Novembre
La Porcelaine Blanche (porcelain)
30 Rue du Vieux Marché aux Poissons
Lancel (baggage & travel accessories)
Place Kléber
Trendel (food and beverages)
13 Avenue des Vosges
Weber (perfumery)
25 Rue des Grandes Arcades
Kiefer (sausages)
20 Rue d'Austerlitz
Henri, Albert (foie gras)
5 Rue du Chaudron
Riss (confiserie)
33 Rue du 22 Novembre

THE BEST OF ART
L'Expression (modern art)
4 Rue de l'Eglise, Tel. 88 32 83 63

The City

The cradle of the world's status Pegasus, the Concorde, and Europe's most avant-garde satellite-city, Le Mirail (executed by Le Corbusier's disciple Georges Candilis), may not attract as many pilgrims as the processions in Lourdes or the light-show of Carcassonne, maybe not even as many devotees as France's culinary Mozart, Michel Guérard in Eugénie-Les-Bains, but Toulouse, the country's fourth-largest metropolis (after Paris, Lyons, Marseilles), is not only of greater economical and intellectual importance to La Grande Nation, but by far richer in antiquity, sights and attractions than its not-too-distant touristy neighbours. One of the centres of religious, artistic and literary life in western Europe for centuries, Toulouse is rich in traces of its glorious past and guards well the quaintness of its Vieux Quartier as well as the douceur de vie after hours. You can wander through the decorative mews, the luxurious shopping avenue, Rue d'Alsace-Lorraine, along the River Garonne, stopping here for the opulent Romanesque basilica of Saint-Sernin, there for the palm-vaulted Jacobin Convent, for the Hôtel d'Assézat, the prettiest building of them all (where the Académie des Jeux Floraux has held its troubadour contests of music and poetry for over six hundred years, with contenders like Voltaire, Lamartine and Victor Hugo) – and many more landmarks worth a trip by themselves, finally relaxing on Place Wilson over an Armagnac Vieil Age. As you indulge in the lightness of life breathing already the nearness of the Pyrenees and Iberia, and the magic of the ever-changing light, you will agree that this is one of the most unexpectedly interesting cities of France, and in a lyrical mood, you may remember the troubadour's words: ›Ville rose à l'aube, ville rouge au soleil cru, ville mauve au crépuscule.‹ Don't visit Toulouse as if in a Concorde.

Founded: as a Celtic settlement, of uncertain date; Toulouse (French) – from the Latin.

Far-reaching events: 121 B.C. – the Celtic settlement becomes a Roman city, Tolosa; 3rd century, A.D. – bishops bring Christianity to Toulouse; 419–506 – Visigoth rule; 630 – Toulouse the capital of Aquitaine; 11th century – Toulouse follows the Albigensian heresy – religious wars and final defeat in 1229 leads to the foundation of the Dominican order to combat infidelity; 13th century – Toulouse the home of the Inquisition; 1271 – union with France; 15th–17th century – Toulouse one of the last cities to offer a haven to the Huguenots during the period of religious intolerance; the next centuries filled with increasing prosperity; 1976 – the first scheduled flight of the Concorde puts Toulouse back on the map.

Population: 450,000 (urban area); capital of the Haute-Garonne department and 4th largest city in France.

Postal code: F–31000   **Telephone code:** 61 (incorporated in number since 1986)

Climate: warm, dry summers; cold winters.

Calendar of events: *Fête de la Violette* (Easter) – folkloristic festival; *Grand Fénétra* (May) – more of the same; *Académie des jeux floraux* (1–3 May) – festival competition amongst local bards; *Week of Organ Music* (Jun); *Académie Internationale de Chant* (Sep) – festival of song from around the world; *Holiday on Ice* (end of Sep); *Music Festival* (Jun–Sep) in the Dominican monastery.

Fairs and exhibitions: *TOULOUSE INTERNATIONAL FAIR* (Apr/May); *SALON AERONAUTIQUE ET SPATIAL* (Jun); *SALON DU MEUBLE ET DE LA DECORATION* (Sep) – furniture and interior decorating; *SALON DU TEMPS LIBRE* (Oct) – sports and recreation; *SITEF* (Oct, biennial) – international exhibition of technologies and energy of the future; *HOUSEHOLD AND CHILDREN'S GOODS FAIR* (Oct); *GARLIC FAIR* (Oct); *AUTOMOBILE FAIR* (Oct); *REGIONAL ANTIQUES FAIR* (Nov); *VILLAGE GOURMAND SALON* (Nov); *SALON DES ARTISANS CREATEURS* (Nov).

Historical sights: *Abbey and Church of St. Sernin* (11th–13th century) – Romanesque perfection; *Jacobin Monastery* (13th–14th century) – founded by St. Dominic to counter heretical influences; *St. Etienne Cathedral* (12th–15th century) – late Gothic; *Notre-Dame la Daurade* (18th century) – gilded mosaics from the original 5th-century sanctuary; *Notre-Dame-de-la Dalbade* (16th century) – southern Gothic with an Italian Renaissance portal; *Augustinian Monastery* (14th century) – museum with sculptures and a large collection of works by Delacroix and non-native son Toulouse-Lautrec; *Jean de Berny House* (15th century) – typical Toulousain patrician house, with Gothic and Renaissance elements; *Hôtel d'Assezat* (16th century) – another magnificent patrician house with a lovely inner courtyard.

Modern sights: *Grand Rond* – oval English garden, decorated with bronze sculpture; *Le Mirail* and *Colombiers* – the new, super-modern suburbs; *Parc des Expositions* – the convention and congress centre; *Science Centre* – France's largest scientific research centre, covering 400 acres.

Special attractions: an excursion into the Pyrenees to see the *prehistoric cave-paintings* at Niaux; a supersonic joyride in *Concorde.*

Important companies with headquarters in the city: *A.B.G. Semca* (aviation equipment); *Airbus Industrie* (aircraft); *Central Pneu* (tyres); *Extralco* (aluminium and plating); *Malet* (roads and construction); *Motorola* (semi-conductors); *S.N.I.A.S.* (aircraft); *Union Laitière Pyrénées Aquitaine Charente* (dairy products).

Airport: Toulouse-Blagnac, TLS; Tel.: 61 71 11 14; 8 km/5 miles; Air France, Tel.: 61 62 84 04.

The Headquarters

GRAND HOTEL DE L'OPERA

1 Place du Capitole
F–31000 Toulouse
Telephone: 61 21 82 66
Telex: 521 998 espi
General Manager: Philippe Espitalier
Number of rooms: 49 (3 suites)
Price range: FF 330–1,070
Credit cards: AE, DC, CB
Location: city centre, 6 km/4 miles from the airport
Built: 17/18th century (renovated 1981)
Style: classic and luxurious
Hotel amenities: valet parking, outdoor swimming pool, air conditioning
Main hall porter: José Ferrer
Room amenities: colour tv, mini-bar/refrigerator, radio (pets allowed)
Bathroom amenities: radio
Room service: 24 hours
Laundry/dry cleaning: same day
Conference rooms: 6 (up to 100 persons) secretarial services
Bars: ›L'Orangerie‹ (8.00/a.m.–24.00/12.00 a.m.), Jean-Luc Carmeni and Bernard Larroque (barmen)
Restaurants: ›Les Jardins de l'Opera – D. Toulousy‹ (12.00/a.m.–14.00/2.00 p.m. and 20.00/8.00 p.m.–22.30/10.30 p.m.), Dominique Toulousy (chef), regional and modern cuisine, traditional décor, open-air dining

Tucked away in one corner of the famous Place du Capitole, opposite the imposing classical edifice which today houses the Town Hall and the municipal theatre, stands a fine patrician palais which has been converted into a city-centre hotel of considerable charm. The building itself dates from the seventeenth and eighteenth centuries, and retains many architectural features which recall this period of economic and social prosperity for the city. The recently-renovated intérieur is furnished in a style which blends classic and modern form with local touches. Traditional Toulousain designs are used for the floral wallpaper in the lounge, whilst the bedrooms are furnished in restful shades, with coordinated fabrics for bedspreads, chairs and curtains. Strategically-placed antiques and objets d'art enhance the atmosphere of quiet refinement – here a fine old painting, there a display cabinet containing attractively-arranged ceramic vases. The six pretty dining rooms which form the gourmet restaurant Les Jardins de l'Opéra are aptly named, since chef de cuisine Dominique Toulousy serves innovative specialities – from iced gazpacho with scampi to foie gras ravioli – amidst a riot of greenery which provides an aura of spring on even the greyest winter's day. The Orangerie bar recalls the winter-gardens of yesteryear and is a favourite evening rendezvous of the local Haute Bourgeoisie, who gravitate towards the lovely inner courtyard-garden surrounding the swimming pool in summer.

The Hideaway

DIANE

3 Route de St-Simon
F–31100 Toulouse
Telephone: 61 07 59 52
Telex: 530 518 diane
Owner/Managers: Michel and Patricia Chagnon
Number of rooms: 35
Price range: FF 260 – 350
Credit cards: Access, AE, DC, EC, MC, Visa
Location: 8 km/5 miles south-west of city centre
Built: 19th century
Style: Toulousain rural
Hotel amenities: car park, garden
Room amenities: tv, mini-bar
Conference rooms: for up to 30 guests
Sports: swimming, tennis, minigolf
Restaurants: ›Le Saint-Simon‹ (12.00/a.m.–22.00/10 p.m.) René Pollentier (chef de cuisine), nouvelle and local cuisine, elegantized rustic décor (closed on Sunday and public holidays)

The prettiest hideaway between Toulouse and the Pyrenees is half hidden from the road by a copse of fine old trees. The Hôtel de Diane is a late nineteenth-century country house with white shutters at the windows and neatly-trimmed shrubs by the door. Although it is only five miles from the fourth largest city in France, this attractive auberge de campagne is a veritable haven of peace and tranquillity, surrounded by a beautiful private park with lovely flowerbeds, complete with swimming pool and tennis courts. The interior is a rural period piece of great nostalgic charm. The salon is reminiscent of an antique doll's house – lace curtains at the windows, fauteuils and an oriental rug. The thirty bedrooms are similarly old-fashioned. By contrast the dining room, although also retaining an old-world air, manages to strike a refreshingly modern note thanks to the dark blue ceiling and floral wallpaper. The picture windows overlook the garden. René Pollentier's personal and inventive cuisine – duck's liver and oysters in puff pastry, and duck casserole with fruits, together with the attentive professionalism of the staff under the direction of Michel and Patricia Chagnon, complete the atmosphere of refinement and quiet distinction. Diane is as popular amongst local industrialists as amongst national and international celebrities, including astronaut James Irving.

Lunch

VANEL
22 Rue Maurice-Fonvielle
Telephone: 61 21 51 82
Owner/Manager/Chef de cuisine: Lucien Vanel
Closed: Sunday; Monday/lunchtime; August
Open: 12.00/a.m.–14.00/2 p.m. and 19.30/7.30 p.m.–22.00/10 p.m.
Cuisine: nouvelle – classique – régionale
Specialities: scrambled eggs with brains, chicken livers and green pimento; calves' sweetbreads in orange sabayon sauce with carrots; wing of pigeon with duck's liver and artichokes au jus vinaigré; mille feuille aux fraises des bois
Location: in the heart of the city
Setting: small house; understated elegance in the modern idiom, yet warm and friendly
Amenities: air conditioning
Atmosphere: bursting with good humour and joie-de-vivre
Clientèle: hommes d'affaires mingle with hommes de lettres
Dress: easy come, easy go
Service: welcoming
Reservations: advisable (pets permitted)
Price range: medium
Credit cards: AE, Euro

Lunch

ORSI (Le Bouchon Lyonnais)
13 Rue de l'Industrie
Telephone: 61 62 97 43
Owner/Manager: Laurent Orsi
Closed: never
Open: 12.00/a.m.–14.00/2 p.m. and 19.00/7 p.m.–22.30/10.30 p.m.
Cuisine: seafood; Lyonnaise
Chefs de cuisine: Michel Arsuffi and Bernard Bordaries
Specialities: salade lyonnaise; salad of Norway lobster with vegetables; fricassée of squid; fillets of hog-fish with tomato sauce; saumon au gros sel; pike dumpling (quenelle de brochet) sauce Nantua; pear flan with cream of fromage blanc; charlotte au chocolat et crème anglaise
Location: central; next to the headquarters of Sud-Radio
Setting: elegantized bistro; old-fashioned style décor; luxurious and comfortable
Amenities: private dining room (20 persons); air conditioning; attended car park (fee paying) down the road
Atmosphere: lively and alert, yet relaxing
Clientèle: favourite venue for journalists, media-men, local politicians and radio personalities, plus the occasional Lyonnais in exile

Dress: jeans to jacket and tie
Service: good
Reservations: advisable (dogs permitted)
Price range: moderately expensive
Credit cards: AE, DC, Carte Bleue

Dinner

PUJOL
21 Avenue du Gal-Compans
Blagnac (5 km/3 miles)
Telephone: 61 71 13 58
Affiliations: Maîtres Cuisiniers de France
Owner/Manager/Chef de cuisine: Marcellin Pujol
Closed: Saturday; Sunday evening; one week in February; three weeks in August
Open: 12.00/a.m.–13.45/1.45 p.m. and 19.30/7.30 p.m.–21.30/9.30 p.m.
Cuisine: classic and local
Specialities: according to season; foie de canard; confit d'oie; médaillons of veal with morel mushrooms; suprême of sea-perch with sauce Béarnaise; grilled fillets of wood-pigeon; venison; game; local dishes; cassoulet
Location: at Blagnac; 5 km (3 miles) west of Toulouse; 2 km (1 mile) from Toulouse-Blagnac airport
Setting: old country house; parkland; several dining rooms of varying sizes decorated in contemporary style
Amenities: private dining room (35 persons); open-air dining on terrace; car park
Atmosphere: a temple of culinary delights which is as much a part of the local scene as the Basilica or Aérospatiale
Clientèle: Gascon gourmets; business-men tired of Toulouse; Concorde captains and foreign visitors from Buenos Aires to Bahrain
Dress: within reason, anything goes
Service: personal and professional; supervised by the wife of the proprietor
Reservations: advisable (pets permitted)
Price range: fairly expensive
Credit cards: DC, Visa

Lunch

DARROZE
19 Rue Castellane
Telephone: 61 62 34 70
Owner/Manager: Pierre Darroze
Closed: Saturday lunchtime; Sunday; public holidays
Open: 12.00/a.m.–13.30/1.30 p.m. and 20.00/8 p.m.–21.30/9.30 p.m.
Cuisine: Landaise – créative
Chef de cuisine: Viviane Darroze
Specialities: salad of truffles and foie gras; casserole of pigeon; wild salmon marinated in coriander; red mullet in tomato; tureen of calves' sweetbreads braised with wild mushrooms

Location: central; near Place Wilson
Setting: small dining room; recently renovated Louis XV cameo in shades of brown; fauteuils and round tables
Amenities: private dining room (15 persons); air conditioning
Atmosphere: a family restaurant directed with great enthusiasm and devotion by Pierre Darroze, whose family have been stars in the culinary firmament of Aquitaine for four generations
Clientèle: strong contingent of local admirers of the talents of the Darroze family, leavened by a fair sprinkling of discriminating tourists
Dress: no special requirements
Service: Pierre, Viviane and Henri Darroze
Reservations: advisable (pets prohibited)
Price range: philanthropic
Credit cards: AE, DC, Visa, Carte Bleue

Specialities: saumon au foie de canard; cassoulet de Toulouse
Location: in the very heart of the city, on one of France's most beautiful squares
Setting: bar and restaurant; antique columns; fin–de–siècle glamour
Amenities: private room (up to 35 guests); open-air dining on large terrace
Atmosphere: one of Toulouse's most popular meeting points; rather elegant . . .
Clientèle: international connoisseurs of the arts of living, actors, writers, and readers of business and pleasure
Dress: whatever you like
Service: welcoming, charming and very friendly indeed
Reservations: advisable (pets permitted)
Price range: medium-high
Credit cards: AE, DC, Carte Bleue

Dinner

LA MARMITE EN FOLIE
28 Rue Paul Apinleue
Telephone: 61 42 77 86
Owner/Manager/Chef de cuisine: Marc Brandolin
Closed: Sunday; Saturday and Monday lunchtime; September
Open: 12.00/a.m.–13.30/1.30 p.m. and 19.30/7.30 p.m.–22.30/10.30 p.m.
Cuisine: ›au goût du jour‹; ›selon le marché‹
Specialities: duck's liver; duck salad; John Dory with rhubarb; pigeon in Saint-Emilion
Location: in a somewhat unprepossessing suburb of Toulouse; 3 km (2 miles) from city centre
Setting: intimate décor
Amenities: open-air dining on terrace; private dining rooms (15 persons) on first floor
Atmosphere: warm and welcoming
Clientèle: discriminating visitors join local habitués impressed by Marc Brandolin's highly individual brand of nouvelle cuisine
Dress: no special requirements
Service: irreproachable
Reservations: advisable
Price range: medium
Credit cards: AE, Carte Bleue

Meeting Point

BIBENT
5 Place du Capitole
Telephone: 61 23 89 03
Owner/Manager: Max Candoulive
Closed: Sunday
Open: 8.00/a.m.–1.00/a.m.
Cuisine: that of a typical French brasserie
Chef de cuisine: Philippe Duregne

Bar

LONDON PUB
4 Rue Austerlitz
Telephone: 61 21 53 38
Owner/Manager: René Manenc/Jean-Pierre Dur
Closed: Sunday
Open: 16.00/4 p.m.–2/a.m.
Location: near the Place Wilson
Setting: reminiscent of an English pub
Amenities: air conditioning; 100 different whiskies
Atmosphere: comfortable mixture of Anglo-Saxon charm and Gallic flair
Clientèle: heterogeneous; industrialists, academics, students and solicitors
Service: to perfection
Reservations: not necessary
Credit cards: not accepted

Nightclub

L'UBU
16 Rue Saint-Rome
Telephone: 61 23 26 75
Owner/Manager: Emile Fernandez
Closed: Sunday
Open: 23.00/11 p.m. – dawn
Location: near the Town Hall (Mairie) and the Place du Capitole
Setting: cellar nightclub, unrendered brick walls, black armchairs
Amenities: bar, restaurant (open 20.00/8 p.m.–2/a.m.; traditional cuisine); air conditioning; parking facilities on the Place du Capitol
Atmosphere: sophisticated and chic
Clientèle: Toulouse's Top Ten
Service: competent and charming
Reservations: recommended
Credit cards: AE, DC, Carte Bleue

Shopping

EVERYTHING UNDER ONE ROOF
Galeries Lafayette
77 Rue Alsace Lorraine

FOR HIM
Miceli   3 Rue Victor-Hugo

FOR HER
Perry   3 Place Esquirol

BEAUTY & HAIR
Queralto Inter-Coiffure   6 Place Wilson

JEWELLERY
Nuel   41 Rue Croix Baragnon

LOCAL SPECIALITIES
Sonia Fernandez (women's fashion)
2 Rue Victor-Hugo
Francesco Smalto (men's fashion)
3 Rue Victor-Hugo
Pomme (children's fashion)
31 Rue Lafayette
Max Gurgel (leather fashion)
20 Rue du Languedoc
Kopetski (furs)
27 Rue Alsace-Lorraine
Privat et Cie Libraire Editeur (books)
14 Rue des Arts
Lumi-Cado (gifts)
15 Rue de Rémusat
Felix Frères (porcelain)
1 Rue Alsace-Lorraine
Maï Na (baggage & travel accessories)
15 Place Wilson
Porcher (bathroom accessories)
7 Rue de Rémusat
Germain (food and beverages)
6 Rue de Rémusat
Jaques Rebeyrol (perfumery)
14 Rue Alsace-Lorraine
Charles Jourdan (shoes)
11 Rue Alsace-Lorraine

THE BEST OF ART
Axe Art Actuel   (contemporary art)
11 Place de la Daurade, Tel. 88 25 37 17
Protée   (contemporary art)
23 Rue Croix-Baragnon, Tel. 88 53 84 44

The City

As a compensation for being exploited by their victors after the war, it seems, this part of the divided city was left, at least, with the grander ruins and the more beautiful setting than across the Wall. Today, forty years and many more watchtowers later, the majority of the masterpieces of Prussian monumentalism – the architectural landmarks that once brought Berlin the title of ›Athens on the Spree‹ – have been meticulously restored to their former splendour without lending East Berlin the ›Glamour and Glory‹ of yesteryear. The treasures of history and art (foremost the Museum Island) are magnets for tourists as are the two opera houses and – assuming linguistic competence – the many theatres, with the Berliner Ensemble specializing in Brecht the most interesting. Life on the ›other side‹ is a bit crampy when you frequent the so-called luxury hotels, restaurants and bars, but dissolves into warm and jovial spontaneity when you meet the people at their habitué haunts. Business is correct but complicated, officials are polite but hyper-sensitive and Western joys are generally reduced to human relations. The administrative, industrial, cultural and intellectual hub of the ›German Democratic Republic‹ will render a perfect view and notion of society à la socialiste (how they see it). Compared to Gorki it appears free and well-to-do, even though you won't find a Speaker's Corner or potable grand crus, and when you behave apolitically, prudishly and as crampily polite as the officials you are dealing with, there is no danger for your comfort – except, maybe, your idealistic one. ›East is East, and West is West, ...‹ It is hoped that Rudyard Kipling is wrong for once!

Founded: 12th century, along with Cölln and Spandau; Berlin (German) – ›a bear‹.

Far-reaching events: 1240 – Berlin receives a city charter; 1415 – Berlin becomes part of the principality of Brandenburg under the Hohenzollern dynasty; 1486 – Berlin becomes the residence of the Electors; 1701 – the Kingdom of Prussia is founded by Frederick I – Berlin, as capital, becomes an intellectual centre for Europe; 1806–8 occupied by Napoléon; 1809 – foundation of the University; 1871 – founding of the German Empire with Berlin as capital; 1890 – Berlin has a population of 1.9 million; 1910 – population of 3.7 million; 1918 – the Empire ends in revolution – Berlin capital of the new Weimar Republic; 1933 – Hitler comes to power; 1939–45 – heavy bombing during World War II; 1945 – East Berlin the Russian zone in the Allied division; 1946 – first and last free elections in all four zones; 1949 – founding of the German Democratic Republic, with Berlin as capital; 1953 – workers' rebellion suppressed; 1961 – building of the Wall; 1970s – *Ostpolitik* slowly begins reopening borders between the two halves of Berlin.

Population: 1.2 million; capital of East Germany.

Postal code: DDR–1020 to 1197   **Telephone code:** 2

Climate: cold winters, pleasant, dry summers, just like on the other side.

Best time to visit: May to October.

Calendar of events: *May Day* (1 May) – parades, banners and demonstrations of solidarity; *Berlin Festival* (Sept/Oct) – concerts, ballet and folk art; *Christmas Market* (Dec) – a folk festival with booths, rides and amusements without brash commercialism, at the Alexanderplatz.

Fairs and exhibitions: no annual fairs; information on the current programme of symposia, presentations and colloquia through the *International Trade Centre*, Friedrichstrasse, DDR-1086 Berlin; Tel.: 2 06 22 41; Tx.: 1 14381-84 ihz bda.

Best view of the city: from the *Television Tower*, with a view of both halves of the city.

Historical and modern sights: *Brandenburger Tor* (1791) – landmark gate, cut off by the wall, symbolically enough; *Unter den Linden* – linden-lined promenade with many of the former Prussian capital's finest buildings; *Museum Island* – on the Spree, with the *Pergamon Museum* (antiquities), the *National Gallery* (paintings and sculpture) and the *Bode Museum* (Egyptian collection); *St. Hedwig's Cathedral* (1747–93) – built for Frederick the Great; *Ermelerhaus* (1762) – the most beautiful non-aristocratic home of old Berlin; *Köpenick Palace* (17th century); *French Cathedral* (1705) – built on the model of the church in Charenton, for the Huguenots; *Palace of the Crown Prince* (1678) – where Hitler proscribed exhibitions of modern art in his Germany; *Zeughaus* (1706) – former arsenal, now housing the *Historical Museum* of the German Democratic Republic; *Nikolaikirche* (1379) – Berlin's oldest parish church; *Old Palace* (1837) – former palace of Kaiser Wilhelm I; *Dorotheenstadt Cemetery* – graves of Hegel, Fichte, Heine and Brecht; *Comic Opera* – received its current form in 1967; *Palace of the Republic* – seat of the People's Chamber and Congress Hall; *State Council Building* – the façade is a copy of the portal of a Baroque palace; *Television Tower* – a landmark of East Berlin.

Special attractions: a flight to *West Berlin*; a night out at *Klärchens Ballhaus*; the *May Parade* – a cautionary tale; the cabaret at the *Distel* (language permitting).

Important companies with headquarters in the city: *Fashion Institute of the GDR; VEB Bergmann-Borsig* (turbines); *Kabelwerk Oberspree* (formerly AEG Electronics); *Werkzeugmaschinenkombinat ›7. Oktober‹* (machinery); *VEB Berlin-Chemie Adlershof* (chemicals).

Airport: Berlin-Schönefeld, SXF; Tel.: 67 20, 18 km/12 miles.

The Headquarters

METROPOL

150–153 Friedrichstrasse
DDR-1036 Berlin
Telephone: 2 20 40
Telex: 114 141/42
Owning Company: Interhotel DDR
General Manager: Wolfgang Krüger
Affiliation/Reservation System: Supranational Hotel Reservations (SNR), Golden Tulip Hotels
Number of rooms: 327 (31 suites)
Price range: DM 140 (single)
　　　　　　　DM 180–200 (double)
　　　　　　　DM 210–250 (apartments)
　　　　　　　from DM 350 (suites)
Credit cards: AE, DC
Location: city centre
Built: 1977
Style: modern
Hotel amenities: car rental, garage with servicing workshop, house limousine service, health club, swimming pool, solarium, massage, séparée sauna, boutique, florist, intershop (western products for western currency), hairstylist, piano, ballroom, interpreters, guides, sightseeing tours by carriage
Room amenities: air conditioning, colour tv, mini-bar/refrigerator, direct-dial telephone (pets allowed)
Bathroom amenities: bathrobe
Room service: 24 hours
Laundry/dry cleaning: same day
Conference rooms: 2 (up to 100 persons), all necessary equipment
Lobby-Bar: (24 hours) modern style
Restaurant: ›Friedrichstadt‹ (6.00/a.m.–24.00/12.00 p.m.) modern style, pianist, open-air dining
›Spezialitätenrestaurant‹ (11.00/a.m.–24.00/12.00 p.m.) rustic décor, live music, open-air dining, international cuisine, regional and grill specialities

East Berlin's best address is strategically situated opposite the International Trade Centre, which makes it perfect for businessmen. It is also only a short walk from the legendary boulevard ›Unter den Linden‹ – ideal for tourists – and from the Friedrichstrasse frontier checkpoint – convenient for a quick getaway when your visa runs out. Scandinavian in its conception, the Metropol's bright modern décor makes it an appropriate retreat after the rigours of a day in Marxist Disneyland. Leisure facilities and services are almost overwhelming, as is the friendliness of the staff. With enough vodka in the restaurant, or when sweating it out in the séparée sauna on the twelfth floor, one can look back nostalgically to the grand old days of which this part of the city was the stage.

Lunch

GANYMED
5 Schiffbauerdamm
Telephone: 28 29 5 40
Owner/Manager: HO-Gaststätten
Closed: Monday lunchtime
Open: (Monday) 17.00/5 p.m.–1.00/a.m.; (Tuesday-Sunday) 11.00/a.m.–1.00/a.m.
Cuisine: French bourgeoise, local and international
Chef de cuisine: Dieter Bongé
Specialities: duck with red cabbage; nasi goreng; pasta asciutta; pork steak ›Singapore‹; pancakes with lemon and whipped cream (Menschiki)
Location: a short walk (across the iron bridge) from the Friedrichstrasse station (Bahnhof Friedrichstrasse)
Setting: charming décor; pink table-linen; matching lampshades
Amenities: bar
Atmosphere: a luxurious brothel in the 1920s – now rather more respectable!
Clientèle: favoured by actors, producers and backstage-boys from the nearby Theater am Schiffbauerdamm (following in the footsteps of former habitués Bertold Brecht and Helene Weigel
Dress: within reason, come-as-you-please
Service: friendly waiters dressed in black, with aprons
Reservations: recommended
Price range: medium
Credit cards: not accepted

Dinner

PALAST
Marx-Engels-Platz
Telephone: 2 38 23 64/5
Owner/Manager: VEB; HO Gaststätten
Closed: Tuesday
Open: 11.00/a.m.–24.00/12 p.m.
Cuisine: international and local
Specialities: large portions of grilled fish kebabs; pike-perch (Zander) or salmon steaks; Soljanka; ice-cream with fruits flambés; salads
Location: in the Palace of the Republic
Setting: on the second floor of one of East Germany's show buildings; marble, bronze and monumental pictures, smoked glass picture windows overlooking the Foreign Ministry and the Building of State (Staatsgebäude)
Amenities: live music in the evenings (Thursday-Monday); two further restaurants on the same floor
Atmosphere: East German twentieth-century pomp and circumstance
Clientèle: senior government officials; men from the ministries; visiting delegations

Dress: conservative (pin-stripes allowed)
Service: courteous and correct
Reservations: absolutely essential
Price range: medium
Credit cards: not accepted

Lunch

MÜGGELSEE-PERLE
Am Grossen Müggelsee
Telephone: 6 57 14 85
Owner/Manager: Konsum Berlin
Closed: the third Tuesday in the month
Open: (Oct–Apr) 11.00/a.m.–19.00/7 p.m. (May–Sep) 10.30/a.m.–22.00/10 p.m.
Cuisine: local, of an unusually high standard
Chef de cuisine: Herbert Diessel
Specialities: fish; game; poultry; home-cured fillet of pike-perch (Zander) with mustard and dill sauce; lentil soup with sausages; snails; steaks; knuckle of pork (Eisbein) with apple and onion salad and creamed horseradish
Location: on a lake (the Grosser Müggelsee); approximately 30 minutes' drive south-east of Berlin
Setting: in attractive countryside; a large restaurant with even larger terrace for open-air dining in summer
Amenities: private dining rooms; bar; car park
Atmosphere: a gem amongst East German restaurants, in spite of its size
Clientèle: favourite destination for family excursions – especially at weekends
Dress: Sunday casual to Sunday best
Service: way above average
Reservations: recommended
Price range: fairly expensive
Credit cards: not accepted

Dinner

OFFENBACH-STUBEN
8 Stubbenkammerstrasse
Telephone: 4 48 41 06
Chef de cuisine: Lutz König
Closed: Sunday; Monday; lunchtime every day
Open: 18.00/6 p.m.–1.00/a.m.
Cuisine: international and local
Specialities: dishes with titles appropriate to the restaurant's name; veal steak with ham, mushrooms, chipped potatoes and quail's egg (›Prince of Arkady‹); Schaschlik with curry sauce and rice (›Joys of Hades‹); pork steak with ham, cheese and peas (›Orpheus in the Underworld‹)
Setting: owes much to the Berlin Comic Opera and the Metropol Theatre, which supplied much of the décor as well as the props
Atmosphere: a privately-owned restau-

rant reminiscent of the scenario for an Offenbach operetta
Clientèle: expatriate West Germans; artists; intellectuals
Dress: fairly elegant – sometimes eye-catchingly so
Service: good team-work
Reservations: essential
Price range: fairly inexpensive

Bar

ZENNER
14–17 Alt-Treptow
Telephone: 27 27 11
Owner/Manager: HO   Gaststätten/ Rainer Behrendt
Closed: never
Open: 11.00/a.m.–20.00/8 p.m. (Monday, Friday and Saturday until 1.00/a.m.
Setting: Berlin's largest and oldest beer-garden; view of the river Spree; tavern in a classic-style building
Amenities: tavern with various rooms ranging from the café (upstairs) to the Intershop offering a rather limited range of goods to those with foreign currency to pay for them; discothèque (Mondays); dance (Friday/Saturdays); music on Sunday afternoons; boats for hire
Atmosphere: a Berlin institution; gemütlich to gay at times
Clientèle: obligatory stopover for West Berliners doing the rounds; popular amongst East Berlin's Sunday-afternoon crowd en fête and en famille
Dress: high-fashion; low-fashion; no-fashion; anything goes
Service: rather casual but cheerful
Reservations: advisable
Price range: inexpensive

Meeting Point

AUF DEM FERNSEHTURM
29a Littenstrasse, Am Alexanderplatz
Telephone: 2 10 40
Closed: never
Open: 8.00/a.m.–22.00/ p.m.
Location: 200 m up the television tower (Fernsehturm)
Setting: rotating café-restaurant with glass picture windows; on a fine day panoramic view of the divided city (the restaurant completes one rotation in an hour, which is the maxiumum duration of visit allowed)
Amenities: entrance tickets (5 Mark) on sale in the foyer of the television tower
Atmosphere: fairly business-like, but comfortable
Clientèle: as popular amongst Berliners from East and West as amongst visitors wanting a bird's eye view of both sides of the Wall
Service: efficient
Reservations: recommended; Telephone: 2 12 33 33 (10/a.m.–14.00/2 p.m.)

Café

AM PALAST
Karl-Liebknecht-Strasse
Telephone: 24 10
Closed: never
Open: 10.00/a.m.–24.00/12 p.m.
Location: in the Palasthotel
Setting: octagonal extension to the main hotel building; coffee-brown ceiling; central column with mirrors; furnishings in Viennese coffee-house style; picture-postcard panorama of the Spree, the parliamentary building (Palast der Republik) and the towers of the city's churches
Amenities: hotel (600 bedrooms); three restaurants; bar; private dining rooms; open-air dining on terrace; garage; snacks and light meals as well as cakes, desserts and ice-creams
Atmosphere: modern; bright; cheerful and almost chic
Clientèle: predominantly visiting industrialists and tourists
Service: professional

Shopping

LOCAL SPECIALITIES
Meissen (porcelain)
Unter den Linden
Intershop (records)
Bahnhof Friedrichstrasse
(Railway-Unterground Station
Friedrich Street)
Museum bookshops (art books)
Museumsinsel

THE BEST OF ART
Staatlicher Kunsthandel der DDR (modern art), 62–68 Unter den Linden, Tel. 2 29 27 70

The City

The ›secret capital‹ of the ›German Democratic Republic‹ to some, the showcase of German socialism to others, the industrial heart of the country, the most industrious city to most and to the ones who lived here or knew Saxony's metropolis before the war it is related to world history, higher learning, music and books. Gotthold Ephraim Lessing, student at the city's famous university like Goethe, claimed that ›in Leipzig one can observe the whole world en miniature‹. Not quite, today, any more, but many facets of the German national character (from negative cliché to respectable traits) can be witnessed among the people of Leipzig, and it is not just by chance that the ›other‹ Germany's élite is mainly recruited from Saxons, mostly from Leipzig itself. The city, twice a year the turntable of products and processes at its renowned industrial fair, has none of the beauty and glory of Dresden (not even attractive natural surroundings), but apart from production and trade, politics and sports (another form of politics here), self-portrayal and self-affirmation there is still the tradition of publishing, printing, graphics and ›book-keeping‹ (one of the largest archives in the world – ten million volumes in the German language alone), as well as the active music life that Johann Sebastian Bach institutionalized with his Thomaner-Choir, and the Gewandhaus-Orchestra with its sound (concerts and performances are staged almost every week.) The opera, again world-class, and the two political-literary cabarets add to the intellectual climate as much as the academy of arts – today Leipzig is the artistic centre of East Germany, with names like Tübke, Mattheuer, Heisig, Stelzmann, Gilles et al. crossing the border (which isn't so easy for the artists themselves). The cradle of Leibniz, Wagner and Ulbricht has become an entity not only in its own half-country but to be reckoned with on the ›other side‹ as well, which is shown each year at its famous fair. With some fine examples of Baroque, Rococo, Renaissance and ›Wilhelminia‹, with all the smoke stacks smoking around, and the socialist trophies for achievements (in the name of world peace, of course), with the respectable past and the continuation of many traditions, Leipzig is definitely the prime example of the ›young republic‹ – a workers' paradise.

Founded: 1015 as ›urbs Libzi‹ – ›city of lindens‹.

Far-reaching events: chartered 1165; 1409 – foundation of the university; 1497 – Maximilian I grants the annual Easter Market imperial status, marking the beginning of a centuries-old tradition; 1539 – the Reformation; 1642 – late in the Thirty Years War, Leipzig falls to the King of Sweden; 1723 – Johann Sebastian Bach becomes leader of the choir at St. Thomas' Church; 1765–68 – Goethe a student at Leipzig's world renowned university; 1813 – defeat of Napoleon outside Leipzig by the combined armies of Russia, Austria and Prussia (the Battle of the Nations); 1843 – Mendelssohn and Schumann found the Conservatory; 1939–1945 – 13 air raids leave Leipzig in ruins; 1945 – restoration work begins.

Population: 600,000; 2nd largest city in East Germany.

Postal code: DDR-7000 to 7045   **Telephone code:** 41

Climate: continental; extreme; often cloudy.

Calendar of events: *International Bach Festival* (Mar) in honour of the great Johann Sebastian, son of Leipzig; *Cabaret Festival* (May); *Gewandhausfesttage* (Oct) – celebrations in music of Leipzig's world famous Gewandhaus Orchestra; *International Leipzig Documentation and Short Film Festival* (Nov) – politically engaged film festival.

Fairs and exhibitions: *SPRING INDUSTRIAL FAIR* (Mar) – consumer goods fair where East meets West; *BOOK FAIR* (Mar); *TECHNICAL FAIR* (Mar); *GDR AGRICULTURAL EXHIBITION* (Mar); *AUTUMN INDUSTRIAL FAIR* (Sep).

Historical sights: *Church of St. Thomas* (1222) – where Johann Sebastian Bach was cantor between 1723 and 1750; *Alte Börse* (1678–87) – old commodity market, restored 1955–62, now a Baroque setting for chamber orchestra concerts; *Barthels Hof* (1523) – oldest remaining convention hall in the city; *Georgi Dimitroff Museum* (1888–95) – formerly an imperial court-house where Georgi Dimitroff was tried for setting fire to the Reichstag; one of the city's landmarks; *Old Town Hall* (16th century) – completely restored; *Haus zum alten Kloster* (1753) – beautiful German rococo; *Nikolaikirche* (12th cent) – late Roman buttressed basilica, superbly restored; *Romanushaus* (1701) – beautiful Baroque; *Russian Memorial Church* (1912) – gilded onion-shaped dome.

Modern sights: *Opera House* (1956–60) – one of East Germany's most important theatres; *Schauspielhaus* – the new state theatre into which the remains of the old one have been incorporated: *Karl Marx University* – with a three-sided tower.

Special attractions: an evening in *Auerbachs-Keller* – traditional inn, immortalized in Goethe's ›Faust‹; a concert by the *Gewandhaus* orchestra or a visit to the *opera*; a recital by the *Thomaner Choir*; an evening at cabaret ›Pfeffermühle‹; an outing to *Dresden*.

Important companies with headquarters in the city: *Insel Verlag Anton Kippenberg* (publishing); *Interdruck* (printing); *Ph. Reclam* (publishing); *BSB B.G. Teubner Verlagsgesellschaft* (publishing); *VEB Breitkopf & Härtel Musikverlag* (music publishing); *VEB F.A. Brockhaus* (publishing); *VEB Chemiealagen* (chemicals); *VEB Drehmaschinenwerk* (turbines); *VEB Druckmaschinenwerke* (printing machines); VEB Leipziger Baumwollspinnerei (cotton spinning); *VEB Leipziger Wollkämmerei* (wool combing); *VEB Verlade- und Transportanlagen* (transport systems).

Airport: Leipzig (LEJ); Tel.: 27 65, 13 km/8 miles.

The Headquarters

MERKUR

15 Gerberstrasse
DDR–7010 Leipzig
Telephone: 79 90
Telex: 512 609
Owning Company: Interhotel DDR
General Manager: Günter Bragulla
Affiliation/Reservation Systems: Supra-National Hotel Reservations, Golden Tulip/KLM
Number of rooms: 454 (14 suites)
Price range: DM 140 (single)
　　　　　　　 DM 200 (double)
　　　　　　　 suites (on request)
Credit cards: AE, DC
Location: city centre, near botanic garden
Built: 1981
Style: modern
Hotel amenities: parking, car rental desk, beauty salon, hairstylist, shopping arcade, air terminal of Interflug, travel office, exchange office, newsstand, drugstore, tobacconist, florist, boutique

Room amenities: air conditioning, colour tv, radio, direct-dial telephone, mini-bar, alarm clock, balcony in appartments and suites, judas in all rooms
Bathroom amenities: separate shower cabin, bathrobe, hairdrier, telephone in bathroom of appartments, towel warmer, scales, cosmetics
Room service: 24 hours
Laundry/dry cleaning: same day
Conference rooms: 3 (up to 350 persons), 5-channel-simultaneous translating installations, secretarial services
Sports: health centre, bowling, massage, sauna, solarium, indoor swimming pool (12 m × 6 m with jet stream), riding, tennis, bicycles for rent
Lounge Bar: (8.00/a.m.–23.00/11.00 p.m.) panoramic view over the city
Restaurants: ›Arabeske‹ (Art Déco style); ›Milano‹ (Italian restaurant); ›Sakura‹ (11.00/a.m.–24.00/12.00 p.m.) Japanese specialities, pianist
Nightclub: ›Merkur‹ (20.30/8.30 p.m.–4.00/a.m.) live bands
Private dining rooms: five

On the twenty-seventh floor of this modern tower block, built by the Western Easterners, the Japanese, guests at Leipzig's foremost hotel have not only a lively discothèque in the air but also the city of Leibniz, Wagner and Bach at their feet. The décor of this prestigious hard-currency establishment is remarkable by East German standards – a variety of styles, from Tiffany-nostalgic in the Arabeske *restaurant to Scandinavian-functional in the fitness centre, whilst the comprehensive range of facilities for individual travellers and conference visitors, from the bowling alley to the shoeshine machines, is remarkable by any standards in the socialist world. German efficiency blends here with East-German ›savoir-vivre‹.*

Lunch

SAKURA
Hotel Merkur
Gerberstrasse
Telephone: 79 90
Open: 11.00/a.m.–24.00/12 p.m.
Cuisine: international and Japanese
Chef de cuisine: H. Reinhardt
Specialities: oriental dishes – fillet of pork (Ton Hire); fish in various forms (Umino Sachi), rice; seaweed; soya bean curd; Teppanyaki Japanese specialities prepared at the bar
Location: in the Hotel Merkur
Setting: light, unfussy décor; cherry-wood, coloured prints, fans, beige light fittings; two séparées with Japanese-style low tables and Ikebana flower arrangements
Amenities: hotel; three further restaurants; private dining rooms; bar; night club; car park (garage)
Atmosphere: characteristic East German luxury hotel ambience, with a hint of Far Eastern exoticism
Clientèle: cosmopolitan; Western expense-account industrialists and senior managers from Osaka to Yokohama
Service: professionally welcoming
Reservations: recommended
Price range: expensive, especially by East German standards

Dinner

AUERBACHS KELLER
Mädlerpassage
Telephone: 20 91 31
Manager: Wolf-Dietrich Meinel
Closed: never
Open: 10.00/a.m.–24.00/12 p.m.
Cuisine: local unpretentious and international
Chef de cuisine: Kurt Hensch
Specialities: traditional Saxon dishes, often with Faustian names; ›Mephistopheles' meat‹ (Mephisto-Fleisch); ›Devil's Toast‹ (Teufelstoast); Students' dish
Location: in the heart of the town, near the old Market Place
Setting: an inn for more than 450 years; four dining rooms furnished in varying styles – ›Alt-Leipzig‹; ›Goethe-Zimmer‹; ›Böttger-Zimmer‹; ›Fass-Keller‹; painted ceilings, historic paraphernalia and old engravings
Atmosphere: an institution in the town; an essential stopover for all visitors to the Trades Fair, especially those who have read Goethe's ›Faust‹
Clientèle: citizens of Leipzig from students to senior managers – plus professional and commercial birds of passage
Service: anxious-to-please
Reservations: necessary (no dogs)
Price range: inexpensive

Lunch

STADTPFEIFFER
Im Neuen Gewandhaus
Telephone: 7 13 23 89
Owner/Manager: Wolfgang Mädel
Closed: Sunday
Open: 11.00/a.m.–15.00/3 p.m. and 18.00/6 p.m.–24.00/12 p.m.
Cuisine: international
Specialities: sliced fillet of veal in cream sauce with buttered ham rice and salad; stuffed loin of pork in mushroom cream sauce with buttered peas and croquette potatoes
Setting: modern restaurant (opened in 1982) in the Leipzig theatre (Gewandhaus); décor linked to the musical tradition of the town, notably the travelling performers of the 15th century; painted glass windows, menu and even the ground plan in the form of a ›Pfeiffe‹, an old woodwind instrument
Atmosphere: attractively welcoming
Clientèle: publishers, businessmen and musical visitors to the town of J. S. Bach
Service: particularly friendly
Reservations: recommended
Price range: medium

Dinner

VIETNAMESE RESTAURANT
Hotel Bürgerhof
3 Grosse Fleischergasse
Telephone: 20 94 96
Open: 16.00/4 p.m.–20.00/8 p.m.
Cuisine: Vietnamese
Chef de cuisine: Thuy
Specialities: typical Vietnamese dishes – fried, steamed and baked meat and fish served with rice wine, coffee liqueur and ginger wine
Location: in the Hotel Bürgerhof
Atmosphere: lively and yet unhurried
Clientèle: mixture of local lovers of Oriental food, expatriate orientals and Western businessmen
Service: friendly and attentive
Reservations: essential
Price range: fairly inexpensive

Café

VISAVIS
33, Rudolf-Breitscheid-Strasse
Telephone: 29 27 18
Owner/Manager: Helmut Renelt
Closed: Sunday.
Open: 7.00/a.m.–23.00/11 p.m.; Saturday 14.00/2 p.m.–23.00/11 p.m.
Location: central, near the main station
Setting: 1930s Art Deco-style intérieur; walls serve as an art gallery with frequently changing exhibitions of contemporary paintings; pleasant lighting; unobtrusive background music

Amenities: hot meals (7.00/a.m.–22.30/10.30 p.m.) as well as typical coffee-house fare; bar; car park
Atmosphere: casual; invariably full; lively and popular meeting place for the exchange of news, views and the latest gossip
Clientèle: predominantly youthful mélange of students, intellectuals, artists and journalists
Service: efficient

Bar

HALLENBAR
Hotel Merkur
15 Gerberstraße
Telephone: 79 90
Owner/Manager: Interhotel DDR/Günter Bragulla
Closed: never
Open: 8.00/a.m.–23.00/11 p.m.
Location: in the Hotel Merkur
Setting: on the 27th floor overlooking the city
Amenities: TV
Atmosphere: cosy small bar
Clientèle: businessmen; hotel guests
Dress: casual
Service: barkeeper and waiter
Reservations: not possible
Price range: moderate
Credit cards: all major

Nightclub

CLUB MERKUR
Hotel Merkur
15 Gerberstraße
Telephone: 79 90
Owner/Manager: Interhotel DDR/Günter Bragulla
Closed: never
Open: 20.30/8.30 p.m.–4.00/a.m.
Location: in the Hotel Merkur
Setting: bar atmosphere; overlooking the Japanese Garden
Amenities: live music; bar with barkeeper
Atmosphere: busy big-city bar
Clientèle: noctambule businessmen
Dress: as you like it
Service: fairly efficient
Reservations: not possible
Price range: moderate
Credit cards: all major

Shopping

LOCAL SPECIALITIES
Breitkopf und Hertel (music)
10 Karlstrasse
Hotel Merkur (Intershop) (gifts)
Gerberstrasse
Interhotel Astoria (gifts)
Platz der Republik
Eger (books)
Thomaskirche
Volksbuchhandlung (books)
Karl-Marx-Platz and Neue Universität

THE BEST OF ART
Galerie Theaterpassage (modern art)
(Staatl. Kunsthandel der DDR)
180 Karl-Marx-Strasse, Tel. 20 07 25

The City

Some cities are far more important than they sound – Brno and L'vov are among the others. Over one thousand years ago, Germany's westernmost metropolis already had a glorious past before Berlin was even thought of, and with the greatest emperor of his time, Charlemagne, making the ex-Roman spa his main residence, Aquisgranum was accorded global importance as well as imperial edifices: the cathedral with its treasure and Karl's tomb is one of the historical Lourdes north of the Alps and attracts at least as many travellers as the antique taverns or the avant-garde casino. For hundreds of years German kings were crowned here in the Town Hall; today titles are bestowed for intellectual power on professors of the renowned university or the ›Order of Beastly Earnest‹ on politicians and public figures during the famous folkloric carnival. But Aachen is not only on the map for its antiquity. True, the monuments of grandeur and gingerbread Gemütlichkeit have been restored after the last war's raids – lending the Old Town the particular air that moves nostalgic wanderers from Great Falls and Little Rock to tears – but with local maestro Mies van der Rohe in mind, modern times have been the force behind the clinical centre (the city's own Mayo luring stressed managers from Düsseldorf for a check-up by top specialists as well as Arab royalty for cures and the excuse to gamble) and the Eurogress conference centre which is one of the most advanced of its kind, hosting international conventions throughout the year. Aachen is situated at a point where three borders intersect (half of the city's boundary stretches along the frontier with Belgium and Holland) which adds to the European esprit the city has always been known for – the annually awarded Karl's Prize is for an outstanding politician having furthered the cause of the continent's unity. As a business city, Aachen can also hold its own despite the vicinity of Cologne and Düsseldorf. Once the textile centre of the land, many more industrial branches have followed suit, with mining and machinery the classic pillars, but chemicals, plastic, rubber, asbestos, glass and paper runners-up in the economic life of the city. Of economic value as well – although of pleasure to most – is the art collection of Aachen's very own tycoon (of chocolate and modern canvases) Peter Ludwig. Even cultural hippies need not despair – in this equestrian capital you don't have to offer a kingdom for a horse.

Founded: 3 B.C., as a spa by the Romans; Aachen (German) – from the Roman name for the town; Aix-la-Chapelle (French).

Far-reaching events: 2nd century – ›Aquae Grani‹ is a well-known resort; 794 – Charlemagne chooses Aachen as his residential city; 936–1531 – Aachen the coronation place of 28 kings and emperors; 1166 – Emperor Barbarossa names Aachen the capital and Charlemagne the patron saint of the Holy Roman Empire; 1748 – Peace of Aachen signed here ends the War of Austrian Succession; 1774 – Napoléon occupies the city; 1818 – Congress of Aachen ends the occupation of France by the Holy Alliance; 1939–45 – Aachen badly damaged; 1945 – reconstruction.

Population: 250,000.

Postal code: D-5100   **Telephone code:** 241

Climate: changeable.

Calendar of events: *Karneval* (Jan/Feb) – culminating with the bestowal of the ›Order of Beastly Earnest‹ on politicians, presidents or other public personalities; *International Horseback Riding Tournament (CHIO)* – a meeting of the international equestrian élite; *Studentischer Frühschoppen* (May) – the students of Aachen at an early morning gala against the historic backdrop of the market place; *Sommerabend* (Aug) – folk festival; *European Handicrafts Day* (Sep) – handmade in Europe; *Christmas Market* (23 Nov–22 Dec) – magical market in the snow.

Historical sights: *Cathedral* (13th–15th century) – Gothic splendour, adjorning the *Palatine chapel* of Charlemagne (796–805); *Town Hall* (13th century) – twin-towered Gothic, with vaulted halls, on the site of Charlemagne's palace; *Cathedral Treasury* – Charlemagne's sword and a reliquary bust; *Frankenberg Castle* (13th century) – museum of the city's history and for ancient art; *Suermont-Ludwig-Museum* – art from the late Middle Ages to the beginning of the 18th century, with a large collection of medieval sculpture and stained-glass windows; *Abteikirche St. Johann* – holding the great ›abbey treasure‹; *Propsteikirche St. Kornelius* – the former imperial abbey.

Modern sights: *Neue Galerie* – the Ludwig Collection of avant-garde painters and sculptors from Europe and America; *Spielcasino* in the old spa – the sparkling atmosphere of luck in a highly fashionable ambience (roulette, baccarat, blackjack); *Internationales Zeitungsmuseum* – yesterday's headlines preserved for posterity.

Special attractions: a gala at *Gala*; Carnival Ball at the *Quellenhof*; a check-up at the medical centre (negative check-up).

Important companies with headquarters in the city: *Philips* (light bulbs); *Granus Glasfabrik* (glass); *Vegla* (glass); *Uniroyal Englebert* (tyres); *Talbot* (railway carriages); *Schumag* (metal); *Junghans Wollversand* (wool); *Königsberger* (fabrics); *Wilhelm Becker* (fabrics); *Lambertz* (chocolates and Printen); *Franz Zentis* (jams); *Leonhard Monheim AG*; *Vereinigte Glaswerke* (glass).

Airport: Köln-Bonn (Wahn), CGN; Tel.: 22 03/40 23 03–5, 80 km/50 miles; Düsseldorf-Lohausen, DUS; Tel.: 2 11/42 12 23, 90 km/55 miles; Brussels National, BRU; Tel.: 33-2/7 51 80 80, 140 km/87 miles; (private planes only) Aachen-Merzbrück, Tel.: 24 05/7 25 87; Lufthansa, Tel.: 4 83 68.

The Headquarters

**STEIGENBERGER
HOTEL QUELLENHOF**

52 Monheimsallee
D–5108 Aachen
Telephone: 15 20 81
Telex: 8 32 864 quhof
Owning company: Steigenberger
Hotels AG
General Manager: Kurt F. Seidler
Affiliation/Reservation System: SRS
(Steigenberger Reservation Service)
Number of rooms: 200 (5 suites)
Price range: DM 195–500
Credit cards: AE, DC, EC, JCB, Visa
Location: central
Built: 1914–1916 (renovated 1974–1984)
Style: elegant
Hotel amenities: garage, valet parking,
beauty salon, massage, florist, thermal
swimming pool (pets allowed)
Main hall porter: Marcel Kever
Room amenities: colour tv, radio
Bathroom amenities: separate shower
cabin, bidet, bathrobe, hairdrier
Cures: fango-packs, underwater massage,
carbonated baths, Iontophorese
Room service: 6.30/a.m.–23.30/11.30 p.m.
Conference rooms: 19 (up to 2000 persons)
Bar: ›Nationenbar‹ (see Bars)
Restaurants: ›Parkrestaurant‹ (12.00/
a.m.–14.00/2 p.m. and 18.30/6.30 p.m.–
21.45/9.45 p.m.), Norbert Mahlberg (maître), Michael Görres (chef de cuisine);
›Parkstube‹ (17.00/5 p.m.–1.00/a.m.)

*Thirty German kings were crowned in the
cathedral here, and almost as many have
laid their royal heads down in the suites of
the Quellenhof since. One of Germany's
prestigious Steigenberger group's foremost
bridgeheads of hospitality, this traditional
house serves as a headquarters not only for
the pilgrims to Charlemagne's treasures,
the ruinous casino and the healing springs,
but also for the upper echelon business
world of the three countries meeting here –
Germany, Belgium and Holland. The generosity of space in the halls and salons is as
impressive as the efficiency and warmth of
the service is overwhelming. Functionality
meets comfort in the pleasant interior of
the rooms and suites extending to the
swimming pool and fitness area and reach-
ing an appealing symbiosis in the two restaurants. The cuisine, with its sensible
tendency towards the Nouvelle, is as much
a forte as the atmosphere at the* Nationenbar *which is a favourite rendez-vous before
and after business or pleasure activities.
The location is literally ideal: central but
surrounded by parkland, tranquil, yet only
a few steps away from the main attractions
of today – the Eurogress-Congress Centre,
linked directly to the hotel and the Casino-
entertainment complex, just across the
square. For large conventions or grand galas the Quellenhof is as recherché by the
neighbouring nations as it is for le-rouge-
et-le-noir excitement or sheer relaxation by
the burghers of the Rhineland.*

KASTEEL WITTEM

Zuid Limburg
3 Wittemer Allee
NL–6286 AA Wittem (8 km/5 miles)
Telephone: (31-44 50) 12 08
Telex: 56 287 kawit
Owner: P. Ritzen Senior
General Manager: P. Ritzen Junior
Affiliation/Reservation System: Relais et Châteaux
Number of rooms: 12 (1 suite)
Price range: DM 170 (double)
Credit cards: AE, DC, EC, Visa
Location: between Aachen and Maastricht, 20 km/12 miles from Maastricht airport
Style: medieval castle with period furnishings
Hotel amenities: parking, newsstand, tobacconist
Room amenities: tv, radio
Bathroom amenities: hairdrier
Room service: 8.30/a.m.–24.00/12 p.m.
Laundry/dry cleaning: on demand
Conference rooms: 1 (up to 50 persons)
Sports: golf, cycling
Sports nearby: golf, riding, tennis
Restaurants: ›Salle de Prince‹ (12.00/a.m.–14.30/2.30 p.m.), Teus van Schaik (chef de cuisine), nouvelle cuisine; ›Tower Room‹ (18.00/6.00 p.m.–21.30/9.30 p.m.), Teus van Schaik (chef de cuisine), nouvelle cuisine; classic style, open-air dining
Private dining rooms: two (up to 50 persons)

Despite its border proximity to Aachen and a Michelin star for its splendid cuisine, there's no danger of this former fortress of the Julémont knights falling to hordes of German gourmands. The knights themselves took care of that several centuries ago by setting a deep moat around it. The history of Kasteel Wittem can, in fact, be traced back to 1100 A.D., although the building in its present form dates from the fifteenth century. The once-redoubtable citadel has been lovingly converted into a charming and peaceful hotel set in a private park. Swans now glide gracefully across the still waters of the moat, whilst inside the castle will be found twelve luxurious apartments with oaken beams and bartizans, all appropriately finished with choice antiques. Seigneur of this beguiling architectural anachronism Peter Ritzen rules his domain with a masterly blend of savoir-vivre and savoir-faire, aided by chef de cuisine Teus van Schaik, who spoils guests with cold consommé of melon, shrimps, Aberdeen Angus steaks specially flown in, and strawberry gratin.

Lunch

RATSKELLER
Am Markt
Telephone: 3 50 01
Affiliations: Chaîne des Rôtisseurs
Owner/Manager: Willi Vonderbank/
Waldemar Küchemeister
Closed: Christmas Eve; Christmas Day
Open: 12.00/a.m.–15.00/3 p.m. and
18.00/6 p.m.–24.00/12 p.m.
Cuisine: international
Chef de cuisine: Hubert Leifgen
Specialities: steak (8 variations); Helgo-
land herring salad; home-pickled silver
salmon; Alsatian snail soup; Ostend sole
›Küchenmeister Art‹
Location: in the Town Hall (Rathaus)
Setting: in the 14th-century predominantly Gothic Town Hall, built on the
foundations of Charlemagne's audience
room (800 A.D.); five rooms with period
or rustic furnishing from the Kurfürstenstube, named after the electors who once
attended the coronations of the Holy Roman Emperors in the cathedral, to the
vaulted cellar with festively laid tables
and candlelight
Amenities: private dining rooms (50–100
persons); bar; outdoor dining; air conditioning; car park (market place)
Atmosphere: as representative of 1200
years of Aachen's history as the cathedral
itself
Clientèle: camera-toting tourists from Texas to Thailand rub shoulders with
burghers of Aachen en fête and en famille
Dress: high-fashion; low-fashion; no-
fashion
Service: capably directed by Günther
Nussbaum
Reservations: advisable (dogs allowed)
Price range: relatively inexpensive
Credit cards: AE, DC, Euro, Visa

Lunch

PARKRESTAURANT
Hotel Quellenhof
52 Monheimsallee
Telephone: 15 20 81
Affiliations: Chaîne des Rôtisseurs,
Rastatter Kreis, IHA, DEHOGA, Fritz
Gabler Schulverein
Owner/Manager: Steigenberger Hotelge-
sellschaft/Kurt F. Seidler
Closed: never
Open: 12.00/a.m.–14.00/2 p.m. and
18.30/6.30 p.m.–21.45/9.45 p.m.
Cuisine: blend of classic and nouvelle ›au
goût du marché‹
Chef de cuisine: Michael Görres
Specialities: terrine of morel mushrooms
and chanterelles in Parma ham on wal-
nut-flavoured beurre blanc; turbot with

courgettes and champagne and grapefruit
sauce; Aachener Printen ice-cream
(spiced Christmas biscuits) with fruits
marinated in rum
Location: in the Steigenberger Hotel
Quellenhof
Setting: harmonious elegance; warm
tones of natural wood, comfortable upholstery, impeccably-laid tables; view of
the pretty terrace offering open-air dining
overlooking the gardens in summer
Amenities: hotel; second restaurant; bar;
valet car parking service
Atmosphere: festive; rather formal, but
not forbiddingly so
Clientèle: princes, premiers, presidents,
potentates; a king or two; august or aris-
tocratic visitors to Aachen, from Henry
Kissinger to Sheik Zayed
Dress: couturier casual to designer original
Service: unobtrusive perfection
Reservations: advisable (pets permitted)
Price range: fairly expensive
Credit cards: AE, DC, Euro, Visa, JCB

Dinner

GALA
44 Monheimsallee
Telephone: 15 30 13
Affiliations: Relais et Châteaux
Owner/Manager/Chef de cuisine: Ger-
hard Gartner
Closed: Monday
Open: 19.00/7 p.m.–1.00/a.m.
Cuisine: French (classic)
Specialities: salmon and turbot in caviar
stock; asparagus with truffle sabayon,
white beans with crabs; rye noodles
›Walter Scheel‹; ravioli with lobster;
19th–century clarets and ports
Location: in the casino; city-centre
Setting: classical style building; fin-de-
siècle glamour – crystal chandeliers, mir-
rored walls; open fireplace
Amenities: private dining rooms (25–90
persons); bar; terrace
Atmosphere: elegant, with a touch of the
theatrical
Clientèle: Aachen aristocrats; businessmen; culinary journalists and other devotees of Gartner's cuisine
Dress: couturier and conservative predominate
Service: punctilious, charming and part
of the show; long black dresses, white
aprons and fishnet gloves
Reservations: essential (miniature poodles, dachshunds and King Charles spaniels permitted)
Price range: inevitably expensive
Credit cards: AE, DC, Euro, Visa

Lunch

ST. BENEDIKT
12 Benediktusplatz
Telephone: 28 88
Owner/Manager: Hans-Joachim Kreus
Closed: Monday; Tuesday; annual holiday (not fixed)
Open: 18.30/6.30 p.m.–23.30/11.30 p.m. (last orders 21.00/9 p.m.)
Cuisine: mixture of classical French and nouvelle
Chef de cuisine: Gisela Kreus
Specialities: salmon in champagne; casserole of calves'sweetbreads with asparagus; rabbit in three kinds of mustard; dessert ›St. Benedikt‹. 150 wines including 1928 Domaine de Chevalier
Location: outskirts of Aachen; 10 km (6 miles) from city centre
Setting: in a house built in 1755; small dining room; a synthesis of baroque elegance and prosperous middle-class comfort
Amenities: car park
Atmosphere: intimate; harmonious
Clientèle: businessmen; historians; congressmen; conference visitors; admirers of Gisela Kreus' culinary skills
Dress: no special requirements
Service: pleasantly solicitous
Reservations: advisable (only 5 tables!)
Price range: moderate
Credit cards: not accepted

Dinner

SCHLOSS FRIESENRATH
46 Pannekoogweg
Telephone: 8 00 21
Owner/Manager/Chef de cuisine: Wolfgang Alheit
Closed: Monday; January 1–15th
Open: 12.00/a.m.–14.00/2 p.m. and 18.00/6 p.m.–21.00/9 p.m.
Cuisine: mélange of classical French and nouvelle with regional undertones
Specialities: seasonal dishes fit for a châtelain; lobster soup; poached carp with root vegetables; loin of pork in puff pastry; casserole of lobster and calves' sweetbreads
Location: 12 km (7 miles) from city centre; quiet rural surroundings
Setting: formerly a nobleman's country villa; antique furnishing in three rooms overlooking the gardens
Amenities: three apartments for overnight guests; conference rooms; outdoor dining on terrace; car park
Atmosphere: cultivated; aristocratic
Clientèle: industrialists; managing directors; bankers
Dress: no special requirements

Service: friendly and helpful with a hint of deference
Reservations: advisable (pets allowed)
Price range: moderately high
Credit cards: Euro

Café

VAN DEN DAELE
18 Büchel/1–3 Körbergasse
Telephone: 3 57 24
Owner/Managers: Christa Loreth and Hildegard Wehren
Closed: never
Open: (Monday–Saturday) 9.00/a.m.–18.30/6.30 p.m.; (Sunday) 13.00/1 p.m.–18.00/6.00 p.m.
Specialities: Aachener Printen (spiced Christmas biscuits); Belgische Reisfladen (rice cakes); Obstfladen (fruit cakes)
Location: central
Setting: in the heart of the old city; traditional café established in 1765
Amenities: dining terrace in summer
Atmosphere: an institution in the city – an excellent choice for a quick coffee, or the perfect place to while away a rainy afternoon
Clientèle: footsore suburban housewives after a day at the sales; tired tourists after a morning on the town; students, senior citizens, secretaries and shopgirls
Service: cheerful and obliging

Bar

NATIONENBAR
Hotel Quellenhof
52 Monheimsallee
Telephone: 15 20 81
Owner/Manager: Steigenberger Hotelgesellschaft/Kurt Seidler
Closed: never
Open: 18.00/6 p.m.–3.00/a.m.
Location: in the Steigenberger Hotel Quellenhof
Setting: piano bar (live music) with elegant décor in the classic English idiom
Amenities: hotel; restaurant; brasserie with open-air dining; valet car parking service
Atmosphere: vaguely club-like; stylish and confidential
Clientèle: cosmopolitan; chic; confident; discriminating and successful
Service: professional and friendly; under the supervision of chief barman Peter Förster
Reservations: advisable only for Saturday night
Credit cards: AE, DC, Euro, Visa, JCB

Nightclub

ZERO
44 Monheimsallee
Telephone: 15 30 11
Owner/Manager: Peter Le Jeune
Closed: Sunday, Monday, Tuesday, Wednesday, Thursday
Open: during the rest of the week ... – 22.00/10.00/p.m.–4.00/a.m.
Location: in the Casino
Setting: outrageously expensive interior décor; black columns, black mirrors and fascinating lighting effects
Amenities: private ›salon‹ for up to 80 guests, air conditioning, car-parking facilities (those of the Casino)
Atmosphere: a nightclub, where Queens of the Night and noble spirits relax and let it be
Clientèle: the Aachen In-Crowd, all those who feel young at heart, curious businessmen on an adventure-trip, distinguished foreigners and gamblers from the nearby Casino
Dress: individual elegance, sometimes with a certain flair of expensive eccentricity
Service: amazingly efficient
Reservations: advisable to essential
Price range: medium
Credit cards: all major

Shopping

EVERYTHING UNDER ONE ROOF
Kaufhof   20–30 Adalbertstrasse

FOR HIM
Wienands   20 Alexanderstrasse

FOR HER
Ley, Robert   9 Dahmengraben

BEAUTY & HAIR
Rommé   2 Monheimsallee

JEWELLERY
Guenter Ulrich & Giesela Knorren
9–13 Dahmengraben

LOCAL SPECIALITIES
Pfeifen-Schneiderwind
(tobacco)
Krämerstraße 13
La Silhouette (women's fashion)
3 Schmiedstrasse
Oehl (men's fashion)
3–5 Dahmengraben
59–63 Grosskölnstrasse
Mini Twen (children's fashion)
14a Krämerstrasse
Pour Elle (leather fashion)
14 Holzgraben
Robert Stein (furs)
26 Heinrichsallee
Mayer'sche Buchhandlung (books)
17–19 Ursulinenstrasse

Haus der Geschenke (gifts/porcelain)
Kapuzinergraben/1   Wirichs-Bongard-Strasse
Delikatessen Dorn (food and beverages)
45 Theaterstrasse
Blumen Brings (flowers)
40 Peterstrasse
Alt Bruessell (confiserie)
City Passage

THE BEST OF ART
Bardenheuer (18th/19th-century antiques), 6/8 Hof, Tel. 3 96 77

When one thinks of Germany, one remembers Berlin, Hamburg or Munich, a Baltic Sea beach, Rhine-Romanticism and Bavarian folklore – whether one be a thinker or not. (Businessmen perhaps think of Stuttgart for production, Düsseldorf for trade and Frankfurt for merchandising.) The ones who have travelled here will never forget about Baden-Baden. The idyllic town (capable of being the backdrop for a soap-opera and world history at the same time) cannot quite decide whether she should live more for Kur-leisure or casino-glamour, whether walks in Lichtentaler Allee or horse races at Iffezheim serve the image better. Baden-Baden is as German as a novelle by Eichendorff and a requiem by Brahms and yet as cosmopolitan as a fashionable spa of our century – and one of the most beautiful and lovable places in the Old World. (No wonder the New World is so attracted to it.) Since Baden-Baden is so human, the people, too, are pleasant. Despite health-spa – no ›pensionopolis‹, despite tourism – no caravanserai, despite nostalgia – no kitsch. Even during the last century – before all, in the Romantic Age – Baden-Baden was the cultural centre between Berlin and Paris. Carl Maria von Weber (his works are honoured with a special festival), Franz von Liszt, Albert Lortzing and Richard Wagner (who only at the very last minute decided in Bayreuth's favour and against Baden-Baden), Georges Bizet, Giacomo Meyerbeer and Jacques Offenbach have composed here; Hector Berlioz conducted here and the Diva of the world, Pauline Viardot sang – and Vassily Andrejevich Shukovskij composed the Russian national anthem. Here wrote novelists and philosophers such as Clemens Brentano, Theodor Storm, Victor Hugo, Alexandre Dumas, Gustave Flaubert, Anatole France and the great Russian writers Nikolai Gogol, Ivan Turgenev (who even declared himself a German), Leo Tolstoy and Fedor Mikhailovich Dostoievski (who met his Waterloo in Baden-Baden). The genius loci has remained, and many festivals and guest performances offer a wide range of intellectual and artistic entertainment. Even the sybaritic pleasures are not forgotten in this one-time ›Capitale d'Eté de l'Europe‹; only a champagne-cork's flight away is Germany's Gallic neighbour with its gourmet temples and oenological streams. Baden-Baden is always in season. This slogan, for once, can be taken quite literally. The lustrous period of the blossoming of trees, the legendary summer in the Black Forest, the vintage and the snowy Christmas weeks, the turf meetings, the glorious ball nights in the Kurhaus and the galas at Brenner's Park-Hotel form the most noteworthy events and highlights of the Baden-Baden year. If you look for gaiety and peace at the same time, if you want to witness High Society soirées or retreat in introverted intellectuality (after or instead of business), if you like the affectionate character of the people in Germany's south-west as well as the cosmopolitan flair of a world-historic place, then you are – at any time, in any season – better off in Baden-Baden than you would be in Stuttgart, Frankfurt or Bremen. So much lends meaning to the slogan of romantic writer Gérard de Nerval – ›One has to visit Switzerland, but one should live in Baden-Baden.‹

Founded: end of 1st century A.D., by the Romans; Baden-Baden – from the Franconian ›Badin‹ – ›a spa‹.

Far-reaching events: 1st century – a Roman spa, ›Aquae Aureliae‹; 260 – Alemanni destroy the city and its baths; 10th century – Franks build a settlement called either ›Badin‹ or ›Badon,‹; 12th century – the Margraves of Baden take up residence and build the castles; 1507 – local byelaws governing the use of the thermal baths instituted; 1632–4 – Swedish occupation during the Thirty Years' War; 1689 – the French set fire to the city; 19th century – European high society discovers Baden-Baden and turns it into one of the continent's leading resorts; 1832 – casino opens; 1872 – closure of casino causes a temporary setback in the town's fortunes; 1933 – Hitler has the casino reopened; after 1945 – Baden-Baden a leading tourist centre, once again.

Population: 50,000.

Postal code: D-7570 **Telephone code:** 7221

Climate: practically Italian; beautiful summers, mild winters.

Calendar of events: *Rose Show* (Jun–Sep) – flower power, Baden-Baden style; *Musical Summer* (Jul) – classical music; *Grand Week of Horse Racing* (late Aug, early Sep) – truly grand.

Fairs and exhibitions: None. Baden-Baden is a congress city.

Historical and modern sights: *Altes Schloss* (12th century) – romantic castle ruins; *Neues Schloss* (14th–15th century) – Renaissance style, now housing museums; *Lichtental* (13th century) – fine old monastery with church and chapel, exhibiting religious art and handicrafts on the inside and a 15th-century wall on the outside; the *Roman Baths* (117 A.D.) – an Imperial legacy; *Stiftskirche* – Gothic and Baroque, with the tombs of the margraves; *Russian Church* (19th century) – Byzantine refuge for gambling aristocrats.

Special attractions: a session at the *Casino* or at the *Iffezheim race track*; a stroll through *Lichtentaler Allee*; a cure at *Brenner's Park & Spa*; a *balloon trip* over the Black Forest.

Important companies with headquarters in the city: *Korf-Stahlgruppe* (steel), *Südwestfunk* (broadcasting), *Juvena Cosmetics, Parker Pen* (pens).

Airport: (international) Strasbourg-Entzheim, SXB; Tel.: 33-88 78 40 99, 60 km/38 miles; (planes up to 20 metric tons only) Baden-Baden, Tel.: 6 18 48/49, 5 km/3 miles.

The Headquarters

BRENNER'S PARK & SPA

4–6 Schillerstrasse
D–7570 Baden-Baden
Telephone: 35 30
Telex: 7 81 261 brho
Owner: Rudolf August Oetker
General Manager: Richard Schmitz
Affiliation/Reservation Systems: The Leading Hotels of the World, Preferred Hotels Worldwide
Number of rooms: 108 (8 suites)
Price range: DM 170–1,750
Credit cards: not accepted
Location: city centre
Built: 1872 (recently renovated)
Style: grand
Hotel amenities: valet parking, limousine service, solarium, sauna, hairstylist, beauty farm, spa programme

Main hall porters: Gustav Treu, Gaetano Moretti
Room service: 7.00/a.m.–24.00/12 p.m.
Laundry/dry cleaning: same day (weekend service)
Conference rooms: 5 (up to 200 persons)
Cures: medical, revitalizing, anti-stress and diet programmes, check-up
Bars: ›Hallenbar‹, Kwatra Madhu Sudan (barman), pianist; ›Oleander-Bar‹, H. Horn (barman), pianist
Restaurants: ›Hotelrestaurant‹ (12.00/a.m.–14.00/2 p.m. and 19.00/7 p.m.–21.00/9 p.m.) V. Campanelli (maître), Albert Kellner (chef de cuisine), classic cuisine; ›Schwarzwald-Stube‹ (12.00/a.m.–14.00/2 p.m. and 18.30/6.30 p.m.–23.00/11 p.m.) H. Zacher (maître), Albert Kellner (chef de cuisine), nouvelle cuisine

To many it may appear the incarnation of the Grand-Hotel-Resort-Spa par excellence, some describe it not only as the most beautiful, but also the best hotel in the world, and for the habitués, past and present, it is one of the last bastions of ›living in style‹. For the revered owner, Rudolf August Oetker, and the distinguished director, Richard Schmitz, this 100-odd-year -old mansion in one of the world's most magnificent locations is a life engagement, and the service proves it. In a subtly grand manner, everything is right. Why mention the Roman-tent-like baldachin entrée, the Old-Master-hung marble halls, the glassed-in palazzo-pool looking onto the park, the splendour of the restaurant and the club atmosphere of the bar, let alone the harmonious décor and the recherché amenities in the rooms and baths – here you are as much at home as you could possibly be outside your own. The framework is unique, but the staff is overwhelming. With the fabulous cuisine, the limitless events and individual pastimes and the various possibilities for diets, cures and checkups, there is hardly an equal to this living legend in hotel history.

The Hideaway

MÖNCHS POSTHOTEL

D–7506 Bad Herrenalb, Schwarzwald (22 km/14 miles)
Telephone: (70 83) 74 40
Telex: 7 245 123 poho
Owner: the Mönch Family
Affiliation/Reservation System: Relais et Châteaux
Number of rooms: 50 (12 suites)
Price range: DM 115–250
Credit cards: AE, DC
Location: Black Forest, 60 km/38 miles from Stuttgart airport, 150 km/90 miles from Frankfurt, 60 km/40 miles from Strasbourg
Built: 1890 (renovated 1984)
Style: Black Forest grandeur; period furniture
Hotel amenities: garage, valet parking, newsstand, boutique, tobacconist, hairstylist, solarium, massage, manicure, swimming pool
Main hall porter: H. Schmidt
Room amenities: colour tv
Room service: 7.00/a.m.–24.00/12 p.m.
Conference rooms: 2 (up to 60 persons), overhead projector, video, conference equipment, secretarial services, ballroom
Sports: indoor tennis, squash
Sports (nearby): golf, tennis, swimming, fishing, squash, bowling, hunting, riding
Hotel-Bar: (11.00/a.m.–14.00/2.00 p.m. and 18.00/6.00 p.m.–24.00/12.00 p.m.) ›Sir Henry‹ (barman), records
Restaurant: ›Klosterschänke‹ (12.00/a.m. –24.00/12.00 p.m.) Peter Baunacke (chef de cuisine), French cuisine, 14th-century -building, open-air dining
Private dining rooms: three

Bad Herrenalb owes its uncontested position as one of the bastions of fine living in the Black Forest in no small part to Mönchs Posthotel. For eight hundred years, travellers have been offered bed and board here, but only since the Mönch family took over from the monks have gourmets made a detour to sample the fresh fish from les Halles, the lobster and crayfish from the seawater tanks and local apple pie from a medieval recipe in the fourteenth-century oak-beamed restaurant of the gabled and turreted timber-framed house. This elegant auberge on the outskirts of town also seduces the well-travelled and well-known wanderers who arrive on its doorstep to linger by its cosy fireplaces, in its comfortable salons or beside the swimming pool in the park-like garden. With the Black Forest on your doorstep – countryside reminiscent of a Claude Lorrain painting, luxury à la Louis XIV. and lucullian delights to compete with the best bistros in Lyons (and the chance, with careful planning, of giving day-trippers from Basle to Frankfurt and passing tourists from big cities all over the world a wide berth), you could find yourself hiding away here for longer than you intended.

Lunch

POSPISIL'S (Merkurius)
2 Klosterbergstrasse
Telephone: (72 23) 54 74
Owner/Manager: Pavel Pospisil
Closed: Monday; Tuesday lunchtime
Open: 12.00/a.m.–15.00/3 p.m. and
19.00/7 p.m.–24.00/12 p.m.
Cuisine: French (nouvelle) and traditional Bohemian
Chef de cuisine: Pavel Pospisil
Specialities: carp in paprika sabayon;
garlic croûtons with goose liver (Topinky); summer salad with pigeons'
hearts; salmon trout in chive cream
sauce; strawberry dumplings with grated
gingerbread and melted butter
Location: 6 km (4 miles) south-west of
city centre; in the suburb of Varnhalt
Setting: small dining room furnished in
elegant country-house style
Amenities: small hotel; private dining
room (12–15 persons); bar; open-air dining on terrace; car park
Atmosphere: chic; relaxed
Clientèle: local dignitaries; visiting celebrities from the worlds of politics, show-business and the arts
Dress: designer casual to designer elegant to what-you-will
Service: good
Reservations: recommended
Price range: fairly expensive
Credit cards: AE, DC, Euro

Dinner

ZUM ALDE GOTT
10 Weinstrasse
Neuweier (10 km/6 miles)
Telephone: (72 23) 55 13
Owner/Managers: Wilfried and Ilse Serr
Closed: Thursday; Friday lunch time;
January
Open: 12.00/a.m.–15.00/3 p.m. and
18.00/6 p.m.–24.00/12 p.m.
Cuisine: sophisticated modern, with a local accent
Chef de cuisine: Wilfried Serr
Specialities: sorrel soup with pike dumplings (quenelles de brochet); guinea
fowl in goose liver sauce with fresh vegetables; salmon in aspic with chive
sauce; poached beef in basil sauce with
home-made tomato pasta (Spätzle); terrine of fresh plums
Location: 10 km (6 miles) from town centre
Setting: modern building; view of vineyards through large picture windows; elegantized rustic furnishings
Amenities: private dining rooms; outdoor
dining on terrace; car park; air conditioning
Atmosphere: welcoming, homely and
comfortable without loss of style

Clientèle: local habitués; admirers of
Wilfried Serr's cuisine; politicians and
show business personalities from Minister Schiller to Udo Jürgens
Dress: casually elegant to elegantly casual
Service: conscientious and anxious-to-please
Reservations: advisable (dogs allowed)
Price range: high, even by Baden-Baden
standards
Credit cards: DC, Euro, Visa

Lunch

SCHLOSS NEUWEIER
21 Mauerbergstrasse
Neuweier (10 km/6 miles)
Telephone: (72 23) 57 9 44
Owner/Manager/Chef de cuisine: Karl-Heinz Beck
Closed: Tuesday; Wednesday lunchtime;
February
Open: 12.00/a.m.–15.00/3 p.m. and
18.00/6 p.m.–2.00/a.m.
Cuisine: local and international
Specialities: angler fish in saffron with
coloured noodles and leaf spinach; fillet
of wild boar in pepper cream with wild
mushrooms and local pasta (Schupfnudeln)
Location: at Neuweier; 10 km (6 miles)
south-west of Baden-Baden
Setting: historic former moated castle;
various dining rooms, mostly rather dark
and tucked-away; collection of antique
weapons; very picturesque
Amenities: bar; outdoor dining in castle
courtyard; garden; car park
Atmosphere: vaguely Sleeping Beauty;
rustic and homely, with a touch of the
medieval
Clientèle: Baden-Baden's Haute Bourgeoisie en fête and en famille, plus tourists from Boston to Brisbane
Dress: casually elegant to elegantly casual
Service: friendly, knowledgeable and
good; directed by the wife of the proprietor, Barbara Beck
Reservations: advisable
Price range: fairly expensive
Credit cards: Euro

Lunch

BURG WINDECK
104 Kappelwindecker Strasse
Bühl (16 km/10 miles)
Telephone: (72 23) 23 6 71
Affiliations: Relais et Châteaux (Relais
Gourmand)
Owner/Manager/Chef de cuisine: Peter
Wehlauer
Closed: Monday; Tuesday; January-February
Open: 12.00/a.m.–14.30/2.30 p.m. and
18.30/6.30 p.m.–21.30/9.30 p.m.
Cuisine: modernized traditional German
and nouvelle

Specialities: artichoke hearts with crab cassoulet; breast of pigeon on foie gras with blanched celery; saddle of rabbit with leeks and morel mushrooms; breast of guinea-fowl with orange and mustard sauce; spiced coffee mousse on two sauces with sliced peaches
Location: at Bühl; 16 km (10 miles) south of Baden-Baden
Setting: perched high above the Rhine; panoramic views of the river valley; half-timbered former castle converted into a gourmet's refuge
Amenities: hotel; private dining rooms (45 persons); terrace for apéritifs; car park
Atmosphere: beguilingly romantic ambience which mirrors the excellence of the food
Clientèle: businessmen tired of Baden-Baden; growing numbers of pilgrims to this temple of German culinary excellence drawn by Peter Wehlauer's reputation as a pioneer of the Neue Deutsche Küche – and a fair number of lovers of any age, nationality and sex
Dress: informal
Service: charmingly directed by Marianne Wehlauer
Reservations: advisable (dogs permitted)
Price range: inevitably expensive
Credit cards: DC

Dinner

STAHLBAD
2 Augustaplatz
Telephone: 2 45 69
Owner/Managers: Elisabeth Schwank; Ursula and Siegfried Mönch
Closed: Sunday evening; Monday;
Open: 11.30/a.m.–14.30/2.30 p.m. and 17.30/5.30 p.m.–22.00/10 p.m.
Cuisine: classic, international and nouvelle
Chef de cuisine: Elisabeth Schwank
Specialities: angler fish (Lotte) in tarragon butter; fillet steak ›Rossini‹; fresh lobster with two sauces; pancakes with mushrooms; sabayon with ice cream and strawberries
Location: on the edge of the park
Setting: historic rotunda building; small, sumptuous and stunningly beautiful dining room
Amenities: outdoor dining on terrace
Atmosphere: unashamedly luxurious
Clientèle: Baden-Baden ›In-Crowd‹, resident and visiting sheikhs, tycoons and millionaires
Dress: appropriately elegant, expensive and exclusive
Service: courteous, attentive and elegant in red and black tail-coats
Reservations: recommended (pets allowed)
Price range: cheap only if you're an oil sheikh, a tycoon or a millionaire
Credit cards: AC, DC, Visa, Euro

Meeting Point

OXMOX
4 Kaiserallee
Telephone: 2 99 00
Owner/Managers: Elke and Peter Kamp
Closed: never
Open: 18.00/6 p.m.–1.00/a.m.
Location: town centre, near the Kurhaus
Setting: elegantized French bistro in the former dining room of the Tsars; ceiling clad in straw matting; dark, ornately-carved wood and velvet
Amenities: Griffin's Club Discothèque in cellar (closed Monday and Tuesday); bar; winter garden; car park
Atmosphere: roaring 20's nostalgia; exuberantly youthful without sacrificing elegance
Clientèle: Baden-Baden Beau Monde; a sprinkling of aristocracy; jeunesse dorée; politicians en passant; actors – and the occasional sober citizen
Dress: jeans to dinner jacket; way-out to way- in
Service: charming
Reservations: advisable for restaurant
Price range: moderately high
Credit cards: AE

Café

KÖNIG
12 Lichtentaler Strasse
Telephone: 2 35 73
Owner/Manager: Heinz König KG / Herbert Fischer
Closed: Christmas Day
Open: 9.00/a.m.–20.00/8 p.m.
Specialities: home-made chocolates (90 varieties); cakes (80 varieties); ice-cream (36 varieties)
Location: central; on Baden-Baden's ›High Street‹
Setting: appropriately stylish intérieur; antique furnishing and accessoires; old paintings
Amenities: outdoor dining on terrace
Atmosphere: a post-war institution in the town which nevertheless seems to epitomise in a most bewitching manner the charm, gaiety and elegance of Baden-Baden's heyday as a spa of world renown
Clientèle: when in Baden-Baden . . . rich, famous and beautiful people who want to see, be seen, while away an hour or more over a cup of coffee or indulge in some of the calorie-laden treats prepared by chef pâtissier Herbert Fischer
Service: old-world charm; waitresses with black bows in their hair who still serve a glass of iced water with the coffee

Bar

PIT'S CLUB
92 Lange Strasse
Telephone: 2 32 94
Owner/Manager: Pit Fiolka
Closed: never
Open: 22.00/10 p.m.–4.00/a.m.
Location: opposite the old station
Setting: elegant intérieur; comfortable corners for a soirée à deux and an inviting dance floor for those wishing to work-off a few inches or inhibitions
Amenities: en-vogue discothèque
Atmosphere: the Annabel's (or Castel's, or Gil's) of Baden-Baden; the Number One nightspot
Clientèle: polyglot; invariably in a good mood; beautiful, charming, witty and original night owls plus incognito insiders
Dress: designer elegant to definitely kinky
Service: ›grande classe‹ – with Millie and the attractive starlets to take care of lonesome individuals from all over the world
Reservations: admittance by recognition only; recommended
Price range: high, even for Baden-Baden
Credit cards: all major

Nightclub

GRIFFINS CLUB
4 Kaiserallee
Telephone: 2 43 40
Owner/Manager: Elke and Peter Kamp
Closed: Monday; Tuesday
Open: 22.00/10 p.m.–3.00/a.m.
Location: in the cellar of ›Oxmox‹ restaurant
Setting: Jugendstil bistro serving gourmet snacks and light meals from ›Oxmox‹; beyond, somewhat Hades-like beneath a vaulted ceiling, the discothèque
Amenities: restaurant (upstairs); two bars
Atmosphere: young; exciting; with-it; loud to noisy at times
Clientèle: affluent, attractive and arrogant; chauffeured heirs, young hopefuls and a bevy of beautiful hangers-on
Dress: Gucci, Pucci and co.
Service: efficient
Reservations: essential for groups of 5 or more; smaller parties well advised to arrive in good time
Price range: adequately expensive
Credit cards: AE

Shopping

EVERYTHING UNDER ONE ROOF
Wagener   25 Lange Strasse

FOR HIM
Herrenkommode   16 Sofienstrasse

FOR HER
Kleinmann 9 Lange Strasse

BEAUTY & HAIR
Linkenheil   6 Sofienstrasse

JEWELLERY
Friedrich   Kurhaus Collonaden

LOCAL SPECIALITIES
Sieveking (women's fashion)
Gernsbacherstrasse
Céline (men's fashion)
6 Sofienstrasse
Braun (fashion for him and her)
3 a Sofienstrasse
Gassmann (leather fashion)
4 Lichtentaler Strasse
Kuhnert (furs)
Sofienstrasse
Wild (books)
1 b Sofienstrasse
Gaiser (gifts)
22 Lange Strasse
Hoehner (porcelain)
Lange Strasse
Etienne Aigner (baggage & travel accessories) 22 Sofienstrasse
Das Weisse Haus (interior decorating)
4 Sofienstrasse
Lauer (perfumery)
Am Leopoldsplatz

THE BEST OF ART
Apfelbaum-Galerie   (modern art)
10 Kaiser-Wilhelm-Strasse,
Tel. 3 14 82
Fischer, Suzanne   (modern art)
Altes Dampfbad, 13 Marktplatz,
Tel. 26 9 46/2 39 30
Franke, Kunstsalon   (18th/19th-century antiques)
14 Lichtentaler Strasse,
Tel. 2 50 09

The City

Munich is Germany's ›Secret Capital‹, Hamburg the ›Gateway to the World‹, Frankfurt is the turntable of the country for its airport and physical location and Düsseldorf is the desk of the ›Economic Wonderland‹, but deep down inside, every German has to admit that Berlin is the heart in both bodies, East and West. Berliners act faster than Bavarians can think, outwit even the Rhinelanders who are famous for their humour, work harder than Hamburgers and snob Frankfurters as ›Tyrolians; – when they don't swallow them at fast-food stalls – literally. The most important city in the world – politically, creatively and culturally, only a few decades ago – the absurd split-up has left traces, still visible today, that evoke a mélange of nostalgia, melancholy and optimism. Yet, Berlin is still the biggest city in Germany, with the strongest economy (with a little help from her friends), the latest and most swinging nightlife, the grandest and most exciting boulevard, an outstanding university and academy of arts, a great theatre and jazz life, the best orchestra of all time (and its Salzburgian maestro, Herbert von K.), and the most intelligent Germans, including the ones who emigrated to the New World and the others who are locked up behind the Iron Curtain. With its own lake district, deep forests, rivers and mini-villages all within the city boundaries, this metropolis also has more churches than Rome, more bridges than Venice and more flair than any other Teutonic city, from Zurich to Vienna to Cologne. When you have the sensitivity to appreciate the ›Berlin Air‹ you can claim, as President John F. Kennedy did, ›Ich bin ein Berliner‹.

Founded: 12th century, along with Cölln and Spandau; Berlin (German) – ›a bear‹.
Far-reaching events: 1240 – Berlin receives a city charter; 1415 – Berlin becomes part of the principality of Brandenburg under the Hohenzollern dynasty; 1486 – Berlin becomes the residence of the Electors; 1701 – the Kingdom of Prussia is founded by Frederick I – Berlin, as capital, becomes an intellectual centre for Europe; 1806–8 – occupied by Napoléon; 1809 – foundation of the University; 1871 – founding of the German Empire with Berlin as capital; 1910 – population of 3.7 million; 1918 – the Empire ends in revolution – Berlin capital of the new Weimar Republic; 1933 – Hitler comes to power; 1939–45 – heavy bombing during World War II; 1945 – division of the city into four sectors; 1948 – Berlin airlift; 1961 – construction of the Wall.
Population: 2.3 million.
Postal code: D-1000   **Telephone code:** 30
Climate: Prussian, somewhat tempered by the sea.
Calendar of events: *Berlin Music Days* (Jan); *Berlin Film Festival* (Feb) – one of the most respected in the world; *Art Days* (Apr) – a festival of the fine and the performing arts, throughout the city; *World Cultures Festival* (Jun) – international folklore, music, singing, dancing and handicrafts; *Bach Days* (Jul) – fugues for the masses; *Berlin Festival* (Sep/Oct) – a different theme is chosen each year for concerts, opera, ballet, theatre, films and art exhibitions; *Berlin Jazz Days* (Nov) – singing and playing the blues.
Fairs and exhibitions: *GRÜNE WOCHE* (Feb) – international agricultural fair, a ›Green Week‹; *INTERNATIONAL TOURIST EXCHANGE* (Mar) international tourism exhibition; *FREE BERLIN ART EXHIBITION* (May); *SHOWTECH* (May) – international congress for entertainment technology, in conjunction with *VIDEO* exhibition; *OVERSEAS IMPORT FAIR* (Sep); *INTERNATIONAL BROADCASTING EXHIBITION* (Sep); *BÜRO-DATA BERLIN* (Oct) – office organization exhibition; *CAMP* (Sep/Oct) – computer graphics exhibition; *ANTIQUA* (Nov/Dec) – antiques.
Historical and modern sights: *Charlottenburg Palace* (1695–99) – the only Hohenzollern Palace still remaining, with crown jewels and art gallery with some of Rembrandt's greatest masterpieces; *Reichstag* (1884–94) – the famous former seat of the German Parliament, where Hitler was democratically voted into power; *Bellevue* (1785) – reconstructed after the war, now the Berlin residence of the President of the Federal Republic; *Jagdschloss* (1545) – elegant Baroque former royal hunting lodge, in Grunewald, the most elegant part of town; *Bauhaus Archive* – the plans for this museum were drawn by architectural maestro Walter Gropius; *Gedächtsniskirche* – Kaiser Wilhelm memorial church, newly built out of the ruins; *Olympic Stadium* – built by Hitler, for his 1936 propaganda spectacle; *Broadcasting Tower* (1925) – landmark eyrie; the *Berlin Wall* – impressively depressing; the *Egyptian Museum* (Nefertiti's head).
Special attractions: a concert with *Karajan*; the *Kurfürstendamm*, day and night; the *Tuntenball* – carnival in drag; Friday night at *Chez Alex*; the *riverboat shuffle* through Berlin's waterways; an *aerobics session* with Sydney Rome.
Important companies with headquarters in the city: *Siemens* (electrical appliances); *Boettger* (pharmaceuticals); *Dorland* (advertising); *Gillette Deutschland*; *DETEWE* (electrical appliances); *Deutsche Vergaserbau* (automobile parts); *Borsig* (machinery); *Berthold* (machinery); *BMW* (motorcycle division); *Kraftwerk Union* (machinery); *OSRAM* (electrotechnology); *Schering* (chemicals, pharmaceuticals); *Schindler Aufzüge* (lifts); *Schultheiss Brauerei* (beer); *Krone* (electrotechnology); *Core Herlitz* (paper goods); *AEG-Telefunken* (electrotechnology) *Spinnstoffabrik Zehlendorf* (synthetic fabrics); *Rodaprint* (office machinery); *Orenstein & Koppel* (machinery); *Gödecke* (chemicals); *Flohr-Otis* (lifts); *Axel Springer* (printing/publishing); *Sender Freies Berlin & RIAS* (radio/television broadcasting).
Airport: Berlin-Tegel, TXL; Tel.: 41 01 31 45; 8 km/5 miles; Lufthansa, Tel.: 8 87 51.

The Headquarters

STEIGENBERGER

1 Los Angeles-Platz
D–1000 Berlin 30
Telephone: 2 10 80
Telex: 181 444 stbl
Owning Company: Steigenberger Hotels AG
General Manager: Jean K. van Daalen
Affiliation/Reservation System: SRS (Steigenberger Reservation Service)
Number of rooms: 400 (29 suites)
Price range: DM 195–1,500
Credit cards: AE, DC, EC, Visa
Location: city centre
Built: 1981
Style: contemporary
Hotel amenities: valet parking, indoor swimming pool, sauna, massage, fitness room, newsstand, boutique, confiserie
Room amenities: tv/video, mini-bar
Room service: 6.00/a.m.–24.00/12 p.m.
Conference rooms: 11 (up to 450 persons)
Bars: ›Piano-Bar‹ (11.00/a.m.–2.00/a.m.) pianist; ›Cocktail-Bar‹ (12.00/a.m.–15.00/3.00 p.m. and 18.30/6.30 p.m.–24.00/12.00 p.m.) Uri Gabrielli (barman), pianist; ›Hallen-Bar‹ (as Cocktail Bar)
Restaurants: ›Parkrestaurant‹ (see Restaurants); ›Berliner Stube‹ local specialities; ›Destille‹ (15.00/3.00 p.m.–4.00/a.m.) typical Berlin pub
Private dining rooms: three

Despite the central location around the corner of the grands boulevards, the unobtrusively elegant link in the renowned German hotel dynasty's chain is the quietest grande résidence in Berlin. Good comfort with all necessary amenities, appealing décor in warm colours, flawless service from the voiturier welcome to the housekeeping care and an excellent cuisine making the hotel a favourite restaurant for the natives, reflect the perfect management of Jean K. van Daalen (ex-Nassauer Hof, Wiesbaden) and make the hotel the prime choice amongst top-class businessmen and companies alike. (Presidents and stars are regulars here.) Friendly reception, efficient check-in, ample staff, all-day maid service and tight security make this hotel stand out among its local competitors. Conference and convention facilities are of international standard, swimming pool and fitness room of small dimensions yet tasteful ambiance. The Park-Restaurant under the direction of popular Maître Giuseppe Rosso, is one of Berlin's finest, while the Destille serves hearty snacks in pub surroundings and the Berliner Stube forges links between the international house guests and local habitués with menu and mood. The Hallen-Bar is the last stop for many guests and Berliners who like the pianist, the occasional band, the drinks and the strangers-cum-acquaintances.

Lunch

PARKRESTAURANT
Hotel Steigenberger
Los-Angeles-Platz
Telephone: 2 10 80/2 10 88-55/Telex:
18 14 44
Owner/Manager: Jean K. van Daalen
Maître: Giuseppe Rosso
Closed: never
Open: 12.00/a.m.–15.00/3 p.m. and
18.30/6.30 p.m.–24.00/12 p.m.
Cuisine: French-oriented
Chef de cuisine: Detlef Kortenhoff
Specialities: terrine of turbot and salmon; shin of veal with ginger sauce; breast of Barbary duckling with redcurrant sauce; calves' kidneys in champagne mustard sauce; fillet of lamb with ratatouille
Location: in the Hotel Steigenberger
Setting: elegant modern dining room in the bel-étage of the hotel; earthy tones; floral glass partitions; exquisitely laid, well-spaced tables; English-style apéritif bar; pianist (evenings); art gallery with regularly-changing exhibitions
Amenities: hotel; private dining rooms (up to 360 persons); two bars; bistro with outdoor dining on terrace; pub; café; swimming pool; air conditioning; car park; garage; shopping arcade
Atmosphere: understated chic; refreshing, refined and not in the least oppressive
Clientèle: intelligent; discriminating; self-confident; successful
Dress: tie not essential; jeans not desirable
Service: first class
Reservations: recommended (no dogs)
Price range: fairly expensive
Credit cards: AE, DC, Euro, Visa

Lunch

ANSELMO
17 Damaschkestrasse
Telephone: 3 23 30 94
Owner/Manager: Anselmo Bufacchi
Closed: Monday; Tuesday lunchtime
Open: 12.00/a.m.–15.00/3 p.m. and
18.00/6 p.m.–24.00/12 p.m.
Cuisine: Italian Haute Cuisine
Chef de cuisine: Peppino Esposito
Specialities: home-made pasta, especially spaghetti, rigatoni, fettucine; scampi alla mozzarella; lamb chops; fillet of veal with ham and sage (saltimbocca alla romana); carpaccio; zabagione; crêpes Rothschild
Location: west of centre – near the Egyptian Museum
Setting: Milanese avant-garde; reminiscent of a space station; spring green and purple, white and chrome; artistic lighting
Amenities: open-air dining on terrace; bar; car park
Atmosphere: coolly attractive
Clientèle: serious, successful
Dress: informal chic
Service: personal
Reservations: recommended (no dogs)
Price range: rather expensive
Credit cards: not accepted

Lunch

WIRTSHAUS SCHILDHORN
4a Am Schildhorn, Berlin-Grunewald
Telephone: 3 04 04 63
Owner/Managers: Volker Thomas/Manfred Stocker
Closed: 24. 12.
Open: 10.00/a.m.–1.00/a.m.
Cuisine: Neue Deutsche Küche
Chef de cuisine: Lutz Thurmann
Specialities: salad of kidney beans with shrimps and rabbit liver in raspberry vinegar dressing; veal steak veal in lemon sauce with dates, broccoli with hazelnuts and rice
Location: in the suburb of Grunewald; a short drive west of the city centre
Setting: on the Havel; half-timbered restaurant complex in a garden shaded by chestnut-trees; two large dining rooms furnished in the Art Déco style, with mirrors and objets d'art
Amenities: piano bar; open-air dining in garden; soirées musicales in summer; sailing boats and surf-boards for hire; other sports in the vicinity; car park
Atmosphere: depending on the occasion; festive and almost formal to a stylized fête champêtre
Clientèle: favourite destination for Berlin's Haute Bourgeoisie en fête and en famille, especially during the summer months
Dress: Sunday casual to Sunday best
Service: knowledgeable and efficient
Reservations: advisable
Price range: medium
Credit cards: AE, EC, Visa

Lunch

PARIS BAR
152 Kantstrasse
Telephone: 3 13 80 52
Owners: Michel Würthle and Reinald Nohal
Manager: Georges Golfier
Closed: Sunday
Open: 12.00/a.m.–1.00/a.m.
Cuisine: French bistro
Chef de cuisine: Jacques Lecœur
Specialities: vegetable soups; pâtés; leg of lamb; entrecôte; seafood; oysters; mussels; tarte tatin; mousse au chocolat
Location: near the city centre

Setting: classic bistro in an L-shaped room; impressive collection of modern art
Amenities: small bar; attended car park (fee-paying) acrosse the road
Atmosphere: intellectual to informal
Clientèle: businessmen, artists, intelligentsia
Dress: casual to conservative
Service: very French; professional
Reservations: recommended (no dogs)
Price range: moderate to expensive
Credit cards: not accepted

Dinner

HEINZ HOLL
26 Damaschkestrasse
Telephone: 3 23 14 04/3 23 29 93
Owner/Manager: Heinz Holl
Closed: Sunday; three weeks during local school summer holidays
Open: 19.00/7 p.m.–2.00/a.m.
Cuisine: unpretentious
Chef de cuisine: Egon Dirschhauer
Specialities: stuffed cabbage (Kohlroulade) ›Heinz Holl‹; gefilter Fisch (during the carp season); home-cured fresh salmon with potato fritters (Kartoffelpuffer); goose (4 persons; advance order necessary)
Location: west of centre
Setting: comfortable bourgeois living room décor
Amenities: private dining room (20 persons); bar; air conditioning
Atmosphere: an oasis of intimate bonhomie and a true Berlin original; a stage for many who are used to standing on one
Clientèle: Berlin's prominenti – political leaders, actors, singers, television personalities and journalists, from Richard von Weizsäcker to Udo Jürgens
Dress: what you will
Service: inspired; hosted by the inimitable Heinz Holl
Reservations: recommended
Price range: medium
Credit cards: not accepted

Dinner

ESTIATORIO (›Foffi‹)
70 Fasanenstrasse
Telephone: 8 81 87 85
Owner/Managers: Foffi and Vassile Costa
Closed: lunchtime
Open: 19.00/7 p.m.–1.00/a.m.
Cuisine: bourgeoise, with a Greek accent
Chef de cuisine: Peter Hagen
Specialities: Hellenic hors d'œuvres; lamb steamed in pergament (exochiko); fresh vegetables
Location: off the Kurfürstendamm

Setting: chic and lively street-side café/bar/pub in a neo-classic building; white walls; reminiscent of an art gallery with exhibition of paintings
Amenities: open-air dining on terrace; bar; air conditioning; car park
Atmosphere: unique
Clientèle: obligatory stopover for Beau Monde, demi-monde and visitors with sophistication, self-assurance and a suite at the ›Kempi‹
Dress: jeans, frock or carnival costume – nobody cares
Service: welcoming and friendly
Reservations: advisable
Price range: medium
Credit cards: not accepted

Dinner

GUIDO'S TESSINER STUBEN
33 Bleibtreustraße
Telephone: 8 81 36 11
Owner/Manager: Guido Kren
Closed: Saturday and Sunday lunchtime
Open: 12.00/a.m.–15.00/3 p.m. and 18.00/6 p.m.–2.00/a.m.
Cuisine: nouvelle
Chef de cuisine: Achim Plesow
Specialities: ›Salade Nouvelle‹; home-marinated salmon with king prawns; wild salmon trout in Normandy butter; médaillons of different meats in sauces (Panachés aus Fleisch); mixed wild berries
Location: in a side-street off the Kurfürstendamm
Setting: two dining rooms furnished in elegantized rustic style, separated by an archway; dusty pink décor
Amenities: bar for apéritifs; air conditioning; car park; terrace planned
Atmosphere: friendly and welcoming in the main room to confidential or intimate (depending on your companion) in the ›Karajan-Ecke‹
Clientèle: expense-account gourmets, members of the liberal professions and a sprinkling of famous names as familiar faces from the world of politics, show-biz or the media
Dress: as you like it
Service: good
Reservations: recommended
Price range: moderately expensive
Credit cards: AE, DC, EC, Visa

Meeting Point

GUIDO'S MAXWELL
1 Meyer-Otto-Straße
Telephone: 8 81 22 32
Owner/Manager: Gerd Wasmund
Closed: never
Open: 11.00/a.m. – 1.00/a.m.

Cuisine: à la mode and local, with a Swiss accent
Chef de cuisine: Heinz Härrn
Specialities: caviar potato; scampi in Chablis sauce; chocolate mousse
Location: good residential area, a few minutes from the Headquarters
Atmosphere: vaguely transatlantic, lively and casual in the bistro; slightly more formal in the restaurant
Amenities: bistro bar (snacks and light meals); air conditioning; car park
Setting: two neo-classic dining-rooms with colonial style furnishings
Clientèle: chic, showy and egocentric (le m'as-tu vu de Berlin)
Dress: tailored jeans, see-through et al
Service: highly personal
Reservations: a must (delays may still occur)
Price range: moderately expensive
Credit cards: all major

Café

LEYSIEFFER
218 Kurfürstendamm
Telephone: 8 82 78 20
Owner/Manager: the Leysieffer family
Closed: never
Open: 8.00/a.m.–19.00/7 p.m.
Specialities: confiserie – café
Location: city centre
Setting: historic building; beautifully renovated; precious stucco ceiling; modern and elegant interior
Amenities: small balcony (15 persons) with Jugendstil tiles and a birds' eye view of the Kurfürstendamm
Atmosphere: coolly attractive
Clientèle: coffee-house habitués, ladies beyond the midlife crisis in the majority
Service: friendly

Bar

CHEZ ALEX
160 Kurfürstendamm
Telephone: 8 91 60 22
Owner/Manager: Alex Kozulin
Closed: Monday; Tuesday
Open: 22.00/10 p.m.–4.00/a.m. (in summer 16.00/4 p.m.–4.00/a.m.)
Location: city centre
Setting: cool bistro-look
Amenities: bar; air conditioning; cocktails on open-air terrace in summer
Atmosphere: animated, crowded, noisy – with boy-wonder pianist-singer Alex as the life and soul of the party
Clientèle: conservative to kinky
Service: astonishingly professional
Reservations: recommended (few tables)
Credit cards: AE, DC

Bar

TASTY
53 Kurfürstendamm
Telephone: 8 83 94 44
Owner/Manager: Walter Schuber
Closed: never
Open: 11.00/a.m.–22.00/10 p.m.
Cuisine: Franco-Austrian (nouvelle)
Chef de cuisine: Wolfgang Schallek
Specialities: large buffet with lobster, salmon, caviar and oysters; Russian beetroot soup (Borschtsch); foie gras; lobster soup; whitefish fillets (Egli) with tomatoes; artichoke hearts with dill potatoes; saddle of veal in herb and cream sauce with spinach noodles
Location: on Berlin's most famous and elegant shopping street
Setting: elegantized bistro; Art Déco; black leather armchairs and shiny chrome tables
Amenities: air conditioning; open-air dining
Atmosphere: chic, lively and relaxed
Clientèle: fashionable and popular meeting-place for men-and-women-about-town; Berlin's Beau Monde; businessmen; elegant, rich and beautiful people
Dress: Armani and Co. to Yves St. Laurent
Service: efficient
Reservations: not necessary
Price range: surprisingly moderate
Credit cards: all major

Nightclub

FIRST
26 Joachimstalerstrasse
Telephone: 8 82 26 86
Owner/Manager: Joachim Strecker (ex-Komma Bar)
Closed: Monday (except public holidays)
Open: 23.00/11 p.m.–6.00/a.m.
Location: off the Kurfürstendamm, between the German Federal House (Bundeshaus) and the Kaiser Wilhelm Memorial Church (Gedächtnis-Kirche)
Setting: an architectural ruin with American styling
Amenities: air conditioning
Atmosphere: a place where everybody talks to everybody, mostly because he/she is so close; any language, mostly body language and smiles
Clientèle: Berlin's elegant bohemians and personalities passing through – Robert de Niro, Lino Ventura and Pele
Dress: sporty; elegant
Service: with a smile
Reservations: advisable
Credit cards: AE, DC, Euro, Master Card

Shopping

EVERYTHING UNDER ONE ROOF
Ka De We 21–24 Tauentzienstrasse

FOR HIM
Selbach 195–196 Kurfürstendamm

FOR HER
Horn (women's fashion)
213 Kurfürstendamm

BEAUTY & HAIR
Walz Udo 27 Kurfürstendamm

JEWELLERY
Huelse 42 Kurfürstendamm

LOCAL SPECIALITIES
Mientus (men's fashion)
52 Kurfürstendamm
Boom (children's fashion)
91 Kurfürstendamm
Schrank Pelzhaus (furs)
197 Kurfürstendamm
Kiepert (books)
4–5 Hardenbergstrasse
Present Goldberg (gifts)
12 Kurfürstendamm
KPM (porcelain)
26a Kurfürstendamm
Goldpfeil (baggage & travel accessories)
16 Kurfürstendamm
Ka De We (food and beverages)
21 Tauentzienstrasse
Douglas (perfumery)
9 Tauentzienstrasse, Europa Center
Monica Bauer-Schlichtegroll (socks)
66 Kurfürstendamm

THE BEST OF ART
Brusberg (contemporary art)
213 Kurfürstendamm, Tel. 8 82 76 82
Fahnemann (contemporary art)
61 Fasanenstrasse, Tel. 8 83 98 97
Haas, Michael (Fine and contemporary
art) 5 Niebuhrstrasse, Tel. 8 82 70 06
Lietzow (contemporary art)
32 Knesebeckstrasse, Tel. 8 81 28 95
Nothelfer (contemporary art)
184 Uhlandstrasse, Tel. 8 81 44 05
Pels-Leusden (Fine Art)
58–60 Kurfürstendamm, Tel. 3 23 20 46
Poll (contemporary art)
7 Lützowplatz, Tel. 2 61 70 91
Redmann, Hans (contemporary art)
30 Fasanenstrasse, Tel. 8 81 11 35
Springer (contemporary art)
13 Fasanenstrasse, Tel. 3 13 90 88
Wewerka (contemporary art)
41a Fasanenstrasse, Tel. 8 82 67 39
Zellermayer-Lorenzen (contemporary
art) 14 Ludwigkirchstrasse
Tel. 8 83 41 44
Bethmann-Hollweg Antiquitäten GmbH
(works of art, furniture, paintings)
26 Fasanenstrasse, Tel. 8 82 11 62
Bredow Antiquitäten GmbH (antiques
and Art Nouveau)
13 Kalckreuthstrasse, Tel. 2 13 88 77
Dürlich u. Schwarzbaum (furniture,
works of art)
5 Keithstrasse, Tel.: 24 36 60
Faehte, Barbara (jewellery)
69 Fasanenstrasse, Tel. 8 81 67 83
Kunsthaus Klewer (furniture, paintings,
works of art)
12a Viktoria-Luise-Platz, Tel. 2 11 43 02
Spik, Leo (auctioneers)
66 Kurfürstendamm, Tel. 8 83 61 70

The City

When Konrad Adenauer from nearby Cologne managed to lobby his favourite retreat into becoming the capital of the Federal Republic, ambassadors and attachés around the world had to search for it on the map to find out where they were going. Bonn after Berlin – a decision comparable only to shifting the French government from Paris to Pau, or the Italian one from Rome to Rapallo. (In a few other countries, however, the power centres are not identical with the true capital cities either: Berne, The Hague, Ottawa, Canberra, Brasilia, Pretoria, even Washington without Kennedy or Reagan.) Bonn is beautiful, civilized and safe, at least. The romantic Rhine flowing by, fairy-tale castles and pilgrimage chapels looking down from the rolling hills, caravans of escorted limousines gliding through the avenues, and a multitude of races promenading across the market and through the quaint shopping streets of the historic centre produce a colourful potpourri of power and provincialism. John Le Carré called Bonn ›a small town in Germany‹, and the description fits. The capital of one of the world's leading industrial nations has maintained the character of a cosy Rhineland village, disturbed here and there by functional architecture that would insult Gropius and make E.M. Pei giggle. Beethoven's birthplace (he ist taken almost as seriously here as Mozart in Salzburg) is true to its cultural heritage – chamber concerts, castle concerts, music festivals honour Ludwig the Great, but also the opera house, the theatres and the Bahnhof Rolandseck (where engaged artists have created a unique home for festivals, exhibitions and parties) are pillars of the capital which is trying hard to live up to its title. More profane pleasures are not neglected, but for cosmopolitan elegance and swinging nightlife one will have to move on to Cologne and Düsseldorf. The receptions, dinners and galas given by the President, the Chancellor and – even more so – by the extrovert emissaries of some nations count as the favourite pastimes amongst the crème. The others can go VIPeople-watching through the bistros and gourmet restaurants around town. The lowest-keyed of the world's high-powered capitals is slowly coming of age and proving to businessmen and tourists alike that politics is not the only game in town.

Founded: B.C., as a Roman fort; first mentioned 69 A.D. by Tacitus – ›Castra Bonnensia‹; Bonn (German) – from the Latin.

Far-reaching events: 4th century – the first church is built; 1238–1794 – residence of the electors of Cologne – construction of the city walls; 1583 – the Bavarian Wittelsbachs become Electors; 1601 – Bonn the capital of the prince-bishops of Cologne; 18th century – Prince Clement August makes the city his residence and Bonn acquires her Baroque countenance; 1770 – Ludwig van Beethoven is born; 1798 – occupied by the French; 1815 – annexed by the Prussians; 1939–45 – old city fully destroyed; 1949 – Bonn becomes provisional capital of the Federal Republic and home of the Bundestag (and official capital in 1973).

Population: 300,00; capital of the Federal Republic

Postal code: D–5300   Telephone code: 228

Climate: mild; rather humid

Calendar of events: *Karneval* (Nov to Mar) – culminating in the days before *Ash Wednesday*, when the Chancellor turns his office over to a Carnival clown and nobody notices the difference; *Bonner Sommer* (May to Oct) – folklore, concerts and street theatre; ›*Pützchens Markt*‹ – folk festival and fair on the other side of the Rhine; *Beethoven Festival* (triennal, 1986, 1989, etc.).

Fairs and exhibitions: None. Bonn is a congress city with preferred themes of phosphorus chemistry, anaesthesia, neuro-surgery, gynaecology, etc.

Historical sights: *Münster* (11th–13th centuries) – landmark Romanesque-Gothic collegiate church; *Beethoven House* – the composer's birthplace, with the Beethoven archive in the *Haus zum Mohren* next door; *Rathaus* (1737) – rococo Town Hall; *Poppelsdorfer Schloß* (1715–56) – Franco-Italianate palace, now a geological museum; *Villa Hammerschmidt* – official residence of the President of Germany; *Alter Zoll* – souther bastion of the old city fortress.

Modern sights: *Kanzleramt* – a bronze statue by Henry Moore decorates the building from which the Chancellor of Germany rules; *Beethovenhalle* (1956–59) – the city's concert hall; *Stadttheater* – Bonn's daringly modern cultural centre; *Kasimir-Hagen-Sammlung* (1962) – with paintings and sculptures from the 14th to the 20th century; *Bahnhof Rolandseck* – cultural centre; *Museum Alexander König* – natural history.

Special attractions: a glimpse of the *score of the Eroica Symphony*, or a performance of it at the Beethovenhalle; dinner and political gossip at *Maternus*; an invitation to a reception at *Villa Hammerschmidt*; a chamber concert evening or a gala reception at *Schloß Brühl*; an evening of Arts and Music at *Bahnhof Rolandseck*; a stroll through the *Old Cemetery* – the German capital's Père-Lachaise; to glide down the *Balthasar Neumann staircase* at Schloß Brühl.

Important companies with headquarters in the city: *Agrob Wessel Servais* (import/export – at Alfter Witterschlick); *Bonner Zementwerk* (concrete); *Haribo* (sweets); *Klais* (organs); *Klöckner-Moeller* (electrical appliances); *Vereinigte Aluminium-Werke* (aluminium); *Verpoorten* (egg liqueur).

Airport: Köln–Bonn (Wahn), CGN; Tel.: 2203/402303–5; 28 km/18 miles; Lufthansa, Tel.: 2203/402404; VIP-Lounge, Tel.: 2203/402252

The Hideaway

STEIGENBERGER HOTEL

2–10 Bundeskanzlerplatz
D–5300 Bonn 1
Telephone: 2 01 91
Telex: 886 363 steib
Owning Company: Steigenberger Hotels AG
General Manager: Wolfgang D. Wehr
Affiliation/Reservation System: SRS (Steigenberger Reservation Service)
Number of rooms: 160 (8 suites)
Price range: DM 179–800
Credit cards: AE, DC, Visa, EC, Access, MC
Location: 2 km/1 mile from city centre
Built: 1967–1969 (renovated 1982)
Style: modern
Hotel amenities: garage, newsstand, shop, tobacconist, florist, hairstylist, house doctor, swimming pool

Main hall porter: Christa Reinartz
Room amenities: colour tv, mini-bar/refrigerator (pets allowed)
Bathroom amenities: bathrobe, hairdrier
Room service: 6.30/a.m. to 22.30/10.30 p.m.
Laundry/dry cleaning: same day
Conference rooms: 7 (14 to 280 persons), flip charts, overhead projector, slide projector, ballroom (up to 500 persons)
Bar: ›Ambassador‹ (12.00/a.m.–14.30/2.30 p.m. and 18.30/6.30 p.m.–24.00/12.00 p.m.) Rolf Ott (barman), English style

Restaurants: ›Ambassador‹ (12.00/a.m.–14.30/2.30 p.m. and 19.00/7.00 p.m.–23.00/11.00 p.m.) Julio Sanchez (maître), Uwe Trautmann (chef de cuisine), international cuisine, records, refined and exclusive style
›Im Atrium‹ (6.30/a.m.–21.00/9.00 p.m.) Wilfried Rasqui (maître), Bernd Raths (chef de cuisine), international cuisine, open-air terrace-café
Private dining-rooms: on request

Guests at the Steigenberger in Bonn are at the hub of events in the German capital. The hotel is located opposite the Federal Parliament buildings, the chancellor's offices and the Palais Schaumburg. The Steigenberger's functional façade conceals a comfortable intérieur which provides a setting good enough for capital tourists and anonymous VIPs from all walks of life. Red carpets are rolled out at the inner courtyard entrée as often as across the street, but in order to arrive at your Presidential Suite you will either have to take a flying carpet or the direct lift to the top, for the hotel occupies the upper floors allowing relative quiet and a splendid view. The eagle's nest bar and restaurant is among the best culinary locales as well as the city's best lookout.

KAISER KARL

56 Vorgebirgsstrasse
D–5300 Bonn 1
Telephone: 65 09 33
Telex: 886 856 k karl
Owner: Evelyn Koenigs
General Manager: Frieder C. Papsdorf
Affiliation/Reservation Systems: Best
Western Germany, Utell
Number of rooms: 52 (3 suites)
Price range: DM 140–200 (single)
DM 190–250 (double)
from DM 350 (suite)
Credit cards: AE, DC, EC, Visa, JCB
Location: central, 12 km/8 miles from
Cologne airport
Built: 1905 (opening in 1983)
Style: English classic
Hotel amenities: valet parking, garden,
indoor swimming pool
Room amenities: colour tv, mini-bar, safe,
video
Bathroom amenities: bathrobe, hairdrier,
telephone
Room service: 24 hours
Laundry/dry cleaning: same-day service
Conference rooms: 3 (up to 100 persons)
Bars: piano bar with pianist (16.00/4.00
p.m.–1.00/a.m.)
Restaurant: as of 1987
Private dining rooms: three (up to 100
guests)

*As if by appointment only, you will be let in
here after ringing the bell at this city palais.
If the initial impression of the Kaiser Karl
recalls the building's original function as a
turn-of-the century town-house of distinction and charm, the second must be that
the intérieur has been designed to combine
touches of Milanese design with the flair of
a country home. The overall feeling is one
of lightness and freshness, created by the
marble-floored and mirrored public areas,
which reflect the light from the glittering
chandeliers in the nooks and niches. The
bedrooms continue the theme with their
Venetian mirrors and distinctly Japanese
murals above the bed. To this have been
added fine English-style antiques, Oriental
carpets and numerous exquisite touches
which mark this small relais as an establishment of distinction. The service is as
familiar as the ambience. Breakfast is
served on Limoges porcelain in the bed-
room, the veranda-like dining room or – on
fine days – under white Italian sunshades
in the pretty inner courtyard. When you do
finally – and regretfully – have to depart,
you will happily find that the motorway
network or the international airport for
your onward journey are only minutes
away.*

Lunch

LE PETIT POISSON
23a Wilhelmstrasse
Telephone: 63 38 83
Owner/Manager/Chef de cuisine: Rudolf
Ludwig Reinarz
Closed: Sunday; Monday; four weeks in
July/August
Open: 12.00/a.m.–14.30/2.30 p.m. and
18.00/6 p.m.–22.00/10 p.m.
Cuisine: French (nouvelle)
Specialities: mushroom soup with garlic
croutons; salad of calves' sweetbreads
with chanterelles; fish with tarragon
sauce; fillet of venison in vermouth sauce
with pickled cherries
Location: near the district court (Land-
gericht)
Setting: Jugendstil bistro; occasional live
music (piano)
Amenities: air conditioning
Atmosphere: friendly and fashionable
Clientèle: judges; gentlemen of the jury;
politicians; premiers and presidents – not
to mention stars of stage and screen
Dress: fairly conservative
Service: skilful and unobtrusive
Reservations: essential (dogs allowed)
Price range: moderately high
Credit cards: DC, Euro

Lunch

SCHAARSCHMIDT
14 Brüdergasse
Telephone: 65 44 07
Owner/Manager/Chef de cuisine: Michael Schaarschmidt
Closed: Sunday; Saturday lunchtime;
three weeks in August
Open: 12.00/a.m.–15.00/3 p.m. and
18.00/6 p.m.–24.00/12 p.m.
Cuisine: French (nouvelle)
Specialities: surprise menus; fish pot-au-
feu; turbot in champagne; calves' sweetbreads with chanterelles and sweet basil;
medaillons of angler fish (Lotte) on leaf
spinach in paprika butter; saddle of rabbit in mustard and tarragon sauce with
spinach noodles; breast of duckling à
l'orange
Location: pedestrian precinct
Setting: small dining room; Biedermeier
furnishing; view of kitchen
Amenities: wood-panelled bar; terrace
(June–August, weather permitting)
Atmosphere: welcoming and business-
like, without sacrificing comfort
Clientèle: local habitués; unsung celebri-
ties; nice people; passers-by; men-about-
town
Dress: casual to conservative
Service: charmingly directed by Birgit
Schaarschmidt
Reservations: essential
Price range: moderate
Credit cards: DC, Euro

Dinner

LE MARRON
35 Provinzialstrasse
Lengsdorf (4 km/3 miles)
Telephone: 25 32 61
Owner/Manager: Hans-Josef Schlösser
Closed: Saturday; Wednesday evening;
Sunday lunchtime
Open: 12.00/a.m.–14.00/2 p.m. and
19.00/7 p.m.–20.30/8.30 p.m.
Cuisine: French with a German accent
Chef de cuisine: René Sautement (ex-
Chez Alex in Cologne)
Specialities: terrine of guinea-fowl; con-
sommé with bone marrow dumplings;
saddle of veal in morel mushroom cream
sauce; salmon on cress sauce; fillet of
beef with snails
Location: in Lengsdorf, 4 km/3 miles
south-west of Bonn
Setting: rustic; unrendered bricks,
wooden beams, open fireplace, pretty
tableware
Amenities: private dining rooms; bar
Atmosphere: picture-postcard charm with
a hint of romance
Clientèle: businessmen tired of Bonn; diplomats tired of Bad Godesberg; media-
men tired of both – plus a few local lovers
with cause for celebration
Dress: not too outlandish or untidy
Service: very pleasant without being ob-
trusive
Reservations: advisable to essential
Price range: moderately high
Credit cards: AE, DC, Euro

Dinner

KORKEICHE
104 Lyngsbergstrasse
Telephone: 34 78 97
Owner/Manager/Chef de cuisine: Rainer-
Maria Halbedel
Closed: Monday; four weeks in July
Open: 18.00/6 p.m.–24.00/12 p.m.
Cuisine: French (nouvelle)
Specialities: surprise menus; fish dishes;
calves' kidneys with green beans; terrine
of ham with caramelized onions; rabbit
in aspic with cucumber sauce; raspberry
and redcurrant mould (Rote Grütze) with
vanilla sauce; sorbet of blood orange
Location: Bad Godesberg – 6 km (4
miles) south of city centre
Setting: historic timbered building; prettily rustic; antique paraphernalia, Ches-
terfield with dolls, scatter cushions, lace
tablecloths and dried-flower arrangements
Amenities: open-air dining in courtyard
(restricted menu); car park
Atmosphere: nostalgic; homely
Clientèle: diplomats; members of parliament; civil servants
Dress: no special requirements
Service: dresses à la Laura Ashley and
plenty of charm

Reservations: essential
Price range: moderate
Credit cards: none

Lunch

MATERNUS
3 Löbestrasse
Bad Godesberg (8 km/5 miles)
Telephone: 36 28 51
Owner/Manager: Ria Maternus
Closed: Sunday
Open: 12.00/a.m.–15.00/3p.m. and 18.00/6 p.m.–24.00/12 p.m.
Cuisine: traditional dishes of a very high standard
Chef de cuisine: Erwin Drescher
Specialities: sole Nantua; wolf-fish in Chablis with shrimps; duckling with orange sauce; lamb
Location: in Bad Godesberg, 8 km (5 miles) south of Bonn
Setting: German Renaissance; comfortable but elegant – well-chosen antiques
Atmosphere: the non-plus-ultra among meeting places for the stars on the political horizon, imbued with the all-pervasive charm of its legendary owner
Clientèle: prime ministers, cabinet ministers, permanent under-secretaries, ambassadors – men in high places and those aspiring to join them
Dress: conventional (pin-stripes allowed)
Service: superlative
Reservations: recommended
Price range: moderate
Credit cards: AC, DC, Euro

Dinner

WIRTSHAUS ST. MICHAEL
26 Brunnenallee
Bonn 2 – Bad Godesberg
Telephone: 36 47 65
Owner/Managers: Jürgen Martin and Friedrich Braunbarth
Closed: Sunday; public holidays; three weeks during the local school summer-holidays
Open: 19.00/7 p.m.–23.00/11 p.m.
Cuisine: French
Chef de cuisine: Friedrich Braunbarth
Specialities: saddle of lamb; pepper steak; poularde à la viennoise
Location: in Bad Godesberg, near the park (Stadtpark)
Setting: historic building; comfortable mélange of periods and styles; antique furnishing
Amenities: private dining rooms (100 persons); bar; outdoor dining on terrace; car park
Atmosphere: intimate
Clientèle: colourful and cosmopolitan – with the occasional local habitué
Dress: as you like it
Service: professionally welcoming
Reservations: advisable (no dogs)
Price range: moderately high
Credit cards: not accepted

Café

BONNER KAFFEEHAUS
Remigiusplatz
Telephone: 65 55 59
Owner/Manager: Bonner Kaffeehaus Gastronomiebetriebe GmbH/Rudolf F. Nottrodt, Ute Brümmer
Closed: never
Open: 9/a.m.–24.00/12 p.m. and Sunday: 10.30/a.m.–24.00/12 p.m.
Specialities: home-made cakes and gâteaux
Location: in the central mall between Marktplatz and Münsterplatz
Setting: small tables, wall-to-wall carpet, lots of plants
Amenities: downstairs the „Römerkeller", a wine bar in an old wine cellar
Atmosphere: elegant; soothing background music by Beethoven, the city's most famous son
Clientèle: from students coming for a quick expresso from the university around the corner to elderly ladies meeting for their afternoon coffee and cake
Service: students as waiters/waitresses

Meeting Point

BONNGOUT
4 Remigiusplatz
Telephone: 63 72 12
Closed: never
Open: 8.30/a.m.–3.00/a.m.
Location: central, in the capital's attractive and bustling pedestrian district
Setting: the all-day/all-night café in Bonn; understated décor
Amenities: café, tea-room, snacks available
Atmosphere: informal; lively and yet relaxing; a perfect spot if you want to take a break and have a chat with your colleague, your companion or the occupant of the next table
Clientèle: anybody who wants to see and wants to be seen
Dress: anything goes
Service: friendly and efficient

Bar

PRO-CONTRA
12 Josefstrasse
Telephone: 63 31 77
Owner/Manager: Stephan Huschban
Closed: never
Open: 21.00/9 p.m.–3.00/a.m.
Location: central; near Bertha-von-Suttner-Platz

Setting: elegant English-style bar with gallery and collages on the walls
Amenities: snacks and light meals; live music every day except Monday
Atmosphere: welcoming, nostalgic and relaxing
Clientèle: local habitués; discerning, discriminating and successful
Service: feminine charm
Reservations: for large groups only
Credit cards: AE

Nightclub

OCTAGON
Mallwitzstrasse
Telephone: 33 44 52
Owner/Managers: Reiner Meschede, Horst Prill
Closed: Monday, Wednesday, Sunday
Open: 21.00/9 p.m.–2/a.m.; weekend 22.00/10 p.m.–5/a.m.
Location: Bad Godesberg, next to the stadium
Setting: warm; exclusive; high ceiling; like a huge living room; Bistro-setting with lots of windows
Amenities: 2 bars: one Caribbean, one for champagne, 150 seats on different levels
Atmosphere: very elegant and chic
Clientèle: all ages; politicians, embassy people, celebrities
Dress: no jeans and sneakers
Service: fast and friendly
Reservations: advisable
Price range: very moderate
Credit cards: DC

Shopping

EVERYTHING UNDER ONE ROOF
Kaufhof 20 Remigiusstrasse

FOR HIM
Daniels & Co. 31 Markt, City-Passage

FOR HER
Exclusivité Waltzinger J.M.H.
2a Martinsplatz

BEAUTY & HAIR
Michels P. 7 Oxfordstrasse

JEWELLERY
Dix J. 1 Remigiusstrasse

LOCAL SPECIALITIES
Cigarrenhaus Schultz (tobacco)
Sternstraße 2
Moderaum Kersting (women's fashion)
4a Am Michaelshof, Bonn 2 – Bad Godesberg
Carrussell – Mode für Kinder (children's fashion)
4a Am Michaelshof, Bonn 2 – Bad Godesberg
Boecker (furs)
17 Wenzelgasse
Universitatsbuchhandlung Bouvier (books)
32 Am Hof
Kleine Vitrine (gifts)
52 Moltkestrasse, Bonn 2 – Bad Godesberg
Schugt (baggage & travel accessories)
3 Am Neutor
Spanischer Garten (food and beverages)
6 Theaterplatz, Bonn 2 – Bad Godesberg
Ruedell, Herbert (perfumery)
10 Am Fronhof, Bonn 2 – Bad Godesberg
& 1a Alte Bahnhofstrasse
Stendebach, Klaus (bakery/confisérie)
27 Friedrichallee

THE BEST OF ART
Hennemann (modern art)
17 Poppelsdorfer Allee, Tel. 22 37 69
Linssen (modern art)
47 Prinz-Albert-Strasse, Tel. 21 89 09
Magers, Philomene (contemporary art)
13 Händelstrasse, Tel. 65 05 75
Pudelko (fine art)
11 Heinrich-von-Kleist-Strasse, Tel. 22 42 30

The City

Germany's ›other‹ gateway to the world hardly collects any of the sparkle flying off the brilliant galaxy of North-Sea neighbour Hamburg. Beauty, grandeur, power, culture and the attitude to go along seem all assembled ›over there‹, a short sail eastward. But Bremen keeps her head up with Hanseatic dignity and tradition, perfectly in line with the free spirit she has demonstrated throughout her 1200-year-old history, allegorically represented by the Grimm Brothers' ›Town Musicians of Bremen‹ (a quartet of animals revolting against slavery), founded in bronze on the market place. The country's second largest port city – and smallest state within the federation – lacks nothing of the worldliness of her big sister and can claim a few superlatives of her own (largest container terminal of Europe, biggest storage for coffee and cotton, production site for Europe's Eureka Spacelab), but the visitor is more likely to be attracted by the sizzling harbour activities, the artistic Renaissance architecture of the patrician merchants' homes and the refined intérieurs, by the innumerable parks, the world's richest rhododendron grounds and the romantic heather hinterland as well as by the northern functionality embedded in a sincere warmth and hospitality. The air is inspiring, the cuisine is hearty, the communication is correct – and promises are kept. No frills, no show, no disappointment. (Even the weather is better than prophesied by the burghers.) The social Mount Everest is the all-male, all-prestige Schaffermahlzeit in February (a ritual dinner at the magnificent 15th-century town hall for men of power and influence) to which one can be invited but once in a lifetime; less climbing is necessary to reach an invitation to the Eiswette dinner in January (commemorating a traditional test-crossing of the frozen river), and no effort is required in order to indulge in the popular pleasures of the autumn Freimarkt (the city's own funfair Oktoberfest). Bremen is not only genuinely beautiful, but also authentically gay – at second sight. Business, however, is sacred and loved as dearly as the stroll through the bohemian Schnoor quarter and museum-like Böttcher Street, the nordic snacks à la nouvelle at Bremen's bistro-Bocuse, Grashoff, the leisure hours at the lakeside Bürgerpark, the stately festivities at the splendid Parkhotel. Weekends are spent at picturesque artists' colony Worpswede, established as one of the corner pillars of the Expressionist triangle (next to Berlin and Munich) by local daughter Paula Becker-Modersohn whose most important – and beautiful – works adorn her one-time private residence in Böttcher Street. Ultima ratio for this unpretentiously noble city, however, remains the open sea – perspective of the world.

Founded: 787, as a bishopric.

Far-reaching events: 845 – the bishopric becomes an archbishopric; 965 – Emperor Otto I grants the city market privileges; 1358 – Bremen joins the Hanseatic League; 1646 – Bremen a free imperial city; 1654 and 1666 – wars with Sweden; 1783 – start of direct trade with North America; 1810 – occupied by Napoléon's troops; 1815 – independent status restored; 1827 – building of the new harbour, Bremerhaven, at the mouth of the Weser River; 1866 – joins the North German Confederation; 1871 – constituent member of the German Empire; 1939–45 – heavy damage; 1947 – becomes a Free Hanseatic City and capital of the smallest German state.

Population: 550,000; capital of the state of Bremen.

Postal code: D–2800   **Telephone code:** 4 21

Climate: temperate but rather wet (maritime influence); sea breeze in summer.

Calendar of events: *Schaffermahlzeit* (Feb) – gala dinner for local social élite; *Osterwiese* (Mar/Apr) – folkloric celebration of Spring; *Flea Market* (May to Oct); *Spring Market* (May) – in the Vegesack district; *Vegesack Harbour Festival* (Aug/Sep); *Maritime Week* (Sep) – a navigational extravaganza; *Bremen Free Market* (last two weeks in Oct) – a north German folk festival; *Christmas Market* (Dec).

Fairs and exhibitions: *BOOT-BREMEN* (Feb/Mar) – boat show; *AUTOVISION* (Mar/Apr) – motor show; *HAFA-BREMEN* (May) – home and family; *TIER + NATUR/BIOTA* (Aug/Sep) – animals, nature and health; *IMMOBILIA* (Sep) – construction and housing; *BAUEN & WOHNEN* (Sep/Oct) – building, living, furnishing.

Historical sights: *Market Square* – dominated by the Gothic *City Hall* (15th century) – with a Weser Renaissance transformation; *Schütting* (1536–38) – across from the City Hall, former merchant's guild house, with a much gabled façade; *St. Peter's Cathedral* (1042) – Romanesque and Gothic grandeur; *Kunsthalle* – contemporary art museum with 19th and 20th-century French and German paintings; *Gerhard Marcks House* – classicistic building with a museum of modern sculpture; *German Maritime Museum* (in Bremerhaven); *Focke Museum* – Hanseatic mementoes and local archaeology.

Special attractions: a stroll through the *Old Town*, the *Schnoor Quarter* and *Böttcher Street*; dinner and a wine-tasting to sample some of the 600 German wines at the *Ratskeller*; an afternoon in the *Rhododendron Park* in season; an excursion to *Worpswede*.

Important companies with headquarters in the city: *Beck & Co* (brewery); *Bremer Vulkan* (container shipbuilding); *Daimler Benz* (small car division); *Eduscho* (coffee); *Erno* (aerospace); *HAG General Foods* (coffee); *Jacobs* (coffee); *Kellogg* (food); *Klöckner* (steel); *Krupp Atlas Elektronik* (electronics); *Lloyd Dynamo* (electricity); *Martin Brinkmann* (tobacco); *Messerschmitt-Bölkow-Blohm* (airbus planes); *Nordmende* (electrical appliances); *Nordsee* (fishing, food); *Seebeck* (dockyards – at Bremerhaven); *Wilkens* (silverware).

Airport: Bremen-Neustadt, BRE; Tel.: 5 59 51, Lufthansa, Tel.: 5 59 25; 6 km/4 miles.

The Headquarters

PARK HOTEL

Im Bürgerpark
D-2800 Bremen
Telephone: 3 40 80
Telex: 244 343 park
Owning Company: Park Hotel GmbH
General Manager: Wilhelm Wehrmann
Affiliation/Reservation Systems: The
Leading Hotels of the World, Steigen-
berger Reservation Service
Number of rooms: 150 (12 suites)
Price range: DM 195–235 (single)
           DM 250–280 (double)
           DM 390–550 (suite)
Credit cards: AE, DC, EC, MC, Visa
Location: 1.5 km/1 mile from city centre;
10 km/6 miles from airport
Built: 1956; recently renovated
Style: European
Hotel amenities: garage, valet parking,
grand piano, beauty salon, hairstylist,
newsstand, boutique, tabacconist (pets al-
lowed)
Room amenities: colour tv (remote con-
trol), video, mini-bar/refrigerator, radio
Room service: 6.00/a.m.–24.00/12 a.m.
Laundry/dry cleaning: same day
Conference rooms: 10 (up to 800 persons),
flip-chart, simultaneous translation facilities, secretarial services, ballroom
Bar: ›Halali Bar‹ (18.00/6.00 p.m.–
2.00/a.m.), Johannes Bak (barman), pianist, records, dance bar
Restaurant: ›Park Restaurant‹ (12.00/
p.m.–15.00/3.00 p.m. and 18.00/6.00
p.m.–23.00/11.00 p.m.), Henri Precht
(maître), Hans-Jürgen Rupp (chef de cuisine), nouvelle cuisine, traditional style
décor, open-air dining

*The Hanseatic metropolis never had to suf-
fer under the dubious image of being the
epicentre of joie de vivre, but no-one can
deny the dignified style of this Nordic city,
even when it comes to frolics and festivities.
And no-one, native or visitor would dream
of any other arena for a conference, a family affair or a gala but the stately Park. The
landscaped ›jardin anglais‹ behind the hotel calls to mind the surroundings of a patrician residence, complete with artificial
lake, fountains, swans and boats for hire,
while on the other side it's only a short walk
to the shopping malls, the conservative
branch offices of shipbuilders, container
companies and traditional trading houses.
Bremen's Park Hotel, one of the leading
hotels in the land, is the only place in town
you would want to be, for business and
pleasure. La grande entrée gives you the
right feeling, the view puts you into the
right mood and the service is provided by
the right people. Wilhelm Wehrmann sees
to it that nothing is overdone while keeping
the standard of comfort, cuisine and calm
at the highest level – Hanseatic average.*

Meierei im Bürgerpark
under the management of the Park Hotel

Lunch

LE BISTRO
80 Contrescarpe
Telephone: 1 47 49
Owner/Manager: Jürgen Schmidt
Closed: Sunday
Open: (Monday–Friday) 10.00/a.m.–
18.30/6.30 p.m., (Saturday) 10.00/a.m.–
13.00/1 p.m.
Cuisine: French (nouvelle) with a regional touch
Chef de cuisine: Rüdiger König
Specialities: North Sea shrimp soup; ragoût of North Sea fish with fresh herb sauce; saddle of rabbit in mustard sauce; salmon in sorrel sauce; peaches in redcurrant sabayon; walnut parfait
Location: in the Hillmann-Passage of the Plaza Hotel; near the main station (Hauptbahnhof)
Setting: typical small bistro with closely-packed tables and waiters in shirtsleeves; wine bar with small delicatessen counter
Amenities: delicatessen food store; bar; fine view
Atmosphere: casually chic
Clientèle: businessmen, gourmets and Bremen Beau Monde
Dress: come-as-you-please
Service: confident, knowledgeable and efficient
Reservations: essential (no pets)
Price range: moderately high
Credit cards: DC

Dinner

MEIEREI IM BÜRGERPARK
Im Bürgerpark
Telephone: 3 40 86 19
Affiliations: Châine des Rôtisseurs; Food and Beverage Management Association; Club zu Bremen
Owner/Manager: Park Hotel GmbH/ Wilhelm Wehrmann
Closed: never
Open: 11.00/a.m.–22.30/10.30 p.m.; Lunch 12.00/a.m.–14.30/2.30 p.m.; 18.00/6 p.m.–22.00/10 p.m.
Cuisine: nouvelle
Chefs de cuisine: Bernhard Koller and Joachim Himmelskamp
Specialities: according to season; Bremen fish soup; pickled herring (Matjes) with green beans; calves' liver in cassis sauce; partridge with Weinkraut; homemade noodles with gorgonzola; cranberry parfait with cassis sauce mousseline
Location: in the Bürgerpark, 2 km (1 mile) from city centre; 2 km (1 mile) from the Park Hotel
Setting: historic building (former nobleman's residence) in park landscape with artificial lakes; four dining rooms furnished in understated Hanseatic style; open fireplace
Amenities: private dining rooms (60 persons); outdoor dining on large terrace; car park
Atmosphere: typically North German; unostentatious, but with a certain comfortable stylishness
Clientèle: Bremen's Haute Bourgeoisie en fête and en famille; Hanseatic merchants and visitors from Stockholm to Strasbourg
Dress: tends towards the conservative
Service: friendly and willing, but sometimes run off their feet
Reservations: advisable
Price range: moderate
Credit cards: AE, DC, Euro, Visa

Lunch

COMTUREI
31 Ostertorstrasse
Telephone: 32 50 50
Owner/Manager: Harms Sebbes
Closed: Sunday
Open: 11.30/a.m.–14.30/2.30 p.m. and 17.00/5 p.m.–0.30/12.30 p.m.
Cuisine: French
Chef de cuisine: Jan Sebbes
Specialities: ›au goût du marché‹; weekly changing menu of fresh fish, meat and vegetables prepared according to the wishes of individual customers
Location: in the heart of the old city (Altstadt)
Setting: one of the oldest restaurants in Bremen; 13th-century cellar with vaulted ceiling
Amenities: air conditioning; car park
Atmosphere: friendly and welcoming
Clientèle: local High Society and tourists
Dress: casual but stylish (no running shorts, ancient track suits or down-at-heel tennis shoes)
Service: professional and courteous
Reservations: advisable
Price range: average to rather expensive
Credit cards: AE, DC, Euro

Dinner

RATSKELLER
Am Markt
Telephone: 32 09 36
Owner/Manager: Bremer Ratskeller Gastronomie/Lothar Plewnia
Closed: never
Open: 11.30/a.m.–15.00/3 p.m. and 18.00/6 p.m.–22.30/10.30 p.m.
Cuisine: unpretentious, with a strong local accent
Chef de cuisine: Walter Böschen
Specialities: Bremen chicken casserole (Bremer Kükenragout); Bremen rasp-

berry and redcurrant mould (Rote Grütze); game; over 600 different wines (500,000 bottles; ½ million litres in barrels) – the oldest (but not necessarily the most drinkable) being vintage 1727
Location: in the heart of the city, by the old market place
Setting: in the cellars of the 15th-century town hall; vaulted ceilings; spacious main hall and ›Bacchus-cellar‹; long wooden tables; wood-panelled séparées (Priölken)
Amenities: private dining rooms (150 persons)
Atmosphere: steeped in tradition – an institution in the town for more than 500 years; companionable to noisy
Clientèle: tinker, tailor, soldier, tourist ... popular meeting-place for all and sundry; essential stopover for all visitors to the town
Dress: jeans to jacket and tie
Service: fast but never furious
Reservations: advisable (dogs allowed)
Prive range: inexpensive to moderate
Credit cards: AE, DC, Euro

Henseler (gifts)
56 Sögestrasse
Meissen (porcelain)
162 Am Wall
Sonnek (baggage & travel accessories)
26–27 Schüsselkorb
Schmidt Grashoff (food and beverages)
Hillmann Passage
Teehaus Weyh (tea)
30 Martersburg/›Schnoor‹
Eickhoff Schuhe (shoes)
20 Hillmannplatz

THE BEST OF ART
Graphisches Kabinett
Wolfgang Werner (Fine Art)
la Rembertistrasse, Tel. 32 74 78
Michael, Uwe (modern art)
106 Fedelhören, Tel. 32 38 60
Neuse (18th/19th-century antiques)
2 Franz-Liszt-Strasse, Tel. 32 56 42
Trüjen, Monica (glass)
73 Parkstrasse, Tel. 34 70 35
Bolland & Marotz (auctioneers)
19 Fedelhören, Tel. 32 82 82

Shopping

EVERYTHING UNDER ONE ROOF
Karstadt   5–33 Obernstrasse

FOR HIM
Stiesing   35 Sögestrasse

FOR HER
Toelke, Dieter 5–7 Grosse Undestrasse/Kramerzeile

BEAUTY & HAIR
Intercoiffeur Kroupa, Roman
62/64 Ostertorsteinweg

JEWELLERY
Wilkens & Danger   61 Sögestrasse

LOCAL SPECIALITIES
M. Niemeyer (tobacco)
5 Knochenhauerstrasse
Bischof, Rolf (women's fashion)
47 Sögestrasse
L'uomo (men's fashion)
41 Knochenhauerstrasse
Hennes & Mauritz (children's fashion)
31–33 Sögestrasse
Harms (leather fashion)
157 Am Wall
Graupner (furs)
2 Kramerzeile
Melchers, Otto (books)
60 Sögestrasse
Lilac (gifts) 153 Am Wall

The City

The city does not smell of 4711. Large, loud, lively and devoid of the sophistication of Düsseldorf, the stylishness of Hamburg and the splendour of Munich, Germany's oldest and holiest metropolis is nevertheless as cosmopolitan and captivating as the others, with neon-light realism, down-to-earth life style and an overwhelming nonchalance, adorned with the best sense of humour – a quality the country is not exactly famous for. Ex-mayor and Father of the Federal Republic, Konrad Adenauer, brightened many a parliamentary confrontation with it, while Nobel-Prize laureate Heinrich Böll's writings reflect the refined lightness at heart coupled with profoundly human warmth, and during the endless carnival season, Rhenish joie de vivre seems to win a final victory over Teutonic formal stodginess. For the professional visitor, there is enough business to keep him busy: Cologne is the fourth largest city in the country and lives up to its position in production and commerce (from cars to cologne, of course); for the traveller in search of culture, comfort and entertainment, there is more to experience than he will have time for. The imposing cathedral's spires beckon the way for the stranger from afar and from all corners of the city – everything of interest, fame and fun lies within the chime of the bells of this greatest Gothic grail, anyhow. Grand hotels, haute cuisine and fine arts blend with local folklore, exotic pleasures and historic affluence in a carousel around the temple, with pedestrian shopping malls full of status boutiques and beer bistros allowing for superficial joys. Cologne is also the mecca for avant-garde music – from Karl-Heinz Stockhausen to rock and pop à l'allemande, and for nouvelle-vague art – from the Ludwig collection to the galleries to the fairs; Cologne is the centre of modern art in Europe. As the headquarters of the church, secular joys and les beaux arts, this stronghold of pleasures within the nation of severity attracts the whole world – and converts sceptics to enthusiasts.

Founded: 38 B.C. as ›oppidum ubiorum‹; Köln (German) – ›colony‹ (from the Latin-Colonia Claudia Ara Agrippinensi).

Far-reaching events: 462 – conquered by the Franks; 785 – an archbishopric and increased commercial prosperity; 13th–17th centuries – power-struggle between the ruling prince-bishops and the bourgeoisie; Albertus Magnus, Thomas Aquinas and Meister Ekkehard make Cologne an intellectual and cultural capital; 1388 – founding of the university; 1794 – conquered by the French; 1815 – returned to Prussia; 1880 – the cathedral is completed; 1939–45 – 95% of the city destroyed in the Second World War; 1945 – cathedral and city restored and rebuilt.

Population: 1 million, fourth largest city in the Federal Republic.

Postal code: D–5000   **Telephone code:** 2 21

Climate: generally mild; rather wet; almost no snow in winter.

Calendar of events: *Carnival* (Feb–Mar) – one of the biggest pre-Lenten celebrations in Germany, full of folklore and topical satire; *Easter Festival* (Easter to beginning of May) – Easter fair; *Mühlheim Corpus Christi* (Jun) – procession on the Rhine; *Kölner Sommer* (Jun–Sep) – changing cultural programmes; *Cologne Press Ball* (autumn) – international journalists' gala; *Europe Prize Cup* (Oct) – horse race.

Fairs and exhibitions: *INTERNATIONAL FURNITURE FAIR* (Jan&Jul); *ITS COLOGNE* (Jan) - international fashion trends; *ISM* (Jan) – international sweet fair; *DOMOTECHNICA* (Feb) – household appliances; *INTERNATIONAL MEN'S FASHION FAIR; INTER-JEANS KÖLN* (Feb & Aug) – jeans and sportswear fashions; *INTERNATIONAL IRON GOODS FAIR* (Mar); *WIRE* (Apr) – cables; *IN-ATEC* (Apr) – food and nutrition; *OPTICA* (Apr) – optometrics; INTERNATIONAL COMPUTER EXHIBITION (Jun); *PHOTOKINA* (Sep, biennial) – film, photography video; *IFMA* (Sep) – bicycles and motorcycles; *SPOGA* (Sep) – sports, camping and garden exhibition; *ORGATECHNIK* (Oct) – office equipment and systems; *ART COLOGNE* (Nov) – international art market.

Historical sights: *Cathedral* (1248–1880) – the first and biggest Gothic edifice in Germany – a city landmark, with the *Three Kings' Shrine*; *Roman-Germanic Museum* – the Dionysos Mosaic and other antiquities; *Wallraf-Richartz and Ludwig Museum* – Cologne masters, from the 14th century to Pop Art; *Römerturm* (50 A.D.) – fully preserved corner tower of the old city wall; *Overstolzenhaus* (13th century) – with a monumental gabled staircase and Gothic wall paintings inside.

Moderns sights: *Rheinseilbahn* – Europe's only electric monorail, a good way to view the city; *KEFKA-Theatre* – Europe's only pantomime theatre.

Special attractions: the *Carnival* season; mass at the *Cathedral*; a *gallery tour*; a night browse through the *avant-garde pop arenas*; the old waiting room of the *Main Station*.

Important companies with headquarters in the city: *Bayer* (pharmaceuticals, at Leverkusen); *Citroën* (cars); *Colonia* (insurance); *EMI-Electrola* (records); *Felten & Guilleaume* (cables, telecommunications); *Ford* (cars); *Gerling Konzern* (insurance); *Kaufhof* (department stores); *Klöckner-Humboldt-Deutz* (lorries and machinery); *Kölnisch Wasser 4711* (cosmetics); *Lufthansa* (airline); *Madaus* (pharmaceuticals); *Nattermann* (pharmaceuticals); *Pfeifer & Langen* (sugar); *Renault* (cars); *Reynolds Tobacco* (cigarettes); *Sony* (audio-visual equipment); *Stollwerck AG/Imhoff* (sweets); *Toyota* (cars); *Villeroy & Boch* (porcelain); *Wolff, Otto* (industrial production).

Airport: Köln-Bonn (Wahn), CGN; Tel.: 2203/402303–5, Lufthansa, Tel.: 2203/402404–5; VIP Lounge, Tel.: 2203/402252.

The Headquarters

EXCELSIOR HOTEL ERNST

1–5 Trankgasse,
D–5000 Cologne 1
Telephone: 27 01
Telex: 8 882 645 exce
Owner: The Kracht Family
General Manager: Siegfried Breunig
Affiliation/Reservation Systems: The
Leading Hotels of the World, SRS (Steigenberger Reservation Service), Preferred Hotels Worldwide
Number of rooms: 146 (16 suites)
Price range: DM 216–275 (single)
            DM 285–340 (double)
            DM 800–900 (suite)
Credit cards: AE, DC, EC, MC
Location: central, opposite the Cathedral
Built: 1863 (recently renovated)
Style: elegant (interior by Count Pilati)
Hotel amenities: garage, valet parking,
house limousine service, beauty salon,
massage, newsstand, boutique
Main hall porter: Hans Brehm
Room amenities: colour tv (remote control), minibar (pets allowed)
Bathroom amenities: bidet, bathrobe,
hairdrier in some rooms, telephone
Room service: 6.00/a.m.–24.00/12 p.m.
Conference rooms: 9 (up to 100/120 persons), ballroom
Bar: ›Piano‹ (10.00/a.m.–1.00/a.m.) Arnaldo Bonetti (barman), pianist, interior
with honey mahogany and leather seating
Restaurant: ›Hanse-Stube‹ (12.00/a.m.–
14.30/2.30 p.m. and 18.30/6.30 p.m.–
22.30/10.30 p.m.) Wolfgang Nestler (chef
de cuisine), French and international cuisine, Hanseatic style, open-air dining;
›Excelsior-Keller‹ (17.00/5.00 p.m.–
24.00/12.00 p.m., closed Saturday and
Sunday) light meals, informal

*Cologne's stately residence across from the
majestic Dom was opened 120 years ago by
the interior decorator to the court – twenty
years before the official inauguration of
the cathedral itself. The re-decorator of the
present, Count Pilati, has continued the
aristocratic path of this private Grand Hotel and given it the obligatory luxury, from
marble baths to silken salons. When you
are used to the exemplary style and service
of Family Kracht's other auberge de renommé, the Baur au Lac in Zurich, you
will not be astonished about the Excelsior-
Ernst's standards and Siegfried Breunig's
staff. Voiturier and concierge, location and
lobby, bar and restaurant are in line with
the image, light colours, soft materials,
space. The spontaneity of the personnel
keeps you joyful and in a wordly mood –
despite the intimidating divinity next door.*

The Hideaway

SCHLOSS AUEL

D–5204 Lohmar 21, Wahlscheid,
Siegkreis (24 km/15 miles)
Telephone: (22 06)20 41/43
Telex: 88 75 10 auel
General Manager: Baron de la Valette
Affiliation/Reservation System: Gast im
Schloß, ADAC, AvD, Automobilclub
Belgium and Switzerland
Number of rooms: 23 (3 suites)
Price range: DM 80–140 (single)
           DM 120–200 (double)
           DM 130–200 (suite)
Credit cards: AE, DC, EC
Location: 7 km//4 miles from city centre,
15 km/9 miles from airport
Built: 1763 (renovated 1950, 1972)
Style: castle; antique, historical
Hotel amenities: indoor swimming pool,
sauna, heliport
Room amenities: (pets allowed)
Room service: 7.00/a.m.–23.00/11 p.m.
Laundry/dry cleaning: on request
Conference rooms: 5 (10 to 150 persons),
flip charts, overhead projector, slide pro-
jector, screen, ballroom
Sports (nearby): riding, tennis, swim-
ming, fishing, walking
Restaurant: ›Rôtisserie St. George‹
(12.00/a.m.–22.30/10.30 p.m.) W. Dieck-
mann (maître), M. Flinzner (chef de cuisine), French, regional and international
cuisine, open-air dining
Private dining rooms: two

*Half-hidden amongst the trees and the
rolling hills of the Aggertal, only twenty minutes' drive from Cologne or Bonn, is a
hideaway castle which combines an authentic Baroque ambience with twentieth-
century amenities. Built in the eighteenth
century on the site of a medieval moated
fortress, Schloss Auel has been in the
hands of the de la Valette family for more
than two hundred years. From the curving
staircase in the black-and-white flagged
hall to the gilt-and-marble altar in the private chapel, from the four-poster in which
Napoléon slept to the huge fireplace in the
restaurant, this aristocratic auberge exudes historic charm. Once here, you can
shake off the city dust and the three-piece
grey flannel. For active relaxation, the hotel can offer a swimming pool, tennis courts
and a bowling alley. Guests with a more
leisurely approach can enjoy delightful
walks in the private park and the countryside around the castle, or take a fishing rod
to the river. You have to do justice to the excellent food served in the Rôtisserie St.
George with its tiled floor and log fire. On
a sunny Sunday there are few places in the
vicinity as popular – and pretty – for lunch
and dinner, al fresco dining. It's best to
stay altogether. Each of the hotel rooms
and suites has an individual style, but all
are utterly comfortable. Besides being the
ideal place for a brief break, Schloss Auel
could be an excellent venue for a conference without distractions.*

Lunch

HANSESTUBE
Excelsior Hotel Ernst
1–5 Trankgasse
Telephone: 27 01/Telex: 8 88 26 45
Owner/Manager: Romain Witt
Closed: never
Open: 12.00/a.m.–14.30/2.30 p.m. and
18.30/6.30 p.m.–23.30/10.30 p.m.
Cuisine: French and international
Chef de cuisine: Wolfgang Nestler
Specialities: médaillons of veal in morel
mushroom cream sauce; parfait ›Grand
Marnier‹; rabbit liver in Calvados with
tarragon sauce; bourride; salmon in sour
cream sauce; raspberry and redcurrant
mould (Rote Grütze) with vanilla sauce
Location: in the Excelsior Hotel Ernst
Setting: worthy of Cologne's most distinguished hotel; Hanseatic-style décor;
dark mahogany, claret-red velvet upholstery; exquisite procelain and silver
Amenities: hotel; private dining rooms
(3–120 persons); cellar restaurant; bar;
open-air dining; air conditioning; car
park
Atmosphere: sumptuous; refined; utterly
civilized
Clientèle: fairly cosmopolitan; Cologne's
classic costume and cashmere brigade
leavened by hotel guests from Hawaii to
Hong Kong
Dress: casually elegant for lunch; more
formally so (jacket and tie) for dinner
Service: exemplary
Reservations: advisable (no dogs)
Price range: fairly expensive
Credit cards: AE, DC, Euro, Master Card

Lunch

BADO – LA POELE D'OR
50–52 Komödienstrasse
Telephone: 1 37 04/13 41 00
Owner/Manager/Chef de cuisine: Jean
Claude Bado
Closed: Sunday; Monday lunchtime;
public holidays; two weeks at Christmas;
three weeks during school summer holi-
days
Open: 12.00/a.m.–14.00/2 p.m. and
18.30/6.30 p.m.–22.00/10 p.m.
Cuisine: French (nouvelle)
Specialities: lobster salad; truffles in puff
pastry; liver pâté; lamb kebabs in sherry
sauce; rabbit salad with mixed woodland
berries. 250 different wines
Location: city centre, a stone's throw
from the Romano-Germanic Museum
Setting: two small, stylish dining rooms
Amenities: conference rooms; car park
Atmosphere: subdued elegance
Clientèle: managers, industrialists, foot-
sore museum visitors

Dress: no special requirements
Service: adroit and cordial
Reservations: advisable (no dogs)
Price range: moderately high
Credit cards: DC, Euro

Dinner

FRANZ KELLER'S
21 Aachener Strasse
Telephone: 25 10 22-3
Owner/Manager/Chef de cuisine: Franz
Keller
Closed: lunchtime; Sunday; public holidays
Open: 19.00/7. p.m.–22.00/10 p.m.
Cuisine: French, with south-west German
regional undertones
Specialities: quail and truffle salad; Atlantic ray with limes; roast kid with ro-
semary, gratiné potatoes, mushrooms and
vegetables; saddle of young wild boar
with fresh vegetables
Location: west of centre
Setting: rather resembles a passageway
between the bar in front and the kitchen
behind, with an attractive inner courtyard
for al fresco dining in summer
Amenities: bar; private dining room; bistro in basement ›Keller's Keller‹ (open
for lunch as well as dinner); car park
Atmosphere: trendy; crowded; lively
Clientèle: disciples of Wunderkind Franz
Keller's innovative cuisine from Dort-
mund, Düsseldorf and Duisburg, plus
francophile gourmets who remember him
from his days under Paul Bocuse at
Collonges-au-Mont-d'Or and Michel
Guérard at Eugénie-les-Bains
Dress: elegantly casual to casually ele-
gant
Service: agile and alert
Reservations: strongly recommended (no
dogs)
Price range: inevitably expensive
Credit cards: AE, DC, Euro

Lunch

RINO CASATI
3–5 Ebertplatz
Telephone: 72 11 08
Affiliations: Buon Ricordo; Catarina de
Medice; Chaîne des Rôtisseurs
Owner/Manager/Chef de cuisine: Gue-
rino Casati
Closed: Sunday; first three weeks of the
local school summer holidays
Open: 12.00/a.m.–14.30/2.30 p.m. and
18.00/6 p.m.–22.00/10 p.m. (last orders)
Cuisine: creative Italian
Specialities: baby turbot (Buon-Ricordo-
Teller); duck in plum sauce; carpaccio
with white truffles and Parmesan cheese;
spinach noodles with mussels and toma-

toes; shin of veal (osso buco) with morel mushrooms; home-made pasta; home-made liver terrine
Location: on the inner ring road; between Hansaring and Theodor-Heuss-Ring
Setting: elegantly opulent dining room in shades of blue, grey and pink with carefully-chosen accessoires
Amenities: air conditioning
Atmosphere: distinguished and yet not daunting
Clientèle: growing numbers of Rhinelanders converted to Guerino Casati's highly personal cuisine; Italian gourmets in exile; visiting industrialists
Dress: designer jeans to designer cashmere
Service: highly personal advice from the chef-proprietor, assisted by maître Angelo Tavera
Reservations: advisable (no dogs)
Price range: expensive
Credit cards: DC, Euro, Visa

Dinner

CHEZ ALEX
1–3 Mühlengasse
Telephone: 23 05 60/24 99 70
Owner/Manager: Rachel Silberstein
Closed: Sunday; Saturday lunchtime; public holidays
Open: 12.00/a.m.–15.00/3 p.m. and 19.00/7 p.m.–1.00/a.m.
Cuisine: French (classic and nouvelle)
Chef de cuisine: Marc Meynenc
Specialities: pheasant consommé with truffles; Poularde de Bresse in a salt crust; lasagne with lobster; warm goose liver on an apple ring
Location: city centre; by the old market
Setting: reminiscent of an Offenbach operetta; spacious reception rooms – red velvet, highly polished mahogany, leather armchairs and oil paintings; dinner by candlelight; fine porcelain and silver
Atmosphere: unashamedly luxurious; evocative of La Belle Epoque
Clientèle: bankers, bishops, chief executives, cardinals; connoisseurs of good food with a penchant for the romantic
Dress: conservative (pin-stripes allowed)
Service: very reliable; friendly and unobtrusively helpful
Reservations: advisable
Price range: inevitably high
Credit cards: AE, DC, Euro

Beergarden

FRÜH AM DOM
12–14 Am Hof
Telephone: 23 66 18/21 26 21
Owner/Manager: Cölner Hofbräu/P. Josef Früh

Closed: never
Open: 10.00/a.m.–24.00/12 p.m.
Cuisine: unpretentious, with a local accent
Chef de cuisine: Heiner Jehle
Specialities: cured knuckle of pork (Hämchen) with sauerkraut and mashed potato; braised beef marinated in vinegar (Sauerbraten) with dumplings and sweetsour sauce; rye bread roll with Dutch cheese, butter and (optional) mustard (Halver Hahn); smoked blood sausage with raw onion rings and rye bread roll (Kölsch Kaviar) – and, of course, the beer
Location: behind the ›Heinzelmännchen‹ fountain
Setting: typical brewery inn style; original painted ceilings; wood panelling; rooms of varying sizes
Amenities: beer garden (Biergarten) in summer; private dining rooms (150 persons)
Atmosphere: Cologne in a beer glass
Clientèle: heterogeneous cross-section of local habitués, politicians, economists, men from the media and tourists en passant
Dress: jeans and camera to what you will
Service: quick and efficient; clad in traditional ›uniform‹ of the Köbes (brewery worker) – knitted jacket, apron and purse
Reservations: advisable (pets permitted)
Price range: medium
Credit cards: not accepted

Bar

PIANO BAR
Excelsior Hotel Ernst
1–5 Trankgasse
Telephone: 27 01/Telex: 88 82 645
Owner/Manager: Siegfried Breunig
Closed: never
Open: 10.00/a.m.–1.00/a.m.
Location: in the Excelsior Hotel Ernst
Setting: elegant hotel bar; honey-coloured mahogany woodwork; yellow leather upholstery; pianist
Amenities: hotel; private dining rooms (3–120 persons); restaurant; cellar restaurant; open-air dining; air conditioning; car park
Atmosphere: discreetly relaxing, but not dull
Clientèle: top executives from Düsseldorf to Djakarta; international celebrities from Shirley Bassey to Jerry Lewis
Dress: what you will (within reason!)
Service: under the expert guidance of chef barman Arnaldo Bonetti
Reservations: only for groups of more than five
Credit cards: AE, DC, Euro, Master Card

Bar

MÄXWELL
25–27 Pfeilstrasse
Telephone: 24 16 24
Owner/Manager: David Sporn
Closed: Sunday from 16.00/4 p.m.
Open: 12.00/a.m.–14.00/2 p.m. and
18.00/6 p.m.–22.45/10.45 p.m.
Chef de cuisine: Ralph Hauffen, Wilhelm
Niedenhof
Location: near the ›Neumarkt‹
Setting: a comfortable café-restaurant
with Art Nouveau décor
Amenities: bar; café; restaurant
Atmosphere: friendly; expansive
Clientèle: Cologne's In-Crowd; jeunesse
dorée (or at least argentée) and distin-
guished or interesting birds of passage
Dress: whatever you wear is all right (as
long as it fits)
Service: anxious-to-please, efficient
Reservations: advisable
Credit cards: DC, EC

Shopping

EVERYTHING UNDER ONE ROOF
Kaufhof 41 Hohe Strasse

FOR HIM
Daniels Men Shop 18 Neumarkt

FOR HER
Saint-Laurent, Rive Gauche
Am Neumarkt, Im Hause Lempertz

BEAUTY & HAIR
Michaelis 107 Komödienstrasse

JEWELLERY
Mueller R. & C. 134c Hohe Strasse
Dix 2 Domkloster

LOCAL SPECIALITIES
Tabac-Collegium (tobacco)
12 Richartzstrasse
Offentier (women's fashion)
8–10 Neumarkt
Allermann & Niessen (men's fashion)
2–4 Breite Strasse
Gigi's Kinderladen (children's fashion)
20 Pfeilstrasse
Offermann (leather fashion)
135 Hohe Strasse
Herbst (furs)
115 b Hohe Strasse
Bücherstube am Dom (books)
2 Neumarkt
5th Avenue Galerie (gifts)
20–24 Mittelstrasse
Wilker (porcelain)
1 Mittelstrasse
Offermann (baggage & travel accessories)
135 Hohe Strasse

Pesch (interior decorating)
22 Kaiser-Wilhelm-Ring
Hoss (food and beverages)
25–27 Breite Strasse
Dr. Bataille (perfumery)
148 Hohe Strasse
Koenig (books & art)
4 Ehrenstrasse
Raphael (shoes)
136 Hohe Strasse
4711 (Eau de Cologne)
Glockengasse

THE BEST OF ART
Abels (Fine Art)
32 A Stadtwaldgürtel, Tel. 40 76 03
Gmurzynska (Fine Art and Russian
vant garde) 21 Obermarspforten,
Tel. 23 66 21/22
Holtmann (contemporary art)
10 Richartzstrasse, Tel. 21 51 50
Jöllenbeck (contemporary art)
53 Maastrichter Strasse, Tel. 51 58 52
Maenz, Paul (contemporary art)
50 Bismarckstrasse, Tel. 51 50 88
Orangerie-Reinz (Fine and modern art)
2 Helenenstrasse, Tel. 23 46 84/85
Reckermann (contemporary art)
16 Albertusstrasse, Tel. 21 20 64
Stolz (Fine Art)
15 Am Römerturm
Wentzel, Bogislav von (contemporary art)
26 St. Apernstrasse, Tel. 24 24 00
Werner, Michael (contemporary art)
24/28 Gertrudenstrasse, Tel. 21 06 61
Wiegand (contemporary art)
12–14 Mittelstrasse, Tel. 24 95 24
Wilbrand (contemporary art)
20 Lindenstrasse, Tel. 24 49 04
Zwirner, Rudolf (contemporary art)
18 Albertusstrasse, Tel. 23 58 37/38
Fahrbach, Georg (18th/19th-century
antiques)
1c Neumarkt, Tel. 21 13 73/74
Klein, H. G. (18th/19th-century
antiques)
2 St.-Apern-Strasse,
Tel. 21 75 96
Krings, Antonio (18th/19th-century
antiques)
27 Richmondstrasse,
Tel. 21 69 80
Kunsthaus am Museum
Carola van Ham (auctioneers)
1–5 Drususgasse, Tel. 23 81 37
Kunsthaus Lempertz (auctioneers)
3 Neumarkt, Tel. 21 02 51/24 59 52

The westward look of West Germany's most elegant, vain and snobbish metropolis is unmistakable, not only since the revered Elector ›Jan Wellem‹ dreamed of building a Versailles on the Rhine and Napoléon made it a capital of sorts. The Rhinelanders' guiding star has always been the ›City of Light‹, never the Prussian capital. (And next-door neighbour Cologne is frowned upon as proletarian while Bonn, the nation's capital, is discarded as provincial, altogether.) The all-too-often-abused sobriquet of ›Little Paris‹ may be justified for once, and her ›Daughter-of-Europe‹ label isn't sheer flattery either, even though there are more Japanese residing here than Italians. At the ›longest bar-counter in Europe‹, the city's tavernous Old Town, all the world congregates nightly. Desk and showcase of the ›Economic Wonderland‹ (and board room for the all-important Ruhr district), the regional capital of North Rhine-Westphalia (the country's most populous county) is not only rich but highly civilized and even culture-minded beyond charity level. Opera, theatre, concert and museum life, even cabarets are of international standard. The proverbial joyfulness and joviality are omnipresent, and next to administering the billions from industry, big spending and boisterous feasting mark the routine on both sides of the Rhine. For fashion, accessoires and luxury living en miniature the natives don't have to cross the border – their own Faubourg Saint-Honoré, named Königsallee, has 812 metres of Haute Couture, Haute Joaillerie, Haute Fourrure and Haut Monde indulging in it. And there are many reasons and possibilities for exhibiting one's acquisitions, even if not everybody can be invited by Germany's uncrowned, yet undisputed queen, Gabriele Henkel (chemistry-Konrad's wife), whose dinners, parties and galas carry more weight than an audience with the chancellor. As one of the modern-art centres of the continent, with galleries of world standard and vernissages throwing glamour onto genius, the city is a stage for many plays and players, and when the fashion fairs hit town, Düsseldorf becomes a symbiosis of beauty, superficiality and exhibitionism only Munich can match. If ›art is life – and life art‹, as local genius Joseph Beuys used to say, then Düsseldorf is one of the most artful towns of all. And if, according to the city's deity, Heinrich Heine, ›the fundamental evil of the world derives from the fact that the Good Lord did not create enough money‹, then Düsseldorf must have a pact with heaven.

Founded: first mentioned in 1135; Düsseldorf (German) – ›the village on the Düssel‹.

Far-reaching events: 1288 – chartered by Count Adolf von Berg; 1380 – the county becomes a duchy and Düsseldorf gets a castle; 17th century – Elector Jan Wellem rules the duchy and makes Düsseldorf a city of the arts; 1795 – French occupation; 19th century – Düsseldorf ceded to Prussia and the industrial revolution makes the city a centre of the iron and steel industries; 1939–45 – severe damage; 1946 – Düsseldorf becomes capital of North Rhine-Westphalia.

Population: 580,000; capital of North Rhine-Westphalia.

Postal code: D–4000   **Telephone code:** 211

Climate: temperate; humid; rather wet – bring two umbrellas!

Fairs and exhibitions: *JEWELLERY AND WATCHES* (Jan); *BOOT* (Jan) – boats; *IGEDO-JUNIOR* (Feb) – fashion trade fair for the young; *TRAVEL MARKET* (Feb); *ENVITEC* (Feb) – environmental protection; *ARTS AND ANTIQUES FAIR* (Mar); *IGEDO* (Mar); *PRÄVENTA* (Mar) – health education; *GDS* (Mar) – footwear; *IGEDO* (Apr) with *IGEDO-ACCESSORIES; WIRE* (Apr) – wire and cables; *DRUPA* (May) – printing and paper; *METAV* (Jun) – metalworking; *IGEDO-JUNIOR* (Aug); *HI FI VIDEO* (Aug); *IGEDO* (Sep); *K* (Nov, biennial) – plastics and rubber; *DISCO-TEC* (Nov) – entertainment catering; *MEDICA* (Nov); *INTERBAD* (Nov) – swimming pools, saunas; *ONLINE* (Feb, biennial) – communications; *INTERPACK* (May, biennial) – packaging machinery.

Calendar of events: *Karneval* (Feb/Mar) – the Monday preceding Ash Wednesday; *Schützenfest* (Jul) – marksmen's festival and *Kirmes,* a huge amusement fair; *St. Martin's Day* (10 Nov) – children parade through the streets, bearing lanterns; *Hoppediz Erwachen* (11 Nov) – start of the carnival season, in front of the Town Hall.

Historical and modern sights: *Rathaus* – the Town Hall, the oldest part of which dates from the 16th century; *Alt-St. Martin* – 11th-century church, the oldest building in Düsseldorf; *Schloss Jägerhof* (1750) – former hunting lodge of the Electors built by Couven; *Benrath Palace* – rococo palais; *Kunstsammlung Nordrhein-Westfalen* – Paul Klee and action painters; *Kunstmuseum* – modern art, graphics and sculptures; the *Hofgarten* park; *Hetjens Museum* – with an unique collection of porcelain.

Special attractions: a pub crawl through the *old town;* a shopping spree on *Königsallee;* a *Hans Mayer* vernissage; a *Henkel* party; the *Rose Monday carnival procession.*

Important companies with headquarters in the city: *Rheinische Kalksteinwerke* (chemicals); *Mannesmann* (steel); *Georg Fischer* (metal); *August Engels* (metal), *Rheinmetall; ARG* (mineral mining); *Balke-Dürr* (railway carriages); *Schiess* (machinery); *Siemens* (electrical and electronics equipment), *DuPont* (chemicals), *Henkel* (chemicals); *Hermann Wiederholt* (chemicals); *Feldmühle* (wood and papers); *PKL* (papers and plastics); *Pahlsche Gummi- & Asbestgesellschaft* (rubber and asbestos); *Thyssen* (steel); *Veba* (chemicals); *Johnson & Johnson* (chemicals).

Airport: Düsseldorf-Lohausen, DUS; Tel. 421223, Lufthansa, Tel. 4216111; VIP Lounge, Tel.: 4216190; 8 km/5 miles.

The Headquarters

STEIGENBERGER PARKHOTEL

1 Corneliusplatz
D–4000 Düsseldorf
Telephone: 86 51
Telex: 8 582 331 pho
Owning Company: Industrieclub
General Manager: Robert A. Schaller
Affiliation/Reservation System: SRS
(Steigenberger Reservation Service)
Number of rooms: 160 (12 suites)
Price range: DM 179–1,180
Credit cards: AE, DC, JCB, EC, Visa
Location: city centre
Built: 1902 (renovated 1985)
Style: Italian Renaissance, classical
Hotel amenities: car park, valet parking, hairstylist, newsstand
Main hall porter: Friedrich Wilhelm Schmitt
Room amenities: colour tv, mini-bar/refrigerator (pets allowed)
Bathroom amenities: hairdrier, telephone
Room service: 6.00/a.m.–24.00/12 p.m.
Conference rooms: 9 (up to 200 persons)
Bar: ›Etoile‹ (11.00/a.m.–1.00/a.m.)
Restaurant: ›Rôtisserie‹ Detlev Methner (maître), Hugo Kruck (chef de cuisine)

Pastorale and Swan Lake laid out in front of your balconied Schumann Suite – the Park in Düsseldorf can be a symphony of many composers. Only a top C across from the opera house, an extended tremolo away from Germany's avenue de luxe, Königsallee, and a few bars further from the endless row of pubs and tavernas of the Old Town, the ornate turn-of-the-century building is so ideally located that it would probably be successful even as a sanatorium. Instead it is the Headquarters for the movers and shakers of big business and for the elegantsia of the arts and fashion. When you miss someone of importance at the many fairs, openings and first nights you will most likely find him here after hours. Steigenberger's management led this fine establishment to the top of Düsseldorf's hôtellerie, enlarging, renovating, and beautifying every bedchamber while improving the service to luxury level. Lots of light, precious materials, brass and chrome and natural woods and intelligent accessoires without demonstrative flashiness characterize the intérieur. The cuisine, one of the fortes of the prominent company in all of their houses, is praised in the parkside terraced Rôtisserie by the discriminating international clientèle as much as by the pampered snobs of the city, and the Etoile bar is one of the cosiest corners after a confrontation at the green table or a shopping crusade through the Königsallee. From the moment you step onto the thick carpet of the expansive foyer to the last farewell by the liveried voiturier, you won't have to do anything you don't feel like doing – save some. Helping hands, smiles and discreet politeness underline the efficiency here.

SCHLOSS HUGENPOET

51 August-Thyssen-Strasse
D–4300 Essen 18
(Kettwig, 22 km/13 miles)
Telephone: (20 54) 60 54
Owner: Jürgen Neumann
General Managers: Jürgen Neumann, Ulrich Grudda
Affiliation/Reservation Systems: Relais et Châteaux, Gast im Schloß, IHA
Number of rooms: 20 (1 suite)
Price range: DM 110–300
Credit cards: AE, DC, EC
Location: between Düsseldorf and Essen, 18 km/11 miles from Düsseldorf airport
Built: 1650 (modernized and renovated in 1950 and 1986)
Style: a Renaissance château
Hotel amenities: car park, ballroom, newsstand, garage, tennis court
Room amenities: colour tv, mini-bar (pets allowed)
Room service: 7.00/a.m.–23.00/11 p.m.
Laundry/dry cleaning: same day
Conference rooms: 4 (up to 60 persons)
Sports (nearby): golf (5 km/3 miles), swimming pool (6 km/4 miles)
Restaurant: ›Schloß Hugenpoet‹ (12.00/a.m.–21.30/9.30 p.m.) Hans-Dietrich Marzi (chef de cuisine), nouvelle and classic cuisine, antique furnished salons with renaissance fireplaces, open-air dining on terrace
Private dining rooms: for up to 150 persons

Everyone who loves history, mythology and fairy-tales and all who travel to the industrial Ruhr district for business – or to Düsseldorf for pleasure – should spend some time in this water-castle haunted by beauty, allure and the best traits for which Germany is famous. Over 1200 years of turbulent past, from Charlemagne to the Fürstenbergs, have marked this venerable citadel to become one of the most recherché retreats for its medieval flair and nouvelle cuisine, for the unique hospitality and personal service: the work – and life – of châtelain Jürgen Neumann who belongs amongst the most dedicated hosts in the country. The handful of rooms are of apartment size, full of valuable antiques, some with four-poster beds, some with furnishings from the 16th century, all with comfort and warmth to spend the rest of your life in. (Which one famous theatrical star did, in fact.) Whatever season, whatever the event or excuse, if just for one night or your holidays, this is a hideaway par excellence – and so near to German industry's epicentre. Therefore Hugenpoet is a favourite forum for functions and festivities and claims its fame at least as much from its outstanding culinary art as from the art d'hospitalité. A tennis court is on the premises, all sports are close by, and nature à la Novalis is abundant beyond the moat.

Lunch

VICTORIAN
3a Königstrasse
Telephone: 32 02 22
Owner/Manager: Vortmann Gaststätten
and Co. KG/Günter Scherrer
Closed: Sunday; public holidays (lounge
open every day)
Open: 12.00/a.m.–15.00/3 p.m. and
19.00/7 p.m.–24.00/12 p.m. (lounge
12.00/a.m.–24.00/12 p.m.)
Cuisine: French (classic and nouvelle)
with Japanese undertones
Chef de cuisine: Günter Scherrer
Specialities: carpaccio of baby tuna with
caviar; terrine of goose liver; fillet of venison in Savoy cabbage with mushrooms,
home-made noodles, Brussels sprouts
and cinnamon pear; quail stuffed with
goose liver; plum tart with cinnamon parfait and plum sabayon
Location: very central, near the ›Kö‹
(Königsallee)
Setting: ultra-modern; white façade with
gold lettering; inside, a three-storey culinary multi-media object; restaurant (first
floor) – elegantized bistro with dark hard-
wood, brass, chrome and mirrors
Amenities: lounge with gourmet snack-
bar, afternoon tea and pianist on ground
floor; private dining rooms (6–50 persons); air conditioning
Atmosphere: vaguely English; Düssel-
dorf-chic; cramped, rather noisy and hectic at times but decidedly stylish
Clientèle: jet-set; affluent, attractive
Dress: designer casual to designer elegant, with a sprinkling of dark suits
Service: informative, authoritative and
friendly
Reservations: essential
Price range: appropriately expensive
Credit cards: AC, DC, Euro, Visa

Dinner

ORANGERIE
30 Bilker Strasse
Telephone: 13 18 28
Affiliations: Ordre des Coteaux de
Champagne; la Ronde des Gourmets
Owner/Manager: Horst Weigandt
Closed: Sunday (except during Trades
Fairs)
Open: 12.00/a.m.–23.30/11.30 p.m.
Cuisine: international
Chef de cuisine: Harald Schmitt
Specialities: lobster and goose liver par-
fait; turbot and scallops with braised chi-
cory; saddle of rabbit with spinach; ven-
ison in juniper cream sauce with Savoy
cabbage and baby carrots; plums in Ar-
magnac and figs with fresh berry fruits
and vanilla cream
Location: between the Karlplatz and the
Schwanenmarkt

Setting: spacious dining room; fin-de-
siècle accessoires – dark mahogany panelling, velvet banquettes, rattan chairs;
orange-red walls with narrow mirrors and
modern paintings; candlelight
Amenities: private dining rooms (18 persons); bistro; bar; air conditioning
Atmosphere: vaguely club-like; confidential or intimate, depending on your companion
Clientèle: cosmopolitan; successful, self-
confident and stylish
Dress: consciously fashionable
Service: unobtrusively impeccable
Reservations: essential (no pets)
Price range: fairly expensive
Credit cards: AE, DC

Lunch

SCHLOSS HUGENPOET
51 August-Thyssen-Strasse
Essen-Kettwig (22 km/13 miles)
Telephone: (20 54) 60 54
Affiliations: Relais et Châteaux
Owner/Manager: Jürgen Neumann
Closed: Christmas Eve
Open: 12.00/a.m.–14.30/2.30 p.m. and
18.30/6.30 p.m.–21.30/9.30 p.m.
Cuisine: French (classic and nouvelle)
Chef de cuisine: Hans-Dietrich Marzi
Specialities: cream of sorrel soup; goose
liver parfait with gourmet salad; saddle
of lamb; saddle of venison; pheasant;
pike dumplings in lobster sauce; fillet of
veal in spinach with cognac sauce
Location: in Essen-Kettwig, 22 km/13
miles from Düsseldorf
Setting: 17th-century castle surrounded
by moat; fairy-tale parkland setting; antique furnishings, Old Masters, sandstone
fireplaces; quiet (no background music)
Amenities: hotel; private dining rooms
(10–150 persons); open-air dining on terrace; car park
Atmosphere: seigneurial; festive
Clientèle: as popular a venue for entertaining premiers, presidents, princes and
plenipotentiaries as for family celebrations amongst the Ruhr District's Haute
Bourgeoisie
Dress: no track suits, cut-off jeans, sun
tops or T-shirts with dubious slogans
Service: professional
Reservations: advisable (no dogs in res-
taurant)
Price range: aristocratic
Credit cards: AE, DC, Euro

Dinner

IM SCHIFFCHEN
9 Kaiserswerther Markt
Telephone: 40 10 50
Owner/Manager/Chef de cuisine: Jean-
Claude Bourgeuil
Closed: Sunday; public holidays

Open: 12.00/a.m.–14.00/2 p.m. and 19.00/7 p.m.–21.30/9.30 p.m.
Cuisine: mixture of traditional French and nouvelle
Specialities: Breton lobster steamed with camomile flowers; carpaccio of salmon with creamed horseradish; ice-cream soufflé with fresh mountain herbs
Location: 12 km (8 miles) north of city centre; conveniently near airport
Setting: nautical, behind a picturesque historical façade; on the first floor; ship's galley décor complete with portholes; tables fairly close together
Amenities: second restaurant (›Aalschokker‹; Tel.: 40 39 48) – German cuisine of a very high standard
Atmosphere: gemütlich
Clientèle: Upper Crust; steel magnates; managing directors; Jumbo captains
Dress: elegant, conservative; dinner jacket or dark suit
Service: expert, rather friendly; definitely superior
Reservations: essential – preferably a year in advance
Price range: expensive
Credit cards: DC, Euro

Dinner

DAMPFNUDEL
2 Hohe Strasse
Telephone: 13 15 94
Affiliations: La Ronde des Gourmets; Ordre des Coteaux de Champagne
Owner/Manager: Horst Weigandt
Closed: Sunday (except during Trades Fairs)
Open: 12.00/a.m.–15.00/3 p.m. and 18.00/6 p.m.–23.30/11.30 p.m.
Cuisine: local
Chef de cuisine: Harald Schmitt
Specialities: trout mousse on cold crab sauce; stuffed quail with Savoy cabbage; lamb with broccoli; angler fish in tomato and basil butter; fruits on Marsala sabayon with hazelnut ice-cream; dumplings (Dampfnudeln) with apricots, bilberries, plums or fruits and raspberry ice-cream
Location: a short walk or a shorter taxi ride from the Mannesmann skyscraper (Hochaus)
Setting: café-bar-restaurant with elegant décor
Amenities: open-air dining on terrace; air conditioning; affiliated restaurant ›l'Orangerie‹ at Bilker Strasse 30
Atmosphere: cheerful, uncomplicated and chic
Clientèle: some of the city's best-known personalities from the worlds of fashion, films, politics and the press
Dress: from the relatively sober to the decidedly eye-catching
Service: Düsseldorf charm
Reservations: advisable (dogs permitted)
Price range: moderately expensive
Credit cards: not accepted

Café

CAFE HEINEMANN
32 Martin-Luther-Platz &
47 Berliner Allee
Telephone: 13 25 35/13 13 50
Owner/Manager: Bernd and Heinz-Richard Heinemann
Closed: never
Open: 9.00/a.m.–19.00/7 p.m.; (Saturday) 10.30/a.m.–19.00/7 p.m.; (Sunday) 9.00/a.m.–18.00/6 p.m.
Specialities: delicious cakes; Baumkuchen, Apfeltorten, Champagnertruffels, Schneider-Wibbel-Garn
Location: in the Kö-centre
Setting: modern, cool and pleasant interior decoration; Germany's smallest but most distinguished Confiserie-Café
Amenities: splendid roofed terrace; small snack bar
Atmosphere: familiar and pleasant
Atmosphere: a place of pilgrimage for connoisseurs with a sweet tooth
Dress: casual
Service: excellent

Bar

TINO'S
21 Königsallee
Telephone: 32 64 63
Owner/Manager: Vittorio Bazzo
Closed: Sunday, public holidays
Open: 12.00/a.m.–3.00/a.m.
Location: on the ›Kö‹, Düsseldorf's most famous boulevard
Setting: chic; Venetian styling
Amenities: piano-bar, snack restaurant/café
Atmosphere: for many Düsseldorfers the place to find out what's going on in town; for visitors in the know, the first port of call after depositing their Vuittons at the Parkhotel
Clientèle: local chiceria and beautiful or wealthy birds of passage en route from Berlin to the Bahamas
Dress: selected, elegant
Service: fast but never furious
Reservations: not necessary
Price range: medium
Credit cards: AE

Meeting Point

NACHRICHTEN-TREFF
(›NT‹) (›Ente‹)
27 Königsallee
Telephone: 13 23 11
Owner/Manager: Restaurationsbetriebe Stockheim GmbH & Co. KG
Closed: never
Open: (Monday-Thursday) 9.00/a.m.–24.00/12 p.m.; (Sunday and public holidays) 11.00/a.m.–24.00/12.p.m.; (Friday–Saturday) 9.00/a.m.–1.00 a.m.

Location: inside the publishing house of Düsseldorf's daily newspaper (West-deutsche Zeitung)
Setting: bar-bistro; rather reminiscent of an English pub
Amenities: telex-ticker for the latest news; screen-monitored news; slide-screen; newsstand and library on the first floor; al fresco apéritifs on boulevard terrace overlooking the ›Kö‹
Atmosphere: typical quick-drink esta-blishment; chic for a pre-dinner apéritif or a high-class pick-up
Clientèle: advertising executives and bro-kers from the banks; journalists and local politicians; mannequins, models and stars-in-the-making
Dress: jeans to jacket and tie
Service: well-informed
Reservations: recommended
Credit cards: AE, DC, Euro, Visa

Nightclub

SAM'S CLUB PRIVE
48 Königsallee
Telephone: 32 81 71
Affiliations: Club of Clubs
Owner/Manager: Charly Büchter
Closed: never
Open: 22.00/10 p.m.–4.00/a.m.
Location: at the centre of things
Setting: elegant disco-style
Amenities: discothèque; bar
Atmosphere: glitteringly glamourous; Düsseldorf's most fashionable club
Clientèle: Upper Crust noctambules; the Meerbusch society; travelling trading ty-coons, current stars of the model agencies and hangers- on with some other claim to fame
Dress: disco elegance
Service: welcoming to those with the right charisma or the prestigious Club of Clubs membership insignia
Reservations: advisable
Credit cards: AE, DC, EC, Visa

Shopping

EVERYTHING UNDER ONE ROOF
Horten Im Carsch Haus
1 Heinrich-Heine-Platz

FOR HIM
Selbach 88 Königsallee, 57 Berliner Allee

FOR HER
Eickhoff 56 Königsallee

BEAUTY & HAIR
Strerath – Blue Corner
23 Schanzenstrasse

JEWELLERY
Kern 26 Königsallee

LOCAL SPECIALITIES
Peter Linzbach (tobacco)
78 Graf-Adolf-Straße
Herpich (women's fashion)
30 Königsallee
Stock (men and women's fashion)
82 Königsallee
Pinocchio (children's fashion)
66 Königsallee
Heinemann (leather fashion)
18 Königsallee
Lipsia (furs)
28–30 Königsallee
Linke (books)
96 Königsallee
Casa Nova (gifts)
27 Königsallee
Franzen (porcelain)
42 Königsallee
Lambertz & Herkenberg
(baggage & travel accessories)
Kö-Galerie, 14–15 Königsallee
Floeck, Klaus (interior decorating)
37 Marienstrasse
Arnold (bathroom accessories)
28–30 Königsallee
Muenstermann (food and beverages)
11 Hohestrasse
Karl Lagerfeld (fashion for her)
Kö-Galerie
Steiger, Walter (shoes)
Kö-Galerie

THE BEST OF ART
Blaeser (Fine Art)
5 Bilkerstrasse, Tel. 32 31 80
Boerner (Fine Art)
13 Kasernenstrasse, Tel. 13 18 05
Curtze, Heike (contemporary art)
11 Citadellstrasse, Tel. 32 68 00
Gmyrek (contemporary art)
5 Mutter-Ey-Strasse, Tel. 32 77 70
Neumann, Michael (Fine Art)
13 Kasernenstrasse, Tel. 32 55 50
René, Denise and Mayer, Hans
(contemporary art) 2 Grabbeplatz,
Tel. 36 59 72
Strelow, Hans (contemporary art)
3 Luegplatz, Tel. 5 39 73
Wittrock, W. (Fine Art)
42 Sternstrasse, Tel. 48 00 35
Zimmer, Elke and Werner (contempor-ary art)
27 Oberbilker Allee
Tel. 33 29 19
Bröhan, Torsten (Art Déco, Bauhaus)
9 Südstrasse, Tel. 13 25 06
Keats Antiquitäten (English Furniture)
53 Flachskampstrasse, Tel. 20 18 36

The City

Krupp's cannons not only delivered the coup de grace to The Reich's adversaries, but also sounded a triumphant salute for its armoury, Essen – and her hinterland, Europe's greatest industrial complex. The three olympic rings are but one symbol of Germany's Nibelungen treasure hoard, the Ruhr Valley, with its endless natural resources the perpetual mainspring of the country's Economic Miracle. Krupp, Thyssen, Stinnes, Klöckner, Hoesch and other grand entrepreneur dynasties have shaped the nation and its image – for better, for worse – as much as Bismarck, the Kaiser, Adolf H. and K. Adenauer. The capital of the Ruhr Valley, where ten percent of the country's population resides, is the fifth largest city in Germany and primus inter pares amongst the dozen strongholds of the area – Dortmund, Duisburg, Bochum, Recklinghausen, Gelsenkirchen, Oberhausen, Bottrop, Hagen, Unna, Hamm and Herne each ranging from 100,000 to over half a million inhabitants. In the minds of the passing generation Essen may retain an image of coal and steel, of soot and smog, of black-faced miners and despotic captains of industry. Essen's physiognomy has undergone radical cosmetic surgery, however: no blast furnaces, no steel mills, no imperialist exploiters, no Marx-children, either, and definitely no Dickensian atmosphere. Essen is one of the most human industrial cities today, one of the greenest in the land, with a favourable climate, parks and lakes and fairgrounds and playgrounds and polished office buildings where much of the new republic's wealth is administered. Attractive pedestrian districts with elegant shops and art galleries lighten the cosmopolitan scene, while fashionable residential quarters border on pastures and woods. The industry has been diversified with machinery, precision engineering, optical goods, glass, plastics and graphical laboratories replacing the traditional production, and even though Essen remains the centre of energy of the continent, the crude product is only marketed here. Ten of the top one hundred companies in Germany are based here, and the profits are reflected in the city life and in its attractions as well. The Gruga Hall hosts the largest fairs in the country but also the biggest names in entertainment, and the Folkwang Institute of Theatre, Music and Dance (Pina Bausch) enjoys world fame for its avant-garde productions and its picture gallery. Villa Hügel, the Krupp's regal residence, has become a museum, too. Krupp's cannons should not intimidate the world again, but his home town should rather attract the world – and not for business only.

Founded: 852 A. D., around a Benedictine convent.

Far-reaching events: 1041 – a market town; 1243 – a fortified town; 15th–16th centuries – a prosperous trading community; 17th–18th centuries – decline; 1811 – Friedrich Krupp opens his first small steel plant and founds an empire 1939–45 – city badly damaged during World War II, rebuilt after 1945; 1972 – opening of university.

Population: 700,000.

Postal code: D-4300   **Telephone code:** 201

Calendar of events: *Karneval* (Jan/Feb) – parades, music and non-stop nonsense throughout the city; *Maitember* (May to Sep) – five months of fun, from circus to fireworks, jousting knights, and Essen's own Hawaiian luau; *Essener Lichtwochen (Dec)* – the ›weeks of lights‹; Christmas lights; *Old Essen* (Dec) – Christmas market.

Fairs and exhibitions: *INTERSCHAU* (Jan – bi-annual) – fairground equipment and leisure; *PFLANZEN-MESSE* (Feb) – horticultural fair; *EQUITANA* (Mar – bi-annual) – equestrian sports; *CAMPING + TOURISTIK* (Mar/Apr) – camping, tourism and leisure; *BRIEFMARKEN* (Apr – bi-annual) – postage stamps; *ANIMEX* (May – bi-annual) – animal welfare and breeding; *EUROFLOOR/EUROCARPET* (Sep) – floor coverings; *SECURITY* (Sep) – security exhibition with congress, alternating annually between Essen and Utrecht/Netherlands; *CARAVAN-SALON* (Oct) – caravans; *IKK* (Oct – bi-annual) – refrigeration and air conditioning; *ANTIQUITÄTEN* (Nov) – antiques and art; *MOTOR-SHOW* (Nov/Dec) – sports and racing cars with international classic car and oldtimer exchange.

Historical sights: *Münster* (852) – one of Germany's most venerable churches with valuable medieval church treasures; *Old Synagogue* (1911) – largest synagogue north of the Alps; special exhibition relating to Nazi persecution of the Jews; *Borbeck Palace* – late Baroque with a 42 acre park; *Villa Hügel* (1868–72) – Krupp family villa in parkland – antique furnishings and Gobelin tapestries and industrial museum; *Museum Folkwang* – art from 1800.

Modern sights: *Rathaus* – star-shaped city hall, the tallest in Germany; *Haus Industrieform* – industrial products as things of beauty; *Gruga* – central park.

Special attractions: a vernissage or a chamber concert at *Villa Hügel;* an evening of modern dance at the *Folkwang Institute.*

Important companies with headquarters in the city: *Rheinisch Westfälisches Elektrizitätswerk* (electricity); *Ruhrkohle* (mining); *Krupp* (steel and machinery); *Ruhrgas* (gas energy); *Karstadt* (department stores); *RAAB Karcher* (energy, machinery); *Aldi/Mülheim* (supermarkets); *Thyssen* (steel, machinery); *Hochtief* (construction); *Steag* (energy); *Ferrostaal* (financing German industries); *Westdeutsche Allgemeine Zeitung* (publishing); *VEBA* (energy); *Fahrzeugwerke Lueg* (vehicles).

Airport: Düsseldorf-Lohausen, DUS; Tel.: 42 12 23, Lufthansa, Tel.: 42 16 11, VIP Lounge, Tel.: 42 16 1 90; 30 km/20 miles.

The Headquarters

SHERATON

55 Huyssenallee
D–4300 Essen
Telephone: 20951
Telex: 8571266/8571291 esh
General Manager: Peter Kunze
Affiliation/Reservation System: Sheraton Hotels
Number of rooms: 210 (13 suites)
Price range: DM 185–305 (single)
　　　　　　　DM 230–355 (double)
　　　　　　　DM 410–875 (suite)
Location: city centre; 33 km/21 miles from Düsseldorf airport
Built: 1981
Style: modern exterior; modern and English style interior
Hotel amenities: swimming pool, sauna, solarium, car park
Room amenities: air conditioning, colour tv, video, radio, mini-bar
Bathroom amenities: hairdrier, separate shower (some)
Laundry/dry cleaning: same day
Conference rooms: for up to 100 persons
Bars: ›Bar am Park‹ (11.00/a.m. till late); pianist
Restaurants: ›Restaurant am Park‹ (12.00/a.m. – 15.00/3 p.m. and 18.00/6 p.m. – 22.30/11.30 p.m.)
Nightclub: ›Club Papageno‹ (21.00/9 p.m. – the small hours)

The singular glass-and-concrete façade of Essen's dépendance of the rapidly expanding American chain is enhanced by its attractive location next to the lawns and artificial lake of the public gardens. The group's well-established reputation for comfort and efficiency makes it here, as in Istanbul, the only headquarters of choice in town. Apart from the hotel's own comprehensive facilities for all encounters from a summer meeting to a full-scale conference, it stands next door to the Saalbau congress complex and is only a few steps from the town centre. The no-frills décor is predominantly neutral but not nondescript; the suites have attractive English-style furnishings and the bedrooms are restful in beige and brown. The spring-like yellows and greens of the dining room, one of the favourite places in town for a business lunch or a festive family affair, provide a stylishly individualistic setting for the international and German cuisine. The Bar am Park *is a popular rendezvous amongst the local noctambule chiceria, who gather here for cocktails to the strains of the piano. The music of Mozart will not be heard in the* Papageno *nightclub, but as the night wears on, the company chairmen of the Nineties can be observed gyrating on the dancefloor to the sounds of the Eighties.*

The Hideaway

LANDHAUS LEICK

67 Bochumer Strasse
D–4322 Sprockhövel 1
(Niedersprockhövel) (15 km/9 miles)
Telephone: (23 24) 76 15
Owner/General Manager: The Leick family
Affiliation/Reservation System: Relais et Châteaux
Closed: January
Number of rooms: 6 (2 suites)
Price range: DM 78–210
Credit cards: AE, DC, EC
Location: in Sprockhövel, 15 km/9 miles south-east of Essen, 45 km/28 miles from Düsseldorf airport
Built: 1950
Style: formerly a private villa converted into a lovely country house inn
Hotel amenities: car park; vinothèque; private gardens (pets welcome)
Room amenities: colour tv, mini-bar
Bathroom amenities: separate shower, bidet
Room service: 7.00/a.m.–22.00/10 p.m.
Conference rooms: for up to 18 persons
Restaurants: ›Rôtisserie‹ (12.00/a.m.–15.00/3 p.m. and 18.00/6 p.m.–24.00/12 p.m.), elegant gourmet restaurant; ›Pfannenschmiede‹: (11.00/a.m.–15.00/3 p.m. and 17.00/5 p.m.–24.00/12 p.m.), regional cuisine; Günter Kepp (chef de cuisine)

Nestling amidst well-kept gardens in one of the oases of green amongst the factories and steelworks of Europe's most densely concentrated industrial area is a country -house relais which has become an open secret amongst local gourmets and visiting epicures in a region where temples of culinary excellence are even rarer than Cartier dépendances. The spirit of Günter Leick, the philanthropic mentor of this attractive villa, lives on, and impeccable French cuisine – crab bisque, pike with caviar and tomato sauce, and eel pâté – is still served in the pretty pink dining room or on the terrace overlooking the lawns. The wine list is as distinguished as the food, and for those who prefer local specialities there is a second little inn, Pfannenschmiede, in a cottage in the grounds. Many guests just book a table for dinner, but insiders reserve simultaneously one of the six bedrooms, each a cameo lovingly furnished with taste by châtelaine par excellence, Edith Leick. One room is decorated in rustic farmhouse style with gingham curtains round the four-poster bed; there is also an Art Nouveau room and a Milanese avant-garde room – all offering comfort and service in an atmosphere which remains essentially that of a gracious private house. Landhaus Leick has no need of sauna, swimming pools and solaria. Its guests come here to escape from the concrete jungle, and they find the tranquillity of the setting and warmth of the hospitality the perfect antithesis to twentieth-century stress.

Lunch

SAALBAU
53 Huyssenallee
Telephone: 22 18 66/Telex: 8 57 11 90
Owner/Manager: Hubert Imhoff GmbH
Closed: never
Open: 11/a.m.–13.00/1 p.m.
Cuisine: traditional and innovative
Chef de cuisine: Karl Schmitz
Specialities: local specialities from the Rheinland and Westphalia; menu specialities depend on the season
Location: in the Congress and Cultural Centre (Kongress- und Kulturzentrum)
Setting: dining rooms of different sizes decorated in various styles, ranging from the wood-panelled, vaguely club-like pub (Bierstube) to the cool and classic main restaurant
Amenities: conference facilities (up to 1,800 persons); bar; open-air dining on terrace in summer; car park
Atmosphere: latest addition to the gastronomic empire of the Imhoff family of Parkhaus Hügel renown
Clientèle: heterogeneous; conference delegates, local top brass and visiting VIPs from the worlds of finance, the arts and industry
Dress: according to season and circumstance
Service: very professional
Reservations: advisable
Price range: medium
Credit cards: AE, DC, Euro

Lunch

LA BUVETTE
30 An der Altenburg
Essen 16 (Werden) (10 km/6 miles)
Telephone: 40 80 48
Owner/Managers: Wilfried and Monika Hansel
Closed: never
Open: 12.00/a.m.–14.00/2 p.m. and 18.30/6.30 p.m.–21.30/9.30 p.m.
Cuisine: French (›au goût du jour‹)
Chef de cuisine: Wilfried Hansel
Specialities: leek soup; rabbit olives with herb stuffing; sweetbreads; veal chop with cheese sauce; breast of pigeon with elderberry sauce; fillet of turbot with lime sauce; peach champagne sabayon
Location: 10 km (6 miles) south of city centre
Setting: a quiet woodland; old country house; stylish table-settings in rustic dining room; quarry tiles, beamed ceiling, gallery and welcoming open central fireplace; contrasting modern paintings
Amenities: private dining rooms; lovely view; outdoor dining in inner courtyard and by pond; car park
Atmosphere: comfortable and home-like, without loss of elegance

Clientèle: cross-section of men of commerce, managers, managing directors and men-about-town
Dress: no special requirements
Service: very friendly
Reservations: essential (dogs allowed)
Price range: moderately high
Credit cards: DC

Dinner

BONNE AUBERGE
92 Witteringstrasse
Telephone: 78 39 99
Owner/Manager: Giorgio Mazzoli
Closed: Sunday
Open: 12.00/a.m.–15.00/3 p.m. and 18.00/6 p.m.–23.00/11 p.m.
Cuisine: French
Chef de cuisine: Thierry Eidenweil
Specialities: fresh mushrooms in cream; salmon in champagne sauce; guinea fowl in cream sauce; breast of duckling with shallots; peppermint cream in kiwi sorbet; surprise menu
Location: city centre
Setting: mediterranean – white roughcast walls with Italian-style accessoires
Amenities: car park; solarium
Atmosphere: lively and cheerful
Clientèle: businessmen; bankers; mining executives; metallurgists
Dress: come as you please
Service: friendly and accommodating, even at busy times
Reservations: advisable
Price range: medium
Credit cards: all major

Lunch

PARKHAUS HÜGEL
203 Freiherr-vom-Stein-Strasse
Bredeney (6 km/4 miles)
Telephone: 47 10 91
Affiliations: Chaîne des Rôtisseurs
Owner/Manager: the Imhoff family
Closed: never
Open: 11.00/a.m.–22.00/10 p.m.
Cuisine: French (nouvelle) and local
Chef de cuisine: Ulrich Werner
Specialities: duck liver parfait with cassis sauce and fresh salads; beef consommé with stuffed marrow bones; gratiné of seafood in saffron; breast of wild pigeon in puff pastry with parsley purée; iced coffee mousse on cherry purée
Location: 6 km (4 miles) south of city centre
Setting: in attractive countryside near Lake Baldeney (Baldeney-See); late 19th-century (Gründerzeit) villa; summerhouse style; small dining room with view of the lake furnished with carefully-selected antiques
Amenities: hotel; four private dining rooms (up to 120 persons); open-air

dining on terrace overlooking the lake; car park; woods; tennis and golf in the vicinity
Atmosphere: that of an elegant country house whose owner understands the art of gracious living
Clientèle: Essen's social élite with cause for celebration, plus distinguished visitors wishing to remain incognito, knowing they can rely on the Imhoff family's discretion
Dress: fairly formal to fairly casual, depending on the circumstances
Service: very personal and hospitable
Reservations: advisable (pets permitted)
Price range: rather expensive
Credit cards: AE, DC, Euro

Dinner

ANGE D'OR
326 Ruhrtalstrasse
Essen-Kettwig (11 km/7 miles)
Telephone: 23 07
Owner/Manager: Claude Huppertz
Closed: Sunday; Monday; between Christmas and New Year
Open: 19.00/7 p.m.–22.00/10 p.m.
Cuisine: Italian with French touches
Chef de cuisine: Rolf Schmidt
Specialities: breast of duckling in Bouzy-Rouge sauce; lobster with breast of poularde; potato pancakes (Kartoffelpuffer) with smoked salmon and caviar; carpaccio with warm artichoke salad
Location: 11 km (7 miles) from city centre; attractive woodland
Setting: country-house atmosphere; rose garden with statues; small rooms decorated in various styles ranging from the rustic to the sophisticated; prettily elegant table settings; different china for each course
Amenities: terrace with a view for summer evenings; conference rooms; car park
Atmosphere: intimate, friendly, comfortable
Clientèle: industrialists; hommes d'affaires; celebrities tired of being celebrated
Dress: no restrictions or requirements
Service: welcoming and friendly
Reservations: advisable (no pets)
Price range: appropriately expensive
Credit cards: AE, DC, Euro

Dinner

BISOU DE MER (Bredeney)
5 Theodor-Althoff-Strasse
Telephone: 71 40 81
Owner/Managers: K. B. Gobel and J. P. Troillet
Closed: never
Open: 11.00/a.m.–15.00/3 p.m. and 18.00/6 p.m.–23.00/11 p.m.

Cuisine: French
Chef de cuisine: Daniel Freu
Specialities: seafood; salmon fillet; turbot in Chablis with morel mushrooms and wild rice
Location: near the Essen–Düsseldorf motorway; quiet suburb 8 km (5 miles) from city centre
Setting: in Hotel Bredeney; quiet woodland; reminiscent of a Spanish resort hotel; wall paintings and picture-window overlooking swimming-pool
Amenities: hotel; bar; open-air dining on terrace; car park and garage
Atmosphere: pleasantly elegant
Clientèle: fish fans; chemists; sportsmen and industrialists
Dress: no special requirements
Service: attentive
Reservations: advisable (dogs allowed)
Price range: moderate
Credit cards: AE, DC, Euro, Visa

Dinner

LANDHAUS LEICK
67 Bochumer Strasse
4322 Sprockhövel (15 km/9 miles)
Telephone: (23 24) 7 34 33
Affiliations: Relais et Châteaux
Owner/Manager: The Leick Family
Closed: Sunday; Monday lunchtime; two weeks at Christmas
Open: 12.00/a.m.–15.00/3 p.m. and 18.00/6 p.m.–24.00/12 p.m.
Cuisine: French (classic)
Chefs de cuisine: Dieter Schaumburg and Günther Kepp
Specialities: warm asparagus salad with lobster slices and truffle vinaigrette; salmon dumplings on parsley purée; fried suckling lamb's liver with glazed apples; stuffed breast of guinea-fowl with leek cassoulet and potato pancake in port wine sauce; whisky parfait with mango and kiwi
Location: in Sprockhövel, 15 km/9 miles south-east of Essen
Setting: a country villa more reminiscent of a private house than a hotel; terrace overlooking flower-filled garden; two dining rooms; one decorated in rustic style; the other more classically elegant
Amenities: hotel; private dining room (30 persons); bar; car park
Atmosphere: an oasis of tranquillity and good taste
Clientèle: connoisseurs of good food and gracious living
Service: unobtrusively painstaking and professional
Reservations: recommended (pets permitted)
Price range: fairly expensive
Credit cards: AE, DC, Euro

Café

TAPAS
2 Rathenaustrasse
Telephone: 23 74 16
Owner/Manager: Olaf Cuno
Closed: never
Open: 10/a.m.–1.00/a.m.;
weekend till 3.00/a.m.
Location: in the new ›Theater-Passage‹
Setting: a Roman garden with a riot of plants; grey and pink décor; water cascade
Amenities: air conditioning; bar, snacks
Atmosphere: reminiscent of an open air garden
Clientèle: heterogeneous collection of locals and visitors to the city
Service: efficient

Bar

JIMMY'S
2 Am Hauptbahnhof
Telephone: 1 70 80
Owner/Manager: Handelshof Hotel
Closed: never
Open: 17.00/5 p.m. – the last guest has left
Location: in the Handelshof Hotel
Setting: comfortable small hotel bar
Amenities: hotel; private dining rooms; restaurant; car park
Atmosphere: confidential or intimate, depending on your companion
Clientèle: businessmen and hotel guests predominate
Service: efficient
Reservations: not necessary
Credit cards: AE, DC, Visa, Master Card

Nightclub

MISSISSIPPI
2 Am Hauptbahnhof
Telephone: 1 70 80
Owner/Manager: Mövenpick/Siggi Ornot
Closed: Monday, Tuesday
Open: 21.00/9 p.m.–2 a.m.; weekend: 20.00/8 p.m.–4/a.m.
Location: in the Handelshof Hotel; entrance via side door of hotel
Setting: nautical; like a ship's cabin
Amenities: air conditioning; bar
Clientèle: heterogeneous; hotel guests from far and near, plus local jeunesse dorée
Dress: fairly casual
Price range: medium
Credit cards: AE, DC, Euro, Visa

Shopping

EVERYTHING UNDER ONE ROOF
Karstadt   Limbecker Platz

FOR HIM
Klasmeyer
2 Rathenau Strasse, Theaterpassage

FOR HER
Elle Boutique
Acazienallee/Allianzhaus & 87 Rüttenschneider Strasse

BEAUTY & HAIR
Klaus Wolf   31 Kettwiger Strasse

JEWELLERY
Deiter   22 Kettwiger Strasse

LOCAL SPECIALITIES
Pfeifen-Schilde (tobacco)
14 Kastanienallee
Lilo Bögner (fashion for her)
112 Bredeneyer Strasse
Il mondo (fashion for him)
7 Rathenaustrasse
Boecker (children's fashion, fashion and furs)
6 Am Markt
Neher (books)
75 Ruttenscheider Strasse
Delbruegger & Klingen (gifts)
Haus am Kettwiger Tor
Koester (porcelain)
37 Hagen III.
Belker (interior decorating)
82 Huyssenallee
Heinemann (food and beverages)
103 Bredeneyer Strasse
Moerchen (ice-cream)
202 Rüttenschneider Strasse
Tina Beltz (antiques)
3 Markuspfad

THE BEST OF ART
Heimeshoff   (modern art)
5 Kennedyplatz, Tel. 23 04 90 &
5 Moltkeplatz, Tel. 26 37 47
Neher   (Fine Art)
75 Rüttenscheider Strasse,
Tel. 78 20 71

The City

When the world thinks of West Germany, of the ›Economic Miracle‹ and the ›Fräulein-Wunder‹, of dynamic development, surprising success and liberal joys, of fairytale folklore amongst reconstruction splendour, Frankfurt on the Main is likely to symbolize this cliché image more than any other city in the Federal Republic. Gateway to the country (with the continent's busiest airport and rail system), geographical centre of central Europe (with daily return shuttles to every major city between Lisbon and Helsinki), one of the most important industrial showcases in the world (for books, furs, textiles it's even the biggest), centre of banking, stocks and red-light business, but also of culture and tourism, Frankfurt – nicknamed ›Mainhattan‹, ›Bankfurt‹, Chicago on the Main‹ – represents the future of this half-nation more than Hamburg or Munich. Home town of Germany's genius par excellence, Johann Wolfgang von Goethe, and a few others like Werner von Siemens and Willy Messerschmitt, as well as the legendary Rothschilds, there is enough historic notability in the cradle of Germany's democracy, but also nostalgic eminence dispersed among the silvery skyscrapers, from the gingerbread-and-apple-wine-gemütlichkeit of singing-and-swinging Sachsenhausen to the picture-postcard villages dotted around the city between the Taunus hills and the Rhine valley. Struwwelpeter, Schopenhauer and Fassbinder; nightlife à l'américaine, world jazz and international crime; big money and great ideas, concentrated city stress and luxurious leisure in the vicinity make Frankfurt – contrary to its reputation – a true capital of Germany, which it almost became twice. Maybe next time.

Founded: 1st century A.D., by the Romans; Frankfurt – ›Franconian ford‹.

Far-reaching events: 794 – Frankfurt a royal residence, under Charlemagne; 1152 – Frederick Barbarossa elected King in Frankfurt; 1240 – first reference to the Frankfurt Fair; 1356 – Frankfurt chosen as centre for election of the kings of Germany; 1525 – Frankfurt accepts the Reformation; 1562–1806 – German emperors crowned in Frankfurt instead of Aachen; 18th century – ascendancy of Frankfurt as a banking capital (Rothschilds, Bethmanns); 1806 – the town becomes a Grand Duchy under Napoléon; 1815 – declared a Free City and seat of the German parliament at the Congress of Vienna; 1866 – part of Prussia; 1939–45 – the city largely destroyed in World War II; post-1945 – reconstruction of the city earns it the name of ›Mainhattan‹.

Population: 700,000; largest city in the state of Hessen.

Postal code: D-6000   **Telephone code:** 69

Climate: unpredictable; often cloudy; warm summers.

Calendar of events: *Dippemess* (Holy Week & Sept) – ceramics and pottery market; *Wäldchestag* (May/Jun) – the Tuesday after Whitsuntide finds the streets filled with Frankfurters, music and apple wine, a local speciality; *Jazz in the Palmengarten* (biweekly, from May to Sep); *Main Festival* (1st Sun in Aug) – fireworks on the banks of the Main; *Fountain Festival* (Mid-Aug) – folk festival with a 500 year tradition; *October Music and Theatre Festival* – plays and concerts, from classical to jazz; *Christmas Market* (Dec) – seasonal fair – candles, baubles and gifts.

Fairs and exhibitions: *HOME FABRICS FAIR* (Jan); *MUSIC FAIR* (Feb) – musical instruments; *INTERNATIONAL TRADE FAIR* (Feb, Mar, Aug); *FUR TRADE FAIR* (Apr); *INFOBASE* (May) – data processing; *INTERSTOFF* (Aug) – textiles; *IAA* (Sep, biennial) – international automobile exhibition; *INTERAIRPORT* (Sep) – airport construction fair; *INTERNATIONAL BOOK FAIR* (Oct); *PUBLIC DESIGN EXHIBITION* (Oct); *FBA* (Nov) – office supplies; *TOURISTICA* (Nov) – tourism; *DO-IT-YOURSELF* (Nov); *AGRITECHNICA* (Nov) – agricultural technology.

Historical sights: *Cathedral* (852) – with a tall Gothic tower and fine choir-stalls; *Römer* (1405) – the city's landmark city hall; *Hauptwache* (1729) – former station of old city militia, now a café and the heart of the city; *Old Opera House* (1873) – modern concert and congress hall, behind a monumental façade; *Nikolai Church* (13th century) – the roof gallery was a favourite place for watching medieval jousting matches; *Goethe's House* – a walk through the life of Germany's great genius; *Städel Museum* – Flemish primitives and 16th century paintings; *Senckenberg Museum* – natural history.

Special attractions: a tour of the *apple wine taverns* in Sachsenhausen; one of *Dorian Gray's* parties; an evening of *jazz*, the Zoo.

Important companies with headquarters in the city: *AEG Telefunken* (electrics); *Bank für Gemeinwirtschaft* (banking); *Binding* (brewery); *Braun* (electrical appliances); *Commerzbank* (banking); *Control Data* (data processing); *Danzas* (transport); *Degussa* (precious metals); *Deutsche Bank* (banking); *Deutsche Bundesbahn* (railway); *Deutsche Lloyd* (insurance); *Diesterweg, Moritz* (publishing); *Dresdner Bank* (banking); *Hartmann* (cotton, fabrics); *Henninger* (brewery); *Hertie* (department stores); *Hoechst* (chemicals and pharmaceuticals); *Holzmann, Philipp* (construction); *McCann-Erickson* (advertising); *Merz* (pharmaceuticals); *Milupa* (food); *NUR* (travel); *Preussag* (steel); *Salomon Oppenheimer* (banking); *Sarotti* (chocolate); *Schenker* (transport); *Schindler* (lifts); *Standard-Elektronik-Lorenz* (electronics); *Suhrkamp* (publishing); *Telefonbau und Normalzeit* (telephone systems and measuring devices); *Teves, Alfred* (brakes); *VDO* (speedometers); *Villeroy & Boch* (ceramics); *Young & Rubicam* (advertising).

Airport: Frankfurt am Main–Rhein-Main, FRA, Tel.: 6902595; Lufthansa, Tel.: 6902111; VIP Lounge, Tel.: 6902106/6903277; 10 km/6 miles.

The Headquarters

STEIGENBERGER HOTEL FRANKFURTER HOF

Kaiserplatz
D–6000 Frankfurt/Main 1
Telephone: 2 02 51
Telex: 411 806 fraho
Owning Company: Steigenberger Hotels AG
General Manager: Bernd O. Ludwig
Affiliation/Reservation Systems: SRS (Steigenberger Reservation Service), Nikko Hotels Int., SAS
Number of rooms: 400 (14 suites)
Price range: DM 189–980
Credit cards: AE, CB, EC, Visa, JCB
Location: city centre
Built: 1876 (renovated 1982/83)
Style: elegant with antique furniture
Hotel amenities: valet parking, limousine service, grand piano, newsstand
Main hall porter: Herbert Nathal
Room amenities: colour tv (remote control), mini-bar/refrigerator (pets allowed)
Bathroom amenities: bidet, bathrobe, hairdrier, telephone
Room service: 24 hours
Laundry/dry cleaning: same day (weekend service)

Conference rooms: 15 (up to 300 persons), all modern facilities, ballroom
Bars: ›Aperitif‹ (12.00/a.m.–24.00/12 p.m.), Josef Schubert (barman), pianist ›Lipizzaner‹ (17.30/5.30 p.m. to 1.00/a.m.), Karl-Heinz Eifert (barman)
Restaurants: ›Français‹ (12.00/a.m.–14.00/2 p.m. and 19.00/7 p.m.–23.00/11.00 p.m.), Wolfgang Werner (maître), Bernhard Stumpf (chef de cuisine), French cuisine, pianist, Empire style décor; ›Grill‹ (12.00/a.m.–14.45/2.45 p.m. and 18.30/6.30 p.m.–22.00/10.00 p.m.), Wolfgang Werner (maître), Bernhard Stumpf (chef de cuisine), international cuisine, pianist, open-air dining, English country house style; ›Frankfurter Stubb‹ (12.00/a.m.–24.00/12 p.m.); Frau Reuter (maître); Bernhard Schuster (chef de cuisine); regional-rustic cuisine; ›Kaiserbrunnen-Bistro‹ (12.00/a.m.–24.00/12 p.m.)
Private dining rooms: fifteen

Steigenberger Hotels has become the synonym for excellence in hôtellerie despite its complicated name and the diversification of its properties, ranging from a forest spa to a prominent modern palace. The Frankfurter Hof is the flagship and Frankfurt's first. Heads of state and stars would only reside in the grand suites here, while the bosses of big companies reserve room, restaurant and conference chamber a year in advance for the grand fairs. City-palais architecture with fountain-courtyard for quiet moments in the heart of the metropolis blends with realistic luxury and personalized service, from the famous concierge, Herbert Nathal, to the famous barman, Karl-Heinz Eifert. If you want to know who – of some importance – is in town, come and stay at the Frankfurter Hof.

The Hideaway

SCHWEIZER STUBEN

12 Geiselbrunnweg
D–6980 Wertheim-Bettingen
(90 km/56 miles)
Telephone: (9342) 4351
Telex: 689123 halit
Owner/General Manager: Adalbert Schmitt
Affiliation/Reservation System: Relais et Châteaux
Number of rooms: 16 (1 suite)
Price range: DM 155–350
Credit cards: DC
Location: 95 km/60 miles from airport
Built: 1971
Style: elegant country-style
Hotel amenities: valet parking, sauna, solarium, boutique, tobacconist, outdoor swimming pool
Room amenities: colour tv; mini-bar/refrigerator (pets allowed)
Bathroom amenities: hairdrier, telephone
Room service: 8.00/a.m.–22.00/10 p.m.
Conference rooms: 1 (up to 12 persons)
Sports: indoor tennis court
Sports (nearby): golf (50 km), horse riding
Restaurants: ›Schweizer Stuben‹ (12.00/a.m.–14.00/2.00 p.m. and 19.00/7.00 p.m.–22.00/10.00 p.m.) Georg Bonefas (maître), Dieter Müller (chef de cuisine), nouvelle cuisine, elegant style décor (closed in January, and on Sunday and Monday for lunch)
›Schober Landgasthof‹ (12.00/a.m.–22.00/10.00 p.m.) Jean-Jacques Lamboley (maître), Thomas Müller (chef de cuisine), international cuisine

On the banks of the River Main some sixty miles upstream of Frankfurt stands a small family-run hotel which merits not only a detour from the motorway but even a much longer journey – from Gütersloh, Garmisch or Gibraltar. For more than a decade Adalbert Schmitt, self-styled ›last romantic of the century‹ and entrepreneurial realist, has taken an interest in dumplings and ducklings in his native village as well as in plastics in Kreuzwertheim. The energetic bon-vivant with a penchant for epic challenges constructed a stylized chalet with a country-château character (claiming at the time that it was intended as a restaurant for his tennis court), exhorted his élite team in the kitchen, led by maître cuisinier Dieter Müller, to create Grande Cuisine and encouraged his front-of-house staff under the direction of son Andreas to aim for perfection. Perfection can be found here, in every facet of this incomparable little Grand Hotel. The sixteen bedrooms are prettier than the chicest mountain retreat from Grindelwald to Gstaad, particularly the ones in the newly-opened dépendance chalet. Whilst the immediate view encompasses the daily menu and the tennis courts, the longer perspective stretches from the meadows by the river to the wooded hillsides in the distance.

Lunch

HUMPERDINCK
95 Grüneburgweg
Telephone: 72 21 22
Owner/Managers: H.-Willi Tetz and Edmund Teusch
Closed: Saturday lunchtime; Sunday
Open: 12.00/a.m.–14.00/2 p.m. and 19.00/7 p.m.–22.30/10.30 p.m.
Cuisine: French (nouvelle and classic)
Chef de cuisine: H.-Willi Tetz
Specialities: 8-course set menu; crab consommé with yellow lentils; saddle of lamb with leeks; saddle of rabbit with liver in chive cream sauce; angler fish (Lotte) in saffron sauce or balsam vinegar with Spanish onions; almond girdle cake with fruit purée
Location: near botanic garden; business and residential area to the west of the city centre
Setting: historic town palazzo; formerly residence of composer Engelbert Humperdinck and ›Struwwelpeter‹ author Dr. Hoffmann; no-expense-spared classic elegance in dove grey and ivory; crackle-wood panelling
Amenities: pianist; baroque music
Atmosphere: refined but légère; understated; harmonious
Clientèle: music-loving expense-account gourmets
Dress: fairly conservative
Service: well-trained and irreproachable
Reservations: advisable (dogs permitted)
Price range: very expensive
Credit cards: AE, DC, Euro, Visa

Lunch

BISTRO 77
1–3 Ziegelhüttenweg,
Frankfurt-Sachsenhausen
Telephone: 61 40 40
Owner/Manager: Chester Sauri
Closed: Sunday; Saturday lunchtime; June
Open: 12.00/a.m.–15.00/3 p.m. and 19.00/7 p.m.–1.00/a.m.
Cuisine: French
Chef de cuisine: Dominique Mosbach
Specialities: salade trompe-l'oeil; warm goose liver with forest mushrooms; truffle ravioli; crayfish salad; wolf-fish in basil sabayon; calves' sweetbreads in mustard sauce; raw salmon in puff pastry with ginger and mint; duck in honey; ›Festival de desserts‹
Location: in Frankfurt-Sachsenhausen; 1 km (⅝ mile) from city centre
Setting: modern building complex; contemporary neo-classic dining room with white tiles, white paint and white imitation marble; contrasting red neon lights and luxuriant pot plants

Amenities: outdoor dining; air conditioning
Atmosphere: highly individualistic
Clientèle: Frankfurt's francophile crème de la crème, plus visiting geniuses from Goscinny and Giscard d'Estaing to Jeanne Moreau
Dress: correspondingly witty and elegant
Service: friendly and knowledgeable; supervised by Guy Mosbach, brother of the chef
Reservations: advisable (pets allowed)
Price range: top
Credit cards: AE, DC, Euro, Visa

Dinner

NEUER HAFERKASTEN
4 Löwengasse
Neu-Isenburg (7 km/4 miles)
Telephone: (61 02) 3 53 29
Owner/Manager/Chef de cuisine: Pasquale Lavorato
Closed: Sunday; during the school summer holidays
Open: 12.00/a.m.–14.00/2 p.m. and 18.00/6 p.m.–22.30/10.30 p.m.
Cuisine: Italian
Specialities: antipasti; kidneys in red wine sauce; poularde de Bresse; homemade pasta; ragoût of venison; saddle of lamb; duck; squid in ›ink‹ sauce with noodles; desserts
Location: in Neu-Isenburg
Setting: elegantized Italian; well-spaced tables; domestic paraphernalia
Amenities: private dining room (30 persons); open-air dining on terrace; bar; air conditioning; car park
Atmosphere: très à la mode
Clientèle: businessmen tired of Frankfurt; Hessen's Haute Societé
Dress: elegantly fashionable
Service: con brio; stage-managed by Luigi Brunetti
Reservations: advisable to essential
Price range: fairly expensive
Credit cards: AE, DC, Euro, Visa

Lunch

SCHLOSSHOTEL KRONBERG
25 Hainstrasse
Kronberg/Taunus (15 km/9 miles)
Telephone: (61 73) 70 11
Telex: 4 15 424 shlod
Telefax: 7 01 267
Owner/Manager: Klaus Fischer
Closed: never
Open: 12.30/p.m.–15.00/3 p.m. and 18.30/6.30 p.m. to 22.00/10 p.m.
Cuisine: classic French-oriented
Chef de cuisine: Günther Ledermüller
Specialities: various terrines on three sauces; essence of mushrooms with truffles; saddle of lamb with herbs, ratatouille and potato waffles

Location: in the Schlosshotel Kronberg, 15 km (9 miles) north-west of Frankfurt
Setting: in a Tudor-style castle built in 1890 by Dowagen Empress Victoria, widow of Emperor Friedrich III; restaurant in the former royal dining room; furnished, like the rest of the castle, in regal style with valuable paintings and priceless antiques
Amenities: hotel; private dining rooms; park with private golf-course; car park
Atmosphere: as if time had stood still almost a century ago; nostalgic grandeur almost (but not quite) à la folie
Clientèle: predominantly a many-splendoured collection of well-heeled overseas visitors on a Grand Tour of Europe – plus Frankfurt industrialists wishing to impress foreign delegations
Service: superior
Reservations: advisable (no dogs in restaurant)
Price range: fairly regal
Credit cards: AE, DC, Euro, Visa

Dinner

GUTSSCHÄNKE NEUHOF
Dreieich-Götzenhain (12 km/8 miles)
Telephone: (61 02) 32 14
Affiliations: Hotel und Gaststättenverband; IHA; Chaîne des Rôtisseurs
Owner/Managers: Dr. Egon Schumacher/Walter Uhrig
Closed: December 23rd–24th
Open: 12.00/a.m.–13.30/1.30 p.m. and 18.00/6 p.m.–21.30/9.30 p.m.
Cuisine: regional – specialities and nouvelle cuisine on request
Chef de cuisine: Ralph Heerklotz
Specialities: hors d'œuvres ›Neuhof‹; smoked fillet of trout with horseradish; steaks, médaillons; salmon in Riesling
Location: 12 km (8 miles) south of Frankfurt
Setting: 500-year-old country house surrounded by woodland and open countryside; beamed ceiling, open fireplace and period accessoires – grandfather clock, pewter and old prints
Amenities: outdoor dining on terrace; banquets and receptions; facilities for the disabled; farm produce shop (Alte Backstube); car park; footpaths for those who wish to walk off the excess calories after lunch
Atmosphere: rustic and homely, but with a certain stylishness
Clientèle: popular venue for weddings and similar festivities amongst Frankfurt's Haute Bourgeoisie; a sprinkling of distinguished visitors from Prince Philip and Chancellor Kohl, not to mention Japanese, Russian and American businessmen and tourists
Dress: casual for lunch; tie for dinner
Service: attentive and efficient

Reservations: advisable to essential
Price range: fairly expensive
Credit cards: AE, DC, Visa

Café

EINS ZWEI
48 Hochstrasse
Telephone: 28 51 66
Owner/Managers: Gerd Schüler and Michael Presinger
Closed: never
Open: (Monday–Friday) 17.00/5 p.m.–1.00/a.m. (Saturday/Sunday) 19.00/7 p.m.–1.00/a.m.
Location: next to the Opera House (Alte Oper)
Setting: ultra-modern but not impersonal; dark green leather and chrome furnishings
Amenities: live piano music
Atmosphere: outgoing; free and easy
Clientèle: Frankfurt's Younger Set; the after-hours office crowd
Service: good
Credit cards: AE, DC

Café

LAUMER
67 Bockenheimer Landstrasse
Telephone: 72 79 12
Owner/Manager: Michael Rimbach
Closed: December 25th; December 26th
Open: 8.00/a.m.–19.00/7 p.m. (Sunday and public holidays; 11.00/a.m.–19.00/7 p.m.)
Specialities: lunch menus and one of the largest selections of cakes in the land; Herrentorte Laumer, Baumkuchen, Frankfurter Brenten et al.
Location: between the Old Opera House and the Palmengarten
Setting: marble tables, mahogany and exhibitions of works by local artists
Amenities: open-air dining on large terrace
Atmosphere: typical coffee-house; lively, nostalgic and vaguely Viennese
Clientèle: 9 months to 99 years
Service: feminine and friendly
Reservations: only for lunch

Meeting Point

PLASTIK
34 Seilerstrasse
Telephone: 28 50 55
Owner/Managers: Gerd Schüler and Michael Presinger
Closed: Saturday
Open: 21.00/9 p.m.–4.00 a.m.
Cuisine: American
Specialities: ›Plastik‹-burger
Location: in the heart of Frankfurt, near Bethmanns Park

Setting: classical-style nobleman's town house, furnished and fitted entirely in plastic – from the chairs to the plates and ›glasses‹
Amenities: restaurant with discothèque on the first floor; car park (can be reserved in advance)
Atmosphere: totally cool; understated, but fun
Clientèle: young; with-it; approachable
Reservations: for dining or large groups
Price range: inexpensive – moderate
Credit cards: AE, DC, Euro, Master Card

Bar

DIE LEITER
11 Kaiserhofstrasse
Telephone: 29 21 21
Closed: Sunday
Open: 11.00/a.m.–1.00/a.m.
Location: central
Setting: bistro-café with twentieth-century décor in black and white, with strategically-placed mirrors
Amenities: bistro-type meals (warm goats' cheese with vinaigrette and pine kernels to lobster or ripeye-steak); open-air dining on terrace; bar; air conditioning
Atmosphere: sophisticated, fashionable, fun and inevitably full to bursting – especially at lunchtime
Clientèle: publicity managers; jeunesse dorée; artists; men of letters
Dress: conservative to casual
Service: quick and capable
Reservations: advisable
Price range: medium
Credit cards: AE, DC, Euro

Nightclub

DORIAN GRAY
Flughafen, Terminal C
Telephone: 6 90 22 12/6 90 47 35
Owner/Manager: Gerd Schüler and Michael Presinger
Closed: Monday; Tuesday
Open: (Wednesday/Thursday) 21.00/9 p.m.–4.00/a.m.; (Friday) 21.00/9 p.m.–6.00/a.m.; (Saturday/Sunday) 12.00/a.m.–6.00/a.m.
Location: in the catacombs of Frankfurt International Airport
Setting: a vast communications centre consisting of Art Nouveau elegantized French-style bistro, club room with comfortable lounge areas and discothèque with 4–D music and light synthesizer
Amenities: VIP lounge; pianist, orchestra or whatever – depending on the occasion
Atmosphere: ›atmospheric gastronomy‹; a nightclub for those for whom a discothèque should consist of more than ear-splitting music, dance-floor and dim lighting
Clientèle: Jet-Set and VIPs

Dress: in accordance with the occasion
Service: amazingly efficient
Reservations: essential for major events
Credit cards: AE, DC, Euro

Shopping

EVERYTHING UNDER ONE ROOF
Kaufhof 116–126 Hauptwache Zeil

FOR HIM
Henry 13 Goethestrasse

FOR HER
Riffel-Moden 25 Goethestrasse and 3 Rathenauplatz

BEAUTY & HAIR
Troendle Frankfurt Airport

JEWELLERY
Wempe 7–8 An der Hauptwache

LOCAL SPECIALITIES
Davidoff Laden-Galerie am Theater (tobacco)
2 Theaterplatz
La Casetta (men's fashion)
17 Schneckenhofstrasse
Moeller & Schaar (men and women's fashion) 4 Steinweg and 35 Goethestrasse
Pfueller (children's fashion)
12 Goethestrasse
Zorbach (leather fashion)
15 Rossmarkt
Blazek & Bergmann (books)
1 Goethestrasse
Selection (gifts)
10 Goethestrasse
Pfeifer (baggage & travel accessories)
Fressgasse

THE BEST OF ART
Ehrhardt, Heinrich (contemporary art)
36 Myliusstrasse, Tel. 72 50 80
Frankfurter Kunstkabinett (Fine Art)
13–15 Börsenplatz, Tel. 28 10 85
Gering-Kulenkampff (Realism)
77 Schweizer Strasse, Tel. 61 58 89
Grässlin, Bärbel (contemporary art)
42 Staufenstrasse, Tel. 72 40 7 88
Lüpke, Klaus (contemporary art)
37 Braubachstrasse, Tel. 29 11 34
Meyer-Ellinger (contemporary art)
22 Brönnerstrasse, Tel. 29 29 94
Bienert, Erich (18th/19th-century antiques)
10 Domplatz, Tel. 28 89 80
Döring, Dr. Karl-Heinz (Art Nouveau)
10 Goethestrasse, Tel. 28 25 42
Ritter-Antik (early Victorian)
26 Berliner Strasse, Tel. 29 39 76; 28 20 40
Schneider, Carl, KG. (18th/19th-century Antiques)
4 Eschersheimer Landstrasse
Tel. 55 67 26
Arnold (auctioneers)
42 Bleichstrasse, Tel. 28 27 79
Döbritz (auctioneers)
10–12 Braubachstrasse,
Tel. 72 11 18/28 77 93

The City

Why is Lucas in Birmingham and not in London? Why can't Michelin produce in Nice instead of Clermont-Ferrand? Wouldn't it be lovely if Volkswagen's headquarters were in Munich, not in Wolfsburg, Siberia! Unfortunately, not all important business can be conducted in the capitals and places of culture and joy. In fact, many of the key industries are located in areas where you wouldn't want to be found by the Tatler's reporter. On the other hand, industry has more often than not created cities which, in turn, attracted intelligentsia, entertainment and social pleasures. Gütersloh is one such place, and Bielefeld is another. And little sister Paderborn a third. All three form the so-called Teutoburg Triangle (being triangularly situated around the Teutoburg Forest), one of Germany's industrial cradles such as the not-too-distant Ruhr Valley (Essen, Dortmund, Bochum, Duisburg, Oberhausen, Recklinghausen, et al.), the Rhine-Main Confluence (Frankfurt, Wiesbaden, Mainz, Darmstadt, Offenbach), or the Heidelberg-Mannheim-Ludwigshafen-Frankenthal quartet. The least centralized of European states, Germany has more such interwoven industrial formations than any other country, and sometimes you cross a few cities when you think it's one. The Teutoburg Triangle is a new growth area with Gütersloh being the secret primus inter pares for its attractive physiognomy and surroundings as well as the close connection to the Ruhr district, Düsseldorf and the fairy-tale Münsterland. (Gütersloh lies on the Paris-Warsaw rail link and on the Cologne-Berlin motorway.) So, even when you have business in Bielefeld, reside in Gütersloh. World famous for its yarn for almost two centuries and known today even more for the world's largest media concern, Bertelsmann, most of the firms here are family enterprises – foodstuffs, clothing, furniture and domestic appliances go on the road from here around the globe. And when the name of Dr. Oetker comes up, one may remember Bielefeld – in that order, while Nixdorf computers are most certainly of greater renown than their home, Paderborn. All three towns offer an architectural pot-pourri of timbered houses, ninteenth-century villas and contemporary office buildings, picturesquely grouped around the church green in Gütersloh, dominated by the Sparrenburg Castle in Bielefeld and the Romanesque-Gothic cathedral in Paderborn. Forming a natural boundary to the east of the Teutoburg Triangle, separating the German-Polish and the Westphalian plains, the Hansel-and-Gretel woodland of the forest also represents a strategic barrier historically. In nine A.D. the Roman legions of Varus met their Waterloo at the hands of the local peasantry, led by Arminius ›Hermann‹, Germany's William Tell, thereby shaping the future of the Teutons who might, otherwise, have become the slaves of Rome, instead of the Romans being employed as guest workers up here, today. The Teutoburg Triangle is in many ways the epitome of what Germany stands for: industriousness and industry, discipline and artisanry, sober matter-of-factness and jovial gemütlichkeit. For business, you're in heaven – the paradise of pleasure it is not.

Founded: Gütersloh: first mentioned in 1184; Bielefeld: 1214 by the Count von Ravensburg; Paderborn: 777 as the Imperial Court of Charlemagne.

Population: Gütersloh: 80,000; Bielefeld: 313,000; Paderborn: 120,000.

Postal code: Gütersloh: D-4830; Bielefeld: D-4800; Paderborn: D-4790

Telephone code: Gütersloh: 5241; Bielefeld: 521; Paderborn: 5251.

Calendar of events: Gütersloh: *Town Centre Festival* (May); *Gütersloher Sommer* (summer holidays) – art exhibition; *Trade Fair* (Sep, bi-annual); *Christmas Market* (Dec); Bielefeld: *Linen Weavers' Market* (May) – town festival; *Summer Festival* (May–Sep); *Pig Market* (Aug) – folk festival; *Sparrenburg Festival* (Aug) – medieval festival; *Bielefeld Wine Market* (Sep); Paderborn: *Puppet Festival* (Jan/Feb); *Lunapark* (Apr); *Easter Run; Spring Festival* (May); *Organ Summer* (Jul); *Shooting Fair* (Jul); *Libori Festival* (Jul–Aug); *Autumn Libori Festival* (Oct).

Historical sights: Gütersloh: *Old Church Square* – fine timbered buildings, notably the *Veerhoffhaus*, now a museum; Bielefeld: *Old Market; Crüwell House; Aschoff Angel Apothecary* (1640) – where Dr. Oetker first developed his baking powder; *Church of St. Nicholas* – Gothic; *Sparrenburg* – medieval castle; *Linen Weavers' Memorial* – the city's landmark; Paderborn: *Adam and Eve House* (16th century); *Cathedral* (13th–16th centuries); *Town Hall* (1613–20) – magnificent façade; *Heisingsches Haus* (around 1600) – built for a local nobleman; *Schloss Neuhaus* (16th century); *Archbishop's Court* (1716) – by the Baroque master Schlaun; *Carolingian Imperial Palace* (9th century).

Modern sights: Gütersloh: *Civic Hall* and *Theatre;* Bielefeld: *Rudolf Oetker Hall* – a concert hall with excellent acoustics; *Art Gallery* – modern art.

Special attractions: *Maritime museum* – Ernst Josef Weber's private collection of 5000 model ships (Schulstrasse – by private appointment only).

Companies with headquarters in the city: Gütersloh: *Bertelsmann* (books and records); *Miele* (kitchen appliances); *Mohndruck* (printing); Bielefeld: *ADS-Anker* (cash registers); *Alcina* (perfumery); *Asta-Werke* (chemicals); *Bielefelder Keksfabrik* (sweets); *Claas Guss* (steel); *Deutsche Granini* (soft drinks); *Gildemeister* (tool machinery); *Jobis* (clothes); *Dr. August Oetker* (food, spices); *Seidensticker* (shirts); *Windsor* (men's clothes); Paderborn: *Benteler Werke* (steel); *Nixdorf* (computers); *Stute* (foodstuffs); *Welle* (furniture).

Airport: Hanover, HAJ; Tel.: (511) 7305614, Lufthansa, Tel.: (511) 7305614, 130 km/85 miles.

The Headquarters

PARKHOTEL

27 Kirchstrasse
D–4830 Gütersloh
Telephone: 850
Telex: 933641 parkh
General Manager: Arwed Sparber
Number of rooms: 84 (3 suites)
Price range: DM 155 (single)
          DM 195 (double)
          DM 390 (suite)
Credit cards: Visa, AE, EC, DC
Location: central
Built: 1983
Style: Tiffany, luxurious, elegant
Hotel amenities: parking, air conditioning, wheelchair accessibility
Room amenities: colour tv, mini-bar (pets allowed)
Bathroom amenities: all rooms with private bathroom facilities
Room service: 7.00/a.m.–23.00/11 p.m.
Laundry/dry cleaning: same day
Conference rooms: 7 (up to 250 persons)
Sports: bowling
Bar: ›Kamin-Bar‹ (20.00/8.00 p.m.–2.00/a.m.)
Restaurant: (7.00/a.m.–10.30/a.m.; 12.00/a.m.–18.00/6.00 p.m. and 18.30/6.30 p.m.–23.00/11.00 p.m.) elegant style; Martino Porcelli (manager), Pierre Luigi Giraldin (maître), Bernhard Büdel (chef de cuisine); French and international cuisine
Private dining rooms: five

The name, in this case, is appropriate, for the terrace of the Parkhotel – in spite of its conveniently central location – overlooks a pool complete with fountain, surrounded by venerable trees, rhododendrons and flowering shrubs. The charming inner courtyards continue with more self-conscious artifice the harmonious rapport between the well-proportioned brick-and-tile structure and its setting. Architecturally, the modern building is all-of-a-piece, with gabled roof and oriel windows echoing traditional features of the numerous fine old houses which grace the town. The interior, too, is a good example of a perfect symbiosis of latter-day twentieth-century functionalism and unapologetic Tiffany-style nostalgia, from the fine mirrored and pillared hall with its welcoming open fireplace to the pièce de résistance, the stained-glass cupola in the panelled formal dining room. Comfort in the pretty bedrooms, camaraderie in the bar, plus sauna, solarium and bowling alley – since its opening in 1983 the Parkhotel has shown its paces convincingly enough to persuade East Westphalians, Southern Bavarians and even North Americans alike that it has a right to consider itself Gütersloh's finest address.

WALDHOTEL KRAUTKRÄMER

173 Am Hiltruper See
D–4400 Münster-Hiltrup
(53 km/33 miles)
Telephone: (0 25 01) 80 50
Telex: 892 140 wald
Owning Company: Hans Krautkrämer GmbH
General Manager: Hans Joachim Krautkrämer
Affiliation/Reservation System: Relais et Châteaux
Closed: December 23–25
Number of rooms: 75 (3 suites)
Price range: DM 135–180 (single)
DM 180–210 (double)
DM 320–360 (suite)
Credit cards: AE, DC, EC, Visa
Location: 6 km/4 miles south of Münster facing lake Hiltrup
Built: 1968 (renovated 1982)
Style: modern
Hotel amenities: car park, solarium, sauna, indoor swimming pool, tennis court, fitness room, bikes for rent
Room amenities: colour tv, radio, balcony or terrace, mini-bar
Bathroom amenities: all rooms with private bathroom facilities
Room service: 7.00/a.m.–22.00/11 p.m.
Laundry/dry cleaning: same day
Conference rooms: for up to 200 persons
Bar: ›Lobby-Bar‹
Restaurant: ›Krautkrämer‹: (12.00/a.m.–14.30/2.30 p.m. and 18.00/6 p.m.–22.15/10.15 p.m.), Wolfgang Stein (chef de cuisine), nouvelle and Westphalian cuisine, elegantized rustic style

From the charming sylvan setting to the innovative cuisine, Waldhotel Krautkrämer is an establishment of contrasts but not contradictions. There's something for everyone here, but – thanks to the high-precision planning and highly skilled organization of Hans Joachim Krautkrämer – no danger of the managers from Münster or elsewhere impinging on the wishes and whims of other guests. The modern chalet-style buildings overlooking Lake Hiltrup are tastefully decorated in elegantized rustic style – open fireplace in the foyer, exposed beams in the dining rooms and open house in the bar. Oriental carpets and fine antique furnishings add exclusivity to the ambience whilst Wolfgang Stein's blend of traditional Westphalian dishes and French nouvelle cuisine adds variety to the menu. Keen sportsmen and keep-fit enthusiasts will be fully occupied sampling the astonishing gamut of activities available – after a work-out in the gymnasium, a swim in the pool and a session in the sauna they may well be too tired for fox-hunting, windsurfing or even a gentle walk in the woods. Habitués know that there is only one solution to the problem – to stay longer next time!

Lunch

ENTE
18 Niedernstrasse (Bielefeld)
Telephone: (5 21) 55 54 55
Owner/Manager: Roland Barbach
Closed: Sunday, Monday; public holidays
Open: 12.30/p.m.–14.30/2.30   p.m.;
18.30/6.30 p.m.–12.00/a.m.
Cuisine: au goût du jour
Chef de cuisine: Marly Hartrumpf-van der Sluis
Specialities: asparagus parfait, smoked fish pâté; salad of smoked breast of duck; poached salmon on tomato sauce with stuffed scallops in spinach leaves; calves' sweetbreads in port wine sauce
Location: two bars away from the old market (Alter Markt) in Bielefeld
Setting: newly-opened gourmet restaurant with stylish modern décor in pastel shades with an abundance of mahogany
Amenities: private dining room; bar; car park in the vicinity
Atmosphere: sophisticatedly relaxing
Clientèle: Bielefeld's Beau Monde, plus discriminating or distinguished birds of passage
Dress: according to season and circumstance
Service: charming and anxious-to-please
Reservations: recommended
Price range: fairly expensive
Credit cards: AE, DC, Euro

Lunch

SCHWEIZER HAUS
99 Warburger Strasse (Paderborn)
Telephone: (52 51) 6 19 61
Owner/Manager/Chef de cuisine: Kurt Pfeiffer
Closed: Sunday; Saturday lunchtime; three weeks during local school holidays
Open: Mo–Fr: 11.30/a.m.–14.30/2.30 p.m. and 17.30/5.30 p.m.–22.00/10 p.m.
Cuisine: Swiss
Specialities: gratin of fillet of sole in Gewürztraminer with spinach; fondue bourguignonne
Location: near the university
Setting: alpine chalet-style building; two dining rooms decorated in contrasting styles
Amenities: car park
Atmosphere: welcoming and homely
Clientèle: local Haute Bourgeoisie en fête and en famille, plus the occasional tourist intent on seeing the Pader, the shortest river in Germany (4 km/2.5 miles long) or the cathedral
Dress: casual
Service: personal and professional
Reservations: advisable
Price range: moderately expensive
Credit cards: Euro

Dinner

LANDHAUS ALTEWISCHER
36 Avenwedder Strasse
Gütersloh-Avenwedde (3 km/2 miles)
Telephone: 7 66 11
Owner/Manager: Roland Burbach
Closed: lunchtime every day; Thursday; three weeks during the local school summer holidays
Open: 19.00/7 p.m.–23.00/11 p.m.
Cuisine: inventive, with an Italian accent
Chef de cuisine: Karl-Heinz Mersmann
Specialities: baked gold-head bream (Dorade) on vegetable noodles; calf's head in white butter sauce; leek and potato soup with caviar; veal carpaccio with Parmesan cheese; sauté of lamb with noodles and paprika; turbot on cress purée with champagne butter
Location: 3 km/2 miles north-east of Gütersloh in the suburb of Avenwedde
Setting: lovingly cared-for timbered manoir half-hidden by oak-trees; large dining hall with exposed beams; a few strategically-placed cupboards and elegantly-laid tables
Amenities: open-air dining on terrace; car park
Atmosphere: a scenario fit for a châtelain; redolent of history; one of the most attractive restaurants in the country
Clientèle: expense-account connoisseurs of the finer things of life; disciples of Karl-Heinz Mersmann's cuisine from his days under Eckart Witzigmann at ›Aubergine‹ in Munich
Dress: elegantly formal to formally elegant
Service: attentive and painstaking
Reservations: recommended
Price range: rather expensive
Credit cards: DC, Euro

Dinner

ZUR DEELE
13 Kirchstrasse (Gütersloh)
Telephone: 2 83 70
Owner/Manager: Horst-Dieter Sieweke
Closed: lunchtime every day; Saturday; second half of local school holidays
Open: 17.30/5.30 p.m.–1.00/a.m.
Cuisine: international; sea food
Chef de cuisine: Ulrich Pohlmeyer
Specialities: according to season and market availability; fish; game; asparagus; fresh boiled potatoes with piquant curd cheese (Quark; Weisskäse); grandmother's green cabbage with fresh sausage and bacon
Location: near the church of the Apostles (Apostelkirche)
Setting: recently-renovated 17th–century timbered house; small dining rooms on ground floor with appropriate décor and

furnishings; the day's specialities written on a large slate
Amenities: bar; tavern
Atmosphere: charmingly nostalgic and intimate
Clientèle: Gütersloh's gourmet élite; publishers, printers and members of the liberal professions
Dress: casual
Service: friendly and efficient
Reservations: recommended
Price range: medium

Lunch

LENNHOF
20 Menglinghauser Strasse
(Dortmund-Barop) (80 km/50 miles)
Telephone: (231) 7 57 26/Telex: 8 22 602
Affiliations: Romantik Hotels and Restaurants
Owner/Managers: Nina and Willi Ascheuer
Closed: never
Open: 12.00/a.m.–15.00/3 p.m. and 18.00/6 p.m.–23.30/11.30 p.m.
Cuisine: modern (German nouvelle)
Chefs de cuisine: Ulrich Manfrass and Detlef Bieder
Specialities: pickled herring (Matjes); snail soup; scampi; lamb provençale; steaks
Location: 6 km (4 miles) from city centre of Dortmund; 80 km/50 miles from Gütersloh
Setting: timbered building; converted threshing barn and stables; dark wood and period furniture; elegantized rustic
Amenities: conference rooms (one with open fireplace); garden; outdoor dining on terrace; bar; hotel (sauna, indoor swimming pool); car park; garage
Atmosphere: ›gemütlich‹
Clientèle: businessmen; brewery chiefs; managing directors and manufacturers
Dress: no special requirements
Service: friendly
Reservations: advisable
Price range: moderately high
Credit cards: AE, DC, Euro, Visa

Dinner

LE COQ D'OR
Harsewinkel (Gütersloh)
Telephone: 81 09
Owner/Manager: Monique Seyffart
Closed: Monday
Open: 11.00/a.m.–15.00/3 p.m. and 18.00/6 p.m.–23.30/11.30 p.m. (last orders; clients can stay till 2.00/a.m.–3.00/a.m.)
Cuisine: French (classic)
Chef de cuisine: Detlef Lübecke
Specialities: monthly changing menu; fish; mixed seafood platter; dessert, Caroline's hat (pancake with ice cream, fruits and cream)

Location: between Gütersloh und Harsewinkel
Setting: 18th-century house with rustic décor; dining room on two floors; niches for séparée dining, large fish tank to facilitate choice of menu, accessoires according to season
Amenities: car park
Atmosphere: informally stylish
Clientèle: predominantly middle-aged, comfortably-off, self-assured and discriminating
Service: welcoming and personal; supervised by the proprietor
Price range: fairly expensive
Dress: dungarees to dinner-jacket
Reservations: essential at weekends (dogs permitted)
Credit cards: all major

Dinner

AU CYGNE NOIR
3 Mühlenstrasse, Paderquellgebiet (Paderborn)
Telephone: (52 51) 2 30 26
Owner/Manager: Hansdieter Berens
Closed: never
Open: lunchtime by prior arrangement only and 18.00/6.00 p.m. until the last guest has left
Cuisine: French (nouvelle) and local
Chef de cuisine: Johannes Brackhaus
Specialities: fillet of sole with salad; beef consommé with dumplings and creamed cress soup; poached salmon in champagne sauce; local specialities; pig's tail in aspic; prawns; oxtail and carrot ragoût; vanilla ice-cream with figs and strawberry purée
Location: in the Hotel zur Mühle, a psalm away from the cathedral of Paderborn
Amenities: hotel; open-air dining on terrace; car park
Atmosphere: stylishly comfortable
Clientèle: Paderborn's princes of industry plus a sprinkling of well-heeled but footsore visitors to the town after ›doing‹ the cathedral and the source of the Pader
Dress: as you like it
Service: knowledgeable and courteous
Reservations: essential for lunch
Price range: cheap by Paris standards only
Credit cards: AE, DC, Euro, Visa

Café

CAFE RIDDER
14–16 Hohenzollernstrasse (Gütersloh)
Telephone: 2 09 07
Owner/Manager: Walter Müller
Open: Monday–Saturday 9.00/a.m.–18.30/6.30 p.m.; Sunday 11.00/a.m.–18.00/6 p.m.

Location: just outside the pedestrian precinct
Setting: recently renovated; vaguely Art Nouveau décor; predominantly white, with marble counter area and mahogany and white chairs
Amenities: two salons; open-air dining on garden terrace with fountain in summer
Atmosphere: a tradition in the town; owned by the same family for 125 years
Clientèle: suburban housewives, shopgirls, secretaries, students, solicitors, stockbrokers and senior citizens
Service: cheerful and helpful

Café

KONDITOREI ROGGENKAMP
23 Königstrasse (Gütersloh)
Telephone: 2 00 97
Owner/Manager: Georg Roggenkamp
Closed: Monday
Open: 7.00/a.m.–18.30/6.30 p.m. (Saturday – 18.00/6 p.m.); (Sunday and public holidays 11.00/a.m.–18.00/6 p.m.)
Location: a few steps from the civic centre (Stadthalle)
Specialities: Baumkuchen (sponge cake baked so that when cut it looks like the annual rings of a tree), home-made chocolates; gâteaux;
Setting: elegant coffee-house with Chippendale-style décor
Amenities: terrace; air conditioning
Atmosphere: perfect for a quick cup of coffee en passant
Clientèle: fashionable
Service: helpful and welcoming

Bar

BAR IM PARKHOTEL
27 Kirchstrasse (Gütersloh)
Telephone: 8 50
Owner: Parkhotel
Closed: never
Open: 17.00/5 p.m. – until the last guest has left
Location: in the Parkhotel
Setting: domed ceiling with hand-painted frescoes; open fireplace

Amenities: hotel; restaurant; live piano music (twice a week); air conditioning; car park
Atmosphere: stylishly refined
Clientèle: Gütersloh's Upper Crust; visiting top brass; local chiceria
Service: good
Reservations: not necessary
Credit cards: all major

Shopping

EVERYTHING UNDER ONE ROOF
Spiekergasse

FOR HIM
Le Monsieur   7 Münsterstrasse, Gütersloh

FOR HER
Elle   7 Berliner Strasse, Gütersloh

BEAUTY & HAIR
Riewenherm   74 Münsterstrasse, Gütersloh

JEWELLERY
Laumann   42 Berliner Strasse, Gütersloh

LOCAL SPECIALITIES
Vogue (fashion for her)
Münsterstrasse, Gütersloh
Peterburs, Rolf (fashion for him)
6 Spiekergasse, Gütersloh
Finke GmbH (fashion for him and her)
20 Königstrasse, Gütersloh
Herzog Kindermoden (children's fashion)
5 Berliner Strasse, Gütersloh
Kremers-Maas (leather fashion)
5 Spiekergasse, Gütersloh
Schoeller, Klaus (furs)
8 Spiekergasse, Gütersloh
Osthus (books)
2 Königstrasse, Gütersloh
Schlink (baggage & travel accessories)
12 Berliner Strasse, Gütersloh

THE BEST OF ART
Kurze   (contemporary art)
12 Spiekergasse, Gütersloh, Tel. 2 79 71

The City

›The best city in Germany‹, said The Times. But then, Hamburg is the most British city on the Continent, and no-one would expect The Times to award this title to a whistle-stop in the Black Forest, anyhow. Hamburg is as British as the City, Fleet Street, parks and docks all put together, complete with the private clubs, the social sports, the manly look, the conservative attitudes and the stiff-upper-lip understatement. Cosmopolitan, liberal and tolerant – yes, but suspicious and disapproving of joviality and fast friends. Quality, reliability and fairness are the trademarks of Hamburgers in business and pleasure. For the Free and Hanseatic City, the country's largest (save the island of Berlin), business is the credo (if possible shipping or trading), but not every parvenu with buying power is automatically accepted by the commercial élite, let alone invited to the Overseas Club, the Anglo-German Club, the Matthiae Dinner or even the Rothenbaum Tennis Club, the Falkenhain Golf Club, the Polo Club in Klein-Flottbek, the North-German Regatta Club; the Haute Bourgeoisie's villas along the Alster, on the Elb-chaussee and in Blankenese are holy shrines of discretion, anyway. Away from the inner circles of the refined, yet purist business Upper Crust, Hamburg is one of the most beautiful, lively cities imaginable, with the pulsating harbour, picturesque markets, elegant shopping arcades and a cultural life of world dimensions. Rolf Liebermann's opera, John Neumeier's ballet, theatres galore and a fair share of museums set the tone for the locals as much as ›Sin City‹, the notorious Reeperbahn, magnetizes millions of visitors to sex and crime and rock 'n roll. (What you don't find here, just doesn't exist – not even in anyone's fantasy.) Poet Klopstock, composer Brahms and sculptor Barlach adorn the annals of the city, but today the likes of statesman Helmut Schmidt, media-mogul Axel Springer and fashion-prophet Jil Sander have labelled Hamburg with their names. And if it isn't Germany's best city in the eyes of a Ludwig-lover from Paris, it certainly has the best hotel in the country, the Vier Jahreszeiten, where in a microcosmic way you can experience overnight all the Hamburgian traits of dignity, respect and efficiency wrapped in near-Victorian splendour.

Founded: 7th/8th century; Saxon and Slavic settlements.

Far-reaching events: 1188 – commercial league with Lübeck; 1202–25 – Danish rule; 1225 – under counts of Holstein; 1241 – foundation of the Hanseatic League with Lübeck; 1365 – privilege of fair city; 1460 – Hamburg ceded to Denmark; 1510 – imperial city; 1669 – end of Hanseatic League; 1768 – Danish accept Hamburg's independence; 1783 – trading connections with the United States; 1806–14 – French occupation; 1815 – status of a ›free and sovereign city‹; 1871 – part of the German Empire; 1943 – almost completely destroyed; post-1945 – reconstruction.

Population: 2 million, second largest city in Germany.

Postal code: D–2000 **Telephone code:** 40

Climate: maritime; bring an umbrella! In autumn the notorious ›Hamburger Schmuddelwetter‹ (light drizzle) cloaks the town in grey mist.

Calendar of events: *Matthiae-Mahlzeit* (Feb) – gala dinner given by the Senate for politicans, diplomats and prominenti; *Frühlings-Dom* (Mar/Apr) – folk festival, *Overseas Day* (7 May) – commemoration of open navigation on the Elbe; *International Tennis Masters Tournament* (Apr/May); *German Steeplechase* (May) – the longest steeplechase course in Germany; *Harbour Anniversary* (May) – all the ships fully decked out in celebration; *Hamburg Ballet Days* (May/Jun) – the world-renowned Hamburg ballet; *Gallop-Derby-Woche* (Jun/Jul) – Ascot in Hamburg.

Fairs and exhibitions: *ELECTROTEC* (Jan; bi-annual, 1988) – electronics; *GARDEN, TRAVEL AND LEISURE* (Feb); *INTERNORGA* (Mar) – restaurants and catering convention; *VITALIS* (Apr) – nature and health; *PORTEX* (May) – harbour convention; *NORDBÜRO* (Sep) – office technology; *INTERNATIONAL FAIR FOR SHIPS, MACHINES AND MARITIME TECHNOLOGY* (Sep); *EMTC* (Oct) – trade convention for the boating industry; *DEUTSCHE BOOT* (Oct) – boats and equipment; *NORDPOSTA* (Nov) – a philatelic paradise.

Historical sights: *St. Michaelis* (1751–62) – the city's landmark; *Chilehaus* (1922–24) – typical North German brick architecture; *Town Hall* 1896–97) – Renaissance façade; *Elbchaussee* (19th century) – façades in classicistic style, manors of the wealthy trading families.

Special attractions: a tour of the *Reeperbahn's* hard core kaleidoscope; *social events* – tennis, riding, polo; one night at the *Vier Jahreszeiten*; the *fish market* on Sunday morning; a *dress rehearsal* with Jil Sander; *Pöseldorf* – any time.

Important companies with headquarters in the city: *Axel Springer* (publishing); *BAT-Cigaretten Fabriken* (cigarettes); *Beiersdorf* (pharmaceuticals and cosmetics); *Blohm & Voss* (shipbuilding); *Brinkmann, Wirtz & Co* (banking); *Colgate-Palmolive* (cosmetics, chemicals); *EDEKA-Zentrale* (supermarket chain); *Gruner + Jahr* (publishing); *Heinrich Bauer-Verlag* (publishing); *Helm, Karl O.* (import/export); *Holsten Brauerei* (brewery); *Howaldt* (shipbuilding); *Kistenmacher, E. G.* (import/export); *Langnese-Iglo* (food); *Lever Sunlicht* (chemicals, cosmetics); *Marcard & Co* (banking); *Otto Versand* (mail order); *Philips* (electrical goods); *Reemtsma* (cigarettes); *Schwarzkopf* (cosmetics); *Tchibo* (coffee); *Toepfer, August C.* (import/export); *Warburg* (banking).

Airport: Hamburg-Fuhlsbüttel, HAM; Tel.: 50 80; Lufthansa, Tel.: 5 09 41 41; VIP Lounge, Tel.: 5 09 22 19; 13 km/9 miles.

The Headquarters

VIER JAHRESZEITEN

9–14 Neuer Jungfernstieg
D–2000 Hamburg 36
Telephone: 3 49 41
Telex: 21 16 29 jahr
Owner: The Haerlin Family
Managing Director: Gert Prantner
Affiliation/Reservation System: The Leading Hotels of the World
Number of rooms: 175 (37 suites)
Price range: DM 230–1,290
Credit cards: all major
Location: city centre
Built: 1897 (recently renovated)
Style: traditional patrician style
Hotel amenities: garage, valet parking, limousine service, beauty salon, hairstylist
Main hall porter: Gerhard Beyer
Room service: 24 hours
Laundry/dry cleaning: same day (weekend service)
Bars: ›Simbari‹ (see Bars); ›Jahreszeiten-Keller‹; Jürgen Prill (barman)
Restaurants: ›Jahreszeiten-Keller‹; Günther Harm (maître); ›Haerlin‹ (see Restaurants); ›Jahreszeiten-Grill‹; Herbert Kröger (maître), Peter G. Hinz (chef de cuisine)
Café: ›Condi‹ (see Cafés)

Call it the best hotel in Germany, the best hotel in Europe or the best hotel in the world – in neither case will you be frowned upon for euphemistic exaggeration. And yet, the luxury is not as obvious as in most Parisian palaces or London's leading grands. Of course, the silhouette of the Inner Alster patrician house is quite majestic, and the public halls demand a certain dignity, but there is no awe-inspiring glamour, no film-set frills, no intimidation by the liveried servants whom you notice only when doors are opened, gestures rendered and smiles exchanged at crossings. Here, the luxury is deeply-rooted, authentic and radiates from the quality of products and procedures without the shine. Hanseatic understatement in the traditional intérieur, round-the-clock service with a self-understood attitude, seemingly no restriction on the fulfilment of individual wishes. The antique furniture is hand-repaired in the house, the laundry is scientifically treated and the private tailor will widen trousers or shorten skirts overnight, if you please. Breakfast is brought on leathered trays not to disturb the morning peace by the rattling porcelain, the fresh flowers are rearranged and watered twice daily, and the telephone will be plugged from bed to desk according to the times. Concierge Beyer, barman Prill, maîtres Mrugalska and Kröger, and director Gissinger are the pillars of service – world-standard. And hotelier Gert Prantner directs this German Académie de l'art d'hospitalité as an example to the world. The world élite thanks him with habitué patronage, for business and pleasure, for lunch and dinner, for coffee, drinks or family fêtes. The Vier Jahreszeiten may, after all, be the best hotel in the world.

The Hideaway

GARDEN HOTELS PÖSELDORF

60 Magdalenenstrasse
D–2000 Hamburg 13
Telephone: 44 99 58
Telex: 212621 gard
Owners: Reinhard Rudel/Karsten Rutt-
kamp
General Manager: Claudius Zwein
Number of rooms: 62 (4 suites)
Price range: DM 140–180 (single)
        DM 180–280 (double)
        DM 280 (suite)
Credit cards: AE, DC, EC, Visa
Location: 2 km/1 mile from city centre,
10 km/6 miles from airport
Built: 1890
Style: turn-of-the-century
Hotel amenities: car park, private gar-
dens, terrace
Room amenities: colour tv, video, mini-
bar (pets welcome)
Bathroom amenities: hairdrier
Room service: 24 hours
Bar: hotel bar adjoining the winter gar-
den (11.00/a.m.–1.00/a.m.)

*Not so much a traditional auberge, more a
philosophy of life – and one which has
earned for the pretty turn-of-the-century
villas in Harvestehude a place amongst the
legendary IN World Guide's Top Twenty
Charm Hotels. The Garden Hotels also
possess, of course, the traditional attributes
of comfort, standard and service which discerning descendants of the Hanseatic merchants and latter-day temporary visitors to
the most British city in Germany require.
Situated in the media and publishing district on the western side of the Outer Alster,
the three spick-and-span town-houses have
a welcoming, understated air. The intérieur
is a masterpiece of Hamburg understatement, too. The friendly but quiet décor by
interior-designer-turned-hôtelier Carsten
Ruttkamp is Italian-inspired and acts as a
perfect foil for the profusion of pot plants
which help to justify the hotel's name. Contemporary paintings and selected antiques
in the bedrooms, and mirrors and concealed lighting in the bar create an ambience which is a symbiosis of the private
apartment of an arbiter of taste and a sybarite's cloistered cell. The eponymous gardens, an immaculate profusion of climbing
and trailing plants and shrubs, are lovingly
tended by co-owner Reinhard Rudel; their
omnipresent greenery transforms this city
hotel into an oasis of rural peace. The advertising executives, journalists and film directors who stay here find breakfast in the
charming greenhouse-like jardin d'hiver an
excellent start to the day, and a nightcap in
the civilized bar after a flirtatious marathon along the Reeperbahn a fitting conclusion.*

Lunch

HAERLIN
Hotel Vier Jahreszeiten
9–14 Neuer Jungfernstieg
Telephone: 3 49 41/Telex: 21 16 29
Owner: The Haerlin Family
Maître: Alfred Mrugalska
Closed: Sunday; public holidays; January
Open: 12.00/a.m.–15.00/3 p.m. and 18.00/6 p.m.–22.00/10 p.m.
Cuisine: international
Chef de cuisine: Peter G. Hinz
Specialities: seafood in herb stock; cassoulet of Norway lobster; wolf-fish in butter sauce; poached salmon; chicken (Stubenküken) stuffed with goose liver and calves' sweetbreads
Location: in the Hotel Vier Jahreszeiten
Setting: understated classic elegance in the white mansion on the Binnenalster lake; Gobelin tapestries, fine porcelain
Amenities: hotel, private dining rooms (16–100 persons); grill restaurant (open every day); café (open Monday–Saturday); bar; nightclub with live music; car park/garage (valet parking service); air conditioning
Atmosphere: patrician; dignified
Clientèle: company presidents, financiers and shipping magnates passing through, plus a considerable number of local habitués with well-upholstered bank accounts
Dress: rather conservative; tie de rigueur for men; ladies in trouser suits (but not jeans or Bermuda shorts) admitted
Service: suave perfectionism
Reservations: advisable (pets prohibited)
Price range: appropriate
Credit cards: all major

Lunch

FISCHEREIHAFEN-RESTAURANT HAMBURG
43 Grosse Elbstrasse, Altona
Telephone: 38 18 16
Owner/Manager: Rüdiger Kowalke
Closed: never
Open: 11.30/a.m.–22.30/10.30 p.m.
Cuisine: seafood – nouvelle, classic and regional
Chef de cuisine: Wolf Dieter Klunker
Specialities: the freshest fish in Europe; carpaccio of salmon and turbot; smoked mirror carp on horseradish mousseline sauce; turbot with salmon mousse in a green ›jacket‹ with Pommery mustard mousseline sauce
Location: overlooking the fishing harbour
Setting: elegant Hanseatic-style dining room
Amenities: private dining room; bar; car park

Atmosphere: Hamburg in a nutshell
Clientèle: local habitués; men from the media, men of commerce and the occasional politician
Dress: not too casual
Service: efficient
Reservations: essential, especially for a coveted window table with a view of the harbour traffic
Price range: fairly expensive
Credit cards: AE, DC, Euro

Dinner

LE CANARD
11 Martinistrasse, Eppendorf
Telephone: 4 60 48 30
Owner/Manager/Chef de cuisine: Josef Viehhauser
Closed: Sunday
Open: 12.00 p.m.–23.00/11 p.m.
Cuisine: French (nouvelle)
Maître: Martial Bourgoin
Specialities: spring salad with marinated calf's tongue; rolled fillets of sole in saffren sauce; creamed peas with lobster; orange mousse with wild strawberries
Location: in the suburbs of Eppendorf, north of city centre
Setting: small French style dining room in shades of white, pink and claret; wall dominated by modern work of art made of 1000 champagne corks; tables fairly close together
Amenities: bar; classical background music
Atmosphere: harmonious; confidential to romantic; depending on your mood (and that of your companion!)
Clientèle: gourmets; admirers of Josef Viehhauser's skills as restaurateur and chef
Dress: appropriately exclusive, expensive (or at least expensive looking) and elegant
Service: polished and charming
Reservations: recommended for dinner (pets allowed)
Price range: decidedly expensive
Credit cards: AE, DC

Dinner

LANDHAUS SCHERRER
130 Elbchaussee, Altona
Telephone: 8 80 13 25
Affiliations: Relais et Châteaux (Relais Gourmand)

Owner/Manager: Emilie Scherrer
Closed: Sunday
Open: 12.00/a.m.–22.30/10.30 p.m.
Cuisine: German (nouvelle)
Chef de cuisine: Heinz Wehmann
Specialities: Matjes herrings à la tartare; filleted oxtail; stuffed cabbage with pike-perch; gratinée of truffled Brussels sprout leaves with salmon in chive sauce; calf's head in aspic with red and yellow lentils
Location: 6 km (4 miles) from city centre
Setting: country-house style; somewhat feudal; ›Armin's Bistro‹ in functional French style with Tiffany lampshades; wood panelling; tables without cloths (but with fine china and glass); main dining room housing erotic paintings collected by the late Armin Scherrer
Amenities: private dining rooms (50 persons); car park; facilities for the disabled; catering service
Atmosphere: beguiling
Clientèle: Hamburg High Society converts to modern Haute Cuisine; discriminating, self-confident and chic
Dress: Jil Sander to Gianni Versace, and vice-versa
Service: excellently directed by Siegfried Marner
Reservations: advisable (pets allowed)
Price range: naturally, very high
Credit cards: AE, DC

Lunch

MÜHLENKAMPER FÄHRHAUS
1 Hans-Henny-Jahnn-Weg
Hamburg-Uhlenhorst
Telephone: 2206934
Owner/Manager: the Hillesheim Family
Closed: Saturday evening (from 18.00/6 p.m.); Sunday; public holidays; Christmas Eve; New Year's Eve
Open: 12.00/a.m.–23.00/11 p.m.
Cuisine: North German traditional
Chef de cuisine: Christoph Riedl
Specialities: seafood; fresh lobster tails with beef marrow; eel in dill jelly; fillet of salmon in champagne mousseline sauce; pork chop in aspic; very comprehensive wine list
Location: near the Alster Fleet
Setting: town house; club-like interior with an abundance of brass, wood and tiles
Amenities: private dining room; car park; open-air dining on terrace
Atmosphere: an institution on the Hamburg culinary scene for more than half a century
Clientèle: local habitués and visiting cognoscenti
Dress: tends towards the conservative
Service: dignified
Reservations: advisable (pets permitted)
Price range: fairly expensive
Credit cards: AE, DC, Euro, Visa

Dinner

PETIT DELICE
(Restaurant in der Galleria)
21 Grosse Bleichen
Telephone: 327727
Owner/Managers: Axel Henkel and Werner Henssler
Closed: Sunday; public holidays
Open: 12.00/a.m.–15.00/3 p.m. and 18.00/6 p.m.–22.00/10 p.m.
Cuisine: modern German (Neue Deutsche Küche)
Chef de cuisine: Reinhold Apfelbeck
Specialities: cucumber soup; salmon tartare with potato pancakes (Kartoffelpuffer); fillet of veal; lamb with green sauce; John Dory in Savoy cabbage; carp fricassée; venison pot-au-feu
Location: behind the main station (Hauptbahnhof)
Setting: elegantized bistro; décor in dusty pink with marble, bronze, chrome and neon lights; picture windows; spacious, light and open
Amenities: bar; outdoor dining on terrace directly overlooking the Fleet; air conditioning; car park
Atmosphere: totally different; discriminating and sparkling
Clientèle: heterogeneous; favourite rendezvous for Hamburg's gourmets
Dress: casual; come as you please
Service: unconventional but good
Reservations: advisable (pets allowed)
Price range: moderately expensive
Credit cards: not accepted

Bar

SIMBARI
Hotel Vier Jahreszeiten
9–14 Neuer Jungfernstieg
Telephone: 34941
Owner/Manager: The Haerlin Family/ Gerd Prantner
Closed: never
Open: 11.00/a.m.–2.00/a.m.
Location: in the Hotel Vier Jahreszeiten
Setting: mahogany-clad walls; fine inlaid wood ceiling and bar counter; red patent leather-upholstered chairs; spiral staircase; modern pictures and posters of circus performer Nicola Simbari
Amenities: hotel; second bar (Keller-Bar); air conditioning; car park
Atmosphere: vaguely reminiscent of an English club; classic and confidential; as perfect for a pre-lunch cocktail as for a post-dinner cognac
Clientèle: élite; exclusive; elegant; expensive
Service: as sophisticated as the surroundings; supervised by chief barman Jürgen Prill
Credit cards: all major

Café

CONDI
Hotel Vier Jahreszeiten
9–14 Neuer Jungfernstieg
Telephone: 3 49 46 42
Closed: Sunday
Open: (Monday–Friday) 10.30/a.m.–
18.30/6.30 p.m., (Saturday) 10.30/a.m.–
15.00/3 p.m.
Specialities: hand-made chocolates
(more than 40 varieties); short menu with
15 suggestions for lunch or a snack
Location: in the Hotel Vier Jahreszeiten
Setting: on two levels; Biedermeier-style
Atmosphere: elegantly élitist
Clientèle: crème de la crème
Service: to perfection

Nightclub

DIE INSEL
35 Alsterufer
Telephone: 41 81 55
Owner/Manager: Charles Grendl/Horst
Rave
Closed: Monday
Open: 20.00/8 p.m.–2.00/a.m.
Location: central; near Kennedy Bridge
(Kennedy-Brücke), directly on the Aus-
senalster
Setting: old feudal villa; three floors; sophisticated chic; metallic wallpaper,
spotlights, chrome, leather and marble
tables; open fireplace (in use in the even-
ings); regularly changing display of con-
temporary art
Amenities: restaurant (chef de cuisine
Wolfgang Richter, ex-Magnum); garden;
terrace; bar; discothèque; private dining
rooms; art gallery; from autumn onwards, entertainment in the form of classical music or circus
Atmosphere: lively, elegant, witty and heterogeneous
Clientèle: young and on-the-way-up to
middle-aged but definitely not moribund
Dress: fashionable and emphatic
Service: excellent
Reservations: advisable (no dogs)
Credit cards: AE, DC, Euro

Shopping

EVERYTHING UNDER ONE ROOF
Alsterhaus   16–20 Jungfernstieg

FOR HIM
Wormland   4–5 Jungfernstieg

FOR HER
Jil Sander   8–9 Milchstrasse

BEAUTY & HAIR
Marlies Möller   20 Tesdorpfstrasse

JEWELLERY
Brahmfeld & Gutruf   Jungfernstieg

LOCAL SPECIALITIES
Thomas Timm (tobacco)
Jungfernstieg/Hamburger Hof
Penndorf (women's fashion)
10 Mönckebergstrasse
Ihr Herrenausstatter (men's fashion)
10 Fonteney
Hamburger Kinderstuben (children's fash-
ion) 30–34 Jungfernstieg
Selbach (leather fashion)
32 Neuer Wall
Zoern (furs)
25 Colonnaden
Thalia Buchhandlung (books)
15 Hermannstrasse
Design Galerie (gifts)
26 Magdalenenstrasse, Hamburg 13
Lattorf (porcelain)
35 Dammtorstrasse
Gruenewaldt (baggage & travel accesso-
ries) 27 Alsterarkaden
Bornhold (interior decorating)
70 Neuer Wall
Michelsen L.W.C. (food and beverages)
10–14 Grosse Bleichen
Godiva Chocolatier (confiserie)
Hamburger Hof, 26 Jungfernstieg
Prange (women's and men's shoes)
38 Jungfernstieg
Stewen, Holger (antiques)
28 Milchstrasse

THE BEST OF ART
Brockstedt   (modern art)
11 Magdalenenstrasse, Tel. 4 10 40 91
Crone, Ascan   (contemporary art)
121 Isestrasse, Tel. 47 90 67
Dröscher, Elke (Kunstraum Falken-
stein)   (contemporary art)
79 Grotiusweg, Tel. 81 05 81
Levy   (contemporary art)
54 Magdalenenstrasse, Tel. 45 91 88
Loeper, Gabriele von   (contemporary
art) 152 Mittelweg, Tel. 45 32 92
Munro, Vera   (contemporary art)
64 Heilwigstrasse, Tel. 47 47 46
Westenhoff, Klauspeter   (Fine Art)
4/IV Milchstrasse, Tel. 44 02 93
Azadi, Siawosch   (carpets)
24 Deichstrasse, Tel. 34 32 12
Brinkama, Edda   (17th–19th-century antiques) 23 Hohe Bleichen, Tel. 34 26 70
Hennig, Dr. Karl   (oriental art)
20 Hohe Bleichen, Tel. 35 25 85
F. K. A. Huelsmann   (16th–18th-century
works of art) 15 Hohe Bleichen,
Tel. 34 20 17
Kratz, Edmund-Joachim   (18th-century
works of art, furniture)
25 Dockenhudener Strasse, Tel. 86 14 45
Kunstkabinett Werner Kittel (18th/
19th-century and Art Déco works of art)
Neuer Wall 43, Tel. 36 59 33
Dörling   (auctioneers)
40 Neuer Wall, Tel. 36 46 70
Hauswedell & Nolte   (auctioneers)
1 Pöseldorfer Weg,
Tel. 44 83 66/4 10 36 22

The City

Nowadays the cradle of English kings and queens since George I is better known as the arena for the world's largest industrial fair, but the Anglo-Saxon connection remains in the form of a friendly rivalry between the capitals of Albion and Lower Saxony. Apart from losing its rulers to the Court of St. James, Hanover also lost its most illustrious court musician, George Frederick Handel, who not only anglicized his name but actually tipped the scales in favour of London. Today he rests, as an Englishman to the English, amongst monarchs and bishops, in Westminster Abbey. Still, his abandoned compatriots celebrate his genius with operas, pageants and son-et-lumière ›Music for the Royal Fireworks‹ in the Baroque gardens of Herrenhausen Castle during the summer festival. In spite of this pompous and circumstantial backdrop, Hanover is an unpretentiously hard-working city, supplying tyres, batteries and brakes for the car factories of the Ruhr and pens and pencils for the nation's schoolchildren. The city itself has shunned picture-postcard postwar reconstruction, combining twentieth-century functionalism with the undamaged timbered and gabled houses and a cheerfully extrovert collection of pop art sculptures. Following the red line here leads not to the East (close enough for a first-hand impression through barbed wire) but via the River Leine, the neo-Gothic Town Hall and the main artery, the Georgstrasse, to the equestrian statue of the city's founding father, Duke Ernst-Augustus. It's the favourite tryst for all local lovers who are not waiting expectantly by the Kröpcke Clock. Visitors are welcomed with a cautious blend of lively interest and Nordic sincerity at all times. Wilhelm Busch, local son and creator of Germany's twin heroes of the Victorian moralist epic, Max and Moritz, left a museum of memorabilia in his home town. Adopted son, philosopher-librarian Wilhelm Gottfried Leibniz, must have lived in paradise here for most of his life, leaving Hanover – and the world – the ›Best of All Possible Worlds‹.

Founded: 950 A.D. first settlements; Hannover (German) – ›high bank‹.

Far-reaching events: 1241 – chartered; 1367 – joins the Hanseatic League; 16th century – develops into a main trading centre; 1626 – Danish troops invade; 1636 – Georg von Calenberg proclaims Hanover as his residence; 1638 – Herrenhausen Castle is built; 1696 – marriage of Duke Ernst-Augustus with Princess Palatine Sophia, grand-daughter of James I of England, thus establishing a claim to the English throne; 1714 – Elector Georg Ludwig of Hanover becomes King George I of England; 1756–63 – Seven Years War, French occupation; 1815 – sovereign kingdom; 1831 – founding of university; 1866 – Hanover becomes a Prussian province; 1940–45 – heavy bombing; 1946 – capital of Lower Saxony; 1947 – first Export Fair.

Population: 550,000.

Postal code: D–3000   **Telephone code:** 511

Climate: warm and mild; not too hot.

Calendar of events: *Spring Festival* (Apr) – annual fair, with booths, amusements and fireworks; *Swinging Hanover* (Ascension Day) – jazz in the city; *Festival of Lights* (Jun, Aug, Sep) – music, dance, theatre and parades in Herrenhausen; *Marksmen's Festival* (Jun, Jul) – the world's largest shooting spree; *Summer Festival* – black and white garden party in the *Stadtpark; October Festival* – like the Spring Festival, but a little bigger; *Jazz Days* (Dec) – jazz festival in Hanover; *Christmas Market* (Dec).

Fairs and exhibitions: *ABF* (Feb) – cars, boats and tourism; *ART AND ANTIQUES FAIR* (Apr); *CE BIT/HANNOVER MESSE* (April) – world's largest industrial fair; *LIGNA* (May) woodworking machines and equipment; *EMO* (Sep) tool machinery; *INTERRADIO* (Oct) – computer technology and electronics for the home; *PFERD & JAGD* (Nov) – riding and hunting, with an indoor riding tournament.

Historical sights: *Herrenhausen Castle* (17th century) – former royal residence with large parks, Europe's highest garden fountain and a mausoleum of the kings of Hanover; *Kreuzkirche* (1333) – altar by Lucas Cranach; *Old Town; Opera* (1845–52) – neoclassic, designed by Georg Ludwig Laves; *Kestner Museum* (19th century) – Egyptian collection; *Waterloo Column* (1832) – in memory of the Hanoverian soldiers assisting England in its war against Napoléon; *Marktkirche* (1359) – Hanover's landmark church; *Altes Rathaus* (1455) – old city hall in Gothic brick; *Leine Castle* (1678) – house of Lower Saxony; *Leibniz House* (1652) – home of the inventor of the binary counting system parliament; *Welfenschloss* (1878) – former Tudor home of kings, now a university.

Modern sights: *sculptures* by Nanas de Saint Phalle.

Special attractions: a weekend at the *Fürstenhof* in Celle; *Handel's Fireworks Music* accompanied by fireworks in Herrenhausen Gardens.

Important companies with headquarters in the city: *Bahlsen* (biscuits); *Continental* (tyres); *Geha-Werke* (writing utensils); *Hanomag* (lorries and heavy machinery); *Kali-Chemie* (chemicals); *Pelikan* (writing utensils); *Preussenelektra* (electricity); *Raffinerie Deurag-Nerag; Sprengel* (sweets); *Telefunken* (appliances); *Teutonia Zementwerke* (cement); *Varta* (batteries); *Vereinigte Leichtmetall* (light metals); *Volkswagen* (transporters); *TUI* (travel); *Hapag-Lloyd* (charter airline); *Polygramm* (records); *Wabco Westinghouse* (automobile brakes).

Airport: Hanover-Langenhagen, HAJ; Tel.: 7 30 51, VIP Lounge, Tel.: 7 30 56 12; 13 km/9 miles; Lufthansa, Tel.: 7 30 56 14/5.

The Headquarters

MARITIM

34–40 Hildesheimer Str.
D–3000 Hanover
Telephone: 1 65 31
Telex: 9 230 268 maha
General Managers: Rolf E. Binnecker and Bernd Beer
Affiliation/Reservation Systems: Utell, Hotelbank
Number of rooms: 291 (6 suites)
Price range: DM 148–800
Credit cards: AE, DC, EC, MC, Visa
Location: central, 1.5 km/1 mile from city centre
Built: 1984
Style: modern, elegant
Hotel amenities: parking, wheelchair accessibility, car rental, house limousine service, newsstand, sauna, solarium, health club, indoor swimming pool
Room amenities: colour tv, mini-bar, radio, air conditioning
Bathroom amenities: bathrobe, hairdrier
Room service: 24 hours
Conference rooms: for up to 600 persons
Bar: cocktail bar (15.00/3.00 p.m.–3.00/a.m.) pianist, modern décor
Restaurant: ›Maritim‹ H. Schoknecht (maître), H. Schantl (chef de cuisine), international cuisine, candlelight dinner with piano entertainment on Saturdays
Private dining rooms: banqueting facilities for up to 500 persons

The Maritim dépendance in Hanover stands out amongst the quality hotels belonging to this expanding German group. It's certainly not as old as Schloß Herrenhausen, and it doesn't stand in the middle of one of the most beautiful Baroque gardens in the world. But since the former summer palace of the Hanoverian kings of England doesn't offer accommodation to visiting industrialists, international lawyers and insurance brokers, the Maritim has a legitimate claim to be considered as the city's first address. The restrained modern extérieur conceals a temple of twentieth-century comfort and good taste; countless the glittering, sparkling reflections in the mirrors of the hall, comprehensive the menu for the dinner by candlelight in the restaurant and myriad the exotic cocktails in the bar. The bedrooms are thoughtfully appointed, the staff take care of you well and – at the end of the stay – the airport is only fifteen minutes away. The chances are, however, that after a stay at the Maritim you may well be more reluctant to leave town than Handel once was. If you are satisfied here, you will most likely be in Maritim's other outposts – in Timmendorfer Strand, Kiel, Travemünde, Braunlage, Bad Salzuflen, Gelsenkirchen, Hamm, Bad Sassendorf, Fulda, Bad Homburg, Darmstadt, Mannheim, Würzburg, Malta, Teneriffe and Mauritius.

The Hideaway

FÜRSTENHOF

55 Hannoversche Strasse
D–3100 Celle (45 km/28 miles)
Telephone: (51 41) 20 10
Telex: 925 293 cehols
General Manager: Horst Brühl
Affiliation/Reservation Systems: Relais et Châteaux, Gast im Schloß, IHA, Hotel Mosaik
Number of rooms: 70 (5 suites)
Price range: DM 90–190 (single)
DM 150–320 (double)
from DM 300 (suite)
Credit cards: AE, DC
Location: in Celle, 40 km/25 miles from Hanover airport
Built: 17th century and modern (renovated 1970)
Style: manor house
Hotel amenities: garage, beauty salon, sauna, solarium, massage, boutique, indoor swimming pool
Room amenities: colour tv, minibar/refrigerator (pets allowed in hotel, only)
Bathroom amenities: bathrobe
Room service: 6.00/a.m.–24.00/12 p.m.
Laundry/dry cleaning: same day
Conference rooms: for up to 100 persons, all facilities, secretarial services, ballroom
Sports (nearby): tennis, riding
Bar: ›Hallenbar‹ (15.00/3.00 p.m.–23.00/11.00 p.m.)
Restaurants: ›Endtenfang‹ (12.00/a.m.–14.00/2.00 p.m. and 18.30/6.30 p.m.–21.30/9.30 p.m.) Manfred Althammer (maître), Ernst Rissmann (chef de cuisine), nouvelle cuisine; ›Kutscherstube‹ (17.00/5.00 p.m.) Manfred Althammer (maître), Ernst Rissmann (chef de cuisine), nouvelle cuisine, brasserie
Nightclub: ›Celler Grotte‹ (21.00/9.00 p.m. till late), discothèque
Private dining rooms: three

The medieval town of Celle, on the edge of the Lüneburg Heath, is less than an hour's drive from Hanover. Long a mecca for historians, it has become a promised land for aesthetes and connaisseurs since Christian, Count von Hardenberg, rescued the dilapidated ducal palace and transformed it, with the aid of manager Horst Brühl, into a nonpareil amongst aristocratic retreats. The décor is worthy of a castle; wood panelling, a Baroque staircase, stucco ceilings, chandeliers and classical statues adorn the public rooms – whilst the modern bedrooms, the swimming pool, the sauna and the grand piano, provide all the comfort of a grand hotel. With service to match that of a nobleman's country mansion and the cuisine of a francophile guesthouse prepared by Ernst Rissmann in the celebrated Endtenfang where duck (of course!) is the speciality, the Fürstenhof is an auberge de renommé for sober northerners and a hideaway for selective southerners as well as a goal for neglected gourmets from the surrounding area.

Lunch

ZUR BRÜGGES
29 Bödekerstrasse
Telephone: 31 90 05
Owner/Manager: Ralf and Annelore zur Brügge
Closed: Sunday; second half of August
Open: 12.00/a.m.–15.00/3 p.m. and 18.30/6.30 p.m.–24.00/12 p.m.
Cuisine: French (nouvelle); seafood
Chef de cuisine: Karl-Heinz Wüstefeld
Specialities: lambs' lettuce (Feldsalat) with calves' sweetbreads; saffron soup with turbot and lobster; quails in Madeira sauce; foie gras with blackberries and cassis sauce; sauté of calves' kidneys in Beaujolais with chive and potato pancakes (Kartoffelplätzchen); marzipan ice-cream; sorbets of redcurrant, Campari-orange and grapefruit
Location: a short taxi-ride or a slightly longer walk from the main station (Hauptbahnhof)
Setting: rustic; hunting green and warm red
Amenities: bistro with small delicatessen store; open-air dining on terrace
Atmosphere: cosy; confidential or intimate – depending on your companion
Clientèle: admirers of the Zur Brügge family's gastronomic talents of ›Bakkarat‹ fame
Dress: jeans to jacket and tie
Service: exceptionally attentive
Reservations: appreciated
Price range: medium (dogs allowed)
Credit cards: not accepted

Lunch

SCHU'S
6 Hinüberstrasse
Telephone: 3 49 50
Owner/Manager: Uwe Flechsig
Closed: Saturday lunchtime; Sunday; one month during the summer
Open: 12.00/a.m.–14.30/2.30 p.m. and 18.00/6 p.m.–24.00/12 p.m.
Cuisine: nouvelle
Chef de cuisine: Norbert Schu
Specialities: salad of scampi tails and squid with melon balls; creamed chestnuts with herb pancakes; salad of lobster, walnuts, avocado mousse and pine kernels; fillet of turbot with chive butter and beetroot; médaillons of angler fish with thyme butter and stuffed courgettes; calves' kidneys and sweetbreads with redcurrant sauce and marrow; cinnamon ice-cream with poached plums
Location: in the Hotel Schweizerhof
Setting: near the city centre, but in a quiet side-street; luxurious décor with Jugendstil accessoires
Amenities: hotel; bar; ›Gourmet's Buffet‹ bistro; private dining rooms (45 persons); pianist; car park; garage

Atmosphere: prestigious; elegant; refined – and yet not intimidating
Clientèle: expense-account epicures; Hanover's Top Ten, plus visiting celebrities from ex-President Scheel to Ephraim Kishon
Dress: according to season and circumstances
Service: as good as the food
Reservations: advisable (pets permitted)
Price range: rather expensive
Credit cards: AE, DC, Euro, Visa

Dinner

WITTEN'S HOP
4 Gernsstrasse, Bothfeld
Telephone: 64 88 44
Owner/Manager: Andreas Lüssenhop
Closed: first three weeks in January
Open: (Monday–Saturday) 18.00/6 p.m. – when the last guest has finished; (Sunday and public holidays) 12.00/a.m.–14.00/2 p.m. and 19.00/7 p.m. – ›closing time‹ (see above)
Cuisine: French (nouvelle) with local accents; ›au goût du marché‹
Chefs de cuisine: Andreas Lüssenhop and Dieter Grubert
Specialities: according to season; lamb salad (das Beste von der Heidschnucke); soufflé of cheese from the Harz on caraway sauce; pike-perch (Zander) with truffles and leeks in puff pastry; warm lobster soufflé on two pimento sauces; pigeon de Bresse with green asparagus
Location: 15 minutes' drive from the city centre along Podbielskistrasse (northeast)
Setting: 300-year-old timbered Lower Saxon farmhouse with antique and rustic furniture, wrought-ironwork, pots and pans and fresh cottage-garden flowers; two timbered dining rooms
Amenities: garden; pleasant view; terrace; car park
Atmosphere: stylish, comfortable and not a little nostalgic
Clientèle: discriminating gourmets during and after business hours; young and on-the-way-up to middle-aged and successful; local politicians
Dress: correspondingly
Service: under the aegis of Andreas Lüssenhop; very personal and knowledgeable
Reservations: advisable
Price range: expensive (but worth it)
Credit cards: not accepted

Lunch

CLICHY
31 Weisse Kreuzstrasse
Telephone: 31 24 47
Affiliations: Gaststättenverband Hannover

Owner/Manager: Ekkehard Reimann and Peter Bücker
Closed: Sunday; Saturday lunchtime
Open: 12.00/a.m.–15.00/3 p.m. and 18.30/6.30 p.m. 24.00/12 p.m. (last orders 22.30/10.30 p.m.)
Cuisine: French (nouvelle) with a local accent
Chef de cuisine: Ekkehard Reimann
Specialities: salmon in aspic; pigeon with garlic; saddle of lamb on paprika butter; breast of pheasant in juniper sauce; sautéed calves' kidneys with mangold; char (Saibling) in lime butter with julienne of vegetables; white peach with pistachio ice-cream and champagne sabayon
Location: central
Setting: tricolour in entrance; Parisian street-café tables; wall candelabras with yellow candles; antique bric-à-brac
Amenities: private dining rooms (12 persons); bar; car park
Atmosphere: francophile; comfortable, homely and with the food itself taking pride of place
Clientèle: architects, bankers, clerics, doctors; the electors and the elected
Dress: no special requirements
Service: efficiently supervised by Peter Bücker
Reservations: advisable
Price range: rather expensive
Credit cards: AE

Dinner

HOPFENSPEICHER
16 Dorfstrasse
Isernhagen (15 km/9 miles)
Telephone: (51 39) 8 76 09
Owner/Manager: Wilhelm Strohdach
Closed: January 1st – 20th
Open: 18.00/6 p.m.–24.00/12 p.m.
Cuisine: nouvelle – ›au goût du marché‹
Chef de cuisine: Renzo Pilazzi
Specialities: tartare de chanterelles with cress in raspberry vinegar dressing; fillet of baby turbot in mustard mousseline sauce with buttered potatoes; rabbit in champagne mousseline sauce with home-made pasta and fresh vegetables; quails' eggs with cress, crème fraîche and Beluga caviar; blackberry ice-cream roulade with fresh fruits
Location: 15 km (9 miles) north of Hanover; 1 km (5/8 mile) past church on left-hand side when driving towards Grossburgwedel
Setting: timber-framed converted hop barn with no sign or name-plate other than the legally-required (handwritten) menu card affixed to the wall of this historic building; interior stylized rustic; exposed beams, granite-tiled floor, light wood; round tables and rush-seated chairs; vaguely Scandinavian in its simplicity, adorned by pewter candlesticks and huge vases of lilies, tulips or sunflowers

Amenities: garden terrace for al fresco dining; car park
Atmosphere: casually chic and happily relaxing
Clientèle: Hanoverian High Society; hommes d'affaires; artists, architects and journalists
Dress: come-as-you-please
Service: stylishly casual
Reservations: advisable
Price range: fairly expensive
Credit cards: not accepted

Dinner

LANDHAUS AMMANN
185 Hildesheimerstrasse
Telephone: 83 08 18/Telex: 92 30 900
Affiliations: Relais et Châteaux
Owner/Manager: Helmut and Frieda Ammann
Closed: never
Open: 12.00/a.m.–14.00/2 p.m. and 19.00/7 p.m.–23.00/11 p.m.
Cuisine: French (nouvelle)
Chef de cuisine: Helmut Ammann
Specialities: according to season; daily changing menu; home-made pasta with truffles and Savoy cabbage; mixed shellfish soup; poached pear with croquant ice-cream and praliné sauce; more than 500 wines
Location: 2 km/1 mile from city centre; a quiet woodland
Setting: two-storey manor-house with mansard roof and small-paned windows; interior elegant in the classic idiom
Amenities: hotel; banqueting hall; ›Nudelstubb‹ bistro (famous traditional pasta dishes from SW Germany); winter garden; outdoor dining on terrace; car park
Atmosphere: that of a luxurious country house whose owner understands the art of gracious living
Clientèle: affluent, conservative; businessmen and ardent followers of Ammann's cuisine of ex-Nörten-Hardenberg renown
Dress: as you like it (provided they like you)
Service: pleasantly home-like, yet courteous
Reservations: advisable (no pets)
Price range: cheap by Paris standards only
Credit cards: AE, DC, Euro

Café

OPERNCAFE + OSCAR'S BAR
38 Georgstrasse
Telephone: 1 66 06 70
Owner/Manager: Opern-Café Betriebs-GmbH/Brigitte Haack
Closed: never
Open: 8.30/a.m.–24.00/12 p.m.

Specialities: lunches and light meals in addition to home-made pâtisserie and traditional coffee-house fare
Location: opposite the Opera House (Oper)
Setting: old English-style décor; vaguely ecclesiastical, with altar serving as cupboard and matching chairs; Parisian crystal chandeliers; picture gallery on first floor with regularly changing exhibitions
Amenities: restaurant; bar; bistro
Atmosphere: sophisticated and stylish
Clientèle: musicians; music lovers; men--about-town; ladies lunching their best girl-friends; businessmen seeking refuge from the rigours of the boardroom
Service: with a smile

Bar

PIANO BAR
Hotel Maritim
34–40 Hildesheimer Straße
Telephone: 1 65 31
Owner/Manager: Maritim Hotel-Gesellschaft/Mr. Beer and Mr. Binnecker
Closed: never
Open: 15.00/3 p.m.–3.00/a.m.
Location: in the Hotel Maritim
Setting: luxurious piano bar with judiciously-placed mirrors and a small dance floor; live piano music (17.00/5 p.m.–20.00/8 p.m.) followed by discothèque
Amenities: hotel; restaurant; snacks and full meals until 24.00/12 p.m.; air conditioning; car park
Atmosphere: cosmopolitan
Clientèle: well-informed, well-heeled, well-dressed, well-travelled and (occasionally) well-known
Service: attentive and anxious-to-please; directed by chief barman Franco Brutagno
Price range: medium to high
Dress: casual but not careless
Reservations: only for large groups (no pets)
Credit cards: all major

Shopping

EVERYTHING UNDER ONE ROOF
Kaufhof   9–11 Bahnhofstrasse

FOR HIM
Hemdenstube
42 Georgstrasse

FOR HER
Hellborn   1 Theaterstrasse

BEAUTY & HAIR
Roggendorf   12 Luisenstrasse

JEWELLERY
Brinkmann & Lange   9 Rathenaustrasse

LOCAL SPECIALITIES
Zigarren Brunkhorst (tobacco)
71 Lavesstrasse
Ted's alta moda (women's fashion)
35 Georgstrasse
Mantelhaus Kaiser (men's fashion)
27–29 Karmarschstrasse
Bonbon (children's fashion)
12 Am Markt
Agatha (leather fashion)
16 Theaterstrasse
Stoll (furs)
23–29 Kurt-Schumacher-Strasse
Sachse & Heinzelmann (books)
34 Georgstrasse
Estetico (gifts)
44 Karmarschstrasse
Weitz (porcelain)
46 Georgstrasse
Exquisite (baggage & travel accessories)
30 Karmarschstrasse
Schaaf, Folkert Ludwig (interior decorating)
12 Am Markt
Backhaus (food and beverages)
49 Königstrasse
Liebe (perfumery)
25 Karmarschstrasse
Tee-Seeger (tea)
15 Rathenaustrasse
Klingenspor-Mode (haute couture)
18 Berliner Allee

THE BEST OF ART
Koch, Jürgen   (Fine Art)
50 Königstrasse, Tel. 32 20 06
Kö 24   (contemporary art)
24 Königsworther Strasse,
Tel. 1 77 83/32 06 20
Beckmann, Erich   (18th/19th-century antiques)
48 Georgstrasse, Tel. 32 30 74
Degener, L.   (18th/19th-century antiques)
33 Hindenburgstrasse,
Tel. 81 20 68
Friedleben, U.   (glass)
8 & 14 Kramerstrasse, Tel. 32 52 89;
4 Am Holzmarkt, Tel. 32 38 71
Mooshage, H.-G.   (18th/19th-century antiques)
23 Kramerstrasse,
Tel. 32 01 73/77 28 24

The City

Next time you get stuck in a traffic jam, spare a thought for Karlsruhe. Were it not for local son Carl Benz, who built the world's first car, you could still be living in the age of the train. Of course, Greenpeace ecologists and potential cardiac-case managers may have already changed over to bicycles. In which case the idea goes back to Karlsruhe, too, since Karl Friedrich Drais, Baron von Sauerbronn, pioneer of the bicycle, was also a native of the city. Karlsruhe, in fact, is the secret Akademgorodk of the Federal Republic, albeit with an infinitely more congenial climate in every respect than its Siberian counterpart, since it lies in the southern Rhine valley. Home of the country's first technical university, with physicist Heinrich Hertz and Nobel Laureate chemist Fritz Haber amongst its most illustrious alumni, the city also houses alchemist epicentres for nuclear physics, nutrition and air purification as well as a broad spectrum of manufacturing industries typical for the area, reflecting the industrious nature of the local population. But Karlsruhe assumes national importance above all as the headquarters of the Federal Constitutional and Surpreme Courts (the mountains of files in the archives reflect, it seems, the conscientious German's pedantic determination to pursue every case to the very highest instance). Margrave Karl Wilhelm von Baden-Durlach's country retreat provides a suitably dignified setting, with elegant Baroque houses and gracious neo-classical buildings, from Friedrich Weinbrenner's Protestant church to his State Mint, which line the boulevards radiating like a fan from the imposing symmetry of the palace. The city's parks provide a luxuriant backdrop for a proliferation of statues and fountains, mythological and humourous, with museums full of dinosaurs, galleries full of works by Lucas Cranach and local son Hans Thoma, concert halls and theatres, premières and cabarets rounding out the cultural palette. Here Wagner's Tristan broke his heart and moved everyone to tears for the first time. Restrained maestro Johannes Brahms from Hamburg considered Karlsruhe an essential stopover for an understanding of the classical repertoire. But the local citizens do not live on culture alone. Karlsruhe is a bastion of unpretentious good living. ›Karl's Rest‹'s founding father didn't originally intend building a town at all, but he found his home-from-home so irresistible that he moved his court from nearby Durlach. Foreign visitors will not be able to resist Karlsruhe's good life either. In the heart of one of Germany's fairy-tale landscapes, food, wine and jovial-conviviality have found a stronghold which the hospitable and generous citizens will be happy to share.

Founded: 1715 – as a retreat for Count Karl Wilhelm von Baden-Durlach; Karlsruhe – ›Karl's rest‹.

Far-reaching events: 1765 – first extension of the city; 1825 – Technological High School founded; first quarter of the 19th century – construction of many of the classical buildings by Friedrich Weinbrenner; heavy damage during World War II; post-1945 – rebuilt in the original style with many parks.

Population: 280,000.

Postal code: D-7500   **Telephone code:** 721

Climate: mild winters; warm to hot summers.

Calendar of events: *Spring Market* (May–Jun); *Handel Festival* (Jun–Jul); *Ettlingen Castle Festival* (Jul–Aug); *Lichterfest* (Aug); *Kulturmarkt* (Sep); *International Music Parade* (autumn); *Autumn Market* (Nov); *Christkindlesmarkt* (Dec).

Fairs and exhibitions: *SELEX* (Mar&Dec) – trade fair; *LEISURE TIME EXHIBITION* (Mar); *FIT UND GESUND* (Apr) – health exhibition; *KOMMTECH* (Jun, biennial – 1987) – German communications fair for microcomputer, videotext and office communications; *FENSTERBAU* (Jun) – international exhibition of the window industries; *PHARMACEUTICAL EXHIBITION* (Aug–Sep); *HOLZVERARBEITUNG* (Sep) – wood and plastic-working trade fair; *HORTEC* (Sep) – professional technology in horticulture; *OFFERTA* (Oct–Nov) – consumer goods fair; *ANTIKMA* (Oct–Nov) – art and antiques exhibition; technical aids for rehabilitation, with workshops.

Historical sights: *Castle* (1715–19th century) – housing the Baden Regional Museum; *Town Square* (1773–76) – with mausoleum; *Town Hall* (1805–21); *Lutheran Church* – pure Jugendstil; *St. Stephen* (1808–14); *Hans Thoma Museum; Fine Arts Museum* – works of old masters; *Orangerie* (1853–57) – works of modern masters; *Castle Ettlingen* – with Dolphin Fountains and Asam Room; *Bruchsal Castle* – with staircase by Balthasar Neumann; *Schloss Favorite* – with the ›Sala Terrena‹.

Modern sights: *Botanic gardens* with redoubtable cactus collection; *Baden State Theatre*.

Special attractions: a concert at *Ettlingen Castle*; dinner at *Erbprinz*.

Important companies with headquarters in the city: *ACUM* (electronic media); *Badenia* (printing); *Badische Maschinenfabrik* (heavy plant); *Grebau – Greschbach Industrie* (heavy plant); *Haake* (control engineering); *Heine, Heinrich* (mail order); *Holtzmann, E. & Cie* (paper and carton); *Kniel System-Electronic* (electronic components); *Michelin Reifenwerke* (tyres); *Moninger Brauerei* (brewery); *Pfaff* (sewing machines); *Pfizer* (chemicals); *Pharma-Allergan* (pharmaceuticals); *Ragolds, Rachengold* (sweets); *Tubus Metall* (import/export metal).

Airport: Stuttgart, (STR); Tel.: (711) 7 90 11, 80 km/50 miles, inter-city connection; Strasbourg, SXB; Tel.: (3 38 86) 68 92 12/8; 80 km/50 miles; Karlsruhe airport only for sports and private planes, Tel.: 51 06 59.

The Headquarters

RAMADA RENAISSANCE

Mendelssohnplatz
D–7500 Karlsruhe
Telephone: 3 71 70
Telex: 7 825 699 rrhk
Owning Company: Fluek GmbH
General Manager: Kurt Berndt
Affiliation/Reservation Systems: Ramada Hotels, Ramada Roomfinder 2
Number of rooms: 215 (8 suites)
Price range: DM 165–205 (single)
     DM 205–265 (double)
     DM 450–900 (suite)
Credit cards: DC, EC, Visa, AE, En Route
Location: city centre, a short walk from the city's historic market place
Built: 1982
Style: modern, luxurious
Hotel amenities: valet parking, garage, car rental desk, wheelchair accessibility, hotel shops, hairstylist, beauty salon, sauna, solarium, massage, boutique, newsstand, drugstore, ballroom, house doctor

Room amenities: air conditioning, colour tv, mini-bar, radio, video, trouser press (pets allowed)
Bathroom amenities: hairdrier, telephone, bidet (in some)
Room service: 24 hours
Laundry/dry cleaning: same day
Conference rooms: 10 (up to 300 persons), flip charts, overhead projector, microphone, screen
Bar: ›Weinbrenner‹: (9.00/a.m. till dawn), pianist, Gianni Bonettin (barman)
Restaurants: ›Zum Markgrafen‹ (6.15/a.m.–15.00/3 p.m. and 18.00/6 p.m.–1.00/a.m.) Pierro Serfaini (maître), Rudolph Pichl (chef de cuisine), international cuisine with local specialities, pianist, Biedermeier style; ›Zum Brigande‹: (18.00/6 p.m.–3.00/a.m.) rustic beer and wine cellar, Beate Wöhrle (maître)

Private dining rooms: one (14 persons)

In a city whose public image is so definitely characterized by the classical formality of its public buildings, the Ramada Renaissance stands out with its modern clinker-clad façade and its barrel roof in the skyline as well as for its standard and service within the American hotel chain. In fact, along with its sister establishments in Düsseldorf and Hamburg, it has made itself an astonishing reputation. (The trail was clearly blazed by the heritage of the one-time Hilton.) The Margraves of Baden would not have objected to the marble floors, the light and spacious rooms, the practical comfort and the attractive colour scheme, let alone the menu in the namesake restaurant and the mood in the cosy Brigande wine tavern. However old-fashioned you may be – live à la moderne in Karlsruhe. Renaissance-style.

The Hideaway

ERBPRINZ

1 Rheinstrasse
D–7505 Ettlingen (8 km/5 miles)
Telephone: (72 43) 1 20 71
Telex: 782 848 erbe
Owner/General Managers: Uschi and Lutz Werner
Affiliation/Reservation Systems: Relais et Châteaux, Traditions & Qualité
Number of rooms: 49 (5 suites)
Price range: DM 120–155 (single)
DM 170–200 (double)
DM 290–310 (suite)
Credit cards: AE, DC, EC
Location: in the centre of Ettlingen, between Karlsruhe and Baden-Baden, 60 km/37 miles from Stuttgart airport
Built: 1788 (modernized)
Style: classical
Hotel amenities: car park, lift, terrace (pets welcome)
Room amenities: colour tv
Room service: 6.00 a.m.–22.00/10 p.m.
Laundry/dry cleaning: same day
Conference rooms: for up to 60 persons
Sports (nearby): tennis, swimming (1 km/0.6 miles)
Bar: one
Restaurant: ›Erbprinz‹ (12.00/a.m.–14.00/2.00 p.m. and 18.30/6.30 p.m.–22.00/10.00 p.m.), Paul Schmidt (chef de cuisine), classic cuisine, antique décor
Private dining rooms: three (up to 80 persons)

The sleek carriages which pull up these days outside the ›Erbprinz‹ in Ettlingen keep their horse-power under their bonnets rather than on display, but apart from that, superficially, at least, it's a question of ›plus ça change . . .‹ Napoleon stayed here, and would have little difficulty recognizing the former post-house today, since châtelains Uschi and Lutz Werner ensure the continuity of the relais' long-standing tradition of high-quality hospitality. Aristocracy of rank and wealth who have wined, dined and slumbered here for the past two hundred years would certainly approve the retention of all the finest period features of this distinguished auberge, from the wood-panelled dining room with its valuable old paintings and tapestries to the ornately gilt lamp-post by the front door. They would endorse the eulogies of latter-day gourmets for the cuisine of Paul Schmidt which, from the consommé to the crêpes au Calvados to the coffee, is bound to be a memorable experience – enhanced, of course, by the sort of service which will make you feel like a prince.

Lunch

ZUM KRANZ
210 Neureuter Hauptstrasse
Neureut (7 km/4 miles)
Telephone: 70 57 42
Owner/Manager: the Nagel family
Closed: Sunday; public holidays; first
week in April; second half of July
Open: 12.00/a.m.–14.00/2 p.m. and
18.00/6 p.m.–23.00/11 p.m.
Cuisine: German
Chef de cuisine: Wolfgang Nagel
Specialities: cress soup; salad; tripe in
Noilly Prat; fillet of pike-perch (Zander)
in Riesling sauce
Location: in Neureut; 7 km/4 miles north
of city centre
Setting: an old country inn on the main
road of what was once a village; comfor-
table seating; festive décor and attrac-
tively-laid tables
Amenities: private dining room; open-air
dining on terrace; car park
Atmosphere: old-world charm
Clientèle: Karlsruhe's In-Crowd; bank-
ers; businessmen, the local Saturday af-
ternoon crowd en fête and en famille
Dress: as you like it (as long as they will
like you!)
Service: friendly and welcoming
Reservations: recommended
Price range: moderately expensive
Credit cards: AE

Dinner

ERBPRINZ
1 Rheinstrasse
Ettlingen (8 km/5 miles)
Telephone: (72 43)1 20 71
Owner/Manager: Lutz Werner
Closed: Sunday; public holidays (except
for hotel guests)
Open: 12.00/a.m.–14.30/2.30 p.m. and
18.30/6.30 p.m.–21.30/9.30 p.m.
Cuisine: local; ›au goût du marché‹
Chef de cuisine: Paul Schmidt
Specialities: calf's tail consommé; fillet
of lamb with spices; stuffed sole; pâtés
and terrines; duck with orange and pepper sauce; fillet of veal with morel mushroom sauce; pike dumplings in white
wine with lobster au gratin; cinnamon
parfait with figs
Location: in Ettlingen; 8 km/5 miles
south of Karlsruhe
Setting: spacious, elegant dining room
with well-chosen furnishings and accessoires and exquisitely-laid tables
Amenities: hotel; private dining rooms;
bar; open-air dining on terrace; car park
(garage)
Atmosphere: a beguiling mixture of aristocratic tranquillity and rural charm
Clientèle: discerning and discriminating
hotel guests; industrialists tired of Karls-
ruhe; travellers en route from Bremen to
Basle
Dress: rather conservative
Service: solicitous
Reservations: advisable
Price range: fairly expensive
Credit cards: AE, DC, Euro

Dinner

DA PINO
22 Mathystrasse
Telephone: 81 39 49
Owner/Manager: Pino Melani
Closed: Thursday
Open: 12.00/a.m.–14.30/2.30 p.m. and
18.00/6 p.m.–23.30/11.30 p.m.
Cuisine: highly individual, Italian
Chef de cuisine: G. Disario
Specialities: home-made pasta to go with
unorthodox but excellent sauces; fresh
salmon in dock leaves; duckling breasts
in vinegar and sherry sauce; charcoal
grilled steaks; seafood
Setting: large dining room for up to 80
guests, elegant Italian décor
Amenities: restaurant, conference rooms,
car park
Atmosphere: refined, warm and friendly;
Italian charm
Clientèle: heterogeneous; local habitués
mingle with homesick Italian gourmets
and foreign visitors
Dress: as you like it (as long as they will
like you!)
Service: attentive, friendly, efficient
Reservations: essential
Price range: medium
Credit cards: AE, DC, EC

Lunch

DUDELSACK
79 Waldstrasse
Telephone: 2 21 66
Owner/Manager/Chef de cuisine: Heinz
Hügel
Open: 12.00/a.m.–14.00/2 p.m. and
18.00/6 p.m.–23.00/11 p.m.
Cuisine: local, unpretentious
Specialities: fillet of calf in morel mushroom sauce; crêpes with smoked salmon
and fresh herbs; low-calorie menu
Location: in the building of ›Kammerspiele‹ (Karlsruhe's theatre)
Setting: bistro-like restaurant, comfortably furnished in local style
Amenities: open air dining on garden terrace in summer, cocktail bar, pets permitted
Atmosphere: very ›Badisch‹, lively and
yet relaxing, rather crowded
Clientèle: sales managers, members of
the liberal professions and tourists during
lunch-time, followed by actors and the

usual after-theatre-crowd before and after performances at the ›Kammerspiele‹
Dress: elegant and eye-catching
Service: efficient and smiling
Reservations: advisable to essential
Price range: medium

Dinner

KÜNSTLERKNEIPE
(Gasthof zur Krone)
18 Pfarrstrasse
Daxlanden (5 km/3 miles)
Telephone: 57 22 47
Owner/Manager/Chef de cuisine: Hugo Schwall
Closed: Sunday; Monday; December 24th – 28th
Open: 12.00/a.m.–14.00/2 p.m. and 18.00/6 p.m.–23.00/11 p.m.
Cuisine: local; ›au goût du marché‹
Specialities: terrine of goose liver; mushroom soup (Steinpilzsuppe); pike dumpling soup (Hechtklösschensuppe); lobster pâté with caviar cream sauce; kidneys in Pinot Noir; Strasbourg-style noodles; ice-cream parfait with strawberry purée
Location: in Daxlanden, 5 km/3 miles west of Karlsruhe
Setting: timbered country auberge amidst vineyards; run by the same family for 125 years; attractively old-fashioned dining rooms with paintings and drawings by local artists of the Karlsruhe school, who frequented the establishment at the turn of the century
Amenities: private dining rooms; open-air dining on terrace
Atmosphere: prettily nostalgic
Clientèle: local politicians; civic dignitaries; expense-account art-lovers
Dress: within reason, come-as-you-please
Service: individual and attentive
Reservations: essential
Price range: moderately expensive

Meeting Point

LUDWIG'S (›Café Wichtig‹)
61 Waldstrasse
Telephone: 2 33 49
Owner/Manager: Udo Glaser and Heinz Hügel
Closed: never
Open: 8.00/a.m.–1.00/a.m.
Cuisine: Italian
Chef de cuisine: Alfredo Gala
Specialities: pasta, pasta pasta . . ., but also Bavarian white sausages (Weisswürstchen), brought fresh every day from Munich
Location: in the centre of the Ludwigsplatz
Amenities: café, bar and restaurant (60 persons); small terrace

Atmosphere: favourite meeting point for the exchange of news, views and local gossip by those in the know and those who would like to be
Clientèle: a scintillating cocktail of local personalities, visiting celebrities and those who enjoy the company of the former or the latter
Dress: what you will
Service: Italianissimo
Reservations: advisable
Price range: medium
Credit cards: Euro

Café

FELLER
Am Marktplatz
Telephone: 2 59 98
Owner/Manager: Feller GmbH
Closed: December 25th/26th, January 1st, February 11th, March 30th/31st
Open: (Monday–Friday) 7.00/a.m.–23.00/11 p.m.; (Saturday) 8.00/a.m.–23.00/11 p.m.; (Sunday) 9.00/a.m.–23.00/11 p.m.
Location: central, on the market place, near the chateau
Setting: stylish; light and bright; modern décor with large picture windows
Amenities: café for up to 160 guests, also offering light meals and a restaurant; open-air dining in summer, car parks nearby
Atmosphere: comfortable and elegant
Clientèle: heterogeneous
Dress: whatever you like
Service: charming, professional and friendly
Reservations: advisable (especially for lunch)
Price range: medium
Credit cards: not accepted

Shopping

EVERYTHING UNDER ONE ROOF
Schneider Kaiserstrasse

FOR HIM
Therkatz 223 Kaiserstrasse

FOR HER
Donna 193 Kaiserstrasse

BEAUTY & HAIR
Kiefer 16 Herrenstrasse

JEWELLERY
Bertsch GmbH 165 Kaiserstrasse

LOCAL SPECIALITIES
Epoque (women's fashion)
66 Waldstrasse
Reif Exquisit Moden (men's fashion)
41–43 Karlstrasse
Pünktchen und Anton (children's fashion)
37 Amalienstrasse
Gassmann, Karl Mode Leder (leather fashion)
13 Herrenstrasse
Arzt (furs)
239 Kaiserstrasse
Müller und Schlicht (books)
Kaiserstrasse
Wohlschlegel (gifts/porcelain)
173 Kaiserstrasse
Gold Pfeil (baggage & travel accessories)
104 Kaiserstrasse
Kaefer's-Schlemmerinsel (food and beverages)
23 Herrenstrasse
Mütschelle (perfumery)
66 Waldstrasse
Cinderella da Felice GmbH (shoes)
53 Amalienstrasse

THE BEST OF ART
Rottloff (contemporary art)
105 Sophienstrasse, Tel. 84 32 25

It's not among the secret capitals of the continent, has hardly a superlative attraction to compete with Hamburg, Frankfurt or Munich, is not quite of Rhine Valley dreaminess, and most travellers in search of culture and pleasure bypass it for the lack of an international airport as well as for the proximity of Heidelberg. Yet Mannheim, centre of one of the country's largest industrial agglomerations, is not only living up to its commercial importance but also creating an image for itself as a city of artful joys. Second largest river port in Europe, with one of the most significant oil refineries, production of chemicals, pharmaceuticals, electro-technical goods, cellulose and paper, Mannheim is also proud of its electoral past – with its castle the biggest Baroque palace in Germany – even though much of the architectural heritage fell prey to conquistadores from all sides in the past five centuries of its planned existence. Conceived down to the geometrical détail of a chessboard by the Palatine sovereign, Mannheim's inner-city layout is still avant-garde in the Old World, today. Chimneys and office buildings may mark the skyline, along with the ones across the river, in Ludwigshafen, but the hinterland on both sides of the Neckar and the Rhine is the landscape of fairy tales and love poems. In times past, Voltaire was pleased by Mannheim as well as Goethe, and regional prophet of freedom, Friedrich Schiller, had all his dramas inaugurated at the Elector's court. Of unexpectedly refined artistic greatness, this metropolis was even the stage for the forerunners of post-Baroque classical music, influencing maestri like Haydn and Mozart. And as a fairly new city compared to the medieval strongholds in the vicinity – Worms, Speyer and Heidelberg – new ideas were often translated into action here, such as Karl Drais' bicycle, Karl Benz's motor car and Heinrich Lanz's tractor. This city remains the arena of industry and business, however much one points to the historic traces and ecological achievements, but one of the great advantages of Mannheim is the suburban closeness of Heidelberg, showcase of romanticism, embedded in a wonderland of idealized nature. (It takes less time to reach Heidelberg Castle from the landmark Water Tower than to get from the Tower of London to Earl's Court.) The intellectual-informal-intimate climate in town (the oldest university in Germany has an atmospheric influence beyond Gemütlichkeit), the walks along the hillside Philosophenweg across the river (with Novalis or lover in hand), and the floodlit fortress with fireworks as a backdrop in sight (dwarfing all the Son-et-Lumière productions), you may forget everything irritating about Germany – and maybe business in Mannheim as well.

Founded: 766 – first mentioned as ›Maninheim‹ – ›home of Manno‹.

Far-reaching events: 1606 – city founded under Elector Friedrich IV; 1688/89 – destroyed in Wars of Succession; 1692 – city rebuilt on a grid pattern; 1720 – Elector Palatine Carl Philipp moves his residence to Mannheim following the sacking of Heidelberg – the city becomes a home of the arts; 1795 – destroyed in the Revolutionary Wars; 1799 – castle built; 1802 – part of the Electorate of Baden; 19th century – Mannheim develops as an important trade centre; 1944/45 – heavily damaged; post-1945 – city reconstruction retaining the 17th-century grid pattern.

Population: 302,000; second largest city in the state of Baden-Württemberg.

Postal code: D–6800 **Telephone code:** 621

Climate: mild; spring comes early on the Upper Rhine.

Calendar of events: *Carnival Parade* (Shrove Sunday) – spectacular procession, alternating with the neighbouring city Ludwigshafen; *Amusement Fair* (May) – huge festival concurrent with the *May Market; Schwetzingen Castle Festival* (May) – in the Baroque theatre of the castle; *German Formula One Grand Prix* (Jul) – at Hockenheim; *Heidelberg Castle Festival* (Aug); *International Film Week* (Oct).

Fairs and exhibitions: *MAY MARKET* (May and Oct) – industrial exhibition.

Historical sights: *Castle of the Electors Palatine* (1720–60) – one of the most magnificent Baroque palaces in the world; *Old City* – the grid-like plan was drawn up in 1698; *Water Tower* (1889) – Mannheim's landmark; *Reiss Museum* – municipal history and Baron Drais' first bicycle; *Jesuit Church* (1733–60) – most important Baroque church in southern Germany; *Old Observatorium* (1774), next door to the *Old City Hall*.

Modern sights: *Planetarium; National Theatre* – three stages with 1900 seats; *Fine Arts Museum* – Jugendstil, 19th and 20th century art; *Augusta Park* (1933) – park setting for a monument to Carl Benz, the man who brought the automobile to Mannheim.

Special attractions: any festivity as long as it's in the *castle;* the *romantic surroundings* on both sides of the Rhine (left bank – Speyer to Worms; right bank – the Bergstrasse); *Heidelberg* (castle concerts, summer fireworks, Old Town tavern life); *Schwetzingen* (castle concerts, asparagus gluttony in season).

Important companies with headquarters in the city: *Bibliographisches Institut* (dictionaries); *Boehringer, Bopp & Reuther* (engines, electronics); *Brown, Boveri & Cie* (electrotechnology); *Daimler Benz* (buses); *Deere & Company* (tractors); *Goldschmidt* (chemicals, copper); *Lanz, Heinrich* (machinery); *Motorenwerke Mannheim* (engines); *Papierwerke Waldhoff-Aschaffenburg* (hygienic paper products); *Pressluft Goetz* (machinery); *Schildkröte* (dolls); *Siemens* (electronics); *Süddeutsche Zucker AG* (sugar); *Vögele, Joseph* (heavy plant).

Airport: Frankfurt-Rhein-Main, FRA; Tel.: 69/6901; Lufthansa: 69/6902111; 80 km/50 miles; Mannheim-Neuostheim (connection to Munich); Tel.: 621/413041.

The Headquarters

DER EUROPÄISCHE HOF – HOTEL EUROPA/KURFÜRSTENSTUBE

1 Friedrich-Ebert-Anlage
D–6900 Heidelberg (16 km/10 miles)
Telephone: (6221) 271 01
Telex: 461 840
Managing Owner: Ernst-Friedrich von Kretschmann
Manager: Peter-A. Rübartsch
Affiliation/Reservation Systems: The Leading Hotels of the World; SRS (Steigenberger Reservation Service); Hotel-Mosaik; Hotels de Grande Classe
Number of rooms: 154 (14 suites)
Price range: DM 189–440
Credit cards: AE; DC; EC; Visa
Location: town centre; 80 kilometres/55 miles from airport
Built: 1865; annexes 1928, 1977 and 1986
Style: traditional
Hotel amenities: garage (pets allowed)
Room amenities: colour tv, radio, safe
Room service: 6.00/a.m. to 24.00/12 p.m.
Conference rooms: 10 (up to 400 persons)
Bar: ›Europa Bar‹ Herr Balla (barman)
Restaurant: ›Kurfürstenstube‹ (12.00 p.m.–14.30/2.30 p.m. and 18.30/6.30 p.m.–23.00/11 p.m.); Herr Breitschaft/Herr Goss (maîtres); Herr Leiendecker (chef de cuisine); nouvelle cuisine

The reasons for taking up headquarters in Heidelberg when doing business in Mannheim or its sister-city Ludwigshafen on the other Rhine embankment are manifold. The main one – without underrating the natural delights of Germany's romantic résidence – is the Headquarters itself: Der Europäische Hof. Neither in the twinned metropolis nor anywhere near will the discerning manager or discriminating globetrotter find a hotel as beautiful and luxurious, yet cosy and personal at the same time, making it not only the logical choice for all activities – from base to meetings, from conferences to festivities – but also the ideal hideaway from the industrial centres in the proximity. (Even in bad weather and during rush-hour traffic you won't drive longer than from King Street to the Bank of England.) Ernst-Friedrich von Kretschmann runs this traditional family-auberge-cum-grand-hotel in a symbiotic fashion between efficient practicality and historic splendour, with a professional staff only found in cosmopolitan capitals. When you enter the grande-entrée driveway you can decide to reside either in the historic wing or in one of the avant-garde suites. Views are guaranteed from most rooms and modern comfort, pleasant colours and materials in all. Highlight of the hotel and the city is the renowned Kurfürstenstube *with its coffered ceiling and marquetry wall panelling, and – above all – its cuisine, international and local, known as the best at the foot of the fairy-tale castle. Do business in Mannheim, but enjoy all the pleasures in Heidelberg. At the Europäischer Hof!*

Lunch

BLASS
30 Langlachweg
Mannheim-Friedrichsfeld
Telephone: 47 20 04
Owner/Manager: Kurt Blass
Closed: Monday; Saturday lunchtime
Open: 11.30/a.m.–13.30/1.30 p.m. and
18.30/6.30 p.m.–21.00/9 p.m.
Cuisine: innovative
Specialities: terrine of pheasant with foie
gras d'oie and pistachio kernels; fish pâté
with salad; quenelles de brochet with
crabs' tails, leeks and spinach; stuffed
quail with salsify and creamed potatoes
Location: a 15-minute drive south-east of
city centre
Setting: on the fourth floor of a furniture
shop in a shopping centre which seems
totally abandoned at night; leather armchairs, plenty of greenery
Amenities: bar; private dining room; terrace with a view; car park
Atmosphere: that of a private club; chic
and rather exclusive
Clientèle: gourmets-in-the-know (no one
else would guess of the existence of this
restaurant)
Dress: tends towards the conservative
Service: rather superior
Reservations: recommended
Price range: fairly high

Dinner

L'EPI D'OR
H 7, 3
Telephone: 1 43 97
Owner/Chef de cuisine: Günter Lorenz
Closed: Monday; Saturday lunchtime;
three weeks in June
Open: 11.30/a.m.–14.30/2.30 p.m. and
18.00/6 p.m.–23.00/11 p.m.
Cuisine: French (classic)
Specialities: gourmet menu; warm lob-
ster salad with seaweed; pigeons' breast
with chanterelles; brain in chervil butter;
angler-fish soufflé in lobster sauce; lamb
with rosemary; breast of duck with
thyme; peaches with cinnamon ice-cream
Location: central – just inside the Luisen-
ring
Setting: rather unprepossessing exterior;
inside, rustic granny-style front-room
parlour décor
Amenities: air conditioning; car park
Atmosphere: comfortable and friendly
Clientèle: local gourmet habitués and for-
eign businessmen
Dress: informal
Service: particularly warm and welcom-
ing; under the direction of Fräulein
Hauss
Reservations: essential (no dogs)
Price range: fairly high
Credit cards: AE, DC, Euro, Visa

Lunch

KOPENHAGEN
2a Friedrichsring
Telephone: 1 48 70
Owner/Manager/Chef de cuisine: Man-
fred Bantle
Closed: Sunday; public holidays; 3
weeks in June
Open: 12.00/a.m.–15.00/3 p.m. and
18.00/6 p.m.–24.00/12 p.m.
Cuisine: fish specialities
Specialities: seafood terrine; sea snails in
Italian sauce; home-made spinach ravioli
(Maultaschen) with turbot mousse fill-
ing; coquilles St. Jacques in Pernod; eel
in red wine; sole filled with truffles; tur-
bot in champagne mustard sauce
Location: near the Water Tower (Wasser-
turm)
Setting: elegantized rustic; long narrow
dining room with view of kitchen at end
Amenities: bar; air conditioning
Atmosphere: bustling and cheerful, but
stylish
Clientèle: cross-section of men of com-
merce, men from the media, industrialists
and fish gourmets
Dress: no special requirements
Service: pleasant and friendly; directed
by the wife of the patron
Reservations: advisable
Price range: moderately high
Credit cards: AE, DC, Euro, Visa

Dinner

DA GIANNI R 7, 34
Telephone: 2 03 26
Owner/Manager: Gianni Julita
Closed: Monday; one week at New Year;
3 weeks in summer
Open: 12.00/a.m.–14.00/2 p.m. and
18.00/6 p.m.–22.30/10.30 p.m.
Cuisine: nuova cucina italiana
Chef de cuisine: Lillo Bisaccia
Specialities: foie gras with bean salad;
Scotch wild salmon in saffron sauce;
Mediterranean fish and shellfish; quail in
Parma ham;
Location: city centre, near Water Tower
Setting: subdued Mediterranean ele-
gance; pink wallpaper and table linen,
fine porcelain, silver, glass; original pain-
tings; large fish tank
Amenities: conference room
Atmosphere: luxurious, with a hint of
romance
Clientèle: heads of state; famous faces
from the world of politics, sport and
show business; Mannheim's Top Ten
Dress: elegantly casual to casually ele-
gant, with a sprinkling of dinner jackets
Service: friendly and welcoming
Reservations: advisable
Price range: moderately high
Credit cards: AE, Euro

Bar

MÜNZ CHALET
1 P 7
Telephone: 2 82 62
Owner/Manager: Bob Haag
Open: 19.00/7 p.m.–4.00/a.m.
Location: central; a champagne cork's trajectory from the Maritim Hotel
Setting: chalet-style intérieur with an abundance of light old wood; antique furnishings and accessoires
Amenities: restaurant upstairs (French and local cuisine); late snacks available until midnight; cocktail lounge
Atmosphere: typical friendly bar ambience
Clientèle: mostly well-heeled, well-travelled, well-dressed and fairly well-off
Service: very efficient
Price range: medium
Dress: no sneakers, fairly elegant
Reservations: essential
Credit cards: AE, DC, Euro, Visa, Master

Nightclub

TIFFANY
7–9 Hortenpassage
Telephone: 1 26 50
Owner/Manager: Thomas von Esselborn
Open: 22.00/10 p.m.–5.00/a.m.
Location: central
Setting: modern; vaguely Art Déco with original lamps and accessoires; unusual lighting effects; octagonal dance floor surrounded by tables and bar counter; two lounges with separate bar
Amenities: discothèque; air conditioning
Atmosphere: from fortissimo con fuoco in the main hall to a decibel level which permits normal conversation or even whispered sweet nothings in the bar-lounges
Clientèle: young and self-assured to middle-aged and successful, with a sprinkling of glittering and glamourous visitors – from the King of Sweden and Udo Jürgens to Alice and the Rolling Stones
Dress: designer casual to disco elegant
Service: amiable and efficient
Reservations: advisable
Price range: fairly expensive
Credit cards: AE, DC

Shopping

EVERYTHING UNDER ONE ROOF
Kaufhof   Paradeplatz

FOR HIM
Axel's Club   Q 5,6

FOR HER
Busch   P 7,20–23 An den Planken

BEAUTY & HAIR
Salon Rainer + Rosi
4 Stresemannstrasse

JEWELLERY
Braun   O 7,10 An den Planken

LOCAL SPECIALITIES
Sepp Guetinger (tobacco)
7 An den Planken
Klemm (men's fashion)
O 7,12 An den Planken
Robinson (men & women's fashion)
P 6,3–4
Ellen Cola (children's fashion)
16 Friedrichsplatz
Leonhard Weber (leather fashion)
P 6,22 Plankenhof
Kunze (furs)
N 2,6 Paradeplatz
Otto's Buchhandlung (books)
O 7,11 An den Planken
Hermès Boutique (gifts)
O 7,10 An den Planken
Manz (porcelain)
P 6,26
Leder Doering (baggage & travel accessories)
P 7,16–17 An den Planken
Suedlandhaus (food and beverages)
P 3,8

THE BEST OF ART
Bausback   (oriental carpets)
N 3,9, Tel. 2 58 08

›Munich is the Paradise of which all Germans dream‹, wrote restless Thomas Wolfe, whose Homeward-looking Angel would have hovered very happily on its cloud above the capital of the Free State of Bavaria. From whatever perspective it is viewed, it is commonly agreed that Germany's much-extolled and much-envied ›Secret Capital‹ is a jewel among Europe's glittering centres of cosmopolitan activity, blending an all-pervading Bavarian Gemütlichkeit with Italian farniente and French promiscuité. But Munich, with her world-renowned music life, museums and ›Mädchenwunder‹, with her fashion fairs, film studios and beer festivals, is not all play. Some of Germany's status industries have their headquarters here, and as a city of fairs and exhibitions, Munich has gained a reputation of its own. If ever there were an ideal symbiosis of business and pleasure, you could find it here.

Founded: former monk community; 1158 – incorporated as a town by the Duke of Saxony and Bavaria, Henry The Lion; München (German) – from the founding monks.

Far-reaching events: from 1180 – residence of the House of Wittelsbach; 14th century – seat of government for Emperor Ludwig the Bavarian (the town expands fivefold); 17th century – occupation by Swedish King Gustav Adolf (Thirty Years War) and decimation of one third of the population by the plague; 19th century – Ludwig Era (grand architecture and the arts under Ludwig I, architecture à la folie and fairy-tale nostalgia under Ludwig II); after World War I – foundation of the Free State of Bavaria; Third Reich – Hitlermania reigns in the Führer's favourite city; 1939–45 – half the city is destroyed during World War II; 1972 – Olympic Games; from here to eternity – Munich one of the fun cities of the world.

Population: 1.4 million; third largest city in Germany.

Postal code: D–8000 **Telephone code:** 89

Climate: very fickle (warm winds – the Föhn– create heat waves in winter and headaches throughout the year); it may snow in May, but you may also enjoy a beergarden in late October.

Best time to visit: June until October; January until March (carnival/skiing).

Calendar of events: *Fasching* – galas, balls and artists' parties (Jan, Feb); *Theatre Festival* (May–Jun); *Castle Concerts* in Nymphenburg, Schleissheim, Blutenburg (Jun, Jul); *Opera Festival* (end-Jul, Aug); *Oktoberfest* (Sep–Oct) – largest public festival in the world/beer funfair; *Christkindlmarkt* (Dec) – Christmas market.

Fairs and exhibitions: *HADROFA* (Jan) – drugs and cosmetics; *INHORGENTA* (Feb) – watches and jewellery; *ISPO* (Feb) – sports articles; *IHM* (Mar) – international crafts and trade; *FASHION WEEK* (Mar); *BAUMA* (Apr) – building fair; *ELECTRONICS* (Jul); *ISPO* (Sep); *IGAFA* (Sep) – hotel and restaurant trade; *INTERMONTEC* (Sep) – sports and pastimes; *FASHION WEEK* (Oct); *CERAMITEC* (Oct) – ceramics machinery; *SYSTEMS* (Oct) – computers; *PRODUCTRONICA* (Nov).

Best views of the city: from the *Television Tower* at the Olympic Stadium; *St. Peter's* church tower (landmark bell tower); *Bavaria statue* on the Theresienhöhe.

Historical sights: *Frauenkirche* (15th century), cathedral – Munich's landmark; *Asam Church* (mid-18th century) – rococo reverie; the *Residenz* – royal palace since the 14th century, treasure vault and valuable collections; *Theatiner Church* – impressive Baroque; *Cuvilliés Theatre* – one of the most beautiful rococo interiors in the world; *Old Pinakothek* – one of the most important picture galleries in the world; *New Pinakothek* – pictures 18th to 20th centuries; *Glyptothek* – antique sculptures of world renown in a striking classicistic building; *Bayerisches Nationalmuseum* – art and artefacts, interior design and paraphernalia dating back to medieval times; *Nymphenburg Castle* (mid–17th century) – summer residence of the Wittelsbach – largest Baroque castle in Germany.

Modern sights: *Olympic Stadium* (1972) – best for sports events, open-air theatre or rock concerts; *Deutsches Museum* – biggest and best-equipped technical museum in the world; *Bavaria Film Studios* – Hollywood en not-so-miniature; *BMW Museum* – striking architecture and the history of cars; the *English Garden* – Hyde Park of Munich.

Special attractions: a première at the *Opera;* a candlelight concert at *Nymphenburg Castle;* a pop concert at the *Olympic stadium; Hofbräuhaus* (most famous beer hall in the world); *beergardens* (Augustiner, Aumeister, Hirschgarten, Salvator, English Garden); the *girls* of Ipanema this side of the Atlantic.

Important companies with headquarters in the city: *Allianz* (insurance); *Augustiner* (brewery); *Bayerische Motoren-Werke* (cars); *Bayerische Vereinsbank* (banking); *Bogner* (fashion); *Burda* (publishing); *Hacker-Pschorr* (brewery); *Hypo Bank* (banking); *Krauss Maffei* (heavy plant); *Langenscheidt KG* (publishing); *Löwenbräu* (brewery); *Messerschmitt-Bölkow-Blohm* (aerospace); *Münchener Rückversicherung* (insurance); *Siemens* (electronics); *Spaten-Franziskaner* (brewery); *Togal* (pharmaceuticals); *Wacker* (chemicals); *Wamsler* (heating systems).

Airport: München-Riem, MUC; Tel.: 9 21 10; Lufthansa; Tel.: 9 21 21; VIP/Senator Lounge, Tel.: 9 21 22 29; 10 km/6 miles.

The Headquarters

GRAND HOTEL CONTINENTAL

5 Max Joseph-Strasse
D–8000 Munich 2
Telephone: 55 15 70
Telex: 5 226 603 conti
Owner/Manager: Hermann Prinz von Sachsen
Affiliation/Reservation Systems: Utell, Best Western, Lufthansa, Swissair, Pan American World Airways
Number of rooms: 159 (14 suites)
Price range: DM 190–1,000
Credit cards: AE, DC, EC, Visa
Location: city centre
Built: 1945 (renovated 1985)
Style: individualistic, luxury, antiques
Hotel amenities: garage, valet parking, house limousine service (Mercedes 600), beauty salon, hairstylist, newsstand, tobacconist, florist
Main hall porter: Hans Muderlak
Room amenities: colour tv (remote control), video, mini-bar

Bathroom amenities: bidet, bathrobe
Room service: 6.00/a.m. to 24.00/12 p.m.
Conference rooms: 4 (up to 250 persons), ballroom
Bar: ›Conti‹ (21.00/9 p.m.–2.00/a.m.), Paolo Amadio (barman), pianist
Restaurants: ›Kaminrestaurant‹ (11.30/a.m.–15.00/3.00 p.m. and 18.00/6.00 p.m.–24.00/12.00 p.m.) Dietmar Haller (maître), Rudi Staiger (chef de cuisine), French-international cuisine, antique castle-décor, open-air dining, zither-playing in the evening; ›Conti-Grill‹ (11.30/a.m.–15.00/3.00 p.m. and 18.00/p.m.–24.00/12.00/p.m.) Alfred Vorleiter (maître), regional-international cuisine, zither-playing
Private dining rooms: three

New by Grand Hotel standards, but world-renowned for decades, this unobtrusive city palace in a quiet part of the city centre attracts the conservative élite among the travellers (and the citizens for lunch, dinner and meetings). The Prince of Saxony preserves the aristocratic flair, the tasteful décor, the good cuisine and the perfect service. The suites to the inner court radiate the atmosphere of a private mansion enjoyed by the refined clientèle who are used to the other ›Grands‹ of the world. The liveried voiturier receives you at the elevated driveway with courtesy, and Hans Muderlak arranges your life from that moment onwards. Spacious halls and salons adorned with valuable antiques and elegant Bavarica make the hotel an ideal meeting point as well as the perfect place for conferences, parties and galas. And the Conti-Grill in the castle cave has no equal as a rendez-vous for sentimental tête-à-têtes. In summer you can lunch and dine al fresco in the quiet inner court while the Conti-Bar awaits its guests with cosy cachet and fiery concoctions. The ›Conti‹ is everything to everyone – with grandeur.

The Hideaway

BACHMAIR AM SEE

47 Seestrasse
D–8183 Rottach-Egern (55 km/35 miles)
Telephone: (80 22) 64 44
Telex: 526 920 bmair
Owners: The Bachmair-Rauh Family
General Manager: Klaus W. Scheerke
Number of rooms: 230 (54 suites)
Price range: DM 135–570
Credit cards: AE, DC
Location: south of Munich on the lakeside of Tegernsee
Built: 1826
Style: pre-alpine luxury; antique and elegantly rustic
Hotel amenities: garage, valet parking, car rental in the hotel, beauty salon, health club, indoor/outdoor swimming pool, sauna bath, solarium, massage, hairstylist, newsstand, tobacconist, boutiques, house doctor
Main hall porter: Klaus Stein
Room amenities: colour tv, mini-bar, terrace
Bathroom amenities: some rooms with Roman baths, separate shower cabin
Room service: 7.00/a.m. to 23.00/11 p.m.
Laundry/dry cleaning: same day
Conference rooms: 5 (up to 220 persons), ballroom
Sports: bowling, boccia, table-tennis, gymnastics, shooting, badminton, tennis, rowing, curling
Sports (nearby): indoor tennis, riding, minigolf, 18-hole golf course 6 km/4 miles (Bad Wiessee); sailing, mountaineering, skiing in winter
Cures: various medical, revitalizing, anti-stress and diet programmes
Bar: (10.00/a.m.–3.00/p.m.) Jürgen Friedmann (barman), pianist
Restaurants: ›Bartlmästub'n‹ and ›Bierstube‹ (12.00/a.m.–23.00/11.00 p.m.) Georg Herbst (maître), H. Dürr (chef de cuisine), open-air dining in summer
Nightclub: ›Bachmair‹ (21.00/9.00 p.m.–4.00/a.m.) Uwy Heens (manager), elegant-rustic décor, live bands and pianist, discothèque

Bachmair is one of the world's international oases, where you can hide in splendour as well as indulge in a limitless number of sports, cures, pastimes and relaxations. The luxurious Bavarian picture-postcard retreat is a ›must‹ for the first-time traveller to the country as well as for the travelling businessman with a spare moment or weekend. The charm Germany's favourite land is famous for has been condensed here to perfection. Every angle, niche and nook is a delight to the disciples of Rousseau and Wordsworth – and the followers of Kneipp and Pritikin. Health and wealth meet here in natural and man-made splendour.

Lunch

KÄFER-SCHENKE
1 Schumannstrasse
Telephone: 4 16 81
Owners: Gerd and Helmut Käfer
Managers: H. Hase; H. Klier; J. Schmidt
Closed: Sunday; public holidays
Open: 11.00/a.m.–24.00/12 p.m.
Cuisine: international-sophisticated
Chef de cuisine: Peter Wesle
Specialities: French, Italian, Bavarian; regional and seasonal delicacies; hors d'œuvres-and-salad buffet
Location: on lively avenue, half-way between airport and city centre; 10 minutes from The Headquarters
Setting: beautiful renovated city palais; highly stylized, elegant Bavarian Disneyland with fairy-tale séparées for tête-à-têtes, parties or conference meals
Amenities: one of the best food stores in the world; private salons; champagne bar, bistro bar; gift shop; world famous catering service; open-air dining on small terrace
Atmosphere: lively; elegantly casual for lunch – casually elegant for dinner; a touch of snob appeal
Clientèle: affluent, jovial, conservative
Dress: from designer jeans to designer dirndl to designer cashmere
Service: impeccable (waiters en masse)
Reservations: advisable to obligatory (no pets)
Price range: appropriately expensive
Credit cards: AE, DC, Euro

Lunch

AUBERGINE
5 Maximiliansplatz
Telephone: 59 81 71
Affiliations: Traditions et Qualité
Owner/Manager/Chef de cuisine: Eckart Witzigmann
Closed: Sunday; Monday; public holidays
Open: 12.00/a.m.–14.00/2 p.m. and 19.00/7 p.m.–24.00/12 p.m.
Cuisine: nouvelle et classique
Specialities: French dishes; daily changing menu according to season and market availability
Location: central
Setting: light, modern and elegant
Amenities: salon for apéritifs
Atmosphere: stylishly sophisticated
Clientèle: connoisseurs of the finest things in life
Dress: no special requirements or restrictions
Service: impeccable
Reservations: essential
Price range: understandably expensive
Credit cards: Euro

Dinner

TANTRIS
7 Johann-Fichte-Strasse
Telephone: 36 20 61
Affiliations: Traditions et Qualité
Owner: Fritz Eichbauer
Manager: Peter Kluge
Closed: Monday lunch, Saturday lunch; Sunday; public holidays; 2 weeks at Whitsun
Open: 12.00/a.m.–15.00/3 p.m.; 18.30/6.30 p.m.–1.00/a.m.
Cuisine: French Haute Cuisine (nouvelle)
Chef de cuisine: Heinz Winkler
Specialities: wild salmon in parsley sauce with chanterelles; duckling à la Nantaise in mustard seed sauce; soufflé of nuts with white mousse-au-chocolat and raspberry sauce
Location: solitary concrete structure on the outskirts of town; 15 minutes from The Headquarters
Setting: modernistic glassed-in hall on different levels
Amenities: private parking; large bar; open-air dining in small courtyard
Atmosphere: pleasantly cool avant-garde; elegantly detached; no-frills décor; view into the kitchen
Clientèle: strictly business
Dress: grey flannel prevails
Service: to perfection; multilingual
Reservations: advisable for lunch – obligatory for dinner
Price range: naturally very high
Credit cards: AE, DC, Euro

Lunch

BOETTNER
8 Theatinerstrasse
Telephone: 22 12 10
Owner/Manager: Roland Hartung
Maître d'hôtel: Adolf Luber
Closed: Sunday; Saturday evening; public holidays
Open: 11.00/a.m.–24.00/12 p.m.
Cuisine: sophisticated French-Italian-German
Chef de cuisine: Ernst Soldan
Specialities: the finest variations of the finest products of every season; lobster, truffles, caviar
Location: in the centre of Munich's elegant shopping district
Setting: subdued elegance; conservative décor; small (8 tables); entrance through delicatessen bar
Amenities: miniature bar; exclusive delicatessen (best caviar in town)
Atmosphere: exclusive, elegant, unobtrusive – off-putting for the ›wrong‹ people
Clientèle: conservative (jacket and tie)
Service: old school perfection
Reservations: absolutely necessary (no pets)
Price range: very high
Credit cards: AE, DC, Visa, Euro

Lunch

FRANZISKANER–FUCHS'N STUB'N
5 Perusastrasse / Residenzstrasse
Telephone: 22 50 02
Owner: Eduard Reinbold
Maître d'hôtel: Karl Stauder (Herr Karl)
Closed: New Year's Day
Open: 8.00/a.m.–24.00/12 p.m.
Cuisine: Bavarian
Chef de cuisine: Hans Mühleck
Specialities: white sausages (Weiß-
würste), liver dumpling soup (Leber-
knödelsuppe), cooked meat pâté (Leber-
käs'), roast knuckle of pork (Schweins-
haxn), boiled beef with fresh horseradish
(Tellerfleisch), sugared, cut-up pancake
with raisins (Kaiserschmarrn)
Location: in the centre of Munich's elegant shopping area; at the end of Maximilianstrasse, across from the opera
house
Setting: typically Bavarian bourgeois;
various halls, salons and niches; special
decorations according to seasons
Amenities: snack-bar; private salons;
open-air dining in small courtyard
Atmosphere: lively, casual, communica-
tive
Clientèle: cross-section of men of commerce, tourists, aristocrats, local habitués
and casual passers-by
Dress: no requirements or restrictions
Service: hectic, Bavarian-moody
Reservations: only weekend lunch; pets
allowed
Price range: average
Credit cards: AE

Dinner

LA MER
24 Schraudolphstrasse
Telephone: 2 72 24 39
Owner/Manager: Alfred Kirsch
Closed: Monday; end-July to end-August
Open: 19.00/7 p.m.–23.30/11.30 p.m.
Cuisine: French
Chef de cuisine: Othmar Schweiger
Specialities: seafood
Location: in a quiet area, 10 minutes from
the city centre
Setting: impressively beautiful cellar res-
taurant, full of flowers, porcelain and de-
corative paraphernalia; candles and clas-
sic music; the city's lovers' retreat par ex-
cellence
Atmosphere: romantic
Clientèle: sentimental Upper Crust gour-
mets
Dress: floating gowns and dark suits
Service: impeccable
Reservations: obligatory (no pets)
Pricer range: very expensive
Credit cards: AE, DC, Euro

Dinner

KAY'S BISTRO
1 Utzschneiderstrasse
Telephone: 2 60 35 84
Owner/Managers: Kay Wörsching and
Achim Neumann
Closed: lunchtime every day; Sunday
Open: 19.00/7 p.m.–1.00 a.m.
Cuisine: nouvelle à l'internationale
Chef de cuisine: Manfred Duci (disciple
of Eckart Witzigmann)
Specialities: gourmet salad; Barbary
duckling; fillet of sole in champagne
sauce; médaillons of lamb with ratatouille; assiette surprise (according to
season)
Location: off Munich's most colourful
market, the Viktualienmarkt
Setting: theme-based décor, changing
every two months (à la Yves Saint Laurent in the old days)
Amenities: background music; live entertainment – especially when famous stars
take the floor
Atmosphere: Kunst & Kitsch, in the most
attractive way possible – calling to mind
the heyday of Paris–Berlin; a touch of
Hollywood and a soupçon of La Cage
aux Folles
Clientèle: famous or beautiful exhibitionists celebrating Carnival every night of
the year (introverted recluses seeking
tranquil intimacy have been warned)
Dress: Beach Boys nostalgic to Mae West
Service: part of the show
Reservations: highly advisable (pets permitted)
Price range: fairly expensive
Credit cards: not accepted

Café

CAFE LUITPOLD
11 Brienner Strasse (Luitpoldblock)
Telephone: 29 28 65
Owner/Manager: Paul Buchner
Closed: Sunday; public holidays; during
Christmas and New Year
Open: 9.00/a.m.–20.00/8 p.m.
Specialities: world-famous ›Luitpold-
torte‹; home-made chocolates prepared
in Luitpold's own confiserie
Location: central, just round the corner
from Marienplatz
Setting: stylish; elegant coffee-house
built in 1962 on the grounds of the café
opened in 1888 and named after Prince
Luitpold of Bavaria
Amenities: café, grill-restaurant
(11.45/a.m.–20.30/8.30 p.m.), open-air
dining on terrace, confiserie air conditioning
Atmosphere: comfortable; fairly sophisticated

Clientèle: the young and young-at-heart and those who wished they were . . ., Munich's Haute Bourgeoisie mingles with elegant birds of passage; journalists
Dress: conservative Haute Couture
Service: anxious-to-please
Reservations: advisable to essential

Café

EXTRABLATT
7 Leopoldstrasse
Telephone: 33 33 33
Owner: Michael Graeter
Manager: Joachim Schmitt and Dagmar Schuler
Open: Monday–Friday 7.00/a.m.–24.00/12 p.m.; Saturday 9.00/a.m.–1.00/a.m.; Sunday 9.00/a.m.–24.00/12 p.m.
Location: on Munich's Bohemian boulevard; university quarter; 10 minutes from city centre
Setting: French bistro-café with Parisian paraphernalia, celebrities' photo gallery and the international press
Amenities: 2 bars (inside and outside), open-air dining (snacks)
Atmosphere: busy, pleasantly light, fresh; ideal for singles of both sexes
Clientèle: from shopgirls to shopkeepers
Service: surprisingly agreeable
Reservations: not necessary
Prive range: average
Credit cards: none

Meeting Point

MUNICH (restaurant – bar – café)
9 Leopoldstrasse
Telephone: 39 64 38
Owners: Michel Blanchard and Gérard Rideau
Manager: Michel Blanchard
Open: 18.00/6 p.m.–3.00/a.m.; Saturday from 13.00/1 p.m.; Sunday and public holidays from 11.00/a.m.
Cuisine: French
Chef de cuisine: Gérard Rideau
Specialities: Tuesday couscous; Sunday brunch
Location: on Munich's Bohemian boulevard
Setting: ice-cream parlour chic with neon art inside; Côte-d'Azur-inspired streetside terrace with Caribbean bar
Amenities: bar inside, bar outside; separate dining section
Atmosphere: a voyeur's paradise; jazzy, jumpy, jolly
Clientèle: on the young side; exhibitionistic, sparkling, light-hearted
Dress: the wilder the better; anything goes
Service: pretty makes up for professional
Reservations: for dining (pets allowed)
Price range: medium high
Credit cards: none

Meeting Point

MADRIGAL
Herzog-Rudolph-Strasse/Ecke Maximilianstrasse
Telephone: 22 33 55
Owner: Peter Cramer
Manager: Roger Baranda
Closed: 10 days at Christmas
Open: (Monday–Friday) 12.00/a.m.–2.00/a.m. (Saturday–Sunday and public holidays) 19.00/7 p.m.–2.00/a.m.
Cuisine: French
Specialities: according to season
Location: central
Setting: typical bistro; closely-packed tables
Amenities: piano bar (downstairs); cocktail bar; separate video room; bowling in an exclusive atmosphere
Atmosphere: lively, extrovert and exhibitionistic
Clientèle: Kir Royal – frequently more attractive, amusing and interesting than elsewhere
Dress: eye-catchingly à la mode
Service: under the personal supervision of Roger Baranda
Reservations: essential
Credit cards: AE, EC, Visa

Beergarden

SEEHAUS
3 Kleinhesselohe, Schwabing
Telephone: 39 70 72
Affiliations: Chaîne des Rôtisseurs
Owner/Manager: Dr. Erich Kaub/Roland Kuffler
Closed: never
Open: 10.00/a.m.–1.00/a.m.
Cuisine: local and international
Specialities: fish, seafood; home-butchered meat; home-made cakes and pâtisserie
Location: in Schwabing; in Munich's best-loved park (Englischer Garten)
Setting: a newly built beergarden/café overlooking the lake (Kleinhesseloher See); piano bar and dining room for inclement weather; idyllic beergarden and lakeside terrace for sunny summer afternoons and evenings
Amenities: private dining room (up to 90 persons)
Atmosphere: a good place to see and to be seen; perfect vantage point for surveying the swans, society belles taking the air with their beaux or their Borzois and the local Sunday-afternoon crowd en fête, en famille and en masse
Clientèle: local chiceria, jet-setters en passant, sculptors, poets, students, philosophers, local Haute Bourgeoisie and a sprinkling of ordinary mortals
Dress: sundress and sandals to mink coat and moonboots

Service: with a smile
Reservations: not necessary
Price range: moderate – high
Credit cards: AE, EC, Visa

Bar

HARRY'S NEW YORK BAR
9 Falkenturmstrasse
Telephone: 22 27 00
Owner/Manager: William ›Bill‹ Deck
Closed: Sunday
Open: 17.00/4 p.m.–3.00/a.m.
Location: city centre, off Maximilian-
strasse; around the corner from the Hof-
bräuhaus
Setting: what you would expect from an
American bar; on three floors
Amenities: piano-bar downstairs; snacks
Atmosphere: from quiet to frenzied as the
evening moves on; crowded before mid-
night
Clientèle: habitués from the media, busi-
nessmen, after-dinner crowd
Dress: casual
Service: quick and friendly
Reservations: for a favourite table al-
ways; for any seat after 11 p.m. (no pets)
Price range: very reasonable
Credit cards: AE

Bar

SCHUMANN'S
36 Maximilianstrasse
Telephone: 22 90 60
Owners: Peter Cramer and Karl Schu-
mann
Manager: ›Charles‹ Schumann
Closed: Saturday
Open: 17.00/5 p.m.–3.00/a.m.
Location: on Munich's most fashionable
shopping street; 10 minutes from The
Headquarters
Setting: 2 halls; long bar; avant-garde
non-décor
Amenities: street-side terrace
Atmosphere: cool, detached, egocentri-
cal, intellectual, experienced
Clientèle: media; nouvelle-vague aristoc-
racy; intelligentsia; upstart decadence
Dress: light and designer-sloppy
Service: fickle, according to the inrush
Reservations: not required
Price range: regular
Credit cards: not accepted

Nightclub

MAXIMILIAN'S (discothèque)
16 Maximiliansplatz
Telephone: 22 32 53
Owner/Manager: Niko Niessen
Open: 22.00/10 p.m.–4.00/a.m.
Location: city centre; 1 minute from The
Headquarters

Setting: elegant downstairs discothèque
with elevated seating arrangements
around the floor-lit dance-floor; top floor
designer-chic
Amenities: 2 bars
Atmosphere: typical nightclub snobbery;
good music (something for everyone)
Clientèle: affluent, attractive and arro-
gant; well-dressed, well-behaved visitors
Dress: Armani & Co.
Service: existent
Reservations: for more than two
Price range: high (no entrance fee, no
cover charge)
Credit cards: AE, DC, Euro

Nightclub

P 1 (discothèque)
1 Prinzregentenstrasse
Telephone: 29 42 52
Owner/Manager: Michael Käfer
Open: 23.00/11 p.m.–4.00/a.m.
Location: in the Haus der Kunst (Modern
Art Museum); on a prominent avenue
leading from the State's guest house to
the seat of the Bavarian Premier; on the
periphery of the English Garden – Mu-
nich's Hyde Park
Setting: large empty duplex hall with
large square bar downstars and more inti-
mate bar upstairs; 2001 décor
Amenities: 4 bars
Atmosphere: railway station charm
Clientèle: young, detached, with-it-hip,
approachable
Dress: way-out
Service: astonishingly wonderful in this
pandemonium
Reservations: not possible
Price range: modest
Credit cards: not accepted

Shopping

EVERYTHING UNDER ONE ROOF
Hertie 7 Bahnhofplatz

FOR HIM
L. H. van Hees 3 Brienner Strasse

FOR HER
E. Braun & Co. 1 Wittelsbacher Platz

BEAUTY & HAIR
Le Coup 23 Theatinerstrasse/Odeons-platz, Tel. 22 23 27

JEWELLERY
Gebrüder Hemmerle 14 Maximilian-strasse

LOCAL SPECIALITIES
Max Zechbauer (tobacco)
10 Residenzstraße
Ludwig Beck am Rathauseck (fashion/accessories) 11 Marienplatz
Bernheimer (interior decorating)
3 Lenbachplatz
Dallmayr, Alois (food & beverages)
14 Dienerstrasse
Dietl, Max (fashion for him and her)
16 Residenzstrasse
Et Cetera (gifts)
11 Wurzerstrasse
Hugendubel (books)
22 Marienplatz
Leder-Walter (leather fashion)
9 Amalienstrasse
Lodenfrey (Bavarian fashion & accessoires)
7 Maffeistrasse
MCM, Moderne Creation München (baggage & travel accessories)
11 Nikolaistrasse
Moshammer, Rudolf (fashion for him)
14 Maximilianstrasse
Nymphenburger Porzellanmanufaktur (porcelain)
1 Odeonsplatz
Pilati (interior decorating)
3 Amiraplatz
Stange-Erlenbach, Dieter (furs)
21 Maximilianstrasse
Vereinigte Werkstätten (interior decorating)
1 Amiraplatz
Wallach (Bavarica)
3 Residenzstrasse
Objekte: Gert M. Weber
(interior design/furniture)
24–26 Feilitzsch-Str.

THE BEST OF ART
Artcurial   (modern art)
10 Maximilianstrasse, Tel. 29 41 31
Charlotte   (naive art)
8 Falkenturmstrasse, Tel. 22 71 66
Friedrich, Six   (contemporary art)
15 Maximilianstrasse
Gunzenhauser, Dr. Alfred   (Fine Art)
10Maximilianstrasse, Tel. 22 30 30
Jahn, Fred (modern art)
10 Maximilianstrasse, Tel. 22 07 14
Keller, Dany (modern art)
11 Buttermelcherstrasse, Tel. 22 61 32
Klüser, Bernd (modern art)
15 Georgenstrasse, Tel. 33 21 79
Knust, Sabine (modern art)
36 Maximilianstrasse, Tel. 29 21 13
Tanit (modern art)
36 Maximilianstrasse, Tel. 29 22 33
Thomas   (contemporary and Fine Art)
25 Maximilianstrasse, Tel. 22 27 41
van de Loo   (contemporary art)
27 Maximilianstrasse, Tel. 22 62 70
Wittenbrink   (contemporary art)
8 Ohmstrasse, Tel. 39 23 50
Antic-Haus   (18th/19th-century works of art)
1 Neuturmstrasse, Tel. 29 73 17
Arnoldie-Livie (18th/19th-century drawings and paintings)
36 Maximilianstrasse, Tel. 22 59 20
Bernheimer   (17th/18th-century Chinese porcelain, tapestries, works of art)
3 Lenbachplatz, Tel. 59 66 43–45
Kunsthandel Oscar Labiner   (18th/19th-century jewellery, silver)
3 Ferdinand-Miller-Platz, Tel. 1 29 55 72
Ness, Ferdinand W.   (Art Déco, Art Nouveau)
19 Franz-Joseph-Strasse
Scheidwimmer, Xaver   (16th-18th-century paintings)
3 Barer Strasse
Karl & Faber   (auctioneers)
2 Amiraplatz, Tel. 22 18 65
Ketterer, Wolfgang   (auctioneers)
25 Brienner Strasse, Tel. 59 11 81
Neumeister   (auctioneers)
37 Barer Strasse, Tel. 28 30 11

The City

The Golden Age of the fifteenth and sixteenth centuries has left traces of architectural grandeur, the golden past of craftsmanship, science and Les Beaux Arts lives on in many industries, and the dubious image as the arena of the Third Reich's hypnotical propaganda rallies has evaporated by now and given way to the symbiosis of capitalist reality embedded in medieval nostalgia. Not only as a commercial entity and an historical landmark but also as one of the country's playgrounds of intellectuality and ›Lebenslust‹ does Nuremberg stand out – and not necessarily in the shadow of its glittering Big Brother Munich, 150 kilometres away. Favourite son Albrecht Dürer is of paramount importance in the museums. The Nuremberg Mastersingers belong to the world repertoire of the great opera houses, but the city's leading industry is more playful than its past – toys. The yearly Toy Fair attracts more visitors than the castle Kaiserburg, the Old Town's ramparts and the site of the infamously famous International Military Tribunal of the Second World War's aftermath. Nuremberg is a prime example of Germany's Wirtschaftswunder, housing manufacture of heavy machinery, cars, electronics, business machines and graphic materials, as well as one of the picture-postcard townships reminding critical travellers not only of Renaissance and Romanticism (which originated in this country), but also of the southern German charm unfairly overruled by the Prussian image accredited to the whole nation.

Founded: 1050, near the tomb of St. Sebald; Nürnberg (German).

Far-reaching events: 1219 – chartered, Kaiser Karl IV grants the Imperial Constitution in Nuremberg; 1520s – Martin Luther's Reformation strikes home; 1526 – Melanchthon founds first German science university; 1650 – the Thirty Years War ends with the Dinner of Peace in Nuremberg; 1806 – Nuremberg joins the Kingdom of Bavaria; 1835 – the first railroad in Germany runs between the cities of Nuremberg and Fürth; 1933–45 – Nuremberg becomes a shrine of National Socialism; 1945 – 90% of the Old City destroyed by bombs; 1945–49 – Nuremberg site of the War Crimes Tribunal; 1966 – reconstruction of the Old City completed.

Population: 500,000.

Postal code: D-8500   **Telephone code:** 911

Climate: beautiful spring; pleasant summer; golden autumn; rainy winter.

Calendar of events: *Spring Festival* (Mar/Apr); *Summer in Nuremberg* (May to Sep) – cultural programmes; *Kaiserburg Concerts* (May to Aug) – held inside/outside the city's landmark castle; *International Organ Week* (Jun/Jul) – the churches resound; *Old City Festival* (Jun) – dancing in the streets; *Bards' Reunion* (Aug) – festival of singing minstrels; *Autumn Folk Festival* (Aug/Sep); *Christkindlmarkt* (Nov/Dec) – Nuremberg's toys go to market – literally – along with the best of German Gemütlichkeit.

Fairs and exhibitions: *INTERNATIONAL TOY FAIR* (Jan/Feb) – concurrent with trade fair for models, hobby and do-it-yourself materials; *KUNST UND ANTIQUITÄTEN* (Mar/Apr) – art and antiques fair; *NUREMBERG MINERAL AND FOSSIL MARKET* (Sep/Oct) – international fair; *IKK* (Oct) – international trade fair for cooling and climate control technologies; *CONSUMENTA* (Nov) – consumer goods fair; *IENA* (Nov) – international exhibition for ›ideas and inventions‹; *BRAU* (Nov) – brewing and beverages; *KUNST UND ANTIQUITÄTEN* (Nov) – art and antiques fair.

Best views of the city: from the *Kaiserburg* – a beautiful view of the ›pointed gables and the rooks that round them throng‹ (Longfellow); from the Telegraph Tower over the entire Old City.

Historical sights: Church of *St. Lawrence* (1252–1477) – Gothic, two towers and Veit Stoss' famous ›Angel's Greeting‹ sculpture; *Church of Our Lady* (1352–61) – with a ›Glockenspiel‹ at noon; *Church of St. Sebald* (1225–1579) – its twin towers are Nuremberg's most famous; *Schöner Brunnen* – at the main market, legendary fountain with a ›Ring of Fortune‹ for lovers; *Old Town Hall* (14th–17th century) – the old city hall and the ›Gander Fountain‹ in front of it are two of the city's main landmarks; *Germanic Museum* – particularly good on goldsmith artistry; *City Walls* (15th century) – 5 km/3 miles long with 80 towers; *Albrecht Dürer House* (1450–60) – at the Zoo Gate, the city's prettiest square, is the home of the city's greatest artist.

Modern sights: *Toy Museum* – for children of all ages; *Meistersinger Hall* – for congresses and festivals; *Zeppelin Field* – where the ›Party‹ held its parties, home of Hitler's huge mass rallies; *Traffic Museum* – where the first railway in Germany is on view.

Special attractions: a browse through the *Christkindlesmarkt* – at the Market Square, Germany's best and best known Christmas Market, usually with a light cover of snow and about as picturesque as Christmas can be; a visit to the *Historische Wurstbraterei* – for the world-famous Nuremberg sausages; a festival performance at *Bayreuth;* a weekend at *Pflaums Posthotel.*

Important companies with headquarters in the city: *Grundig* (TV, radio); *Triumph-Adler* (office electronics); *Diehl* (machinery); *Staedtler Mars* (drawing equipment); *Foto-Quelle* (photographic equipment); *Faber-Castell* (artists' needs); *M.A.N.* (lorries, tractors); *Gebr. Fleischmann* (toys); *Schwan-Stabilo* (drawing and artists' needs); *Otto Schmidt* (gingerbread); *Schöller* (ice cream and gingerbread); *Tucher* (brewery).

Airport: Nuremberg Airport, NUE; Tel.: 52 10 11; Lufthansa, Tel.: 52 40 50, 7 km/4 miles.

259

The Headquarters

FORSTHAUS

20 Zum Vogelsang
D–8510 Fürth-Dambach
Telephone: 77 98 80
Telex: 626 385 hofor
Owning Company: Max-Grundig-Stiftung
Manager: Walter Möllmann
Number of rooms: 100 (11 suites)
Price range: DM 145–160 (single)
　　　　　　　DM 180–200 (double)
　　　　　　　DM 300–600 (suite)
Credit cards: AE, DC, EC, Visa
Location: in the beautiful forest of Fürth, 3 km/2 miles from the city centre of Nürnberg, 10 km/6 miles from airport
Built: 1978
Style: modern
Hotel amenities: garage, house limousine service, car rental desk, ballroom, hotel shops, travel agency, wheelchair accessibility (pets welcome)
Room amenities: colour tv, video, minibar, alarm clock
Room service: 6.30/a.m. to 24.00/12.00 p.m.
Laundry/dry cleaning: same day (weekend service)
Conference rooms: hyper-modern facilities for up to 350 persons
Sports: indoor swimming pool, health club, sauna, solarium, massage
Bar: cocktail bar (18.00/6.00 p.m.–1.00/a.m.) elegant décor, pianist (occasionally)
Restaurants: ›Jäger- und Bauernstube‹ (12.00/a.m.–14.30/2.30 p.m. and 18.00/6.00 p.m.–23.00/11.00 p.m.) local Franconian specialities; ›Wald-Restaurant‹ and ›Französisches Restaurant‹, specializing in venison and seafood, French cuisine, high-quality wines, open-air dining for up to 220 persons
Private dining rooms: banqueting facilities available on request

The ›Forest House‹ at the outskirts of Fürth (today just another arm of octopussying Nuremberg) is not to be confounded with a Ritz in the woods, but beats by far all city-centre chalets in quiet, comfort, amenities and surroundings (And with a chauffeured limousine there is hardly time enough to read The Times from here to the airport, the station or any of the Bratwurst-institutions). Fairy-tale landscape nearby, swimming-pool and health club under the same roof; hearty German fare al fresco or refined francophile gourmandises in warm intérieur; lots of space from the entrée to the rooms and perfect management and service from the desk to the bar – electronics magnate Dr. Max Grundig's pet project in his native town lives up to standards here. To avoid mediocrity and mass-market hospitality, retreat to the Forsthaus for business – and pleasure.

The Hideaway

PFLAUMS POSTHOTEL

14 Nürnberger Straße
D–8570 Pegnitz (60 km/40 miles)
Telephone: (92 41) 72 50
Telex: 642 433 ppp
Owner: Andreas and Hermann Pflaum
General Manager: Andreas Pflaum
Affiliation/Reservation Systems: Relais et
Châteaux
Number of rooms: 40 (15 suites)
Price range: DM 135 – 680
Credit cards: AE, DC, EC, MC
Location: in a little village in the Franco-
nian mountains, 57 km/36 miles from air-
port Nuremberg
Built: 1707 (renovated 1983)
Style: private country house
Hotel amenities: garage, valet parking,
house limousine service, swimming pool,
health club, sauna, solarium, massage,
newsstand, boutique, tobacconist, house
doctor, car service to Bayreuth Festspielhaus and Nuremberg toy fair (pets allowed)
Room amenities: colour tv (remote control), satellite tv, video, mini-bar/refriger-
ator
Bathroom amenities: separate shower
cabinet, bidet, bathrobe, hairdrier
Laundry/dry cleaning: same day (weekend service)
Conference rooms: 3 (up to 60 persons)
Sports: table-tennis, billiards, bowling alleys
Sports (nearby): golf, riding, tennis, gliding club
Bar: ›Zum Säbel Napoleons‹ (19.00/7.00
p.m.–1.00/a.m.) pianist (Saturday), records
Restaurant: ›Rôtisserie Pflaums Speise-
garten‹ (12.00/a.m.–14.00/2.00 p.m. and
18.00/6.00 p.m.–21.00/9.00 p.m., till
12.00/p.m. after Festspiel performances)
elegant style, Andreas Pflaum (maître),
Hermann Pflaum (chef de cuisine),
French cuisine; ›Posthalter Stube‹
(12.00/a.m.–1.00/a.m.) open-air dining
Private dining rooms: two

*Ever since the Brothers Pflaum (Andreas,
the worldly host and Hermann, the ingeni-
ous chef) took over the 300-year-old family
staging inn, Pegnitz, that sleepy little nowhere in the Franconian hinterland, has
been marked in Cartier calendars and Dior
diaries of the Beautiful People, gourmet
snobs and élitarian Wagnerians alike.
During the Bayreuth Festival it is the hub
of cultural and social action outside the opera house (French Presidents, Prince Amyn
Aga Khan, the world tenors and tycoons,
Le Tout Bayreuth), but throughout the
year it is one of Germany's foremost resorts, retreats and grand cuisines. No matter, what weather – plenty of intellectual
and sportive pastimes are on the premises;
no matter, what reason – the warmth and
hospitality of the Pflaums are proverbial.*

Lunch

BAMMES (GOLDENER ADLER)
63 Hauptstrasse, Nuremberg-Buch
Telephone: 39 13 03
Owner/Manager: Karl-Bernd Sperber
Closed: Sunday; public holidays
Open: 11.30/a.m.–14.00/2 p.m. and
17.00/5 p.m.–21.30/9.30 p.m.
Chefs de cuisine: Rainer Vockentänzer
and Karl-Bernd Sperber
Specialities: fillet of angler fish (Seeteufel) with rye noodles and white summer
truffles; poached salmon steak in champagne sauce; cassoulette of sole in Noilly
Prat; fillet of veal with Périgord truffles;
sautéed calves' kidneys; poppy-seed and
cinnamon ice cream
Location: near the airport
Setting: historic Franconian village hostelry; chestnut trees and sunshades; red
tablecloths, attractive floral arrangements; dining rooms rustic in style, with
wood predominating
Amenities: terrace; car park
Atmosphere: cheerfully casual and relaxed
Clientèle: a large and devoted following
of discriminating local burghers, leav-
ened by a sprinkling of tourists from
Prague to Oporto
Dress: shirtsleeves the norm (in summer,
anyway)
Service: praiseworthy if unconventional
Reservations: recommended (pets allowed)
Price range: moderate
Credit cards: DC, Euro

Lunch

ROTTNER
15 Winterstrasse, Grossreuth
Telephone: 61 20 32
Owner/Manager: Konrad Rottner
Closed: Sunday; Saturday lunchtime;
August; part of December and January
Open: 11.30/a.m.–14.30/2.30 p.m. and
17.00/5 p.m.–22.00/10 p.m.
Cuisine: regional
Chef de cuisine: Stefan Rottner junior
Specialities: Knoblauchsländer vegetable
soup (nothing to do with garlic!); venison
liver; wild duck with apple slices; salmon
trout in basil sauce; apple cake with apple ice-cream; home-grown asparagus;
freshwater fish and venison from pri-
vately owned rivers and hunting-grounds
Location: west of city centre; just off the
road to Rothenburg, outside the motorway ring road
Setting: picture-postcard country inn behind church; flower, vegetable and herb

gardens; two-storey building (top half
timber-framed); wooden beams separating the various dining rooms; rustic accessoires
Amenities: private dining rooms (2–40
persons); bar; outdoor dining in garden
(open-air grill); car park
Atmosphere: from a peaceful haven to a
cheerful camp-fire
Clientèle: favourite venue for Nuremberg
industrialists wishing to impress visiting
businessmen during or after working
hours
Dress: what you will
Service: ably directed by Frau Rottner
junior and Werner Meyer
Reservations: advisable to essential
Price range: moderate
Credit cards: AE, Euro

Dinner

SCHWARZER ADLER
166 Kraftshofer Hauptstrasse
Kraftshof (10 km/6 miles)
Telephone: 39 21 21
Owner: Günther Hertel
Managers: Michael and Karin Noack
Closed: December 23rd–January 10th
Open: 12.00/a.m.–14.30/2.30 p.m. and
18.00/6 p.m.–24.00/12 p.m.
Cuisine: French and local (classic and
nouvelle)
Chef de cuisine: Peter Wagner (ex-Land-
haus Scherrer in Hamburg)
Specialities: stuffed zucchini flowers with
pimento; terrine of calves' liver with redcurrant mousseline sauce; creamed celery with salmon; entrecôte steak with sorrel
Location: 10 km (6 miles) north of city
centre in a village suburb; 2 km (1 mile)
from airport
Setting: renovated historic building;
Franconian style elegantized rustic;
wood panelling; antique paintings; damask tablecloths, silver, glass and white
porcelain
Amenities: private dining rooms (12–70
persons); outdoor dining in beergarden;
air conditioning; car park
Atmosphere: harmonious and restful;
prettily picturesque, but without a hint of
kitsch
Clientèle: disciples of Peter Wagner's culinary skills of Landhaus Scherrer renown mingle with local expense-account
gourmets with a penchant for the romantic
Dress: as you like it (as long as they will
like you)
Service: excellent, well-rehearsed team-
work
Reservations: advisable (dogs allowed)
Price range: fairly expensive
Credit cards: DC, Euro

Lunch

BRATWURSTHÄUSLE BEI ST. SEBALD
1 Rathausplatz
Telephone: 22 76 95
Owner/Manager: Werner Behringer
Closed: Sunday
Open: 09.30/a.m.–21.30/9.30 p.m.
Cuisine: unpretentious, with a strong local accent
Chef de cuisine: Klaus Böhm
Specialities: grilled food, especially Nuremberg small grilled pork sausages (Rostbratwürstchen) – a tradition in the town since 1313; roast shoulder of pork (Schäuferle), sour pigs' trotters (Knöchle); Franconian wines
Location: close to the main market square
Setting: two 500-year-old Tyrolean farmhouses; rustic furnishings; open beechwood grill in the centre of the restaurant
Amenities: open-air dining
Atmosphere: lively and casual meeting-place for all and sundry; popular with locals and visitors alike
Clientèle: local habitués; foreign visitors; journalists, politicians, artists
Dress: high fashion; low fashion
Service: very efficient (it has to be!)
Price range: inexpensive
Credit cards: not accepted

Dinner

LUTZGARTEN
113 Grossreuther Strasse
Telephone: 35 80 00
Owner/Manager: Salvatore Scarlata
Closed: Sunday
Open: 11.30/a.m.–14.30/2.30 p.m. and 18.00/6 p.m.–22.30/10.30 p.m.
Chef de cuisine: Klaus Rauch
Specialities: calves' kidneys in wine with young vegetables; terrine of smoked salmon with basil sauce; saddle of lamb in a herb crust; breast of duckling on Savoy cabbage; selection of desserts ›Lutzgarten‹
Location: on the northern outskirts of the city, just outside the motorway ring-road
Setting: historic village inn, lovingly restored; low ceilinged rooms with nineteenth-century dolls' house décor; subdued lighting; rustic accessoires
Amenities: private dining rooms; terrace; car park
Atmosphere: a hint of romance
Clientèle: formerly a favoured destination for excursions amongst Nuremberg's Haute Bourgeoisie; now also the preserve of lovers of any age, nationality and sex
Dress: not too outrageous or outlandish
Service: very attentive
Reservations: advisable (no dogs)
Price range: medium high
Credit cards: AE, Euro

Dinner

ESSIGBRÄTLEIN
3 Weinmarkt
Telephone: 22 51 31
Owner/Manager: Heinzrolf Schmitt
Closed: Sunday; public holidays
Open: 18.30/6.30 p.m.–1.00/a.m.
Cuisine: French (nouvelle) with local undertones
Chef de cuisine: Claudia Simone Schmitt
Specialities: mousse of smoked char (Saibling); salmon in pink champagne; brown trout in chive sauce; fillet of lamb in a mild mustard sauce or with ratatouille; gingerbread soufflé in Franconian Riesling Sabayon
Location: in the heart of the old city
Setting: the oldest existing hostelry in Nuremberg; building dates from 1550; accessoires include old engravings, candlesticks and pottery, with eighteenth-century cookery books on display
Amenities: outdoor dining; car park; medieval banquets arranged on request
Atmosphere: a lucullian paradise steeped in history
Clientèle: connoisseurs of good food and drink; culinary historians; fellow-Canadians drawn by Claudia Simone Schmitt's highly original and inventive cuisine
Dress: no special requirements
Service: in line with the excellence of the food and the exquisite ambience
Reservations: strongly recommended (no pets)
Price range: fairly expensive
Credit cards: AE, DC, Euro

Café

KARL NEEFS CAFE-CONFISERIE
29 Winklerstrasse
Telephone: 22 51 79
Owner/Managers: Karl and Ingrid Neef
Closed: Sunday
Open: (Monday–Friday) 8.30/a.m.–18.00/6 p.m. (Saturday) 8.30/a.m.–14.00/2 p.m.
Specialities: the best gingerbread (Lebkuchen) in Germany – and delicious cakes and gâteaux, especially strudel with a variety of fillings
Location: near the toy museum (Spielzeugmuseum)
Setting: small, attractively modern dining room
Amenities: light lunches; car park
Atmosphere: the antithesis of the traditional coffee-house atmosphere, but refreshing and cheerful
Clientèle: sweet-toothed men-(and women!)-about-town; students, solicitors, secretaries and shop-girls
Service: personal and professional

263

Beergarden

GARASCH
91–93 Bahnhofstrasse
Telephone: 49 39 99
Owner/Manager: Rudi Brandl
Closed: never
Open: summer: 16.00/4 p.m.–1.00/a.m.
winter: 18.00/6 p.m.–1.00/a.m.
Location: by the Wöhrder See; on the
edge of the city, but very accessible
Setting: bar with small tables; in summer,
an attractive beergarden with sunshades
Amenities: champagne bar; snacks and
light meals; brunch on Sunday mornings
Atmosphere: légère; heterogeneous; an
essential stopover for all who wish to see
or be seen.
Clientèle: the young; the not-so-young
Dress: anything goes
Service: rather variable
Reservations: not necessary
Credit cards: EC, AE, DC

Bar

VOGEL BAR
Pirkheimer Strasse
Telephone: 36 11 01
Owner/Manager: Martin Vogel
Closed: never
Open: 17.00/5 p.m.–1.00/a.m.
Location: on the outskirts of the city, but
easily reached
Setting: unfussy décor in black and
white, with judiciously-placed mirrors
and marble tables
Amenities: car park
Atmosphere: raffinée
Clientèle: local Top Twenty; intelligent,
outgoing and well-dressed; the ones who
have made it
Service: solicitous
Reservations: advisable
Credit cards: EC, DC, Visa

Nightclub

LE BATEAU
Adlerstrasse
Telephone: 22 23 44
Owner/Manager: Babs Ewe
Closed: never
Open: 21.00/9 p.m.–4.00/a.m.
Location: central
Setting: old English ship style
Amenities: discothèque; nightclub
Atmosphere: considered by many to be
the best discothèque in Nuremberg
Clientèle: local chiceria, celebrities and
hangers-on; young and on the way up to
middle-aged but not moribund
Dress: no cut-off jeans, Bermuda shorts,
T-shirts or training shoes
Service: good
Reservations: not usually necessary
Price range: expensive
Credit cards: AE, DC

Shopping

EVERYTHING UNDER ONE ROOF
Karstadt   14 Königstrasse

FOR HIM
Stamm's Boutique   16 Hauptmarkt

FOR HER
Fellner 1a Karolinenstrasse

BEAUTY & HAIR
Schrepfer   60 Königstrasse and
52 Obere Schmiedgasse

JEWELLERY
Schott   27 Karolinenstrasse

LOCAL SPECIALITIES
Schuler Moden   (women's fashion)
23 Kaiserstrasse
Gordon   (men's fashion)
7 Kaiserstrasse
Mutter und Kind   (children's fashion)
4 Josephsplatz
Ostermeier Boutique   (leather fashion)
6–8 Hauptmarkt
Unbehauen   (furs)
2 Karlsbrücke
Universitätsbuchhandlung   (books)
10 Adlerstrasse
Herzog Volkskunsthaus   (gifts)
17 Königstrasse & In der Mauthalle
Gordon   (baggage & travel accessories)
2 An der Fleischbrücke
Engelbrecht   (food and beverages)
13 Karolinenstrasse
Haeberlein & Metzger   (gingerbread)
43 Karolinenstrasse, Im Handwerkhof,
46 Kaiserstrasse
Der Töpferladen   (pottery)
18 Hauptmarkt

THE BEST OF ART
Defet   (modern art, prints)
33 Gustav-Adolf-Strasse, Tel. 61 29 24
Ricard, Johanna   (Russian avant-garde)
33–37 Königstrasse, Tel. 22 50 20

The City

No-one would confuse the capital of Germany's conservative south-west with an Alemannic nest of light-heartedness, lust for life and laisser-faire. The silvery shine of its
status-symbolic tri-pointed guiding star is brighter than the glitter of its social life, but
the Swabians' much respected and ridiculed diligence (mixed with discipline, efficiency and stamina) is not exclusively spent building Mercedes motor cars – or
Porsches. Stuttgart, embedded in the lush valley of the River Neckar, with vineyards
growing in the middle of town and Roman springs in suburban Bad Cannstatt making
it into a fully-fledged spa, also takes everything else in life so seriously and tries even
harder to reach success, that the city and its attractions profit greatly from this spirit.
Englishman James Stirling's new structure for the State Gallery is only the latest example of the burghers' sense for quality and innovation of form (as with their cars), putting the monumental museum in line with the Centre Beaubourg in Paris. (The largest
German collection of Picassos is enriched by local greats, Schlemmer and Baumeister).
Brazilian choreographer Marcia Haydée's ballet (built up to world fame with Romeo
and Juliet, et al. by American John Cranko) is one of the leading groups in the world,
while more profane enjoyment has an outstanding stronghold in the Perkins Park discothèque high above the city in a fancy palais. Destroyed in the war, but built up again
as a symbiosis of pragmatism and the past, Stuttgart does not rival Munich or Hamburg
for beauty and style, yet the landscape around is sheer tourist-land, and with castles
and parks, al-fresco cafés and elegant shopping galleries, there are enough pastimes for
the overnight businessman. And with some of the country's best restaurants and lively
wine taverns dotting the streets, even the monoglot men of commerce from faraway
places won't have to retire with local son Hegel's aphorisms.

Founded: 1st century A.D. – as a Roman settlement; Stuttgart – from ›a mares‹ garden.
Far-reaching events: 260 – raids by Alemanni; 950 – established as Duke Luitlof's resi-
dence; 1160 – Stuttgart first appears in documents; 1219 – chartered; 1321 – Count
Eberhard moves his residence to Stuttgart; 1482 – capital and court residence of the
Duke of Württemberg; 19th century – growth of the city and its industries; 1952 – capi-
tal of Baden-Württemberg.
Population: 560,000; capital of Baden-Württemberg.
Postal code: D-7000   **Telephone code:** 711
Climate: mild and sunny.
Calendar of events: *Fastnacht* (Jan–Mar) – Stuttgart's carnival celebrations; *Porsche
Grand Prix for Tennis* (in neighbouring Filderstadt); *Mercedes-Benz Tennis Cup* (at the
Weissenhof grounds); *Wine Village* (Aug) – street festival with ›Gemütlichkeit‹ all over
Schillerplatz and Marktplatz; *Cannstatt Festival* (Sep/Oct) – famous outdoor festival
with 4–5 million visitors each year.
Fairs and exhibitions: *SÜDDEUTSCHER MUSTERMARKT* (Jan) – design exhibi-
tion; *CMT* (Jan) – camping and tourist industry; *DIDACTA* (Feb/Mar) – school, edu-
cation and vocational training; *PROSANITA* (May) – health and nature; *IWB* (May) –
weapons fair; *WINDOW CONSTRUCTION* (Jun); *OFFICE SUPPLIES EXHIBI-
TION* (Sep); *ELTEFA* (Oct) – electrotechnology; *HOBBY ELEKTRONIK* (Sep) –
microcomputers for model building; *HAFA* (Nov) – sport for the whole family; *VKA*
(Dec) – antiques convention.
Historical sights: *Altes Schloss* (1553–70) – Renaissance, home of the Württemberg
crown jewels, idyllic outdoor concerts in summer, housing the Regional Museum;
Neues Schloss (1747–68) – late Baroque, former residence of the kings of Württemberg,
now seat of the Ministry of Finance; *Königsbau* (1856–60) – shopping arcade behind
an elegant columned façade; *Alte Kanzlei* (1544) – library and kitchen of the Altes Schloss;
Stiftskirche (12th–16th century) – church with unequal towers, a Stuttgart landmark.
Modern sights: *City Hall* – striking modern architecture; *Kunstgebäude* (1910) – art collection of the Württemberg Art Association; *Calwer Passage* – modern shopping mall
in reconstructed 15th-19th-century buildings; *Planetarium* – one of the most modern in
the world; *Staatsgalerie* – art museum designed by London's leading architect, James
Stirling; *Württemberg State Theatre* – known both for its striking architecture and as
the home of the world-renowned Stuttgart Ballet; *Weissenhof Colony* (1927) – part of
the Werkbund Exhibition by 16 leading European architects including Le Corbusier,
Gropius and Mies van der Rohe; *Daimler Benz Automobile Museum* – at Untertürk-
heim, old and new dreams.
Special attractions: a *ballet performance*; a special night at *Perkins Park*; personal
pick-up of your *Porsche 959* or *Mercedes 560*; a *country tour* between the Swabian Jura
and the Black Forest.
Important companies with headquarters in the city: *Auwester, Gottlob* (buses); *Bosch*
(photographic material, batteries); *Daimler-Benz* (cars); *Dinkelacker* (brewery); *IBM
Deutschland* (computers); *Jacobi* (brandy) at Weinstadt; *Klett* (publishing); *Kodak*
(photographic material and processing); *Leitz* (office equipment); *Mahle* (automobile
accessories); *Porsche* (cars); *Standard-Elektronik-Lorenz* (electronics); *Süddeutsche
Kühlerfabrik Julius Behr* (car parts); *Werner & Pfleiderer* (machine manufacturing);
Züblin, Ed. (construction).
Airport: Stuttgart-Echterdingen, STR; Tel. 790 11, Lufthansa, Tel.: 790 14 67, VIP
Lounge, Tel.: 790 19 71; 14 km/9 miles.

The Headquarters

**STEIGENBERGER HOTEL
GRAF ZEPPELIN**

7 Arnulf-Klett-Platz
D–7000 Stuttgart
Telephone: 29 98 81
Telex: 722 418 zepp
Owning Company: Steigenberger Hotels AG
General Manager: Robert P. Herr
Affiliation/Reservation System: SRS (Steigenberger Reservation Service)
Number of rooms: 260 (20 suites)
Price range: DM 219–1,020
Credit cards: AE, BA, DC, EC, Visa, MC, JCB
Location: opposite main station
Built: 1929–1931 and 1969–1971
Style: modern
Hotel amenities: garage, valet parking, newsstand, swimming pool, sauna
Main hall porter: Dominique Servan
Room amenities: cable tv (remote control), minibar/refrigerator, radio (pets allowed)
Bathroom amenities: bathrobe, hairdrier
Room service: 6.00/a.m.–24.00/12 p.m.
Conference rooms: 11 (up to 500 persons), secretarial services, ballroom
Bars: ›Aperitif-Bar‹ (see Bars); ›Scotch Club‹ (21.00/9 p.m.–3.00/a.m.) Peter Olufsen (manager)
Restaurants: ›Graf Zeppelin‹ (12.00/a.m.–14.30/2.30 p.m. and 18.00/6.00 p.m.–22.30/10.30 p.m.) Wolfgang Mack (maître), Adolf Niefer (chef de cuisine); ›Zeppelin-Stüble‹ (11.00/a.m.–24.00/12.00 p.m.) Wolfgang Hausmann (maître), Gert Herzog (chef de cuisine); ›Maukenescht‹ as Zeppelin-Stüble, open-air dining

One of the flagships of Germany's prominent Steigenberger group, this unadorned edifice proves its standing and modernistic grandeur the moment you pass through its gates, across from the city's main station. Corresponding well with the land's renowned philosophy of hard work-no show -excellence as the fundamental principle, it is a Mercedes of the hôtellerie, so to speak. And the welcome is as warm as the hospitality is sincere. Named after one of Stuttgart's favourite sons, rebuilt after the war and recently renovated to shiny perfection, there is absolutely nothing you will miss – from fast communications and room service to varied cuisine of the highest quality, from avant-garde conference facilities to secretarial services, from an early limousine to a late massage after a swim in the pool. Herr Herr manages this aristocratic residence behind the bourgeois façade as well as his president-habitués from Bosch, Porsche and Daimler-Benz their industrial companies which hold all their meetings here. So, when you come to Germany's most hard-working city for business – or ballet – you don't have to move on to Munich to live in style. Graf Zeppelin will carry you on a cloud.

TRAUBE-TONBACH

237 Tonbachstrasse
D-7292 Baiersbronn 1-Tonbach
(100 km /63 miles)
Telephone: (7442) 4920
Telex: 764394 trto
Owner: Willi Finkbeiner
General Manager: Erdmann Degler
Affiliation/Reservation Systems: Relais et
Châteaux (Restaurant) Relais Gourmand
Number of rooms: 200 (18 suites)
Price range: DM 85–350
Credit cards: only in restaurant
Location: in the Black Forest, between
Stuttgart and Baden-Baden
Built: 1789, modernized and converted
into a luxury hotel
Style: elegant country house hotel
Hotel amenities: car park, lounges, li-
brary, three swimming pools (one with
seawater), whirl-pool, indoor tennis
courts, health club, sauna, solarium (no
pets allowed)
Room amenities: colour tv, telephone
Bathroom amenities: all rooms with pri-
vate bath or shower, hairdrier
Room service: 7.00/a.m.–23.00/11 p.m.
Conference rooms: two
Sports (nearby): shooting, skiing, cross-
country skiing, skating
Bars: three
Restaurants: ›Schwarzwaldstube‹,
(12.00/a.m.–17.00/5 p.m. and 18.30/6.30
p.m.–00.30/a.m., Dieter Kalweit (maître),
Harald Wohlfahrt (chef de cuisine), nouvelle cuisine; ›Köhlerstube‹ and ›Eich-
bergstube‹, international cuisine; ›Bauernstube‹, local specialities

*Nestling in an emerald-green oasis amidst
the awe-inspiring conifer-clad inclines of
the Black Forest on the outskirts of the picture-postcard town of Baiersbronn, the
Traube-Tonbach impresses immediately by
virtue of its location, its look of permanence and its carousel of endless possibilities
of activities and entertainment. Willi Finkbeiner's family established the first
›Traube‹ almost 200 years ago, and whilst
it is unlikely that his ancestors would recog-
nise the luxurious auberge today, they
would certainly approve the emphasis laid
on personal and friendly service which remains a hallmark of the house. They would
no doubt also endorse the choice of predominantly local furnishings throughout
this haven for refugee millionaires, tired
car manufacturers and sport-loving international tycoons – and would be the first to
dive into the swimming pool or work up an
appetite on the tennis courts (if they were
not indulging in the more traditional local
pastimes of ski-ing, skating or shooting)
before the gourmet gala performance of
Harald Wohlfahrt's fêted and rosetted cuisine in the famous Schwarzwaldstube.*

Lunch

HIRSCH-WEINSTUBEN
3 Maierstrasse, Stuttgart-Möhringen
Telephone: 71 13 75
Owner/Manager: Heiderose Frietsch
Closed: Sunday; Saturday lunchtime
Open: 12.00/a.m.–14.00/2 p.m. and
18.00/6 p.m.–22.00/10 p.m.
Cuisine: French (nouvelle) with a Swabian accent
Chef de cuisine: Martin Frietsch
Specialities: Menu Gastronomique; rabbit in aspic with green sauce; basil soup with brain and quail's egg; terrine de foie gras; salmon with Chablis sauce and paprika; calves' sweetbreads in Riesling sauce with basil and leaf spinach
Location: in the suburb of Möhringen; near motorway exit
Setting: small dining room in elegantized rustic style; lace curtains; predominantly neutral colour-scheme
Amenities: car park
Atmosphere: stylish but légère
Clientèle: disciples of Martin Frietsch's cuisine of Sindelfingen renown including a sprinkling of Stuttgart's social élite
Dress: casually elegant to elegantly casual
Service: enthusiastic and charming
Reservations: usually necessary (no dogs)
Price range: moderately high
Credit cards: AE, DC, Euro

Lunch

COME PRIMA
3 Steinstrasse
Telephone: 24 34 22
Owner/Manager: Maurizio Olivieri
Closed: Monday
Open: 12.00/a.m.–14.30/2.30 p.m. and
18.00/6 p.m.–23.30/11.30 p.m.
Cuisine: Italian
Chef de cuisine: Antonio Patriarca
Specialities: duck livers with spinach; fillet of angler fish with asparagus; salmon in cognac
Location: next door to the Town Hall (Rathaus)
Setting: rather functional and business-like, but quite stylish
Amenities: private dining rooms (25 persons); outdoor dining on terrace; car park
Atmosphere: mixture of Teutonic reliability and Italian flair
Clientèle: pasta-loving locals, homesick Italians and tourists from Gothenburg to Glasgow
Dress: fairly casual to fairly formal
Service: Italianissimo
Reservations: advisable (dogs allowed)
Price range: moderate
Credit cards: AE, DC, Euro

Dinner

ALTE POST
43 Friedrichstrasse
Telephone: 29 30 79
Owner/Manager: Siegfried Riegger
Closed: Sunday; public holidays; Saturday and Monday lunchtime; end of Juli–mid-August
Open: 12.00/a.m.–14.30/2.30 p.m. and
18.00/6 p.m.–22.45/10.45 p.m.
Cuisine: Franco-Swiss with local undertones
Chefs de cuisine: Wolfgang Pfeiffer and Siegfried Riegger
Specialities: saddle of venison (Rehrücken); canard de Challans; stuffed guinea-fowl; filleted oxtail in port wine sauce; asparagus tips with calves' sweetbreads; ravioli filled with pike-perch (Zander)
Location: central, near Palace Gardens (Schlossgarten)
Setting: walnut panelling and furniture; rustic with a hint of sophistication
Amenities: guest house (2 bedrooms); private dining room (20–25 persons)
Atmosphere: conservative, comfortable and comforting
Clientèle: publishers; industrialists; businessmen; prosperous and dependable
Dress: nothing too outrageous or untidy
Service: excellent
Reservations: essential (no pets)
Price range: fairly expensive
Credit cards: DC

Dinner

LAMM
24 Mühlstrasse
Telephone: 85 36 15
Owner/Manager: Walter Engel
Closed: Sunday; Saturday lunchtime; public holidays; between Christmas and New Year
Open: 12.00/a.m.–14.00/2 p.m. and
18.00/6 p.m.–21.00/9 p.m.
Cuisine: nouvelle
Chef de cuisine: Hermann Engel
Specialities: fish and game pâtés; clear tomato soup; salmon with sorrel; breast of Barbary duckling; desserts
Location: near the Killesberg park
Setting: small dining room; newly renovated; velvet upholstered benches; new chairs and curtains
Atmosphere: confidential or intimate, depending on your companion
Clientèle: expense-account gourmets wanting to get away from it all
Dress: according to circumstances
Service: ably supervised by Margarita Engel and Ernst Nothdurfter
Reservations: essential (only 20 places)
Price range: moderately high
Credit cards: not accepted

Lunch

BARON DE LA MOUETTE
11 Kleiner Schlossplatz
Telephone: 22 00 34
Owner: Mövenpick Restaurantbetriebs-
und Handels GmbH
Manager: Norbert Neidenbach
Closed: never
Open: 12.00/a.m.–14.00/2 p.m. and
18.00/6 p.m.–24.00/12 p.m.
Cuisine: French (nouvelle) and Swiss
Specialities: fish dishes; scampi with
herb butter; fresh grilled salmon; Valai-
san steak with chanterelles and Swiss
fried potato (Rösti); carpaccio of turbot;
cassoulet of lobster with asparagus tips;
fillet of rabbit with chive mousseline
sauce and vegetable noodles
Location: central; on one of Stuttgart's
best-known squares
Setting: elegantized rustic décor; oak
beams; one wall with wood cladding; attractive side walls
Amenities: bar; air conditioning; car
park; garage
Atmosphere: chic, cheerful and uncomplicated
Clientèle: predominantly businessmen at
lunchtime give way to a younger, more
pleasure-loving set at night
Dress: what you will
Service: under the expert direction of
maître d'hôtel Giulio Giovannacci
Reservations: recommended
Price range: moderately high
Credit cards: AE, DC, Euro, Visa

Dinner

ÖXLE'S LÖWEN
2 Veitstrasse
Mühlhausen (10 km/6 miles)
Telephone: 53 22 26
Owner/Manager: Martin Öxle
Closed: Sunday; Monday and Saturday
lunchtime; public holidays
Open: 12.00/a.m.–14.30/2.30 p.m. and
18.30/6.30 p.m.–24.00/12 p.m.
Cuisine: Neue Deutsche Küche; ›au goût
du marché‹
Specialities: smoked ham with fig and
mango; veal stock soup with cream, fish
and mangold; breast of pigeon with foie
gras, champagne sauce and artichoke
hearts; saddle of lamb with fresh vegetables; melon with mousse au chocolat
and three sorts of ice-cream
Location: in Mühlhausen, 10 km/6 miles
north of Stuttgart
Setting: an auberge de campagne with
dining rooms decorated in rustic style
Amenities: air conditioning; car park in
the vicinity
Atmosphere: attractive but basically unpretentious surroundings somewhat at
variance with the delicacy and sophistication of the cuisine

Clientèle: growing numbers of gourmet
habitués attracted by Martin Öxle's
highly original and inventive cuisine
Dress: elegantly casual
Service: enthusiastic
Reservations: recommended
Price range: moderately high
Credit cards: AE, EC

Dinner

TRAUBE
2 Brabandtgasse
Plieningen (13 km/8 miles)
Telephone: 45 48 33
Affiliation: Châine des Rôtisseurs
Owner/Manager: Friedrich Recknagel
and family
Closed: Saturday; Sunday; 3 weeks in
August; between Christmas and New
Year
Open: 12.00/a.m.–14.15/2.15 p.m. and
18.00/6 p.m.–22.00/10 p.m.
Cuisine: French (nouvelle) with a Swa-
bian accent
Chef de cuisine: Theodor Weber
Specialities: Barbary duckling consommé
with vegetables; ragôut of fresh Breton
lobster; medaillons of veal fillet with sau-
téed mushrooms; orange ice-cream par-
fait with Grand Marnier
Location: at Plieningen – 13 km (8 miles)
south of city centre (10 minutes from mo-
torway)
Setting: newly-renovated 17th-century
timbered country inn; small dining-
rooms; Swabian rustic with local bric-à-
brac
Amenities: hotel, conference room; bar;
outdoor dining on terrace (restricted
menu); car park; garage
Atmosphere: welcoming and comfortable
Clientèle: men from the media; men of
commerce
Dress: no special requirements
Service: friendly and anxious-to-please
Reservations: advisable (pets allowed)
Price range: moderately expensive
Credit cards: not accepted

Café

SCHAPMANN
14 Feuerseeplatz
Telephone: 62 35 50
Owner/Manager: Wilhelm Schapmann
Open: (Monday–Saturday) 8.00/a.m.–
18.30/6.30 p.m.; (Sunday) 13.00/1 p.m.–
18.30/6.30 p.m.
Specialities: marzipan and hazelnut gâteau (Marzipan-Nusstorte)
Location: at the ›Feuersee‹
Setting: various salons on two floors furnished with valuable antiques and Old
Masters; fine china; excellent view of the
world passing by from the coveted window-seats on the first floor
Amenities: dining room overlooking the
lake; outdoor dining on terrace

Atmosphere: a tradition in the town for more than 50 years; as perfect for a quick cup of coffee as for a leisurely (and excellent) ice-cream after a shopping spree
Clientèle: ladies from Stuttgart's suburbia; Swabian chiceria; students, sociologists and senior citizens
Service: efficient

Bar

ZEPPELIN
Hotel Graf Zeppelin
7 Arnulf-Klett-Platz
Telephone: 29 98 81
Owner/Manager: Steigenberger Hotels AG/Robert Herr
Open: 11.00/a.m.–23.00/11 p.m.
Location: in the Hotel Graf Zeppelin
Setting: English-style décor
Amenities: hotel; valet parking service
Atmosphere: understated; discreet; rather club-like
Clientèle: mostly middle-aged, comfortably-off, discriminating and successful
Dress: within reason
Service: efficiently supervised by chief barman Werner Winter
Reservations: advisable
Credit cards: AE, DC, Euro, Visa, Bank America, Master Charge, JCB

Nightclub

PERKINS PARK
39 Stresemannstrasse
Telephone: 25 20 62
Affiliations: Dehoga
Owner/Manager: Gerd Schüler and Michael Preisinger
Closed: Monday; Tuesday
Open: 20.00/8 p.m.–5.00/a.m.
Location: 5 km/3 miles north of city centre, in Stuttgart-Killesberg; near the Exhibition Centre (Messegelände)
Setting: lobby with marble and potted palms; Art Nouveau bistro; large discothèque, small clubroom
Amenities: video room; billiards; pianist
Atmosphere: sophisticated; companionable to decidedly crowded at times
Clientèle: young, successful and definitely not moribund
Dress: disco elegance
Service: amazingly efficient
Reservations: advisable for dining
Credit cards: AE, DC, Euro, Visa

Shopping

EVERYTHING UNDER ONE ROOF
Breuninger 1–3 Marktstrasse

FOR HIM
Widmann 5 Alte Poststrasse

FOR HER
Angela Grashoff 26 Calwerstrasse

BEAUTY & HAIR
Hörmann Lautenschlagerstrasse

JEWELLERY
Krauss 21 Kronprinzenstrasse

LOCAL SPECIALITIES
Bührle Pfeifenarchiv (tobacco) Calwerpassage
Modehaus Fischer (women's fashion) 19b Königstrasse
Brunett (men's fashion) 20 Königstrasse
Koelble & Brunett (men & women's fashion) 20 Königstrasse, Marquardt Passage
Firma Uli's (Uli Knecht) (men & women's fashion) 1–3 Stiftstrasse
Happy Kids (children's fashion) 1 Stiftstrasse
Waldbaur (leather fashion) 29 Königstrasse
Pelz Maier (furs) 8 Kleine Königstrasse, Wilhelmsbau
Wittmer (books) Königsplatz
Galerie Valentin (gifts) Königsbau
Maercklin (porcelain) 39 Königstrasse
Boehm (food and beverages) Calwerstrasse
Iris Kirschke (décor) 41 Olgastrasse

THE BEST OF ART
Haderek, Tilly (contemporary art) 1 Römerstrasse, Tel. 60 90 40
Kunsthaus Fischer (20th-century paintings) 23 Torstrasse, Tel. 24 41 63
March, Brigitte (contemporary art) 254 Solitudestrasse, Tel. 88 45 35
Schurr, Dr. Ursula (contemporary art) 153 Alexanderstrasse, Tel. 60 54 64
Valentien (Fine Art) Königsbau, 28 Königstrasse, Tel. 22 16 25
Wahlandt, Edith (contemporary art) 6 Werastrasse, Tel. 24 23 55
Lörcher, Margot (oriental art) 42 Heubergstrasse, Tel. 46 12 48
Schaller KG (Fine Art) 3 Marienstrasse, Tel. 29 66 46
Schoettle Ostasiatica, Joachim Baader (oriental art) 21 Hohenstaufenstrasse, Tel. 60 03 33
Nagel, Dr. Fritz (auctioneers) 17–19 Mörikestrasse, Tel. 60 80 00–02

High up on the scale of favourite cities in Germany (for climate and natural beauty, historical traces and architectural aestheticism, wide avenues and luxuriant parks, elegant shopping boulevards and romantic walks, year-round festivities and cultural highlights – and a rare cosmopolitan esprit seldom found in a town of this size), Wiesbaden is a worthy capital, if only of the Duchy of Nassau and, more recently, of the Federal State of Hesse, only a few miles away from the continent's largest airport, closer still than big, brash neighbour Frankfurt after which it is named. Residential paradise for the lucky locals (envied by the twin-capital of the Palatinate, Mainz, across the Rhine, which received a larger portion of the national television as a consolation), the ›Bath in the Meadows‹ is not only Lourdes to the health-spa addicts for its twenty-six hot springs (or for Germany's mini-Mayo clinic for diagnostics) but also goal-line to many a gambler for the splendid casino (the Waterloo for Dostoievski, however, who immortalized the city as ›Rouletteburg‹ in a novel). Some visitors come for the Belle-Epoque splendour so caringly preserved by the city, some for the theatre, the opera or the May Festival, so civilized and untouched by proletarian avant-garde (the burghers of Wiesbaden hardly take notice of the red-green coalition in the State parliament around the corner), and many just come for fun to Germany's grandest small-city auberge with the country's sacred shrine of culinary extravaganza, the Nassauer Hof, where almost every day of the year some gala, tastevin, charity dinner, show or party takes place. Joie de vivre is a household word in this mini-metropolis, which was not only the preferred summer retreat of Emperor Wilhelm II, but beloved home town for thousands of Czarist emigrés and adopted son Alexey von Jawlensky, whose works adorn the city's picture gallery. Starting point for the most beautiful stretch of the fabled Rhine valley and capital of Germany's champagne land, the Rheingau, dotted with castles, fortresses and villages à la Brothers Grimm, Wiesbaden even enchanted the restrained Queen of England on her visit: ›What an extraordinarily lovely city!‹ (She may just have translated good old Goethe who said the same, two centuries before).

Founded: 1st century – as a Roman settlement; Wiesbaden – ›spa in the meadow‹.

Far-reaching events: 259 A.D. – Alemanni invade and destroy the city; about 370 – city walls built; about 500 – Franks invade; 1123 – imperial court; 1242 – archbishop of Mainz takes the city from Friedrich II; 1270 – Wiesbaden becomes the capital of the counts of Nassau; 1282 – Gottfried von Eppstein invades and destroys the city; 1644 – fire destroys the city; 1744 – residence of the Dukes of Nassau-Usingen; Biebrich Castle is built; 1841 – new ducal palace built in the centre of town; 1866 – becomes part of Prussia; 1874 – Bismarck prohibits gambling; 1918–30 – occupied by foreign troops; 1946 – capital of the state of Hesse

Population: 300,000; capital of the state of Hesse

Postal code: D–6200   **Telephone code:** 61 21

Climate: hot and sunny in the summer, cold in the winter – typical for the Rhine Valley.

Calendar of events: *Fastnacht* (Feb) – Carnival in Wiesbaden; *Casino Ball* (spring) – a party in the grand style for those who love glamour; *Midnight Party* (Feb/Mar) – after the Ball des Sports, at the Nassauer Hof; *May Festival* (May) – theatre, opera and art festival; *International Riding Tournament* (Whitsuntide) – in Biebrich Castle; *Wilhelm Street Festival* (Jun) – high living takes to the streets; *Rhine Valley Wine Festival* (Aug) – the jewel of the Rhine Valley celebrates its noble potables in the palace courtyard; *Vintagers' Festival* (autumn) – the region celebrates the new grape harvest; *St. Andrew's Festival and Christmas Market* (Dec) – ringing in the Christmas holidays.

Fairs and exhibitions: *EDE* (Jan&Aug) – German iron merchants' congress; *INTERKON-DI-CA* (Feb) – bakers and confectioners convention; *INTERBIOLOGICA* (Mar) – German homeopathy convention; *CONGRESS OF PHYSICIANS* (Apr); *AN-SPO* (Sep) – fishing equipment; *HAFA* (Oct) – home economics convention.

Historical sights: *Castle* (1840) – classicistic, former residence of the counts of Nassau, now seat of the State Parliament; *Old Town Hall* (1609) – oldest house in Wiesbaden; *Greek Chapel* (1855) – a golden shimmering mausoleum for Russian princesses; *Marktbrunnen* (1537) – fountain with a gilded lion and the Nassau family coat of arms, in the palace courtyard; *Biebrich Castle* (1700) – Baroque summer residence of the Dukes of Nassau, on the banks of the Rhine; *Hessian State Theatre* (1894) – rococo on the inside, Baroque on the outside; reconstructed after World War II and reopened in 1978; *Kaiser-Friedrich-Bad* (1913) – bath with luxurious tiled Roman swimming area, for taking the waters in style.

Special attractions: a chamber concert in *Castle Biebrich*; life at the *Nassauer Hof* and the *Ente*; a tour of the *champagne country*; a boat trip downstream on the *Rhine* with a stopover dinner at *Die Krone* at Assmannshausen; an evening at the treasure-box *Opera House*.

Important companies with headquarters in the city: *Abbot Diagnostic Products* (medical instruments, pharmaceutical products); *Bilfinger & Berger* (construction); *Didier-Werke* (heat-resistant materials); *Henkell & Co* (wine, champagne); *Perennatorwerk Alfred Hagen* (seals); *Linde AG* (refrigeration technology); *Söhnlein Rheingold* (wine, champagne).

Airport: Frankfurt-Rhein-Main, FRA; Tel: (69) 69 01, Lufthansa, Tel.: (69) 6 90 21 11, VIP Lounge, Tel.: (69) 6 90 21 06, 35 km/23 miles; Lufthansa, Tel.: 3 91 95 97.

The Headquarters

NASSAUER HOF

3–4 Kaiser-Friedrich-Platz
D–6200 Wiesbaden
Telephone: 13 30
Telex: 4 186 847 hnh
Owning Company: Stinnes AG
General Manager: Karl Nüser
Affiliation/Reservation Systems: The Leading Hotels of the World, Preferred Hotels Worldwide, SRS (Steigenberger Reservation Service)
Number of rooms: 188 (21 suites)
Price range: DM 210–1,700
Credit cards: AE, DC, EC, Visa
Location: opposite the casino
Built: 1819 (renovated 1984)
Style: Wilhelminian Baroque
Hotel amenities: valet parking, thermal swimming pool, sauna
Main hall porters: Heino Reichard, Hermann Mayr
Room service: 24 hours
Laundry/dry cleaning: same day (weekend service)
Bar: ›Kamin Bar‹ (see Bars)
›Entenkeller‹ (see Meeting Points)
›Entenbistro‹ (see Restaurants)
Restaurants: ›Die Pfanne‹; H. W. Kniesbeck (maître), W. Carle (chef de cuisine)
›Die Ente vom Lehel‹ (see Restaurants)

Amongst the advantages pertaining to Frankfurt and its universal airport must be counted the proximity of Wiesbaden with its Nassauer Hof, one of the best and newest hotels in the world, if in a 150-odd-year-old grandiose city palais. Amidst casino, state opera, thermal springs and elegant shops, this Olympus of refined hospitality, cuisine and service is the carousel for business and pleasure, the turntable for meetings and conferences, the magnet for society, gourmets and spoiled globe-trotters. Every detail is a reason for joy: the roses in the bathroom – along with separate shower-cabin, non-standard hairdrier, scale, bathrobe and cosmetic accessoires; the evening sweet – as the final touch after the day-long continuous bedchamber service; the self-understood helpfulness without the pourboire philosophy; the uniquely tasteful décor – furniture, lamps, textiles, even the coat hangers are of a special quality; spaciousness – even in the smallest single room you could camp with two lovers or your family; the intelligent concept of hiding mini-bars, stereo equipment, television sets and baggage racks; the undemonstrative glamour allowing a very personal atmosphere despite the size and, finally, the landmark attractions in the house: the penthouse-pool spa, the city's chicest rendez-vous, the chimney-bar, and – of world renown – the restaurant empire of Hans-Peter Wodarz' Ente, the most famous Duck since Donald. Omnipresent court marshal Karl Nüser's magic touch – and innkeeper professionalism – has turned this hotel into a world address.

The Hideaway

KRONE

20 Rheinuferstrasse
D–6220 Assmannshausen/Rüdesheim
(30 km/20 miles)
Telephone: (67 22) 20 36
Owner/General Managers: Ernst and
Liselotte Hufnagel
Closed: mid-Nov – mid-Mar
Number of rooms: 86 (2 suites)
Price range: DM 40–225
Credit cards: AC, DC, EC, Visa
Location: in Assmannshausen, 30 km/20
miles from Wiesbaden
Built: 1541
Style: German romantic idyll
Hotel amenities: garage, car park, garden,
swimming pool
Room service: breakfast only
Conference rooms: 2 (up to 60 persons)
Restaurants: ›Krone‹ (12.00/a.m.–
14.30/2.30 p.m. and 18.30/6.30 p.m.–
21.30/9.30 p.m.), Herbert Pucher (chef de
cuisine), classic French and local cuisine

*Boating enthusiasts who plan to leave
Wiesbaden in a downstream direction
would do as well to consider continuing
their journey by train when they reach Assmannshausen. Apart from thereby avoid-
ing the dangers of shipwreck and a watery
grave after being lured onto the rocks just
north of the town by that most vindictive of
Rhinemaidens, the Loreley, they will also
have a perfect excuse to stop at one of the
most celebrated inns in Germany. For almost 450 years the Krone has stood directly on the bank of one of the most picturesque stretches of the river – a timber
framed building with a multi-gabled roof,
oriel window and geraniums in the window-boxes. The meticulous extensions and
renovations over the years have only added
to the charm of this historic auberge – in
particular, the pretty vine-covered terrace
which offers an unobstructed view of the
passing barges as well as goose liver pâté,
fish specialities or stuffed breast of guinea-
fowl. (You have a choice between becoming
inebriated by the intoxicatingly romantic
atmosphere, or the full body of the Hufnagel family's own wines). Inside, the
Krone is everything you would expect – exposed beams, antiques with the patina of
the centuries, fresh flowers and hunting trophies. The old-world charm continues upstairs into the bedrooms, which vary in size
and in some cases have a balcony overlooking the waters of the river and the swimming
pool (make sure you specify a room with
private bathroom!). The Hufnagel family,
dedicated custodians of this august hostelry for almost a hundred years, are justifiably proud of the Krone's venerable tradition. Small wonder that the guest list
ranges from local Romantic poets (Freilig-
rath, Otto Roquette, et al.) to international
bards (Engelbert Humperdinck), from Presidents (Scheel, Sukarno, et al.) to stars
and sheer gourmands – sometimes all in
one like Robert Morley.*

273

Lunch

ENTENBISTRO
3 Kaiser-Friedrich-Platz
Telephone: 13 36 61
Manager: Hans-Peter Wodarz
Maîtres: Günther Kaufmann and Hubert Kleinfercher
Closed: Sunday; Monday; public holidays; January 1–12; four weeks in summer
Open: 12.00/a.m.–1.00/a.m.
Cuisine: Nouvelle (German and French)
Chefs de cuisine: Hans-Peter Wodarz and Herbert Langendorf
Specialities: roulade of turbot and salmon with lobster sauce; smoked freshwater char (Saibling) on summer salad; roast Bavarian duckling with Savoy cabbage and bread dumpling; fresh fig with cassis and poppy-seed ice-cream
Location: in the Hotel Nassauer Hof
Setting: elegantized bistro; arched ceiling and pillars; picture windows with view of promenade
Amenities: hotel; restaurant (private dining rooms); bar; gourmet boutique; outdoor dining on terrace; car park; garage
Atmosphere: cheerfully and uncomplicatedly stylish
Clientèle: men (and women)-about-town; for business or pleasure; pre-conference or post-shopping
Dress: casual suit to designer jeans
Service: pleasantly efficient
Reservations: advisable to essential
Price range: moderately expensive
Credit cards: AE, DC, Euro, Visa

Dinner

DIE ENTE VOM LEHEL
3 Kaiser-Friedrich-Platz
Telephone: 13 36 66
Manager: Hans-Peter Wodarz
Maître: Johannes M. van Toorn
Closed: Sunday; Monday; public holidays; January 1–12; four weeks during summer
Open: 17.00/5 p.m.–1.00/a.m.
Cuisine: nouvelle (German and French)
Chefs de cuisine: Hans-Peter Wodarz and Herbert Langendorf
Specialities: duck liver parfait; soufflé of salmon and trout with Riesling sauce; goose with morel mushrooms in cream and carrots; fillet of turbot with lobster in champagne sauce; saddle of venison in two sauces with purée of celery and broccoli; poached white peach with whisky sauce and various sorbets; artistic design of fruit purées (›Dialog der Früchte‹)
Location: in the Hotel Nassauer Hof
Setting: historic building; domed ceiling with fresco; gallery; well-spaced tables; predominantly neutral colour-scheme with a proliferation of the eponymous ducks in all sizes and forms
Amenities: hotel; private dining rooms; bistro; bar; gourmet boutique; car park; garage
Atmosphere: harmonious and pleasing, with a hint of showmanship
Clientèle: local bons-vivants; businessmen from Baltimore to Brisbane; disciples and admirers of Hans-Peter Wodarz' multi-talented genius
Dress: fairly formal
Service: impeccable
Reservations: essential (no dogs)
Price range: appropriately expensive
Credit cards: AE, DC, Euro, Visa

Lunch

LANTERNA
3 Sedanplatz/3 Westendstrasse
Telephone: 40 25 22/40 75 22
Affiliations: Vereinigung Deutscher Sommeliers; Associazione Italiana Sommeliers; President of Ciao Italia (Association of Italian Gastronomes in Germany)
Owner/Manager: Angelo and Monika Gennaro
Closed: Friday; Saturday lunchtime
Open: 12.00/a.m.–14.00/2 p.m. and 18.00/6 p.m.–23.00/11 p.m.
Cuisine: nuova cucina italiana
Chef de cuisine: Carmine Carvelli
Specialities: cannelloni with herbs and curd cheese (ricotta); wolf-fish salad with lemon sauce; calf's tongue with orange salad; stuffed artichokes; passion fruit sorbet; daily changing menu
Location: central
Setting: small dining room; elegantized rustic style; candlelight and soft music
Amenities: tiny bar; terrace
Atmosphere: intimate (a rose for each lady)
Clientèle: local congressmen; businessmen tired of Frankfurt anonymity; Sekt manufacturers
Dress: no Bermuda shorts and sloganed T-shirts
Service: attentive
Reservations: essential
Price range: medium
Credit cards: AE, DC, Euro, Visa

Dinner

LANDHAUS DIEDERT
9 Am Kloster
Klarenthal (5 km/3 miles)
Telephone: 46 02 34
Owner/Manager: Peter and Karin Diedert
Closed: Monday; Saturday at lunch
Open: 12.00/a.m.–15.00/3 p.m. and 18.00/6 p.m.–22.00/10 p.m.
Cuisine: local; ›au goût du marché‹
Chef de cuisine: Peter Diedert
Specialities: John Dory in lemon sauce

with wild rice; strawberry salad with vanilla ice-cream
Location: in Wiesbaden-Altklarenthal; 5 km/3 miles north-west of town centre
Setting: idyllic countryside; 700-year-old former monastery, lovingly converted into a luxurious manoir; gabled roof, open fireplace, carefuly chosen antique rustic accessoires; candle-lit at night
Amenities: hotel; open-air dining on terrace; car park
Atmosphere: warm and welcoming; that of an attractive country house whose owner understands the art of gracious living
Clientèle: managing directors hoping to clinch a deal; modern men seeking a respite from the twentieth century
Dress: fairly conventional
Service: exceptionally welcoming and hospitable
Reservations: advisable

Dinner

LE VAL D'OR
3 Hauptstrasse
Guldental (8 km/5 miles)
Telephone: (67 07) 17 07
Owner/Manager: Silvia Buchholz
Closed: Monday; two weeks in January; two weeks in summer
Open: 12.00/a.m.–14.00/2 p.m. (Sunday only) and 18.00/6 p.m.–22.00/10 p.m.
Cuisine: nouvelle, with a local accent
Chef de cuisine: Johann Lafer
Specialities: terrine de foie gras with bean sprouts; Norway lobster in curry coating; lamb with pounded basil; venison; desserts; curd cheese girdle cake (Topfengalette) with fresh raspberries; apricot dumplings with curd cheese ice-cream (Aprikosenknödel mit Quarkeis)
Location: 8 km (5 miles) north of Bad Kreuznach; 30 minutes' drive from Wiesbaden
Setting: sleepy village amidst vineyards bordering the River Nahe; whitewashed house with small-paned windows and window-boxes; two small connecting dining rooms; Jugendstil; beige and terracotta; mahogany, brass and old prints on walls
Amenities: car park
Atmosphere: festive but intimate
Clientèle: gourmet habitués, culinary journalists and other pilgrims to this shrine of lucullian delights; local congressmen and businessmen tired of Wiesbaden
Dress: casually stylish to stylishly casual
Service: friendly and very knowledgeable
Reservations: essential – preferably well in advance (dogs allowed)
Price range: fairly expensive
Credit cards: DC, Euro

Café

BLUM
44–46 Wilhelmstrasse
Telephone: 30 00 07
Owner/Manager: Wessinger GmbH/Hildegard Wessinger
Closed: never
Open: (Monday–Saturday) 8.00/a.m.–20.00/8 p.m. (Sunday) 10.00/a.m.–20.00/8 p.m.
Location: in Wiesbaden's most elegant shopping street
Setting: recently-renovated traditional-style café; luxurious intérieur with lavish use of expensive materials
Amenities: open-air dining on boulevard terrace
Atmosphere: post avant-garde; cool but friendly
Clientèle: heterogeneous; local habitués and casual visitors
Service: very good

Meeting Point

ENTENKELLER
3 Kaiser-Friedrich-Platz
Telephone: 13 36 66
Manager: Hans-Peter Wodarz
Closed: Sunday; Monday; public holidays; January 1–12; four weeks during summer
Open: 17.00/5 p.m.–1.00/a.m.
Location: in the Hotel Nassauer Hof
Setting: greens and beiges; pillars, fountain and ceiling lighting; stone ducks, china ducks and stuffed ducks
Amenities: hotel; restaurant; bistro (with terrace); snacks à la Wodarz (duck liver parfait with hazelnut bread; Atlantic fish soup)
Atmosphere: sophisticated and relaxing
Clientèle: locals mingle with well-dressed, well-behaved visitors; pre-dinner drinks crowd gives way to discriminating post-theatre crowd in search of refreshment as the evening wears on
Service: professional
Reservations: necessary
Credit cards: AE, DC, Euro, Visa

Bar

KAMIN
Hotel Nassauer Hof
3 Kaiser-Friedrich-Platz
Telephone: 13 30
Manager: Georg Schütz (Sir George)
Closed: never
Open: 10.00/a.m.–after midnight

Location: in the Hotel Nassauer Hof
Setting: comfortable hotel bar with traditional English-style décor, open fireplace and a pianist, should you prefer meditation to conversation
Amenities: hotel; private dining rooms; restaurant; bistro; second bar; gourmet boutique; air conditioning; car park; garage
Atmosphere: perfect for a pre-pandial cocktail or a late-night cognac
Clientèle: international lawyers, megamagnates, journalists and globe-trotters plus a sprinkling of Wiesbaden's resident crème de la crème
Service: unobtrusive and reliable
Price range: high
Dress: elegant to casual
Reservations: advisable in the evenings
Credit cards: AE, DC, Euro, Visa

Nightclub

PARK WIESBADEN
Tanzpalast Park
Telephone: 3 93 21
Closed: never
Open: 21.00/9 p.m.–4.00/a.m.
Location: on the Wilhelmstrasse; a dice throw from the casino
Setting: recently renovated; stylish Art Nouveau décor, complete with potted palms and trailing plants
Amenities: five bars; dancing to live orchestra; shows every week; gala evenings on Thursdays; air conditioning
Atmosphere: international; chic; spontaneous; invigorating
Clientèle: familiar faces and famous names from the worlds of politics, television and the arts, plus a liberal sprinkling of trades fair exhibitors and local industrialists
Dress: no tennis shoes
Service: very good
Reservations: advisable
Credit cards: AE, DC, Euro, Visa

Shopping

EVERYTHING UNDER ONE ROOF
Hertie   6 Kirchgasse
FOR HIM
Kurowski   34 Wilhelmstrasse
FOR HER
Mode Schmidt   52 Wilhelmstrasse
BEAUTY & Hair
Wittmer   56 Wilhelmstrasse
JEWELLERY
Stoess   34 Wilhelmstrasse

LOCAL SPECIALITIES
Tabak-Shop (tobacco)
10 An den Quellen
Annabel of Koenigstein (women's fashion)
3a Webergasse
Modehaus Gerich (men & women's fashion)
35 Louisenstrasse
Max & Moritz (children's fashion)
35 Webergasse
Adam (leather fashion)
42 Wilhelmstrasse
Lachmann (furs)
32 Wilhelmstrasse
Koerr (books)
48 Wilhelmstrasse
Behagel (gifts)
10 Wilhelmstrasse
Letschert (baggage & travel accessories)
Kirchgasse
Danker (interior decorating)
14 Friedrichstrasse
Feikert (food and beverages)
Marktstrasse

THE BEST OF ART
Brumme   (Fine Art prints)
40 Taunusstrasse, Tel. 52 66 63
Keul & Sohn   (18th-century antiques)
33–35 Taunusstraßse, Tel. 52 26 61
Ott-Heydendahl OHG   (18th/19th-century antiques) 15 Taunusstrasse,
Tel. 52 28 18
Weichmann   (auctioneers)
24 Luisenstrasse, Tel. 30 70 60

The City

Athens itself is no museum, but it's full of them, repositories of many a ›group that's quite antique, half naked, loving, natural, and Greek‹. And yet the glory that was Greece still pervades the city, crystallized for all time in the serene classicism of the Temple of Theseus on the Agorá, the former forum where Diogenes philosophized and democracy was born, and in the cornucopia of monuments and statues culminating in the Acropolis. Despite the ravages of time, plundering English archaeologists and twentieth-century self-destruction, the Parthenon stands on its mini-Olympus above the man-made pandemonium like a ›still unravish'd bride of quietness‹, a ›foster-child of silence and slow time‹; it is the indestructible symbol of ephemeral splendour which so poignantly imbues the city with the essence of western civilization. Shelley's paean of praise of the moment ›when o'er the Aegean main Athens arose; a city such as vision builds from the purple crags and silver towers of battlemented cloud‹ shines like a lode star amongst the galaxy of panegyrics which the capital of the world's first democracy has inspired. For the descendants of the eighteenth-century Grand Tourists coming to Greece today it's a case of plus ça change . . . The magnetism exerted by the cradle of Aeschylus, Aristotle, Homer, Hippocrates, Pericles, Pythagoras et al. is as strong as it ever was, despite concrete-box architecture à l'extrème, cacophonous traffic chaos and the uncivilized effects of civilization. Small wonder – one third of the country's population lives here, half the cars in the land are driven here and the city, including the port at Piraeus and the hinterland of Attica, is also the factory and market place for three quarters of the nation's industry. The legendary renommé of the shipping dynasties – Goulandris, Livanos, Onassis, Niarchos – is echoed by the glittering trendsetters in fashion (Polatoff), jewellery (Lalaounis), films (Cocoyannis) and music (Theodorakis), with film-star-turned-politician Melina Mercouri combining social engagement with her dramatic roles. Pallas Athene's namesake protégée is a cross between a quintessential European metropolis and a Turkish bazaar – pulsating, temperamental and resilient. The streets exude a mixture of oriental mystery and Latin never-on-Sunday (if Monday will do) philosophy, bursting forth at night in a riot of ouzo, bouzouki and neon in the Plaka district, whilst the remnants of antiquity jostle with the Byzantine churches, the neo-classical banks and the nondescript public buildings. Syntagma Square is the modern amphitheatre, with palm-fringed cafés the stage and the Parliament building the backdrop for Platonic dialectic by the children of Aristophanes.

Founded: 10th century; B.C., by Theseus; Athênai (Greek) – after Athene, goddess of wisdom, daughter of Zeus and patroness of the city.

Far-reaching events: 776 B.C. – first official celebration of the Olympic Games; 621 B.C. – Drakon; first written laws; 461 – Pericles; arts flourish; 431–404 – Peleponnesian War; surrender to Sparta; 146 – Roman occupation; 395 – Greece becomes part of the Eastern Roman Empire; 1453 – Turkish invasion; 1687 – Venetian attack; 1821 – Greece independent; 1825 – Turkish invasion; 1832/33 – Contract of Constantinople; Greece independent; 1833–62 – Otto I of Bavaria king; 1864 – George I of Denmark chosen by British to be king; 1896 – first Olympic Games of modern times; 1897 – war against Turkey; 1913–16 – Constantine king; 1923 – revolution ends King George II's reign; 1935 – monarchy restored; 1940 – Italian invasion; 1941–44 – occupation by foreign forces; 1964 – Constantine II crowned; 1967 – military government under Papadopoulos, Constantine in exile; 1974 – democratic republic; 1981 – member of the EC.

Population: 3.2 million.   **Postal code:** GR–10000 to 18000   **Telephone code:** 1

Climate: sunshine 300 days per year.

Calendar of events: *Carnival* (Feb) – food and fêtes; *National Day* (25 Mar) – military parade; *Theatre and Music Festival* (Jun–Sep) – classical drama on modern stages with historic backdrops; *Folk Dancing* and *Wine Festivals* fill the city in the late summer.

Fairs and exhibitions: *EUROMODE* (Jan) – clothes; *XENIA* (Jan/Feb) – hotel equipment; *NAUTIKO* (Mar) – boats; *HOBBY* (Mar) – sports equipment; *DEFENDORY* (Oct) – arms industry.

Historical and modern sights: *Propylaea* (437 B.C.) – monumental entrance; *Parthenon* (5th century B.C.) – constructed under Phidias' direction, Athene's temple; *Erechtheion* (421–405 B.C.) – Ionic, the most intricate of the temples; *Areopagus* – former government and court of justice; place of St. Peter's sermon; *Agora* – antique market square; *Roman Agora* (1st century); *Temple of Olympic Zeus* – with Hadrian's Arch (2nd century); *Museum of Archaeology* – representing the 5,000 years of Greek's history; *Plaka* – picturesque part around the Acropolis.

Special attractions: a performance at the amphitheatre during the *Athens Festival;* an evening at *Turkolimano* (›Turkish harbour‹); climbing the *Acropolis* before sunrise; sunset at *Cap Sourion;* a weekend at *Hydra*.

Important companies with headquarters in the city: *Aluminium de Grèce* (aluminium); *Chemical Industries of Northern Greece* (chemicals); *Eleusis Bauxite Mines* (bauxite); *General Cement* (cement); *Greek Powder and Cartridge* (explosives); *Hellenic Shipyards* (shipbuilding); *Helleniki Techniki Group* (technology); *Olympic Airways* (airline); *Titan Cement* (cement).

Airport: Athens-Hellenikon, ATH; Tel.: 9 69 91; 12 km/8 miles; Olympic Airways, Tel.: 9 81 12 01.

The Headquarters

GRANDE BRETAGNE

Constitution Square
GR–10210 Athens
Telephone: 3 23 02 51
Telex: 215 346 and 219 615 hbrt
Owning Company: Hellenic Hotels Lampsa
Managing Directors: Apostolos Doxiadis/Pericles Petracopoulos
Affiliation/Reservation System: The Leading Hotels of the World
Number of rooms: 384 (25 suites)
Price range: Drs 8,204 – 23,409
Credit cards: all major
Location: city centre
Built: 1862 (recently renovated)
Style: traditional – regal style
Hotel amenities: parking, beauty salon, newsstand, boutique
Main hall porter: D. Mossios
Room amenities: colour tv, mini-bar/refrigerator, radio (small pets allowed)
Bathroom amenities: bidet, telephone
Room service: 24 hours
Laundry/dry cleaning: same day (weekend service)
Conference rooms: 4 (up to 450 persons)
Bars: ›Main Bar‹ (10.00/a.m.–24.00/12.00 p.m.) pianist; ›G. B. Corner‹ (see Meeting Point)
Restaurants: ›Grande Bretagne‹ (see Restaurants); ›G. B. Corner‹ (11.30/a.m. to 2.00/a.m.) as Coffee Shop and Bar
Private dining rooms: three

The GB is the epicentre of Athens' high life, the business foyer and conference centre, the crossroads of the diplomatic corps, the regal address, the starting point for culture pilgrimages, the most luxurious resting place, the liveliest watering hole, the best restaurant, the social parade ground, the Grand Hôtel par excellence, the grandest in Greece. Across from the King's-Palace -cum-House-of-Parliament, the GB was built as the Royal Guest House by Danish architect Theophile Hansen 125 years ago and has more than guarded its style and greatly improved in standard since. The spacious rooms and suites are comfortably furnished and appointed with the necessities of Western civilization as well as with touches from Antiquity and local colour, and the bathrooms are all marble and mirrors. From the balconies you have the most breathtaking view over Athens and the Acropolis and since everything – official, sensational or scandalous – happens on Constitution Square, you have a ring-side seat at the GB around the clock. Downstairs, at the GB Corner, you are in the midst of Athens' fashionable life à huis clos, and in the bar you will hear the latest gossip to make you an insider of the city instantly. Even though Aristotle O. doesn't stop here any more, all the other tanker tycoons, the stars of industry and show business are regulars for breakfast, lunch and dinner. There is no business like business at the GB.

The Hideaway

ASTIR PALACE

Vouliagmeni Beach, Attica
(23 km/14 miles)
GR-166 71 Athens
Telephone: (21) 8 96 02 11/8 96 03 11
Telex: 215 013 aspa
General Manager: Chronis Stergiopoulos
Affiliation/Reservation Systems: AHC, RFW, Citel Space Bank
Number of rooms: 550 (34 suites)
Price range: Drs 9,600–53,000
Credit cards: AE, DC, Visa, MC, CB, EC
Location: 13 km/8 miles from airport
Built: 1967 (renovated 1979–1984)
Style: modern
Hotel amenities: garage, valet parking, house limousine service, health club, beauty salon, sauna, massage, newsstand, drugstore, boutique, tobacconist, florist
Room amenities: air conditioning (in some rooms), colour tv, mini-bar/refrigerator (some)
Bathroom amenities: bathrobe, telephone
Room service: 24 hours
Laundry/dry cleaning: same day (weekend service)
Conference rooms: 11 (up to 500 persons)
Sports: water skiing, windsurfing, tennis
Bars: ›37‹ (8.00/a.m.–17.30/5.30 p.m.) snacks on the beach; five further bars (12.00/a.m.–24.00/12 p.m.)
Restaurants: six restaurants, serving Greek and international specialities
Club House: (13.00/1.00 p.m.–15.00/3.00 p.m. and 20.00/8.00 p.m.–24.00/12.00 p.m.) 9 maîtres, 4 chefs de cuisine, international and Greek specialities
Nightclub: (June to September) modern style, pianist, orchestra

Not only during the summer months, when a pall of heat hangs over Syntagma Square and waves of tourists threaten to engulf the Acropolis, but also on every sunny weekend or even, quieter still, during the week in off-season, there ist no better place to be, in and around Athens, than this sea resort not farther away than the airport. Vougliameni is not Cap d'Antibes and Astir Palace is not Eden Roc, but what it lacks in architecture, luxury and glamour is made up by the rugged nature softened with groves of pine trees, the Aegean Sea with its unique light and the overwhelming service by the lovable staff. A scenic coastal road leads you in less than an hour to the modern main building encircled by seventy-odd little bungalows dotted around the grounds, offering total privacy and still the same fast and friendly assistance. Contemporary furnishing and no-frills comfort favour the eternal holiday ambiance and the moods go from carefree around the pools and the beach to romantic in the evening, on the terrace restaurant or in the country's chicest summer discothèque, the ›Nine Muses‹.

Lunch

ATHENAEUM
8 Amerikis Street
Telephone: 3 63 11 25
Owner/Manager: Board of Directors
Closed: Sunday
Open: 12.00/a.m.–16.00/4 p.m. and 20.30/8.30 p.m.–2.00/a.m.
Cuisine: international
Chef de cuisine: George Avranas
Specialities: prosciutto with melon; sea-food pancakes; grilled chicken; prunes with whipped cream
Location: central, close to Constitution Square
Setting: turn-of-the-century
Amenities: air conditioning
Atmosphere: sophisticated charm and elegance
Clientèle: stylish judges en fête and en famille; a president or two; distinguished foreigners; well-to-do burghers of Athens
Dress: conservative
Service: very good
Reservations: advisable
Price range: fairly expensive
Credit cards: DC, EC, MC, Visa

Lunch

GRANDE BRETAGNE
Sintagma Square
Telephone: 3 23 02 51
Owner/Manager: Hellenic Hotels Lampsa/Pericles Petracopoulos
Closed: never
Open: 7.00/a.m.–11.00/a.m.; 13.00/1 p.m.–15.00/3 p.m. and 19.00/7 p.m.–22.00/10 p.m.
Cuisine: international and Greek
Specialities: Greek dishes
Location: in the Hotel Grande Bretagne, on the main Constitution Square
Setting: timeless luxury; classic décor befitting Athens' ›best address‹
Amenities: hotel; air conditioning
Atmosphere: formally elegant but not forbiddingly so
Clientèle: when in Greece ... visiting monarchs, presidents, plenipotentiaries and prominenti from the worlds of industry, politics and the arts
Dress: casually stylish to stylishly casual
Service: professional and knowledgeable
Reservations: advisable
Price range: fairly expensive
Credit cards: all major

Dinner

CORFU
6 Kriezotou
Telephone: 3 61 30 11
Closed: never
Open: 12.00/a.m.–1.00/a.m.
Cuisine: Corfiote
Specialities: beef Pastitsada, beef Sofrito; prawn and lobster; traditional Greek specialities and dishes from the island of Corfu
Location: in the very heart of the city close to Syntagma Square and King's Palace Hotel
Setting: modest décor
Atmosphere: an ever-crowded Greek taverna, vivacious, informal
Clientèle: businessmen, politicians, lawyers and birds of passage from all over the world
Dress: informal to elegant
Service: amazingly efficient
Reservations: not necessary
Price range: moderate

Dinner

DIONISIOU LYCABETTUS
Telephone: 7 22 63 74
Owner/Manager: the Dionysos-chain
Closed: never
Open: 9.00/a.m.–23.45/11.45 p.m.
Cuisine: Greek
Specialities: charcoal-grilled shrimps; lamb
Location: on Lycabettus Hill
Setting: elegant restaurant offering breathtaking views over the entire city
Atmosphere: an elegant brunch-, lunch- and dinner-restaurant with good food and unique panorama
Clientèle: international; foot-sore tourists mingle with businessmen en fête and en famille
Dress: as you like it
Service: multilingual, efficient and rather busy all the time
Reservations: essential
Price range: expensive

Dinner

GEROFINICAS
10 Pindarou Street
Telephone: 3 63 37 10/3 62 27 19
Owner/Manager: J. Roggenbucke
Closed: never
Open: 12.00/a.m.–1.00/ a.m.
Cuisine: Greek and oriental
Chef de cuisine: G. Georgopoulos
Specialities: Doner kebab with oriental rice; lamb; veal; fresh vegetables; friut and rich desserts

Location: central
Setting: rustic; indoor terrace overgrown with shrubbery; open kitchen where the day's specialities can be scrutinized and chosen in true Greek fashion
Amenities: air conditioning
Atmosphere: informal; very ›in‹ (within its sphere); probably the best local introduction to Greek cuisine
Clientèle: resident foreigners; tourists from Helsinki to Hamburg – and a sprinkling of genuine Greeks
Dress: as you like it
Service: friendly and good-natured
Reservations: advisable
Price range: medium
Credit cards: AE, DC, Visa

Dinner

TAVERNA MYRTHIA
35 Markou Mousouri-Metz
Telephone: 701 22 76
Closed: Sunday; June to September
18.00/6 p.m.–23.45/11.45 p.m.
Cuisine: Greek
Specialities: a wide variety of traditional hors d'œuvres; roast chicken; lamb in lemon sauce
Location: on the hill behind the Olympic Stadium
Setting: typical Greek taverna; serenading guitarists and other musicians play – for those in love only of course – whilst others concentrate on the excellent food
Amenities: restaurant; live music entertainment
Atmosphere: full of life and spirit, informal and vivacious
Clientèle: Athenian citizens, artists, journalists and lovers from Los Angeles to Luxembourg
Dress: informal
Service: unobtrusive efficiency
Reservations: advisable to essential
Price range: medium high

Dinner

VASSILENAS
72 Etolikou Street
Piraeus (10 km/6 miles)
Telephone: 461 24 57
Owner/Manager: Georg Vassilenas
Closed: lunchtime every day; Sunday
Open: 19.00/7 p.m.–24.00/12 p.m.
Cuisine: local
Specialities: Greek dishes; a sixteen-course selection of traditional foods (minute portions!)
Location: in Piraeus; 10 km (6 miles) from Athens
Setting: typical Greek tavern with traditional décor

Atmosphere: à la mode but still authentic
Clientèle: Hellenic Haute Bourgeoisie in fête and en famille, plus international celebrities from Melina Mercouri to Jeanne Moreau
Dress: casual
Service: helpful and anxious-to-please
Reservations: advisable
Price range: medium
Credit cards: not accepted

Dinner

BAJAZZO
10 Ploutarchous Street, Kolonaki
Telephone: 7 29 14 20
Owner/Manager/Chef de cuisine: Klaus Feuerbach
Closed: Sunday
Open: 19.30/7.30 p.m.–2.00/a.m.; last orders 24.00/12 p.m.
Cuisine: Greek, oriental and nouvelle
Specialities: ›bouzouki frivolities‹ – vine leaves filled with mousse of sea-bass, octopus filled with pine-nuts and aubergine filled with minced lamb and mint on ouzo sauce; carpaccio of lamb fillet in sherry garlic sauce
Location: at the foot of the Lycabettus Hill – between the best boutiques
Setting: palm trees at the entrance; four flower-filled salons; understated décor in tones of pastel rosé by Dave Keller (designer of the interior of the Sultan's Palace in Brunei)
Amenities: bar (upstairs)
Atmosphere: undeniably chic
Clientèle: the occasional shipping magnate (Stavros Niarchos) or star of stage or screen (Anouk Aimée), plus local habitués and visiting businessmen
Dress: soignée
Service: well-informed
Reservations: advisable
Price range: on the expensive side

Café

MAYEMENOS AVLOS
(›The Magic Flute‹)
4 Kalevkou Aminda
Telephone: 7 22 31 95
Closed: never
Open: 10.00/a.m.–23.00/11 p.m.
Specialities: lemon pie; special sauerkraut
Location: close to the Truman Statue
Atmosphere: lively and informal, a meeting point for the theatre- and after-theatre-crowd
Clientèle: all those secret lovers of Mozart's Queen of the Night, Papagenos and Papagenas mingle with other interesting birds of passage
Service: friendly
Reservations: not necessary
Price range: medium

Meeting Point

G. B. CORNER
Hotel Grande Bretagne
Sintagma Square
Telephone: 3 23 02 51
Owner/Manager: Hellenic Hotels
Lampsa/Pericles Petracopoulos
Closed: never
Open: 11.30/a.m.–2.00/a.m. (approx.)
Location: in the Hotel Grande Bretagne,
on the main Constitution Square
Setting: comfortably Edwardian; vaguely
club-like – dark wood, leather
Amenities: hotel; air conditioning
Atmosphere: informal, friendly and so-
phisticated café-restaurant serving every-
thing from drinks to sandwiches to five-
course dinners until the wee small hours
Clientèle: hotel guests from Gettysburgh
to Glasgow mingle with the Athenian so-
cial élite and the younger jet-set during
the late hours
Dress: informal
Service: cheerful
Reservations: advisable during High Season; otherwise unnecessary
Credit cards: all major

Meeting Point

STAGE DOOR
14 Voukourestiou Street
Telephone: 3 63 51 45
Open: 9.30/a.m.–1.00/a.m. (upstairs dining room 13.00/1 p.m.–16.00/4 p.m. and
20.00/p.m.–1.00/a.m.)
Cuisine: Greek and international
Location: in the Voukourestiou pedestrian area (close to Panepistimiou Ave-
nue)
Setting: on two floors; attractively stylish
décor
Amenities: fully air-conditioned café, res-
taurant, bar, including take-away-service
Atmosphere: one of the city's cosmopoli-
tan meeting points; informal to elegant
Clientèle: mostly well-informed, well-travelled, well-dressed and (occasionally)
well-known
Dress: whatever kind of elegance you like
Service: helpful and friendly and very efficient
Reservations: advisable
Price range: medium to expensive

Nightclub

NINE PLUS NINE
5 Agras
Telephone: 7 22 22 58
Open: 22.00/10 p.m.–2.00/a.m.
Location: Platia Stadiou

Setting: jet-set discothèque, simple but
tasteful décor
Atmosphere: charmingly understated,
very intimate
Clientèle: disco-freaks mingle with the
most beautiful of beauties
Dress: paradise-like disco-elegance
Service: impeccable
Reservations: essential – well in advance
Price range: expensive

Shopping

EVERYTHING UNDER ONE ROOF
Minion   Patisia Street

FOR HIM
Ascot   6 Kapsali Street

FOR HER
Travassaros, Yannis
46 Vassilissis (Hilton Hotel)

BEAUTY & HAIR
Angelus   Academia Street

JEWELLERY
Lalaounis, Ilia   6 Panepistimiou

LOCAL SPECIALITIES
Nikos & Takis (women's fashion)
10 Panepistimiou Avenue (Plaka)
Gianetos (men's fashion)
15 Valaoriton Street
Bambina rose (children's fashion)
Hermès Street
Lizard (leather fashion)
14 Kriezoto Square
Sistovaris (furs)
Hermès Street
Eleftheroukis (books)
Sintagma Square
Gallani, Gianari (baggage & travel acces-
sories)
Kolonaki Square
Haritakis, C. (interior decorating)
7 Valaoritou Street
Mouriades (shoes)
4 Stadiou Street

THE BEST OF ART
Bernier, Jean   (contemporary art)
51 Marasli, Tel. 7 23 56 57

The City

If Budapest is really situated over the entrance to Hell, as the myth asserts, then the descendants of legendary founder Arpád must have a pact with Lucifer. Belle Epoque glamour, haunting melancholy, a trace of exoticism and a soupçon of kitsch – the citizens of Budapest restored their capital to its former glory out of the ruins of the Second World War, presenting the world with an image to be taken at face value by unashamed romantics, or with a metaphysical pinch of salt by those who share the Hungarians' fine sense of irony. This city on the seven hills is not merely a repository of souvenirs of vanished empires, but also the economic and industrial centre of a land which today is finding its own equilibrium within the socialist imperium; Pal Maleter's spirit of defiance still lives on, as the citizens resort to guile to maintain their way of life under the new régime. Their revenge lies in a mordantly satirical assessment of themselves and the rest of the world on both sides of the rather moth-eaten but still efficacious Curtain, coupled with an unrepentant enjoyment of palatschinken, whipped cream and coffeehouse nostalgia for the good old days. Love of luxury, love of life and a devil-may-care nonchalance are as Hungarian as her most glamourous ›gypsy baronesses‹, Eva, Magda and Zsa Zsa Gabor, or her most famous culinary exports, from salami and paprika to all those goose livers for the world's foie gras. Here in Budapest, as in Warsaw, Vienna or Salzburg, the genius loci finds its most striking expression in music, from the light-hearted operettas of Franz Lehár or the works of Zoltán Kodály and Béla Bartók to those of Franz Liszt. His Hungarian Rhapsodies evoke the pathos and the passion, the cosmopolitan brilliance and the folkloric syncopations which permeate the city, summarizing for all people and all time the enigmatic smile on the face of turbulent, resilient, bewitching, magnetic Budapest.

Founded: as a Celtic settlement; Budapest (Hungarian) – from Buda – ›an oven‹, and Pest – ›a lime kiln‹.

Far-reaching events: 1st century – Roman rule, capital of Pannonia; 376 – barbarian invasion; 896 – Magyar occupation; 1001–1038 – Stephen I, first crowned king; 1241 – Mongolian invasion; 1247 – construction of castle in Buda under Bela IV; 1458–90 – Mathias I; Renaissance and humanism flourish; 1465 – founding of university in Buda; 1541–1686 – Turkish occupation; 1686 – Hungary becomes part of the Hapsburg Empire; 1703–11 – Ferenc II Rákoczi; uprisings against Hapsburgs; 1848/49 – revolution; 1867 – full partnership in the Austro-Hungarian Empire, although an independent state; 1873 – union of Buda and Pest; 1918 – revolution – Republic proclaimed under Bela Kun; 1920 – Contract of Trianon – Hungary loses two thirds of its territories; 1944 – German occupation; 1944 – Russian ›liberation‹; 1949 – constitution voted; 1956 – popular uprising against Stalinist puppet régime under Imre Nagy – Russian intervention; 1968 – economic reconstruction – beginning of liberalization – autonomy of some sections of the economy – birth of private sector (Maszek).

Population: 2.1 million.

Postal code: H–Budapest   **Telephone code:** 1

Climate: mild – July is the hottest month.

Best time to visit: May to late September.

Calendar of events: *Budapest Spring Festival* and *Budapest Autumn Festival* – concerts, operas, ballet and folklore fill the city's cultural temples.

Fairs and exhibitions: *INTERNATIONAL TOURISM FAIR* (Mar); *AUTOSERVICE* (Apr) – car service and maintenance; *AVIAEXPO* (Apr) – aviation; *CONSTRUMA* (Apr) – construction industry; *INTERNATIONAL SPRING FAIR* (May) – technology; *AGROMASEXPO* (Aug) – agriculture, food machinery and equipment; *HOVENTA* (Sep) – restaurants and catering; *PROTENVITA* (Sep) – ecology and water conservation; *INTERNATIONAL AUTUMN FAIR* (Oct) – consumer goods; *BUDATRANSPACK* (Oct) – packaging and transport; *INTERPLAYEXPO* (Oct) – toys.

Historical and modern sights: *Aquincum* (1st century) – relics of the Roman settlement, museum and amphitheatre; *St. Stephen's Basilica* (19th century) – Italian Renaissance; *Mount Géllert* – with *Citadel* (1851) and Budapest's *Statue of Liberty; Royal Palace* – Gothic, now the National Gallery of Budapest; *Castle* – Renaissance; *Fishermen's Bastion* – Romanesque houses; *St. Mathias* (13th century) – Gothic coronation church of the Hungarian kings; *St. Nikolaus* – Gothic chapel, tower and walls included in the Hilton Hotel; *National Museum* (1836–46) – Hungary's 1,000 years of history with St. Stephen's crown on display; *Parliament* (19th/20th centuries) – neo-Gothic, façade reflected in the Danube; *Chain Bridge* (1848) – first connection between Buda and Pest; *Váca utca* – meeting and shopping centre; *Turkish Baths*.

Special attractions: good, clean tourist fun but with the best gypsy bands in the country at the *Mathias Cellar*; a *gluttonous tour* through Budapest's coffee-houses and confiseries – *Hungaria, Gerbeaud, Ruszwurm* et al.; a trip to *Szentendré* – an artists' colony (look for the Kovacs Margit exhibition); a stroll across *Heroes' Square* and *Elizabeth Bridge*; rejuvenating thermal therapy on *Margaret Island*; a night at the *Opera* (depending who is guest star).

Important companies with headquarters in the city: *Icarus Buses* (vehicles); *Ganz-Mávag* (locomotives); *Medicor* (medical equipment); *Pálma* (rubber).

Airport: Budapest-Ferihegy, BUD; Tel.: 570290/MALEV, Tel.: 572122; 16 km/10 miles.

The Headquarters

HILTON

1–3 ter Hess Andras
H–1014 Budapest
Telephone: 751 000
Telex: 225 984
Owning Company: Hilton Hotels Corp.
General Manager: Dr. György Nemedi
Affiliation/Reservation Systems: Danubius, Hilton Reservation Service
Number of rooms: 323 (28 suites)
Price range: US$ 54–84 (single)
               US$ 74–104 (double)
               US$ 131–177 (suite)
Credit cards: AE, DC, Visa, CB, EC, MC, JCB
Location: city centre
Built: 1977
Style: modern with historical remains
Hotel amenities: car park, car rental desk, travel office, shopping gallery, hairdresser, newsstand, open-air theatre, casino, beauty parlour, wheelchair accessibility, shuttle to city centre (on weekdays) and airport
Room amenities: air conditioning, colour tv, mini-bar, direct-dial telephone, in-house films, radio
Laundry/dry cleaning: same day (weekdays)
Conference rooms: for up to 600 persons
Sports: jogging
Sports (nearby): swimming pool and sauna at Thermal Hotel on Margaret Island – free entrance, free shuttle service
Bars: ›Dodex‹; ›Corner Lobby Bar‹; ›Café Margareta‹; open-air dining
Restaurants: ›Kalocsa‹; ›Coffee Shop‹; ›Fishermen's Bastion‹; international and local cuisine; gypsy violinists
Private dining rooms: 8 (up to 600 persons)

A Hilton is a Hilton is a Hilton. Not here. True, you can expect modern tones, standardized systems and 24-hour efficiency. And the beds are equally as large as in Strasbourg or Rotterdam. But apart from the New World achievements and acquisitions, atmosphere, service and flair are Hungarian. Which means life at the top. Despite the political reality. Charm, smiles, helpfulness, joy – all that lets you forget about what you want to forget about, anyway. Perched on a hillside near the mediaeval royal fortress on the Buda side of the Danube, with remains of the walls and tower of a 13th-century Dominican church and a Jesuit monastery incorporated into the structure, no-one here is interested in archaeology, but rather in the goose liver, the gypsy musicians and the czsardas princesses in the bars and restaurants. Business in Budapest should best be done at the Hilton – from the objective ouverture to the festive finale.

Lunch

KISKAKUKK ETTEREM
(›Little Cuckoo‹)
XIII. Pozsonyi út 12
Telephone: 32 17 32
Closed: Tuesday
Open: from 10.00/a.m. to 23.00/11 p.m.
Cuisine: Hungarian
Specialities: venison; wild duck on steamed apple; roast pork with cherry sauce; calf's loin on ananas; famous plum schnapps apéritif
Location: just round the corner from Margaret-Bridge
Setting: rather spartan interior décor; 14 tables
Atmosphere: relaxed and informal
Clientèle: local habitués and visitors-in-the-know
Dress: whatever you like (as long as it's not too outrageous)
Service: anxious-to-please
Reservations: advisable
Price range: medium high

Dinner

VADRÓZSA
(›Wild Rose‹)
Pentelei Molnár Ut. 15
Telephone: 35 11 18
Owner/Manager: Margo Vetter and Kati Horvath
Closed: lunchtime; Monday; three weeks in August
Open: 18.00/6 p.m.–24.00/12 p.m.
Cuisine: Hungarian and international
Specialities: charcoal-grilled goose liver; pike-perch; saddle of venison; saddle of wild boar; Beluga and Malossol caviar; cold goose liver
Location: 2 km (1 miles) north-east of city centre in an attractive suburb on the Rosenhügel; one of the prettiest squares in Budapest
Setting: small Baroque villa with a dining room furnished in Baroque style
Amenities: open-air dining in attractive garden; pianist
Atmosphere: civilized; nostalgic, with a hint of romance
Clientèle: bankers and businessmen from Buda and Pest, with a fair sprinkling of tourists
Dress: neat attire requested
Service: helpful and welcoming
Reservations: essential (no dogs)
Price range: expensive by Budapest standards
Credit cards: AE, DC, Euro, Visa

Lunch

KÁRPÁTIA
4–8 Károlyi Mihály Street
Telephone: 17 35 96

Owner/Manager: Hungar Hotels/Mihály Gonda
Closed: never
Open: 12.00/a.m.–15.00/3 p.m. and 18.00/6 p.m.–23.00/11 p.m.
Cuisine: international and Hungarian
Chef de cuisine: László Lepp
Specialities: goulash soup; paprika chicken with gnocchi; médaillons of pork Hungarian style; grilled trout; crisp roast duck; venison ragoût; Morello cherry strudel; pancakes
Location: city centre; round the corner from the Hotel Astoria
Setting: neo-Baroque intérieur with matching décor; vaulted ceilings, genre-paintings and custom-designed furniture; five dining rooms (main one with excellent gipsy orchestra during the evening)
Amenities: 4 private dining rooms (each 24–40 persons); beer restaurant in same building (open 11.00/a.m.–23.00/11 p.m.); bar; open-air dining on two covered terraces
Atmosphere: quiet and confidential for lunch; gregariously relaxing for dinner
Clientèle: local politicians, ambassadors and private citizens entertaining on a public or personal scale; visiting celebrities from Willy Brandt to Leonard Bernstein
Dress: casual
Service: personal and professional
Reservations: advisable (pets permitted)
Price range: four stars
Credit cards: AE, DC, Euro, Visa, Access, Master Card, JCB

Meeting Point

GERBEAUD CUKRASZDA
V. Vörösmarty tér
Telephone: 18 13 11
Open: 9.00/a.m.–21.00/9 p.m.
Specialities: the most tempting pastries on offer in Budapest; the recipes of the specialities of this renowned Budapest café going back to Emil Gerbeaud, a Swiss confectioner who took over the café in 1884
Location: near the Vörösmarty tér underground station
Setting: a beautiful café; fin-de-siècle interior décor with two ›salons‹, marble tables, chandeliers
Amenities: café, confiserie
Atmosphere: just a little bit rétro; charmingly understated elegance
Clientèle: an institution in town, where intellectuals and others from Budapest meet and mingle with visitors from all over the world
Dress: rather conservative
Service: ladies in black and white; friendly and impeccable
Reservations: advisable

Bar

BELVAROSI LIDO
Szabadsajtó u.5
Telephone: 18 24 04
Owner/Manager: Árpád Szücs
Closed: never
Open: 10.00/a.m.–4.00/a.m.
Cuisine: Hungarian and international
Specialities: consommé Lido-style;
stuffed apple Tokay–style
Location: on the Pest side of the Elizabeth bridge
Setting: neo-Baroque building; Belle
Epoque intérieur; stained glass windows,
chandeliers and black lacquered furniture
Amenities: folklore programmes (12.00/
a.m.–15.00/3 p.m); live jazz (15.00/3
p.m.–18.00/6 p.m.); roulette salon (slot
machines; 16.00/4 p.m.–4.00/a.m.); show
programmes (21.00/9 p.m.–4.00/a.m.)
with ice-skating clowns, topless dancers,
glitter, glamour and go-go girls galore;
dance orchestras; open-air dining on terrace; air conditioning; car park
Atmosphere: from the gipsy romantic to
the sophisticated spectacular as the evening progresses
Clientèle: frequent haunt of visiting cultural, technical and business delegations,
plus a minority of Hungarian habitués
Dress: no special requirements
Service: unobtrusive by comparison
Reservations: advisable
Price range: rather expensive
Credit cards: all major

Nightclub

HOROSCOP
41–43 Krisztina krt
Telephone: 56 63 33
Owner/Manager: Balázs Farkas
Closed: never
Open: 22.00/10 p.m.–4.00/a.m.
Location: in the Hotel Buda Penta
Setting: on the ground floor of the hotel;
bar/nightclub in shades of brown with
imaginative tubular lighting system; zodiac signs decorating the walls; séparées;
large dance floor
Amenities: hotel; two restaurants; café
with open-air dining on terrace; non-stop
music – live, discothèque and show programme with singers and dancers; air
conditioning; car park
Atmosphere: youthful; stylish
Clientèle: almost cosmopolitan; self-confident and comfortably-off
Dress: casual but not careless
Service: under the capable direction of
chief barman Ernö Székler
Reservations: advisable
Credit cards: AE, DC, Euro, Visa, Master
Charge, JCB, Carte Blanche, Access

Shopping

EVERYTHING UNDER ONE ROOF
Skala-Metro
Nyugati Palyaudvar/Marx tér

FOR HIM
Divatáru 8 Váci utca

FOR HER
Aranypók Konsumee Váci utca

JEWELLERY
Rubin 2 Parizsi utca

LOCAL SPECIALITIES
Knitwear (women's fashion)
4–6 Kigyó utca
Skala (men's fashion)
6–10 Schoenherz Zoltán utca
S-Modell (furs) 9 Galamb utca
Gondolat (books)
10 Váci utca
Haas & Czjzek (gifts)
23 Bajcsy Zs utca
Gerbeaud (food and beverages)
7 Voeroesmarty tér
Hungaroton (records)
1 Voeroesmarty tér

THE BEST OF ART
Artbureau-Artex (modern art)
31 Muennich F. U., Tel. 5 30–2 22
Art Galerie (modern art)
5 Táncsis Mihály ucta
Gulácsy Galéria (modern art)
4a Fürj utca
Bizományi Aruház (antiques)
3–5 Felszabadulás

The City

History credits Englishman Simon de Montfort with laying the foundation stone of modern parliamentary democracy but, strictly speaking, the ›Mother of Parliaments‹ had a predecessor on another island. The Icelandic Althing first met on the desolate moss-covered plain of Thingvellir, thirty miles away from the present capital, in 930 A.D., over three centuries before the grander English assembly. Today, this nirvana nook of Wagnerian mystery has become a place of pilgrimage for twentieth-century fugitives in search of solitude, peace of mind and communion with nature's elements, while the descendants of those Dark-Age Norse refugees hold their political sessions in the city. Reykjavik is the most remote capital on the continent (unless you judge it from the perspective of a Shetland islander), but not the smallest (if you include Vaduz, Valletta and Monte-Carlo). Nestled around the sheltered inlet on Faxa Bay at the south-western tip of the island, the mini-metropolis stands out with its functional architecture in the dramatic natural surroundings like a tanker among fishing boats, but some Scandinavian period buildings give relief to the utilitarian setting. Having grown from a fishing village in the middle of nowhere to a political, economic and strategic entity in only a few decades, Reykjavik has still retained its modest image as a peaceful port, even though the hotly contended cod and the equally disputed herring stocks of the North Atlantic constitute the country's most important industry. Catching, freezing, salting and canning the rich fauna around its shores are raison d'être for most burghers of the capital, with shipbuilding, aluminium smelting and textiles rounding out the industrial life of the city; famous, useful and of trade importance are the fine leather goods and the knitwear made from the local wool. All-out attraction to everyone coming to Reykjavik, be it for fishing rights, NATO duties or adventurous ambitions, is the bizarre beauty of the city's surroundings. The ever-changing sea and sky, from hurricanes to midnight sun to Aurora Borealis, provide the scenic backdrop for volcanic eruptions violent enough to alter the profile of the mountains or to throw up the island of Surtsey from the depths of the ocean. The endless moors, surrounded by glaciers, waterfalls and geysers, are home to an ornithological Noah's Ark of rare species and compensate each spring for the paucity of trees by blossoming forth in a riot of sub-arctic flora. The Icelanders' nature is in line with their island's – rough-cut, open, hospitable, worldly in a basic sense, proud, patriotic and sincere. Whoever built a home and a nation up here, just outside the Arctic circle, withstanding the weather, the waves and the not so splendid isolation, just has to be all that and more. Paradise to the pure, purgatory to the snob.

Founded: 874 A.D. by Norse Vikings; Reykjavik – ›smoky bay‹ – so named because of the hot stream nearby.

Far-reaching events: 930 – founding of the Althing, the Icelandic parliament, the oldest in Europe; 982 – Eric the Red discovers Greenland; 1000 – Christianity comes to Iceland; 1264 – Iceland under Norwegian rule; 1380 – the Danish occupation; 1550 – Reformation; 1786 – Reykjavik chartered Danish monopoly on trading in Iceland; 1874 – constitution; 1904 – autonomous; 1911 – founding of university; 1918 – sovereign state; 1940 – British occupation; 1941 – American occupation; 17 May 1944 – founding of the Republic of Iceland; 1949 – membership of NATO.

Population: 90,000 capital and largest city of Iceland.

Postal code: IS–101 to 110   **Telephone code:** 1

Climate: cool summers; relatively mild winters due to the influence of the Gulf Stream; very changeable.

Calendar of events: *Film Festival* (Feb); *Sumardagurinn fyrsti* (3rd Thurs in Apr) – processions and dancing in the streets to greet the advent of summer; *Labour Day* (1 May) – brass bands and speeches; *Seamen's Day* (late May) – rowing competitions; *Arts Festival* (Jun); *National Day* (17 Jun) – processions and amusements in the streets; *New Year's Eve* (31 Dec) – bonfires and fireworks brighten the winter darkness.

Fairs and exhibitions: None.

Best views of the city: from the cathedral, the *Hallgrímskirkja*; *Sjómannaskólinn* (nautical school); *Hafnarshúsith* (harbour building).

Historical sights: *Althing* (1881) – parliament building; *Dómkirkjan* (19th century) – Lutheran cathedral with marble font; *Statue of Jón Sidurthsson* – national hero; *Stjórnarráthshúsith* – once a prison, now home of the Cabinet Offices; *Arnarhóll* – with statue of Ingólfur Arnarson, founder of Reykjavik; *Thjóthleikhúsith* (1923) – national theatre; *Háskólinn* (1911) – university, overlooking the airport; *Menntaskólinn* (19th century) – the oldest high school in the country; *Einar Jónsson Museum* – containing sculptures by Iceland's best known sculptor.

Modern sights: *Thjóthminjasafnith* – national museum; *Hallgrímskirkja* – cathedral of distinctive Icelandic design; *Háskólabíó* – the concert hall, excellent acoustics; *Neskirkja* – contemporary ecclesiastical architecture.

Special attractions: a swim in *Sundlag Vesturbaejar* thermal pool; a *low-altitude flight* over the island's volcanoes; an excursion to *Thingvellir.*

Important companies with headquarters in the city: *Loftleidir* (airline); *Alu-Suisse* (metal); *IBM; Icelandic Cold Water Corporation* (fisheries).

Airport: Reykjavik-Keflavik, REK; Tel.: 2 60 11, Icelandair, Tel.: 2 66 22/2 60 11; 45 km/30 miles.

The Headquarters

SAGA

Hagatorg
IS-107 Reykjavik
Telephone: 299 00
Telex: 22 55 hosaga
Owning Company: Farmers Association of Iceland
General Manager: Konrad Gudmundsson
Affiliation/Reservation Systems: British Airways/Concordia, Golden Tulip, SAS, Icelandair
Number of rooms: 106 (7 suites)
Price range: US$ 54–70 (single)
US$ 68–93 (double)
US$ 128–175 (suite
Credit cards: AE, DC, Access, Visa, EC, MC
Location: city centre
Built: 1962 (renovated permanently)
Hotel amenities: parking, car rental, ballroom, outdoor swimming pool heated with geothermal water, massage, beauty salon, manicure, hairstylist, boutique, tobacconist, florist, bank, souvenir shop, travel agent; healt club, sauna, solarium
Main hall porter: Karl Thorsteinsson
Room amenities: colour tv, mini-bar, radio, some rooms with balcony
Bathroom amenities: hairdrier
Room service: 8.00/a.m. to 23.30/11.30 p.m.
Laundry/dry cleaning: same day
Conference rooms: 7 (up to 350 persons) overhead and slide projectors, video, film projector
Bars: ›Astra‹ and ›Mimi's‹ (19.00/7,00 p.m. to 23.00/11.00 p.m.) with pianist
Restaurants: ›The Grill‹ (8.00/a.m.–23.30/11.30 p.m.) on top floor; international and continental cuisine with Icelandic specialities, pianist;
›Garden Restaurant‹ (7.00/a.m.–22.00/10.00 p.m.)
Nightclub: ›Sulnasalur Ballroom‹ (19.00/7.00 p.m.–3.00/a.m.) live music
Private dining rooms: banqueting facilities for up to 600 guests

On a clear day you can see to the centre of the earth. Or, more precisely, from the rooftop restaurant of the Saga, the panoramic view of Iceland's capital includes the peak of Snaefellsjökull Glacier which provided the setting for Jules Vernes' epic journey – just one of the unexpected delights offered by this cosmopolitan and yet intensely patriotic modern hotel. With wild goose and reindeer on the menu, friendly staff on call and comprehensive executive services on request, the Saga is rapidly acquiring a reputation as the lighthouse for Nordic hospitality and the agreeable blend between wild nature and tamed civilization.

Lunch

SAGA
107 Hagatorg
Telephone: 2 99 00
Owner/Manager: Farmers' Association of Iceland/Konrad Gudumndsson
Open: 8.00/a.m.–22.30/10.30 p.m.
Cuisine: international and Icelandic
Chef de cuisine: S. Fridjonsson
Specialities: Icelandic dishes
Location: in the Hotel Saga
Setting: modern dining room on the top floor of the hotel; panoramic view of the city and surroundings
Amenities: hotel; private dining rooms (20–350 persons)
Atmosphere: welcoming but stylish
Clientèle: cosmopolitan; visitors to Reykjavik for business or pleasure, official delegations and participants in the Art Festival
Dress: not too outrageous or outlandish
Service: knowledgeable and professional; directed by maître d'hôtel W. Wessman
Reservations: advisable
Price range: moderately expensive
Credit cards: AE, DC, Euro, Visa, Master Card, Access

Dinner

ARNARHOLL
8–10 Hvefisgata
Telephone: 1 88 33
Owner/Manager: Mr. Hansen/Guðbjörn Karl Olaffson
Open: from 12.00/p.m. to 22.30/10.30 p.m.
Cuisine: Icelandic with a French accent
Chef de cuisine: Mr. Hansen
Specialities: fillet of pork with blue cheese; sole cutlets with lemon sauce
Location: central
Setting: modern; wooden tables
Amenities: 3 bars; private dining room; air conditioning; parking
Atmosphere: cosy; the best restaurant in Reykjavik
Clientèle: local gratin; top industrialists and visiting VIPs
Dress: very formal
Service: always perfect; well trained
Reservations: necessary for dinner and weekends (no dogs)
Price range: medium
Credit cards: AE, DC, Euro, Visa

Lunch

LAEKIARBREKKA
2 Bankastraeti
Telephone: 1 44 30
Owner/Manager: Mrs. Klobrun
Closed: never
Open: 10.00/a.m.–23.30/11.30 p.m.
Cuisine: Icelandic and French
Chef de cuisine: Mr. Gudnundur
Specialities: mixed seafood platter; shrimps, lobster, scallops; flounder, mussels
Location: in the centre on the main street
Setting: modern touch to an old-style setting
Amenities: air conditioning; bar
Atmosphere: cosy
Clientèle: in summer a lot of tourists; in winter mostly local
Dress: casual
Service: good
Reservations: always necessary in summer, in winter only at weekends (no dogs)
Price range: medium
Credit cards: DC, Euro, Visa

Dinner

I KVOSINNI
22 Austurstraeti
Telephone: 1 13 40
Owner/Manager: Vinein Dodnundson
Closed: never
Open: 18.00/6 p.m.–1.00/a.m.
Cuisine: French
Chef de cuisine: François Fons (Commandeur du Cordon Bleu)
Location: central
Setting: opened in 1922; Reykjavik's most intimate restaurant, with nostalgic décor
Amenities: bar; air conditioning; car parking in the vicinity
Atmosphere: attractively old-fashioned
Clientèle: francophile gourmets, expatriate Parisians and local lovers with cause for celebration
Dress: formally elegant in winter (jacket and tie); more casually so in summer
Service: welcoming
Reservations: recommended, particularly at the weekend
Price range: medium
Credit cards: AE, DC, Euro, Visa

Café

FJARKINN
4 Austurstraeti
Telephone: 1 02 92
Owner/Manager: Mr. Orm
Closed: Sunday
Open: 9.00/a.m.–18.30/6.30 p.m.; Saturday 10.00/a.m.–14.00/2 p.m.
Location: central
Setting: bar/restaurant complex on two floors; old-fashioned intérieur, with lots of natural wood
Amenities: no alcohol; hamburgers; soft drinks; live band occasionally

Atmosphere: refreshingly different
Clientèle: students, secretaries, teetotal senior executives and a sprinkling of cheerleaders from Bible Belt colleges
Service: engagingly friendly
Reservations: not necessary
Credit cards: AE, DC, Euro

Bar

ASTRA
Hotel Saga
107 Hagatorg
Telephone: 2 99 00
Owner/Manager: Farmer's Association of Iceland/Konrad Gudumndsson
Closed: never
Open: 19.00/7 p.m.–23.00/11 p.m.
Location: in the Hotel Saga
Setting: comfortable international hotel bar with live piano music
Amenities: hotel; grill restaurant; private dining rooms (20–350 persons); second bar (›Mimi's‹); nightclub; outdoor swimming pool in the vicinity
Atmosphere: comfortable and relaxing
Clientèle: Iceland's In-Crowd; hotel guests
Service: expert
Reservations: advisable
Credit cards: AE, DC, Euro, Visa, Master Card, Access

Nightclub/Bar

BROADWAY
8 Alfabakki
Telephone: 7 75 00
Owner/Manager: Mr. Laodan
Closed: Monday to Thursday; Sunday
Open: Friday, Saturday 20.00/8 p.m.–3.00/a.m.
Location: in the Breidholt area
Setting: modern nightclub/discothèque with cool, understated décor
Amenities: restaurant; 8 bars; snacks and desserts; air conditioning
Atmosphere: fashionable
Clientèle: Iceland's Younger Set plus a selection of young (or not-so-young) birds of passage
Dress: boutique chic
Service: good
Reservations: essential for dining
Credit cards: AE, DC, Euro, Visa, Access

Nightclub

SULNASALUR
Hotel Saga
107 Hagatorg
Telephone: 2 99 00

Owner/Manager: Farmer's Association of Iceland/Konrad Gudumndsson
Closed: never
Open: 19.00/7 p.m.–3.00/a.m.
Location: in the Hotel Saga
Setting: modern nightclub with discothèque and live orchestra
Amenities: hotel; grill restaurant; private dining rooms; two bars; outdoor geothermal swimming pool in the vicinity
Atmosphere: sophisticated
Clientèle: young, self-assured and on-the-way-up to middle-aged and successful but definitely not moribund
Dress: disco elegance
Service: unobtrusively efficient
Reservations: advisable
Credit cards: AE, DC, Euro, Visa, Master Card, Access

Shopping

FOR HIM
Herrahúsið 7a Bankastræti

FOR HER
EVA 42 Laugavegi

BEAUTY & HAIR
Salon VEH Húsi Verslunarinnar, Kringlumýrarbraut

JEWELLERY
Jens Guðjónsson 13 Posthússtrr ti

LOCAL SPECIALITIES
Icelandic arts and craft centre (Islenskur heimilisiðndaður)
3 Hafnarstræti (fashion for her)
3 Hafnarstræti
Rammagerdin (fashion for him)
19 Hafnarstræti
Sævar Karl Olafsson (fashion for him and her)
9 Bankastræti
Bangsi (childrens fashion) 11 Bankastræti
Sdrydda (leather fashion)
1 Bergstadarstræti
Eggert Jóhannsson feldskeri (furs)
66 Laugavegi
The bookstore of Sigfús Eymundsson (books)
18 Austurstræti
Rammagerdin (gifts)
19 Hafnarstræti
Tekk-Kristall
15 Laugavegi
Gullfoss (cashmere)
9 Austurstræti

The City

›Action is the last resource of those who know not how to dream‹. Dreamer-dandy Oscar Wilde judged his compatriots well, who – loved and envied for this luxury – are masterful builders of castles, not only around their island, but also in the air. However, when it comes to it, Dubliners can act decisively too – as Englishman-by-choice George Frederick Handel discovered. Had it not been for the Lord Lieutenant's invitation, the struggling composer might never have been able to put on the ›Messiah‹. The ›town of the ford of hurdles‹, lying on the eastern coast of Ireland where the River Liffey meets the sea, is indelibly stamped with the Baroque imprint of that economic Golden Age. Eloquent testimony to the ›plaguy twelvepenny weather‹, the ›fourty shades of green‹ of Phoenix Park and the rolling arc of the Wicklow Mountains on the horizon provide an iridescent backdrop to James Gandon's pillared and porticoed public buildings, from the Italianate Four Courts to the Custom House. The clear-eyed Georgian perspectives of the broad streets of terraced patrician houses open onto the harmonious vistas of Merrion Square or St. Stephen's Green, adorning the city with a leisurely eighteenth-century aura as tangible as the magical ›pinkish sun-charged gauze‹ which shimmers over the spire of St. Patrick's Cathedral when it stops raining. The industrial and commercial arena of the divided island – and its main link to exoverlord England as well as the rest of the world – Dublin's economy today rests on its shipyards. It also floats metaphorically on a sea of Guinness and whiskey, with the export of Irish brood mares to the racing stables of the élite as a profitable spin-off of equestrian High Society's August showcase, the Dublin Horse Show. But the Irish capital's mysterious spell, most comprehensible to the outsider in the philosophical camaraderie of her pubs, is woven above all by her citizens, whose Gaelic forefathers jealously guarded their myth-laden traditions and superstitions whilst helping St. Patrick to save Christianity from extinction in the Dark Ages. A multi-faceted heritage, the gift of the Blarney and the blessing of the Little People has enabled the island race to preserve, throughout its tumultuous and troubled history, a fine sense of humour and a beguilingly satirical charm, coupled with a lacrymose sentimentality which makes even waiting for Godot tolerable. The ›Humptydumpty Dublin‹ of James Joyce, Brendan Behan, Oscar Wilde, George Bernard Shaw, Sean O'Casey, Samuel Beckett, William Butler Yeats and Jonathan Swift has also produced history-makers like the Duke of Wellington. But it is her men of letters whom she remembers with particular affection and who, with their wit, their irony, their poetry and their pessimism best sum up the ›endearing young charms‹ of the ›indomitable Irishry‹.

Founded: 841, by Danes; Dubh Linn – ›black pool‹; Baile Atha Cliath (Gaelic) – ›town of the ford of the hurdles‹.

Far-reaching events: 1014 – the Danes finally driven out by the local inhabitants; 1169 – the Anglo-Norman invasion puts Ireland under English rule; the Irish fight unsuccessfully for their freedom in a series of wars against Richard II (1394–99), Henry VII (1494), Oliver Cromwell (1649–50) and William III (1690); 18th century – Dublin's economic Golden Age; 1803 – birth of the Fenian movement under Robert Emmet and nationalism under Daniel O'Connel; 1846 – outbreak of the potato famine, 1.5 million Irishmen die of hunger; 1916 – the Easter Rebellion; continued bloodshed forces the English to grant Ireland its liberty (Home Rule); 1921 – partition – Ulster under British rule; Eire independent; 1939–45 – Ireland remains neutral in World War II; 1949 – the Republic of Ireland leaves the Commonwealth.

Population: 600,000, capital of the Republic of Ireland.

Postal code: IRL–Dublin **Telephone code:** 1

Climate: maritime; equable; bring at least two umbrellas!

Calendar of events: *St. Patrick's Week* (Mar) – celebrations in honour of Ireland's patron saint; *Opera Festival* (Apr); *Feis Ceoil* (May) – folklore festival; *Organ Festival* (Jun); *International Folklore Festival* Jul) – songs, music, dancing and handicrafts from all corners of the globe; *Dublin Horse Show* (Aug) – the country's main equestrian event; *Polo Games* (May–Sep) – at the All-Ireland Polo Club in Phoenix Park; *Antiques Fair* (Aug) – Old Ireland for sale; *Theatre Festival* (Sep); *Dublin City Marathon* (Oct) – endurance test; *International Opera Festival* (Dec).

Fairs and exhibitions: *HOLIDAY AND RECREATION FAIR* (Feb); *SPRING INDUSTRIAL FAIR* (May); *FOREX* (May) – foreign exchange dealers conference.

Historical sights: *Christ Church Cathedral* (1038) – Gothic grandeur; *Merrion Square* (18th century) – Georgian graciousness and the homes of Oscar Wilde and William Butler Yeats; *St. Patrick's Cathedral* (1191 – built by a power-hungry archbishop; *National Museum* – Irish antiques; *Trinity College Library* – illuminated manuscripts including the Book of Kells; *Phoenix Park* – the third largest park in the world.

Special attractions: the *pubs*; an evening with the boys at the *Horseshoe Bar*; the *Horse Show;* *castle-hopping* round the island; a musical performance at the *Hibernian Catch* or a dramatic one at the *Abbey Theatre; golf, fishing, sailing; horse* or *greyhound racing.*

Important companies with headquarters in the city: Bord Bainne (export marketing); Smurfit Group (printing); Cement Roadstone (construction); Aer Lingus (airline); Dunnes Stores (retailing); Guinness Ireland (beer); Purcell Exports (live cattle); CIE (transport).

Airport: Dublin Airport, DUB; Tel.: 37 99 00; 11 km/7 miles, Aer Lingus, Tel.: 77 49 06.

The Headquarters

SHELBOURNE

27 St. Stephen's Green
IRL Dublin
Telephone: 76 64 71
Telex: 93 653 slbn
Owning Company: Trusthouse Forte
General Manager: Alan Blest
Affiliation/Reservation Systems: Trusthouse Forte, SAS, Golden Tulip
Number of rooms: 172 (19 suites)
Price range: IR£ 80–300
Credit cards: AE, DC, Visa, Access, MC, CB, EC
Location: in the heart of the business, cultural and social life of the city
Built: 1824 (fully refurbished in 1986)
Style: aristocratic with aura of 18th-century charm
Hotel amenities: beauty salon, hairdresser, car park, doctor on call, car hire, wheelchair accessibility
Room amenities: colour tv, radio, minibar
Bathroom amenities: bidet, telephone, toiletries kit, hairdrier
Room service: 24 hours
Conference rooms: 14 (up to 600 persons), translating, audio-visual equipment
Bar: ›Horseshoe Bar‹ Dublin's most famous meeting place
Restaurant: ›The Aisling Restaurant‹ (12.30/p.m.–14.30/2.30 p.m. and 18.30/6.30 p.m.–22.30/10.30 p.m.) French/international with Irish flavour; ›The Causerie‹ (11.00/a.m.–23.00/11 p.m.)
Private dining rooms: 14 (up to 450 persons)

From some of the most picturesque village inns and country-town hotels of England to the venerable Ritz in Madrid and the fashionable Plaza-Athénée in Paris, the name Trusthouse Forte is the coat of arms of establishments of quality, standing and character. The Shelbourne in Dublin is one of the jewels in the company's crown in the Irish capital – ›magnificently conducted‹ according to William Thackeray, beloved of Victorian writer Elizabeth Bowen, and equally popular today amongst the disciples of James Joyce as well as amateur genealogists from the New World alike. The fine red-brick façade with its white stucco trim echoes nineteenth century civic pride as well as embellishing the periphery of lovely St. Stephen's Green; inside, this historic auberge has been completely renovated but happily retains its enchanting period quality. It may seem something of a paradox that in a city where the pubs are legion, the Shelbourne's Horseshoe Bar should be the favourite tryst of both Dublin's hommes de lettres and the local rugger club. In this city of contrasts and contradictions, however, such antitheses merely add to life's rich pattern and confirm the complexity of the Celtic spirit which permeates the Emerald Isle.

The Hideaway

ASHFORD CASTLE

IRL–Cong, Mayo County (240 km/160 miles)
Telephone: (94) 7 14 44
Telex: 53 749 ashc
Owning Company: Dowmar Securities
General Manager: Rory Murphy
Number of rooms: 82 (6 suites)
Price range: IR£ 60–200
Credit cards: AE, DC, Access, Visa
Location: in the town of Cong, 40 km/25 miles from Galway; 125 km/80 miles from Shannon Airport
Built: 19th century
Style: historic castle
Hotel amenities: shopping arcade
Room amenities: tv with satellite station/video
Room service: 24 hours
Laundry/dry cleaning: laundry – same day; dry cleaning – next day
Conference room: up to 140 persons
Sports: golf, tennis, shooting
Sports (nearby): fishing; lake trips on private cruiser
Bars: ›Cocktail Bar‹ (10.30/a.m.–12.00/a.m.); ›Dungeon Bar‹ (22.00/10 p.m.–after midnight); Irish music and sing-alongs with the resident musicians
Restaurants: ›Ashford Castle‹ (13.00/1 p.m.–14.15/2.15 p.m. and 19.00/7 p.m.–21.15/9.15 p.m.); ›Sun Lounge‹ (12.30/p.m.–17.00/5 p.m.) snack luncheon and afternoon tea; ›Gourmet Restaurant‹ (19.00/7. p.m.–22.30/10.30 p.m.)

Among the many castles, fortresses and manoirs, this is the most splendid for the spoiled mystery tourist – and therefore worth the scenic detour as the hideaway of Dublin, and of Eire altogether. The grey stone turrets of Ashford Castle give the impression of having dominated the inlets and islets of Lough Corrib since time immemorial. In fact, parts of this Celtic château do date back to medieval times; the craftsmen employed by Lord Ardiluan in the nineteenth century skilfully incorporated the ruins of the original building into the impressive façade which still bears the coat of arms of the original châtelains. Today, worldly wanderers come to seek recreation, refreshment and rejuvenation amidst the Mountains of Mayo. No-one is prepared to promise that you will see a ghost, although fertile imaginations could picture some long-dead ancestor haunting the antique-lined corridors or the baronial halls. Fortunately, however, the bedrooms are sufficiently light, bright and friendly to ensure the sweetest of dreams – particularly after a leisurely dinner following an idyllic afternoon golfing, shooting or fishing – or simply strolling through the woods amongst some of the most splendid scenery the country has to offer.

Lunch

LOCKS
1 Windsor Terrace, Portobello
Telephone: 75 20 25/53 83 52
Owner/Managers: Claire and Richard Douglas
Closed: Sunday; Saturday lunchtime; one week at Christmas
Open: 12.00/a.m.–14.00/2 p.m. and 19.15/7.15 p.m.–23.00/11 p.m.
Cuisine: French (cuisine moderne)
Chef de cuisine: Kevin McCarthy
Specialities: baked mussels au gratin; crisp strips of roast duck breast in sweet and sour sauce with mange-tout peas; chocolate pudding
Location: between Clanbrassil Street and Richmond Street, just north of Grove Road
Setting: overlooking the Grand Canal; pretty French provincial décor
Amenities: two private rooms
Atmosphere: charming, comfortable and quiet
Clientèle: mixture of businessmen at work and at leisure
Dress: no special requirements
Service: helpful
Reservations: advisable
Price range: moderately expensive
Credit cards: AE, DC, Visa, Access

Lunch

LE COQ HARDI
35 Pembroke Road
Telephone: 68 90 70/68 41 30
Owner/Manager: John Howard
Closed: Sunday; Saturday lunchtime; 2 weeks in August; 2 weeks at Christmas
Open: 12.00/a.m.–15.00/3 p.m. and 19.00/7 p.m.–23.00/11 p.m.
Cuisine: French creative, classic and bourgeoise
Chefs de cuisine: John Howard and James O'Sullivan
Specialities: fish mousse with lobster cream and cognac sauce; salmon sauce Nantua; ›Symphonie de la Mer‹; salade de homard ›Roger Vergé‹; ›Coq Hardi‹; veal cutlet with Calvados and Dauphin potatoes; foie de veau au vinaigre de cassis
Location: in the fashionable surburb of Ballsbridge; 2 km (1 mile) south-east of city centre
Setting: beautifully-restored Georgian house; high, ornate ceilings, antique furniture, original oil paintings, brass and mirrors; fine linen, silver and porcelain
Amenities: two suites for overnight guests; small lounge bar (restaurant patrons only) in basement; air conditioning
Atmosphere: harmonious in the classic idiom; aristocratic but welcoming
Clientèle: bishops, businessmen, politi-

cians and prelates; popular venue for wining and dining stars and celebrities or impressing visiting industrialists
Dress: soignée
Service: discreet and very personal; under the direction of Catherine Howard
Reservations: essential
Price range: rather expensive
Credit cards: AE, DC, Visa, Mastercard

Dinner

PATRICK GUILBAUD
46 James Place
Telephone: 60 17 99/76 41 92
Owner/Manager: Patrick Guilbaud
Closed: Sunday; Saturday lunchtime; Bank Holidays
Open: 12.30/p.m.–14.00/2 p.m. and 19.30/7.30 p.m.–22.15/10.15 p.m.
Cuisine: French (nouvelle)
Chef de cuisine: Guillaume Lebrun
Specialities: beetroot consommé; terrine de poissons aux pistaches; fillets of John Dory with chive sauce; steamed chicken with exotic fruits; mignon of lamb with parsley mousse and garlic sauce; magret de canard au pamplemousse rose; sabayon d'orange aux fraises
Location: behind the Bank of Ireland, off Baggot Street
Setting: chic; modern
Amenities: private parking
Atmosphere: sophisticated
Clientèle: gourmet habitués; celebrities tired of being celebrated; francophile Dubliners and Gallic visitors to the Emerald Isle
Dress: jacket and tie
Service: friendly and very French
Reservations: advisable (no pets)
Price range: inevitably expensive
Credit cards: all major

Dinner

CELTIC MEWS
109a Lower Baggot Street
Telephone: 76 07 96/68 23 27
Owner/Managers: The Grey Family
Closed: lunchtime; one week at Christmas
Open: 18.30/6.30 p.m.–23.45/11.45 p.m.
Cuisine: Irish and international
Chef de cuisine: William Woods
Specialities: seafood; lobster Thermidor; prawns meunière; Irish stew; roast pheasant; fillet steak in whiskey cream sauce; boeuf Stroganoff
Location: 1 km (5/8 mile) south-east of city centre
Setting: original mews house; old-world décor; beamed ceiling; open fire in lounge area; white table-linen
Amenities: private dining room (4–20 persons); air conditioning

Atmosphere: intimate; friendly, warm and very relaxed
Clientèle: visiting and resident personalities from the worlds of entertainment, sport and business – plus a fair number of diplomats
Dress: jacket and tie preferred
Service: welcoming; ably directed by Anthony Conlon
Reservations: advisable (no pets)
Price range: moderately expensive
Credit cards: AE, DC, Visa, Access, Master Card

Lunch

KING SITRIC
East Pier
Howth (15 km/9 miles)
Telephone: 32 52 35/32 67 29
Affiliations: Restaurant Association of Ireland
Owner/Managers: Aidan and Joan MacManus
Closed: Sunday; Saturday lunchtime; Bank Holidays; 10 days at Christmas; 10 days at Easter
Open: 12.30/p.m.–14.30/2.30 p.m. and 18.30/6.30 p.m.–23.00/11 p.m.
Cuisine: French/Irish
Chef de cuisine: Aidan MacManus
Specialities: fresh, locally-caught fish; avocado à la King; calmar frit; lobster thermidor; black sole à la meunière; sole soufflé; turbot Nantua; fresh crab with fennel; steaks; game in season; ice cream
Location: 15 km (9 miles) east of Dublin; on the quayside at Howth Harbour, near the marina
Setting: the Old Harbour Master's house, named after an 11th-century Norse king of Dublin; Georgian features of house emphasised by period furnishings and pictures; fine china, cutlery and table linen
Amenities: private dining room (16–18 persons); lounge with magnificent sea views overlooking Balscadden Bay; fires in winter
Atmosphere: elegantly relaxing
Clientèle: affluent northside Dubliners; ambassadors, men from the ministries – and industrialists seeking a respite from Dublin's fair city
Dress: informal but neat
Service: welcoming and professional
Reservations: advisable (no dogs)
Price range: moderately high
Credit cards: AE, DC, Visa, Access, JCB

Dinner

MIRABEAU
Marine Parade`
Sandycove (11 km/7 miles)
Telephone: 80 98 73
Owner/Managers: Eoin and Doreen Clarke

Closed: Sunday; Monday; second half of February
Open: 19.30/7.30 p.m.–22.00/10 p.m. (last orders); Friday open for lunch from 12.30/p.m. on; lunchtime: open for special parties by arrangement only
Cuisine: French (nouvelle)
Chef de cuisine: Michel Flamme (ex-Arbutus Lodge and Lovetts)
Specialities: fresh fish; game in season; fillet of turbot topped with a fish mousse, spiked with Meaux mustard in a saffron sauce
Location: 11 km (7 miles) south of Dublin, on the seafront at Dun Laoghaire
Setting: classic Victorian villa, completely refurbished under new management; false low ceilings removed, original cornices revealed; two linked dining rooms evocative of 1930s – light, warm colours, stained glass screens and lampshades; fireplace, trompe-l'oeil painting
Amenities: cocktail bar
Atmosphere: warm, intimate and friendly
Clientèle: fans of the ›Mirabeau‹ of Sean Kinsella's era; disciples of Michel Flamme's cuisine; curious culinary journalists; celebrities relying on Eoin and Doreen Clarke's discretion – and favourably-impressed local lovers of good food and fine wine
Dress: neatly informal to informally neat
Service: blend of Gallic and Irish charm
Reservations: essential (pets prohibited)
Price range: rather expensive
Credit cards: AE, DC, Visa, Access, Mastercard

Dinner

THE LORD EDWARD
23 Christchurch Place
Telephone: 75 25 57
Affiliations: Irish Restaurant Owners Association
Owner/Manager: Tom Cunniam
Closed: Sunday; public holidays; between Christmas and New Year
Open: 12.30/a.m.–14.30/2.30 p.m. and 18.00/6 p.m.–22.45/10.45 p.m.
Cuisine: classic French with an Irish brogue
Chef de cuisine: Liam Murray
Specialities: seafood (no meat dishes on menu); creamy fish chowder; oysters; sole bonne femme; sole ›Lord Edward‹; prawns provençale
Location: in the oldest part of the city; beside Dublin Castle, opposite Christchurch Cathedral
Setting: turn-of-the-century house built by the present owner's grandfather; small dining room on the second floor with Edwardian-style décor and portraits of generations of Irish rabble-rousers on the stairs
Amenities: pub (on ground floor); bar (on first floor) serving light lunches, with an open fire

Atmosphere: warm and homely; drawing-room
Clientèle: comfortable mixture of businessmen, local habitués with cause for celebration
Dress: neat attire
Service: courteous and Dublin-charming
Reservations: advisable
Price range: fairly expensive
Credit cards: all major

Meeting Point

HORSESHOE BAR
Shelbourne Hotel
27 St. Stephen's Green
Telephone: 76 64 71
Owner/Manager: Alan Blest
Closed: never
Open: 10.00/a.m.–15.00/3 p.m. and 16.00/4 p.m.–23.30/11.30 p.m.
Location: in the Shelbourne Hotel
Setting: large, comfortably furnished room dominated by the eponymous horseshoe-shaped bar counter
Amenities: hotel; two restaurants; car park
Atmosphere: Dublin in a nutshell – the city's most famous meeting place
Clientèle: local bankers, business travellers and personalities from the world of sport and horse racing, leavened by a liberal sprinkling of writers, poets and artists
Dress: what you will
Service: engagingly professional
Reservations: not necessary
Credit cards: all major

Bar

THE BAILEY
2–4 Duke Street
Telephone: 77 30 55/77 06 00
Owner/Manager: Brown & Thomas Ltd./ Brendan Green
Closed: Sunday; Bank Holidays; December 24th
Open: 12.30/a.m.–14.30/2.30 p.m. and 18.30/6.30 p.m.–23.00/11 p.m.
Location: on the famous Duke Street – Leopold and Molly Bloom lived here
Setting: a 19th-century eating house and bar – renowned for being mentioned in Joyce's Ulysses; leather booths; mirrors; paintings; hanging plants
Amenities: restaurant, light meals, sandwiches and salads
Atmosphere: Dublin's most historic tavern; stylish; convivial
Clientèle: writers, journalists and cosmopolitan intellectuals
Dress: whatever you like
Service: anxious-to-please
Reservations: advisable
Price range: medium high
Credit cards: all major

Bar

CASPER & GIUMBINI'S
6–8 Wicklow Street
Telephone: 77 51 22
Owner/Manager: Kevin and Murph O'Driscoll/Donald Ballance
Closed: June 6th; August 8th; December 25th/26th
Open: 12.00/a.m.–24.00/12 p.m.
Location: central
Setting: individualistic décor; comfortable and charming bar; separate dining area
Amenities: both pub and restaurant
Atmosphere: relaxed and informal
Clientèle: cosmopolitan Dubliners and those who would like to be considered as such
Dress: as you like it
Service: professional
Reservations: advisable
Credit cards: Access, DC, Visa

Nightclub

ANNABEL'S
Upper Lesson Street
Telephone: 60 52 22/68 88 38
Owner/Manager: P. V. Doyle Group/Adrian Doyle
Closed: Sunday; Monday; Christmas
Open: 22.00/10 p.m.–2.00/a.m.; Saturday 20.30/8.30 p.m.–1.00/a.m.
Location: in the Burlington Hotel
Setting: a large but luxurious night club
Amenities: bar; dancing; light meals
Atmosphere: intimate and elegant
Clientèle: the young, the not-so-young, the young-at-heart and those who wish they were
Dress: rather elegant
Service: efficient
Reservations: advisable
Price range: medium high
Credit cards: all major

Shopping

EVERYTHING UNDER ONE ROOF

Powercourt
Grafton Street

FOR HIM
Bron Thomas
Grafton Street

FOR HER
Bron Thomas
Grafton Street

JEWELLERY
Weir's
Grafton Street

The City

Rome, Milan, Naples, Florence and Venice are all household names – even amongst those who haven't been there. Trieste, Turin, Genoa, Verona and Bologna have an international renommé outside the Sahara desert. And who has not heard of Palermo, headquarters of a highly overrated, misinterpretated and romanticized club? But Bari, on the other hand, may mystify the international traveller because it has only recently become one of the rising business centres of the country. The Apulian capital, situated where the cavalier would affix his spurs on the boot of Italy, lies geometrically at the centre of the Monte-Carlo – Mykonos pleasure axis. From Naples it's just as quickly reached by motorway as Capri is by slow steamer. Latter-day adventurers with lots of time to spare may even wander from one civilization's cradle to the other by using Brindisi, next door to Bari down the Adriatic coast, as the jumping-off point. Virgil, in his time, had no other choice (unfortunately he never made it back home, dying in Brindisi after a trip to Greece). Nor did Phileas Fogg, Jules Verne's globe-trotting hero, who boarded the India Mail there on his eighty-day world trip. But for businessmen, it has to be Bari. The second most important city south of Rome, its commercial significance in times past lay primarily in its two harbours. Tankers have supplanted the sailing ships which carried the crusaders to the Holy Land in medieval times; gone, too, are the raiding fleets and armies of occupation of the Greeks, Byzantines, Saracens, Normans, Swabians, Spaniards, French, Venetians and Lombards who came, saw and conquered over the centuries. Traces of their cultures can be found if you look – in the Swabian castle, the Romanesque basilica with a Byzantine madonna image and Venetian-style frescoes, and in the Greek exhibits in the archaeological museum. The ethnic kaleidoscope has produced an outgoing, adventurous breed of citizens whose enterprise in stealing the relics of St. Nicholas from Myra, in Asia Minor, is commemorated by an annual pilgrimage flotilla of fishing boats and processions through the city. Traditions are preserved above all in the time-honoured crafts of the region – spinning, lace-making and embroidery – and in the net-making and mending of the local fishermen. And yet, the citizens know how to keep abreast of the times, adapting centuries-old manual skills to the marketing demands of the future – computers. Bari's microchip revolution is about to transform the city into an Italian version of California's Silicon Valley. Despite twentieth-century super-technology, however, Bari remains essentially unchanged. It's true that the demands of the expanding population have led to the construction of a chessboard pattern of concrete-box blocks of flats, but the old city centre huddled around the promontory separating the old harbour from the new is still a labyrinth of cool arched alleyways between tall whitewashed houses, a shady refuge from the heat of the noonday sun. The dolce-far-niente sleepiness gives way, as the sun sets, to a convivial Mediterranean cheerfulness in the cafés and bars on the Piazza Garibaldi, the Corso Vittorio Emanuele, or around the harbours. Musical son of the city Niccolò Piccinni left home for Paris and a claim to modest fame as Christoph Willibald Gluck's arch-rival. Nowadays his statue stands in front of the Prefecture in Bari, greeting the increasing numbers of visitors who come for the Levantine Fair and find themselves attracted to the city for its own sake.

Founded: 2nd century B.C.; Bari – from the Latin Barium.

Far-reaching events: 841 – Arab occupation; 875 – Byzantines invade and make Bari a stronghold in southern Italy; 1071 – Norman conquest under Robert Guiscard; 11th–13th centuries – one of the main departure points for the crusades; 15th century – the Sforza dynasty from Milan takes over in Bari; 1558 – annexed by Naples; 1923 – founding of the university.

Population: 370,000, capital of the region of Apulia.

Postal code: I-70100   **Telephone code:** 80

Climate: very warm in summer, especially in August; the winters are mild, the temperatures never below freezing.

Calendar of events: *Holy Week* – processions through the streets; *Festival of St. Nicholas* (7–8 May) – pilgrims arrive in a procession of fishing boats to honour the city's patron saint.

Fairs and exhibitions: *EXPO-SPORT LEVANTE* (Mar) – leisure, sports, tourism; *MOBILEVANTE* (Apr) – furniture fair; *FIERA DEL LEVANTE* (Sep) – international fair; *AGRILEVANTE* (Sep) – agricultural fair; *EDIL LEVANTE* (Sep) – building; *MODALEVANTE* (Sep) – fashion fair; *OROLEVANTE* (Oct) – jewellery gold, silverware, watches.

Historical sights: *Basilica San Nicola* (1087–1197) – Romanesque, dedicated to the patron saint of children and seafarers; *San Gregorio* – noble Romanesque church; *Pinacoteca* – art gallery with an excellent collection of Venetian masters; *Castello* (1233) – reconstructed by the Swabian Emperor, Friedrich II on the foundations of a Norman fortress; *Museo Archeologico* – Greco-Roman finds.

Modern sights: *Lungomare Nazario Sauro* – seafront promenade.

Special attractions: a *tour à la nature* south into the heel of Italy; the *harbour.*

Important companies with headquarters in the city: *Laterza* (publishing); *Pasta Granoro* (noodles – at Corato).

Airport: Bari-Palese (domestic), BRI; Tel.: 37 46 54, Alitalia, Tel.: 21 66 09, 9 km/6 miles.

The Headquarters

**PALACE HOTEL &
PALACE CONGRESSI**
13 Via Lombardi/Corso Vittorio
Emanuele
I-70122 Bari
Telephone: 21 65 51
Telex: 810 111 palace
Owning Company: S.A.I.G.A. SpA Turin
General Manager: Dr. Simone di Cagno
Abbrescia
Affiliation/Reservation Systems: Space
Hotels, Italhotels
Number of rooms: 203 (14 suites)
Price range: Lit. 103,000–295,000
Credit cards: AE, DC, Visa, EC
Location: city centre
Built: 1975 (renovated 1984)
Style: modern
Hotel amenities: garage, valet parking,
house limousine service, health club, so-
larium, massage, hairstylist, grand piano
in the hotel
Main hall porters: Antonio Verini, Mario
Andriano, Oronzo Sciavilla

Room amenities: air conditioning, colour
tv (remote control), mini-bar/refrigerator
(pets allowed)
Bathroom amenities: bidet, hairdrier, telephone, bathrobe
Room service: 7.00/a.m. to 24.00/12.00
p.m.
Laundry/dry cleaning: same day
Conference rooms: 18 (5 to 700 persons),
complete public address system, simultaneous translation via radio, tape recorder, overhead projectors, video recorder,
secretarial services, specialized technical
assistance, ballroom
Bar: ›Palace Bar‹ (10.00/a.m. to
24.00/12.00 p.m.) Domenico Di Ridolfo
(barman)
Restaurant: ›Palace Restaurant‹
(13.00/1.00 p.m.–15.00/3.00 p.m. and
20.00/8.00 p.m.–22.30/10.30 p.m.)
Mauro Pansini (chef de cuisine) regional
and international cuisine, pianist, ele-
gant-traditional style, open-air dining
Private dining rooms: four

*The rather stark modern building at the
junction of two of bustling Bari's principal
thoroughfares gives no hint of the sound-
proofed, high-technology, air-conditioned
comfort which awaits you within. In the understated,   uncluttered,   predominantly
modern reception rooms the valuable antique paintings are displayed to perfect advantage, no doubt, in marked contrast to
some of the incumbents of the marbled and
mirrored en-suite bathrooms. With an attractive ambiente to accompany your apéritif in the bar and soothing piano music to
go with your pesce in the restaurant, plus
friendly service from the foyer to the conference room, your business trip to Bari will
certainly be made a more pleasurable experience when staying here.*

Lunch

VECCHIA BARI
47 Via Dante Alighieri
Telephone: 21 64 96
Owner/Managers: Anna Lagrasta Pilone and Giuseppe Lagrasta
Closed: Saturday (except public holidays); 15 days in August (Ferragosto)
Open: 12.00/a.m.–15.00/3 p.m. and 19.00/7 p.m.–22.00/10 p.m.
Cuisine: local
Chef de cuisine: Anna Lagrasta Pilone
Specialities: traditional local hors d'œuvres (antipasto tradizionale barese con panzerottini e focaccia); noodles with broccoli (orechiette e cime di rape); local meat stew (terrina di carne alla barese); beef olives (brasciole al ragù barese); charcoal-grilled kebabs (spiedino misto di carne al carbone)
Location: near the Piazza Umberto I
Setting: the former oil storage depot in the centre of town; rustic décor; vaulted ceiling; attractively-laid tables; appetising array of desserts in main dining room
Amenities: parking facilities (with a bit of luck) on the Piazza Moro
Atmosphere: typical family-owned restaurant; welcoming and friendly
Clientèle: expense account industrialists during the week; the local Sunday afternoon crowd at weekends
Dress: Sunday casual to Sunday best
Service: friendly
Reservations: advisable (pets prohibited)
Price range: medium
Credit cards: AE, DC, Visa

Dinner

LA PANCA – DA NANUCCIO
8 Piazza Massari
Telephone: 21 60 96
Owner/Manager: Giuseppe Virgilio
Closed: Wednesday
Open: 9.00/a.m.–17.00/5 p.m. and 19.00/7 p.m.–24.00/12 p.m.
Cuisine: traditional and local
Chef de cuisine: Salvatore Novembrini
Specialities: insalata di mare; stuffed squid (seppiette ripiene); lasagne al forno; roast scampi; home-made Bari-style noodles (orecchiette alla barese); charcoal-grilled mixed kebabs (spiedino misto alla brace); typical local desserts (dolci vari regionali)
Location: near the old city (Città Vecchia) and the castle (Castello); opposite the Piccinni Theatre
Setting: two dining rooms; one a traditional restaurant furnished in elegantized rustic style; the other a typical pizzeria with a wood-burning stove
Atmosphere: intimate to cheerfully welcoming and relaxing

Clientèle: Bari businessmen and expense-account gourmets give way to hungry theatre-goers as the evening progresses
Dress: rather formal and conservative
Service: ceremonious (restaurant) or unfussy (pizzeria)
Reservations: advisable to essential
Price range: medium
Credit cards: AE, DC, Visa

Lunch

TABERNA MEDIOEVALE
6 Via Ospedale di Venere, Carbonara di Bari
Telephone: 35 05 57
Owner/Managers: Maria and Filippo Carella
Closed: Monday; July; August
Open: 12.30/p.m. – the last client has finished and 18.00/6 p.m. – ditto
Cuisine: local
Chef de cuisine: Pietro Abbaticchio
Specialities: the best lamb ›alla carbonara‹ in Bari province; goat (capriata); prosciutto alla barese; spaghetti al cartoccio; curd cheese dessert (la Svizzera)
Location: at Carbonara di Bari, 7 km (4 miles) south of Bari
Setting: in the vaults of a former ›trappeto‹ (cellar where the grapes were crushed); ceiling and fireplace of solid rock; white walls, red brickwork, wrought iron lamps; wooden benches and old upholstery
Amenities: car park (two minutes' walk)
Atmosphere: redolent of history; nostalgic; plenty of local colour
Clientèle: popular venue for entertaining visiting delegations, plus a fair sprinkling of tourists from Turin to Tampa
Dress: casually elegant during the week; more formally so on Saturdays
Service: accurate and courteous – even at busy times
Reservations: usually advisable (no dogs)
Price range: average
Credit cards: DC, Visa

Dinner

LA PIGNATA
9 Via Melo
Telephone: 23 24 81
Owner/Manager: Antonio and Franco Vincenti
Closed: Wednesday; August
Open: 12.00/a.m.–16.00/4 p.m. and 20.00/8 p.m.–1.00/a.m.
Cuisine: casalinga and local
Chef de cuisine: Antonio Vincenti
Specialities: octopus (polipo) alla Luciana; anchovy flan; tortiera alla barese; soufflé of curd cheese (ricotta); squid kebabs (spiedino di aglivi); roast lamb

with potatoes and Murgia mushrooms;
delicia Pignata
Location: near the old city (città vecchia)
and the old harbour (porto vecchio)
Setting: attractive classic-style décor –
modern and elegant
Amenities: air conditioning; car park (in
the vicinity)
Atmosphere: characteristic Apulian fam-
ily restaurant; warm-hearted and relaxing
Clientèle: gourmets from Paris, Rome
and Milan – and, of course, from Bari
Dress: within reason
Service: irreproachable; directed by
Franco Vincenti
Reservations: advisable (no pets)
Price range: medium
Credit cards: AE, DC, Euro, Visa

Bar

PALACE
13 Via Lombardi
Telephone: 21 65 51
Owner/Manager: S.A.I.G.A. Spa (Turin)
Dr. Simone di Cagno Abbreschia
Open: 10.00/a.m.–24.00/12 p.m.
Location: in the Palace Hotel
Setting: elegant and comfortable, with
antique accessoires
Amenities: hotel; restaurant with open-
air dining on roof-garden terrace; air con-
ditioning; car park
Atmosphere: cosmopolitan and very civi-
lized
Clientèle: the Who's Who of distin-
guished visitors of the town; from Lu-
ciano Pavarotti and Susannah York to
delegates to the Council of Europe and
international congresses
Service: impeccable
Reservations: advisable
Credit cards: AE, DC, Euro, Visa

Meeting Point

VILLARI 54
54 Via Villari
Telephone: 21 08 79
Owner/Manager:
Closed: lunchtime; Monday; August
Open: 20.30/8.30 p.m. till the last cus-
tomer leaves
Location: central
Setting: ground-floor bar with club-like
furnishings; dark upholstery, stone walls
and a buffet table displaying salads and
snacks for consumption with the 60 types
of beer available
Amenities: restaurant (first floor); open
two hours longer than the other bars
Atmosphere: restrained; vaguely Anglo-
Saxon
Clientèle: bankers; barristers; top indus-
trialists, managing directors; chief execu-
tives
Service: reliable
Reservations: advisable at the weekend

Shopping

FOR HIM
L'Uomo   25a Via de Rossi
FOR HER
Valentino Boutique   45a Via Putignani
BEAUTY & HAIR
Scarpa   inside the building of famous
Petruzelli theatre
JEWELLERY
Alfredo Trizio   81 Via Sparano

LOCAL SPECIALITIES
Luciana Boutique (women's fashion)
27 Via Dante
Jet (men's fashion)
Via Abate Gimma
Rione Baby (children's fashion)
Via Dante
Alaska (furs) Via Putignani
Laterza (books) 137 Via Sparano
›**Il Pozzetto**‹ (gifts) 29 Via Cairoli
Ambrosini (baggage & travel accessories)
Corso Vittorio Emanuele II
Gucci (baggage & travel accessories)
105 Via Sparano
Misura (interior decorating)
7 Via Abate Gimma
De Carne (food and beverages)
Corso Vittorio Emanuele II
Coratella Cavaliere Alfredo (food and
beverages)
217 Via Fenelli
Pepe – Cose belle (perfumery)
105 Via Sparano
Star (decorating materials)
146 Via Sparano
›**Foyer**‹ **libri d'Arte** (antique books)
8 Viale Giovanni XXIII
Pintucci (shoes) Via Dante
Rossetti (shoes) Via Sparano
Stoppani (sweets)
Via Roberto da Bari

THE BEST OF ART
Bonomo   (contemporary art)
19 Via Nicolò dell'Arca
Tel. 21 01 45 / 48 13 53

Every time you switch on the radio, you unconsciously pay tribute to Bologna's favourite son. Scientist-genius and Nobel Prize winner Guglielmo Marconi's first transatlantic wireless link was admittedly set up in Land's End, England, but he is still remembered in his home town with a mixture of pride, affection and a museal mausoleum. Thanks to its university (the oldest in Europe), ›Bologna the Learned‹ can claim associations with a long line of distinguished scientists and scholars, from Nicholas Copernicus and Luigi Galvani to Dante Alighieri, Francesco Petrarca and Torquato Tasso. Lying on the Via Emilia where the fertile plain of the River Po meets the Appenine chain, this former papal dominion and cradle of pontiffs enjoys a reputation as a city of learning which is only rivalled by its culinary renown. ›Bologna the Fat‹, having given the world mortadella sausage and bolognese sauce, proceeds to show visitors that you still can't beat home cooking. Food products figure prominently amongst the city's industries, dwarfing the shoes, steel and electrical equipment. An important arena for international conventions and conferences, ›Bologna the Turreted‹ has preserved her medieval heritage in the mellow brick buildings around the Piazza Maggiore and the Piazza del Nettuno. Dominated by the vast, unfinished Basilica of St. Petronius, the skyline is pierced by numerous steeples and campaniles, from the leaning Asinelli and Garisenda towers to the belfry of St. Stephen's church. The vaulted arcades of the city centre are rendezvous, lovers' trysts and vantage points for people-watching against a colourful backdrop of cheerfully chaotic traffic and Latin exuberance tempered with Northern Italian efficiency. Bologna's appeal is inseparable from that of her citizens; ›it is a pleasant thing being with them, a delightful thing coming among them, and a very pleasant thing living where they are living‹.

Founded: approx. 3,000 B.C. by the Ligurians; Bologna – from the Roman colony Bononia (Latin).

Far-reaching events: 189 B.C. – following the Etruscans and the Celts, the Romans colonize the settlement; 5th century A.D. – barbarian invasions; 6th century – Byzantine rule spreads from Ravenna to Bologna – the city comes under papal jurisdiction; 771 – Bologna part of Lombardy; 1088 – home of Europe's first university and a free city; 1167 – membership of the Lombardy Confederation; 1256 – Bologna guarantees its inhabitants civil rights; 13th–15th century – the Pepoli and Visconti families involved in the Ghibelline dispute, but the city flourishes; 1506–1860 – following victory by the Guelphs, the popes control Bologna which is second only to Rome as a centre of Church power; 1796 – conquered by Napoleon; 1815 – returned to jurisdiction of the Church; 1860 – Bologna joins the Piedmont region of the newly unified Italy; 1939–45 – heavily damaged during World War II; 1970 – seat of the Emilia-Romagna regional government.

Population: 450,000.

Postal code: I–40100   **Telephone code:** 51

Climate: hot and humid summers; relatively cool winters with occasional heavy fog.

Calendar of events: *International Film Festival* (summer); *Independence Day* (25 Aug) – celebrations; *Opera Season* (Nov–May).

Fairs and exhibitions: *PACKAGING* (Feb) – packaging machinery and materials exhibition; *SAEIDUE* (Mar) – international salon for construction renovation equipment; *INTERNATIONAL CHILDREN'S BOOK FAIR* (Mar); *SHOE FAIR* (Mar); *ARTE FIERA* – international trade market for contemporary art; *COSMOPROF* (Apr) – international perfumes and cosmetics show; *INTERNATIONAL SAMPLES FAIR* (Jun); *SIA* (Jun) international food convention; *MICAM* (Sep) – international shoe fair; *TECHNO TM 4* (Sep) – quadrennial exhibition of technologies and machinery for the textile, knitting and clothing industries; *CERSAIE* (Oct) – international exhibition for building industrialization; *SAIE SITEL* (Oct) – Italian exhibition of technology and organization for local concerns and public services; *EIMA* (Nov) – international agricultural machinery manufacturers fair; *FASHION SHOW* (Nov); *EXPO HI-FI* (Dec) – hi-fi equipment; *INTERNATIONAL MOTORING EXHIBITION* (Dec).

Historical sights: *Basilica of St. Petronius* (14th century) – fifth largest church in the world, fine sculptures and reliefs; *Torri Pendenti* (12th century) – two leaning towers built by rival families; *Basilica of St. Stephen* (11th century) – picturesque group of church buildings; *Piazza del Nettuno* with *Neptune Fountain* (16th century); *Piazza Maggiore* – with the *Palazzo Communale* (13th century); *City Hall* (now home of the *Municipal Art Gallery)* and the *Palazzo del Podestà* (13th century) – with arcades and Corinthian columns; *Palazzo Bevilacqua* (15th century) – prettiest palace in town, pure Florentine Renaissance; *Sanctuary of the Madonna of St. Luke* (18th century) – with the Byzantine image of the black madonna (5 km/3 miles).

Special attractions: lunch at *San Domenico* (Imola) and dinner at *Pappagallo*; a rejuvenating stay at *Montecatini Terme*.

Important companies with headquarters in the city: *Arcotronics Italia* (electrics and electronics); *Bertagni Industria Alimentari* (noodles); *Fochi, Filippo* (heavy metal construction); *G.D.* (packaging machines); *Gio. Buton* (wines and liqueurs); *Panigal* (food and cosmetics); *Sasib* (machinery).

Airport: Bologna-Borgo Panigale, BLQ; Tel.: 31 15 78, Alitalia, Tel.: 55 85 85; 7 km/4 miles.

The Headquarters

ROYAL HOTEL CARLTON

8 Via Montebello
I–40121 Bologna
Telephone: 55 41 41/55 41 43
Telex: 510356 royala
Owning Company: E.G.A. Emiliana Grandi Alberghi S.p.A.
General Manager: Orazio Biglietti
Affiliation/Reservation Systems: SRS (Steigenberger Reservation Service), Utell
Number of rooms: 250 (22 suites)
Price range: Lit. 180,000 (single)
                Lit. 240,000 (double)
                Lit. 400,000 (suite)
Credit cards: AE, DC, EC, Visa
Location: city centre
Built: 1973
Style: modern
Hotel amenities: garage, valet parking, house limousine service, car rental desk
Room amenities: air conditioning, colour tv, mini-bar, balcony
Bathroom amenities: bathrobe, telephone
Room service: 6.30/a.m. to 22.30/10.30 p.m.
Conference rooms: 11, up to 600 persons
Bars: ›American Bar‹ (8.30/a.m.–1.00/a.m.)
Restaurant: ›Royal Grill‹ (12.00/a.m.–14.30/2.30 p.m. and 19.30/7.30 p.m.–22.30/10.30 p.m.) Italian and international cuisine

The architects responsible for the design of the Royal Carlton must have deliberately chosen mellow ochre tones so that its clean-cut countenance would blend harmoniously with the time-worn stones of the medieval buildings which characterize the capital of Emilia Romagna. The intérieur is unobtrusive enough to appeal to both visiting professors to Europe's oldest university (and still one of the most esteemed), and to the industrial élite passing through for more materialistic intellectual business, such as the famous Children's International Book Fair. From the curving staircase in this conference centre to the comfortable leather armchairs in the lobby, from the well-designed bedrooms to the glittering ballroom for functions for up to 600 persons, the hotel exhibits that timeless flair which has brought Italian designers fame, even for buildings as functional as this. Don't worry if your business engagements leave you with no time to sample the culinary delights the city has to offer; the hotel's Royal Grill lives up to alta cucina expectations.

The Hideaway

GRAND HOTEL E LA PACE

1 Via della Toretta
I–51016 Montecatini Terme
(110 km/70 miles)
Telephone: (572) 75801
Telex: 570005 paceot
Owner/Managing Director: Ricciardo Pucci
General Manager: Gino Degli Innocenti
Affiliation/Reservation System: The Leading Hotels of the World
Closed: November to March
Number of rooms: 150 (20 suites)
Price range: Lit. 170,000–350,000
Credit cards: AE, DC, EC
Location: between Pisa and Florence
Built: 1870
Hotel amenities: valet parking, air conditioning, swimming pool, sauna, beauty parlour, tennis court
Room amenities: colour tv (pets allowed)
Conference rooms: for up to 220 persons
Cures: diets, physiotherapy, mudbaths, manual and underwater massages, lifting, ozonised baths, gymnastics, cosmetic algae treatments, aesthetics treatments
Bars: two
Restaurants: three, open-air dining

You will find both in abundance: grandeur and peace. Florence is closest, but after business in Bologna, La Pace is the only solution. (Why not do business here?) Away from it all – culture caravans and humid smog adieu – this is the Arcadian resort to retreat to. In the very centre of Tuscany's most famous spa city, yet walled in against any average disturbance, the palatial hotel leads a life of its own, with gardens, pool and tennis to distract a little from the imposing dignity of the high-ceilinged halls, the Old-Master-hung couloirs, the antique-filled salons and lounges radiating tranquillity and protection from the plebeian pleasures of the outside world. Many a guest may sneak out to the casino for a fortune or a glamourous show at the Kursaal, some may go to the races at night, but most habitués just indulge in the grandiose beauty of their luxurious ashram and the dolce vita culinaria renowned for its seasonal specialities, international dishes and – praised by bon-vivants on a diet as well as gourmets on leave – for the health restaurant. The Natural Health Spa of La Pace is another prominent reason why myriads of managers and mesdames à la Begum and Rose Kennedy make the pilgrimage to Montecatini Terme. Various massages and baths, cosmetic treatments and beautifying procedures, medical therapies or sheer relaxation as a remedy for the sins of the good life belong to the gentle programme of this heavenly hideaway. D'Annunzio and the Duke of Windsor were already satisfied clients and everyone else seemed to be magnetized by La Pace, too. Ever since 1870. Unfortunately, Ricciardo Pucci, the owner, and his director, Gino degli Innocenti, lock this Belle Epoque asylum during the winter.

Lunch

BACCO – VILLA ORSI
Al Centergross
Telephone: 86 24 51
Owner/Manager: Gianni Sarti
Closed: Saturday; Sunday; August
Open: 12.00/a.m.–16.00/4 p.m.
Cuisine: classic and modern ›au goût du marché‹
Chef de cuisine: Alberto Reecato
Specialities: gratin of vineyard snails; kebab with mortadella and cheese; prawns in white wine; lasagne al forno; lasagne with casserole of duck; tortellini with herbs; veal goulash with mushrooms; cutlet alla bolognese
Location: in Centergross
Setting: 18th-century villa in park with ancient trees; elegant dining room in the classic idiom
Amenities: car park
Atmosphere: restrained; dignified; serenely harmonious
Clientèle: fans of Gianni Sarti's skills as sommelier and restaurateur from his previous restaurant at Borgo Panigale
Dress: soignée
Service: knowledgeable; ably assisted by Giovanni Tabacchi
Reservations: advisable
Price range: medium
Credit cards: AE, DC, Visa

Lunch

ANTICA TRATTORIA DEL CACCIATORE
25 Via Caduti
Casteldebole (6 km/4 miles)
Telephone: 56 42 03
Owner/Managers: Domenico, Eugenio and Stefano Ferrari
Closed: Monday; ten days in August
Open: 12.00/a.m.–15.00/3 p.m. and 19.00/7 p.m.–23.00/11 p.m.
Cuisine: local and international
Chef de cuisine: Albano Valentino
Specialities: according to season; warm hors d'œuvres (antipasti caldi); risotto with strawberries (fragole); lasagne with game stew (pappardelle alla caccia); truffle flan (tortino al tartufo); wild duck with fruits; breast of pheasant in Barolo wine
Location: at Casteldebole, 6 km (4 miles) west of Bologna
Setting: singularly attractive elegantized rustic; quarry tiles, wood panelling and luxuriant pot plants
Amenities: outdoor dining on covered veranda; large garden; bar; air conditioning; car park
Atmosphere: warm and welcoming
Clientèle: businessmen and journalists during the week give way to Bologna's

Sunday-afternoon crowd en famille at weekends
Service: molto simpatico – expertly stage-managed by the Ferrari brothers
Reservations: advisable (no dogs)
Price range: medium
Credit cards: AE, DC, Euro, Visa

Dinner

DANTE
2 Via Belvedere
Telephone: 22 44 64/23 95 10
Affiliations: Association of Italian Sommeliers; Association of Italian Maîtres d'Hôtel
Owner/Manager: Dante Casari
Closed: Monday and Tuesday lunchtime; August; December 23rd–January 10th
Open: 12.30/p.m.–14.30/2.30 p.m. and 19.30/7.30 p.m.–22.30/10.30 p.m.
Cuisine: nuova cucina italiana
Chefs de cuisine: Michael Paulaski and Domenico Cirigliano
Specialities: according to season; fish; risotto ›1001 Nights‹; fillet of veal in balsam vinegar with fresh shallot; escalope of goose liver in Marsala; rabbit stew with prunes; fresh salmon with peas; fillet of turbot with paprika cream; terrine of rabbit
Location: central
Setting: emphatically elegant; comfortable in the classic idiom; décor harmonious down to the last detail – nothing superfluous, nothing out of place
Amenities: air conditioning; car park
Atmosphere: refined; intimate
Clientèle: visiting gourmets; local industrialists and stars of the international film scene – Marcello Mastroianni to Franco Fellini
Dress: as emphatically elegant as the décor
Service: under the expert eye of Dante Casari
Reservations: essential (only 40 places); (no dogs)
Price range: fairly expensive
Credit cards: AE, DC, Visa

Lunch

SAN DOMENICO
1 Via Gaspare Sacchi
Imola (33 km/21 miles)
Telephone: (5 42) 2 90 00
Affiliations: Traditions et Qualité; Relais et Châteaux (Relais Gourmand)
Owner/Manager: Gianluigi Morini
Closed: Monday
Open: 12.30/p.m.–14.30/2.30 p.m. and 20.00/8 p.m.–22.30/10.30 p.m.
Cuisine: traditional and creative
Chef de cuisine: Valentino Marcattillii (ex-pupil of Nino Bergese, cook to the last king of Italy)

Specialities: terrine of calves' liver with white truffles from Piedmont; fried tagliolini with spinach and freshwater crayfish; lobster with artichokes; breast of duck in red wine; escalope of salmon with hazelnut cream; guinea-fowl in port; saddle of veal ›Nino Bergese‹; cassata with dried woodland fruits in raspberry sauce; bitter chocolate fondant in vanilla sauce
Location: at Imola, 33 km (21 miles) south-east of Bologna
Setting: on the site of the former Dominican convent (1501); small dining room in reds and pinks; black leather upholstery; ceiling with floral wallpaper and toning modern pictures; fine china, silver and glass
Amenities: air conditioning; opposite a beautiful public garden
Atmosphere: intimate; elegant; a haven of peace, tranquillity and impeccable good taste created by former banker and gastronome par excellence, Gianluigi Morini
Clientèle: businessmen tired of Bologna; aesthetes and connoisseurs of the art of good living from New York to New South Wales
Dress: according to season and circumstance
Service: to perfection; personal welcome by Gianluigi Morini, assisted by maître d'hôtel Natale Marcattillii; waitresses in black dresses with white aprons; waiters in livery
Reservations: essential (no dogs)
Price range: justifiably expensive
Credit cards: AE, DC, Visa

Dinner

PAPPAGALLO
30 Piazza della Mercanzia
Telephone: 23 28 07
Affiliations: Consorzio Ristoratori Bolognesi
Owner/Manager: Gianluigi Morini (from the Restaurant San Domenico in Imola)
Closed: Monday
Open: 12.30/p.m.–14.30/2.30 p.m. and 20.00/8 p.m.–22.30/10.20 p.m.
Cuisine: international and creative
Chef de cuisine: Roberto Mongardi
Specialities: ham in balsam vinegar with lambs' lettuce; médaillons of turkey; home-made pasta; pancakes (crespelle); shrimps and pink chicken livers with spring salad; tagliatelle with mushrooms and basil; stuffed chicken legs braised in white wine
Location: a psalm away from the cathedral
Setting: superb Art Déco dining room; fine china, glass and silver; lobster-pink table linen, fresh flowers, luxuriant plants and mirrors
Amenities: air conditioning

Atmosphere: welcoming, intimate and elegant
Clientèle: erstwhile haunt of Toscanini, Einstein, Hitchcock and King Gustav of Sweden; more recently, discriminating managing directors, doctors and dons from home and abroad
Dress: designer jeans to dark suit
Service: professionally directed by Franco Lazzari
Reservations: advisable
Price range: on the expensive side
Credit cards: AE, DC, Visa

Dinner

NOTAI
1 Via de Pignattari
Telephone: 22 86 94/26 58 72
Owner/Manager: Nino Castorina
Closed: Sunday; second half of August
Open: 12.00/a.m.–15.00/3 p.m. and 20.00/8 p.m.–24.00/12 p.m.
Cuisine: Italian (creative) and international
Chef de cuisine: Giuseppe Garofolo (exchez Gualtiero Marchesi)
Specialities: according to season; tagliatelle perfumed with cedarwood; tortellini with curd cheese (ricotta) and mushrooms; escalope of veal with ham and mozzarella; calves' liver with fresh grapes
Location: in the pedestrian precinct; on the corner of the Piazza Maggiore; near the Basilica San Petronio
Setting: turn-of-the-century elegance; Liberty-patterned wallpaper; toning prints; Tiffany lampshades and subdued lighting
Amenities: American piano bar and singing pianist on first floor; outdoor dining on terrace
Atmosphere: confidential or romantic – depending on your companion
Clientèle: artists, artistes, bishops and local celebrities; mayors and museum directors, professors and town planners
Dress: fairly conservative
Service: attractive, feminine and attired in black
Reservations: advisable to obligatory
Price range: moderately expensive
Credit cards: AE, DC, Euro, Visa

Meeting Point

SAMPIERI
3 Via Sampieri
Telephone: 22 26 50
Closed: Monday
Open: at night
Setting: splendid antique interior décor; sculptures; paintings
Amenities: piano-bar, restaurant, pizzeria, bar, nightclub

Atmosphere: convivial, lively and very stylish
Clientèle: Gerry Mulligan and Ray Charles (playing the sax or piano) and their followers from Italy and the rest of the world; Bologna's In-Crowd
Dress: anything goes
Service: excellent
Reservations: only if you want the 14th-century private dining room with only one table in it reserved for you and your companion
Price range: medium high

Bar

AMERICAN BAR
36 Via Aurelio Saffi
Telephone: 43 74 17
Owner/Manager: Demo S.R.L./Pierantonio Zarotti
Closed: never
Open: 7.00/a.m.–2.00/a.m.
Location: in the Grand Hotel Elite
Setting: rather business-like modern hotel bar; wood panelling, parquet floor, dark brown leather upholstery and a pianist or soft music to fill in any awkward gaps in the conversation
Amenities: hotel; restaurant; private dining rooms (120 persons); air conditioning; valet parking service
Atmosphere: soothing but not soporific
Clientèle: mostly conservative, comfortably-off, middle-aged and self-assured
Service: capably supervised by Nicola Sassano and Enrico Baldini
Reservations: advisable
Credit cards: AE, DC, Euro, Bank Americard, Comites

Shopping

EVERYTHING UNDER ONE ROOF
Croff   Via Ugo Bassi

FOR HIM
Tozzi   38/7 Via San Felice

FOR HER
Papillon   7 Galleria Cavour

BEAUTY & HAIR
Adriana Gherardini ›Lifestyles‹
1 Piazza Bonazzi

JEWELLERY
Veronesi   4 A Piazza Maggiore

LOCAL SPECIALITIES
Polvere di Stelle (women's fashion)
3 Via Indipendenza
Ritz Saddler (men & women's fashion)
4 Via Farini
›Alla cicogna‹ (children's fashion)
49 E Via Murri
Sarti (furs)
1/3 Galleria del Leone
Parolini (books)
14 Via Ugo Bassi
Cervellati Mario (gifts)
29 Via Santo Stefano
Rossi (baggage & travel accessories)
8 Via Indipendenza and 9 Via Rizzoli
Fabbri (interior decorating)
15 Via Chisiliera
Gazziero Giampaolo (interior decorating)
98 Via Lame
Tamburini (food and beverages)
3 Piazza Maggiore
Tamburini (food and beverages)
1 Via Capraia
Murri (perfumery)
49 Via Murri
Zucchelli (jewellery, silver, antiques)
2 A Galleria Cavour
Magli (shoes)
33 Via Larga and 2 Piazza Mercanzia
For you by Saddler (shoes)
22 Via Murri
Majani (café + sweets)
6 Via Carbonesi

THE BEST OF ART
Fabjbasaglia   (contemporary art)
26 C via Farini, Tel. 23 49 22
G7/Ginevra Grigolo   (contemporary art)
7G via Val d'Aposa,
Tel. 26 64 97
Pellegrino,   Fernando   (contemporary art) 8 Via Belle Arti,
Tel. 22 70 54
Studio Cavalieri   (contemporary art)
18 via Guerrazzi, Tel. 26 12 19

The City

Florence the Divine is a museum, albeit a living one. The first thing you wonder is whether you have stepped out of a magic time machine: this, one of the world's most beautiful cities, has been celebrated across the centuries by local bard Dante and countless visiting literati – Shelley, Dickens, Lamartine, Anatole France. It is the most masculine of Italian cities, the most enchanting, stunning, chaotic and wild. Perhaps a bit too beautiful to be true or too true to be really beautiful. During the Renaissance no city on earth came close to rivalling the brilliance of Florence's creative genius, encapsulated in the works of the artists who lived and worked here (Cimabue, Giotto, Masaccio, Fra Angelico, Fra Filippo Lippi, Botticelli and Raphael), the sculptors (Ghiberti, Donatello, della Robbia, Verrocchio and Cellini), the architects (Brunelleschi, Buontalenti, Guardi and Ghirlandaio), composers (Cherubini, Lully), scientists (Galileo), politicians (Machiavelli), explorers (Vespucci) – and consummated in the work of the giants of the Golden Age, Leonardo da Vinci and Michelangelo Buonarroti. The very stones of the town on the Arno breathe its two-thousand-year history – the marbled geometricity of the Duomo, the Ponte Vecchio where Dante silently worshipped his Beatrice, and the serenely proportioned palazzi of the princely merchant dynasties under whose aegis the city flourished – the Medici, Pitti, Rucellai, Strozzi, Pazzi and Bardi-Peruzzi. But Florence is not simply a city for art lovers. Business plays a prominent role here too – wool and glass, cars and chemicals, crafts and Alta Moda. Some people come to Florence just to shop at Gucci, Pucci, Ferragamo, Carrano, Ginori, Gherardi, Turrini and Piccini. Others come for the food – the costata alla fiorentina or the truffles. Or the wine – the Chianti or the grands crus from the vineyards of the Antinori family. Then there are the parks – the magnificent Boboli Gardens, the bustling Straw Market, the medieval festivals and the Piazza della Signoria, the city's busy heart. The hills of Tuscany are on the doorstep – fabled Fiesole, where Boccaccio wrote his ›Decameron‹, with its most beautiful enclave, the Villa San Michele; medieval San Gimignano, Lucca, Pisa and Siena (The Beloved) – a gentle landscape of vineyards, olive groves and oleanders, of villas and villages, intact and unspoilt; a land where time has all but stood still for centuries. Florentines are taciturn, wary of the myriads of tourists but treating them with amused and amicable reserve. After all, the ›lily of Florence, blossoming in stone‹, is a peerless city, possessing the fatal gift of beauty – where angels fear to tread.

Founded: 200 B.C. by the Romans; Firenze (Italian) – ›the flourishing‹

Far-reaching events: 50 B.C. – Roman colony; 3rd–10th century – Florence passes through the hands of the Goths, the Byzantines and the Lombards; 11th–12th century – increasing wealth as the trades guilds flourish; 13th century – the city a centre of Guelph and Ghibelline strife – Florence a silk trading centre; 1348 – population decimated by the Black Death; 15th–18th century – power and wealth under the Medici family; 16th century – many of the city's Renaissance buildings are constructed; 1737–1860 – Florence ruled by the House of Lorraine apart from 1799–1814 – French occupation; 1860 – Florence becomes part of the United Kingdom of Italy (and capital from 1865–71); 1944 – severe bomb damage; 1966 – severe flooding; 1970 – Florence awarded the fourth gold medal ›for civil valour‹.

Population: 500,000. **Postal code:** I–50100 **Telephone code:** 55

Climate: the winters are mild, the summers hot and humid.

Calendar of events: *Festival of the Chariot* (Easter Sunday) – a wagon laden with fireworks goes up in smoke; *Iris Show* (May) – largest European collection of the symbolic ›lily of Florence‹ on the Piazzale Michelangiolo; *Musical May* (mid-May to Jun) – opera, ballet and concerts; *Historic Football Match* (24 Jun) – football in historic costumes in honour of the city's patron saint, San Giovanni; *Grasshoppers' Festival* (15 Aug) – grasshoppers, symbols of luck, displayed in the Cascine Park in various cages; *Festa delle Rificolone* (7 Sep) – parades with lanterns; *Birds' Fair* (last Sunday in Sep) – birds' market; *Documentary Film* Festival (Dec).

Fairs and exhibitions: *ALTA MODA* (Mar & Sep) – fashion; *INTERNATIONAL ARTS AND CRAFTS FAIR* (May); *CAMPIONARIA DI FIRENZE* (May/Jun; Oct/Nov) –leather goods exhibition; *MOSTRA MERCATO INTERNAZIONALE DELL'ANTIQUARIATO* (Sep/Oct, biennial) – seventh heaven for antique lovers; *PRESELEZIONE ITALIANA MODA* (Nov) – leather and shoe fashions made in Italy.

Historical sights: every palazzo, every house, every stone.

Special attractions: be a *tourist* for once; exploration of the *hinterland* – Siena, Lucca et al.; a *shopping spree* à la banquerotte; a tastevin tour at the *Antinoris* (with the Antinoris); many quiet days and romantic nights at *Villa San Michele*.

Important companies with headquarters in the city: *Antinori* (wine); *Calzaturificio Rangoni* (shoes); *Emerson Electronics* (optical instruments); *Ginori, Richard* (porcelain); *Gucci* (leather fashion); *Industria Filati Calenzo* (yarns); *Magona d'Italia* (sheet metals); *Manetti, Gabbriello* (bags); Nuove Pignone (machinery); *Officine Galileo* (optical instruments); *O.T.E. Biomedica* (medical instruments); *Pontello* (construction); *Pucci* (fashion); *Roller* (caravans); *Superpila Industriale* (batteries); *Targetti Sankey* (lighting systems).

Airport: Pisa-Galileo Galilei, PSA; Tel.: 26106, 95 km/62 miles; Alitalia, Tel.: 263051–3.

The Headquarters

EXCELSIOR

3 Piazza Ognissanti
I–50123 Florence
Telephone: 26 42 01
Telex: 570 022 excefi
Owning Company: Cigahotels
General Manager: Massimo Rosati
Affiliation/Reservation System: Hello-ciga
Number of rooms: 189 (19 suites)
Price range: Lit. 180,000–1,100,000
Credit cards: AC, DC, MC, JCB, CB, Visa
Location: city centre
Style: Florentine/Empire style
Hotel amenities: garage, valet parking, house limousine service, hairstylist, newsstand (pets allowed)
Room amenities: colour tv
Bathroom amenities: separate shower cabinet, bidet, bathrobe, hairdrier, phone
Room service: 24 hours
Conference rooms: 4 (up to 200 persons)
Bar: ›Donatello‹ (11.00/a.m.–1.00/a.m.), pianist
Restaurant: ›Il Cestello‹ (12.00/p.m.–15.00/3 p.m. and 19.00/7 p.m.–22.30/10.30 p.m.), Fausto Monti (chef de cuisine), international and local cuisine

Erstwhile residence of Napoleon's sister, Carolina Bonaparte, the favourite Florentine address for more than a century for transatlantic luminaries since its conversion into a hotel is the Tuscan jewel in the Ciga clan diadem. It stands on the banks of the Arno a few Gucci steps from the Municipal Theatre and the fashionable shops, on one of the city's most historic squares. Here, in the thirteenth century, a monastic order laid down the foundations of the city's wealth with their weaving, succeeded by the great merchant families who built the Renaissance palazzi which adorn the area. The Excelsior is the pre-eminent headquarters for business encounters of every magnitude, offering every reliable and professional service, modern facilities and a congenial ambience. The imposing décor sets the tone; marble-floored and pillared reception hall under a carved and painted ceiling, salons with local thirteenth-century baronial motifs and stained glass, aristocratic bedrooms and accessoires fit for a prince – Persian carpets, ornate chandeliers and Old Masters. The Donatello bar is the favourite meeting point in town for the fashion crowd during the Pitti fairs, and a fashionable crowd at any time of year. Even the Cestello roof-garden terrace, with international and regional specialities, is eclipsed in summer by the breath-taking view of the Ponte Vecchio and the rolling hills of Fiesole. Here, dining to the haunting sounds of the piano is as evocative of nostalgic splendour for Old World descendants of local sons Jacopo Bellini, Sandro Botticelli, Dante Alighieri and all the Medicis as for the New World visitors who come to Florence for the Uffizi, the leather goods or to meet their Beatrice.

The Hideaway

VILLA SAN MICHELE

4 Via Doccia
I–50014 Fiesole (5 km/3 miles)
Telephone: 5 94 51–52
Telex: 570 643 sanmic
Owning Company: Cipriani S.P.A
General Manager: Maurizio Saccani
Affiliation/Reservation Systems: The Leading Hotels of the World, Relais et Châteaux
Closed: November–February
Number of rooms: 28 (2 suites)
Price range: Lit. 375,000–1,280,000
Credit cards: AE, DC, EC, MC
Location: Fiesole–Florence, 100 km/65 miles from Pisa airport
Built: early 1400 (renovated 1952–1983)
Style: Florentine tradition, elegant
Hotel amenities: house limousine service, solarium, hairstylist, heated open-air swimming pool
Room amenities: colour tv, minibar, radio (small pets allowed)
Bathroom amenities: shower cabin, bidet, bathrobe, hairdrier, telephone, jacuzzi
Room service: 7.00/a.m.–24.00/12 p.m.
Laundry/dry cleaning: 24 hours
Conference rooms: 1 (up to 40 persons)
Sports (nearby): golf course (14 km), tennis (7 km), horse racing (7 km)
Bar: ›San Michele‹ (10.00/a.m.–24.00/12 p.m.) Pino Fornaroli (barman), pianist, elegant style
Restaurants: ›The Loggia‹ (12.30/p.m.–15.00/3 p.m.); ›San Michele‹ (19.30/7.30 p.m.–22.30/10.30 p.m.) Giuseppe Dalla Rosa (chef de cuisine), Tuscan and Italian regional cuisine, pianist, open-air dining
Private dining rooms: one

The world's foremost charm hotel (according to the bible of Le Beau Monde, the IN World Guide) is also one of the most luxurious since container king James Sherwood acquired this Franciscan monastery of Etruscan traces and with a façade designed by Michelangelo from the Teissier family and had grandseigneur-hotelier Natale Rusconi rejuvenate this hermitage on the hillside of Fiesole overlooking Florence. The monks' cells now boast marble baths, couture lingerie and castle antiques, and the terraced gardens serve as a miniature spa with pool and bar and liveried service. The inner sanctum courtyard with its Donatello coat of arms, and the vaulted loggia with alfresco restaurant, keep many San Michele worshippers within these holy walls untormented about not setting out on the pilgrimage to the mecca of the Renaissance. Instead, they indulge in the natural panorama and the man-made beauty, in the cucina toscana and in the charm of ›the world's foremost charm hotel‹.

Lunch

SABATINI
9a Via Panzani
Telephone: 28 28 02
Owner/Manager: Società Five di Quinte' Franca
Closed: Monday
Open: 12.30/p.m.–15.00/3 p.m. and 19.30/7.30 p.m.–22.30/10.30 p.m.
Cuisine: local and international
Chef de cuisine: Rosario Santoro
Specialities: red mullet en papillote (triglia del Tirreno al cartoccio); trippa fiorentina; bistecca di manzo chianino; minestrone; truffle noodles; fillet of beef with tarragon; bread; strawberry tart
Location: behind the church of Santa Maria Novella; between the main station and Cathedral Square
Setting: sober, restrained elegance; wood panelling, softened by draperies; valuable paintings
Amenities: bar; open-air dining in garden; car park (50 metres); air conditioning
Atmosphere: the classic place to eat; reminiscent of lunch at the United Nations – as much a part of the Florentine scene as Maxim's is in Paris
Clientèle: popular with Florence's Top Twenty and illustrious visitors from all corners of the globe
Dress: informal
Service: courteous and discreet
Reservations: recommended
Price range: fairly expensive
Credit cards: AE, DC, Euro

Lunch

CELESTINO
4r Piazza Santa Felicita
Telephone: 29 65 74
Closed: Sunday; April 17th; August; Christmas
Open: 12.00/a.m.–14.30/2.00 p.m. and 19.00/7.00 p.m.–22.30/10.30 p.m.
Cuisine: local and regional
Specialities: fiocchetti (type of pasta) alla fiorentina con piselli; ravioli; fresh salmon with butter and sage; Piedmontese fondue with truffles; buttered asparagus; fruit flans
Location: near the Galleria Palatina (Palazzo Pitti)
Setting: unpretentious but attractive décor
Amenities: air conditioning
Atmosphere: comfortably unassuming, with more emphasis placed on the quality of the food than on the wallpaper
Clientèle: discriminating connoisseurs of art and fine food mingle with Florentine families en fête and en masse
Dress: within reason, come as you please

Service: exemplary
Reservations: advisable
Price range: medium
Credit cards: not accepted

Dinner

HARRY'S BAR
22 Rosso, Lungarno A. Vespucci
Telephone: 29 67 00
Owner/Manager: Leo Vadorini
Closed: Sunday; December 10th–January 10th
Open: 12.00/a.m.–15.00/3 p.m. and 17.30/5.30 p.m.–24.00/12 p.m.
Location: central
Setting: classic, with plenty of natural wood and comfortable upholstery
Amenities: restaurant
Atmosphere: vaguely transatlantic
Clientèle: resident aristocracy and élite expatriates for lunch; American tycoons and Japanese jet-setters for dinner
Dress: Armani to Valentino to Burberry's and Halston
Service: friendly and efficient
Reservations: advisable for restaurant
Credit cards: AE

Dinner

ENOTECA PINCHIORRI
87 Via Ghibellina
Telephone: 24 27 77/24 27 57
Affiliations: Traditions et Qualité; Relais et Châteaux (Relais Gourmand)
Owner/Managers: Giorgio Pinchiorri and Annie Feolde
Closed: Sunday; Monday lunchtime; August
Open: 12.30/p.m.–13.30/1.30 p.m. and 20.00/8 p.m.–22.00/10 p.m.
Cuisine: Italian and French
Chef de cuisine: Annie Feolde
Specialities: carrot mousse with broccoli sauce; shrimp salad with asparagus tips and spinach, sauce foie gras; curd cheese (ricotta) ravioli with cream; suprême de pigeon with rosemary sauce; chicken breast with ginger; steamed turbot with fresh tomatoes and basil; dark chocolate and peppermint mousse
Location: less than a Rossini aria from the Piazza Santa Croce
Setting: nobleman's town-house dating from the 15th century; leaded windows and open fireplace; dining rooms furnished à l'ancienne, enlivened by an eye-catching collection of modern paintings
Amenities: wine bar; al fresco dining in inner courtyard
Atmosphere: refreshingly cool and uncluttered without being stark
Clientèle: well-heeled but footsore pilgrims to the tombs of Michelangelo, Macchiavelli, Galileo and Rossini in the nearby Chièsa de Santa Croce mingle

with disciples of Annie Feolde's cuisine from far and wide
Dress: suitably elegant
Service: faultless
Reservations: essential (pets permitted)
Price range: understandably expensive
Credit cards: AE, Carte Bleue

Lunch

LE CAVE DI MAIANO
16 Via delle Cave, Maiano di Fiesole
San Domenico (8 km/5 miles)
Telephone: 5 91 33
Owner/Manager: Ottone Rosai
Closed: Thursday; Sunday evening; August
Open: 12.00/a.m.–15.00/3 p.m. and 19.00/7p.m.–22.00/10 p.m.
Cuisine: local
Chef de cuisine: Romeo Berti
Specialities: ›Russian‹ salad; cannelloni stuffed with pork; tortellini verdi; charcoal-roasted chicken with polenta and fried artichokes; lamb; torta della nonna; caramelized pears in wine
Location: at Maiano de Fiesole, 8 km/5 miles north-east of Florence
Setting: a Tuscan auberge de campagne on a hillside, flanked by cypress trees; panoramic view of Florence from the top of the hill for those who wish to walk off a few excess calories after dinner
Amenities: shady terrace with stone tables, linden and mulberry trees
Atmosphere: a Tuscan idyll only 10 minutes' drive from the Piazza della Signoria
Clientèle: businessmen and tourists seeking a respite from the heat of Florence in summer – following in the footsteps of Michelangelo (according to the legend, anyway!)
Dress: cool and casual, especially in summer
Service: on the slow side at busy times, but friendly
Reservations: recommended (especially for dinner)
Price range: moderate
Credit cards: AE, DC

Dinner

COCO LEZZONE
26 r. Via Parioncino
Telephone: 28 71 78
Owner/Manager: Franco Paoli
Closed: Sunday; August
Open: 12.00/a.m.–14.00/2 p.m. and 19.30/7.30 p.m.–22.30/10.30 p.m.
Cuisine: local – casalinga
Chef de cuisine: Piero Paoli
Specialities: bean soup (ribollita); roast pork with herbs (arista al forno); braised beef; spaghetti with shin of veal stock; tripe à la Florentine; chestnut cake (castagniccio) in winter

Location: city centre
Setting: old taverna (established 1890); two whitewashed dining rooms; simple rustic décor
Atmosphere: family kitchen; surroundings somewhat at odds with the elegant and discriminating regular customers drawn by the excellence of the food
Clientèle: cross-section of men of commerce, actors, aristocrats and tourists – local habitués and casual passers-by
Dress: jeans to jackets (to be thrown off)
Service: ›alla buona‹ – ably supervised by Gianluca Paoli
Reservations: impracticable (always full)
Price range: medium
Credit cards: not accepted

Dinner

CANTINETTA ANTINORI
3 Piazza Antinori
Telephone: 29 22 34
Owner/Manager: Marchesi L&P. Antinori/Mr. Gioffredo Giusti
Closed: Saturday; Sunday; August
Open: 12.30/a.m.–14.30/2.30 p.m. and 19.00/7.00 p.m.–22.30/10.30 p.m.
Cuisine: local; ›casalinga‹
Chef de cuisine: Franco Rovilli
Specialities: salads; onion soup; braised beef; casseroles; tripe alla fiorentina; veal goulash; bean soup (ribollita)
Location: in the Palazzo Antinori
Setting: small ground-floor dining room in patrician palais; large picture windows; balcony section for groups or on busy days
Amenities: snack bar; air conditioning
Atmosphere: bustling and friendly
Clientèle: Florentines en passant mingle with English, Americans and Swiss
Dress: as you like it
Service: attentive and friendly
Reservations: recommended
Price range: moderately inexpensive
Credit cards: AE, Visa

Café

GIACOSA
83 Via de Tornabuoni
Telephone: 29 62 26
Owner/Manager: Bruno Bardelli
Closed: Monday
Open: 7.00/a.m.–23.00/11 p.m.
Specialities: the best cappuccino in town; hand-made chocolates; sandwiches; hot snacks and mouth-watering cakes
Location: in the heart of the city
Setting: modern styling with a sensible touch of classic
Atmosphere: crowded at times, but always chic
Clientèle: the younger generation of the Beautiful People
Service: faultless

Meeting Point

PROCACCI
64 Via Tornabuoni
Telephone: 21 16 56
Owner/Manager: Giuliana Procacci
Closed: Monday
Open: 8.00/a.m.–13.00/1 p.m. and
16.00/4 p.m.–23.00/11 p.m.
Location: near the Palazzo Strozzi
Setting: a small delicatessen shop with
three tables and a few chairs
Amenities: gourmet foods; bar (cold
drinks only); truffle rolls
Atmosphere: pure turn-of-the-century
nostalgia
Clientèle: Florence's crème de la crème,
and those who would like to be consid-
ered as such
Service: old-fashioned charm
Credit cards: not accepted

Bar

FOLL-UP
21r della Vigna Vecchie
Telephone: 29 30 06
Owner/Manager: Roberto Cecconi
Closed: Tuesday
Open: 22.00/10 p.m.–2.30/a.m.
Location: near from the Piazza della
Signoria
Setting: piano bar with classic décor
Atmosphere: youthful; refreshing
Clientèle: the young; the not-so-young;
the young-at-heart and those wishing to
recapture their lost youth
Dress: fairly conventional but chic
Service: with a smile
Reservations: recommended
Credit cards: not accepted

Nightclub

YAB YUM
5 Via Sassetti
Telephone: 28 20 18
Owner/Manager: Bruno Cherici and Ar-
mando Carzodi
Closed: Monday
Open: 22.00/10 p.m.–3.30/a.m.
Location: near the Piazza della Repub-
blica
Setting: large discothèque with modern
décor, laser beams, artificial fog, count-
less mirrors and an enormous dance floor
Amenities: two bars
Atmosphere: avant-garde; from feverish
to frenzied as the night wears on
Clientèle: a preponderance of energetic,
attractive and arrogant members of Flor-
ence's younger In-Crowd
Dress: way-out to way-in
Service: amazingly efficient and friendly
Reservations: advisable
Credit cards: AE, Euro

Shopping

FOR HIM
Zanobetti
18–28r Via Calimala

FOR HER
Emilio Pucci 6 Via del Pucci

BEAUTY & HAIR
P.A. 10 Via delle Terme
Arelli Alda 6r Via Barbadori

JEWELLERY
Settepassi 1/3r Ponte Vecchio
Arenti 93r Via Tornabuoni

LOCAL SPECIALITIES
Valentino (women's fashion)
Via della Vigna
Old England Store (men's fashion)
28r Via dei Vecchietti
Ferragamo (men and women's fashion)
12/16r Via Tornabuoni
Principe (children's fashion)
21/29r Via Strozzi
Cioni (furs) 1 Via Ricasoli
Seeber (books)
70r Via Tornabuoni
Poggi (gifts)
114/118r Via Calzaiuoli
Richard Ginori (porcelain)
7r Via Rondinelli
Gucci (baggage & travel accessories)
73/75r Via Tornabuoni
Arredo Tex (interior decorating)
4/6r Via dei Gonzi
Vera (food and beverages)
3r Piazza Frescobaldi
Aline (perfumery)
11r Via Vaccereccia
Giacosa (sweets, chocolatier)
83 r Via Tornabuoni
Farmacia (special pharmacy/cosmetics)
Via della Scala
Bellini (antiques)
3/5 Lungarno Soderini
Pratesi (linen)
8/10 Lungarno Vespucci
Sutor-Mantellassi (shoes)
3r Via Rondinelli and 25r Piazza Repub-
blica

THE BEST OF ART
Bitterlin, Fina (contemporary art)
2 Via de Cerretani, Tel. 26 50 68
Centro Tornabuoni (contemporary art)
5 Via Tornabuoni, Tel. 29 60 45
Finck, Michèle & Catherine (oriental
art)
15 Via della Vigna Nuova

The City

It must have been the Midas dream, coupled with a spirit of adventure, which lured young Christopher Columbus from his native Genoa to India. ›Gold constitutes treasure, and he who possesses it has all he needs in this world‹ he observed, before sailing into the sunset almost five hundred years ago in search of wealth, fame and a ›brave new world‹. The descendants of the Genoese he left behind have remained disciples of his thoughts to this day. Their city's historical role as one of the great trading republics of the Mediterranean, vying for supremacy with Valencia, Barcelona, Marseilles, Naples and Venice, has been confirmed in the twentieth century. Nowadays Genoa is Italy's principal port, second only in regional importance to Marseilles. As the chief outlet for industrial titans Milan and Turin, Genoa herself contributes oil refining, iron and steel and shipbuilding to the economic budget, with one of the country's most important pipelines linking it to the countries of central Europe. The city is the hub of the Ligurian coast – from the Riviera dei Fiori to the Riviera di Levante, from San Remo to Portofino – without succumbing to the instamatic hordes of budget trippers who threaten to overrun the more immediately accessible charms of her neighbours. Genoa's marble Renaissance palazzi, homes of the merchants who brought her fame and fortune, the Dorias, the Spinolas, the Fieschis and the rulers-to-be of Monte-Carlo, the Grimaldis, rise tier upon tier above the shady cobbled streets of the medieval town around the harbour, surmounted by the wide boulevards and spacious squares of the new city. Steep stairs, sharp angles and unexpected perspectives, fountain courtyards and noble statues, characterize the town's physiognomy, with the sixteenth-century landmark lighthouse counterbalancing the Gothic-Renaissance cathedral. Artists have always loved the setting; Van Dyck and Rubens worked here, recording the city's dignitaries for posterity, whilst today centre-Beaubourg-architect Renzo Piano has a grandiose plan to save his city from the inexorable encroachment of the motor car. Beloved of local son and one of the masterminds behind the Risorgimento, Giuseppe Mazzini, for visiting literatus Gustave Flaubert Genoa was ›a marble town with luxuriant rose gardens, a beauty who breaks your heart‹. For the visitor with a bit of time and understanding she still is – Genoa; La Superba.

Founded: prehistoric Ligurian settlement; 180 B.C. – a Roman colony; Genova (Italian).

Far-reaching events: 5th–9th century – invaded in turn by Goths, Byzantines, Lombards and Charlemagne – Genoa a free commune; 11th century – Genoa a maritime power and dominant city in Liguria; 13th century – with help from crusaders, Genoa expands its trade network to the Levant – conflict with Venice; 1380 – Genoa defeated in battle by Venice; 1407 – founding of the Bank of St. George, one of the first ›modern‹ banking institutions (the first to work with cheques), which soon develops into a state within the city-state; 1522 – Genoa an independent republic; 1528 – Admiral Andrea Doria becomes virtual dictator of Genoa – alliance with Charles V of Spain; 1684 – attacked by the French; 1746 – occupied by the Austrians; 1797; Liguria a French dependency; 1815 – Genoa passes to the Duchy of Piedmont-Sardinia; 1861 – comes to new prosperity following unification of Italy; 1939–45 – damage during World War II; post – 1945 – reconstruction.

Population: 750,000; capital of the province of Liguria and 7th largest city in Italy.

Postal code: I-16100   **Telephone code:** 10

Climate: exceptionally mild.

Calendar of events: *Theatre & Opera Season* (Nov–Dec).

Fairs and exhibitions: *ORCHIDEA* (Jan/Feb) – orchid show; *FIORARTE* (Jan/Feb); *PRIMAVERA* (Mar) – household, gifts, holidays and leisure; *RIABITAT* (May); *SIC* (Sep) – international coffee exhibition; *INTERNATIONAL BOAT SHOW* (Oct); *INTERNATIONAL EXHIBITION OF UNDERWATER EQUIPMENT* (Oct); *TECN-HOTEL* (Nov) – international exhibition of hotel equipment; *BIBE* (Nov) – international beverage exhibition; *INTERFOOD* (Nov) – international exhibition of food and fast food.

Historical sights: *Palazzo Bianco* (16th century) – containing the *Art Gallery,* with Dutch, Flemish and local masterpieces; *Via Garibaldi* – Genoa's luxury street, lined with palazzi from the 16th century, including the Palazzo Bianco, the *Palazzo Rosso,* with a fine art gallery, the *Palazzo Cataldi,* with Drescolo and a gilded gallery and the *Palazzo Doria Tursi,* the magnificent home of the pirate-hunting Andrea Doria, now the city hall; *Via Balbi* and *Palazzo dell'Università* – elegant inner courtyard; *Palazzo Doria-Pamphilii* – with a water garden; *Villa Durazzo Pallavicini* – an exotic park with an atmosphere of mystery; *Cathedral of St. Lawrence* (11th–18th century) – Gothic, with a Renaissance dome; *Porta Soprana* and *Porta dei Vacca* – the medieval city gates; *Lighthouse* – a city landmark; *Centro Storico* – Europe's largest intact medieval city.

Special attractions: as much time as you have at *Portofino*; embarking on a world cruise from the *harbour.*

Important companies with headquarters in the city: *Ansaldo* (nuclear and electrotechnical engineering); *Electronica San Giorgio Elsag* (electronic systems); *Eridania Zuccherifici Nazionali* (sugar); *Industria Italiani Petroli* (petrol); *Italimpianti* (construction); *Mira Lanza* (detergents); *Nuova Italsider* (metals); *Piaggio, E. C.* (vehicles).

Airport: Genoa-Christoforo Colombo-Sestri Ponente, GOA; Tel.: 60 08 61, Alitalia; Tel.: 54 93, 7 km/4 miles.

The Headquarters

COLOMBIA

40 Via Balbi
I–16126 Genoa
Telephone: 26 18 41
Telex: 2 70 423
Owning company: Cigahotels
General Manager: Gianfranco Baroncelli
Affiliation/Reservation System: Hello-ciga
Number of rooms: 172 (10 suites)
Price range: Lit. 120,000–600,000
Credit cards: AE, DC, EC, Visa
Location: central, opposite the main railway station
Built: 1929
Style: Art Nouveau
Hotel amenities: parking, beauty salon, hairdresser, babysitting, interpreter
Room amenities: air conditioning, tv, radio, mini-bar
Room service: 7.00/a.m.–23.00/11 p.m.
Conference rooms: up to 350 persons
Bars: ›The Library‹ American Bar
Restaurants: ›L'Ammiraglio‹ national and regional cuisine
Private dining rooms: for up to 300 guests

The only de luxe hotel in this world seaport, too often overlooked, neglected or misinterpreted, is by itself worth booking a cruise for. Many exclusive Atlantic crossings starting from Genoa therefore include a night here before departure and after landing, anyway. The Colombia, prime example of Art Déco architecture and design, sports many elements reflecting the Belle Epoque and the opulence of yesteryear, when lavish vessels sailed into the harbour, with pleasure cruisers, adventurers and mysterious personalities exchanging their unwanted past for a hopeful future on the other side of the ocean. Even today, the glass-domed, marble-floored foyer still fills with glamour and gossip from the wide and wonderful world. The curved and colonnaded façade on the corner of one of the city's principal thoroughfares is the entry to Genoa's liveliest museum and one of the noble members of the Aga Khan's CIGA hotel group. The service is as worldly as the clientèle, and the rooms and suites make a good antichambre for the prodigally installed bedchambers of the luxury liners. Conferences and banquets of standing and international importance are all held here, meetings and high-level talks have found in the Colombia the only other platform possible. Forte of the hotel – and true to the philosophy of CIGA – is the L'Ammiraglio dining room with its dignified intérieur and elegant air and, above all, with a cuisine unmatched by many restaurants in the city. Tableware, porcelain and crystal are of the same precious quality as the gourmet victuals in their own right. And when you meet for a drink at The Library, you will run into everybody who is anybody from out of town.

The Hideaway

SPLENDIDO

13 Viale Baratta
I–16034 Portofino (36 km/22.5 miles)
Telephone: (185) 69551
Telex: 331057 splend
Owning Company: Sea Containers
General Manager: Antonio Marson
Affiliation/Reservation System: Relais et Châteaux
Closed: November – end of March
Number of rooms: 55 (12 suites)
Price range: Lit. 198,000–258,000
Credit cards: AE, Visa, EC
Location: overlooking bay of Portofino
Built: 15th century
Style: old patrician mansion
Hotel amenities: garage, valet parking, house limousine service, beauty salon, swimming pool, sauna, solarium, massage, boutique, florist, tennis court
Main hall porter: Fausto Allegri
Room service: 7.30/a.m.–23.00/11 p.m.
Conference rooms: 1 (30 persons)
Bars: ›Piano Bar/Pool Bar‹ (10.00/a.m.–24.00/12.00 p.m.) Antonio Beccali (barman), pianist, orchestra
Restaurants: ›La Terrazza‹ G. Tognazzi (maître), G. Pizzi (chef de cuisine)
›Grill Il Barbecue‹ (13.00/1.00 p.m.–14.30/2.30 p.m.) M. Cuzzoni (maître), G. Pizzi (chef de cuisine), charcoal grill

Nomen est omen. And the future looks more splendid still. James Sherwood's generosity, Natale Rusconi's style and Antonio Marson's direction will eventually lift this hillside ›Villa d'Ovest‹ onto the Olympus of hôtellerie. High above Portofino (yet linked to the harbour by a private path), embraced by botanical beauty and flanked by some of the most prominent summer residences in the land, the albergo is already one of the most fashionable hideaways in the world, but under the new ownership luxury and finesse will penetrate every angle of this cream-coloured terrace building. The location alone – with one of the world's most charming port-towns at its feet – is overwhelming. The air, the view, the history; and now the elegance, the people and the service. Richard Lionheart never had it so good when he stopped here on the way to Syria. Arriving at the hotel demands skilful driving, but being here requires nothing except the ability to see, hear, feel and taste – you don't even have to talk, unless you have individual desires that Agnelli-look-alike Fausto, the concierge, will arrange, or you want to learn about anything from the annals of this house to the pearls of wisdom from Signore Marson. There is a swimming pool à la Eden Roc, a tennis court amidst pines, a piano player in the bar with a repertoire of everyone's romantic youth and a cook who seduces you with his creations as much as the charm of the servants. To misinterpret a misinterpreted aphorism: see Portofino and live! But only at the Splendido.

Lunch

VITTORIO AL MARE
1 Belvedere Firpo
Telephone: 31 28 72
Owner/Manager: Giorgio Rivelli
Closed: Monday; annual holiday not fixed
Open: 9.00/a.m.–2.00/a.m.
Cuisine: local
Chef de cuisine: Nicola Sicarra
Specialities: seafood salad; anchovies either stuffed or with lime juice; risottos with various sauces; taglierini; fish dishes (also some meat, mushrooms or game); lobster à l'armoricaine
Location: overlooking the fishing cove of Boccadasse
Setting: a light attractive dining room with large windows providing a panoramic view of the rocks, the shoreline and the Ligurian coast as far as the headland of Portofino
Amenities: air conditioning; car park
Atmosphere: one of the most typically Mediterranean restaurants in Genoa
Clientèle: gentlemen (and ladies) of Genoa, who appreciate the setting and the food just as much as do the businessmen from the frozen and foggy North
Dress: as you like it – as long as they will like you
Service: somewhat capricious
Reservations: advisable (pets prohibited)
Price range: medium
Credit cards: AE, DC

Dinner

LA SANTA
1r Via Indoratori
Telephone: 29 36 13
Owner/Managers: Fulvio Tommasi and Sergio Pallavicini
Closed: Sunday
Open: 12.15/p.m.–15.00/3 p.m. and 19.00/7 p.m.–21.30/9.30 p.m.
Cuisine: international and local
Chef de cuisine: Ottavio Corrado
Specialities: classic antipasti; duckling à l'orange; fish ravioli; taglierini with lobster sauce; local-style roast meats; timbale of Creole-style rice with prawns; rice with beef sauce and cheese (riso mantecato)
Location: in the maze of alleyways behind the Piazza Caricamento
Setting: attractively old-fashioned restaurant in a medieval building named after Saint Catherine Fieschi who was born in the palais opposite
Amenities: air conditioning
Atmosphere: warm; romantic or confidential, depending on your companion
Clientèle: local dignitaries, shipping magnates passing through – and Genoa's

Haute Bourgeoisie with cause for celebration
Dress: fairly casual to fairly formal, depending on the occasion
Service: courteous, solicitous and multilingual (English, German, Spanish and French spoken)
Reservations: essential for groups of more than 10 people
Price range: medium (Yorkshire terriers allowed, but not Irish wolfhounds)
Credit cards: AE, DC, Visa

Dinner

CARDINALI (Da Ermanno)
6r Via Assarotti
Telephone: 87 03 80
Owner/Managers: Enrico and Ermanno Ghiorzo
Closed: Sunday; August 10th–25th
Open: 12.00/a.m.–14.30/2.30 p.m. and 20.00/8.00 p.m.–22.15/10.15 p.m.
Cuisine: international
Chef de cuisine: Enrico Ghiorzo
Specialities: the best meat in Genoa; stuffed courgettes; frogs' legs à la provençale; hot flans (tortini caldi); gnocchi di Ermanno; fruits flambés (frutta alla fiamma); crêpes Suzette
Location: near the Piazza Corvetto
Setting: typical tavernetta; small dining room
Amenities: bar; air conditioning
Atmosphere: chic but not chichi
Clientèle: Genoa's social élite en fête, plus top industrialists celebrating a signed contract or hoping to clinch a deal
Dress: according to season and circumstance
Service: knowledgeable and helpful; directed by Ermanno Ghiorzo
Reservations: advisable
Price range: moderate
Credit cards: AE, DC, Carte Bleue

Lunch

ANTICA OSTERIA DEL BAI
12 Via Quarto, Quarto dei Mille
Telephone: 38 74 78
Owner/Managers: Renata Luppi and Giuseppe Malagoli
Closed: Monday; one week in February and 3 weeks in summer
Open: 12.00/a.m.–14.30/2.30 p.m. and 19.30/7.30 p.m.–22.30/10.30 p.m.
Cuisine: local
Chef de cuisine: Renata Luppi
Specialities: razor-clam soup; marinated squid; croûtons with hazelnut sauce; (pasta with basil and garlic sauce); fish ravioli; lobster and king prawns all'armoricana; braised squid; semifreddo alla nocciola with raspberry sauce

Location: on the coast road towards Nervi
Setting: historic coaching-inn in an old fort on the coast; décor a mixture of the rustic and the nautical, with a panoramic view of the sea
Amenities: bar; outdoor dining on terrace; car park
Atmosphere: the history and geography of Genoa in miniature
Clientèle: stopover for a succession of historic personages, from Garibaldi to Pius VII; nowadays, favourite locale for Genoese Sunday-afternoon crowd en famille
Dress: Sunday casual to Sunday best
Service: expertly supervised by Giuseppe Malagoli
Reservations: recommended
Price range: medium
Credit cards: AE

Dinner

ZEFFIRINO
20 Via XX Settembre
Telephone: 59 59 39
Owner/Manager: Zeffirino Belloni
Closed: Wednesday
Open: 12.00/a.m.–15.30/3.30 p.m. and 19.00/7 p.m.–24.00/12 p.m.
Cuisine: local and Emilian; Italian classic and international
Chefs de cuisine: Paolo, Odino and Giorgio Belloni
Specialities: seafood; home-made pasta – tagliatelle, maccheroncini, tortellini, lasagne with sauces; mushrooms; game; rabbit; poultry; fish soup; sautéed breast of chicken and skylarks in puff pastry
Location: central
Setting: modern stylized rustic; panelled ceiling; large dining room; wrought iron, wine bottles, marine and domestic paraphernalia
Amenities: private dining room (130 persons); bar; air conditioning
Atmosphere: characteristic family establishment; warm, imaginative and intimate
Clientèle: Genoese habitués, tourists and celebrities en passant; lovers of any age, nationality and sex
Dress: what you will
Service: welcoming and courteous; supervised by Luciano and Alberto Belloni
Reservations: essential
Price range: medium
Credit cards: AE, DC, Euro, Visa, Comites

Dinner

ANTICA OSTERIA PACETTI
22r Via Borgo degli Incrociati
Telephone: 89 28 48
Owner/Manager: the Pacetti family
Closed: Monday; three weeks in August

Open: 12.00/a.m.–14.00/2.00 p.m. and 19.00/7 p.m.–22.00/10.00 p.m.
Cuisine: local
Chef de cuisine: Antonio Maffini
Specialities: salad of cooked vegetables with fish and shellfish (cappon magro); ravioli di mare; sardelle soup (minestrina di bianchetti); braised squid; fricassée of kid with artichokes; milk and apple dessert (fritto di latte dolce e mele)
Location: near Brignole station
Setting: in a narrow cul-de-sac characteristic of old Genoa; typical trattoria; rustic décor, with bric-à-brac and memorabilia; arched ceiling, benches
Amenities: bar; air conditioning
Atmosphere: a family-run restaurant (established by the father-in-law of the present owner in 1908); picturesque and authentic
Clientèle: aficionados of genuine Genoese cuisine
Dress: within reason, anything goes
Service: ›familiare‹
Reservations: advisable (no dogs)
Price range: moderate
Credit cards: not accepted

Dinner

HARRY'S BAR
13r Via Donato Somma
Nervi (9 km/5 miles)
Telephone: 32 60 74
Owner/Manager: Mario Sessarego
Closed: Tuesday; July 1st–15th
Open: 12.00/a.m.–15.00/3.00 p.m. and 20.00/8.00 p.m.–24.00/12.00 p.m.
Location: at Nervi; 9 km/5 miles east of Genoa
Setting: small bar-restaurant; elegant in the classic idiom, with sunblinds
Amenities: restaurant offering Franco-Italian-international cuisine; outdoor dining on terrace
Atmosphere: cheerfully cosmopolitan
Clientèle: comfortable and heterogeneous mixture of loyal regulars and international birds of passage
Service: charming welcome from Lucia Sessarego
Reservations: essential
Credit cards: AE

Café

MOODY
12 Largo Ottobre 51
Telephone: 59 54 31
Owner/Manager: Esposito and Giovanni Foglini
Closed: Sunday
Open: 7.30/a.m.–21.30/9.30 p.m.
Location: close to Pica Pietra
Setting: café-bar and restaurant on two floors; classic décor
Amenities: piano-bar (16.00/4 p.m. to 19.45/7.45 p.m.), garden terrace; air conditioning

Atmosphere: huge but elegant café – perfect for writing novels or reading the Sunday Times
Dress: whatever you like, if they like it, too
Service: self-service
Credit cards: not accepted

THE BEST OF ART
Chisel   (contemporary art)
6/1 Salita S. Caterina, Tel. 58 14 14
La Polena   (contemporary art)
24 Largo XII Ottobre, Tel. 56 23 38

Shopping

EVERYTHING UNDER ONE ROOF
Coin   4/5 Via XII Ottobre

FOR HIM
Devoto & Vitale   46/r Via XXV Aprile

FOR HER
Abolaffio   43/r Via Roma

BEAUTY & HAIR
J. L. David Group   1 Via Ceccardi

JEWELLERY
Parodi   3/r Via Ceccardi

LOCAL SPECIALITIES
Coveri (women's fashion)
50/r Via Roma
Paganello (men's fashion)
39/r Galleria Mazzini
Cicogna Life (children's fashion)
112/r Via XII Ottobre
Torlaschi (leather fashion)
50/r Salita Santa Caterina
Fausto Carlino (furs)
48/r Via Fiasella
Di Stefano (books)
40/r Via Roccatagliata Ceccardi
Prisma (gifts and porcelain)
Largo XII Ottobre
Contini (baggage & travel accessories)
25/r Via XXV Aprile
Obelisco (interior decorating)
1 Piazza Rovere (near Salita Santa Caterina)
Croff Centro Casa (bathroom accessories)
225/r Via XX Settembre
Pattono (bathroom accessories)
448 Via Casoni/Cancello
Primizie (food and beverages)
44/r Via Galata
Glamour (perfumery)
25/r Salita Santa Caterina
Fratelli Rossetti (shoes)
69/r Via Roma
Magli (shoes)
135/r Via XX Settembre
Tomasoni Yachting Sport (boat utilities)
117/r Piazza della Vittoria

The City

If there were a contest for greatness among the continent's metropolises today, Milan would have to be awarded the bronze medal. Next to London and Paris (and despite the frown from Rome, the objection from Madrid and the astonishment by Zurich, Vienna, and a few other world villages like Munich) there is no other competitor on the continent surging to the skies with such genius, energy and brio as this volcanic agglomeration in the Lombardian plains. Business takes on a new dimension here, and all the clichés about the Italians – romantic to ridiculous – should be discarded before you enter the 14th-century ramparts. Centre of industry, trade and banking, Milan stands out for motors and machines, electromechanics and chemicals, fibres and pharmaceuticals, for art and antiques, design and publishing, couture and cuisine, music and style and for the most elegant men and women in the world. Only petit-bourgeois souls will lament about the fog and the smog, the chaos, costs and crime rate. Milan is the stage for people in search of success in sophistication, for new ideas and talents, too tough for Romans. (In the eyes of the Milanese, their city has remained the capital of Italy ever since Napoléon endowed it with this title, anyhow.) Il Duomo, La Scala, Leonardo's Cena, Via Montenapoleone, Gallerie Vittorio Emanuele, Giorgio Armani, Gualtiero Marchesi, the vernissages, the premières, the shows, the galas, the hinterland Lake District and the quick excursions to the Riviera, St. Moritz and Venice – what could be missing? (The only thing, as with New York – a safe-full of Lire in the palazzo.) The visitor, for business and pleasure, enters a kaleidoscope ranging from antiquity to avant-garde, from intellect to superficiality, from hard facts to an atmosphere only Italians can create – which will make your forget the fog and the smog, and . . .

Founded: 222 B.C. – Celtic settlement conquered by the Romans; Milano (Italian).

Far-reaching events: 286 A.D. – Milan the capital of the western Roman Empire; 539 A.D. – sacked by barbarians – part of Langobard kingdom; 1158 – invaded by Frederick Barbarossa, who takes the shrine of the Three Magi to Cologne; 1277–1447 – Milan ruled by the Visconti family; 1450–1530 – the city flourishes under the Sforzas; 1535–1706 – Spanish rule – Borromes family patronizes the arts; 1714 – Hapsburg domination; 1797 – conquered by Napoléon; 1815 – returned to Hapsburgs – one of the music centres of Europe; 1859 – part of the Kingdom of Italy; 1919 – Fascist party founded here; 1939–45 – heavy damage during World War II; post-1945 – emergence as Italy's main commercial centre.

Population: 1.7 million; Italy's second largest city and capital of Lombardy.

Postal code: I–20100   **Telephone code:** 2

Climate: mild to warm; from November to February often covered in a blanket of fog.

Best time to visit: May to June and September to October.

Calendar of events: La Scala: *Opera season* – December to the end of May, June to mid-July, October; *Concert season* – mid-November; *Ballet* – September.

Fairs and exhibitions: *TOY FAIR* (Jan); *SICOF* (Mar) – film, photography and laboratory technology; *IPACK-IMA* (Mar) – packaging material and machinery; *COVER-FLEX* (Mar/Apr) – paper production machinery; *INTERNATIONAL TRADE FAIR* (Apr); *INTEL* (May) – electrotechnology and electronics.

Best views of the city: from the roof of the *Duomo*, the central cathedral.

Historical sights: *Cathedral* (1386–1809) – Gothic, third largest cathedral in the world, colossal white marble, stained glass and rose windows, 135 spires; *Palace of the Sforzas* (1368) – paintings, sculptures, ivory and tapestries; *Basilica of St. Ambrose* (11th century) – Lombard Romanesque; *St. Mary of Grace* (1465–90) – Renaissance, Leonardo's ›Last Supper‹; *Municipal Cemetery* – the last retreat for Milan's tycoons; *Brera Palace* and *Picture Gallery* (17th century) – local and north Italian artists; *Leonardo da Vinci Museum of Science and Technology* (16th century).

Special attractions: A night at *la Scala*; a shopping spree along the *Via Montenapoleone*; life in and around the *Piazza del Duomo*; an ice-cream creation at *Café Sant' Ambroeus*; a première at *Armani, Versace* et al.; lunch at *Savini*; a night out at *Nepentha*.

Important companies with headquarters in the city: *Acciaierie Ferr. Lombarde Falck* (metals); *Adelphi* (publishing); *Alfa Romeo* (cars); *Armani, Giorgio* (fashion); *Bompiani* (publishing); *Borletti* (cars and car parts); *Campari* (vermouth); *Crespi* (fabrics); *Ercole Marelli* (mechanical engineering); *Fabbri* (publishing); *Farmitalia-Carlo Erba* (pharmaceuticals); *Feltrinelli* (publishing); *Garzanti* (publishing); *Innocenti* (vehicles); *Locatelli* (furniture); *Longanesi* (publishing); *Magneti Marelli* (mechanical engineering); *Mondadori* (publishing); *Montedison* (chemicals); *Olympia Press* (publishing); *Pirelli* (tyres); *Rizzoli* (publishing); *Sagar* (publishing); *Saras Raffinerie* (petrol); *Sirti* (pharmaceuticals).

Airport: Milan-Linate, LIN; Tel.: 71 71 15; 8 km/5 miles; Milan-Malpensa, MXP; Tel.: 86 80 29, 50 km/30 miles; Alitalia, Tel.: 28 37.

The Headquarters

**PRINCIPE DI SAVOIA
CIGAHOTEL**

17 Piazza Della Repubblica
I–20124 Milano
Telephone: 62 30
Telex: 310 052 prinmi
Owning Company: Cigahotels
General Manager: Paolo Biscioni
Affiliation/Reservation System: Hello-ciga
Number of rooms: 262 (18 suites)
Price range: Lit. 285,000–1,100,000
Credit cards: AE, DC, EC, Visa
Location: central
Built: 1927 (renovated 1956/57)
Style: modern and Empire style
Hotel amenities: garage; valet parking, house limousine service, beauty salon, newsstand; tobacconist, florist
Main hall porter: Giovanni Santangeletta
Room service: 24 hours
Laundry/dry cleaning: same day; weekend service
Conference rooms: up to 1,200 persons
Bars: ›Il Principe‹ (9.00/a.m to 1.00/a.m.); Luciano Fusi (barman); ›Il Glicine‹ (summer): as Il Principe Bar
Restaurants: ›Il Principe‹ (12.00/a.m.–15.30/3.30 p.m. and 19.00/7.00 p.m.–24.00/12.00 p.m.); Pancrazio Mendolia (maître); Luciano Orio (chef de cuisine), Mediterranean and Italian cuisine; ›La Bella Fontana‹ (summer)

Since the Sforzas left no palaces to be converted into Grand Hôtels, the Aga Khan's CIGA-hotels flagship is the most palatial address in town. Piazza Repubblica is no castle park and the Principe's architecture not starred in the Guide Bleu either, but once you have stepped inside this imposing stock exchange of business encounters, social affairs and luxurious amenities, you realize why everybody who is anybody resides only here – or at least comes for meetings, drinks, lunch and dinner. Concierge Giovanni Santangeletta is yet another reason – and the surest guarantee of a successful stay. Voiturier, porters, room service and management are of world standard, and Italian at that. The intérieur is pure Art Déco with many beautiful elements and Venetian lamps. The bathrooms are marbled to the ceiling and spacious, whilst every bedchamber reflects the lavish generosity of this country in the furniture, the linen and the accessoires. Communications – one of the most important factors for the upper-management habitués – are perfect, and the cuisine of Il Principe *is as haute as anywhere in this gourmet capital. Tête-à-tête dinners alfresco in the little front garden belong to the fashionable summer pleasures of Milan, whereas the hotel bar can safely be called the meeting point of the metropolis for the media, design and couture. With the new CIGA in the galaxy of grandezza, this mansion will only rise to greater heights.*

The Hideaway

VILLA D'ESTE

40 Via Regina
I–22010 Cernobbio, Lake Como
(53 km/33 miles)
Telephone: (31) 51 14 71/51 24 71
Telex: 380 025 Vilest
General Manager: Mario Arrigo
Closed: end of October – March 20th
Affiliation/Reservation System: The Leading Hotels of the World
Number of rooms: 181 (32 suites)
Price range: Lit. 237,000–840,000
Credit cards: AE, DC, Visa
Location: on Lake Como
Built: 16th century
Style: palatial
Hotel amenities: car park, house limousine service, shopping gallery
Room service: 7.00/a.m.–23.00/11 p.m.
Conference rooms: 9 (up to 250 persons)
Sports: tennis, swimming, squash
Sports (nearby): golf
Bars: ›Canova Bar‹: piano bar band for dancing; ›Pool Bar‹
Restaurants: ›Verandah‹: (7.00/a.m.–10.30/a.m., 12.30/p.m.–14.30/2.30 p.m. and 20.00/8 p.m.–22.00/10 p.m.) Italian cuisine; ›The Grill‹: (19.30/7.30 p.m.–24.00/12 p.m.) informal atmosphere
Nightclubs: ›The Night Club‹, dancing after 22.00/10 p.m.

The Renaissance palace right on the water's edge of one of Europe's most marvellous lakes (originally built in 1568 as Villa Gàrrovo by Pellegrino Pellegrino) was for centuries a congregating point for privileged eccentrics who indulged their artistic inclinations in the solitude of the surrounding countryside and their social proclivities in the staging of orgiastic festivities. The opulent Villa passed through the hands of macchiavellists, monks and maîtresses, all of whom shared the predilection for grandiose buildings, glorious intérieurs, majestic parks and superb service, in short, a Babylonian way of life in the western world. Shelley and Stendhal never managed to be invited by Caroline of Brunswick, wife of George IV of England and her Italian lover, to walk the grounds full of pine and cypress trees, fountains, cascades and mosaic walls – let alone to the princely halls, salons and bedrooms (kept in full splendour along with grand hotel amenities by the owning Droulers family), but Sir Winston Churchill was one of the first history greats and paying guests to take advantage of the conversion into one of the paradisiac summer resorts of the world. All the trappings of grandeur remain (complete with pools and tennis, yachts and golf), guided in the grand manner by grandseigneur Mario Arrigo, and comments on beauty, luxury, service and atmosphere – from the bedchambers to the bar, from the restaurant to the nightclub – are quite superfluous: summa cum laude, what else. The only handicap of the Villa d'Este is that it closes in winter.

Lunch

SAVINI
Galleria Vittorio Emanuele II
Telephone: 8 05 83 43/8 05 83 64
Owner/Manager: Alfio Bocciardi/Giancarlo Guancioli
Closed: Sunday; August 10th–19th; December 22nd–January 4th
Open: 12.00/a.m.–15.00/3 p.m. and 19.30/7.30 p.m.–23.00/11 p.m.
Cuisine: local and international
Chef de cuisine: Sergio Torelli
Specialities: scampi Savini con riso pilaf or risotto all'onda; saffron rice with white truffles; risotto al salto (with paprika and peas); veal cutlet alla milanese; osso buco con risotto alla milanese; fillet of beef with Armagnac; charlotta alla milanese
Location: between the cathedral (Duomo) and La Scala
Setting: dining rooms with crimson velvet upholstery; crystal chandeliers, mirrors and convenient niches; antique silver and damask tablecloths
Amenities: winter-garden under the glass-roofed Galleria in summer; air conditioning
Atmosphere: the Grand Véfour of Milan; as much a landmark as the Duomo or La Scala
Clientèle: stars from La Scala, from Puccini to Pavarotti; princes of the church and princes of industry, from Agnelli to Pirelli
Dress: from Valentino to Ken Scott to Mila Schoen
Service: skilfully directed by maître d'hôtel Albini Oreste, aided by an impeccable team including a sommelier who will choose a wine and taste it from a silver bowl around his neck as in days gone by
Reservation: advisable to essential
Price range: inevitably expensive
Credit cards: all major

Lunch

GUALTIERO MARCHESI
9 Via Bonvesin de la Riva
Telephone: 7 38 66 77
Affiliations: Traditions et Qualité; Relais et Châteaux (Relais Gourmand)
Owner/Manager/Chef de cuisine: Gualtiero Marchesi
Closed: Sunday; Monday lunchtime; public holidays; January
Open: 12.30/p.m.–14.00/2 p.m. and 19.30/7.30 p.m.–23.30/11.30 p.m.
Cuisine: classic and modern
Specialities: continually changing menu; raviolo aperto; rice with herbs and scampi; rib of beef au gratin; escalope alla milanese in sweet and sour sauce; pear in red wine with cinnamon mousse
Location: city centre

Setting: ultra-modern; a subterranean culinary art gallery with unique sculptures by famous artists on the dozen tables
Amenities: air conditioning
Atmosphere: sober and elegant, with a touch of brio
Clientèle: worthy of a Scala première; adventurous gourmets from all over the world
Dress: appropriately chic
Service: à la Savini
Reservations: advisable (no dogs)
Price range: inevitably expensive
Credit cards: AE

Dinner

EL TOULÀ
6 Piazza Paolo Ferrari
Telephone: 87 03 02/8 69 05 75
Affiliations: El Toulà Group
Owner/Manager: Mario Benedetti
Closed: between Christmas and New Year; three weeks in August
Open: 12.00/a.m.–14.30/2.30 p.m. and 20.00/8 p.m.–22.30/10.30 p.m.
Cuisine: Venetian and international
Chef de cuisine: Brocca Raminin
Specialities: risotto with courgette flowers; coulibiac alla Russa; spaghetti Nataschia (with caviar); octopus in oil; gnocchi with prosciutto; asparagus flan; filet mignon of veal with mustard seeds; fegato alla veneziana; iced zabaglione with coffee; fregolata (girdle-cake from Treviso)
Location: in the former foyer of the Teatro Filodrammatici, two top C's away from La Scala
Setting: operetta décor with many original paintings by contemporary artists
Amenities: bar; air conditioning
Atmosphere: very sophisticated and chic
Clientèle: financiers and managing directors for lunch; glitterati, litterati, operastars, opera-producers and opera-lovers for dinner
Dress: from Armani to Versace, and vice-versa
Service: very elegant
Reservations: advisable
Price range: naturally high
Credit cards: AE, DC, Euro, Visa

Dinner

ST. ANDREW'S
23 Via Sant'Andrea
Telephone: 79 31 32/79 82 36
Owner/Manager: Piero Vezzulli
Closed: Sunday; August
Open: 12.00/a.m.–16.00/4 p.m. and 19.00/7 p.m.–2.00/a.m.
Cuisine: international and local
Chef de cuisine: Giuliano de Cillis

Specialities: risotto au champagne; fillet Cossack (steak tartare with caviar); Norway lobster soufflé; fillet Mornay; smoked pheasant; tangerine soufflé; crêpes
Location: round the corner from the Via Montenapoleone, home of the big couturiers and the small jewellers (size of shop only)
Setting: English furniture and décor; leather armchairs and sofas; bookshelves as room dividers; dim lighting and background music
Amenities: bar; private dining room (25 persons); air conditioning
Atmosphere: reminiscent of a London club
Clientèle: Milan's Top Ten; bijoutiers and couturiers; celebrities incognito and the hungry after-theatre crowd
Dress: jacket and tie
Service: excellent and discreet
Reservations: advisable
Price range: fairly expensive
Credit cards: AE, DC, Euro, Visa, Carte Blanche, Comites

Lunch

SCALETTA
3 Piazzale Stazione Genova
Telephone: 8 35 02 90
Owner/Manager: Pina Bellini
Closed: Sunday; Monday; August; two weeks at Christmas; two weeks at Easter
Open: 12.30/p.m.–15.00/3 p.m. and 20.00/8 p.m.–24.00/12 p.m.
Cuisine: nuova cucina italiana
Chefs de cuisine: Pina Bellini and Ernesto Maestri
Specialities: smoked eel pâté; dumplings with marrow, herbs and saffron; risotto with nettles and strawberries; fillet with bone marrow and peppermint; asparagus and white truffle ravioli; cinnamon ice-cream with melon mousse
Location: on the somewhat unprepossessing square in front of the Genova railway station
Setting: small restaurant (8 tables) with exquisite modern décor by wunderkind of design Gianfranco Frattini
Amenities: bar; air conditioning
Atmosphere: suave; refined; and yet warm-hearted – reflecting the charms of mother-and-son team Pina and Aldo Bellini
Clientèle: friendly, trendy and discriminating – pilgrims to the court of Pina Bellini, one of the best cooks in Italy
Dress: casual but chic
Service: utterly disarming
Reservations: essential
Price range: decidedly expensive, but cheap at the price
Credit cards: not accepted

Dinner

ANTICO RISTORANTE BOEUCC
2 Piazza Belgioioso
Telephone: 79 02 24/79 28 80
Owner/Manager: Paolo Brioschi
Closed: Friday evening; Saturday; August; Christmas
Open: 12.30/p.m.–14.30/2.30 p.m. and 19.30/7.30 p.m.–22.30/10.30 p.m.
Cuisine: traditional
Chef de cuisine: Dino Musio
Specialities: hot fisherman's hors d'œuvre (antipasto caldo del pescatore); scampi and lobster raviolini; fresh fettucine with nettles and mushrooms; quail and partridge in season
Location: on one of Milan's most beautiful piazzas; not far from La Scala
Setting: established in 1682; attractive dining room with classic-style décor
Amenities: plant-filled terrace for open-air dining in summer; air conditioning
Atmosphere: restrained yet relaxing
Clientèle: affluent; conservative
Dress: no special requirements
Service: under the expert guidance of the owner as sommelier, aided by maître Piero Berzero
Reservations: recommended
Price range: fairly expensive
Credit cards: AE

Café

SANT'AMBROEUS
7 Corso Matteotti
Telephone: 79 00 29
Owner/Manager: Hans Werner Pauli
Closed: Saturday; Monday evening
Open: 8.00/a.m.–19.30/7.30 p.m.
Specialities: the best rolls in Milan – with truffles, ham, tuna pâté ......
Location: in the heart of the city
Setting: exceptionally attractive Venetian-style salon; fine table-linen, exquisite porcelain and silver
Amenities: air conditioning; bar; summer garden
Atmosphere: raffinée
Clientèle: well-dressed Milanese ladies and gentlemen
Service: old-fashioned charm

Bar

COVA
8 Via Montenapoleone
Telephone: 79 31 87/70 05 78
Owner/Manager: Franco Traversa
Closed: Sunday
Open: 8.00/a.m.–20.00/8 p.m.
Location: on the Via Montenapoleone, Milan's most elegant shopping street

Setting: elegant turn-of-the century décor
Amenities: bar; pasticceria; confetteria
(established in 1817); air conditioning
Atmosphere: ideal for a quick carpano
Clientèle: cosmopolitan; VIPs, and hangers-on from the Bahamas to Biarritz
Service: very Milanese
Credit cards: not accepted

Nightclub

NEPENTHA
1 Piazza A. Diaz
Telephone: 80 48 37/87 36 52
Affiliations: Club of Clubs
Owner/Manager: Carlo Gattoni
Closed: Sunday; August
Open: 21.00/9 p.m.–3.00/a.m.
Location: central
Setting: new décor à la Michael Folon replaces overworked Rousseau-style
Amenities: dining club; air condition
Atmosphere: an oasis of beauty, youth, elegance and good living
Clientèle: jeunesse dorée – affluent
Dress: Armani and Co.
Service: friendly
Reservations: advisable for dining
Credit cards: AE

Nightclub

CHARLYMAX
2 Via Marconi
Telephone: 87 14 16
Owner/Manager: Ugo Cristina
Closed: Sunday; August
Open: 21.00/9.00 p.m. – dawn
Location: a champagne cork's trajectory
away from the Cathedral Square
Setting: sophisticated bar-restaurant
Amenities: discothèque (good music)
Atmosphere: the brightest star in the nocturnal firmament in this part of town
Clientèle: high-born, youthful, witty
Dress: fairly conservative to rather kinky
Service: slick
Reservations: advisable
Credit cards: AE, DC, BA

Shopping

EVERYTHING UNDER ONE ROOF
Rinascente
Galleria Vittorio Emanuele II

FOR HIM
Larusmiani   43 Via Manzoni

FOR HER
Ferré   11 Via della Spiga

BEAUTY & HAIR
Rolando   31 Via Manzoni
Cappola   25 Via Manzoni

JEWELLERY
Calderoni   8 Via Montenapoleone

LOCAL SPECIALITIES
Smart Lady   (women's fashion)
42 Via della Spiga
Riccardo Prisco (women's fashion)
Via Orefici
Tincati (men's fashion)
2 Piazzale Oberdan
Bardelli (men & women's fashion)
13 Corso Magenta
Pasini (children's fashion)
46 Via Manzoni
Marilena Cervo (furs)
19 Via Bigli, 1st floor
Tabak Pellicce (furs and leather)
4 Via Bigli
Cavour Libreria Internazionale (books)
1 Piazza Cavour
Napoleon (baggage & travel accessories)
25 Via Montenapoleone
De Padova (interior decorating)
14 Corso Venezia
Mobilia (bathroom accessories)
30 Via Manzoni
Il Salumaio di Montenapoleone (food and
beverages)
12 Via Montenapoleone
Cantarelli (perfumery)
Via Manzoni/Via Montenapoleone
Baratti (perfumery and beauty treatment)
46 Via Manzoni
Noé (toys)
40 Via Manzoni
Fiumi – Orologiaio in Milano dal 1867
(horlogerie, clocks, watches)
39 Via Manzoni
Guido Pasquali (shoes)
1 Via Sant Andrea & 6 Via Gèsu
Diego della Valle (shoes for men)
22 Via della Spiga

THE BEST OF ART
Blu, Dr. Giuseppe Palazzoli (contemporary art) 18 Via Senato, Tel. 79 24 04
Marconi   (contemporary art)
15 Via Tadino, Tel. 22 55 43
Naviglio   (modern art)
45 Via Manzoni, Tel. 6 55 15 38
Stein   (contemporary art)
15 Via Lazzeretto, Tel. 6 70 47 54
Studio d'Arte Cannaviello   (contemporary art) 10/7 Via Cusani, Tel. 80 79 91
Toselli, Franco   (contemporary art)
9 Via del Carmine, Tel. 8 05 04 34
Longari, Nella   (18th-century works of
art, furniture, Old Master paintings)
15 Via Bigli, Tel. 79 42 87/78 03 22

The City

›The Queen of Sirens‹ is justly famed for her elemental beauty – for the disposition at the foot of magic mountain Vesuvius, the embracing bay of azure waters, the caressing air of eternal Sole Mio and the fiery nature of La Bella Italia's most passionate people – best embodied by local daughter Sophia Loren. Almost three thousand years of history have left their mark – waxing empires and waning fortunes, foreign powers and local disasters. The arc of the coastline stretches from Ischia, the Emerald Isle, to Capri, the Island of Dreams, and round the Punta della Campanella to the orange groves and rocky inlets of the Amalfi Coast, from Positano to Salerno. No wonder the area was the favourite winter resort of Augustus, Tiberius, Nero, Virgil and Horace, who indulged here in orgies of bacchanalia or balladry, and the live stage for Eduardo de Filippo's dramatic comedies as well as for Curzio Malaparte's *Skin*. The classical past, miraculously excavated for posterity from the volcanic lava at Pompeii and Herculaneum, merely provides the backdrop for Naples' development, via Spanish and French colonization and the Kingdom of the Two Sicilies, to its present position as the third largest city in Italy, an important industrial centre and port with oil refining, chemicals, glass, rubber and engineering (from aircraft to typewriters). The monuments to the city's venerable past remain in the forbidding Castel Nuovo fortress and the gracious sixteenth- and seventeenth-century palazzi around the Piazza del Plebiscito, which once enchanted the Grand Tourists from the Marquis de Sade to Goethe. Now they provide an anachronistic background for a melting-pot of peoples and cultures, aristocrats and proletarians, world citizens and local peasants, insiders and outsiders, cartels and Camorra. Local son and musical maestro Riccardo Muti is fêted as much as adopted son, football star Diego Maradona. Naples seems about to be engulfed in an apocalypse of the uncivilizing results of civilization, and yet – crumbling monuments and traffic chaos notwithstanding – it is perhaps the only metropolis on earth where earthquakes, man-made pandemonium and sheer neglect enhance the chiaroscuro effect of the teeming vitality in the streets. Here family loyalties – especially to ›Mamma‹, native wit and an innate instinct for survival are characterized by Pulcinella, the local harlequin, for this is the ›permanent playhouse of Italy‹.

Founded: 8th–7th century, B.C. – as a Greek colony; Napoli (Italian) – ›new city‹ (from the Greek).

Far-reaching events: 326 – links with Rome, under Greek constitution; 89 – becomes a Roman city; 553 A.D. – Byzantine Emperor Justinian conquers the city; 7th century – under ducal rule, successful resistance against Langobards, Saracens and Normans; 1139 – Normans take the city under Roger II; 1224 – Friedrich II founds university; 1265 – Charles I of Anjou; 1442 – Alfonso I of Aragon conquers Naples; 1501–1713 – Spanish rule; 1656 – plague kills 60% of the population; 1713 – Treaty of Utrecht, Naples becomes Austrian; 1735 – to Spanish Bourbons, centre of Reformation; 1806–15 – French rule under Joseph Bonaparte and Joachim Murat; 1815 – under Bourbon rule again; 1860 – joins united Kingdom of Italy; 1904 & 1950 – special laws for the support of Naples; 1980 – earthquake.

Population: 1.3 million; capital of Campania, 3rd largest city in Italy.

Postal code: I–80100   **Telephone code:** 81

Climate: typically Mediterranean hot summers and mild winters; dry, sandy Sahara winds (the sirocco) in spring and autumn.

Calendar of events: *Festival of St. Gennaro* (1st Sun in May & 19 Sep) – sumptuous religious festival in honour of the martyr; *Festival of Our Lady of Songs* (15 Jul); *Festival of Piedigrotto* (8 Sep) – barefoot procession to Madonna dell'Arco; *Neapolitan Song Festival* (Sep) – bel canto at its best.

Fairs and exhibitions: *EXPOSUDHOTEL* (Feb) – international exhibition of hotel, tourist and licensed trade equipment; *NAUTICSUD* (Mar) – international nautical exhibition; *BI-MI-SUD* (Apr) – biennial machine tool exhibition; *EXPO-SPORT* and *VACANZA* (Apr/May) – sports and recreation exhibition; *SALON INTERNAZIONALE DELL'OROLOGERIA* (May) – watches and jewellery; *SIR* (May) – international show of gift articles, silverware, glass and ceramics; *INTERNATIONAL HOUSING FAIR* (May); *FIERA INTERNAZIONALE DELLA CASA* (Jul) – international house and garden fair; *TECNOMESU* (Sep) – trade fair for machinery, equipment and leather for shoe production; *SUDPEL* (Sep) – leather goods exhibition; *OPTICA* (Nov) – international optics fair.

Historical and modern sights: *New Castle* (1279–82) – former residence of the Anjou and Aragon rulers, the city's landmark; *St. Gennaro's Cathedral* (14th century) – Gothic, with *St. Restituta*, Naples' oldest basilica and *Baptisterium* where St. Gennaro's blood is preserved; *Castle dell'Ovo* (1st century) – Lucullus' villa, a fortress since Norman times; *Catacombs* – under St. Gandioso and St. Gennaro; *Pompeii* and *Herculaneum* – buried Roman cities; *Capri* – the Isle of Dreams.

Special attractions: a slow boat to *Capri*; a night at *Santa Lucia*; a season at *Positano's San Pietro;* a *football game* with Maradona; an authentic *pizza*.

Important companies with headquarters in the city: *Aeritalia* (aircraft); *Aerotransporti Italiai* (transport); *Alfasud* (cars); *Caremar* (shipping); *Olivetti* (business machines); *Olio Rocco* (olive oil); *Tramontano* (leather).

Airport: Naples-Capodichino, NAP; Tel.: 31 22 00, Alitalia, Tel.: 32 53 25, 8 km/4 miles.

The Headquarters

EXCELSIOR

48 Via Partenope
I–80121 Naples
Telephone: 41 71 11
Telex: 71 00 43 excena
Owning Company: Cigahotels
General Manager: Giuliano Corsi
Affiliation/Reservation System: Hello-ciga
Number of rooms: 139
Price range: Lit. 145,000–750,000
Credit cards: AE, DC, BA, Visa
Location: on the Bay of Santa Lucia
Built: 1909
Style: neo-classic
Hotel amenities: parking, beauty salon, safe deposit boxes, sauna, massage (pets allowed)
Room amenities: colour television, radio, mini-bar, air conditioning
Bathroom amenities: hairdrier, bidet, bathrobe on request
Room service: 7.00/a.m.–23.00/11.00 p.m.
Laundry/dry cleaning: same day
Conference rooms: 4 (up to 300 persons), photocopies, interpreters
Casanova Bar: (21.00/9.00 p.m.–1.00/a.m.)
Restaurant: ›Casanova Grill‹: (12.00/p.m.–15.00/3.00 p.m.; 19.00/7.00 p.m.–23.30/11.30 p.m.), Neapolitan specialities
Private dining rooms: up to 20 persons

If you really want to follow the misinterpreted motto ›See Naples and die‹, do it in style – at the Excelsior. Across from Santa Lucia and Castel dell'Ovo, that fortress harbour where countless romances were struck up between American tourists, with a panoramic view of Vesuvio, the Amalfi Coast and Capri (if you're lucky) and embedded in the Aga Khan's Cigahotels group – standing for classic traditions and modern efficiency – the Excelsior is the classiest framework one could die in. Much rather live, for that matter. Life is extremely lively at this seaside residence, and the lapping of the waves is not the only music heard throughout the day. Private lunches, grand receptions and large conferences are held at the Excelsior regularly, and all the dignitaries, stars and luxury tourists stop over here, for business and pleasure. At the small driveway you will be received with that winsomeness you will remember from Marcello Mastroianni films, and the amiable service doesn't stop there. The rooms are large, high-ceilinged and air-conditioned, have an original mixture of interior styles, and most of them that precious view over the ›egg-castle‹ and into the most beautiful sunsets you can imagine. There is hardly need to go across to one of the various restaurants built on piles around the ›borgo marinaro‹, because the food in the Casanova Grill *outdoes them all. Here, at last, you will think about the good life, better times and the excellent Excelsior.*

The Hideaway

SAN PIETRO

2 Via Laurito
I–84017 Positano (60 km/38 miles)
Telephone: 87 54 55/87 54 54
Telex: 770 072 hsp
Owner: Salvatore Attanasio e Co.
General Manager: Salvatore Attanasio
Number of rooms: 60 (11 suites)
Price range: Lit. 160,000–900,000
Credit cards: all major
Location: 67 km/42 miles from airport
Built: 1970
Style: Mediterranean
Hotel amenities: valet parking; limousine service, solarium, newsstand, tobacconist, swimming pool, tennis court (pets allowed)
Room amenities: colour tv, mini-bar/refrigerator
Bathroom amenities: bidet, bathrobe, hairdrier
Room service: 24 hours
Laundry/dry cleaning: same day
Conference rooms: 1 (up to 50 persons)
Bar: (8.00 a.m. to 24.00/12 p.m.)
Restaurant: (13.00/1. p.m. to 14.30/2.30 p.m. and 20.00/8. p.m. to 21.30/9.30 p.m.) Amendola (maître), De Lucia(chef de cuisine), pianist, open-air dining
Private dining rooms: two

The patron saint could very well hold the keys to this Xanadu on the Costiera Amalfitana nestling on a rocky promontory just outside Positano. The name derives from the eighth-century chapel on top of the hill, however, but San Pietro is the gate to paradise for aesthetes, eccentrics and bon-vivants, ever since bel-esprit Carlo Cinque realized his fantasy which has become the dreamland of his guests-cum-friends. Carlino is no more, sad to say, but his spirit lives on in this terraced labyrinth of natural beauty and interior-design delirium. Many styles mix with the Mediterranean flair; floral-tile benches and marble baths blend with gilded wooden headboards and torch-holding statues; wintergarden salons extend some of the rooms whereas every bedchamber commands the extensive panorama of Positano or Praiano. Plants and flowers everywhere, Old Masters and antiques galore, accessoires and decorative paraphernalia as for a mythopoetical party – and the whole show run by Carlino's nephew and niece Salvatore and Virginia Attanasio like a grand little club, welcoming stars incognito and unknowns arriving by private yacht. You can take the lift from the hall through the mountain to the platform-beach for a lazy day or boating and water-skiing; you can also play tennis in this latter-day Semiramis; best of all is still complete immotion absorbing the scented air, viewing the sea and Positano and only coming to life at lunchtime and dinner. Werther disciples are warned not to jump across the balustrade for Weltschmerz after a romantic evening at San Pietro.

Lunch

LA CANTINELLA
42 Via Cuma
Telephone: 40 48 84
Owner/Manager: Giorgio Rosolino
Closed: Sunday; August
Open: 12.00/a.m.–15.00/3 p.m. and
19.00/7 p.m.–24.00/12 p.m.
Cuisine: local, classic and international
Chefs de cuisine: Bruno Salvatore and
Bruno Aldo
Specialities: noodles (linguine) with
scampi and seafood; seafood risotto;
penne (pasta) alla Cantinella; grilled
fish; steak Châteaubriand
Location: just off the seafront; near most
of the main hotels
Setting: dining room furnished in elegan-
tized rustic style
Amenities: air conditioning
Atmosphere: understated elegance, yet
warm and welcoming
Clientèle: heterogeneous; Campania's
In-Crowd, local Haute Bourgeoisie leav-
ened by a liberal sprinkling of artists, wri-
ters and political journalists
Dress: elegantly casual
Service: attentive
Reservations: advisable
Price range: fairly expensive
Credit cards: AE, DC, Visa

Lunch

GIUSEPPONE A MARE
13 Via Ferdinando Russo, Capo Posillipo
Telephone: 7 69 60 02
Owner/Manager: Mario Della Notte
Closed: Sunday; between Christmas and
New Year
Open: 12.30/a.m.–15.30/3.30 p.m. and
19.30/7.30 p.m.–23.30/11.30 p.m.
Cuisine: local; seafood
Chef de cuisine: Giacomo Trani
Specialities: prawn cocktail; fish; shell-
fish; linguine (pasta) ›Riva Fiorita‹;
squid ›alla pignatiello‹; charcoal-grilled
fish of all shapes and sizes
Location: Capo Posillipo
Setting: by the sea; large restaurant with
characteristic décor and a panoramic
view of Sorrento, Mount Vesuvius and
the Mediterranean
Amenities: outdoor dining on shady ter-
race; car park
Atmosphere: rather commercialized but
still chic and very popular
Clientèle: Campania's In-Crowd; local
businessmen; a certain number of Eu-
rope-at-the-double tourists
Dress: casual but not careless
Service: sometimes a little on the slow
side, especially at busy times
Reservations: advisable (no dogs)
Price range: medium
Credit cards: AE, DC, Euro, Visa

Dinner

IL GALLO NERO
466 Via Tasso
Telephone: 64 30 12
Owner/Managers: Gianpaolo and An-
gela Fortini
Closed: lunchtime (except Sunday); Sun-
day evening; Monday; August
Open: 18.00 p.m.–23.30/11.30 p.m.
Cuisine: local and imaginative
Chefs de cuisine: Angela Fortini, Anna
Gorgone and Giancarlo Schettini
Specialities: according to season; shellfish pâté; insalata alla pirata; noodles
(linguine) with scampi; green noodles
with brains ragoût; charcoal-grilled fish;
kebabs; fillet steak with red wine; orange
pudding
Location: above the Golf of Naples
Setting: a patrician villa; fin-de-siècle
grandeur, with white colonnade; inside,
small salons and elegant dining room
with period furnishings
Amenities: open-air dining on garden terrace overlooking the Bay of Naples; car
park
Atmosphere: welcoming; aristocratic; not
a little romantic
Clientèle: discerning; discriminating; local expense-account gourmets and visiting industrialists with a penchant for the
finer things in life
Dress: no special requirements
Service: distinguished
Reservations: yes, please!
Price range: moderately expensive
Credit cards: AE, Visa

Dinner

HARRY'S BAR
11 Via Lucilio
Telephone: 40 78 10
Owner/Manager: Vincenzo Esposito
Closed: Sunday; August
Open: 18.00/6 p.m.–1/a.m.
Cuisine: international and national
Chef de cuisine: Ciro Montella
Specialities: ›Risotto al Caviale‹ (rice
with caviar); fish in all guises
Location: near the Headquarters
Setting: small dining room
Amenities: air conditioning; piano bar;
capacity: 50 seats
Atmosphere: stylish but welcoming
Clientèle: local crème de la crème
Dress: elegant
Service: excellent
Reservations: essential (no dogs)
Price range: medium
Credit cards: AE

Lunch

LA SACRESTIA
116 Via Orazio
Telephone: 66 41 86
Owner/Managers: Arnaldo and Marco Ponsiglione
Closed: Wednesday; July
Open: 12.30/p.m. – the last customer has left
Cuisine: local
Chef de cuisine: Michele Verrina
Specialities: croûtons with salmon; sardines with lemon; oyster salad; risotto ›1001 Nights‹; timbale ›alla cardinale‹; swordfish rolls in sauce; fillet steak with curry; rum baba; profiteroles with chocolate sauce
Location: near the harbour of Nergelline; where the streamers to Capri and Ischia are moored
Setting: on a hill overlooking the Bay of Naples; large, stylishly-furnished dining room with a spacious garden for outdoor dining in summer
Amenities: air conditioning
Atmosphere: Neapolitan sophisticated
Clientèle: local Haute Bougeoisie en fête and en famille, plus fair numbers of foreign visitors from Fort Worth to Fremantle
Dress: fairly formal
Service: knowledgeable and helpful
Reservations: preferable
Price range: moderately expensive
Credit cards: AE, Carte Bleue

Dinner

ROSOLINO
5–7 Via N. Sauro
Telephone: 41 58 73
Owner/Manager: Antonio and Giorgio Rosolino
Closed: Sunday; August
Open: 12.00/a.m.–15.00/3 p.m. and 19.00/7 p.m.–24.00/12 p.m.
Cuisine: local; classic; international
Chef de cuisine: Italo Postiglione
Specialities: rigatoni ›Rosolino‹; maccheroncelli ›maison‹; seafood risotto; steak ›Châteaubriand‹; veal chop ›Caruso‹; fish en papillote; soufflés
Location: near the Headquarters
Setting: newly-established restaurant on the sea front; attractive 1950s décor
Amenities: piano bar; video; discothèque; air conditioning
Atmosphere: friendly and chic
Clientèle: increasingly popular meeting place for Neapolitan politicians, businessmen and men-about-town
Dress: way-out to way-in; anything goes
Service: high-class
Reservations: advisable
Price range: fairly expensive
Credit cards: AE, DC, Visa

Café

GAMBRINUS
1–2 Via Ghiaia
Telephone: 41 75 82
Owner/Manager: Arturo Sergio
Closed: Tuesday
Open: 6.00/ a.m.–1.00/a.m.
Specialities: apéritifs; the most famous gâteaux and pâtisseries in Naples
Location: close to the Palazzo Prefettura and the ›San Carlo‹ theatre
Setting: 3 salons for up to 70 guests, all decorated with 18th-century frescoes
Amenities: garden terrace
Atmosphere: very elegant and rather intellectual – Naples' oldest traditional café
Clientèle: artists, noblemen with their noble ladies and a handful of foreigners
Service: Italianissimo

Meeting Point

HAPPY ROCK
51 Via Bausan
Telephone: 41 17 12
Owner/Manager: Giuseppe de Simone
Closed: Tuesday; July 15th – September 1st
Open: 19.00/7.00 p.m.–1.00/a.m.
Location: central
Setting: bar-restaurant on two floors; black tables; red-gold walls with strategically-placed mirrors and 30s-style pictures
Amenities: restaurant serving international dishes and very good ice-cream
Atmosphere: young; cheerful; à la mode
Clientèle: youthful; self-assured and on-the-way up to middle-aged, successful and definitely not moribund
Service: friendly
Reservations: advisable
Credit cards: AE, BA

Bar

VERDI
23 Via G. Verdi
Telephone: 32 08 36
Owner/Manager: Carlo Compagnone
Closed: Sunday
Open: 19.30/7.30 p.m.–1.30/a.m.
Location: next to the Palazzo San Giacomo
Setting: on 3 levels; 17th-century building
Amenities: air conditioning; car park; piano bar; tea room
Atmosphere: elegant, romantic
Clientèle: select
Dress: elegant
Credit cards: AE, DC

Shopping

EVERYTHING UNDER ONE ROOF
Rinascente   340 Via Roma

FOR HIM
I. H. Cose da Maschi   62 Via Chiaia

FOR HER
Carrano   40 Via Bellini

BEAUTY & HAIR
Antoine Coiffeur   132 Via Chiaia

JEWELLERY
Antica Gioielleria Gallotta
139 Via Chiaia and 251 Via Toledo

LOCAL SPECIALITIES
Coppola (women's fashion)
114 Via Scarlatti
Coppola (men's fashion)
114 Via Scarlatti
Harnald (men and women's fashion)
10 Galleria Vanvitelli
Siola (children's fashion)
111/115 Via Chiaia
Pepe (furs)
3 Vico d'Afflitto and 189 Via Chiaia
De Simone (books)
30/31 Via B. Croce
Frezzetti (gifts)
76 Via Scarlatti
La Cappelli (gifts)
146 Via Chiaia
›Porcellane e Vetri antichi‹
(Guiseppe Giolio) (porcelain)
Via Carlo Poerio
Tramontano Marietta (baggage & travel
accessories)
149E Via Chiaia (Palazzo Cellamare)
Studio Riviera (interior decorating)
(La Cappelli S.P.A.)
64 Via Dei Mille
Idrosanitaria di Mosca (bathroom acces-
sories)
Via Nuova & 161 Poggio Reale
La Botteghina (food and beverages)
1 and 4 Via Orazio
Pepino (perfumery)
352 Via Toledo and 223 Via Chiaia
Enoteca Partenopea (wines)
2 Viale Augusto
Scaturchio (café and sweets)
19 Piazza San Domenico Maggiore
Bottega artigiana del libro e
della carta (books and hand-made paper)
4 Calata Trinità Maggiore
Maria Martin (shoes)
157/8/9 Via Roma
Pempinello e d'Arcangeli (shoes)
Via Chiaia

THE BEST OF ART
Amelio, Lucio   (contemporary art)
58 Piazza dei Martiri, Tel. 42 20 23
Rumma, Lia   (contemporary art)
12 Via Vannella Gaetano,
Tel. 39 93 39
Trisorio   (contemporary art)
215 Riviera di Chiaia,
Tel. 41 43 06

The City

Timbuktu to the Milanese. Cradle of an exaggerated, overestimated and possibly apocryphal coterie to the world at large. La Terra Santa to Sicilians the world over. The deformed football at the toe of Italy's boot is still shrouded in a cloak of mystery, even though nowadays Alitalia will whisk you there in minutes from most mainland cities. Its geographical remoteness has made Sicily a treasure chest of archaeological relics left behind by a succession of aspiring colonial powers. Phoenicians, Romans, Vandals, Byzantines, Greeks, Saracens, Normans, Germans and Spaniards have all considered it a point of honour since time immemorial to try to hold this strategic outpost between Europe and Africa against the next would-be incumbents, enriching the countryside with temples and mosaic-lined villas and world literature with a proliferation of myths. Honour and tradition, fatalism and passion, a sense of the theatrical and a love of la dolce vita alla simplice are the foundation stones of life in Palermo. The provincial capital and largest city, sharing its patroness, Saint Rosalia, with Naples and Nice and challenged only by Catania for economic supremacy, is the market place and port for the products of the agricultural hinterland, the ›Golden Conch Shell‹ – wine, almonds, citrus fruit and cotton. The city was until recently the Cinderella amongst manufacturing centres in Italy; however, in the vanguard of Palermo's recent commercial renaissance are electronics industries and a new atomic research centre. Music plays an important note in la vita alla siciliana; local son Vincenzo Bellini's operas charmed audiences in Paris, whilst Germany's maestro Richard Wagner found in Palermo the way to the Holy Grail for his opera Parsifal. This most southerly of Italy's major cities is also the most typically Latin; the monuments and historic buildings – the Romanesque-Gothic cathedral, the Baroque palazzi and the contemporary concrete shoeboxes – not only recall the turbulent past, but act as a backdrop for the tumultuous present. Much business here is conducted after hours, as the ›violent, impudent‹ sun sinks in the west and the citizens emerge from their midday hibernation. The bars and restaurants by the harbour or surrounding the floodlit ›Four Corners‹, the Piazza Pretoria and the Piazza Bellini, are the stage for encounters more public but no less dramatic than the fabled family gatherings of the Bonannos, the Liggios, the Grecos and the Corleones amongst the Beau Monde at Charleston's. Time takes on a different dimension here than in Milan, as you contemplate the scene from the waterfront palazzo de renommé, the Grand Villa Igiea. It's only a couple of hours by fast Ferrari to the San Domenico Palace, the sybaritic retreat in lovely Taormina, in the shadow of Mount Etna. Here, you can reflect on the enchantment of the island-home of Nobel prize-winner Luigi Pirandello, Salvatore Quasimodo and Gattopardo-author Giuseppe Tomasi di Lampedusa – for whom ›soft Sicily‹ lies in a time capsule, ›cradled by violent dreams‹.

Founded: 9th century B.C. – by the Phoenicians; Palermo – from the Phoenician ›Panormos‹.

Far-reaching events: 3rd century A.D. – city becomes Roman; 6th–9th centuries – ruled in turn by Vandals, Ostrogoths and Byzantines; 9th century – 1072 – under Saracen rule; 11th century – Norman capital under Roger II; 12th century – under the Hohenstaufen kings Henry IV and Frederick II; 1266 – Charles I of Anjou invades, becomes king of Naples and Sicily; 1282 – rebellion (Sicilian Vespers) against French, Sicily becomes Spanish; 13th–17th centuries – Spanish reign; 1860 – annexed by Italy under Garibaldi; 1946 – independent region of Sicily.

Population: 710,000; capital and largest city of Sicily.

Postal code: I–90100   **Telephone code:** 91.

Climate: typical Mediterranean, with hot summers and rainy winters; the sirocco (hot dry wind from North Africa) is occasionally present.

Calendar of events: *St. Rosalia Festival* (mid-Jul) – with processions, street parties and fireworks in honour of the city's patron saint; *International Underwater Meeting* (Jul) – on Ustica; *Giro Aereo di Sicilia* (Jul) – international flying contest; *Pilgrimage* to the statue of St. Rosalia (4 Sep).

Fairs and exhibitions: *INTERNATIONAL MEDITERRANEAN FAIR* (May); *MEDI-VINI* (Oct) – international exhibition market for wine advertising.

Historical sights: *Cathedral* (12th century) – Norman and Gothic, with tombs of Henry IV and Frederick II; *Cathedral of Monreale* (begun in the 12th century) – magnificent columned cloisters and mosaics; *St. John of the Hermits* (1132) – Arab influence, with five domes; *La Martorana* (1143) – Baroque façade, Byzantine mosaics; *Norman Palace* (restored 17th century) – Baroque façade, with *Palatine Chapel* (1130–40), mosaics, now the seat of the Sicilian government; *Piazza Pretoria* – with a fountain by Francesco Camilliani from the 16th century; *Chinese Palace* (18th century) – small but with a lovely garden; *Great Theatre* (18th century) – seating 3,200, one of the largest theatres in the world; *National Gallery* – documenting Sicily's colourful history in paintings and sculptures.

Special attractions: one night at *Villa Igiea* and a weekend at *San Domenico Palace*; lunch, dinner, drinks and coffee at *Charleston*.

Important companies with headquarters in the city: *Migliore* (electrical appliances); *Siremar Regione Marritima* (shipping).

Airport: Palermo-Punta Rais, PMO; Tel.: 59 14 14, Alitalia, Tel.: 58 45 33.

The Headquarters

GRAND HOTEL VILLA IGIEA

43 Salita Belmonte
I–90142 Palermo
Telephone: 54 37 44
Telex: 910092 igieah
Owning Company: Atahotels
General Manager: Antonio Croci
Affiliation/Reservation Systems: Atahotels, Utell International
Number of rooms: 128 (9 suites)
Price range: Lit. 158,000–394,000
Credit cards: AE, DC, MC, Visa
Location: central, from airport
Built: turn-of-the-century
Style: Art Nouveau
Hotel amenities: valet parking, house limousine service, swimming pool, tennis court

Main hall porter: Napolitano Spadafora
Room service: 7.00/a.m.–23.00/11 p.m.
Conference rooms: 4 (up to 400 persons)
Bars: ›La Terrazza‹ (21.00/9.00 p.m.–2.00/a.m.); ›Arcade‹ (21.00/9.00 p.m.–2.00/a.m.) Crisci (barman), pianist
Restaurants: ›Villa Igiea‹ (12.30/p.m.–15.30/3.30 p.m.) Catalano (maître), Sorrentino (chef de cuisine), pianist, Art Nouveau style; ›La Terrazza Mare‹ (19.30/7.30 p.m.–23.30/11.30 p.m.) Agro (maître), Sorrentino (chef de cuisine), open-air dining, pianist, Liberty style

Gabriele D'Annunzio, forever obsessed by beauty and grandeur, loved the seaside palazzo also for its creative tranquillity, its fin-de-siècle capriccio, its luxuriant park and the mellow mood pervading this erstwhile lovers' tryst where an English nobleman and a Sicilian Cinderella re-enacted a Romeo-Juliet romance. King Constantine of Greece, grandfather of the émigré sovereign, even died here, but most lovers and kings come to live in this mild air and sensual ambiance. Planned by former magnate-maecenas Ignazio Florio and his architect Basile as a clinic, the guests leave this fashionable resort as if they had undergone the therapy of the nearby sacred spa of the Acquasanta springs. Perfect as the headquarters for business in Palermo – and all the meetings, conferences and invitations – Villa Igiea is the ideal sanatorium de luxe as well, complete with a seawater swimming pool next to an Ionic gazebo and a tennis court amidst pine and palm trees. Single rooms have the spaciousness of a suite, bathrooms are Roman in dimension, and cupboards and desks are made for long stays and lots of luggage. But even if you come just for the Massimo Opera festival – sharing the house with all the primadonnas and tenor idols – or the mosaics of Monreale, there is no other place in Palermo worth staying at. The cuisine is in line with the graciousness of the hotel, the little nightclub swings alla siciliana and the starry sky over the Terrazza Bar will evoke memories of D'Annunzio's – and your own – Piacere.

The Hideaway

SAN DOMENICO PALACE

5 Piazza San Domenico
I–98039 Taormina (260 km/162 miles)
Telephone: (942) 237 01
Telex: 980 013 domhot
Owning Company: Atahotels S.p.a.
General Manager: Stefano Bàccara
Number of rooms: 117 (10 suites)
Price range: Lit. 145,000–304,000
Credit cards: AE, DC, Visa
Location: in Taormina, 60 km/38 miles
from Catania airport
Built: 1430
Style: former monastery; antique style
Hotel amenities: garage, valet parking,
house limousine service, swimming pool
Main hall porter: Mr. Lo Re
Room service: 7.00/a.m–23.00/11 p.m.
Conference rooms: 6 (up to 500 persons)
Bar: (10.00 a.m.–24.00/12 p.m.) Mr. Ar-
rigo (barman); antique style décor
Restaurants: ›Bougainville‹ (8.00 a.m.–
22.00/10 p.m.); Mr. Bereti (maître); Mr.
Caco Pardo (chef de cuisine), pianist, or-
chestra; ›Mosé‹ (12.30/p.m.–14.30/2.30
p.m.; closed in winter) ›Grill‹ (19.30/7.30
p.m.–21.00/9.00 p.m.), open-air dining

*The Dominican friars who in 1430 selected
the hilltop above Taormina Bay for their
convent displayed an unerring sense of the
dramatic and the beautiful. Perched between Mount Etna and the sea amidst a
riot of hibiscus and orange blossom, these
finely-proportioned Renaissance-style
buildings house the Sicilian hideaway par
excellence. There is nothing ascetic about
the San Domenico Palace, although traces
of its ecclesiastical origins remain; the
modern conference centre was once a
ruined chapel, and the monks' cells have
been converted into bedrooms whose bou-
gainvillea-framed windows overlook the
sub-tropical gardens. The lovely vaulted
cloister gallery is lined with ancient choir
stalls, whilst an ornately carved altar
serves as counter in the bar where, at night,
can be heard the romantically nostalgic
strains of the guitar. From pillared hall to
spacious lounge, this erstwhile monastery
has a distinctly palatial air, enhanced by
the valuable carpets, the antique tapestries
and the Oriental vases. The unadorned
white walls of the bedrooms evoke the cloistered cells of yesteryear whilst acting as a
foil for the wrought-iron bedsteads and the
chinoiseries of the chests of drawers. In its
heyday as a winter resort the San Domenico was frequented by crowned heads
(Kaiser Wilhelm II, King Edward VII),
celebrated men of letters (Luigi Pirandello,
John Steinbeck) and international film-
stars (Marlene Dietrich, Sophia Loren).
Nowadays the unique ambiente of this
bastion of la Belle Epoque attracts unashamed romantics and individual travellers who come to savour, on the creeper
-clad terrace overlooking the Ionian Sea,
the hotel's unique blend of meditative spir-
ituality and joyful worldliness.*

Lunch

L'APPRODO-RENATO
28 Messina Marine
Telephone: 47 01 03
Owner/Manager: Gianrodolfo Botto
Closed: Wednesday
Open: 12.30 p.m.–15.00/3 p.m. and
20.00/8 p.m.–23.00/11 p.m.
Cuisine: local and international, with a
hint of ›Nouvelle‹
Chef de cuisine: Francesca Botto
Specialities: ›good mood‹ spaghetti (del
buon umore); fettucine verdi con fanta-
sia; fish soup; fish in white sauce; grilled
meats; roast kid with potatoes; beef
olives; excellent wine list
Location: in the harbour area
Setting: sea view; comfortable, stylishly-
furnished dining room with antique accessoires; wood panelling; fine china,
glass and silver
Amenities: private dining rooms (70–80
persons); open-air dining on terrace; car
park
Atmosphere: a temple of the Sicilian culinary arts
Clientèle: expense-account gourmets, executives and Sicily's social élite
Dress: conservatively elegant to elegantly
conservative
Service: smooth; knowledgeably directed
by Gianrodolfo Botto, assisted by Con-
stanzo Cosmo and Rizzo Marcello
Reservations: recommended (essential for
Friday and Saturday night)
Price range: moderately expensive
Credit cards: not accepted yet (DC in fu-
ture)

Lunch

CHARLESTON
30 Piazzale Ungheria
Telephone: 32 13 66
Owner/Manager: Angelo Ingrao
Closed: Sunday; June 10th–September
30th
Open: 12.00/p.m.–15.30/3.30 p.m. and
20.30/8.30 p.m.–24.00/12 p.m.
Cuisine: international, national and local
Chef de cuisine: Antonino Tantillo
Specialities: aubergines ›Charleston‹;
cannelloni ›alla favorita‹ (with artichokes, beans and black pepper); noodles with anchovies; crayfish risotto; fish
(spit-roasted, grilled or lightly gratinéed)
garden-fresh vegetables; almond parfait
with hot chocolate; excellent desserts
from Pasticceria Mazzaro, where di
Lampedusa wrote ›The Leopard‹
Location: in the business centre of Palermo
Setting: large restaurant furnished in Lib-
erty/Art Déco style
Amenities: pianist; air conditioning; replaced during summer months by Char-

leston le Terrazze in Mondello, 12 km (7
miles) from Palermo
Atmosphere: Sicilian sophistication with
a hint of the cosmopolitan
Clientèle: discriminating; local dignita-
ries and jet-set birds of passage
Dress: what you will
Service: charmingly reliable and friendly
Reservations: advisable
Price range: moderately expensive
Credit cards: AE, DC, Euro, Visa

Dinner

LA BOTTE
186 Strada Statale
Monreale (7 km/4 miles)
Telephone: 41 40 51
Owner/Manager: Giuseppa Priulla
Closed: Monday; August; September
Open: 12.30/p.m.–15.00/3.00 p.m. and
20.00/8.00 p.m.–23.00/11.00 p.m.
Cuisine: local
Chef de cuisine: Salvatore Cascino
Specialities: spaghetti with tuna fish, cap-
ers, olives, tomatoes and white wine;
spaghetti with herbs and spices (alla ca-
pricciosa); grilled fish; venison
Location: 7 km (4 miles) from Palermo
Setting: typical Sicilian restaurant; din-
ing room furnished in elegantized rustic
style; well-spaced tables, open fireplace
and domestic bric-à-brac
Amenities: open-air dining on terrace;
car park
Atmosphere: a stronghold of Sicilian culture and culinary traditions; intimate,
with a hint of romance
Clientèle: local connoisseurs and discriminating but footsore tourists usually in
equal numbers
Dress: casual but not untidy or outlandish
Service: discreet
Reservations: advisable to essential
Price range: medium
Credit cards: AE

Dinner

LE GOURMAND'S
37 Via della Libertà
Telephone: 32 34 31
Owner/Managers: Rosario Guddo and
Antonino Ferro
Closed: Sunday; ten days in August
Open: 9.30/a.m.–15.30/3.30 p.m. and
19.30/7.30 a.m.–23.30/11.30 p.m.
Cuisine: local
Chef de cuisine: Rosario Guddo
Specialities: grilled fish kebabs; pasta
with herb sauces; meat croquettes; char-
coal-grilled rolls of swordfish; mille-
feuille with oranges; dessert ›aly pachà‹
Setting: on an elegant tree-lined avenue;
comfortable modern décor with salmon-
pink walls

Amenities: air conditioning; car park in the vicinity
Atmosphere: Sicilian chic, with just a hint of snob-appeal
Clientèle: Palermo's Beau Monde; top industrialists; financiers, politicians and government officials
Dress: rather elegant
Service: irreproachable; directed by Antonino Ferro
Reservations: advisable
Price range: moderate
Credit cards: AE, DC, Euro, Visa

Lunch

CHARLESTON LE TERRAZZE
Viale Principe Scalea
Mondello (11 km/7 miles)
Telephone: 45 01 71
Owner/Manager: Angelo Ingrao
Closed: October 1st–June 10th
Open: 12.30/p.m.–15.30/3.30 p.m. and 20.30/8.30 p.m.–24.00/12 p.m.
Cuisine: international, national and local
Chef de cuisine: Antonino Tantillo
Specialities: risotto with basil; salad of sardelles with oranges; spaghetti cooked in seawater; charcoal-grilled swordfish rolls; braised squid; almond parfait with hot chocolate; home-made ice-cream; iced melon flan
Location: at Mondello, 11 km (7 miles) from Palermo
Setting: on the esplanade at Mondello; incomparable sea views; Belle Epoque villa evocative of Mondello's past fame as a seaside resort frequented by the high and mighty of Europe; Liberty style décor
Amenities: pianist (evenings); shady terrace for al fresco dining
Atmosphere: nostalgic and yet légère and fashionable; ›Charleston‹ in holiday mood
Clientèle: Palermo's Beau Monde, anxious not to miss out on Antonino Tantillo's cuisine during the summer recess
Dress: as you like it – as long as they will like you
Service: under the impeccable guidance of Carlo Assan, one of the best and most famous maîtres d'hôtel in the world
Reservations: advisable (no dogs)
Price range: fairly expensive
Credit cards: AE, DC, Euro, Visa

Dinner

LA SCUDERIA
9 Viale del Fante
Telephone: 52 03 23
Owner/Manager: Giuseppe Stancampiano
Closed: Sunday evening
Open: 12.00/a.m. – until the last guest has left and 20.00/8 p.m. – ditto
Cuisine: local

Chef de cuisine: Franco Lo Verso
Specialities: seafood salad with American sauce; noodles (magliette) messinesi; fettucine ›Blue Sea‹; mixed grill; perch rolls ›Neptune‹; flan with noodles (bucatini); partridge ›all'erotica‹ (in season); sorbet ›Sicilian Sun‹
Location: in the La Favorita Park
Setting: amidst fountains and luxuriant foliage; spacious dining room with expensive modern décor
Amenities: outdoor dining on large terrace with flowers in profusion; attended car park
Atmosphere: à la mode; exuberant and enthusiatic
Clientèle: fashionable; horse-loving; extrovert and yet elegant
Dress: elegantly expensive
Service: remarkable
Reservations: not necessary
Price range: rather expensive
Credit cards: AE, DC, Carte Bleue

Dinner

FRIEND'S BAR RESTAURANT
138 Via Filippo Brunelleschi
Borgo Nuovo (5 km/3 miles)
Telephone: 20 14 01
Owner/Manager: Friend's Bar SRL/Antonino Reginella
Closed: Monday; August
Open: 13.00/1 p.m.–15.00/3 p.m. and 20.30/8.30 p.m.–24.00/12 p.m.
Cuisine: Mediterranean and ›alternative‹
Chefs de cuisine: Salvatore Alterno and Croce Tortorici
Specialities: risottino ›Sicilia‹; rigatoni concimati; king prawns with orange; squid au gratin; cutlets with almonds or olives; coffee and orange jelly; coconut ice-cream
Location: in the suburb of Borgo Nuovo, 5 km (3 miles) from city centre
Setting: English-style decor inside, with a gazebo in front of the main entrance for open-air dining
Amenities: air conditioning
Atmosphere: refreshing, harmonious and intimate
Clientèle: le Tout-Palermo; chic, enthusiastic and modish
Dress: classic
Service: knowledgeable and welcoming
Reservations: advisable
Price range: average
Credit cards: AE, DC

Café

MAZZARA
15 Via Generale Magliocco
Telephone: 32 13 66
Closed: Sunday
Open: 12.00/a.m.–15.00/3 p.m. and 20.00/8 p.m.–24.00/12 p.m.

Specialities: the best whipped cream in town
Location: next to the Massimo Theatre
Setting: historic coffee-house with period furnishings
Amenities: dispatch service at Christmas and Easter for sending gift parcels of local wines to absent friends
Atmosphere: a place to see and be seen in; the most famous café in Palermo
Clientèle: local celebrities and visiting personalities since the days when di Lampedusa was wont to visit the café whilst working on his novel ›The Leopard‹ (Il Gattopardo)
Service: unhurried but efficient

Meeting Point

CAFÉ
7 Via Parisi
Telephone: 32 80 54
Owner/Manager: Pietro Carrubba
Closed: Wednesday
Open: 8.00/a.m.–24.00/12 p.m.
Location: in the centre; near the Piazza Politeama
Setting: a triumph of Art-Déco in shades of grey and pink
Amenities: live piano music
Atmosphere: a nostalgic and slightly decadent evocation of bygone days
Clientèle: youthful, self-assured and on-the-way-up to middle-aged, comfortably-off and successful
Service: mostly with a smile
Reservations: advisable
Credit cards: not accepted

Bar

HARRY'S BAR
74 Via Ruggero Settimo
Telephone: 32 81 97
Closed: Monday; August
Location: a few steps from the Piazza Politeama
Setting: small city-centre bar-restaurant; a handful of tables and chairs
Amenities: meals and light meals as well as drinks, ices and snacks
Atmosphere: buzzing with activity and invariably packed
Clientèle: discerning; discriminating; distinguished; obligatory stopover for anyone who is anyone
Service: agile
Reservations: essential

Nightclub

SPEAK EASY
34 Viale Strasburgo
Telephone: 51 84 86
Open: 22.30/10.30 p.m.–2.30/a.m.
Amenities: discothèque

Atmosphere: one of the most-frequented night-spots in town during the winter months; tends to be abandoned in favour of the Mondello Lido in summer
Clientèle: a parade of some of Palermo's most beautiful people – young, attractive and affluent – with gentlemen of rather more mature years
Service: Sicilian
Reservations: advisable

Shopping

EVERYTHING UNDER ONE ROOF
Croff Centro Casa   79/87 Via R. Settimo

FOR HIM
Battaglia   97 Via R. Settimo

FOR HER
Valentino Haute Couture
31A Via Libertà

BEAUTY & HAIR
Agulia   59 Via Ricasoli

JEWELLERY
Fiorentino   11/B Via Libertà

LOCAL SPECIALITIES
Boudoir (women's fashion)
9 Piazza Crispi
Alongi (men's fashion)
46 Via R. Settimo
Giglio In (men & women's fashion)
44 Via Libertà
Baby chic (children's fashion)
30 Via Notarbartolo
Fendi (leather fashion)
37 Via Libertà
Guarneri (furs)
68 Via R. Settimo
Libreria Ciuni (books)
459 Via Verdi
Bart shop (gifts)
131 Via L. da Vinci
Fendi (baggage & travel accessories)
37 Via Libertà
Valentino Più (interior decorating)
16 Via XX Settembre
Mangia and Mannino (food and beverages) 116 Via Principe del monte
Hugoni (perfumery)
89/95 Via R. Settimo
Magli (shoes)
19 Via R. Settimo
Calfisch (sweets)
35 Via Libertà
Gulì (sweets)
208/214 Via Stabile

The City

The Eternal City – eternal sunshine, caressing breezes, music in the air; a world carousel for hedonists, bel-esprits, belles de jour and de nuit, historians, worshippers, tramps, exhibitionists and voyeurs; the cradle of Christianity, dolce vita and decadence; al-fresco museum for world treasures, careless everyday life among holy shrines of antiquity, palazzi by the thousands; a worldly pope, charming nuns, religious pilgrims by the millions; cathedrals, churches, chapels, monasteries, museums, collections, historic landmarks, fountains, sculptures – unnoticed by free-lance grand-prix drivers, demonstrators, strikers, starlets, gigolos; Piazza di Spagna, Via Condotti, Caffé Greco, Fendi, Valentino, Brioni; Moravia, Fellini, Mastroianni, Vitti; paparazzi, politics, scandals, gossip, gesture-talk; Via Veneto, Trastevere, Via Appia Antica, Fregene, Tivoli; Grand, Hassler, Inghilterra, Lord Byron; Bolognese, Tre Scalini, Hostaria dell'Orso, Tartarughino, Jackie O. – here today, gone tomorrow; life for the moment, dressed to the minute, fettucine al dente, basta. Mamma Roma.

Founded: 8th century B.C. by Latin and Sabine tribes; Roma (Latin) – from its legendary foundation by Romulus in 753 B.C.

Far-reaching events: 509 B.C. – republic founded; 3rd–1st century – Punic wars, enlargement of territory; 59 – Caesar consul; 27 – Octavius becomes ›Augustus‹, arts flourish; 1st and 2nd century A.D. – zenith of territorial power; 305–37 – Constantine, Christianity state religion; 4th century – Empire split into East and West; 476 – Odoaker victorious over the last emperor; 6th and 6th century – barbarian invasions; Papal rights increase; 756 – capital of the Church; 800 – Charlemagne crowned; 1144 – Senate re-established; 15th century – arts flourish under Sixtus IV; 1527 – Charles V conquers Rome; rise of Protestantism; 17th century – Counter-Reformation; 1789/99 – French invasion, Rome a French republic, Pius IV in exile; 19th century – confrontations between papal and state forces; 1870 – Italy united under Victor Emmanuel II, Rome capital, Pope retreats into the Vatican; 1922 – Mussolini's march on Rome; 1929 – Lateran Agreements settling the conflict between Italy and the Church; 1957 – founding contract of the Common Market; 1960 – Olympic Games.

Population: 3 million; capital and largest city in Italy.

Postal code: I-00100   **Telephone code:** 6

Climate: variable spring, very hot summer; rainy winter.

Calendar of events: 5 Jan – before *Epiphany* – a huge celebration at the Piazza Navona; *St. Joseph's Day* (19 Mar) – a celebration of spring; *Easter* – all Rome, especially the Vatican, celebrates the resurrection of Christ; from Maundy (Holy) Thursday to Easter Sunday – hundreds of thousands of pilgrims from around the globe; *Valentino Haute Couture Show* (Jul) – on the Spanish Steps; *Noiantri* (15 to 29 Jul) – the people of Trastevere celebrate; *Immaculate Conception* (8 Dec) – in Spanish Square.

Fairs and exhibitions: *ROMA ALTA MODA* (Jul) – fashion fair; *EUROPHILA* (Oct) – stamps and telecommunications.

Best views of the city: from the terrace restaurant of the *Hassler Villa Medici*; from the dome of *St. Peter's*; from the *Capitol*; *Pincio*; *Monte Testaccio.*

Historical and modern sights: *Forum* – ancient centre of Roman civilization with the most important palaces and ruins and the *Coliseum* (1st century) – where the morituri saluted Caesar; *Palatine Hill* – site of Domitian's imperial palace; *St. Peters' Basilica* (17th century) – biggest cathedral in the world, with Michelangelo's Pietà; *Vatican Museums* (13th century) – Rome's ancient history with the *Sistine Chapel* (15th century) and Michelangelo's paintings; *Picture Gallery* – a collection of Roman masterpieces; *Capitoline Hill* with Piazza del Campidoglio (16th century) – by Michelangelo, with the statue of Marcus Aurelius, and the *Palazzo dei Conservatori* (15th century) – Renaissance, museum with the famous She-Wolf; *Arch of Constantine* (2nd century) – reliefs depicting scenes of Roman history; *Pantheon* (1st century) – entrance through granite columns, tombs of the kings of Italy and of Raphael; *Castel Sant'angelo* (2nd century) – Hadrian's mausoleum with a quadriga on top; *Piazza Navona* – with Bernini's Fountain of the Four Rivers (17th century); *Via Appia Antica* (4th century B.C.) – one of Christian Rome's main centres with *Catacombs* (2nd century); *St. Mary Major* (5th century) – mosaics, on the Esquiline Hill; *Spanish Steps,* with the church of *Trinità dei Monti* and *Keats' House; monument to Victor Emmanuel II* – wedding-cake architecture and the house on the *Piazza Venezia* from whose balcony Mussolini used to address the crowd; the *Borghese Gardens* – Rome's loveliest park.

Special attractions: an audience with the *Pope*; breakfast at *Caffé Greco*; a shopping spree along the *Via Condotti*; an aperitivo – espresso tour along the *Via Veneto*; an Alta Moda show by *Valentino*; a night in *Trastevere*; a tête-à-tête fiacre ride through the *Borghese Gardens.*

Important companies with headquarters in the city: *Agip Petrol* (petrol); *Cantina Sociale Cooperativa di Marino* (wines – at Marino); *Consorzio Moda Roma* (fashion); *Construzioni Meccaniche Bernardini* (machinery); *Covalca Plastici* (plastics, chemicals); *Italstrada* (construction); *Selenia Industrie Elletroniche* (electronic systems); *Serono Industria Farmaceutica* (pharmaceuticals); *Valentino* (fashion).

Airport: Rome – Leonardo da Vinci/Fiumicino, ROM; Tel.: 60 12; 30 km/20 miles; Alitalia, Tel.: 46 88.

The Headquarters

GRAND

3 Via V. E. Orlando
I–00185 Rome
Telephone: 47 09
Telex: 610 210 granro
Owning Company: Cigahotels
General Manager: Nadio Benedetti
Affiliation/Reservation System: Hello-ciga
Number of rooms: 168 (35 suites)
Price range: Lit. 180,000–850,000
Credit cards: AE, DC, EC
Location: city centre
Built: 1894 (renovated 1983)
Style: elegant, luxurious
Hotel amenities: garage, limousine service, car rental, beauty salon, solarium, sauna
Main hall porter: Renzo Chiaranda
Room amenities: colour tv, mini-bar
Bathroom amenities: bathrobe, telephone
Room service: 24 hours
Conference rooms: 6 (up to 600 persons)
Bar: ›Le Grand Bar‹ (11.00/a.m.–2.00/a.m.) harpist at tea time, pianist in the evening, Mauro Lotti (barman)
Restaurants: ›Le Rallye‹ (12.30/p.m.–15.00/3.00 p.m. and 19.30/7.30 p.m.–24.00/12.00 p.m.) C. Arti (maître), Adelio Pagani (chef de cuisine); ›Le Pavillon‹ (as Le Rallye) F. Giannitrapani (maître), Adelio Pagani (chef de cuisine)

›The refined meeting point of the international élite‹ has only continued on former director César Ritz's path for nearly one hundred years since the days when it was already declared ›the favourite resort of European and American Society in Rome‹. Le Grand is grand not only for its history, its architecture by Cavaliere Podesti, its service from the good old times and the guests who keep changing everything but their standard; class and renommé at this Roman palace also stem from the owning CIGA's rejuvenation under Nadio Benedetti, the adaptation to the faster pace of life demonstrated in the modern luxury, the lighter intérieur and the two restaurants, once under the supervision of Auguste Escoffier, of which Le Rallye, in fact, is among the handful of gourmet galleries and snob stops of the city. The location close to the station, the Quirinal, Via Veneto and even Piazza di Spagna put it within walking distance of the business centres, the embassies, the pleasure alleys and stylish shopping – and behind these walls you feel much securer than anywhere else. The comfort, too, is real: uniformed helpers at every step, wide corridors and extensive halls (with lots of little corners for an intimate espresso encounter), marble columns, Murano lustres, antique tapestries, and princely bedchambers and bathrooms with king-size beds and regal accessoires. The Grand's suites are the finest accommodations in town, available only when the arrival of presidents and the departure of monarchs don't coincide.

The Hideaway

INGHILTERRA

14 Via Bocca di Leone
I–00187 Rome
Telephone: 67 21 61
Telex: 614 552 hoting
General Manager: Avv. Francesco de Simone Niquesa
Manager: Nushin Mozaffari
Number of rooms: 105 (12 suites)
Price range: Lit. 185,000 (single)
Lit. 240,000 (double)
Lit. 370,000 (suite)
Credit cards: AE, DC, EC, Visa
Location: city centre, between Via Condotti and Via Borgognana
Built: 1850
Style: historic building, modernized in 1978
Hotel amenities: car park
Room amenities: air conditioning, colour tv, mini-bar
Room service: 7.00/a.m.–24.00/12 p.m.
Laundry/dry cleaning: same day
Conference rooms: for up to 12 persons
Bars: (11.00/a.m.–24.00/12.00 p.m.)
cocktail bar, Mario Pinchetti (barman), 18th century English style

When in Rome, don't do as the Romans would when hiding away at weekends during summer or for a short holiday, going to Castelgandolfo or Porto Ercole. Stay right here – at the prettiest hermitage in town. There is nothing English about the Inghilterra, except, maybe, the quality of the textiles and the tea. The former guest house of the Torlonia Palace across the street is a little palazzo in itself, flanked by the most high-sounding names in fashion and accessoires – Valentino, Fendi, Gucci, et al. Piazza di Spagna, Caffè Greco, bistros and galleries form a kaleidoscope of distractions around this enclave which, once you have stepped onto the black-marbled floor of the club-like foyer, embraces you with serenity and warmth, and the smiling servants of Rome's most fashionable small hotel treat you as if you were coming home to your private residence. Many public figures who search for this privacy and tranquillity stay only here – from Catherine Deneuve to Harry Ward Bailey – following in the footsteps of Franz Liszt, Hans Christian Andersen and Ernest Hemingway. The latter's favourite place, of course, was the tiny bar where, at times, you will find more prominent personalities crammed in one corner than on the whole Spanish Steps. Nushin Mozzafari, who conducts this harmony of aesthetical beauty and l'art d'hospitalité with a touch of eastern femininity, reigns over one-hundred-odd rooms and suites that are among the most recherché chambers in Rome. No wonder, this treasure-chest residence was elected one of the Top Twenty Charm Hotels in the world.

Lunch

EL TOULÀ
29 b Via della Lupa
Telephone: 6 78 11 96/6 78 64 71
Affiliations: El Toulà Group
Owner/Manager: Vinicio Carlon
Closed: Saturday lunchtime; Sunday; August
Open: 13.00/1 p.m.–15.00/3 p.m. and 20.00/8 p.m.–23.00/11 p.m.
Cuisine: Venetian and international
Chef de cuisine: Paolo Preo
Specialities: salad ›El Toulà‹; blinis; pasta and beans alla Veneta; risotto with squid ›ink‹; tagliolini bianchi with scallops; turbot with almonds; shin of veal with cumin; fillet of beef with artichokes; tirami su; crema Catalana
Location: two Gucci steps from the Pantheon
Setting: three small dining rooms (the last is the most desirable); period décor; fabric-lined walls, comfortable fauteuils and banquettes; old pictures, chandeliers, valuable silverware and snowy napery
Amenities: private dining room (20 persons); bar; air conditioning
Atmosphere: the Maxim's of Rome; lively, sought-after, prestigious and unashamedly luxurious in the style of the ›El Toulà‹ chain of restaurants founded by Alfred Beltrame
Clientèle: a parade of Cinecittà's children mingle with Rome's Haute Bourgeoisie, resident aristocracy and elegant birds of passage
Dress: jacket and (possibly) tie
Service: superior
Reservations: essential
Price range: appropriately high
Credit cards: AE, DC, Euro, Visa

Dinner

HOSTARIA DELL'ORSO
25 Via dei Soldati/93 Via Monte Brianzo
Telephone: 6 56 42 50
Owner/Manager: Claudio Giorgioni
Closed: lunchtime; Sunday; August
Open: 19.00/7. p.m.–24.00/12 p.m.
Cuisine: Italian; international
Chef de cuisine: Guiseppe Chessa
Specialities: caviar; foie gras; smoked salmon, crêpes alla valdostana (with ham and cheese); sole with almonds
Location: between the Piazza Navona and the Ponte Umberto I
Setting: 15th-century palazzo; gilt stucco, frescoes, lapis lazuli pillars, silver chandeliers and golden cutlery
Amenities: Blue Bar (Blubar); air conditioning
Atmosphere: one of the most exquisitely lovely restaurants in the city, if not in the world

Clientèle: the occasional beautiful and elegant resident of the Eternal City surrounded by tourists from Ohio to Osaka
Dress: couturier-chic to check trousers and blue rinse
Service: efficient
Reservations: recommended (no dogs)
Price range: decidedly expensive
Credit cards: AE, DC, Euro, Visa

Dinner

DAL BOLOGNESE
1–2 Piazza del Popolo
Telephone: 3 61 14 26
Owner/Manager: Alfredo Tomaselli
Closed: Sunday night; Monday; three weeks in August; one week at Christmas
Open: 12.45/p.m.–15.00/3 p.m. and 20.15/8.15 p.m.–23.00/11 p.m.
Cuisine: Italian
Chef de cuisine: Sesto Rossi
Specialities: pasta dishes; tortellini alla panna (with cream); tortellini di ricotta (with curd cheese); tagliatelle alla bolognese
Location: on one of Rome's most famous squares
Setting: classic
Amenities: overgrown terrace
Atmosphere: extrovert
Clientèle: actors in search of an audience; foreign film fanatics – plus a more sober selection of businessmen, bankers and brokers, chargés d'affaires and senior government officials
Dress: rather eye-catching to fairly conventional
Service: quick and industrious
Reservations: advisable
Price range: fairly expensive
Credit cards: AE, DC

Lunch

ROMOLO
(nel Giardino di Raffaello e della Fornarina)
8 Via di Porta Settimana
Telephone: 5 81 82 84/5 81 38 73
Affiliations: Associazione Ristoranti Romani
Owner/Manager: Marisa Casali
Closed: Monday; August
Open: 12.00/a.m.–15.30/3.30 p.m. and 19.30/7.30 p.m.–24.00/12 p.m.
Cuisine: Roman
Chef de cuisine: Mario Cardoni
Specialities: spaghetti with tomatoes, tuna fish and dried mushrooms (alla boscaiola); steamed marinated veal with tomatoes and red wine (bocconcini di vitello); tripe alla Romana; shoulder of lamb; mozzarella alla Fornarina; prawns alla Luciana; roast pork
Location: in Roma Trastevere (on the right bank of the Tiber); between the

Ponte Mazzini and the Ponte Sisto
Setting: 16th-century house; typical Roman trattoria (established 1848); important collection of modern paintings; terracotta-framed window from which la Fornarina (the baker's daughter) first looked down and saw the painter Raphael, whose model and confidante she became; inner courtyard
Amenities: outdoor dining on large terrace, guitarist
Atmosphere: romantico alla Vittorio de Sica classic
Clientèle: monarchs; ministers and the media; Roman High Society; globe-trotters en passant – and a sprinkling of ordinary mortals
Dress: easy-come, easy-go
Service: sometimes a little on the slow side
Reservations: advisable (dogs allowed)
Price range: medium
Credit cards: AE, Visa

Dinner

LE SANS SOUCI
20 Via Sicilia
Telephone: 49 35 04; 49 34 27
Owner/Manager: B. Bruno Borghesi
Closed: Monday; August
Open: 19.30/7.30 p.m.–1.30/a.m.
Cuisine: Italian and international
Chefs de cuisine: Alfonzo Carnazzola and B. Bruno Borghesi
Specialities: risotto; soufflés; Sardinian lobster in champagne and strawberries
Location: central; off the Via Veneto, just before the Porta Pinciana
Setting: Belle Epoque; ornate furnishings, mirrors, period accessoires; subdued lighting and chandeliers
Amenities: bar; guitar player in restaurant
Atmosphere: fashionable and elegant, with a hint of snob appeal
Clientèle: lords ecclesiastical and lords temporal; prelates and presidents; princes; pop singers and primadonnas from Cinecittà; from Sophia Loren to Liza Minelli
Dress: jacket and tie de rigueur
Service: solicitous and friendly
Reservations: advisable
Price range: expensive (unless you're a plutocrat)
Credit cards: AE, DC, Euro, Visa

Dinner

PASSETTO
14 Via Zanardelli
Telephone: 6 54 36 96; 6 54 05 69
Owner/Manager: Tonino di Giammarco
Closed: Sunday
Open: 12.30/p.m.–15.00/3 p.m. and 19.30/7.30 p.m.–23.30/11.30 p.m.
Cuisine: local and international

Chef de cuisine: Luigi Serantoni
Specialities: saltimbocca alla romana; spigola fish; lombatina di vitello al cartoccio; tagliatelle with white truffles; abbachio al forno; fettucine with mushrooms; risotto with fish; pilaff Indiana
Location: just off the Piazza Navona
Setting: a trattoria established over 100 years ago; three slightly cramped dining rooms furnished in old-fashioned style
Amenities: open-air dining on terrace; air conditioning
Atmosphere: comfortable but elegant ambiance
Clientèle: from Carlo Ponti en famille to a pair of princesses, plus a handful of awed Americans
Dress: casually stylish to stylishly casual
Service: exceptionally friendly
Reservations: not necessary
Price range: medium
Credit cards: AE, DC, Visa

Café

ANTICO CAFFE GRECO
86 Via Condotti
Telephone: 67 17 00; 6 78 25 54
Closed: Sunday; Saturday afternoon (July-August); one week in August
Open: 8.00/a.m.–21.00/9 p.m.
Specialities: the most fashionable quick breakfast and luncheon snack
Location: on Rome's most elegant shopping street, leading from the Spanish Steps
Setting: 18th and 19th century; dark wood panelling; red velvet, marble and mahogany; old paintings and neo-classic sculptures
Amenities: bar; air conditioning
Atmosphere: old-fashioned but still popular
Clientèle: the world of the world-ever since Goethe, Berlioz and Cézanne
Service: Roman

Meeting Point

OPEN GATE
4 Via San Nicola da Tolentino
Telephone: 4 75 04 64/ 4 74 66 70
Affiliations: Club of Clubs
Owner/Manager: Principe Barberini
Closed: never
Open: 20.30/8.30 p.m.–4.00/a.m.
Location: off the Via XX Settembre
Setting: very modern
Amenities: restaurant; piano bar; one private room
Atmosphere: Roman fun behind closed doors
Dress: elegant
Service: impeccable
Reservations: essential
Credit cards: AE

Bar

BLUBAR
25 Via dei Soldati
Telephone: 6 56 42 50
Closed: never
Open: 19.30/7.30 p.m.–3.30/a.m.
Location: between the Piazza Navona
and the Ponte Umberto I; in the same
building as the Hostaria dell'Orso
Setting: piano bar with excellent music
(occasionally other instruments too)
Amenities: restaurant
Atmosphere: lively to fairly frenzied on
occasion
Clientèle: familiar faces and famous
names, following in the dancing footsteps
of former habitués Aristotle Onassis (ac-
companied by first Maria Callas and then
Jacqueline Kennedy); Roman Polanski
and Liza Minelli
Service: polished and professional
Reservations: advisable

Nightclub

JACKIE O
11a Via Boncompagni
Telephone: 46 14 01
Affiliations: Club of Clubs
Closed: never
Open: 23.00/11 p.m.–3.30/a.m. (restau-
rant from 20.00/8 p.m.)
Location: off the Via Veneto
Setting: Liberty-style décor
Amenities: discothèque; restaurant; pia-
no bar (in cellar)
Atmosphere: exclusive; despite its some-
what jaded name, still regarded by many
as the smartest club in Rome; almost an
institution
Clientèle: glitterati from the world of
films and fashion; scions of Europe's no-
ble houses and stars of the suntan set
Dress: Valentino to Gianni Versace, and
vice-versa
Service: suave
Reservations: recommended
Credit cards: AE, DC

Shopping

EVERYTHING UNDER ONE ROOF
Rinascente   Via del Corso/Piazza Colonna

FOR HIM
Valentino Uomo   12 Via Condotti

FOR HER
Ferré Boutique   42B Via Borgognona
Marislain   Via Condotti

BEAUTY & HAIR
Sergio Valente   11 Via Condotti

JEWELLERY
Petochi   23 Piazza di Spagna

LOCAL SPECIALITIES
For You (women's fashion)
Via Frattina
Piattelli Donna (women's fashion)
Via Condotti
Polidori (fashion)
Via Borgognona
Piattelli Uomo (men's fashion)
Via Borgognona
Roland's (men & women's fashion)
Piazza di Spagna/on the corner of Via
Condotti
Massoni (children's fashion)
Via Condotti/Via del Corso
Fendi (furs)
39 Via Borgognona
Rizzoli (books)
Piazza Colonna
Fornari (gifts)
Via Frattina
Stilvetro (gifts)
Via Frattina
Saddler (baggage & travel accessories)
Via Condotti
Design 2000 (interior decorating)
Vivai del Sud, Via Claudio Monte-
verdi 20
Castroni (food and beverages)
Via Cola di Rienzo
De Paola (perfumery)
Via della Croce
Saddler (shoes)
Via Condotti

THE BEST OF ART
D'Ascanio, Anna   (contemporary art)
29 Via del Babuino, Tel. 6 78 59 20
Ferranti, Ugo   (contemporary art)
26 Via di Tor Millina, Tel. 6 54 21 46
Il Ponte   (contemporary art)
6 Via S. Ignazio, Tel. 6 79 61 14
Pieroni   (contemporary art)
203 Via Panisperna, Tel. 46 57 06
Sprovieri, Paolo   (contemporary art)
3 Piazza del Popolo, Tel. 3 61 09 75
Toninelli   (modern art)
86   Piazza di Spagna, Tel. 6 97 34 88
Monetti   (fine art)
169 Via Giulia, Tel. 65 74 36

The City

James Joyce never did get to the bottom of the riddle. Why did Archduke Maximilian, brother of Emperor Franz Joseph – like the sphinx who greets you so enigmatically from her pedestal by Miramar Castle – turn his back on the lovely mock-Tudor capriccio he had built on the promontory? Why did he, accepting the empty promises and hollow crown offered by Napoléon III, set sail for Mexico and death before a firing squad, when he could have remained in his palatial home contemplating the author's favourite view of the Gulf of Trieste, ›from swerve of shore to bend of bay‹? Pine-forested granite cliffs, the Dinaric Alps beyond the shimmering reflections of the Adriatic – such is the setting of Trieste, erstwhile maritime outpost of the Hapsburg empire and principal port for Austria today. Nowadays the capital of Italy's easternmost mainland province marks the last spaghetti stronghold before the poor people's riviera as once she defended the Pax Romana against the barbaric incursions of the Ostrogoths. Relics of the proud imperium remain, from the amphitheatre on the former Capitoline Hill to the ruined basilica, interwoven into the fabric of the city alongside the medieval fortress eyrie and the starkly Romanesque cathedral. But Trieste owes her urbanely harmonious physiognomy above all to those dynastic empire-builders, the Hapsburgs. They embellished their Mediterranean outlet with the noble classicistic and Renaissance-style mansions which line the Riva seafront promenade in red-roofed arcaded splendour. The symmetry of the grid layout culminates in the balanced perspectives of the Piazza dell' Unità d'Italia, the city's living theatre, uniting the cafés and the most beautiful palazzi with the Hotel Duchi d'Aosta, the best address in town – complete with sea view and the sound of bells; a forum here – as in Venice's St. Mark's Square across the water – for local literati (Umberto Sava, Italo Svevo et al.) and visiting prominenti following in the footsteps of archaeologist Johann Winckelmann, consular penman Henri Beyle dit Stendhal, poet Rainer Maria Rilke and military bandmaster Franz Léhar. Vienna's territorial eminence is no more, but Trieste is still the crossroads for the northern Adriatic. The port, with its associated industries – shipbuilding and oil refining (much of central Europe's oil is pumped through the pipelines of Trieste's docks) – assumes greater importance today than that of her serene rival across the lagoon, and is still the city's focal point. Here northern Italian efficiency meets Latin nonchalance in a purposeful, open-minded ambiente enhanced and enjoyed by the cavalcade of migrants from all points of the compass for whom the city has been a stopover or embarcation point for two thousand years. The city's contrasting legacy, mirrored by the alternation between the bracing bora wind from the north, and the indolent warmth of the southerly sirocco, summarizes her elusively contrary grace. Trieste, the geometrical heart of Europe, epitomizes the meeting of the ways, a microcosm of ›the now, the here, through which all future plunges to the past‹.

Founded: first mentioned in 3rd century B.C.; Trieste (Italian) – from Tergeste.

Far-reaching events: 52 B.C. – conquered by Julius Caesar – important east-west trade centre; 5th century – barbarian invasions and plundering; 7th–8th century – reorganization of city by Charlemagne; 1382 – menaced by Venice, Trieste places itself under the protection of the Austrian Habsburgs; 1719 – Trieste a free port; 1797–1813 Napoleon occupies the city on three occasions; 19th century – most important Austrian port on the Adriatic; 1919 – Trieste annexed by Italy, along with its province; 1947–54 – Trieste and province a free territory under UN protection; 1954 – London Accord: Trieste city goes to Italy, Trieste province to Yugoslavia.

Population: 260,000; capital of the province of Friuli-Venezia Giulia.

Postal code: I–34100   **Telephone code:** 40

Climate: Alpine, with maritime influence; periodically the bora, a dry cold wind from the north, causes a drop in temperature.

Calendar of events: Carnival (Feb); ›Light and Sound‹ (Jun to Sep) – dramatic tragedies performed daily at the Miramar castle; Folk Festival (Jul) – the city celebrates.

Fairs and exhibitions: INTERNATIONAL FLOWER EXHIBITION (Apr); TRANSADRIA (May and Oct) – international exhibition and conference on sea and roll-on, roll-off-transport; INTERNATIONAL SAMPLES FAIR (Jun).

Historical and modern sights: San Giusto Cathedral (10th to 14th century) – Trieste's main landmark, with mosaics of the Venetian School; Teatro Romano (2nd century, B.C.); Arco di Riccardo (33 B.C.) – a section of the Roman city wall; the Citadel (15th century) – ruined fortress; San Giovanni (15th century) – Gothic church; Miramar Castle (19th century) – built for Archduke Maximilian of Austria; Faro della Vittoria – Europe's tallest lighthouse; Museo del Mare – excellent collection of maritime objects; Grotto Gigante – cave with natural illumination (13 km/8 miles).

Special attractions: Piazza dell'Unità d'Italia day and night; the harbour and the promenade along the sea front.

Important companies with headquarters in the city: Barbieri, E. C. (import/export); Eurospital Pharma (medical instruments); Fincantieri Navale (shipbuilding); Fincantieri-Grande Motori (ship engines); Friulgiulia (foodstuffs, machinery); Melingo, Paolo (import/export); Petrucco, Pietro (import/export); Stock (liqueurs); Universal (import/export).

Airport: Trieste-Ronchi dei Legionari, TRS; Tel.: 481/777001; 34 km/21 miles; Alitalia, Tel.: 615 06.

The Headquarters

DUCHI D'AOSTA

2 Piazza Unita D'Italia
I–34121 Trieste
Telephone: 6 20 81
Telex: 460 358 duchi
Owning Company: Cigahotels
General Manager: Giancarlo di Matteo
Affiliation/Reservation Systems: Hello-
ciga
Number of rooms: 48 (2 suites)
Price range: Lit. 100,000–290,000
Credit cards: AE, DC, BA, EC
Location: city centre
Built: 1873 (renovated 1973)
Style: central European atmosphere
Hotel amenities: garage; valet parking
Room amenities: air conditioning, colour
tv, mini-bar/refrigerator (pets allowed)
Bathroom amenities: bidet, bathrobe,
hairdrier, telephone
Room service: 7.00/a.m.–24.00/12.00
p.m.
Conference rooms: 2 (up to 25 persons),
slide and overhead projector
Bar: ›Harry's Bar‹ (see Bars)
Restaurant: ›Harry's Grill‹ (12.00/a.m.–
15.00/3 p.m. and 19.30/7.30 p.m.–
23.00/11.00 p.m.), Aldo Cesselli (maître),
Ernesto Casalis (chef de cuisine), international cuisine with regional specialities,
open-air dining in summer

*Arrive at night, and you will understand
why this stately little city palais belongs to
the favourite hotels of artists, bel-esprits
and men of commerce à la recherche du
temps perdu: the setting on one of the loveliest squares in the world, across from the
old harbour and the open sea, lit as for a
scene in a Visconti movie and embraced by
a mild breeze scented with wanderlust and
adventure, with the bells of City Hall vis-à
-vis chiming as in a Pink Floyd overture.
The CIGA grand hotel chain's easternmost
outpost certainly lives up to standard and
even to expectations of spoiled hedonists
turning a blind eye to the lack of some of
the luxury they are used to from the Gritti,
the Grand, et al. The Duchi d'Aosta (the
mountain peers never had it so good)
evokes nostalgia and melodrama, but also
grandeur and dolce vita in style. Foyer,
staircase, salons and lounges are as in a
private house, and the rooms, comfortable
and in subtly tasteful colour schemes if
without glamour, set the final tone for the
feeling of being at home. Appropriately, the
service is extremely personable and will arrange for anything with evident pleasure.
The restaurant is one of the best in the city
and certainly the most beautiful. Sitting on
the wooden benches of the terrace in summer, indulging in carpaccio, fresh fish
caught a few hours before, dolce and vino
and watching the world pass by will pacify
you for not having lived here in the Belle
Epoque, when the Duchi d'Aosta was built
by Viennese architect Greininger, and give
you the then-habitué James Joyce's notion
of ›all space in a nutshell‹.*

Lunch

NASTRO AZZURRO
12 Riva Nazario Sauro
Telephone: 30 57 89
Owner/Manager: Guido Braico
Closed: Saturday evening; Sunday; Christmas and New Year; Assumption (August 15th)
Open: 12.00/p.m.–15.00/3 p.m. and 19.00/7 p.m.–23.00/11 p.m.
Cuisine: local
Chef de cuisine: Davide de Grassi
Specialities: seafood; hors d'oeuvres; fish or shellfish soups; risotto or spaghetti in various guises; fritto misto; apple strudel; curd cheese flan
Location: on the seafront
Setting: large dining room with well-spaced tables; wood panelling, ornate ceiling and elegantly-laid tables
Amenenities: bar; air conditioning; open air dining for up to 50 persons
Atmosphere: the most stylish fish restaurant in Trieste; intimate and quiet in spite of its size
Clientèle: cross-section of expense-account gourmets, men from the media, advertising executives and local habitués
Dress: elegant
Service: courteous and helpful in the old tradition
Reservations: advisable
Price range: medium
Credit cards: AE, DC

Dinner

ANTICA TRATTORIA SUBAN
2 Via Comici
Telephone: 54 368
Owner/Manager: Mario Suban
Closed: Monday; Tuesday; August; December 26th–January 7th
Open: 10.00/a.m.–16.00/4 p.m. and 18.00/6 p.m.–1.00/a.m.
Cuisine: local and Eastern European
Chef de cuisine: Mario Suban; chef pâtissier: Giuseppe Milazzi
Specialities: ham in pastry crust; insalata alabarda; cabbage and bean hot-pot (jota triestina); risotto with mountain herbs (alle erbe del Carso); crespelle alla mandriera (shepherd-style noodles); leek pie; roast shin of veal; fillet steak ›Claudia‹
Location: in the San Giovanni suburb of Trieste
Setting: on a hillside; a trattoria established by the Suban family in 1865; originally in the country, now (thanks to urbanization) within the city but as charming es ever; pergola-covered terrace with view of Trieste; attractively-furnished dining rooms of varying sizes in characteristic local style

Amenities: private dining room (80 persons; Russian, Indian or Hungarian meals available on request); outdoor dining on terrace; car park
Atmosphere: elegantized typical trattoria which has lost none of its charm by keeping abreast of the times
Clientèle: Trieste's Top Twenty; homesick Hungarians; travellers en route from Prague to Palermo for business or pleasure
Dress: casual
Service: charmingly old-fashioned and cordial
Reservations: advisable (no dogs)
Price range: medium
Credit cards: AE, DC, Euro, Visa

Lunch

OSTERIA ALLA MASCHERE
57a Via Giulia
Telephone: 5 46 02
Owner/Manager: Arrigo Spessot
Closed: Tuesday; July
Open: 11.00/a.m.–15.00/3 p.m. and 17.00/5 p.m.–1.00/a.m.
Cuisine: exotic and international
Chefs de cuisine: Livio and Elda Spessot
Specialities: mulligatawney soup; Indonesian rice (nasi goreng); timbale of tagliatelle in pastry; Thai-style noodles (mi krob); couscous; paella valenciana; Peking duck; halva (Turkish dessert)
Setting: small dining room, traditionally furnished in local style
Amenities: air conditioning
Atmosphere: imbued with the spirit of faraway places by founder Arrigo Spessot, father of the present owner
Clientèle: sailors and other restless souls seeking a hint of the exotic, plus a fair number of ›exiled‹ foreigners seeking memories of home
Dress: normal
Service: expertly stage-managed by Giuliano Spessot
Reservations: essential
Price range: inexpensive
Credit cards: not accepted

Dinner

HARRY'S GRILL
2 Piazza Unità d'Italia
Telephone: 6 20 81
Owner/Manager: Cigahotels SpA/Giancarlo di Matteo
Closed: never
Open: 12.00/a.m.–15.00/3 p.m. and 19.30/7.30 p.m.–23.00/11 p.m.
Cuisine: international
Chef de cuisine: Ernesto Casalis
Specialities: carpaccio; artichoke flan; baked sea-perch with spices and white

wine; scampi à l'impériale; steak Châteaubriand; home-made ice-cream
Location: in the Hotel Duchi d'Aosta
Setting: pure Belle Epoque; very elegant;
soft lighting
Amenities: hotel; bar; open-air dining on
terrace; car park
Atmosphere: stylish; fashionable, cosmo-
politan and with a hint of romance; a
place to see and be seen
Clientèle: le Tout Trieste; local aristoc-
racy; wealthy and beautiful birds of pas-
sage
Dress: designer casual to designer ele-
gant
Service: impeccably supervised by maître
Aldo Cesselli
Reservations: advisable
Price range: moderately expensive
Credit cards: AE, DC, Euro, Bankameri-
card

Café

SAN MARCO
18 Via Battisti
Telephone: 72 72 16
Closed: Wednesday
Open: 9.00/a.m.–24.00/12 p.m.
Location: central
Setting: turn-of-the-century splendour;
small pink marble tables, hat-stands,
gleaming brass lamps; light but comfortable chairs; two salons (the first being
the more lively)
Amenities: newspapers
Atmosphere: an ideal lookout-post for
watching the world go by
Clientèle: retired naval types and professors before lunch; local ladies after a
shopping expedition in the afternoon;
students, secretaries and shopgirls in the
evenings
Service: allegretto moderato

Bar

HARRY'S BAR
2 Piazza Unità d'Italia
Telephone: 6 20 81
Owner/Manager: Cigahotels SpA/Gian-
carlo di Matteo
Closed: never
Open: 11.00/a.m.–24.00/12 p.m.
Location: in the Hotel Duchi d'Aosta
Setting: luxuriously-appointed hotel bar
furnished in the Central European idiom
Amenities: hotel; car park
Atmosphere: as perfect for a pre-prandial
sherry as for a post-dinner cognac
Clientèle: obligatory stopover for all dis-
tinguished visitors to the town
Service: faultless; directed by chief bar-
man Luciano Pietrini
Reservations: advisable
Credit cards: AE, DC, Euro, Bankameri-
card

Shopping

FOR HIM
Trussardi   27 Via San Nicolò

FOR HER
Il Bagaglio   15 Piazza della Borsa

BEAUTY & HAIR
Marisa   18 Via Mazzini

JEWELLERY
Margari   3 Via Roma

LOCAL SPECIALITIES
Gucci (women's fashion)
21 Corso Italia
Tommasini (men & women's fashion)
37 Via Mazzini
Trussardi (men & women's fashion)
27 Via San Nicolò
3 A (furs)
8 Piazza Borsa
Internazionale ›Italo Svevo‹ (books)
9r Corso Italia (Galleria Rossoni)
Opiglia (gifts)
8 Via Roma
Rossi Dario, (baggage & travel accessories)
3 Via Ponchielli
Fedele (interior decorating)
16 Via Mazzini
Mario Delicatezze (food and beverages)
3/1 Rotonda Boschetto
Cillia (perfumery)
20 Via Roma

THE BEST OF ART
Torbandena   (contemporary art)
1 Via di Tor Bandena, Tel. 6 05 98

The City

The cradle of the Italian male's second-favourite pastime – just before dandyism – provides more than three quarters of those mobile toys that serve him as carriage, rocket, macho totem, status symbol or even means of locomotion, but it would be doing this regal city an utter injustice to compare it with Birmingham or Detroit solely for that technical degree of relationship. The Fabbrica Italiana Automobili Torino (along with adopted son Lancia) keeps the majority of the citizens alive (not only with cars, but also tractors, locomotives, underground trains, ships, aeroplanes, banks, steel mills, power stations, publishing houses and hotel corporations), yet the formative influence of the royal House of Savoy – from Umberto the Whitehanded to Umberto II – has marked Turin's beauty, culture and wealth, if not its image among travellers, over nine centuries. Residence of the Italian kings for over two hundred years, but capital of the Kingdom of Italy only for a few, this aristocratic metropolis – which Baron de Montesquieu called ›the most beautiful village in the world‹ – remains to the cognoscenti a magnet for the enrichment of the eye and the mind, and no thought is spared for the Agnelli Empire. (›Gianni Nazionale‹, third-generation ›duce‹ of the dynasty and one of the most brilliant men of the epoch, is a worthy follower of the city's patrons, however, and an invitation to his hillside fortress is the ascent of the social Mount Everest.) Olivetti's elegant office equipment and Pinin Farina's avant-garde designs may deviate further from the wealthy essence of Turin, and Cinzano, Carpano and Martini steal the city's thunder among the cocktail crowd, but once you have stepped onto Piazza San Carlo, walked the fashionable shopping streets under arcades and whiled away some time in the magnificent cafés on the Via Po, you will absorb an atmosphere unexpected in Italy's industrial centre. Much of the inner city seems to be constructed exclusively of palazzi, and with the innumerable religious monuments adding to the serenity of the atmosphere, it is no wonder that Turin has always been an attractive point of pilgrimage, mainly for the (disputed) Holy Shroud of Christ in St. John's Cathedral. But also geniuses of all arts and trade fell in love with the city, unexpectedly as their records prove. Casanova philandered through the silk factories full of young seamstresses, Friedrich Nietzsche saw in Turin ›the first place in which I am possible – and carry the courage to the extreme!‹, and Giorgio De Chirico discovered here ›the melancholy of the beautiful autumn afternoons in town‹. Crossed by the River Po, and surrounded by capital mountains (on the slopes of which grow the best crus of the country – Barolo, Barbera, Nebbiolo, et al.), Turin is, for business – inevitably, and pleasure – surprisingly, one of the most worthwhile destinations on the continent.

Founded: 3rd century B.C. – by Taurini tribes; Torino (Italian).

Far-reaching events: 1st century B.C. – Roman colony Augusta Taurinorum; 6th century – seat of counts of Lombardy; 9th century – seat of Franconians; 1281 – House of Savoy; 1404 – founding of university; 1418 – capital of the dukes of Savoy; 1536–62 – annexed by France after victory by Francis I; 1566 – Duke Emanuele Filiberto wins it back for Savoy and makes it the capital; 1640 – French occupation by Turenne; 1706 – Prince Eugene liberates the city; 1720 – residence of the house of Savoy; 1800–04 – capital of the Po region; 1861–4 – capital of the newly unified Italy.

Population: 1.2 million; capital of Piedmont.

Postal code: I–10100   **Telephone code:** 11

Climate: generally mild, protected by the Alps.

Calendar of events: *St John's Day* (Jun 24th) – riotous celebrations in honour of the city's patron saint.

Fairs and exhibitions: *S.A.M.I.A.* (Feb & Sep) – international clothing; *EXPOVACANCE* (Feb/Mar) – vacation, tourism and sports fair; *OSCAR PRIZE SHOW* (Apr) – best footwear; *INTERNATIONAL PERFUMERY AND COSMETICS* (Apr); *INTERNATIONAL TECHNICS* (Oct); *INTERNATIONAL MOTOR SHOW* (Nov).

Historical sights: *Cathedral* (1492–98) – Renaissance, with *Chapel of the Sacred Shroud* (1668–95) – by Guarini – black marble dome and gilded bronze floor decorations; *Royal Palace* (1646–60) – brick architecture, built on the site of the old Roman theatre; *Palatine Towers* – the only remnants of Roman times; *Piazza San Carlo* (1619–38) – with the Monument of Emanuel Filiberto; *Piazza Castello* – scene of the Risorgimento; *City Hall* (1663) – by Granchi, tablets commemorating the different wars of independence; *Palazzo Carignano* (1680) – Baroque, museum of the Risorgimento.

Modern sights: *Automobile Museum* – 160 cars from the beginning to the present.

Special attractions: a day of cruising, browsing and pausing in the cafés around *Piazza San Carlo;* a look at the *Holy Shroud* (only rarely shown) in St. John's Cathedral; a romantic rendez-vous at the *Villa Sassi;* a *discovery tour* through the Piemontese hinterland and Langhe province – with tastevin and gluttony of *tartufi bianchi, gorgonzola, sweetmeats, stuffed pastries,* et al.; an audience with *Gianni Agnelli.*

Important companies with headquarters in the city: *Fiat* (cars); *Lancia* (cars), *Cinzano* (vermouth); *Martini e Rossi* (vermouth); *Carpano* (vermouth); *Olivetti* (at Ivrea – office equipment); *Cartiere Burgo* (paper); *Teksid* (steel); *Gruppo Finanziario Tessile* (clothes); *Indesit* (household appliances); *ATI MEC* (car parts); *S.I.E.T.T.E.* (car parts).

Airport: Turin-Caselle, TRN; Tel.: 5 77 81; 16 km/10 miles, Alitalia, Tel.: 5 59 11.

The Headquarters

TURIN PALACE

8 Via Paolo Sacchi
I–10128 Turin
Telephone: 51 55 11
Telex: 221411 turinpal
Owning Company: S.T.E.A. S.P.A.
General Manager: P. Moreggio
Affiliation/Reservation Systems: Italhotels, SRS (Steigenberger Reservation Service)
Number of rooms: 125 (1 suite)
Price range: Lit. 145.000 (single)
Lit. 182.000 (double)
Lit. 302.000 (suite)
Credit cards: AE, DC, Visa, EC
Location: city centre
Built: 1873 (renovated 1972)
Style: classic
Hotel amenities: garage, valet parking, beauty salon, hairstylist, grand piano
Main hall porter: Camillo Faure
Room amenities: colour tv (remote control), mini-bar/refrigerator (pets allowed)
Bathroom amenities: separate shower, bidet, bathrobe, hairdrier, telephone
Room service: 6.30/a.m. to 1.00/ a.m.
Laundry/dry cleaning: same day
Conference rooms: 5 (up to 300 persons), ballroom
Bar: (9.00/a.m.–1.00/a.m.) records
Restaurant: ›Turin‹ (12.30/p.m.–14.00/2 p.m. and 19.30/7.30 p.m.–22.00/10 p.m.) international and regional cuisine, classic style décor
Private dining rooms: two

The first-time visitor to Turin will not only be surprised at the visible culture of Fiat-Town, but also at the style and service of its leading hotel, which here – at least – is quite worthy of its name. No palatial promenade, no Belle Epoque splendour and no four-poster beds under stuccoed ceilings, yet all the flair of antiquity combined with the facilities no aristocrat would want to live without today. Across from the ›stazione‹ (which must not be confounded with regular train stations in other countries, but rather be regarded as a colourful spinning wheel with bazaar bustle), the Palace is the centre of action for the cultivated businessman of the city as well as for the upper echelon of the management world from all over the world, for whom the staff of the hotel are prepared. Camillo Faure distinguishes easily the buyers from the bosses, but handles perfectly the wishes of all guests. The Old-World restaurant rates highly among gourmets and the avant-garde bar attracts many an arcade shopper for a cocktail. The rooms are intelligently conceived and gently coloured, some with precious woods, others with ›quietening‹ art. (All windows are sound-proofed, anyway.) Bathrooms bristle and what you miss in ritzy décor and romantic views will be made up for in efficiency, friendliness and attention, largely due to the care of the owning family.

The Hideaway

VILLA SASSI RESIDENCE

47 Strada Traforo del Pino
I–10132 Turin (7 km/4 miles)
Telephone: 89 05 56/7
Owner: Toulà Spa
General Manager: Arturo Filippini
Affiliation/Reservation Systems: Relais et
Châteaux, El Toulà
Closed: August
Number of rooms: 10 (1 suite)
Price range: Lit. 160,000 (single)
              Lit. 210,000 (double)
              Lit. 370,000 (suite)
Credit cards: AE, DC, Visa, Access, CB,
EC, MC
Location: 7 km/4 miles from the centre of
Turin, on the road to Genoa, 13 km/10
miles from airport
Built: a 17th-century château, (renovated
1976)
Style: elegant country house style
Hotel amenities: car park, 5 acres of pri-
vate gardens (no pets allowed)
Room service: 7.00/a.m.–22.00/10 p.m.
Conference rooms: for up to 200 guests
Sports (nearby): swimming pool (10 km/6
miles), tennis club (8 km/5 miles), 18 hole
golf course (20 km/12 miles)
Bar: American Bar
Restaurant: ›El Toulà‹ (closed on Sun-
days) open-air dining on garden terrace
Private dining rooms: banqueting facili-
ties for up to 200 persons

What Palais Schwarzenberg is to the Vien-
nese, Villa Sassi is to the Turinese – simply
the most delightful place to run away to, for
a stroll, a chat, a meeting, a flirt or an en-
counter for eternity. Some would come for
just the cucina raffinata. The 17th-century
country-castle turned relais-royal par ex-
cellence (after having changed hands from
cardinals to counts) is only minutes away
from the desks of Fiat and Olivetti, from
the shopping arcades and the convention
halls, so that even a quick collazione di ne-
gozii seems sensible – and sensational – to
the captains of Italy's flagship industries.
The five acres of private park around clear
the air and the mind, the regal intérieur
creates an aura of dignity and the chef's
specialities justify the culinary euphoria
only Italian businessmen are capable of.
The dozen rooms are almost wasted on
men of commerce with only business in
mind, but more than one pin-striped square
has turned into a mellow reveller after be-
ing infused with the Sassi scent. Maria
Callas and Guiseppe di Stefano spent
many a night here, on the hill above Turin,
and many others still return with their idols
in mind or a fond recollection of the former
mentor, Alfredo Beltrame, one of the spiri-
tus rectores of ›la dolce vita‹.

Lunch

VILLA SASSI (El Toula)
47 Strada Traforo del Pino (7 km/4 miles)
Telephone: 89 05 56
Affiliations: Relais et Châteaux
Owner/Manager: Toulà Spa/Arturo Filippini
Closed: Sunday; August
Open: 12.00/a.m.–14.00/2 p.m. and 20.00/8 p.m.–22.30/10.30 p.m.
Cuisine: local and international
Chef de cuisine: Mr. Ibba
Specialities: warm hors d'œuvres; onion soup; salmon marinated in paprika; green risotto with champagne; breast of duck with herbs
Location: on the road to Chieri
Setting: on a hillside; 17th-century villa set in a lovely park; dining rooms with picture windows; elegant décor and luxurious table-settings
Amenities: bar; outdoor dining on terrace; air conditioning; car park
Atmosphere: aristocratic at all times; delightful for lunch on a fine day; romantic at night
Clientèle: expense-account diners; Piedmont's chiceria; Turin's social élite with something to celebrate – from baptisms and confirmations to weddings
Service: exemplary
Reservations: advisable (dogs permitted in hotel only)
Price range: rather expensive
Credit cards: AE, DC, Visa, Access, Master Card

Lunch

TIFFANY
16/h Piazza Solferino
Telephone: 54 05 38
Owner/Manager: Perino Wilmo Marzini, Domenico Pisu and Antonio Chirone Teresio
Closed: Sunday; August
Open: 12.00/a.m.–15.00/3 p.m. and 20.00/8 p.m.–23.00/11 p.m.
Cuisine: local and international
Chefs de cuisine: Teresio Chirone and Antonio Pisu
Specialities: antipasti caldi piemontese; Alba-style meat salad; rice flan; risotto ›Tiffany‹; old Piedmontese-style ragoût of chicken giblets; fillet of sole ›Tiffany‹; stuffed escalope of veal ›Delizia‹; fruit sorbets
Location: central
Setting: two dining rooms elegantly furnished in the English style; chandeliers, red moquette; fabric-lined walls
Amenities: private dining room; bar; air conditioning; parking available on the Piazza

Atmosphere: imposing; distinguished; well-established
Clientèle: bankers, businessmen and industrialists at lunchtime give way to a more cosmopolitan set for dinner
Service: molto accurato
Reservations: advisable
Price range: moderately expensive
Credit cards: AE

Dinner

AL GATTO NERO
14 Corso F. Turati
Telephone: 59 04 14/59 04 77
Owner/Manager: Luca Grassi
Closed: Sunday; Monday lunchtime; August
Open: 12.30/p.m.–15.00/3 p.m. and 20.00/8 p.m.–23.00/11 p.m.
Cuisine: Tuscan
Chef de cuisine: Luca Grassi
Specialities: hors d'œuvres (antipasti); fish salad ›Gatto Nero‹; fish roe with potato (bottarga sulla patata lessa); taglione with vegetables in season; spaghetti with white wine, onions and herbs (alla marinara); mixed charcoal-grilled seafood; charcoal-grilled steak (costata alla fiorentina)
Location: 1.5 km (1 mile) from city centre
Setting: unrendered brickwork; dining room dominated by large table with arrangements of shellfish, vegetables and fresh fruits
Amenities: air conditioning
Atmosphere: welcoming; an institution in Turin (established 40 years ago)
Clientèle: large faithful following amongst the well-heeled citizens of Turin
Dress: usually jacket-and-tie
Service: very friendly
Reservations: advisable to essential
Price range: moderately expensive
Credit cards: not accepted

Dinner

VECCHIA LANTERNA
21 Corso Re Umberto
Telephone: 53 70 47
Affiliations: Chaîne des Rôtisseurs; Discepolato Caterina de Medici Orpi; Ristorante del Buon Ricordo; Commanderie des Cordons Bleus
Owner/Manager: Armando Zanetti
Closed: Saturday lunchtime; Sunday; August
Open: 12.00/a.m.–15.00/3 p.m. and 20.00/8 p.m.–24.00/12 p.m.
Cuisine: local and international

Chefs de cuisine: Armando Zanetti and Casarotto Eda
Specialities: monthly changing gourmet menu; croûtons Medici with creamed mushrooms; rice savarin with shellfish; duck agnolotti in truffle sauce; tortellini ›Vecchia Lanterna‹; snail soup; bass with salt or Catalan-style with potatoes and onions; dolci di Bruno
Location: central
Setting: Venetian-style luxury; brocade, pictures, moquette and carpeted floor
Amenities: bar; pianist; air conditioning
Atmosphere: chic; comfortable; not overpowering
Clientèle: connoisseurs, business tycoons, Turin's Top Ten and tourists from Toulouse to Teheran
Dress: fairly casual to fairly formal
Service: dinner-jacketed, unobtrusive and professional; directed by the son-in-law of the patron, Luciano Antonioli
Price range: fairly expensive
Credit cards: AE, Euro, Visa

Lunch

LA CLOCHE
106 Strada Traforo del Pino
Telephone: 89 42 13
Owner/Manager: Pasquale Bello
Closed: Monday
Open: 12.30/p.m.–14.30/2.30 p.m. and 20.00/8 p.m.–22.00/10 p.m.
Cuisine: local
Chef de cuisine: Rosa Cico, wife of the proprietor
Specialities: hot and cold antipasti; risottos; home-made tagliatelle; dumplings (gnocchi) filled with cheese; braised beef; guinea-fowl with grapes; fillet steak with green butter
Location: 10 minutes' drive from city centre
Setting: on a hillside; typical décor with an abundance of wood; attractive pictures; large glassed-in terrace (heated in winter) with panoramic view of the city
Amenities: bar (pianist); air conditioning
Atmosphere: family-run establishment; warm and welcoming without loss of style
Clientèle: Turin's Haute Bourgeoisie en fête and en famille, plus a sprinkling of visitors from Verona, Vaduz and Las Vegas
Dress: Sunday casual to Sunday best
Service: under the watchful eye of Pasquale Bello, charmingly aided by daughters Angela and Pinuccia
Reservations: essential on Saturday and for public holidays in summer
Price range: medium
Credit cards: AE, DC

Dinner

DEL CAMBIO
2 Piazza Carignano
Telephone: 54 66 90
Owner/Manager: Teresio Mo
Closed: Sunday; August
Open: 12.30/p.m.–15.00/3 p.m. and 19.30/7.30 p.m.–22.30/10.30 p.m.
Cuisine: local and international
Chef de cuisine: Angelo Maionchi
Specialities: raw meat with mushrooms; agnolotti alla piemontese; green risotto with sparkling wine; beef braised in Barolo wine; fritto misto alle piemontese; fondue with white truffles from Alba; ›Santa Vittoria‹ pudding
Location: opposite the former local parliament
Setting: 18th-century building, lovingly restored in Second Empire style; mirrored walls, red velvet, gilt, marble and crystal chandeliers
Amenities: bar; private dining rooms; air conditioning
Atmosphere: the oldest restaurant in Turin (opened in 1757); elegant, civilized and vaguely museum-like; the ›Florian‹ or ›Savini‹ of Turin
Clientèle: national figures and local dignitaries from Cavour onwards; essential stopover for anybody who is anybody from local aristocracy to self-confident and stylish visitors from overseas
Dress: suitably seemly and sober
Service: black suit, white apron and plenty of charm
Reservations: advisable
Price range: fairly expensive
Credit cards: AE, DC

Café

TORINO
204 Piazza S. Carlo
Telephone: 54 51 18
Owner/Manager: Dante Baudino
Closed: Tuesday
Open: 8.00/a.m.–1.00/a.m.
Location: central
Setting: sumptuous Piedmontese Baroque salons with appropriate accessoires
Amenities: restaurant; bar; café; ice salon
Atmosphere: a grandiose (but not forbidding) evocation of the heyday of the café society
Clientèle: local ladies after gruelling afternoons at the sales; senior executives after a gruelling conference in the boardroom; shopgirls, secretaries, students and senior citizens
Service: appropriately accomplished
Dress: elegant; dernier cri
Reservations: not necessary
Credit cards: AE, EC, Euro, Visa

Nightclub

CHATHAM
3 via Teofilo Rossi
Telephone: 54 53 18
Owner/Manager: Claudio Albanese
Closed: Monday
Open: (nightclub) 22.30/10.30 p.m.–4.30/a.m.
(piano bar) 18.00/6 p.m.–2.00/a.m.
Location: near the Via Roma
Setting: exclusive and elegant discothèque/nightclub complex
Amenities: restaurant; American bar; live music; cabaret; air conditioning; car park
Atmosphere: elegant, intimate
Clientèle: discriminating local night-owls and visiting noctambules from Naples to Nova Scotia
Dress: disco chic
Service: professional and painstaking
Reservations: advisable
Credit cards: AE, DC

Scilp (bathroom accessories)
2 Corso Galileo Ferraris
Steffanone (food and beverages)
2 Via Maria Vittoria
Thesaura (perfumery)
12 Via Gramsci
Borbonese (handbags)
Via Monte Pietà
Bruschi (shoes)
212 Piazza San Carlo
Sacchetti (shoes)
17 Via Pietro Micca
Peyrano Fine Chocolates (chocolatier)
76 Corso Vittorio E II

THE BEST OF ART
Persano, Giorgio (contemporary art)
29 via dei Mille, Tel. 83 55 27/83 08 86

Shopping

EVERYTHING UNDER ONE ROOF
Rinascente   15 Via Lagrange

FOR HIM
De Candia   175 Piazza San Carlo

FOR HER
San Carlo Dal 1973
169–173 Piazza San Carlo

BEAUTY & HAIR
Angelo Cappellini   1 Via Monte Pietà

JEWELLERY
Fasano   325 Via Roma

LOCAL SPECIALITIES
San Lorenzo – Alta Moda/Couture (women's fashion)
Corso Vittoria, 68 Emanuele II
Top Ten (men's fashion)
1 Via Cavour
Olympic (men & women's fashion)
182 Piazza San Carlo
Rosa Azzurro (children's fashion)
4 Piazza Bodoni
Conbipel (leather fashion)
4 Via Amendola
Tiviolo Carlo Furs (furs)
9 Via Pietro Micca
Luxembourg (books)
7 Via C. Battisti
Babele (gifts)
51 Piazza Castello (in the courtyard)
Ginori (porcelain)
95 Via Roma
Laurence (baggage & travel accessories)
15H Via Gramsci
Gurlino Arreda/Gurlino Illumina (interior decorating)
38 Via Carlo Alberto

The City

›Venice is the closest man has come to reconstructing paradise – with its Piazza the world's most beautiful anti-chambre.‹ Napoléon

›If the Earthly Paradise where Adam dwelt with Eve were like Venice, Eve would have had a hard time to tempt him out of it with any apple.‹ Pietro Aretino

›Venice can only be compared with itself.‹ Johann Wolfgang von Goethe

›One of the most marvellous prospects which the human eye can behold.‹ Théophile Gautier

›So, o'er the lagoon we glided; and from that funereal bark I leaned, and saw the city, and could mark how from their many isles, in evening's gleam, its temples and its palaces did seem like fabrics of enchantment piled to heaven.‹ Percy Bysshe Shelley

›Venice is a folding picture-postcard of itself.‹ Mary McCarthy

›When I went to Venice, my dream became my address.‹ Marcel Proust

›Venice seems to personify itself, to become human and sentient, and conscious of your affection. You desire to embrace it, to caress it, to possess it; and finally, a soft sense of possession grows up, and your visit becomes a perpetual love affair.‹ Henry James

›I am a man that has five home towns, Oak Park, Paris, Key West, Havana . . . and Venice.‹ Ernest Hemingway

›Existence is still so easy at Venice, where I begin to feel life through every pore.‹ George Sand

›Venice – the most magnificent fête in the world.‹ Mark Twain

›In Venice the pedestrian is master of the ground as he will be in the new town of our time.‹ Le Corbusier

›Venice is like eating an entire box of chocolate liqueurs at one go.‹ Truman Capote

›Venice – such a magical platform for an amourous encounter.‹ Casanova

›Que c'est triste, Venise, aux temps des amours mortes . . .‹ Charles Aznavour

›Oh Venice! Venice! When thy marble walls are level with the waters, there shall be a cry of nations o'er thy sunken halls, a loud lament along the sweeping sea!‹ Lord Byron

Save Venice! (The Author)

Founded: 421 A.D., according to legend; Venezia (Italian) – from the founding tribe, the Veneti.

Far-reaching events: 639 – Torcello colonized; 727–1797 – rise of Venice as a trading republic ruled by the Doges – Selvo, Dandolo, Foscari et al.; 1003 – St. Mark's Basilica built to house the relics of the saint stolen from Alexandra; 1204 – sack of Constantinople by crusaders under Doge Dandolo – Venice as co-ruler; 15th–16th centuries – Venice's Golden Age in painting concides with gradual loss of political power; 1453 – Constantinople recaptured by the Turks, ending Venice's supremacy in the Levant; 1498 – Vasco da Gama rounds the Cape of Good Hope, ending Venice's monopoly in trade with the Orient; 1516 – the world's first Jewish ghetto established in Venice; 1797 – fall of the Venetian republic to Napoleon's army 1815 – ceded to Austria; 1866 – the Risorgimento – unification of Venice with the Kingdom of Italy; 1966 – the worst flooding in Venice's history; 1973 – worldwide ›Save Venice‹ appeal launched.

Population: 350,000, capital of Venetia.

Postal code: I–30100   **Telephone code:** 41

Climate: extremely mild; some snow in the winter; lovely spring; very warm summer.

Calendar of events: *Carnival* (Feb/Mar) – classical, mystical, Europe's best masked balls and most élite carnival celebrations; *Festival of the Redeener* (3rd Sunday in July) and *Festival of St. Mary of Salvation* (21 Nov) – grand celebrations in memory of deliverance from the plague; *Regatta Storica* (1st Sun in Sep) – a gondola regatta with the gondoliers in historical costumes; *Venice Film Festival* (Aug/Sep) – one of the most respected in the world, on the Lido; *Biennale of Modern Arts* – biennial (Jun to Oct) – art exhibition featuring living artists.

Best views of the city: from the top of *St. Mark's Basilica.*

Historical sights: *St. Marks' Basilica* (1063–73) – Byzantine treasure chest; *Doge's Palace* (12th century) – Gothic, with *Bridge of Sighs; St. Mary of Salvation* (17th century) – by Longhena after an epidemic of plague; *St. George Major* (1566–1610) – Tintorettos and a fine view of the city from the campanile; *Academy of Fine Arts* (15th and 18th century) – Venetian paintings by the Bellinis, Giorgione, Titian, Veronese, Tintoretto, Canaletto, Guardi et al.; *Scuola di San Rocco* (16th century) – Renaissance, canvasses by Tintoretto; *Church of the Friars* – masterpieces by Titian and Florentine Donatello; *Ca d'Oro* (1421–40) – Gothic, former private house with gold façade, now a museum.

Special attractions: *St. Mark's Square* – twenty-four hours a day; a boat trip to Torcello and lunch at *Locanda Cipriani;* a guided water tour along the *Grand Canal;* a trip to the islands of the lagoon – *Giudecca, Murano* (glass-blowing), *Burano* (atmosphere); an evening at the opera at *La Fenice;* a daily routine of breakfast at *Florian's,* lunch at *Harry's Bar,* dinner at *Antico Martini* and the night at *Gritti* or *Cipriani.*

Important companies with headquarters in the city: *Assicurazioni Generali* (insurance); *Coin* (department stores); *Deltasider* (steel); *Dreamland Costruzioni* (shipbuilding); *Fincantieri* (shipbuilding); *Metallotecnica* (shipbuilding); *Sava* (electrochemical processing, aluminium products); *Sirma* (heat-resistant materials).

Airport: Venice-Marco Polo, VCE; Tel.: 66 11 11; 13 km/8 miles, Alitalia, Tel.: 70 03 55.

The Headquarters

GRITTI PALACE
2467 Campo S. M. del Giglio
I–30124 Venice
Telephone: 79 46 11
Telex: 410 125 gritti
Owning Company: Cigahotels
General Manager: Nico Passante
Affiliation/Reservation System: Hello-ciga
Number of rooms: 78 (9 suites)
Price range: Lit. 350,000 (single)
               Lit. 450,000 (double)
Credit cards: AE, DC, EC, Visa
Location: on the Grand Canal, near St. Mark's Square
Built: 15th century (renovated 1948, 1958, 1969)
Style: palatial
Hotel amenities: beauty salon, newsstand, motor launch, private jet rentals
Main hall porter: Mario Varnier
Room amenities: air conditioning, colour tv, minibar/refrigerator (small pets allowed)
Bathroom amenities: bidet, bathrobe, hairdrier, telephone
Room service: 6.30/a.m.–23.30/11.30 p.m.
Conference rooms: 3 (up to 120 persons)
Bar: ›Al Gritti‹ (10.00/a.m.–1.00/a.m.) Giorgio Gasperuzzo (barman), guitarist in winter
Restaurant: ›Club del Doge (Doge's Club; see Restaurants)
Private dining rooms: three

Nico Passante must be a very happy man: he spends most of his life at the Gritti. Few hotels have been immortalized as often as this 15th-century Doge's palazzo on the Canal Grande, across from the church of Santa Maria delle Salute and only a few paddle-strokes away from Piazza San Marco and Harry's Bar – and it would be a formidable undertaking to quote all the poets, novelists and playwrights, the composers, conductors and soloists, the actors, dancers and directors and the countless personalities whose claim to fame derived from the genius to absorb great wealth and the quality to spend some of it here. The guests, for once, try to live up to the standard of the house which embraces everyone with an almost mythological air as well as with the unique beauty, taste and refinement which reigned here before this water castle became the flagship hotel of Italy's prestigious CIGA group. The antiques, materials, colours and paraphernalia are so enchanting, that even the inevitable necessities of our uniform times could not obstruct the nobility and grandeur of this stately landmark as represented by its history, architecture, art and style. And after the most sceptical cynic has seen for himself that the luxury is real from the carpeted boat-landing to the thermostatic-control air conditioning, everyone must join in the laudatio of Ernest Hemingway, Somerset Maugham and Noel Coward, of Arturo Toscanini, Isaac Stern and Cole Porter, of Greta Garbo, Princess Grace and Wallis Windsor – and me.

The Hideaway

CIPRIANI

10 Giudecca (Giudecca Island)
I–30123 Venice (3 minutes by launch
from St. Mark's Square)
Telephone: 70 77 44
Telex: 410 162 ciprve
General Manager: N. Rusconi
Affiliation/Reservation Systems: The
Leading Hotels of the World, Relais et
Châteaux
Closed: December–mid February
Number of rooms: 98 (28 suites)
Price range: L 370,000–620,000
Credit cards: AE, DC, EC, Visa
Location: on the island of Giudecca
Built: 1958; grand hotel style
Main hall porter: S. Cavallarin
Conference rooms: 5 (up to 200 persons)
Bars: ›Pool Bar‹ Guido Fusaro (barman),
pianist; ›Cocktail Bar‹; ›Il Gabbiano‹
(20.30/8.30 p.m.–1.00/a.m.), piano bar
Restaurants: ›Poolside‹ (12.30/p.m.–
15.00/3.00 p.m.) Antonio Pandin (maî-
tre), Giovanni Spaventa (chef de cuisine);
›Cipriani‹ (19.30/7.30 p.m.–22.30/10.30
p.m.)

*How to describe paradise to an atheist?
You can debate the beauty of Cathérine
Deneuve, the genius of Andrew Lloyd
Webber and the value of a Warhol, but not
even the spoiled snob would disparage this
quintessential masterwork of modern ho-
tellerie – priceless beauty to perfection.
With Guidecca lending the stage, the Palladian magnificence of cupolas and spires
providing the backdrop and the skyline of
the world's most breathtakingly resplendent city forming the panorama, the site
alone is heavenly. With the late Commend-
atore Guiseppe Cipriani as the master-
mind, the Guinness family the partners in
the execution of this villa-palace-Eden, the
owning bel-esprit-tycoon James Sherwood's generosity and grandseigneur-hotelier Natale Rusconi's refined direction,
the Cipriani just has to be the most blessed
hotel in the world. It is also the only one in
Venice with a tennis court and a scenic
swimming pool most Riviera resorts would
envy. True to its name, the Cipriani's three
restaurants live up to alta cucina standard
(pasta, pâtisserie and croissants are made
daily in the house), and its antipasti buffet
rates as the most outstanding in the country. A high-level business dinner at the Ca-
baret-Grill* Il Gabbiano *or a candle-light
tête-à-tête on the lagoon terrace are events
souvenirs and historic moments are made
of. And when you enter your poolside suite
or just any other room, you will understand
why the world loves Italy beyond the Antiquity. Luxury from bed to bath, from door-
handles to writing paper. The servants
seem to have been palazzo-trained and
know your idiosyncrasies by your physiognomy. And if ever you want to go to Piazza
San Marco, there is the Cipriani's private
launch to whisk you across the water at any
given moment – don't look back when you
are finally carried to the mainland: you
will sink into an Aschenbach melancholy.*

Lunch

LOCANDA CIPRIANI
Isola di Torcello (40 minutes by launch
from St. Mark's Square)
Telephone: 73 01 50
Owner/Manager: Carla Cipriani
Closed: Tuesday (except July–September); November 4th–March 18th
Open: 8.00/a.m.–24.00/12 p.m.
Cuisine: Italian classic and local à la Cipriani
Specialities: polenta; semolina dumplings (gnocchi); seafood risotto; meat
and fish dishes accompanied by vegetables and salads from the garden; carpaccio alla Carlina; filetti di sogliola alla
Waleska; crêpes à la crème
Location: on the island of Torcello (40
minutes from Venice) by water taxi (expensive) or 50 minutes by vaporetto
(cheaper); next door to the Byzantine basilica
Setting: country-style inn set in well-
cared-for gardens; dining room Italian
rustic with cane-seated chairs, exposed
beams and hurricane lamps; most tables
on shady porches and vine-covered terraces with views of the garden and the basilica
Amenities: 6 exquisite bedrooms for overnight guests; perfect for writing novels
(like Hemingway), for painting pictures
(like Churchill) or for merely basking in
the idyllic peace of Torcello once the day-
trippers have left
Atmosphere: from an elegantized fête
champêtre to a romantic idyll
Clientèle: visiting royalty to resident millionaires; favourite venue for wedding
receptions amongst Venice's bourgeois
élite; devotees of the culinary achievements of the Cipriani clan wishing to
sample its delights far from the madding
crowd of Harry's Bar
Dress: Sunday casual to Sunday best
Service: quick and smiling
Reservations: recommended (no dogs)
Price range: justifiably expensive
Credit cards: AE, Visa

Dinner

ANTICO MARTINI
Campo San Fantin 1983 San Marco
Telephone: 2 41 21
Owner/Manager: Emilio Baldi
Closed: Tuesday; Wednesday lunchtime;
December–February
Open: 12.00/a.m.–15.00/3 p.m. and
19.00/7 p.m.–1.00/a.m. (last orders at
14.30/2.30 p.m. and 23.30/11.30 p.m.)
Cuisine: classic and local, with own spe-
cialities
Chef de cuisine: Dino del Puppo
Specialities: cannelloni Nizzarda; filetti
di soglia Martini; grilled scampi; calves'

liver with polenta; fillet of John Dory alla
Betty; involtini di salmone (with whipped
cream, horseradish, caviar and Tabasco
sauce); filetto di bue del chef (fillet steak
with chicken liver, sauce béarnaise and
sauce Marsala); chocolate cake; marzipan tart; tiramisù
Location: next to La Fenice theatre
Setting: established in 1720 – run by the
present owner's family since 1921; elegant 18th-century décor; in summer, a
pretty covered terrace overlooking the
imposing façade of the theatre
Amenities: bar; nightclub with terrace
and orchestra; air conditioning
Atmosphere: elegant, civilized and almost
too beautiful to be true
Clientèle: from Karajan to Sir Laurence
Olivier; conductors, performers and
spectators who can dine during the interval and dash back in time for the next act
thanks to the bellboy who patrols the restaurant to ensure that no-one comes too
late
Dress: jacket and tie
Service: excellent
Reservations: advisable
Price range: rather expensive
Credit cards: AE, DC, Euro, Visa, Master
Charge

Lunch

CIPRIANI
10 Isola della Giudecca (3 minutes by
launch from St. Mark's Square)
Telephone: 70 77 44
Owner/Manager: Hotel Cipriani S.p.A./
Antonio Pandin
Closed: November 24th – February 28th
Open: 7.30/a.m.–22.30/10.30 p.m.
Cuisine: Italian (regional) and interna-
tional
Chef de cuisine: Giovanni Spaventa
Specialities: antipasti Cipriani; fillet of
John Dory (San Pietro) with artichokes;
risotto with vegetables or fish; spinach
tagliolini with ham; calves' liver with po-
lenta; soufflé Nerone; pâtisserie; hors
d'œuvres; buffet at lunch time (May–
Sept.)
Location: in the hotel Cipriani, on the is-
land of Giudecca
Setting: spacious dining room; luxuri-
ously appointed; reminiscent of Boris
Godunov rather than the Doges of Venice
Amenities: hotel; private dining rooms
(20–100 persons); buffet lunches by the
swimming pool (May–Sept.); cabaret-
grill; pianist; air conditioning
Atmosphere: elegantly escapist
Clientèle: jet-setters in search of relative
seclusion; jeunesse dorée; admirers of
Palladio's architecture seeking suste-
nance after viewing the ›Redentore‹
Dress: informal at lunch; tie and jacket
de rigueur for dinner
Service: appropriately professional;

pool-side waiters dressed in naval-type uniforms
Reservations: yes (pets prohibited)
Price range: fairly expensive
Credit cards: AE

Dinner

CLUB DEL DOGE (Doge's Club)
2467 Campo Santa Maria del Giglio
Telephone: 79 46 11 (2 60 44)
Owner/Manager: Cigahotels / Giovanni Gava
Closed: never
Open: 8.00/a.m.–11.00/a.m.; 12.30/p.m.–15.30/3.30 p.m. and 19.30/7.30 p.m.–23.30/11.30 p.m.
Cuisine: Italian, regional and international
Chef de cuisine: Carlo Ciccarelli
Specialities: ham mousse Wally; vegetable risotto; spinach noodles au gratin; fried scampi with greens (in Erbaria); sliced raw beef with shrimps and celery (Gran Maestro); zabaione
Location: in the Gritti Palace Hotel
Setting: 15th-century Doge's palace; in winter in the dining room with decorated wooden beam ceiling; old Venetian style; marble floor and oriental carpets; in summer on the terrace overlooking the Grand Canal towards Santa Maria della Salute
Amenities: private dining rooms (15–120 persons); pianist in winter; air conditioning
Atmosphere: palatial; inimitable recreation of a unique lifestyle
Clientèle: tourists and Venice lovers; lovers of any age, nationality and sex; politicians, artists and writers from the Old World and the New; Aga Khan; Gore Vidal; Yehudi Menuhin; Robert de Niro and Paul Newman
Dress: according to season and circumstance
Service: in line with the décor and the ambiente
Reservations: recommended
Price range: aristocratic
Credit cards: AE, DC, Euro, Visa

Meeting Point

GRAN CAFFE RESTAURANT QUADRI
120 Piazza San Marco
Telephone: 5 22 21 05
Owner/Manager: Antonio Fulgenzi
Closed: Monday (except July–September); (café) mid-December–end of January; (restaurant) November–April/May
Open: 12.00/a.m.–14.30/2.30 p.m. and 20.00/8 p.m.–22.30/10.30 p.m.
Location: opposite Caffè Florian, on the Piazza San Marco
Setting: 17th–century Venetian inside;

outside, plenty of tables in the ›world's most beautiful salon‹ with a view of St. Mark's, the Campanile, the tourists, the locals – and the pigeons
Amenities: restaurant; orchestra
Atmosphere: as essential a stopover for all visitors to Venice since the era of the Grand Tour as the Doge's Palace and the Rialto Bridge
Clientèle: writers from Byron to Cocteau; composers from Liszt to Wagner; artists, aristocrats and visiting royalty from Braque to Princess Margaret – in short, everyone who is anyone who is not at Florian's – and vice-versa
Service: surprisingly cordial, even at busy times
Reservations: advisable for restaurant
Prices: appropriately exorbitant
Credit cards: AE, DC, Euro, Visa

Café

FLORIAN
Piazza San Marco
Telephone: 8 53 38
Owner/Manager: Giovanni Lorenzoni
Closed: Wednesday
Open: 9.00/a.m.–24.00/12 p.m.
Location: on the Piazza San Marco
Setting: mid-19th century grandeur; mirrors, wall paintings on various themes giving the different salons their names (Chinese, Persian etc.): Murano glass chandeliers; fine china, glass and silver
Amenities: large terrace on the Piazza San Marco; orchestra; restaurant
Atmosphere: the oldest and most famous café in Europe (established 1720); the foyer of the ›world's most beautiful salon‹
Clientèle: Casanova, Madame de Staël, Goethe, Proust; mélange of foreign aristocracy, Venetian nobility, artists, sculptors, writers and tourists from Pasadena to Penang – not to mention the resident pigeons
Service: remarkably friendly
Reservations: essential for dinner
Prices: appropriately exorbitant (surcharge on first order when the orchestra is playing)

Bar

HARRY'S BAR
1323 Vallaresso
Telephone: 5 23 67 97
Owner/Manager: Arrigo Cipriani
Closed: Monday; January 8th–21st
Open: 10.30/a.m.–0.30/12.30 a.m.
Cuisine: Italian classic and local à la Cipriani
Chef de cuisine: Alfredo Del Peschio
Specialities: carpaccio with sauce tartare; taglierini verdi; the best risotto in Italy, with changing accompaniments accord-

ing to season; squid with polenta; calves' liver with onions (fegato di vitello alla veneziana); millefeuille
Location: two gondoliers' poles from the San Marco landing stage
Setting: swinging door; tiny restaurant upstairs; elegant, closely-packed tables
Amenities: grey marble-topped bar downstairs (the best vantage point); air conditioning
Atmosphere: vaguely American and yet reminiscent of a Venetian Commedia dell'Arte; cheerful, lively, rather noisy at times – but never dull
Clientèle: essential port of call for the Who's Who of literature, high society and the arts since the days of Somerset Maugham, Ernest Hemingway and Charlie Chaplin
Dress: elegantly casual to casually elegant
Service: good-humoured, acrobatic and multilingual
Reservations: essential (it's always packed)
Price range: inevitably expensive
Credit cards: DC, Euro, Visa

Mobili Boselli (interior decorating)
3540 Castello San Antonin
Aliani (food and beverages)
644/5 San Polo
Mariani (perfumery)
1291 Salizada San Moisé – San Marco
La Fenice (shoes)
2255 Via XXII Marzo – San Marco
Jesurum (lace)
4310 Ponto Canonica – San Marco
Arianna da Venezia (hand-painted velvet)
3130 Campo San Barnaba – Dorsoduro
Monovo (masks)
Dorsoduro – Campo San Barnaba – Ponte dei Pugni

THE BEST OF ART
Il Traghetto (modern art)
2460 San Marco, Tel. 2 11 88
Ravagnan (contemporary art)
50A Piazza San Marco, Tel. 70 30 21
Casellati, Pippo (18th-century antiques)
2404 San Marco, Tel. 3 09 66
Scarpa, Pietro (fine Old Master paintings and drawings)
2089 2155 v. XXII Marzo, Tel. 2 71 99/70 44 24

Shopping

EVERYTHING UNDER ONE ROOF
Coin Cannareggio – Ponte dell'Ogio 5788

FOR HIM
Elite 284 Calle larga San Marco

FOR HER
Elisabetta alla Fenice
196 Campo Teatro Fenice

BEAUTY & HAIR
Umberto 5024 San Marco – Mescerie

JEWELLERY
Missiaglia 125 Piazza San Marco

LOCAL SPECIALITIES
Rossella (women's fashion)
4600 San Marco – Teatro Goldoni
Al Duca d'Aosta (men & women's fashion)
4922/3 San Marco – Mercerie
Tato e Tata (children's fashion)
4488 San Marco – San Luca
Camerino, Roberta di (leather fashion)
1256 Calle dell' Ascensione
Ferro (furs)
San Marco – Campo San Bartolomeo
Libri d'Arte Electa (books)
4221 Campo San Luca – San Marco
Vetri Murano (glass)
175 San Gregorio – Dorsoduro
Salviati (porcelain)
195 San Gregorio
Vugini (baggage & travel accessories)
1292 Calle dell' Ascension – San Marco

The City

William Shakespeare never made it this far south (in fact, he never left the shores of his scepter'd isle). Giuseppe Verdi never showed great interest in the ›scene of the crime‹, either. And yet, their twin geniuses hover as possessively over ›fair Verona‹ as Mozart over Salzburg or Wagner over Bayreuth. The summer festival season lures Aida-addicts and Macbeth-maniacs from the Old World and the New – couturier-clad Beautiful People who stay at the ›Two Towers‹, dine at the ›Twelve Apostles‹ and sip espressi or the fine local wines at the boulevard cafés of the Piazza Brà before taking their place in the vast Roman Arena. La Traviata's consumptive arias alternate with the despairing suicides of those ›star-cross'd lovers‹, Romeo and Juliet, in an atmosphere of high drama and grand passion where once gladiators fought and chariots raced. Verona has always been a stage for business encounters and commercial meetings as well, her location on the banks of the Adige at the junction of the Brenner Pass and the Plains of the River Po making the city a natural focal point for the region. Monuments to this mercantile prosperity abound, from the arcaded Piazza dei Signori to the bustling Piazza delle Erbe, the secular palazzi and Gothic mausolea of the Montecchi, the Capuleti and the Scaligeri vying for glory with each other and with the less profane splendours of the cathedral and churches. Dominating the marbled red-and-ochre medieval and Renaissance splendour by virtue of antiquity and scale, the Roman monuments, from the stone bridge to the Porta Borsari to the amphitheatre, recall the city that Latin love-poet Catullus, local-born writer Scipione Maffei and painter Paolo Veronese – and even exiled Florentine Dante Alighieri – loved so well. In fact, everyone loves Verona – sun-hungry Nordic hordes en route to the coasts as much as élitarian globe-gallopers from around the world. It goes without saying that Verona loves herself, too. With beautiful Lake Garda and the Dolomites behind and the ›sunny plains and deep indigo transparent skies of Italy‹ before her, Verona is a symphony of colours, forms and emotions crystallising the myriad moods of two millenia of the peninsula's history.

Founded: 5th–4th century B.C. by Celts; Verona – from the Roman colony.

Far-reaching events: 1st century B.C. – colonia Augusta Verona, an important Roman colony; 312 – taken by Constantine; 4th century – archbishop Zeno; 489 – Theodorich wins over Odoaker; 952 – part of German empire; 1107 – free city; 1164 – Union of Verona against Friedrich I; 1260–1387 – Princes of the Scala; 1302 – Romeo and Juliet; 1308 – Cangrande I rules the city; arts flourish; 1387 – annexed by Milan; 1405–1801 – Venetian rule; 1797–1805 – under Austrian rule; 1805 – reverts to Italy; 1814 – Austrian again; 1882 – Congress of Verona; 1866 – becomes part of the united Italy; 1882 – the River Adige floods the city; 1939–45 – heavy damage during World War II.

Population: 275,000.

Postal code: I-37100   **Telephone code:** 45

Climate: mild spring and autumn; relatively mild winters, hot in summer.

Calendar of events: *Bacchanal de Guocchi* (Feb) – the closing festivities of Carnival in Verona; *Opera Festival* in the Arena (Jul/Aug) – a variety of cultural events including ballet, concerts, exhibitions and opera from June to September; *Shakespeare Festival* (Sep) – in the Roman theatre; *Sagra dei Osei* (Sep) – a festival of birds.

Fairs and exhibitions: *INTERNATIONAL AGRICULTURAL AND ZOOTECHNICAL FAIR* (Mar); *NINITALY* (Apr) – wine industry fair; *REGALIT* (Apr) – food gifts exhibition; *EUROFORESTA* (May, biennial) – forestry fair; *MOBILARTE* (May) – designer furniture fair; *HERBORA* (May) – plants for medicinal use; *MARMORAC* (Sep) – international fair for the marble, granite and stone processing industry; *EUROCARNE* (Oct) – international exhibition for the meat processing industry; *INTECSOL* (Oct, biennial) – agricultural energy convention; *SAMOTER* (Oct, biennial) – earth moving and building machinery exhibition; *INTERNATIONAL HORSE AND RIDING ACCESSORIES SALON* (Nov).

Historical sights: *San Zeno Major* (1120) – Romanesque, bronze plated doors, triptych (1459) by Mantegna; *Arena* (1st century) – one of the largest in the Roman world; *Piazza Brà*; *Cathedral of Our Lady of Miracles* (12th century) – Romanesque chancel, Gothic nave, classical tower; Titian's ›Assunta‹; *Piazza delle Erbe* – former Roman forum, with winged Lion of St. Mark (1523); *Palazzo Maffei* (1668) – Baroque; *Tombs of the Scaligers* (14th century) – Gothic mausoleum; *Old Castle and Bridge of the Scaligers* (14th century) – with museum containing works by Veronese and Venetian artists; *St. Anastasia* (1290–1481) – Gothic, doorway with frescoes and sculptures; *Juliet's House* (13th century) – with the famous balcony; *Piazza dei Signori* with the *Loggia del Consiglio* (1476–1793) and the *Café Dante* (19th century); *St. Laurence* (founded 17th century) – Romanesque, typical Veronese architecture.

Special attractions: a night at the opera in the *Arena*; a Shakespeare play at the *Roman Theatre* (it sounds so much better in Italian!); a night at the *Due Torri*; a drive through the *gardens* at Valeggio Sul Mincio and lunch at the *Antica Locanda Mincio*.

Important companies with headquarters in the city: *Abital* (men's clothes); *Auto Germa* (car import); *Bertani* (wine); *Bolla* (wine); *Cartiere Fedrigoni* (paper); *Fro Saldatura* (electrical appliances); *Hero Verona* (tinned fruits, marmelade); *Mazzi* (construction).

Airport: Verona-Villafranca, VRN; Tel.: 51 37 00, 12 km/7 miles; Alitalia, Tel.: 59 42 22.

The Headquarters

DUE TORRI

5 Piazza Santa Anastasia
I–37121 Verona
Telephone: 59 50 44
Telex: 480 524 duetor
Owner: The Wallner Family
General Manager: Raimondo Giavarini
Affiliation/Reservation Systems: The
Leading Hotels of the World, Steigen-
berger Reservation Service
Number of rooms: 86 (14 suites)
Price range: Lit. 170,000–260,000
Credit cards: AE, DC, EC
Location: city centre
Built: 14th century (renovated 1958)
Style: antique and modern
Hotel amenities: garage, valet parking,
house limousine service
Main hall porter: Angelo Varnier
Room amenities: air conditioning, colour
tv, mini-bar/refrigerator (pets allowed)
Bathroom amenities: bidet, bathrobe,
hairdrier
Room service: 24 hours
Conference rooms: 5 (up to 250 persons)
Bars: ›American Bar‹ (see Bars); ›Boîte‹
(20.00/8.00/p.m.–2.00/a.m., open Sept.
to May) pianist
Restaurant: ›Due Torri‹ (see Restaurant)

*Long before Romeo and Juliet came to
tragic world fame and idolization by all
lovers ever since, the Scaligeri Princes,
Lords of Verona, built this house as the
Foresteria for their guests; over 100 years
ago, known as the Grand Hôtel Impérial
aux Deux Tours, it returned to modesty by
name but more than lived up to the imperial grandeur on its coat-of-arms, and with
châtelain Raimondo Giavarini continually
restoring the past and simultaneously rejuvenating the rooms and amenities for the
future, the Due Torri has become one of the
living legends in world hôtellerie. Goethe
doesn't stop here any more, nor does Amadeus M. and not even la Callas, but for
Placido Domingo and Luciano Pavarotti it
is one of the favourite residences, and royal
families, sheikhs and the Gettys don't continue on to Venice for the very reason that
there is the Due Torri. Few hospitable fortresses in the world have the beauty, the
flair and the warmth of service that you
find here, fewer still could claim such tasteful and harmonious bedchambers, lounges
and one of the most glamourous foyers
anywhere. The perfection is completed by
the efficiency and flexibility of the staff,
combining northern exactness with Latin
charm. The location, across from a museal
cathedral and only steps away from the elegant shopping streets and flamboyant market places, is as splendid as the innumerable antiques and personal touches
throughout the palace as well as the superb
cuisine alla italianissima. Whether for a
sombre commercial dealing or a charis-
matic performance in the Arena, there is always one highlight more to look forward to
in Verona: the Due Torri.*

The Hideaway

VILLA CORTINE

12 Via Grotte
I–25019 Sirmione
(Lombardy; 45 km/28 miles)
Telephone: (30) 91 60 21/2
Telex: 300 171 vicopa
General Manager: Roberto Cappelletto
Closed: end of Oct – end of March
Number of rooms: 54
Price range: Lit. 190,000–280,000
Credit cards: AE, DC, EC, MC, Visa
Location: Lake Garda, 130 km/80 miles
from Milan airport
Built: 1900, renovated in 1981 and 1985
Style: Renaissance-style 19th-century
villa
Hotel amenities: car park, air conditioning, wheelchair accessibility, swimming
pool, private beach, formal garden, tennis
court

Main hall porter: Maurizio Luise
Room amenities: balcony; tv, mini-bar
(some), (pets allowed)
Bathroom amenities: hairdrier (some),
bidet
Room service: 7.30 a.m.–24.00/12 p.m.
Laundry/dry cleaning: laundry same day;
dry cleaning 2 days
Conference rooms: 2 (up to 40 persons)
Sports nearby: golf
Bars: ›American Bar‹
Restaurant: (12.30 p.m.–14.30/2.30 p.m.
and 19.30/7.30 p.m.–21.30/9.30 p.m.) Mr.
Jukich (maître), international and Italian
cuisine, open-air dining, ›Beach Restaurant‹, barbecue lunch and buffet
Private dining rooms: upon request

*When, in summer, the heat haze shimmers
over the plains of Lombardy and the descendants of all the Montagues and Capulets take to the hills, abandoning their city
to the opera lovers from the Old World and
the New, the Villa Cortine is a cool and
peaceful base for those wishing to sketch
the mountain scenery or explore the nearby
grottoes of Catullus. The exquisite Renaissance-style palazzo stands amidst olive
trees and cypresses on the outskirts of
Sirmione, a picturesque little town with a
crenellated medieval fortress at the tip of a
narrow peninsula jutting out into the southern end of Lake Garda. Built at the turn of
the century, it stands in a magnificent formal garden adorned with fountains and
statues, a swimming pool surrounded by
palm trees and a tennis court. The classical
dignity of the porticoed and pillared façade
is continued in the entrance hall with its
marble-flagged floor and imposing Doric
columns. The bedrooms, by contrast, have
modern lamps and furnishings, and when
you step out onto the balcony you have a
magnificent view of the grounds and the
lake. The ambiente on the lovely terrace as
dusk falls is unashamedly romantic; the
staff are charming without being obsequious, and the cuisine is good. In spite of the
addition of such modern refinements as air
conditioning, the Villa Cortine retains essentially an air of unhurried elegance more
characteristic of a bygone era.*

Lunch

LE ARCHE
6 Via Arche Scaligere
Telephone: 2 14 15
Owner/Manager: Giancarlo Gioco
Closed: Sunday; Monday lunchtime;
first three weeks in June/July
Open: 12.30/p.m.–14.30/2.30 p.m. and
20.00/8 p.m.–22.00/10 p.m.
Cuisine: local traditional and creative;
seafood
Chef de cuisine: Paola Gaspari and Bi-
anca Busini
Specialities: mussel salad with black truffles ›Vivaldi‹; sea-bass ravioli with shellfish sauce; baked scorpion-fish with
black olives; sea-bass and seafood en papillote; John Dory with artichokes alla
Marco Polo; orange Bavarian cream
Location: near the Piazza delle Poste
Setting: next to former home of the Montagues (Montecchi); a tavern, inn and restaurant since 1420 – directed by the
owner's family for a century; old Veronese style; painted porcelain, silver, fine
linen and Murano chandeliers
Amenities: small bar for restaurant customers' use
Atmosphere: charming; civilized
Clientèle: gentlemen of Verona with their
ladies; Shakespeare scholars; expense-
account gourmets
Dress: as you like it
Service: knowledgeably directed by Giancarlo Gioco
Reservations: advisable to essential (pets
permitted)
Price range: moderately expensive
Credit cards: not accepted

Dinner

DUE TORRI
4 Piazza Santa Anastasia
Telephone: 59 50 44
Owner/Manager: Raimondo Giavarini
Closed: never
Open: 12.30/p.m.–14.30/2.30 p.m. and
19.30/7.30 p.m.–22.00/10 p.m.
Cuisine: local, national and international
Chef de cuisine: Onorio Clama
Specialities: antipasto ›Gourmet‹ (kiwi,
shrimps and grapefruit); involtino di
crêpes ›Due Torri‹ (with ham and aspara-
gus); veal cutlet en papillote (with mush-
rooms, ham and white wine)
Location: in the Hotel Due Torri
Setting: in an aesthetically beautiful pa-
lazzo; modern décor; porcelain and
dishes of the ›Company of the Indies‹
dating back to 1700
Amenities: hotel; private dining rooms;
air conditioning
Atmosphere: quiet, refined and dignified
Clientèle: when in Verona ... hotel
guests including – in the past – Mozart,

Goethe, Tsar Alexander I and Maria Cal-
las – plus more recent visitors to the Fes-
tival – opera-stars, opera-producers and
opera-fans
Dress: elegant
Service: palatial
Reservations: advisable (no dogs)
Price range: de luxe
Credit cards: AE, DC, Euro, Master Card

Dinner

RE TEODORICO
Piazzale Castel San Pietro
Telephone: 4 99 90
Owner/Manager: Rodolfo Florean
Closed: Wednesday; 15 Nov–15 Dec
Open: 12.00/p.m.–15.00/3 p.m. and
18.30/6.30 p.m.–24.00/12 p.m.
Cuisine: local; ›au goût du marché‹
Chef de cuisine: Ernesto Regolin
Specialities: risotto di zucca; home-made
pasta; scaloppa Teodorico (veal escalope
with ham, cheese and foie gras)
Location: near Juliet's tomb
Setting: stylish dining room; harmoni-
ously finished; red stone fireplace; fine
silver; magnificent views of the city and
the river Adige
Amenities: outdoor dining in courtyard
(floodlit at night)
Atmosphere: stylish; luxurious; rather
festive
Clientèle: Verona's Haute Bourgeoisie
with cause for celebration; local industrialists, members of the liberal professions
and the occasional tourist en passant
Dress: according to season and circum-
stance
Service: courteous and efficient
Reservations: advisable (no dogs)
Price range: moderate
Credit cards: AE, DC, Carte, Bleue

Lunch

ANTICA LOCANDA MINCIO
12 Via Michelangelo, Borghetto di
Valeggio sul Mincio (20 km/13 miles)
Telephone: 7 95 00 59
Affiliations: SKAL Club, Touring Club
Owner/Manager: Gabriele Bertaiola
Closed: Thursday; November–March
Open: 12.30/p.m.–15.00/3.00 p.m. and
19.00/7 p.m.–22.00/10 p.m.
Cuisine: regional – casalinga
Chef de cuisine: Angelo Rossi
Specialities: pasta; tortellini in butter;
tortellini with marrow; fettucine with
mushrooms; charcoal-grilled meat and
fish from Lake Garda; peaches in syrup;
home-made desserts (the best zabaione in
world)
Location: half-way between Verona and
Mantua; 12 km (8 miles) from Villafranca
Airport

Setting: idyllic historic country inn on the banks of the Mincio, surrounded by picturesque old bridge, Romanesque church, ruined castle; stylish but comfortable period furnishing
Amenities: shady terrace under linden trees, with tubs of hibiscus, oleander and hydrangeas
Atmosphere: welcoming and friendly
Clientele: Italian Sunday morning crowd en famille; all the descendants of the Montagues and the Capulets; aesthetes from Cinecitta to La Scala, from Monica Vitti to Mirella Freni
Dress: Sunday casual to Sunday best
Service: Italian charm
Reservations: advisable (dogs allowed)
Price range: philanthropic for what it offers
Credit cards: AE

Dinner

IL DESCO
7 Via Dietro San Sebastiano
Telephone: 2 38 27
Owner/Manager: Elia Rizzo and Natale Spinelli
Closed: Sunday; 1–16 Jan
Open: 12.00–15.30/3.30 p.m. and 19.30/7.30–23.00/11 p.m.
Cuisine: nuova cucina italiana
Chef de cuisine: Elia Rizzo
Specialities: fish pudding with parsley and herb vinegar sauce; hot squid with shallots and beetroot; curd cheese and nut ravioli; jack-knife clams with paprika; sea-bass with fennel; fillet of beef with Amarone wine; calf's kidneys with Savoy cabbage and raspberry vinegar; chocolate mousse with peppermint sauce
Setting: small, intimate restaurant in a lovingly-restored Veronese palazzo
Amenities: air conditioning; car park in the vicinity
Atmosphere: a bright new star in the town's culinary firmament; raffiné
Clientèle: connoisseurs of fine food from Copenhagen to Cannes, attracted by Elia Rizzo's growing reputation as a chef of originality and distinction
Dress: within reason, what you will
Service: punctilious and professional; supervised by Natale Spinelli
Reservations: recommended (no dogs)
Price range: moderately expensive
Credit cards: AE, DC, Euro, Visa

Dinner

I DODICI APOSTOLI
3 Corticella San Marco
Telephone: 59 69 99
Owner/Managers: Franco and Giorgio Gioco
Closed: Sunday evening; Monday: June 15th–July 8th; December 25th–31st

Open: 12.30/a.m.–15.00/3 p.m. and 19.30/7.30–22.00/10 p.m.
Cuisine: local
Chef de cuisine: Giorgio Gioco
Specialities: salmon or ham en croûte; fish from Lake Garda; cheese and truffle flan; meat from the trolley; the best selection of cheeses in Italy; unusual wines
Location: in the historic town centre; just off the Piazza delle Erbe
Setting: ancient taverna established nearly 300 years ago; Renaissance décor with frescoes relating the story of Romeo and Juliet; two dining rooms, the recent renovation of which revealed the walls of an ancient Roman temple – now preserved for inspection by visitors
Amenities: air conditioning; terrace
Atmosphere: as much an institution in Verona as the Arena and the Due Torri
Clientèle: latter-day lovers; visitors to Verona from Valparaiso to Port Vila – and a moderate sprinkling of Veronese en fête
Dress: elegant to casual
Service: to perfection – supervised by Franco Gioco aided by sommeliers Raimondo Sergio and Gianni Rossin
Reservations: recommended
Price range: fairly expensive
Credit cards: DC

Café

DANTE
Piazza dei Signori
Telephone: 3 01 44
Closed: never
Open: 9.00/a.m.–20.00/8 p.m.
Location: on the Piazza dei Signori (›Piazza Dante‹)
Setting: a traditional 19th-century-style café on one of Verona's most architecturally harmonious squares; open-air dining on terrace with an uninterrupted view of the tourists being pensively surveyed by the author of the ›Divine Comedy‹ from his pedestal in the centre
Atmosphere: a more tranquil alternative to the bustling cafés surrounding the Piazza delle Erbe
Clientèle: heterogeneous; local Veronese between home and office or market, plus an assortment of footsore foreigners between Juliet's House and the Arena
Service: friendly

Bar

AMERICAN BAR
4 Piazza Santa Anastasia
Telephone: 59 50 44
Owner/Manager: Raimondo Giavarini
Closed: never

Open: 8.00/a.m.–1.00/a.m.
Location: in the Hotel Due Torri
Setting: sumptuously-appointed hotel bar decorated with modern frescoes
Amenities: hotel; restaurant; private dining rooms (30–250 persons); air conditioning
Atmosphere: unashamedly luxurious
Clientèle: the Who's Who of distinguished visitors to Verona; Middle-Eastern potentates; international politicians; financiers; superstars – from Burt Lancaster to Luciano Pavarotti
Service: impeccable; directed by chief barman Tony Dolfo
Reservations: advisable
Credit cards: AE, DC, Euro, Visa

Bar

LA CAPPA
Piazza Bra Molinari
Telephone: 3 45 16
Owner/Manager: Rolando Cestaro
Closed: Sunday
Open: 11.30/a.m.–1.00/a.m.
Location: in the central pedestrian area of the town
Setting: typical Veronese bar on a little piazza, with a shady terrace overlooking the River Adige
Atmosphere: the unofficial communications centre of Verona; buzzing with all the latest news (or gossip), especially during the ›Happy Hour‹
Clientèle: attractively approachable; from local aristocracy to the man-in-the-street and the task force of the local carabinieri
Service: Italianissimo
Reservations: advisable

Shopping

EVERYTHING UNDER ONE ROOF
Coin   30 Via Cappello

FOR HIM
Battistoni   18 Corso IV Novembre

FOR HER
Novella   18 Via C. Cattaneo

BEAUTY & HAIR
Luisa   18 Via Cappello

JEWELLERY
Pozzo   70 Via Mazzini
Bordegnoni F.   12 Via Rosa

LOCAL SPECIALITIES
BeC (women's fashion)
4 Via Cantore
Il Bagaglio (women's fashion)
8 Via Catullo
Al Ducca d'Aosta (men & women's fashion) 31 Via Mazzini
Birilli (Baby Shop) (children's fashion)
3 A Via Ponte Nuovo
Castelli (furs)
32 Via Mazzini
Cortina (books)
8 Via Cattaneo
Richard-Ginori (gifts and porcelain)
74 Via Mazzini
Cordovano (baggage & travel accessories)
2/A Galleria Mazzini
Aedes (interior decorating)
11 Via Redentore
Sinico (food and beverages)
5 Via Leoni & 29 Corso di Porta Borsari
Fadini (perfumery)
7 Piazza Erbe
Cordioli (sweets)
39 Via Cappello
Principe (shoes)
80 Via Mazzini

THE BEST OF ART
Dello Scudo   (modern art)
2 Via Scudo di Francia, Tel. 59 01 44
Studio La Città   (modern art)
10 vicolo Samaritana, Tel. 2 57 28

The City

It's highly advantageous to carry a Swiss passport, but it's so much more fashionable to acquire a Liechtensteinian one, even though it may be as difficult as purchasing a luxury dacha on the Crimea. Since the mini-state only has a population of some 26,000 (of whom one third are foreigners – and that's more than enough in the eyes of the natives) and boasts one of the lowest birth rates in Europe, being born a Liechtensteiner takes some arranging. Being elected one is even more difficult, with the whole Parliament having to agree, and has only been achieved by a handful of illustrious outsiders like publisher Richard Gruner. Fortunately, spending one night in the capital, Vaduz, poses no such problems. If you approach the micro-metropolis via Switzerland you may even erroneously succumb to the temptation of regarding the principality as a supernumerary canton of the Confederation since there are no visible borders. It's true that the neighbours have more in common than a tradition of political neutrality, stunning Alpine scenery, and an Alemannic variant of the German language. Currency in both countries is the Swiss franc, and the Berne government acts for its tiny neighbour in foreign affairs. (Liechtenstein has recently applied for independent representation at the United Nations.) Within the country's boundaries, encompassing an area one tenth the size of Greater London, the fifteen-man parliament upholds the constitution under the benevolent aegis of Prince Hans Adam (acting on behalf of his father, Prince Franz Joseph II), whilst the 40-strong Princely Liechtenstein Police Force maintains law and order and doubles up as army and air force (which leaves them with no time to organize a navy on the Rhine). Vaduz is a diminutive town on the edge of the river valley, set against the rugged panorama of the Vorarlberg Mountains and dominated by the medieval walled and turreted castle built by the Austrian ancestors of the Royal Family. The houses, clustered around the graceful spire of the Parish Church, are built in harmonizing traditional and contemporary styles, exhibiting the shuttered and be-window-boxed gaiety typical of the Alpine regions. Tucked away amongst the vineyards are the world monopoly denture laboratories which contribute to the country's wealth, as well as small-scale industrial enterprises, whilst low rise office blocks house the administrations of important holdings profiting from Liechtenstein's liberal taxation regulations. The world-famous postage stamps, displayed in the Postal Museum, often feature chefs d'œuvre from the Prince's priceless collection of Flemish paintings. Perennial stars of the hôtellerie scene in this understated microcosm of world commerce are the Real brothers, hosts to star executives from all the corners of the globe. In winter the visiting prominenti are outshone on the ski slopes of Malbun by the local stars, brother and sister Wenzel. But despite the increasing importance of tourism, business – conducted in an atmosphere of utter discretion under a mysterious cloak of anachronism – is the ultima ratio of life in Vaduz.

Founded: first mentioned in documents of 1150.

Far-reaching events: 12th century – Vaduz Castle is built by Field Marshal Johann Adam von Liechtenstein, of Austrian descent; 13th century – Vaduz a county, almost as big as today's principality; 1719 – creation of the Principality of Liechtenstein, as a fief of the Holy Roman Empire; 1806 – the principality gains its sovereignty under Napoléon; 1815 – membership in the German Confederation; 1866 – declaration of independence, trade agreement with Austria; 1868 – the army is disbanded; 1921 – passage of the current constitution; 1923 – a customs treaty links the country to Switzerland; 1924 – Swiss Franc is adopted as the local currency; 1985 – Liechtenstein, although represented abroad by Switzerland, seeks direct representation at the UN.

Population: 5,000.   **Postal code:** FL–9490   **Telephone code:** 75 (Switzerland)

Climate: Alpine; unpredictable; the Föhn (south wind) brings a sharp rise in temperature in winter and headaches all the year round.

Calendar of events: *Fastnacht* (Feb/Mar) – celebrations before the start of Lent; *International Master Classes* (mid-Jul) – musicians from around the world teach and give concerts; *National Holiday* (15 Aug) – fireworks; *Annual Fair* (Oct).

Fairs and exhibitions: *LIHGA* (Sep) – light industry, commerce and trade exhibition, in the neighbouring town of Schaan.

Historical and modern sights: *Royal Castle* (12th century) – landmark regal residence; *Liechtenstein National Museum* – in a beautifully restored 18th-century inn; *Liechtenstein State Art Collection* – owned by the Royal Family – works by Hals, Breughel, van Dyck and Rubens; the *Parish Church* – graves of the ruling princes and a landmark tower; *Liechtenstein Postal Museum* – one of the world's best stamp collections.

Special attractions: an invitation to the *Castle;* dinner at *Real;* registration of a *company.*

Important companies with headquarters in the city: *Abnox* (technical appliances); *Balzers AG* (optics, electronics, semi-conductors); *Hilti* (fittings for the construction industry); *Ivoclar* (artificial teeth); *Pavatex* (construction materials); *Press- & Stanzwerk* (press-casting); *Hoval-Werke* (heating tanks); *PAV Präzisions-Apparatebau* (precision instruments); *Baumwollspinnerei Jenny, Spoerry & Cie* (textiles); *Perkin-Elmer Censor Anstalt* (microelectronics); *Plissana* (embroidered and knitted goods); *Gravo-Optic* (photochemical products); *Liechtensteinische Landesbank* (banking); *Bank in Liechtenstein* (banking); *Verwaltungs- und Privat-Bank* (banking).

Airport: Zürich-Kloten, ZRH; Tel.: 01/8 12 71 11, 130 km/80 miles.

The Headquarters

REAL

21 Städtle
FL–9490 Vaduz
Telephone: 2 22 22
Telex: 779 484 real
Owner: Felix Real
General Manager: Felix Real
Affiliation/Reservation System: Relais et Châteaux (restaurant: Relais Gourmand)
Number of rooms: 10 (1 suites)
Price range: Sfr 90–180
Credit cards: AE, DC, Visa, EC
Location: city centre, 120 km/72 miles from Zurich airport
Built: 1921 (renovated 1969/1978)
Style: modern
Room amenities: colour tv (remote control, mini-bar/refrigerator, radio (pets allowed)
Room service: 7.00/a.m.–24.00/12 p.m.
Laundry/dry cleaning: same day
Conference rooms: 2 (for up to 12 persons), secretarial services
Restaurant: ›Au Premier‹ (11.00/a.m. to 23.00/11.00 p.m.) Therese Real (maître), Felix Real (chef de cuisine), classic and modern cuisine
Private dining rooms: one (8 persons)

Real, Liechtenstein's most famous hotel, stands in the middle of the high street of the mini-capital Vaduz, its whitewashed and shuttered façade decorated in summer by window-boxes of geraniums and matching red awnings. Cognoscenti know that tucked away upstairs are ten attractive bedrooms which offer the fortunate few – mainly chairmen of international companies or directors of firms with more employees than the Principality has inhabitants – an opportunity to enjoy to the full the renowned hospitality of this celebrated relais. The conference room is small enough for a confidential tête-à-tête to conclude a multi-million deal, whilst the friendly familiar atmosphere in the bar is leavened by the big-business small-talk amongst the miniature state's locals and the foreign magnates. Above all, Real is also a fêted restaurant. Therese Real stage-manages the daily gala performance in the wood-panelled dining room ›Au Premier‹ with flowers from the garden on the tables and fine wines in the cellars. Owner-manager-chef Felix Real and son Martin create menus for all tastes and all seasons – breast of duck in orange sauce, calf's kidneys ›Henri IV‹, a coq au vin which made Prince Rainier forget the pigeon dish the Grand Véfour named after him, and even (by special request) lobster with sauerkraut, served with an ice-cold Haut-Brion. Small wonder that everyone who is anyone, from the local Royal Family to the Prince and Princess of Wales to maestro of the pan-pipes Georghi Zamphyr, all make a point of visiting Real when they are in town. Many come to town for Real alone.

The Hideaway

PARK-HOTEL SONNENHOF

29 Mareestr.
FL–9490 Vaduz
Telephone: (75) 2 11 92
Telex: 889 329 sohof
Owners: Emil Real and family
General Managers: Emil and Jutta Real
Affiliation/Reservation Systems: Relais et
Châteaux; Ambassador Swiss Hotels
Closed: mid-January to mid-February
Number of rooms: 29 (12 suites)
Price range: from Sfr 120–270
Credit cards: AE, DC, Visa; EC; MC
Location: 2 km/1.2 miles from city cen-
tre; 120 km/75 miles from airport
Built: 1952/1972
Style: modern, rustic
Hotel amenities: garage; valet parking;
sauna; solarium; swimming pool
Room amenities: colour tv; mini-bar/
refrigerator; safe; radio (pets allowed)
Bathroom amenities: bidet; bathrobe;
hairdrier; cosmetic bar
Room service: 7.00 a.m. to 23.00/11 p.m.
Conference rooms: 1 (up to 16 persons)
Restaurant: (only for hotel guests,
7.00/a.m. to 24.00/12 p.m.); Jutta Real,
Silvia Brunner (maîtres); Emil Real (chef
de cuisine); international and classic-
modern cuisine

*Prince Charles and Lady Di, the dream-
land duo for millions, were welcomed as
warmly in the royal château as everyone
else who makes a stop at this sunny relais
or chooses it as the hideaway in the Alps –
after all, this is a princely inn, if with a very
democratic house policy. In fact, even an
unobservant new arrival in Vaduz would
soon discover one of the delightfully pecul-
iar coincidences which underline the intimate character of this bourgeois principality – the fact that Liechtenstein owes its
reputation as a diminutive oasis of hedo-
nistic joys almost entirely to the Real family – Felix at the hotel-restaurant of the
same name, and Emil at the Sonnenhof. As
the owners of the twin members of the prestigious ›Relais et Châteaux‹ group in the
land, the brothers could be said to have a
monopoly on the local laurels for hospitalité et cuisine. The whitewashed Alpine hostelry with a slate roof and a majestic panoramic view of vineyards, the encircling
mountains and the Rhine valley, lies in a
lovingly-tended garden in a smart residential area a short walk from the town centre.
It's a welcoming family-run hotel which
manages to achieve a perfect symbiosis between an informal atmosphere and the
standard of proficiency and congeniality
expected by an international clientèle.
Jutta Real's attractive rustic décor, the kitchen's agreeable cuisine, the pleasant
swimming pool with patio doors leading to
the garden and the courteous care for the
guests all endorse the choice of the Sonnenhof as the base or retreat for meetings, conferences, festivities or sheer relaxation.*

Lunch

REAL (Au Premier)
21 Städtle
Telephone: 2 22 22
Affiliations: Relais et Châteaux (Relais Gourmand)
Owner/Manager: Felix Real
Closed: never
Open: 11.30/a.m.–13.45/1.45 p.m. and 18.15/6.15 p.m.–21.30/9.30 p.m.
Cuisine: French Swiss and Austrian
Chef de cuisine: Felix and Martin Real
Specialities: turbot mousse; salmon dumplings; coq au vin with noodles; roast lamb with green beans; breast of duckling in orange sauce; gratin of sole and shrimps; goose liver with purée of peas; lobster with lemon noodles
Location: central; on the High Street (Hauptstrasse)
Setting: directly beneath the royal residence; two dining rooms (that on the first floor affording a view of the main street of the capital of the mini-principality); restrained modern middle-class décor
Amenities: hotel; private dining rooms (2–12 persons); bar; open air dining on terrace; car park
Atmosphere: a bastion of gastronomic excellence in this mini-principality at the heart of Europe
Clientèle: German tax exiles; conservative refugees from the twentieth century; resident gourmets from the prince and his consort downwards
Dress: rather conservative
Service: chatty, persuasive and charming – a warm welcome from Theresia Real
Reservations: advisable to essential
Price range: fairly expensive
Credit cards: AE, DC, Euro, Visa

Lunch

WIRTHSCHAFT ZUM LÖWEN
Schellenberg
Telephone: 3 11 62
Owner/Manager: Andreas Biedermann
Closed: Thursday
Open: 8.00/a.m.–23.00/11 p.m. (–24.00/12 p.m. on Friday and Saturday)
Cuisine: unpretentious, with a strong local accent
Chef de cuisine: Ursula Biedermann
Specialities: traditional dishes; cheese ›buttons‹ (Käsknöpfli); home-made brawn (Schwartemagen)
Location: at Schellenberg, 10 km/6 miles north of Vaduz
Setting: traditional Alpine auberge situated at one of the country's best vantage-points in the midst of particularly beautiful countryside; near the ruined castle of Schellenberg
Amenities: mountain walks in all directions

Atmosphere: redolent of history; full of local colour
Clientèle: favourite destination for local citizens en fête and en famille; the Vaduz Sunday afternoon crowd
Dress: Sunday casual to local costume
Service: solicitous
Reservations: advisable – especially at weekends
Price range: medium

Dinner

TORKEL
Vaduz
Telephone: 2 44 10
Owner/Manager: Fürst von Liechtenstein-Stiftung / Rolf Berger
Closed: Sunday evening; Monday; 22 Dezember–22 Januar
Open: 10.00/a.m.–23.00/11 p.m.
Cuisine: ›au goût du marché‹
Chef de cuisine: Rolf Berger
Specialities: according to season and market availability; buffet-style businessman's lunch
Setting: a lovingly restored old house set amidst the royal vineyards
Amenities: open-air dining on terrace; car park
Atmosphere: refined; refreshing
Clientèle: connoisseurs of good food; disciples of Rolf Berger's cuisine of ›Ochsen‹ in Bäretswil renown
Dress: fairly elegant to fairly casual
Service: professional and knowledgeable
Reservations: recommended
Price range: fairly expensive
Credit cards: AE, DC, Euro,, Visa

Lunch

GASTHAUS ENGEL
Balzers
Telephone: 4 12 01
Owner/Manager: M. and E. Brunhart
Closed: Monday
Open: 9.00/a.m.–12.00 p.m.
Cuisine: unpretentious
Chef de cuisine: M. Brunhart
Specialities: finely-sliced meat in sauce (Geschnetzeltes) with Swiss fried potato (Rösti); farm sausages (Bauernwurst)
Location: in Balzers, 8 km/5 miles south of Vaduz
Setting: a historic inn in the oldest part of the village
Atmosphere: rustic
Clientèle: Liechtenstein's Haute Bourgeoisie with cause for celebration
Dress: as you like it
Service: anxious-to-please
Reservations: advisable
Price range: medium

Dinner

REAL (Au Premier)
21 Städtle
Telephone: 2 22 22
Affiliations: Relais et Châteaux (Relais Gourmand)
Owner/Manager: Felix Real
Since the real reason for many a visit to Vaduz is Real, it's really logical to use any opportunity to sample Felix Real's renowned cuisine

Dinner

WALDHOF
Schaanwald (5 km/3 miles)
Telephone: 3 11 38
Owner/Manager/Chef de cuisine: Peter Meier
Closed: Sunday evening; Monday; January 6th – February 1st
Open: 10.00/a.m.–24.00/12 p.m.
Cuisine: traditional and nouvelle
Specialities: snacks and four-course meals, according to season and market availability; smoked trout with horseradish; cream of parsley soup; scampi salad, saddle of venison; Grand Marnier mousse; comprehensive wine list (predominantly French wines)
Setting: comfortably stylish dining room with an abundance of wood
Amenities: private dining room; car park; open-air dining on terrace
Atmosphere: welcoming and friendly
Clientèle: followers of Peter Meier's culinary career since his days at Real
Dress: according to season and circumstance
Service: well-dressed, feminine and welcoming
Reservations: advisable
Price range: moderately expensive
Credit cards: AE, DC, Euro, Visa

Dinner

LANDHAUS RHEINECK
73 Appenzeller Strasse
Rheineck (45 km/28 miles)
Telephone: (71) 44 12 60
Owner/Managers: Pius and Marianne Schnider
Closed: Monday
Open: 11.30/a.m.–14.30/2.30 p.m. and 18.30/6.30 p.m.–22.00/10 p.m. (last orders)
Cuisine: nouvelle
Chef de cuisine: Pius Schnider
Specialities: according to season and market availability; salad of chanterelles and bacon; lobster; red cabbage salad with quail; lamb curry; breast of duckling; turbot in champagne sauce with chives; gratinée of raspberries with vanilla petits fours
Location: at Rheineck, 45 km/28 miles north of Vaduz
Setting: above the village; 400-year-old Appenzeller country house; pretty rustic dining room with an abundance of wood
Amenities: car park; terrace for apéritifs
Atmosphere: particularly welcoming
Clientèle: local habitués; cognoscenti and businessmen en passant
Dress: no special requirements or restrictions
Service: attentive
Reservations: essential (only 9 tables!)
Price range: moderately expensive
Credit cards: AE, DC, Euro, Visa

Café

AMMANN
Äulistrasse 56
Telephone: 2 34 11
Owner/Manager: Peter Amman
Closed: Sunday; Public Holidays
Open: 7.00/a.m.–19.00/7.00 p.m.
Location: vis-à-vis the Post Office
Setting: rustic style with an abundance of natural wood
Amenities: car park in the vicinity
Atmosphere: cosy and warm in winter; light, airy and lively in summer
Clientèle: housewives with their children after shopping sprees in the mornings; students, secretaries and a sprinkling of jeunesse dorée in the evenings
Service: fast and efficient
Price range: moderate
Dress: everybody comes as she/he pleases
Reservations: not necessary
Credit cards: not accepted

Bar

APERO-BAR WOLF
29 Städtle
Telephone: 2 23 21
Owner/Manager: Albrecht Wolf Jnr.
Closed: Monday
Open: 9.00/a.m.–1.00 a.m.
Location: a few steps from the Headquarters
Setting: luxurious; mirror ceiling and carpeted walls
Atmosphere: confidential, intimate and rather exclusive
Clientèle: local businessmen, visiting industrialists, young people
Service: friendly and fashionably dressed
Reservations: advisable
Credit cards: AE, DC, Euro, Visa

Bar

MASCHLINA-BAR
Triesen
Telephone: 2 26 90
Owner/Manager: the Negele family
Closed: Monday
Open: from 20.00/8 p.m. to 2.00 a.m.
Location: at Triesen; 2 km/1 mile south
of Vaduz; practically on the main road
Setting: dance floor and bar-restaurant
decorated in rustic style
Amenities: dinner menu (grills) as well as
drinks and snacks; orchestra; car park
Atmosphere: sedately sophisticated
Clientèle: international; businessmen
from ›over the Border‹ and from Ohio to
Osaka mingle with the local In-Crowd
Service: good; supervised by Rosita
Kindle
Reservations: recommended for Friday
and Saturday evenings
Credit cards: AE, DC, Euro, Visa

Nightclub

CLUB 1
Schaanwald
Telephone: 3 38 11
Owner/Manager: Johnny Wachter
Closed: never
Open: 18.00/6 p.m.–2.00/a.m.
Location: in Schaanwald, on the border;
12 km/8 miles north of Vaduz
Setting: modern décor with white leather
upholstery
Amenities: discothèque; live music; res-
taurant ›Waldhof‹ (classic and modern
cuisine) with open-air dining in summer
Atmosphere: chic but not chi-chi
Clientèle: Vaduz' jeunesse dorée; resi-
dent aristocracy; a prince or two; jet-set
birds of passage
Dress: disco elegant
Service: friendly and welcoming
Reservations: advisable
Price range: medium
Credit cards: AE

Shopping

EVERYTHING UNDER ONE ROOF
Jelmoli, Buchs Bahnhofstrasse

FOR HIM
Boutique Nino Im Städtlemarkt

FOR HER
Boutique Nina Schaan, Landstrasse

BEAUTY & HAIR
Salon de Beauty Brosi, 7 Herrengasse
Salon Nigg 12 Lettstraße

JEWELLERY
Diamanthaus 27 Herrengasse

LOCAL SPECIALITIES
Dünser Hans (tobacco)
38 Hauptstraße
Boutique Nina (women's fashion)
Landstraße
Wanger Mode (men's fashion)
20 Landstraße
Ludwig Aspelt (children's fashion)
2 Städtle
Domé Buchhandlung (books)
30 Landstraße
Boutique Graf G. Andrassy (gifts)
Städtle
Heimdekor Oehri (porcelain)
35 Städtle
Hofkellerei des Fürsten von Liechtenstein
(food and beverages)
4 Feltstraße
Vendôme, Institut de Beauté (perfumery)
36 Städtle
Rechtsteiner, Alois (shoes)
33 Städtle

THE BEST OF ART
Perspective Etablissement (contemporary art, prints) 1 Kirchstrasse
Studer, Alfred Carl (17th/18th-century
paintings) 11 Herrengasse, Tel. 26540

The City

A Solomonic decision by the European Community's mentor, French statesman Robert Schuman, to elect his birthplace as one of the headquarters of the ›Economic League of Nations‹, has brought more world importance and worldliness to the small Grand Duchy than all the alliances between France and Austria over the past millenium put together. Its central location (a Learjet's lap from Paris and Bonn and equidistant from the other Euro-capitals, Brussels and Strasbourg), its neutral position and its international past and spirit precluded any protests of nepotism from the remaining five founder-members. Today, Luxembourg justifies its awarded function as the turntable for the Secretariat of the European Parliament and the Council of Ministers with a plethora of acronymic commissions within the enclave on the Kirchberg. They have endowed the city – and the country – with the highest percentage of foreign residents on the continent infusing it with a cosmopolitan cachet unrivalled amongst the other miniature nations and many larger ones. The heart of Duke Sigefroi's 1000-year-old ›Little Fortress‹, daringly perched on a precipitous rocky outcrop and almost encircled by the Alzette and the Pétrusse rivers, can easily be reached nowadays by one of the ninety-nine bridges spanning the gorges. Modern, future-minded, yet with many historic traces, Luxembourg is an attractive pot-pourri of business and pleasure. A Sleeping-Beauty aura pervades some quarters of town, while the visiting princes of industry, trade and finance engage in commercial megalomania in the city centre where banks are outnumbered only by the cheerful cafés, bars and bistros. Competing with other Lilliputian states, Luxembourg is also a favourite residence and market place for its advantageous tax legislation, and for the multi-lingual genius of its citizens. In every language and around the world, night by night, Radio Luxembourg puts the city-country's name on the map and the latest sounds in the air, magnetizing the new generation more than Liechtenstein does with its stamps, whilst the flagship airline offers them a mainland base for bargain flights to the New World. Luxembourg does not persist in national chauvinism, but combines the better qualities of its neighbours in an urbane mix: Belgian bourgeois solidity, German disciplined efficiency and French light-hearted nonchalance. Any foreign visitor will feel welcome here. And anyone adding natural delights to the scheduled business will rejoice in the vine-covered hills of the Moselle valley and the castle-clad pine forests of ›Little Switzerland‹, realizing that the Grand Duke Jean's 999-square-mile micro-imperium (fitting 99 times into the United Kingdom) is an insider's tip away from the Grand Tour.

Founded: 4th century, as a Roman watch-tower; Luxembourg (French) – from ›Lützelburg‹, ›a little fortress‹.

Far-reaching events: 926 – the fortress ›Castellum Lucilinburhu‹ is built; 12th century – ruled by Henry the Blind, Duke of Namur; 1308 – Henry's grandson becomes Holy Roman Emperor; 1443 – Luxembourg goes to the House of Burgundy; 1477 – the Habsburgs assume power; 1555 – the Spanish take the city; 1684 – Luxembourg taken by the French under Vauban; 1698 – back to the Spanish; 1701 – back to the French; 1713 – to the Dutch; 1795 – to the French again; 1814 – to Prussia; 1839 – to Belgium; 1867 – Luxembourg becomes neutral; 1914–18 and 1939–45 – German occupation; 1952 – seat of the European Coal and Steel Authority; 1957 – seat of the secretariat of the European Parliament; 1973 – European Court of Justice.

Population: 100,000.

Postal code: L–Luxembourg   **Telephone code:** 352

Climate: temperate, without extremes; the North Sea provides a moderating influence.

Calendar of events: *Emaischen* (Mar/Apr) – Easter Monday celebrations; *Octave of Our Lady of Luxembourg* (5th Sunday after Easter) – festive religious procession; *Musical Spring* (May to Jun) – music festival; *International Festival of Classical Music* (Jun to Jul); *National Day* (23 Jun); *Schobermesse* (last 2 weeks of Aug) – amusement fair.

Fairs and exhibitions: *EXPOGAST* (Jan/Feb) – equipment and installations for the hotel and catering industries; *EUROPLEINAIR* (Feb/Mar) – European leisure and recreation exhibition; *SPRING FAIR* (May/Jun); *AUTUMN FAIR* (Oct).

Historical sights: *Casemates* (1745) – subterranean defensive labyrinth; *Chemin de la Corniche* – panoramic views; *Grand Ducal Palace* (16th and 18th century); *Citadel of St. Esprit* – the remains of the 19th-century fortress, carved into the cliffs; *Villa Vauban* – Dutch and Flemish masters.

Special attractions: an outing and a dinner in the *countryside*.

Important companies with headquarters in the city: *Arbed* (iron and steel); *Creditbank* (banking); *Paul Wurth* (metal); *Cleveland Crane & Engineering* (overhead handling equipment); *Banque Internationale à Luxembourg* (banking); *SECALT* (hoists and lifting accessories); *Villeroy & Boch* (porcelain); *Betons Feidt* (pre-cast concrete goods); *Luxair* (transport); *Cargolux* (air freight); *DuPont* (chemicals); *Heintz van Landewyck* (tobacco); *Brasseries Réunies de Luxembourg* (brewery); *Société Luxembourgeoise d'Entreprises et de Constructions* (building and engineering); *CDC* (bridges, joint ventures, earth movements); *Georgetti Eustache & Fils* (civil engineering); *Caisse d'Epargne* (banking); *Pierre Pérard & Fils* (building contracting); *RTL – Radio & Télévision Luxembourg* (broadcasting).

Airport: Luxembourg-Findel (LUX), Tel.: 4 79 81; Luxair, Tel.: 4 79 81, 7 km/4 miles.

The Headquarters

LE ROYAL

12 Boulevard Royal
L–Luxembourg
Telephone: 4 16 16
Telex: 2979 royho
General Manager: Jean Bibauw
Affiliation/Reservation Systems: SRS (Steigenberger Reservation Service), The Leading Hotels of the World, Keytel, Hotels de Grande Classe Internationale, Utell
Number of rooms: 170 (15 suites)
Price range: BF 5,200–8,700
Credit cards: AE, DC, MC, EC, JCB, Visa
Location: 1.5 km (1 mile) from the station
Built: September 1984
Style: modern
Hotel amenities: garage, fitness club swimming pool, sauna, solarium
Room service: 24 hours
Conference rooms: 4 (up to 800 persons)
Bar: ›Piano Bar‹ (11.00/a.m.–1.00/a.m.)
Restaurants: ›Le Jardin‹ (7.00/a.m.–22.30/10.30/p.m.); ›Le Relais Royal‹ (12.00/a.m.–14.30/2.30 p.m. and 18.30/6.30 p.m.–22.00/10 p.m.)
Nightclub: ›Club Arlequin‹

After the signing of the Treaty of Rome in 1957 the Grand Duchy of Luxembourg's position at the geographical epicentre of the Common Market was underlined by the decision to base various institutions – notably the Secretariat of the European Parliament and the European Court of Justice – in the mini-capital. Amongst the older hotels in the city and the chain-gang giants which have mushroomed during the past few years to cater to the ceaseless stream of dignitaries and diplomats who descend with their retinues, Le Royal stands out for quality, standard and service. Its convenient location on one of the principal boulevards near the commercial and banking centre of town makes it the headquarters of choice for visiting financiers and international lawyers as well as official delegations. The rather austere modern façade is broken up by arches over the windows and by the large canopy over the main entrance. Inside, the hotel offers a good level of comfort and a wide range of amenities. The décor is rather traditional, from the light and spacious atrium with its oriental rugs and luxuriant pot-plants to the welcomingly attractive suites. The informal terrace restaurant Le Jardin is a riot of flowers and greenery, whilst the Relais Royal's more sober atmosphere makes it a good alternative to the gourmet rallying points in town for an undisturbed business lunch. After-hours relaxation is catered for by the swimming pool and sauna as well as the quiet Piano Bar and the Arlequin nightclub, which is a kaleidoscope of lights and live music. The brightest star on the horizon amongst hotels in Luxembourg is undoubtedly Le Royal.

The Hideaway

AUBERGE DU MOULIN HIDEUX

1 Route de Dohan
B–6831 Noirefontaine (108 km/86 miles)
Telephone: (3261) 467015
Telex: 41989 hideux
Owner: Charles and Martine Lahire
Affiliation/Reservation Systems: Traditions et Qualité, Relais et Châteaux
Closed: end Nov – mid-March
Number of rooms: 13 (3 suites)
Price range: BF 2,500–3,500
Credit cards: AE, CB, Visa
Location: at Noirefontaine, 148 km/93 miles south of Brussels, 108 km/86 miles from Luxembourg
Style: converted water mill; elegant country-house décor
Hotel amenities: car park
Room amenities: small lobby for storage of suitcases, radio, tv, mini-bar (pets allowed in bedrooms only)
Bathroom amenities: separate shower; separate WC (most rooms), bathrobe
Room service: 7.00/a.m.–22.00/10 p.m.
Conference rooms: one (up to 12 persons)
Sports: tennis
Sports (nearby): fishing (with licence), riding, golf, swimming
Restaurant: ›Auberge du Moulin Hideux‹, Christian Ulweling (chef de cuisine), nouvelle cuisine, elegantized rustic décor (closed on Wednesday, except Jul–Aug–Sep)

The tree-lined road meanders between the densely wooded slopes of the Ardennes. At last it arrives at the white wrought-iron fence and the bridge across the fast-flowing stream which once powered the mill-wheel, formerly the raison d'être of this loveliest of rural hideaways. The name is an intentional misnomer, a corruption of ›Y deux‹, since there were once two water-mills on this spot. The Moulin Hideux, surrounded by manicured lawns, flower-beds and stands of ash and beech trees, is a pretty pink building with a black mansard roof. Charles and Martine Lahire, second-generation châtelains of this romantic relais, practise l'art d'hospitalité with the same loving attention to detail as their parents. The intérieur is a cameo of rural charm; exposed beams and roaring fires in the lounge, pastel fabrics and king-size beds in the thirteen guest rooms, and pretty wallpapers and antique porcelain vitrines adding touches of individuality throughout the house. Christian Ulweling's double-starred nouvelle cuisine – warm lobster salad, or John Dory with chervil – draws gourmet day-trippers from three countries to the cheerful orange and beige dining room, whilst pampered overnight guests can breakfast in bed with hand embroidered napkins which match the sheets. After a week – or a weekend – at the beautiful Moulin Hideux you will emerge sufficiently refreshed to put the twentieth century in its true perspective.

Lunch

AU GOURMET
8 Rue Chimay
Telephone: 2 55 61
Owner/Manager: Marie Weber-Gambini
Closed: Sunday evening; Monday; January 23rd–February 15th; July 28th–August 14th
Open: 12.00/a.m.–14.00/2 p.m. and 19.00/7 p.m.–22.00/10 p.m.
Cuisine: French
Chef de cuisine: Jempy Boden
Specialities: trout in Riesling; gratin d'écrevisses; baked turbot; calves' sweetbreads Jempy; game; saddle of lamb ›gourmet‹; pigs' trotters in vinaigrette; rognons de veau liégeoise
Location: central
Setting: historic house (1673); three main dining rooms with period furnishings plus three private dining rooms in Louis XVI style
Amenities: private dining rooms (60 persons)
Atmosphere: relaxed and relaxing
Clientèle: fairly cosmopolitan – government ministers, diplomats and bankers plus a selection of local habitués
Dress: tenue de ville
Service: generously welcoming
Reservations: advisable (no dogs)
Price range: quite expensive
Credit cards: AE

Dinner

SAINT MICHEL
32 Rue de l'Eau
Telephone: 2 32 15
Affiliations: Relais et Châteaux (Relais Gourmand)
Owner/Manager: Pierrick and Lysiane Guillou
Closed: Saturday; Sunday; August
Open: 12.00/a.m.–14.00/2 p.m. and 19.00/7 p.m.–22.00/10 p.m.
Cuisine: ›au goût du marché‹
Chef de cuisine: Pierrick Guillou
Specialities: mosaic of salmon and Norway lobster; sea-perch with mussels; turbot and salmon with vegetable lasagne; fillet of mullet with crisp cauliflower; steamed rabbit with fresh pasta and basil; honey-roast Bresse duckling and leg of duck with walnut-oil salad; farandole de desserts; soufflé à la mirabelle
Location: opposite the Grand Ducal Palace
Setting: 16th-century building; low wooden ceiling, unrendered bricks, open fireplace; small-paned windows, period furnishings, pot plants and flowers
Amenities: private dining room (25 persons)
Atmosphere: a temple of gastronomic excellence created by Breton Pierrick Guillou

Clientèle: ambassadors, resident aristocracy, francophile foreigners, local gourmets and visiting VIPs
Dress: suitably soignée
Service: smiling, welcoming and attentive – under the supervision of Lysiane Guillou
Reservations: essential
Price range: fairly expensive
Credit cards: AE, Euro, Visa

Lunch

HOSTELLERIE DU GRUNEWALD
10–16 Route d'Echternach,
Dommeldange (5 km/3 miles)
Telephone: 43 18 82/43 60 62
Affiliations: Romantic Hotels and Restaurants; Chaîne des Rôtisseurs
Owner/Manager: Louise Decker
Closed: Saturday lunchtime; Sunday; January 7th–22nd
Open: 12.00/a.m.–14.00/2 p.m. and 19.00/7 p.m.–21.00/9 p.m.
Cuisine: French
Chef de cuisine: Walter Gerhards
Specialities: homard fin Bec; shrimps à la luxembourgeoise; venison in Chablis; ham mousse
Location: 5 km (3 miles) from city centre
Setting: elegant dining rooms in Louis XVI style plus a third rustic salon
Amenities: hotel (open all the year round); terrace (drinks and apéritifs only – dinner by special request); air conditioning; swimming, golf and riding 2 km (1 mile) away
Atmosphere: that of a luxurious country house whose owner understands the art of gracious living
Clientèle: comfortable mixture of men of politics, men of commerce, financiers and television celebrities
Dress: tenue de ville (no bikinis, Bermuda shorts or cut-off jeans)
Service: pleasantly courteous
Reservations: advisable (dogs smaller than a spaniel and shorter than a basset hound admitted)
Price range: moderately expensive
Credit cards: AE, DC, Euro, Visa, Mastercard

Dinner

LA BERGERIE
1 Geyershof (25 km/17 miles)
Telephone: 7 94 64
Owner/Manager/Chef de cuisine: Claude Phal
Closed: Sunday evening; Monday; February
Open: 12.00/a.m.–13.30/1.30 p.m. and 19.00/7 p.m.–21.00/9 p.m.

Cuisine: French (classique et nouvelle)
Specialities: andouillette of wolf-fish; sole fumée Minute; lamb en croûte; salad of warm Norway lobster with avocado pear and hazelnut oil; vacherin au moka; home-made breads
Location: 25 km (17 miles) north of Luxembourg along E42 towards Echternach; turn right at Michelshof (towards Geyershof)
Setting: lovingly-renovated mid-19th century whitewashed farmhouse; small dining room; fine antique furnishings, silver and glass
Amenities: private dining room (20–60 persons) on first floor; terrace with views across countryside; car park
Atmosphere: welcoming, luxurious and relaxing
Clientèle: disciples of Claude Phal's cuisine of the Luxemburg golf club fame; Belgian, French and German gourmets; financiers, government officials and international delegates
Dress: ›correcte‹
Service: discreetly charming and friendly; supervised by the wife of the patron
Reservations: advisable (dogs tolerated)
Price range: fairly expensive
Credit cards: AE, DC, Euro, Visa

Meeting Point

BRASSERIE JACQUES
21 Rue des Bains
Telephone: 2 88 88
Owner/Manager: Jacques Engel
Closed: Sunday
Open: 7.00/a.m.–1.00/a.m.
Location: not far from the Hotel Royal
Setting: the longest bar counter in Luxembourg (19 metres); old-world exposed beams and modern décor glass-and-marble cocktail lounge
Amenities: car park (5 minutes walk)
Atmosphere: bon chic; bon genre
Clientèle: very mixed; bank clerks, bank managers, brokers, international barristers and visitors from Brussels, Bahrain and Berlin
Service: cordial
Reservations: not necessary (well-behaved whippets and wolf-hounds admitted)
Credit cards: AE

Café

LE BISTROT
31 Rue du Fort Elisabeth
Telephone: 48 57 75
Owner/Manager: Henri Ewerard
Closed: never
Open: 7.00/a.m.–1.00/a.m.
Location: a short walk (or a shorter taxi ride) from the station (la gare)

Setting: turn-of-the-century café; nostalgic
Amenities: bar; open-air dining on large terrace; air conditioning; car park on the square
Atmosphere: bustling but not impersonal
Clientèle: heterogeneous; local citizens with a few international celebrities from the theatre and show business
Service: fast and friendly

Bar

LE TRIANON
29 Boulevard Roosevelt
Telephone: 2 19 75
Owner/Manager: the Cravat family
Closed: never
Open: 12.00/p.m.–14.00/2 p.m.; 18.00/6 p.m.–12.00/a.m.
Location: in the Hotel Cravat, next to the cathedral
Setting: sumptuous hotel bar decorated in Louis XV style, with period fauteuils and an abundance of natural wood
Amenities: hotel; snacks; car park
Atmosphere: a haven of elegance; raffineé
Clientèle: local company chairmen, international tycoons, members of the liberal professions and their well-dressed companions
Service: directed with great charm and aplomb by Eddie, chief barman for over 25 years
Reservations: not necessary (pets permitted)
Price range: medium
Credit cards: AE, DC, Euro, Visa

Nightclub

GOLDEN CLUB
75 Route d'Esch
Telephone: 44 29 31
Owner/Manager: José Juvillier and Mme Juvillier
Closed: Sunday
Open: 21.00/9 p.m. till dawn
Location: central
Setting: exclusive and luxurious nightclub with nostalgic style décor and crystal chandeliers
Amenities: restaurant; air conditioning
Atmosphere: intimate and romantic (if you're feeling so inclined)
Clientèle: the crème de la crème of Luxembourg society, plus distinguished, interesting or witty birds of passage
Dress: strictly elegant and rather formal
Service: observant and attentive

Reservations: recommended at the weekend (no dogs)
Price range: rather expensive
Credit cards: AE, DC, Euro, Visa

THE BEST OF ART
Tableaux d'Art   (modern art)
19 Rue de Bonnevoie, Tel. 2 78 61

Shopping

EVERYTHING UNDER ONE ROOF
Rosenstiel   Rue Philippe II

FOR HIM
Gilbert   89–93 Grand-Rue

FOR HER
Boutique Lady Shop   Grand-Rue

BEAUTY & HAIR
Salon de Coiffure Alexandre de Paris   6–12 Place d'Armes

JEWELLERY
Bijouterie Alain Welter
36–38 Centre Brasseur

LOCAL SPECIALITIES
Romain Terzi (tobacco)
20 Route d'Arlon
Boutique Epoque (women's fashion)
Rue Philippe II
Boutique Richy (men's fashion)
12 Rue des Capucins
Boutique Dujardin (children's fashion)
58 Grand-Rue
Boutique Frieden (leather fashion)
47 Grand-Rue
Fourrure Jenny (furs)
8 Rue Notre-Dame
Librairie Francaise (books)
1 Place d'Armes
Cadeaux Exclusifs ›Monogram NHS‹ (gifts)
20 Rue Notre-Dame
Frising Henri (porcelain)
10 Rue Louvigny
Maroquinerie Keller (baggage & travel accessories)
63 Grand-Rue
Maroquinerie Sandam Gaston (baggage & travel accessories)
53 Grand-Rue
Ameublement Roch Bobois (interior decorating)
8 Avenue de La Porte Neuve
Kaempff Kohler (food and beverages)
Place Guillaume
Schnekert (food and beverages)
15 Rue du Fossé
Parfumerie Opera (perfumery)
Avenue Monterey
Chaussures Bally (shoes)
2 Rue des Capucins
Villeroy & Boch (faiences), 330 Rue de Rollingergrund

The City

Not another Verdi heroine, but the capital of the southernmost European country, named after a real-life hero, the Grand Master of the Maltese Order – and today one of the Mediterranean resorts off the Marbella-Monte-Carlo-Mykonos trail. A briefcase is a relatively rare object amongst the beach bags, tennis holdalls and yachting gear toted by the international northerners who arrive in hordes during the numerous summer months. Business is definitely not on the agenda of most visitors to the island, who cannot wait to shed their grey flannel and bourgeois inhibitions in favour of a fortnight's subscription to the pleasure-oriented world of this biblical archipelago. In fact, the half-dozen islands of Malta seem to be the holiday paradise of which all Anglo-Saxons who can't afford the Costa Smeralda dream, from the predictably perfect weather to the cliché kodachrome contrasts of South-Seas sky, Sahara sand and Mayfair fashion. The hotels lining the beaches won't be mistaken for Jacques-Coelle creations, and Côte-d'Azur sophistication seems to be barred from import, but natural joys are aplenty and natural charm epidemic among the people. The old town of Valletta, overlooking the fine Grand Harbour from its hillside position, has retained its predominantly Baroque countenance, from the Italianate Co-Cathedral to the Grand Master's Palace. Here, within the Knights Hospitallers' sixteenth-century fortifications, the city's grid layout acquires a third dimension by virtue of the ›streets of stairs‹ so abhorred by arch-globetrotter Lord Byron. Tourism is still the main business of the city, with shipbuilding and harbour services the logical industrial entity. (The explosives factories are kept at a safe distance, fortunately.) The overall ambiente reflects the proximity of Italy, with shades of an exotic kaleidoscope stemming from all the Phoenicians, Greeks, Carthagians, Romans, Goths, Arabs and Normans who have fought over this strategic stronghold lying virtually half-way between Europe and Africa since the dawn of recorded time. The most recent incumbents, the British, awarded the ›George Cross Island‹ its independence some twenty years ago, but show responsibility for their protégés with money and men. Language and left-hand driving are not the only marks the friendly colonizers left on Maltese life, and with the pale invasion each summer, one is led to believe that nothing has changed after all. Politically, however, Dom Mintoff is not exactly clinging to the apron-strings of Margaret Thatcher. When St. Paul was shipwrecked on Malta, before the two islands ever knew of each other, he lost no time in converting the local chiefs to Christianity. Had he realized their successors would ever turn their eyes left instead of looking upwards, he might well have annexed the islands for the Vatican.

Founded: 7th century B.C., by the Phoenicians; Valletta – from the founding Grand Master of the Order of Knights Hospitallers, Jean Parisot de la Valette.

Far-reaching events: 8th century B.C. – a Greek colony; 6th century – occupied by the Carthaginians; 218 – annexed by Rome; 60 A.D. – St. Paul, shipwrecked on the island, brings Christianity to Malta; 533 – Byzantine conquest; 870 – the Arabs; 1090 – the Sicilian Normans; 1530 – Holy Roman Empire gives Malta to the Knight Hospitallers; 1565 – Grand Master Jean de la Valette supervises the construction of the town's fortifications; 1798 – Napoleonic invasion; 1800 – the British take the island after a two-year siege; 1964 – Malta independent

Population: 15,000.   **Postal code:** none   **Telephone code:** 356

Climate: always pleasant, with a light breeze; January–March rather cool.

Calendar of events: *Holy Week* (Mar/Apr) – festive celebrations, culminating with a grand procession on Good Friday; *Independence Day* (31 Mar) – jubilation, jubilation; *Carnival* (2nd weekend in May) – processions, parades and parties; *Festa* (summer) – each village on the island(s) celebrates its very own patron saint with processions and fireworks; *Liberation Day* (1st weekend in Sep) – celebrating the end of the occupations in 1565 and 1943, a large regatta sails by.

Historical sights: *St. John's Co-Cathedral* (1573–77) – the hospital order's monastery chapel and museum, the latter containing Caravaggio's ›Beheading of St. John‹; *Grand Masters' Palace and Armoury* (1574) – frieze depicting the history of the Order of St. John; *National Museum of Fine Arts* – in an 18th-century palace including works by Tintoretto and Tiepolo; the *Folk Museum* in the Inquisitor's Palace; *National Museum of Archaeology* – main exhibits from local prehistoric sites housed in the *Auberge de Provence*; *Paola* and *Tarxien* (7 km/4 miles) – megalithic temples; *Mdina* (12 km/8 miles) – walled medieval ›Silent City‹; *Rabat* (12 km/8 miles) – catacombs; *Gozo* (40 km/25 miles) – Circe's island; *Comino* and *Cominetto* – small islands.

Special attractions: a performance at the *Manoel Theatre;* being made a knight of the *Order of St. John;* a romantic night on uninhabited *Cominetto.*

Important companies with headquarters in the city: *Amalgamated Engineers Supplies* (industrial tools); *Aluminium Ltd* (aluminum); *Agio Tobacco* (tobacco); *Atlas Tool and Engine* (light engineering works); *Blue Bell* (jeans); *Fildex* (office files); *Malta Drydocks* (shipbuilding); *Pharmamed* (pharmaceuticals); *Polyfoam* (polyurethane foam); *Pulvic* (explosives); *Air Malta* – Luqa (airline); *Consolidated Biscuits* (biscuits); *Simonds Farsons Cisk* (beer and soft drinks).

Airport: Valletta-Luqa (MLA); Tel.: 2 35 96/6 22 90; Air Malta, Tel.: 88 29 16–26 or 6 20 062–4; 8 km/5 miles.

The Headquarters

PHOENICIA

M–The Mall, Floriana
Telephone: 2 12 11/2 52 41
Telex: MW 1 240 otphen
Owning Company: Trusthouse Forte
General Manager: Anthony J. Gatt
Affiliation/Reservation System: Trusthouse Forte
Number of rooms: 110 (4 suites)
Price range: Lm 27 (single)
                Lm 37 (double)
                Lm 70 (suite)
Credit cards: AE, DC, THF, Access, Visa, MC
Location: just outside the walls of the historic centre of Valletta, 8 km/5miles from airport
Built: 30s (opened: 1947)
Style: traditional Maltese architecture
Hotel amenities: parking, hairdresser, private gardens, boutique, newsagent, shopping arcade
Room amenities: private balcony, radio, air conditioning, tv on request
Room service: 24 hours
Laundry/dry cleaning: same day
Conference rooms: 5 (up to 500 persons) ballroom
Sports: swimming pool, mini-golf, table-tennis, boccia
Bars: ›Cocktail Bar‹, ›Pegasus Piano Bar‹
Restaurants: ›Main Restaurant‹, ›Pegasus Snack Bar‹, ›Swimming Pool Restaurant‹; live music and entertainment every day in the Main Restaurant and Pegasus Bar
Private dining rooms: up to 500 guests

The seafarers of old who gave their name to this Grande Dame among Maltese hotels would have approved the location on the Floriana promontory, from where it boasts a commanding view of the twin harbours of Valletta. Of the successive nationalities who have left their stamp on the George Cross Island, however, it is the British who have had the greatest influence on this attractively traditional auberge – particularly since it is now a member of the well known Trusthouse Forte group. All the ingredients for a successful conference or a perfect holiday are here – attractively furnished rooms with a view of the private gardens, fine food, friendly staff – plus a swimming pool to laze by, a sports club in the vicinity to keep fit and live music for dancing during the long summer evenings. In such congenial surroundings no one will blame you for concluding your contract negotiations as quickly as possible in order to enjoy the holiday ambience to the maximum.

The Hideaway

TA'CENC

M–Sannat – Gozo (40 km/25 miles)
Telephone: 55 68 30/55 68 19/55 15 20
Telex: 1 479 refinz
Owning Company: Real Finanz AG
General Manager: Giuseppe De Muro
Number of rooms: 48 (10 suites)
Price range: Lm 18 h.b. (double)
              Lm 22 h.b. (suite)
Credit cards: AE, DC, Visa, Access, MC, EC
Location: on the island of Gozo, 3.5 km/2 miles from town centre, 40 km/25 miles from airport
Built: 1971
Style: Mediterranean and modern
Hotel amenities: valet parking, house limousine service, library/gaming room, solarium, newsstand, boutique, outdoor swimming pool (heated), house doctor
Main hall porter: Franco Tabone
Room amenities: tv, mini-bar/refrigerator
Bathroom amenities: bidet, pool/beach towels
Room service: 24 hours
Laundry/dry cleaning: same day (weekend service)
Conference rooms: 1 (up to 70 persons), flip charts, overhead and slide projector, video, secretarial services, ballroom
Sports: table-tennis, darts, billiards, table-soccer, 2 tennis courts (1 floodlit), boccia courts
Bar: ›Ta'Cenc‹ (9.30 a.m.–24.00/12.00 p.m.) Joe Sciberras (barman), guitarist
Restaurant: ›Ta'Cenc‹ (13.00/1.00 p.m.–15.00/3.00 p.m. and 19.30/7.30 p.m.–23.00/11.00 p.m.) Sammy Rapa (maître), Saviour Muscat (chef de cuisine), Italian and international cuisine, folk music duo, open-air dining
Ta'Cenc Discotheque: (21.00/9.00 p.m.–1.00/a.m.) Pepe Sciberras (manager)

In the corner-cutting, price-paring world of sunshine-for-all tourism the Ta' Cenc hotel complex on the Mediterranean island of Gozo stands out like a Dior original at a jumble sale. The honey-coloured limestone bungalows grouped around the swimming pool seem to grow naturally out of the hillside itself and offer – apart from an exceptional degree of luxury, by Maltese standards – private terraces or gardens for séparée sunbathing, oleanders and bougainvillea to delight the eye, Italian cuisine to delight the palate, and for those who find that even sun-worshipping under such idyllic conditions palls eventually, sports facilities and sightseeing excursions to delight even the most energetic. Whether you come with the family or come with a friend, the Ta'Cenc is exactly what you want it to be – a lively resort, a romantic retreat, a base for outings or an end in itself.

Lunch

MDINA
Holy Cross Street
Mdina (5 km/3 miles)
Telephone: 67 40 04
Affiliations: Winston Restaurants
Owner/Manager: Noel Debono
Closed: Sunday
Open: 12.00/a.m.–14.30/2.30 p.m. and
18.30/6.30 p.m.–21.30/9.30 p.m.
Cuisine: Continental
Chef de cuisine: John Borg
Specialities: duck, lamb and steaks
Location: at Mdina, 5 km/3 miles west of
Valletta
Setting: arched ceiling and unrendered
brickwork; neutral colour scheme; white
table-linen; rush-seated chairs
Amenities: open-air dining in courtyard
Atmosphere: businesslike; discreetly con-
fidential
Clientèle: industrialists and export ma-
nagers hoping to clinch a deal or to cele-
brate a signed contract; local couples
celebrating an anniversary, a birthday or
an engagement
Dress: according to season and circum-
stance
Service: friendly
Reservations: advisable

Lunch

PHOENICIA
The Mall, Floriana
Telephone: 2 52 41/2 12 11
Owner/Manager: Trusthouse Forte
Closed: never
Open: 13.00/1 p.m.–14.30/2.30 p.m. and
20.00/8 p.m.–22.30/10.30 p.m.
Cuisine: international and Maltese
Chef de cuisine: Mr. Attard
Specialities: Maltese fish soup (aljotta);
pasta with meat, tomatoes, hard-boiled
eggs and chicken livers in a puff pastry
case (timpana); swordfish; Maltese beef
olives (bragoli); stewed rabbit (fenek)
Location: in the Phoenicia Hotel
Setting: rather regal dining room with ta-
pestry-covered wall; in summer, meals
served on the open-air terrace by the
swimming pool
Amenities: hotel; ›Malta Night Extravaganza‹ (Thursday) with traditional dishes
and folklore entertainment by the pool
Atmosphere: an international hotel restaurant making a genuine effort to recapture for its guests the picturesque customs, songs and dances associated with
Malta's history
Clientèle: predominantly visitors to Valletta for business or pleasure – with a
sprinkling of Maltese Haute Bourgeoisie
with cause for celebration
Dress: within reason, come-as-you-
please
Service: friendly

Lunch

TUNNY NET
Ghadira Bay (10 km/6 miles)
Telephone: 57 43 38/9
Owner/Manager: Patrick Dally
Closed: Monday in winter
Open: 12.00/a.m. to 6.00/4 p.m.
Cuisine: seafood
Chef de cuisine: M. Joseph Galia
Specialities: local fish (of course); hors
d'oeuvres; meat and poultry
Location: at Ghadira Bay; 10 km/6 miles
north-west of Valletta
Setting: whitewashed, rather gaunt build-
ing; dining room affording a panoramic
view of the bay – one of the most popular
places in Malta during high season
Amenities: lido – perfect for a quick dip
before lunch
Atmosphere: leisurely; relaxed; informal
Clientèle: tourists from Manchester to
Mannheim; honeymoon couples; fami-
lies – and the occasional businessman
Dress: summery, sporting and preferably
chic
Service: attentive
Reservations: advisable

Dinner

PALAZZO PESCATORE
St Paul's Bay (6 km/4 miles)
Telephone: 57 31 82/57 37 96/57 12 95
Owner/Manager: Ben and Maria Muscat
Closed: Monday
Open: 19.30/7.30 p.m. to 22.30/10.30
p.m.
Cuisine: international; seafood
Chef de cuisine: M. Victor Casha
Specialities: Adriatic cocktail; fish soup
(aljotta); giant prawns; cernia ›meunière‹; duckling à l'orange; Steak Châteaubriand; crêpes
Location: at St Paul's Bay; 6 km/4 miles
from Valletta
Setting: 18th-century palazzo; dining
rooms furnished in varying styles; from
the stylish vaulted cellar to the Mediterranean rustic ground-floor area with ceiling
beams and red string-seated chairs
Amenities: private dining rooms; piano
bar with live entertainment; air conditioning; car park; ›Summer Garden Restaurant‹ – also offering seafood, weighed
and cooked at your table – in the gardens
of the Palazzo
Atmosphere: from the elegant (cellar) to
the homely (ground floor)
Clientèle: local habitués en fête and en
famille
Dress: casual but not careless
Service: efficient and multilingual
Reservations: advisable
Price range: moderately expensive
Credit cards: all major

The City

Only parochial hypocrites would object to calling the Principality of Monaco the earthly paradise for privileged mortals, but then, the miniature nation's minuscule capital, Monte-Carlo – the Magic Mountain of the Riviera – wasn't made for plebeians, puritans and Philistines, anyway. Despite the decline of monarchies and manners, this regal retreat (a few minutes by helicopter away from Nice International Airport) remains one of the last civilized enclaves – and one of the safest – where you won't risk stumbling over strikers, demonstrators or yokels. Even cocottes and gigolos are well behaved here, while day-tripping polyester-clad pilgrims from the hinterland camping grounds are intimidated into parading in amazement around La Place du Casino with its Rolls-to-Rolls carpeting, shunned by the aristocratic institutions of pleasure – *La Salle Privée* of Garnier's glorious gambling citadel; dreamland of travellers, *L'Hôtel de Paris* and fin-de-siècle ecstasy, *L'Hermitage*; the Beautiful People's beauty spa, *California Terrace*; summer fortress of La Vie en Rose, *Le Sporting d'Eté*, with the world's most dazzling clubs, Régine's *Jimmy'z* and *Maona*; *Monte-Carlo-Beach* with the Roman-emperor tent camp and the seaside hideaway, the *Monte-Carlo-Beach Hotel*. Exhibition site of Belle Epoque and Le Beau Monde, of Grand Hôtels and glittering galas, of Haute Couture and profound passions, of stars under the sun and philanderers after dark, the aesthetical framework breeds a sensuous atmosphere where every moment becomes a memorable highlight. International rallies and Grand-Prix races, tennis championships and golf Tournaments, charity balls and fireworks festivals, opera premières and castle concerts, treasure auctions, parties à la Great Gatsby and boat life à la Cockaigne adorn the calendar throughout the year, with many world companies organizing their conventions, conferences and incentives during the quieter months at the fabulous Congress Centre, combining business and pleasure at the most elevated niveau possible. In fact, Rainier III's Lilliputian state lives off industry, trade and services rather than off the profits from the Société des Bains de Mer's ›amusement park‹, let alone the casino's winnings and the stamps, and not only the favourable taxes attract firms and even some ecological industries such as cosmetics. Amongst the imposing skyscrapers marking the open boundaries to France (which acts as a godfather-guardian for Monaco) you will also find the life of a small Côte-d'Azur town with a picturesque market, gay bistros and still a few idyllic places and walks. Monte-Carlo is no South-Seas resort and introvert intellectuals had better go to Athos, but you must come here in summer when you long for the world's most elegant beach, chicest crowd and best service, as well as for the most luxurious hotels, fantastic yachts, fancy cars, extravagant gowns, precious jewellery – and prominent events and encounters. A healthy climate for the body, the mind, business and fantasy, coupled with style and sophistication, make Monte-Carlo the most attractive place for a day, a season or a lifetime. (Before Paradise).

Founded: 4th century B.C. – by the Ligurian Monoikos; Monte-Carlo – ›Charles' mountain‹.

Far-reaching events: 1215 – first building started by Genoese; 1297 – castle built under François Grimaldi; 1308 – principality bought from the Genoese; 1524–1641 – Spanish occupation; 1641–1814 – French occupation; 1814 – the Grimaldis regain sovereignty; 1793 – principality connected with France; 1856 – Prince of Monaco authorizes opening of a gambling house; 1861 – treaty proclaiming Monaco's sovereignty; François Blanc, director of the Bad Homburg casino, founds the Société des Bains de Mer and the Cercle des Etrangers, beginning of tourism; 1867 – railway between Nice and Ventimiglia opened; 1869 – opera built; 1942–44 – German occupation; 1949 – Prince Rainier of Monaco.

Population: 30,000.

Postal code: MC–98000   **Telephone code:** 93 (incorporated in number since 1986)

Climate: exceptionally mild all year round, with sunshine and light breezes.

Calendar of events: *St. Dévote* (26 Jan) – a ship is burnt commemorating a legend; *Rallye Monte-Carlo* (Jan) – car race; *International Television Festival* (Feb); *Bal de la Rose* (Mar) – royal reception for High Society; *International Tennis Tournament* (Apr); *Spring Arts Festival* (Apr) – concerts and ballets; *Grand Prix* (May) – the city's streets provide the race track; *Red Cross Gala* (Aug) – dinner-dance for le Beau Monde; *National Holiday* (Nov); *International Circus Festival* (Dec).

Historical sights: *Prince's Palace* (15th–16th centuries) – Italian Renaissance, with Moorish tower; *Cathedral* (1875–1903) – neo-Romanesque, interior decorated with white marble and mosaics; *Casino* (1878) – oldest part by Charles Garnier, architect of the Paris opera; *St. Dévote's Chapel* (1075).

Modern sights: *Oceanographic Museum* – aquarium and collection of oceanographic zoology objects, directed by Jacques Cousteau; *National Museum* – historic slot machines and doll collection; *Tropical Gardens* – large cactus collection and grottoes.

Special attractions: the *social routine*.

Important companies with headquarters in the city: *Lancaster* (cosmetics); *Honeywell; Monte Carlo Parfum; Laboratoires Wellcome* (pharmacy); *General X-Ray Company; Christian Dior Fourrure* (furs); *Ajax; Biobie Monaco; Ingram International*.

Airport: Nice-Côte d'Azur, NCE; Tel.: 93 72 30 30; Héli-Air, Tel.: 93 30 80 88; 7 min by helicopter.

The Headquarters

DE PARIS

Place du Casino B.P. 309
MC–98000 Monte-Carlo
Telephone: 93 50 80 80
Telex: 469 925 parihot
Owning Company: Société des Bains de Mer
General Manager: Dario dell'Antonia
Manager: Karl-Heinz Vanis
Number of rooms: 260 (38 suites)
Price range: FF 1,000–1,400 (single)
           1,100–1,600 (double)
           3,000–8,000 (suite)
Credit cards: AE, DC, EC, Visa
Location: city centre
Built: 1863
Style: Belle Epoque
Hotel amenities: valet parking, beauty parlour, hairdresser, boutique, tobacconist, florist, swimming pool, health club, sauna, solarium, massage
Room amenities: air conditioning, colour tv, mini-bar (pets allowed)
Bathroom amenities: bidet, bathrobe, hairdrier, telephone
Room service: 24 hours
Conference rooms: 3 (for up to 80 guests)
Bar: ›Bar Américain‹ (10.00/a.m.–4.00/a.m.) Roger Girardi (barman), pianist
Restaurants: ›La Salle Empire‹ (12.00/a.m.–14.00/2.00 p.m. and 20.00/8.00 p.m.–22.30/10.30 p.m.) P. Orrigo (maître), S. Buonsignore (chef de cuisine), French cuisine, orchestra, open-air dining; ›Le Grill‹ (see Restaurants)
Nightclubs: ›Le Jimmy'z‹ and ›Le Cabaret‹ (23.00/11.00 p.m. to 4.00/a.m.) orchestra (Sporting d'Eté)

Glory, glory for the last 120 years, and hallelujah from the High Society habitués and the fashionable hangers-on ever since. Palace of all palaces, stage of super-stars and sensations, fortress of a life-style that has long vanished from the rest of the earth, ›Le Paris‹ is, incidentally, one of the best hotels in the world. You will fall into raptures about its architecture, décor and amenities; you will be mesmerized by the high concentration of haute couture, haute coiffure and haute bijouterie; you will be romanticized by all the memories, stories and legends – but, most of all, you will be surprised about the routine efficiency, the amiable service and the standard of cuisine. Marble splendour, lustre shine and the venerability of antiques and accessoires are balanced by an air of joy, most likely stemming from the fact of being here. Whatever room you occupy, it will be luxurious, and the view will be breathtaking; whatever you order will be near-to-perfect, and most everything self-understood; and when you move between Le Bar (bar of bars), the penthouse Grill (the most beautiful observatory in the world), or the terraced Salle Empire (Belle Epoque à la folie) – you are always in the right place. The Palace's palace is the epitome of elegant leisure and grande hôtellerie à l'extrême.

HERMITAGE

Square Beaumarchais
P.O. Box 277
MC–98000 Monte-Carlo
Telephone: 93 50 67 31
Telex: 479 432 hermit
Owning Company: Société des Bains de Mer
General Manager: Dario dell'Antonia
Manager: Jean Rauline
Number of rooms: 260
Price range: FF 800–1,200 (single)
FF 1,000–1,400 (double)
FF 2,500–5,000 (suite)
Credit cards: AE, DC, CB, EC
Location: city centre, 30 km/19 miles from airport
Built: 1900 (renovated 1980–1984)
Hotel amenities: valet parking, limousine service, beauty salon, health club, sauna, solarium, massage, grand piano, swimming pool
Room amenities: air conditioning, colour tv, video, mini-bar/refrigerator
Room service: 24 hours
Conference rooms: 5 (up to 70 persons)
Bar: ›La Terrace‹, pianist
Restaurant: ›Belle Epoque‹ (see Restaurants)
Nightclubs: ›Le Jimmy'z‹ (23.00/11.00 p.m. to late) orchestra, ›Cabaret‹ (as Jimmy'z), orchestra (Sporting d'Eté)

Living up to the standard and standing of its St. Petersburg namesake in its own way, this regal retreat in the princely enclave is the equally glorious twin to the Hôtel de Paris across the little park square, with its majestic cream-colour colonnaded façade surveying the sea. Belle Epoque splendour receives you here with psychedelic force, from the fin-de-siècle jardin d'hiver under a floral glass dome to the delirious dining room, rightfully carrying the lavish period's name, Salle Belle Epoque, *and competing only with its neighbouring Salle Empire for the title of the world's most beautiful restaurant. Marble rosé, ornately mirrored walls, diamond glitter from the lustres and table accessoires and the ceiling fresco by Gabriel Ferrier lend this oval salon an ambiance which Hollywood and Cinecittà couldn't re-enact together. The intimate bar leading to the terrace lets you tip-toe from the pianist to the panorama, and vacillate between the harbour view and the sentimental repertoire. But the time you spend in your own room will be alluring enough – every detail is either antique or redesigned in the Art Nouveau fashion. The service to come with it is à la hauteur, and the amenities – from California Terrace pool-and-spa to the Monte-Carlo Beach – are all of the same family. With the stage set for illusionary luxury, the choice where to reside or do business or not do anything at all, will be one between heaven and paradise.*

The Hideaway

MONTE-CARLO BEACH

Avenue du Bord de Mer
MC–06190 Roquebrune-Cap-Martin
Telephone: 93 78 21 40
Owner: Société des Bains de Mer
General Manager: George Maillet
Closed: mid-Oct.–mid-March
Number of rooms: 50 (7 bungalows)
Price range: FF 1,100–1,250 (single)
FF 1,200–1,400 (double)
FF 2,400–2,800 (suite)
Credit cards: AE, DC, EC, Visa
Location: directly on the beach, near city centre
Hotel amenities: car park, swimming pool, 200 dressing cabins, 144 cabanas, 34 private solaria, 2 swimming pools, private beach
Room amenities: tv, air conditioning
Bathroom amenities: bidet, telephone, bathrobe, hairdrier
Room service: 24 hours
Laundry/dry cleaning: same day
Conference rooms: 2 (up to 30 persons)
Sports: tennis, swimming, windsurfing, water-skiing, diving, sailing
Sports (nearby): Monte-Carlo Country Club
Bars: ›Beau Rivage‹ (12.00/a.m.–15.00/3 p.m. and 20.00/8 p.m.–22.00/p.m.); ›La Potinière‹ (12.00/a.m.–15.00/3 p.m. and 20.00/8 p.m.–22.00/10 p.m)
Restaurant: ›La Potinière‹; French cuisine, fish specialities, M. Fusero (chef de cuisine)

Some dream about an island in the South Seas, others about a yachting cruise through the Caribbean and the more modest ones may yearn for a frivolous fortnight on the shores of Ibiza. When you desire the best-groomed beach with the sleekest yachts dropping anchor, luxurious cabanas with grand-hotel service and the Upper Crust of many worlds in couture tangas and designer accessoires – there is only one place on the continent (and the chicest in the world): Monte-Carlo Beach. The pastel-coloured half-circle edifice overlooking the elegant pool area, the ritzy terrace restaurant and the Côte d'Azur's dearest speck of land is also the most desirable retreat between the blossoming of the mimosas and the fading of the suntans. Cornerstone of the Société des Bains de Mer, no word has to be lost about the supremacy of hospitalité. If you want to be unnoticed for the length of your stay, you will be protected from suite to beach-tent, receive your meals on your private terrace and be shuttled to town from a separate entrance. If you want to take part in the dance on the volcano, you can be sure that there is no other place where you meet as many stars skin-to-skin. Spending the summer at Monte-Carlo Beach (which is based on French soil, curiously enough) is among the last possible ways to pretend the Belle Epoque is still in full swing.

Lunch

LA COUPOLE
1–3 Avenue Princesse Grace
Telephone: 93 25 45 45
Affiliations: Société des Bains de Mer, Monte-Carlo
Owner/Manager: Georges Maillet
Closed: never
Open: 12.00/a.m.–14.30/2.30 p.m. and 19.30/7.30 p.m.–22.30/10.30 p.m.
Cuisine: nouvelle
Chef de cuisine: Yves Garnier
Specialities: soupière de poissons de roche safranée en croûte; three fish on mullet mousse in puff pastry with morel mushroom sauce; salade d'aiguillettes de canard fumé; panier de nougatine glacée aux fruits
Location: next to the casino; in the Hotel Mirabeau
Setting: bright, attractive modern décor with trompe-l'œil à la Toulouse-Lautrec
Amenities: hotel; outdoor dining in summer (buffet by swimming pool); bar; private dining rooms (up to 150 persons); air conditioning; car park (attended)
Atmosphere: chic et chaleureuse
Clientèle: jeunesse dorée (or at least argentée); princes, princesses and a plentitude of international celebrities
Dress: jacket de rigueur
Service: dinner jackets indoors; T-shirts by the pool – and always smiling
Reservations: advisable (no dogs)
Price range: expensive (except for those born with a silver spoon in their mouths)
Credit cards: AE, DC, Euro, Carte Bleue

Dinner

LA BELLE EPOQUE
Square Beaumarchais
Telephone: 93 50 67 31
Owner/Manager: Société des Bains de Mer, Monte-Carlo
Closed: never
Open: 12.00/a.m.–15.00/3 p.m. and 20.00/8 p.m.–22.30/10.30 p.m.
Cuisine: classic, with a modern accent
Chef de cuisine: François Fusero
Specialities: lobster bisque with vintage Armagnac; steamed turbot with saffron and basil; viennoise of fresh salmon with watercress; blanquette of scampi and scallops; fillet of lamb with cream and fresh mint, served with fried courgettes; sautéed ducks' liver with red currants; piccata de veau with lemon thyme; gratin of raspberries with sabayon; iced chocolate and peppermint parfait
Location: in the Hôtel Hermitage
Setting: in a beautiful Belle Epoque palais, perched on a cliff overlooking the sea and the royal palace; dining room with trompe-l'œil ceiling by Gabriel Fer-

rier, chandeliers on gleaming sconces, pink marble pillars and what is probably the most lovely terrace in the principality
Amenities: hotel; pianist; open-air dining on terrace; air conditioning; car park
Atmosphere: even more evocative of Edwardian splendour (if that is possible) than the Salle Empire
Clientèle: some of the most beautiful people on the planet
Dress: rather elegant at all times; jacket and tie de rigueur for dinner
Service: particularly anxious-to-please
Reservations: advisable to essential (no dogs)
Price range: rather expensive – even by Monégasque standards
Credit cards: AE, DC, Euro, Visa

Lunch

LE GRILL
Place du Casino
Telephone: 93 50 80 80
Affiliations: Groupements des Palaces de la Côte d'Azur
Owner/Manager: Société des Bains de Mer/Karl Vanis
Closed: Monday; December 8th – 23rd; lunchtime from June 1st – September 5th
Open: 12.00/a.m.–15.00/3 p.m. and 20.00/8 p.m.–24.00/12 p.m.
Cuisine: classic
Chef de cuisine: Claude Jeanneret
Specialities: spit-roasted fish and meat on a charcoal grill; noix de St. Jacques au caviar à la marinière; escalope of turbot with winkles and leek fondue; guinea-fowl in Provençal honey and Sauternes
Location: in the Hôtel de Paris; near the casino
Setting: penthouse; recently completely renovated; royal barge décor
Amenities: roof opens to enhance the feeling of ›A Night in Monte-Carlo‹ – especially impressive during the international firework display in August; bar; air conditioning
Atmosphere: romantic
Clientèle: familiar faces and famous names from Liza Minelli to Yehudi Menuhin
Dress: jacket and tie
Service: perfect
Reservations: advisable (pets prohibited)
Price range: rather expensive
Credit cards: AE, DC, Euro, Visa, Carte Bleue

Meeting Point

LE BISTROQUET (Galerie Charles III)
22 Avenue Princesse-Grace
Telephone: 93 50 65 03/93 51 71 68
Owner/Manager: Rolf Palm
Closed: never

Open: 12.00/a.m.–8.00/a.m.
Cuisine: French
Specialities: baby lamb in red wine and pepper sauce; ›Bistroquet Festival‹ (shrimps, salmon and caviar are some of the many ingredients)
Location: close to the Casino
Setting: Belle Epoque
Amenities: restaurant; piano-bar on the first floor; open-air dining on terrace, cocktail bar, air conditioning
Atmosphere: relaxed and lively elegance; here you spend the fortunes you make at the nearby Casino – and if you're a gentleman (or gentle lady . . .): invite the losers too
Clientèle: upper middle class, middle upper class as well as the lower higher upper class – and of course all sorts of cosmopolitan beauties and businessmen
Dress: as you like it, as long as you like it elegant . . .
Service: personal, professional and multilingual
Reservations: advisable
Price range: medium
Credit cards: AE, CB, DC, EC, Visa

Nightclub

JIMMY'Z DE LA MER (Chez Régine)
Monte-Carlo Sporting Club
Avenue Princesse-Grace
Telephone: 93 30 71 71
Closed: October – May (replaced during winter closure by Jimmy'z, Place du Casino/Telephone 50 80 80)
Open: 23.00/11 p.m. – dawn
Location: in the bay of the artificial island of the Sporting d'Eté
Setting: a breathtaking Japanese garden; a mixture of Hollywood fantasy and Art Déco nostalgia; half-open sky-roof; view over the sea; fountains; low-slung armchairs (the fresh-air tables on the lagoon are best)
Amenities: discothèque; affiliated nightclubs from Rio to London, including the sister establishment on the Place du Casino open during the winter months
Atmosphere: the most magnificent club under the moon; sparkling, romantic, sensual and piquant – the brightest star in the firmament of the empire ruled by Queen of the Night Régine; really the only place to see and be seen
Clientèle: youthful; beautiful; rich; exhibitionistic; monarchs, tennis kings, millionaires and mannequins
Dress: St-Laurent and Lagerfeld rather than Levis and loafers (quelle horreur!)
Service: impeccable
Reservations: essential
Price range: fairly expensive
Credit cards: all major

Shopping

FOR HIM
Lanvin 2   Place du Casino
FOR HER
Scherrer, Jean-Louis   Terrasses de l'Hôtel de Paris, Avenue de Monte-Carlo

BEAUTY & HAIR
Nogues, Robert   Place Beaumarchais (Hôtel Hermitage)

JEWELLERY
Fabergé   Avenue de Monte-Carlo

LOCAL SPECIALITIES
Marie-France Couture (women's fashion)
37 Boulevard des Moulins
Façonnable (men's fashion)
23 Boulevard des Moulins
Bootega, La-L'Estoril (men & women's fashion) 31 Avenue Princesse-Grace
Hermès (leather fashion)
Avenue de Monte-Carlo
Dior, Christian (furs)
Hôtel Métropole, Avenue de la Madonne
British library (books)
30 Boulevard des Moulins
Cartier (gifts)
Place du Casino
Palais du Cristal, Au (porcelain)
3 Avenue Princesse-Alice
Vuitton, Louis (baggage & travel accessories)
6 Rue des Beaux-Arts
Renwick (interior decorating)
2 Rue Honoré Labande, (Avenue St. Charles)
Galleria (bathroom accessories)
Avenue Princesse-Grace
Maison du Caviar, La (food and beverages)
Avenue de Monte-Carlo
Parfum Caroline (perfumery)
8 Avenue Princesse-Caroline
Jourdan, Charles (shoes)
18 Boulevard des Moulins
Björn Borg Sportshop (tennis equipment)
L'Estoril, Avenue Princesse-Grace
Narmino (flowers)
27 Avenue de la Costa

THE BEST OF ART
Galerie d'Art Ancien et Moderne
21 Boulevard Princes-Charlotte
Tel. 93 30 76 22
Sotheby's Parke Bernet (auctioneers)
Place du Casino, Tel. 93 30 88 80

Amsterdam is beautiful in a bourgeois rather than an aristocratic sense; it exudes respectability – despite the red-light and blue-film prejudices – rather than recklessness, conventionally solid taste rather than elegance. In the museums and galleries the Rembrandts and the Vermeers, the Hals and the Van Goghs encapsulate the glorious past. The ornately gabled merchants' houses lining the concentric rings of canals – Singel, Herengracht, Keizersgracht, Prinsengracht – which keep Amsterdam's head above water (literally), reflect the city's Golden Age and the image tourists have of it in the mirror-like surface. Clichés of the most pleasantly picturesque kind all materialize before your eyes – tiled roofs, cobbled streets, church spires, arched bridges, houseboats, hurdy-gurdy men, bicycles galore and the notorious tulips at every street corner. Antwerp has the bigger diamond centre, but Amsterdam makes the more important deals. The Hague is the country's administrative and political arena, but Amsterdam is the lobby for more far-reaching decisions. Rotterdam has the bigger port, but all the most important personalities are shipped in through Schiphol. Amsterdam is, above all, the country's economic turntable and undisputed showcase. From the famed Concertgebouw to the Fifties-style jazz clubs around the Leidseplein, from the doll's house restaurants to the smoke-filled cafés, redolent of sailors' yarns and faraway places, the city stands out amongst world capitals for multilingual ability, open-hearted friendliness and down-to-earth tolerance. And even though Amsterdam has lost its influence over its former colonial empire, the local Heineken dynasty's national ›champagne‹ has regained Dutch supremacy all over the world.

Founded: 12th century as a fishing village; Amsterdam (Dutch) – ›dyke on the Amstel‹.

Far-reaching events: 1275 – first mentioned as ›Amsteldamme‹; 1300 – receives City Rights; 1317 – annexed to the County of Holland; 1369 – joins the Hanseatic League; 1535 – the Reformation; Hapsburg Charles V comes for support; 1556 – Philip II of Spain succeeds Charles V; 1567 – Duke of Alba occupies Amsterdam by order of Philip II; 1572 – William of Orange, leader of the revolt in the northern provinces; 1578 – Amsterdam surrenders to William's troops; 1610 – the first principal canals are constructed; 1648 – Contract of Münster, independence of the Republic; 17th century – Amsterdam flourishes as an important trade centre; 1780–84 – loses its pre-eminence at sea in the British Sea Wars; 1795 – French occupation; 1806 – capital of a French kingdom under Napoléon's brother Louis; 1810 – integrated into France; 1813 – victory over the French, monarchy under William of Orange-Nassau, seat of government moves to The Hague; 1876 – North Sea canal, direct access to the sea; 1940 – German troops invade; 1940–45 – heavy bombing; 1945 – reconstruction starts.

Population: 850,000.

Postal code: 1100 NA   **Telephone code:** 20

Climate: fresh and clear, sometimes with very cool sea breezes.

Calendar of events: *Queen's Birthday* (30 Apr) – fairs and fireworks, with the city decorated in the national colours; *Rijtuigendag* (2nd Sun in Jul) – festival of coaches; *Holland Festival* (Jun to Jul) – ballet, street theatre, symphonies and more, a cultural cornucopia; *Jordaan-Festival* (Sep) – folk festival; *Arts Festival* (end of Sep–Oct) – a ten-day open-house in the city's museums, galleries, theatres and opera house – free of charge, with peeks behind the scenes encouraged; *St. Nicholas* (5 Dec) – the city's patron saint.

Fairs and exhibitions: *AUTOVAK* (Mar) – international trade fair for garage equipment; *INTERCLEAN* (May) – international trade fair of professional maintenance and cleaning; *REIMATO* (May) – cleaning machinery for towns and municipal refuse destruction; *EUROFINISH* (May) – technical and maintenance services; *AUTOBUS RAI* (Sep) – international autobus and touring cars exhibition; *W + G* (Sep) – national trade fair for wine and spirits; *EFFICIENCY BEURS* (Oct) – office machines and equipment; *SALE* (Oct) – sales promotion trade fair; *COMDEX EUROPE* (Oct) – Europe international computer trade show; *SPEELGOED* (Nov) – international exhibition of toys and hobby articles; *HOLLAND OFFSHORE* (Nov) – international offshore technology and service exhibition; *ENERGY ECONOMY* (Dec) – energy control and management, equipment and systems; *TOUR* (Dec) – tourism trade fair.

Historical sights: *Royal Palace* (1648–65) – former city hall atop 13,659 oak piles, constructed by Jacob van Campen; *Rijksmuseum* (1877–85) – neo-classic, Dutch painters of the past four centuries; *Rembrandt House* (1606); *Munttoren* – city tower with beautiful carillon, on the *Muntplein*, one of the liveliest spots in the city; *Oude Kerk* (1300) – decorated arches and an 18th-century organ; *Westerkerk* (1620) – Renaissance style, with Rembrandt's grave.

Modern sights: *Van Gogh Museum* (1973) – specially built to house his works.

Special attractions: look at the *Flemish Masters* in their own home; a tour through the *bars, pubs* and *jazz clubs*; a tour through the *canals of the city* in a gondola brought in from Venice.

Important companies with headquarters in the city: *Amsterdam Rotterdam Bank* (banking); *Ballast Nedam Groep* (construction); *Bührmann Tetterode* (packing materials); *Cindu-Key & Kramer* (roofing); *Delta Lloyd* (insurance); *Fokker* (aeroplanes); *Heineken* (brewery); *KLM* (airline); *N.V. Centrale Suiker Maatschappij* (sugar); *Otra* (books); *VMF-Stork* (steel, iron, machinery).

Airport: Amsterdam-Schiphol, AMS; Tel.: 5110432; 15 km/10 miles.

The Headquarters

L'EUROPE

2–4 Nieuwe Doelenstraat
NL–1012 CP Amsterdam
Telephone: 23 48 36
Telex: 12 081 europ
General Manager: Adriaan W. Grandia
Affiliation/Reservation Systems: The Leading Hotels of the World, Hotels de Grande Classe Internationale, Alliance Gastronomique Néerlandaise
Number of rooms: 79 (4 suites)
Price range: Hfl 275–950)
Credit cards: AE, DC, CB, EC, Visa
Location: opposite the flower-market
Built: 1896 (renovated 1984)
Style: traditional, classic
Room amenities: colour tv, mini-bar
Bathroom amenities: bathrobe, telephone
Room service: 24 hours
Laundry/dry cleaning: same day (weekend service)
Conference rooms: 3 (up to 64 persons)
Bars: ›Le Bar‹ (11.00/a.m.–1.00/a.m.) cocktail bar, ›La Terrasse‹ (10.00/a.m.–22.00/10.00 p.m., open in summer only) private boat jetty
Restaurants: ›Excelsior‹ (12.30/p.m.–14.30/2.30 p.m. and 19.00/7.00 p.m.–22.30/10.30 p.m.), French cuisine; ›Le Relais‹ (12.00/a.m.–24.00/12.00 p.m.) French and Dutch cuisine
Private dining rooms: up to 64 persons

The Dutch do not only have a knack for grandiose nature, but also for animating interiors with natural grandeur. The hospitable canal-corner ›Palais de l'Europe‹ is one eminent example where the fortunate guests, from hurried men of commerce to timeless bel-esprits, are surrounded by the home-away-from-home atmosphere with many pleasant surprises you always missed at home itself. The intimately cosy bar, the elegant bistro-restaurant Le Relais *and the below-the-water-level* Excelsior *dining room allow for some of the joys even when you are not residing here. The building, restored, renovated and resplendent as one of Amsterdam's prettiest – complete with beflagged gables and spires and red-canopied windows as for a royal regatta alla Venetiana – has somewhat become a landmark in this city. Not only for its physical appearance, however, but also for the luxuriously beautiful intérieur, the lightness, the warmth, the material and quality of every ordinary item, for the homey rooms with that worldly view, for the pleasant service and the self-understood efficiency overlooked by youthful and personable Adriaan Grandia and for the renowned cuisine in one of the best, most attractive and elegant restaurants in the country. Dîner-à-deux, tête-à-tête, hand-in-hand at the Excelsior is among the highlight pleasures here. And when you retire to the Bridal Suite with four-poster bed and whirlbath in the right company, embraced by water and a thousand lights, and… – you may forget about the rain, the cold, the Caribbean and business.*

The Hideaway

PULITZER

315–331 Prinsengracht
NL–1016 GZ Amsterdam
Telephone: 22 83 33
Telex: 16 508 pulam
Owning Company: Hotelmij Oud Amsterdam
General Manager: Alfred Egli
Affiliation/Reservation Systems: Golden Tulip Hotels/Best Western
Number of rooms: 200 (5 suites)
Price range: Hfl 250–700
Credit cards: AE, DC, EC, Visa
Location: central, near the Palace and the shopping area
Built: 16th and 17th century (renovated 1970)
Style: modern interior in an antique house
Hotel amenities: gardens; valet parking; car rental, newsstand, tobacconist
Main hall porter: Mr. van Kooten
Room amenities: colour tv, video, minibar (pets allowed)
Bathroom amenities: hairdrier
Room service: 6.00 a.m.–24.00/12 p.m.
Laundry/dry cleaning: same day (weekend service)
Conference rooms: 5 (up to 45 persons)
Bar: ›Pulitzer‹ (11.00 a.m.–1.00 a.m.) Jerry Kooyman (barman), pianist
Restaurant: ›Pulitzer‹ (11.00 a.m.–22.30/10.30 p.m.); Bert Clewitz (maître)
Private dining rooms: two

In the heart of the Dutch capital, a carillon away from the Westerkerk where Rembrandt is buried, stands a city-centre hideaway of great originality, sophistication and charm. The Pulitzer bears the name of its mentor, an American entrepreneur of vision and courage who, with the help of architect Van Kasteel, transformed the enclave of nineteen seventeenth-century homes, workshops and warehouses standing back to back on the Prinsengracht and Keizersgracht canals into an auberge which appeals to visitors from both sides of the Atlantic. In accordance with Holland's strict conservation laws the distinctive façades, including the neck, spout or clock gables, have been maintained, whilst the intérieur has become a fascinating rabbit -warren of interconnecting corridors and half-landings linking rooms whose bright, modern furnishings contrast refreshingly with the wooden beams, the arched windows, the attic nooks and the skylights of the original houses. Some have a canal view, whilst others overlook the enchanting garden courtyard where, in summer, you can sip Heineken amidst cotoneaster and laburnum under a hundred-year-old chestnut tree to the song of birds and the chimes of church bells. Although the Pulitzer is larger than many rural hideaways the staff, under manager Alfred Egli, foster the tradition of discreet personal service associated with small hotels. Which explains why James Stewart and Danny Kaye choose to stay here when in Amsterdam.

Lunch

DE BOERDERIJ
69 Korte Leidsdwarsstraat
Telephone: 23 69 29
Owner/Manager/Chef de cuisine: Ruud
Wunneberg
Closed: Saturday lunchtime; Sunday:
second half of July
Open: 12.00/12 a.m.–14.00/2 p.m.;
18.00/6 p.m.–22.00/10 p.m.
Cuisine: French (nouvelle)
Specialities: fish; shellfish; poularde de
Bresse; classic meat dishes; calves' sweet-
breads with morel mushrooms
Location: near the Leidseplein; opposite
the ›t' Schwarte Schaep‹
Setting: Old Dutch front-room parlour
décor with antique paraphernalia and an
attractive fireplace
Amenities: car park at Raamplein
Atmosphere: Netherlands nostalgia with
a soupçon of Gallic wit (due at least in
part to the excellent food)
Clientèle: expense-account gourmets
from Gouda, Glasgow and Guatemala,
plus the occasional local lovers celebrating anniversaries, engagements or reun-
ions
Dress: informal
Service: knowledgeable and attentive
Reservations: necessary (no dogs)
Price range: rather expensive
Credit cards: AE, DC, Euro, Visa

Lunch

LES QUATRE CANETONS
1111 Prinsengracht
Telephone: 24 63 07
Owner/Manager/Chef de cuisine: Wy-
nand Vogel
Closed: Saturday lunchtime; Sunday;
December 30 – 31st; New Year's Day;
Easter
Open: 12.00/a.m.–14.00/2 p.m. and
18.00/6 p.m.–22.00/10 p.m.
Cuisine: French (classic and nouvelle)
Specialities: cold and warm goose liver;
crab tureen; eel mousse; truffle soup;
lobster with leek sauce; smoked plaice;
escalope of duckling marinated in red
pepper sauce; Dutch fillet of beef with
Genever sauce
Location: on the Prinsengracht canal; a
champagne cork's trajectory away from
the Carré Theatre; not far from Rembrandt Square (Rembrandtsplein)
Setting: a converted and renovated warehouse; neutral colour scheme with indirect lighting; spotlit pictures; well-spaced
tables; podium at rear with tables for
groups
Amenities: private dining room ›de Plan-
tenzaal‹ (10–30 persons)
Atmosphere: peaceful and relaxing to romantic, especially during candlelit dinners at Christmas
Clientèle: mixture of francophile Royal
Dutch subjects, homesick French businessmen and tourists from Guadeloupe
to the Gilbert and Ellice Islands
Dress: jacket and tie preferred
Reservations: advisable
Price range: fairly expensive
Credit cards: AE, DC,, Euro, Visa, Bank
Americard, Master Charge, Access

Dinner

›T SCHWARTE SCHAEP‹
(›The Black Sheep‹)
24 Korte Leidsedwarsstraat, 1 hoog
Telephone: 22 30 21
Owner/Manager: Wim Liefting
Closed: Saint Nicholas (December 6th);
Christmas Day and Boxing Day (Decem-
ber 25th–26th); New Year's Eve; New
Year's Day
Open: 12.00/a.m.–21.00/9 p.m.
Cuisine: French (traditional and nou-
velle)
Chef de cuisine: Ton van den Boogard
Specialities: regularly changing menu;
caviar; lobster ravioli; salpicon de caille
with garlic, basil and tomato sauce with
saffron and aniseed; minute of smoked
salmon with leek butter; angler-fish salad
with shrimps; suckling lamb with balsam
vinegar
Location: near the Leidseplein; on the
first floor
Setting: old Dutch interior; pretty stair-
case; dark oakwood panelled dining
room; plenty of brass accessoires
Amenities: air conditioning
Atmosphere: cosy Dutch; not without a
hint of romance
Clientèle: comfortable mixture of local
habitués and foreign visitors at work or at
leisure
Dress: from jeans and camera to cash-
mere and pearls
Service: welcoming and helpful
Reservations: advisable
Price range: fairly expensive
Credit cards: AE, DC, Euro, Visa, Master
Charge

Lunch

OESTERBAR
10 Leidseplein
Telephone: 23 29 88
Owner/Managers: Hans and Wim Hoop-
man
Closed: never
Open: 12.00/a.m.–1.00/a.m.
Cuisine: seafood
Chef de cuisine: Henk Böhmer
Specialities: fresh fish – lobster, Irish sal-
mon, Dover sole, turbot – and, of course,
oysters; fresh fish pâté of turbot, salmon

and shrimp; fillets of sole ›Danoise‹; poached or grilled salmon with sauce hollandaise

Location: a short taxi-ride or a slightly longer walk from the Rijksmuseum

Setting: fish tanks, copper fish-kettles and tiled scenes of old Amsterdam and the sea; menu on blackboard and bar for snacks in the corner

Amenities: restaurant (upstairs) – quieter but less fun; air conditioning; car park

Atmosphere: lively; not to be confused with its namesake in New York's Grand Central Station, but to Amsterdam just as famous and frequented

Clientèle: heterogeneous; fish fanciers of all ages, shapes, sizes and sex tackle the squid, shrimps and sole

Dress: as you like it – as long as they will like you

Service: cheerful

Reservations: advisable

Price range: medium

Credit cards: AE

Dinner

D'VIJFF VLIEGHEN (›Five Flies‹)
294–302 Spuistraat
Telephone: 24 83 69

Owner/Manager: Hotel Krasnapolsky / Robert de Vries

Closed: St. Nicholas (December 6th); Christmas Day; Boxing Day; New Year's Eve

Open: 17.00/5 p.m.–24.00/12 p.m.

Cuisine: international and Dutch

Chef de cuisine: Jan Biegelaar

Specialities: smoked eel soup; Dutch brown bean soup; Dutch sole; Dutch smoked fish; macaroon pudding

Location: central, near the Spui

Setting: five small townhouses, the oldest dating from 1627; seven dining rooms each furnished in a different Renaissance style; oak beams, unrendered brick, tiles and dark wood; antique memorabilia; glass, copper, brass and two original Rembrandt etchings

Amenities: bar

Atmosphere: a national monument (but very much alive and well); an international curiosity; dinner by candlelight in a setting steeped in Amsterdam's history

Clientèle: sprinkling of local burghers and artists, plus tourists from Alaska to Adelaide; celebrities whose names adorn the chairs they once sat in; Françoise Sagan, Rudolf Nureyev, Danny Kaye and Vera Lynn

Dress: no special requirements or restrictions

Service: efficient

Reservations: advisable

Price range: moderately expensive

Credit cards: AE, DC, Euro, Visa, JCB

Café

CAFE AMERICAIN
97 Leidsekade
Telephone: 24 53 22

Owner/Manager: Heinz Strobel/John Cats

Closed: never

Open: 11.00/a.m.–24.00/12.00 p.m.

Location: near the theatre

Setting: built by W. Kromhout at the turn of the century; a listed historic monument; ornate Art Nouveau décor; 1920s sculptures and furnishings

Atmosphere: Amsterdam's Café de la Paix; a nostalgic evocation of a graciously unforgotten era; a haven of style

Clientèle: would not disgrace a Garbo film; elegant and expensive

Dress: casual

Service: black-suited and very suave

Reservation: recommended for larger groups at busy times

Credit cards: AE, DC, Visa

Meeting Point

HOPPE
12–20 Spui
Telephone: 24 07 56

Owner/Manager: Hoppe B. V./Han Bos

Closed: Christmas, New Year

Open: 8.00/a.m.–1.00/a.m.

Location: central

Setting: an authentic brown café (bruine kroeg); established 300 years ago; traditional, predominantly brown décor with an abundance of wood providing a neutral background for the colourful clientèle

Amenities: fresh beer from the tap and generation-old Genever

Atmosphere: still has the somewhat mystifying sobriquet ›the P. J. Clarke's of Amsterdam‹; heterogeneous; usually rather smoky; a good place to catch up on the latest news (or gossip) – especially in the ›Happy Hour‹ between 17.00/5 p.m. and 20.00/8 p.m.

Clientèle: colourful mixture of entrepreneurs, publishers, journalists, men of letters and those who would have one believe they fit into one or another of these categories

Dress: mostly rather casual

Service: friendly

Reservations: not required

Credit cards: not accepted

Meeting Point

CONTINENTAL BODEGA (›The Sherry Bodega‹)
246 Lijnbaansgracht
Telephone: 23 90 98

Owner/Manager: Bols Liquer Company/A. F. Steeneken

Closed: Sunday; public holidays
Open: 15.00/3 p.m.–21.00/9 p.m.
Location: near the Leidseplein
Setting: cosy, cask-lined warehouse
Amenities: grill/bistro serving light snacks and the season's first oysters – as well as sherry, port and wine
Atmosphere: very chic for a Fino and nibbles at lunchtime; equally so for an amontillado before dinner at Dikker en Thijs or De Boerderij
Clientèle: Amsterdam's High Society habitués; jet setters and other social tourists en passant
Dress: casual
Service: efficient
Reservations: not necessary
Credit cards: not accepted

Bar

OBLOMOW
40 Reguliersstraat
Telephone: 24 10 74
Owner/Manager: S. Kooistra/
T. MacKenzie
Closed: never
Open: 12.00/a.m.–1.00/a.m.; weekends till 2 a.m.
Location: near Munt; behind the Flower Market
Setting: modern, very light, old fashioned ceramic stone work
Amenities: parking only in the street
Atmosphere: trendy bar for people in their 20s
Clientèle: business, advertising people, artists
Dress: casual
Service: friendly and efficient
Reservations: recommended
Price range: moderate
Credit cards: AE, DC, Euro, Visa

Nightclub

BIOS
12 Leidseplein
Telephone: 27 65 44
Owner/Manager: Rian Hausinfeld/Julian van der Kamp
Closed: never
Open: 22.00/10 p.m.–3.00/a.m.; weekends till 4.00/a.m.
Setting: old cinema (Bioscope) luxury
Amenities: air conditioning, TV screens; 3 bars
Clientèle: no teenies; upper class
Dress: stylish
Price range: expensive

Shopping

EVERYTHING UNDER ONE ROOF
De Bijenkorf 90a Damrak

FOR HIM
Maison de Vries 125–129 Kalverstraat

FOR HER
Maison de Vries 125–129 Kalverstraat

BEAUTY & HAIR
Boendie, Haute Coiffure
89 P.C. Hooftstraat

JEWELLERY
Siebel Juweliers 121–123 Kalverstraat

LOCAL SPECIALITIES
Davidoff-Shop (tobacco)
Van Baerlestraat 84
Maison de Bonneterie (women's fashion)
183 Kalverstraat
Jaques d'Ariege (men's fashion)
P.C.142 Hooftstraat
Leeserstudie (children's fashion)
117 P. C. Hooftstraat
Zumpolle (leather fashion)
157 Kalverstraat
W. de Ruiter (furs)
91 P. C. Hooftstraat
E. Pronk (furs)
124 PC Hooftstraat
J. de Slegte (books)
48–52 Kalverstraat
Geschenkenhuis de Vyzel (gifts)
47 Vyzelstraat
Focke & Meltzer (porcelain)
176 Kalverstraat
Zumpolle (baggage & travel accessories)
157 Kalverstraat
Abraham Kef (cheese)
192 Marnixstraat
H. Keyzer (coffee and tea)
180 Prinzengracht
Boonebakker & Zoon (diamonds)
88 Rokin

THE BEST OF ART
Brinkman (contemporary art)
105 Kerkstraat, Tel. 22 74 93
d'Eendt (contemporary art)
272–270 Spuistraat, Tel. 26 57 77/24 30 64
Farber, Barbara (contemporary art)
340 Herengracht, Tel. 27 63 43
Wending (contemporary art)
60 Rubensstraat, Tel. 71 86 30
Waterman (17th/18th-century Old Master paintings) 116 Rokin
Brandt, B.V., Paul (auctioneers)
738 Keizersgracht, Tel. 24 86 62/23 03 01

The City

Sue Great Britain for closing the pubs before midnight! Argue with the Greek government about their puritanical sex laws! Try to persuade Los Cortes in Madrid to liberalize their drug regulations! It may not get you very far, but at least it will get you as far as The Hague – the seat of the International Courts of Justice and Arbitration, providing an arena where countries clash in a peaceful way. It's also the administrative capital of The Netherlands, home of the States General, residence of diplomats and the Dutch Royal Family – and one of the prettiest mini-metropolises in the world. The city surrounding the former nobleman's hunting lodge (S'Gravenhage) stands serene amidst tulip fields and windmills, shunning deliberately the more extrovert attractions of big brother Amsterdam as Washington scorns New York. The medieval heart of the city, the austerely sumptuous Binnenhof, is surrounded by gracious eighteenth-century patrician houses bordering canals or broad, tree-lined roads along which glide the sleek pennanted limousines of the emissaries, ambassadors, delegates and lawyers who contribute an air of understated cosmopolitanism to the scene. Although friendships may be forged and bargains struck over a Heineken or a Genever in the convivial atmosphere of one of the city's cheerfully crowded bars, most deals here are concluded in camera. Local industry is unobtrusive too, with craft furniture, pharmaceuticals and plastics as the principal products. The Hague today still retains the air of genteel tolerance which made it, during the Golden Age, a favourite haunt amongst the political philosophers who shaped modern thinking, from Spinoza to Descartes. Scheveningen, the seaside suburb with the Belle Epoque resort aura, offers, by contrast, distractions of a less abstract nature to Dutch burghers and hardy visitors who prefer the bracing North Sea air on the beach or a session at the casino to comparing the present-day view of nearby Delft to Vermeer's original hanging amidst the Rembrandts and the Van Dycks in the Mauritshuis. With Amsterdam the pleasure carousel and Rotterdam the business turnable of the United Provinces, The Hague is an underrated showcase for the traditional Dutch virtues of comfort, bourgeois conventionality and solidity, offering visitors tired of enclaves of more worldly entertainments a refreshing gamut of attractions of subtler kind.

Founded: 10th century – a hunting palace on the site of Celtic and Roman colonies; Den Haag or s'Gravenhage (Dutch) – ›the count's hedge‹

Far-reaching events: 1248 – William, Count of Holland, builds a palace here; 1598 – seat of the States General of the United Provinces of the Netherlands; 1795 – treaty of the Hague between France and Holland; 1815 – founding of the Kingdom of the Netherlands under William I.; 1899 and 1907 – international peace conferences held here (the Hague Conferences); 1980 – Queen Beatrix ascends the throne.

Population: 445,000; 3rd largest city of the Netherlands.

Postal code: NL–2500   **Telephone code:** 70

Climate: maritime; temperate, but rather damp; sea breezes

Best time to visit: May to September.

Calendar of events: *der Haagse Vloienmarkt* (Apr and Oct); *National Sporting Day of the Netherlands* (May 1); the *Residence Orchestra of the Hague* and the *Netherlands Dance Theatre seasons* (May and Sep); *Holland Festival* (May-Oct) – music, opera, ballet, jazz, folk music, theatre and the visual arts, in cities throughout the country; *Prinsjesdag* (3rd Tues in Sep); – celebratory concert; *Thuiskunstmarkt* (end of Nov).

Fairs and exhibitions: *AVICULTURA* (Jan); *WOONTEXTIEL* (Jan); *FOVIAM* (Mar); *HOVIMEX* (Apr); *BOVAG* (Jun); *DAMESBEURS* (Sep); *MICRO COMPEX* (Nov); *MANNENBEURS* (Dec).

Historical and modern sights: *Binnenhof* (17th century) – with the ›Knight's Hall‹ (13th century) where the Dutch Parliament meets; *Royal Palace* (1550); *Peace Palace* (19th century) – neo-Gothic, on the Old Chaussee – founded by Andrew Carnegie, the seat of the International Court of Justice; *Huis ten Bosch* (17th century) – the residence of the Queen, a Baroque pleasure palace with magnificent Japanese and Chinese salons; the churches *Groote Kerk* (1539) and *Nieuwe Kerk* (17th century); the *Mauritshuis* (17th century) – once the residence of princes, now the home of the royal art collection including Vermeers and Rembrandts; *Municipal Museum* – Mondriaan, plus 19th-century paintings and silverware; *Huis Schluylebusch* – a lordly 16th-century residence; *Panorama Mesdag* – the beach at Scheveningen in 1881 - 360° landscape, trompel'oeil at its most illusory; *Delft* (13 km/8 miles) – compare Vermeer's view in the Mauritshuis with the original; *Madurodam* – miniature village; *United States Embassy* – by Marcel Breuer in the ›Bauhaus‹ style; *Haagse Passage* – a covered shopping arcade in Venetian style.

Special attractions: a night tour of the countless little *bars* in the town centre; a night at the *Kurhaus* at Scheveningen; the *antique* market on Lange Voorhout in summer.

Companies with headquaters in the city: *Badger* (machines and equipment for medicine and chemistry); *Hercules* (chemicals); *IBM* (computers); *KLM* (airline); *Laurens Sigarettenfabriek* (cigarettes); *Lummus* Nederland (industrial equipment); *Norfolkline* (transport); *Schottel* (shipbuilding).

Airport: Amsterdam-Schiphol, AMS; Tel.: (20) 5 11 04 32, KLM, Tel.: (20) 74 77 47, 40 km/24 miles; Rotterdam-Zestienhoven, RTM; Tel.: (10) 15 76 33, 17 km/11 miles; KLM, Tel.: 46 94 66.

The Headquarters

STEIGENBERGER KURHAUS HOTEL SCHEVENINGEN

30 Gevers Deynootplein
NL–2586 CK The Hague
Telephone: 52 00 52
Telex: 33 295 khau
Owning Company: EMHK vof
General Manager: Walter Mankel
Affiliation/Reservation System: SRS (Steigenberger Reservation Service)
Number of rooms: 240 (10 suites)
Price range: HFl 145–300
Credit cards: AE, DC, EC, MC, Access, Visa
Location: 5 km/3 miles from city centre
Built: 1885 (renovated 1979)
Style: rooms contemporary, public rooms turn-of-the-century
Hotel amenities: garage, valet parking, sauna, solarium, financial information centre, casino, swimming pool
Main hall porter: J. Bink
Room amenities: colour tv, mini-bar/refrigerator, radio, trouser press, safe
Room service: 6.00/a.m.–24.00/12 p.m.
Conference rooms: 14 (up to 450 persons)
Bars: ›Kurhaus Bar‹ (17.00/5 p.m.–1.00/a.m.) Peter Schregel (barman), modern; ›Louis Davids‹ (17.00/5 p.m.–24.00/12 p.m.) Kees Janssen (barman)
Restaurants: ›Kurzaal‹ (12.00/a.m.–14.00/2 p.m. and 18.00/6 p.m.–21.00/9 p.m.) J. Wakkermans (maître), J. A. M. Bragonje (chef de cuisine)
›Kandinsky‹ (12.30/p.m.–14.30/2.30 p.m. and 18.30/6.30 p.m.–24.00/12 p.m.) L. Judels (maître), A. J. Hekkelman (directeur des cuisines), modern cuisine
Private dining rooms: fourteen

When you do business in The Hague, stay in Scheveningen. In fact, try to deviate all meetings, conferences, lunches and dinner to the Kurhaus. It is closer to the capital than Chelsea is to the East End; it has more facilities for dealings, discussions and demonstrations than any other hotel in town; points of reunion are so numerous and diversified that you can retreat to splendid isolation or entertain in splendour with cuisine and service to match; last, but not least, the Kurhaus is linked to the Casino, to the swimming pool–spa with artificially induced waves and to the wide private beach on the North Sea. The air is even better here, so is the food, and the comfortable accommodations, if not ritzy, provide modern interior and the timelessly marvellous view over the ocean. The convention-centre-sea-resort-deluxe-hotel has had a 100-year-old eventful history and continues to host concerts, shows and festivals, but still succeeds in catering to the individual on business or pleasure in a very personal way, a tradition kept intact by the Steigenberger group. Shops, more restaurants and clubs embrace the sea-side palace, and even on rainy days (not too few) there will be no reason to long for downtown. In the Kurhaus you are in the midst of things. Let your people come – here.

Lunch

SAUR
47–53 Lange Voorhout
Telephone: (Restaurant) 46 33 44, (Oyster Bar) 46 25 65
Affiliations: Les Etapes du Bon Goût
Owner/Manager: Frits Saur B.V./A.L. Abbink
Closed: Sunday; public holidays
Open: 12.00/a.m.–22.30/10.30 p.m.
Cuisine: French
Chefs de cuisine: Ad van Wel and Han Nelck
Specialities: seafood; sole Lafayette; lobster ›98‹; turbot braised in champagne
Location: a lobster quadrille from the Mauritshuis
Setting: long dining room on first floor; beamed ceiling; classic décor with chandeliers, antique furniture and old masters
Amenities: oyster bar; air conditioning; fish delicatessen on ground floor
Atmosphere: refined and harmonious
Clientèle: government ministers; officials from the International Court; shipping magnates tired of Rotterdam – and a fair sprinkling of local fish fans
Dress: fairly sober
Service: knowledgeable and unobtrusive
Reservations: advisable (no dogs)
Price range: fairly expensive
Credit cards: AE, DC, Euro, Visa

Dinner

BOERDERIJ DE HOOGWERF
20 Zijdelaan
Telephone: 47 55 14
Owner/Manager: Lambert Tannemaart
Closed: Sunday
Open: 12.00/a.m.–15.00/3 p.m.; 18.00/6 p.m.–22.00/10 p.m.
Cuisine: French
Chef de cuisine: Eric Vergne
Specialities: scallops; wolf-fish; médaillons of Texel lamb with rosemary
Location: in the residential area near the Royal Palace
Setting: 350-year-old farmhouse, beautifully furnished in typical old Dutch style
Amenities: 4 private dining rooms; garden; 4 open fire places; car park
Atmosphere: comfortable and cosy, but decidedly stylish
Clientèle: politicians; government ministers; Common Market Top Brass; chairmen of multinational companies situated in The Hague
Dress: rather conservative (pin-stripes allowed)
Service: exemplary
Reservations: essential (no pets)
Price range: expensive
Credit cards: AE, DC, Visa, Euro

Lunch

ROYAL
44 Lange Voorhout
Telephone: 60 07 72
Closed: Sunday
Open: 12.00/a.m.–15.00/3 p.m. and 18.00/6 p.m.–21.30/9.30 p.m.
Cuisine: French
Chef de cuisine: Rideau Bouchard
Specialities: veal; game
Location: central
Setting: 16th-century style maintained; an abundance of wood
Atmosphere: nostalgic and homely without sacrificing elegance
Clientèle: successful, self-assured, discriminating and distinguished
Dress: suit and tie
Service: very good
Reservations: recommended (no dogs taller than a spaniel or longer than a dachshund)
Price range: medium
Credit cards: AE, DC

Dinner

AUBERGERIE
17 Nieuwe Schoolstraat
Telephone: 64 80 70
Owner/Manager: Tom Boerboom and Olaf Weissmann
Closed: Tuesday
Open: 18.00/6 p.m.–23.00/11 p.m.
Cuisine: French (nouvelle)
Chef de cuisine: Tom Boerboom
Specialities: baked fillet of sole; guinea-fowl with different types of mushrooms
Location: next to the Theater Pepign
Setting: classic; French paintings from ›le Monde Illustré‹
Amenities: air conditioning; car park
Atmosphere: confidential to intimate, depending on your mood (or your companion)
Clientèle: The Hague's social élite with cause for celebration
Dress: elegant and usually rather formal
Service: always good, friendly and efficient
Reservations: essential (well-behaved Yorkshire terriers and chihuahuas permitted)
Price range: rather expensive
Credit cards: AE, DC, Visa

Café

BODEGA DE BOSTHOORN
39a Lange Voorhout
Telephone: 60 49 06
Owner/Manager: Hans Meeuwisse
Closed: Sunday
Open: 8.00/a.m.–1.00/a.m.
Specialities: brandcafés; cakes; drinks

Location: opposite the American Ambulance
Setting: old fashioned; rather unpretentious
Amenities: air conditioning; Happy Hour 17.00/5.00 p.m.–19.00/7.00 p.m.
Atmosphere: typical café; lively and popular meeting place for a drink and a chat
Clientèle: business, government and embassy people mingle with artists and radio and TV personalities
Service: good
Reservations: recommended for large groups (pets permitted)

Bar

SCHLEMMER CAFE TABAC ANIME
17 Lange Houtstraat
Telephone: 60 90 00
Owner/Manager: Dorine de Vos
Closed: never
Open: (Monday–Wednesday) 9.30/a.m.–20.00/8 p.m.; (Thursday and Sunday) 9.30/a.m.–1.00/a.m.; (Friday and Saturday) 9.30/a.m.–1.30/a.m.
Location: near the Royal Theatre and the government buildings
Setting: theatrical evocation of the archetypal European coffee-house; separate dining and café areas within the same room
Amenities: lunch and dinner menu as well as snacks and drinks; live show most evenings at 21.00/9.00 p.m.; outdoor dining on Italian terrace in summer
Atmosphere: lively; trendsetting (indoors) to peaceful (on the terrace)
Clientèle: heterogeneous; youthful, with-it and fun-loving to not-so-young but young-at-heart and those wishing to recapture temporarily their lost youth
Service: friendly
Reservations: recommended for dining (pets permitted)
Credit cards: not accepted

Nightclub

LEE POWER'S PLACE
155–159 Strandweg
Scheveningen
Telephone: 54 11 54
Owner/Manager: Lee Powers/Tom Danner
Closed: (summer) never; (winter) Monday – Thursday
Open: (restaurant) 12.00/a.m.–15.00/3 p.m. and 18.00/6 p.m.–1.00/a.m.; nightclub: 22.00/10 p.m.–4.00/a.m.
Location: in Scheveningen
Setting: modern classic; cosy; lots of plush

Amenities: air conditioning, valet parking; live music every night; soft dancing music/soft rock; show bands
Atmosphere: chic
Clientèle: business people; very stylish
Dress: suit and tie de rigueur
Service: ›unique‹
Reservations: essential (pets allowed)
Price range: rather expensive
Credit cards: AE, DC, Euro, Visa

Shopping

EVERYTHING UNDER ONE ROOF
De Bijenkorf   32 Wagenstraat

FOR HIM
Weiss Wertheimer   5 Kneuterdyk

FOR HER
Meddens   11 Hofweg

BEAUTY & HAIR
Heym Ryken   1 Noordeinde

JEWELLERY
Siebel Juweliers   9–11 Lange Poten

LOCAL SPECIALITIES
Cigarhouse Vorstenbosch (tobacco)
94 Van Hoytemastraat
Maison de Bonneterie (men & women's fashion) 2 Gravenstraat
Zumpolle (leather fashion)
29 Venestraat
Fred van Wordragen (furs)
36 Hoogstraat
J. de Slegte (books)
9 Spuistraat
Focke & Meltzer (gifts, porcelain)
33 Hoogstraat
Delicashop Louisa (food and beverages)
408 Deltaplein
Rimmel (perfumery)
25 Hoogstraat

THE BEST OF ART
Roode Boom (contemporary art)
500 p/a Beeklaan, Tel. 60 20 95
Bouwman, Ivo (17th/18th-century Old Master paintings) 20 Lange Vijverberg, Tel. 46 66 13
Cramer, G. (17th/18th-century Old Master paintings) 38 Javastraat, Tel. 63 07 58

The City

All glory, laud and honour to Rotterdam, only comparable to Dresden in its fate –
razed to the ground by bombs during the Second World War. Its resilient citizens have
built out of the ruins of 1945 an efficiently functional and functioning city with the biggest harbour in the world (ahead of New York, London and next-door neighbour Antwerp). You will not, of course, find here the Holland which greeted Byron on his
Grand Tour, the ›water-land of Dutchmen and of ditches‹, a Vermeer landscape of medieval houses and windmills enlivened in spring by the inevitable tulips – for such stuff
as dreams are made of, it suffices to travel a few miles inland. This, the kingdom's second city, linked to the North Sea since 1872 by the Nieuwe Waterweg, is part of a vast
urban complex offering, with the coastal Europort, ultra-modern facilities for mega-
tankers and conventional vessels, around which have sprung up oil refineries and car
assembly lines, chemical plants and shipbuilding wharves. The city reveals itself as a
child of our times, where post-war devastation has been replaced by expanses of parkland, above which tower glass, concrete and steel edifices jostling with the cranes and
gantries of the dock areas. The historic buildings, so familiar to local son Desiderius
Erasmus, and with interiors so lovingly portrayed by townsman Pieter de Hooch, remain only in the meticulously restored Delfshaven area, where local craftsmen maintain proudly the traditions of their forefathers, and in the Grote Kerk, the Great
Church, which blends with the contemporary scene as harmoniously as the Rubens
with the Picassos in the Boymans-van Beuningen Museum. During the summer months
the De Deulen concert hall is a popular venue for the nationwide Holland Festival, but
its acoustics are, according to maestrissimo Herbert von Karajan, almost perfect – even
on wet winter evenings. Cultural offerings notwithstanding, Rotterdam's pulse – determined, purposeful, industrious – can best be felt as her citizens stream harbourwards in
the grey half-light of the early morning, for the city's aorta, the interlaced waterway of
the Rhine-Meuse delta, infuses this brave new metropolis with a power of endurance
and a vitality as remarkable as it is exemplary.

Founded: 1228; Rotterdam – ›dyke on the Rotte‹

Far-reaching events: 1340 – Rotterdam receives its charter; 1489 – annexed by Maximilian of Austria; 1572 – plundered by the Spanish; 17th century – Holland's most important trading centre; 1872 – the opening of the ›New Waterway‹ gives ocean vessels
access to the port; 1939–45 – heavy damage during World War II; from 1945 Rotterdam's 20,000 acre harbour grows to become the most important in the world.

Population: 1 million (urban area); second largest city in the Netherlands.

Postal code: NL–3000   **Telephone code:** 10

Climate: maritime; humid, often foggy in winter.

Best time to visit: May to July.

Calendar of events: *Film Festival* (Jan/Feb) – featuring both commercial and more serious films; *Holland Festival* (May–Oct) – arts festival in towns throughout the country;
Poetry International (Jun) – bards from around the world; *Open Havensdag* (Sep) – a
look behind the scenes of the harbour; *Heineken Jazz Festival* (Sep) – hot jazz and cool
beer; *Rotterdam Organ Month* (Sep) – concerts in churches throughout the city; *Kerst-
land* (Dec) – a Christmas spectacle.

Fairs and exhibitions: *BINNENHUIS* (Feb/Mar) – home furnishings; *ANTIEK-
BEURS AHOY* (Mar) – antiques fair; *VISMA AHOY* (Mar/Apr) – angling fair;
PORTS AND TRANSPORT (Apr) – international trade fair on harbours, transport facilities and service; *SKI HAPP* (Oct) – winter sports fair; *FEMINA* (Oct) – international consumer goods fair; *TOTAL ENERGY* (Oct/Nov) – energy control, production
and insulation; *HOUT* (Nov) – international trade fair for timber and woodworking
machinery.

Best view of the city: from the *Euromast Spacetower.*

Historical sights: *St. Laurenskerk* (15th century; restored 1952) – the only large historic
building left in Rotterdam; *Delfshaven* – historic port area with craftsmen's ateliers,
from which the Pilgrim Fathers set sail; *De Dubbelde Palmboom* – museum devoted to
old crafts; *Museum Ship Buffel* – a restored ship from 1868; *Museum Boymans-van-
Beuningen* – van Gogh, Hieronymus Bosch, Rembrandt, modern masters and objets
d'art; *Zakkendragers Huisje* – pewter workshop; *Spice Mill* ›De Ster‹ (1866) – produces
spices and snuff; *Gouda* (23 km/15 miles) – cheese market and the country's oldest and
most beautiful Town Hall.

Modern sights: *De Doelen* – modern concert hall, the biggest on the continent; *Lijnbaan* – enclosed shopping area in the centre of town; *Europort* – a huge construction
project to adapt Rotterdam's port to the ever increasing size of modern tankers; *Delta
Works* (›Storm Surge Barrier‹) – the world's largest sluices; *L'homme qui marche* –
sculpture by Rodin; *Monument to the Destroyed City;*

Special attractions: a concert in the *De Doelen Hall;* a circuit of the *bars* in the harbour
area.

Important companies with headquarters in the city: *De Rotterdamsche Droogdok* (shipbuilding); *Ferro* (chemicals); *Hunter-Douglas* (aluminium and alloys); *ICI-Holland*
(chemicals); *Koninklige Volker Stevin* (construction); *Mobil Oil* (petrol).

Airport: Rotterdam-Zestienhoven, RTM; Tel.: 15 76 33; 9 km/6 miles; KLM, Tel.:
74 77 47.

The Headquarters

HILTON

10 Weena
NL–3012 CM Rotterdam
Telephone: 4 14 40 44
Telex: 22 666 hilr
General Manager: Rudy Bausch
Affiliation/Reservation Systems: Hilton
Reservation Service
Number of rooms: 263 (15 suites)
Price range: Hfl 215–315 (single)
        Hfl 245–365 (double)
        Hfl 550 (suite)
Credit cards: AE, CB, DC, EC, MC,
Access
Location: city centre, near main station
Built: 1963 (renovated 1985)
Style: modern
Hotel amenities: garage, valet parking,
hairstylist, shops, casino
Room amenities: air conditioning, colour
tv, mini-bar
Room service: 24 hours
Laundry/dry cleaning: same day
Conference rooms: 10 (up to 200 persons)
Bars: ›Lobby Lounge Bar‹ (10.00/a.m.–
1.00/a.m.)
Restaurant: ›Le Restaurant‹ (12.00/
a.m.–15.00/3 p.m. and 17.00/5 p.m.–
22.30/10.30 p.m.), French and interna-
tional cuisine, Mr. Briolas (chef de cui-
sine), Walter Willemsen (maître)
Nightclub: ›Le Bateau‹ (22.00/10.00
p.m.–5.00/a.m.), discothèque

*Conrad's ›children‹ don't all look alike,
and even if their physiognomy reflects the
creator to a degree, their personalities are
quite different from one another. Only the
philosophy is the same: pragmatism on the
highest level possible and reasonable. The
Hilton in Rotterdam is a successful symbiosis of this New World Weltanschauung
and the forward-looking spirit of one of the
Old World's most realistic cities. The Sixt-
ies' high-rise between the Central Station
and the stock exchange won't bedazzle you
with charm, but soon after you have experienced the service in this modern appealing
intérieur you will warm to the sales-fever
atmosphere in the duplex foyer which over-
flows into the Lobby-Lounge bar and the
swinging Bâteau discothèque after hours.
In contrast, Le Restaurant restaurant is of
a dignified niveau and a calm bastion
within the business fortress. The newly installed casino is the latest focal point of the
city's entertainment carousel, while most
private entertaining is done in the perfectly
equipped conference and banquet rooms.
Not every guest is an oil sheikh or a supertanker captain, yet the habitué clientèle is
of the highest standard because the Hilton
is not only the biggest, but also the best hotel in Rotterdam.*

The Hideaway

DE SWAEN

47 De Lind
NL–5061 HT Oisterwijk
(90 km/60 miles)
Telephone: (42 42) 1 90 06
Telex: 52 617 swaen
Owner: Henk A. Aan de Stegge
General Manager: Piet C. J. Rutten
Affiliation/Reservation System: Relais et
Châteaux
Closed: 2 weeks in Jan., 3 weeks in July
Number of rooms: 19
Price range: Hfl 175 (single)
                Hfl 225 (double)
Credit cards: AE, EC, DC, Visa
Location: 90 km/60 miles from Rotter-
dam airport
Built: rebuilt 1978
Style: classic
Hotel amenities: terrace
Room amenities: colour tv, air condition-
ing, mini-bar/refrigerator
Room service: 7.00/a.m.–21.30/9.30 p.m.
Conference rooms: 2, seminar facilities
Sports nearby: tennis, golf
Bars: (17.00/5.00 p.m.–1.00/a.m.), classic
décor
Restaurant: ›De Swaen‹ (closed Mon-
day; open 12.00/p.m.–15.00/3.00 p.m.
and 18.00/6.00 p.m.–21.00/9.00 p.m.),
Piet C. J. Rutten (maître), Cas Spijkers
(chef de cuisine)
Private dining rooms: two

*The small country town of Oisterwijk, situ-
ated half-way between Tilburg and s'Her-
togenbosch, one and a half hour's drive
from Rotterdam, has been a landmark on
the culinary horizon of the Netherlands
since local industrialist Henk Aan de
Stegge appointed Piet Rutten and gave
him carte blanche to transform the newly
renovated Swaen into one of the leading
auberges in the country. The long whitewashed façade of the spick-and-span relais
on the tree-lined main street is relieved by
the wrought-iron balcony which overhangs
the black-and-white flagged boulevard terrace with its cheerful red cane furniture.
The public rooms are spacious and traditionally furnished, with crystal chandeliers,
stucco ceiling and well-chosen accessoires.
There are only nineteen bedrooms, each of
them stylish and comfortable enough for
the succession of potential habitués, once
they have stayed one night or sampled one
meal in the dining room. The pièce de résistance is the star-spangled restaurant
with its pretty patio overlooking the rather
formal garden, where Cas Spijkers serves
nouvelle cuisine eulogized by Gallic gourmets and German gourmands alike – salmon stuffed with asparagus, fillet of sole
with lobster and saffron-flavoured spinach
ravioli, and cinnamon ice-cream with
plums. De Swaen's understated comfort
and aura of unhurried gentility make it the
hideaway of choice for a weekend away
from Rotterdam.*

Lunch

LE COQ D'OR
25 V. Vollenhovenstraat
Telephone: 36 64 05
Affiliations: Romantic Restaurants
Owner/Manager: Ferdinand Cats
Closed: Christmas–New Year, Sunday
and Saturday
Open: 12.00/a.m.–14.30/2.30 p.m. and
18.00/6 p.m.–23.00/11 p.m.
Cuisine: classic
Chef de cuisine: Raymond Wellauer
Specialities: mousse de canard et foie
d'oie;scallops in champagne; gratin of
lobster Thermidor; monthly changing
menu
Location: a short walk or a shorter taxi
ride from the Museum Boymans van Beuningen
Setting: entrance hall with welcoming red
carpet and glass chandelier; lounge area
with leather armchairs and open fireplace: first-floor dining room with
wooden beams, subdued lighting, pink
table-linen and candles; catholic art collection ranging from old tapestries and
Old Masters to old photographs and
›naughty Nineties‹ prints
Amenities: bar with quick meals service;
private dining room (40 persons); outdoor dining on terrace (60 persons); air
conditioning
Atmosphere: intimate
Clientèle: expense-account gourmets at
work or at leisure; businessmen with a
penchant for the romantic
Dress: no special requirements or restrictions
Service: reliable and helpful
Reservations: advisable
Price range: fairly expensive
Credit cards: AE, DC, Euro, Visa

Dinner

FESTIVAL
53 Schouwburgplein
Telephone: 33 38 88
Owner/Manager: Maison van den Boer
B.V./Ohhia Wassanbarg
Closed: Sunday; two weeks in summer;
Saturday lunchtime
Open: 12.00/a.m.–15.00/3 p.m. and
18.00/6 p.m.–23.00/11 p.m.
Cuisine: French-oriented
Chef de cuisine: Ruud de Paauw
Specialities: soupe de poissons de mer;
red mullet with fondue of green cabbage;
Barbary duckling with sweet and sour
shallots; roast quail with cherries
Location: in the ›de Doelen‹ concert hall;
two bars away from the Lijnbaan shop-
ping area
Setting: modern sophisticated; U-shaped
dining bar; round tables; rattan chairs;
stainless steel, glass, concealed lighting,

potted plants and modern paintings
Amenities: air conditioning; multi-storey
car park next door
Atmosphere: luxurious; stylishly semi-
formal but welcoming
Clientèle: international, especially during
the concert season; musicians, men-and-
women-about town; pre-conference,
post-shopping or during the interval
Dress: Jil Sander to Gianni Versace, and
vice-versa
Service: attentive and helpful
Reservations: advisable (dogs allowed)
Price range: moderate
Credit cards: AE, DC, Euro, Access, Mas-
ter Charge

Dinner

DE HERBERGE
591 Overschiese Kleiweg
Telephone: (4) 65 24 71
Owner/Manager: Nicolas Bergmann
Closed: never
Open: 12.00/p.m.–22.00/10 p.m. and Sa-
turday 17.00/5 p.m.–22.00/10 p.m.
Cuisine: French
Chef de cuisine: René Tortlend
Specialities: saumon cru à l'Annette (raw
salmon with white wine and peppers);
crème de moutarde (soup); mousse au
chocolat blanc; crêpes with ice-cream
and cassis
Location: 10 minutes' drive from city;
near the San Francisco Hospital
Setting: eighteenth-century house; clas-
sic style
Amenities: car park; private dining room
for about 30 people
Atmosphere: elegant
Clientèle: business people mostly
Dress: suit and tie
Service: very personal
Reservations: advisable (pets allowed)
Price range: very expensive
Credit cards: AE, DC, EC

Lunch

IN DEN RUSTWAT
96 Honingerdijk
Kralingen (4 km/2½ miles)
Telephone: 13 41 10
Owner/Manager: Johan van der Horst
Closed: Saturday; public holi-
days; two weeks in July/August
Open: 12.00/a.m.–15.00/3 p.m. and
17.30/5.30 p.m.–22.00/10 p.m.
Cuisine: French
Chef de cuisine: Jacob Turfboer

Specialities: saddle of rabbit; venison; suprême de turbot aux écrevisses; noisette de veau pays d'Auge; excellent choice of wines with a large number of rare vintages
Location: in Kralingen; 4 km (2½ miles) south-west of city centre
Setting: 16th-century inn in woodland setting; small-paned shuttered windows; dining room in elegantized farmhouse style with wooden beams, tiled floor, rush-seated chairs, domestic bric-a-brac and white tablecloths
Amenities: pianist; outdoor dining on terrace; air conditioning; car park
Atmosphere: rustic
Clientèle: tanker captains and shipping tycoons rub shoulders with Rotterdam regulars in search of a breath of the countryside
Dress: fairly conservative
Service: welcoming; very personal – and quick if time presses
Reservations: advisable
Price range: moderately expensive
Credit cards: AE, DC, Euro

Lunch

DE HOEFSLAG
28 Vossenlaan
Zeist (Bosch en Duin) (65 km/40 miles)
Telephone: (30) 78 43 95
Affiliations: Relais et Châteaux (Relais Gourmand)
Owner/Manager: Gerard Fagel
Closed: Sunday; Monday
Open: 12.00/p.m.–14.30/2.30 p.m. and 18.00/6 p.m.–21.30/9.30 p.m.
Cuisine: French (nouvelle)
Chef de cuisine: Wulf Engel
Specialities: marinated scallops with caviar; terrine of duck's liver with green beans; poached oysters with finely-cut vegetables in stock; lamb chops in shallot sauce; lightly-smoked turbot with caviar; quail with truffle cream; lobster in white cabbage with chive sauce; desserts from the trolley
Location: at Zeist; 11 km (7 miles) from Utrecht; 65 km (40 miles) from Rotterdam; 55 km (34 miles) from Amsterdam
Setting: pretty countryside; elegant country villa; dining room decorated in pastel tones; exquisitely-laid tables, with fine porcelain, silver and glass
Amenities: private dining room (35 persons); open-air dining on terrace; car park
Atmosphere: festive and yet légère; indubitably one of the brightest stars on the Dutch culinary scene; directed by Gerard Fagel, member of a gastronomic dynasty which runs a good half dozen establishments in the country
Clientèle: as beloved of the more conservative members of the local populace as of their more adventurous counterparts
Dress: rather conservative

Service: courteous and patient, even with difficult customers
Reservations: recommended
Price range: fairly expensive
Credit cards: AE, DC, Euro

Dinner

SPECIALITEITEN RESTAURANT KEIZERSHOF
7 Martin Luther Kingweg,
Rotterdam-Oud Verlaat (3 km/2 miles)
Telephone: 55 13 33
Owner/Manager: Bernhardt Leeftink
Closed: New Year's Eve (December 31st)
Open: 11.00/a.m.–24.00/12 p.m.
Cuisine: French (traditional, with a soupcon of nouvelle)
Chef de cuisine: Christian Grootenboer
Specialities: regularly changing menu; specialities according to season and market availability; surprise menus
Location: at Oud Verlaat, 3 km (2 miles) north-east of Rotterdam city centre
Setting: Saxon farmhouse – built 1780 in Bentheim and re-erected on its present site as a restaurant and party centre; half-timbered buildings; interior (unrendered brickwork and beamed ceiling) dominated by large circular open stone fireplace in centre; rush-seated chairs, pink tablecloths and period accessoires from the linen cupboard to the boar's head
Amenities: bar; pianist; private dining rooms (20–250 persons); receptions (600 persons) new conference centre (60 persons); catering service; outdoor dining on terrace; car park; bowling alley; air conditioning (planned)
Atmosphere: old-world nostalgia combined with modern comfort
Clientèle: Rotterdam's Haute Bourgeoisie en fête and en famille; government ministers, oil company managers, KLM jumbo captains and men from the media
Dress: fairly conservative
Service: welcoming and friendly
Reservations: advisable (pets permitted)
Price range: moderately expensive
Credit cards: AE, DC, Euro

Shopping

EVERYTHING UNDER ONE ROOF
De Bijenkorf   105 Coolsingle

FOR HIM
The Saint   46 Coolsingle

FOR HER
Meddens   51 Lynbaan

BEAUTY & HAIR
Robert Limburg   4a Coolsingle

JEWELLERY
Siebel Juweliers   24–28 Stadthuisplein

LOCAL SPECIALITIES
Fa. van Dalen Rookartikelen
(tobacco)
17 Meent
Maison de Bonneterie (men's fashion)
83 Lynbaan
Zumpolle (leather fashion)
25k Lynbaan
Van As (furs)
112–116 Nieuwe Binnenweg
J. de Slegte (books)
83 Coolsingle
Meyer en Blessing (gifts)
68 Lynbaan
Hulst BV (porcelain)
69 Coolsingle
Zumpolle (baggage & travel accessories)
25k Lynbaan

THE BEST OF ART
Delta   (contemporary art)
113 Oude Binnenweg, Tel. 14 54 56

The City

Peer Gynt – wilful, intemperate, anarchistic – is not typically Norwegian. Henrik Ibsen – individualistic, idealistic, freedom-loving – was. And so was Edvard Grieg – attached to nature, folklore and patriotism. If Europe ever fell prey to decadence, Oslo would be the last bastion to succumb. Norway's film-set capital amidst dramatic mountains, fairy-tale forests and sagaesque fjords, enwrapped in the twilight of the gods and injected with an elysian atmosphere, is not all picture-postcard idyll, however. Modern times have marked this Nordic metropolis with all consequences, but despite the avant-garde genius of this energetic people and the Black-Gold Rush into the North Sea there is no danger of decay, here, neither of the traditions nor of the purity of this showcase model-town where more than half of the area is bedecked with pastures, parks and woods. The pioneering spirit of the Norwegians – documented by national heroes Eric the Red and his son Leiv Eriksson as well as Roald Amundsen, Fritjof Nansen and Thor Heyerdahl – has always nurtured an open mind and a wide perspective whilst retaining a conservative solidity at home. The traders of oil, ships, wood or salmon coming here are best advised to bring their fishing rod, walking boots, skis and sleep shades in summer, instead of black tie and great expectations. Nevertheless, there is more to Oslo fun-life than fresh air and outdoor sports. The opera, in fact, stages prominent productions as often as the concert hall (and not always Grieg), and at weekends the city reverberates with life, without much sophistication, but also without the rat-race of the accessoire philosophy. Nature in and around Oslo offers so much – from the Oslofjord to Holmenkollen, from Gustav Vigeland's sculpture park to Studenterlunden's living theatre – that you won't miss la dolce vita. Oslo is as beautiful as Sonia Henie and as genuine as Liv Ullmann. There is a grand hotel in town (literally), the restaurateurs are exporting graved lax and importing nouvelle cuisine, the local Beatles – A–HA – fill the clear air with music, and the Osloite hospitality will make you feel completely at home, here. Especially because everyone speaks English.

Founded: c. 1050 by Harold III.

Far-reaching events: 1066–93 – Viking King Olav Kyrre; Oslo becomes an ecclesiastical centre; 1299–1319 – King Haakon V Magnusson declares Oslo capital and has Askershus Castle built; 1349 – the city is decimated by plague; 1624 – city destroyed by fire, rebuilt by King Christian IV, named Christiana; 1811 – founding of university; 1814 – separation of Denmark and Norway, Oslo Norwegian capital; 1925 – named Oslo again.

Population: 490,000.

Postal code: N–Oslo   **Telephone code:** 2

Climate: mild summers, but cold winters.

Best time to visit: July and August; winter sports enthusiasts may disagree.

Calendar of events: *Constitution Day* (17 May) – colourful ceremonies; *Holmenkollen Ski Festival* (Mar) – jumping programmes; *Karneval* (beginning of June) – Norway welcomes the summer; *23 June* – midsummer festival, the longest day of the year; *Maridal Drama* (mid-August) – open-air historical theatre; *Nobel Peace Prize Ceremony* (Nov).

Fairs and exhibitions: *CONFUR* (Jan) – international contracts furniture fair; *GAVE-EXPO* (Jan) – Norwegian gift and decoration fair; *MOTEUKEN* (Feb & Sep) – fashion fair; *BELYSMING* (Mar) – lighting; *THE SEA FOR ALL* (Mar) – boat and engine show; *NOR-SHIPPING* (May) shipping industry exhibition (bi-annual); *TRADE FAIR OF THE FURNITURE INDUSTRY* (Oct); *BYGG-REIS DEM* (Oct, bi-annual) building exhibition; *HJEM OG HOBBY* (Nov) – consumer goods fair.

Best view of the city: from the nearby *Holmenkollen Ski Jump* tower.

Historical sights: *Akershus Castle* (13th century) – Renaissance, now used for government affairs; *Cathedral* (17th century) – stained-glass windows by Emanuel Vigeland; *Viking Ship House* – relics of the Viking age; *Fram Museum* – Fridtjof Nansen's ship; *Royal Palace* (1825); *Storting* (19th century) – parliament building.

Modern sights: *Munch Museum* – displaying the painter's donation to the city; *Kon-Tiki Museum* – Thor Heyerdahl's vessels; *Frogner Park* – sculptures by Gustav Vigeland.

Special attractions: *Holmenkollen World Ski Jumping Championships; sailing* in the Oslo Fjord; *midsummer*..

Important companies with headquarters in the city: *Aschehoug, H & Co* (publishing); *Ardag og Sunndal Verk* (aluminum and alloys); *Block Watne Byggfornyelse* (construction); *Den Norske Creditbank* (banking); *Elkem* (metal, steel, chemicals); *Fieldhammer Brus* (concrete and plastic); *Frionor Norsk Frossenfisk* (frozen food); *Kreditkassen Christiana Bank* (banking); *Landteknikk* (agricultural machinery); *Norkem* (concrete and bricks); *Norsk Data* (data processing); *Norsk Hydro* (chemical products); *Norsk Olje* (oil); *Tandberg Data* (data processing).

Airport: Oslo-Fornebu, OSL; Tel.: 59 33 40; 8 km/5 miles, SAS, Tel.: 42 75 00/42 79 00; Oslo-Gardermoen, Tel.: (6) 97 80 20; 50 km/30 miles.

The Headquarters

GRAND HOTEL

31 Karl Johans Gate
N–0159 Oslo 1
Telephone: 42 93 90
Telex: 71 683 grand
Telefax: 42 12 25
General Manager: Helge Holgersen
Manager: Alan Moxon
Affiliation/Reservation Systems: Inter
Nor Hotels, SRS (Steigenberger Reserva-
tion Service)
Number of rooms: 308 (30 suites)
Price range: NKr 950–3,600
Credit cards: AE, DC, EC, Visa
Location: opposite the Parliament
Built: 1874 (recently renovated)
Style: traditional
Hotel amenities: garage, indoor swim-
ming pool, sauna, fitness centre, solar-
ium, hairstylist, newsstand, bank
Main hall porters: Jan Naevestad
Room amenities: mini-bar, video
Bathroom amenities: bidet, bathrobe
Room service: 6.30/a.m.–23.30/11.30
p.m.
Conference rooms: 6 (up to 300 persons)
Bars: ›Limelight‹, (see Bars)
Restaurants: ›Grand Café‹ ›Grand
Grill‹; ›Etoile‹; ›Palmen‹; ›Bonanza‹;
Thor Stangeland (maître)
Nightclub: ›Bonanza‹ (see Nightclubs)

*Henrik Ibsen, one of the hotel's habitués at
the turn of the century, did not use this
stately home as a model for his Doll's
House, but he appreciated and immortalized it by his long standing patronage, well
recorded in the annals. (His home-away-
from-home immortalized Norway's favourite son by naming a lounge after him.) Today, everyone who is anyone stays at the
Grand, from Queen Elizabeth to Bishop
Tutu, from Henry Ford to Eartha Kitt. The
name rightfully implies not only the style,
but also the location, the service, the cuisine and the carousel of attractions and
distractions ranging from the Penthouse
Etoile restaurant – where you are enrap-
tured between the midsummer-night sky
and the Haute Cuisine –, to the Bonanza
discothèque – where you can dance with
the town's movers and shakers into the
morning –, from the cheerful Grand Café
with its St. Germain atmosphere to the
slightly evocative Palmen – where you can
have your morning tea, a quick lunch or
drinks through the day. The possibilities of
atmospheric surroundings are just limitless
here, and even realists who come strictly for
business may be seduced by the imposing
Christian Radich Suite, the club-like Hogarth Lounge or the roof-garden swimming pool with keep-fit facilities. Aficionados of the stage may sneak into the nightly
productions of the Oslo Nye Teater by way
of the Limelight Bar, and to the ones who
have really come for one night only Oslo
presents itself at its best and liveliest right
outside the door.*

The Hideaway

HOLMENKOLLEN PARK

26 Kongeveien
N–0390 Oslo
Telephone: 14 60 90
Telex: 72 094 holm p
Owning Company: Hoeghe Shipping Co.
General Manager: Ivar Hasselknippe
Affiliation/Reservation System: Preferred Hotels Worldwide
Number of rooms: 200
Price range: NKr 795–1,053
Credit cards: AE, DC, EC, Visa
Location: 6 km/4 miles from city centre and from Fornebu airport
Built: 1894 and 1982
Style: traditional log-beam building; modern interior
Hotel amenities: house limousine service, indoor swimming pool, whirl-pools, fitness equipment, sauna bath, solarium
Room amenities: colour tv, mini-bar/refrigerator, balcony (in some rooms)
Room service: 6.00/a.m.–24.00/12 p.m.
Laundry/dry cleaning: same day
Conference rooms: for up to 150 persons
Bar: ›Atrium‹
Restaurants: ›De Fem Stuer‹ rustic gourmet cuisine, open fire-places; ›The Bakeriet‹ Scandinavian cuisine
Nightclub: discothèque

One thousand feet above the hustle and bustle of the Norwegian capital stands a hideaway hotel of historic charm and modern comfort. The view of the city and the fjord below, with the mountains on the far side, is breath-taking at all times of the year, but especially so when the first snow turns the scene into a picture-postcard landscape of great beauty and unlimited winter-sports possibilities. The older section of Holmenkollen Park is a traditional log-beam tower dating from 1894, meticulously renovated and skilfully integrated into the contemporary wing. The dramatic foyer could be a latter-day Hall of the Mountain King, with stainless steel stalactites and a gigantic three-dimensional snowflake structure dominating the earth-brown décor. The main formal restaurant, De Fem Stuer (the Five Rooms), has timbered walls and serves local specialities amidst antique accessoires, whereas the Bakeriet has contemporary pine furniture and a popular salad buffet at lunch-time. The bedrooms in the new wing are light and cheerful, with pretty pastel colour schemes and a sunny balcony. There are excellent facilities for two-men summits and their 150-man entourages, plus a swimming pool, sauna and the best ski-jumping hill in the world just outside the door. In winter Holmenkollen Park becomes a sports paradise par excellence where the Arctic fairyland outside contrasts with the open fires and Nordic Gemütlichkeit within. During the long summer evenings the air is heavy with birdsong and the scent of pine forests. This resort hotel on the outskirts of Oslo is an auberge for all seasons.

Lunch

BLOM
41b Karl Johansgt.
Telephone: 42 73 00
Owner/Managers: Inni-Carine and Gunnar Holm, plus their children Camilla and Carl Christian
Closed: Sunday; one week at Christmas
Open: 11.40/a.m.–15.00/3 p.m. and 17.00/5 p.m.–23.00/11 p.m.
Cuisine: French and international
Chef de cuisine: Ortwin Kulmus
Specialities: seafood; fish; grilled reindeer; famous sandwich buffet lunch (gravlax; shrimps; beef tartare; Brie . . .); salads; cakes; business lunches à la carte; late-night snacks
Location: in Oslo's main street, between the Royal Castle and the Parliament building
Setting: historic tavern painstakingly dismantled and reassembled in the middle of a modern theatrical and shopping complex; intact antique décor; fountain; columns and heraldic shields representing awards to outstanding artists and contributors to the art of our time; valuable collection of paintings by Dégas, Utrillo and Toulouse-Lautrec
Amenities: wine bar (bodega) serving snacks and light meals; air conditioning
Atmosphere: an Oslo tradition, lovingly maintained and very much alive and kicking in spite of the changes in its surroundings
Clientèle: international lawyers closing multi-national contracts; composers discussing worldwide premières; artists, local citizens and a sprinkling of tourists from Tokyo to Tampa
Dress: casual in the bodega; rather more formal in the restaurant
Service: very expert and professional; under the guidance of maître d'hôtel Thorleif Haug and the Holm family
Reservations: advisable
Price range: medium to high
Credit cards: AE, DC, Euro, Visa

Dinner

BAGATELLE
3 Bygdøy Allee
Telephone: 44 63 97
Owner/Managers: Ole Rostad and Eyvind Hellstrøm
Closed: Sunday; Saturday and Monday lunchtime; Christmas; Easter; July
Open: 11.30/a.m.–14.00/2 p.m. and 17.30/5.30 p.m.–21.30/9.30 p.m.
Cuisine: French (nouvelle) ›au goût du marché‹
Chef de cuisine: Eyvind Hellstrøm (ex-l'Archestrate and Chapel)

Specialities: daily changing menu; fish and seafood; salad of Norway lobster; filets de turbot au coulis de tomate; paupiettes de sole with chives; fillet of monkfish with basil; calf's head with tarragon butter
Location: 1 km (half a mile) west of city centre
Setting: modern dining room; mirrors, contemporary paintings and elegantly-laid tables
Amenities: air conditioning
Atmosphere: stylishly informal
Clientèle: growing number of local gourmet habitués plus a fair sprinkling of fans of Eyvind Hellstrøm's cuisine from his periods in France under Alain Chapel at Mionnay and Alain Senderens at l'Archestrate in Paris
Service: charming and helpful
Reservations: advisable (dogs permitted)
Price range: fairly expensive
Credit cards: AE, DC, Euro, Visa

Lunch

FROGNESETEREN
200 Holmenkollveien, Voksenkollen (Postbox 40)
Telephone: (Maître d'hôtel) 14 37 36/ (office) 14 08 90
Owner/Manager: Knut Thune
Closed: never
Open: 10.00/a.m.–23.30/11.30 p.m. (main meals from 12.00/a.m.)
Cuisine: Norwegian
Chef de cuisine: Espen Dahl
Specialities: marinated salmon; reindeer; typical Norwegian dishes; apple pie
Location: on a hillside overlooking the city
Setting: traditional Norwegian timber building on the edge of the forest; breathtaking views of the harbour, the fjord and the city; dining rooms furnished in various styles from the homely ›Peisestua‹ to the elegantized rustic ›Storstua‹ with hunting trophies; open fireplaces and traditional accessoires
Amenities: private dining rooms (up to 320 persons); open-air dining on terrace in summer; sports facilities, from mountain walks to trout fishing and slalom skiing
Atmosphere: quiet (no background music)
Clientèle: businessmen seeking a respite from Oslo; sportsmen and walkers seeking refreshment after exertion; Oslo Sunday-afternoon crowd en famille
Dress: sporting to semi-formal
Service: good
Reservations: advisable
Price range: medium
Credit cards: DC, Euro, Visa, Nøkkelkonto

Dinner

LUDVIG
16 Torg'g't
Telephone: 42 88 80
Owner/Manager: Paul Jelseth/Tom Erik Andreasin
Closed: Sunday lunchtime
Open: 11.30/a.m.–22.30/10.30 p.m. (Sunday) 16.00/4 p.m.–22.00/10 p.m.
Cuisine: Norwegian and international
Chef de cuisine: Tom Magnusen
Specialities: monthly changing menu; fish; vegetarian buffet; vanilla ice-cream (the best in the city!); almond gâteau with ice-cream, chocolate sauce and the national flag of the guest in question
Location: next to the Landsbank
Setting: former bus station with public transport paraphernalia, model aeroplane, wind instruments, old-fashioned motorcycle and – above the kitchen door – a pendulum clock from which emerges on the hour the eponymous Ludvig, a Canadian elk who solemnly pronounces ›Cuckoo!‹ in an appropriately bass voice
Amenities: three niches providing séparée dining; air conditioning
Atmosphere: unique
Clientèle: as popular amongst the under-10s as amongst the over-80s (not to mention those between)
Dress: as you like it (as long as Ludvig will like you!)
Service: with a smile
Reservations: recommended (no pets)
Price range: moderately expensive
Credit cards: all major

Dinner

MØLLA AS
32 Sagveien/Telephone: 37 54 50
Owner/Manager: Luigi Valente
Closed: lunchtime; Sunday; public holidays
Open: 15.00/3 p.m.–24.00/12 p.m.
Cuisine: French
Chef de cuisine: Joel Albin Amiot
Specialities: fish; game
Location: 2 km (1 mile) from city centre; in Sagene – an old quarter of Oslo
Setting: an old spinning mill (1850) overlooking the floodlit waterfalls of Akerselva which formerly turned the mill wheels; thick stone walls and spinning memorabilia; three dining rooms
Amenities: separate Grill Room (70 persons); pianist
Atmosphere: nostalgic; historic; romantic or confidential, depending on your companion
Clientèle: favourite venue for impressing visiting industrialists, foreign politicians and Middle-Eastern potentates
Dress: no special requirements

Service: discreet
Reservations: advisable
Price range: exclusive
Credit cards: AE, DC, Euro, Visa

Meeting Point

THEATERCAFEEN
24–6 Stortingsgaten
Telephone: 41 90 60
Manager: Martes Berg
Closed: never
Open: 11.00/a.m.–23.00/11 p.m.
Cuisine: Norwegian and international
Chef de cuisine: Willi Wissenbach
Specialities: according to season and market availability; seafood; pepper steak
Location: in the Hotel Continental
Setting: light and comfortable, with an old-fashioned air
Amenities: hotel; two restaurants; café; discothèque
Atmosphere: welcoming
Clientèle: local habitués and visitors from all the corners of the globe
Service: friendly
Reservations: essential for large groups (pets permitted)
Price range: medium
Credit cards: AE, DC, Euro, Visa

Bar

LIMELIGHT
31 Karl Johansgt.
Telephone: 42 93 90
Owner/Manager: Grand Hotel (Public Ltd. Co.)/Helge Holgersen
Closed: Sundays
Open: 15.00/3. p.m.–24.00/12 a.m.
Location: in the Grand Hotel
Setting: direct access to the theatre next door; wood panelling; warm colour scheme in dark wood and leather
Amenities: hotel; restaurants; private dining rooms; café; two further bars
Atmosphere: steeped in the atmosphere of the stage
Clientèle: local businessmen; Oslo citizens; hotel guests; actors, actresses, producers and backroom-boys; drama critics; theatre-goers
Service: presided over by cocktail wizard Eric, the chief barman
Reservations: advisable
Credit cards: AE, DC, Euro, Visa

Nightclub

BONANZA
31 Karl Johansgt.
Telephone: 42 93 90
Owner/Manager: Grand Hotel (Public Ltd. Co.)/Helge Holgersen
Closed: Sundays
Open: 20.00/8 p.m.–3.00/a.m.
Location: in the Grand Hotel

Setting: night restaurant and bar with dancing (discothèque); neutral modern décor in tones of white, blue and red; in the basement of the hotel
Amenities: hotel; restaurant; café, three bars; car park
Atmosphere: popular in the classic idiom
Clientèle: favourite rendezvous for Oslo's night owls and insomniac birds of passage
Dress: disco elegance
Service: with a smile
Reservations: advisable
Credit cards: AE, DC, Euro, Visa

Shopping

EVERYTHING UNDER ONE ROOF
Steen & Strøm   23 Kongensgatan

FOR HIM
Herman Mehren   4 Rosenkratzgate

FOR HER
Anna-Bella   16 Rosenkratzgate

BEAUTY & HAIR
Head & Hair   30 Drammensvägen

JEWELLERY
Gullsmed Blom   Drammensvägen

LOCAL SPECIALITIES
Desirée (women's fashion)
10 Haakon VII-s Gate
Men Only (men's fashion)
14 Karl Johansgate
Fru Lyng (children's fashion)
47 Akkersgate
Henry Olesen (leather fashion)
20 Universitetsgate
Henry Olsen (furs)
20 Universitetsgate
Tanum-Cammermeyer (books)
41–43 Karl Johansgate
Colseth A/S (gifts)
Karl Johansgate
Norsk Rosenthal A/S (porcelain)
17 Øvre Slottsgate
Interdesign (interior decorating)
12 Rosenkrantzgate
Scandinavian Souvenirs (gifts, handicrafts)
30 Holbergsgate
Bally – Paul Braaten A/S (shoes)
16 Øvre Slottsgate

THE BEST OF ART
Galerie K   (modern art)
6 Bjørn Farmannsgatan, Tel. 56 84 09
Galerie Riis   (modern art)
T.H.S. Heftyesplass, 11 Elisenbergvägen, Tel. 56 49 54

The City

The Little Mermaid gazing down on the Vistula from her pedestal on the Kościuszko embankment is no gentle maiden with flowing tresses like her Danish counterpart, but rather a stern-faced silver-grey warrior Siren, her sword raised above her head in defence of Poland's proud capital. Battlefield of nothern Europe for almost four hundred years, Warsaw has been fought over, invaded, bombed, annexed, razed, occupied by successive aspiring Napoléons from Stockholm to Moscow to Berlin without surrendering her indomitable spirit to her oppressors. The latest reconstruction has brought back the fourteenth-century houses of the Stare Miasto old town surrounding Zamkowy Square to a Cinecittàesque be-flowered and be-gabled Baroque-Renaissance grandeur, which once more forms the backdrop for bar-and-coffee-house encounters, impromptu business deals and displays of solidarity over barszcz and vodka. Modern Warsaw is a youthful city with a venerable past jealously preserved in the neo-classic palaces where Bonaparte once danced with Countess Walewska. The monumentally lowering presence of the Stalinist wedding-cake House of Culture dwarfs even the shoe-box high-rise office blocks housing the headquarters of the empty banks and the struggling businesses, the machinery and car firms which form the basis of the economy (what economy). The pragmatic determination with which Nicholas Copernicus and Marie Curie pursued their theories to world-shattering conclusions imbues Varsovians of today with that indestructible soul so admired by Churchill and so admirably summarized in the city's motto: ›Defies the Storm‹. Not yet defying the tempest of communist suppression but showing a sign of hope like the Prague Spring, Solidarnoscz is continuing to unite the freedom-thirsty people, if underground. Best-loved local son Fryderyk Chopin, leaving his homeland before the tsar's brutal repression of the 1830 nationalist uprising – foreshadowing Big Brother's treatment of the country in more recent years – lamented that Warsaw was full of ›cannon concealed by flowers‹, before composing the polonaises and mazurkas which have captivated the world ever since with the syncopated rhythms, the haunting melancholy and the ethereal gaiety which best convey the mood of his native land.

Founded: 1260, on the site of an 11th-century settlement; Warszawa (Polish) – ›Warsz' town‹ after the legendary fisherman who founded the city.

Far-reaching events: 1594 – Warsaw replaces Cracow as official residence of the King of Poland; 1596 – capital of Poland; 1607 – city destroyed by fire; 1656 & 1702 – atacked by Sweden; 18th century – prosperity and a cultural renaissance under Stanislaus II, last king of Poland; 1793 – Russian occupation; 1795 – under Prussian rule; 1806 – annexed by Napoléon; 1815 – Russia rules in Poland, nationalist uprisings (1830, 1863); 1919 – bombs destroy 90 % of the city; 1945 – entry of the Red Army and founding of the People's Republic with Warsaw as capital.

Population: 1.6 million; capital and largest city in Poland.

Postal code: PL – 00   **Telephone code:** 22 (for seven digit numbers, 2 for numbers beginning with 622 or 677)

Climate: continental; extreme – bring two fur coats in winter

Best time to visit: April–June; September–mid-November.

Calendar of events: *Student Theatre Drama Festival* (May); *Warsaw Autumn* (Sep) – international contemporary music festival; *International Jazz Festival* (Sep); *Warsaw Poetry Autumn* (Sep); *Graphics Festival* (Oct) – biennial graphic arts fair; *Chopin Piano Contest* (Sep) – every five years.

Fairs and exhibitions: *AGPOL* (Mar) – consumer goods exhibition; *INTERNATIONAL BOOK FAIR* (May); *INTERNATIONAL EXHIBITION FOR BABY GOODS* (Nov); *CONTROLA* (Nov) –·scientific research materials and equipment.

Best view of the city: from the observation platform of the *Palace of Culture.*

Historial sights: *Royal Castle* (14th–18th century) – reconstructed Baroque symbol of Polish history overlooking the statue of *Sigismund III* (1644); *Stare Miasto* – the Old Town – Baroque houses surrounding the Market Square; *Church of St. Mary* (15th century) – Gothic, for the Jesuits; *Radziwell Palace* (17th century) – neo-classical home of the Council of Ministers; *Potocki Palace* (18th century) – Saxon rococo; the classicistic *Grand Opera House* (19th century); *Theatre Square* – with the National Theatre for Opera and Ballet; *Krakowski Przedmiescie* – the ›Royal Route‹, bordered by many of Warsaw's most famous public buildings; *Lazienski Palace* (18th century) – neo-classic, with beautiful gardens and summers concerts in front of the Chopin monument; *Wilanow* – the royal residence, a jewel among Poland's Baroque palaces, with a magnificent garden, fountains and sculptures; *Chopin's birthplace* at Zelazowa Wola (53 km/33 miles).

Modern sights: *Palace for Culture and Science* – Stalinistic architecture at its most monumental; *Intraco Building* – ultra-modern Swedish architecture; *Central Railway Station* – much glass; *East Wall* – a shopping and office centre of mammoth proportions.

Special attractions: a Chopin concert in *Kazienki Park;* a *chat* with one of Walesa's aides-de-camp; a *tour de jazz.*

Important companies with headquarters in the city: *Agromet-Motoimport; Agros; Bomis; Bumar; Ciech; Dal; Energopol; Elektrim; Impexmetal; Pezetel; Paged; Pewex; Polmot; Polservice; Poltel; Intraco; Agpol; Varimex; Rolipex; Metronex; Polexpo; Warta; Universal; Labimex; Antimex; DESA.*

Airport: Warszawa-Okecie, WAW; Tel.: 46 96 70; LOT, Tel.: 21 70 21; 7 km/4 miles.

The Headquarters

VICTORIA INTER-CONTINENTAL

11 Krowlewska
PL–Warsaw
Telephone: 27 92 71/27 80 11
Telex: 812 516 ihc
Owner: S. Wcislo
Affiliation/Reservation System: Worldwide Inter-Continental Reservation System
Number of rooms: 410
Price range: Zloty 15 640 (single)
              Zloty 17 680 (double)
Credit cards: AE, DC, EC, CB, MC
Location: on Warsaw's famous Victoria Square, 15 minutes' drive from airport
Built: 1973
Style: modern
Hotel amenities: garage, boutique, travel agent, car hire, sauna, massage, health club, indoor swimming pool
Room amenities: colour tv, radio, minibar
Room service: 24 hours
Laundry/dry cleaning: same day
Conference rooms: for up to 1,000 guests, audio-visual aids, simultaneous translation

Bar: cocktail bar
Restaurants: ›Canaletto‹ (13.00/1.00 p.m.–24.00/12.00 p.m.) Polish and international cuisine, American Colonial-style décor; ›Rôtisserie Hettmánska‹: international cuisine; ›Brasserie‹: informal restaurant
Nightclub: ›Czarny Kot‹ (Black Cat) (22.00/10.00 p.m.–3.00/a.m.), velvet and mirrors, discothèque, show (24.00/12.00 p.m.)

Although it lacks the classical elegance of the Opera House around the corner, and the Baroque splendour of Wilanow Palace at the other end of the ›Royal Route‹, the clean-cut silhouette of Warsaw's dépendance of the renowned American hotel chain is a prominent landmark on one of the city's principal squares. Thanks to its location near the commercial district, the Victoria is the excellent headquarters for visiting businessmen: there are facilities for a two-man summit with an entourage of up to one thousand. The intérieur displays the even more no-frills comfort which is in any case a hallmark of the Inter-Continental's establishments from Helsinki to Auckland, with capitalist refinements including a marble floor, concealed lighting and leather armchairs in the foyer, bright green floral carpet and matching tables in the bar, neutral furnishings in the bedrooms and a wide range of extra amenities, including a swimming pool and a sauna. You can sample Polish specialities in the Colonial-style Canaletto before dancing the night away after the cabaret at the Czerny Kot discothèque. Should you encounter any minor difficulties during your stay, the solidarity of the friendly staff will help you to overcome them with a minimum of inconvenience.

Dinner

WILANOW
Ul. Wiertnicza
Telephone: 42 13 63
Closed: Monday; after a public holiday
Open: 11.00/a.m.–23.00/11 p.m.
Cuisine: Polish
Specialities: roast suckling pig; hare in sour cream sauce
Location: in the grounds of Wilanow Palace
Setting: in the former servants' house of a beautifully-restored Baroque palais, once the home of Polish royalty and aristocracy; attractive and comfortable dining room furnished in rustic style
Amenities: second restaurant (›Hetmanska‹); café; bar; car park
Atmosphere: welcoming, friendly and popular
Clientèle: local citizens en fête, en famille and (at weekends in summer) en masse, plus a sprinkling of footsore museum visitors
Dress: nothing too outrageous or outlandish
Service: with a smile
Reservations: not necessary (pets permitted)
Price range: medium
Credit cards: AE, Euro

Lunch

ZAYAZD NAPOLEONSKI
83 Ptowiecka (10 km/6 miles)
Telephone: 15 30 68
Closed: never
Open: 13.00/1 p.m.–24.00/12 p.m.
Cuisine: Polish
Specialities: steak ›Napoleon‹; fresh trout (from the pool) in various guises
Location: 10 km (6 miles) from city centre
Setting: recently-opened restaurant in a historic former coaching inn where Napoleon met Countess Walewska whilst on his way to Moscow (according to the legend, anyway)
Amenities: bedrooms for overnight guests; open-air dining on beautiful terrace in summer; small pond; car park
Atmosphere: seductively romantic
Clientèle: sentimentally-inclined local top industrialists plus a selection of lovers of any age, sex or nationality
Dress: elegantly casual to casually elegant
Service: exceptionally helpful and friendly
Reservations: recommended at the weekend
Price range: moderately high
Credit cards: not accepted

Lunch

CANALETTO
11 ul. Królewska
Telephone: 27 80 11/27 92 71
Owner/Manager: S. Wcislo
Closed: never
Open: 13.00/1 p.m.–24.00/12 p.m.
Cuisine: Polish and international
Specialities: roast mutton with vegetables (Baranina); pork in various traditional forms (Polejvia)
Location: in the Hotel Victoria Inter-Continental
Setting: American Colonial-style décor; wood-panelled ceiling and screens between tables affording extra privacy; brown upholstery; orange tablecloths
Amenities: hotel; grill restaurant; brasserie; coffee shop; bar; nightclub; air conditioning
Atmosphere: exclusive; confidential to intimate, depending on your mood (or that of your companion!)
Clientèle: predominantly visiting manufacturers and men of commerce
Dress: tends towards the conservative
Service: elegant in tail-coats and suavely professional
Reservations: recommended
Price range: cheap by Paris standards only
Credit cards: AE, DC, Euro, Carte Blanche, Master Card

Nightclub

CZARNY KOT (Black Cat)
11 ul. Królewska
Telephone: 27 80 11/27 92 71
Owner/Manager: S. Wcislo
Closed: never
Open: 22.00/10 p.m.–3.00/a.m.
Location: in the Hotel Victoria Inter-Continental
Setting: sophisticated nightclub with bar, discothèque and show (at midnight); mirrored walls, comfortable velvet-upholstered armchairs, dance-floor and stage
Amenities: hotel; two restaurants; brasserie; coffee shop; bar; air conditioning
Atmosphere: party-like but refined
Clientèle: local night owls and a miscellaneous collection of birds of passage
Dress: disco-elegance
Service: efficient
Reservations: recommended
Credit cards: AE, DC, Euro, Carte Blanche, Master Card

411

Nightclub

KONGRESOWA
Ul. Emilii Plater
Telephone: 20 85 23
Closed: never
Open: 20.00/8 p.m.–3.00/a.m.
Location: central; in Warsaw's House of Culture
Setting: 1950s-style décor; discothèque with bar and dance-floor
Amenities: restaurant (dinner menu; snacks at midnight); show with charmingly modest strip-tease; car park
Atmosphere: cheerful, uncomplicated and almost chic
Clientèle: mostly young and approachable, plus one or two middle-aged optimists hoping to recapture – albeit temporarily – their lost youth
Dress: glad rags to dressed-to-kill
Service: reliable and helpful
Reservations: not necessary
Price range: medium

Shopping

EVERYTHING UNDER ONE ROOF
Junior   Sawa, Wars – Marszatkowska

FOR HIM AND FOR HER
Moda Polska   Swietokrzyska

JEWELLERY
Silver   Nowy Świat

LOCAL SPECIALITIES
Ksiegarnia   (books)
Swietokrzyska
Cepelia   (gifts)
Swietokrzyska

THE BEST OF ART
Ars Polonia Gallery   (modern art)
2 Al. Jerozolimskie
Tel. 27 87 75

Europe's ›Serene Harbour‹ on the Tagus estuary is ›where winter comes to spend its summer‹. The gateway to the New World, firmly anchored to the Old, is one of the most unexpectedly splendid cities on earth, if lacking the grandeur of London, the glamour of Paris and the flamboyance of Rome. The richest metropolis on the continent and stronghold of international commerce at the time of the Great Discoveries (Vasco da Gama, Pedro Alvares Cabral, Fernão de Magalhães, et al.), this regal city has replaced the shine of luxury with the authenticity of nobility, warmth and charm. Here, you can still live like a king. Many kings did – French would-be king, Le Comte de Paris, Italian ex-king, Umberto II and Juan Carlos as the Spanish King-in-waiting, as well as assorted aristocracy of capitalism like Bolivian tin king, Antenor Patiño and Armenian oil king, Calouste Sarkis Gulbenkian who bequeathed his private collections to Portugal to form the city's most eminent museum. (Today, the Princes of Polignac, foremost family and hosts to the world in their stately residence, are among the last ›royalists‹ in town.) Revolution, recession and grande entrée into the Common Market have shaken traditions but signal a new awakening for the country, epitomized in high concentration in its capital. There is still fado saudade in the antique labyrinth of Alfama, historic splendour in the palaces and parks, romantic atmosphere in the Sintra hills and in the quaint fishing village of Cascais, but the fast pulse of the modern business centre of Baixa, with the Rossio its nucleus for traffic, trade and trysts, rules Lisbon's new life. The structures of the Portuguese avant-garde wunderkind, Tomas Taveira, bear witness to the future, while this sunny, nonchalant metropolis still lives up to the title bestowed upon it by Renaissance poet Luis de Camões in the Lusiad epic – ›Princess of the world before whom even the ocean bows.‹

Founded: ca. 1200 B.C., by the Phoenicians; Lisboa (Portuguese) – ›serene harbour‹.

Far-reaching events: 3rd and 2nd centuries B.C. – Roman occupation; 5th century A.D. – Sueves and Visigoths' occupation; 8th century – Moorish invasion; 1249 – Alfonso III ends Moorish occupation; 1260 – Lisbon capital; 1495–1521 – Manuel I king, architect Boytac designs important buildings in the Manueline style; 15th and 16th centuries – city of the explorers da Gama, Cabral and Magellan; 1580 – Philip II invades; 1668 – Portugal independent; 1755 – earthquake destroys large parts of the city; Marquis of Pombal rebuilds Lisbon; 1807 – French invasion; 1808 – liberation by the British; 1810 – Wellington constructs the Lines of Torres Vedras as defence against the French; 1910 – Manuel II abdicates; republic proclaimed; 1932–68 – Antonio Salazar's dictatorship; 1968–74 – Caetano's rule; 1974 – coup d'état, ›Carnation Revolution‹, by a military junta; 1974/75 – colonies independent.

Population: 860,000; capital and largest city of Portugal.

Postal code: P–1000 to P–1900   **Telephone code:** 1

Climate: mild; moderately warm in summer, rather wet in winter.

Best time to visit: May to October, though July and August may be rather hot.

Calendar of events: *Holy Week* (Mar/Apr) – processions; *Carnival* (Feb) – four days of parades and flowers; *St. Anthony's Festival* (13 Jun); *St. John* (23 Jun); *St. Peter* (29 Jun) – colourful parades and folk dancing.

Fairs and exhibitions: *INTERCASA* (Sep) – electrical appliance exhibition; *FIL* (May) – international fair.

Best views of the city: from the *Suspension Bridge*; from the pedestal of *Cristo Rei*; from the *Santa Justa Lift*, constructed by Eiffel.

Historical and modern sights: *Cathedral* (12th century) – Romanesque with Gothic nave; former fortress with *Sacristy* – Baroque, museum, objects of religious art; *Castle Sao Jorge* (5th and 6th centuries) – ten towers linked by massive walls; *Mosteiro do Jeronimos* (16th century) – Gothic, architect Boytac's style modified in Renaissance and Classical style; *Rossio* (13th century) – square bordered by the *National Theatre*; *Chapel of St. John the Baptist* (1742) – Italian Baroque, constructed in Rome, transferred to Lisbon in 1750, interior rich in valuable gems and metals; *Alfama* – oldest area of the city; *Baixa* – reconstructed old city; *Belem Tower* (16th century) – fortress with Manuel I's arms; *Museum of Ancient Art* – Portuguese Primitives, polyptych-panels by Nuno Goncales; *Calouste Gulbenkian Museum* – the most significant private art collection in the world; *Bridge of 25 April* (1962–66) – first direct connection to the southern province, longest span in Europe; the *Royal palaces* at Queluz and Sintra; *Pena Park* in Sintra.

Special attractions: an evening of *Fado* in Alfama; a *bullfight*; a drive to *Estoril, Cascais, Guincho,* and *Sintra,* and a night or a weekend at *Palacio dos Seteais.*

Important companies with headquarters in the city: *Petrogal* (oil); *Quimigal* (textiles, chemicals); *Transportes Aeros Portugueses* (air transport); *Correios e Telecomunicacoes de Portugal* (communications); *Tabaqueira* (tobacco); *Portucel* (paper); *Rodoviaria Nacional: Efacec* (electrical appliances); *CTM* (shipping); *Caminhos de Ferro Portugueses* (transport).

Airport: Lisbon, LIS; Tel.: 889191; Navigator Lounge, Tel.: 899121; 13 km/7 miles; TAP, Tel.: 889185.

The Headquarters

TIVOLI

185 Avenida da Liberdade
P–1298 Lisboa 2
Telephone: 53 01 81/52 11 01
Telex: 12 588 tivoli
General Manager: Antonio Gonçalvez Machaz
Affiliation/Reservation System: SRS (Steigenberger Reservations Service)
Number of rooms: 344 (15 suites)
Price range: Esc 10,500 (single)
　　　　　　　Esc 12,000 (double)
　　　　　　　Esc 18,000 (suite)
Credit cards: AE, BC, DC, EC, Visa, Access, MC
Location: city centre
Built: 1958 (renovated 1982)
Style: modern
Hotel amenities: car park, air conditioning, shopping arcade, boutique, hairdresser, swimming pool, tennis court
Room amenities: colour tv, mini-bar, radio
Room service: 24 hours
Conference rooms: for up to 200 persons
Bar: ›American Bar‹
Restaurants: ›O Zodiaco‹, local specialities; ›Terrace Grill‹, panoramic view

Despite its high-sounding name, the Portuguese capital's pre-eminent residence for upper-echelon businessmen and individual tourists alike is not related to the Roman namesake and hardly comparable to the Villa d'Este, but the modern hotel on ›High Street‹ has all the amenities and attractions you would expect in a luxury establishment here, and – even though in the very heart of the city – it claims a reposeful garden with a circular swimming pool amidst tropical vegetation and a tennis court on the premises. The imposing pillared lobby lounge is the turntable for encounters, short meetings and pre-all rendez-vous with the little bar to the side a famous in-between and after-hours watering hole, while the classy O Zodiaco restaurant is the best Sesame for first-time visitors to get acquainted with Portuguese specialities such as the unusual fish and seafood variations, smoked, sweet or hot. In the Terrace Grill, *one of the magnificent vantage points for the panorama of one of Europe's most beautiful metropolises, a festive or romantic dinner in the warm season will carry you on a silver tray into a golden night. The 300-odd rooms are comfortably equipped, the suites with a touch of style; communications and conference facilities are the best in town and with a handful of practical additions such as a boutique, a hairstylist and a well-guarded garage, the Tivoli is definitely the superlative headquarters in Lisbon.*

The Hideaway

PALACIO DE SETEAIS

8 Rua Barbosa do Bocage, Seteais
P–2710 Sintra (28 km/18 miles)
Telephone: 9 23 32 00
Telex: 14410 hopase
Owning company: Tivoli Hotels
General Manager: Joaquim Machaz
Number of rooms: 18 (1 suite)
Price range: Esc 7,500–12,650
Credit cards: AE, DC, EC, MC, Visa
Location: in Sintra, 28 km/18 miles from Lisbon airport, 10 km/6 miles from the beach
Built: 1787; converted into a luxury hotel in 1955 (renovated in 1983)
Style: palatial
Hotel amenities: parking, gardens
Room amenities: balcony
Room service: 7.00/a.m.–23.00/11 p.m.
Sports: riding
Sports (nearby): golf
Bar: (12.00/a.m.–23.00/11 p.m.)
Restaurant: (12.30/p.m.–14.30/2.30 p.m. and 19.30/7.30 p.m.–21.30/9.30 p.m.)

For George Gordon, Lord Byron, the lovely hilltop town of Sintra was a ›glorious Eden‹. One mile north of the centre stands the ›Palace of Seven Sighs‹ where he stayed, working on ›Childe Harold‹ in the park-like gardens. Today, since its conversion into the most luxurious hideaway in the country, this magnificent eighteenth-century château is the goal for other pilgrims – grand tour Americans and holidaying Europeans as well as businessmen seeking a temporary respite from the capital. The symmetrical grey stone residential wings stand four-square on either side of a triumphal arch which hints at the noblesse of the intérieur. The public rooms are on a grand scale, with high ceilings, marble floors, monumental staircases, velvet curtains, chandeliers, hand-painted frescoes and elaborate antique furniture. The eighteen bedrooms are equally cavernous, with enormous bathrooms and views of the mountains or the sea. Only the bar is relatively small, which lends it an agreeable air of intimacy amidst so much splendour. In the dining room, decorated in restful shades of beige and green, local specialities including the famous acepipes variados (hors d'œuvres), are served on delicate Portuguese Vista Alegre porcelain. The Tivoli hotel group and manager Joaquim Machaz have successfully brought the Palacio dos Seteais through a transitional period into a new epoch of grace and favour. The Duke of Wellington, who signed an armistice here with Napoleon's generals during the Peninsular War, would find the stately mansion little changed apart from the unobtrusive addition of modern amenities. This, no doubt, is the reason for the hotel's popularity amongst such celebrities as Brigitte Bardot and Melina Mercouri.

Lunch

TAVARES
37 Rua da Misericórdia
Telephone: 32 11 12
Owner/Manager: Fernando A. M. Lopes
Closed: Saturday; Sunday lunch
Open: 13.00/1 p.m.–15.00/3 p.m. and
20.00/8 p.m.–22.30/10.30 p.m.
Cuisine: French (classic) and Portuguese
Specialities: crayfish au gratin ›Tavares‹;
shrimp kebabs with herbs; filet mignon
with pimentos; vichyssoise; sole (lin-
guado) Newburg; crab (santola) re-
cheada a Tavares; soufflés
Location: in the heart of the old city
Setting: dining room with mirrored
walls; gilt; ecru; crystal chandeliers;
sconces; Louis XV fauteuils; elegantly-
laid tables with fresh flowers
Amenities: reception lounge; air conditioning
Atmosphere: the oldest restaurant in Lisbon (founded in 1784; acquired by the
eponymous Tavares brothers in the 19th
century), and a star on Lisbon's culinary
horizon ever since
Clientèle: a Who's Who of visitors to Lisbon for 200 years; gourmet-minded politicians, exiled royalty (and vice-versa);
diplomats; glitterati; litterati
Dress: appropriately glamourous
Service: good
Reservations: definitely advisable (no
dogs)
Price range: rather expensive
Credit cards: AE, Visa, Master Card

Dinner

GAMBRINOS
25 Rua das Portas de Santo Antão
Telephone: 32 14 66
Owner/Manager: Socedade de represen-
tações gambrinus, LDA
Closed: never
Open: 12.00/a.m.–1.30/a.m.
Cuisine: seafood
Chef de cuisine: Antonio Joaquim da
Silva Rocha
Specialities: ultra-fresh fish, oysters and
shellfish
Location: in the heart of the city
Setting: typical Portuguese restaurant
with a bar counter for quick meals
Amenities: air conditioning
Atmosphere: reflects Portugal's proximity
to the sea
Clientèle: fish gourmets; heterogeneous
mixture of businessmen, media-men jour-
nalists and local habitués
Dress: as you like it
Service: efficient
Reservations: advisable
Price range: fairly expensive
Credit cards: AE, Visa

Dinner

TAGIDE
18–20 Largo da Academia Nacional de
Belas Artes
Telephone: 32 07 20/36 05 70/71 88 80
Owner/Manager: Alvaro Rodrigues; Al-
varo Silva-Manuel; Marques de Car-
valho-Simao
Closed: Saturday evening; Sunday
Open: 12.00/a.m.–14.30/2.30 p.m. and
19.30/7.30 p.m.–22.30/10.30 p.m.
Cuisine: Portuguese and international
Chef de cuisine: Alvaro Rodrigues
Specialities: seafood; fish and shellfish
(the day's selection is displayed on a
large table to facilitate choice); salmon
pâté; smoked swordfish; cold stuffed
crab; grilled lamb with herbs; baked cod
›Tagide‹; halibut with coriander; crêpes
Location: central
Setting: in a building overlooking the
river and the harbour; distinguished inté-
rieur with 18th-century sculptures, an-
tique-style chairs and crystal chandeliers
Amenities: private dining room (50 per-
sons); air conditioning
Atmosphere: refined; luxurious but not
forbidding
Clientèle: expense-account gourmets;
Lisbon's Haute Bourgeoisie with cause
for celebration; academics; members of
the liberal professions; bankers
Dress: fairly subdued
Service: quick and friendly
Reservations: recommended
Price range: fairly expensive
Credit cards: AE, Visa

Lunch

PALACIO DE SETEAIS
8 Rua Barbosa do Bocage
Seteais, Sintra (28 km/18 miles)
Telephone: 9 23 32 00
Owner/Manager: Joao Clemente
(owner); Joaquim Machaz (manager)
Closed: never
Open: 8.00/a.m.–11.00/a.m.; 12.30/
p.m.–14.30/2.30 p.m.; 16.30/4.30 p.m.–
18.00/6.00 p.m.; 19.30/7.30 p.m.–21.30/
9.30 p.m.
Cuisine: French, international and local
Specialities: hors d'œuvres; shrimps;
Russian salad; fish mousse; turbot Florentine; meat dishes with fresh vegetables;
desserts(!); in spring, the best strawberries in the world
Location: at Sintra; 28 km/18 miles north
of Lisbon
Setting: an exquisite 18th-century palais;
dining room overlooking the hillside with
villas and orchards; luxurious décor with
carefully-chosen accessoires
Amenities: hotel; bar; car park
Atmosphere: that of a nobleman's country château – raffiné; refreshing; rejuvenating – and romantic

Clientèle: businessmen tired of Lisbon; top managers, local social élite and celebrities in search of seclusion
Dress: soignée
Service: skilful and polite
Reservations: recommended
Price range: rather expensive
Credit cards: AE, DC, Euro, Visa

Dinner

AVIZ
12 Rua Serpa Pinto
Telephone: 32 83 91/2–32 53 72
Owner/Manager: Pietro Rapetti
Closed: Saturday lunchtime; Sunday
Open: 12.00/p.m.–14.00/2 p.m. and 17.00/5 p.m.–22.00/10 p.m.
Cuisine: French (classic)
Chef de cuisine: Armando Valente
Specialities: smoked swordfish with lemon; roast duck with bitter-sweet orange sauce and potato croquettes; ›Scampi-Fritti‹, ›Kief de Volaille Aviz‹; crêpes Suzette
Location: central
Setting: reception lounge with green marble columns, deep black leather armchairs, crystal chandeliers; three interconnected dining rooms with wood panelling and grained silk wallcovering; gilt sconces; life-size statue of an American Indian girl
Amenities: air conditioning
Atmosphere: animated (the main dining room) to intimate (the smaller ones); an attractive old-world aura
Clientèle: royalty; international tycoons; jet-set; globe-trotters and other exotic birds of passage
Dress: rather conservative, elegant and expensive
Service: attentive
Reservations: recommended (no dogs)
Price range: rather expensive
Credit cards: AE, DC, Visa, Access, Master Card

Dinner

O PAGEM
20 Largo da Trinidade
Telephone: 37 31 51
Owner/Managers: Fernanda Farinha/ Ursula MacTisell
Closed: two weeks in August
Open: 12.00/a.m.–15.00/3 p.m. and 19.30/7.30 p.m.–24.00/12 p.m.
Cuisine: Portuguese and international
Location: central
Setting: intimate and elegant piano bar on the ground floor; two romantic dining rooms upstairs

Amenities: pianist; air conditioning
Atmosphere: comfortable and confidential, with good music to mask any awkward silences in the conversation
Clientèle: intelligent, discriminating and well-informed – and those who would like to be considered as such
Service: professionally directed by chief barman Jorge Costal
Reservations: advisable (pets permitted)
Credit cards: AE, DC, Visa, Master Charge

Café

A BRASILEIRA
120 Rua Garrett
Telephone: 36 95 41
Owner/Manager: Jaime Foaris Silva and Francisco Silva
Closed: Sunday
Open: 12.00–14.00/2 p.m. and 19.00/7 p.m.–21.00/9 p.m.
Location: in the Chiado district of Lisbon
Setting: Art Nouveau façade; minuscule tables; tooled leather chairs; marble pilasters; mirrored walls; collection of impressionist and cubist paintings; oversize clock
Amenities: shoe-cleaning by old men who give the impression of having been here since the café opened
Atmosphere: unhurried turn-of-the-century nostalgia; the last old coffee-house in Lisbon
Clientèle: artists; writers; showgirls; shopgirls; shopkeepers; students; respectable matrons
Service: old-fashioned charm
Reservations: only for groups
Credit cards: all accepted

Bar

LISBOA A NOITE (Fado Café)
69 Rua das Gáveas
Telephone: 36 85 87; 36 85 57 (for reservations)
Owner/Manager: Romao Martins
Closed: Sunday
Open: 12.00/a.m.–16.00/4 p.m. and 20.00/8 p.m. to 3.00/a.m.
Location: near the Largo da Chafariz
Setting: re-creation of a 17th-century tavern; several open rooms separated by thick stone arches; leather and brass-studded chairs, blue-tiled walls, old engravings and prints; open fire in winter; domestic paraphernalia
Amenities: dinner menu as well as drinks (for which there is a minimum charge); some of the best fado in Lisbon, performed by the owner of the café, Fernanda Maria

Atmosphere: comfortable and relaxed to electric as the performance is about to begin
Clientèle: fado fans from far and wide – local devotees and tourists from Rio de Janeiro to Macao
Service: waitresses in black and white, and waiters in black and brown
Reservations: advisable for groups
Credit cards: not accepted

Nightclub

BANANA POWER
51 Rua de Cascais
Telephone: 64 73 02/63 18 15
Affiliations: Club of Clubs
Owner/Manager: Tomás Taveira/José Manuel Simoes
Closed: never
Open: 23.00/11 p.m.–4.00/a.m.
Setting: unashamedly luxurious
Amenities: restaurant; bar; discothèque
Atmosphere: a kaleidoscope of nocturnal revelry
Clientèle: distinguished local night-owls and insomniac fun-loving globe-trotters
Dress: tie de rigueur
Service: smiling and helpful
Reservations: advisable

Nightclub

STONE'S
1 Rua do Olival
Telephone: 66 45 45
Affiliations: Club of Clubs
Owner/Manager: Tomás Taveira/Dr. Costa Duarte
Closed: never
Open: 23.00/11 p.m.–4.00/a.m.
Location: in the centre near the ›Janelas Virdes‹ – Museum for Antique Arts
Setting: elegant; individualistic
Amenities: discothèque
Atmosphere: the most expensive and exclusive discothèque in Portugal for the past ten years; reminiscent of a club; very fashionable, especially in the wee small hours
Clientèle: affluent and attractive – or at least attractively dressed
Dress: appropriately eye-catching but elegant
Service: hospitable
Reservations: advisable
Price range: the highest door charge in Lisbon (can be used up in ordering drinks)
Credit cards: AE, DC

Shopping

EVERYTHING UNDER ONE ROOF
Centro Comercial Amoreiras
Av. Eng. Duarte Pacheco

FOR HIM
Rosa & Teiceira
204–r/c D Av. da Liberdade

FOR HER
Loja das Meias   1 Rossio

BEAUTY & HAIR
Ayer   12 Rua Manuel Castilho

JEWELLERY
Torraes   123–31 Rua da Prata
Ourivesaria Torres   253/5 Rua Aurea

LOCAL SPECIALITIES
Loja das Meias (women's fashion)
1 Rossio
Rosa & Teixeira (men's fashion)
204–r/c D Av. da Liberdade
Cenaoura (children's fashion)
39–6° Rua Castilho
O Rei das Peles (leather fashion)
88–2° Rua Assuncao
Samco (furs)
12 Rua Mouzinho da Silveira
Casa das Malas (baggage & travel accessories)
180 Rua Ouro
Galerias Vitoria Decoracoes Lda. (interior decorating)
227–A Av. da Liberdade
Map-Materias Plasticas (bathroom accessories)
80–1° Dto. Rua Passos Manuel
Martins & Costa Lda. (food and beverages)
41 Rua do Carmo
Charcuatria Moy (food and beverages)
6–8–Lj. 72/3 Pc. Alvalade
Casa Monteiro (perfumery)
259/85/69 Rua Ouro
Casa Macario (wines)
272 Rua Augusta
Casa da Madeira (local specialities)
65 Rua do Século
Centro Turismo e Artesanato (local specialities) 61–8 Rua Castilho
Helin (shoes and accessories)
41 Rua Garrett
Casa Havaneza (smoker's requisites)
24/25 Largo da Chiado

THE BEST OF ART
Comicós (contemporary art)
18 Rua Tenente Raúl Cascais

The Emperor Chia Ching would no doubt have resorted to a Confucian aphorism to express his surprise at discovering that Portuguese craftsmen had infringed Chinese copyright. The seafaring descendants of Prince Henry the Navigator who had ventured as far as Cathay returned to their native shores with cobalt-blue-and-white Ming porcelain, providing local artisans with colour and design inspiration for the azulejos, the tiles which so characteristically and picturesquely adorn the façades and intérieurs of the public buildings, houses and churches of the city on the Douro. Oporto and Cale, its left-bank twin in Roman times, eventually gave the entire country its name, reflecting the commercial importance of Portugal's second city in the past, and underlining her crucial role in the country's economy today. The hinterland supports a range of key industries – textiles, metal foundries, chemicals, food canning, leather and ceramics, whilst small family-run firms are responsible for many of the traditional craft products, from silverware to hand-embroidered rugs, for which the area is renowned. The main harbour – Portugal's second largest – is at Leixões on the Atlantic coast, thus keeping tankers discreetly at bay and providing a convenient base for the sardine fleet. Oporto is, in fact, an industrious city, as borne out in the local proverb which asserts that ›Coimbra sings, Braga prays, Lisbon shows off, and Porto works‹. Its spectacular location, rising like an amphitheatre on the granite cliffs overlooking the river spanned by Gustave Eiffel's bridge, has produced a crowded central area in which the four-and-five-storey houses compete for space in an ambience of forceful determination and industrious seriousness not usually associated with southern climes. The architecture is a synthesis ranging from Italian Renaissance and Spanish Baroque to pillared Mauresque geometricity in the hall of the Stock Exchange. And yet, Oporto has an undeniably Anglo-Saxon air about it, due at least in part to the large British community whose involvement in Portugal stretches back six hundred years, beyond the eighteenth-century trade agreements. The treaty of perpetual peace and friendship of 1373 repeatedly prompted England to send reinforcements to support the struggle against adversaries, pretenders and aspiring empire builders from the Moors to Napoléon Bonaparte, and Winston Churchill to describe the country as ›our oldest ally‹. The life-blood nurturing this age-old friendship is ruby, tawny, vintage, or (occasionally) white, matured in casks in the vaults of Vila Nova de Gaia before being shipped to the shores of Albion. In the egalitarian twentieth century it is no longer just a case of ›port for men‹ as in Samuel Johnson's day, and plans to paint the globe pink are no lǫnger hatched over a carafe of Cockburn's or Sandeman's in the panelled dining rooms of the Carlton Club, but despite industrial diversification the fortified wine remains fundamental to and characteristic of the city which has bred the ›freest, most human, most responsible and most capable‹ citizens of all Portugal.

Founded: 2nd century A. D. by the Romans on the site of an ancient settlement, ›Porto‹ (Portuguese) – ›a port‹.

Far-reaching events: 8th century – Mohammedan invasion; 1095 – given to Henry of Burgundy as part of dowry; 1415 – Oporto equips the fleet of Prince Henry the Navigator to free Ceuta from the Moors; 1703 – Methuen Treaty, facilitating trade between England and Portugal; 1717 – English trading centre; 1808 – French invasion; 1809 – British invasion, Wellington captures the town; 1820 – rebellion against British; 1822 – liberal constitution; 1828 – Miguel I ascends the throne; 1833 – liberal monarchy; 1891 – Republican rebellion

Population: 340,000; Portugal's second largest city.

Postal code: P-4000–4300   **Telephone code:** 2

Climate: sunny and temperate.

Best time to visit: May to October.

Calendar of events: *Saint's Festival* (23 Jun) – high life in Oporto; *Cortejo de Papel (24 Aug)* procession with papier-maché figures.

Fairs and exhibitions: *PROTEX LAR* (Nov) – household textiles; *PORTEX* (Dec) – ready–to–wear–fashion.

Historical and modern sights: *Cathedral* (12th century) – Romanesque rose window and Baroque doorway; Gothic cloister adjoining; *St. Francis* (17th century) – Baroque interior; *Maria Pia* bridge (19th century) – railway bridge designed by Eiffel; *Convent of Nossa Senhora da Serra do Pilar* (16th/17th centuries) – rotunda building with Renaissance cloister; *Soares dos Reis Museum* (18th century) – Portuguese Primitives, sculptures by one of the country's best-known artists; *Estacao de Sao Bento* – interior walls covered with azulejos describing local everyday life; *Monument to the Peninsular War* (1909–45) – Portugal's victory against Napoleon's army; *Palacio da Bolsa* (19th century) – stock exchange.

Special attractions: walk through Vila Nova de Gaja and a visit to the *wine stores;* an evening at *Twin's.*

Important companies with headquarters in the city: *Refinarias de Acucer Reunidas* (sugar refineries); *Sociedade de Construcoes da Costa Sarl* (construction); *Manufactura Nacival de Borracha* (shipbuilding); *Comp. Port. do Cobre* (copper); *Indus. Jomar Madeiras & Derivados Sarl* (wood and wood products); *Armazens da Matinha* (machinery).

Airport: Porto-Pedras Rubras, OPO; Tel.: 9 48 21 41; 15 km/10 miles; TAP, Tel.: 69 60 41.

The Headquarters

INFANTE DE SAGRES
62 Praca D. Filipa de Lencastre
P–4000 Oporto
Telephone: 2 81 01
Telex: 26 880 sagres
Owning Company: Empresa Textil D. Ferreira
General Manager: Fernando de Sousa
Number of rooms: 84 (4 suites)
Price range: Esc 9,000–33,000
Credit cards: AE, DC, Visa, Access, CB, EC, MC, Standard Bank
Location: city centre
Built: 1951 (renovated 1984)
Style: traditional
Hotel amenities: solarium, newsstand, tobacconist, terraces, lifts (pets allowed)
Main hall porter: Ernesto Silva
Room amenities: colour tv, mini-bar
Bathroom amenities: bidet
Room service: 24 hours
Conference rooms: 2 (up to 80 persons)
Bar: ›Infante‹ traditional style (10.00/a.m.–1.00/a.m.)
Restaurant: ›Dona Filipa‹ (12.30/p.m.–14.30/2.30 p.m. and 19.30/7.30 p.m.–22.00/10.00 p.m.), Cipriano Teixeira (chef de cuisine)
Private dining rooms: up to 164 persons

The pale pink of the façade blends as perfectly with the historic buildings of Oporto as a glass of Cockburns would with Stilton. The patrician town-houses and the churches, which rise tier upon tier on the granite cliffs above the Douro river, cradle the city's aristocratic inn. Since 1951 the hotel has established a good tradition of comfort and service, which is in evidence from the wide wood-panelled foyer to the well-appointed bedrooms. The public rooms are furnished in Renaissance style; the lounge, with its white walls and mirrors, creates an impression of lightness and space, whilst the Dona Filipa *restaurant has a coffered ceiling, ornate chandeliers and wood-framed tapestries which lend it a rather formal air. Chef de cuisine Cipriano Teixeira produces a menu which contains a range of French and Portuguese specialities including tripe Oporto style – a dish which recalls the occasion in 1415 when local son Prince Henry the Navigator's armada of ships set sail from the town to capture Ceuta from the Moors, taking all the cattle in the region to victual the squadron and leaving the burghers only the offal, thus endowing them with the nickname ›tripeiros‹ (tripe eaters). There is also a quiet inner courtyard for drinks, high tea, or just basking in the Mediterranean sunshine, if you don't feel like going to the beach having been infected by the siesta virus. English wine importers and businessmen from both sides of the Atlantic will find the Infante de Sagres a convenient headquarters for their assignments in Oporto.*

The Hideaway

VERMAR DOM PEDRO

Av des Banhos
P–4490 Póvoa de Varzim
(30 km/18 miles)
Telephone: (52) 68 35 01
Telex: 25 261
Owner: SOPETE
General Manager: Eduardo J. Salgado
Costa Duarte
Number of rooms: 208 (12 suites)
Price range: Esc. 6,500–15,000
Credit cards: Access, AE, CB, DC, EC,
MC, Visa
Location: 30 km/18 miles north of
Oporto
Built: 1975
Style: modern
Room service: 24 hours
Conference rooms: 2 (up to 350 guests)
Restaurant: ›Grill Room‹ M. Rodriguez
(chef de cuisine)

Slightly off the Marbella-Monte-Carlo-Mykonos trail, and not even on Portugal's Côte d'Azur, the Algarve, this modern seaside hotel north of Oporto can neither claim a regal history nor a palatial architecture, but is still one of the most outstanding hotels in the country and a ›must‹ for everyone coming to Oporto for business or trying to hide away from it. The answer lies in the hands and hearts of the employés who provide a service that is almost incomparable. Despite the size of this unostentatious year-round resort, the individual guest is met with such attention, courtoisie, restrained familiarity and respect that, for once, the so-called VIP-status receives a meaning here. The warmth and efficient helpfulness make up for the grand-hotel splendour, and after a short stay you won't long for the fashionable frills and their secret side-effects. Master-mind of this atmosphere embracing everyone spending a day or his life's holiday here, is a man of culture and finesse who set out to invert the rules of commercial hôtellerie – with immense success, nonetheless –, the hotel's director Eduardo Salgado Costa Duarte. The place he manages so idiosyncratically is not without charm and attraction itself. The halls, salons and corridors are tastefully furnished and adorned with luxuriant greenery, lending an air of sub-tropical allure while the rooms and suites lack nothing in comfort and charm. Colours, materials and very personal touches contribute to the home-away-from-home philosophy, and with a panoramic view from your balcony, you wish home were here. The possibilities for an eventful or relaxing sojourn are limitless: restaurants and bars from the pool to the penthouse, gymnasium, sauna and tennis courts; card room, children's playground (just in case), and folklore programmes throughout the year; a swinging discothèque frequented by the Oporto jeunesse dorée as well as the casino with international entertainment around the corner. And the raison d'être for many of the habitués, the beach, is just across the street.

421

Lunch

ORFEU
928 Rua Julio Dinis
Telephone: 6 43 22
Owner/Manager: Messrs. Pereira and Ramos
Closed: never
Open: 8.00/a.m.–24.00/12 p.m.
Cuisine: Portuguese and international
Chef de cuisine: Jose Oliveira
Location: in the commercial district of town
Setting: attractive restaurant in one of the newer parts of Oporto
Amenities: air conditioning
Atmosphere: convivially relaxing
Clientèle: expense-account businessmen, bankers, brokers and local bons-vivants
Dress: mostly fairly casual
Service: welcoming
Reservations: advisable
Price range: medium
Credit cards: AE, DC, Visa, Sottomayor, Unibanco

Dinner

MEMBER'S RESTAURANT
(›Twins‹)
Rua do Passeio Alegre
Telephone: 68 57 40
Affiliations: Club of Clubs
Owner/Manager: Tomás Taveira and Jose Manuel Simoes/Jose Carlos Amorim
Open: 12.30/p.m.–15.00/3 p.m. and 19.30/7.30 p.m.–23.00/11 p.m.
Cuisine: Portuguese and international
Chef de cuisine: Maria Eugenia Esteves
Location: near the beach
Setting: elegantly exclusive dining room
Amenities: private nightclub; air conditioning; car park
Atmosphere: raffinée
Clientèle: Oporto crème de la crème plus distinguished and discriminating visitors
Dress: tie de rigueur
Service: knowledgeable and proficient
Reservations: essential
Price range: fairly expensive
Credit cards: AE, DC, Euro, Unibanco

Lunch

PORTUCALE
598 Rua da Alegria
Telephone: 57 07 17
Owner/Manager: Manuel Hernesto de Azevedo
Open: 12.30/p.m.–14.30/2.30 p.m. and 19.30/7.30 p.m.–22.00/10 p.m.
Cuisine: Portuguese and international
Chef de cuisine: Antonio Vieira
Specialities: goat cooked in local red wine sauce, tripe with white beans; steak with mushrooms
Location: central penthouse restaurant view of the city
Setting: view of the city and the river; sculptured walnut ceiling with concealed spotlights; central service area
Amenities: air conditioning; car park
Atmosphere: unashamedly luxurious
Clientèle: discriminating, sophisticated, self-assured and stylish
Dress: casual but elegant
Service: suave professionalism
Reservation: recommended (no pets)
Price range: high
Credit cards: AE, DC, Unibanco

Dinner

MESA ANTIGA
208 Rua de St. Ildefonso
Telephone: 2 64 32
Owner/Manager: Joaquim T. Oliveira
Closed: Sunday
Open: 12.00/a.m.–15.00/3 p.m. and 19.00/7 p.m.–22.00/10 p.m.
Location: central
Setting: typical Portuguese restaurant
Amenities: air conditioning; car park
Atmosphere: rather intimate; authentic local colour
Clientèle: Oporto's Top Brass; visiting delegates from Liverpool to Lyons; local Haute Bourgeoisie en fête and en famille
Dress: casual but not careless
Service: charming
Reservations: recommended
Price range: average
Credit cards: AE, DC, Unibanco

Nightclub

TWIN'S
Rua do Passeio Alegre
Telephone: 68 57 40
Affiliations: Club of Clubs
Owner/Manager: Jose Manuel Simoes/ Tomás Taveira
Open: 22.00/10 p.m. to dawn
Location: in the chicest part of Oporto, the Foz
Setting: on three floors: 1st floor: discothèque in modern style; 2nd floor: bar and taverna with piano player, open fire place, British atmosphere; 3rd floor: Restaurant ›Member's‹, classic, nouvelle cuisine
Amenities: discothèque
Atmosphere: the baby brother of Lisbon's ›Stone's‹; lively, sophisticated and chic
Clientèle: Oporto's In-People – youthful, attractive
Dress: elegant
Service: unobtrusively professional
Reservations: recommended
Credit cards: AE, DC, Visa

The City

Superficially, the city that Dracula named is an inappropriate setting for a Hollywood horror film – except for a different kind of horror. You will have to travel a long way northwards into the mountains of Transylvania, to reach the fortress of Bran. Perched on an eminence, above the pine-forested slopes, Vlad the Impaler's weekend retreat stands turreted and foreboding – a perfect backdrop for Polanski's perverted fantasies. But even here, appearances can be deceiving; the blueprint hero for all those blood-curdling spine-chillers only visited the castle occasionally, and, despite his gruesome nickname, he made a valuable contribution to the unification of Romania in the fifteenth century. Many nightmarish legends, several bloody skirmishes and two world wars later, little remains of the medieval town the count loved so much, although more recent monuments – from the Curtea Veche imperial palace to the Coltea church – have been renovated and are proudly preserved. They form a marked contrast to the twentieth-century monumental and functionalist buildings which have mushroomed since the war to meet the demands of the population explosion (Romania has the highest birth rate in Eystern Europe), and to house the various socialist organizations based here. Bucharest is the country's economic turntable, manufacturing over a quarter of the nation's industrial output, including consumer goods, chemicals, petrochemicals, fuel, electrotechnology, textiles and leather, thus providing a broad spectrum of businessmen from both sides of the invisible ›curtain‹ with a compelling reason for spending one night in the capital. The polluted air is counterbalanced by enough parks to qualify the city as one of the greenest east of Dublin. Being the international business stage and therefore the showcase of the People's Republic, the cultural palette is as impressive as you would expect from the capital of an Eastern Block country, not only for its managed spectacle but also for artistic quality. Apart from the classical repertoire, the highlight would be to witness a performance by wunderkind gymnast Nadia Comaneci at the parallel bars. It is unlikely that the nightlife of Bucharest will draw more than a yawn from those accustomed to Annabel's, Castel's, et al., although after-hours establishments provid basic entertainment and good clean fun à la socialist along with bars offering beer-and-slivovitz camaraderie. Visitors travelling westwards, wearing rose-tinted spectacles or even walking with a white cane, have described Bucharest as the ›Paris of the Balkans‹, a sobriquet only Nicolae Ceaucescu would be happy to endorse. The Romanian Duce's subjects would much rather endorse the mysterious angst instigated by the Carpathian aristocrat than the realistic terror exerted by the proletarian Big Brother next door.

Founded: first settlements in the Stone Ages; Bucuresti (Romanian) – from a shepherd called Buca.

Far-reaching events: 1368 – first mentioned as ›Citadel Dimbovit‹; 1459 – renamed Bucharest by Prince Vlad Tepes; 16th century – Emperor Mircea Ciobanul builds the palace Curtea Veche on the grounds of the old fortress; 1659 – capital of Turkish-ruled Wallachia; 1861 – founding of the united principalities of Romania, with Alexandre Cuzas premier Prince; 1881 – capital of the Romanian kingdom; 1916–18 – occupation by the Central Powers; 7 May 1918 – Contract of Bucharest; loss of territories; 1944 – Russian invasion; 1977 – heavy earthquake damage in the old city.

Population: 2 million; 9th largest city in Europe.

Postal code: R–70000   **Telephone code:** 90

Climate: short, hot summer; long, mild autumn; cold winters, with the icy east wind the ›Criveti.‹

Calendar of events: *International Music Festival ›Georg Enescu‹* (Sep) – every three years; *Folklore Festival* (Aug) – magnificent historic costumes.

Fairs and exhibitions: *TIB* (mid-Oct) – international fair.

Best views of the city: from the high-rise building at *University Square;* from the tower of the *Grand Publishing House;* from the *TV tower.*

Historical and modern sights: *Curtea Veche* (15th century) – royal palace in the heart of the old city; *Mihai Vodă* (16th century) – monastery and architectural monument; *Stavropoleos Church* (18th century) – outside wall ornamentation; *Mogosaia Palace* (18th century), *St. Iosif* (1883) – by Viennese architect Schmidt; *Hunul Manuc* (18th century) – a traditional inn with much history, near the flower market; *Athenaeum* – Baroque and neo-classical concert hall; the *Museum of Art* – a collection of 70,000 works by native and foreign artists; *Museum of History* (1894–1900) – neo-classic, displays of people and culture of the Romanian countries; *Herastru* – public park with lakes, an open-air theatre, pavilions, sculptures, libraries, restaurants and the *Village Museum,* the most amusing spot in Bucharest; *Bucharest State Circus* – in its own, non-travelling, home; *Jewish State Theatre* – the only one of its kind in Europe.

Special attractions: following the trail of *Count Dracula;* a performance by *Nadia Comaneci;* a quick shuttle to *Istanbul.*

Important companies with headquarters in the city: *Technoforest* (furniture); *Prodexport* (food); *Chimica* (chemical products); *Exportlemn* (wood products); *Masinexport* (industrial facilities); *Metalimportexport* (metals).

Airport: Bucharest-Otopeni, BUH; Tel.: 33 31 37; Tarom, Tel.: 16 33 46; 18 km/ 11 miles.

The Headquarters

INTER-CONTINENTAL

4 Boulevard Nicolae Balcescu
R–70121 Bucharest 1
Telephone: 14 04 00/13 70 40
Telex: 11 541/2/34 inter
Owner: Romanian Ministry of Tourism
General Manager: Marin Stancu
Affiliation/Reservation System: Worldwide Inter-Continental Reservation System
Number of rooms: 423 (35 suites)
Price range: $ 69–79 (single)
$ 85–99 (double)
$ 148–300 (suite)
Credit cards: ACC, AE, BC, CB, DC, EC, MC, Visa
Location: central, 18 km/11 miles from airport
Built: 1971 (modernized 1983)
Style: modern and antique-style interior
Hotel amenities: parking, car rental desk, house limousine service, travel agent, hotel shop, beauty salon
Room amenities: air conditioning, colour tv, balcony (pets welcome)
Room service: 24 hours
Laundry/dry cleaning: same day
Conference rooms: all modern conference facilities for up to 500 persons
Sports: indoor swimming pool, health club, sauna and solarium, massage
Bars: ›Belvedere‹ (8.00/a.m.–21.00/9.00 p.m.); ›Luna‹ (18.00/6.00 p.m.–23.00/11.00 p.m.)
Restaurants: ›Balada‹ (12.00/a.m.–16.00/4.00 p.m. and 18.00/6.00 p.m.–23.00/11.00 p.m.) Romanian and international cuisine; traditional; ›Madrigal‹ (6.30/a.m.–9.30/a.m., 12.00/a.m.–16.00/4.00 p.m. and 18.00/6.00 p.m.–23.00/11.00 p.m.); ›Corso‹ (6.30/a.m.–21.00/9.00 p.m.) international cuisine, Romanian specialities and wines, orchestra
Private dining rooms: three (›Ronda‹, ›Hora‹, ›Rapsodia‹)

The Inter-Continental skyscraper on Bucharest's impressive Nicolae Balcescu boulevard dwarfs all the buildings in the vicinity and stands head and shoulders above the other hotels in the Romanian capital. Here can be found the familiar standards of comfort, service and practicality for which the world-wide chain is renowned. Inside, the décor ranges from the spacious modern lobby to the antique-style Madrigal *restaurant where international and local dishes are served amongst chandeliers and vaguely Louis-something chairs. Visiting businessmen can discuss preliminary proposals in the cheerful* Belvedere *bar and conclude negotiations in one of the conference rooms. A central location, comprehensive recreational facilities, charming staff and – from the* Balada *restaurant or the panoramic bar – a splendid view at the city – make the Inter-Continental the hotel of choice when visiting the ›Paris of the Balkans‹.*

Lunch

ATHENEE PALACE
1–3 Episcopieistraße
Telephone: 14 08 99
Open: 12.00/p.m.–21.00/9 p.m.
Cuisine: continental and Romanian traditional
Specialities: excellent soups; small cheese rolls roasted in bread crumbs; meat dishes; crêpes flambées
Location: in the hotel Athenée Palace, across the Atheneum
Setting: at the corner of the hotel; excellent view through panorama windows of the newly-renovated Atheneum and of the Republic Palace
Amenities: small bar for special desserts; summer garden terrace (also for drinks and snacks); two-shaped dining rooms
Atmosphere: businesslike, solid and correct
Clientèle: businessmen
Dress: formal
Service: reliable
Reservations: not accepted
Price range: medium to high
Credit cards: not accepted

Dinner

BALADA
4 Nicolae Balcescu Boulevard
Telephone: 14 04 00
Owner/Manager: Romanian Ministry of Tourism/Marin Stancu
Closed: never
Open: 12.00/a.m.–16.00/4 p.m. and 18.00/6 p.m.–23.00/11 p.m.
Cuisine: Romanian and international
Chef de cuisine: Julian Staneiu
Specialities: cabbage leaves stuffed with minced meat; spicy minced meat balls; fish; salads
Location: in the Hotel Inter-Continental
Setting: traditional Romanian décor in a modern de-luxe hotel building with a panoramic view of the city
Amenities: hotel; private dining rooms (20–450 persons); two further restaurants; two bars; orchestra; air conditioning
Atmosphere: local colour without sacrificing modern conveniences
Clientèle: fairly cosmopolitan mixture of local businessmen, visiting industrialists and up-market package tourists – with the occasional distinguished VIP, from Yehudi Menuhin and Demis Roussos to Bjorn Borg
Dress: elegant
Service: well-schooled and professional
Reservations: advisable
Price range: fairly expensive
Credit cards: AE, DC, Visa, Carte Blanche, Master Card

Lunch

HANUL LUI MANUC
(the Inn of Manuc)
62 str. 30. Decembrie
Telephone: 13 14 15
Closed: never
Open: 10.00/a.m.–21.00/9 p.m.
Cuisine: Romanian
Specialities: Romanian caviar (excellent); different kinds of ›ciorba‹ (national sour soup with meat or vegetables); ›pui la ceaun‹ (chicken cooked slowly in a rich spiced sauce, in a cast-iron pot); ›mititei‹ (skinless sausages blistered over an open fire with a flavour that will keep you alert); Romanian fruits or Turkish pies adapted to Romanian taste
Location: in the heart of the old city
Setting: in a gracious historic building in Byzantine style; the former inn of the horse-dealer Manuc, built in 1808, now a complex of one hotel and three different restaurants surrounding an inside courtyard; very rustic
Amenities: two ground-floor restaurants; one cellar-restaurant ›Crama‹ and a very noisy but pleasant open-air dining terrace with live folklore entertainment
Atmosphere: very Romanian; relaxed and joyful
Clientèle: popular venue for entertaining visiting delegations
Dress: no rules at all
Service: overworked but very adroit
Reservations: not necessary (pets allowed and welcomed)
Price range: medium
Credit cards: not accepted

Dinner

LIDO
5 Bd. Magheru
Telephone: 14 49 39
Open: 12.30/p.m.–22.00/10 p.m.
Closed: never
Cuisine: Romanian and continental
Specialities: one of the best ›saramura‹ in town (grilled fish in a hot pepper and garlic sauce); delicious mixed grill; fruit-filled pancakes
Location: in the hotel Lido
Setting: very modern interior
Amenities: one main restaurant; in summer two open-air dining terraces around the wave-bath swimming pool; dancing in the evenings; live band
Atmosphere: holiday-like
Clientèle: upper-class; journalists; intellectual people
Dress: from bathing-suit to jacket and tie
Service: friendly
Reservations: advisable
Price range: rather high
Credit cards: not accepted

Meeting Point

CAPSA
1 Edgar Quinet
Telephone: 13 44 82
Closed: never
Open: 12.00/a.m.–21.00/9 p.m.
Cuisine: Romanian and continental
Specialities: open continental buffet, but also typical Romanian dishes; fish – grilled or marinated; sarmalute in foi de vita (ground meat wrapped in vine leaves sprinkled with bortsch and served with cream or yoghurt); desserts from the café
Location: near the University and across from the Architectural Academy
Setting: dark-red walls with golden columns; round tables and red velvet chairs
Amenities: hotel; two dining rooms; a café next to it
Atmosphere: old meeting place for local artists; everybody interested in who's coming in and who's going out
Clientèle: artists, good looking young women, noisy tourists and businessmen of any kind
Dress: casual
Service: prompt and polite
Price range: moderate
Reservations: not necessary
Credit cards: not accepted

Bar

BELVEDERE
4 Nicolae Bălcescu Boulevard
Telephone: 14 04 00
Owner/Manager: Romanian Ministry of Tourism/Marin Stancu
Closed: never
Open: 8.00/a.m.–21.00/9 p.m.
Location: in the Hotel Inter-Continental
Setting: tea/cocktail lounge and bar
Amenities: hotel; private dining rooms (20–450 persons); three restaurants; second bar (›Luna‹; open 18.00/6 p.m.– 23.00/11 p.m.); air conditioning
Atmosphere: pleasantly informal
Clientèle: Bucharest bankers and brokers seeking a respite from the rigours of the boardroom mingle with overseas visitors from Ohio, Osaka and Oporto
Dress: elegant
Service: pleasantly efficient
Reservations: not necessary
Credit cards: AE, DC, Visa, Carte Blanche, Master Card

Shopping

EVERYTHING UNDER ONE ROOF
Confectia   Calea Victoriei

FOR HIM
Magazinul Adam   1 Piata Palatului

FOR HER
Magazinul Eva   Bulevardul magęhru

BEAUTY & HAIR
Casa de Modă   Calea Victoriei

LOCAL SPECIALITIES
Magazinul Victoria (women's fashion)
Calea Victoriei
Adam (men's fashion)
1 Piata Palatului
Vulturul de mare (children's fashion)
Piata Unirii
Romarta (leather fashion)
Calea Victoriei
Nord-Comturist (furs)
137 Calea Grivitei
Librăria mihail sadoveanu (books)
Strada Libscani
Hanul lui Manuc (gifts)
Piata Unirii
Casa de Modă (porcelain)
Calea Victoriei
Magazinul Bucureşti (baggage & travel accessories)
Boulevard Magheru
Magazinul Cocorul (food and beverages)
Boulevard Anul 1848
Casa de Modă (perfumery)
Calea Victoriei
Bucur Obor (shoes)
2 Strada Colentina
Miorita (records)
Calea Victoriei

THE BEST OF ART
Galeria de artă   (modern art)
20 Bd. Magheru

The City

›The city's situation und beauty are without parallel‹. For once, Don Quixote was not lost in the realms of chivalrous fantasy; he was merely endorsing the claims of the aristocratic city to be mentioned in the same breath as arch-rival Madrid. The economic and commercial supremacy of Barcelona – Spain's second largest city and one of the principal ports in the Mediterranean, industrial giant and publishing best-seller – is beyond dispute, the efficiency and diligence of its citizens an Iberian legend. The most important political decisions may be made in the Cortes, but the best business deals are made in the boardrooms and gourmet temples of the Catalan capital. Barcelona, airport for the Saxon suntraps on the Costa Dorada and Brava, transatlantic rest-and-recreation stop for the Sixth Fleet and grandiose operatic stage for Montserrat Caballé, Placido Domingo, José Carreras, et al., has also been the melting-pot of local post-Expressionist painters, from Juan Gris and Joan Miró to Pablo Picasso and Salvador Dalí. Artist-architect extraordinaire Antonio Gaudí's Art Nouveau fantasies transformed the city into an Alice-in-Wonderland townscape, where the kodachrome mosaics of the Güell Park and the dizzy spires of the unfinished ›Holy Family‹ cathedral stand in witty counterpoint to the medieval buildings of the Gothic Quarter and the neo-classicistic monuments on the magnificent Avenida de la Diagonal. The blend of cosmopolitan sophistication and Latin traditionalism is crystallized in Las Ramblas, a Champs-Elysées in the sun – the ›most beautiful street in the world‹ for Somerset Maugham – whilst the impromptu Sabbath-day celebrations of the serene rhythms and circling movements of the sardana recall the centuries-old folkloric customs of the ›city of cities‹. Cervantes may have ›smiled Spain's chivalry away‹, but even the Knight of the Sorrowful Countenance would have to concede that Barcelona, today, is rightfully the country's Secret Capital.

Founded: 1st century B.C. – by Greeks; Barcelona – from the ›House of Barca‹.
Far-reaching events: 201 B.C. – Romans take the province from the Carthagians; 414 – capital of the Visigoths' empire; 713 – Moorish invasion; 801 – Charlemagne takes the city from the Moors and makes it the capital of his Spanish dominions; 1137 – union between County of Barcelona and the Aragon empire; 15th century – centre of trade, banking and clothing manufacturing; 16th century – Barcelona's importance as a main port declines because of diminishing trade with the colonies; 1640–52 – centre of Catalan revolt against Spain, Louis of Bourbon viceroy; 1659 – integrated into Spain; 1701–1714 – King Philip V occupies the city in the Spanish War of Succession; 1714 and 1808–14 – Napoleon invades; 1888 and 1929 – World Trade Fairs; 1936–1939 – resistance against Nationalists; 1978 – Catalan is taught in schools.
Population: 1.8 million, capital of Catalonia; second largest city in Spain.
Postal code: E–8000   **Telephone code:** 3
Climate: mild, under the influence of the Mediterranean Sea.
Best time to visit: at any time of the year.
Calendar of events: *Holy Three Kings* (6 Jan) – procession; *Les Tres Tombs* (17 Jan) – parade on horseback; *Saint Jordi* (23 Apr) – books and roses galore at the Ramblas; *St. John's* (23 Jun), *St. Peter's* (29 Jun) – fireworks and dancing in the streets; *Our Lady of Mercy* (last week of Sep) – bullfights, folk dances and ceremonies in honour of the city's patron saint.
Fairs and exhibitions: *INTERNATIONAL BOATS AND CARAVANING FAIR* (Jan); *CONSTRUMATA* (Mar) – construction fair; *MOSTRA DE HILADOS INTERNACIONAL* (Mar) – yarn and thread exhibition; *SALON GAUDI MUJER INTERNACIONAL; SALON GAUDI HOMBRE INTERNACIONAL* (spring & autumn) – women's and men's fashions; *SPORT* (Mar) – international sporting goods fair; *EXPOTRONICA* (Apr) – computer and data processing; *FOIM* (Jun) – international trade fair; *EXPOMOGA* (Sep) – gift show; *SONIMAG* (Sep/Oct) – tv, sound and electronics fair; *BARNAJOYA* (Oct) – jewellery and watches; *EXPOMATEX* (Nov) – textile machinery exhibition; *TECNOCLINIC* (Oct/Nov) – international exhibition of hospital techniques and equipment.
Best view of the city: from the *Tibidabo* hill.
Historical and modern sights: *Cathedral* (14th and 15th centuries) – Catalan-Gothic, relics of St. Eulalia, the city's patron saint; *Church of the Holy Family* (1898–1915); *Guëll-Palace* (1885–89) – designed by modernist architect Antonio Gaudi; *Museum Frederico Marés* – sculptures by Marés; *Picasso Museum; Montjuich Park* – buildings for the 1929 World Fair with the *Spanish Village* displaying local styles of architecture and craftsmanship; *Barrio Gotico* – Gothic houses on the site of the former Roman settlement; *Columbus Monument* – in memory of his return from the West Indies.
Special attractions: an architectural spree of *Gaudi's fantasies*; a stroll through *Las Ramblas*; dinner at *Agut d'Avignon*; after dinner at *Up & Down*; a holiday at *Hostal de la Gavina*.
Important companies with headquarters in the city: *SEAT* (cars); *Fomento de Obras y Construcciones* (construction); *Iberia* (transport); *Motor Iberica* (cars); *Danone* (food); *Pirelli* (tyres); *Oleaginosas Españolas* (oil).
Airport: Barcelona, BCN; Tel. 3 79 37 or 3 79 43 67; 15 km/10 miles; Iberia, Tel.: 3 25 60 00.

The Headquarters

PRINCESA SOFIA

4 Plaza de Pio XII
E–08028 Barcelona
Telephone: 3 30 71 11
Telex: 51 032 sofi
Owning Company: City Grand Hoteles, S.A.
General Manager: José Maria Cuñat
Affiliation/Reservation System: Husa Hotels, HUS, NHI, UIL
Number of rooms: 512 (26 suites)
Price range: Ptas 11,550 (single)
Ptas 14,500 (double)
Ptas 30,500 (junior suite)
Ptas 45,000 (suite)
Credit cards: AE, DC, EC, Visa, MC
Location: at the western end ot the Diagonal boulevard, 20 minutes from airport
Built: 1975
Style: modern
Hotel amenities: garage, car rental desk, hairstylist, airline office, shopping gallery, heated swimming pool, sauna, massage, gymnasium
Room amenities: air conditioning, colour tv, private video channel, mini-bar
Bathroom amenities: infra-red unit
Room service: 24 hours
Laundry/dry cleaning: same day
Conference rooms: 25 (up to 1250 persons), audio-visual and multi-lingual equipment
Sports: indoor swimming pool, sauna, gymnasium
Bars: four
Restaurants: ›Le Gourmet‹, Salvador Saiz (chef de cuisine), French and international cuisine; ›Top City‹, panoramic view from 19th floor, music and dance; ›L'Empurda‹, typical Catalan dishes
Nightclubs: Régine's

Biggest is best in Barcelona, at least as far as the skyscraper-Princesa Sofia goes – and as long as the Ritz still waits for renovation and new splendour. For the past decade the imposing twenty-floor tower at the western end of the famous Diagonal Boulevard has dominated the architectural skyline and the social stage of Spain's secret capital. Spaciousness, décor and ambiance are distinctly transatlantic, from the atrium-foyer to the Top City *restaurant where you can dine and dance the night away with Barcelona 19 floors below. Le Tout Barcelona assembles on the walled-in lawns by the swimming pool for cocktails and galas, whilst the elegant* Mayfair *piano bar is the meeting point for upper echelon managers and tourists alike. When heads of state or corporations come to town, they will most likely reside at the vast* ›Super Suite‹ *where nothing is missing, except, maybe, nostalgic touches for romantic melancholics.*

The Hideaway

HOSTAL DE LA GAVINA

Plaza de la Rosaleda
E S'Agaró (Gerona), Costa Brava
(110 km/70 miles)
Telephone: (72) 32 11 00
Telex: 57 132 host
Owner: D. Jose Ensesa Monsalvatge
General Manager: Gustavo Jean-Mairet
Affiliation/Reservation Systems: Relais et Châteaux, The Leading Hotels of the World
Closed: 1 Nov–31 March
Number of rooms: 74 (16 suites)
Price range: Ptas 10,000–50,000
Credit cards: AE, DC, Visa, CB, EC, MC
Location: between two lovely beaches on a small peninsula surrounded by the Mediterranean, 25 km/15 miles from Gerona airport
Built: 1932
Style: country palatial
Hotel amenities: swimming pool, 2 tennis courts, sauna, massage, hairdresser, shopping gallery, terrace, park, (pets welcome)
Room amenities: colour tv on request
Bathroom amenities: bathrobe, hairdrier (suite)
Room service: 24 hours
Laundry/dry cleaning: same day
Conference rooms: for up to 150 persons
Sports: swimming, tennis, boating, watersports
Sports (nearby): golf (3 km/2 miles), riding
Bars: two
Restaurants: ›Villa d'Este‹ and ›Las Conchas‹, continental cuisine with Catalan specialities; ›Garbi‹ poolside restaurant

Far from the madding crowd of the ›wrong‹ tourists invading the Costa Brava with bravour, camping cars and their picnic-philosophy, stands a country-castle Shangri-La for the Happy Few who succeed in reserving a terrace room, a suite onto the luxuriant gardens or one of the grand apartments adorned with antiques, boiseries and precious carpets. One of the luxury lodges on the Mediterranean coast, La Gavina is the only alternative to Marbella within Spain, and most definitely more dignified and understated. There is no lack of life and entertainment, however, and the service could well live up to Grand Hotel standards. Kept à la hauteur by the owning family and run like a country club by Swiss Gustavo Jean-Mairet, there is no mañana attitude among the staff, no accessoire missing here, from the bathroom to the beach. Instead, you will find works of art, Haute Cuisine and guests you would love to have as neighbours or friends. For lovers, fathers, sportsmen, aesthetes, gourmets, mono-linguists or taciturn voyeurs – La Gavina spoils them all. When you leave Barcelona, don't leave without stopping over in S'Agaró.

429

Lunch

RENO
27 Tuset
Telephone: 2 00 91 29/2 00 13 90
Affiliations: Traditions et Qualité; Restaurantes de Buena Mesa
Owner/Manager: José and Antonio Juliá
Open: 13.00/1 p.m.–15.30/3.30 p.m. and 20.30/8.30 p.m.–23.30/11.30 p.m.
Cuisine: French and Catalan, with an individual flair
Chef de cuisine: Isidro Martin
Specialities: terrine de foie gras ›Reno‹; shrimp kebabs with herbs; civet of lobster Catalan-style; fillets of sole ›Reno‹; double entrecôte with truffles; crêpes flambées ›Reno‹; home-made pastries and ice-cream
Location: off the Avenida de la Diagonal; 2 km (1 mile) from city centre
Setting: elegant English; an abundance of wood; black leather upholstery; oriental carpets; floral china and matching flower arrangements
Amenities: private dining rooms (6–45 persons); bar; closed terrace; air conditioning; car park
Atmosphere: select, classical and prestigious locale run by 5th-generation restaurateurs
Clientèle: large faithful following amongst the business community for lunch giving way to a younger, more informal set in the evening
Dress: business-like and fairly conservative for lunch; casually elegant for dinner
Service: discreet
Reservations: advisable
Price range: fairly expensive
Credit cards: AE, DC, Visa, Master Charge

Lunch

AMA-LUR (›Mother Earth‹)
275 Mallorca
Telephone: 2 15 30 24
Owner/Manager: Nieves de Ormaolea and José Luis Carles
Closed: Sunday; public holidays; Holy Week (the week before Easter); August; Christmas
Open: 13.30/1.30 p.m.–15.30/3.30 p.m. and 21.00/9 p.m.–23.30/11.30 p.m.
Cuisine: Basque and modern
Chef de cuisine: Mikel Ezcurra
Specialities: rice with clams (arroz con almejas); kidney beans (judías) de Goyerri; sole with truffles (lenguado con trufas); rodaballo (turbot-like fish) en papillote ›Ama-Lur‹; sirloin of beef with peaches; ice-creams and sorbets
Location: central
Setting: luxurious dining room with magnificent furnishings in the tradition of the classic Basque noble houses
Amenities: private dining rooms; open-air dining on terrace overlooking garden; air conditioning
Atmosphere: vaguely club-like; very chic
Clientèle: expense-account gourmets; homesick Basque businessmen; discriminating visitors from Dallas to Düsseldorf
Dress: conventional but elegant
Service: feminine and clad in attractive uniforms
Reservations: recommended
Price range: rather expensive
Credit cards: AE, DC, Euro, Visa

Dinner

FINISTERRE
469 Diagonal
Telephone: 2 30 91 14/2 39 55 76
Closed: never
Open: 13.00/1 p.m.–17.00/5 p.m. and 21.00/9 p.m.–1.00/a.m.
Cuisine: classic and modernized local
Chef de cuisine: Francisco Gorro
Specialities: turbot with sauce hollandaise; casserole of veal in wine sauce with mushrooms from the woods of Catalonia; ragoût of dried cod; pâté of langoustines; gâteau ›Corona‹
Location: on one of Barcelona's main thoroughfares
Setting: timeless; dignified décor; panelled walls with white gloss paint; equestrian pictures and old Dutch paintings portraying the gastronomic partnership between cook and diner
Amenities: air conditioning
Atmosphere: distinguished but not daunting
Clientèle: predominantly the preserve of top executives and visiting delegations for weekday lunches; Barcelona's Haute Societé at night and at weekends
Dress: fairly conventional
Service: welcoming and helpful
Reservations: essential (no dogs)
Price range: rather expensive
Credit cards: AE, DC, Euro, Visa

Dinner

AGUT D'AVIGNON
3 Trinidad (Avinyo 8)
Telephone: 3 02 50 34/3 17 36 93
Affiliations: Cofradia Internacional del Arroz – Confrérie de la Chaîne des Rôtisseurs – Restaurantes de Buena Mesa – Miembro fundador del Consejo Espagñol de Gastronomia – Miembro fundador Confederacion Mundial Gastronomia
Owner/Manager: Mercedes Giralt Salinas

Closed: Sunday; Holy Week (the week before Easter)
Open: 13.00/1 p.m.–15.30/3.30 p.m. and 21.00/9 p.m.–23.30/11.30 p.m.
Cuisine: Spanish (Catalan) and Provençal
Chef de cuisine: Julian Telleria
Specialities: thrush soup; casserole ›Agut d'Avignon‹; turbot with saffron; sirloin of beef in red wine; crème brûlée (crema Catalana)
Location: city centre
Setting: Catalan rural
Amenities: bar; private dining room (14 persons); banqueting facilities (100 persons); catering service
Atmosphere: congenial and relaxing
Clientèle: politicians; executives; mediamen; men of art and men of leisure
Dress: casual but correct to correct but casual
Service: good
Reservations: advisable
Price range: moderate
Credit cards: AE, DC, Euro, Visa, Mastercard, Access, JCB.

Lunch

JAUME DE PROVENÇA
88 Provenza
Telephone: 2 30 00 29
Owner/Manager/Chef de cuisine: Jaume Barguès (Premio Nacional de Gastronomía)
Closed: Sunday evening; Monday; public holidays (evenings only); Holy Week (the week before Easter); August; Christmas
Open: 13.00/1 p.m.–16.00/4 p.m. and 21.00/9 p.m.–23.30/11.30 p.m.
Cuisine: local and nouvelle
Specialities: gratin of clams and spinach (gratinado de almejas con espinacas); spaghetti with vegetables (con verduras); sole with mushrooms in port (lenguado con setas al Oporto); cod with saffron; peppermint sorbet; iced Catalan cream with hazelnut sauce (helado de crema catalana con salsa de avellanas)
Location: three bars away from Sants Station
Setting: small dining room decorated in country style
Amenities: bar; air conditioning
Atmosphere: invariably crowded, but friendly and cheerful
Clientèle: young, self-confident and on-the-way-up to middle-aged, successful and definitely not moribund
Dress: what you will (as long as they will like you!)
Service: painstaking and anxious-to-please
Reservations: essential – preferably well in advance
Price range: fairly expensive
Credit cards: AE, DC, Euro, Visa

Dinner

LA ODISEA
7 Copons
Telephone: 3 02 36 92
Owner/Manager/Chef de cuisine: Antonio Ferrer Taratiel
Closed: Sunday; Holy Week (the week before Easter); August
Open: 13.30/1.30 p.m.–16.00/4 p.m. and 21.00/9 p.m.–24.00/12 p.m.
Cuisine: French and local
Specialities: frequently changing menu; sirloin with vegetables in Calvados (solomillo villete con hortalizas al'Calvados); brains flan with truffles ›Teresa‹ (flan de sesos con trufas ›Teresa‹); seabass with oysters (lubina con ostras); warm duck's liver salad (ensalada de hígado de pato templada)
Location: in a narrow street near the cathedral
Setting: a rather run-down façade; entrance hall dominated by a life-size portrait of the patron; dining room furnished with a charming mixture of antique accessoires and granny's memorabilia; mirrors, pictures and statues (even in the cloakrooms!); hand-painted plates, lovely flower arrangements and candles at night
Amenities: air conditioning
Atmosphere: beguiling; gastronomic and visual poetry reflecting the versatile talents of proprietor-chef Antonio Ferrer, a John Lennon-lookalike who has already published three volumes of verse
Clientèle: Barcelona's In-Crowd; local top brass and visiting dignitaries; gourmet globe-trotters and a sprinkling of lovers with or without cause for celebration
Dress: as you like it
Service: charming
Reservations: advisable (pets permitted)
Price range: fairly expensive
Credit cards: AE, Visa

Meeting Point

CAFETERIA LA OCA
10 Plaza Francesco Macia
Telephone: 3 21 10 19
Affiliations: Club of Clubs
Owner/Manager: Señor Lozano
Open: from 19.30/7.30/a.m. to 2.00/a.m.
Location: on one of the principal city squares
Setting: large dining room with an abundance of natural wood; classic décor
Amenities: restaurant serving full meals; bar; open-air dining on terrace; air conditioning; valet parking; newsstand
Atmosphere: refined but not repressive
Clientèle: top industrialists, men from the ministries and men of letters
Service: courteous and correct
Reservations: necessary
Credit cards: all major

Bar

IDEAL
89 Aribau
Telephone: 25 10 28
Owner/Manager: José Ma Gotarda Quintilla
Closed: Sunday; public holidays
Open: 12.00/a.m.–2.30/a.m.
Location: central
Setting: classic English; wood; important collection of Spanish paintings
Amenities: air conditioning; good music
Atmosphere: the oldest cocktail bar in Barcelona; aristocratic yet cosy
Clientèle: well-frequented by a cross-section of journalists, advertising executives
Dress: no special requirements
Service: directed by cocktail wizard, author and television personality José Ma Gotarda Quintilla
Reservations: not necessary
Credit cards: not accepted

Bar

SANDOR
5 Plaza Francesco Macià
Telephone: 2 00 81 08
Owner/Manager: Sociedad Toncar S.A./ Juan Llort
Closed: never
Open: 20.30/8.30 p.m.–2.00/a.m.
Location: in the Hotel Cadena Hosa
Setting: vaguely Anglo-Saxon décor, with a terrace which is pleasant even in winter
Amenities: hotel; air conditioning
Atmosphere: a must – the place to see and be seen
Clientèle: when in Barcelona ... resident aristocrats, artists et al., plus visiting BPs wanting to catch up on the social scene
Service: mostly efficient
Reservations: not necessary
Credit cards: not usual

Nightclub

UP AND DOWN
179 Numancia
Telephone: 2 04 88 09/2 04 85 03
Affiliations: Club of Clubs
Owner/Manager: Ignacio Ribo
Closed: Sunday
Open: 22.00/10 p.m.–5.00/a.m.
Location: central
Setting: ›Up‹ – gourmet restaurant with discreet background music; ›Down‹ – ultra-modern discothèque
Amenities: air conditioning

Atmosphere: relaxing (Up) to energetic (Down), but always chic
Clientèle: Barcelona's crème de la crème
Dress: jacket de rigueur
Service: good
Reservations: advisable, especially for dining

Shopping

EVERYTHING UNDER ONE ROOF
El Corte Ingles   14 Plaza Catalunya

FOR HIM
Furest   19 Paseo de Gracia

FOR HER
Pertegaz   580 Calle Diagonal

BEAUTY & HAIR
Llongueras   16 Rbla. Catalunya (for her)
Iranzo   100 Paseo de Gracia (for him)

JEWELLERY
Roca   18 Paseo de Gracia

LOCAL SPECIALITIES
Todo Para La Mujer (fashion for her)
56 Rbla. Catalunya
Fancy Men (fashion for him)
463 Calle Diagonal
Santa Eulalia (fashion for him and her)
93 Paseo de Gracia
Loewe (leather fashion)
35 Paseo de Gracia
Christian Peletero (furs)
1 Fernando Angulló
Grife & Escoda (porcelain)
484 Calle Diagonal
Loewe (baggage & travel accessories)
35 Paseo de Gracia
Muebles Rossell (interior decorating)
417 Calle Diagonal

THE BEST OF ART
Ediciones Poligrafa (contemporary art)
54 Balmes, Tel. 3 01 91 00
Eude   (contemporary art)
278 Consejo de Ciento, Tel. 3 17 78 73
Maeght, Adrien (contemporary and fine art) 25 Calle Montcada,
Métras   (contemporary art)
331 Consejo de Ciento, Tel. 3 02 05 39
Prats, Joan   (contemporary art)
54 Rambla de Catalunya, Tel. 2 16 02 84

The City

Spain's ›Gateway to the Oceans‹, largest commercial port of the country, and so much more important as an industrial and trading centre than its sixth position among the Iberian capital cities may reflect, is not only the centre of the individualistic-independent Basque province (separatism is such an old-fashioned expression and not even used amongst the French Canadians any more), but one of the unjustifiably neglected places along the Cantabrian Coast. Santander may be more fit as a seaside resort, and San Sebastian in relation to Bilbao like Marbella to Málaga, but the political and economic headquarters of the north of Spain is also the magnet for ideas and activity, for intellectual entertainment and as a sociological mirror of this part of the peninsula. During the Semana Grande in August, Bilbao is also the arena for the most Spanish of pastimes, corridas, and as a tribute to its local nationalism, pelota championships, which attract the crème of the Basque hinterland. (Many Spaniards claim that bullfighting is of even greater niveau here than in the rings of Madrid.) North of Hemingway's Spain and Carmen-clichés, Bilbao indulges more in a progressive future than in the glorious past, realizing that the sun does set on this empire – quite beautifully, in fact, over the Bay of Biscay. The city is a dynamic amalgam of tradition and modernity, with an industrial palette including – apart from shipbuilding – iron and steel, chemicals and fertilisers. Tankers are tactfully tucked away at Abra and oil refineries at a safe distance at Somorrostro. Its twin faces are in evidence in its architecture too, with the broad boulevards of the El Ensanche district contrasting but not conflicting with the medieval cluster round the Gothic cathedral, where the countless tiny restaurants, bistros and bars provide a setting for siesta encounters, promising deals ending in a mañana-philosophy somewhat less illusionary here than in Seville.

Founded: 1300 as the capital of Vizcaya province, on the site of a 9th century fishing village.

Far-reaching events: 14th–16th century – the town develops as a wood port for Castile; 1511 – Bilbao has its own consulate with sovereign powers; 1718 – the citizens refuse to pay port taxes to the king, and win the day; 19th century – increasing prosperity based on iron and steel industry; 1808 – the French plunder the town; 1936–39 – centre of Basque resistance to Franco; 1960 – industrial expansion.

Population: 440,000; 6th largest city in Spain.

Postal code: E–48000 **Telephone code:** 4

Climate: maritime; mild, pleasant summers, mild winters; equable.

Best time to visit: May to October.

Calendar of events: *Semana Santa* (Holy Week, Mar/Apr) – a week of festivities, with processions and masses; *Nuestra Señora del Carmen* (16 Jul) – festive celebrations in honour of Our Lady: *Festivales de España in Portugalete* (Jul/Aug); *Basque Dance Festival* (Aug/Sep); *Semana Grande* (Aug) – bullfights in the ›Vista Alegre‹ and the local ›Pelota‹ championships.

Fairs and exhibitions: *INTERARK* (Feb) – interior decoration exhibition; *BIMO* (Feb) – furniture fair; *ANTICUARIOS* (Mar) – antiques fair; *AMBIENTE* (Apr) – international industrial equipment fair; *PROMA* (Apr) – international environmental protection exhibition; *ARTEDER* (Apr) – international art fair; *EXPOCONSUMO* (May) – consumer goods; *EXPOVACACIONES* (May) – tourism and recreation; *FERROFORMA* (Oct, biennial) – international hardware exhibition; *SIDUROMETALURGICA* (biennial, Oct) – international trade fair; *FOSMINER* (Nov) – international exhibition of minerals and fossils; *SINAVAL* (Nov) – international shipbuilding and harbour industries fair.

Best views of the city: from the terrace of the *Nuestra Señora Church*; from the *Punte de la Victoria,* the central bridge connecting the old and new cities; from the *Algorta* – the observation point on the old harbour.

Historical and modern sights: *Santiago Cathedral* (14th century) – with Gothic cloister; *Nuestra Señora de Begona* (10th century) – pilgrimage church with fine wood carvings; *Town Hall* (19th century) – with a Mudéjar ceiling; *San Antón* (15th century) – church with Renaissance portal and intricate Baroque tower; *San Nicolás de Bari* (18th century) – octagonal church; *Teatro Campós* (1901) – with magnificent Art Nouveau façade; *Casilda Iturrizar* – the city's best loved park, with the *Museo de Bellas Artes y de Arte Moderna* – El Greco, Goya, Rembrandt and Basque masters; *International Exhibition Centre* in Basurto-San.

Special attractions: a visit to the *bullfight* or the *pelota championships* during the Semana Grande; a *football match* at the ›cathedral‹ stadium.

Important companies with headquarters in the city: *Altos Hornos de Vizcaya* (steel); *Astilleros Españoles* (shipbuilding); *Banco de Bilbao* (banking); *Banco de Vizcaya* (banking); *Refineria de Petroleos del Norte* (petrol refining); *Manufacturas Generales de Ferreteria* (iron and steel); *La Papelera Espanola* (paper); *Ind. Reunidos Minero-Metalurgicas* (metals); *Union de Centros Farmaceuticos* (pharmaceuticals).

Airport: Bilbao, BIO; Tel.: 4 53 06 40, 11 km/7 miles; Iberia, Tel.: 4 24 43 00.

The Headquarters

VILLA DE BILBAO

87 Gran Vía de López de Haro
E–4800 Bilbao
Telephone: 441-6000, 441-8150
Telex: 32164 chare
Owning Company: Cadena Hotelera Aranzazu
Owner: Aranzazu S. A.
General Manager: Julio Egana
Number of rooms: 142 (3 suites)
Price range: Ptas 9,680 (single)
            Ptas 12,100 (double)
            Ptas 17,500 (suite)
Credit cards: AE, DC, EC, Visa
Location: central; 7 km/4 miles from Sondica Airport
Built: 1975
Style: modern superior first class hotel
Hotel amenities: valet parking, hairdresser, boutique, house doctor
Room amenities: air conditioning, radio, mini-bar, colour tv, video
Bathroom amenities: hairdrier, bathrobe, bidet
Room service: 24 hours
Laundry/dry cleaning: same day
Conference rooms: 5 (up to 350 persons), simultaneous translation on request
Bars: ›American Bar‹ (11.00/a.m.–2.00/a.m.), pianist (sometimes); ›Cafeteria‹ (7.00/a.m.–18.00/6 p.m.)
Restaurants: ›Artagan‹ (1.00/p.m.–15.30/3.30 p.m.; 21.00/9 p.m.–22.30/11.30 p.m.), regional and international cuisine
Private dining room: one

Academics interested in separatist political movements come to Bilbao to study the Basques; art-loving historians turn their steps towards the cathedral; aficionados of blood sports want to see the bullfighting, and shipping magnates and export managers set a course for the harbour. The first stop for all of them, however, is invariably the Villa de Bilbao. The name might suggest some historic manoir in the country, but the hotel is actually a modern structure with a concrete-and-glass façade on Bilbao's principal thoroughfare. The intérieur is predominantly contemporary without being anonymous; potted plants add a welcoming touch to the cavernous foyer with its marble, wood and black leather armchairs, whilst striking abstract paintings in the bedrooms harmonize with the colour scheme of the soft furnishings. When the long Spanish siesta is over and the town reawakens for the second, more pleasurable part of the day, the lively American Bar *becomes a focal point for Bilbao's Beau Monde, especially when their animated discussions are accompanied by the strains of live piano music. As night falls they join hotel guests and local couples with cause for celebration for the fine local specialities – chiefly fish – in the stylishly elegant restaurant.*

The Hideaway

LANDA PALACE

Carretera de Madrid Km. 236,
E-Burgos (150 km/90 miles)
Telephone: (47) 20 63 43/20 63 44
General Manager: Maria-Victoria Landa
Affiliation/Reservation System: Relais et Châteaux
Number of rooms: 42 (9 suites)
Price range: Ptas 9,300 (single)
               Ptas 10,400 (double)
Credit cards: Visa
Location: 2 km/1.2 miles from Burgos city centre; 150 km/90 miles from Bilbao airport
Built: an antique castle renovated in 1964
Style: XIVth century
Hotel amenities: garage; valet parking; house doctor; garden
Room amenities: colour tv, air conditioning
Laundry/dry cleaning: 24 hours
Sports: indoor swimming-pool
Sports (nearby): tennis; fishing; hunting
Restaurants: ›Hostal Landa‹ (13.00/1 p.m.–23.00/11.00 p.m.); Basilio Perez (chef de cuisine)

The crenellated keep of the majestic fourteenth-century castle with the El Cid atmosphere towers four-square and forbidding above the pink-tiled, whitewashed villa wing beside the road from Burgos to Madrid. Beautifully restored by Carmela Landa, the cadre is indeed a noble one, from the marble-flagged and pillared foyer with its ornamental staircase to the suite reserved for King Juan Carlos, which has English tapestries, Isabel II's bed and gold taps in the bathroom. Everywhere there are exquisite status fittings to delight the eye and ego of prosperous and prominent guests. Even the swimming pool with its graceful arched windows and a breathtaking view of the Sierra assumes a vaguely ecclesiastical air, whilst the greenhouse gallery houses collections of antique clocks, teapots and other museum-pieces. The glittering chandelier in the vaulted dining room offsets the starkness of the stone walls, and provides an appropriately opulent setting for the elegant cuisine of Bocuse-trained Basilio Perez. On a sunny morning the breakfast room with its pretty pink table-linen and unpretentious country-style accessoires is infused with a joie-de-vivre guaranteed to put balance-sheets, circulation figures and export quotas into perspective.

Lunch

BERMEO
37–39 c Ercilla
Telephone: 4 43 88 00
Owner/Manager: Agustin Martinez Bueno
Closed: Sunday evening
Open: 13.00/1 p.m.–16.00/4 p.m. and 21.00/9 p.m.–23.00/11 p.m.
Cuisine: Basque, traditional and international ›au goût du marché‹
Chef de cuisine: Angel Lorente
Specialities: daily changing menu; salad of goose liver; stuffed peppers; haddock; flan of pine kernels (tarta de piñones); blackberry sorbet
Location: in the Gran Hotel Ercilla complex, but independent from it
Setting: English nautical style; ceiling beams, wood panelling; well-spaced tables; uncluttered and unfussy; well-chosen and strategically-placed bric-à-brac – ship's bell, coral and turtle-shells
Amenities: hotel; private dining rooms; air conditioning
Atmosphere: businesslike, yet warm and welcoming
Clientèle: cross-section of men of commerce, men of industry and men from the media, leavened by a generous sprinkling of actors, bullfighters and local politicians
Dress: tends towards the conservative
Reservations: adivsable
Price range: medium expensive
Credit cards: AE, DC, Euro, Visa, Master Card

Lunch

MACHINVENTA
26 Ledesma
Telephone: 4 24 84 95
Owner/Manager: Maria Castra/Dionisio Lasa
Closed: Sunday
Open: 13.00/1 p.m.–16.00/4 p.m. and 21.00/9 p.m.–23.30/11.30 p.m.
Cuisine: local traditional
Chef de cuisine: Carlos Castellanos
Specialities: deliciao de lenguado (sole); piperade; eels; peppers stuffed with lamb; sea-bass (lubina) with green peppers; haddock in green sauce; fish ›Machinventa‹; plum ice-cream; kiwi soufflé
Location: central
Setting: classic English-style décor
Amenities: private dining rooms (6–16 persons); air conditioning
Atmosphere: charmingly civilized
Clientèle: as popular with top executives, industrialists and members of the liberal professions for business at lunchtime, as with their wives (or girlfriends) for pleasure at night

Dress: fairly casual to rather formal
Service: impeccable; charming waitresses
Reservations: recommended for lunch
Price range: fairly expensive
Credit cards: AE, DC, Euro, Visa

Dinner

EL TOLEDO
Gran Vía de López de Haro
Telephone: 4 42 04 97/4 42 04 47
Owner/Manager: Javier Artaso del Rio/ Mr. Laria
Closed: never
Open: 19.30/7.30 a.m.–24.00/12 p.m.
Cuisine: regional and traditional
Specialities: salads – ensalada Toledo, ensalada primavera (Spring); ensalada mixta
Location: on Bilbao's main street
Setting: large dining room with classic décor
Amenities: private dining room (40 persons); outdoor dining on terrace; bar
Atmosphere: fairly formal
Clientèle: favourite meeting-place for all and sundry; Bilbao's Upper Crust; doctors, dentists, managing directors and shipping agents
Dress: jacket and tie
Service: efficiently directed by maître d'hôtel Abel Lozano
Reservations: essential (no dogs)
Prive range: moderate to rather expensive
Credit cards: all major

Lunch

GOLZEKO-KABI
4–6 Particular de Estraunza
Telephone: 4 41 50 04
Owner/Manager: Jesús Santos
Closed: Sunday
Open: 13.15/1.15 p.m.–16.00/4 p.m. and 20.30/8.30 p.m.–24.00/12 p.m.
Cuisine: local; ›au goût du marché‹
Chefs de cuisine: Carmelo Gorrochategui and Jesús Santos
Specialities: Basque dishes; marmitako; squid (chipirones); Biscay-style fish (pescados a la vizcaína) or fish in green sauce (salsa verde); sweetbreads with mushrooms (mollejas con hongos); puff pastry in various forms, sweet and savoury
Location: central
Setting: attractively-furnished dining room; antique accessoires combined with modern comfort
Amenities: air conditioning; car parking in front
Atmosphere: stylish; sophisticated yet not awe-inspiring
Clientèle: Bilbao's social élite with cause for celebration; bankers, brokers and businessmen at work or at leisure

Dress: as you like it – as long as they will like you
Service: expertly directed by the proprietor, Jesús Santos
Reservations: desirable – preferably in advance
Price range: fairly expensive
Credit cards: AE, DC, Euro, Visa, JDC

Dinner

GURIA
66 Gran Vía de López de Haro
Telephone: 4 41 05 43
Owner/Manager/Chef de cuisine: Jenaro Pildain Urraza
Closed: Sunday
Open: 13.30/1.30 p.m.–16.00/4 p.m. and 20.30/8.30 p.m.–24.00/12 p.m.
Cuisine: Basque and international
Specialities: sea-bass (lubina) with oranges; goose liver with grapes; Biscay-style cod (bacalao vizcaína); partridge; pigs' trotters; rice pudding; pancakes with caramelized oranges
Location: central
Setting: elegant dining room with subtle colour scheme which blends well with the collection of paintings adorning the walls
Amenities: air conditioning; car park
Atmosphere: attractively harmonious and chic
Clientèle: Bilbao's Beau Monde; gourmets from Granada to Gothenburg
Dress: high-fashion; low-fashion; no-fashion
Service: appropriately charming team of waitresses supervised by Nati Pildain
Reservations: advisable (no dogs)
Price range: rather expensive
Credit cards: AE, DC, Euro, Visa, JCB, Master Card

Meeting Point

OLD TAVERN (English Pub)
3 Calle Rodriguez Arias
Telephone: 4 15 07 44
Owner/Manager: Angel Marugan
Closed: never
Open: 12.30/p.m. to 3.00/a.m.
Location: opposite the local House of Deputies
Setting: typical comfortable English pub-style décor
Amenities: snacks (sandwiches, sausages, tortillas etc.) as well as drinks and cocktails; air conditioning or heating (depending on the time of year)
Atmosphere: elegant but unaffected
Clientèle: heterogeneous; youngish; self-assured and dynamic to middle-aged, comfortably-off and well-informed
Service: under the personal supervision of Angel Marugan
Reservations: not necessary (no dogs)
Credit cards: not accepted

Café

ERCILLA
39 Via Ercilla
Telephone: 4 43 88 00
Owner/Manager: Hotel Ercilla/Senor Andres
Closed: never
Open: 7.00 a.m.–1 a.m.
Location: in the Hotel Ercilla
Setting: elegant
Amenities: air conditioning, car park
Atmosphere: informal, lively and constantly on-the-move
Clientèle: mostly hotel guests, some visiting business people
Service: good and efficient
Price range: moderate
Dress: elegant
Reservations: not necessary
Credit cards: all major

Bar

MONTERREY
Gran Vía/Diego L. Haro
Telephone: 4 24 84 90
Owner/Manager: Dionisio Lasa/Maria Costro Lasa
Closed: Sunday
Open: 19.00/p.m.–1.00/a.m.
Location: opposite the Corte Inglés department store
Setting: small bar with only seven tables
Amenities: air conditioning
Clientèle: judges; gentlemen of the jury; clerks; reporters; a sprinkling of tourists and casual passers-by
Service: friendly
Reservations: impracticable (dogs prohibited)
Credit cards: not accepted

Nightclub

BLUESVILLE
1 Telesforo Aranzadi
Telephone: 4 43 70 56
Affiliations: Club of Clubs
Owner/Manager: Fernando Baneta/Gabriel Santa Maria
Closed: Sunday
Open: (Monday–Thursday) 16.30/4.30 p.m.–4.00/a.m.; (Friday/Saturday until 3/a.m.)
Location: central
Setting: nightclub decorated in English style; large dance-floor; music to suit all tastes
Amenities: discothèque; air conditioning
Atmosphere: moderately loud to fortissimo at times; friendly, fashionable and fun

Dress: casually elegant to casual
Service: helpful; under the watchful eye
of assistant manager Gabriel Santa Maria
Reservations: recommended
Credit cards: all major

Shopping

EVERYTHING UNDER ONE ROOF
El Corte Inglés   9 Gran Vía

FOR HIM
José Luís   39 Ercilla

FOR HER
Courrèges, André   9 Dr. Achucarro

BEAUTY & HAIR
Alhoa   5, Avenida J. A. Zunzunegui

JEWELLERY
Joyería-Relojería Genève
22 Rodríguez Arias

LOCAL SPECIALITIES
Veritas (women's fashion)
46 Rodríguez Arias
Smith and Smith (men's fashion)
2 Bandera Vizcaya
Muecos (children's fashion)
30 Rodríguez Arias
Loewe, Hnos. SAC (leather fashion)
39 Gran Vía
Villar, Librería Papelería (books)
22 Gran Vía
Guerra San Martín (gifts)
Bilbao – Galcano Bolveta
Guerra San Martin, S.A. (porcelain)
10 Rodríguez Arias
Artipiel (baggage & travel accessories)
12 Buenos Aires
Artespana (interior decorating)
45 Colón de Larreategui
Indauchu (perfumery)
43 Ercilla
Bourguignon Hijo (flowers)
15 Rodríguez Arias

THE BEST OF ART
  Windsor-Kulturgintza   (contemporary
art) 10 Marqués del Puerto, Tel. 4 15 03 37

The City

A regal capital of a stately kingdom situated and structured for presidential visits, pilgrimage-promenades and galas galore; an architecturally impressive layout with hundreds of landmarks, monuments to world history and its own grandeur over centuries, Madrid has one of the most beautiful settings in the world. Plaza Mayor, Palacio Real, Retiro Park with the Crystal Palace, the Gran Vía for espresso strolls, the Serrano for shopping and the Paseo del Prado for the namesake museum and the grandest habitable palace next-door, the Ritz. The sun is Californian, the air forever leisurely, the life-style aristocratic. As the centre of politics, economy, banking, higher learning, the arts, society and the Royal Family, Madrid is today's Spain, however Barcelona may pout or Seville frown. From the first café to the last drink, from a cocktail to a corrida, Madrid is exciting, breathtaking, creative. Business, on the other hand is done in a graceful way, with long lunches and eternal dinners. With more than just one night to spend, Aranjuez, Toledo, El Escorial and Avila lie within easy reach for a visit – when your local associates are holding a siesta. When in Madrid, live twenty-four hours a day and recuperate north of the Pyrenees.

Founded: 852 A.D., by Mohammed I, emir of Córdoba; Madrid (Spanish) – from the Arabic ›Majrit‹.

Far-reaching events: 1083 – Alfonso VI conquers and christianizes; 1390 – Henry III celebrates coronation in Madrid; 1561 – Philip II chooses Madrid, with its 20,000 inhabitants, as the capital of his empire; 1516 – the Hapsburgs rule, followed by the Bourbons in the 18th century, who give the city its dignified, geometric countenance; 1808 – rebellion against the occupation of Napoleon, as depicted by Goya in his ›Second of May‹; 1936–39 – Madrid the bastion of Republican resistance to Franco; virtually the last town to surrender.

Population: 3.7 million; capital and largest city of Spain.

Postal code: E-28000 **Telephone code:** 1

Climate: continental; extreme.

Best time to visit: April to June; August to September.

Calendar of events: *Carnival* (Feb); *Madrid Theatre and Cinema Festival* (Mar/Apr); *Grand Prix of Spain* (May) – Formula One Racing; *Festival of Patron St. Isidor* (8–15 May) – with bullfights, processions, fireworks, theatre and concerts; *Madrid Open Tennis Championships* (May); *Folk Festival in Honour of St. Antonio* (Jun); *Festival of the Patroness Carmen* (Jul); *Verbena de la Paloma* (15 Aug) – bullfights; *Madrid Jazz Festival; Autumn Festival* (Sep/Oct); *Juvenalia* (Dec) – international youth festival.

Fairs and exhibitions: *IBERJOYA* (Jan) – international jewellery fair; *GEGALO FAMA* (Jan) – gift fair; *SICUR* (Feb) – trade exhibition for safety and fire prevention; *FITUR* (Feb) – tourism fair; *IBERDISCO* (Apr) – recording industry fair; *FINART* (Jun) – handicrafts fair; *FIDEC* (Sep) – sporting goods fair; *INTERMODA* (Sep) – international ready-to-wear fashion fair; *LIBER* (Oct) – international book fair; *EXPO PLASTICA* (Nov) – plastic manufacture fair; *VINTER* (Nov) – international wine fair; *IBERPIEL* (Nov) – leather goods fair; *SIMO* (Nov) – international trade fair for office equipment and data processing; *FERIARTE* (Nov) – Spanish antiques fair.

Best views of the city: from the suspension cable-car terrace on the *Casa del Campo*; from the skyscrapers ›*Torre de Madrid*‹ and ›*Edificio España*‹.

Historical sights: *Palacio Real* (18th century) – 1,000 rooms of regal Bourbon splendour – pomp, painted ceilings and portraits; *Plaza Mayor* (17th century) – scene of ceremonies and autodafés then, of a market, family outings and folklore festivals now; *Museo del Prado* – neo-classical, one of the world's greatest museums within; *Alcalá Gate* (18th century) – Madrid's main landmark, at Independence Square; *Palacio de Cristal* – a glass palace in the city's most beautiful garden; *Parque del Retiro* (16th century) – the royal pleasure garden with fields of roses, a lake, fountains, an observatorium and sculptures; *San Isidoro del Real* (17th century) – Baroque cathedral; *Convento de la Encarnación* (17th century) – Augustinian monastery, with magnificent works of art and the aura of religious life at the Spanish court; *El Escorial* (55 km/35 miles) – monastery with tombs of the kings of Spain.

Modern sights: *Plaza Colón* – with modern skyscrapers and gigantic park fountains; *Congress and Exhibition Palace.*

Special attractions: a shopping spree on the *Gran Vía*; an international football match involving *Real Madrid*; a browse through the *El Rastro flea market*; the *Saint Isidor* or *Verbena de la Paloma* bullfights; a grandstand view of the *Grand Prix*; one night at the *Ritz.*

Important companies with headquarters in the city: *Banco Hispana Americana; Empresa Nacional del Petroleo* (petrol); *Hidroelectrica Española* (hydroelectricity); *Hispanica de Petroleos* (petrol); *Petroleos del Mediterraneo* (petrol); *Renfe* (railway); *Union Explosivos Rio Tinto* (explosivos).

Airport: Madrid-Barajas, MAD; Tel.: 2 22 11 65, 14 km/8 miles.

The Headquarters

RITZ

5 Plaza de la Lealtad/E–28014 Madrid
Telephone: 2 21 28 57/5 21 28 57
Telex: 43 986 ritz
Owning Company: Trusthouse Forte
Executive Director: John M. Macedo
Affiliation/Reservation Systems: The Leading Hotels of the World, Trusthouse Forte Hotels, Utell
Number of rooms: 155 (27 suites)
Price range: on request
Credit cards: AE, DC, Visa, THF
Location: city centre
Built: 1910 (renovated 1985)
Style: turn of century – Belle Epoque
Hotel amenities: valet parking, house limousine service, beauty salon, newsstand
Main hall porter: Jesus Sarrionandia

Room amenities: air conditioning, colour tv, mini-bar/refrigerator, radio, linen sheets (pets allowed except in restaurant)
Bathroom amenities: separate shower cabin, bidet, bathrobe, telephone
Room service: 24 hours
Laundry/dry cleaning: same day (Sunday; laundry only)
Conference rooms: 5 (up to 450 persons)
Bar: ›Upper and Lower Halls‹ (12.30/p.m. to 0.30/a.m.) pianist, harpist, Belle Epoque style
Restaurant: ›The Ritz‹ (7.30/a.m.–11.00/a.m., 13.00/1.00 p.m.–15.15/3.15 p.m. and 20.30/8.30 p.m.–23.15/11.15 p.m.) Patrick Buret (chef de cuisine), international, French and Spanish regional cuisine

The Ritz Garden: breakfast, lunch, dinner, drinks (al fresco): spring–autumn.
Private dining rooms: five

The Diana-the-Huntress sculpture is back in its niche in the hall, once more one of the most elegant public rooms in the world, and the air of La Belle Epoque has been reincarnated by Anglo-Spaniard John Michael Macedo along with a rejuvenation programme comparable to the transfiguration of the Kon-Tiki into the Sea Goddess. The Ritz of the Eighties – and thereafter – is again worthy of the Ritz of 1910, and the kings and stars keep coming anew, just for the Ritz. The driveway is palatial, the foyer a salon, the restaurant a gallery of aestheticism, the terrace-garden a Manet painting and the rooms embrace you with château-furniture, couturier linen, valuable antiques blended with designer accessoires – this place is so beautiful, luxurious and provides such rare individual service that you wouldn't even mind falling ill here. The cuisine lives up to that of the best restaurants in town, a drink in the hall is certainly more fashionable than at any other address in Madrid – save a cocktail in the Palacio Real – and the people passing by, meeting here or residing upstairs could make up a royal reception. Even with a full programme – business, culture or social events – spend as much time here as possible: tomorrow you may have to set up camp in a Holiday Inn.

The Hideaway

HOSTAL DEL CARDENAL

24 Paseo de Recaredo
E–45004 Toledo (90 km/56 miles)
Telephone: (25) 22 49 00
Owning Company: I.N.T.V.R.I.S.A
General Manager: José Gonzales Martin
Number of rooms: 27 (3 suites)
Price range: Ptas 7,000
Credit cards: AE, DC, EC, Visa
Location: Toledo
Built: 1790 (renovated 1972)
Style: neoclassic – Baroque
Main hall porter: Armando Sepulveda
Room service: breakfast only
Laundry/dry cleaning: same day
Conference rooms: for up to 50 persons
Restaurant: ›Hostal Del Cardenal‹ (13.00/1 p.m.–16.00/4 p.m. and 20.30/8.30 p.m.–24.00/12 a.m.) José Gonzalez Martin (maître); Emilio Sanchez Morcillo (chef de cuisine)

When staying at the Ritz in Madrid, it's hard to believe that there's a place worth leaving for. However, lovers with a penchant for the romantic, the authentic and the artful will find a perfect hideaway in one of Spain's most important centres of les Beaux Arts. One and a half hours' drive away is the historic city of Toledo, its mellow biscuit-coloured walls and buildings contrasting with the effulgent blue of the Castilian sky. Its rises from a granite eminence, almost encircled by a precipitous gorge carved out by the River Tagus as it flows across the central Iberian Montes Universales towards Lisbon and the Atlantic Ocean. El Greco immortalized it, and art-lovers have been coming to admire the view – and to see the master's chef d'œuvres in the cathedral – ever since. Cognoscenti always stay at the Hostal del Cardenal when visiting Toledo. The former residence of Cardinal Lorenzo is as redolent of history as the town itself. Built during the eighteenth century, this elegant palais stands in tranquil seclusion, thanks to the medieval wall which shelters it from the street, near one of the former gates of the old city, the Puerta de Bisagra. The intérieur is a neo-classic and Baroque period piece of considerable charm and distinction, with aristocratic vaulted ceilings and corridors displaying antiques worthy of a place in the Prado. There are fewer than thirty air-conditioned bedrooms, each one furnished in a different style. The dining room has a Mudéjar ceiling reflecting the earlier Moorish influence in Spain, but during the summer months it is particularly pleasant to dine on the shady walled patio, where Castilian specialities, ranging from the local soup, stuffed partridge and marzipan to fresh asparagus and strawberries are served in season. The gracious private -house ambiance and the unhurried siesta tempo at the Hostal del Cardenal will appeal even to those who arrive fresh from a grand hôtel sojourn at the Ritz.

Lunch

HORCHER
6 Alfonso XII
Telephone: 2220731/2323596
Owner/Manager: Gustavo Horcher
(›Moppy‹)
Closed: Sunday
Open: 13.30/1.30 p.m.–15.30/3.30 p.m.
and 20.00/8 p.m.–23.30/11.30 p.m.
Cuisine: international, with a Central European accent
Chef de cuisine: Carlos Horcher
Specialities: Wiener Schnitzel (escalopa vienesa); consommé Don Victor; stuffed artichokes; game; partridge; ragoût of venison with Spätzle (Swabian pasta); Boeuf Stroganoff; crayfish salad; crêpes; Viennese desserts
Location: a flamenco dance away from the Prado
Setting: recently-renovated dining room; elegant in the classic idiom; panelled ceiling; prettily-draped curtains; restful shades of blue and pink; fine collection of porcelain figures of soldiers in regimental dress
Amenities: air conditioning
Atmosphere: unashamedly luxurious and yet not daunting
Clientèle: cosmopolitan; homesick Hungarians; hungry Austrian aristocrats and a sprinkling of Spanish grandees
Dress: tie de rigueur; elegant
Service: under the expert guidance of prize-winning maître d'hôtel Cristobal López, assisted by Victor Clemente
Reservations: essential (no dogs)
Price range: expensive
Credit cards: AE, DC

Lunch

JOCKEY
6 Amador de los Rios
Telephone: 4192435/4191003
Affiliations: Traditions et Qualité
Owner/Manager: Luis-Eduardo Cortés
Closed: Sunday; August
Open: 13.00/1 p.m.–16.00/4 p.m. and
21.00/9 p.m.–24.00/12 p.m.
Cuisine: French and international
Chef de cuisine: Clemencio Fuentes
Specialities: marrow-stuffed potatoes; pheasant in grape sauce; duck with fresh figs; bone marrow on milk bread; artichoke hearts with fresh goose liver à la Jockey; salad of Norway lobster; lambs' kidneys with tarragon; jus et mousse de mandarine en surprise
Location: in the aristocratic quarter
Setting: English-style club décor; wood panelling, green velvet upholstery and racing prints
Amenities: air conditioning
Atmosphere: utterly civilized; Madrid's Numéro Uno luxury restaurant

Clientèle: the rendezvous par excellence for businessmen for lunch and for le Tout Madrid élégant for dinner
Dress: jacket and tie
Service: discreetly attentive
Reservations: advisable (pets prohibited)
Price range: predictably expensive
Credit cards: AE, DC, Euro, Visa

Dinner

ZALACAÍN
4 Alvarez de Baena
Telephone: 2614840
Affiliations: Relais et Châteaux (Relais Gourmand)
Owner/Manager: Jesús María Oyarbide
Closed: Saturday lunchtime; Sunday; public holidays; August
Open: 13.15/1.15 p.m.–16.00/4 p.m. and
21.00/9 p.m.–2 a.m.
Cuisine: Basque and French
Chef de cuisine: Benjamín Urdiaín (Premio Nacional de Gastronomía; ex-Plaza Athénée in Paris)
Specialities: haddock with clams; salad of pigeon's legs and foie gras; salad of artichokes and fresh truffles; bream in red pepper sauce; steamed haddock suprême with basil; calves' sweetbreads with spinach and paprika; desserts
Location: 15 minutes' drive from the city centre
Setting: polished mahogany woodwork; beautiful salmon-pink fabric-covered walls; handsome paintings, fine napery, china, glass and silver
Amenities: private dining rooms; air conditioning; open air dining on terrace, car park
Atmosphere: distinguished; refined; perfect harmony from the apéritif to the coffee; one of Spain's most outstanding restaurants
Clientèle: expense-account gourmets from Alicante to Zaragoza, with increasing numbers of foreign visitors from Frankfurt, Florence and Santa Fe
Dress: jacket and tie de rigueur
Service: suave perfectionism under the direction of Liberto Campillo
Reservations: essential
Price range: expensive
Credit cards: AE, DC, Euro, Visa

Dinner

CASA LUCIO
35 Cava Baja
Telephone: 2653252
Owner/Manager: Luciano Blázquez
Closed: Saturday lunchtime; August
Open: 13.00/1 p.m.–16.00/4 p.m. and
21.00/9 p.m.–1.00/a.m.
Cuisine: traditional and regional
Chef de cuisine: Aurelio Calderón

Specialities: Jabugo ham; shellfish; carne de buey; fish
Location: in the heart of the old city
Setting: restored Segovian-style house; dining room with rustic décor
Amenities: bar; air conditioning; valet parking service
Atmosphere: cheerful; chic but not cliquey
Clientèle: the Madrid crowd; Castilian noblemen, princes, poets and politicians; Geraldine Chaplin, the Garrigues Walkers and the occasional ordinary man-in-the-street
Dress: casually elegant to elegantly casual
Service: jovial and hearty
Reservations: essential
Price range: medium
Credit cards: AE, DC, Visa

Lunch

EL AMPARO
8 Puigcerdá
Telephone: 4 31 64 56
Owner/Manager: Ramón Ramirez Miquel
Closed: Saturday lunchtime; Sunday; Holy Week (the week before Easter); August
Open: 13.30/1.30 p.m.–15.30/3.30 p.m. and 21.30/9.30 p.m.–23.30/11.30 p.m.
Cuisine: Basque and French
Chef de cuisine: Ramón Ramirez Miquel
Specialities: according to season; pastry entrées and sorbets
Location: central
Setting: intimate, elegant and welcoming
Amenities: air conditioning
Atmosphere: one of the most à la mode spots in the Spanish capital – always full
Clientèle: heterogeneous; Basques in exile, businessmen at large and a fair sprinkling of Madrid's Beau Monde
Dress: ›correcta‹
Service: ditto
Reservations: advisable (dogs prohibited)
Price range: moderately expensive
Credit cards: AE, Visa

Dinner

BOTIN (Antigua Casa Sobrina de Botín)
17 Calle Cochilleros
Telephone: 2 66 42 17
Owner/Manager: Antonio Gonzalez Martin
Open: 13.00/1 p.m.–16.00/4 p.m. and 20.00/8 p.m.–24.00/12 p.m.
Cuisine: traditional Spanish
Chef de cuisine: Rafael Lorenzo
Specialities: roast suckling pig (roasted over an oakwood fire in a brick stove almost as old as the house itself)
Location: in the old city, just off the Plaza Mayor

Setting: ancient building (1725); vaulted cave; wine cellar (Bodega); typical 18th and 19th-century décor
Amenities: traditional ballads after midnight in the wine cellar; air conditioning
Atmosphere: as vital a part of Madrid's scene for hungry tourists as the Prado is for art-loving ones
Clientèle: favourite haunt of foreign writers from Hemingway (who mentioned it in ›Death in the Afternoon‹ and ›The Sun Also Rises‹) to Truman Capote, James Michener and Graham Greene
Dress: come-as-you-please
Service: very Spanish
Reservations: advisable
Price range: average
Credit cards: AE, DC, Visa

Dinner

CLUB 31
58 Alcalá
Telephone: 2 31 00 92
Owner/Manager: the Cortés family
Closed: public holidays; August
Open: 13.00/1 p.m.–16.00/4 p.m. and 20.45/8.45 p.m.–24.00/12 p.m.
Cuisine: traditional
Chef de cuisine: Angel Paracuellos
Specialities: pheasant with grapes (faisán a las uvas); trout ›au bleu‹; ham; oysters; home-made pastries; sorbets
Location: near the Puerta de Alcalá
Setting: stylish but unfussy dining room with abstract tapestries made by local craftsmen
Amenities: air conditioning; valet car parking service; affiliated restaurant ›Le Jockey‹ (6 Amador de los Rios/Telephone 4 19 24 35/4 19 10 03)
Atmosphere: comfortable and rather homely, but nevertheless casually chic
Clientèle: the expense-account crowd at lunchtime; couples with cause for celebration at night, giving way to the hungry after-theatre set as the evening wears on
Dress: casually elegant to elegantly casual
Service: particularly charming
Reservations: advisable
Price range: fairly expensive
Credit cards: AE, DC, Euro, Visa

Bar

RITZ
5 Plaza de la Lealtad
Telephone: 2 21 28 57
Owner/Manager: Trusthouse Forte / John M. Macedo
Open: 12.30/p.m.–00.30/12.30 a.m.
Location: in the Hotel Ritz
Setting: Upper and Lower Halls; spacious, light and bright; Belle Epoque Décor; stucco ceiling; pillars, French win-

443

dows, potted plants and comfortable
fauteuils; pianist (bar area in lower hall);
(spring-autumn) drinks served in the Ritz
Garden
Amenities: hotel; air conditioning; valet
parking service
Atmosphere: turn-of-the-century ele-
gance in the Upper and Lower Halls; per-
fect for a drink, a coffee, an apéritif or the
legendary afternoon tea
Clientèle: International High Society,
Heads of State and Top Executives
Dress: the most elegant in town
Service: excellent and very personal
Reservations: advisable
Credit cards: AE, DC, Visa, THF

Bar

JOSE LUIS
11 Raffael Sagado
Telephone: 4 57 50 36
Owner/Manager: José Luis Ruiz Solag-
uren/José Luis Garcia
Closed: Sunday; August
Open: 12.00/a.m.–1.00/a.m.
Specialities: hot champagne; dry Martini
Location: next to the stadium of Real Ma-
drid
Setting: large bar with plants in profu-
sion; terrace for outdoor apéritifs
Amenities: 2 private dining rooms; air
conditioning; car park
Atmosphere: lively but civilized
Clientèle: football stars; football fans; ta-
lent scouts; top managers
Service: very efficient
Reservations: not necessary (no pets)
Credit cards: AE, Visa, DC

Nightclub

MAU MAU
83 Padre Damián
Telephone: 4 57 78 00
Owner/Manager: Paco de Rivera
Open: 23.00/11 p.m.–5.00/a.m.
Closed: never
Location: in the Hotel Eurobuilding
Setting: large nightclub with discothèque
in a big modern hotel complex
Amenities: hotel; air conditioning; car
park
Atmosphere: big enough to lose an ex-
lover in; small enough to find a new one
Clientèle: jazzy; jumpy; jolly; aristo-
cratic teens and their acquaintances,
friends and hangers-on
Dress: tie essential
Service: amazingly amiable
Reservations: obligatory
Credit cards: AE, DC, Visa

Shopping

EVERYTHING UNDER ONE ROOF
Corte Inglès
3 calle Preciados
FOR HIM
Yufty   20 Ayala
FOR HER
Rango   19 Carrera San Hironimo
JEWELLERY
Sanz   17 Serrano

LOCAL SPECIALITIES
Ello Berhanver (women's fashion)
25 Juan De Mena
Denif (men's fashion) 29 Serrano
Nancy (children's fashion)
35 Nonez Balboa
Friky Midas (children's fashion)
35 Velasquez
Loewe (leather fashion)
26 Serrano
Arturo (furs) 22 Argensola
Espasa Calpe (books)
29 Gran Vía
Loewe (gifts)
26 Serrano
Domo (porcelain)
22 Serrano
Hispano-Inglèsa (porcelain)
13 Ayala
Loewe (baggage & travel accessories)
26 Serrano
Casa y Jardin (interior decorating)
21–32 Padella
Ibelart (interior decorating)
17–30 Fernando el Santo
Mallorca (food and beverages)
59 Velazquez
Alva Rez Comez (perfumery)
14 Serrano
Bravo (shoes)
42 Serrano
Eureka (shoes)
6 Serrano

THE BEST OF ART
Aele   (contemporary art)
28 Claudio Coello, Tel. 2 75 66 79
Aizpuru, Juana, de   (contemporary
art) 44 Barquillo, Tel. 4 10 55 61
Buades   (contemporary art)
43 Claudio Coello, Tel. 4 31 42 82
Mordó, Juana   (contemporary art)
7 Villanueva, Tel. 4 31 05 28/4 35 84 42
Theo   (contemporary art)
2 Marqués de la Ensenada, Tel. 4 10 26 51
Tórculo   (contemporary art)
17 Claudio Coello, Tel. 2 75 86 86
Vijande   (contemporary art)
65 Nuñez de Balboa, Tel. 4 35 80 25

The City

›For many visitors to Málaga the city's raison d'être is its international airport and the only view they have of the city is through their rear-view mirror as they head south along the Carretera de Cádiz, the erstwhile Via Augusta, pausing to adjust their sunglasses before accelerating through Torremolinos in a cloud of dust on the last stage of the Mykonos – Monte-Carlo – Marbella trail. Indeed the businessman whose work brings him to the largest city on the Costa del Sol, whether for the town's industries – machinery, chemicals, oil refineries, shipbuilding, or cotton, or to attend one of the scientific congresses at the new convention centre, may be tempted to follow the Suntan Society's example without pausing to consider the counter-attractions of this ancient metropolis. More than three thousand years before Prince Alfonso von Hohenlohe put the fishing village surrounding the Puento Romano on the map for the Cartier crowd, Málaga was a Phoenician trading centre and port. A cavalcade of nations and civilizations has passed through the city since then – Carthaginians and Romans, Visigoths and Moors, leaving traces of their cultures in the ruined amphitheatre, the Alcazaba or the Gibraltaro fortresses and turning it into a kaleidoscopic microcosm of Spanish history and culture, best seen in the rabbit-warren of narrow streets surrounding the fine Baroque cathedral or the Plaza Constitución. Here whitewashed stone houses gay with flower-filled window-boxes jostle with buildings whose delicate tracery reveals their Arab ancestry, broken up by balconies and backyards where washing hangs heavy in the midday heat and only a stray cat, a mad dog or the occasional Englishman disturbs the sacred siesta calm. In this atmosphere of sun-drunk lethargy decisions may best be left until the day after mañana, but the cool of evening brings a new vitality to the little taverns, restaurants and tascas where, over a gazpacho and a glass of the eponymous, sweet, full-bodied wine meetings, encounters and assignments take place in an atmosphere of Mediterranean camaraderie always tinged with that flamenco passion and melancholic pathos which characterize the Andalusian temperament. The changing moods of the corridas are echoed in the latter-day dramas acted out in the seafront discothèques or in the sub-tropical public gardens of the town with greater intensity than along the coast. Marbella shows the world the sunny countenance of Spain. Sunshine, sea, sand, Ambre Solaire and a hint of Diorissimo overlay the scent of orange-blossom, and the brilliantly coloured local costumes at the tablaos de flamenco are matched by the Armani casuals and Mic Mac sundresses of the bronzed Adonises and the cosmopolitan butterflies in the audience. Go to Marbella, of course, for the sun, the fun and the social scene, but if you want a taste of the Spain which nurtured Pablo Picasso, you must go to Málaga, the ›darling of poets and the gods.‹

Founded: ca. 1200 B.C., as a Phoenician settlement.

Far-reaching events: 600–500 B.C. – major trade centre for minerals and fish; 2nd century B.C. – the Romans follow the Greeks and Carthaginians as rulers; 571 A.D. – invasion of the Visigoths; 711 – the Arabs conquer the city and remain in power for some 800 years, building palaces and fortresses and making Málaga the centre of their Moorish empire; 1487 – Spanish Christians take control; 16th–17th century – increasing prosperity as a result of Spain's colonial policy; 1936–39 – a *falange* bastion during the Civil War; 1955 – rapid development as a tourist centre.

Population: 500,000.

Postal code: E-29000   **Telephone code:** 52

Climate: Mediterranean; mild winters and long, hot summers; little rain.

Best time to visit: February to June; September to November.

Calendar of events: *Great Riders Parade* (5 Jan) – equestrian show; *Winter Festival* (Jan/Feb) – tennis, golf, riding, rowing and shooting contests; *Semana Santa* (Holy Week, Mar/Apr) – processions, liturgical celebrations and passion plays; *Bullfights* – the great traditional ones are held on Easter Sunday and Corpus Christi Day; *Evening Procession in Honour of the Holy Virgin* (16 Jul) – along the coast; *Carmen Darma Festival* (15–20 Jul); *Velaiha* (Jul) – folkloristic festival of St. John; *Memorial Services for the Expulsion of the Moors* (27 Jul); *Ballet Festival* (Aug) – in the caves of Nerja; *Summer Festival* (Aug) – with bullfights; *Festivales de España* (Aug).

Best views of the city: from the *Gibralfaro* and *Alcazaba* fortresses; from the *cathedral.*

Historical and modern sights: *Cathedral* (16th century) – Renaissance, with magnificent choir stalls; the Moorish fortress *Alcazaba* (11th century) – former palace of Arabian kings, with a museum of Moorish art; *El Sagrario* (16th century) – late Gothic-Isabellan church with beautiful portal; *Gibralfaro* (14th century) – castle cum lighthouse and citadel; *Roman Theatre* (1st century, B.C.); *Palace of the Archbishop* – with a Baroque façade and a magnificent, garden-like inner courtyard; *Museo de Bellas Artes* – in the Italian marble palace of the Count of Buenavista, containing works of Picasso and Murillo.

Special attractions: *a hydrofoil trip* to Tangiers or Ceuta; one night in *Marbella.*

Airport: Málaga-García Morato, AGP; Tel.: 31 19 44; 8 km/5 miles.

The Headquarters

GUADALMAR

Urbanización Guadalmar
E–29004 Málaga
Telephone: 31 90 00
Telex: 77 099 himal
General Manager: Carmelo Doña
Number of rooms: 195 (10 suites)
Price range: Ptas 4,500 (single)
    Ptas 6,500–6,950 (double)
    Ptas 11,450–12,665 (suite)
Credit cards: AE, DC, EC, Visa
Location: 5 km/3 miles from city centre, in the residential area between Málaga and Torremolinos
Built: 1972
Style: modern
Hotel amenities: swimming pool, car park, boutique, hairdresser, house doctor, air conditioning, bar/discothèque; tennis
Room amenities: radio, balcony, terrace, tv
Bathroom amenities: bathrobe, hairdrier, some with separate shower
Room service: 7.30 a.m.–23.30/11.30 p.m.
Laundry/dry cleaning: same day
Conference rooms: 1 (up to 175 persons)
Bar: ›La Corrida‹ (6.00/a.m.–1.30 a.m.)
Restaurant: ›La Bodega‹ (13.00/1.00 p.m.–15.30/3.30 p.m. and 19.30/7.30 p.m.–22.30/10.30 p.m.)

In a city such as Malaga it is often difficult to draw a clear boundary between the realms of business and pleasure. The trappings of industrialization – factories, oil refineries and chemical works – are in evidence, it is true, but the countenance which this ›earthly paradise‹ presents to the outside world is a joyous amalgam of sun, sea, scenic beauty and that infectiously happy -go-lucky nonchalance combined with a hint of melancholy so characteristic of the Mediterranean. In such an atmosphere it is appropriate that even a hotel as admirably suited to the needs of visiting businessmen as the Guadalmar should have a seaside location and an ambience appropriate to a holiday resort. Situated in a newly-erected residential area between Málaga and Torremolinos, the plain modern concrete façade is relieved by balconies from which guests can overlook the lawns surrounding the swimming pool. Sailing and windsurfing are available on the beach by the hotel for those who prefer to be active whilst acquiring a tan after working hours. The hotel's interior is contemporary with local touches, the bedrooms are well equipped and the food in the restaurant a mixture of Spanish and international cuisine. Comprehensive conference facilities and the delights of the seaside are at your disposal – in short, for a business trip to Málaga, the Guadalmar is the hotel of choice.

The Hideaway

PUENTE ROMANO

Carretera de Cádiz
E–Marbella (56 km/40 miles)
Telephone: (52) 77 01 00
Telex: 77 399 puro
Owner: Prince Alfonso von Hohenlohe and associates
General Manager: Willi Dietz
Affiliation/Reservation System: The Leading Hotels of the World
Number of rooms: 200
Price range: Ptas 11,500–43,000
Credit cards: AE, CB, DC, EC, MC, Visa
Location: west of Marbella
Built: 1978
Style: Andalusian
Hotel amenities: drugstore, sauna, beach club, car park, swimming pool, tennis courts, stadium
Room service: 24 hours
Conference rooms: up to 150 persons
Bars: ›Cascada‹ Piano Bar
Restaurants: ›El Puente‹; ›La Tasca‹
Nightclub: ›Régine's‹

This other Eden, Paradise Regained lies in a shady oasis of palm trees on the beach at Marbella, one hour's drive along the coastal road from Málaga. Next to his famous Marbella Club, for years the most prestigious resort amidst the sleepy fishing hamlets of the as yet undiscovered Costa del Sol, maecenas Prince Alfonso von Hohenlohe has created a hideaway Elysium which is all the more enchanting for being earth-bound. Puente Romano is a luxurious re-creation of an Andalusian village. Whitewashed, russet-tiled houses grouped around the swimming pools cascade down the hillside towards the sea amidst lush flower-bedecked tropical gardens of bougainvillea, oleander, jasmine and hibiscus, through which a stream meanders underneath the trees, criss-crossed by bridges, footpaths, and archways. The two hundred apartments – most with very private balconies for séparée sunbathing – set new standards of individuality and taste amongst the peseta-paring production-line hotels which dot the Iberian shore; marble floors, Moroccan rugs and boldly-patterned fabrics, plus service à la perfection, Spanish style. The ruins of the eponymous Roman bridge separate this haven of peace and privilege from the commercial area, where the daytime focal point is the buffet lunch at the beach pavilion. As night falls and the mini-village reawakens from the somnolence of the afternoon siesta, attention shifts to the seafood specialities of the El Puente and La Tasca, preceded by a Campari at the Cascada piano bar, with the private outpost of Régine's as postlude for those who choose to dance the night away. In between, a multiplicity of sports, from tennis at Bjorn Borg's school, to deep-sea fishing, vie with mañana philosophy and the Mediterranean sun to encourage the upper echelon managers and jet-set celebrities to procrastinate a little longer in this abode of the blest.

Lunch

TABERNA DEL PINTOR
Maestranza
Telephone: 21 53 15
Owner/Manager: Trinidad Lopez Merida/Jose Antonio Sanchez Lopez
Closed: Sunday
Open: 12.40/p.m.–16.00/4 p.m. and 20.00/8 p.m.–24.00/12 p.m.
Cuisine: local and French
Chef de cuisine: Luis Zamora
Specialities: charcoal-grilled meats; salad of sweetcorn and palm hearts (ensalada de maíz y palmitos); mushroom and avocado salad (ensalada de aguacate con champignones); sirloin of beef; entrecôte steaks
Location: a ten-minute walk from the centre of town
Setting: rustic-style dining room with German décor
Amenities: private dining rooms (35–65 persons); bar; air conditioning
Atmosphere: stylish; rather formal
Clientèle: local Haute Bourgeoisie with cause for celebration, plus tourists from Oslo to Osnabrück
Dress: jacket and tie
Service: friendly and welcoming; supervised by Antonio Sanchez Lopez
Reservations: necessary (pets permitted)
Price range: medium
Credit cards: AE, DC, Euro, Visa

Lunch

ANTONIO MARTÍN
Paseo Marítimo
Telephone: 21 10 18/22 21 13
Owner/Manager: Alvaro Martin Segura
Closed: Sunday evening (in winter only)
Open: 13.00/1 p.m.–16.00/4 p.m. and 20.00/8 p.m.–24.00/12 p.m.
Cuisine: local
Specialities: fritura malagueña; oxtail (rabo de toro)
Location: near the harbour (puerto)
Setting: seafront restaurant; dining room furnished in elegant style; open-air dining on terrace with panoramic view of the sea
Amenities: two bars; private dining rooms; air conditioning; car park
Atmosphere: fashionably chic but not chi-chi
Clientèle: favourite rendezvous for local artists, actors, writers and bullfighters
Dress: nothing too outrageous or outlandish
Service: efficiently supervised by maître Francisco Sanchez
Reservations: advisable
Price range: medium
Credit cards: AE, DC, Visa

Dinner

CASA PEDRO
Plaza de El Palo (5 km/3 miles)
Telephone: 29 00 13
Owner/Manager: Lorenzo Martinez
Closed: Monday (except public holidays); November
Open: 13.00/1 p.m.–16.15/4.15 p.m. and 20.00/8 p.m.–23.45/11.45 p.m.
Cuisine: local and international
Specialities: sardine kebabs (espetón de sardinas); fritura malagueña; ›servana‹ (fish with ham and mushrooms); paella
Location: at El Palo; 5 km (3 miles) north-east of Málaga
Setting: typical seafront restaurant; view of the Mediterranean
Amenities: car park
Atmosphere: friendly
Clientèle: mixed; resident businessmen and holidaymakers from Hamburg to Halifax
Dress: casual
Service: friendly
Reservations: necessary (especially on Sundays)
Price range: medium
Credit cards: AE, DC, Visa

Dinner

LA HACIENDA
Carretera de Cádiz, km 200 (Las Chapas), Marbella (50 km/30 miles)
Telephone: (9 52) 83 12 67/83 11 16
Affiliations: Relais et Châteaux (Relais Gourmand)
Owner/Managers: Paul and Thérèse Schiff
Closed: Monday all year round; Tuesday (except during August)
Open: 13.00/1 p.m.–15.30/3.30 p.m. and 20.30/8.30 p.m.–23.30/11.30 p.m.
Cuisine: Belgian and local; ›au goût du marché‹
Chef de cuisine: Paul Schiff (Premio Nacional de Gastronomía)
Specialities: green gazpacho; sweetcorn and cockle crêpes; caille flambée; duck's liver with crisp-fried pork (chicharros) in Muscatel; escalope of duck with figs; red mullet with rosemary; roast partridge with vine leaves; sorbets; puff pastry desserts
Location: on Sierra Las Chapas; on the road from Málaga to Marbella; 50 km (30 miles) from Málaga; 11 km (7 miles) from Marbella
Setting: whitewashed villa in a lush garden; dining room with beamed ceiling; Andalusian rustic style in white and terra-

cotta; domed glassed-in patio offering a panoramic view of the Mediterranean and – on a clear day – the African continent

Amenities: open-air dining in garden; air conditioning; car park

Atmosphere: a haven of good food and gracious living

Clientèle: gourmet businessmen tired of Málaga, plus Marbella's social élite; sheikhs, starlets, Swiss financiers and Spanish noblemen

Dress: boutique chic to designer original

Service: under the expert direction of maître Miguel Estrugo

Reservations: recommended (chihuahuas and cocker spaniels allowed, but no Great Danes or greyhounds)

Price range: fairly expensive

Credit cards: AE, DC, Visa, ICB

Lunch

LA MERIDIANA
Camino de la Cruz, (La Lomas)
Marbella (60 km/38 miles)
Telephone: 52/77 61 90
Owner/Manager: Paolo Guirelli
Closed: lunchtime in August; November 20–December 20
Open: 13.30/1.30 p.m.–15.30/3.30 p.m. and 20.30/8.30 p.m.–1.00/a.m. August 21.00/9 p.m.–1.00/a.m.
Cuisine: ›au goût du marché‹
Chef de cuisine: Luis Hernandez
Specialities: goose liver pâté; garlic soup; sweetcorn pancakes filled with quail; roast duck with cherries; casserole of shrimps with wild mushrooms and truffles; shin of veal with saffron; calves' sweetbreads with grapefruit
Location: 1 km (5/8 mile) above the mosque in Marbella; 60 km (38 miles) from Málaga
Setting: flat-roofed modern pinkish brick-built house; a blend of Moorish and contemporary architecture; comfortable lounge-bar in shades of red and beige; collection of abstract paintings; dining room with tiled floor, crystal chandeliers, chrome chairs and classical statues
Amenities: open-air dining on roof-top terrace; air conditioning; car park
Atmosphere: très à la mode
Clientèle: resident fans of Paolo Guirelli's skills as restaurateur from his days at ›Don Leone‹ in Puerto Banus, plus growing numbers of visitors attracted by this relatively new but glittering addition to the Andalusian culinary scene
Dress: appropriately elegant, exclusive and expensive (or at least expensive-looking)
Service: friendly white-jacketed waiters
Reservations: essential – preferably 2–3 days in advance during the season
Price range: fairly expensive
Credit cards: AE, DC, Euro, Visa

Dinner

LA FONDA
9 Plaza Santo Cristo
Marbella (60 km/38 miles)
Telephone: 77 25 12/77 25 16
Owner/Manager: Gustavo Horcher Weber
Closed: lunchtime every day; Sunday
Open: 20.00/8 p.m.–24.00/12 p.m.
Cuisine: local and Central European
Chef de cuisine: José Ramos Torres
Specialities: broccoli mould with shrimp sauce; vegetable pâté with pepper sauce; sole with clam sauce; veal Berlin-style; pancake with sardine mousse; ragôut of calves' kidneys in mustard sauce with home-made pasta (Spätzle); Viennese strudel; cheesecake
Location: in the heart of the old town
Setting: historic building; attractive Nouvelle Epoque dining room with open fireplace
Amenities: summer patio for al fresco dining; garden; car park
Atmosphere: beguiling amalgam of Mediterranean romantic joie-de-vivre and Central European charm
Clientèle: homesick Hungarian aristocrats; conservative German connoisseurs of good food; Málaga's Beau Monde and Marbella's suntan set
Dress: Armani and Mic Mac to Ted Lapidus
Service: impeccably directed by maître d'hotel Ramón Ballesteros Ayerza
Reservations: recommended
Price range: fairly expensive
Credit cards: AE, DC

Dinner

PUENTE ROMANO
Marbella (60 km/38 miles)
Telephone: 52/4 77 01 00
Owner/Manager: Hung Kui Lee
Closed: lunchtime every day
Open: 20.00/8 p.m. – the last guest has left
Cuisine: Chinese
Chef de cuisine: Simón Padilla
Specialities: prawns in spring roll wrappers; spare ribs in chili sauce; Cantonese roast duck; fried noodles
Location: in the garden suburb of Puente Romano in Marbella, 60 km (38 miles) from Malaga
Setting: luxurious but uncluttered modern dining room and bar; striking wood ceiling, white walls and tiled floor; patio doors leading to lush sub-tropical garden and swimming pool (floodlit at night); well-spaced immaculately-laid tables
Amenities: bar where ›Tiger‹ Lee serves a colourful array of exotic cocktails before or after the meal; open-air dining on terrace
Atmosphere: understated finesse; pre-

sided over by the genial and courteous
Mr. Lee, founder and erstwhile proprie-
tor of the original ›Tiger Lee‹ in London
Clientèle: discriminating lovers of Canto-
nese cuisine from Manchester, Milwau-
kee, Manila and Melbourne
Dress: rather elegant but not necessarily
formal
Service: Mediterranean charm and orien-
tal hospitality; hot towels before the meal
and a rose for each lady afterwards
Reservations: recommended (no dogs)
Price range: moderate by Marbella stand-
ards
Credit cards: AE, DC, Visa, Master Card,
EL

Café

EL GALLO DE INDIAS
2 Canovas del Castillo
Telephone: 22 78 42
Owner/Manager: Francisco de Besa
Closed: never
Open: 8.30/a.m.–2.00/a.m.
Location: opposite the castle (Castillo)
Setting: dining room with furnishings in
shades of green and blue; open-air dining
on terrace overlooking a small garden
Amenities: weekly changing lunch menu
as well as drinks and snacks; private din-
ing room (60 persons); bar; air condition-
ing; car park
Atmosphere: distinguished but not daunt-
ing
Clientèle: local crème de la crème and
discerning visitors
Service: good

Shopping

EVERYTHING UNDER ONE ROOF
El Corte Inglès   Alameda Principal

FOR HIM
Rally   2 Plaza de las Flores

FOR HER
Rocamar   3 Marques de Larios

BEAUTY & HAIR
Benjamin   2 Plaza Marina

JEWELLERY
Aurelio Marcos   2 Marques de Larios

LOCAL SPECIALITIES
Menfis (women's fashion)
15 Plaza Constitución
Cortes España (men's fashion)
24 Calle Granada
La gran boutique (men & women's fashion) 25 Calle Sevilla
Huguette's (children's fashion)
8 Calle Arango
Ruiz, Pepe (leather fashion)
12 Sanchez Pastor
Peleteria Salido (furs)
4 a. Principal
Negrete Montiel (books)
43 Calle Granada
Orly (gifts)
10 Molina Larios
Exposicion, La (porcelain)
12 Calle Granada

The City

Love and death, jealousy and violence, even sex and crime could not have a more sentimental and dramatic stage than Carmen's cradle, the capital of Andalusia – where self-
affirmation and lethargy can so beautifully explode into masochism and theatrical ag-
gression. Home town of Velázquez, Pacheco, Zurbarán and Murillo, port of origin for
the New World expeditions of Amerigo Vespucci and Magellan, playground of Figaro
and Don Juan and dream-come-true for fantasy pilgrims by the dozen and culture tourists by the million, Seville fulfills every dream of all of her visitors. Fourth largest city
of Spain, largest inland harbour on the River Guadalquivir, market place of agriculture
and centre of industries such as textiles, food processing and metallurgy (all assembled
on the ›other‹ side of the water, in Triana, well away from the historic centre, the business area and the romantic plazas), Seville magnetizes even the men of commerce and
the visitors to the April Feria. It weaves its spell of enchantment with its cathedral
(third largest in the world after St. Peter and St. Paul), a fortress of high Gothic grandeur, with the Alcázar (the nearest substitute if you don't reach Granada or Córdoba),
a brilliant example of Mudejar architecture and terraced gardens, with the fabled Santa
Cruz Quarter – the cachet of minute mews adorned with wrought iron grills, flower-
filled patios oozing ›flamenco‹ mood and with the omnipresent folklore, coming to a
kaleidoscopic crescendo in the Semana Santa – one of the events not to miss in life.
With its glorious past alive in every corner (built by Hercules, fortified by Caesar, embellished by Yacoub Al Mansur and freed for Christian refinement by Ferdinand III of
Castile – and saved by General Queipo de Llano from destruction in the Civil War),
with 300 days of azure skies and ›music in the air‹ and with the exotic beauty of the city,
the surroundings and the people – it's hard not to invent some kind of business in order
to come to Sevilla – La Maravilla.

Founded: by the Carthaginians; Sevilla (Spanish).

Far-reaching events: 45 B.C. – Caesar fortifies the first Roman city outside Italy, Sevilla; 411 – the Vandals drive out the Romans and are themselves driven out in 441 by
the Visigoths; 712 – conquest by the Moors; 1248 – Ferdinand III takes the city and
resides here as King of Spain; Seville the administrative centre of Spain's colonial empire in the next centuries, and the port of departure for Amerigo Vespucci and Ferdinand Magellan; 1771 – decline in the city's importance following the silting up of the
Guadalquivir; 1803–13 – centre of resistance to Napoleon; 1936 – Franco's troops begin their conquest of Spain in Andalusia; post 1945 – re-dredging of the deep-water
channel re-opens the harbour and paves the way for industrial expansion.

Population: 660,000.

Postal code: E-4100   **Telephone code:** 54

Climate: mild, because of its proximity to the coast; hot during the summer months.

Calendar of events: *Three Kings* (Jan) – procession through the city in honour of the
Wise Men of the East; *Semana Santa*/Holy Week (Mar/Apr) – the last week of Lent is
Seville's biggest festival with processions and street celebrations; *Feria de Abril* (Apr) –
parades, illuminations, bullfights and dancing; *Romeria de Rocio* (May) – pilgrimage
to Rocio; *Mayo Musical Hispanlense* (May) – classical music festival; *Corpus Christi
Procession* (Jun/Jul); *Festival of the ›Virgen de los Reyes‹* (15 Aug) – in honour of the
city's patron saint; *Bullfights* (Sep).

Fairs and exhibitions: *VIBEXPO* (Mar) – wine and beverage fair; *MOBILARIA* (Mar)
– furniture and machinery; *FERIA DE ANTIQUEDADES* (Apr) – antiques fair; *FE-
RIA DE MUESTRAS IBERICOAMERICANA* (Apr) – industrial fair; *AGROMEDI-
TERRANEA* (Oct) – national exhibition and fair for the agricultural industry; *SANI-
TARIA* (Nov) – hospital and surgical supplies, pharmaceuticals; *FLORANDALUCIA*
(Nov) – measuring and testing systems; *EXPOARTA* (Dec) – Andalusian handicrafts

Historical sights: *Cathedral* (15th century) – Gothic, the third largest in Christendom;
Giralda (12th century) – formerly a minaret, a landmark of the city; *Alcázar* (1350–69)
– Mudejar palace based on the Alhambra; *Barrio de Santa-Cruz* (17th century) – noblemen's houses and gardens in the former Jewish quarter of town; *Fabrica de Tobacos*
– the old tobacco factory, the largest building in Spain, next to the Escorial – and the
scene of Act I of ›Carmen‹; *Torre del Oro* (13th century) – tower of the old city wall,
reputedly plated with gold ceramic in earlier times; *Santa Anna* (13th century) – the
oldest church, in the ›Triana‹ district, named for local son the Roman Emperor Trajan;
La Magdalena – grand Baroque church; *El Salvador* – the second largest cathedral in
the city; the Renaissance church of the *Old University* – a pantheon of Seville's most
famous sons; *Casa Lonja* (16th century) – built by the architect of the Escorial; *Casa de
Pilatos* – prototype of an Andalusian palace; *City Hall* (1534); *Fine Arts Museum* – in a
former friary – Golden Period paintings

Modern sights: *Calle de las Sierpes* – the main street; *Galle de Feria* – flea market;
Parque de Maria Luisa – the most popular park

Special attractions: Seville en fête, from the *Three Kings Procession* to *Holy Week* to the
April Fair to the *Romeria de Rocio*; a *bullfight*; a *tablaos de flamenco*; an evening on the
Plaza Nueva and a night in *Santa Cruz*; getting locked in the *Giralda* at night.

Important companies with their headquarters in the city: La Cruz del Campo (brewery);
Sevillana de Electricidad (electrical energy).

Airport: Seville-San Pablo, SVQ; Tel.: 51 65 98; 14 km/9 miles.

The Headquarters

ALFONSO XIII

2 San Fernando
E–41004 Seville
Telephone: 22 28 50
Telex: 72 725 has
Owning company: Hoteles de Lujo
Director: Manuel Martinez Cornejo
General Manager: Mr. Martinez
Number of rooms: 149 (21 suites)
Price range: Ptas. 9,000–11,000 (single)
　　　　　　 Ptas. 12,000–15,000 (double)
　　　　　　 Ptas. 33,000–38,000 (suite)
Credit cards: AE, DC, EC, MC, Visa
Location: central
Built: 1929 (recently renovated)
Hotel amenities: car park, garage, shopping arcade, courtyard, garden, swimming pool
Room amenities: air conditioning, tv, mini-bar
Bathroom amenities: separate shower, bidet, bathrobe, telephone
Room service: 24 hours
Laundry/dry cleaning: same day
Conference rooms: 8 (up to 500 persons); banqueting rooms (up to 1,200 persons)
Bars: two
Restaurants: ›Itálica‹, international cuisine; ›Real‹

The palm-fringed palace at the junction of two of Seville's principal boulevards a few flamenco steps from the former royal residence of the Alcázar, is – like the Plaza Espana – a relic from the international fair of 1929. Alfonso XIII bears the name of the last pre-Franco King of Spain, who officially dedicated this distinctive auberge and whose grandson, the present monarch, reopened it after five years of extensive renovations in 1979. Its position as the headquarters in the city has been unassailable ever since. The décor is inimitable; an unashamedly mock-Moorish palacio of grandiose proportions, the hotel is a showcase for the art of Andalusian Spain. The grand entrance-hall is built cloister-like around a central fountain courtyard. Monumental pillars, inlaid tiles, colonnades and intricate sculpturing stamp this latter-day Alhambra of hôtellerie. The bedrooms are large and luxurious enough for the procession of businessmen and prominence. The former are met by facilities for the most regal of conferences; the latter find it an ideal base for the exploration of this most Spanish of cities. The original dining room, with its lustres, frescoes and panelled ceiling, is festive enough for the most dignified of banquets; the cuisine of the less formal Itálica, however, serves as the city's most attractive quick lunch between boardroom and bullfight. The staff is at par with the overall standard of the regal house. The Alfonso XIII is the liveliest museum of the Belle Epoque à l'espagnole – a tradition in the town and an exuberant testimony to the variegated history of Spain.

The Hideaway

OROMANA

E Alcala de Guadaira, Sevilla
(14 km/9 miles)
Telephone: 70 08 04
Owner/General Manager: Francisco
Martinez Ramires
Number of rooms: 30
Price range: Ptas 4,000 (single)
             Ptas 5,000 (double)
Credit cards: AE, Visa, EC
Location: 14 km/9 miles outside Seville
Built: 1929
Style: Moresque
Hotel amenities: air conditioning, garden,
car park, garage (no pets allowed)
Room service: from 7.00/a.m. to
23.00/11.00 p.m.
Laundry/dry cleaning: next day
Conference rooms: for up to 200 persons
Sports: swimming pool
Bar: ›Los Pinares‹ (8.00/a.m.–11.00/a.m.
and 13.00/1.00 p.m.–15.30/3.30 p.m.),
cafeteria/snack-bar
Restaurant: ›Oromana‹: Rafael de la Fu-
ente (maître), Antonia Roman (chef de
cuisine), traditional Spanish cuisine.

*Living – or staying – in Seville resembles in
some respects taking up residence in the
middle of an epic film set. It's photogenic,
facinating, festive and frequently tumultu-
ously noisy; small wonder, then, that visitors of a more contemplative disposition in
search of peace and quiet should take refuge in the Hotel Oromana. Perched on a
hillside a short drive from the city, this luxurious relais provides a tranquil rural retreat in which devotees can relax and enjoy
the charm of the Andalusian countryside.
Standing in park-like woodland near the
River Guadaira, the colonnades of the red
-roofed white-washed building reflect the
centuries-old Moorish influence in this part
of Spain. Thanks to the thick walls and
marble floors – not to mention the air conditioning, of course – the ferocity of the
midday sun is kept at bay throughout the
elegant intérieur, from the comfortable
bedrooms to the vaulted lounge. Most
guests find a gentle stroll through the gardens or a few lengths of the swimming pool
the ideal way to work up an appetite for the
fine local cuisine served in the restaurant.
In fact, thanks to the friendly and caring
staff, the Oromana provides everything
you're likely to need for a lazy weekend –
or a week – away from it all.*

Lunch

LA ALBAHACA
12 Plaza Santa Cruz
Telephone: 22 07 14
Owner/Manager: Don Bartolome Sanchez Coto
Closed: Sunday
Open: 13.00/1 p.m.–16.00/4 p.m.; 20.00/8 p.m.–12.00/a.m.
Cuisine: regional and international
Chef de cuisine: Enrique Lozano Heredia
Specialities: according to season and market availability; fish dishes; sole with oranges; mixed salads white garlic (ajo blanco); desserts
Location: near the French Consulate
Setting: classic; renovated patrician townhouse; three dining rooms furnished in the style of a Sevillian nobleman's residence; half-tiled walls, period accessoires and original paintings
Amenities: air conditioning; private dining rooms (up to 60 persons) bar; outdoor dining on terrace
Atmosphere: classic in the Spanish idiom; peaceful and coolly relaxing
Clientèle: cross-section of hommes d'affaires, hommes de lettres, artists, actors and politicians
Dress: elegantly informal
Service: helpful
Reservations: advisable (no pets)
Price range: medium
Credit cards: AE, DC, Visa, Euro, Access, Mastercard

Lunch

LA DORADA
6 Virgen de Aguas Santas
Telephone: 45 51 00
Owner/Manager: José Felix Cabeza
Closed: Sunday evening; July 15th – August 15th
Open: 13.00/1 p.m.–16.30/4.30 p.m. and 20.00/8 p.m.–2.30/a.m.
Cuisine: local
Chef de cuisine: Antonia Bueno
Specialities: seafood; fritura malagena; flan de la casa; soufflé au chocolat
Location: central
Setting: dining room decorated in nautical style
Amenities: air conditioning; two dining rooms (130–270 persons)
Atmosphere: lively and cheerful, but stylish
Clientèle: mostly young, fashionable, self-confident and successful
Dress: elegant to informal
Service: very quick and efficient; supervised by a maître in the uniform of a yachting captain
Reservations: essential
Price range: moderately expensive
Credit cards: AE, Visa

Dinner

SAN MARCO
6 Cuna
Telephone: 21 24 40
Owner/Manager: the Ramacciotti brothers
Closed: Sunday; August
Open: 13.00/1 p.m.–16.00/4 p.m.; 20.00/8 p.m.–24.00/12 p.m.
Cuisine: Franco-Italian and local
Chef de cuisine: Ansano Ramacciotti
Specialities: gazpacho; baked gilt-head bream (dorada); home-made pasta dishes prepared before the eyes of the customer; lasagne; noodles (tallarines) with truffles; poularde with mushrooms; tarts, sorbets and ice-creams
Location: central
Setting: historic nobleman's town palais; spacious dining room and exceptionally attractive glassed-in patio; marble pillars; wrought iron screen; classical statues and reliefs
Amenities: air conditioning
Atmosphere: chic but not chi-chi; comfortably à la mode
Clientèle: expense-account gourmets; top industrialists, bankers, brokers and bullfighters
Dress: fairly elegant
Service: charmingly hospitable; directed by Angelo Ramacciotti
Reservations: advisable
Price range: medium
Credit cards: AE, DC, Visa

Lunch

OR-IZA
61 Betis
Telephone: 27 95 85
Owner/Manager/Chef de cuisine: José Maria Egaña
Closed: Sunday; August
Open: 13.00/1 p.m.–16.30/4.30 p.m. and 21.00/9 p.m.–0.30/12.30/p.m.
Chef de cuisine: José Maria Egaña
Cuisine: local and nouvelle
Specialities: squid; haddock with clams; goose liver with truffles
Location: off the Plaza de Cuba; near the San Telmo bridge (Puente de San Telmo)
Setting: on one of Seville's loveliest boulevards, lined with orange trees
Amenities: air conditioning
Atmosphere: one of the brightest lights on the Sevillian culinary horizon
Clientèle: comfortable mixture of Andalusians en fête and en famille, discerning company directors and men-in-the-street
Dress: elegant
Service: smiling and friendly
Reservations: advisable
Price range: fairly expensive
Credit cards: AE, DC, Euro, Visa

Dinner

MESON DEL MORO
6 y 10, Mesón del Moro
Telephone: 21 43 90
Owner/Manager: Domingo Romero
Closed: Sunday; January
Open: 13.00/1 p.m.–16.00/4 p.m. and
20.00/8 p.m.–24.00/12 p.m.
Cuisine: local (traditional and modern)
and international
Chef de cuisine: Manuel Gomez
Specialities: fish from Punta Umbria;
Andalusian-style swordfish (pez espada a
la andaluza); Andalusian-style symphony of shellfish (zarzuela de mariscosa
a la andaluza); salads; chicken a la sevillana; quail (codórnices) ›Mesón del
Moro‹; Arabian-style desserts including
nuts and dates with honey and cream
Location: in the Barrio de Santa Cruz district of town
Setting: in a 12th-century Moorish-style
building which once housed thermal
baths; dining rooms on three floors decorated with bullfighting posters and paintings by the well-known Moroccan artist
Ben Yessef; Sevillian-style patio
Amenities: air conditioning
Atmosphere: a charming and nostalgic
amalgam of Andalusian charm and Ara-
bian exoticism reflecting the colourful
history of the town
Clientèle: Seville's High Society and
Haute Bourgeoisie plus discerning tour-
ists attracted by the ambience almost as
much as the food
Dress: boutique chic to designer elegant
Service: friendly and welcoming
Reservations: essential in springtime (no
dogs)
Price range: rather expensive
Credit cards: DC, Euro, Visa

Dinner

REAL VENTA DE ANTEQUERA
PLAZA DE TOROS
(SUPERRESTAURANT)
2 Avenida de Jerez
Telephone: 69 06 60
Owner/Manager: Domingo Romero
Closed: November–February
Open: 10.00/a.m.–24.00/12 p.m.
Cuisine: local traditional and interna-
tional
Chef de cuisine: Manuel Soria
Specialities: Fish a la marinera; venison;
partridge a la sevillana; avocado salad;
endive salad
Location: a short walk (or a shorter taxi
ride) from the city centre
Setting: large traditional Sevillian res-
taurant offering equestrian displays, pa-
rade of bulls, flamenco (prior reservation
only), carriage rides; bullfighting arena

Amenities: private dining rooms (24–750
persons); bar; open-air dining on terrace;
air conditioning; car park
Atmosphere: informal but not imper-
sonal; stylish in spite of its size
Clientèle: bullfighters, businessmen, bar-
risters and bankers – plus a sprinkling of
tourists from Porto to Passau
Dress: as you like it (as long as they will
like you)
Service: welcoming and courteous
Reservations: essential (dogs allowed)
Price range: rather expensive
Credit cards: AE

Meeting Point

CASA ROMAN
1 Plaza de los Venerables
Telephone: 22 84 83
Owner/Manager: Roman Castro Medina
Closed: Sunday
Open: 8.00/a.m. to 15.00/3 p.m. and
17.30/5.30 p.m. to 2.00/a.m.; Sundays:
10.00/a.m. to 15.00/3 p.m.
Location: in the Barrio Santa Cruz district of town
Setting: tiny; typical Andalusian bar of-
fering a good selection of snacks (tapas)
to go with Valdepenas de la casa
Amenities: delicatessen shop renowned
for the quality of its ham and cheeses
Atmosphere: as popular amongst the
town's permanent residents as amongst
visitors on a tapa-tour (the Sevillan equiv-
alent of a pub-crawl)
Clientèle: journalists, matadors, torea-
dors, poets, painters and those who con-
sider themselves as such
Service: hospitable
Price range: moderate
Dress: légère
Reservations: impracticable (no pets)
Credit cards: not accepted

Shopping

EVERYTHING UNDER ONE ROOF
Corte Inglès, El   10 Plaza de Duque

FOR HIM
Elite   7 Santa Maria Gracia

FOR HER
Tip–Top, Boutique   2 Plaza de Cuba

BEAUTY & HAIR
Koupas   22 Bailen

JEWELLERY
Ignacio   63 Sierpes

LOCAL SPECIALITIES
Stilo (men's fashion)
42 Sierpes
Mi ropa (children's fashion)
13 Rioja
Loewe Hermanos (leather fashion)
12 Plaza Nueva
Akissy (furs)
2 Plaza Duque Victoria
Libreria San Pablo (books)
17 Calle Sierpes
Sajonia (gifts)
18 O'Donnell
Dolmen (porcelain)
4 Gral. Moscardo
Velasco Dominguez (baggage & travel
accessories)
27 Santa Clara
Carballo Anerez (perfumery)
12 Plaza Salvador

THE BEST OF ART
Aizpuru, Juana, de   (contemporary art)
10 Canalejas, Tel. 22 85 01

The City

Put a fresh carnation in your buttonhole twice a day when in Valencia – the fertility of La Huerta, Spain's garden surrounding the Levant Region's capital produces millions of them in three yearly harvests, along with the notorious oranges and all the other ingredients for a subtropical fruit salad, which could come as a welcome alternative to the local diet of paella. And yet, the country's third largest city is not only the tool-shed of the Iberian orchard and canteen of the rice paddies, but one of the most industrialized centres as well, sporting shipyards (at the nearby port of El Grao) and factories for chemicals, textiles, metallurgical goods, furniture and toys. Not many of the seasonal 40 million tourists this side of the Mediterranean come to Valencia for its beauty, sights and entertainment, therefore offering more peace and space to the visitors to the city and to the holidaymakers on the northern Costa del Azahar. Two thousand years of turbulent history have left their traces, and – inhabited by the most engaged people in the multiple wars – many wounds as well: during the Civil War Valencia was twice the headquarters of the Republicans, and the last place to surrender to Franco's Nationalists, even after Madrid. The fighting spirit of local hero Rodrigo Diaz de Vivar, better known through Corneille as le Cid, did not always help Valencia in its efforts for independence, and ever since the Greeks founded it, Carthaginians, Romans, Visigoths, Arabs and Aragonians resided here as masters, not without leaving imprints in many ways, from irrigation to industries, from cathedrals to ceramics. Even its carnival, the Fallas, dates back to medieval times while the most attractive buildings as well as the local school of painting go back to the 15th and 16th centuries, with José de Ribera, Francisco de Ribalta and Jerónimo Jacinto de Espinosa well represented in the Fine Arts Museum. For business or pleasure, for red carnations (dandies should be habitué clients) or for culture, the expected values and attractions of Spain are all represented here as well – bullfights, flamenco, women, wine and song.

Founded: 1st cent B.C., by the Greeks; Valencia (Spanish) – from Valentia Edetanorum (Latin).

Far-reaching events: 2nd century A.D. – a Roman colony; 5th century – overrun by Visigoths; 714 – conquered by the Arabs; 1094 – recaptured by El Cid; 1102 – retaken by the Arabs; 1238 – conquered by James I of Aragón; 13th–15th century – gains first commercial, then cultural and finally intellectual prominence; 15th–17th century – decline in the city's fortunes; 1808 – rebellion against French rule; 1812 – French under Suchet recapture the city; 1939 – last bastion of Republican resistance during the Civil War.

Population: 800,000, 3rd largest city in Spain.

Postal code: E-46023 **Telephone code:** 6

Climate: Mediterranean – mild, sunny and with a sea breeze.

Calendar of events: *Fallas* (Mar) – celebration of the advent of spring, with bonfires and effigy-burning à la Guy Fawkes (19 Mar); *Feria* (Jul) – flower processions, fireworks and sports, with the *Corridas* (25 Jul) – bullfights.

Fairs and exhibitions: *TEXTILHOGAR* (Jan) – fabrics for the home; *INDUFERIAS* (Jan) – betting and gaming machines, stage machinery; *FEJU* (Feb) – toys and games; *FIMI* (Feb and Sep) – fashions for children and teenagers; *MAICOP* (Feb/Mar) – baking fair; *EXPOCARNE* (Feb/Mar) – meat industry fair; *CEVISAMA* (Mar) – ceramics, glass and facings for the construction industry; *FIAM* (Apr) – jewellery, lamps and metal art; *CEVIDER* (Apr) – decorative articles; *FIV* (May) – industrial trade fair; *SALON INTERNATIONAL DE LA MUSICA* (May) – musical instruments; *MUNDO BELLEZA* (May) – perfumes, cosmetics and hairdressing articles; *DROGUEXPO* (May) – drugstore articles; *EXPOFARMACIA* (May) – congress and exhibition of pharmaceutical specialities; *FIM* (Sep) – furniture fair; *IBERFLORA* (Oct) – gardening; *EUROGARDO* (Oct) – agricultural production; *INTERARTE* (Nov) – art fair; *FIMMA MADERALIA* (Nov) – wood processing machines; *EXPOJOVEN* (Dec/Jan) – youth fair.

Historical sights: *Cathedral* (14th–15th centuries) – landmark, on the site of a former mosque, with three portals (Romanesque, Gothic and Baroque) and works by Goya, Jacomart and Cellini; *Basilica Vergen de los Desamparados* – dedicated to the city's patron saint; *Palace of the Marques de dos Aguas* – housing the *Ceramics Museum*; *Lonja* (1483–98) – flamboyant Gothic silk merchants' hall; *Torres de Serranos* (1398) arch of triumph cum fortress; *La Generalidad* (15th–16th century) – coffered ceilings; *Santos Juanes* – with one of the most extensive ceiling frescoes in the world; *Colegio del Patriarca* (1603) – Spanish Renaissance; *Santa Catalina* (1705) – elegant church with a slender Baroque bell tower; *Torres de Quart* (1441) – city gate; *Santo Domingo* – monastery; main portal of Philip II, Gothic elegance on the inside; *Almudin* – formerly a grainhouse, now a palaeontological museum.

Modern sights: *Jardines del Real, Alameda Garden, Monforte Garden, Glorieta* – parks which justify Valencia's name as the ›Garden of Spain‹.

Special attractions: Valencia's folklore festivals, from the medieval *Fallas* to the *Feria* and the *Corridas.*

Important companies with headquarters in the city: *Altos Hornos del Mediterraneo* (steel); *Ford España* (cars).

Airport: Valencia-Manises, VLC; Tel.: 3 25 53 32/3 25 61 59; 12 km/8 miles.

The Headquarters

REY DON JAIME SOL

2 Avenida Baleares
E–46023 Valencia
Telephone: 3 60 73 00
Telex: 64 252 hoja
Owning Company: Hoteles Sol
General Manager: Angel Pando Tarilonte
Affiliation/Reservation Systems: Keytel, Utell
Number of rooms: 314 (6 suites)
Price range: Ptas 7,200–10,400 (single)
Ptas 9,000–13,000 (double)
Credit cards: AE, DC, Visa, EC
Location: a few minutes away from city centre
Style: modern
Hotel amenities: valet parking, solarium, beauty salon, hairstylist, newsstand, drugstore, boutique, tobacconist, house doctor; executive floor
Room amenities: air conditioning, colour tv (remote control), mini-bar/refrigerator, video
Bathroom amenities: separate shower cabin, bidet, bathrobe, hairdrier
Room service: 24 hours
Laundry/dry cleaning: same day
Conference rooms: 7 (up to 200 persons), audio-visual equipment, simultaneous translations and closed-circuit tv with automatic recording of video-tapes
Sports: outdoor swimming pool
Bars: ›Sherry Bar‹ (18.00/6.00 p.m.–1.00/a.m.) Rubio (barman), English style; ›Trident's Bar‹ (Coffee Shop)
Restaurant: ›Albufeira‹ (14.00/2.00 p.m.–16.00/4.00 p.m. and 20.30/8.30 p.m.–23.30/11.30 p.m.) Boquer (maître), Francisco De Miguel (chef de cuisine), local and international cuisine, modern style

The colourful gamut of architectural styles which characterizes Valencia today ranges from Romanesque to high-rise – a category exemplified by the clean-cut silhouette of the Rey Don Jaime. The principal town in the ›Garden of Spain‹, which once lurked strategically, if rather untidily, in a bend of the Turia, has put out tentacles in all directions in recent years, appropriating even areas beyond the once all-important defensive boundary of the river. The hotel's location on the ›other‹ bank, in pleasantly peaceful surroundings, bodes well for an undisturbed night's sleep, and the taxi ride into town is hardly long enough for you to consult your diary before proceeding to your first appointment. Should you prefer, however, to conduct your business at the hotel itself, you have a choice between an elegant lounge, a convivial pub-style bar, and a fine gourmet restaurant. With conference rooms for large-scale gatherings and a swimming pool to relax by when it's all over, plus friendly service before, during and after, your visit to Valencia is bound to be an agreeable amalgam of business and pleasure.

The Hideaway

HOTEL-CASINO MONTE PICAYO

E-46000 Urbanizacion Monte Picayo
Valencia-Puzol (18 km/11 miles)
Telephone: 1 42 01 00
Telex: 62 087 hmp
Owner: Jesali S. A.
General Manager: Jose M. Aranda
Affiliation/Reservation System: Hotels of Distinction
Number of rooms: 79 (4 suites)
Price range: Ptas 8,140–23,540
Credit cards: AE, DC, EC, Visa
Location: 18 km/11 miles from city centre, 25 km/16 miles from airport
Built: 1968 (renovated 1984)
Style: modern; antique interior
Hotel amenities: garage, valet parking, library/games room, beauty salon, boutique, tobacconist, florist, massage, manicure, sauna, hairstylist, house doctor
Main hall porter: Mr. Perez or Mr. Martinez

Room amenities: air conditioning, colour tv, video, mini-bar/refrigerator
Bathroom amenities: separate shower cabin, bidet, bathrobe, telephone
Room service: 6.30/a.m.–24.00/12 p.m.
Laundry/dry cleaning: same day
Conference rooms: 3 (up to 350 persons)
Sports: tennis, swimming pool
Sports (nearby): mini-golf, riding
Bar: (6.30/a.m.–1.00/a.m.), classic style
Restaurant: ›Grand‹ (13.30/1.30 p.m.–16.00/4.00 p.m. and 21.00/9.00 p.m.–23.30/11.30 p.m.) Alfonso Cantero (maître), Jacinto Mares (chef de cuisine), Spanish and international cuisine; classic style décor, open-air dining in summer
Nightclub: ›Taska‹: (19.00/7.00 p.m.–3.00/a.m.), discothèque, classic style

A short drive north of Valencia stands the perfect hideaway for business travellers to Spain's third largest city and industrial centre as well as one of the few luxurious resorts between Monte-Carlo and Marbella. The eponymous ›mountain‹ – actually a rocky outcrop – is surrounded by groves of orange trees. The hotel itself – a modern building with picture windows and balconies affording a panoramic view of the Mediterranean sea with its harbours and beaches – seems to grow directly out of the hillside. The public rooms are furnished in medieval style, with stone walls; the bedrooms – some with picture windows overlooking the swimming pool – are furnished in similar, if less martial style, with elaborate headboards and lace bedspreads. By day, apart from the pool and the sunshine, there's tennis in the hotel grounds and a variety of sports nearby. At night, a culinary tête-à-tête on the terrace could be followed by a few gyrations round the dance-floor in the nightclub or by a session in the ›Monte Picayo‹ casino. And, in season, the relaxing guest may want to enliven his leisure on the private Plaza de Toros.

Lunch

RESTAURANTE COMODORO
C11 Transits N. 3, Junto Hotel Astoria
Telephone: 3 51 38 15
Owner/Manager: Enrique Monto Quilis
Closed: Saturday lunchtime; Sunday; public holidays; August
Open: 13.30/1.30 p.m.–15.30/3.30 p.m. and 21.00/9 p.m.–23.30/11.30 p.m.
Cuisine: international
Chef de cuisine: José Vigo
Specialities: salad ›Comodoro‹; lobster garni; steak tartare; rape with prawns and mushrooms; desserts; pancakes ›Raquel‹
Location: central
Setting: English-style décor
Amenities: air conditioning
Atmosphere: chic; stylish
Clientèle: cross-section of politicians, men of commerce, artists and intellectuals
Dress: cool, casual and sporting to cool, casual and elegant
Service: under the friendly guidance of Vicenti Lopez Gimeno
Reservations: advisable
Price range: medium
Credit cards: AE, DC, Visa, JCB

Dinner

LA HACIENDA
12 Navarro Reverter
Telephone: 3 73 18 59
Owner/Manager: Antonio Larranz
Closed: Saturday lunchtime; Sunday; Holy Week (the week before Easter)
Open: 13.30/1.30 p.m.–16.00/4 p.m. and 21.00/9 p.m.–24.00/12 p.m.
Cuisine: traditional and regional
Chef de cuisine: Juan Morgado
Specialities: frequently changing menu; oxtail in the style of Córdoba (rabo de toro cordobesa); local-style rice (arroces locales); cattle rancher's aubergines (berenjenas del macendado); smoked salmon pancakes; Grand Marnier soufflé
Location: near the river Furia
Setting: two dining rooms (one a recent addition); elegant ameublement, including antique cupboards and fine engravings
Amenities: private dining rooms (17–50 persons); bar for restaurant clients only; garden; air conditioning; car park
Atmosphere: distinguished but not daunting
Clientèle: businessmen entertaining visiting delegations at lunchtime give way to local Haute Bourgeoisie with cause for celebration at night
Dress: suitably elegant and correct
Service: professional and helpful
Reservations: advisable
Price range: medium
Credit cards: AE, DC, Visa

Lunch

RESTAURANTE ›EL CONDES-TABLE‹
7 Artes Gráficas
Telephone: 3 69 92 50
Owner/Manager: Vicente Granelli Pavia
Closed: Sunday
Open: 13.30/1.30 p.m.–16.30/4.30 p.m. and 21.00/9 p.m.–23.30/11.30 p.m.
Cuisine: international
Chef de cuisine: Francisco Gil Moreno
Specialities: salad ›Condestable‹; lobster salad; foie gras d'oie; fresh salmon; eels; sirloin with foie gras; chop ›Avila‹; steak Châteaubriand with sauce Béarnaise
Location: near the Jardines de Monforte public gardens
Setting: medieval Castillian; antique furnishings, an abundance of wood panelling; oriental rugs; open fireplace; tapestries, stained glass and suits of armour
Amenities: private dining room (5–20 persons); bar; air conditioning
Atmosphere: vaguely feudal, without sacrificing mod cons
Clientèle: Valencia's industrial élite, plus a liberal sprinkling of foreign visitors from Oporto to Osaka
Dress: within reason, what you will
Service: well-schooled and efficient
Reservations: advisable
Price range: medium
Credit cards: AE, DC, Euro, Visa, Master Card

Dinner

MA CUINA
49 Gran Vía Germanías
Telephone: 3 41 77 99
Owner/Manager: Juan José Pache
Closed: Sunday
Open: 13.30/1.30 p.m.–15.30/3.30 p.m. and 21.00/9 p.m.–23.30/11.30 p.m.
Cuisine: imaginative Basque, plus local and international
Chef de cuisine: Peter Rhode
Specialities: stuffed salmon with crayfish sauce; mushroom flan in season; stuffed haddock; baked sea-bass with apples and cider
Location: near the Town Hall
Setting: main dining room with stylish décor plus bistro/bar ›La Taberna Vasca‹ serving a variety of snacks and light meals
Amenities: private dining rooms (15–25 persons); lounge; bar; air conditioning; car park
Atmosphere: lively and popular meeting-place for exchange of news and views; a hint of romance, especially at night
Clientèle: fairly heterogeneous; local gourmets and homesick Basques rub shoulders with artists, journalists and media-men

Dress: casually elegant to elegantly casual
Service: attentive and painstaking
Reservations: necessary at the weekend
Price range: medium
Credit cards: AE, DC, Visa

Café

CAFE AQUARIUM
57 Gran Via Marquès del Turia
Telephone: 3 51 00 40
Affiliations: Sociedad de Barmen Espanoles
Owner/Manager: Aquarium S. L./Santiago Llovedas
Closed: never
Open: 7.00/a.m.–1.00/a.m.
Location: a short walk from the city centre
Setting: large bar-café decorated in maritime style, with nautical furnishings and accessoires
Amenities: a wide variety of ice-creams as well as the usual drinks and cocktails; air conditioning
Atmosphere: welcoming and relaxing but still fashionable
Clientèle: all and sundry; advertising executives and office workers before, during and after working hours; students, secretaries, shopkeepers and senior citizens at any time of the day
Service: good; supervised by the manager, Santiago Llovedas

Bar

BAR CAFETERIA MURANO
59 Camino de la Gran Vía Marquès del Turia
Telephone: 3 51 61 05
Owner/Manager: Gran Via 59 S.A./Antonio Sanchez Collado
Closed: never
Open: 18.30/6.30 p.m.–3.00/a.m.
Location: south of centre
Setting: large bar with classic modern décor and an attractive terrace for summer evenings
Amenities: air conditioning; valet parking
Atmosphere: fairly glamourous; confidential or intimate, depending on your mood (and that of your companion!)
Clientèle: Valencia's High Society – resident aristocrats, a millionaire or two and the occasional exotic stranger
Service: quick and friendly; usually supervised by the patron
Reservations: necessary at the weekend (no dogs)
Credit cards: Visa

Nightclub

DISCOTECA SUSSO'S
4 Taquigrafo Marti
Telephone: 3 33 65 09
Owner/Manager: Showval S. A./Don Jesus Barrachina Luna
Closed: never
Open: 19.00/7 p.m.–21.00/9 p.m. and 23.30/11.30 p.m.–3.00/a.m. (or later)
Location: central
Setting: large discothèque/nightclub; marble floor; mirrored walls
Amenities: dinner menu; live shows (Thursday); air conditioning; valet parking service
Atmosphere: fashionably elegant; rather romantic as the night wears on
Clientèle: Valencia's Upper Crust; youthful, self-confident and on the way up to middle-aged and successful (the ones who've made it)
Dress: disco elegance
Service: smiling and cheerful
Reservations: only for major attractions (no dogs)
Credit cards: AE, DC; Visa

Shopping

EVERYTHING UNDER ONE ROOF
Corte Inglès, El   19–26, Pintor Sorolla

FOR HIM
Gran Estil   13, Roger de Lauria

FOR HER
Celia   41 Colón

BEAUTY & HAIR
Ramona, Edificio Valencia
3 Plaza San Augustin (entry: Pasajes)

JEWELLERY
Jimenez   16 Plaza Pais Valencia

LOCAL SPECIALITIES
Doble (women's fashion)
11 Jorge Juan
Lopez Criado (men's fashion)
5 Pascual y Genis
Cocco, Boutique (children's fashion)
41 Colon
Loewe (leather fashion)
7 Avenida Puerta Querol
Creaciones Safari (furs)
24 Don Juan de Austria
Libreria Madrilëa (books)
6 Lonja
Mariana (gifts)
31 Colón
Marnur (porcelain)
17 Jorge Juan
Valenpiel (baggage & travel accessories)
1 Paz
Valenti (interior decorating)
4 Isabel la Católica
Castillo (food and beverages)
1 Gran Vía Marques Turia
Las Bracas, Perfumeria (perfumery)
15 Moratin
Riera (shoes)
3 Lauria

THE BEST OF ART
Punto   (contemporary art)
37 Av. Barón de Cárcer, Tel. 3 21 46 23
Val i 30   (contemporary art)
1 Almirante, Tel. 3 31 88 66

The City

Ever since Wilbur and Orville Wright finally solved the Icarus problem in 1903 it might seem that half-way houses like Zaragoza, 1000-year-old staging post between the Spanish capital and the Pyrenees or the Costa Brava, are in danger of losing their raison d'être. Businessmen not involved in the local industries of sugar refining, textiles, glass and machinery may well not give Spain's fourth largest city (after Madrid, Barcelona and Seville) a second thought as Iberia whisks them across the Cordillera. Those who do stop over here, however, will find a bridge between the Castilian and Catalonian cultures, albeit with a penchant in favour of the latter. Zaragoza wears her rôle as go-between easily. A warm red brick city on the banks of the Ebro, this ›Mistress of Four Cultures‹ still bears traces of the quartet of civilizations which formed her. You will have to search for reminders of the Iberian settlement and the rest-and-recreation base for Roman legionaries, but the city of today is indelibly stamped with the Moorish imprint of the Benihud dynasty, from the mudejar minaret adorning the La Seo cathedral to the delicate tracery and carved capitals of the Alhambra-like Aljaferia palace. Side by side within the same building, the Gothic flamboyance recalls the Spain of El Cid, Ferdinand of Aragon and the Golden Age of voyages of discovery, literature and the arts. The past is omnipresent, in the architecture and in the citizens' proud maintenance of local customs, best seen in the festivals of Holy Week or of Nuestra Señora del Pilar, when the costumed dancers celebrate in the whirling rhythms of the jota the plaisirs et chagrins d'amour to the click of castanets and the strains of the guitar on the plaza before Francisco Herrera's neo-classic basilica. Such tales of love and passion have inspired dramas (Victor Hugo's ›Hernani‹) and operas (Giuseppe Verdi's ›Il Trovatore‹), whilst local son Francisco de Goya y Lucientes preferred to leave his frescoes on the cupolas of the church and his statue in the park before heading for Madrid and a place in the Prado. Zaragoza today is a vital link in Spain's industrial chain, but it remains a city where the undercurrents of the past are inextricably interwoven into the fabric of life, enriching the present with the history and traditions of this exuberant and passionate region.

Founded: by the Phoenicians; mentioned in 3rd century B.C.; Saragossa – Zaragoza (Spanish) – from Caesaraugusta (Latin).

Far-reaching events: 1st century, B.C. – Roman legionary colony; 3rd century, A.D. – seat of bishops; 406 – the Visigoths; 452 – the Swabians; 476 – Visigoths again; 712 – the Moors conquer the city; 1118 – Alphonse I recaptures the city and makes it the royal residence of the House of Aragon; 1437 – the first printing establishment in Spain in Zaragoza; 1583 – Philip II founds the university of Zaragoza; 17th century – Zaragoza's Golden Age; 1808–9 – revolts against Napoleonic rule; 1936 – Zaragoza taken by the Nationalists during the Civil War.

Population: 590,000, 5th largest city in Spain.

Postal code: E-50000   **Telephone code:** 76

Climate: Mediterranean; long, hot summers; less precipitation than in most other regions of Spain.

Best time to visit: April to October.

Calendar of events: *Semana Santa* (Holy Week, Mar/Apr) – religious celebrations and bullfights; *Fiestas de Primavera* (May) – spring celebrations with biennial art fair; *Festival of the Patron Saint Pilar* (Oct) – masked processions, flower festivals, bullfights; *Day of the Hispanic Race* (12 Oct) – traditional dances in front of the basilica.

Fairs and exhibitions: *ENOMAQ* (Jan) – international biennial wine-cellar machinery and equipment fair; *SMOPYC* (Feb) – international fair for public works and construction machinery; *SMAGUA* (Feb) – international water exhibition; *ROBOTICA* (Mar) – international robot techniques exhibition; *FIMA* (Apr) – international technical fair for agricultural machinery; *NATIONAL GARDEN AND FLORAL ART COMPETITION* (May); *EXPOARAGON* (May) – regional popularization fair; *FORESTAL* (Sep) – national biennial show of forestry use; *METROMATICA* (Oct) – biennial international show of measurement, testing and control; *INTERIORISMO* (Dec) – interior decoration and furnishings fair.

Historical and modern sights: *Nuestra Señora del Pilar* (17th century) – Francisco Herrera the Younger's neo-classic basilica decorated with frescoes by Goya, the world's first church dedicated to Virgin Mary; *Cathedral de la Seo* (14th century) – Castilian Gothic with Renaissance and Baroque elements; *Lonja* exchange (16th century) – highly decorative example of the Spanish Renaissance, with Corinthian columns; *Aljaferia* (9th century) – Moorish castle, later a royal residence, with typical horseshoe-shaped arches; *San Pablo* (16th century) – Romanesque-Gothic, brick construction with a 60 m octagonal tower; *Magdalena Church* (14th century) – Mudejar style; *Roman City Wall* (1st century B.C.) – ruined but still visible; *Carthusian Monastery of Aula Dei*, housing an important collection of works by native son Goya.

Special attractions: the celebrations for the *festival of Nuestra Señora del Pilar;* a night at *Monasterio de Piedra.*

Important companies with headquarters in the city: *Piensos y Ganados; Distribuciones Gimenez y Cia; Banco Zaragonano.*

Airport: Zaragoza-Sanjuro, ZAZ; TEL.: 349050, 9 km/6 miles; Iberia Airlines, Tel.: 218250 or 218257.

The Headquarters

CORONA DE ARAGON

13 Avenida Cesar Augusto
E-50004 Zaragoza
Telephone: 43 01 00
Telex: 58 828 hcna
Owning Company: Hoteles SOL
General Manager: Mr. Morales
Affiliation/Reservation System: SOL
Number of rooms: 249 (9 suites)
Price range: Ptas 6,100–7,800 (single)
              Ptas 8,600–12,000 (double)
              Ptas 20,000–25,000 (suite)
Credit cards: AE, DC, EC, MC, Visa
Location: central, 12 km/7 miles from
Sanjurjo airport
Built: 1968 (renovated in 1982)
Style: modern
Hotel amenities: air conditioning, ›businessmen's floor‹, newsstand, sauna, health club, beauty salon, valet parking, car rental, piano
Room amenities: air conditioning, colour tv, video, mini-bar
Bathroom amenities: bidet, bathrobe, telephone
Room service: 24 hours
Laundry/dry cleaning: same day (weekend service)
Conference rooms: 13 (up to 400 persons), secretarial services
Sports: outdoor swimming pool, gymnasium
Bars: ›Piccadilly's‹ American Bar (18.00/6.00 p.m.–1.30/a.m.), modern setting; ›Trident's‹ cafeteria (8.00/a.m.–24.00/12.00 p.m.)
Restaurant: ›El Bearn‹ (13.00/1.00 p.m.–15.00/3.00 p.m. and 21.00/9.00 p.m.–24.00/12.00 p.m.) international and regional cuisine; modern style
Nightclub: ›El Coto‹ discothèque

Historically speaking, the architecture of Zaragoza exhibits a heterogeneous mixture of Iberian, Roman, Moorish and Spanish styles – a fact which has earned the city the affectionate sobriquet ›The Mistress of Four Cultures‹. The architects of the Corona de Aragon decided on a functional modern exterior for this city -centre hotel, which consequently blends in with other contemporary buildings in the town without overshadowing the varied ancient landmarks, except by virtue of its size. Since this is primarily a businessman's hotel, one floor has been equipped to cater to their particular needs; these facilities, together with the cheerful dining room and the welcoming bedrooms – both decorated in warm orange tones – guarantee an atmosphere of congenial efficiency. And adherents of the ›all work and no play‹ philosophy can unwind at the end of the day in the sauna, by dancing the night away in the discothèque, or simply by soaking up some Spanish sunshine by the swimming pool.

The Hideaway

MONASTERIO DE PIEDRA

E–5000 Nuévalos (120 km/80 miles)
Telephone: (76) 84 90 11
Owning Company: Monasterio de Piedra S.A.
General Manager: Julian Adradas
Number of rooms: 61 (7 suites)
Price range: Ptas 300 (single)
Ptas 400 (double)
Credit cards: AE, DC
Location: Western Aragon, 120 km/80 miles from Zaragoza, 100 km/65 miles from airport
Built: late 12th century
Style: monastery; Romanesque, Gothic
Hotel amenities: valet parking, newsstand, tobacconist, florist, gardens
Room amenities: veranda (pets allowed)
Bathroom amenities: bidet
Room service: 8.00/a.m. to 10.30/a.m. (breakfast only)
Laundry/dry cleaning: 24 hour/48 hour service
Conference rooms: 2 (up to 75 persons)
Bars: ›Monasterio de Piedra-Plaza‹ (9.00/a.m.–19.00/7.00 p.m.); ›Monasterio de Piedra‹ (18.00/6.00 p.m. –23.30/11.30 p.m.)
Restaurants: two; (13.00/1.00 p.m.–16.00/4.00 p.m. and 21.00/9.00 p.m.–23.00/11.00 p.m.) classic cuisine, classic style and (13.00/1.00 p.m.–17.00/5.00 p.m.) classic cuisine, modern style

The remote and rugged setting in the mountains of Aragon, with its hidden lakes and secret waterfalls, would have prompted a rêverie from Cervantes or an impromptu sonnet from Ortega y Gasset. The Cistercian monks who chose to build their monastery here in the twelfth century found the seclusion an aid to their contemplation of God, whilst for today's tired men of commerce it is a welcome refuge from the pursuit of Mammon. To the structural embellishments which bear witness to the changing architectural precepts over the years – the Byzantine-Romanesque tower, the Gothic staircase and cloisters and the Renaissance filigree façade of the former kitchen and guest-house – have been added the basic accoutrements of twentieth-century comfort; the former monks' cells are now attractive if unadorned bedrooms with a sunny gallery overlooking the lovely gardens, and the hotel also provides a variety of sports facilities for twentieth-century keep-fit aficionados. But the Monasterio de Piedra's unique appeal lies in its all-pervading atmosphere of quietude. The inner peace gained here by ascetics so long ago still haunts the nobly vaulted dining room and is, perhaps, their greatest legacy to their successors in this infinitely less spiritual age.

465

Lunch

ROGELIO'S
10 Eduardo Ibarra
Telephone: 35 89 50
Owner/Manager: Alonso Gonzalo
Open: 8.00/a.m.–1.00/a.m.
Chef de cuisine: Abril Dicente
Specialities: fish according to season; cream desserts; ›pêche au vent‹
Location: behind the soccer stadium
Setting: 13th century; Romanesque arches, pillars and columns
Amenities: four private dining-rooms (100–300 persons); open-air dining on terrace; bar and cafeteria (independently run); car park
Atmosphere: intimate; redolent of history
Clientèle: heterogeneous; local politicians, government officials, bankers
Dress: fairly informal
Service: extremely friendly
Credit cards: Visa

Dinner

COSTA VASCA
13 Tte. Coronel Valenzuela
Telephone: 21 73 39
Affiliations: Chaîne des Rôtisseurs
Owner/Manager: Antonio Mur
Closed: Sunday; Christmas
Open: 13.00/p.m.–16.00/4 p.m. and 20.30/8.30 p.m.–23.00/11 p.m.
Cuisine: international ›au goût du marché‹
Chef de cuisine: Jesus Bollo
Specialities: haddock; rolls of sole with salmon; lamb with artichokes; sirloin of beef in red wine; chestnut croquettes
Location: central
Setting: large, elegant dining room
Amenities: private dining rooms (10–40 persons); bar; air conditioning; car park
Atmosphere: dominated by the discriminating, genial and lively presence of proprietor Antonio Mur – chef, maître and public relations officer rolled into one
Clientèle: Zaragoza's social élite; lovers of good food
Dress: chic and fairly conservative
Service: personally
Reservations: essential (no dogs)
Price range: medium to expensive
Credit cards: AE, Visa, Master Card

Lunch

CASA TENA
8 Plaza de San Francisco
Telephone: 35 80 22
Owner/Manager: David Diez
Closed: Sunday evening
Open: 7.00/a.m.–24.00/12 p.m.
Cuisine: local and classic
Chef de cuisine: David Diez (son of the owner)

Specialities: roast meats; clams with artichokes; stuffed peppers; peaches in wine; ›musician's tart‹
Location: central
Setting: the former Slaughterhouse Tavern (Tasca del Matadero) – now a sophisticated modern restaurant; dining room in cellar furnished in Aragonese style
Amenities: private dining rooms; bar; open-air dining (boulevard terrace); air conditioning
Atmosphere: as friendly and lively as it ever was, but nowadays with considerably more style than in days gone by
Clientèle: cross-section of hommes d'affaires
Dress: elegantly informal
Service: welcoming
Reservations: during the season
Price range: medium
Credit cards: AE, DC, Euro, Visa

Dinner

EL CACHIRULO
Autovía de Logroño
Telephone: 33 16 74
Owner/Manager: Mr. Rausell
Closed: Sunday evening (except by prior arrangement)
Open: 13.00/1 p.m.–16.00/4 p.m. and 21.00/9 p.m.–1.00/a.m.
Cuisine: local classic and international
Chef de cuisine: Alfonso Pastor
Specialities: roast lamb; garlic soup; egg dishes; peach with wine
Location: west of the city centre; on the road to the airport
Setting: dining rooms of varying sizes furnished in typical Aragonese style
Amenities: private dining rooms (10–400 persons); bar; open-air dining on terrace; air conditioning; car park
Atmosphere: informal and welcoming
Clientèle: businessmen en route for Madrid or Malaga during the week
Dress: informal but not untidy
Service: anxious-to-please
Reservations: not usually necessary
Price range: medium
Credit cards: AE, DC, Euro, Visa

Shopping

EVERYTHING UNDER ONE ROOF
Corte Inglès   3 Paseo Sagasta

FOR HIM
Mino Bay   8–10 Paseo de Pamplona

FOR HER
Cachet   44 San Miguel

BEAUTY & HAIR
José Manuel   15 Bolonia

JEWELLERY
Perlat   13 Royo

Had Goethe sent Faust this far north he could have depicted to good advantage the Walpurgis Night bonfires celebrating the advent of spring after the long, dark northern winter as they blaze out on the hilltops overlooking the Kattegat. Gothenburg owes more than just its name to its Viking forebears. The pioneering spirit which drove the warriors' long ships of yore across the seas to Britain, Iceland and beyond, and the eighteenth-century Swedish East India Company to trade iron for Spanish doubloons in Cadiz or to barter for Chinese silks, porcelain, tea and spices in Canton, makes the city primarily an outward-going port – Sweden's largest – today, with worldwide oceanic connections from its largely ice-free harbour as well as a waterway linking it to big brother Stockholm. The Dutch, Scottish, English and German merchants of the past left their imprint on Gustavus Adolphus' neo-classic ›Gothic fortress‹ – canniness and Gründlichkeit, the Hamnkanal in front of the Kristine Church and the Picassos and Cézannes in the art gallery. But the town – impregnable in days of old thanks to those fortifications – has tempered these foreign influences with its own essentially Swedish character. On land, prestige industries, from Volvo to Hasselblad, are the focal point, with engineering, petrochemicals and surgical equipment enlarging the commercial perspective. The breathtaking scenery of the fjords lies to the north and the country's best beaches to the south – and with the untamed wilderness of the mountains an enticing hinterland, there is plenty of scope for trying out the new Volvo and the new Hasselblad.

Founded: 1619 by Gustavus II Adolphus; Gothenburg – Göteborg (Swedish) – ›castle on the Gota‹.

Far-reaching events: 17th century – German, Scottish, English, and Spanish-Dutch settlers and merchants build up the city, including a Dutch system of canals; 1665 – the bishops take up residence; 1731 – the East India company handles the administration of all Swedish colonies from its base in Gothenburg; 1732 – sea traffic with China; 1778 – founding of the Royal Academy; 1806 – Napoleon's blockade turns Gothenburg into the principal entrepôt port for the import of English goods for the whole of Europe; 1891 – founding of the university.

Population: 700,000; Sweden's second largest city.

Postal code: S–40000 to 42590 **Telephone code:** 31

Climate: less extreme than elsewhere in Sweden, but bring two umbrellas!

Calendar of events: *Gothenburg Scandinavian Horse Show* (Apr); *Garden Party* (Apr) – horticultural show; *Walpurgis Night* (30 Apr) – bonfires, songs and speeches in praise of the advent of spring; *Liseberg Amusement Park* (Apr–Sep) – concerts, entertainment, theatre, dancing; *Happy Gothenburg* (Jun) – music festival; *Midsummer* (21–23 Jun); *Santa Lucia's Day* (13 Dec) – Lucia procession of the Queen of Light.

Fairs and exhibitions: *SCANDINAVIAN LIGHTING FAIR* (Jan); *INTERNATIONAL BOAT SHOW* (Feb); *INFOTRANS* (Feb) – computer aided information systems in transport; *MAINTENANCE* (Feb) – industrial maintenance; *EXHIBITION OF STORAGE MATERIALS HANDLING* (Mar); *TUR* (Mar) – international tourism and travel fair; *AUTO* (Mar) – motor, workshop, service station and garage equipment; KEMI (Apr) – trade fair for chemistry; *ISM* (Apr) – industrial trade fair – machine tools; *NURSING CARE AND HEALTH EXHIBITION* (May); *RORO* (May) – roll-on/roll-off and ferry transport; *KOMMUN* (autumn) – municipality techniques; *LANGEDRAG* (Sep) – floating boat show; *DAGENS HUSHALL* (Sep) – international consumer goods fair; *DATA INFO* (Oct) – computer and information technology; *INTERNATIONAL TIMBER, WOOD PRODUCTS AND WOODWORKING MACHINERY INDUSTRY TRADE FAIR* (Oct); *INTERFOOD/INTEREST* (Oct) – food products and machinery, restaurant equipment, shop fitting; *ELFACK* (Nov) – electrotechnical trade fair – power, production, distribution; *SCAN AUTOMATIC* (Nov) – hydraulics, pneumatics, electronics, transmission equipment, control technology.

Historical sights: *Radhus* (17th–20th century) – the city hall and centre of the old and modern city; *Kronhuset* – oldest secular building in the city; *Gustavi Domkyrka* – cathedral consecrated in 1633 and rebuilt in classic style; *Klippan* – houses from the 17th century; *Viking* – old, four-masted barque in the city's guest harbour; *Drottning Kristinas Jaktslott* (17th century) – coffee and waffles are now served in the former queen's hunting lodge; *Kronhusbodarna* – turn-of-the century shops and handicrafts; *Götaplatsen* – modern centre of the Lorensberg district, with the famous *Poseidon Fountain* and an art museum with everything from Rembrandt to Picasso; *Skeppsbron* – landing place for the large passenger ships; *Antikhallarna* – Scandinavia's largest antiques and collectors' centre; *Slottsskogen* – a park and zoo with Scandinavian animals; *Scandinavium* – Gothenburg's Madison Square Garden; *Historical Museum* – former home of the East India Company; *Järntorget* – historic site where the iron market was formerly located; *Gunneby in Möndal* – an elegant little palace.

Special attractions: a trip into the interior with a night at *Hooks Herrgård*.

Important companies with headquarters in the city: *Volvo* (cars); *Svenska Varv* (ships); *SKF* (steel and machinery); *Hasselblad* (cameras); *Swedyards* (petrochemicals); *Lindholmen Motoers* (power machines); *ESAB* (welding equipment); *Mölnlycke* (surgical equipment, sanitary products); *Gätaverken* (offshore engineering).

Airport: Gothenburg-Landvetter, GOT; Tel.: 94 11 00; 25 km/16 miles.

The Headquarters

PARK AVENUE

36–38 Kungsportsavenyn
Box 53 233
S–40016 Gothenburg
Telephone: 17 65 20
Telex: 2320 parkave
Owning Company: Scandinavian Airline System
General Manager: Karl Otto Skogland
Affiliation/Reservation Systems: Scanvest Ring A/S
Number of rooms: 320 (11 suites)
Price range: SEK 795–875 (single)
SEK 950–1,115 (double)
Credit cards: AE, DC, Visa, MC, EC
Location: city centre, 25 km/16 miles from airport
Built: 1950 (renovated 1985)
Style: modern
Hotel amenities: garage, valet parking, grand piano, beauty salon, sauna, solarium, massage, hairstylist, newsstand, house doctor

Room amenities: colour tv, minibar, trouser press, hairdrier, safe (pets allowed)
Bathroom amenities: separate shower cabin, bathrobe and telephone in Royal Club rooms
Room service: 24 hours
Landry/dry cleaning: same day (weekend service)
Conference rooms: 14 (up to 600 persons), conference equipment and secretarial services, ballroom
Sports: indoor swimming pool
Restaurants: ›Belle Avenue‹ gourmet restaurant, classic French cuisine;; ›Harlequin‹ charcoal grill, steaks, spare-ribs, salads
Nightclubs: ›Lorensberg‹ with restaurant and two bars

International managers may experience a sensation of déjà vu during their first visit to the Park Avenue Hotel, since this link in the prestigious SAS chain offers their renowned standards of style, service and comfort. Far from being a production-line replica of some archetypal prototype, however, the establishment on Gothenburg's principal boulevard is imbued with a unique character and charm of its own. From the upper floors it vouchsafes stunning views of the towers and tiled roofs of the city, whilst Swedish design skills provide for mirrored walls in the bedrooms, a modern fireplace in the bar, carefully chosen antiques and contemporary paintings – plus a choice of restaurants, sports facilities and an exclusive nightclub. It's hardly surprising that Henry Kissinger, David Rockefeller, the Beatles, the Rolling Stones and Diana Ross all chose to stay here when they were in town.

The Hideaway

HOOKS HERRGÅRD

S–56013 Hook (180 km/110 miles)
Telephone: (393) 2 10 80
Telex: 70 419 hook
Owner: Stefan Edberg
General Manager: Stefan Edberg
Affiliation/Reservation System: Relais et Châteaux
Number of rooms: 82 (·12 suites)
Price range: SEK 450 (single)
           SEK 620 (double)
           SEK 820 (king-size room)
           SEK 1,240 (suite)
Credit cards: all major
Location: on lake Hook in the highlands of southern Sweden, 30 km/18 miles from Joenkoeping airport
Built: 1778 (recently renovated)
Style: Swedish country manor-house
Hotel amenities: car park, car rental, sauna, health club, outdoor swimming pool (heated; salt water), solarium, tobacconist, newspaper stand (no dogs allowed)
Room amenities: colour tv (some rooms), minibar/refrigerator
Bathrom amenities: separate shower cabin, bathrobe on request
Room service: on request
Laundry/dry cleaning: on request
Conference rooms: separate conference building; facilities for 25–140 persons
Sports: gymnasium, 18-hole golf course with modern clubhouse, tennis court, boats, canoes, windsurfing, fishing
Bar: ›Pub‹ (17.30/5.30 p.m.–0.30/a.m.); English style décor, Robert (barman) and Wieno (lady bar tender)
Restaurant: (Monday to Friday: 12.00/a.m.–14.00/2.00 p.m. and 18.00/6.00 p.m.–20.00/8.00 p.m.; weekends: 12.00/a.m.–15.00/3.00 p.m. and 18.30/6.30 p.m.–21.00/9.00 p.m.) Bernd Strehlow (chef de cuisine), Swedish and international specialities, Swedish 17th century style décor
Private dining rooms: three (up to 60 persons)

A relais de campagne where time takes on a new dimension; where quartz crystal punctuality suddenly seems of no import – Hooks Herrgård, an eighteenth-century manoir amongst the lakes and forests of the south Swedish highlands. The setting is awe-inspiringly beautiful, the intérieur comfortable and pleasant. The salons are graciously formal, but life in the manor is leisurely and family-style. The bedrooms, all different, are inviting. There are jacuzzis in some bathrooms and apart from the Swedish Smörgasbord served daily, there are French specialities in the restaurant. You can row across to one of the islets on the lake or try your hand at windsurfing, fishing or tennis; the golf course is renowned and the swimming pool heated. Leave some time for an unhurried walk in the woods if you really want to put the twentieth century into perspective.

Lunch

KAJUTAN
7 Stigbergslidan
Telephone: 42 25 20
Owner/Manager: Iris Stolberg
Closed: never
Open: 11.30/a.m.–14.00/2 p.m.; 18.00/6
p.m.–24.00/12 p.m.
Cuisine: French (nouvelle) and Swedish
(classic)
Chef de cuisine: Karl Loefgren
Specialities: sole with lobster sauce and
mashed potatoes; various dishes ›au
gratin‹; selection of desserts; parfaits
Location: 10 minutes from the centre of
Gothenburg; near Stenalina harbour and
museum
Setting: uninterrupted view of the har-
bour and the cargo trains; nautical–style
décor
Amenities: veranda for open-air dining;
dancing downstairs
Atmosphere: a romantic hint of harbours,
the sea and faraway places with strange-
sounding names
Clientèle: predominantly affluent, con-
servative, middle-aged and successful
Dress: no restrictions or requirements
Service: fast and friendly
Reservations: advisable (pets permitted)
Price range: fairly astronomic
Credit cards: AE, DC, Euro

Dinner

TRADGARDSFORENINGEN
Nya Allen
Telephone: 13 31 11/13 82 98 (office)
Owner/Manager: Pelle Lundberg
Closed: lunchtime every day; December
19th – June 19th
Open: 19.30/7.30 p.m.–2.00/a.m.
Cuisine: local and international
Chef de cuisine: Manfred Berghaus
Specialities: very varied menu, changing
according to the seasons and market
availability
Location: near Gothenburg's main boule-
vard
Setting: large dining room decorated in
shades of blue; modern furnishings; pic-
ture windows
Amenities: bar; excellent cabaret shows;
nightclub (open until 3 a.m.); open-air
dining on terrace; air conditioning; car
park (3 minutes' walk from restaurant)
Atmosphere: civilized and stylish
Clientèle: shipping magnates, export managers and financiers; on the first day of
each month national celebrities from the
media, the arts and politics
Dress: jacket de rigueur
Service: efficient and professional
Reservations: essential, preferably well in
advance (no dogs)
Price range: decidedly expensive
Credit cards: AE, DC, Euro, Visa

Lunch

WHITE CORNER
43 b Vasag
Telephone: 81 28 11
Owner/Manager: John Fredlund
Closed: never
Open: 11.00/a.m.–14.00/2 p.m. and
18.00/6 p.m.–2.00/a.m.
Location: a two minute walk or a five minute saunter from the Rubinen
Setting: ground-floor bar serving drinks,
light meals and meals at popular prices;
downstairs, a grill restaurant with rôtisserie, fireplace and comfortable armchairs; room divided into booths for extra privacy; blue- and grey-check tablecloths; pewter place plates
Amenities: bar
Atmosphere: alert and lively upstairs;
confidential to romantic downstairs, depending on the occasion or your companion (or both!)
Clientèle: youthful, self-confident and
well-informed in the bistro; middle management and marketing executives in
the steak house
Service: very good
Reservations: advisable (no pets)
Credit cards: AE, DC, Euro, Master Card

Dinner

JOHANNA
41 S. Harng.
Telephone: 11 22 50
Affiliations: Relais et Châteaux (Relais
Gourmand)
Owner/Manager/Chef de cuisine: Crister
Svantesson
Closed: lunchtime every day; Sunday
Open: 18.00/6 p.m.–23.30/11.30 p.m.
Cuisine: French and Scandinavian (tradi-
tional and nouvelle)
Specialities: according to season; turbot,
sole, salmon, scallops, crabs and lobster
in crab and champagne sauce (grand col-
lage de fruits de mer); pâtés; dessert ›Jo-
hanna‹; fresh and preserved fruits with
ice-cream; sorbets; parfaits; pastries
Location: near the Central Station
Setting: elegantized rustic dining room
with an impressive collection of old paint-
ings
Amenities: first-floor bar for apéritifs and
coffee
Atmosphere: welcoming and friendly, but
with an air of chic
Clientèle: glittering and glamourous
globe-trotters; jet set; millionaires;
Ralph Siegel, Mick Jagger, David Bowie
and Colin Chaplin
Dress: designer jeans to designer cash-
mere
Service: knowledgeable and helpful
Reservations: advisable (no pets)
Price range: unashamedly expensive
Credit cards: AE, DC, Euro, Visa

The cradle of Greta Garbo and myriads of long-legged blondes who adorn the fashion capitals of the world is physically just as beautiful as her children. Embraced by water as clear as Swedish crystal and bathed in light as effulgent as a gleam of hope in a Bergman film, ›The City between the Bridges‹ presents herself to the aesthetical voyeur like a backdrop to a nordic fairy-tale. The buildings are attractive, the streets are clean, the air is fresh and the people are polite – and multi-lingual. Neutral, but not sober; efficient, but not Germanic; outgoing, but not theatrical – the burghers are a pleasant lot. (And when the night draws in over Café Opera, Alexandra's, et al., August Strindberg's disciples can even turn wild.) The Royal Palace, the regal opera, the arts and profane pleasures, the princely life style and the aristocratic surroundings – Stockholm is a midsummer night's dream – even in winter.

Founded: 1255, by Birger Jarl; Stockholm (Swedish) – ›log island‹.

Far-reaching events: 13th century – intensive trade with the Hanseatic League; 1523 – residence of the Swedish king; 1634 – Stockholm the capital of the empire; 1710 – the plague wipes out one third of the city's population; 1720 – ›Peace of Stockholm‹ regulates the tensions between Sweden and Prussia peacefully; 18th–19th century – industrial and commercial expansion; 1815 – loss of Finland but alliance with Norway following Napoleonic Wars; 20th century – Sweden becomes independent of Norway but remains neutral during the two World Wars; 1971 – parliamentary reform.

Population: 1.5 million (urban area); capital and largest city of Sweden.

Postal code: S–10005 to 12612   **Telephone code:** 8

Climate: variable; more sunshine than in any other city in Sweden.

Calendar of events: *Walpurgis Night* (30 Apr) – bonfires, songs and speeches to welcome the long-awaited advent of spring; *National Day* (6 Jun) – big celebrations at Skansen; *Midsummer Night* (Friday closest to 21 Jun) – all Stockholm dances through the shortest night of the year; *Nordic Music Festival* (Jun–Jul) – classical concerts at Riddarhuset; *July Festival* – everything from sports to street theatre; *Summer Evening Concerts* (Jul–Aug) – usually Tuesdays in the National Museum; *Nobel Prize Awards Ceremony* (10 Dec) – a gala for great minds; *Santa Lucia Day* (13 Dec) – maidens in white robes and the longest night of the year bearing candelabras and breakfast in bed.

Fairs and exhibitions: *INTERNATIONAL MOTORCYCLE FAIR* (Jan); *INTERNATIONAL SWEDISH FURNITURE TRADE FAIR* (Feb); *INTERNATIONAL FASHION TRADE FAIR* (Feb); *STOCKHOLM INTERNATIONAL BOAT SHOW* (Mar); *INTERNATIONAL SHOE TRADE FAIR* (Mar); *NORDIC BUILDING* (Apr) – building industry; *INTERNATIONAL ANTIQUES FAIR* (Apr); *INTERNATIONAL ELECTRONICS PRODUCTION TRADE FAIR (EP)* (Apr); *INTERNATIONAL TRADE FAIR OF CONTROL SYSTEMS IN PULP, PAPER, BOARD, PARTICLE BOARD, FIBREBOARD AND CONVERTING INDUSTRY* (May); *INTERNATIONAL MEDICAL LABORATORY AND TECHNOLOGY CONGRESS* (Aug); *POSTTEC* (Sep) – international post technics exhibition; *INTERNATIONAL FASHION TRADE FAIR* (Sep); *INTERNATIONAL SHOE TRADE FAIR* (Sep); *INTERNATIONAL ELECTRICAL TRADE FAIR* (Oct); *INTERNATIONAL TECHNICAL TRADE FAIR* (Oct); *EDUCATION* (Nov) – trade fair for education; MEDICINE (Dec) – international trade fair for doctors.

Historical sights: *Kungliga Slottet* – royal palace with changing of the guard ceremony; *Riddarhuset* (17th century) – Swedish Baroque, houses the coats of arms of 2,600 aristocratic families; *Storkyran* (13th century) – church where the Reformation got its start in Sweden and where Swedish kings are still crowned; *Drottningholm Castle* (16th century) – the ›Versailles of the North‹ and home of the Swedish royal family; *German Church* (1642) – Gothic on the outside, Baroque on the inside; *Helgeandsholmen* – small island in the middle of the city where the Swedish parliament meets in the old *Riksdaghus*; *Riddarholmskyrkan* (13th century) – church where Swedish kings have been buried since the 17th century; *Börshus* (18th century) – home of the Nobel Library; *Wasavaret* – wharf, with the flagship of Gustav II's fleet; *Skansen* (1891) – the world's first open-air museum; *Stadshuset* (20th century) – the town hall, where the Nobel Prizes are presented; *Nationalmuseum* – 16th–19th century art; *Ostasiatiska Museet* – oriental art; *Moderne Museet* – modern and avant-garde paintings.

Modern sights: *Nordiska Kompaniet* – Stockholm's answer to Bloomingdale's; *Gamla Stan* – a former fortress, now the city's elegant shopping zone.

Special attractions: an evening of ballet or opera at *Drottningholm Palace*; an *outdoor concert* on a summer evening at Skansen; an invitation to the *Nobel Prize ceremony*; a reception in the *Grand Hotel's* Hall of Mirrors; a night at the *Café Opera*; a *royal reception* by Sweden's favourite couple.

Important companies with headquarters in the city: *Ericsson* (electronics); *Christer Ericsson* (oil-drilling platforms); *Electrolux* (appliances); *Axel Johnson Group* (trading, electronics, engineering, shipping); *Statsföretag* (building, chemicals, engineering); *Saab Svenska Stal* (steel); *Atlas Copco* (exploring, mining equipment); *Svenska Philips Företagen; Bahco* (machines); *Swedevelop* (hospital projects); *Boliden* (metal); *Svenska Handelsbanken; Swedish Match* (matches).

Airport: Stockholm–Arlanda, STO; Tel.: 7530265; 40 km/25 miles; SAS, Tel.: 7803030.

The Headquarters

GRAND HOTEL

8 S. Blasieholmshamnen, P.O. Box 16424
S–103 27 Stockholm
Telephone: 22 17 20
Telex: 19 500 grand   **Telefax:** 218 688
Owning company: Stockholm Saltsjön AB
General Manager: Tord Smidt
Affiliation/Reservation Systems: The
Leading Hotels of the World, Steigen-
berger Reservation Service
Number of rooms: 335 (19 suites)
Price range: SKr 995–10,000
Credit cards: AE, DC, EC, MC, Visa,
JCB
Location: city centre
Built: 1874 (renovated continously)
Style: old European
Hotel amenities: valet parking, house li-
mousine service, beauty salon, sauna,
hairstylist, massage, manicure, news-
stand, drugstore, boutique, florist, tobac-
conist, house doctor
Room amenities: air conditioning; colour
tv (remote control); video; mini-bar/ ref-
rigerator (pets allowed)
Bathroom amenities: bidet, bathrobe;
hairdrier; telephone
Room service: 24 hours
Laundry/dry cleaning: same day
Conference rooms: 19 (up to 700 persons); secretarial services; ballroom
Bar: ›Cadier‹ (12.00 p.m.–2.00 a.m.); pianist
Restaurants: ›French Dining Room‹
(12.00 p.m.–24.00/12.00 a.m.); French
and international cuisine; classical
French and Art Nouveau décor; ›Grand
Café‹ (7.00 a.m. to 24.00/12 a.m.), traditional Swedish cuisine, Swedish style dé-
cor

*The Changing of the Guard across the wa-
ter, barges and steamboats passing under
your suite, the walls of this crowned nordic
palazzo echoing world history and the
restrained luxury continuing after a century of élite hospitality make the Grand
what its name implies. Times have changed
since Sarah Bernhardt cast her hourglass
figure onto the satin sheets in the Grand,
but the stars keep coming here more frequently than to the Royal Palace on the
other bank. In fact, whenever there is a
chance, the royalty glides across the waves
to indulge in the many glittering events at
Stockholm's grandest public establishment.
But you will not only stumble over Gotha
Gods, Nobel Prize winners and title page
smiles when staying here – life at the
Grand is as much business as usual, despite all the balls and board meetings and
big shots demanding extra attention. The
bar is a carousel of encounters, the restaurant one of the most elegant dining rooms
in the country, and the neighbouring Bo-
linder Palace, the suite-and-banquet dépendance of the hotel is the stage for most
affairs not held in the Palace or the Parliament. In short, the Grand is the Grand is
the Grand . . .*

The Hideaway

GRAND HOTEL SALTSJOEBADEN

P.O. Box 329
S–13 303 Saltsjoebaden, Stockholm
(15 km/9 miles)
Telephone: 7 17 00 20
Telex: 10 210 seahot
Owning Company: Saltsjoebadens Hotel-lab
General Manager: Ulf von Roth
Number of rooms: 103 (10 suites)
Price range: SKr 730–805 (single)
SKr 970–1,140 (double)
SKr 1,350–1,550 (suite)
Credit cards: Access, DC, EC, MC, Visa
Location: 62 km/35 miles from Stockholm Arlanda airport
Built: 1893 (renovated 1984)
Style: castle; traditional, solid, comfortable
Hotel amenities: car rental, gaming room, piano, wheelchair accessibility, sauna, newsstand
Room amenities: air conditioning, colour tv, most rooms with balcony (pets allowed)
Bathroom amenities: separate shower cabin in some rooms, bidet
Room service: 16 hours
Laundry/dry cleaning: same day
Conference rooms: for up to 275 persons, all equipment available, foreign TV standards (NTSC-SECAM), simultaneous translation, wide-angle screen
Sports: 18-hole golf course, outdoor swimming
Sports (nearby): tennis, mini-golf, watersports, skiing, bobsleigh
Bars: cocktail bar (18.00/6.00 p.m.–1.00/a.m.) Peter Fuchs (barman)
Restaurants: ›French Dining Room‹ (6.30/a.m.–23.30/11.30 p.m.) Curt Blomberg (chef de cuisine); ›Grand's Grill‹ (10.30/a.m.–21.00/9.00 p.m.) Haridas Nayar (chef de cuisine)
Private dining rooms: two

The most romantic way to approach the Grand Hotel Saltsjoebaden, the prettiest hideaway in the environs of Stockholm, is to glide in a boat along the bay to the landing-stage in front of the white Edwardian façade. Inside, the décor of this nineteenth-century castle strikes a balance between an appropriately formal elegance in the dining room and a comfortable private-house intimacy in the lounges. You can jump straight into the waters of the Baltic Sea after a session in the sauna, but this yachtsmen's paradise also offers a fine golf course, a beach, and ample opportunity to relax and enjoy the excellent food in enchantingly beautiful surroundings.

Lunch

OPERAKÄLLAREN,
Operahuset
Telephone: 24 27 00/11 11 25
Affiliations: Traditions et Qualité
Owner/Manager/Chef de cuisine: Werner Vögeli
Closed: Christmas Day; July 5th – August 5th
Open: 12.00/a.m.–23.45/11.45 p.m.
Cuisine: Swedish and French (nouvelle)
Specialities: smorgasbord; fish; game; iced seafood from the North Sea; smoked or home-marinated salmon; salmon mousseline in puff pastry ›Queen Silvia‹; baked turbot ›Charles XII‹; hazel grouse and reindeer from the Northern Forests; desserts ›North Pole gala‹; frozen Arctic raspberry mousse
Location: opposite the Royal Palace
Setting: an historic monument; sumptuous dining room with wood panelling, painted ceiling and red velvet upholstery; glittering veranda; view over the Strömmen; torchlit at night
Amenities: bar; Café Opera bistro; private dining rooms; snack bar; gourmet take-away meals (all in same complex); live orchestra; open-air dining on terrace
Atmosphere: unashamedly and extravagantly luxurious in the style of a royal court banquet of the end of the nineteenth century
Clientèle: connoisseurs of the finer things of life; francophile gourmets from Gothenburg to Granada; admirers of Werner Vögeli's cuisine and organisational talents from his days at Maxim's and Le Grand Véfour
Dress: suitably festive; mostly rather formal
Service: impeccable; from the blue-liveried doorman to the white-jacketed waiters
Reservations: advisable
Price range: moderately expensive

Lunch

COQ BLANC
111 Regeringsgatan
Telephone: 11 61 53
Owner/Manager: Uno Hedman and Erwin Hug
Closed: Sunday; Bank Holidays; Saturday lunchtime; July
Open: 11.30/a.m.–23.00/11 p.m.
Cuisine: international Haute Cuisine
Chef de cuisine: Erwin Hug (winner of numerous culinary awards, including the Gastronomiska Akademins Gold Medal)
Specialities: an excellent collection of quality selected wines from all over the world
Location: city centre

Setting: in a modern theatre complex; attractively laid tables surrounding the stage; séparées for intimate dining
Amenities: air conditioning, banqueting facilities for up to 40 persons
Atmosphere: a theatre-restaurant; polished, informal elegance
Clientèle: businessmen, ambassadors together with their secretaries and other embassy staff, distinguished tourists
Dress: casual for lunch; dinner-jacket for dinner
Service: professional, helpful, friendly
Reservations: advisable
Price range: fairly expensive
Credit cards: AE, DC, Euro, Visa

Dinner

PAUL & NORBERT
9 Strandvägen
Telephone: 63 81 83
Owner/Manager: Paul Beck/Norbert Lang
Closed: Saturday; Sunday; official holidays; last week in March; July 7th – August 3rd; December 24th – January 6th
Open: 12.00/a.m.–14.30/2.30 p.m. and 17.30/5.30 p.m.–22.30/10.30 p.m.
Cuisine: French (nouvelle)
Chef de cuisine: Norbert Lang
Specialities: according to season – selected French wines
Location: city centre
Amenities: tastevin cellar
Atmosphere: sophisticated, refined but nevertheless relaxing
Clientèle: insiders, outsiders and those on top of everything, gourmets, wine-connoisseurs and a sprinkling of distinguished tourists
Dress: no special requirements or restrictions
Service: impeccable
Reservations: advisable
Price range: medium to expensive
Credit cards: AE, DC, Euro, MC, Visa

Lunch

WÄRDSHUSET STALLMÄSTEREGÅRDEN
11347 Norrtull
Telephone: 24 39 10
Affiliations: Relais et Châteaux (Relais Gourmand); Châine des Rôtisseurs
Owner/Manager: TWRAG / Horst Hantzel
Closed: Christmas Eve (December 24th); Christmas Day
Open: 11.30/a.m.–23.00/11 p.m.
Cuisine: French and Swedish
Chef de cuisine: Jörg Dössegger

Specialities: charcoal-grilled meat and fish; baked eels; Smörgåsbord in summer; gastronomic weeks with well-known French restaurants
Location: 3 km (2 miles) north of Stockholm, at Norrtull on Brunnsvik Bay
Setting: early 17th-century inn; well-preserved wooden coaching house; built by an illegitimate member of the Swedish Royal Family for his stable-master; a hostelry for private travellers since 1660; garden, lake, water lilies, fountains and willow trees; trees with fairy lights in winter
Amenities: private dining rooms (up to 150 persons); terrace for drinks and coffee; in summer, entertainment including 18th-century Swedish songs – sometimes in English; car park; sports facilities in the vicinity
Atmosphere: ancient, romantic, traditional – a rural idyll in one of the most delightful auberges in the whole of Scandinavia
Clientèle: members of the Swedish Royal Family; Stockholm's Sunday lunchtime crowd en famille
Dress: shirt and tie
Service: efficient and helpful
Reservations: advisable
Price range: medium
Credit cards: all major

Dinner

BLA GÅSEN
28 Karlavägen
Telephone: 10 02 69
Owner/Manager: Gert Lindberg
Closed: Saturday; Sunday; public holidays
Open: 11.00/a.m.–23.00/11 p.m. (except July) 17.00/5 p.m.–23.00/11 p.m.
Cuisine: Swedish and French
Chef de cuisine: Mats Vinestrand
Specialities: fish; meats and shellfish; daily changing menu
Location: in Östermalm; 1 km (5/8 mile) east of Stockholm
Setting: rustic bistro; flowery and romantic
Amenities: bar; open-air dining on veranda
Atmosphere: trendy; relaxing and refreshing when the grander places pall
Clientèle: men (and women) – about-town, with a fair number of celebrities incognito
Dress: no bikinis, Bermuda shorts or T-shirts with dubious slogans
Service: excellent
Reservations: advisable
Price range: medium
Credit cards: AE, DC, Euro, Visa

Meeting Point

OPERABAR
Operahuset
Telephone: 10 79 35
Owner/Manager: Jam Ling
Closed: never
Open: 12.00/a.m.–24.00/12 p.m. and 17.00/5 p.m.–24.00/12 p.m. (Sunday)
Location: opposite the Royal Palace
Setting: breathtaking Nordic Art Nouveau – stained glass domed ceiling; mahogany, marble and leather upholstery
Amenities: restaurant ›Operakällaren‹; Café Opera bistro; private dining rooms; snack bar; gourmet take-away meals (all in same complex)
Atmosphere: nostalgic evocation of the heyday of café society; the oldest meeting-place in the city, and still the most fashionable
Clientèle: chic, self-confident, discriminating and well-informed
Service: to perfection
Reservations: advisable
Credit cards: AE, DC, Euro, Visa

Café

GATEAUX
2 Norrlandsgatan
Telephone: 20 61 20
Owner/Manager: Claes Christianson
Open: (Monday–Friday) 7.30/a.m.–19.00/7 p.m.; (Saturday) 10.00/a.m.–19.00/7 p.m.; (Sunday) 11.00/a.m.–19.00/7 p.m.
Location: central
Setting: newly-opened café in an indoor piazza; elegant décor in a blend of traditional and modern styles
Amenities: salads, sandwiches, snacks and light meals as well as home-made cakes and pastries; pianist; air conditioning
Atmosphere: a bright, cheerful, up-to-date version of a classic coffee-house
Clientèle: heterogeneous; young and trendy students and secretaries; young-at-heart senior citizens with a sweet tooth
Service: cheerful and enthusiastic

Meeting Point

CAFE OPERA
Operahuset
Telephone: 24 27 07/11 00 26
Owner/Manager: Tore Wretman Restauranter AB/Per Vriger
Closed: April 30th; June 20th; December 24th–25th; New Year's Eve
Open: 11.30/a.m.–3.00/a.m.
Location: in the Opera House complex

Setting: French-style brasserie; one room in 1970s style; the other pure 1880s nostalgia; grandiose vaulted stucco ceiling with turn-of-the-century frescoes; tables cleared after midnight to make way for a sea of gyrating bodies as the discothèque warms up
Amenities: restaurant (Operakälleren) with open-air dining; bar; private dining rooms; snack bar; gourmet take-away meals; live orchestra
Atmosphere: colourful amalgam of 19th century grandeur, 20th century decadence, French flair and Swedish laissez-faire
Clientèle: punks to black tie; Stockholm's chiceria and stylish strangers from 19 to 99
Service: charming
Reservations: essential for lunch
Credit cards: all major

Location: central
Setting: two-storeyed bar/restaurant/nightclub; Art Déco style
Amenities: bar; restaurant (11.30/a.m.–14.00/2 p.m. and 18.30/6.30 p.m.–23.30/11.30 p.m.); casino; shows (every Monday); open-air dining in summer; pianist; air conditioning
Atmosphere: the Régine's of Stockholm; warm, stylish and casual
Clientèle: young (but not necessarily innocent); King Carl Gustav and Queen Silvia; tennis idols Björn Borg and Ilie Nastase; movie queen Britt Eklund; transatlantic guests from Jack Nicholson to Andy Williams
Dress: elegant; expensive and designer-chic
Service: expertly supervised by Sweden's uncontested ›Queen of the Night‹
Reservations: advisable
Credit cards: all major

Nightclub

VALENTINO
24 Birger Jarlsgatan
Telephone: 14 27 80
Owner/Managers: Paolo and Sergio Montanari
Closed: Sunday
Open: 11.30/a.m.–14.30/2.30 p.m. and 18.00/6 p.m.–3.00/a.m.
Location: central
Setting: stylish blend of Roman and Venetian décor
Amenities: discothèque (soft music); gourmet restaurant serving French and international food; bar/café; air conditioning; affiliated restaurant ›Martini‹ (4 Normalmstorg/Telephone 20 04 20) with Italian cuisine
Atmosphere: a shining new star in Stockholm's nocturnal firmament
Clientèle: cosmopolitan; jet-set, jeunesse dorée, local luminaries and visiting dignitaries
Dress: Gucci, Pucci and co. (no blue jeans)
Service: suave and solicitous
Reservations: advisable
Price range: average
Credit cards: all major

Shopping

EVERYTHING UNDER ONE ROOF
Nordiska Kompaniet   NK, Hamngatan

FOR HIM
Dirigent Herrmode   24–26 Sveavaegen

FOR HER
Boutique Madame   7 Nybrogatan

BEAUTY & HAIR
Hairport   PK Huset 10 Hamngatan

JEWELLERY
Georg Jensen Silver AB
13 Birger Jarlsgatan

THE BEST OF ART
Galleri 16   (contemporary art)
16 Karlavägen, Tel. 20 78 07/20 78 34
Konstruktiv Tendens (contemporary art)
69 Nybrogatan, Tel. 61 13 65
Olsson, Gunnar   (modern art)
6 Jungfrugatan, Tel. 62 28 68
Ståhle, Leif   (contemporary art)
Täby/11 Karlsholmsvägen, Tel. 7 56 40 10
Bukowski   (auctioneers)
8 Wahrendorffsgatan, Tel. 8 24 81 65

Nightclub

ALEXANDRA'S
29 Birger Jarlsgatan
Telephone: 10 48 64/10 46 46
Affiliations: Stockholm Plaza Hotel; Club of Clubs
Owner/Manager: SSRS and Alexandra Charles
Closed: Christmas Eve; Christmas Day; New Year's Day
Open: 11.30/a.m.–14.00/2 p.m. and 18.30/6.30 p.m.–3.00/a.m.

The City

Whenever you swallow a Valium, pre-fabricated peace of mind will set in – made in Basle. CIBA-Geigy, Hoffmann-La Roche, Sandoz & Co. dominate the skyline, the image and the economy of this tranquillizing town. Second-largest city in ›Europe's centre of gravity‹, serious, sincere and Swiss to the core (despite its bordering Germany and France – sharing the goods depot with the former and the international airport of Mulhouse with the latter), Basle has always been a bastion of conservatism with avant-garde philosophers enlivening the scene. Erasmus of Rotterdam found his stage here in the Renaissance to work and preach his ideas in freedom, followed over the centuries by countless scientists and free spirits whom Basle received as generously as her burghers kept to a bourgeois style of life marked by correct manners rather than revolutionary esprit. Business is the religion here, and art (as another form of business) the pastime. When the Basle Art moves to town, the world seems an auction house with the New Wild Ones not the misfits as one would expect, but the hottest tickets to reach for. Basle has its fair share of medieval charm, Old World antiquity and quaint corners for the peace of mind without a Valium, but, by and large, Vitamin C, DDT and LSD are the greater force behind the city's future. Rudolf Steiner had his success here, Karl Jaspers took refuge at the local university and Jeannot Tinguely even decorated his hometown with a few masterpieces, yet Basle remains the small brother of Zurich, in the cosmopolitan shadow of Geneva and away from the Alpine glamour of the St. Moritz-Gstaad routine.

Founded: 44 B.C., by Munatius Plancus; Basle – Basel (German) – from Basilia (Latin).

Far-reaching events: 7th century – Basle becomes an episcopal see; 11th century – free imperial city and residence of prince bishops; 1225 – first stone bridge over the Rhine; 1431–48 – Council of Basle elects Felix V as antipope; 1460 – foundation of University; 1501 – entry into the Swiss Confederation; 1516 – Erasmus publishes New Testament; 1523 – Basle accepts the Reformation and the rule of the prince bishops ends; 1648 – Basle independent of Switzerland following Treaty of Westphalia; 18th century – prosperity based on silk industry; 1833 – Basle becomes an independent canton.

Population: 180,000 – second largest city in Switzerland and capital of the Canton of Basle.

Postal code: CH-4000   **Telephone code:** 61

Climate: changeable but mild.

Calendar of events: *Fasnacht* (Feb/Mar) – world famous ›Mummenschanz‹ – pantomime with fantastic disguises, bands, dancing and processions; *Basle Autumn Fair* (Oct–Nov) – Switzerland's oldest and largest annual fair.

Fairs and exhibitions: *MUBA* (Jan) – coins; *EUROPEAN CLOCK AND JEWELLERY FAIR* (Feb); *SWISSBAU* (Feb) – building machinery fair; *EUROCAST* (Mar) – international cable and satellite television exhibition; *SWISS INDUSTRIES FAIR* (Mar); *SWISSPACK* (Apr) – packaging industry; *CIBBO* (Apr) – international association of jewellery, silverware, diamonds, pearls and gems; *ART AND ANTIQUES FAIR OF SWITZERLAND* (Apr); *FAWEM* (Jun) – machine tool and tools exhibition; *ART 17* (Jun) – international art fair (20th-century art); *EURO-DESIGN* (Sep); *VIDEO-EUROPA* (Sep) – Swiss videotex congress and exhibition; *INTERFEREX* (Sep) – international trade fair for hardware, tools and household goods; *FABRITEC* (Sep) – trade fair for fabrication installations in electronics; *SAMA* (Sep) – international exhibition of advanced techniques: production, automation, industrial robotics and surface treatment; *SWISSDATA* (Sep) – exhibition of data processing in technical application and research; *AIR CARGO FORUM* (Sep); *HOLZ* (Oct) Swiss woodworking trade fair; *PRO AQUA – PRO VITA* (Oct) – engineering in environmental protection and ecology; *BASLE WINE FAIR* (Oct–Nov) – in connection with the Basle autumn market; *AUTUMN TRADE FAIR* (Oct/Nov); *SNOW* (Nov) – winter sports and recreation show; *COLLECTOR'S EXCHANGE* (Nov) – art and antiques.

Best view of the city: from the tower of the *Münster*, the central cathedral.

Historical sights: *Münster* (12th–14th centuries) – Basle's Romanesque and Gothic landmark cathedral; *Fine Arts Museum* – a valuable collection of works by Holbein and modern artists from Monet to Mondriaan; *Rathaus* (1504–14) – late Gothic city hall with gilded turret; *Preacher Church* (1269) – elegantly Gothic, with the famous ›Dance of Death‹ series of paintings; *Casino* – with a large concert hall for the city's two symphony orchestras; *Holbein Fountain; Barefoot Church* (14th century); *Spalentor* (14th century) – city gate.

Modern sights: *Church of St. Anthony* (1931) – designed by Karl Moser; *Bank for International Balance of Payments* – elegant modern tower and office building; *Barfüsserplatz* – the city's vibrant centre, for pedestrians only; *Convention Centre* – an aesthetic place to do business.

Special attractions: a festival concert in *Römerbad* (in Badenweiler); dinner at *Donati's* during the Arts Fair; a private party at *Schloss Binningen*.

Important companies with headquarters in the city: *Kühne & Nagel* (transport); *Sandoz* (pharmaceuticals); *Ciba-Geigy* (chemicals, pharmaceuticals); *Hoffmann-La Roche* (chemicals, pharmaceuticals); *Lonza* (chemicals); Schweizer Bankverein (banking).

Airport: Basle-Mulhouse, BSL (on French territory); Tel.: 57 31 11; 12 km/8 miles.

The Headquarters

DREI KOENIGE AM RHEIN

8 Blumenrain
CH–4001 Basle
Telephone: 25 52 52
Telex: 962 937 roib
Owning Company: Societe d'Exploitation et Gestion Hôtelière
Managing Director: Paul Bougenaux
Director: Roman M. Steiner
Affiliation/Reservation Systems: The Leading Hotels of the World, Utell International, Leading Hotels of Switzerland
Number of rooms: 80 (7 suites)
Price range: Sfr 150–215 (single)
　　　　　　　Sfr 230–355 (double)
　　　　　　　Sfr 450–710 (suite)
Credit cards: Access, AE, BC, CB, DC, EC, MC, Visa
Location: city centre
Built: 1026 (renovated 1983)
Style: traditional and distinguished
Hotel amenities: limousine service, secretarial services
Main hall porter: Walter Plebiscita
Room service: 6.30/a.m.–24.00/12 p.m.
Laundry/dry cleaning: same day
Conference rooms: 5 (up to 100 persons)
Bar: ›Dreikönigs-Bar‹ (17.00/5.00 p.m.–24.00/12.00 p.m.)
Restaurants: ›Rôtisserie des Rois‹ (11.30/a.m.–14.00/2.00 p.m., 18.30/6.30 p.m.–23.00/11.00 p.m.); ›Rhy-Deck‹ (7.00/a.m.–24.00/12.00 p.m.)
Chef de cuisine: Bernard Muller
Nightclub: ›King's Club‹

Forty years before the Battle of Hastings an inn stood here on the banks of the fast -flowing Rhine. Originally called ›At the Sign of the Flower‹, this oldest hostelry in Switzerland can claim pre-eminence as headquarters in the city since, soon after its foundation, it acquired its present name following an early summit meeting between three crowned heads, who redrew the political boundaries in the area. For nine hundred years since then the ›Three Kings‹ has provided bed and board to countless late and ci-devant emperors, monarchs, princes and businessmen, from Napoléon Bonaparte to King Farouk. The un-adorned, vaguely francophine building dates from 1026; the intérieur ranges from stucco ceilings and period furniture in the bedrooms to wood panelling and concealed lighting in the Dreikönigs-Bar, the city's chicest after-hours rendez-vous. The high-ceilinged lounge, dominated by a huge historical mural, is as popular for preliminary discussions amongst visiting managers as is the riverside terrace of the Rôtisserie des Rois – glassed-in in spring and autumn – for a quick lunch or a leisurely dîner-à-deux. Almost a millenium of experience and the guiding hand of hôtelier extraordinaire Paul Bougenaux maintain the Trois Rois' unchallenged position as the city's only regal address.

The Hideaway

RÖMERBAD

1 Schloßplatz
D–7847 Badenweiler (40 km/25 miles)
Telephone: (49–76 32) 700
Telex: 772933 roeb
Owner: The Fellmann-Lauer family
General Manager: Klaus Lauer
Affiliation/Reservation System: The Leading Hotels of the World
Number of rooms: 112 (11 suites)
Price range: DM 115–330
Credit cards: AE, Visa
Location: southern Black Forest, 40 km/25 miles from city centre, 45 km/28 miles from airport
Built: 1825 (recently renovated)
Style: traditional Grand Hotel
Hotel amenities: garage, valet parking, house limousine service, indoor swimming pool, beauty salon, sauna, solarium, massage, newsstand, tobacconist, library, grand piano, house doctor
Main hall porter: Lino Chierchia
Room amenities: colour tv (pets allowed)
Bathroom amenities: bidet, bathrobe
Room service: 7.00/a.m.–24.00/12 p.m.
Laundry/dry cleaning: same day (weekend service)
Conference rooms: 3 (up to 80 persons), secretarial services, ballroom
Sports: tennis, table tennis, golf, minigolf, riding, fishing, swimming
Bar: (11.00/a.m.–14.30/2.30 p.m. and 18.00/6.00 p.m. to closing time) Stefan (barman), English style décor, records
Restaurant: (12.00/a.m.–14.00/2.00 p.m. and 19.00/7.00 p.m.–21.00/9.00 p.m.) Ginetto Bucci (maître), Jochen Möhringer (chef de cuisine), international cuisine, records
Private dining rooms: two

The imposing nineteenth-century spa-town décor of the Hotel Römerbad belies its unpretentious origins, some 150 years ago, as a coaching inn. Few traces of this humble beginning remain, although the luxurious auberge set in its own landscaped gardens in the pretty Black Forest town of Badenweiler has been run by the Fellmann-Lauer family since its opening. Echoes of the past there are in plenty – fine antique furnishings, valuable pictures lovingly arranged by connoisseur Klaus Lauer, old-fashioned service and above all an unhurried atmosphere which nostalgically recalls the turn -of-the-century Golden Age. But the Römerbad is no museum-piece; it has managed to integrate modern facilities into a traditional framework in a most effective way. Water from the mineral springs is on tap in the well-equipped bathrooms, and music – most of it modern – performed by international artists is on stage in the magnificent octagonal concert hall during the widely-acclaimed arts festivals in November and March.

Lunch

CHEZ DONATI
48 St. Johanns-Vorstadt
Telephone: 57 09 19
Affiliations: Schweizerischer Wirteverein
Owner/Manager: Franco Donati
Closed: Monday; four weeks in July
Open: 11.30/a.m.–24.00/12 p.m. (kitchen 11.30/a.m.–14.30/2 p.m. and 18.00/6 p.m.–22.00/10 p.m.)
Cuisine: Italo-French
Chef de cuisine: Rolf Muller
Specialities: home-made pasta; shin of veal (osso buco); white truffles (September–December); scampi; sole au beurre; rhubarb meringue tart
Location: on the banks of the Rhine
Setting: typical old brasserie; two high-ceilinged rooms; Jugendstil décor; collection of contemporary paintings
Amenities: open-air dining on terrace overlooking the Rhine
Atmosphere: lively; chic; rather Italian
Clientèle: le Tout Basle; mostly for business at lunchtime and for pleasure at night
Dress: what you will
Service: professional and competent
Reservations: advisable
Price range: rather expensive
Credit cards: not accepted

Lunch

KUNSTHALLE
7 Steinenberg
Telephone: 23 42 33
Owner/Manager: Romano Villa/Peter Wies
Closed: never
Open: 8.30 a.m.–midnight
Cuisine: imaginative
Specialities: antipasto of fillets of sardelles, home-marinated salmon and chilli peppers; boeuf gros sel with bean and potato salad; chocolate mousse; tirami sù (rich Italian coffee and cream cheese dessert)
Location: near the theatre (Stadttheater)
Setting: distinguished; predominantly white dining room with French windows leading to the ›Winter Garden‹
Amenities: open-air dining on terrace shaded by lovely old trees
Atmosphere: fashionable and popular
Clientèle: favoured rendezvous for actors, artists and the town's chiceria
Dress: suitably with-it
Service: welcoming
Reservations: advisable
Price range: quite expensive
Credit cards: Euro

Dinner

STUCKI (›Bruderholz‹)
42 Bruderholzallee
Telephone: 35 82 22
Affiliations: Traditions et Qualité; Relais et Châteaux (Relais Gourmand)
Owner/Manager/Chef de cuisine: Hans Stucki
Closed: Sunday; Monday (except during Trades Fairs); mid-July–early August
Open: 12.00/a.m.–13.30/1.30 p.m. and 19.00/7 p.m.–24.00/12 p.m.
Cuisine: nouvelle, with a French-Swiss accent
Specialities: frequently changing menu; crabs and young vegetables in aspic; lobster with sage and shallots; fillet of mullet in sherry vinegar; truffle ravioli with Roquefort; sautéed frogs' legs in chive cream; quince soufflé
Location: on the Bruderholz, south of city centre
Setting: on a hillside in an elegant residential area; large patrician house in a lovely shady garden; two dining rooms – one with fabric-covered walls, the other with a large painting of a lively banquet; small-paned windows; carefully-chosen period furnishings; well-spaced small round tables with fine damask tablecloths and pretty china
Amenities: private dining room (20–40 persons); terrace overlooking garden for apéritifs
Atmosphere: light, bright and welcoming, but distinguished in the classic idiom
Clientèle: Basle's Beau Monde; expense-account connoisseurs of good food and gracious living
Dress: elegant
Service: quietly knowledgeable
Reservations: essential (pets permitted)
Price range: justifiably expensive
Credit cards: AE, Visa

Lunch

CASANOVA
9 Spalenvorstadt
Telephone: 25 55 37
Owner/Managers: August and Silvia Beerli
Closed: Sunday; Monday; July
Open: 11.00/a.m.–15.00/3 p.m. and 18.00/6 p.m.–24.00/12 p.m.
Cuisine: French – ›à la minute‹
Chef de cuisine: August Beerli
Specialities: foie gras; fresh lobster (fish tanks); saddle of lamb with rosemary; pigeon with black truffle sauce; seasonal specialities
Location: central

Setting: turn-of-the-century brasserie; Jugendstil décor with original furniture from Paris
Amenities: small bar for apéritifs
Atmosphere: elegant but not too formal
Clientèle: comfortable mixture of academics, pharmaceutical experts, bankers, businessmen and burghers of Basle
Dress: not too outlandish or untidy
Service: supervised with great charm by Silvia Beerli
Reservations: essential
Price range: moderately expensive
Credit cards: AE, DC, Euro, Visa

Lunch

SCHLOSS BINNINGEN
5 Schlossgasse
Binningen (3 km/2 miles)
Telephone: 47 20 55
Owner/Manager: Mario Hermann
Closed: Sunday evening; Monday; one week at Fastnacht (Fasching/Shrove Tuesday - pre-Lenten celebrations in February/March); two weeks in July
Open: 12.00/a.m.–15.00/3 p.m. and 18.30/6.30 p.m.–22.30/10.30 p.m.
Cuisine: French
Chef de cuisine: Bernard Rocheray
Specialities: according to season; salmon mousse with raspberry vinaigrette; warm salad of lobster claws with melon and lemon sauce; escalope de foie gras grillée au poivre rouge; coq au Chambertin; extravagant dessert buffet; pears in white chocolate; îles flottantes; caramelized apples
Location: in the gastronomic suburb of Binningen, 3 km (2 miles) east of Basle
Setting: lovingly-renovated and maintained 16th-century Sleeping-Beauty castle in a fairy-tale park; towers and turrets, original furniture and accessoires; rooms decorated in various styles from the medieval (von-Salis-Stube and Great Hall) to Louis XVI and Rococo
Amenities: private dining rooms (8–55 persons); shady terrace overlooking park; car park
Atmosphere: ›ambiance chevaleresque ‹ – festive and nostalgic; redolent of time past with just a hint of Hollywood
Clientèle: gourmets with a penchant for the romantic from Basle, Besançon and Baden-Baden; antiquarians with a sweet tooth; presidents, politicians, personalities and local patricians en fête and en famille
Dress: armour to be left in the cloakroom
Service: impeccable
Reservations: advisable (no pets)
Price range: aristocratic
Credit cards: AE, Euro, Visa

Dinner

WEIHERSCHLOSS BOTTMINGEN
9 Schlossgasse
Bottmingen (4 km/3 miles)
Telephone: 47 15 15
Owner/Manager: René and Ruth Gischig-Steiner
Closed: Sunday evening/Monday; one week at Fastnacht (end of February)
Open: 12.00/a.m.–14.00/2 p.m. and 18.00/6 p.m.–24.00/12 p.m. (last orders at 21.00/9 p.m.)
Cuisine: French
Chef de cuisine: René Gischig-Steiner
Specialities: warm salad of salmon and sole in fruit vinegar with vegetables; creamed chanterelles in puff pastry; turbot with fresh truffles; fricassée of chicken with shrimps and morel mushrooms in cognac sauce; sorbets ›Four Seasons‹ with fresh fruits
Location: at Bottmingen, 4 km/3 miles from Basle
Setting: fairy-tale castle; a lake with swans and weeping willows
Amenities: private dining rooms (8–150 persons); open-air dining on terrace
Atmosphere: a feast fit for a châtelain
Clientèle: local citizens with cause for celebration, plus discriminating tourists from Gothenburg to Genova
Dress: rather conservative
Service: friendly
Reservations: advisable
Price range: fairly expensive
Credit cards: AE, DC, Euro

Café

CAFE DES ARTS
3 Klostergasse
Telephone: 22 36 19
Owner/Manager: Frank Hablutzel/ Christoph Krieg
Closed: never
Open: 9.00/a.m.–24.00/12 p.m. (weekends – 1.00/p.m.); (Sunday) 11.00/a.m.– 24.00/12 p.m.
Location: vis-à-vis the theatre (Stadttheater)
Setting: in the Arts Centre (Kunsthalle); skilfully converted into a glimmering, shimmering locale in shades of green; exotic collection of contemporary paintings on the walls
Amenities: wicker chairs and tables under chestnut trees for outdoor dining in summer; light lunches, salads and snacks; cocktail bar
Atmosphere: unique
Clientèle: the focal point for Basle's Top Ten; the young, the would-be-young and the young-at-heart
Service: cheerful

Bar

ATLANTIS
13 Klosterberg
Telephone: 23 34 00
Owner/Manager: Restaurant Atlantis
AG/Eddie Cassini
Closed: never
Open: 7.30 a.m.–24.00/12 p.m. (Friday
till 1 a.m.); Sunday 10.00 a.m.–12.00/a.m.
Location: vis-à-vis the theatre
Setting: on two levels; walls lined with
mirrors
Amenities: music shows, talk shows, ca-
baret; 2 bars
Atmosphere: légère, elegant
Clientèle: broad range of people from 18
to 80; artists, actors, musicians
Service: fast and very efficient
Reservations: advisable, especially for
live shows
Credit cards: not accepted

Nightclub

STRATOS
20 Freiestrasse/1 Rüdengasse
Telephone: 25 15 35
Owner/Manager: Uli Riesen
Closed: never
Open: 21.00/9 p.m.–2.00/a.m. weekends-
till 3.00/a.m.
Location: across the street from the main
Post Office
Setting: large nightclub; recently reno-
vated; all in dark blue; satin upholstery;
niches for 2–9 persons; golden painting
especially created for the Stratos by a Ba-
sle artist
Amenities: air conditioning; parking in
the vicinity
Atmosphere: ›the nicest nightclub in Ba-
sle‹; cosy and comfortable
Clientèle: bank directors to bohémiens
Dress: jeans to dark suit; anything goes
Service: sometimes hectic, but always
friendly
Reservations: recommended, especially
after midnight
Credit cards: AE, DC, Visa

Shopping

EVERYTHING UNDER ONE ROOF
Globus 2 Marktplatz

FOR HIM
Fein-Kaller 48 Gerbergasse

FOR HER
Aphrodite 4 Dufourstrasse

BEAUTY & HAIR
Beauté Grazia Barblan
45 Steinentorstrasse
Intercoiffure H. Schweizer
2 Freie Strasse

JEWELLERY
Bijouterie Bucherer 40 Freie Strasse

LOCAL SPECIALITIES
Oettinger Cigares (tobacco)
2 Steinenvorstadt
Feldpausch (women's fashion)
19–27 Falknerstrasse
PKZ-Burger Kehl (men's fashion)
5 Freie Strasse
Modehaus Spengler (children's fashion)
5 Steinenvorstadt
Royale Boutique (leather fashion)
105 Freie Strasse
Fourrures Lindner (furs)
88 Freie Strasse
Walter Kueng (gifts)
Fischmarkt
Laeckerli-Huus (local specialities)
57 Gerbergasse

THE BEST OF ART
Beyeler   (Fine and contemporary art)
9 Bäumleingasse, Tel. 23 54 12
Buchmann   (contemporary art)
64 St. Alban-Rheinweg, Tel. 23 99 88
Hummel, Corinne   (contemporary art)
3 Kornhausgasse, Tel. 25 34 13
Littmann   (contemporary art)
16 Bäumleingasse, Tel. 23 87 67
Bieder, Hans   (18th/19th-century an-
tiques) 21 Barfüsserplatz,
Tel. 25 08 69
Cackett, Dr. Christa   (17th–19th-cen-
tury antiques) 59 Spalenberg,
Tel. 25 91 85
Münzen und Medaillen AG.   25 Malz-
gasse, Tel. 23 75 44
Segal   (17th/18th-century works of art,
furniture) 14–16 Aeschengraben,
Tel. 23 39 08

Democracies have nothing exciting about them – no Caesar, no Shah, no glamour, no pomp. The capital of the oldest – and best functioning – democracy in the world is hardly an exception. Here, more importance is accorded to banking than banquets, more time is spent watching the famous namesake bears in their pits than the heads of state passing through this toyland town which has lost virtually nothing of its medieval character. The intact little pearl in the midst of the rugged oyster shell of Europe is by no means boring, unless quiet beauty and a peaceful style of life are considered such. Perched high on a peninsula formed by a loop of the River Aare, the mini-metropolis is bedecked with towers and fountains, churches and patrician houses, arcaded streets and vaulted caves. There is no gambling in the casino (only concerts), there is no gay nightlife (except for joyful drinking in historic cellars and the Schweizerhof's Jaylin's Club), there are no fancy festivals (save the Jazz days – again with Jaylin's as the prime platform and Jean-Jacques Gauer of the Schweizerhof as the mastermind behind it), but there are strings of elegant shops, antique dealers and galleries lining the picturesque alleys. The business of politics does not entrail the glitter of the film world here. (And local daughter Ursula Andress comes home rather unnoticed.) The countryside around town, on the other hand, reconciles for the lack of social highlights and frivolous fun – the beauty here is of such Alpine opulence that one can easily dispense with yearnings for the capitals of the world.

Founded: 1191 by Berthold von Zähringen; Bern (German), Berne (French) – ›a bear‹.

Far-reaching events: 1218 – Berne a free imperial city; 1353 – Berne joins the Helvetic Confederation; 1475 – acquisition of the Emmental, Aargau and other territories, as far as the Rhône; 1528 – Berne accepts the Reformation; 1648 – in the wake of the Thirty Years War, Switzerland independent of the German Empire; 1798 – French occupation – founding of the Helvetian Republic under the Directory; 1815 – Switzerland asserts her neutrality in the Treaty of Paris after Napoleon's downfall; 1848 – capital of Switzerland.

Population: 170,000; capital of Switzerland and of Canton Berne.

Postal code: CH–3000   **Telephone code:** 31

Climate: Alpine; unexpectedly hot in summer, expectedly cold in winter.

Best time to visit: May to October (skiers tend to disagree).

Calendar of events: *Gassenfastnacht* (Feb); *Easter Market* (Mar); *Grand Prix de Berne* (Apr) – World Cup of rapier fencing; *International Jazz Festival* (May); *Erlacher Hoffest,* classical music (May); *International Festival of Small Theatres* (Jun); *International Folk Festival (Jul*-biennial); *Hand-Organ Festival* (Sep); *Gala Show (Nov)* – in aid of Berne's spastic children.

Fairs and exhibitions: *BEA* (Apr/May) – handicraft, agriculture, industry and trade; *LIGAM* (Jun) – furniture; *ORNARIS* (Aug) – modern living and industrial arts; *BESPO* (Sep/Oct) – summer sports and textiles; *MOWO* (Nov/Dez) – fashion, living, household arts.

Best views of the city: from the tower of the cathedral.

Historical and modern sights: *Zytgloggeturm* (1218) – landmark clock tower cum glockenspiel; *Käfigturm* (1250–1350) – city gate and one-time prison; *Berne Historical Museum* – containing the state treasure collection; *Berne Art Museum* – one of the first buildings to be wrapped by Bulgarian packaging artist Christo, with an excellent collection of modern art, from Hodler to Braque, and a unique collection of paintings by local son Paul Klee; *Münster* (1421–1588) – Gothic cathedral, with Switzerland's best stained-glass windows; *Federal City Hall* (1857) – Italian Renaissance style seat of the Swiss parliament; *Natural History Museum* – Ice Age fossils and African mammals; *Bernese Historical Museum* – 18th-century furniture and Flemish tapestries; the *Central Station.*

Special attractions: a walk through the *Lauben,* the 17th and 18th-century shopping arcades, a pot-pourri of sights, sounds and aromas, from flowers to fresh coffee; views of the city from the *Nydegg Bridge* and *Junkerngasse; Bärengraben* – since 1315 a preserve for bears, the city's mascots; *Geranium Market* – held against a medieval backdrop; *Post Museum* – with the world's largest public exhibition of stamps; *Paul Klee Foundation* – an impressive collection of works by the Berne artist; the *Bernese Oberland* – flowers, lakes and a trip up the *Jungfraujoch.*

Important companies with headquarters in the city: *Galenica* (pharmaceutical products); *Hallwag* (printing and publishing); *Hasler* (news technology and electronics); *Kümmerly & Frey* (geographical publications); *Losinger* (construction); *MAPAG* (plastics production machinery); *Schweizer Volksbank* (banking); *Stuag* (roads and underground construction); *Suchard Tobler* (chocolate), *Wabco Westinghouse* (electrical appliances): *Wander* (pharmaceuticals and foodstuffs); *WIFAG* (geographic technology).

Airport: (national) Berne-Belpmoos, BRN; Tel.: 54 34 11, 10 km/6 miles; (international) Zurich, ZRH; Tel.: (1) 8 12 71 11, 125 km/78 miles; Geneva, GVA; Tel.: (22) 99 31 11, 154 km/96 miles; Swissair, Tel.: 22 95 11.

The Headquarters

GAUER HOTEL SCHWEIZERHOF

11 Bahnhofplatz
CH–3000 Berne
Telephone: 22 45 01
Telex: 911 782 shbe
Owner/General Manager: J. J. Gauer
Affiliation/Reservation Systems: The Leading Hotels of the World, The Leading Hotels of Switzerland, Utell International, SRS (Steigenberger Reservation Service), Prohotel of Switzerland
Number of rooms: 120 (7 suites)
Price range: Sfr 165–540
Credit cards: all major
Location: city centre
Built: 1850 (recently renovated)
Style: classic, antique style
Hotel amenities: garage, valet parking, house limousine service, beauty salon, newsstand, massage
Main hall porter: Louis Achermann
Room amenities: colour tv, video, minibar (pets allowed)
Bathroom amenities: bathrobe, hairdrier, telephone
Room service: 6.00/a.m.–24.00/12 p.m.
Conference rooms: 10 (up to 350 persons)
Bar: ›Arcady‹ (see Bars)
Restaurants: ›Schweizerhof‹ (18.00/6.00 p.m.–24.00/12.00 p.m.) J. Woerle (maître), E. Weyermann (chef de cuisine) ›Grill Room‹ (12.00/a.m.–13.30/1.30 p.m. and 19.00/7.00 p.m.–24.00/12.00 p.m.) F. Niklaus (maître), U. Hauri (chef de cuisine)
Nightclub: ›Jaylin's‹ (see Nightclubs)

The Swiss capital is famous for its medieval beauty and three world-famous institutions: the neutral government, the landmark bear-moat and the grand Schweizerhof. Across from the station and a few Bally steps away from the parliament, the boutiques and the galleries, this windowbox-covered city palais shows a touch of class in every detail without frills and pompous paraphernalia. Wide hallways and large rooms are decorated in the style of a private manor house with antiques, Gobelins, Old Masters and hints of the homelike atmosphere the owning Gauer family is so famous for creating in all their hotels. The beds are as comfortable as in a mountain chalet, the baths as luxurious as in a palace; the service is as personal as in a country inn whereas the clientèle is as international as in Basle, Zurich and Geneva combined. The Arcady-Bar is the meeting point of Berne, the two restaurants are the gourmet-stops of the land and the Jaylin's nightclub is one of the foremost jazz scenes on the continent. The sophistication, the fashionable people and the metropolitan flair are largely the result of worldly Jean-Jacques Gauer's universal policy – anachronistic in part to the pretty town's lovable provinciality. The Schweizerhof is the only stop for globe-trotters, for business or pleasure, and the only game in town.

**GRAND HOTEL
VICTORIA – JUNGFRAU**

41 Höhenweg
CH–3800 Interlaken (40 km/25 miles)
Telephone: (36) 21 21 71
Telex: 923121 Vic
Telefax: (36) 22 26 71
Managing Director: Emanuel Berger
Affiliation/Reservation Systems: The Leading Hotels of the World, Utell International, Swissair/Horis, The Leading Hotels of Switzerland
Closed: mid-November to mid-December
Number of rooms: 233 (13 suites)
Price range: Sfr 170–340
Credit cards: AE, DC, EC, Visa, MC, Access, JCB
Location: in Interlaken
Built: 1864/1866
Style: Art Nouveau
Hotel amenities: house limousine service, swimming pool, souvenir shop, hairstylist
Room amenities: colour tv, video, radio, mini-bar, message lamp
Bathroom amenities: hairdrier
Room service: 24 hours
Conference rooms: 8 (up to 380 persons)
Sports: tennis
Bars: ›Victoria‹ (17.00–5.00 p.m. to closing time) Mauro Gramatica (barman); ›Intermezzo‹ (10.00/a.m.–23.00/11 p.m.); Racket-Club‹ (8.00/a.m.–23.00/11 p.m.)
Restaurant: ›La Terrasse‹: 12.00/a.m.–14.00/2.00 p.m. and 19.00/7.00 p.m.–22.00/10.00 p.m.) Raffaele Esposito and Dino Sotgiu (maîtres), Erwin Stocker (chef de cuisine), pianist; ›Jungfraustube‹ (12.00/a.m.–24.00/12.00 p.m.) Hélène Mourelle (maîtresse), Hanspeter Zurflüh (chef de grill)
Nightclubs: three

Interlaken used to be an obligatory stop on last century's Grand Tour. It is again, but less for the Alps' most majestic range than for the grandest auberge de renommé at its feet. So many things have changed since the times of the great Queen lending her name – and her tourists – to this venerable institution (and most of them within the last decade under the entrepreneurial spirit of Emanuel Berger), that former guests will be dazzled by the abundance of amenities, luxury and style – quite anachronistic in this quaint town of renowned boarding schools, seasonal wanderers and lakeside romance. Gourmet restaurant, indoor tennis, swanky nightclub and ritzy suites adorn this bastion of high life in the lowlands as if it were in the middle of Zurich. Small wonder that countless companies of world ranking hold their top-level conferences here. Nevertheless, the spacious areal allows for anonymity, intimacy and hiding away from activists. In summer the surroundings blossom into a Garden of Eden and in winter the ski resorts of Mürren, Wengen and Grindelwald are just up the hill.

Lunch

COMMERCE
74 Gerechtigkeitsgasse
Telephone: 22 11 61
Owner/Manager: Enrique Ros
Closed: Sunday; Monday lunchtime;
July
Open: 9.00/a.m.–24.00/12 p.m.
Cuisine: Spanish
Chef de cuisine: Maria Ros
Specialities: paella; fillet steak; scampi
nature; rice ›Juan‹
Location: near the Fountain of Justice
Setting: a little Spanish-style taberna
with a distinctly Mediterranean air
about it
Amenities: multi-storey car-park (two mi-
nutes' walk away)
Atmosphere: one of the unchanging insti-
tutions on the Berne culinary scene
Clientèle: expatriate Spaniards; conser-
vative, comfortably-off burghers of Berne
who prefer a well-tried and tested menu
to culinary surprises
Dress: nothing too eccentric
Service: friendly waiters in waistcoats
and aprons; supervised by the patron,
Enrique Ros
Reservations: recommended
Price range: moderately expensive
Credit cards: not accepted

Dinner

RÄBLUS
3 Zeughausgasse
Telephone: 22 59 08/9
Owner/Manager/Chef de cuisine: Peter
Pulver
Closed: Sunday
Open: 11.00/a.m.–14.00/2 p.m.; 17.00/5
p.m.–24.00/12 p.m.
Cuisine: classic, unpretentious
Specialities: home-made pâté (Hauspas-
tete); consommé with bone marrow
(Markbouillon); home-
made pasta; scampi; flambéed pepper
steak; Grand Marnier gâteau; crêpes Su-
zette
Location: central; near the French church
Setting: first-floor dining room with com-
fortable rustic décor
Amenities: open-air dining on veranda;
piano bar; car park (multi-storey)
Atmosphere: pleasantly welcoming and
home-like
Clientèle: Berne's Top Twenty; predomi-
nantly for business at lunchtime and for
pleasure at night
Dress: elegant
Service: efficient
Reservations: advisable for dinner
Price range: on the expensive side
Credit cards: AE, DC, Euro, Visa

Lunch

DU THEATRE
7 Theaterplatz
Telephone: 22 71 77
Owner/Manager/Chef de cuisine: Ernesto
Schlegel
Closed: Sunday evening; Monday; July
9th–August 2nd
Open: 9.30/a.m.–24.00/12 p.m.
Cuisine: modernized classic; interna-
tional
Specialities: quail terrine in aspic; stuffed
morel mushrooms in puff pastry; fillet of
sole in Noilly Prat; émincé de filet de
veau with crayfish; soufflé aux poires
Location: near the Clock Tower (Zeit-
glockenturm)
Setting: established in 1903; converted
theatre, with wall paintings illustrating
subjects from la vie du théâtre
Amenities: three private dining rooms (40
persons)
Atmosphere: quietly exclusive
Clientèle: from Businessmen to Beau
Monde
Dress: elegant
Service: charming
Reservations: necessary
Price range: medium to high
Credit cards: not accepted

Lunch

FROHSINN
54 Münstergasse
Telephone: 22 37 68
Owner/Manager: Leonello Rubli
Closed: Sunday; Monday
Open: 8.00/a.m.–14.00/2 p.m.; 18.00/6
p.m.–22.00/10 p.m.
Cuisine: traditional and innovative
Chef de cuisine: Leonello Rubli
Specialities: goulash; goose liver mousse;
liver with Swiss fried potatoes (Rösti); fil-
let of beef in whisky sauce; minute de
boeuf bourguignon; sabayon with straw-
berries
Location: almost in the shadow of the
Clock Tower (Tour de l'Horloge)
Setting: under the famous arcades of
Berne; small restaurant; dining room
with exposed-beam ceiling and checked
tablecloths on the twelve tables
Atmosphere: cheerful and friendly
Clientèle: comfortable mixture of local
businessmen, men from the media, jour-
nalists, politicians and men-in-the-street
Dress: as you like it (as long as they will
like you)
Service: professional and very personal
Reservations: recommended
Price range: moderately expensive
Credit cards: not accepted

Dinner

PIAZZA LORENZINI
3 Marktgass-Passage
Telephone: 22 78 50
Owner/Manager: Judith Adank
Closed: Sunday
Open: 11.30/a.m.–14.00/2 p.m.; 19.00/7
p.m.–23.30/11.30 p.m.
Cuisine: Tuscan
Chef de cuisine: Mr. Berganaschi
Specialities: Tuscan-style rabbit (coniglio
alla toscana con bocconi); steak Floren-
tine; trifle (zuppa inglese)
Location: central
Setting: characteristic Tuscan-style rustic
décor
Amenities: bar; car park in the vicinity
Atmosphere: very colourful
Clientèle: popular meeting place for all,
from government ministers to show-busi-
ness young hopefuls
Dress: come-as-you-please
Service: cheerfully welcoming
Reservations: advisable
Price range: average
Credit cards: Euro, Visa

Dinner

KLÖTZLIKELLER
62 Gerechtigkeitsgasse
Telephone: 22 74 56
Owner/Manager: Isabella Gschwind
Closed: Sunday; lunchtime every day
Open: 16.00/4 p.m.–0.30/12.30 a.m.
Cuisine: Swiss
Chef de cuisine: Kathi Marthaler
Specialities: salads; salad with calf's
liver; macaroni ›Alpler‹; fillet of beef
with morel mushroom cream sauce and
Swiss fried potatoes (Rösti); champagne
sorbet
Location: by the bell clock tower (Zeitglockenturm); near the Bear Pits (Bärengraben)
Setting: a wine cellar since 1635; reached
by means of a steep staircase; eye-catching décor
Amenities: open-air dining on first-floor
terrace in summer; wine cellar and bar
downstairs
Atmosphere: unique old German wine-
bar atmosphere; impromptu entertainment by actors with talent, musicians
with bands, performers with a sense of
humour and local citizens with grudges;
world-famous, too, because only unmar-
ried landladies with children are eligible
to manage the establishment (provided
they do not subsequently marry!)
Clientèle: Berne's Top Ten; bankers, brokers and successful businessmen, plus exotic birds of passage
Dress: as you like it

Service: very good; waiters in local cos-
tume
Reservations: advisable
Price range: medium
Credit cards: AE, Euro

Café

TSCHIREN
73 Kramgasse
Telephone: 22 18 64
Owner/Manager: Haus 8/Rita Tschiren
Closed: Monday morning (before
11.30/a.m.); Sunday
Open: 7.30/a.m.–18.30/6.30 p.m.
Specialities: chocolates; the oldest cake-
shop in town
Location: almost in the shadow of the
Clock Tower (Zeitglockenturm)
Setting: recently-renovated salon with
vaguely nostalgic décor and an abundance of natural wood
Amenities: small tea-room on first floor;
light lunches; catering service; export
service
Atmosphere: an institution in the town; a
guardian of the Swiss coffeehouse tradition, bustling and lively
Clientèle: heterogeneous; resident aristocrats; ambassadors en passant; students, suburban housewives, secretaries
and shopgirls
Service: particularly anxious-to-please

Meeting Point

ARLEQUIN
51 Gerechtigkeitsgasse
Telephone: 22 39 46 (from 10/a.m.)
Owner/Manager: Trudi Wild
Closed: Sunday
Open: 15.00/3 p.m.–00.30/a.m.
Cuisine: local unpretentious and Italian
Specialities: goulash soup; chicken pâté
with morel mushrooms in puff pastry;
farmhouse-style ham with potato salad;
Italian dishes
Location: in the heart of the old city
Setting: elegantized rustic intérieur, with
extensive art collection, bronze castings
and appropriate accessoires
Amenities: bar; outdoor dining on per-
gola-shaded terrace in summer
Atmosphere: welcoming and homely but
with a certain stylishness
Clientèle: Bernese Haute Bourgeoisie en
fête mingles with hommes d'affaires,
hommes de lettres, musicians and artists
Dress: légère
Service: quick and accurate
Reservations: advisable (pets permitted)
Price range: medium
Credit cards: not accepted

Bar

ARCADY
11 Bahnhofsplatz
Telephone: 22 45 01
Owner/Manager: J. J. Gauer
Closed: never
Open: 11.00/a.m.–24.00/12 p.m.
Location: in the Gauer Hotel Schweizer-hof
Setting: vaguely reminiscent of a ship's lounge; leather fauteuils; alternate parquet floor and carpeting; pianist
Amenities: light lunches as well as drinks and snacks; two restaurants; second bar; nightclub; valet parking service
Atmosphere: timelessly elegant; lively and yet relaxing
Clientèle: essential stopover for distinguished visitors to make the acquaintance of local prominence from the worlds of politics, local government and finance
Service: under the capable supervision of chief barman Walter Niederer, assisted by Mademoiselle Marina
Reservations: advisable for lunch (pets permitted)
Credit cards: AE, DC, Euro, Visa, Master card

Nightclub

JAYLIN'S
11 Bahnhofplatz
Telephone: 22 45 01
Affiliations: Club of Clubs
Owner/Manager: Jean Jacques Gauer
Closed: Sunday
Open: 21.00/9 p.m.–4.00/a.m.
Location: in the Hotel Schweizerhof
Setting: traditional; comfortable seating, harmoniously-proportioned dance floor; soft lighting
Amenities: hotel; orchestra; well-known jazz soloists; excellent music at a decibel level calculated not to split the eardrums; partial air conditioning
Atmosphere: attractively civilized; chic without being chi-chi
Clientèle: Berne's Beau Monde; some of the prettiest girls in town; visiting heads of state and stars of stage and screen
Dress: Armani and Co.
Service: attentive and friendly
Reservations: advisable
Credit cards: all major

Shopping

EVERYTHING UNDER ONE ROOF
Loeb   47–57 Spitalgasse

FOR HIM
Loew Boutique   76 Kramgasse

FOR HER
Ciolina   51 Marktgasse

BEAUTY & HAIR
Ryf   70 Lentulusstrasse

JEWELLERY
Guebelin   Schweizerhoflaube and 11 Bahnhofplatz

LOCAL SPECIALITIES
A. Dürr & Co. AG (tobacco)
Spitalgasse 37
Mode Wartmann (women's fashion)
45 Marktgasse
Fein-Kaller (men's fashion)
55 Marktgasse
Claudine & Pierre (children's fashion)
37 Marktgasse
Gygax (leather fashion)
4 Spitalgasse
Roth (furs)
1 Kochergasse
Scherz (books)
25 Marktgasse
Franz Karl Weber (gifts)
52–54 Marktgasse
Steiger (porcelain)
21 Aarberger Gasse
Jelmoli (baggage & travel accessories)
Marktgasse/Baerenplatz
Intraform (interior decorating)
76–80 Rathausgasse
Globus Delicatesse (food and beverages)
Marktgasse/Baerenplatz
Parfumerie Passage (perfumery)
36 Spitalgasse
Bally (shoes)
9 Spitalgasse
Tschirren (confiserie)
73 Kramgasse

THE BEST OF ART
Friedrich, Erika + Otto (contemporary art) 55 Marktgasse, Tel. 22 78 03
Megert, Lydia   (contemporary art)
6 Münstergasse, Tel. 22 73 02/23 06 23
Bloch-Diener, Elsa (Egyptian, Etruscan, Greek and Roman objets d'art and 16–19th-century icons)
60 Kramgasse, Tel. 22 04 06; (home)
7 Obstbergweg, Tel. 44 67 65
H. Schaedeli, E. W. Leuenberger (antiques) 30 Gerechtigkeitsgasse
Zeller & Cie. (18th/19th-century antiques) 29 Kramgasse, Tel. 22 23 54
Kornfeld (auctioneers)
14 Laupenstrasse, Tel. 25 46 73

The City

The most international village in the world – overwhelmingly pretty, clean, safe, social and gay (by Swiss standards) – is everybody's favourite retreat for hiding away, resting, celebrating, shopping, quietly indulging and recovering from Paris, Rome, et al. Conservative cliques and universal organizations determine the élite routine (and the chances of crashing gates are as big as becoming a member of the Golf Club de Genève), but even as a transiting conventioneer or a cultivated introvert you are likely to have a good time and an even better memory. From the Richemond to the Rue du Rhône, from the park Perle du Lac to the one of Eaux-Vives, the city presents itself in natural beauty and haut bourgeois splendour with a touch of Gallic joie de vie. You don't feel the industries as in Basle, the banks as in Zurich and the boarding schools as in Lausanne – not even the Red Cross, the WHO, the ILO and the GATT – but rather the fresh air and the elegant atmosphere. And if native Jean-Jacques Rousseau could look back, he would probably opt for a villa on the Quai Mont-Blanc rather than returning à la nature.

Founded: 2500 B.C., as a settlement built on stilts over the lake; Genève (French) – ›rising out of the waters‹.

Far-reaching events: 2nd century B.C. – a Celtic settlement; 58 B.C. – becomes part of the Roman Empire; 443–461 A.D. – capital of the Kingdom of Burgundy; 534 – conquered by the Franks; 887 – reclaimed by the Kingdom of Burgundy; 1033 – part of Holy Roman Empire; 13th century – annexed by Savoy; 1530 – Geneva's independence recognized – successive treaties with Fribourg, Berne and Zurich to form a republic; 16th century – a focal pont of the Reformation under John Calvin; 1712 – philosopher Jean-Jacques Rousseau is born; 1798 – Geneva annexed by France; 1815 – joins the Swiss Confederation; 1864 – signing of the first Geneva Convention for the humane treatment of combatants and civilians in wartime; the city gradually develops its role as a centre of diplomacy and international affairs; 1880 – International Red Cross committee founded; 1020–46 – seat of the League of Nations.

Population: 300,000 (urban area); capital of the Canton of Geneva.

Postal code: CH–1200   **Telephone code:** 22

Climate: mild to warm, due to the influence of the lake – but cool at night.

Best time to visit: all the year round, for conferences, cosmopolitan atmosphere and shopping.

Calendar of events: *Folklore Festival* (Jun) – in the Bois de la Bâtie; *Fêtes de Genève* (Aug) – the whole city decks itself out in flowers and parties; *Bol d'Or* – Europe's largest and most beautiful lake regatta; *Geneva Music Festival* (Sep); *Vintner's Festival* (autumn) – Switzerland's third largest wine producing area celebrates the new grape harvest; *International Horse Show* (Nov); *Esplanade* (2nd Sunday in Dec) – the city celebrates its liberation from the House of Savoy by parading through the streets at night.

Fairs and exhibitions: *CYCLE AND MOTORCYCLE EXHIBITION* (Feb); *WOMEN'S READY-TO-WEAR AND ACCESSORIES EXHIBITION* (Feb); *INTERNATIONAL COMMERCIAL VEHICLES SHOW* (Feb); *AUTO* (Mar) – international automobile show; *NASCON* (Apr) – international security conference and exhibition; *INTERNATIONAL EXHIBITION OF INVENTIONS AND NEW TECHNOLOGIES* (Apr); *SPEMAC* (Apr) – special technologies; *INDEX* (Apr) – trade fair for the non-wovens and disposables industries; *SITEV* (May) – international exhibition for suppliers of the motor vehicle industry.

Historical sights: *St. Peter's Cathedral* (12th century) – austerely Calvinistic, after the Reformation leader who preached here; *Ancien Arsenal* (16th century) – originally intended for storing grain; once held the weapons to fight for Swiss independence; *Maison Tavel* – oldest private house in the city; *Collège Calvin* (16th century) – founded by the Reformation leader, an academy in Gothic and Renaissance packaging; *Place du Bourge-du-Four* – former Roman forum, the city's main fair centre in the Middle Ages and heart of the old city today; *Ile Rousseau* (1835) – an island at the mouth of the Rhône with a bronze statue of the philosopher; *Jardin Anglais* – with a flower clock and the *Monument National* commemorating Geneva's entry into the Swiss Confederation; *Musée d'Horlogerie et d'Emaillerie* – Swiss timepieces and enamels; *Museum of Art and History* – masterpieces by Konrad Witz, Italian and Dutch artists and local painters; *Ariana Museum* – ceramics; *Monument Brunswick* (1789) – Scaligeric memorial to a benefactor.

Modern sights: *Reformation Monument* (1917) – wall with bas-reliefs commemorating Calvin, Knox, Farel et al.; *Palais des Nations* – extra-territorial headquarters of the European office of the United Nations; *St. Paul's Church* – paintings by Maurice Denis; *Jet d'Eau* – 145 m high water fountain in Lake Geneva, a city landmark.

Special attractions: a shopping spree on the *Rue du Rhône*; a boat trip to the *Château de Chillon*; lunch by the lake or at *Coppet*; a stroll through *Carouge* – a town within the town where time has stood still.

Important companies with headquarters in the city: *La Genevois* (Insurance); *Girardet-Perregaux* (watches); *Mathey-Tissot* (watches); *NOGA* (import/export); *Piaget* (watches); *Montres Rolex* (watches); *SIP* (drilling milling machines).

Airport: Geneva-Cointrin, GVA; Tel. 99 31 11; 5 km/3 miles.

The Headquarters

LE RICHEMOND

Jardin Brunswick
CH–1201 Geneva
Telephone: 31 14 00
Telex: 22 598 rich
Telefax: 316 709
Owner: Jean Armleder
General Manager: Victor Armleder
Affiliation/Reservation Systems: The Leading Hotels of the World, Leading Hotels of Switzerland, Preferred Hotels Worldwide, Horis Swissair, Relais et Châteaux, Hôtels de Grande Classe Int.
Number of rooms: 98 (30 suites)
Price range: SFr 240–600 (suites on request)
Credit cards: AE, DC, EC, MC, JCB, Visa
Location: Rive Droite, on the lake front
Built: 1875 (renovated 1984/86)
Style: Louis XV, Louis XVI, Empire
Hotel amenities: garage, valet parking, house limousine service, beauty salon
Main hall porter: Maurice Tassera
Room amenities: colour tv, video, mini-bar (pets allowed)
Bathroom amenities: separate shower cabin, bidet, bathrobe, telephone
Room service: 24 hours
Bars: ›Gentilhomme‹ Evans Zangas (barman), Napoleon III décor; ›Jardin‹ (8.30/a.m. to closing time) Art Déco style
Restaurants: ›Le Gentilhomme‹; and ›Le Jardin‹ (see Restaurants)

Books have been written on Le Richemond and the Armleder hotelier dynasty, and love-stories and dramas found their stage here, the grandest of the small grand hotels. ›A grand hotel is the last public place on earth where nothing is impossible‹ philosophizes the grandseigneur Jean Armleder, and with the help of his director-son Victor he not only continues the centennial family tradition but sees to it that his motto remains living legend. The city palace with the best location (on the lake, but slightly set back from the main-traffic avenue across a quaint little park) is Geneva's prime address, and the world comes to live here, for business, for the exceptional balance between beauty and luxury in the salons and rooms, for the city's – and country's – most elegant restaurants, Le Jardin and Le Gentilhomme (the latter rightfully declared Switzerland's Maxim's), for the service, for the people, for snob appeal and glamour. Kings and Presidents come here for the security, maybe, ladies love Le Richemond for the right lighting, the velvet floors and the feminine touch in the rooms, but everyone agrees that, for whatever reason, this hotel is in a class of its own, a landmark and, hopefully, an eternal one. The Duke of Edinburgh and the Emir of Qatar, the Rothschilds and the Kennedys, Sophia Loren and Christian Barnard are all in love with this house, its service and the fact that everything is possible here.

The Hideaway

ROYAL CLUB EVIAN

Rive sud du Lac de Genève
F–74500 Evian-les-Bains
(42 km/26 miles)
Telephone: 50/75 14 00
Telex: 385 759 casiroy
Owning Company: Gervais Danone
Managing Director: Robert Lassalle
Affiliation/Reservation System: The Leading Hotels of the World
Closed: mid-December – mid-February
Number of rooms: 200
Price range: SFr 305–2,760
Credit cards: AE, DC, EC, Visa
Location: 48 km/30 miles from airport
Built: 1907
Style: reminiscent of a Grand Hotel
Hotel amenities: parking, sauna, Institute ›Mieux Vivre‹, helipad, casino
Room amenities: terrace/balcony
Laundry/dry cleaning: 48 hours
Sports: tennis, golf, jogging, archery
Bars: ›Tony's Bar‹ (casino), ›The Golf Club House‹; ›Tennis Club House‹
Restaurants: ›Cafe Royal‹, ›Barbecue‹, ›La Rotonde‹, ›Chez Lapierre‹, ›Le Chalet du Golf‹
Nightclub: ›La Toque Royale‹

Travellers accustomed to follow the Lausanne-Montreux trail when circumventing Lake Geneva may find the little French spa town on its southern shores something of a surprise. Connaisseurs, however, see in Evian-les-Bains a Gallic counterbalance to the palace hotel philosophy and the muesli -roesti school, due in no small part to this very unusual hideaway, primus inter pares amongst all the châteaux and palais from Divonne-les-Bains to Talloires. The Royal Club stands perched amidst woods and well-kept lawns overlooking the azure waters of the lake, guarded to the rear by the awesome snow-clad summit of Mont-Blanc. The exterior recalls vaguely the wedding-cake décor so beloved at the turn of the century by the architects of the rivieras from Brighton to Biarritz; the interior is Belle Epoque at its glittering best – prettily pastel bedrooms and a domed and pillared lounge with murals of leaves and garlands as fresh today as when they were painted in 1908. Within this nostalgic framework Managing Director Robert Lassalle conducts a carefully-orchestrated symphony of epicurean pleasures and sybaritic delights, whilst offering subscribers to the ›mens sana in corpore sano‹ tradition, a chance to be pampered and cossetted whilst repairing the ravages of indulgence. You can dine in gourmet luxury under striped sunshades on the lakeside terrace before dancing or playing the night away at the nearby Casino, or you can opt for exercise, massage and cuisine minceur under the auspices of the Institut Mieux-Vivre. You can improve your forehand or your handicap, your figure or your frame of mind; the Royal Club offers something for everyone amidst comfort, luxury and some of the most beautiful scenery in the world.

Lunch

LE BUSINESS
36 Boulevard Helvétique
Telephone: 35 42 06
Owner/Manager: Bernard Grobet
Closed: Sunday; Saturday lunchtime;
December 21st–January 13th
Open: 11.30/a.m.–14.00/2 p.m. and
20.00/8 p.m.–22.30/10.30 p.m.
Cuisine: French
Chef de cuisine: Bruno Bouin
Specialities: celestine of salmon and
wolf-fish with basil; fresh noodles with
crayfish and saffron-flavoured beurre
blanc; aiguillettes of duckling with
orange and lime; rabbit with thyme flow-
ers; almond cake (›l'enfer des anges‹)
Location: central
Setting: a new restaurant (opened June
1984); modern décor; attractive and ele-
gant
Amenities: outdoor dining on terrace; air
conditioning
Atmosphere: soignée; intimate
Clientèle: Geneva's jeunesse dorée; fash-
ionable, chic and self-confident
Dress: as you like it
Reservations: advisable
Service: professional and punctilious
Price range: medium and high
Credit cards: AE, DC, Euro, Visa

Dinner

PARC DES EAUX VIVES
82 Quai Gustave-Ador
Telephone: 35 41 40
Affiliation: Traditions et Qualité
Owner/Manager: François Perret and
family
Closed: Sunday evening; Monday; Janu-
ary 1st–February 15th
Open: 12.00/a.m.–14.30/2.30 p.m. and
19.00/7 p.m.–21.30/9.30 p.m.
Cuisine: French
Chefs de cuisine: Roger Parrot and Jean
Perreard
Specialities: gratin of filleted frogs' legs;
lobster salad with fresh truffles; papillote
de langoustine with leek fondue and
Roquefort sauce; fillet of John Dory (St.
Pierre) with sweet peppers; poulet de
Bresse with anis and fennel; feuilleté aux
fruits frais sauce caramel
Location: 2 km (1 mile) from city centre;
by Lake Geneva, near the fountain
Setting: 18th-century nobleman's residence now owned by the city of Geneva;
beautiful gardens; views of the lake; Empire-style interior with chandeliers; mixture of modern and period accessoires;
fine table-linen, silver and china
Amenities: private dining rooms and
lounges (up to 1000 persons); open-air

dining on terrace (restricted menu); ex-
tensive car-parking facilities
Atmosphere: favourite venue amongst
Geneva's Upper Crust with cause for
celebration, from business contracts to
weddings
Clientèle: as cosmopolitan as the city it-
self; ambassadors, heads of multi-na-
tional organisations, globe-gallopers and
resident patricians
Dress: jacket and tie – of course
Service: cordial and respectful
Reservations: essential
Price range: haut bourgeois
Credit cards: AE, DC, Euro, Visa

Lunch

LE JARDIN
Jardin Brunswick
Telephone: 31 14 00
Affiliations: Relais et Châteaux
Owner/Manager: Jean Armleder/Victor
Armleder
Maître: Carlo Corosu
Closed: never
Open: 6.00/a.m.–24.00/12 p.m.
Cuisine: Franco-Italian
Chef de cuisine: Olivier Bagnoud
Specialities: according to season and
market availability; marinated salmon
with two sorts of pepper; artichoke hearts
and truffle salad; champagne risotto;
pasta (penne) with salmon; banquette de
queues de langoustines
Location: in the Hotel Richemond
Setting: a showcase for décorateur par
excellence Gérard Bach; Art Déco fa-
çades mingling with lianed trellises; rem-
iniscent of the winter-gardens of yester-
year
Amenities: hotel; outdoor dining on terrace; air conditioning; car park
Atmosphere: lively; chic; beguilingly
charming
Clientèle: society aesthetes and visiting
celebrities; anybody who is anybody who
is not at ›Le Gentilhomme‹
Dress: from Ted Lapidus to Lanvin via
Gianni Versace
Service: to perfection
Reservations: advisable (pets permitted)
Price range: moderately expensive
Credit cards: AE, DC, Euro, Visa, JCB

Dinner

LE GENTILHOMME
Jardin Brunswick
Telephone: 31 14 00
Affiliations: Relais et Châteaux

Owner/Manager: Jean Armleder/Victor Armleder
Maître: Frank Pipala
Closed: Saturday lunchtime
Open: 12.00/a.m.–14.30/2.30 p.m. and 19.00/7 p.m.–24.00/12 p.m.
Cuisine: French (nouvelle)
Chef de cuisine: Philippe Bezout
Specialities: according to season and market availability; ragoût of scallops and shrimps with lemon; Périgord truffles in a salt crust; roast Breton lobster with two sauces; blanc de turbot au beurre d'orange
Location: in the Hotel Richemond
Setting: stylized Grand Siècle pomp and circumstance; red velvet, gilt, crystal and fine porcelain
Amenities: hotel; pianist; orchestra; diners dansants; soirées concerts; restaurant ›Le Jardin‹; air conditioning; car park
Atmosphere: the ultimate in elegance and sophistication at lunchtime; a glittering gala reminiscent of 19th-century banquets at night
Clientèle: magnates; multi-moguls; superstars and the private jet-set; from Teddy Kennedy to Sophia Loren
Dress: tenue de ville
Service: impeccable; indulgent
Reservations: advisable (no dogs)
Price range: fairly astronomic (unless you're an oil sheikh)
Credit cards: AE, DC, Euro, Visa, JCB

Dinner

LION D'OR
5 Place Gautier,
Cologny (3 km/2 miles)
Telephone: 36 44 32
Affiliations: Route Suisse ›Plaisirs de la Table‹; Maître Cuisinier de France; Club Prosper Montagné
Owner/Manager/Chef de cuisine: Henri Large
Closed: Saturday; Sunday; December 20th–January 20th
Open: 12.00/a.m.–14.00/2 p.m. and 19.00/7 p.m.–22.00/10 p.m.
Cuisine: classique et moderne
Specialities: salade de homard bleu; escalope of wolf-fish with ginger; Breton lobster in cream of green peas; roast lamb with garlic; casserole of duck with vinegar and maple syrup
Location: in Cologny; 3 km (2 miles) north-east of city centre
Setting: recently-renovated modern Louis XVI; leather, light wood, round tables
Amenities: bistro; large terrace shaded by plane-trees with view of Lake Geneva; car park
Atmosphere: festive – especially at night
Clientèle: le Tout-Genève international; Petula Clark and Alain Delon; Middle-Eastern princes and Jean-Claude Killy

Dress: designer casual to designer elegant
Service: charmingly directed by the wife ot the patron and by Giovanni Ramello
Reservations: advisable (pets permitted)
Price range: inevitably expensive
Credit cards: AE, DC, Euro, Visa

Meeting Point

CLUB 58
15 Glacis-de-Rive
Telephone: 35 15 15
Owner/Manager: Pierre Jaeger/Serge Picco
Closed: never
Open: 20.00/8 p.m.–4.00/a.m.
Location: a short walk from the Place des Eaux-Vives
Amenities: restaurant serving meals until 3 a.m.; air conditioning
Atmosphere: club-like
Clientèle: members and guests
Service: cordial and welcoming
Reservations: advisable (no dogs)
Credit cards: AE, DC, Euro, Visa

Bar

LE GENTILHOMME BAR
8–10 Rue Adhémar-Fabri
Telephone: 31 14 00
Owner/Manager: Jean Armleder/Victor Armleder
Closed: never
Open: 11.00/a.m.–14.00/2 p.m.; 18.30/6.30 p.m.–1.30/a.m.
Location: in the Hotel Richemond
Setting: sumptuous Napoléon III décor
Amenities: hotel; second bar; air conditioning; car park
Atmosphere: luxurious, lively and popular
Clientèle: the Who's Who of illustrious visitors to the mini world-capital, plus all its most distinguished residents
Service: with a smile
Reservations: advisable
Credit cards: all major

Bar

GRIFFIN'S PUB
4 Rue Duchosol
Telephone: 36 11 44
Owner/Manager: Bernard Grobet
Closed: Sunday
Open: 17.00/5 p.m.–1.00/a.m.
Location: next door to Griffin's Club
Setting: old pub style; very English
Amenities: restaurant serving meals to the public until 3 a.m.; nightclub next door

Atmosphere: something of an institution with the local gratin
Clientèle: Beau Monde glitterati and visitors with charm, sophistication and wit
Service: good
Reservations: advisable
Credit cards: all major

Nightclub

GRIFFIN'S CLUB
35 Boulevard Helvétique
Telephone: 35 12 18
Owner/Manager: Bernard Grobet
Closed: never
Open: 20.00/8 p.m.–4.00/a.m.
Location: two bars away from the School of Fine Arts (Ecole des Beaux-Arts)
Setting: designer-delirious interior; mirror columns and halls, with master of ceremonies Bernard Grobet, cigar at the ready, always at his table (first on the left after the bar)
Amenities: discothèque; restaurant serving meals to the public until 3 a.m.; car park
Atmosphere: the Calvin capital's private social Olympus of the night; not only the best nightclub in the country but one of the best in the world
Clientèle: eminent night-owls of the city plus the happy few rotating between London and Los Angeles, Rome and Rio
Dress: elegant
Service: unobtrusively efficient
Reservations: essential
Price range: appropriately expensive
Credit cards: AE, DC, Euro, Visa

Tigre Royal (furs)
60 Rue du Rhône
Payot (books)
2 Rue Adrian Vollent
Hermès (gifts)
60 Rue du Rhône
Kuhn (porcelain)
Rue de la Confédération
Vuitton, Louis (baggage & travel accessories)
40 Rue du Marché
Dupain (interior decorating)
11 Rue du Rhône
Coq d'Or, Au (food and beverages)
5 Place du Molard
Pharmacie Principal (perfumery)
11 Rue du Marché
Nôtre, Le (confiserie) 31 Rue des Alpes

THE BEST OF ART
Calart (modern art)
4bis Rue Prévost-Martin, Tel. 20 40 50
Franck, Eric (contemporary art)
15 Route de Florissant, Tel. 47 08 09
Krugier (fine art)
3 Place du Grand-Mézel, Tel. 28 57 19
Malacorda, Marika (contemporary art)
1 Rue de L'Evêché, Tel. 28 64 50
Weber, S.A. d'Editions (contemporary art prints) 13 Rue de Monthoux, Tel. 32 64 50
Rossire, Paul (18th/19th-century antiques) 18 Corraterie, Tel. 21 26 99

Shopping

EVERYTHING UNDER ONE ROOF
Bon Génie, Au   34 Rue du Marché

FOR HIM
Carneval de Venise
13 Rue du Mont Blanc

FOR HER
Jacquelet, Jean   2 Rue Saint Léger

BEAUTY & HAIR
Carita   22 Rue de Condolle

JEWELLERY
Boucheron   1 Rue de la Tour de l'Ale

LOCAL SPECIALITIES
Davidoff & Cie. (tobacco)
2 Rue de Rive
Smaga, Anita (women's fashion)
51 Rue du Rhône

›The Swiss have managed to build a lovely country around their hotels‹, teased word-smith-critic George Mikes, and rarely will you find a more convincing proof of that humorous theory than in this Swiss resort par excellence. Nestling amongst the hills on the shore of Lake Geneva, it seems the picture-postcard layout was created to form worthy surroundings – of nature, medieval charm and functional institutions to keep the former alive – for all the palaces and pensions where the last Russian czarists, nostalgic nobility from the bygone monarchies and gentlemen of leisure mix with sober men of commerce and parents of high income and broad mind delivering or visiting their children who are being prepared for the good life in style by the élitist boarding schools in town. But Lausanne is more than just another pretty face on the Swiss Riviera – with a lot more to offer than a healthy climate, exclusive sanatoria, schools and hotels – not having to be envious about the regal renommé of its nearby neighbour Geneva, which has all the glamour, the tycoons, the watch companies, the international institutions and the airport. (With a private aeroplane you can touch down here, anyhow.) The city is proud of housing the highest court in the country and the headquarters of the International Olympic Committee as well as prestigious companies of its own. Already settled in Roman times, the Old Town (with Switzerland's most imposing Gothic cathedral in the middle) is still reminiscent of the Middle Ages down to the night-watchman calling out the time every hour on the hour, while the Haute Bourgeoisie villas, the luxurious auberges and the jeunesse dorée about town lend Lausanne a worldly air. No wonder Jean-Jacques Rousseau, Voltaire, Goethe and Napoléon were in love with this elysium, and Lord Byron was not the first, nor will he be the last, looking over the flower-decked quays of Ouchy, to revel: ›Lake Léman woos me with its crystal face.‹

Founded: 5th century, by Bishop Marius on the foundations of a Stone Age and Roman settlement; Lausanne (French) – from Lousanna (Latin).

Far-reaching events: 6th century – bishopric and centre of Church power until the Reformation; 1536 – conquered by the Bernese; 1537 – founding of the Academy, which later became the university; 18th century – prosperity – French influence – the arts flourish; 1803 – Lausanne regains its autonomy and becomes the capital of the Canton of Vaud, a member of the Swiss Confederation; 1874 – Lausanne becomes the seat of the Swiss High Court.

Population: 214,000 (urban area); capital of the Canton of Vaud.

Postal code: CH-1000   **Telephone code:** 21

Climate: mild, sunny and temperate.

Best time to visit: May to October.

Calendar of events: *Festival de la Cité* and *Fête de Lausanne* (Jun) – singing and dancing in the streets; *Lausanne vous offre pour un été* – summer festival of music and theatre; *Festival International* (May/Jun) – world famous dancers and musicians flock to the city and fill its stage.

Fairs and exhibitions: *HABITAT & JARDIN* (Feb/Mar) – home and garden; *CAMPING & CARAVANING* (Feb/Mar); *SERATEX* (Mar) – ladies', gentlemen's and children's wear; *COMPUTER* (Apr) – electronic data processing; *COMPTOIR SUISSE* (Sep) – national fair; *SERATEX* (Oct); *ANTIQUITÄTENMESSE* (Nov) – art and antiques.

Best view of the city: from the *Signal de Sanvabelin* in the north of the city.

Historical sights: *Notre-Dame Cathedral* (1175–1232) – the finest Gothic cathedral in Switzerland; *La Vaudoise* – brigantine lying at anchor, the last reminder of the cargo sailboats which once plied the lake; *Mules' Fountain* – in honour of those who carried the heaviest burden in bulding the city in the Middle Ages, humorously inscribed ›in memory of the Academy‹; *St. Laurent* (18th century) – Baroque: *Ancien Evéché* (11th century) – former bishops' residence; *Hôtel de Ville* (17th century) – beautiful Renaissance Town Hall with hand-painted clockface on the tower, on a square lined with 18th-century burgher houses, with the ›*Fountain of Justice*‹ in the middle; *Escaliers du Marché* – covered stairway leading from the harbour to the market place; *Tour de l'Ale* (13th century) – circular tower, a remnant of the old city fortress; *Grand Pont* (1844) – a granite viaduct; *Château de St. Maire* (15th century) – the ›new bishops‹ residence, now housing the canton's administrative offices; *Fine Arts Museum* – paintings by Swiss artists.

Special attractions: a walk through the *Old Town* (around the cathedral); a stroll at sunset through the lakeside district of *Ouchy*; a *trip in a private yacht* on Lake Geneva; lunch at *Girardet*.

Important companies with headquarters in the city: *André & Cie.* (international trade); *Bobst* (heavy plant); *Fibriver* (isolation materials); *Nestlé* (foodstuffs) at Vevey; *Publicitas* (advertising agency).

Airport: Geneva-Cointrin; GVA; Tel. (22) 99 31 11, 65 km/40 miles; Blécherette and Montricher airports – small private planes only; Swissair, Tel.: 20 50 11.

The Headquarters

LAUSANNE PALACE

7–9 Grand Chêne
CH–1003 Lausanne
Telephone: 2037 11
Telex: 24 171 palas
Telefax: 23 2571
Owning Company: Sodereal Holding SA
General Manager: Georges Fraschina
Affiliation/Reservation Systems: The Leading Hotels of the World, Prohotel, Horis, Alpha 3, Steigenberger Reservation Service
Number of rooms: 171 (23 suites)
Price range: Sfr 160–1,400
Credit cards: AE, DC, Visa
Location: city centre
Built: 1915 (renovated 1950–1970)
Style: classic
Hotel amenities: garage, valet parking, house limousine service, sauna, hairstylist, solarium, massage, newsstand, drugstore, tobacconist, florist, house doctor, shopping gallery, 2 cinemas
Main hall porter: Pierrot Albertelli
Room amenities: colour tv (remote control), mini-bar (pets allowed)
Bathroom amenities: separate shower, bidet, bathrobe, hairdrier, telephone
Room service: 6.30/a.m.–3.30/a.m.
Conference rooms: 8/16 mm film projector, flipcharts, barcovision, simultaneous translation, secretarial services
Bar: ›Le Relais‹ (11.30/a.m.–1.00/a.m.) C. Finini (barman), English bar style, pianist
Restaurants: ›Le Relais‹ (11.30/a.m.–14.30/2.30 p.m. and 18.30/6.30 p.m.–22.00/10.00 p.m.) V. Damizia (maître), F. Taufer (chef de cuisine), neo-classic style, pianist; ›La Veranda‹ (11.30/a.m.–22.30/10.30 p.m.) C. Finini (maître), F. Taufer (chef de cuisine), open-air dining, pianist
Nightclub: ›Le Brummel‹ (20.30/8.30 p.m.–4.00/a.m.) M. Beausire (manager), modern style, international cabaret, records
Private dining rooms: one

The Lausanne Palace could easily be the city's palace were it not for the oath taken on the Rütli Mountain. It stands out for its architecture and palatial air and is so centrally located that you can pop back to your room to change your cologne between business appointment and lunch date. This Belle Epoque mansion has nobly proportioned public rooms and aristocratic amenities in the private ones. Stucco and marble, antiques and chandeliers, panelled ceilings and silver trays, electric-button comfort and that certain-smile attitude let you forget about Geneva, and the view across the lake and the Alps may make you forget about the weather. And when you indulge in a piano-accompanied dîner-à-deux in – and on – La Veranda, you will forget about everything else. (Except, maybe, prolonging the evening in Lausanne's chicest nightspot, Le Brummel.)

The Hideaway

DU LAC

CH–1296 Coppet/Vaud (35 km/22 miles)
Telephone: (22)76 15 21
Telex: 27 639 hlcop
Owner/General Managers: Jacques and Nicole Dallinges-Gottraux
Affiliation/Reservation System: Relais et Châteaux
Number of rooms: 18 (6 suites)
Price range: Sfr 100–140 (single)
          Sfr 140–180 (double)
          Sfr 280–800 (suite)
Credit cards: AE, DC, EC, Visa
Location: on the lake, 10 km/6 miles from Geneva-Cointrin airport
Built: 1750
Style: traditional
Hotel amenities: car park
Room amenities: colour tv (in apartments), mini-bar, radio
Bathroom amenities: all rooms with private bathroom facilities
Room service: 24 hours
Laundry/dry cleaning: same day
Conference rooms: for up to 15 persons; possibility of special arrangements for seminars
Sports: watersports, fishing
Sports (nearby): tennis (10 km/6 miles), golf (4 km/3 miles)
Restaurant: ›Rôtisserie du Lac‹ Bertrand Hubert (chef de cuisine), nouvelle and classic cuisine, open-air dining on terrace
Nightclub: (21.00/9.00 p.m.–2.00/a.m.) exciting
Private dining rooms: for up to 30 persons

That this exquisite eighteenth-century relais in the pretty little medieval town of Coppet is so frequently fully booked is less indicative of the relative merits of big sisters Lausanne and Geneva than of the irresistible charm it exerts. On age grounds alone it is entitled to be treated with respect, since the original inn on this site was awarded the title of ›Grand Logis‹ in 1628. Owner-Managers Jacques and Nicole Dallinges-Gottraux treat each of the inhabitants of the eighteen bedrooms as honoured guests; the ambience, in fact, is that of a gracious country house. With predominantly nouvelle cuisine in the restaurant (or, in summer, on the enchanting shady lakeside terrace with a view of Mont Blanc) and elegantized rustic furnishings including many fine period pieces throughout the house, it's not hard to see why gourmets from both sides of Lake Geneva moor their yachts at the private landing-stage. They are, after all, merely following in the footsteps of Lord Byron and Benjamin Constant, who visited Madame de Staël in her nearby château for philosophy and pleasure. In this less reflective age, the latter is the Du Lac's raison d'être.

Lunch

LA GRAPPE D'OR
3 Cheneau de Bourg
Telephone: 23 07 60
Affiliations: Chaîne des Rôtisseurs; Club Prosper Montagné
Owner/Manager/Chef de cuisine: Peter Baermann
Closed: Sunday; one week in February
Open: 12.00/a.m.–15.00/3 p.m. and 19.00/7 p.m.–23.00/11 p.m.
Cuisine: grande cuisine élaborée
Specialities: warm escalope of foie gras with balsam vinegar; salad of turbot with passion fruit juice; gratin of lobster with port; suprême de cailles; noisettes d'agneau au Bordeaux et fines herbes; passion fruit soufflé; white chocolate mousse
Location: in the heart of the old city
Setting: ancient patrician townhouse; shuttered windows and gay windowboxes; recently-renovated spacious dining room with beamed ceiling and open fireplace; predominant colours red and white, with parquet floor
Amenities: private dining room (10–30 persons)
Atmosphere: harmonious, luxurious and festively welcoming
Clientèle: local gourmets; admirers of Peter Baermann's cuisine of the ›Beau Rivage‹ fame; businessmen tired of Geneva; parents visiting offspring at the various exclusive boarding schools
Dress: fairly conservative
Service: charmingly supervised by Angelika Baermann
Reservations: advisable (pets permitted)
Price range: fairly expensive
Credit cards: AE, DC, Euro, Visa

Dinner

GIRARDET
1 Rue d'Yverdon
Crissier (5 km/3 miles)
Telephone: (21) 34 15 14
Affiliations: Traditions et Qualité
Owner/Manager/Chef de cuisine: Fredy Girardet
Closed: Sunday; Monday; 3 weeks July/August; 3 weeks at Christmas
Open: 12.00/a.m.–14.00/2 p.m. and 19.30/7.30 p.m.–21.00/9 p.m.
Cuisine: haute cuisine du marché
Specialities: daily changing menu; escalope de foie gras de canard à la vinaigrette; cabbage stuffed with Norway lobster (langoustines) with Beluga caviar butter; cassolette de truffes with globe artichokes; saddle of rabbit with basil; poulette de Bresse et foie gras de canard en gelée au fenouil; gratin d'oranges Madame France; passion fruit soufflé
Location: at Crissier; 5 km (3 miles) north of Lausanne
Setting: elegant patrician townhouse with striped sunblinds in summer; dining room a model of understated grace and charm, utterly in keeping with the genuine modesty of the legendary patron, considered by many to be the best cook in the world
Amenities: private dining room (20–27 persons); car park; air conditioning
Atmosphere: a Mecca for anyone who considers food and drink more important than just the best means to fight starvation
Clientèle: religious gourmets; other pilgrims to this temple of culinary perfection from Mougins to Mionnay; celebrities, famous chefs and the occasional taxi-driver who would rather blow his entire annual savings on a meal at Girardet's than waste his money on second-rate imitations
Dress: casually elegant to elegantly casual
Service: attentive and highly personal
Reservations: essential
Price range: philanthropic
Credit cards: not accepted

Lunch

AUBERGE DU RAISIN
1 Place de l'Hotel-de-Ville
Cully (9 km/6 miles)
Telephone: 99 21 31
Owner/Manager: the Blokbergen family
Closed: Thursday; mid-July – mid-August
Open: 12.00/a.m.–14.00/2 p.m. and 19.00/7 p.m.–21.30/9.30 p.m.
Cuisine: French (nouvelle) with a Swiss accent
Chef de cuisine: Adolf Blokberger
Specialities: shrimp salad; minute de saumon with leeks; lobster à la nage with dill; breast of pigeon with young vegetables; Norway lobster ravioli
Location: near the Town Hall (l'Hôtel de Ville) in Cully, 9 km (6 miles) south-east of Lausanne
Setting: on the lake; a romantic auberge de campagne with a homely rustic-style dining room; wooden ceiling and an open fireplace
Amenities: hotel; private dining rooms (10–45 persons)
Atmosphere: comfortable and comforting
Clientèle: predominantly prosperous middle-aged members of the liberal professions
Dress: elegant
Service: exceptionally attentive; supervised by Giacomo Custodero, maître d'hôtel for the past 24 years
Reservations: essential
Price range: fairly expensive
Credit cards: AE, Euro, Visa

Dinner

LE WELLINGTONIA
Place du Général-Guisan, Ouchy
Telephone: 26 38 31
Owner/Manager: Maurice Urech
Closed: Sunday evening; lunchtime every day
Open: 19.00/7 p.m.–24.00/12 p.m.
Cuisine: French
Chef de cuisine: Hans Martin Fopp
Specialities: wolf-fish (loup de mer) with fennel; Bresse guinea-fowl with cream of foie gras; salads
Location: in the Hotel Beau-Rivage Palace at Ouchy, on the shores of the Lake of Geneva
Setting: in a gracious Belle Epoque palais hotel amidst beautiful gardens; wood-panelled walls and ceiling; quarry-tiled floor; Spanish rustic furnishings with yellow upholstery
Amenities: hotel; second restaurant; open-air dining on terrace; bar; orchestra; air conditioning
Atmosphere: pleasantly home-like and welcoming
Clientèle: Lausanne's social élite; conservative and comfortably-off temporary residents form Knoxville to Küsnacht
Dress: rather formally elegant; tie de rigueur
Service: old-school efficiency
Reservations: essential (no pets)
Price range: grande maison
Credit cards: AE, DC, Visa, EC, Carte bleue

Café

MANUEL
5 Place St. François
Telephone: 23 17 64
Owner/Manager: Daniel Manuel
Closed: Sunday
Open: 7.30/a.m.–19.00/7 p.m.
Location: near the Church of St. Francis (Eglise St. François)
Setting: sumptuous Louis XV-style tearoom with fine china and silverware
Amenities: lunch menu as well as delectable calorie-laden pâtisserie; two private salons (15–20 persons); bar; first-floor terrace and boulevard café overlooking the square in summer
Atmosphere: rather genteel but not repressive
Clientèle: very select; resident countesses, passing princes, international aristocracy and the occasional ordinary mortal
Dress: tenue correcte
Service: meticulous
Reservations: advisable (pets allowed)
Price range: medium–high
Credit cards: AE, DC, Visa, EC, Carte bleue

Bar

LE RELAIS
7–9 Grand Chêne
Telephone: 20 37 11
Owner/Manager: Sodereal Holding SA/ Georges Fraschina
Closed: never
Open: 11.30/a.m.–1.00/a.m.
Location: in the Lausanne Palace Hotel
Setting: luxurious hotel bar with English-style décor; pianist
Amenities: hotel; 2 restaurants; private dining rooms; outdoor dining on terrace; nightclub; car park
Atmosphere: rather like a London Club
Clientèle: discriminating globe-trotters; the occasional millionaire; the private jet-set
Service: under the expert guidance of chief barman M.C. Finini
Reservations: advisable
Credit cards: AE, DC, Visa

Bar

LA CRAVACHE
7 Rue du Grand Chêne
Telephone: 22 88 10
Owner/Manager: Claude Manuel
Closed: Sunday; public holidays
Open: (Monday–Thursday) 7.00/a.m.–1.00/a.m.; (Friday–Saturday) 7.00/a.m.–2.00/a.m.
Location: next to the Lausanne Palace Hotel
Setting: English pub-style décor with equestrian bric-à-brac (reminiscent of a stable)
Amenities: second bar on first floor; covered terrace
Atmosphere: légère and lively
Clientèle: cosmopolitan collection of financiers, industrialists, politicians and men of commerce
Dress: as you like it
Service: fast and friendly
Reservations: not necessary (pets tolerated)
Price range: medium
Credit cards: AE, DC, Visa, EC

Nightclub

LE BRUMMEL
7–9 Grand Chêne
Telephone: 20 37 11
Owner/Manager: Sodereal Holding SA/M. Beausire
Closed: never
Open: 20.30/8.30 p.m.–4.00/a.m.

Location: in the Lausanne Palace Hotel
Setting: luxurious hotel cabaret-night-club; striking modern décor
Amenities: discothèque; international cabaret; hotel; 2 restaurants; private dining rooms; outdoor dining on terrace; bar; car park
Atmosphere: exclusive, chic
Clientèle: Lausanne's insomniac crème de la crème plus interesting, wealthy or beautiful birds of passage
Dress: disco elegance
Service: unobtrusively efficient
Reservations: advisable
Price range: fairly expensive
Credit cards: AE, DC, Visa

Nightclub

LE DARLING
Galeries St-François
Telephone: 22 09 35
Owner/Manager: Dad Reynier/Yves Reinhard
Closed: Monday; Tuesday
Open: 22.00/10 p.m.–4.00/a.m.
Location: central
Setting: a nocturnal garden
Amenities: discothèque
Atmosphere: a breath of the countryside; yet chic and sophisticated
Clientèle: jeunesse dorée (or at least argentée) including some of the prettiest girls in town
Dress: eccentric
Service: efficient and friendly
Reservations: advisable
Price range: medium to fairly high
Credit cards: EC, Visa, AE, Diners

Shopping

EVERYTHING UNDER ONE ROOF
Au Bon Génie   11 Place Saint-François

FOR HIM
Excelsior   12 Rue Louvre

FOR HER
Boutique Elle   47 Rue de Bourg

BEAUTY & HAIR
Calane   6 Rue du Grand-Chêne

JEWELLERY
Bucherer   5 Place Saint-François

LOCAL SPECIALITIES
Tabacs Masson (tobacco)
28 Rue de Bourg
La Galoche (women's fashion)
6 Rue Madeleine
Nelson Boutique (men's fashion)
Galerie Saint-François

Koba-Cuir (leather fashion)
14 Rue Madeleine
Canton Fourrures (furs)
20 Rue de Bourg
Payot (books)
4 Place Pépinet
Arts & Maison (gifts)
Galérie Saint-François
Paradis de la table (porcelain)
20 Rue Grand-Saint-Jean
Au Sac-Chic (baggage & travel accessories)
28 Rue de Bourg
Arts et Maison La Reine Blanche SA (interior decorating)
Galerie Saint-François
Piaget & Fils (watches)
29 Rue Saint-Laurent
Manuel (food and beverages)
5 Place Saint-François
Parfums Saint-François (perfumery)
10 Rue Saint-François
Loew Boutique (shoes)
29 Rue de Bourg
Blondel (confiserie)
5 Rue de Bourg
Langenthal SA (embroidery)
8 Rue de Bourg
Fermière, La (cheese)
Rue Saint-François

THE BEST OF ART
Pauli, Alice   (contemporary art)
7 Av. de Rumine, Tel. 22 87 62
La Vieille Fontaine   (18th–19th-century works of art, furniture) 9–13 Cheneau-de-Bourg, Tel. 23 47 87

The City

The Swiss-est Switzerland that even the Swiss fall in love with – a toyland town at the delta of an Alpine river flowing into a mountain lake, criss-crossed by medieval alleyways and nooky mews, dotted with turret-covered wooden bridges, churches, banks, grand hotels, cafés and watchmakers. The epitome of a tourist's dream goal, this cliché paradise is not only one of the ›musts‹ on the Grand Tour and many small ones, but also a hard-working town of production and trade (textiles, metallurgical and electrical goods, paper and tobacco), even though the services to the millions of bypassers and holiday-makers are of the utmost economic importance. The weekend wonderland for Zurich Society and a frequent pleasure destination for the burghers of nearby Zug and not-so-far Berne, Basle and St. Gallen, has not lost one bit of its charm since it was founded by the Benedictine monks over 1000 years ago. During its renowned music festival in late August – one of the most prominent in the world – the quaint little city reaches fashionability not only for Karajan and Co. but also for the international gratin assembling for concerts, cocktails and well-earned rest from social stress. Lucerne is also the cradle of the famous watchmaker dynasties of Gübelin and Bucherer as well as the hideaway for many famous heirs to other dynasties, namely the Flicks from neighbouring Germany. Richard Wagner had already fled to Lucerne and, inspired by the beauty and flair, finished his Götterdämmerung here as well as getting married to Liszt's daughter, Cosima. The Lucerne International Music Festival was originally introduced to honour the maestrissimo and Arturo Toscanini was the one to lift his baton in 1938 for the première. Innumerable writers, painters and composers have come here – and keep coming – for the quiet, the intense inspiration by the unique force of nature and the light over Lake Lucerne, and for the luxury of life that has always had a motivating effect on artists, from Goethe to Nabokov who described this city with euphoria and superlatives. Favourite ex-resident Wagner paid it the greatest tribute of all: ›the sweet warmth of Lucerne is such that it even makes me forget my music!‹

Founded: 8th century, around a Benedictine monstery; Lucerne (French), Luzern (Swiss) – ›city of light‹.

Far-reaching events: 13th century – city purchased by the Austrian Hapsburgs; Lucerne a trading centre between Lombardy and the Lower Rhine; 1332 – Lucerne breaks with Hapsburgs and joins the Swiss Confederation and William Tell to fight for independence; 16th century – the centre of the Counter-Reformation, Lucerne is the seat of a papal nuncio (1601–1873); 1574 – the Jesuits open their first college in the German part of Switzerland; 1798 – French occupation under Napoléon; 19th century – international tourism blooms; 20th century – Lucerne's discreet Industrial Revolution.

Population: 70,000; capital of the Canton of Lucerne.

Postal code: CH–6000 **Telephone code:** 41

Climate: Alpine; clear; fickle, with sudden storms.

Best time to visit: May to October.

Calendar of events: *Fasnacht* (Feb/Mar) – carnival celebrations and revels in the streets; *Volksfeste* (Apr–Oct) – local folklore – costumes, music, dance and handicrafts; *Swiss Rowing Championships* (Jul); *Sea Night Festival* (Aug/Sep) – Lucerne's most enchanting night, with a 250-year tradition; *International Music Festival* (Aug/Sep) – one of the world's best known musical events; *Concours* (Aug/Sep) – horse racing.

Fairs and exhibitions: *ARTISWISS/ORNARIS* (Apr/May) – Swiss handicrafts and international boutique articles; *INTERNATIONAL WEAPONS MARKET* (Apr); *LUGA* (May) – agricultural and industrial fair; *SWISS FORESTRY TRADE FAIR* (Aug); *BUILDING MODERNIZING FAIR* (Sep); *ANTIQUES EXCHANGE* (Nov).

Best view of the city: from one of the nine towers of the city wall.

Historical sights: *Chapel Bridge* 1333) – landmark covered wooden bridge with water tower and ceiling paintings, originally a city defence; *Spreuer Bridge* – covered wooden bridge with a chapel and a painting of the ›Dance of Death‹ on the gable; *Cathedral of St. Léger* (17th–18th centuries) – Swiss Renaissance, with a famous organ; *Jesuit Church* (1667–78) – Swiss Baroque; *Rathaus* (17th century) – Swiss and Italian Renaissance; *Lion Monument* – memorial to the Swiss Guards who died defending Louis XIV at the storming of the Tuileries in Paris on 10 August 1792; *Fine Art Museum* – works by Swiss artists; *Richard Wagner Museum* – for ›Ring‹ fans; *Verkehrshaus der Schweiz* – trains.

Special attractions: a dîner à deux at the round table in the upstairs dining room of the *Old Swiss House;* a visit to the *market* under the arcades by the Town Hall (Tue and Sat); a *boat trip* (of course); the *Garden of Glaciers* – potholes; *summer exhibitions* and *concerts* at the Fine Arts Museum; a trip by rack-and-pinion railway or cable-car to the top of *Mount Pilatus.*

Important companies with headquarters in the city: *Eichhof* (brewery); *Frigorex* (refrigeration and air conditioning); *Gardisette* (home textiles); *von Moos* (steel).

Airport: Zurich-Kloten, ZRH; Tel. (1) 8 12 71 11, 33 km/21 miles; Luzern-Beromünster, Tel.: 45/51 18 66 (small planes only) – Kehrhof-Tringen, Tel.: 45/74 15 98.

501

The Headquarters

PALACE

10 Haldenstrasse
CH–6006 Lucerne
Telephone: 50 22 22
Telex: 865 222 palu
Telefax: 51 69 76
Owning Company: Schweizerische Hotelgesellschaft AG
Managing Director: Jürg Reinshagen
Affiliation/Reservation System: The Leading Hotels of the World
Number of rooms: 157 (4 suites)
Price range: on request
Credit cards: AE, DC, EC, MC, Visa
Location: on the water front, 1 km/0.6 miles from city centre, 60 km/37.5 miles from airport
Built: 1904–1906 (recently renovated)
Style: elegant, traditional
Hotel amenities: garage, valet parking, fitness room, sauna, whirlpool
Main hall porter: Marcel Theler
Room amenities: air conditioning (public rooms only), tv/video, mini-bar (pets allowed)
Bathroom amenities: separate shower cabin (in some rooms), bidet, hairdrier, telephone (in some rooms)
Room service: 24 hours
Laundry/dry cleaning: same day
Conference rooms: 6 (up to 300 persons), conference equipment/built-in screen, convention office with own telephone and telex, secretarial services
Bar: ›Rendez-vous‹ (10.00/a.m.–2.00/a.m.) Silvano (barman), pianist, elegant English style
Restaurants: ›Mignon‹ (12.00/a.m.–14.30/2.30 p.m. and 19.00/7.00 p.m.–23.00/11 p.m.) Giorgio Montella (maître), Peter Schmidt (chef de cuisine), French cuisine, pianist; ›Gourmet‹ (7.00/a.m.–10.00 a.m. and 19.00/7.00 p.m.–22.00/10.00 p.m.) P. Andreoli (maître), Ueli Baumann (chef de cuisine), as Restaurant ›Mignon‹
Private dining rooms: four

The private-public palace has not only been the headquarters of all dignitaries, stars and beaux esprits in Lucerne for the past eight decades, but also the turntable of events and encounters in this, Switzerland's most beloved town. History, tradition and luxury are being kept in balance by Jürg Reinshagen and his staff, from the lakeside promenade to the intimate Mignon restaurant. The Belle Epoque mansion is an oasis of peace as much as a stock exchange of business deals and creativity during the yearly music festival; here you can retire from the world as well as meet it, from Karajan to company heads. The most beautiful countryside at your feet, Swiss Disneyland clichés all around, and the worldly pleasures of the good life within the walls of the Palace.

The Hideaway

PARKHOTEL

CH–6354 Vitznau (25 km/16 miles)
Telephone: (41) 83 13 22
Telex: 862 482 phv
Owner: Rudolf August Oetker
General Manager: Peter Bally
Affiliation/Reservation Systems: Relais et Châteaux, Preferred Hotels Worldwide, Leading Hotels of Switzerland
Number of rooms: 104 (17 suites)
Price range: SFr 235–690
Credit cards: not accepted
Location: on the Vierwaldstättersee; 65 km/40 miles from airport Zurich
Built: 1900 (recently renovated; new wing in same turn-of-the-century style added 1985/86)
Style: château-style and luxurious country-house style
Hotel amenities: garage, valet parking, house limousine service, sauna, newsstand, solarium
Sports: tennis, indoor/outdoor swimming pool, minigolf, water ski-ing
Sports (nearby): golf, boating, fishing, mountaineering
Room amenities: colour tv (remote control), mini-bar/refrigerator (pets allowed in rooms at additional charge)
Bathroom amenities: separate shower cabins, bidet, hairdrier, telephone
Room service: 24 hours
Laundry/dry cleaning: same day (weekend service)
Conference rooms: 10 (up to 100 persons)
Hallenbar: (11.00/a.m. to closing time) pianist
Restaurants: (12.00/a.m.–14.30/2.30 p.m. and 19.30/7.30 p.m.–21.30/9.30 p.m.) Helmut Seelbach (chef de cuisine), French and Swiss cuisine, open-air dining; ›Garden Restaurant‹ (10.30/a.m. till midnight) elegant à la carte dining
Private dining rooms: two (Gotthard, Grill Room and Von Pfeiffer Room)

This is how the world loves Switzerland: mountains, lakes, pasture-land with chalets and chapels, and in the midst of it – romantic and mysterious as well as tidy and well functioning – a fairy-tale castle for illusions, weekends and the confirmation that nothing's rotten in the state of Switzerland. Peter Bally is the happiest châtelain of them all – he receives guests who become fans, provides ›peaceful‹ entertainment (swimming, boating, water-skiing, tennis, minigolf, angling, hiking) or just peace. The rooms are big and comfortable enough to read Conrad Ferdinand Meyer's complete works in, the restaurant atmospheric enough to linger over old reserves until the sun rises again over Lake Lucerne. In German industry magnate Rudolf August Oetker's hotel quartet (Hôtel du Cap, Bristol in Paris, Brenner's Park), it is hardly surprising to find all amenities and perfection from the lakeside park to the turret suite.

Lunch

OLD SWISS HOUSE
4 Löwenplatz
Telephone: 51 61 71
Affiliations: Chaîne des Rôtisseurs;
Route Suisse des Plaisirs de la Table;
Club Prosper Montagné; Chevalier du
Tastevins; Grand-Maître du Bontemps
de Médoc et des Graves; Bier-Convent
International; l'Ordre Mondial des
Gourmets Dégustateurs
Owner/Manager: Willy and Hanny Bu-
holzer
Closed: February
Open: 9.00/a.m.–24.00/12 p.m.
Cuisine: French and Swiss
Chef de cuisine: Max Winzeler
Specialities: calves' sweetbreads ›Tour
d'argent‹; poached turbot; escalope of
veal prepared at table; lobster; oysters (in
fish tanks); freshwater fish (in pond)
Location: opposite the famous Lion
Monument (Löwendenkmal)
Setting: a family enterprise since it was
built in 1859; half-timbered building;
leaded windows (stained glass); rooms in
various styles, mostly 17th-century;
hand-carved doors, antiques (Meissen
porcelain, silver and pewter); Old Masters and a handmade porcelain-tile stove
dated 1636 in the ›Knights' Room‹
Amenities: private dining rooms (30 and
50 persons); boulevard tables for outdoor
dining
Atmosphere: redolent of history; elegant,
yet welcoming
Clientèle: Lucerne's Haute Bourgeoisie,
leavened by a generous sprinkling of superstars, from ›man-in-the moon‹ Neil
Armstrong and ex-President Nixon to
Prince Rainier of Monaco and prince des
cuisiniers Paul Bocuse
Dress: casual
Service: friendly, multilingual waitresses
in local costumes under the efficient su-
pervision of Karl Heinz Schmidt
Reservations: advisable (pets allowed)
Price range: medium (lunch) to medium-
expensive (dinner)
Credit cards: all major

Dinner

ZUM RABEN (›Chez Marianne‹)
5 Kornmarkt
Telephone: 51 51 35
Owner/Manager/Chef de cuisine: Ma-
rianne Kaltenbach
Closed: never
Open: 12.00/a.m.–14.00/2 p.m. and
18.30/6.30 p.m.–22.00/10 p.m.
Cuisine: French-Swiss
Specialities: gratin of scallops with
scampi; émincé of calves' liver in rasp-
berry vinegar; calves' sweetbreads and
kidneys; crème brûlée à la grand-mère
Location: in the heart of the old city

Setting: a beautifully-restored historic
building; four restaurants decorated in
varying styles; from the elegant ›Schult-
heissenstube‹ to the classic ›Reuss-Stube‹
with a view of the river to the comfortable
›Weinstube‹ and the highly original ›Ra-
ben-Beizli‹ with terrace for open-air dining
Amenities: private dining room (26 persons)
Atmosphere: picture-postcard charm
Clientèle: Transatlantic visitors from To-
ronto or Tampa, attracted by Marianne's
reputation and the fabled beauty of the
town, to local burghers en fête and en famille
Dress: however you like it, as long as they
like you
Service: sometimes a little on the slow
side
Reservations: necessary
Price range: moderately expensive
Credit cards: AE, DC, Visa

Lunch

MIGNON
10 Haldenstrasse
Telephone: 50 22 22
Owner/Manager: Jürg Reinshagen/Gior-
gio Montella
Closed: never
Open: 12.00/a.m.–14.00/2 p.m. and
19.00/7 p.m.–22.30/10.30 p.m. (snacks
available until 24.00/12 p.m.)
Cuisine: French (traditional and nouvelle)
Chef de cuisine: Peter Schmidt
Specialities: frequently changing menu;
fish; turbot in Sauternes sauce; duck with
beetroot and horseradish sauce; apple
tart; cheese soufflé; crème caramel, surprise menus; veal médaillons with green
peppercorns and mangoes
Location: in the Palace Hotel
Setting: wood-panelled dining room in
historic hotel building with retaining
walls; circular tower overlooking the
lake; live piano music and candlelight at
night
Amenities: hotel; private dining rooms;
open-air dining on terrace; bar; air conditioning, car park
Atmosphere: refined and distinguished at
lunchtime; with a hint of romance at
night
Clientèle: local High Society; discriminating and well-heeled tourists
Dress: formally elegant for dinner (jacket
or evening dress); rather casual for lunch
Service: professionally directed by Giorgio Montella
Reservations: recommended, especially
for dinner (no pets)
Price range: on the expensive side
Credit cards: AE, DC, Euro, Visa

504

Dinner

ADLER
18 Hauptstraße
Nebikon (40 km/25 miles)
Telephone: (62) 86 21 22
Owner/Manager: Josef and Sylvia Hunkeler
Closed: Tuesday; Wednesday
Open: 8.00/a.m.–00.30/12.30 a.m.
Cuisine: nouvelle
Chef de cuisine: Josef Hunkeler
Specialities: terrine of game with figs, green asparagus and mushrooms; cress soup; freshwater crabs; ragoût of salmon with clover; duck; game in season; tartelettes with fruit according to season
Location: at Nebikon, 40 km/25 miles north-west of Lucerne
Setting: small dining rooms furnished in elegantized rustic style
Amenities: three private dining rooms; car park
Atmosphere: a temple dedicated to les plaisirs de la table
Clientèle: favourite haunt of the Forsters and their numerous international friends
Dress: according to season and circumstance
Service: feminine and friendly
Reservations: advisable to essential, especially at weekends
Price range: rather expensive
Credit cards: AE, DC, Euro, Visa

Dinner

WILDEN MANN
30 Bahnhofstrasse
Telephone: 23 16 66
Owner/Manager: Fritz Furler/Susi Rick
Closed: never
Open: 9.00/a.m.–0.30/12.30 a.m.
Cuisine: French
Chef de cuisine: Eduard Obermad
Specialities: tartare of smoked sturgeon and fresh salmon; Luzern Krügli pastete
Location: near Lucerne's famous wooden bridge (Kapellbrücke)
Setting: historic auberge (1517); antique furnishings and an abundance of wood in the various dining rooms
Amenities: hotel; private dining rooms (12–30 persons); bar; car park (round the corner)
Atmosphere: gemütlich
Clientèle: Lucerne's social élite – local dignitaries, top brass and a sprinkling of tourists from Wisconsin to Winchester
Dress: rather conservative
Service: anxious-to-please
Reservations: recommended
Price range: moderately expensive
Credit cards: AE, DC, Euro, Visa

Bar

BLACK JACK
Kursaal (Casino)
6 Haldenstrasse
Telephone: 51 27 51
Owner/Manager: Kursaal Casino AG/ René Bachmann
Closed: never
Open: 21.00/9 p.m.–2.00/a.m.
Location: in the Casino (Kursaal)
Setting: striking red-gold décor with star-spangled ceiling
Amenities: bar; casino and nightclub in same building
Atmosphere: informal but stylish
Clientèle: Lucerne's jeunesse dorée before midnight gives way to a more mature (but not necessarily more staid) set in the wee small hours
Dress: no jeans, running shorts or training shoes
Service: cheerful and helpful
Reservations: not necessary
Credit cards: all major

Bar

RED ROSE
Kursaal (Casino)
Telephone: 51 27 51
Owner/Manager: Kursaal Casino AG/ René Bachmann
Closed: never
Open: 21.00/9 p.m.–2.00/a.m.
Location: in the Casino (Kursaal)
Setting: red velvet upholstery and subdued lighting
Amenities: nightclub with bar, dancing and daily strip-tease show; ›Black Jack‹ bar; casino in same building
Atmosphere: as sparkling as the champagne on offer
Clientèle: worldly-wise, well-heeled, well-travelled and (occasionally) well-known
Dress: disco elegant to disco casual
Service: observant and friendly
Reservations: not necessary
Credit cards: AE, DC, Euro, Visa

Nightclub

HAZYLAND
21 Haldenstrasse
Telephone: 51 19 61
Owner/Manager: Urs Gribi and Irma Lehmann
Closed: public holidays except with special permit
Open: 21.00/9 p.m.–2.30/a.m.
Location: opposite the Hotel National
Setting: shades of red; Art Nouveau bar and windows; upstairs gallery lounge with bar; light synthesizer
Amenities: discothèque; three bars, live shows

Atmosphere: légère but stylish
Clientèle: mostly young or at least young-
at-heart, plus the occasional middle-aged
manager
Service: cheerful and friendly
Price range: rather high
Dress: disco elegance
Reservations: advisable at weekends and
for special shows and dances (no pets)
Credit cards: all major

Shopping

EVERYTHING UNDER ONE ROOF
EPA, Neue Warenhaus AG
20 Rössligasse

FOR HIM
Fein-Kaller & Co   7 Am Schwanenplatz

FOR HER
Maison de Boer   29 Weggisgasse

BEAUTY & HAIR
Elegante   7 Pilatusstrasse

JEWELLERY
Bucherer   5 Am Schwanenplatz

LOCAL SPECIALITIES
Naegeli zum Tabakfass AG (tobacco)
2 Schwanenplatz
Maison Grieder (women's fashion)
Schweizerhofquai
Jucker & Borner (men's fashion)
4 Alpenstrasse
Hennes & Mauritz (children's fashion)
11 Kappelgasse
Biber (leather fashion)
39 Hertensteinstrasse
Bizzaro (furs)
28 Moesmattstrasse
Raeber (books)
Schweizerhofquai
Cristallhaus (gifts/porcelain)
18 Pilatusgasse
Leder Locher (baggage & travel accesso-
ries) 6 Schwanenplatz
Kraenzlin (interior decorating)
11 Lerdergasse
Leuet (food and beverages)
3 Weggisgasse
Leutwyler (perfumery/boutique)
6 Reussteg
Loew Boutique (shoes)
16–18 Weggisgasse
Coeur Fou, Au (confiserie)
3 Kornmarktgasse
Suter, Marlies (embroideries)
4 Stiftstrasse
Gübelin (Swiss watches)
1 Schweizerhofquai
Schwyzer's Zinn Zentrum (pewter)
3 Seidenhofstrasse

THE BEST OF ART
Fischer   (auctioneers)
19 Haldenstrasse, Tel. 51 57 72/73

Over one hundred, one quarter of all banks in Switzerland have their headquarters in Zurich – no wonder every 300th inhabitant is a millionaire. Contrary to Palm Beach and Palm Springs, however, you could not make out a single one, for the understatement of the burghers here makes even the British seem like pompous squanderers; the villas on Zürichberg are fortresses of discretion and at the public places of social renommé the consumption of carafe wine dwarfs that of champagne; labelled fashion is as frowned upon as status accessoires, and purchases at the jewellers, watchmakers and art galleries are as confidential as the legendary numbered accounts at Leu & Co. Yet, even with the famous stock exchange and the gold market, Zurich is not all money; the industries in and around the city – textiles, silk, machinery, chemicals, hydraulic and electrical equipment, paper and foodstuffs – are equally important for the country and its exports. And with all the transfers and trade and business with the ›gnomes‹, there is still enough room for pleasure, if somewhat more subdued than in Paris or Rome. Music and stage life are of world standard, galleries and auction houses can compete with London and New York, gourmetdom and shopping belong to the best, and watersports on the immaculately clean lake won't make you miss Geneva. The secret capital – and by far the most important city – of Switzerland has magnetized men of commerce as much as gentlemen of the arts: Thornton Wilder (›the only European city I could live in‹), Gottfried Keller (›a heavenly location‹), Victor Hugo (›a miniature paradise with grand views into eternity‹), Thomas Mann, James Joyce, Richard Wagner, Hans Arp and Tristan Tsara who founded Dadaism at the Café Voltaire. Baroque and pragmatism, worldliness and neutrality, high quality and low key mark life in Zurich. Not the gayest – but the safest.

Founded: on a site occupied since Neolithic times; a Roman settlement from 58 B.C.; Zürich (German) – from ›Turicum‹ (Latin).

Far-reaching events: 5th–10th century – occupied by the Alemanni, the Franks and the Swabians; 10th century – a fortified town; 1218 – Zurich a free imperial city; 1351 – Zurich joins the Swiss Confederation; 1519 – Zurich a leader in the Swiss Reformation under the influence of Huldrych Zwingli; 1523 – foundation of the university; 18th century – the capital of German Swiss intellectual life under Gessner, Lavater and Pestalozzi; 19th century – rapid industrial and commercial expansion; 1848 – seat of the Federal Polytechnic School; 1869 – constitution a model for the Confederation.

Population: 675,000; Switzerland's largest city; capital of the Canton of Zurich.

Postal code: CH–8000   **Telephone code:** 1

Climate: less extreme than many Alpine cities.

Calendar of events: *Fasnacht* (Shrove Tuesday) – music, parades and masked balls; *Zurich Spring Festival* (Apr); *Zurich Weapon Race* (Apr); *Zurich Marathon* (Apr); *International Festival Weeks* (Jun) – in the Opera House; *Zurich Night Festival* (mid-Jul) – every three years at the lake, with lots of fireworks; *Knabenschiessen* (autumn); *International Light Athletics Meet* (Aug) – in Letzigrund; *International Jazz Festival* (Oct); *Christmas Market* (Dec); *Zurich New Year's Run* (New Year's Eve).

Fairs and exhibitions: *ORNARIS* (Jan) – trade fair for living design and handicrafts; *INTOOLEX* (Feb) – trade fair for tools of the industrial finishing industry; *BIENNIAL MODERN INDUSTRIAL PRODUCTION TECHNOLOGY TRADE FAIR* (Feb); *MODEXPO* (Mar & Oct) – ladies' fashion fair; *SWISSPO* (Mar) – Swiss winter sports goods fair; *SAFT* (Mar) – syndicate for avant-garde fashion trends; *ANTIC* (Apr) – art and antiques fair; *ZÜSPA* (Sep) – Zurich autumn show for household, home, sport and fashion; *FERA* (Sep) – radio, television and hi-fi exhibition; *BANQUE* (Sep) – European trade fair for techniques and organization in banking; *INTERCOM* (Oct) – trade fair for the communications and information industry; *MICROTECHNIC* (Oct, biennial) – fair for precision technology; *FORUM* (Oct) – art fair; *EXPOVINA* (Nov) – Zurich wine fair; *INTERPHEX* (Nov) – exhibition and conference for the pharmaceutical, cosmetics and toiletry industry.

Historical and modern sights: *Grand Cathedral* (11th–13th century) – Romanesque landmark, with twin metal-covered wooden domes; *Fraumünster* (9th–14th century) – Romano-Gothic cathedral with windows by Chagall; *Wasserkirche* (15th century) – late Gothic church with unusual built-in choir stalls; the *Town Hall* (17th century) – Italian Renaissance, with a Baroque ballroom and magnificent stucco work; *St. Peter's Church* (13th–17th century) – in the old city, with Europe's largest clock face; the *Lindenhof Park* – site of the first settlement in Zurich; *Züricher Kunsthaus* – museum with collections of European painting and sculpture from ancient to modern times; *Swiss National Museum* – Swiss civilization from Roman swords to Carolingian frescoes to local costumes; *Rietberg Museum* – oriental objets d'art, Peruvian pottery and Flemish carpets; *Wohnmuseum* – restored 17th and 18th-century homes.

Special attractions: a shopping spree on the *Bahnhofstrasse*; a drink or a meal amongst the Chagalls and Picassos at the *Kronenhalle*; *Numismatic Auction* at Leu's Bank.

Important companies with headquarters in the city: *Aebi* (heavy plant); *EMS Chemie* (chemicals); *Göhner* (real estate); *Hayek* (industrial consulting); *Leu Bank* (banking); *Schweizerische Bankgesellschaft* (banking); *Schweizerische Kreditanstalt* (banking); *Schweizerische Aluminium* (aluminium); *SRO* (ball bearings), *Swissair* (airline).

Airport: Zurich-Kloten, ZRH; Tel.: 8 12 71 11; 11 km/6 miles; Swissair, Tel.: 8 12 12 12.

The Headquarters

BAUR AU LAC

1 Talstrasse
CH–8022 Zurich
Telephone: 2 21 16 50
Telex: 813 567 bal
Telefax: 2 118 139
Owning Company: H. Kracht's Erben
General Manager: Michel Rey
Affiliation/Reservation Systems: The Leading Hotels of the World, Preferred Hotels Worldwide
Number of rooms: 150 (15 suites)
Price range: Sfr 200–380
                    suites on request
Credit cards: AE
Location: city centre; lake front
Built: 1844 (recently renovated)
Style: classical
Hotel amenities: garage, valet parking, house limousine service, beauty salon, hairstylist, newsstand, house doctor
Main hall porter: Albert Ostertag
Room amenities: air conditioning, colour tv (cable), mini-bar (pets allowed)
Bathroom amenities: bidet, bathrobe, hairdrier, telephone
Room service: 6.15/a.m. to 23.45/11.45 p.m.
Laundry/dry cleaning: same day (weekend service)
Conference rooms: 4 (up to 200 persons), fashion runway, runway lighting, orchestra podium
Bars: ›American‹ (12.00/a.m.–24.00/12.00 p.m.) Tudor style
Restaurants: ›Grill Room‹ (12.00/a.m.–24.00/12.00 p.m.) international cuisine; Tudor style interior; ›French Restaurant‹ (12.00/a.m.–15.00/3.00 p.m. and 19.00/7.00 p.m.–23.30/11.30 p.m., Oct to end of Apr) Bernard Gothuey (chef de cuisine), French cuisine; ›Pavillon‹ (12.00/a.m.–15.00/3.00 p.m. and 19.00/7.00 p.m.–23.30/11.30 p.m., May to Sep), open-air dining
Nightclub: ›Diagonal‹ (22.00/10.00 p.m.–2.00/a.m.) Paul Bernold (manager)
Private dining rooms: for up to 200 persons

Among the world's leading palaces d'hospitalité, two stand out for unobtrusive grandeur and invisible luxury. The ›other‹ is the Baur au Lac. No fanfare, no fuss, no fake – the renommé habitués can enjoy anonymity for once and still be served like kings (which many are) and relax in unpretentious utter comfort. City palais, private garden, elegant restaurant, park pavilion for tea and snacks, club lunch in a waterside villa (for members only) and membership discothèque with the ›right‹ crowd. Michel Rey, court marshal of the owning Kracht family here, reigns the Baur au Lac in style and understatement. The only couleur in the grey-flannel philosophy is the private Rolls shuttling guests to and from the airport. (Many times to their private plane.)

The Hideaway

DOLDER GRAND

65 Kurhausstrasse
CH–8032 Zurich
Telephone: 2 51 62 31
Telex: 816 416 gran
General Manager: Raoul T. de Gendre
Affiliation/Reservation Systems: The
Leading Hotels of the World, Hotel Representative Inc., Preferred Hotels
Worldwide
Number of rooms: 180 (14 suites)
Price range: Sfr 200–800
Credit cards: AE, EC, Visa
Location: 4 km/2.5 miles from city centre,
12 km/8 miles from airport
Built: 1899 (recently renovated)
Style: Victorian
Hotel amenities: outdoor swimming pool
Main hall porters: Gaudenz Soliva, Modeste Follonier
Room amenities: colour tv/videotapes,
mini-bar/refrigerator
Bathroom amenities: separate shower
cabin, bidet (in most rooms)
Room service: 24 hours
Laundry/dry cleaning: same day
Conference rooms: 6 (up to 250 persons),
simultaneous translation facilities
Sports: 9-hole golf course, 3 indoor practice ranges, skating, curling, tennis
Sports (nearby): ice rink, riding
Restaurants: ›La Rotonde‹; French cuisine; ›Lobby‹; snacks; ›Barstübli‹;
snacks, piano music
Private dining rooms: five

*›Within this idyllic framework you are
bound to receive a warm welcome, an extraordinary cuisine, an impeccable service
and the best wines of France‹, noted Auguste Escoffier in 1930. Nothing has
changed in the past few decades – much
has even improved. The location is still the
most romantic in this epicentre of materialism and bourgeois solidity, high above
Lake Zurich, amidst a fairy-tale forest,
with a private golf course laid out in front,
and the rooms and suites are appointed as
in the surrounding villas occupied by the
gnomes and émigré stars from all over the
world. Raoul de Gendre, host to the élite of
hard currency, has found a gentle symbiosis of American ›guest recognition‹ and
European savoir-vivre radiated in every
salon, gable and turret. ›Tradition can only
be maintained with new ideas, today‹, philosophizes the worldly châtelain, and the
result is stunning. From the voiturier via
the concierge to the maître – there is an experienced personality behind every livrée,
and the luxurious amenities are as self-understood as the fulfilment of extravagant
wishes. There is no need to leave the Dolder except when you have to leave – nature
is the freshest, sports are the closest, the
view is the widest, the cuisine is the best
and the guests are the most fashionable
ever since Einstein, Toscanini, Furtwängler, Sauerbruch, Gigli, Chagall, Churchill,
Kissinger and the others.*

Lunch

KRONENHALLE
4 Rämisstrasse
Telephone: 2 51 02 56/(Bar) 2 51 15 97
Owner/Manager: Gustav Zumsteg
Closed: never
Open: 12.00/a.m.–14.00/2 p.m. and
19.00/7 p.m.–23.00/11 p.m.
Cuisine: traditional bourgeoise and
French (classic)
Chef de cuisine: Hans Georg Bay
Specialities: carré d'agneau with garlic
and Provençal herbs; Zurich-style trout
with boiled potatoes; chocolate mousse
Location: central (Bellevueplatz); by the
lake
Setting: elegantized 19th-century central
European bistro; wood panelling; valu-
able collection of modern paintings by Pi-
casso, Matisse, Miró, Bonnard and Cé-
zanne
Amenities: air conditioning
Atmosphere: a Zurich legend since its es-
tablishment in 1863, mirroring both the
history of the city and that of its artists;
light, quiet (no music); elegant but by no
means museum-like
Clientèle: sung and unsung celebrities
from the world of literature, fine arts, fin-
ance and fashion – from Max Frisch to
Joan Miró and from the Rothschilds to
Hubert de Givenchy
Dress: as you like it
Service: personal and professional
Reservations: advisable
Price range: rather expensive
Credit cards: AE, DC, Euro, Visa

Dinner

CHEZ MAX
53 Seestrasse
Zollikon (4 km/2½ miles)
Telephone: 3 91 88 77
Affiliations: Relais et Châteaux (Relais
Gourmand); Traditions et Qualité; Route
Suisse des Plaisirs de la Table
Owner/Manager/Chef de cuisine: Max
Kehl
Closed: Sunday; Monday; two weeks at
Christmas/New Year; three weeks in
July
Open: 12.00/a.m.–14.00/2 p.m. and
18.30/6.30 p.m.–22.00/10 p.m. (Bar open
17.00/5 p.m.–24.00/12 p.m.)
Cuisine: nouvelle
Specialities: Salmon marinated in se-
same; fillet of St. Pierre in champagne;
salad of green asparagus and truffles;
foie gras sauté aux nectarines; suprême
de cailles with artichoke purée; Japanese
menu; balik – coupe spéciale; snails'
eggs on white sweetcorn; lamb with lentil
sprouts
Location: 4 km (2½ miles) south-east of
city centre
Setting: terraced house by the lake; harmonious blend of modern masters' pain-

tings and English antique objets d'art
Amenities: open-air dining on terrace;
car park; bar for drinks and gourmet
snacks
Atmosphere: salon-like; light and refreshing at lunchtime; leisurely, candle-lit and
filled with classical music at night
Clientèle: expense-account gourmets at
lunchtime; in the evenings, pilgrims to
the paradise of lucullian lust created by
prince of cooks and pioneer of nouvelle
cuisine in Switzerland, Max Kehl
Dress: understatedly elegant for lunch;
more emphatically so for dinner
Service: assiduous
Reservations: essential
Price range: high – unless you're a millionaire
Credit cards: AE, DC, Euro, Visa

Dinner

WITSCHI'S REBE
5 Schützengasse
Telephone: 2 21 10 65
Owner/Manager: Heinz Witschi
Closed: Sunday, Saturday
Open: 12.00/a.m.–14.00/2 p.m. and
18.00/6 p.m.–22.00/10 p.m.
Cuisine: nouvelle (⟩au goût du marché⟨)
Chef de cuisine: Heinz Witschi
Specialities: galantine of calves' sweetbreads with woodland berries; escalope
of sea perch (loup de mer) with oysters;
artichoke soup with black truffles; fricassée of lobster; John Dory and scallops
with lime and ginger; sauté of Bresse
pigeon with Médoc
Location: near the railway station
Setting: two dining rooms; colonial style
downstairs, solid bourgeois comfort upstairs
Amenities: car park
Atmosphere: bordering on the elegant;
dominated by the artistic and adventurous spirit of proprietor Heinz Witschi
Clientèle: Zurich's Upper Crust; distinguished, refined, worldly-wise and comfortably-off
Dress: suitably sophisticated
Service: charming and feminine
Reservations: strongly recommended (no
dogs)
Price range: expensive
Credit cards: AE, DC, Euro, Visa

Lunch

WIRTSCHAFT ZUR HÖHE
73 Höhestrasse
Zollikon (8 km/5 miles)
Telephone: 3 91 59 59
Affiliations: Maison de Qualité; Club
Prosper Montagné; Chaîne des Rôtis-
seurs; Ordre des Coteaux de Cham-
pagne; Confrérie de Guillon

Owner/Manager: Robert Haupt
Closed: Tuesday; last Monday in the month; 1 week in February; 3 weeks in July/August
Open: 9.00/a.m.–24.00/12 p.m. (kitchen 12.00/a.m.–14.00/2 p.m. and 18.00/6 p.m.–21.30/9.30 p.m.)
Cuisine: ›au goût du marché‹
Chef de cuisine: Walter Schnetzler
Specialities: according to season; salad of duck's liver with bilberries; mussel soup with saffron; elderberry sorbet; pigeon farci au sauternes; bavarois aux kiwis
Location: 8 km (5 miles) south of Zurich-Bellevue
Setting: 200-year-old whitewashed house with green shutters in a rural setting above the village and the lake; recently renovated; Swiss country-house style
Amenities: private dining room (20 persons); large terrace overlooking garden for open-air dining; car park
Atmosphere: stylish; relaxing without loss of elegance
Clientèle: Lions' Club Zollikon; local businessmen with and without wives; conservative and comfortably off
Dress: no restrictions or requirements
Service: helpful and friendly
Reservations: essential (pets permitted)
Price range: fairly expensive
Credit cards: AE, DC, Euro, Visa

Dinner

AGNES AMBERG
5 Hottingerstrasse
Telephone: 2 51 26 26
Owner/Manager: Agnes Amberg
Closed: Saturday lunchtime; Sunday
Open: 11.30/a.m. – whenever 'the last guest has finished his coffee and 18.30/6.30 p.m.–0.30/12.30 a.m.
Cuisine: ›du marché‹ – light and modern
Chef de cuisine: Michel Finck
Specialities: salad of scallops with truffles; caramelized terrine de foie gras de canard; potato pancake (Reibeküchlein) with home-marinated salmon and caviar; scampi with orange and ginger; salsify soup; excellent pâtisserie; theatre-goers' menu (three courses before the play and three after the final curtain)
Location: near the Peacock Theatre (Pfauen-Theater)
Setting: highly individualistic; pale green draperies covering windows and walls; mirrors, marble, green leather and wood; dominated by art déco dessert tower; modern paintings by Bruce Robbins and Bryan Hunt
Amenities: gourmet boutique; cookery school; catering service; terrace; car-parking service in the evening (park car

on pavement and leave keys at reception); air conditioning
Atmosphere: elegant and luxurious; meticulous attention to detail by the dynamic and versatile ›AA‹
Clientèle: pampered and spoilt connoisseurs; food critics; epicurean theatre-goers, financiers – and the occasional millionaire
Dress: casually elegant to elegantly casual
Service: waiters in black tie; very professional
Reservations: essential
Price range: high – unless you're a millionaire
Credit cards: AE, DC, Euro, Visa

Meeting Point

WIDDERBAR
6 Widdergasse
Telephone: 2 11 31 50
Closed: Sunday evening
Open: 10.30/a.m.–0.30/12.30 a.m.
Location: near St. Peter's church
Setting: four-hundred-year-old-house; piano bar
Amenities: restaurant on the first floor
Atmosphere: elegant; antique; the absolute meeting point in town
Clientèle: a preponderance of serious burghers in Savile Row tweeds
Service: excellent
Reservations: advisable
Price range: medium
Credit cards: AE, DC, Euro, Visa

Bar

KRONENHALLE
4 Rämistrasse
Telephone: 2 51 15 97
Owner/Manager: Gustav Zumsteg
Closed: never
Open: 12.00/a.m.–14.00/2 p.m. and 19.00/7 p.m.–23.00/11 p.m.
Location: central (Bellevueplatz); by the lake
Setting: niche in elegantized 19th-century bistro; collection of original paintings by Picasso, Matisse, Miró, Bonnard and Cézanne which would grace any art gallery
Amenities: restaurant; air conditioning
Atmosphere: as sparkling as the myriad cocktails on offer, from Kronenhalle-Fizz to Lady-Killer
Clientèle: happy habitués and everybody who is anybody in town
Service: efficient
Reservations: advisable
Credit cards: AE, DC, Euro, Visa

Bar

BAUR AU LAC
1 Talstrasse
Telephone: 2 21 16 50
Owner/Manager: Michel Rey
Closed: never
Open: 10.00/a.m.–24.00/12 p.m.
Location: in the Hotel Baur au Lac
Setting: understatedly elegant bar in Zurich's oldest and most famous Grand Hotel
Amenities: hotel; restaurant; open-air dining on terrace; car park
Atmosphere: refined but not repressive
Clientèle: bankers, watchmakers, jewellers and globe-trotting tycoons
Service: punctilious
Reservations: advisable
Credit cards: AE, DC, Euro, Visa

Nightclub

DIAGONAL
8 General Guisan Quai
Telephone: (day) 2 01 35 31/(night) 2 01 24 10
Affiliation: Club of Clubs
Owner/Manager: Paul Bernold
Closed: never
Open: 22.00/10 p.m.–2.00/a.m.
Location: in the Hotel Baur au Lac teahouse in the grounds of the hotel
Amenities: discothèque
Atmosphere: very private and very exclusive
Clientèle: chauffeured heirs, jeunesse Cartier and the occasional fortunate stranger with charm, personality, a winning smile and/or a beautiful companion
Dress: Gucci, Pucci and co.
Service: vigilant but friendly (once you are)
Reservations: recommended
Price range: fairly high

Shopping

EVERYTHING UNDER ONE ROOF
Globus   Loewenplatz/Schweitzergasse

FOR HIM
Weinberg   13 Bahnhofstrasse

FOR HER
Gross, Walter   22 Bahnhofstrasse

BEAUTY & HAIR
Coiffeur Savoy   12 Poststrasse

JEWELLERY
Binder   4 Storchengasse

LOCAL SPECIALITIES
Davidoff (tobacco)
12 Poststrasse

Gassmann, Otto Jacques (women's fashion)
7 Poststrasse
Alfred Day (men's fashion)
12 Bahnhofstrasse
Tom & Tina (children's fashion)
2 Storchengasse
Leder-Locher (leather fashion)
91 Bahnhofstrasse
Pelzparadies (furs)
28 Bahnhofstrasse
Bisang (furs)
15 Storchengasse
Orell Fuessli (books)
10 Pelikanstrasse
Sequin Dormann (gifts)
Bahnhofstrasse/Rennweg
Ditting (porcelain) 35 Rennweg
Maedler (baggage & travel accessories)
26 Bahnhofstrasse
Forma Viva (interior decorating)
9 Oberdorfstrasse
Seiler (food and beverages)
7 Uraniastrasse
Vendôme (perfumery)
5 Pelikanstrasse
Teuscher (confiserie)
9 Storchengasse
Tuerler & Co. (watches)
28 Bahnhofstrasse

THE BEST OF ART
Bischofberger   (contemporary art)
29 Utoquai, Tel. 9 10 43 62
Haftmann, Roswitha   (Fine and modern art) 28 Rütistrasse, Tel. 2 51 24 35
Huber, Semiha   (modern art)
16 Talstrasse, Tel. 2 11 66 61
Knoedler   (contemporary art)
24 Kirchgasse, Tel. 69 35 00
Maeght, Lelong   (modern art)
10–12 Predigerplatz, Tel. 2 51 11 20
Schlégl, Dr. Istvan   (Fine art)
119 Minervastrasse, Tel. 2 51 49 63
Stähli   (contemporary art)
Im Bahnhof Zürich-Enge, Tel. 2 02 79 55
Ziegler, Renée   (contemporary art)
34 Rämistrasse, Tel. 2 51 23 22
Iseli-Mooser, M.   (arts et décors)
22 Kirchgasse, Tel. 47 18 60/47 51 14
Payer   (17th/18th-century works of art)
6 Pelikanstrasse, Tel. 2 21 13 82
Vogt   (country furniture)
13 Neumarkt, Tel. 47 41 55/47 41 58
Koller   (auctioneers)
8 Rämistrasse, Tel. 47 50 40
Ineichen   (auctioneers, clocks)
14 C.-F.-Meyer-Strasse, Tel. 2 01 30 17

The City

Its former names – Byzantium and Constantinople – revive memories of fairy tales of 1001 Nights, of Sultans and princesses, flying carpets and dervishes with magic power, but also of legendary empires with a grandiose court life and equal splendour among the arts. Secret capital of the Turkish democracy – clinging to its European position while its heartbeat is moved by the ›right bank‹ of the Bosphorus – Istanbul has lost little of its historical and mysterious lure and manages with charm and warmth to be the link between the two Old Worlds. It is advisable to shake off German mania for cleanliness, Swiss precision, British Colonial snootiness, French arrogance, Italian exhibitionism and American ›coined liberty‹, in order to enter this Sesame of wonders, only superficially resembling a hectic, loud, disorderly metropolis with a skyline out of a film set. Landmarks, sights and views are aplenty, architectural variety of centuries, treasures of art and objets d'art innumerable, and the human factor – despite its differences from the so-called Western traits – dominates life here more than in other rich centres of the continent. No-one will leave the city without having paid a visit and reference to the Hagia Sophia (Christianity's most beautiful house of worship and most important creation of Byzantine art), to the Topkapi Palace (having gained world fame through Peter Sellers for its Imperial Treasury) and the Sultan Ahmet Camii (named the Blue Mosque for its blue iznik tilework), but no-one should disembark before having walked the bazaar and the streets, taken a terrace lunch on the water and a private boat ride along the Yalis and summer palaces of the moguls of the past and the magnates of today as well as to Prince's Island in summer where you feel the Mediterranean again. Atmosphere, sounds, odours and the eternally changing light over the city are the essence of Istanbul, enthralling even the most sober men of commerce, rushing in for products and profits. Business will probably not be done as smoothly as in Davos, so there will be more time on hand to explore at least some of the labyrinth of this magic mountain, composed of seven hills. If not politically, Istanbul is still economically, culturally and socially the centre of the country –and this part of the world altogether.

Founded: 660 B.C., as Byzantium, by Greeks from Megara; Istanbul (Turkish): from the Greek ›is tin poli‹ – ›into the city‹.

Far-reaching events: 5th century B.C. – under Persian rule; 196 A.D. – conquered by the Romans under Septimus Severus; 330 – the emperor Constantine turns Byzantium into a ›new Rome‹ and renames it ›Constantinopolis‹; 476 – fall of Rome and ascent of Byzantium; 1204 – Enrico Dandolo, Doge of Venice, and an army of crusaders conquer the city; 1261 – won back by the Greeks; 1453 – Constantinople conquered by the Turks, who call it ›Istanbul‹; fire (1453 and 1679) and plague (1812) ravage the city, but the Ottoman Empire flourishes; 18th–19th century – war against Austria and Russia lead to loss of territority; 1846 – slave trade prohibited; 1909–18 – Balkan War and First World War lead to further territorial losses; 1922 – Mustafa Kemal Ataturk overthrows the last Ottoman sultan and is elected president of the Turkish Republic; Constantinople is now officially Istanbul, but no longer capital; 1973 – dedication of the Bosphorus Bridge.

Population: 4 million.

Postal code: TR-Istanbul   **Telephone code:** 1

Climate: surprisingly fickle; the summers are often cooled by the ›Poyraz‹ from Russia and the winters warmed by the ›Lodos‹ from north Africa; snow-capped mosques are not a rarity.

Calendar of events: *Istanbul Festival* (20 Jun to 15 Jul) – folk dancing, concerts at historic sites, ballet, mime, performing arts.

Fairs and exhibitions: *TOURISM FAIR* (Apr).

Historical sights: *Hagia Sofia* (537) – Byzantine splendour; *Sultan Ahmet Camii* (1616) – the ›Blue Mosque‹; *Topkapi Sarayi* (1462–78) – imperial palace seraglio and Pandora's box of exotic treasures; *Dolmabahce Palace* (19th century) – white marble neo-Baroque; *Edirnekapi* (5th century) – the gate through which the Turkish conquerors entered the city in 1453; *Kariye Camii* (14th century) – monastery with late Byzantine mosaics and frescoes; *Süleymaniye Camii* (1577) – mosque built on one of Istanbul's seven hills to rival the Hagia Sophia; *Bozdogan Kemeri* (1375) – bi-level aquaduct bringing water to the sultan's palace; *Rumelihisari* (1492) – fortress dominating the Straits of the Bosphorus; *Yeni Camii* (17th century) – one of the city's landmark mosques; *Ibrahim Paca Palace* – largest palace in the Ottoman Empire housing the *Museum for Turkish and Islamic Art* – ceramics, lamps and prayer rugs; *Hippodrome* (3rd century); *Museum of Mosaics*; the *Sunken Palace Cistern* – pillared vaults

Modern sights: *Bosphorus Bridge* (1973) – the crossing from Europe to Asia

Special attractions: a visit to the *Kapaờiçarşi* bazaar; a session at the *Cağaloğlu Hamam* Turkish baths; an afternoon on the tree-shaded terrace of the café *Beyazit Meydani*; a festival concert in the former *Church of St. Irene* (6th century)

Important companies with headquarters in the city: *Derimod* (leather); *Enka Holding* (construction); *Haci Bekir* (sweets; Turkish lokum); *Koc Holding* (machinery); *Pasabahce* (glass); *Sabanci Holding* (textiles)

Airport: Istanbul – Yesilköy, IST; Tel. 73 73 33/73 41 36, VIP-Lounge: 73 21 75; Turkish Airlines, Tel.: 73 35 10; 25 km/16 miles.

The Headquarters

SHERATON

Taksim Park
TR–Istanbul
Telephone: 13 12 12 1
Telex: 22 729 sher
General Manager: William Bauer
Affiliation/Reservation System: Sheraton Corporation
Number of rooms: 459 (16 suites)
Price range: $ 98–113 (single)
$ 115–145 (double)
$ 155–725 (suites)
Credit cards: AE, CB, DC, EC, MC, Visa, JCB
Location: near Dolmabahce Palace
Built: 1975
Style: modern de luxe
Hotel amenities: garage, valet parking, house limousine, swimming pool, beauty parlour, travel agency, bank
Room amenities: air conditioning, colour tv/in-house video, radio
Bathroom amenities: bidet, bathrobe
Room service: 24 hours
Conference rooms: (up to 1000 persons), all facilities; ballroom
Bars: ›Taksim‹ (10.00/a.m.–24.00/12 p.m.), lobby lounge; ›Aquarius‹ (10.00/a.m.–18.00/6 p.m., summer only), at the swimming pool; ›Sultan‹ (12.00/a.m.–1.00/a.m.), rooftop
Restaurant: ›La Coupole‹ (7.00/a.m.–24.00/12 p.m.), French cuisine; orchestra; ›Revan‹ (12.00/a.m.–1.00/a.m.), coffee shop
Nightclub: ›Disco 2000‹: (22.00/10 p.m.–4.00/a.m.), rooftop; discothèque; video entertainment

The American hotel in Asia's European outpost, directed by an Englishman with a German name, is the biggest and the best and its shopping arcade the most elegant bazaar in town. The hillside tower overlooking the Bosphorus and the neighbouring continent, innumerable mosques and the football-battlefield stadium, is a place for all seasons and moods. As a business arena it provides every facility for a board -of-directors conference or shareholders' meetings, complete with the newest equipment and fastest service – as a pleasure forum it serves something for everyone from everywhere blending the best of three worlds in the spacious labyrinth of twenty-three floors. The multi-level foyer is Istanbul's ideal rendezvous with coffee served in the deep fauteuils or drinks in the adjoining Taksim Bar*; the rooftop* Sultan Bar *is every foreigner's eagle's nest for the most dazzling views of one of the world's most picturesque city-scapes; the* La Coupole *restaurant will even satisfy the chauvinistic French, and the* Disco 2000 *high up in the sky assembles local chiceria and universal tourists used to the Palladium and the Hippodrome. In between the kaleidoscope of attractions and distractions there are hundreds of comfortable bedrooms and suites with that 1001-night view and Oriental service round the clock.*

Lunch

PLAZA
2 Bronz Sok, Maçka
Telephone: 1 41 63 56 / 1 47 54 96
Owner/Manager: Pem Co.; Mr. Meto/
Metin Sarier
Closed: (June–September) Sunday
Open: 12.00/a.m.–16.00/4.00 p. m. and
20.00/8.00 p.m.–24.00/12.00 p.m.
Cuisine: international
Specialities: Bosphorus fish
Location: in the Maçka district of Istanbul (the central business and residential area)
Setting: large dining room reminiscent of a winter-garden; glass roof and luxuriant greenery
Amenities: bar; air conditioning
Atmosphere: charmingly nostalgic
Clientèle: as popular amongst Istanbul's top industrialists entertaining foreign delegations as amongst the local Haute Bourgeoisie with something to celebrate
Dress: tends towards the conservative
Service: professionally welcoming
Reservations: essential for Friday and Saturday
Price range: moderately expensive
Credit cards: AE, DC

Lunch

LE CHALET
Tarabya
Telephone: 1 62 33 15/16
Owner/Manager: Nechettin Attaiylmaz
Closed: never
Open: 12.00/a.m.–the last guest has left
Cuisine: French and international
Chef de cuisine: W. H. Ströhmberg
Specialities: fresh fish; traditional Turkish dishes; home-made bread
Location: in the village of Tarabya; on the European side of the Bosphorus
Setting: chalet-style building vaguely reminiscent of a Swiss mountain village, with overhanging roof and window-boxes; dining room with wooden ceiling and comfortably-upholstered chairs
Amenities: VIP dining room (18 persons) upstairs with private terrace; open-air dining on terrace
Atmosphere: an oasis of Gallic epicureanism thanks to the fine cuisine of the Alsace-born chef, W. H. Ströhmberg; confidential or intimate, depending on your companion
Clientèle: Istanbul's In-Crowd; francophile gourmets from Ankara to Iszmir, plus conservative well-heeled overseas visitors
Dress: within reason, come as you please
Service: multilingual charm
Reservations: necessary
Price range: moderately expensive
Credit cards: AE, JCB

Dinner

CLUB 29
29 Nispetiye, Cad, Etiler (6 km/4 miles)
Telephone: 1 63 54 11 / 1 65 29 25
Affiliation: Club of Clubs
Owner/Managers: Mr. Meto/Mr. Sururi and Mr. Celôl
Closed: June–September
Open: 20.00/8.00 p.m.–2.30/a.m.
Cuisine: Turko-French
Chef de cuisine: Ali (holder of the 1983 Best European Cook Award)
Specialities: kebab with hot yoghurt; grilled jumbo prawns
Location: in the exclusive Etiler residential area; 6 km (4 miles) from the city centre
Setting: Art Déco-inspired dining room
Amenities: affiliated restaurant/club at 29 Vaniköy open during months of summer closure; open-air dining; air conditioning; nightclub
Atmosphere: intimate; sophisticated
Clientèle: crème de la crème; chic, self-confident and cosmopolitan
Dress: elegant; emphatic; eye-catching
Service: helpful and attentive
Reservations: essential for Friday or Saturday evening
Price range: fairly expensive
Credit cards: AE, DC

Bar

ZIHNI
21 Bronz Sokagi, Tesvikiye
Telephone: 1 46 90 43
Owner/Manager: Sardag Zihni
Amenities: lunchtime snacks; a Turkish orchestra playing Baroque music in the evening
Atmosphere: Istanbul's premier bar and in-place, with a genuine ›pub‹ atmosphere fostered by its sculptor/interior decorator/proprietor
Clientèle: lively; witty; with-it; Istanbul's international set mingles with local habitués and tourists from Kashmir to Kansas (it's one of the few places in town where a woman can enter unaccompanied)
Service: efficient

Bar

ZIYA II (›Ziya Lokantasi‹)
109 Muallim Naci Cad., Ortaköy
Telephone: 1 61 60 05
Owner/Manager: Ziya Haznedar
Location: in Ortaköy; on the European side of the Bosphorus
Setting: two open bars
Amenities: discothèque; affiliated restaurant ›Ziya‹ at Mim Kemal Oke Caddesi, Nişanteş (Telephone 1 47 17 08) serv-

ing excellent local dishes including 40 different kinds of hors d'œuvres (meze)
Atmosphere: very touristic
Clientèle: particularly popular amongst Istanbul's younger set – but no upper age limit
Dress: no sports leisurewear
Service: with a smile
Reservations: advisable
Price range: fairly expensive

Bar

PLAZA BAR
2 Bronz Sok, Maçka
Telephone: 1 41 63 56/1 47 54 96
Owner/Manager: Pem Co.; Mr. Meto/ Metin Sarier
Closed: (June-September) Sunday
Open: 12.00/a.m.–16.00/4.00 p.m. and 20.00/8.00 p.m.–24.00/12.00 p.m.
Location: in the Maçka district of Istanbul (the central business and residential area)
Amenities: restaurant; air conditioning
Clientèle: heterogeneous mixture of illustrious visitors
Dress: fairly casual to fairly formal
Service: friendly
Reservations: advisable
Credit cards: AE, DC

Nightclub

CLUB 29
29 Nispetiye, Cad
Etiler (6 km/4 miles)
Telephone: 1 63 54 11/1 65 29 25
Affiliations: Club of Clubs
Owner/Managers: Mr. Meto/Mr. Sururi and Mr. Celôl
Closed: June–September
Open: 20.00/8.00 p.m.–2.30/a.m.
Location: in the exclusive Etiler residential district; 6 km (4 miles) from city centre
Setting: two-floor Turkish wonderland consisting of club/restaurant with discothèque
Amenities: affiliated restaurant/nightclub at 29 Vaniköy open during months of summer closure; restaurant with open-air dining on terrace; air conditioning
Atmosphere: without doubt the most elegant and exclusive club in Istanbul
Clientèle: everybody who is somebody from the small circle of Turkish Society and business
Dress: jacket de rigueur
Service: good
Reservations: advisable; essential at the weekend – preferably in advance
Price range: fairly expensive
Credit cards: AE, DC

Shopping

EVERYTHING UNDER ONE ROOF
Kapali Çarşi   (covered bazaar)

AFOR HIM
Beymen   Şişli, Halâskârgazi C. 230

FOR HER
Alta Moda   Şişli, Halâskârgazi Caddesi

BEAUTY & HAIR
Beauty Parlor   Hilton Hotel

JEWELLERY
Mauromati   Kapalı Çarşı

LOCAL SPECIALITIES
Titiz (women's fashion)
Osmanbey, 60 Rumeli Caddesi
Vakko (men's fashion)
Beyoğlu, 123 Istiklal Caddesi
Pabetland (men & women's fashion)
Maslak, 57 Büyükdere Caddesi
Vakkorama (children's fashion)
Taksim, Etap Hotel
Derimod (leather fashion)
Zeytinburnu, Sahilyolu, 28 Beşkardeşler Durak
Haşet (books)
Beyoğlu, 469 Istiklal Caddesi
Vakko (gifts)
Beyoğlu, 123 Istiklal Caddesi
Nursan (porcelain)
Nişantaş, 18 Abdi Ipekçi Caddesi
Beymen (baggage & travel accessories)
Beyoğlu, Vakif Gökçek Iş Han
Güngör Mobilva ve Dokorasyon (interior decorating)
Nisantas, 26 Emlak Caddesi
Ankara Pazar (food and beverages)
Şisli, 368 Halâskârgazi Caddesi
Goya (shoes)
Beyoğlu, 117 Istiklal Caddesi

THE BEST OF ART
Galeri Baraz   (contemporary art)
191 Kurtulus Cad., Tel. 1 40 47 83
Tiglat Art Gallery   (modern art)
2 Küçük Bebek Cad., Bebek
Urart Sanat Galerisi   (modern art)
21 Abdi Ipekçi Cad., Nişantaşi

Since the construction of the M1 and the expansion of the airport, few visitors to the United Kingdom's second largest city are likely to follow G. K. Chesterton's ›rolling English road‹ and approach Birmingham by way of Beachy Head. Jane Austen may have had ›no great hopes of Birmingham‹, but, emerging from the intricacies of Spaghetti Junction you will discover a pulsating metropolis which, without competing with London for cosmopolitan glamour or Edinburgh for historical charm, nevertheless occupies a vital position in the island nation's economic and social life. Birmingham is the geographic epicentre of England and the very heart of British heavy engineering, from car manufacturing to tyres and batteries. Yet the city is by no means the asphalt-and-concrete jungle one might expect. Dotted with parks, surrounded by a green belt (thanks to the socially-conscious Cadbury family) and interlaced by more canals than Venice (rehabilitated by volunteer groups when superseded by railways as a means of industrial transport), the capital of the Black Country is an effervescent mélange of cultures, races, ethnic groups and tongues which has a characteristic self-confidence distilling its hererogeneous elements into a complex entity. Occasionally tumultuous, baffling at times, and invariably fascinating, Birmingham remains, above all, as inescapably English as the Vale of Evesham, the Cotswolds, or even Stratford-upon-Avon.

Founded: 1066, as a gift from Lord Fitzansculf to his Lord Steward Birmingham.

Far-reaching events: 1156 – Henry II grants Birmingham market privileges; 16th century – a centre for the iron smelting industry; 1662 – a refuge for dissenting priests; 18th–19th centuries – rapid industrial expansion – awarded city status under Queen Victoria; 20th century – redevelopment and remodelling of the city centre.

Population: 2.5 million (urban area); second largest city in the United Kingdom; Birmingham - after the Doomsday Book landlord.

Postal code: confusing; depends upon street, part of the city and house number.

Telephone code: 21

Climate: mild but rather damp.

Best time to visit: May to October.

Calendar of the events: *Lord Mayor's Procession* (May) – Birmingham celebrates the election of the new mayor; *Tulip Festival* (end of May); *Highland Gathering* (Jul) – for expatriate Scots; *Children's Funweek* (Aug); *City of Birmingham Show* (Aug) – parades and street parties; *Guy Fawkes* (5 Nov) – mammoth firework display.

Fairs and exhibitions: *INTERNATIONAL SPRING FAIR* (Feb); *BOAT & CARAVAN SHOW* (Feb); *MARKETING AND PROMOTION SERVICES* (Feb); *ELECTREX* (Feb) – international electrotechnical exhibition; *GLASSEX* (Mar) – glass and glass technology; *MEATEX* (Mar) – meat technology and food processing; *MT* (Mar) – materials testing; *INTERNATIONAL MATERIALS HANDLING FAIR* (Mar); *CAD/CAM* (Apr) – computer-aided design exhibition; *INTERNEPCON* (Apr) – electronic production conference; *BREWEX* (Apr) – brewing, bottling and allied trades; *PAKEX* (Apr) – packaging; *OPTRAFAIR* (May) – optics; *HEVAC* (May) – heating, ventilation, air conditioning; *COMMUNICATIONS* (May) – communications equipment and systems; *ROSPA SAFETY EXHIBITION* (May); *EUROCHEM* (Jun) – chemical and process engineering; *SURFACE TREATMENT AND FINISHING SHOW* (Sep); *METCUT* (Sep) – metal cutting machinery; *SUBCON* (Sep) – subcontracting industries; *GLEE* (Sep) – garden and leisure exhibition; *WOODMEX* (Nov) – woodworking industries; *I.C.E.* (Nov) – construction equipment.

Best view of the city: from the *Post Office Tower.*

Historical sights: *Birmingham Museum and Art Gallery* – with one of the world's best collections of Pre-Raphaelites, and sculptures by Henry Moore and Auguste Rodin; *Museum of Science and Industry* – technology – made in England, and elsewhere; *St. Philip's* (1711) – Italianate Baroque, a cathedral since 1905; *St. Lazar* – a reflection of the 14th-century Serbian Byzantine style; *Council House* (1879) – a reminiscence of Renaissance Italy in Victorian England; *Town Hall* (1834) – a copy of the Castor and Pollux temple; *Sarehole Hill* (1760) – inspirational for J. R. R. Tolkien's ›Hobbit.‹ *Aston Hall* (1618–1635) – Jacobean mansion in a Charles I background.

Modern sights: *National Exhibition Centre* – conference facilities in a park-like setting; *Birmingham Repertory Theatre* – modern building for a company with a long and proud history; *New Central Library* – the biggest in Europe; *Bull Ring Market* – shopping for just about everything.

Special attractions: *narrow boat trip through Birmingham's canals* – more extensive than in Venice, but without the gondolas; an evening at the *theatre*; a tour of the *pubs*; a circuit of the *flea market* or a *golf course*; the last shuttle to *London.*

Important companies with headquarters in the city: *Joseph Lucas Industries* (cars and car parts); *Austin Rover* (vehicles); *Sturge* (chemicals); *Davenports* (brewery); *Dunlop* (rubber); *Cadbury-Schweppes* (foodstuffs).

Airport: Birmingham International, BMX; Tel.: 7 43 62 27; 10 km/7 miles; British Airways, Tel: 2 36 70 00.

The Headquarters

PLOUGH AND HARROW

135 Hagley Road, Edgbaston,
GB–Birmingham B16 8LS
West Midlands
Telephone: (454) 41 11
Telex: 338 074 chbirm
Owning Company: Crest Hotels Ltd.
General Manager: Stuart J. Smith
Affiliation/Reservation Systems: Crest
Hotels, Utell Australia
Number of rooms: 41 (3 suites)
Price range: £ 65–135
Credit cards: AE, DC, Visa, Access, MC,
CB, JCB.
Location: 2 km/1.5 miles west of city cen-
tre
Built: 1835
Style: Victorian – Queen Anne
Hotel amenities: garage, house limousine
service, health club, beauty salon, solar-
ium, massage
Main hall porter: Arthur Foden
Room amenities: air conditioning, video,
mini-bar/refrigerator, radio
Bathroom amenities: telephone
Room service: 7.00 a.m.–22.00/10 p.m.
Conference rooms: 2 (up to 55 persons);
overhead projector; slide projector; VHS
format video; screen
Cocktail Bar: (12.00 a.m.–14.30/2.30
p.m. and 18.30/6.30 p.m. to midnight);
Christopher Edwards (barman)
Restaurant: ›Plough and Harrow‹ (7.00
a.m.–10.00 a.m., 12.30 p.m.–14.30/2.30
p.m. and 19.00/7.00 p.m.–22.30/10.30
p.m.); Giovanni Di Leva (maître); John
Sweeney (chef de cuisine); French traditional cuisine; pianist

*That this handsome red-brick hotel is the
Pole Star amongst the Milky Way of
stereotyped city-centre monoliths is appar-
ent from the moment the uniformed voiturier steps forward at the door of the Plough
and Harrow. Built on the site of a seventeenth-century inn on one of Birmingham's
main arteries, the 24-carat member of the
Crest chain is the outstanding headquarters for business in the West Midlands. The
original Victorian edifice and the modern
extension provide about forty bedrooms
spacious and comfortable enough for visiting executives, furnished in shades of
brown and equipped with luxurious bathrooms with gold-plated taps. The public
rooms have the congenial air of a select
club; panelled foyer, Queen Anne style
lounge and a bar which is a focal point for
the local management élite before they pro-
ceed to sample John Sweeney's chicken
mousse with crab sauce or fillet of lamb
with walnuts, herbs and port in the festively
elegant dining room. There are full facilities for board meetings and swimming
pool, sauna, solarium and smiling service
complete the pleasure picture. Yehudi Menuhin, Lauren Bacall and Jeffery Archer always make the Plough and Harrow their
headquarters when they visit Birmingham.*

LYGON ARMS

GB–Broadway, Worcs. WR 12 7DU
(56 km/35 miles)
Telephone: (3 86) 85 22 55
Telex: 338 260 lygon
Owner: Douglas Barrington, O.B.E.
Managing Director: Kirk Ritchie
Affiliation/Reservation Systems: Relais et
Châteaux, Prestige Hotels, The Leading
Hotels of the World
Number of rooms: 58 (5 suites)
Price range: £ 50–130
Credit cards: AE, DC, MC, Visa, Access
Built: 16th century
Style: antique
Hotel amenities: garage, heliport, jethire,
chauffeur service, tennis, gardens, bal-
looning
Room amenities: radio, remote control tv,
trouser presses
Bathroom amenities: hairdrier, telephone
Room service: 24 hours
Laundry/dry cleaning: laundry: 24 hours,
dry cleaning: same day
Conference rooms: 4 (up to 80 persons)
Sports nearby: golf, squash, riding
Bars: ›Goblets‹, ›Cocktail Bar‹
Restaurants: ›Lygon Arms‹ (12.30/p.m.–
14.00/2.00 p.m. and 19.30/7.30–21.15/
9.15 p.m.)

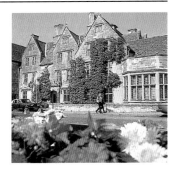

*›Involved, yet tranquil like an epic poem‹
stands Broadway, its wide grass verges
shaded by chestnut trees, its mellow stone
cottages wearing their years as unselfcon-
sciously as the gently rolling Cotswold hills
themselves. In this loveliest of villages at
the very heart of the ›precious stone set in
the silver sea‹, stands a relais de campagne
in which has been distilled the essence of
450 years of Englishness. The Lygon Arms
– honey-coloured, slate-roofed and mul-
lion-windowed – still presents to the curious traveller of today the immutably tranquil countenance with which it has greeted
the ebb and flow of centuries of history.
Even the new extension, brainchild of men-
tor-owner Douglas Barrington, fuses perfectly with the Elizabethan inn to create a
harmonious entity. The interior is a treasure-chest of priceless antiques which bear
the scars of time as proudly as the patina of
loving care; beamed ceilings, inglenook
fireplaces, burnished copper and Windsor
chairs. The past is omnipresent, inescap-
able; the front doorway, where landlord
John Trevis carved his name in 1620, the
year the Mayflower sailed; the Cromwell
room, where the Roundheads' leader slept
before defeating Charles I at nearby Wor-
cester; the Great Hall dining room, scene
of many a banquet then and now, with
hunting trophies, heraldic frieze and minstrels' gallery. And yet, the Lygon Arms is
no museum-piece. Under the sure guidance
of director Kirk Ritchie it continues to
evolve, overlaying the riches of its past with
that spirit of innovation and self-challenge
which is a hallmark of the island race.*

Lunch

SLOANS
Chad Square, Hawthorne Road,
Edgbaston
Telephone: 4 55 66 97
Owner/Manager: John Sloan
Closed: Saturday lunchtime; Sunday;
Bank Holidays; two weeks in July/August
Open: 12.00/a.m.–14.00/2 p.m. and
19.00/7 p.m.–22.00/10 p.m.
Cuisine: French (nouvelle); fish and seafood
Chef de cuisine: John Daniels
Specialities: fish; seafood; fresh lobster;
sea bass in white wine sauce; turbot with
salmon mousse; Grand Marnier soufflé;
seasonally-changing menu; 7-course
Menu Dégustation
Location: past Botanical Gardens on one-way system; turn left and immediately
right
Setting: modern, sophisticated décor
Amenities: private dining room (16 persons)
Atmosphere: relaxing, yet elegant
Clientèle: fairly heterogeneous; predominantly business clients at lunchtime give
way to Birmingham's Beau Monde plus a
sprinkling of visitors from Bristol to Bremen for dinner
Dress: no hard-and-fast rules, but tends
towards the conservative
Service: friendly
Reservations: preferable (no dogs)
Price range: moderately expensive
Credit cards: AE, DC, Visa, Access

Lunch

PLOUGH AND HARROW
Hagley Road, Edgbaston
Telephone: 4 54 41 11
Owner/Manager: Plough and Harrow/
Stuart Smith
Closed: Christmas Day; Bank Holiday;
Mondays
Open: 12.30/p.m.–14.30/2.30 p.m. and
19.00/7 p.m.–22.30/10.30 p.m. (Sundays
until 21.00/9 p.m.)
Cuisine: French traditional
Chef de cuisine: John Sweeney
Specialities: light chicken mousse served
with crab sauce; chicken Kiev; traditional Sunday lunch; breast of duck with
blackcurrant and cassis; tournedos with
morel mushrooms, desserts
Location: in the Plough and Harrow Hotel, 2 km/1.5 miles from the city centre
Setting: elegant, rather formal dining
room in a charming historic inn
Amenities: hotel; private dining room (60
persons); car park
Atmosphere: stylishly festive but not in
the least forbidding

Clientèle: conservative, comfortably-off
epicures from Cheltenham, Canterbury
and Canberra
Dress: mostly rather conventional
Service: knowledgeable and attentive
Reservations: recommended
Price range: relatively expensive
Credit cards: AE, DC, Visa, Access, Master Card, Carte Blanche

Dinner

LORENZO
3 Park Street
Telephone: 6 43 05 41
Owner/Manager: Lorenzo Ferrari
Closed: Saturday lunchtime; Sunday;
Monday evening; Bank Holidays; 3
weeks in July/August
Open: 12.00/a.m.–14.30/2.30 p.m. and
19.00/7 p.m.–23.30/11.30 p.m.
Cuisine: Italian
Specialities: hors d'œuvres; home-made
pasta; fish; meat; tempting desserts
Location: a chorus of Santa Lucia from
the Bullring Shopping Centre
Atmosphere: Italianissimo
Clientèle: expatriate Italians; spaghetti-loving locals; Trades Fair exhibitors from
Texas, Taiwan and Teeside
Dress: within reason, what you will
Service: anxious-to-please
Reservations: advisable for lunch
Price range: moderate
Credit cards: AE, DC, Visa, Access

Lunch

RAJDOOT
12 Albert Street
Telephone: 6 43 88 05
Owner/Manager: S. K. Sharma
Closed: Sunday lunchtime; lunchtime on
Bank Holidays; Christmas Day; Boxing
Day
Open: 12.00/a.m.–14.30/2.30 p.m. and
18.30/6.30 p.m.–23.30/11.30 p.m.
Cuisine: North Indian
Specialities: lassi (yoghurt based drink);
Tandoori dishes; nan bread; lamb pasanda (mild curry); cucumber raita
Location: central
Setting: spacious; split-level dining room
Amenities: private dining room (50 persons)
Atmosphere: epitomises modern Birmingham; cosmopolitan, welcoming and
friendly
Clientèle: heterogeneous mixture of
academics, members of the liberal professions, habitués from Bhopal to Bangalore, ex-Army colonels and casual passers-by
Dress: fairly casual to fairly formal
Service: helpful and good-natured
Reservations: recommended
Price range: average
Credit cards: AE, DC, Visa, Access

Dinner

JONATHANS'
16–20 Wolverhampton Road
Telephone: 4 29 37 57
Closed: never
Open: 12.00/a.m.–14.00/2 p.m. and
19.00/7 p.m.–22.00/10 p.m.
Cuisine: English
Specialities: smoked chicken in sour
cream and caper sauce; beef Wellington;
gung-ho mutton casserole with pickled
mushrooms; venison; pork with cider
and apples; summer pudding; spotted
Dick; Cambridge burnt cream
Location: 6 km/4 miles west of Birmingham; near the M5 (junction 2)
Setting: a maze of dining rooms furnished like a Victorian drawing-room,
with the lighting at the back subdued
enough to please the most lovesick of
couples
Amenities: private dining rooms (2–16
persons); open-air dining on terrace; car
park; late-night supper for theatre-goers
Atmosphere: welcoming and relaxing,
with a hint of romance
Clientèle: industrialists celebrating a contract or clinching a deal during the week
for lunch; the after-theatre crowd at
night; Birmingham's Haute Bourgeoisie
en fête and en famille (provided the
children behave) at weekends
Dress: as you like it
Service: efficient
Reservations: essential
Price range: moderately expensive
Credit cards: AE, DC, Visa, Access

Bar

THE MILLIONAIRE
Centre City Tower, Hill Street
Telephone: 6 43 45 54
Closed: Sunday
Open: 21.00/9 p.m.–2.00/a.m.
Location: a champagne cork's trajectory
from New Street Station
Setting: ultra-luxurious bar/nightclub
with two licensed bars and a cocktail bar
as well as a restaurant
Amenities: discothèque
Atmosphere: leisured; encapsulating;
ultra-chic
Clientèle: local connoisseurs of the finer
things in life
Service: smooth
Reservations: advisable

Nightclub

LIBERTY'S
184 Hagley Road
Telephone: 4 54 44 44
Closed: Sunday
Open: 21.00/9 p.m.–2.00/a.m.; (restaurant from 20.00/8 p.m.)
Setting: super-sophisticated; up-to-the-
minute sound and lighting installations
Amenities: discothèque; piano bar restaurant (French cuisine); cocktail bar;
champagne and seafood bar; shorts bar;
two main bars; car park
Atmosphere: from the intimate and relaxing (restaurant) to the dazzling and energetic (discothèque)
Clientèle: Birmingham's business people,
including a fair proportion of mink-
coated, Rolls-Royce-driving, factory-
owning millionaires
Dress: elegant and exclusive
Service: in keeping with the surroundings
Reservations: recommended – especially
for dinner

Nightclub

BOBBY BROWN'S CLUB
52 Gas Street
Telephone: 6 43 25 73
Closed: never
Open: (Monday–Saturday) 21.00/9
p.m.–2.00/a.m.; (Sunday) 21.00/9 p.m.–
24.00/12 p.m.
Location: central
Setting: in a former canalside warehouse,
which has retained much of its original
character despite the high technology;
sumptuous décor; dance floor areas, secluded nooks and ever-changing lighting
and sound effects
Amenities: discothèque; bars; bistro; restaurant (also open at lunchtime) periodic
live music; three affiliated ›BB‹ restaurants in the Birmingham area
Atmosphere: original; friendly; low-key
to fairly emphatic as the evening progresses
Clientèle: Birmingham's jeunesse argentée – chic, cheerful, uncomplicated and
self-confident
Dress: conservative to kinky
Service: friendly
Reservations: recommended

Shopping

EVERYTHING UNDER ONE ROOF
Rackhams Ltd.
35 Temple Row/Corporation Street

FOR HIM
Austin Reed Ltd.
3 Birmingham Shopping Centre

FOR HER
Smart Susan
4 City Arcade/Union Street

BEAUTY & HAIR
Raymond Art de Coiffure Ltd.
138 New Street

JEWELLERY
Nathan & Co.   31 Corporation Street

LOCAL SPECIALITIES
Miss Selfridge Ltd. (fashion for her)
79 High Street
Horne Bros. Ltd. (fashion for him)
14 New Street
Reiss Fashions Ltd. (fashion for him and
her)
32 a New Street
Persuedes (leather fashion)
11 Burlington Chambers/New Street
Neilsons (furs)
8 Needless Alley
Hamleys Toy Shop (gifts and toys)
Bull Street
Lawleys Ltd. (porcelain)
37 Great Western Arcade
Bradbury, L. F. (baggage & travel accessories)
625 Bearwood Road, Smethwick
Longland, Lee & Co. Ltd. (interior decorating) 224 Broad Street
Rackhams Food Hall (food and beverages)
35 Temple Row/Corporation Street
Shakespeare Clinic (perfumery/beauty
salon)
290 Baldwin's Lane, Hall Green
Cartier, Roland (shoes)
42 New Street

›There were three sailors of Bristol city who took a boat and went to sea. But first with beef and captain's biscuits and pickled pork they loaded she.‹ The adventurous spirit of William Makepeace Thackeray's heroes has left its mark on the town at the mouth of the Avon. For almost a millenium Bristol has been an outward-looking place, its trading links with other west coast European ports – from Oporto to Bordeaux – expanding to include the New World after adopted son John Cabot's discovery of Newfoundland. Cathedral, Georgian houses and Stock Exchange testify without ostentation – thanks to the deep-rooted streak of Quaker puritanism – to the prosperity brought by this early commerce. Today the port – now centred on nearby Avonmouth – is as vibrant as ever. Its hinterland houses a range of industries based on traditional imports – tobacco, wine and sugar, to which have been added brainchildren of twentieth-century technology from computers to jet engines. And yet – university, zoo and Old Vic notwithstanding – Bristol remains for many of its visitors a transit-lounge-cum-business-arena, a backdrop for discussions or a conference en passant. Those leaving by train are reminded of local wunderkind Isambard Kingdom Brunel's pioneering engineering achievements at Temple Meads Station; those who stay can see his versatility in the ›Great Britain‹ or the Clifton Suspension Bridge before crossing the Severn Bridge to Wales or retiring to the Georgian splendours of Bath.

Founded: 10th century, by the Saxons, near a bridge across the Avon.

Far-reaching events: 14th century – a prosperous port due to its wool trade; 1497 – John Cabot sails from Bristol to discover Newfoundland; 1552 – foundation of the Society of Merchant Venturers; 17th century – expansion of trade to the Spanish colonies in South America, Africa and the West Indies; 1809 – creation of the floating harbour; 1879 – opening of Avonmouth harbour; 18th–19th centuries – Industrial Revolution sees the establishment of iron, brass, copper, tin, porcelain and glass industries; 1940–42 – heavy bombing damages much of the city; 1966 – opening of the Severn Suspension Bridge.

Population: 420,000.

Postal code: GB – confusing, depending on part of city, street and house number.

Telephone code: 272.

Climate: temperate – but bring two umbrellas!

Best time to visit: June to August.

Calendar of events: *Bristol Marathon* (Apr); *North Somerset show* (May); *Lorry Driver of the Year Competition* (Jun); *Bristol Power Boat Grand Prix* (Jun); *West of England International Tennis Tournament* (Jun) – Bristol's centre court as centre of the West of England; *International Music Festival* (Jul); *Bristol Horse Show* (Jul); *Harbour Regatta* (Aug); *International Balloon Fiesta* (Aug); *Maritime Carnival* (Aug); *Christmas Illuminated Water Carnival* (Dec).

Fairs and exhibitions: *CARAVAN, CAMPING, HOLIDAY AND TRAVEL EXHIBITION* (Feb); *INDUSTRY AND COMMERCIAL PRODUCTS* (Feb); *WORLD WINE FAIR* (Jul); *ELECTRONICS SHOW* (Sep); *GIFTWARE AND FASHION ACCESSORIES TRADE SHOW* (Sep); *AUTUMN FASHION FAIR* (Sep); *CATERING EXHIBITION* (Oct); *BICYCLE SHOW* (Nov); *FOOD, WINE AND KITCHEN EXHIBITION* (Nov).

Historical sights: *St. Mary Redcliffe* (1280) – one of the largest parish churches in England; *Cathedral* (1140–1888) – former Augustinian monastery hall-church; *City Museum and Art Gallery* – a collection of Bristol, Nailsea, Roman, Pre-Roman and Chinese glass – reflecting the city's former importance as a centre of the glass industry; the *Georgian House* (18th century) – merchant's house, an exquisite period piece; *Red Lodge* (16th century); *St. Stephen's* (13th century) – city parish church; *Merchant Seamen's Almhouse* – the arms of Bristol's leading merchant guild, the Merchant Venturers, are on display here; *St. Nicholas Church Museum* – with a vast Hogarth Triptych; *Quakers Friars* – typical example of Quaker architecture; *Theatre Royal* – the oldest playhouse in the country still in use; *Industrial Museum; Harvey's Wine Museum; Clifton Suspension Bridge* (1830) – by Isambard Kingdom Brunel.

Modern sights: *SS Great Britain* – the world's first iron-built and propeller driven Atlantic liner, made in Bristol and on display in her original dry dock; *Queen Square* – with merchant houses in a quiet area; *Arnolfini* – visual arts centre in a cleverly converted 1830s tea warehouse, overlooking the floating harbour; *University* (1925) – octagonally shaped landmark; *Zoo* – one of the most famous in the country.

Special attractions: a performance at the *Bristol Old Vic*; most of the rest are in Bath, from the *Roman Baths* to an afternoon shopping on *Pulteney Bridge* to an intimate dîner-à-deux in the restaurant of the *Royal Crescent Hotel*.

Important companies with headquarters in the city: *Hewlett Packard* (computers); *British Aerospace* (space systems); *Rolls Royce* (jet engines); *W. D. and H. O. Wills* (cigarette manufacturing); *Bendix* (brake systems); *Cadbury Schweppes* (confectionery); *Newman Industries* (electric motors); *TRW Cam Gears* (motor components); *ICI* (chemicals); *Dupont Electronics; British Telecom* (telecommunications); *Sun Life* (insurance); *Phoenix Assurance; Harvey's* (spirits); *DRG* (publishing); *Carlton Industries.*

Airport: Bristol-Lulsgate, BRS; Tel.: 02 75 87/44 41; 11 km/7 miles; British Airways, Tel.: 29 81 81.

The Headquarters

THE ROYAL CRESCENT

Royal Crescent
GB Bath BA1 2 LS
Telephone: (2 25) 31 90 90
Telex: 444 251 royal
Owning Company: Blakeney Hotels Ltd.
Managing Director: John C. S. Tham
Affiliation/Reservation Systems: The Leading Hotels of the World, Prestige Hotels
Number of rooms: 45 (13 suites)
Price range: £ 68–275
Credit cards: all major
Location: at the centre of the world-famous Royal Crescent, 1.6 km/1 mile from city centre, 144 km/90 miles from London airport
Built: 1767 (renovated 1979)
Style: 18th-century classical style
Hotel amenities: garage, valet parking, house limousine service, jacuzzi pool, croquet
Room amenities: colour tv, video
Bathroom amenities: bathrobe, hairdrier, range of toiletries
Room service: 24 hours
Laundry/dry cleaning: same day (weekend service)
Conference rooms: 4 (up to 60 persons)
Bar: (12.00/a.m.–14.00/2.00 p.m. and 18.00/6.00 p.m.–closing time) Luis Garrido (barman), 18th-century classical style
Restaurant: ›Dower House‹ (18.30/6.30 p.m.–22.00/10.00 p.m.) David McArthur (maître), Michael Croft (chef de cuisine), nouvelle cuisine, 18th-century classical style
Private dining rooms: one (suites can be transformed)

The view of Bath from the Royal Crescent is unforgettable. So, too, is the harmonious perspective of the famous Georgian façade, at the centre of which, in a former royal residence, stands this luxurious and noble hotel – nominated by the Beau Monde's Baedeker, the IN World Guide, as one of the twenty most charming hotels in the world. The lovingly-renovated intérieur is a glorious evocation of eighteenth-century grace and elegance, from the stucco ceilings and the crystal chandeliers to the sweeping horseshoe staircase, above which hangs a priceless Brussels tapestry. In the garden is an exquisite Palladian villa containing sumptuously-appointed suites with thermal water from the hot springs for which the town has been famous since Roman times. The cuisine in the restaurant is, by contrast, refreshingly innovative – a fact which, together with the impeccable service and the stylish ambience, contributes to the creation of an auberge of undeniable finesse and distinction.

The Hideaway

HOMEWOOD PARK

Hinton Charterhouse
GB–Bath, Avon BA3 6BB
(30 km/19 miles)
Telephone: (2 21 22) 37 31
Telex: 44 49 37
Owner/General Managers: Stephen and Penny Ross
Affiliation/Reservation System: Prestige Hotels
Closed: 23 Dec–12 Jan
Number of rooms: 15
Price range: £60–85
Credit cards: all major
Location: 8 km/5 miles from Bath
Built: 18th and 19th century
Style: luxurious country-house style
Hotel amenities: large gardens, car park, tennis court
Room amenities: tv, radio
Room service: 7.30/a.m.–12.30/a.m.
Conference rooms: 2 (for up to 30 persons)
Sports: tennis, croquet
Bar: ›Hotel Bar‹ (10.30/a.m.–12.00/a.m.)
Restaurant: ›Homewood Park‹ (12.00/a.m.–15.00/3.00 p.m. and 19.00/7.00 p.m.–21.30/9.30/p.m. last order)
Private dining rooms: two

Set well back from a quiet lane amidst the rolling Avon countryside to the south of Bath, its sweeping driveway bordered by fine trees and shrubs, stands a rural hideaway of individual character and attractiveness run with dedication and enthusiasm by Stephen and Penny Ross. According to tradition – possibly apocryphal – Homewood Park was once the abbot's house of the ruined thirteenth-century Carthusian priory across the road; today this dignified eighteenth-century house with Victorian and modern extensions has the appearance of an immaculately-kept country vicarage, with a fine arched portico lending an air of distinction to the Bath-stone façade. The extensive gardens, including an arboretum and pretty herbaceous borders, have been cossetted back to their former glory and provide quiet corners for elegiac musings, as well as tennis or croquet. The intérieur is comfortably furnished, and decorated in pretty pastel tones which enhance the impression of lightness and space created by the finely proportioned rooms, echoing the harmony and beauty of the Limpley Stoke valley outside. The bay-windowed dining room with its floral curtains and pink table-linen is an appropriate setting for the proprietor-chef's daily tour de force; marinated salmon and scallops with orange and white wine, stuffed breast of guinea fowl in pastry, or hot mango pancakes with passion fruit sauce. Since there are only fifteen bedrooms, the youthful staff can foster the private country-house intimacy and welcoming informality which constitute the essence of Homewood Park's highly personal charm.

Lunch

HARVEYS
12a Denmark Street
Telephone: 27 76 65
Owner/Manager: F. Sanfiz
Closed: Saturday lunchtime; Sunday;
Bank Holidays
Open: 12.00/a.m.–14.30/2.30 p.m. and
19.30/7.30 p.m.–23.30/11.30 p.m.; (Saturday) 18.30/6.30–23.30/11.30 p.m.
Cuisine: French
Chef de cuisine: Tony Reed
Specialities: crab tart; pink kidneys with
tarragon and mustard sauce; grills
Location: a hymn away from the Cathedral
Setting: in one of England's oldest residential buildings, the Jew's House; formerly Harveys old sherry-bottling cellars
– vaulted ceilings, brickwork, bottle glass
and old rose colour scheme
Amenities: private dining room (40 persons)
Atmosphere: festive; confidential or romantic, depending on your companion
Clientèle: Bristol's social élite with cause
for celebration; top industrialists entertaining visiting delegations; architects
and sherry manufacturers
Dress: rather conventional
Service: knowledgeable and observant
Reservations: essential
Price range: fairly expensive
Credit cards: AE, DC, Visa Access

Lunch

LES SEMAILLES
9 Druid Hill, Stoke Bishop
Telephone: 68 64 56
Owner/Manager: Jillian and René Gaté
Closed: Sunday; Bank Holidays; second
half of July; December 22nd–January 5th
Open: 12.00/a.m.–14.30/2.30 p.m. and
19.00/7 p.m.–22.00/10 p.m.
Cuisine: French
Chef de cuisine: René Gaté (ex-Studley
Grange)
Specialities: sea trout mousseline; stuffed
summer vegetables with a cream and herb
sauce; fillet of lamb with mint and fresh
ravioli; guinea-fowl with truffle sauce
and parsley coulis garnished with liver
mousse; white chocolate gâteau with
orange and bitter chocolate sauce
Location: in the pedestrian precinct at
Stoke Bishop
Setting: newly-opened restaurant situated between a wine merchant's and a
vegetable shop
Amenities: private dining room (20 persons)
Atmosphere: refreshingly chic
Clientèle: mostly young

Dress: no special requirements
Service: efficiently charming
Reservations: usually essential
Price range: moderately expensive
Credit cards: AE, Visa

Dinner

GRANGE AT NORTHWOODS
Old Gloucester Road
Winterbourne (11 km/7 miles)
Telephone: (4 54) 77 73 33
Owner/Manager: J. Cockram
Closed: never
Open: 12.00/a.m.–14.00/2 p.m. and
19.00/7 p.m.–22.00–10 p.m. (Saturday) –
23.00/11 p.m.; (Sunday) – 21.00/9 p.m.
Cuisine: international and English
Specialities: veal and ham terrine with
marinated vegetables; pink trout with
white wine sauce; grilled venison with
orange and fresh ginger; roast leg of
lamb; Malay chicken curry
Location: at Winterbourne; 11 km/7
miles north of Bristol
Setting: a sturdy old house set in attractive countryside; elegantly-furnished dining room
Amenities: hotel; two bars; garden, car
park
Atmosphere: that of a gracious country
manoir whose owner understands the art
of good living
Clientèle: businessmen tired of Bristol;
expense-account gourmets; tourists from
Brisbane, Baltimore and Berlin
Dress: casually conservative for lunch;
more formally for dinner
Service: welcoming and anxious-to-please
Reservations: advisable
Price range: moderately expensive
Credit cards: AE, DC, Visa, Access

Dinner

MASTERS
2 Upper Byron Place, Clifton
Telephone: 2 83 14
Closed: Saturday lunchtime; Sunday;
New Year's Day; Easter; Christmas Day;
Boxing Day; two weeks in August
Open: 12.30/p.m.–14.30/2.30 p.m. and
19.00/7 p.m.–21.30/9.30 p.m.
Cuisine: English
Specialities: scallops with basil butter
and leek purée; rack of lamb baked in
hay; chicken liver pâté; poached salmon;
pan-fried steak; poacher's pie (in season)
Location: west of centre
Setting: small, intimate dining room
Atmosphere: welcoming and relaxing
Clientèle: very popular amongst members of the liberal professions

Dress: nothing too outlandish
Service: friendly
Reservations: essential
Price range: moderately expensive
Credit cards: AE, DC, Visa, Access

Lunch

HOWARDS
14 Avon Crescent
Telephone: 2 29 21
Owner/Managers: Chris and Gillian Howard
Closed: lunchtime (except Sunday); Sunday evening; Monday; Christmas Day; Boxing Day; one week in March; two weeks in September
Open: (Sunday) 12.30/p.m.–14.30/2.30 p.m. (Tuesday – Thursday) 19.00–7 p.m.– 23.00/11 p.m.,, (Friday/Saturday) 19.00/7 p.m.–23.30/11.30 p.m.
Location: south-west of city centre; by the river Avon, just off the road to Avonmouth
Setting: small bistro with typical décor
Amenities: menu including pheasant and apricot pie as well as moussaka, beef Stroganoff and hearty soups; private dining room (12–30 persons)
Atmosphere: cheerful, friendly and lively
Clientèle: a favourite rendezvous for Bristol's Beau Monde, bankers, brokers and budding business executives
Dress: as you like it
Service: good
Reservations: advisable to essential
Price range: medium
Credit cards: not accepted

Dinner

RAJDOOT
83 Park Street
Telephone: 2 80 33
Owner/Manager: S. D. Sharma
Closed: Sunday lunchtime; Bank Holidays (lunchtime only); Christmas Day; Boxing Day
Open: 12.00/a.m.–14.15/2.15 p.m. and 18.30/6.30 p.m.–23.30/11.30 p.m.
Cuisine: Indian
Specialities: Punjabi dishes; tandoori spring chicken; lamb or prawn curry; Basmati rice; sweetmeats
Location: a chapatti away from the Georgian House
Setting: attractively spick-and-span dining room
Amenities: private dining room (30 persons)
Atmosphere: oriental charm and occidental efficiency
Clientèle: expatriate Indians; local sahibs with a yen for an authentic curry; academics, advertising executives and men from the media

Dress: within reason, come-as-you-please
Service: professional and personal
Reservations: recommended
Price range: medium
Credit cards: AE, DC, Visa, Access

Bar

ROYAL CRESCENT
Royal Crescent, Bath
Telephone: (2 25) 31 90 90
Owner/Manager: Blakeney Hotels Ltd./J. C. S. Tham
Closed: never
Open: 12.00/a.m.–14.00/2 p.m. and 18.00/6 p.m. until the last guest has left
Location: in the Royal Crescent Hotel at Bath, 21 km/13 miles south-east of Bristol
Setting: luxurious cocktail bar in a lovingly-renovated Georgian building set in the middle of one of Bath's most famous crescents; elegant 18th-century furnishings
Amenities: hotel; restaurant; private dining rooms (6–60 persons); air conditioning, valet parking service
Atmosphere: classically sumptuous
Clientèle: celebrities from both sides of the Atlantic – Sir Lawrence Olivier to Charlton Heston – visiting monarchs (King Hussein of Jordan) and businessmen tired of Bristol
Service: suave perfectionism
Reservations: advisable
Credit cards: all major

Nightclub

LIGHT SHIP
Welch Back
Telephone: 27 24 02
Owner/Manager: Michael Minn
Closed: never
Open: 12.00/p.m.–15.00/3 p.m.; 18.30/ 6.30 p.m.–12.00/a.m.
Location: next to the Lindroger Crow Pub (where Daniel Defoe wrote ›Robinson Crusoe‹)
Setting: an old light ship; promenade deck with marble tables, wicker chairs and sun lounges; middle deck with wood panelling, leather chairs, mahogany tables and brass railing; discothèque on lower deck amidst ship's engine room machinery and pipework; leather chairs and bar from a former apothecary's shop, with countless tiny drawers
Amenities: air conditioning
Atmosphere: fairly quiet to decidedly loud as one approaches the water-line

Clientèle: upper echelons of industry and banking at lunchtime; Bristol's youthful noctambules and at least one insomniac disco grannie later on
Dress: (Thursday–Saturday) no jeans or training shoes (during the week) casual but not unkempt
Service: with a sense of humour
Reservations: not necessary
Price range: moderate, rather pub than nightclub range
Credit cards: not accepted

Shopping

EVERYTHING UNDER ONE ROOF
Dingles 44–56 Queens Road, Clifton Village

FOR HIM
Austin Reed Embassy House/Queens Road, Clifton Village

FOR HER
Chequers 32 The Mall, Clifton Village

BEAUTY & HAIR
Rudi's Hair Stylist Shop Unit, John Street

JEWELLERY
Chillcott, Alfred 47 Park Street

LOCAL SPECIALITIES
Boules (women's fashion)
68 Queens Road, Clifton Village
Michaels, M., Furrier Ltd. (leather fashion furs)
38 Triangle West, Clifton Village
Georges (books)
89 Park Street, Clifton Village
Fenice (gifts/fashion accessories)
24–28 Princess Victoria Street Clifton Village
Lawley's Ltd. (porcelain)
32 Merchant Street
Salisburys Handbags (baggage & travel accessories)
65 Broadmead
Bristol Guild of Applied Art (interior decorating) 68 Park Street
Millhouse, G. (food and beverages)
12 The Mall, Clifton Village
The Body Shop, Natural Beauty Productions (perfumery)
33 Queens Road
Bally London Shoes Co. Ltd. (shoes)
70–78 Queens Road

The comparison with Salzburg comes to mind – the river, the hills, the castle, the festival; and the complacent capital too far to have any influence on the individualistic life of the city. Mary Stuart comes to mind, of course – she still is the national heroine, more so for the scornful feelings of the Scots toward their southern brethren and as their figurehead of romantic emotions than for her actual popularity at the time. Sir Walter Scott has to come to mind – his 287-step Gothic-spire monument in Princes Street Gardens reminds you of him like no other hero, of the retrieved crown jewels, the kilt made respectable again and maybe even of his writings – his own raison d'être, incidentally. And Adam Smith comes to mind – but you think of him anyway, when you think of money. Scotland's capital, of lesser industrial importance than Glasgow, but undoubtedly the more refined residence, is physically beautiful, historically interesting and culturally enchanting. The Edinburgh International Festival of Music and Drama – happening at the same time as the Film Festival and the Military Tattoo – has something for everyone and, thanks to the foremost directors, conductors, actors and singers and the uniquely romantic setting, draws aficionados from all over the world – and Salzburg. But even when there are no Highland Games, Royal Scottish Academy Art Exhibitions or high-stake golf tournaments on one of the dozens of championship courses, Edinburgh proves to be magnetizing. Edinburgh Castle, offering imposing testimony to the indomitable spirit of the city, looks upon the noble homes along the medieval Royal Mile, the Georgian elegance of Charlotte Square and the pulsating vitality of Prince's Street. Home of one of the most important universities of the island, with a famed law school, and centre of publishing in the country, there is also a fair share of bare-necessities production such as textiles, oil and food. And whisky.

Founded: 7th century; Edinburgh – ›Edwin's fortress‹ (from the Gaelic ›Dun Eideann‹).
Far-reaching events: 1371 – the House of Stuart comes to the throne; 1437 – Edinburgh becomes capital of Scotland; 1530 – fire destroys the city; 1583 – founding of the university; 1603 – union of the English and Scottish kingdoms; 1707 – political union of England and Scotland, following a period of unrest; 18th and 19th centuries – Edinburgh blossoms as a cultural centre; 1968 – oil and gas discovered off the coast.
Population: 500,000; capital of Scotland and royal burgh.
Postal code: confusing; depends upon street, part of the city and house number.
Telephone code: 31
Climate: cool under the influence of the North Sea; October to January very rainy, March to June dry; sudden storms and lots of fog.
Best time to visit: May to August.
Calendar of events: *Folk Festival* (Easter) – music, song and dance from the British Isles; *Edinburgh International Festival of Music and Drama* (Aug) – concerts, ballet and plays plus ›fringe‹ events from revue to poetry reading; *Edinburgh Military Tattoo* (Aug) – bands, marching and displays by the armed forces; *Edinburgh Jazz Festival* (Aug); *Edinburgh Film Festival* (Aug); *Braemar Gathering* (1st Sat in Sep) – the most famous Highland Games, attended by the Royal Family (at Braemar).
Fairs and exhibitions: *SCOTTISH ANTIQUES FAIR* (Feb/Mar)
Best views of the city: from the wall of the fortress.
Historical sights: *Edinburgh Castle* (11th–17th centuries) – the city's landmark on the basalt rock dominating the city – Scottish regalia and a fine view; *St. Giles'Cathedral* (14th–15th centuries) – the Gothic High Kirk of Edinburgh; *Holyroodhouse* (1500) – palace of the Stuarts and official residence of the Queen in Scotland; *Museum of Antiquities* – history and everyday life of Scotland; *National Gallery of Scotland* – paintings from the Renaissance to Cézanne, plus Scottish artists; *Scott Monument* (1844) – a memorial to the novelist; *Royal Mile* – connecting the castle and Holyroodhouse; *Lady Stair's House* (1622) – museum housing manuscripts of works by Sir Walter Scott, Robert Burns and Robert Louis Stevenson.
Modern sights: the two *Bridges* across the Firth of Forth, Victorian iron and concrete construction; *St. James' Centre* – commercial building artfully integrated into the old city.
Special attractions: *Prince's Street* – the city's best shops on one side, and a park on the other; *Highland Games* – tossing the caber and swirling bagpipes; *Military Tattoo; Edinburgh Festival; Beating the Retreat* on Castle Esplanade.
Important companies with headquarters in the city: *Distillers Co.* (whisky); *Scottish Agricultural Industries* (agricultural chemicals); *Scottish and Newcastle Breweries* (beer); *United Wire Group* (cables and wire); *William Thyne* (carton).
Airport: Edinburgh, EDI; Tel.: 333 1000; 11 km/7 miles; British Airways, Tel.: 225 2525.

The Headquarters

CALEDONIAN

Princes Street
GB-Edinburgh, EHI 2 AB
Telephone: 225 2433
Telex: 72179 ghplc
Owning Company: Gleneagles Hotels PLC
General Manager: Dermott Fitzpatrick
Affiliation/Reservation System: The Leading Hotels of the World
Number of rooms: 254 (15 suites)
Price range: £ 55–150
Credit cards: all major
Location: prime situation in the heart of Edinburgh overlooking Edinburgh castle and Princes Street Gardens
Built: 1903
Style: grand Edwardian building of warm pink sandstone, decorated to deluxe but traditional standards
Hotel amenities: valet parking, grand piano, florist, hairstylist, tobacconist
Main hall porter: Jock Docherty
Room amenities: colour tv, mini-bar/refrigerator, in-house films (pets allowed)
Bathroom amenities: separate shower cabin, bathrobe (VIP), hairdrier, telephone (some)
Room service: 24 hours
Laundry/dry cleaning: same day
Conference rooms: 8 (up to 300 persons)
Bars: ›Pullman‹: (11.00/a.m.–23.00/11.00 p.m.) lounge style, pianist; ›Platform 1‹ (19.30/7.30 p.m.–1.00/a.m. and at lunchtime) pub lunches, live entertainment at weekends, pianist

Restaurants: ›Pompadour‹: (7.30/a.m.–10.30/a.m. and 12.30/p.m.–14.00/2.00 p.m.) George Figarrola (maître), Alain Hill (chef de cuisine), French cuisine, pianist, dinner dances Fridays and Saturdays; ›Gazebo‹ (7.30/a.m.–10.00/a.m. and 12.00/a.m.–14.30/2.30 p.m.) Ruari Mackenzie (maître), Alain Hill (chef de cuisine), buffet style, coffee shop, pianist

Don't mistake the United Kingdom's northernmost grand hotel for the castle (which you can see – illuminated at night – from many of the rooms) even though you will be treated like a visiting baron by the courteous staff. Here, the proverbial dourness of the Scots turns into gentle helpfulness, be it to reconcile you for the weather or just to prove that there is also greatness in Britain outside London. ›The Caley‹ guards its Edwardian spirit not only in its beautiful red sandstone façade but also in the generosity of space and service. The décor is not ritzy, but blends perfectly with the land and the unpretentious esprit of the people. The location on Princes Street is perfect, the amenities – from bars to restaurants – are excellent and the extras on request are only a hall porter call away. And only one hour more: sister establishment Gleneagles.

The Hideaway

GLENEAGLES

Auchterarder
GB-Perthshire Scotland PH3 1NF
(72 km/45 miles)
Telephone: (76 46) 22 31
Telex: 76 105 glenho
Owning company: Guinness PLC
General Manager: Peter Lederer
Affiliation/Reservation System: The
Leading Hotels of the World
Number of rooms: 254 (19 suites)
Price range: £ 50–195
Credit cards: Access, AE, DC, Visa
Location: Tayside
Built: 1924
Style: palatial mansion house
Hotel amenities: car hire, helipad
Room service: 24 hours
Conference rooms: 7 (up to 400 persons)
Bars: ›American Bar‹; ›Dormy House
Bar‹
Restaurants: ›Dormy House‹; ›Eagles
Nest‹ (from 19.30/7.30 p.m.); ›The Stra-
thearn‹
Nightclubs: discothèque

*The Perthshire countryside bordering the
River Tay is a landscape of green meadows
and sylvan woodland, its northern frontier
demarcated by the foothills of the rugged
and desolate Grampian Highlands. Here,
an hour's drive north-west of Edinburgh, is
a hideaway resort of world-wide repute.
Gleneagles impresses at first sight by virtue
of its size. An imposing grey stone mansion
built in 1924, it stands in extensive grounds
exuding the same air of permanence as the
Royal castles further north – Glamis,
Braemar and Balmoral. The country house
tradition prevails in the décor and in the atmosphere. The guests come to enjoy the
country walks, the views of the hills and
glens from the hotel's thousand windows,
and to participate in the overwhelming gamut of sports and leisure activities, from
time-honoured Scottish pastimes (trout
fishing, shooting) to more modern pursuits
(squash, billiards). There's an indoor swimming pool in a sub-tropical garden for the
active, a sauna for the less energetic, a
Georgian shopping arcade with a post office and the smallest bank in the world for
those with no inclination to go into town,
and – in the restaurant – an irresistible
combination of French haute cuisine and
fine local products for everyone. You can
learn to wield a rifle at Jackie Stewart's
Shooting Range, and to control a horse at
Captain Mark Phillip's Riding School.
Above all, there is golf – four of the finest
courses in the country which attract stars
from Jack Nicklaus to Tony Jacklin. Gleneagles has something for everyone, successfully blending twentieth-century innovation with old-fashioned graciousness in a
setting of great natural beauty at all seasons of the year.*

Lunch

HOWTOWDIE
27a Stafford Street
Telephone: 2 25 62 91
Owner/Manager: A. R. Fairlie
Closed: Sunday; January 1–2; Christmas
Day; Boxing Day (26 December)
Open: 12.00/a.m.–14.30/2.30 p.m. and
19.00/7 p.m.–23.00/11 p.m.
Cuisine: Scottish
Specialities: mussel and onion stew; roast
duckling in heather-honey sauce; game
in season; desserts; strawberry and
Grand Marnier mousse
Location: a Highland Fling away from
the western end of Princes' Street
Setting: basement; elegant
Amenities: private dining rooms
Atmosphere: very Scottish; rather festive
Clientèle: middle-aged, comfortably-off,
conservative Sassenachs; sixth-genera-
tion American amateur genealogists; a
sprinkling of local Haute Bourgeoisie
with cause for celebration
Dress: kilt not essential
Service: friendly
Reservations: advisable
Price range: moderately high
Credit cards: AE, DC, Visa, Access

Lunch

COSMO
58 a North Castle Street
Telephone: 2 26 67 43
Owner/Manager: Cosmo Tamburro/Al-
fredo Pavone
Closed: Saturday lunchtime; Sunday;
Monday
Open: 12.15/p.m.–14.15/2.15 p.m. and
18.30/6.30 p.m.–22.15/10.15 p.m.
Cuisine: Italian
Chefs de cuisine: Cosmo Tamburro and
James McWilliams
Specialities: seafood; shrimp bisque;
frutti di mare with home-made mayon-
naise; grilled turbot; scallops; veal sal-
timbocca (with Parma ham, cheese, fresh
mushrooms, double cream and lemon);
profiteroles; brandy snaps
Location: a tarantella away from Queen's
Street Gardens
Setting: Georgian traditional; spacious
dining room decorated in shades of
brown; subdued lighting
Amenities: apéritif bar
Atmosphere: warm and welcoming
Clientèle: spaghetti-loving Top People;
expatriate Florentines, Milanese and
Venetians; fish fans from Fort William to
Frankfurt
Dress: no special requirements
Service: Italianissimo
Reservations: advisable to essential
Price range: moderately expensive
Credit cards: Visa, Access

Lunch

VERANDAH TANDOORI
17 Dalry Road
Telephone: 3 37 58 28
Owner/Manager: Tasar Uddin
Closed: Christmas Day
Open: 12.00/a.m.–14.15/2.15 p.m. and
17.00/5 p.m.–23.45/11.45 p.m.
Cuisine: North Indian and Bangladeshi
Chef de cuisine: Sarwar Khan
Specialities: pakura with mint sauce;
lamb pasanda; chicken tikka; chicken
bhuna; nan; vegetarian thali; Bangla-
deshi tea; mango lassi
Location: diagonally opposite Haymar-
ket Station
Setting: well-designed dining room with
pale linen walls
Amenities: Indian music
Atmosphere: serene
Clientèle: managers; marketing direc-
tors; academics; architects; curry fans;
arts critics
Dress: within reason, come-as-you-
please
Service: good-natured but a little slap-
dash at times
Reservations: essential for dinner and at
weekends (no dogs)
Price range: medium
Credit cards: AE, DC, Visa, Access, Carte
Blanche

Dinner

POMPADOUR
Princes Street
Telephone: 2 25 24 33
Owner/Manager: Gleneagles Hotels PLC
Closed: never
Open: 12.30/p.m.–14.00/2 p.m. and
19.30/7.30 p.m.–22.30/10.30 p.m.
Cuisine: French (nouvelle) and local spe-
cialities
Chef de cuisine: Alan Hill (ex-Dorches-
ter)
Specialities: surprise menu ›La Bonne
Bouche‹; ›Legends of the Scottish Table‹
(at lunchtime); barley broth; baked skate
in breadcrumbs, onion and egg with anchovies and mustard; lobster soup with
fish quenelles; loin of lamb in spinach
and pastry; venison; summer pudding
Location: in the Caledonian Hotel
Setting: in a grand Edwardian building;
Louis XVI-inspired décor with stucco
ceiling, archways, delicate floral panels
and chandeliers; pianist on Sundays and
Thursdays; dancing on Friday and Saturday
Amenities: hotel; private dining rooms
(10–300 persons); ›Gazebo‹ buffet-style
restaurant; two bars; garage (valet parking service)

Atmosphere: Caledonian charm with a soupçon of Gallic raffinesse
Clientèle: Edinburgh's most illustrious visitors; royalty from the Duke and Duchess of Kent to the Prince of the Cameroons; premiers and presidents from Margaret Thatcher to Mikhail Gorbatchov; diplomats, show-business personalities and well-heeled holidaymakers
Dress: jacket and tie preferred
Service: knowledgeable dinner-jacketed waiters under the guidance of maître George Figarrola
Reservations: essential (no dogs)
Price range: rather expensive
Credit cards: all major

Lunch

CHAMPANY INN TOWN
2 Bridge Road, Colinton
Telephone: 4 41 25 87
Owner/Manager: Clive and Anne Davidson
Closed: Saturday lunchtime; Sunday
Open: 12.00/a.m.–14.00/2 p.m. and 19.00/7 p.m.–22.00/10 p.m.
Cuisine: international
Specialities: some of the best steaks in Britain – Aberdeen Angus straight from the farm and matured in an ionised refrigerator before being charcoal-grilled and served with a variety of sauces, salads and vegetables
Location: in the suburb of Colinton, south-west of Edinburgh city centre
Setting: small restaurant in a converted butchery
Atmosphere: a recently-opened offshoot of the Davidsons' highly successful restaurant in Linlithgow
Clientèle: local devotees of Clive and Anne Davidson's uncomplicated but excellent cuisine, plus Transatlantic visitors
Dress: jacket and tie preferred
Service: personal and solicitous
Reservations: essential
Price range: moderately expensive
Credit cards: AE, DC, Visa, Access

Dinner

STRATHEARN
Gleneagles Hotel
Auchterarder (72 km/45 miles)
Telephone: (76 46) 22 31

Affiliations: The Leading Hotels of the World
Manager: Peter Lederer
Closed: never
Open: 12.30/p.m.–14.30/2.30 p.m. and 19.30/7.30 p.m.–22.00/10 p.m.
Cuisine: international with a Scottish accent
Specialities: Highland game soup; smoked salmon; Scotch mist; minestrone; pork cutlet ›Zingara‹; mille-feuille
Location: in the Gleneagles Hotel, about one hour's drive from Edinburgh
Setting: 1920s country mansion-style hotel set in a 600-acre estate of breath-taking Perthshire countryside; handsome pillared restaurant with period accessoires, subtle décor and carefully-chosen pictures; live piano music during the evenings
Amenities: hotel; restaurant ›The Eagle's Nest‹; private dining rooms (up to 350 persons); ballroom; leisure complex; golf courses; car park; helicopter pad
Atmosphere: that of an elegant country house whose owner understands the art of gracious living
Clientèle: local lairds; infiltrators from South of the Border; businessmen tired of Edinburgh (or Glasgow); oil tycoons; golf addicts
Dress: jacket and tie for dinner; slightly less formal for lunch
Service: impeccable
Reservations: advisable to essential
Price range: fairly expensive
Credit cards: AE, DC, Visa, Access

Bar

PULLMAN
Princes Street
Telephone: 2 25 24 33
Owner/Manager: Gleneagles Hotel PLC
Closed: never
Open: 11.00/a.m.–23.00/11 p.m.
Location: in the Caledonian Hotel
Setting: in a grand Edwardian building; spacious lounge-style bar with seating areas on two levels; comfortable classic modern décor
Amenities: hotel; two restaurants; ›Platform One‹ pub-style bar; pianist; garage (valet parking service)
Atmosphere: cosmopolitan and civilized
Clientèle: hotel guests from Honduras to Helsinki; Sassenachs, Scots, financiers and Festival visitors
Dress: rather conservative
Service: polished and professional
Reservations: advisable
Credit cards: all major

Nightclub

BUSTER BROWN'S
25–27 Market Street
Telephone: 2 26 42 24
Owner/Manager: Waverley Leisure Ltd/
William Dickson
Closed: never
Open: 21.30/9.30 p.m. till late
Location: central, near railway station
Setting: modern
Amenities: discothèque, reputedly the
best music in town; air conditioning
Clientèle: broad range of people ›from 18
to 60‹
Dress: casual, moderate
Service: good and efficient
Reservations: not needed
Price range: moderate
Credit cards: AE, DC, Euro, Access

Shopping

EVERYTHING UNDER ONE ROOF
Jenners   Princes Street/St. David Street

FOR HIM
Gieves and Hawkes   48 George Street

FOR HER
Browning, Jennifer   12 Randolph Place

BEAUTY & HAIR
Drumm, Brian   37 a George Street

JEWELLERY
Hamilton & Inches   87 George Street

LOCAL SPECIALITIES
Herbert Love (tobacco)
31 Queensferry Street
Gallo, Michael (men & women's fashion)
93 Rose Street
Jaeger Shops Ltd. (men & women's fash-
ion) 119 Princes Street
The Bare Necessities (children's fashion)
60 Thistle Street
Leatherworld Ltd. (leather fashion)
131 a Princes Street
Wilkie's of Edinburgh (furs)
49–61 Shandwick Place
Nisbet's (porcelain)
61 George Street
Jenners (baggage & travel accessories)
Princes Street/St. David Street
Valvona & Crolla Ltd. (food and beverages)
19 Elm Row
Johnston, June (shoes)
5 William Street

The City

›Wee Willie Winkie runs through the town, upstairs and downstairs, in his nightgown‹. William Miller, almost-forgotten nineteenth-century advocate of the early-to-bed philosophy, shares the best view of Glasgow with the incumbents of the other graves on the Necropolis, the hillside cemetery near the University where James Watt revolutionized industry with his steam engine. The second largest city in the pale pink Empire (thanks to those merchants and industrialists whose final resting-place now also commands a prospect of high-rise office blocks and factory chimneys) has since slipped into third place behind London and Birmingham, and the world map has acquired a more variegated colour scheme. But Glasgow's unshakeable civic pride can be seen in her public buildings – from the grandiose arched ceiling and sweeping staircase of the Civic Centre to the self-assuredly pompous Doric-columned façade of the Royal Bank. Her citizens represent in their corporate character a perfect synthesis of the wildness and austerity, the softness and ruggedness, so typical of the Scots. It can be seen in the rather stark Gothic lines of the Cathedral of St. Mungo, but it was local architect Charles Rennie Mackintosh who best expressed this dour charm in his turn-of-the-century Art School, which combines the immutability of a baronial castle with a harmonious assertion of solid middle-class confidence. The Scotch mist – a euphemism for the wet climate which favoured the development of the cotton industry, one of the pillars of Glasgow's prosperity in times past – also produces some of the lushest public gardens outside the Emerald Isle; a damp morning in Linn Park or Rouken Glen evokes the not-so-distant bonnie banks o' Loch Lomond or the Ayrshire countryside home of beloved bard Robert Burns. Over the years other industries have sprung up here – heavy engineering, electronics and printing. Above all, however – recessions notwithstanding – Clydebank shipyards have regularly been the scene for royal launchings, from the Queen Mary to the QE2. A melting-pot of nationalities and cultures, Glasgow is a fine blend of the fruits of Scots canniness overlaid with the mysticism of Celtic charm.

Founded: 543 by St. Mungo (St. Kentigern); Glasgow – ›Dear Green Place‹ (Celtic).

Far-reaching events: 18th century – Glasgow's growth as a commercial port begins with the dredging of a deep-water channel in the Clyde; 1769 – local son James Watt's invention of the steam engine paves the way for the Industrial Revolution; 19th century – Glasgow develops rapidly to become the second largest city in the British Empire; 20th century – massive redevelopment.

Population: 2 million (conurbation); largest city in Scotland, third largest in Great Britain.

Postal code: confusing; depends on street, part of the city and house number.

Telephone code: 41

Climate: mild, due to the influence of the Gulf Stream; rather wet.

Calendar of events: *International Gathering Scotland* (May/Jun) – a typical Scottish celebration, with clan meetings, music, theatre and dance; *American Festival* (May) – music, theatre, art, dance and literature; *Scottish Rally RSAC* (Jun) – in the Scottish Highlands; *Scottish National Tennis Championship* (Aug); soccer, croquet and rugby are played all year round.

Fairs and exhibitions: *SCOTTISH COMPUTER SHOW* (spring); *SCOTTISH TECHNOLOGY WEEK* (Jun); *SCOTTISH FURNITURE SHOW* (Aug); *SCOTTISH AUTUMN GIFT FAIR* (Aug); *SCOTTISH WINE AND SPIRIT FAIR* (Sep).

Historical sights: *St. Mungo's Cathedral* (1136) – the only complete medieval church on the Scottish mainland; *George Square* – magnificent square with a monument to George III; *University* (1451) – James Watt discovered the steam engine here; *Royal Exchange Building* (1775) – majestic columns and wood-panelled ceilings in the former home of Lord William Cunningham of tobacco empire fame; *Royal Bank* – very Victorian; *Provand's Lordship* (1471) oldest house in the city, where Mary, Queen of Scots is reputed to have written the fatal ›Casket Letters‹; *Kelvingrove Art Gallery and Museum,* Scotland's most beautiful collection of British and European masters; *City Chamber* – Victorian Renaissance style; *Burrell collection* – 19th-century French paintings and furniture.

Modern sights: *School of Art* – best example of Art Nouveau in Scotland by Charles Rennie Mackintosh.

Special attractions: *Argyll Arcade* – Glasgow's best shops; *Sauchiehall Street* – Glaswegians' favourite shopping area; *Necropolis* – one of the most fascinating cemeteries in the world, with a panoramic view of the city; *Linn Park; Rouken Glen; the Trossachs, Loch Lomond and the Kyle of Bute* – Scottish scenery at its most spectacular.

Important companies with headquarters in the city: *Anderson Strathclyde* (mining machinery); *Britoil* (oil); *Caterpillar Tractor Co.* (heavy plant); *Coats Patons* (yarns); *William Collins* (books); *Highland Distilleries* (whisky); *IBM* (computers); *F.J.C. Lilley* (construction material and heavy plants); *Scottish Universal Instruments; The Weir Group* (pumps).

Airport: Glasgow, GLA; Tel.: 8 87 11 11; 15 km/10 miles.

The Headquarters

ALBANY

Bothwell Street
GB–Glasgow G 2 7EN
Telephone: 2 48 26 56
Telex: 7 74 40 albgla g
Owning Company: Trusthouse Forte
General Manager: Alberto Laidlaw
Affiliation/Reservation Systems: Tycom Computer, Trusthouse Forte
Number of rooms: 251 (3 suites)
Price range: £ 46–120
Credit cards: AE, DC, MC, THF, Access, Visa
Location: city centre
Built: 1973
Style: modern
Hotel amenities: valet parking, house limousine service, grand piano, health club, sauna, solarium, beauty salon, massage, hairstylist, newsstand, boutique, tobacconist, house doctor
Main hall porter: Felix McCoy
Room amenities: colour tv, video, minibar/refrigerator (pets allowed)
Bathroom amenities: bidet, hairdrier
Room service: 24 hours
Laundry/dry cleaning: same day (weekend service)
Conference rooms: 6 (up to 800 persons)
Bars: ›Albany‹ (10.00/a.m.–closing time); ›Cabin‹ (11.00/a.m.–14.30/2.30 p.m. and 17.00/5 p.m.–23.00/11 p.m.); Brian McGrough (barman), pianist, orchestra, modern décor
Restaurants: ›Four Seasons‹ (12.30/p.m.–14.30/2.30 p.m. and 19.00/7.00 p.m.–23.00/11.00 p.m.), Luis Letelier Lobos (maître), Frank Boggie (chef de cuisine), French and Scottish cuisine, pianist, orchestra, elegant style; ›Carvery‹ (7.00/a.m.–10.00/a.m., 12.00/a.m.–14.30/2.30 p.m. and 17.30/5.30 p.m.–23.00/11.00 p.m.) Gerry McMahon (maître), Frank Boggie (chef de cuisine) pianist, orchestra
Private dining rooms: four

If the Albany had been built four centuries earlier, the tragic Mary Queen of Scots might have written the Casket Letters (which sealed her fate) here instead of at Provand's Lordship, the oldest house in Glasgow. Adam Smith and James Watt couldn't stay here, either, but since its opening in 1973 this Caledonian outpost of the world-wide and world-famous Trusthouse Forte chain has offered the group's renowned standards of comfort and efficiency to visiting celebrities no less known or powerful than the historic dignitaries. No wonder, for in this rising industrial metropolis, the Albany stands out not only by architecture, functional finesse and pleasant décor à la moderne, but most of all by courtesy of staff and niveau de cuisine in its Four Seasons restaurant. The carousel is complete with lively bars and grand conference rooms where all the important meetings take place. Another forte one can trust this house for.

INVERLOCHY CASTLE

Fort William
GB–Torlundy PH33 6SN
(160 km/100 miles)
Telephone: (397) 2177
Telex: 776229
Owner: Grete Hobbs
General Manager: Michael Leonard
Affiliation/Reservation System: Relais et Châteaux
Closed: mid-Nov–mid-March
Number of rooms: 16 (2 suites)
Price range: £ 120–£ 180
Credit cards: Visa, EC
Location: 5 km/3 miles from Fort William
Built: 1863
Style: Scottish Baronial
Hotel amenities: garage, limousine service, grand piano, tennis court
Room service: 24 hours
Conference rooms: for up to 25 persons
Sports (nearby): fishing, golf
Restaurant: (12.30/p.m.–14.30/2.00 p.m. and 19.00/7 p.m.–22.00/10 p.m.) François Huguet (chef de cuisine)

Inverlochy Castle, tucked away in the Western Highlands one hundred miles north of Glasgow, is not only primus inter pares amongst exclusive hideaways north of Hadrian's Wall, but also one of the finest in Europe. The setting is one of solitary, awesome grandeur: heather-clad slopes, swirling Scotch mists, the lowering presence of Ben Nevis. A Victorian Gothic baronial manor house rather than a fortress, built by the first Lord Abinger in 1863, this aristocratic relais stands amidst fifty acres of landscaped gardens on a 500-acre private estate. Focal point of the palatial interior is the two-storey Great Hall, in which ornate chandeliers illumine the ancestral portraits on either side of the carved mantelpiece, surmounted by a lovely frescoed ceiling. The drawing room is prettily feminine in pastel shades of pink and blue, whilst the obligatory stag's heads and other hunting trophies adorn the oak-panelled billiard room at the top of the carved oak staircase. A guest at Inverlochy Castle can sleep like a laird in the satin-and-brocade splendour of one of the sixteen bedrooms after a round of golf or a day's trout fishing followed by a sherry on the rose-and-rhododendron-bordered terrace. Jacket and tie is still de rigueur here for the gourmet banquets presented by ex-Connaught chef François Huguet in the bay-windowed dining-room – best rounded off by a home-distilled Dew of Ben Nevis. Danish-born châtelaine Grete Hobbs and manager Michael Leonard continue the unbroken tradition of élite hospitality offered to only twenty individual guests, thus preserving the gracious country-house atmosphere which prompted the scotophile Queen Victoria to note in her diary after spending a week at Inverlochy Castle in 1873: ›I never saw a lovelier or more romantic spot‹.

Lunch

COLONIAL
25 High Street
Telephone: 5 52 19 23
Owner/Manager/Chef de cuisine: Peter Jackson
Closed: Saturday lunchtime; Sunday; Monday evening
Open: 12.00/a.m.–14.30/2.30 p.m. and 18.00/6 p.m.–22.30/10.30 p.m.
Cuisine: nouvelle, with a strong local accent
Specialities: panache of seafood with saffron pistils; fillet of beef ›Nan Eilean‹
Location: in the historic mercantile district of Glasgow
Setting: elegant, understated décor
Amenities: air conditioning
Atmosphere: warm and welcoming but not overpowering
Clientèle: Glaswegian gourmets, members of the liberal professions and a sprinkling of discriminating Sassenachs from South of the Border
Dress: casually elegant
Service: attentively directed by maître d'hôtel Giuseppe Vita
Reservations: preferred
Price range: fairly expensive by local standards
Credit cards: AE, DC, Visa, Access

Dinner

COOL JADE
107 Waterside Road
Telephone: 6 44 28 64
Closed: Sunday lunchtime; three days at Chinese New Year
Open: 12.00/a.m.–14.00/2 p.m. and 17.00/5 p.m.–24.00/12 p.m. (Friday/Saturday evening until 1.00/a.m.)
Cuisine: Cantonese, plus some Malaysian and European dishes
Specialities: fried squid with ginger and spring onions; crispy roast duck; spicy chicken in a paper bag
Location: just south of Glasgow Bridge over the River Clyde; off the A77 (Bridge Street)
Setting: in a small village on the southern edge of the city; elegant restaurant with modern décor
Amenities: private dining room
Atmosphere: fairly business-like, but welcoming
Clientèle: local government officials, advertising managers and journalists at lunchtime give way to a more heterogeneous and pleasure-seeking assembly at night
Dress: within reason, anything goes
Service: friendly
Reservations: advisable
Price range: medium
Credit cards: AE, DC, Visa, Access

Dinner

BUTTERY
652 Argyle Street
Telephone: 2 21 81 88
Owner/Manager: Ken McCulloch/Suzanne Ritchie
Closed: Saturday lunch; Sunday
Open: 12.00/p.m.–14.30/2.30 p.m. and 19.00/7 p.m.–22.00/10 p.m.
Cuisine: French with a strong Scottish accent
Chefs de cuisine: Ferrier Richardson and Douglas Painter
Specialities: Scottish venison; Scottish seafood; fillet of salmon with cream and orange sauce and seaweed; oysters (served in bar)
Location: on one of Glasgow's main thoroughfares, near the motorway flyover
Setting: black-painted house with gold lettering; Victorian-style dining room; bar with comfortable sofas; cartoon prints; white napery
Amenities: private dining room (8 persons); air conditioning; car park
Atmosphere: nostalgically reminiscent of a gentlemen's club
Clientèle: favourite venue for top industrialists entertaining foreign delegates, celebrating their wife's birthday or turning their butler's night off to good advantage
Dress: rather conservative (jacket and tie preferred)
Service: hospitable
Reservations: essential for dinner (no pets)
Price range: relatively expensive
Credit cards: AE, DC, Visa, Access

Lunch

POACHER'S
Ruthven Lane
Telephone: 3 39 09 32
Owner/Manager: Mo and Peter Scott/Frank and Elaine Bergius
Closed: Sunday; Christmas Day; January 1st; Easter Monday
Open: 12.00/a.m.–14.30/2.30 p.m. and 18.30/6.30 p.m.–23.00/11 p.m.
Cuisine: international
Chef de cuisine: William Orral
Specialities: squid salad; tagliatelle with tomato and seafood sauce; lamb cutlets with garlic, breadcrumbs and herbs; pigeon breasts; desserts(!)
Location: north-west of centre; off Byres Road
Setting: in a converted farmhouse; plants, photographs, umbrellas
Amenities: private dining room (20 persons), outdoor dining on small terrace; car park
Atmosphere: unpretentious; busy, intimate and informal, with the food receiv-

ing most of the attention; one of the main contenders for the title of ›best restaurant in Glasgow‹

Clientèle: Glasgow's gourmet In-Crowd; middle management; media-men; marketing executives
Dress: mostly rather casual
Service: charm itself
Reservations: essential for dinner and at weekends
Price range: moderately expensive
Credit cards: AE, DC, Visa, Access

Dinner

UBIQUITOUS CHIP
12 Ashton Lane
Telephone: 3 34 50 07
Owner/Manager: Messrs. Clydesdale and Brydon
Closed: Sunday; Christmas Day; three days at New Year
Open: 12.00/a.m.–14.30/2.30 p.m. and 17.30/5.30 p.m.–23.00/11 p.m.
Cuisine: international
Specialities: fish (according to availability); fish bisque with fresh ginger; wholemeal cheese and carrot flan; duck with apple, pork and calvados stuffing; one of the best all-round wine lists north or South of the Border; 70 single malt whiskies
Location: off Byres Road, north-west of city centre
Setting: fairly large bistro-style restaurant with batik décor, trailing greenery and a covered courtyard for open-air dining in summer
Amenities: private dining room
Atmosphere: inviting; refreshingly attractive
Clientèle: enthusiastic habitués; wine buffs; local lovers of good food, plus a sprinkling of initiated foreigners from Carlisle, Copenhagen and Cincinnati
Dress: as you like it (as long as they will like you)
Service: not notable for their loquacity
Reservations: essential
Price range: moderately expensive
Credit cards: AE, DC, Visa, Access

Meeting Point

CAFÉ NICO'S
379 Sauchiehall Street
Telephone: 3 32 57 36
Owner/Manager: Caroline Wright
Closed: never
Open: (Monday–Saturday) 8.00/a.m.–24.00/12 p.m.; (Sunday) 9.00/a.m.–23.00/11 p.m.
Location: on one of Glasgow's best-known shopping streets

Setting: late nineteenth-century décor, with French brass and modern tables
Amenities: salad buffet; hot meals
Atmosphere: bustling
Clientèle: cross-section of Glaswegian society
Dress: casual
Service: good-natured and efficacious
Reservations: not required (pets allowed)
Price range: middle of the road
Credit cards: AE, DC, Visa, Access

Café

DE QUINCY'S
71 Renfield Street
Telephone: 3 33 06 33
Owner/Manager: Whitbread Breweries/ Ross Ballantine
Closed: Sunday
Open: Monday–Wednesday 11.00/a.m.–23.00/11 p.m.; Thursday–Saturday 11.00/a.m.–24.00/12 a.m.
Location: central
Setting: classic café/bar with Victorian tiled intérieur and ceiling fans
Amenities: cold buffet at lunchtime (fresh salmon and a wide variety of salads)
Atmosphere: lively and welcoming
Clientèle: bank managers, businessmen and brokers with their colleagues or clients at lunchtime or with their wives (or girlfriends) at night give way to Glasgow's younger crowd towards the weekend
Service: efficient and friendly

Bar

APERITIF
Bothwell Street
Telephone: 2 48 26 56
Owner/Manager: Albany Hotel
Closed: never
Open: 10.00/a.m.–23.00/11 p.m.
Location: in the Albany Hotel
Setting: invitingly comfortable armchairs, oil paintings and a good selection of newspapers and periodicals for those who wish neither to talk nor to listen to the pianist
Amenities: hotel; restaurant; private dining rooms; second bar in basement; air conditioning; parking (limited)
Atmosphere: harmonious and relaxing
Clientèle: conservatively-dressed and comfortably-off businessmen from Birmingham, Bangor and Braemar
Service: good
Reservations: not necessary
Credit cards: not accepted

Bar

CABIN
Bothwell Street
Telephone: 2 48 26 56
Owner/Manager: Albany Hotel
Closed: never
Open: 11.00/a.m.–14.30/2.30 p.m.;
17.00/5 p.m.–23.00/11 p.m.
Location: in the Albany Hotel
Setting: informal public bar in the basement of one of Glasgow's leading hotels; snacks available as well as drinks, plus occasional live music
Amenities: hotel, restaurant; private dining rooms; lounge bar on ground floor; air conditioning; parking (limited)
Atmosphere: cheerful
Clientèle: mostly young, friendly and approachable Glaswegians
Service: with a smile
Credit cards: not accepted

Shopping

EVERYTHING UNDER ONE ROOF
House of Fraser   69 Buchanan Street

FOR HIM
Carswell, A. A.
25 Renfrew Street

FOR HER
Jaeger House   60 Buchanan Street

BEAUTY & HAIR
Taylor Ferguson   106 Bath Street

JEWELLERY
Saul Bercott Ltd.   56 Argyll Arcade

LOCAL SPECIALITIES
Warehouse, The (women's fashion)
61–65 Glassford Street
Next Man (men's fashion)
42 Buchanan Street
Leather & Lace (leather fashion)
Grosvenor Buildings, Byres Road
Karter J. & Co. (Furs Ltd.) (furs)
263–265 Sauchiehall Street
Smith, John (books)
St. Vincent Street
Lawrie Ltd., R.G. (gifts, bagpipes, kilts, tartans)
110 Buchanan Street
Bag & Baggage (baggage & travel accessories)
11 Royal Exchange Square
Habitat Ltd. (interior decorating)
140 Bothwell Street
Epicure Delicatessen (food and beverages)
46 West Nile Street
Thomson's Coffee Roasters, Teablenders (speciality shop)
79 Renfield Street

THE BEST OF ART
D'Offay, Anthony (contemporary art)
9 & 23 Dering Street,
Tel. 4 99 41 00/4 99 46 95
Fischer Fine Art (Fine Art)
30 King Street, Tel. 8 39 39 42
Flowers, Angela (contemporary art)
11 Tottenham Mews, Tel. 6 37 30 89
Gimpel Fils (contemporary art)
30 Davies Street, Tel. 4 93 24 88
Juda, Annely (Fine Art)
11 Tottenham Mews, Tel. 6 37 55 17
Lisson (contemporary art)
66/68 Bell Street, Tel. 2 62 15 39
Marlborough (contemporary and Fine Art) 6 Albemarle Street
The Piccadilly Gallery (Fine Art)
16 Cork Street, Tel. 4 99 46 32
Waddington (contemporary art)
11 & 34 Cork Street,
Tel. 4 37 86 11/4 39 62 62
Arenski (18th/19th-century antiques)
29–31 George Street, Tel. 4 86 06 78
Asprey & Co. (18th/19th-century antiques) 165–169 New Bond Street,
Tel. 4 93 67 67
Barling (early Oriental and European works of art; early European furniture)
112 Mount Street, Tel. 4 99 28 58
Colnaghi Oriental (Michael Goedhuis) (18th/19th-century antiques)
14 Old Bond Street, Tel. 4 09 33 24
Garrard & Co. (jewellery)
112 Regent Street, Tel. 7 34 70 20
Green, Richard (Fine Art; 18th/19th-century paintings) 4 New Bond Street
Harvey, W. R. (18th/19th-century antiques) 5 Old Bond Street,
Tel. 4 99 83 85
Spink (17th/18th-century works of art; furniture, Old Master paintings, oriental art) King Street, St. James's
Wildenstein & Co. (Fine Art)
147 New Bond Street, Tel. 6 29 06 02
Christie's (auctioneers)
8 King Street, Tel. 8 39 90 60
Sotheby's Parke Bernet (auctioneers)
34–35 New Bond Street, Tel. 4 93 80 80

The City

Michelangelo, Bernini and Bramante would turn in their graves if they knew that young Giles Gilbert Scott had set out in 1901 to challenge their combined geniuses. His new Anglican cathedral in Liverpool was to be the second largest church in the world after St. Peter's. Finally completed in 1978, eighteen years after his death, it now stands – like its Catholic twin – on high ground, dominating the office blocks, the warehouses and the Victorian villas and as much a landmark as the legendarily eponymous ›Liver‹ birds or the Mersey itself. The city's aorta, along which a ceaseless stream of vessels of all sizes carried emigrants – willing or unwilling – en route for the Americas in the last century, brings today the raw materials for the area's industries – petroleum, grain, ores, wood and cotton. ›Nobody comes to Liverpool for pleasure‹ remarked Graham Greene, thinking perhaps of the undeniable counter-attractions of Chester next door, before a shock-headed quartet from the Cavern Club rocked the world pop music scene with the sounds of the 60s, glorifying with their insistent rhythms and nasal accents the exuberance of youth and the ›other‹ England north of Watford Gap. Liverpool is like that; vibrant, extrovert, innovative and impossible to ignore – a city which will inexorably work its way under your skin. The Beatles were echoing the sentiments of another illustrious son of the city, four times Prime Minister William Gladstone; ›all my life I will back the masses against the classes‹, revealing himself once more to be ›Oxford on the surface, but Liverpool underneath‹. He would find his audience amongst Liverpudlians today. Business here is always down-to-earth, sometimes arduous and never dull – in short, a ›hard day's night‹.

Founded: 1207 – Liverpool receives its charter; Liverpool – named after the mythical ›Liver‹ bird which carries lyver seaweed in its mouth.

Far-reaching events: 11th century – a fishing village, 17th century – Liverpool expands as sugar, spice and tobacco trade with America grows; 18th century – main centre for slave trade between Africa and America; 1840 – inauguration of the first transatlantic steamship line; 1845 – opening of Albert Dock, one of the earliest to be made entirely of iron and brick; 19th century – departure point for England's emigrants to America and Australia; 20th century – industrial expansion of the Merseyside area following recession in 1929.

Population: 610,000.

Postal code: confusing; depends on street, part of the city and house number.

Telephone code: 51

Climate: mild and humid, due to the influence of the Gulf Stream and the prevailing south-westerly winds.

Best time to visit: May to August.

Calendar of events: *Grand National* (Mar/Apr) – the world's most famous steeplechase; *International Powerboat Race* (Jun 7/8); *Maritime Festival* (Jun 16) – nautical events with visiting Royal Naval vessels; *Mersey River Festival* (Jun 15–29) – non-stop action on the water and on land; *Festival of Comedy* (Jul 12–27); *St. Helen's Show* (Jul 24–26) – flower and cattle show; *Royal Lancashire Show* (Jul 29–31) – cattle and farming show; *Beatles Convention* (Sep) – stars, movies, discussions and entertainment in honour of Liverpool's most famous lads.

Best view of the city: from the Anglican cathedral.

Historical sights: *Anglican Cathedral* (1904–78) – the world's newest and largest Gothic Anglican cathedral, designed by Sir Giles Gilbert Scott, with the highest and heaviest carillon in the world; *Benedictine Monastery* – in Birkenhead (1150) – the monks here used to be in charge of the ferries across the Mersey; *Toxteth Chapel* (1618) – the pastor emigrated to America and his son and grandson were the presidents of Harvard and Yale; *St. George's Hall* (1854) – Victorian classical; *Bluecoat Chambers* (1717) – striking Queen Anne style building, with arts centre; *Town Hall* (1754) – the city's magnificent administrative centre; *Croxteth Hall* – mansion house museum documenting the lives of the aristocracy and their servants; *St. George's Church* – the first church to be built with cast iron; *City Museum* – objets d'art from Egypt to the Far East; Lever Gallery (Port Sunlight) – English Masters and Wedgwood China.

Modern sights: *Catholic Cathedral* (1967) – designed by Sir Frederick Gibberd – circular in form, it shines like a lantern on a hill above the city; the grounds of the *International Garden Festival*.

Special attractions: *Beatle City Exhibition Centre* – from the first guitars to the Yellow Submarine, Beatlemania preserved for the ages; *pubs; Botanic Gardens; Tropical Gardens* (Sefton Park); *Formby foreshore* – seven miles of sand dunes, flora and fauna; *Liver Building* – dominating the waterfront and surmounted by the landmark ›Liver‹ birds; a *ferry trip* on the Mersey; *Chester* – medieval walled town.

Important companies with headquarters in the city: *J. Bibby & Sons* (vegetable oils); *Ellesmere Port* (flour mills); *Ford* (cars); *John Holt & Co.* (cosmetics); *ICI* (chemicals); *Liverpool Daily Post and Echo* (newspaper); *Pilkington Bros.* (plate glass); *Rexmore* (synthetic fabrics); *Vauxhall* (cars).

Airport: Liverpool, LPL; Tel.: 49400 66; 10 km/6 miles.

The Headquarters

CHESTER GROSVENOR

Eastgate Street
GB–Chester CH1 1LT (30 km/19 miles)
Telephone: (244) 2 40 24
Telex: 6 12 40
Owning Company: Grosvenor Estates
Owner: Duke of Westminster
General Manager: Jonathan Slater
Affiliation/Reservation System: Prestige Hotels
Closed: Christmas Day, Boxing Day
Number of rooms: 103 (5 suites)
Price range: £ 52–125
Credit cards: AE, DC, MC, Visa
Location: in Chester; 29 km/18 miles from airport
Built: 1865 (constant renovation)
Style: antique ›Old World‹ style
Hotel amenities: car park, hairdresser
Room service: 24 hours
Conference rooms: for up to 400 persons
Bar: ›Harvey's‹; ›Arkle‹
Restaurant: ›Grosvenor‹; French cuisine, Peter Woodward (chef de cuisine)

The Beatles' cradle could hardly rock its favourite sons to sleep in style today, let alone discerning businessmen of sincere demands for comfort and luxury. But across the Mersey, only a Financial Times ›News in Brief‹ away, stands a regal residence every manager of standing and sense chooses as his headquarters for Liverpool – or even Manchester. The history of Chester, the ancient walled city on the River Dee, stretches back almost two thousand years to the days of the Roman Occupation of Britain. In the heart of this archeological treasure-house of black-and-white timber-framed buildings stands the Grosvenor, an auberge de renommé which successfully combines the attributes of a businessman's city headquarters with authentic period charm. The hotel itself was built in 1865, but matches perfectly its medieval neighbours in The Rows. The interior is comfortable and traditional and sparkles with the patina of years of loving care; the magnificent two-hundred-year-old crystal chandelier above the oak staircase in the foyer reflects prismatically the light, and the brass door-handles shine like mirrors. The bedrooms range from the prettily contemporary, bright and gay with floral wallpaper, to the unashamedly romantic, where pride of place is taken by the magnificent four-poster bed. The stucco-ceilinged and pillared restaurant serves impeccable French cuisine – calf's sweetbreads with spinach or stuffed salmon in wine and lobster sauce – to a discriminating clientèle from both sides of the river, whilst the Arkle bar is dominated by a picture of the legendary racehorse once owned by the Duchess of Westminster. As congenial as a location for discussions as it is to come home to after the day's work is done, the Chester Grosvenor is the headquarters of choice for the Merseyside area.

BODYSGALLEN HALL

GB–Llandudno, Gwynedd, North Wales
LL30 1 RS (110 km/70 miles)
Telephone: (492) 8 44 66
Telex: 617163 hhhg
Owning Company: Historic House Hotels
Ltd., Prestige Hotels
General Manager: Jonathan Thompson
Affiliation/Reservation System: Prestige
Hotels
Number of rooms: 28 (9 suites)
Price range: £ 70–95
Credit cards: AE, DC, Access, Visa
Location: 4 km/2 miles from Llandudno
Style: Elizabethan
Hotel amenities: helipad, car park, valet
parking, house limousine service, library
Room service: 24 hours
Laundry/dry cleaning: same day
Restaurant: ›Bodysgallen Hall‹ David
Harding (chef de cuisine)

*The untamed coast of North Wales near
Llandudno, where the mountains of Snow-
donia meet the Atlantic Ocean, is the setting for a hideaway manoir of great originality and charm. Bodysgallen Hall stands
some miles from Chester on a ridge south
of Great Ormes Head, hidden from view
and sheltered from the westerly gales by an
encircling copse of fine old trees. Architecturally the house, built of pink local sandstone, presents a harmonious if somewhat
austere countenance, despite the numerous
alterations and extensions to the original
part, a thirteenth-century watch-tower built
to prevent a surprise attack on neighbouring Conway Castle. The beautifully restored intérieur also retains elements from
different periods, the staircases becoming
progressively older and narrower as one
climbs from the Victorian entrée to the top
of the medieval tower. In the public and private rooms – in contrast to the somewhat
forbidding façade – all is lightness, brightness and comfort. Focal point in the panelled drawing-room is the fireplace, surmounted by the coat of arms of the original
owners, the Mostyn family, and engraved
with their motto ›Auxilium Meum a Domino‹, whilst the focal point in the bay-windowed dining room is the excellent traditional cuisine prepared by David Harding.
Everywhere there are valuable antiques
and carefully chosen accessoires which be-
stow on the house an aura of distinction.
The service, directed by General Manager
Jonathan Thompson, is unobtrusive perfection. The gardens include a fine rose garden, walled to protect the flowers from the
elements, and a rare Elizabethan knot garden, with neatly-trimmed box hedges filled
with fragrant herbs. Bodysgallen Hall is a
perfect base for exploring the surrounding
castles from Beaumaris to Caernarvon, but
it is also a haven for connoisseurs who wish
to enjoy the atmosphere of a perfect example of a well-appointed, well-administered
country house.*

Lunch

LA GRANDE BOUFFE
48a Castle Street
Telephone: 2 36 33 75
Owner/Manager: Juliette Shield
Closed: Saturday lunchtime, Sunday and
Bank Holidays, Monday
Open: 12.00/p.m.–15.00/3 p.m. and
18.00/6 p.m.–22.30/10.30 p.m.
Cuisine: French
Specialities: aiguillettes de caneton au
poivre vert (filleted duck breast in a sauce
of caramelized apple, white wine and
green peppercorns); strawberry sable bis-
cuit; hazelnut and passion fruit salad;
vegetarian dishes
Location: city centre; near the Town Hall
Setting: bistro-style with wooden pol-
ished floor and wooden tables
Amenities: air conditioning; jazz on Tues-
day and Saturday
Atmosphere: informal and friendly
Clientèle: professionals from the banks
and corporations in the neighbourhood,
accountants and managers as well as secretaries and the local crowd
Dress: anything goes
Service: friendly and attentive
Reservations: advisable (only guide dogs
allowed)
Price range: medium
Credit cards: AE, Access, Visa

Lunch

RISTORANTE DEL SECOLO
36–40 Stanley Street
Telephone: 2 36 40 04
Owner/Manager: Mr. and Mrs. Sciarrini
Closed: Sunday; two weeks in August
Open: 12.00/a.m.–14.30/2.30 p.m. and
18.45/6.45 p.m.–22.15/10.15 p.m.
Cuisine: Italian
Chef de cuisine: P. Butler
Specialities: pasta; steaks; scallops; veal
in a remarkable number of guises
Location: central; near Whitechapel
Setting: up-market Italian restaurant
with plush dining room on the first floor
Amenities: private dining room (25 per-
sons); trattoria ›Villa Italia‹ serving
mainly pasta, and pizzeria ›Casa Italia‹ in
same building
Atmosphere: rather festive but not awe-
inspiring
Clientèle: expense-account spaghetti-
lovers from Birkenhead to Knotty Ash
mingle with homesick Italians from
Rome to Reggio Calabria, plus a fair
number of local lovers with cause for
celebration
Dress: jacket and tie preferred
Service: Italianissimo
Reservations: strongly recommended
Price range: moderately expensive
Credit cards: DC, Visa, Access

Dinner

CHURCHILL'S
Churchill House, Tithebarn Street
Telephone: 2 27 38 77
Owner/Manager: Carl Lewis/Pino Ma-
tissi
Closed: Sunday; Saturday lunchtime,
Bank Holidays
Open: 11.30/a.m.–16.00/4 p.m. and
19.00/7 p.m.–midnight
Cuisine: English and Continental
Chef de cuisine: Stephen Murphy
Location: near Moorfields Station
Setting: restrained elegance; polished
wood, subdued lighting
Amenities: 2 private dining rooms; air
conditioning; car park
Atmosphere: distinguished but not daunt-
ing
Clientèle: top industrialists hoping to
clinch a deal at lunchtime or celebrating a
signed contract or a wedding anniversary
at night
Dress: casual but correct
Service: irreproachable
Reservations: essential – several days in
advance for Saturday evening
Price range: fairly expensive by local
standards
Credit cards: AE, DC, Visa, Access

Dinner

JENNY'S SEAFOOD
Old Ropery, Fenwick Street
Telephone: 2 36 03 32
Owner/Manager: Judy Hinds
Closed: Sunday; Saturday lunchtime,
Monday evening; Bank holidays
Open: 12.15/p.m.–14.15/2.15 p.m. and
19.00/7 p.m.–22.15/10.15 p.m.
Cuisine: seafood
Chef de cuisine: Thomas Parry
Location: central; near James Street Sta-
tion
Setting: cellar restaurant with under-
stated décor; an abundance of wood
Amenities: air conditioning; car park a
few steps away
Atmosphere: welcoming and friendly
Clientèle: Liverpool's social élite and top
management for business at lunchtime
and for pleasure at night
Dress: casual but not careless
Service: a little on the slow side at busy
times, but otherwise quick and efficient
Reservations: recommended, especially
for lunch
Price range: relatively expensive
Credit cards: AE, DC, Visa, Access

Dinner

BODYSGALLEN HALL
Llandudno, Gwynedd
Telephone: (492) 8 44 66
Owner/Manager: Historic House Hotels
Ltd./Jonathan Thompson
Closed: never
Open: 12.30/p.m.–13.45/1.45 p.m. and
19.30/7.30 p.m.–21.00/9 p.m.
Cuisine: classic
Chef de cuisine: David Harding
Specialities: crab, sorrel and tomato flan;
calves' sweetbreads; roast rack of lamb;
venison in juniper berries and herbs;
home-made ice-cream
Location: in the Bodysgallen Hall Hotel
at Llandudno, 80 km/50 miles from the
Headquarters
Setting: in a lovingly-restored 17th-cen-
tury mansion: wood-panelled dining
room with elegant period décor
Amenities: hotel; bar; open-air dining
(weather permitting); valet car parking;
helipad
Atmosphere: that of an elegant country
house whose owner understands the art
of gracious living
Clientèle: shipping magnates tired of
Liverpool; industrialists tired of Man-
chester; international businessmen tired
of both
Dress: rather conventional
Service: unobtrusively friendly
Reservations: advisable (no dogs or child-
ren under 5)
Price range: moderately expensive
Credit cards: AE, DC, Visa, Access

Café

KEG
Ranelagh Place
Telephone: 7 09 72 00
Owner/Manager: Britannia Adelphi Ho-
tel/Stephen Bullock
Closed: Sunday
Open: 12.00/a.m.–14.30/2.30 p.m. and
(Monday – Thursday) 19.00/7 p.m.–
24.00/12 p.m.; (Friday – Saturday)
19.00/7 p.m.–2.00/a.m.
Location: in the Britannia Adelphi Hotel
Setting: small modern hotel café in a Vic-
torian building; décor reminiscent of a
discothèque
Amenities: hotel; two restaurants; private
dining rooms (2–700 persons); snacks;
air conditioning; car park
Atmosphere: perfect for a Campari and
soda before a night on the town
Clientèle: men-about-town; foreign del-
egates; the occasional traveller from Du-
blin, Dortmund or Deauville
Dress: casual but smart
Service: always smiling
Reservations: not necessary
Price range: moderate
Credit cards: AE, DC, Visa, Euro, Access

Bar

ARKLE
Eastgate Street, Chester
Telephone: 2 40 24
Owner/Manager: The Duke of West-
minster/Jonathan Slater
Closed: never
Open: 17.30/5.30 p.m.–23.00/11 p.m.
Location: in the Chester Grosvenor Hotel
Setting: luxurious English-style bar dom-
inated by a picture of the eponymous
Arkle, the legendary racehorse once
owned by the Duchess of Westminster
Amenities: hotel (103 bedrooms); restau-
rant; ›Harvey's‹ bar
Atmosphere: club-like
Clientèle: discerning visitors to Mersey-
side for business or North Wales for plea-
sure
Dress: jacket and tie
Service: good
Reservations: not necessary
Credit cards: AE, DC, MC, Visa

Shopping

EVERYTHING UNDER ONE ROOF
Lee, George Henry   20 Basnett Street

FOR HIM
Austin Reed   27 Bold Street

FOR HER
Jaeger Shop   12 Bold Street

BEAUTY & HAIR
Thatchers   St. Johns Street

JEWELLERY
Boodle and Dunthorne   Boodle House,
Lord Street

LOCAL SPECIALITIES
Next Ltd. (fashion for her)
St. Johns Precinct, Houghton Street
Top Man (fashion for him)
22 Church Street
Watson Pricard Ltd. (fashion for him and
her) North John Street
Academy Unit 10 (children's fashion)
Cavern Walks
Herbert, Kristine (leather fashion)
12 Cavern Walks, Mathew Street
Hiorns, E. T. (furs)
75 a Bold Street
Stonier & Co. Ltd. (porcelain)
25 Williamson Square
Lee, George Henry (baggage & travel
accessories) 20 Basnett Street
Ashley, Laura Ltd., Home Furnishings
(interior decorating) Unit 19 A, Mathew
Street
Lewi's (food and beverages)
1 Ranelagh Street
Amy Jeanne's Shoe Box (shoes)
Unit 1, Albert Dock Village
Bloomers (lingerie)
122 Allerton Road

The City

For grandeur of the Old World, it is a ›Tale of Two Cities‹, the other being Paris. The framework is imperial, the substance lordly, many a superlative evident. World history is palpable everywhere, the culture of centuries omnipresent, the dignity well-earned and the beauty of a subtle, understated nature. London is the only city Paris respects, New York admires and Buenos Aires imitates. No-one would doubt London's supremacy in newspapers and banks, theatre and music life, museums, antiques and auctions, markets, shops and tailors, pubs and clubs, tradition, manners and humour. The world loves London, and many of her lovers come to stay forever, which has turned this insular capital into a patchwork of races, nationalities and types adding to the fascination – and the problems. Conservative London is very much in existence, from the clichés to the attitudes, while Swinging London is just coming back to full swing again, from South Moulton Street to King's Road. Tolerance seems unlimited, the politeness is astonishing, and the worldliness is proverbial. The largest city in Europe, made up of villages, is also the biggest in industry, finance and trade – with an air of devil-may-care. God probably does for this magnificent metropolis, for ›when a man is tired of London, he is tired of life.‹ You are so right, Samuel Johnson.

Founded: first mentioned as ›Londinium‹ in 43 A.D.

Far-reaching events: 150 – London the largest fortress outside Rome; 5th century – Romans withdraw – Celts, Saxons and Danes contest the area; 1066 – William the Conqueror becomes the first Norman king; 1215 – signing the Magna Carta; 1509–47 – Henry VIII rules and breaks with the Roman Catholic Church; 1588 – under his daughter Elizabeth I, England defeats the Spanish Armada and becomes the centre of world trade; 1665 – the Great Plague; 1666 – the Great Fire – London 80% destroyed; 1837–1901 Queen Victoria reigns and London is capital of the British Empire; 1952 – accession of Queen Elizabeth II.

Population: 7.2 million (Greater London area).

Postal code: confusing; depends on area, street, etc.   **Telephone code:** 1

Climate: unpredictable.

Calendar of Events: *Chinese New Year* (Jan/Feb) – fire-breathing dragons and lots of fireworks; *Cruft's Dog Show* (Feb) – 10,000 aristocratic canines; *Maundy Thursday* (Mar–Apr) – the Queen distributes alms; *Easter Parade* (Mar–Apr); *Boat Race* (Mar–Apr) – crews from Oxford and Cambridge race from Putney to Mortlake; *Summer Exhibition* (May) – at the Royal Academy; *Cup Final* (May) – climax to the football season at Wembley Stadium; *Chelsea Flower Show* (May) – four days of flower power; *Trooping the Colour* (Jun) – the Queen's official birthday; *Royal Ascot* (Jun) – horse racing and high fashion; *Lord's Test Match* (Jun) – cricket; *All-England Tennis Championship* (Jun) at Wimbledon; *Henry Wood Promenade Concerts* (Jul–Sep); *Swan Upping* (Jul) – counting of the swans along the Thames; *Notting Hill Carnival* (Aug) – the Caribbean comes to London; *Battle of Britain Day* (15 Sep) – fighter plane formations in the sky; *Guy Fawkes Day* (5 Nov) – fireworks for the not forgotten hero; *Lord Mayor's Day* (Nov) – gilded coaches lead the parade; *State Opening of Parliament* (Nov).

Fairs and exhibitions: *LONDON INTERNATIONAL BOAT SHOW* (Jan); *BRITISH TOY AND HOBBY FAIR* (Jan); *INTERNATIONAL FOOD EXHIBITION* (Feb–Mar); *EXPOSHIP* (Mar); *›DAILY MIRROR‹ PHOTO WORLD EXHIBITION* (Apr); *INTERIOR DESIGN INTERNATIONAL* (May); *GROSVENOR HOUSE ANTIQUES FAIR* (Jun); *COMPUTER FAIR* (Jun); *INTERNATIONAL CERAMICS FAIR* (Jun); *BRITISH DESIGNER SHOW* (Oct); *MOTOR FAIR* (Oct); *CARAVAN CAMPING HOLIDAY SHOW* (Nov).

Historical sights: *Westminster Abbey* (1216–1375) – where kings have been crowned since 1066; *Tower of London* (11th–19th centuries) – ex-prison, museum and home of the Yeoman Warders, the ravens and the Crown Jewels; *St. Paul's Cathedral* (1675–1710) – Sir Christopher Wren's domed classical masterpiece; *Houses of Parliament* (1888) – with the landmark *Big Ben* clock tower; *Tower Bridge* (1894) – landmark of London; *St. Martin's-in-the-Fields* (13th–18th centuries); *Bank of England* (1694); *Cleopatra's Needle* – pink granite obelisk; *10 Downing Street* (17th century) – home of Prime Ministers since 1732; *Kensington Palace* – private home of kings until 1760; *Old Bailey* (1907) – the judges and lawyers still wear wigs; *British Museum* (1823–47) – Magna Carta, the Rosetta Stone and the Elgin Marbles; *Victoria and Albert Museum* (1899) – fine and applied arts; *National Gallery* – all important national schools and almost all major old masters; *Tate Gallery* – modern art; *Wallace Collection*.

Modern sights: *South Bank Arts Centre; Aviary* by Lord Snowden at Regent's Park Zoo; *Barbican* development.

Special attractions: from *Laurence Oliver on stage* to *tea at the Ritz* to an *auction at Christie's*, etc., etc.

Important companies with headquarters in the city: Everybody who is anybody has an office in London – from banks to robber barons.

Airport: Heathrow, LHR; Tel.: 7 59 43 21; 24 km/15 miles; Gatwick, LGW; Tel.: 02 93/2 88 22; 45 km/30 miles; British Airways, Tel.: 3 70 54 11.

SAVOY

The Strand
GB–London WC2R OEU
Telephone: 8 36 43 43
Telex: 24 234 savoy
Telefax: 2 406 040
Managing Director Willy B. G. Bauer
Affiliation/Reservation System: The Leading Hotels of the World
Number of rooms: 202 (48 suites)
Price range: £ 115–440
Credit cards: all major
Location: central
Built: 1889 (renovated continually)
Style: turn-of-the-century nostalgic
Hotel amenities: garage, valet parking, house limousine service, boutique
Main hall porter: Antonio Garcia
Room service: 24 hours
Laundry/dry cleaning: same day service (except Sunday)
Bars: ›Savoy‹ and ›American Bar‹ Gianpiero (Peter) Dorelli (barman)
Restaurants: ›The River‹, Luigi Zambon (maître), Anton Edelmann (chef de cuisine), French cuisine, orchestra; ›The Grill Room‹, Angelo Maresca (maître), Keith Stanley (chef de cuisine) English and French cuisine

›For excellence we strive‹ is their engraved motto. Willy Bauer and his frock-coated men do, indeed. World history was made here, the Golden Twenties gleamed brighter than anywhere else, and even after parting with half of the rooms, the Establishment's favourite London base and playground remains on top. When Richard D'Oyly-Carte, the theatrical impresario, planned ›the perfect hotel‹, he commissioned the most prominent architects and artists of Europe in 1889. One hundred years later, the perfection is complete. There may be no Strauss to conduct the orchestra at one of the celebrated balls still held here, no Caruso to sing, no Escoffier to cook and no César Ritz to overlook the stomping, but Frank Sinatra, Luciano Pavarotti and Mick Jagger, despite their different personalities and demands, are all three fans of the River Suites, the room service and the rest they can enjoy here without being disturbed or publicized. With the same unobtrusive grandeur which met Winston Churchill, Charlie Chaplin and Mae West, the Savoy plays host to every guest individually. The Savoy keeps representatives at Heathrow Airport as well as at the pleasure port of Southampton, so you won't have to cope with plebeians on the way to the mansion, and once you're on the premises there is not much that can't be arranged through Antonio Garcia. It's even wonderful to be here with nothing to do – the bar is a centre of gravity, The Grill is a lunch meeting point for the City and The River restaurant one of the glamourous stages of London's after-hours theatreland.

The Hideaway

LE MANOIR AUX QUAT' SAISONS

Church Road
GB–Great Milton, Oxfordshire OX9 7PD
(49 km/31 miles)
Telephone: (84 46) 88 81
Telex: 837 552 blancr g
Owning Company: Blanc Restaurants Ltd.
Owners: Raymond and Jenny Blanc
General Manager: Alan Desenclos
Affiliation/Reservation Systems: Prestige Hotels; Traditions et Qualité
Closed: last week in December and first three weeks in January
Number of rooms: 10 (2 suites)
Price range: £ 95–180 (double)
           £ 200 (suite)
Credit cards: AE, Access, DC, Visa
Location: 49 km/31 miles from London
Built: 15th century; additions 18th and 19th century (renovated 1984)
Style: country house
Hotel amenities: parking, swimming pool, garden, heliport
Room amenities: tv, radio
Bathroom amenities: jacuzzi (some), hairdrier
Room service: 24 hours
Laundry: next-day service
Conference room: 40 persons
Sports: tennis, swimming, riding
Sports nearby: golf
Restaurant: ›Le Manoir aux Quat' Saisons‹ (12.15/p.m.–14.30/2.30 p.m. and 19.15/7.15 p.m.–22.30/10.30 p.m.; closed Sunday evening, Monday, and Tuesday lunchtime) French cuisine; Raymond Blanc (chef de cuisine)
Private dining rooms: two, for up to 40 persons

At one end of a sleepy village on the Oxfordshire plain between the Chiltern Hills and the city of dreaming spires, nestles the fêted and fabled ne plus ultra of the English gastronomic scene – and it's run as if to the manor born by a Frenchman. The multi-gabled Tudor manoir of mellow Cotswold stone stands in a sylvan setting – a 27-acre estate with manicured lawns, gravel walks and a kitchen garden which Raymond Blanc supervises with almost as much meticulous pride as he does the salmon tartare or the soufflé de crabe, served to perfection in the pretty pink dining rooms. There are only ten bedrooms, each lovingly furnished in exquisite colour-combinations to reflect the name of the flower they bear. The baths are a sybarite's dream – and mostly big enough to sleep in, too. But despite the lure of the country's oldest university town nearby, despite the all-too-apparent attractions of this inn for all seasons, the uncompromising excellence of its cuisine remains its raison d'être – and the reason why the glamourous occupants of the chauffeur-driven Rollses think nothing of cruising up the M 40 in order to roll up the drive in front of this lucullian temple which combines Gallic epicureanism with Anglo-Saxon heritage.

Lunch

SIMPSON'S-IN-THE-STRAND
100 Strand, WC2
Telephone 8 96 91 12
Owner/Manager: Savoy Hotel plc
Closed: Sunday; Bank Holidays
Open: 12.00/a.m.–15.00/3 p.m. and
18.00/6 p.m.–22.00/10 p.m.
Cuisine: English
Chefs de cuisine: J. Curley
Specialities: roast beef and Yorkshire
pudding; roast lamb with redcurrant
jelly; Aylesbury duckling; Dover sole; syrup roll; Stilton and vintage port
Location: a jam roll away from the Savoy
Hotel
Setting: downstairs – immutably Victorian, from the revolving mahogany doors
to the Corinthian columns, the vaulted
ceiling, the candelabra and the enforced
absence of ladies at lunchtime; upstairs –
more elegant and more liberal (in that respect, anyway)
Amenities: private dining rooms (20–140
persons); air conditioning
Atmosphere: a bastion of British tradition
and culture; as if time had stood still
soon after its opening in 1848
Clientèle: illustrious Londoners and distinguished visitors to the metropolis from
Charles Dickens onwards
Dress: jacket and tie essential; pin-stripes
preferred
Service: charmingly anachronistic; morn-
ing coats to ankle-length aprons
Reservations: essential
Price range: appropriate
Credit cards: AE, DC, Visa, Access

Lunch

CECCONI'S
5a Burlington Gardens W1
Telephone: (4 34) 15 09
Owner/Manager: Mr. Cecconi
Closed: Saturday; Bank Holidays
Open: 12.00/a.m.–14.30/2.30 p.m. and
19.30/7.30 p.m.–12.00/p.m.
Cuisine: Italian
Specialities: home-made pasta – taglier-
ini verdi; grilled scampi; veal in tuna fish
sauce (vitello tonnato); fillet of veal; car-
paccio; zabaglione
Location: near Savile Row
Setting: spacious; super-elegant
Amenities: private dining room
Atmosphere: refreshing; the best pasta in
London (albeit at a price) – and some of
the most glittering company – never too
close to be disillusioning
Clientèle: well-known interior decora-
tors; elegant ladies-about-town; musi-
cians and actors from Daniel Barenboim
to Alec Guinness
Dress: predominantly Hardy Amies to
Zandra Rhodes

Service: attentive and friendly
Reservations: essential
Price range: ludicrously expensive
Credit cards: AE, DC, Access

Lunch

**CONNAUGHT GRILL AND
RESTAURANT**
Carlos Place, WI
Telephone: 4 99 70 70
Affiliations: Relais et Châteaux
Owner/Manager: Savoy Hotel plc/J. P.
Chevalier
Closed: (restaurant) never (grill) Satur-
day; Sunday; public holidays
Open: 12.30/p.m.–14.30/2.30 p.m. and
18.30/6.30 p.m.–22.15/10.15 p.m. (grill
until 22.30/10.30 p.m.)
Cuisine: French and international
Chef de cuisine: Michel Bourdin
Specialities: potted crayfish and crab;
zéphirs de sole ›Tout Paris‹; pheasant,
partridge and grouse pâté; noisettes
d'agneau Edward VII; the best bread-
and-butter pudding in London
Location: in the Connaught Hotel
Setting: French-polished Edwardian
wood-panelled walls, mirrors, chandeliers; Grill Room in shades of green, with
stucco ceilings and subdued lighting
Amenities: hotel; private dining room (20
persons); air conditioning
Atmosphere: an exclusive place to see
and be seen in (particularly the far corner
of the restaurant, by the window); dignified, prestigious and utterly memorable
Clientèle: Upper Crust épicures (mostly
masculine) influential, important, illustri-
ous and affluent habitués from Bruton
Square to Baden-Baden
Dress: jacket and tie (jeans prohibited)
Service: consummate courtesy
Reservations: recommended
Price range: unapologetically expensive
Credit cards: Access

Dinner

WILTON'S
55 Jermyn Street, SWl
Telephone: 6 29 99 55
Owner/Manager: Robin Gundry
Closed: Saturday; Sunday; Bank Holi-
days; 3 weeks in July/August
Open: 12.30//p.m.–14.30/2.30 p.m. and
18.30/6.30 p.m.–22.30/10.30 p.m.
Cuisine: English at its best
Chef de cuisine: Alan Gaunt
Specialities: oysters; seafood; fresh De-
von dressed crab; Dover sole; grills;
roasts; game; excellent Stilton
Location: between Piccadilly and Pall
Mall; a short walk from the Ritz in one
direction or St. James' Palace in the other
Setting: plush, formal dining room re-
taining many familiar features from its

previous domicile in Bury Street; elegant
Art Noveau mahogany and glass panels;
reminiscent of grandma's parlour
Amenities: private dining room (16 persons); cosy restaurant for banquets and
other festivites; air conditioning
Atmosphere: very, very British and very,
very Victorian
Clientèle: distinguished; exclusive; conservative; rich; mostly following in the
family footsteps
Dress: jacket and tie de rigueur (will be
supplied if you forget)
Service: indulgently hospitable
Reservations: advisable to essential
Price range: rather expensive
Credit cards: AE, DC

Dinner

SCOTTS
20 Mount Street, W.l.
Telephone: 6 29 52 48
Owner/Manager: Tino Paissoni
Closed: Sunday lunch; Bank Holidays
Open: 12.30/p.m.–14.45/2.45 p.m. and
18.00/6 p.m.–22.45/10.45 p.m. (Sunday)
19.00/7 p.m.–22.00/10 p.m.
Cuisine: English at its best
Chef de cuisine: John Bertram
Specialities: seafood; oysters; smoked
cod roe; skate; sole; mousse of scallops
with champagne sauce and lobster coral;
grills; lamb cutlets; carpet-bag steak
Location: in the heart of Mayfair; near
the American Embassy and the Connaught Hotel
Setting: established over 300 years ago;
understatedly luxurious dining room
Amenities: Oyster Bar for a quick lunch;
private dining room (12 persons); air conditioning; doorman for car parking
Atmosphere: totally civilized; as much a
British institution as the Changing of the
Guard or the Tower of London
Clientèle: very mixed; Prince Charles
and the Anglo-aristocracy, plus more
than a sprinkling of Texan oil millionaires and Bavarian beer barons
Dress: jacket and tie
Service: impeccable; part of the establishment
Reservations: essential (no dogs)
Price range: expensive
Credit cards: AE, DC, Visa, Access

Lunch

KEN LO'S MEMORIES OF CHINA
67 Ebury Street SW 1
Telephone: 7 30 77 34
Owner/Manager: Kenneth and Ann Lo
Closed: Sunday; Bank Holidays
Open: 12.00/a.m.–14.30/2.30 p.m. and
19.00/7 p.m.–23.00/11 p.m.
Cuisine: Chinese

Specialities: ingeniously-named dishes,
many requiring 24 hours' notice; Cantonese triple-fry in black bean sauce; barbecue of lamb in lettuce puffs; snow-flake
prawn balls; Shanghai sea-bass with
ginger and spring onions
Location: a spring roll from Victoria Station
Setting: windows etched with Tang dynasty horses; movable wooden screens to
provide extra privacy
Amenities: private dining rooms (15–90
persons); cookery school; oriental delicatessen in the vicinity
Atmosphere: modern yet oriental; imbued with the multi-faceted personality
of the proprietor-writer, actor, diplomat,
journalist and connoisseur of the finer
things in life, Kenneth Lo
Clientèle: globe-trotting gourmets; oriental diplomats; distinguished, discriminating, intelligent and well-informed
Dress: fairly conventional
Service: pretty waitresses in red silk
gowns supervised by the charming Ann
Lo
Reservations: essential
Price range: fairly expensive
Credit cards: AE, DC, Visa, Access

Lunch

LANGAN'S BRASSERIE
Stratton Street, W1
Telephone: 4 93 64 37/4 91 88 22
Owner/Managers: Peter Langan, Michael
Caine and Richard Shepherd
Closed: Saturday lunchtime; Sunday;
Bank Holidays
Open: 12.30/p.m.–14.45/2.45 p.m. and
19.00/7 p.m.–23.15/11.15 p.m. (Saturday) 20.00/8 p.m.–24.00/12 p.m.
Cuisine: English and international
Chef de cuisine: Richard Shepherd
Specialities: seafood salad; shrimp
bisque; spinach soufflé with anchovy
sauce; roast beef; smoked trout with
horseradish; poached turbot with sauce
hollandaise; suprême of sea bass with
fennel; crème brûlée
Location: just off Piccadilly
Setting: Roaring Twenties brasserie; steel
and mirrors, parquet floor, tropical fans
and a profusion of photographs, prints
and paintings; second dining room upstairs to which unwitting tourists are relegated
Amenities: bar; attended cloakroom; live
music in the evening
Atmosphere: reminiscent of the heyday of
café society; a London institution – buzzing with life and invariably full
Clientèle: le Tout Londres; a glittering
and glamourous procession of personalities; from Ursula Andress to Deborah
Kerr

Dress: suitably eye-catching and expensive
Service: rather superior
Reservations: essential
Price range: fairly expensive
Credit cards: AE, DC, Visa, Access

Dinner

THE ENGLISH HOUSE
3 Milner Street SW3
Telephone: 5 84 30 02
Owner/Manager: Colin M. Livingston
Closed: Christmas Day; Boxing Day
Open: 12.30/p.m.–14.30/2.30 p.m. and 19.30/7.30 p.m.–23.30/11.30 p.m.
Cuisine: English (old recipes adapted to 20th-century taste)
Chef de cuisine: Liam Barr
Specialities: watercress soup; oyster-stuffed chicken; Huntingdon fidget pie; saddle of venison with gin and juniper berries; pork sausage with apple sauce; Devonshire junket with ginger and rum sauce; brown bread ice-cream; chocolate gooseberry cake
Location: a short taxi-ride from the South Kensington museum complex
Setting: white townhouse dating from the 1850s; small dining room; chandeliers, dried flowers, mirrors and Old Masters; sitting-room upstairs with open fireplace
Amenities: private dining room (6–20 persons); séparée for lovers of any sex
Atmosphere: intimate, harmonious
Clientèle: celebrities in search of seclusion; fans of Haute Cuisine Anglaise from both sides of the Atlantic; premiers and politicians from Margaret Thatcher to Michael Foot
Dress: Saville Row to South Moulton Street
Service: suave and very knowledgeable
Reservations: advisable (no pets)
Price range: fairly expensive
Credit cards: all major

Dinner

TIGER LEE
251 Old Brompton Road
Telephone: 3 70 23 23/3 70 59 70
Affiliations: Master Chefs Institute
Owner/Manager: Claudio Cassuto and Hong Kong Partners
Closed: Christmas Day; lunchtime
Open: 18.00/6 p.m.–1.00/a.m.
Cuisine: Cantonese
Chef de cuisine: Cheung Hong
Specialities: lobster with spring onion and ginger; stuffed crab claw; steamed trout in black bean sauce; barbecued sucking pig; stuffed fish; lobster chef's special; yam basket; crispy duck, Cantonese style; stir-fried beef with mango
Location: near Earl's Court

Setting: fish tanks at the entrance; modern classic décor, simple and uncluttered; pastel covers in sea-green and silver; leather chairs
Amenities: air conditioning
Atmosphere: subtle and sophisticated blend of occidental and oriental
Clientèle: cross-section of politicians, bankers, ministers and chairmen of corporations and Quangos, leavened by a fair sprinkling of celebrities from East and West – Miss Hong Kong to Faye Dunaway
Dress: no restrictions or requirements
Service: competent and friendly
Reservations: essential
Price range: moderately expensive
Credit cards: AE, DC, Visa

Café

FORTNUM'S FOUNTAIN
181 Piccadilly, W1
Telephone: 7 34 49 38
Closed: Sunday; public holidays
Open: 9.30/a.m.–23.30/11.30 p.m.
Location: in Fortnum and Mason's store
Setting: large dining room with columns, murals, chandeliers and a bar counter for those in a hurry as well as attractively – laid tables; décor in fruit-flavoured ice-cream colours
Amenities: department store with a world-famous food section; snacks, salads, sandwiches and sweets
Atmosphere: in a category of its own; hopelessly crowded at high noon
Clientèle: ladies in tweed skirts and cashmere cardigans after the rigours of a morning in Regent Street; bankers and brokers in pin-stripes after the rigours of a morning in the boardroom; the hungry after-theatre crowd before facing the drive back to Esher or Surbiton
Service: old-fashioned and excellent

Meeting Point

DRONES
1 Pont Street SW1
Telephone: 2 35 96 38
Owner/Manager: Scott's Ltd/L. D. Leon
Closed: never
Open: 12.30/p.m.–14.45/2.45 p.m. and 19.30/7.30 p.m.–23.30/11.30 p.m.
Location: off Sloane Street; half-way between Knightsbridge and Sloane Square
Setting: pleasant, light décor
Amenities: bar/restaurant
Atmosphere: rather pretentiously and self-consciously chic
Clientèle: the omnipresent magazine and film world at lunchtime – all the Litchfields and Bissets who aren't still in bed – plus all the Public School boys, Sloane Rangers and estate agents – the ›Ooh, I say‹ and ›Rather‹ crowd

Service: reliable
Reservations: necessary
Credit cards: AE, DC, Access, Visa

Bistro

SAN LORENZO
22 Beauchamp Place SW3
Telephone: 5 84 10 74
Owner/Manager: Lorenzo and Mara Berni
Closed: Sunday; Bank Holidays
Open: 12.30/p.m.–14.30/2.30 p.m. and 19.30/7.30 p.m.–23.30/11.30 p.m.
Cuisine: Italian
Chef de cuisine: Gino Arastelli
Specialities: artichokes alla romana; fresh pasta with peas and mushrooms; carpaccio; tripe with mint sauce; crème caramel
Location: off Brompton Road, between Harrods and the Victoria and Albert Museum
Setting: basement winter-garden with a profusion of plants and Marilyn Monroe photos; round tables, comfortable wicker chairs and a sliding roof for semi-al fresco dining on fine days.
Amenities: affiliated restaurant ›San Lorenzo Fuoriporta‹ at Worple Road Mews, Wimbledon (Telephone: 9 46 84 63) with enchanting garden for open-air dining in summer
Atmosphere: chic but not chichi; always full; intimate and relaxing in spite of the tradition that guests leave promptly at the conclusion of their meal in order to allow the waiting hordes a chance to sample some of the best Italian cooking in London
Clientèle: London's Beautiful People from the worlds of theatre, fashion and photography, plus spaghetti-loving gourmets from the provinces and homesick Italian epicures
Dress: Giorgio Armani to Gianni Versace, and vice-versa
Service: exceptionally charming, even when guests outstay their welcome
Reservations: essential
Price range: fairly expensive
Credit cards: not accepted

Dine & Dance

ANNABEL'S
44 Berkeley Square, W1
Telephone: 6 29 23 50
Owner/Manager: Mark Birley
Closed: Sunday
Open: 2.30/8.30 p.m.–3.00/a.m.
Location: in Mayfair; in the basement of John Aspinall's Clermont gambling club
Setting: named after the owner's wife, Lady Annabel Goldsmith; dark; private; understated English country house décor-bar with button-leather chairs

Amenities: discothèque; restaurant (excellent but exceedingly expensive food)
Atmosphere: one of a kind; discreet and (once you are in) surprisingly friendly
Clientèle: Anglo-Aristocracy; assorted American Millionaires; MPs; anyone vouched for by a member (as long as he behaves)
Service: individualistic and excellent, especially the witty and worldly-wise Mabel, custodian of the ladies' cloakroom
Reservations: private club (waiting list for membership; outsiders admitted on personal recommendation of members)
Credit cards: not accepted

Nightclub

TRAMP
40 Jermyn Street, W1
Telephone: 7 34 31 74
Owner/Manager: Jack Gold
Closed: Sunday
Open: 21.00/9 p.m.–4.00/a.m.
Location: a short trek from Piccadilly Circus
Setting: erstwhile staid gentlemen's club; anachronistic stately panelled walls; salon-like dining room with round tables; small, dark and usually crowded dance floor
Amenities: discothèque; restaurant (food rather variable)
Atmosphere: unpredictable; highly entertaining or excruciatingly boring, depending on who happens to be there and how you feel
Clientèle: show-biz nouveaux riches; Upper Class trendies; mostly young, rich and into rock heavies
Dress: trendy to totally outlandish
Service: erratic
Reservations: essential
Price range: expensive
Credit cards: all major

Nightclub

STRINGFELLOWS
16 Upper St. Martins Lane, WC2
Telephone: 2 40 55 34
Owner/Manager: Peter Stringfellow
Closed: Sunday
Open: 23.00/11 p.m.–3.00/a.m. (restaurant from 20.00/8 p.m.)
Location: in the Charing Cross Road area
Setting: one million pounds' worth (according to the legend) of splendiferous High Tech and velvet interior; clear perspex dance floor
Amenities: discothèque; cocktails and flashy à la carte dinner menu

Atmosphere: glittering, glamourous and trendy
Clientèle: executives of advertising and the music biz, plus long-legged models with glossy lips and glossier minds (quite a number of them unattached)
Dress: nothing too understated or conservative
Service: plentiful French-knickered waitresses
Reservations: recommended
Price range: entrance fee for non-members
Credit cards: all major

Shopping

EVERYTHING UNDER ONE ROOF
Harrods   Knightsbridge, SW1

FOR HIM
Anderson and Sheppard (tailor)
30 Savile Row, W1

FOR HER
Bruce OldField
Beauchamp Place, SW3

BEAUTY & HAIR
Vidal Sassoon   44 Sloane Street, SW1

JEWELLERY
Kutchinsky   73 Brompton Road, SW3

LOCAL SPECIALITIES
Alfred Dunhill Ltd (tobacco)
30 Duke Street, St. James, SWI
Renate (women's fashion)
7 Chevalle Place, SW7
Austin Reed (men's fashion)
103 Regent Street, W1
Simpson (men & women's fashion)
203 Piccadilly, W1
White House (children's fashion)
Bond Street
Hawes & Curtis (shirtmakers)
2 Burlington Gardens, W1
Conney, Frank (furs)
23 Avery Row, W1
Foyles (books)
119 Charing Cross Road, WC2
Asprey and Co. (gifts)
165–169 New Bond Street, W1
Wedgwood (porcelain)
158 Regent Street, W1
Nina Campbell (interior decorating)
48 Walton Street, SW3
Fortnum & Mason (food and beverages)
181 Piccadilly, W1
Gidden's (riding equipment)
15d Clifford Street, W1
Christie's (auctioneers)
8 King Street
Lord, D. L. (cashmere)
Burlington Arcade, Piccadilly, W1

THE BEST OF ART
D'Offay, Anthony   (contemporary art)
9 & 23 Dering Street
Fischer Fine Art   (Fine Art)
30 King Street, Tel. 8 39 39 42
Flowers, Angela   (contemporary art)
11 Tottenham Mews, Tel. 6 37 30 89
Gimpel Fils   (contemporary art)
30 Davies Street, Tel. 4 93 24 88
Juda, Annely   (Fine Art)
11 Tottenham Mews, Tel. 6 37 55 17
Lisson   (contemporary art)
66/68 Bell Street, Tel. 2 62 15 39
Marlborough   (contemporary and Fine Art) 6 Albemarle Street
The Piccadilly Gallery   (Fine Art)
16 Cork Street, Tel. 4 99 46 32
Waddington   (contemporary art)
11 & 34 Cork Street
Arenski   (18th/19th-century antiques)
29–31 George Street, Tel. 4 86 06 78
Asprey & Co.   (18th/19th-century antiques) 165–169 New Bond Street
Barling   (early Oriental and European works of art; early European furniture)
112 Mount Street, Tel. 4 99 28 58
Colnaghi Oriental
(Michael Goedhuis)   (18th/19th-century antiques) 14 Old Bond Street
Garrard & Co.   (jewellery)
112 Regent Street, Tel. 7 34 70 20
Green, Richard   (Fine Art; 18th/19th-century Paintings) 4 New Bond Street
Harvey, W. R.   (18th/19th-century antiques) 5 Old Bond Street
Spinks   (17th/18th-century works of art, furniture, Old Master paintings, Oriental art) King Street, St. James's
Wildenstein & Co.   (Fine Art)
147 New Bond Street, Tel. 6 29 06 02
Christie's   (auctioneers)
8 King Street, Tel. 8 39 90 60
Sotheby's Parke Bernet   (auctioneers)
34–35 New Bond Street, Tel. 4 93 80 80

The City

Beethoven's Fifth may well echo these days in the hallowed sanctum where once re-sounded the stirring plaidoyers of the 19th-century pioneers of the laissez-faire philos-ophy. They changed world economic thinking almost as radically as Stephenson's Rocket revolutionized Manchester's industrial fortunes. That the Hallé Orchestra has filled the Free Trade Hall with sound since 1858 is indicative not only of the changing fashions in economics but also of the city's long patronage of the arts. Manchester's 20th-century image is firmly rooted in her Victorian past. Her public buildings, from the Town Hall – a cross between St. Pancras Station and the Houses of Parliament – to the rather grandiose neo-classical Central Library, evince a dignified self-confidence true to the spirit of the times in which they were built and quietly reassuring today. The development of the modest industry established in the 14th century by Flemish weav-ers into one of the bulwarks of British prosperity, is due principally to north-west Eng-land's much-maligned weather; apart from the benefits to the cotton industry, the Old Trafford cricket ground, the city's parks and the surrounding peaks and dales bear wit-ness to William Blake's ›green and pleasant land‹. Fortunately, the ›dark, satanic mills‹ are disappearing in this more environmentally conscious age. With her industries di-versified, her port thriving, and modern buildings adding an air of contemporary dy-namism, Manchester is less a de-Quincey-like hallucination than a slow unfolding of a Lloyd-George dream.

Founded: 79 A.D., as Mancunium, by Agricola; Manchester – from the name of the Ro-man settlement.

Far-reaching events: 14th century – Flemish weavers settle in the small market town; late 18th century – development of cotton manufacturing due to the damp climate and the Industrial Revolution; 1819 – a peaceful civil rights demonstration by workers ends with an invasion of the cavalry (Peterloo); 1830 construction of the railway between Manchester and Liverpool; 1846 – Corn Laws repealed, the age of free trade begins; 1883 – incorporation; 1894 – opening of Manchester Ship Canal; 1951 – Manchester is the first city in Britain to be declared a ›smokeless zone‹.

Population: 2.6 million in Greater Manchester.

Postal code: GB-confusing, depends on street, house number and part of the city.

Telephone code: 61

Climate: mild, but humid and rainy; bring at least two umbrellas.

Best time to visit: May to August.

Calendar of events: *Speedway and Stock Car racing* (Mar–Nov); *Manchester Academy of Fine Art Exhibition* (Apr–May); *Motorcycle Racing* (Apr–Oct); *Manchester Air Show* (May); *Texaco Trophy International Match* (May/Jun) – cricket international; *Ashton Carnival* (Jun); *Lord Mayor's Parade* (Jun); *European Aircraft Championship* (Jul); *The City of Manchester Show* (Aug); *Morris Dancing and Rushcart Festival* (Aug); *Castle-field Carnival* (Sep); *Whitworth Young Contemporaries* (Nov–Dec).

Best view of the city: from the top of the Town Hall.

Historical sights: *Cathedral of St. Mary, St. Denis and St. George* (15th century) – Per-pendicular Gothic with a 19th-century tower; *Town Hall* – neo-Gothic coloured sand-stone, with a magnificent series of paintings illustrating the history of the city; *City Library* – neo-classical; *Main Station* – the oldest train station in the world (for pas-senger travel); *St. Peter's Square* – the city's commercial centre; *Albert Square; Free Trade Hall* – Palladian-style monument to the Manchester-born movement and home of the Hallé Orchestra; *City Art Gallery* – classical-style building by Sir Charles Barry (architect of the Houses of Parliament) – predominantly English paintings; *Whitworth Gallery* – Turner and the Pre-Raphaelites; *John Rylands Library* – neo-Gothic building housing a world-famous collection of early printed books and manuscripts.

Modern sights: *Harbour* – the 56 km/30 miles Manchester Ship Canal connects it with the Irish Sea, navigable for ocean-faring ships; *St. Ann's Square* and *King Street* – the main shopping areas.

Special attractions: *Concerts* by the Hallé Orchestra; the *Peak District* of Derbyshire.

Important companies with headquarters in the city: *Bodycote International* (textiles); *British Aerospace* (aeronautical engineering); *British Vita Group* (foam converters); *Carborundum Abrasives* (industrial abrasives); *Cussons Group* (cosmetics); *East Lan-cashire Paper Group* (paper); *Kellogg* (food products); *Renold* (power transmissions); *Rubber Latex* (rubber); *Sharp Electronics* (electronics engineering); *George H. Scholes* (household appliances); *Tootal* (clothing); *Vantona Viyella* (fabrics).

Airport: Manchester International, MAN; Tel.: 37 17; 16 km/10 miles; British Air-ways, Tel.: 2 28 63 11.

The Headquarters

BRITANNIA

Portland Street
GB–Manchester MI 3 LA
Telephone: 2 28 22 88
Telex: 665 007 rulbri
Managing Director: Alex Langsam
General Manager: Shaun Moriarty
Number of rooms: 360 (57 suites)
Price range: £ 45–225
Credit cards: AE, DC, Access, Visa
Location: city centre
Built: 1851
Style: converted warehouse
Hotel amenities: piano, indoor swimming pool, health club, beauty salon, sauna, solarium, massage, newsstand, hairstylist, doctor on call
Room amenities: colour tv, trouser press
Bathroom amenities: hairdrier, bidet (in suites)
Room service: 24 hours
Laundry/dry cleaning: same day
Conference rooms: 9 (up to 220 persons), ballroom, secretarial services
Bars: ›Spinners‹: (12.00/a.m.–15.00/3 p.m. and 17.00/5 p.m. to midnight), pianist; ›Cromptons‹: (as Spinners Bar) interior of old tobacconist shop, pianist, records
Restaurants: ›Jenny‹: (12.00/a.m.–14.00/2 p.m. and 19.00/7 p.m. to 23.00/11 p.m.), English cuisine, split level, pianist; ›Cromptons‹: (as Jenny), French cuisine, intimate small restaurant, pianist; ›Bobbin Bistro‹: (11.00/a.m.–2.00/a.m.), fast food, basement, wine bar style, pianist
Nightclub: ›Saturday‹: (21.00/9 p.m.–2.00/a.m.), closed Sunday; modern style

The Britannia Hotel represents a perfect symbiosis of Victorian entrepreneurial acumen and Elizabethan adaptability. The former textile warehouse near Piccadilly Station testifies proudly to the key role played by Manchester's businessmen in the Industrial Revolution during the last century. Its skilful conversion, retaining such fine original features as the cantilever staircase and the gold-painted pillars in the foyer, together with the addition of such modern necessities as a health club and a discothèque, has produced a hotel which provides their successors with a suitably elevated environment for their conferences and colloquia, plus recreational facilities for would-be Daley Thompsons and latter-day Gene Kellys alike. In a city where grande hôtellerie belongs to illusion or to the past at most, it is reassuring to know that one doesn't have to flee to Chester's Grosvenor or Birmingham's Plough and Harrow to rest in civilized peace.

RIBER HALL

GB–Matlock Derbyshire DE4 5JU
(74 km/46 miles)
Telephone: (06 29) 27 95
Owner/Managing Director: Alex Biggin
Number of rooms: 11
Price range: £ 47 (single)
          £ 62 (double)
Credit cards: Access, Visa, AE, DC
Location: 74 km/46 miles from Manchester, 48 km/30 miles from airport, in the Peak district, 20 minutes to M1 motorway (Junction 28)
Built: 1400, modernized and converted into country house hotel in 1970
Style: Elizabethan and Jacobean manor house
Hotel amenities: walled garden and orchard, conservatory, all-weather tennis court (no pets allowed)
Room amenities: central heating, colour tv (remote control), mini-bar, radio
Bathroom amenities: bidet, five rooms with jacuzzi
Room service: 7.30/a.m.–22.00/10 p.m.
Laundry/dry cleaning: 24 hours
Conference rooms: one (up to 14 persons), flip charts
Sports nearby: golf, riding (3 km/2 miles)
Bar: one (all day), Jacobean period
Restaurant: ›Riber Hall‹ (7.30/a.m.–9.30/a.m., 12.00/a.m.–13.30/1.30 p.m. and 19.00/7.00 p.m.–21.30/9.30 p.m.), John Brunner (chef de cuisine), French and English cuisine; Jacobean-style décor
Private dining rooms: one (for 14 persons)

Ill-fated Richard II did not live to see the arrival of Riber Hall, and Geoffrey Chaucer never made it up here, either. Maybe he would have immortalized this Decorated manor house built in 1400. Alex Biggin sees to it that this ›Hideaway Break‹ in Derbyshire remains in the annals as well as in the memory of his guests who find their way to the borders of the Peak District National Park, to the peaceful backwater of Riber Village, just outside Matlock. The voyage from Manchester – or Sheffield, Nottingham, Birmingham, or anywhere – is well worth the mystery tour, for there are few relais in the land as authentic in historical interest, personal hospitality and romantic charm. Restored to please a hedonist, a dreamer and a sober aesthete equally, Riber Hall – with its period furniture in the half-timbered rooms – provides just enough luxury not to blind you to the original touches this house is famous for. ›Where excellence is standard‹ for once is a true and therefore forgivable self-praising motto. The salons, lounge and dining room are so cosy you don't want to move anywhere else, but the Jacobean four-poster beds have the same attraction. Sleeping Beauty décor, castle ambiance and the service of angelic maidens tending to every guest as if he had just returned home are as much of an addictive attraction as the candlelight dinners over laudable cuisine and superior wines.

Lunch

TRUFFLES
63 Bridge Street
Telephone: 8 32 93 93
Owner/Manager: John and Ann Steel
Closed: Saturday lunchtime; Sunday;
Monday; Bank Holidays
Open: 12.00/a.m.–14.30/2.30 p.m. and
19.00/7 p.m.–23.00/11 p.m.
Cuisine: French
Specialities: Roquefort and onion tart;
seafood pancake; halibut steak maltaise;
noisettes d'agneau au vin rouge
Location: near the John Rylands Library
Setting: attractive dining room with Vic-
torian-style décor and appropriate acces-
soires
Amenities: private dining room (45 per-
sons)
Atmosphere: welcoming and relaxing
Clientèle: francophile expense-account
gourmets; antiquarian book-lovers; ama-
teur historians; academics and account-
ants
Dress: no special requirements
Service: personal and smiling
Reservations: advisable
Price range: moderately expensive
Credit cards: AE, DC, Visa, Access

Lunch

YANG SING
34 Princess Street
Telephone: 2 36 22 00
Owner/Manager: the Yeung family/
Gerry Yeung
Closed: Christmas Day; three days in
January
Open: 12.00/a.m.–23.30/11.30 p.m.
Cuisine: Cantonese
Chef de cuisine: Harry Yeung
Specialities: dim sum; wun tun soup;
steamed crabmeat balls; lemon and
honey chicken; fried fresh and dried
squid in black bean sauce; octopus and
steamed tripe; stir-fried venison with
winter bamboo shoots and Chinese
mushrooms
Location: central
Setting: recently moved to new premises
in a six-storey building round the corner
from their original restaurant in George
Street
Atmosphere: considered by many to be
Britain's best Cantonese restaurant; a
family-run business which has become an
institution in the Manchester area
Clientèle: large faithful following of regular devotees drawn from Ashton-un-
der-Lyne, Macclesfield and Altrincham –
plus considerable numbers of visitors to
the town attracted by the Yeung family's
culinary reputation

Dress: within reason, come-as-you-
please
Service: proficient and welcoming
Reservations: essential-preferably in ad-
vance
Price range: inexpensive
Credit cards: AE, Access

Dinner

TERRAZZA
14 Nicholas Street
Telephone: 2 36 40 33/2 36 02 50
Closed: Saturday lunchtime; Sunday;
Bank Holidays
Open: 12.00/a.m.–14.30/2.30 p.m. and
19.00/7 p.m.–23.30/11.30 p.m.
Cuisine: Italian
Specialities: pasta (much of it home-
made); calves' liver; deep-fried octopus,
prawn, sole, sardines and baby marrow
(fritto misto di mare); rack of lamb;
stuffed veal; caramelized oranges; hazel-
nut gâteau; profiteroles
Setting: large dining room with luxurious
décor and appropriate accessoires
Amenities: private dining room (60 per-
sons)
Atmosphere: rather sumptuous but not
formidably so
Clientèle: expense-account industrialists
at lunchtime give way to couples with an
anniversary, a birthday or a reunion to
celebrate at night
Dress: jacket and tie de rigueur
Service: friendly
Reservations: essential for dinner
Price range: quite expensive
Credit cards: AE, DC, Visa, Access

Lunch

MOSS NOOK
Ringway Road, Moss Nook
Telephone: 4 37 47 78
Owner/Manager: Pauline and Derek
Harrison
Closed: Sunday; Monday and Saturday
lunchtime; Bank Holidays; two weeks at
Christmas
Open: 12.00/a.m.–14.00/2 p.m. and
19.00/7 p.m.–22.00/10 p.m.
Cuisine: local and European
Chef de cuisine: Robert Thornton
Specialities: chicken pancakes with
mango sauce; scampi with honey; Alas-
kan crab legs; turbot mousse with caviar;
sautéed chicken livers with bacon and apples in red wine sauce with chicory; mussel soup with saffron; salmon and brill
fillets in ginger and cream sauce; Lan-
cashire black pudding with mustard
sauce and chutney
Location: 14 km/9 miles from Manchester; 2 km/1 mile from Manchester Airport

Setting: elegant dining room in shades of red; Edwardian-style décor
Amenities: car park
Atmosphere: nostalgic; stylish and very popular
Clientèle: Manchester's Beau Monde; local government officials, visiting dignitaries, financiers and the occasional ordinary citizen
Dress: jacket and tie
Service: professional and knowledgeable
Reservations: essential
Price range: rather expensive by local standards
Credit cards: AE, DC, Visa, Access

Dinner

LA BONNE AUBERGE
224 Finney Lane
Heald Green (16 km/10 miles)
Telephone: 437 57 01
Owner/Manager: Roger and Cecilia Boutinot
Closed: Sunday; Monday evening; Bank Holidays
Open: 12.00/a.m.–14.00/2 p.m. and 18.30/6.30 p.m.–21.45/9.45 p.m.
Cusine: French (classic)
Chef de cuisine: Roger Boutinot
Specialities: country-style pâté; champignons à la crème; scallops mornay; cassoulet; smoked salmon pancake; ratatouille with Gruyère; raspberry roulade; mille-feuille
Location: 16 km/10 miles south of Manchester along the A5103 and the M56
Setting: set back from the road in a shopping parade; pretty dining rooms on two floors with green check décor, wicker chairs and white table linen
Amenities: private dining room (30 persons), car park
Atmosphere: refreshingly bright and cheerful; a bright star on Manchester's culinary horizon run by the Boutinot family for 25 years
Clientèle: senior executives seeking a respite from the boardroom at lunchtime, entertaining their clients or their wives at night – and local habitués en fête at the weekend
Dress: as you like it
Service: charming
Reservations: essential for lunch and at weekends
Price range: moderately expensive
Credit cards: AE, DC, Access

Café

RUMOURS COFFEE SHOP
Piccadilly Plaza
Telephone: 236 84 14
Owner/Manager: Embassy Hotels Ltd./ D.E. Smith
Closed: never

Open: 10.00/a.m.–24.00/12 p.m.
Location: in the Hotel Piccadilly
Amenities: grills and salads as well as usual café fare; hotel; restaurant; private dining rooms (12–800 persons); car park
Atmosphere: refreshingly genteel
Clientèle: suburban housewives from Cheadle Hulme to Prestbury after the rigours of a day at the sales, plus managing directors and senior executives after the rigours of a morning in the boardroom
Service: cheerfully courteous

Bar

DOWNTOWN
Piccadilly Plaza
Telephone: 236 84 14
Owner/Manager: Embassy Hotels Ltd./D. E. Smith
Closed: never
Open: 11.30/a.m.–14.30/2.30 p.m. and 17.30/5.30 p.m.–22.30/10.30 p.m.
Location: in the Hotel Piccadilly
Setting: luxurious modern piano bar with live music to fill in any awkward gaps in the conversation
Amenities: hotel; restaurant; private dining rooms (12–800 persons); café; car park
Atmosphere: rather transatlantic
Clientèle: hotel guests from Washington to Woomera plus local top industrialists, stockbrokers and businessmen
Service: friendly; supervised by chief barman David Newton
Reservations: advisable
Credit cards: AE, DC, Visa, Access, Master Charge

Nightclub

MILLIONAIRE
West Mosley Street
Telephone: 236 24 66
Owner/Manager: Whitbread Breweries TLC/Richard Drummond
Closed: Tuesday, Sunday
Open: 21.00/9 p.m.–2.00 a.m.
Location: behind Lewis' Department Store
Setting: sophisticated
Amenities: restaurant, discothèque
Atmosphere: soignée; ›the‹ meeting place for the upper class
Clientèle: middle-aged, up market
Dress: dress to impress
Service: impeccable
Reservations: advised for restaurant
Price range: expensive
Credit cards: Access, Visa, DC, AE

Shopping

EVERYTHING UNDER ONE ROOF
Kendal Milne Deansgate

FOR HIM
Austin Reed 4 Exchange Street/
St. Ann's Square

FOR HER
Principles 40 King Street

BEAUTY & HAIR
Razors Edge Fountain Street

JEWELLERY
Boddle and Dunthorne
1 King Street

LOCAL SPECIALITIES
Aston Tobacconist (tobacco)
Royal Exchange Shopping
Centre
Gee, Cecil (men's fashion)
7 St. Ann's Square
Now (children's fashion)
109 Arndale Centre
Marsdens (leather fashion)
43 King Street West
Antony Furs Ltd. (furs)
6 King Street
Willshaw's (books)
16 John Dalton Street
Lawleys Ltd. (porcelain)
Unit F Arndale Centre
Bagatelle (baggage & travel accessories)
Halle Square, Arndale Centre
Habitat Designs (interior decorating)
14 John Dalton Street
Prime Cut (food and beverages)
Unit 125 Arndale Centre
Femme (lingerie)
8 St. Ann's Arcade
Midas (shoes)
22 King Street
Arabica (teas)
Unit G 30, Royal Exchange Shopping
Centre

The City

The image of Southampton which lingers longest in your memory may well be the final one, if you choose as your mode of departure the Queen Elizabeth II, from whose decks you can bid the city a regal farewell as the liner swings majestically out into the Solent on her way to the open sea. Southampton is a town where partings and reunions are part of the fabric of life, from the Pilgrim Fathers en route for Plymouth and a brave New World to the Titanic heading for an iceberg and the bottom of the sea. The town is an important freight harbour as well as Britain's foremost passenger shipping port; sometimes the graceful silhouette of one of Cunard's ships of the line is obscured by the hulk of a supertanker, whilst the Isle-of-White-bound ferries and sailing dinghies tack skilfully between the leviathans of luxury and financial gain. Within the medieval city walls souvenirs of the past jostle with reminders of the present – Saxon artefacts in the God's House Tower Museum, and Graham Sutherland paintings in the Art Gallery. All too often seen as a staging-post on the way to or from London or New York, Southampton – whilst not competing with those cities in terms of size, diversity or cultural attractions – does offer the visitor a congenial insight into the life of a quintessential English seaport. Its industries include computer technology and high-precision engineering, and with the New Forest and the Wessex Downs on the doorstep Southampton is a good base for exploring the countryside of Tess of the d'Urbervilles or Persuasion, for comparing cathedrals at Winchester and Chichester or for investigating the significance of Stonehenge. But the town remains inextricably bound by the ebb and flow of its four high tides a day, overlaying its air of railway-station transience with the faraway-places nostalgia so characteristic of a busy harbour.

Founded: by the Romans as a port, Clausentum, on the River Itchen; Southampton – ›Southern town‹ (from the Saxon)

Far-reaching events: 5th century – a Saxon settlement develops on the ruins of the Roman fort; 12th century – fortified city-port built by the Normans; 12th–16th centuries – development of the port's links with Normandy, Venice and Genoa (spice trade); 1338 – attacked by the French; 1674 – the Titanic started from here on her ill-fated voyage; 19th century – development of Southampton as a major port; 1940 – severe bomb damage during the Blitz.

Population: 215,000.

Postal code: confusing; depends upon street, part of town and house number.

Telephone code: 703; all 5-digit numbers: 7032

Climate: mild.

Best time to visit: May to October.

Fairs and exhibitions: *SOUTHAMPTON INTERNATIONAL BOAT SHOW* (Sep) – largest in-water boat show in the United Kingdom; apart from that Southampton is a congress city.

Best view of the city: from the Clock Tower of the Guild Hall.

Historical Sights: *St. Michael's Church* (11th century) – Norman church, the oldest building in the city; *St. Julian's Church* (1185) – granted by Elizabeth I to the Huguenots who had fled France and Holland; *City Walls* and medieval houses near the *Royal Pier*; *God's House Tower* – Southampton's history from Romans via Saxons to today; *Maritime Museum* – in a medieval warehouse including a large model of the *Queen Mary*; *Eling Tide Mill* – 18th-century mill, the only one in Western Europe still grinding flour; *Bargate* – originally the North Gate of the walled town, now a museum.

Modern sights: *Art Gallery* – British art from 1750, French impressionists, European Old Master paintings of the 17th and 18th centuries; *Hall of Aviation* – museum dedicated to R. J. Mitchell who designed the Spitfire and S6 seaplane in Southampton; *Shamrock Quay,* a vibrant waterfront area where cafés jostle with designer shops and traditional sailing outfitters.

Special attractions: *Harbour* – here the Titanic and the Mayflower started; the Queen Elizabeth II, the Canberra and the Sea Princess are regular visitors; an early evening walk along the *ramparts*; ship-spotting from *Mayflower Park*; *New Forest*; *Broadlands* – gardens landscaped for Lord Palmerston by Capability Brown – home of the late Lord Mountbatten; *Beaulieu Abbey* – National Motor Museum; *Isle of Wight*; *Portsmouth* – Nelson's ›Victory‹, the ›Mary Rose‹ and HMS ›Warrior‹.

Important companies with headquarters in the city: *ARC Marine; B.A.T.* (British American Tobacco); *Chloride Standby Systems* (accumulators, batteries); *Crown House Engineering; Dreamland Electrical Appliances; Esso Chemicals; Mullards* (semi-conductors); *the Ordnance Survey; Pirelli General Cable; Red Funnel Ferries; Skandia Life Assurance; Southern Evening Echo* (newspaper); *Thew Engineering Group; Vero Precision Engineering; Vosper Hovermarine; Westminster Dredging.*

Airport: Southampton-Eastleigh, SOU; Tel.: 61 23 41; 7 km/4 miles.

The Headquarters/The Hideaway

CHEWTON GLEN

Christchurch Road
GB–New Milton, Hampshire BH 25 6QS
Telephone: (42 52) 53 41
Telex: 414 56
Owner: Martin Skan
General Manager: Robin Hutson
Affiliation/Reservation Systems: Relais et Châteaux, The Leading Hotels of the World, Prestige Hotels
Number of rooms: 44 (11 suites)
Price range: £ 50–245
Credit cards: all major
Location: in New Milton
Built: mid-eighteenth century
Style: Georgian-style country manor
Hotel amenities: valet parking, limousine service, swimming pool, tennis court
Room service: 24 hours
Laundry/dry cleaning: same day (weekend service)
Conference rooms: 6 (up to 100 persons)
Bar: ›Marryat‹ François Rossi (barman)
Restaurant: ›Marryat‹ (12.30/p.m.– 19.30/7.30 p.m.) Patrick Gaillard (maître), Pierre Chevillard (chef de cuisine)

Between the squat Norman tower of Winchester Cathedral and the Thomas Hardy memorial in Dorchester lies Southampton's Villa d'Este. From Land's End to London it has no peer for business or pleasure, this Georgian country house on the edge of the New Forest which has earned for its mentor, Martin Skan, a place of honour in the annals of l'Art d'Hospitalité. Chewton Glen stands serene as a Gainsborough painting amidst manicured lawns and fine old trees, its white small-paned windows welcoming against the ivy-clad brick façade. The intérieur is a chef d'œuvre of incomparable antique charm combining historical authenticity with an aura of effulgent freshness which is both jubilant and restful. Every detail, every accessoire reveals a meticulous perfectionism; the wrought-iron carriage lamps and the profusion of pink-and-white flowers before the canopied entrance; the carpeted floor and tapestried fauteuils in the hall; the blithely and romantically chintzy bedrooms, their names recalling the ›Children of the New Forest‹ in honour of Captain Marryat, whose brother once owned the house; the green-and-terracotta dining room, where Troisgros-trained Pierre Chevillard's fine cuisine is served to discriminating businessmen and incognito celebrities from far and wide. They come to Chewton Glen to luxuriate in the all-pervading air of peace and intimacy, to be pampered by the smiling staff, to relax in surroundings which epitomize all that is best in the England everyone dreams about, to enjoy the amenities of one of the Top Twenty summer resort hotels in the world (according to the illustrious IN World Guide). For a paradise of such consummate felicity the final verdict can only be a paean of praise.

Lunch

LA BRASSERIE
33–34 Oxford Street
Telephone: 22 10 46
Owner/Manager: La Luca Group/Antonio Falco
Closed: Saturday lunch; Sunday
Open: 12.00/a.m.–14.00/2 p.m. and 18.30/6.30 p.m.–23.00/11 p.m.
Cuisine: French
Chef de cuisine: Antonio Gentile
Specialities: lobster ›Sofia‹ (lobster and prawns flamed in brandy and glazed with cheese); scampi d'amore (flamed with Pernod and topped with caviar)
Location: central
Setting: light, bright, attractive French-style dining room
Amenities: ceiling fans; bar; car park in the vicinity
Atmosphere: the most exclusive restaurant in town; festive but relaxing
Clientèle: Southampton's social élite; businessmen entertaining prospective customers at lunchtime or celebrating their wedding anniversary at night
Dress: mostly rather formal; jeans not appreciated
Service: friendly and efficient
Reservations: definitely necessary at the weekend (no pets)
Price range: on the expensive side by local standards
Credit cards: AE, DC, Visa, Master Card, Access

Dinner

SIMON'S WINEHOUSE
1 Vernon Walk
Telephone: 3 63 72
Owner/Manager: Simon Foderingham
Closed: never
Open: 10.30/a.m.–14.30/2.30 p.m.; 18.00/6 p.m.–23.00/11 p.m. (weekend till midnight)
Cuisine: international
Specialities: pies; quiches; curries; chilis; home-made sweets plus à la carte menu
Location: near the London Road Post Office
Setting: old world; Dickensian
Amenities: wine bar: 50 different kinds of wines by the glass
Atmosphere: stylish but comfortable
Clientèle: young, self-confident and on-the-way up to middle-aged, successful and decidedly not moribund
Dress: within reason
Service: welcoming
Reservations: advisable for lunch (no pets)
Credit cards: AE, DC, Visa, Access

Lunch

THE OLD HOUSE
The Square
Wickham (17 km/11 miles)
Telephone: (03 29) 83 30 49
Owner/Manager: Richard and Annie Skipwith
Closed: Saturday and Monday lunchtime; Sunday; two weeks in July/August; one week at Christmas; two weeks at Easter
Open: 12.00/a.m.–13.45/1.45 p.m. and 19.00/7 p.m.–21.30/9.30 p.m.
Cuisine: French provincial and modern
Chef de cuisine: Colin Wood
Specialities: weekly changing menu; monkfish in red wine sauce on noodles; salmon with rosemary; fennel and cucumber soup; pot-roasted pheasant with orange sauce; pineapple with black pepper and vanilla ice-cream
Location: in the Old House Hotel at Wickham, 17 km (11 miles) east of Southampton
Setting: high-ceilinged, beamed restaurant in an elegantly uncluttered, beautifully-renovated Queen Anne house overlooking pretty gardens leading down to the River Meon
Amenities: hotel; private dining room (14 persons); bar; car park
Atmosphere: a soupçon of French chic in a welcoming but stylish country house whose owner understands the art of gracious living
Clientèle: Southampton's savants-vivre plus discriminating members of Hampshire's High Society
Dress: elegantly casual for lunch, more formally so for dinner
Service: charming; directed by Annie Skipwith
Reservations: essential (no dogs)
Price range: cheap by Paris standards only
Credit cards: AE, DC, Visa, Access

Dinner

GOLDEN PALACE
17 Above Bar Street
Telephone: 22 66 36
Owner/Manager: Golden Palace Ltd. / Bill Lai
Closed: never
Open: 12.00/a.m.–12/p.m.
Cuisine: Cantonese/Chinese
Chef de cuisine: Y. Lee
Specialities: fillet of beef, Chinese style; dim sum (Cantonese hors d'œuvres)
Location: central
Setting: Chinese Golden Palace décor
Amenities: bar
Atmosphere: cheerfully casual
Clientèle: young and trendy to middle-aged and conventional
Dress: within reason, anything goes
Service: helpful and friendly

Reservations: necessary at the weekend or for large groups (no pets)
Price range: medium
Credit cards: AE, DC, Visa, Access

Bar

SLOANE'S WINE BAR
21 Oxford Street
Telephone: 22 07 85
Owner/Manager: Mr. and Mrs. Coleman
Closed: Sunday
Open: 12.00/a.m.–14.30/2.30   p.m.;
18.00/6 p.m.–22.30/11.30 p.m.
Location: central
Setting: subdued lighting; lots of wood
Amenities: snacks at lunchtime
Atmosphere: unhurried and welcoming
Clientèle: hommes d'affaires; hommes de lettres; hommes de politique; hommes de loisir
Service: with a smile
Reservations: not necessary (pets permitted)
Credit cards: AE, Visa, Access

Nightclub

CASINO SILHOUETTE CLUB
4 St. Michael's Square
Telephone: 22 39 90
Owner/Manager: B. Adamson
Closed: Sunday
Open: 20.00/8 p.m.–2.00/a.m.
Location: in an attractive area of town
Setting: traditional; very comfortable; elegant
Amenities: gambling casino; cabaret with guest artists
Atmosphere: Southampton chic
Clientèle: mostly young, self-assured and on-the-way up
Dress: casually elegant
Service: efficient
Reservations: recommended
Credit cards: AE, DC, Visa, Access

Shopping

EVERYTHING UNDER ONE ROOF
Tyrrel & Green   138 Above Bar

FOR HIM
Wenhams Ltd.   42 Bedford Place

FOR HER
Elaine   80 Bedford Place

BEAUTY & HAIR
Trevor International Ladies Salon
31 Hanover Buildings

JEWELLERY
Parkhouse & Wyatt   96 Above Bar

LOCAL SPECIALITIES
Sergio (men's fashion)
129 Above Bar
Basticks (men & women's fashion)
136 Above Bar
Shrimps (children's fashion)
Unit 2 Shamrock Quay
Clive, Mr. (leather fashion)
6 Bargate
Harley Parish, Court Furrier (furs)
Sable House, 68 Bedford Place
Importers Retail Salerooms Ltd. (gifts: teas)
196 Above Bar
Stoniers & Co. Ltd. (porcelain)
14 The Bargate
Salisbury (baggage & travel accessories)
91 Above Bar
Amalfi (food and beverages)
17 Queens Way
French W. J. & Sons Ltd. (shoes)
40 Bedford Place

The City

Drive up the Sparrow Hills for a first impression. ›Whoever wants to understand Russia must come here and look down on Moscow‹, with Anton Chekov in mind. Or Napoléon. But don't look down on the cradle of Big Brother altogether, even though the hills were renamed after Hawk Lenin. The political reality is as evident as the human warmth – and despite all the shortcomings and the long waits, inconspicuous bystanders with cartoon identities and unfamiliar sounds at night so well-known from the movies, there is nothing you can't have here, at a personalized exchange rate – even though bribing is not in the dictionary of the KGB. It's so much fun to receive a ringside seat for a sold-out Bolshoi performance, an icon for export or caviar for a song. Luxury abounds in the lap of ›Little Mother Moscow‹, as the Russians fondly refer to their cumbersome capital, if only for the Party élite and the partying élite from imperialist lands. Simple pleasures of the businessman are equally rewarding: palaces and churches of all periods, the Red Square with the power-house of sombre socialism, the mausoleum of you-know-who, the Tretjakov Gallery, the Rubljov Museum in the Andronikov Monastery, the decorative Empire mansions where the spirit of Pushkin, Gogol, Turgenyev and Tolstoy comes alive, and the many hidden-away restaurants and bars with wine, women and balalaika bands. Moscow has, with all its might, the personality of a bear learning to dance, ponderous and unwieldy, but somehow lovable in its efforts.

Founded: first mentioned by chroniclers in 1147; Moskva (Russian).

Far-reaching events: 1238 – Mongols set fire to the city, the Tartars conquer it; 1263 – the Principality of Moscow is born; 1326 – seat of the metropolitan (later patriarch) of the Russian Orthodox Church; 1462–1505 – territorial gains by Ivan III result in an end to Tartar domination; 1547 Ivan the Terrible is crowned Tsar; 1571 – Moscow destroyed by the Crimean Tartars; 1613 – the Romanov dynasty begins its rule; 1712 – Peter the Great makes his new city St. Petersburg (now Leningrad) his residence and capital; 1812 – Napoleon in Moscow and the city, largely built of wood, goes up in flames; 1917 – the Revolution; 1918 – Moscow capital once more; 1935 – construction of the subway system begins; 1936–8 – Stalinist Purges; 1941 – German offensive stopped about 32 km/20 miles, from the city centre; 1953 – Khrushchev comes to power; 1961 – Yuri Gagarin is the first man in space.

Population: 8 million; capital of the Union of Soviet Socialist Republics.

Postal code: Moscow 101000–125900.

Climate: very extreme; temperatures as low as $-42°$ C ($-40°$ F) in January and as high as $37°$ C ($98°$ F) in August; July and August are the wettest months.

Calendar of events: *International Women's Day* (Mar 8); *Lenin's Birthday* (Apr 22); *International Labour Day* (May 1) – parades in Red Square; *Moscow Stars Festival of Folk and Classical Music* (May 5–13); *Spring in Moscow* (May) – music festival; *Anniversary of the 1917 Russian Revolution* (Nov 7–8); *Russian Winter Festival* (Dec 25–Jan 5).

Fairs and exhibitions: *TECHNOLOGY* (Mar) – modern technologies in industry and economy; *INTERCON* (Apr) – production and treatment in electronics and microelectronics; *ENERGIE* (Jun) – alternative energy sources; *UPAKOVKA* (Nov–Dec) – packaging techniques.

Historical and modern sights: *Kremlin* – the walled centre of the city – palaces, the Tsars' crown jewels, the parliament of the USSR, the *Cathedrals* of *the Annuciation* (15th–16th centuries), *the Assumption* (1475) and *the Archangel Michael* (1505–9) and the *Bell Tower of Ivan the Great; St. Basil's Cathedral* (1554–60) – built for Ivan the Terrible – the cupolas are a Moscow landmark; *Red Square* – scene of the May Day march-past; *Lenin Mausoleum* – the leader is embalmed in his glass-topped sarcophagus; *Don Monastery* (1591) – one of the city's six fortified monasteries, where services are still held; *Union House* (1784) – one of Moscow's most beautiful former palaces, where prominent dead now lie in state; *GUM* (1888–1894) – what Macy's is to New York, GUM is to Moscow; *House of the Romanov Boyars* (1565–7) – where the dynasty's first members were born, now a samovar museum; *Church of Maria Intercessor and Protectress* (1636) – a prime example of Russian Baroque; *Tretyakov Gallery* (1892) – with 40,000 works by Russian masters of all epochs; *Pushkin Museum* – ancient Oriental and Renaissance art, and French Impressionist paintings; *Lenin Museum.*

Special attractions: the *Metro,* Moscow's artistically decorated subway – the grandest station is at *Komsomolskij Square; Gorki Street* (leading from the airport) and *Kirov Street* (from Dserschinskij Square, home of the KGB, to Komsomolskij Square) – the best streets for admiring Moscow's architecture of old; the *Television Tower* – the second highest in the world; the *Moscow Swimming Pool* – the largest in the world; an evening at the *Bolshoi ballet,* the *Moscow State Opera,* a *concert* or the *circus; ice skating* in winter; the *international departure lounge* at Sheremetyevo Airport.

Important companies with headquarters in the city: *Almasjuwelierexport; Awiaexport; Awtopromimport; Elektronorgtechnika; Exportles; Maschinoimport; Maschpriborimport; Metallurgimport; Promsyrjoimport; Rasnoexport; Rasnoimport; Sojuschimexport; Sojusgasexport; Sojuspromexport; Sojusposchnina; Sojuswneschstrojimport; Stankoimport; Strojmaterialimport; Technointorg; Technopromimport; Traktoroexport.*

Airport: Moscow-Sheremetyevo, SVO; Tel.: 1 55 50 05; 30 km/18 miles.

The Headquarters

MEZHDUNARODNAYA

12 Krasnopresnenskaya Naberzhkaya
USSR–123 610 Moscow
Telephone: 2 53 77 29/2 53 90 00/2 56 63 03
Telex: 411 486 sovin
Owning company: V/O Sovincentr
General Manager: F.K. Kriouchko
Number of rooms: 594
Price range: Rbls 50–250
Credit cards: AE, DC, CB, EC, Visa
Location: close to the Krasnopresnens-
kaya underground station
Built: 1980
Style: modern first class luxury hotel
Hotel amenities: shops, transport ser-
vices, travel office, hairdresser, beauty
parlour, house doctor
Room service: 24 hours
Laundry/dry cleaning: same day (week-
end service)
Conference rooms: for up to 600 persons;
all modern conference facilities including
interpreters, secretarial services
Sports: Health Club, swimming pools,
gym, seven Finnish saunas, massage
Bars: ›Atrium Café‹ (8.00/a.m.–23.00/11
p.m.), ›Cocktail Bar‹ (17.00/5 p.m.–
2.00/a.m.), ›Bier-Stube‹ (11.00/a.m.–
15.00/3 p.m. and 18.00/6 p.m.–23.00/11
p.m.), ›Dolphin Bar‹ (11.00/a.m.–
22.30/10.30 p.m.), integrated into the
Health Club, ›Concert and Terrace Bar‹
(11.00/a.m.–23.00/11 p.m.)
Restaurants: ›Russky‹ (12.00/a.m.–
23.00/11 p.m.), Russian cuisine and
›Continental‹ international cuisine ›Mer-
cury‹ (13.30/1.30 p.m.–24.00/12 p.m.), intimate restaurant with live entertainment,
›Sakura‹ (12.00/a.m.–14.00/2 p.m. and
18.00/6 p.m.–22.00/10 p.m.), Japanese
restaurant, ›Express‹ (8.00/a.m.–
10.00/a.m. and 13.00/1 p.m.–15.00/3
p.m.) unconventional

*The first-time visitor to Moscow is not
likely to be impressed by the Mezhdunarodnaya as deeply as by the Kremlin or St.
Basil's Cathedral, but he will be favourably
surprised that this large modern hotel,
which has been integrated into the WTC
(Moscow Centre for International Trade,
Scientific and Technical Cooperation with
Foreign Countries), offers all facilities
which a Western businessman or holiday-
maker could hope for. Apart from the comfortable bedrooms there are so many bars
and restaurants to choose from that one
could easily meet in a different place for a
week without having to leave the building.
Japanese cuisine, Finnish sauna, French
wines and native company after hours may
make you forget about all the ›wrong‹
propaganda behind the Iron Curtain (seen
from here).*

Lunch

SLAVIANSKII BAZAR
(›The Slavic Fair‹)
13 Ulitsa 25 Oktiabria
Telephone: 2 28 48 45/2 21 18 72
Closed: never
Open: (Monday–Saturday) 11.00/a.m.–
24.00/12 p.m.; (Sunday and public holidays) 13.00/1 p.m.–24.00/12 p.m.
Cuisine: Russian
Specialities: fish soup Slavic style (ukhapo-slavianski); blinis; cucumber salad with sour cream; jellied pike; old-style Moscow meat and potato bouillon with rasstegai; beef cooked in a clay pot (Goviadina porusski gorschochke); ice-cream
Location: near the Dsershinskaja underground station
Setting: established in 1870 but renovated in 1966 after a period of disrepair; décor presumably intended to be reminiscent of the original restaurant, but in fact a basically modern, enormous pink dining room with an ornate fountain in the centre and an electrically illuminated mural depicting an old Russian folk tale
Amenities: second dining room in red; niches and gallery affording the least public (and most coveted) tables; music; dancing
Atmosphere: historically speaking, the most important restaurant in Moscow due to its original inception as the first specifically Russian restaurant; nowadays bathed in neon light and vaguely reminiscent of a waiting-room (due to the slowness of the service, perhaps?)
Clientèle: Moscow's intelligentsia at the turn of the century, including writers (Chekhov and Tolstoy) and composers (Tchaikovsky and Rimsky-Korsakov); nowadays much favoured by courting couples
Dress: rather conservative
Service: Moscow charm
Reservations: recommended
Price range: medium (Intourist coupons accepted)

Dinner

NATSIONAL (›National‹)
1 Ulitsa Gor'kogo
Telephone: 2 03 55 95
Closed: never
Open: 12.00/a.m.–24.00/12 p.m.
Cuisine: Russian
Specialities: English menu; the best bortsch in Moscow (served with crisp cheese pastry); mixed fish hors d'oeuvres with vodka; beef Stroganoff; chicken Kiev; fish salinka; caviar; cream cake (›Tort Natsional‹)
Location: in the Hotel Natsional; near the Ploschtschad Rewoljuzii underground station
Setting: seven dining rooms on the second floor; principal restaurant with understated turn-of-the-century décor, painted ceiling and (from the coveted window-seats) a view of St. Basil's Cathedral and the Kremlin (illuminated until midnight)
Amenities: hotel; fairly subdued music and dancing; foreign currency bar
Atmosphere: quiet and restrained, but not very private
Clientèle: middle-aged, well-dressed and cultured Soviet and foreign customers following in the footsteps of virtually every resident and visiting VIP from Lenin onwards
Dress: fairly decorous (pin-stripes allowed)
Service: Soviet expert
Reservations: necessary (be prepared to share your table with a stranger)
Price range: medium (foreign currency only accepted in two of the dining rooms; Intourist coupons accepted elsewhere)
Credit cards: AE (but check beforehand)

Dinner

PRAGA
2 Arbat Square
Telephone: 2 90 62 00/2 90 61 71/
2 90 62 63 (reservations)
Closed: never
Open: 11.00/a.m.–24.00/12 p.m.
Cuisine: Russian
Specialities: multilingual menu offering (subject to availability!) roast pork (a rarity in Moscow) with dumplings and sauerkraut; hot sausage (vuršty) with potato salad; sturgeon in aspic; bortsch with cheese pastries; rich chocolate cream cake (Tort Praga) – Moscow's Sacher Torte
Location: near the Arbatskaya underground station
Setting: on three floors; main dining room on third floor with wood panelling, murals of Prague, massive columns and gigantic candelabras; two winter-gardens reminiscent of turn-of-the-century palm courts; dining on roof garden terrace in summer
Amenities: café bakery on ground floor; several orchestras for listening or dancing to; partial air conditioning
Atmosphere: an aura of gentility vaguely recalling the old Lyon's Corner House in the Strand; one of the more intimate restaurants in the city
Clientèle: foreign businessmen entertaining Russian delegations (and vice-versa); Soviet army generals; German industrialist, Romanian party bosses and some of the most attractive girls in Moscow

Dress: mostly rather festive
Service: very good
Reservations: essential
Price range: rather expensive (Intourist coupons accepted)

Lunch

ARAGVI
6 Ulitsa Gor'kogo
Telephone: 2 29 37 62
Closed: never
Open: 12.00/a.m.–23.30/11.30 p.m.
Cuisine: Georgian
Specialities spiced cold chicken in walnut sauce (Zatsivi); chicken tabaka; broiled sturgeon; shashlik; deep-fried cheese (sulguni) with fresh bread; Georgian wines, especially Mukuzani; Georgian brandies
Location: near the Pushkinskaja underground station
Setting: cavern-like marble rooms with high ceilings and murals depicting Georgian legends; balcony above main dining room with folk ensemble playing traditional Georgian music
Amenities: private dining rooms; dancing – often Georgian – between the tables
Atmosphere: somewhat staider than in its heyday during the Stalin era, when Cossacks danced with knives between their teeth, but still indisputably one of Moscow's most hospitable and popular restaurants
Clientèle: a favourite rendezvous for Muscovites and visiting Georgians intent upon a gay evening on the town, not to mention top Russians and foreigners from Winston Churchill onwards
Dress: lounge suit to national dress
Service: Georgian waitresses with big brown eyes
Reservations: essential (you may still have to queue!)
Price range: expensive (Intourist coupons accepted)

Lunch

RUS
Blashinskij Rayon
Telephone: 3 08 07 78
Open: 12.00/a.m.–23.00/11 p.m.
Location: east of the motorway ring; approximately 30 km/19 miles from Moscow
Setting: on a lake; surrounded by birch woods; restaurant with bar, attractive terrace and gipsy entertainment in the evenings
Atmosphere: picture-postcard Russia within reach of the capital

Dinner

METROPOL (›Metropole‹)
1 Prospekt Marska
Telephone: 2 28 40 60/2 25 62 04
Closed: never
Open: 11.00/a.m.–24.00/12 p.m.
Cuisine: Russian
Specialities: bortsch; beef Stroganoff; chicken Kiev; chicken tabaka; fish; partridge with jam (Kuropatka Svareniem)
Location: in the Hotel Metropol; near the Prospekt Marksa underground station
Setting: Palm Court glamour à la moscovite – spacious dining room with mirrored walls, enormous crystal chandeliers, angel fountain and the inevitable potted palms; not to mention the eight-piece orchestra – now, alas, just as insistent as most modern dance-bands
Amenities: hotel; tea room (fourth floor); foreign-currency bar
Atmosphere: pre-1914 nostalgia; bright and cheerful at lunchtime; subdued lighting at night
Clientèle: generations of overseas visitors – ambassadors, delegates, resident Americans from John Reed to Lillian Hellman
Dress: not too casual
Service: rather slow and inclined to be blasé
Reservations: not necessary, but try to avoid the rush hours
Price range: medium
Credit cards: AE (but check beforehand)

Dinner

BAKU
13 Ulitsa Shvernika
Telephone: 1 27 32 83
Closed: never
Open: 11.00/a.m.–23.00/11 p.m.
Cuisine: Azerbaidjanian
Specialities: stuffed tomatoes or aubergines; marinated onions or garlic (if you and your companion can stand it!); rice soup; meat and rice cooked in potato soup; shashlik; 20 different pilafs; meat and rice cooked in vine leaves (golubtsy); roast lamb with pomegranates (narkuma)
Location: near the Majakowskaja underground station
Setting: named after the capital of Azerbaidjan, a port on the Caspian Sea; small, intimate rooms with stained-glass windows, brass lamps, carpets on the walls and a small fountain
Amenities: music; dancing
Atmosphere: more than a hint of Eastern exoticism
Clientèle: Azerbaidjani in exile, Muscovites with a penchant for the oriental – and a sprinkling of curious tourists
Dress: nothing too outlandish
Service: quick but unhurried
Reservations: necessary
Price range: medium

Dinner

RUSSKAJA ISBA
(›Russian Peasant Hut‹)
Iljinskaje village
Telephone: 5 61 42 44/2 53 75 04 ext. 44
Open: 12.00/a.m.–23.00/11 p.m.
Location: 20 km/12 miles from Moscow
Setting: ›Russian farmhouse‹ built of
wood with traditional décor overlooking
the River Moskva; dancing at night
Amenities: rural Russia à la Intourist –
popular amongst foreign groups and
delegations

Meeting Point

RUSSKAIA CHAINAIA
(›Russian Tea-Room‹)
1 Prospekt Marksa
Telephone: 2 28 40 60
Closed: never
Open: 14.00/2 p.m.–24.00/12 p.m.
Location: in the Hotel Metropol; near the
Prospekt Marksa underground station
Setting: spacious, domed room on the
fourth floor of the hotel; beautiful folk
décor; samovar and traditional-style
cloth on each table; overhead balcony
with balalaika orchestra at night; the longest line of stacked dolls (Matreshki) you
are ever likely to see
Amenities: hotel; restaurant; foreign currency bar
Atmosphere: a convenient and attractive
spot for a snack or a light meal during the
day or after the theatre, tourist trap/gold-
fish bowl ambience notwithstanding
Clientèle: primarily tourists from Nash-
ville, Nuremberg and Naples who have
the foreign currency available to pay the
bill
Service: multilingual but often mercenary
and inattentive

Meeting Point

ARBAT
29 Prospekt Kalinina
Telephone: 2 91 11 34/2 02 81 58
Closed: never
Open: 12.00/a.m.–17.00/5 p.m.
Location: near the Kalininskaiia underground station
Setting: cavernous restaurant seating
2,000 at a time at the end of the most
modern section of Kalinin Prospekt, a
grandiose modern architectural ensemble
in the centre of Moscow; overhead balcony with neon signs illuminated at
show-time
Amenities: restaurant; orchestra; dancing; floor show (circus acrobats, singers

and chorus girls with some of the shortest
hemlines east of the Urals)
Atmosphere: big; brash; good, clean fun
but not exactly intimate
Clientèle: party members en fête; local
top brass; overseas admirers of Soviet-
style variety shows from Sacramento,
Stockholm and Sofia
Service: at its best before or after (but not
during) the show
Reservations: essential

Bar

LABYRINTH BAR
3–5 Uliza Gorkowa
Telephone: 2 03 13 45
Closed: never
Open: 20.00/8 p.m.–2/a.m.
Location: in the Hotel Intourist; near the
Ploschtschad Rewoljuzii underground
station
Setting: the newest and noisiest of the
foreign-currency bars; Soviet Modern;
maze of interconnecting rooms with raw
concrete walls and massive, precariously-
suspended light fittings with such low-
wattage bulbs that the ambience is almost
sexy
Amenities: hotel; restaurant
Atmosphere: bunker-like charm with
pandemonium at the bar, especially in
the rush hour (1.00/a.m. – closing time)
Clientèle: fellow-travellers; Intourists in
search of company
Service: mini-skirted waitresses and overworked barmen and -maids (erratic pri-
cing of drinks is the norm)
Reservations: you have been warned

Bar

NATIONAL BAR
1 Uliza Gorkowo
Telephone: 2 03 55 66
Closed: never
Open: 13.00/1 p.m.–24.00/12 p.m.
Location: in the Hotel Natsional; near
the Ploschtschad Rewoljuzii underground station
Setting: foreign-currency bar on the second floor of the hotel (turn right at the
top of the stairs and head for the noise);
vaguely café-like décor, with a shortage
of tables and chairs (be prepared to share
the former if not the latter); Polish juke-
box with no song-titles
Amenities: hotel; restaurant; late-night
restaurant across the corridor serving
meals until 1 a.m. (at a price; payable in
hard currency only)
Atmosphere: permanently hung-over, but
reputedly one of the places where the action is
Clientèle: erstwhile home-from-home of
foreign correspondents; now the haunt of
Finnish businessmen, London taxi-driv-

ers, students and ladies with no fixed programme for the evening
Service: friendly barmaids who charge for drinks as they see fit and dispense change in any currency which comes to hand

Shopping

EVERYTHING UNDER ONE ROOF
GUM Krasnaja ploschtschad

FOR HIM
ZUM 2 Ul. Petrowka

FOR HER
ZUM 2. Ul. Petrowka

BEAUTY & HAIR
Hotel ›Mezhdunarodnaya‹
12 Krasnopresnenskaya Nab.

JEWELLERY
›Samozwety‹ 35 Arbat

LOCAL SPECIALITIES
›Swetlana‹ (women's fashion)
9 Kusnezkij most
›Ruslan‹ (men's fashion)
3 Smolenskaja ploschtschad
Detskij mir (children's fashion)
2 Prospekt Marxa
›Berioska‹ (furs)
Hotel ›Mezhdunarodnaya‹
Moskowskij dom knigi (books)
26 Prospekt Kalinina
Russkij suwenir (gifts)
9 Kutusowskij prospekt
Dom farfora (porcelain)
36 Leninskij prospekt
›Moskowskij‹ (baggage & travel accessories)
Komsomolskaja ploschtschad
Gastronom Nr. 1 (food and beverages)
14 Ul. Gorkogo
Berioska (perfumery)
56 Ul. Dorogomilowskaja

THE BEST OF ART
Centralnyi Hudojestvennyi Salon hf SSR (modern art)
6 Ukrainskii Bulvar
Hudojestvennyi Salon n. 1 Hudfonda RSFSR (modern art)
12 Ul. Petrowka
Salon-Magazin Hudojnik RSFSR (modern art) 54 Ul. Dimitrova

The City

The ones believing in poetic justice will have a hard time defending their cause when it comes to qualifying Belgrade as a beautiful, sizzling or amusing city – it is much like entering your mongrel into Cruft's Dog Show. But ask any of the one million Belgradians if they wanted to move to Paris, London or Rome, and they would probably stay put – let alone changing over to Zagreb. Yugoslavia's capital is no showcase for architecture, grandeur, life-style or joie-de-vivre, but, trying hard to manœuvre between the political fronts, its line of sight is directed towards stability and progress rather than competing with Budapest for Number-One status east of Vienna. The ›White Fortress‹ may well be a white spot on the map of the Cartier crowds, but as a sorely tried metropolis for centuries by innumerable wars and occupations, it enjoys peace for once and the beautiful blue Danube waltzing along its shores with the Sava River falling into step right here. There are representative monuments of its recent history – and a few traces of the 2000-year past, if you look hard enough – and all the other achievements functional pragmatism under a stiff rule bring forth. The cafés in the Bohemian Quarter and a few Western-oriented establishments showing signs of joyful decadence enliven the city for the itinerant businessman in search of bargains and slivovitz conviviality.

Founded: first mentioned by Herodotus in the 5th century, B.C.; Beograd (Serbo-Croat); Belgrade – ›white fortress‹

Far-reaching events: 4th century B.C. – a Celtic fortress; 1st century B.C. – conquered by the Romans; 7th century A.D. – a Slav settlement; 10th century – Bulgarian rule; 12th century – Hungarian rule; 1284 – Belgrade invaded by the Serbians, who adopt it as their principal city; 1521–1867 – Belgrade under Turkish rule apart from short periods of Austrian domination; 1806 – the city becomes the official capital of Serbia; 1918 – capital of the Kingdom of Yugoslavia; 1941 – two thirds of the city destroyed in air attack; 1944 – Soviet and partisan troops capture the city; 1946 – capital of the Socialist Federal Republic of Yugoslavia.

Population: 1.4 million; capital and largest city of Yugoslavia and its constituent republic Serbia.

Postal code: YU-11000   **Telephone code:** 11

Climate: continental – hot summers and rather harsh winters.

Best time to visit: April to June and September to October.

Calendar of events: *International Film Festival* (Mar); *Youth Day* (25 May) – with a wide variety of sports events; *International Belgrade Theatre Festival* (Sep) – a world-renowned gathering of avant-garde theatre groups; *Belgrade Music Celebrations* (May and Oct); *Belgrade Jazz Festival* (Nov).

Fairs and exhibitions: *INTERNATIONAL LEATHER GOODS AND SHOE FAIR* (mid-Mar); *INTERNATIONAL AUTOMOBILE SALON* (Apr); *INTERNATIONAL SPORTS, NAUTICAL AND TOURISM FAIR* (Apr); *INTERNATIONAL TECHNICAL FAIR* (May); *INTERNATIONAL EXHIBITION OF SAFETY AT WORK AND ENVIRONMENTAL PROTECTION* (Sep); *INTERNATIONAL FASHION FAIR* (Oct); *INTERNATIONAL BOOK FAIR* (Oct); *INTERNATIONAL FURNITURE, FURNISHINGS AND INTERIOR DECORATION EXHIBITION* (Nov); *INTERNATIONAL FOOD FAIR* (Dec).

Best views of the city: from the *Kalemegdan citadel* overlooking the city; from the top of the high-rise building at Terazije Square.

Historical and modern sights: *Orthodox Cathedral* (1837–45) – with tombs of princes and a valuable collection of icons; the *Kalemegdan Heights* – dominating the confluence of the Sava and the Danube – fortress (1717–39) with churches, museums and gardens; *Royal Palace* (1882), now the seat of Yugoslavia's Executive Council; *Baryak Mosque* (17th century) – the last of the city's 20 mosques; the *Roman Fountain* (15th century); the Doric ›*Victors' Columns*‹ (19th century); *Prince Eugene Gate* (18th century) – Baroque in form; *National Museum* – local history, medieval religious frescoes and icons, and an art gallery containing a fine collection of Impressionist paintings; *Gallery of Frescoes* – 9th–15th-century masterpieces in reproduction; *Ethnographic Museum* – a collection of local costumes, implements and musical instruments revealing the ethnic differences within Yugoslavia; the modern *Congress Centre* ›Sava‹, equipped with the most modern facilities, where the 1977 Conference on Security and Cooperation in Europe was held; the modern *Government Building*; the modern *Neo-Beograd* residential district – housing for 200,000; *House of Flowers* – Tito's tomb.

Special attractions: *Skadarlija* – reconstructed turn-of-the century street with cafés; restaurants and musicians, poets and entertainers; opera at the *National Theatre*; a *hydrofoil trip* on the Danube; early morning open-air *peasant markets*.

Important companies with headquarters in the city: *Energoprojekt* (energy); *Generalexport* (exports); *Hempro* (chemical exports); Jugometal (metals); *Rudnap* (mining); *Yugotours* (travel).

Airport: Belgrade-Surcin, BEG; Tel.: 60 15 55 or 60 55 55, 17 km/10 miles; Yugoslav Airlines, Belgrade, Tel.: 13 13 92 or 13 84 16.

The Headquarters

**BELGRADE
INTER-CONTINENTAL**

10 Vladimira Popovica
YU–11070 Belgrade
Telephone: 13 87 08
Telex: 1 20 09 ichbeg
Owning Company: Generalexport – Belgrade
General Manager: Zoran Kojic
Affiliation/Reservation Systems: Intercontinental Corp. – Panamac
Number of rooms: 420 (30 suites)
Price range: US$ 98 (single)
                US$ 124 (double)
                US$ 195 (suite)
Credit cards: all major
Location: 3 km/2 miles from city centre, 15 km/9 miles from airport
Built: 1979
Style: modern
Hotel amenities: grand piano, health club, beauty salon, sauna, solarium, massage, hairstylist, newsstand, drugstore, boutique, tobacconist, florist, bank, car rental, doctor

Room amenities: air conditioning, colour tv (remote control), video, minibar
Bathroom amenities: bidet, bathrobe, hairdrier
Room service: 24 hours
Laundry/dry cleaning: same day
Conference rooms: 6 (up to 960 persons), overhead projector, film projector, microphones, secretarial services, ballroom
Sports: tennis court
Piano Bar: (9.00/a.m.–24.00/12.00 p.m.) pianist, records, modern, elegantly casual, modern paintings
Restaurants: ›Rôtisserie‹ (12.00/a.m.–16.00/4.00 p.m. and 19.00/7.00 p.m.–23.00/11.00 p.m.) French international cuisine, records, casually elegant; ›Le Club‹ (9.00/a.m.–23.00/11.00 p.m.) snacks, pianist; ›Brasserie‹ (6.00/a.m.–23.00/11.00 p.m.) international and regional cuisine, informal, modern paintings exhibited

Nightclub: (22.00/10.00 p.m.–2.00/a.m.) discothèque, modern décor
Private dining rooms: four

*As the world is getting smaller (way across political and philosophical boundaries) the Western hotels' Eastern dépendances get bigger, not to confront the dealers and wheelers from the decadent occident with the bare necessities of the other side.
The increasing numbers of men of commerce who visit Belgrade and who stay in the Hotel Inter-Continental invariably find that trips into town – despite its proximity – seem superfluous. The green glass edifice next to the Sava Conference Centre is a model of all-embracing modernity; from the bedrooms to the bars, from the secretary to the sauna, you can eat, sleep shop, work and play in twentieth century comfort without leaving the premises.*

Lunch

DVA JELENA (›Two Stags‹)
32 Skardarska
Telephone: 33 48 85
Owner/Manager: Zoran Randjelović
Closed: never
Open: 10.00/a.m.–1.30/a.m.
Cuisine: national
Chef de cuisine: Vlada Opanković
Specialities: grilled meat; noisettes Dva Jelena; Sumadian fillet; steak à la Vlasta Carevac
Location: in Skadarlija, the old bohemian part of Belgrade
Setting: established in 1832; typical rustic Serbian décor
Amenities: pianist; orchestra; outdoor dining in garden; air conditioning
Atmosphere: lively; casual; from quiet to frenzied as the evening progresses; very crowded about midnight
Clientèle: businessmen; celebrities from home and abroad; actors; singers
Dress: as the mood takes you
Service: efficient and helpful
Reservations: advisable (pets in garden only)
Price range: medium to rather expensive
Credit cards: AE, DC

Dinner

KLUB KNJIZEVNIKA
7 Francuska
Telephone: 62 79 31
Owner/Managers: Ivo Kusalic and Budimir Blagojevic
Closed: Sunday; August
Open: 19.00/7 p.m.–2.00/a.m.
Cuisine: Yugoslavian, Italian and French
Chef de cuisine: Mile Brkic
Specialities: steak tartare; lamb; a variety of national dishes
Location: central
Setting: plenty of wood; small, intimate tables for two or (in summer) a lovely garden for alfresco dining
Amenities: private dining room (50 persons)
Atmosphere: confidential, with a hint of romance
Clientèle: a favourite meeting-place amongst the trendier Belgrade politicians, together with fair numbers of artists, painters, writers and actors
Dress: as you like it
Service: anxious-to-please; German and Italian spoken
Reservations: essential – preferably at least two days in advance
Price range: rather expensive by Belgrade standards
Credit cards: not accepted

Lunch

SAVA CLUB
Ada Cigalija
Telephone: 55 85 88
Owner/Manager: Miodrag Mihailović
Closed: Monday
Open: 13.00/1 p.m.–4.00/a.m.
Cuisine: international and traditional Serbian
Chef de cuisine: Rajko Milanović
Specialities: fish (according to availability); freshwater fish steak; fish soup
Location: on an island on the river Sava, not far from the fairground
Setting: classic boat-cruiser
Amenities: outdoor dining
Atmosphere: definitely different
Clientèle: favourite venue for entertaining visiting industrialists, plus resident diplomats and a sprinkling of tourists
Dress: casually elegant for lunch; more emphatically so for dinner
Service: welcoming and professional
Reservations: advisable (pets permitted)
Price range: medium to expensive
Credit cards: not accepted (cash only)

Dinner

CLUB 42
42 Save Kovačeviča
Telephone: 45 68 88
Owner/Managers: the Gavrilović family
Closed: Sunday; July 15th – August 15th
Open: 9.00/a.m.–23.00/11 p.m.
Cuisine: Italian-French
Chef de cuisine: Djordje Djordević
Specialities: pepper steak; Oscar fillet; a variety of Italian pizzas
Location: in Belgrade's residential area
Setting: vaguely Art Nouveau; wood and brass; mostly small tables for two or three; séparées; permanent display of contemporary paintings
Amenities: air conditioning
Atmosphere: pleasantly informal; rather intimate
Clientèle: young; trendy; with-it
Dress: usually fairly casual
Service: engagingly friendly
Reservations: essential (pets prohibited)
Price range: modest
Credit cards: not accepted

Dinner

RESTOTHEQUE ›TOČAK‹ (›Wheel‹)
39 Reljkovićeva, Petrovaradin, Novi Sad
Telephone (21) 43 21 20
Owner/Manager: Stošljević Milorad
Closed: Monday; July
Open: 20.00/8 p.m.–4.00/a.m.
Cuisine: national, international and Italian
Chef de cuisine: Vinka Miholjčić

Specialities: Caré Točak; grilled meat; pancakes and pizzas of all kinds
Location: near Petrovaradin fortress, one hour's drive from Belgrade
Setting: rustic Spanish style restaurant/discothèque with large terrace for open-air dining or drinks
Amenities: orchestra; first-rate entertainment in the shape of a DJ who has twice taken the second prize at a world dancing contest; air conditioning
Atmosphere: attractive in a slightly self-conscious way (le m'as-tu vu de Belgrade)
Clientèle: twentieth-century Vanity Fair
Dress: eye-catchingly casual
Service: polished and professional
Reservations: advisable
Price range: exclusively expensive (membership fee or per night entrance fee)
Credit cards: DC, Visa

Café

GALERIJA
3 Deliska
Telephone: 62 12 90
Owner/Manager: Dragan Kapičić
Closed: Sunday before 17.00/5. p.m.
Open: 8.00/a.m.–22.00/10 p.m.
Location: central
Setting: French-style café
Atmosphere: easy-going; informal; jovial; friendly
Clientèle: youthful, successful, energetic – popular haunt amongst local athletes and sportsmen
Service: with a smile

Bar

TP – TERAZIJE
1 Terazije
Telephone: 33 35 11
Owner/Manager: Hreljac Miomir
Closed: Sunday
Open: 9.00/a.m.–00.30/12.30 a.m.
Location: central
Setting: Renaissance English pub
Amenities: restaurant (Italian cuisine); terrace for open-air dining or drinks; air conditioning
Atmosphere: intimate; légère
Clientèle: young and on-the-way-up to middle-aged but definitely not moribund
Service: charming and attentive
Reservations: advisable (pets permitted)
Credit cards: not accepted

Nightclub

NANA
1 Koste Glavinića
Telephone: 64 87 77
Owner/Manager: Miroljub Kurtović
Closed: July 15th – August 15th
Open: 19.00/7 p.m.–2.00/a.m.
Location: in the residential area near the Belgrade Fair
Setting: modern nightclub with some surrealist details
Amenities: occasional whisky parties and fashion shows; air conditioning
Atmosphere: easy-come, easy-go
Clientèle: artists, models and birds of passage from air hostesses to jet-set tycoons
Dress: anything goes
Service: personal and relaxed
Reservations: advisable (definitely no dogs)
Price range: modest to expensive (depending on what you order)
Credit cards: AE, Visa

Shopping

EVERYTHING UNDER ONE ROOF
Novi Beograd   18 P. komune

FOR HIM
Merkator   7 P. Toljatija

FOR HER
Standard Konfekcija Muski Salon
5 P. Toljatija

BEAUTY & HAIR
Zvonko (hairdresser for men)
Kosovska Street

JEWELLERY
Zlatarna Celje, Terazije 1

LOCAL SPECIALITIES
Jugoslovenska Knjiga (books)
2 Knez Mihajlova
Sebastian (gifts)
29a Knez Mihajlova
Toko (baggage & travel accessories)
Terazijski Prolaz
Centroprom (food and beverages)
27 Maršala Tita

THE BEST OF ART
Galerija Studentskog
Kulturnog Centra   (modern art)
48 Marsala Tita Tel. 65 92 77
ZEL Vuka Icaradžiča 7A
Simonida   Sava Congress Centre
Milentida   (antiques) 9 Popovića

Companies (Headquarters)

A

A.B.G. Semca (Toulouse)
Abbott Diagnostic
    Products (Wiesbaden)
Abital (Verona)
Abnox (Vaduz)
Acciaieri Ferr. Lombarde
    Falck (Milan)
ACEC (Brussels)
Acmat (Paris)
·ACUM (Karlsruhe)
Adambräu (Innsbruck)
Adelphi (Milan)
ADS Anker (Gütersloh)
Aebi (Zurich)
AEG Telefunken (Frankfurt, Berlin)
Aer Lingus (Dublin)
Aeritalia (Naples)
Aerotransporti Italiai (Naples)
Agfa-Gevaert (Antwerp)
Agio Tobacco (Valletta)
Agip Petrol (Rome)
Agpol (Warsaw)
Agrob Wessel Servais (Bonn)
Agromachinaimpex (Sofia)
Agromet-Motoimport (Warsaw)
Agros (Warsaw)
Ahlström, A. (Helsinki)
Air Liquide (Paris, Liège)
Air Malta (Valletta)
Airbus (Toulouse)
Ajax (Monte-Carlo)
Alcina (Gütersloh)
Aldi (Essen)
Alfa Romeo (Milan)
Alfasud (Naples)
Alitalia (Rome)
Allianz (Munich)
Allibert (Paris, Grenoble)
Almasjuwelierexport (Moscow)
Alu-Suisse (Reykjavik)
Aluminium de Grèce (Athens)
Aluminium Ltd (Valletta)
Amalgamated Engineers
    Supplies (Valletta)
·Amey Roadstone Corp (Bristol)
Amsterdam Rotterdam Bank
    (Amsterdam)
Anderson Strathclyde (Glasgow)
André & Cie (Lausanne)
Andritz (Graz)

Ansaldo (Genoa)
Antimex (Warsaw)
Antinori (Florence)
Arbed (Luxembourg)
ARC Marine (Southampton)
Arcotronics Italia (Bologna)
Ardag og Sundal Verk (Oslo)
Arland (Graz)
Armani, Giorgio (Milan)
Armazens da Matinha (Oporto)
Ascheoug, H. & Co (Oslo)
Assicurazioni Generale (Venice)
Ast (Graz)
Asta Werke (Gütersloh)
ATI MEC (Turin)
Atlas Copco (Stockholm)
Atlas Tool and Engine (Valletta)
Atochem (Paris)
Atomic (Salzburg)
Augustiner (Munich)
Austria Philips (Vienna)
Austria Puma (Salzburg)
Austria Tabak (Vienna)
Austrian Airlines (Vienna)
Auto Germa (Verona)
Anwester, Gottlob (Stuttgart)
Awiaexport (Moscow)
Awtopromimport (Moscow)
Axel Johnson Group (Stockholm)
Axel Springer Verlag (Berlin,
    Hamburg)

B

Badenia (Karlsruhe)
Badische
    Maschinenfabrik (Karlsruhe)
Badger (The Hague)
Bahco (Stockholm)
Bahlsen (Hanover)
Balitrand (Cannes)
Balke-Dürr (Düsseldorf)
Ballast Nedam Group (Amsterdam)
Balzers AG (Vaduz)
Banco de Bilbao (Bilbao)
Banco Hispana Americana (Madrid)
Banco de Vizcaya (Bilbao)
Banco Zaragonano (Zaragoza)
Bank für
    Gemeinwirtschaft (Frankfurt)

575

Bank für Tirol und
    Vorarlberg (Salzburg)
Bank in Liechtenstein (Vaduz)
Banque Internationale à
    Luxembourg (Luxembourg)
Banque Nationale de Paris (Paris)
Banque Populaire (Strasbourg)
Banque Veuve Morins-Pons (Lyons)
Barbieri, E. C. (Trieste)
BASF (Antwerp)
BASF Espagnola (Barcelona)
BAT Cigaretten (Hamburg)
B.A.T. Industries (Southampton)
Baumwollspinnerei Jenny, Spoerry &
    Cie (Vaduz)
Bayer (Cologne, Antwerp)
Bayerische Motorenwerke (Munich,
    Berlin-West)
Bayerische Vereinsbank (Munich)
Beck & Co (Bremen)
Becker, Wilhelm (Aachen)
Becton Dickinson (Grenoble)
Behr, Julius (Stuttgart)
Beiersdorf (Hamburg)
Belgian Petroleum (Brussels,
    Antwerp)
Bell Telephone (Antwerp)
Bendix (Bristol)
Benteler Werke (Gütersloh)
Berger Levraut (Nancy)
Bertagni Industrie Alimentari
    (Bologna)
Bertani (Verona)
Bertelsmann (Gütersloh)
Berthold (Berlin)
Berton et Sucard (Marseilles)
Betons Feidt (Luxembourg)
Bibby, J. & Sons (Liverpool)
Bibliographisches
    Institut (Mannheim)
Bichots (Bordeaux)
Bielefelder Keksfabrik (Gütersloh)
Bilfinger & Berger (Wiesbaden)
Billon (Lyons)
Binding (Frankfurt)
Biobie (Monte-Carlo)
Le Blan & Cie (Lille)
Blizzard (Salzburg)
Block Watne Byggfornyelse (Oslo)
Blohm & Voss (Hamburg)
Blue Bell (Valletta)
Bobst (Lausanne)
Bodycote International (Manchester)
Boehringer, Bopp &
    Reuther (Mannheim)
Boettger (Berlin)
Bogner (Munich)

Boliden (Stockholm)
Bolla (Verona)
Bomis (Warsaw)
Bompiani (Milan)
Bonner Zementwerk (Bonn)
Bord Bainne (Dublin)
Borel (Nancy)
Borletti (Milan)
Borsig (Berlin)
Bosch (Stuttgart)
Bové (Nancy)
Brasseries Réunies de
    Luxembourg (Luxembourg)
Braun (Frankfurt)
Bremer Vulkan (Bremen)
Brinkmann, Martin (Bremen)
Brinkmann, Wirtz & Co (Hamburg)
British Aerospace (Manchester,
    Bristol)
British Telecom (Bristol)
British Vita Group (Manchester)
Britoil (Glasgow)
Brown, Boveri & Cie (Mannheim)
Bührmann Tetterode (Amsterdam)
Bulgarcoop (Sofia)
Bulgarkonserv (Sofia)
Bulgartabac (Sofia)
Bumar (Warsaw)
Bundesländerversicherung (Vienna)
Burda (Munich)

C

Cadbury-Schweppes (Birmingham,
    Bristol)
Caisse d'Epargne (Luxembourg)
Caisse Régionale de Crédit
    Agricole (Rheims)
Calzaturificio Rangoni (Florence)
Caminhos de Ferro
    Portugueses (Lisbon)
Campari (Milan)
Cantina Sociale Coop. di Marino
    (Rome)
Carborundum
    Abrasives (Manchester)
Caremar (Naples)
Cargill (Antwerp)
Cargolux (Luxembourg)
Carlton Industries (Bristol)
Carpano (Turin)
Cartier (Paris)
Cartiere Burgo (Turin)

Cartiere Fedrigonialie (Verona)
Caterpillar Tractor (Glasgow)
CDC (Luxembourg)
Cekoslovenska Keramika (Prague)
La Cellulose du Pin (Bordeaux)
Cement Roadstone (Dublin)
Central Pneu (Toulouse)
Centrotex (Prague)
Cerruti 1881 (Paris)
Chanel (Paris)
Chantier Naval de L'Esterel (Cannes)
Chapeaux (Brussels)
Chemapol (Prague)
Chemical Industries of Northern
    Greece (Athens)
Chimica (Bucharest)
Chloride Standby
    Systems (Southampton)
Christian Dior
    Fourrure (Monte-Carlo)
Christiani & Lielsen (Copenhagen)
Ciba-Geigy (Basle)
Ciech (Warsaw)
Cindu-Key & Kramer (Amsterdam)
Cinzano (Turin)
Citroën (Cologne)
Claas Guss (Gütersloh)
Clark Equipment (Strasbourg)
CLBI (Cannes)
Cleveland Crane &
    Engineering (Luxembourg)
C.N.R.S. (Nice)
Coats Patons (Glasgow)
Coin (Venice)
Colgate Palmolive (Hamburg)
Collins, William (Glasgow)
Colonia (Cologne)
Comex (Marseilles)
Commerzbank (Frankfurt)
Comp. Nationale de Rhône (Lyons)
Comp. Port. do Cobre (Oporto)
Comp. des Produits de
    l'Ouest (Nancy)
Confort & Chaleur (Liège)
Consolidated Biscuits (Valletta)
Consorzio Moda Roma (Rome)
Continental (Hanover)
Control Data (Frankfurt)
Cop & Portier (Liège)
Correios e Telecommunicacoes de
    Portugal (Lisbon)
Costruzioni Mecchaniche Bernardini
    (Rome)
Côte d'Or (Brussels)
Crédit Lyonnais (Lyons)
Crédit Mutuel du Nord (Lille)
Creditbank (Luxembourg)

Crepelle & Cie (Lille)
Crespi (Milan)
Crown House
    Engineering (Southampton)
La Cruz del Campo (Seville)
CTM (Lisbon)
Cussons Group (Manchester)

D

Daimler Benz (Stuttgart, Bremen,
    Mannheim)
Daimler-Puch (Graz)
Dal (Warsaw)
Danone (Barcelona)
De Danske
    Zukkerfabriker (Copenhagen)
Danzas (Frankfurt)
Dassler (Salzburg)
La Dauphinoise (Grenoble)
Davenports (Birmingham)
Deere and Company (Mannheim)
Degussa (Antwerp, Frankfurt)
Delta Lloyd (Amsterdam)
Deltasider (Venice)
Deltatex (Nice)
Den Norske Creditbank (Oslo)
Derimod (Istanbul)
Derwa (Liège)
DESA (Warsaw)
Detkachinie (Marseilles)
DeTeWe (Berlin)
Deutsche Bank (Frankfurt)
Deutsche Bundesbahn (Frankfurt)
Deutsche Granini (Gütersloh)
Deutsche Lloyd (Frankfurt)
DFDS (Copenhagen)
Diedier (Wiesbaden)
Diehl (Nuremberg)
Diesterweg, Moritz (Frankfurt)
Digital Equipment (Nice)
Dinkelacker (Stuttgart)
Distillers Co (Edinburgh)
Distribuciones Gimenez y
    Cia (Zaragoza)
Dorland (Berlin-West)
Dow Chemical (Nice)
Dreamland Costruzioni (Venice)
Dreamland Electrical
    Appliances (Southampton)
Dresdner Bank (Frankfurt)
DRG (Bristol)
Dumont-Wautier (Liège)
Dunlop (Birmingham)

Dunnes Stores (Dublin)
DuPont (Düsseldorf, Luxembourg)
Dynafil (Graz)

E

East Lancashire Paper
    Group (Manchester)
Ebes (Antwerp)
Ecole des Mines de Paris (Nice)
EDEKA (Hamburg)
Eduscho (Bremen)
Efacec (Lisbon)
EFCIS (Grenoble)
Eichof (Lucerne)
Eka-yhtymä (Helsinki)
Elan Oil (Vienna)
Elkem (Oslo)
Electrolux (Stockholm)
Elektrim (Warsaw)
Elektroimpex (Sofia)
Elektronorgtechnika (Moscow)
Eleusis Bauxite Mines (Athens)
Eletronica S. Giorgio Elsag (Genoa)
Elleomere Port (Liverpool)
Emerson Electronics (Florence)
EMI Electrola (Cologne)
EMS Chemie (Zurich)
Empresa Nacional del
    Petroleo (Madrid)
Energopol (Warsaw)
Energoprojekt (Belgrade)
Engels, August (Düsseldorf)
Enka Holding (Istanbul)
Enso Gutzeit (Helsinki)
Ericsson (Stockholm)
Ericsson, Christer (Stockholm)
Eridania Zuccherifici
    Nazionale (Genoa)
Erno (Bremen)
ESAB (Gothenburg)
Esso (Antwerp)
Esso Chemicals (Southampton)
L'Est Républicain (Nancy)
Europa (Paris)
Eurospital (Trieste)
Exportlemm (Bucharest)
Exportles (Moscow)
Extralco (Toulouse)

F

Fabbri (Milan)
Faber-Castell (Nuremberg)
Farmitalia-Carlo Erba (Milan)
Fashion Institute of the
    GDR (Berlin-East)
Feldmühle (Düsseldorf)
Felten & Guilleaume (Cologne)
Feltrinelli (Milan)
Ferro (Rotterdam)
Ferromet (Prague)
Ferrostaal (Essen)
Fiat (Turin)
Fibriver (Lausanne)
Fieldhammer Burs (Oslo)
Fildex (Valletta)
Filmbulgaria (Sofia)
Fincantieri (Venice, Trieste)
Fincantieri Navale (Trieste)
Fischer, Georg (Düsseldorf)
Flohr-Otis (Berlin)
Fochi, Filippo (Bologna)
Fokker (Amsterdam)
Fomento de Obras y
    Construcciones (Barcelona)
Ford (Cologne, Glasgow)
Ford France (Bordeaux)
Ford España (Valencia)
De Forenede
    Bryggerie (Copenhagen)
Aux Forges de la Loire (Nantes)
Foto-Quelle (Nuremberg)
Fourcray (Brussels)
Frahuil (Marseilles)
Frigorex (Lucerne)
Frionor Norsk Frossenfisk (Oslo)
Frinlginlia (Trieste)
Fro Saldatura (Verona)

G

G 3 S (Nice)
Gätaverken (Gothenburg)
Galenica (Berne)
Ganz-Mávag (Budapest)
Gardisette (Lucerne)
Garzanti (Milan)
G. D. (Bologna)
Geha (Hanover)
Gelagri Bretagne-Landerneau (Brest)
General Cement (Athens)
General Motors (Paris)

General Motors
Continental (Antwerp)
General X-Ray
Company (Monte-Carlo)
Generalexport (Belgrade)
La Genevois (Geneva)
Georgetti Eustache &
Fils (Luxembourg)
Gerling Konzern (Cologne)
Gervais Danone (Rheims)
Gifrer Barbezat (Lyons)
Gildemeister (Gütersloh)
Gillette (Berlin-West)
Ginori, Richard (Florence)
Gio. Buton (Bologna)
Girardet-Perregaux (Geneva)
Gödecke (Berlin-West)
Göhner (Zurich)
Goldschmidt (Mannheim)
Granus Glasfabrik (Aachen)
Gravo-Optic (Vaduz)
Graz-Köflacher (Graz)
Grebau-Greschbach
Industrie (Karlsruhe)
Greek Powder and
Cartridge (Athens)
Groupe C.D.F. Chimie (Paris)
Grundig (Nuremberg, Vienna)
Gruner + Jahr (Hamburg)
Gruppo Finanziario Tessile (Turin)
Gucci (Florence)
Guinnes Ireland (Dublin)
Gutenbergus Gruppen (Copenhagen)

H

Haake (Karlsruhe)
Haci Bekir (Istanbul)
Hacker-Pschorr (Munich)
Hag (Bremen)
Hallwag (Berne)
Hankkija-yhtymä (Helsinki)
Hanomag (Hanover)
Hapag Lloyd (Hanover)
Haribo (Bonn)
Hartmann (Frankfurt)
Harvey's (Bristol)
Hasler (Berne)
Hasselblad (Gothenburg)
Hauterat & Watteyne (Liège)
Hayek (Zurich)
Heine, Heinrich (Karlsruhe)
Heineken (Amsterdam)
Heinrich Bauer Verlag (Hamburg)

Hellenic Shipyards (Athens)
Helleniki Techniki Group (Athens)
Helm, Karl O. (Hamburg)
Hempro (Belgrade)
Henkel (Düsseldorf)
Henkell (Wiesbaden)
Henninger (Frankfurt)
Hercules (The Hague)
Herlitz (Berlin-West)
Hero Verona (Verona)
Hewlett Packard (Bristol)
Hidroelectrica Española (Madrid)
Highland Distilleries (Glasgow)
Hilti (Vaduz)
Hispanica de Petroleos (Madrid)
Hochtief (Essen)
Hoechst (Frankfurt)
Hoffmann-La Roche (Basle)
Holsten Brauerei (Hamburg)
Holt, John & Co (Liverpool)
Holtzmann, E. & Cie (Karlsruhe)
Holzmann, Philipp (Frankfurt)
Honeywell (Monte-Carlo)
Hoval-Werke (Vaduz)
Howaldt (Hamburg)
Humanic-Schuh (Graz)
Hunter-Douglas (Rotterdam)
Hypo-Bank (Munich)

I

Iberia (Barcelona)
IBM (Bordeaux, Brussels, Glasgow,
Paris, Reykjavik, Stuttgart, The
Hague)
Icarus Busses (Budapest)
Icelandic Cold Water
Corporation (Reykjavik)
ICI (London, Bristol, Rotterdam)
IMI Pacific (Grenoble)
Imperial Hournal (Liège)
Impexmetal (Warsaw)
Ind. Reunidos
Minero-Metalurgicas (Bilbao)
Indesit (Turin)
Induplan Chemie (Salzburg)
Indust. Jomar Madeiras y
Derivados (Oporto)
Industria Eternit (Naples)
Industria Filati Calenzano (Florence)
Industria Italiana Petroli (Genoa)
Infodif (Nice)
Ingram International (Monte-Carlo)

Innerebner & Meyer (Innsbruck)
Insel Verlag (Leipzig)
Institut Mérieux (Lyons)
Intercommerce (Sofia)
Interdruck (Leipzig)
Interescant (Antwerp)
Intergeo (Prague)
Intraco (Warsaw)
Intransmasch (Sofia)
Investa (Prague)
ISS Securitas (Copenhagen)
Italimpianiti (Genoa)
Italstrada (Rome)
Ivoclar (Vaduz)

J

Jacobi (Stuttgart)
Jacobs (Bremen)
J.G.A.O. (Antwerp)
Jobis (Gütersloh)
Johnson & Johnson (Düsseldorf)
Jubilé (Liège)
Jugometal (Belgrade)
Jullian (Marseilles)
Junghans (Aachen)
Juvena (Baden-Baden)

K

Kabelwerke Oberspree (Berlin-East)
Kässbohrer (Salzburg)
Kalichemie (Hanover)
Karl Fazer (Helsinki)
Karstadt (Essen)
Kaufhof (Cologne)
Kellogg (Manchester, Bremen)
Kemira (Helsinki)
Kennedy Smale (Bristol)
Kesko (Helsinki)
Kestner (Lille)
Kistenmacher, E.G. (Hamburg)
Klais (Bonn)
Klett (Stuttgart)
KLM (The Hague)
Klöckner (Bremen)
Klöckner-Humboldt-Deutz
    (Cologne)
Klöckner-Möller (Bonn)
Kniel System-Electronic (Karlsruhe)
KOC Holding (Istanbul)
Kodak (Stuttgart)

Kölnisch Wasser 4711 (Cologne)
Königsberger (Aachen)
Kone (Helsinki)
Koninklige Volker
    Stevin (Rotterdam)
Konsum Österreich (Vienna)
Koospol (Prague)
Korf Stahlgruppe (Baden-Baden)
KOVO (Prague)
Kraftwerk Union (Berlin-West)
Krauss-Maffei (Munich)
Kreditanstalt (Vienna)
Kreditkassen Christiana Bank (Oslo)
Krone (Berlin-West)
Kronenbourg (Strasbourg)
Krupp (Essen)
Krupp Atlas Elektronik (Bremen)
Kühne & Nagel (Basle)
Kümmerly & Frey (Berne)
Kymi-Strömberg (Helsinki)

L

Labimex (Warsaw)
Laboratoire Labaz (Bordeaux)
Laboratoires
    Wellcome (Monte-Carlo)
Laine d'Aoust (Brussels)
Lambertz (Aachen)
Laminois de Strasbourg (Strasbourg)
Länderbank (Vienna)
Lancaster (Monte-Carlo)
Lancia (Turin)
Landeshypothekenbank (Innsbruck)
Landewyck, Heintz
    van (Luxembourg)
Landteknikk (Oslo)
Langenscheidt (Munich)
Langnese-Iglo (Hamburg)
Lanz, Heinrich (Mannheim)
Laterza (Bari)
Laurens Sigarettenfabriek (The
    Hague)
Lauritzen Konzernen (The Hague)
Legia Labo (Liège)
Leitz (Stuttgart)
Leu Bank (Zurich)
Lever Sunlicht (Hamburg)
Lhoist et Leons (Liège)
Liechtensteinische
    Landesbank (Vaduz)
Ligna (Prague)
Lilley, F.J.C. (Glasgow)
Lilly (Strasbourg)

Linde (Wiesbaden)
Lindholmen Motoers (Gothenburg)
Lionel-Dupont (Lyons)
Liverpool Daily Post and
    Echo (Liverpool)
Lloyd Dynamo (Bremen)
Locatelli (Milan)
Löwenbräu (Munich)
Loftleidir (Reykjavik)
Longanesi (Milan)
Lonza (Basle)
Losinger (Berne)
Lucas, Joseph (Birmingham)
Lueg (Essen)
Lufthansa (Cologne)
Lummus Nederland (The Hague)
Lurgi-Benelux (Brussels)
Luxair (Luxembourg)

M

Machinoexport (Sofia)
Madaus (Cologne)
Magona d'Italia (Florence)
Mahle (Stuttgart)
Malet (Toulouse)
Malta Drydocks (Valletta)
Manetti, Gabbriello (Florence)
Mannesmann (Düsseldorf)
Mannesmann Demag (Salzburg)
Manufacturas Generales de
    Ferreteria (Barcelona)
Manufacturas Nacival de
    Borracha (Oporto)
MAPAG (Berne)
Marcard & Co (Hamburg)
Marnier Lapostolle (Paris)
Martin, Arthur (Rheims)
Martini e Rossi (Turin)
Maschinenfabrik Augsburg-
    Nürnberg (Nuremberg)
Maschinoimport (Moscow)
Maschpriborimport (Moscow)
Masinexport (Bucharest)
Mathey-Tissot (Geneva)
Mazzi (Verona)
McCann-Erickson (Frankfurt)
Medicor (Budapest)
Melingo, Paolo (Trieste)
Mercantile-Beliard (Antwerp)
Merkuria (Prague)
Merz (Frankfurt)
Messerschmitt-Bölkow-Blohm
    (Munich, Bremen)

Metalimex (Prague)
Metallotecnica (Venice)
Metallurgie Hoboken
    Overpelt (Antwerp)
Metallurgimport (Moscow)
Metronex (Warsaw)
La Meuse (Liège)
Michelin Reifenwerke (Karlsruhe)
Midest (Nancy)
Miele (Gütersloh)
Milupa (Frankfurt)
Migliore (Palermo)
Mineralimpex (Sofia)
Mira Lanza (Genoa)
Mirabella Küchen (Salzburg)
Mobil Oil (Rotterdam)
Mölnlycke (Gothenburg)
Mohndruck (Gütersloh)
Monberg & Thorsen (Gothenburg)
Mondadori (Milan)
La Mondial (Lille)
Monheim, Leonhard (Aachen)
Moninger (Karlsruhe)
Montana (Vienna)
Monte Carlo Parfum (Monte-Carlo)
Montedison (Milan)
von Moos (Lucerne)
Morteo Soprefini (Genoa)
Motokov (Prague)
Motor Iberica (Barcelona)
Motorenwerke
    Mannheim (Mannheim)
Motorola (Toulouse)
Münchener Rückversicherung
    (Munich)
Mullards (Southampton)
Mumm (Rheims)

N

Nattermann (Cologne)
Nestlé (Lausanne)
Neu (Lille)
Newman Industries (Bristol)
Nixdorf (Gütersloh)
NOGA (Geneva)
Nokia (Helsinki)
Nord-Est Alimentation (Rheims)
Norden et Compagnie (Nancy)
Nordmende (Bremen)
Nordsee (Bremen)
Norfolkline (The Hague)
Norkem (Oslo)
Norsk Data (Oslo)

Norsk Hydro (Oslo)
Norsk Olje (Oslo)
Nuova Italsider (Genoa)
Nuovo Pignone (Florence)
NUR (Frankfurt)
N.V. Centrale Suiker
    Maatschappij (Amsterdam)

O

Oberascher
    Maschinenfabrik (Salzburg)
Österreichische
    Industrieverwaltung (Vienna)
Österreichische Mineralöl (Vienna)
Officina Galileo (Florence)
Dr. August Oetker (Gütersloh)
Oleaginosas Españolas (Barcelona)
Olio Rocco (Naples)
Olivetti (Turin, Paris)
Olympia Press (Milan)
Olympic Airways (Athens)
Omnipol (Prague)
The Ordnance Survey (Southampton)
Orenstein & Koppel (Berlin-West)
OSRAM (Berlin-West)
O.T.E. Biomedica (Florence)
Otra (Amsterdam)
Otto Versand (Hamburg)
Outokumpu (Helsinki)

P

Paged (Warsaw)
Pahlsche Gummi- und
    Asphaltgesellschaft (Düsseldorf)
Palma (Budapest)
Panigal (Bologna)
La Papelera Española (Bilbao)
Papeterie de France (Paris)
Papierwerke Waldhoff-
    Aschaffenburg (Mannheim)
Parker Pen (Baden-Baden)
Pasabahce (Istanbul)
Pascal (Grenoble)
Pasta Granoro (Bari)
PAV Präzisions Apparatebau (Vaduz)
Pavatex (Vaduz)
Pechinery (Paris)
Pelikan (Hanover)

Pérard, Pierre & Fils (Luxembourg)
Perennatorwerk
    Alfred Hagen (Wiesbaden)
Perkin-Elmer Censor Anstalt (Vaduz)
Perusyhtymä (Helsinki)
Petrochim (Antwerp)
Petrofina (Brussels)
Petrogal (Lisbon)
Petroleos del Mediterraneo (Madrid)
Petrucco, Pietro (Trieste)
Peugeot (Paris, Strasbourg)
Pewex (Warsaw)
Pezetel (Warsaw)
Pfaff (Karlsruhe)
Pfeifer & Langen (Cologne)
Pfizer (Brussels, Karlsruhe)
Pharma-Allergan (Karlsruhe)
Pharmamed (Valletta)
Philips (Aachen, Hamburg)
Phoenix Assurance (Bristol)
Piaget (Geneva)
Piaggio (Genoa)
Piensos y Ganados (Zaragoza)
Pilkington Bros (Liverpool)
Piper-Heidsieck (Rheims)
Pirelli (Milan, Barcelona)
Pirelli General Cable (Southampton)
PKL (Düsseldorf)
Plissana (Vaduz)
Polexpo (Warsaw)
Polmot (Warsaw)
Polservice (Warsaw)
Poltel (Warsaw)
Polyfoam (Valletta)
Polygramm (Hanover)
Pommery (Rheims)
Pont & Mousson (Nancy)
Pontello (Florence)
Porsche (Stuttgart, Salzburg)
Portucel (Lisbon)
Pragoinvest (Prague)
Press- und Stanzwerk (Vaduz)
Pressluft Goetz (Mannheim)
Preussag (Frankfurt)
Preussenelektra (Hanover)
Prodexport (Bucharest)
Promogros (Brest)
Promsyrjoimport (Moscow)
Publicitas (Lausanne)
Pucci (Florence)
Pulvic (Valletta)
Purcell Exports (Dublin)

Q

Quimigal (Lisbon)

R

Raab Karcher (Essen)
Radio & Télévision
  Luxembourg (Luxembourg)
Raffinerie Deurag-Nerag (Hanover)
Ragolds, Rachengold (Karlsruhe)
Rasnoexport,
  Rasnoimport (Moscow)
Reclam, Ph. (Leipzig)
Red Funnel Ferries (Southampton)
Reemtsma (Hamburg)
Refinarias de Acucer
  Reunidas (Oporto)
Refineria de Petroleos del
  Norte (Bilbao)
Reims Aviation (Reims)
Renault (Paris, Cologne)
Renault Vehicules
  Industriels (Lyons)
Renfe (Madrid)
Renold (Manchester)
Rexmore (Liverpool)
Reynolds Tobacco (Cologne)
Rheinisch Westfälische
  Elektrizitäts-Werke (Essen)
Rheinische Kalksteinwerke
  (Düsseldorf)
Rheinmetall (Düsseldorf)
RIAS (Berlin-West)
Rivoire et Carret (Marseilles)
Rizzoli (Milan)
Com. Roca Radiadores (Barcelona)
Rodaprint (Berlin-West)
Rodoviaria Nacional (Lisbon)
Roederer (Rheims)
Roghano, Barry (Marseilles)
Rohm and Haas (Nice)
Rolex Montres (Geneva)
Rolipex (Warsaw)
Roller (Florence)
Rolls Royce (Bristol)
Rosner (Grenoble)
De Rotterdamsche
  Droogdok (Rotterdam)
Austin Rover (Birmingham)
Rubber Latex (Manchester)
Rudnap (Belgrade)
Ruhrgas (Essen)
Ruhrkohle (Essen)

S

Saab Svenska Stal (Stockholm)
Sabanci Holding (Istanbul)
Sabca (Brussels)
Sabena (Brussels)
Sagar (Milan)
Sagatrans (Nantes)
Salomon Oppenheimer (Frankfurt)
SAMS (Grenoble)
Sandoz (Basle)
Saras (Milan)
Sarotti (Frankfurt)
Sasib (Bologna)
Sava (Venice)
Savalco (Bristol)
Savic Export (Bordeaux)
Schenker (Frankfurt)
Schering (Berlin-West)
Schiess (Düsseldorf)
Schildkröt (Mannheim)
Schindler (Frankfurt)
Schindler Aufzüge (Berlin-West)
Schmidt, Otto (Nuremberg)
Schoeller (Nuremberg)
Scholes, George H. (Manchester)
Schottel (The Hague)
Schultheiß Brauerei (Berlin-West)
Schumag (Aachen)
Schwan Stabilo (Nuremberg)
Schwarzkopf (Hamburg)
Schwarzkopf, Kurt (Innsbruck)
Schweizer Bankverein (Basle)
Schweizer Volksbank (Berne)
Schweizerische Aluminium (Zurich)
Schweizerische Bankgesellschaft
  (Zurich)
Schweizerische Kreditanstalt
  (Zurich)
Scottish Agricultural
  Industries (Edinburgh)
Scottish and Newcastle
  Breweries (Edinburgh)
Scottish Universal
  Industruments (Glasgow)
SEAT (Barcelona)
SECALT (Luxembourg)
Seebeck (Bremen)
Seidensticker (Innsbruck,
  Gütersloh)
Selenia Industrie Ellettroniche
  (Rome)
Sender Freies Berlin (Berlin-West)
SEP (Bordeaux)
Sergic (Lille)
Serono Industria Farmaceutica
  (Rome)

Sevillana de Electricidad (Seville)
Sharp Electronics (Manchester)
Shell Austria (Vienna)
SIBP (Antwerp)
Siemens (Antwerp, Berlin,
Düsseldorf, Mannheim, Munich,
Vienna)
S.I.E.T.T.E. (Turin)
Simmerling-Graz-Pauker (Graz)
Simonds Farsons Cisk (Valletta)
SIP (Geneva)
Siremar Siciliana (Palermo)
Sirma (Venice)
Sirti (Milan)
Skandia Life Insurance
(Southampton)
SKF (Gothenburg)
Smidth, F.L. (Copenhagen)
Smurfit Group (Dublin)
S.N.I.A.S. (Toulouse)
SNPE (Bordeaux)
Soberma Borghans (Brussels)
Soc. Silva (Brest)
Sociedade de Construcoes da
Costa (Oporto)
Société des Ciments Français (Paris)
Société Luxembourgeoise
d'Entreprises et de
Constructions (Luxembourg)
Söhnlein Rheingold (Wiesbaden)
S.O.G.E.R.I.C. (Marseilles)
Sojuschimexport (Moscow)
Sojusgasexport (Moscow)
Sojusposchnina (Moscow)
Sojuspromexport (Moscow)
Sojuswneschstrojimport (Moscow)
SOK (Helsinki)
Solvay (Brussels, Nancy)
Solyvente-Ventec (Lyons)
Somatrans (Lyons)
Somef (Liège)
Sony (Cologne)
Southern Evening Echo
(Southampton)
Spaten-Franziskaner (Munich)
Spinnstoffabrik Zehlendorf
(Berlin-West)
Sprengel (Hanover)
SRO (Zurich)
Staedtler-Mars (Nuremberg)
Standard Elektronik Lorenz
(Frankfurt, Stuttgart)
Stankoimport (Moscow)
Statsföretag (Stockholm)
Setag (Essen)
Stendhal (Paris)
Steyr-Daimler Puch (Vienna)

Steyrische Brauindustrie (Graz)
Steyrische Ferngas (Graz)
Steweag (Graz)
Stieglbrauerei (Salzburg)
Stock (Trieste)
Stollwerck AG/Imhoff (Cologne)
Store Nodeske Telegraf
Selskab (Copenhagen)
Strojexport (Prague)
Strojmaterialimport (Moscow)
Stuag (Berne)
Sturge (Birmingham)
Stute (Gütersloh)
Suchard Tobler (Berne)
Süddeutsche Zucker AG (Mannheim)
Südwestfunk (Baden-Baden)
Suhrkamp (Frankfurt)
Sun Life (Bristol)
Superfos (Copenhagen)
Superpila (Florence)
Svenska Handelsbanken (Stockholm)
Svenska Philips Företagen
(Stockholm)
Svenska Varv (Gothenburg)
Swarovski (Innsbruck)
Swedevelop (Stockholm)
Swedish Matches (Stockholm)
Swedyards (Gothenburg)
Swissair (Zurich)

T

Tabaqueira (Lisbon)
Tafra Hypermoquettes (Brest)
Taittinger (Rheims)
Talbot (Aachen)
Tambella (Helsinki)
Tandberg Data (Oslo)
Targetti Sankey (Florence)
Tauernautobahn (Salzburg)
Tauernkraftwerke (Salzburg)
Tchibo (Hamburg)
Technoforest (Bucharest)
Technointorg (Moscow)
Technopol (Prague)
Technoproimport (Moscow)
Tecnomatic (Antwerp)
Teekanne (Salzburg)
Teksid (Turin)
Telefonbau und Normalzeit
(Frankfurt)
Telefunken (Hanover)
Télémécanique (Nice)
Teubner, B.G., BSB Verlag (Leipzig)

Teutonia Zementwerke (Hanover)
Teves, Alfred (Frankfurt)
The Weir Group (Glasgow)
Thew Engineering Group
    (Southampton)
Thyssen (Düsseldorf, Essen)
Timken (Strasbourg)
Tiroler Loden (Innsbruck)
Tirrenia di Navigazione (Naples)
Tissmetal (Lyons)
Titan Cement (Athens)
Toepfer, August (Hamburg)
Togal (Munich)
Tootal (Manchester)
Total (Bordeaux, Paris)
Toyota (Cologne)
Traktoroexport (Moscow)
Tramontano (Naples)
Transportes Aeros
    Portugueses (Lisbon)
Triumph-Adler (Nuremberg)
TRW Cam Gears (Bristol)
Tubus Metall (Karlsruhe)
TUI (Hanover)
Tulip (Copenhagen)
TV Flandres (Lille)
Tyrolian Airways (Innsbruck)

U

Ubix (Paris)
UCB (Brussels)
Unilever (Vienna)
Union de Centros
    Farmaceuticos (Bilbao)
Union Explosivos Rio Tino (Madrid)
Union Laitière Pyrénées Aquitaine
    Charente (Toulouse)
Uniroyal Englebert (Aachen)
United Wire Group (Edinburgh)
Universal (Trieste)
Universal (Warsaw)
Universal Versand (Salzburg)

V

Valentino (Rome)
Valexy-Levallois-Perret (Nantes)
Valio (Helsinki)
Valmet (Helsinki)
Vang France (Nantes)

Vantona Viyella (Manchester)
Varimex (Warsaw)
Varta (Hanover)
Vauxhall (Liverpool)
VDO (Frankfurt)
VEB Bergmann-Borsig (Berlin-East)
VEB Berlin-Chemie (Berlin-East)
VEB Breitkopf & Härtel (Berlin-East)
VEB Brockhaus, F.A. (Leipzig)
VEB Chemieanlagen (Leipzig)
VEB Drehmaschinenwerk (Leipzig)
VEB Druckmaschinenwerke
    (Leipzig)
VEB Leipziger
    Baumwollspinnerei (Leipzig)
VEB Leipziger Wollkämmerei
    (Leipzig)
VEB Verlade- und
    Transportanlagen (Leipzig)
Veba (Düsseldorf, Essen)
Vegla (Aachen)
Vereinigte Alu-Werke (Bonn)
Vereinigte Edelstahlwerke (Vienna)
Vereinigte Leichtmetall (Hanover)
Verlagsanstalt Tyrolia (Innsbruck)
Vero Precision Engineering
    (Southampton)
Verpoorten (Bonn)
Verreries Mécaniques Champs
    (Rheims)
Verwaltungs- und Privat-Bank
    (Vaduz)
Veuve Cliquot Ponssardin (Rheims)
Vianora (Graz)
Villeroy & Boch (Luxembourg,
    Frankfurt, Cologne)
VMF-Stork (Amsterdam)
Vögele, Joseph (Mannheim)
Voest Alpine (Vienna)
Voix du Nord (Lille)
Volkswagen (Hanover)
Volvo (Gothenburg)
Vosper Hovermarine (Southampton)

W

Wabco Westinghouse (Berne,
    Hanover)
Wacker (Munich)
Wärtsilä (Helsinki)
Wagnersche Buchdruckerei
    (Innsbruck)
Wamsler (Munich)
Wander (Berne)

Warburg (Hamburg)
Warta (Warsaw)
Welle (Gütersloh)
Welz, Franz (Salzburg)
Werkzeugmaschinenkombinat
›7. Oktober‹ (Berlin-East)
Werner & Pfleiderer (Stuttgart)
Westdeutsche Allgemeine
Zeitung (Essen)
Westminster Dredging
(Southampton)
Wiederholt, Herrmann (Düsseldorf)
Wiener Stadtwerke (Vienna)
WIFAG (Berne)
Wilkens (Bremen)
William Thyne (Edinburgh)
Wills, W.D. and H.O. (Bristol)
Windsor (Gütersloh)
Wolf, Otto (Cologne)
Wurth, Paul (Luxembourg)

Y

Young & Rubicam (Frankfurt)
Yugotours (Belgrade)

Z

Zentis, Franz (Aachen)
ZSE (Prague)
Zublin, Ed. (Stuttgart)

Place	Event	Time

January

Place	Event	Time
Athens	XENIA – Hotel equipment	Jan to Feb
	EUROMODE – fashion fair	
Barcelona	INTERNATIONAL BOATS AND CARAVANING FAIR	
Brussels	LEATHER GOODS FAIR	
	AQUA-EXPO – water technology	
Cologne	INTERNATIONAL FURNITURE FAIR	
	IT'S COLOGNE – internatonal fashion trends	
	ISM – candies and sweets	
Essen	DEUBAU – German construction convention	Jan or Feb
Frankfurt	HOME FABRICS FAIR	
Grenoble	SEA – European antiques fair	Jan or Feb
The Hague	AVICULTURA	
	WOONTEXTIEL	
Helsinki	FINNISH FASHION FAIR	
	INTERNATIONAL FUR AUCTION	
London	LONDON INTERNATIONAL BOAT SHOW	
	BRITISH TOY AND HOBBY FAIR	
Luxembourg	EXPOGAST – equipment and installations for the hotel and catering industries	Jan or Feb
Madrid	IBERJOYA – international jewellery fair	
	GEGALO FAMA – gift fair	
Milan	TOY FAIR	
Oslo	CONFUR – international contracts furniture fair	biennial
	CARAVAN	
	GAVE-EXPO – gift and decoration fair	
Zaragoza	ENOMAQ – international wine-cellar machinery and equipment fair	biennial
Stockholm	INTERNATIONAL MOTOCYCLE FAIR	
Valencia	TEXTILHOGAR – fabrics for the home	Dec or Jan
	INDUFERIAS – betting and game machines, stage machinery	
	EXPOJOVEN – youth fair	
Wiesbaden	EDE – German iron merchant congress	
Zurich	ORNARIS – trade fair for living design	

February

Place	Event	Time
Antwerp	HOLIDAY AND SPRING SHOW	Jan or Feb
	JE HUIS . . .EEN THUIS – home decoration show	
Athens	XENIA – hotel equipment	Jan to Feb
Barcelona	EXPOMATEX – international textile machinery fair	
	SALON GAUDI HOMBRE INTERNATIONAL – mens fashion	
Basle	SWISSBAU – building machinery fair	
Berlin	GRÜNE WOCHE – international agricultural fair, a „green week"	
Bilbao	INTERARK – interior decoration exhibition	Feb 87
	BIMO – furniture fair	
	FORESTA – international forestry exhibition	
Birmingham	INTERNATIONAL SPRING FAIR	
	BOAT & CAR SHOW	
	MARKETING & PROMOTION SERVICES	
	ELECTREX – international electrotechnical exhibition	
Bologna	PACKAGING – packaging machinery and materials	
Bordeaux	ANTIQUES FAIR	
Bremen	BOOT – boat show	

Place	Event	Time
Bristol	CARAVAN, CAMPING, HOLIDAY AND TRAVEL EXHIBITION INDUSTRY AND COMMERCIAL PRODUCT FAIR	
Brussels	BATIBOUW – construction industry	
Cologne	DOMOTECHNICA – household appliances INTERNATIONAL MEN'S FASHION FAIR INTERJEANS KÖLN – jeans and sportswear fashions	
Copenhagen	MIKRODATA	Jan or Feb
	FORMLAND – giftware, handicrafts and applied art	Feb or Mar
	INTERNATIONAL BOAT SHOW FUTURE FASHION SCANDINAVIA	
Dublin	HOLIDAY AND RECREATION FAIR	
Düsseldorf	BOOT – boat show	Jan or Feb
	IGEDO-JUNIOR – first night collections ENVITEC – environmental protection	
Edinburgh	SCOTTISH ANTIQUES FAIR	
Essen	DEBAU – German construction convention IPM – international plant market	
Frankfurt	MUSIC FAIR – musical instruments INTERNATIONAL TRADE FAIR	
Geneva	CYCLE AND MOTORCYCLE EXHIBITION WOMEN'S READY-TO-WEAR AND ACCESSORIES EXHIBITION INTERNATIONAL COMMERCIAL VEHICLES SHOW	
Genoa	ORCHIDEA – orchid show FIORARTE – salon of Italian flower-growers	
Grenoble	SEA – European antiques fair	Jan or Feb
Gothenburg	INTERNATIONAL BOAT SHOW INFOTRANS – Computer aided information systems in transport MAINTENANCE – industrial maintenance	
Hamburg	GARDEN, TRAVEL AND LEISURE EXHIBITION	
Hanover	ABF – automobiles, boats and tourism	
Helsinki	INTERNATIONAL FUR AUCTION	Feb to Mar
	FORMA – giftware trade fair INTERNATIONAL BOAT SHOW	
London	INTERNATIONAL FOOD EXHIBITION	
Luxembourg	EUROGAST – equipment and installations for the hotel and catering industries	Jan or Feb
	EUROPLEINAIR – European leisure and recreation exhibition	Feb or Mar
Madrid	SICUR – trade exhibition for safety and fire prevention FITUR – tourism fair	
Munich	C-B-R-caravan, boat, international travel fair	twice a
	ISPO – international sport articles	year
Naples	EXPOSUDHOTEL – international exhibition of hotel, tourist and licensed trade equipment	
Nuremberg	INTERNATIONAL TOY FAIR concurrent with TRADE FAIR FOR MODELS, HOBBY AND DO-IT-YOURSELF	Jan or Feb
	FREIZEIT – boating, camping, caravans, tourism and recreation GARTEN – for home gardeners and flower friends MOTOR-SPORT-SCHAU – racing, driving, automobiles, motorcycles and equipment	
Oslo	SAFETY EXHIBITION MOTEUKEN – fashion week	
Paris	SEHM – men's and boys' fashion	Jan or Feb
	SALON INTERNATIONAL DU PRET-A-PORTER FEMININ SIPPA – paper and writing articles	
	ARTS MENAGERS – home economics	Jan or Feb
Rotterdam	BINNENHUIS – home furnishings	Feb or Mar

Place	Event	Time
Stockholm	INTERNATIONAL SWEDISH FURNITURE TRADE FAIR	
	INTERNATIONAL FASHION TRADE FAIR	
Stuttgart	DIDACTA – school, education and vocational training	Feb or Mar
Turin	EXPOVACANZE – vacation, tourism and sports fair	Feb to Mar
Valencia	FEJU – toys and games	Feb or Mar
	FIMI – fashions for children and teenagers	
	MAICOP – baking fair	
	EXPOCARNE – meat industry fair	Feb or Mar
Vienna	VIENNA RECREATION FAIR – tourism, camping, boating, flying and tennis	
Wiesbaden	INTER-KONDI-CA – bakers and confectioners convention	
Zaragoza	SMOPYC – international fair for public works and construction machinery	
	SMAGUA – international water exhibition	
Zurich	INTOOLEX – international trade fair for tools of the industrial finishing industry	
	BIENNIAL MODERN INDUSTRIAL PRODUCTION TECHNOLOGY TRADE FAIR	

March

Place	Event	Time
Amsterdam	AUTOVAK – international trade fair for garage equipment	
Antwerp	BUROTIKA – office equipment and computer industry fair	
	ANTWERP MEUBELSALON – building show	
Athens	NAUTIKO – boat show	
	HOBBY – sport equipment	
Barcelona	CONSTRUMAT – construction fair	
	MOSTRA HILADOS INTERNACIONAL – yarn and thread exhibition	
	SALON GAUDI MUJER INTERNACIONAL – women's fashion	
	SPORT – international sporting goods fair	
	ALIMENTARIA – international food fair	
Basle	EUROCAST – international cable and satellite television exhibition	
	SWISS INDUSTRIES FAIR	
Belgrade	INTERNATIONAL LEATHER GOODS AND SHOE FAIR	mid-month
	INTERNATIONAL AUTOMOBILE SALON	
	INTERNATIONAL SPORTS, NAUTICAL AND TOURISM	
Berlin	INTERNATIONAL TOURIST BÖRSE – international tourism exhibition	
Bilbao	ANTICUARIOS – antiques fair	
	ELA – ELEKTRO – international electrical industry, automation and electronics fair	
Birmingham	GLASSEX – glass and glass technology	
	MEATEX – meat technology and food processing MT – material testing	
	INTERNATIONAL MATERIALS HANDLING FAIR	
Bologna	SAEIDUE – international salon for construction renovation equipment	
	INTERNATIONAL CHILDREN'S BOOK FAIR	
	ARTE FIERA – international trade market for contemporary art	
Bremen	BOOT – boat show	Feb or Mar
Brussels	EUROBA – for bakers, chocolatiers and confectioners	
	INTERNATIONAL TRADE FAIR	
	INVEST–EXPOR – investment opportunities	
	SPORT EQUIPMENT FAIR	
Budapest	INTERNATIONAL TRAVEL FAIR	

Place	Event	Time
Cologne	INTERNATIONAL IRON GOODS FAIR	
Copenhagen	FUTURE FASHION SCANDINAVIA	Feb or Mar
Düsseldorf	WEST GERMAN ART FAIR	
	IGEDO – fashion fair	
	GDS – footwear trade fair	
Edinburgh	SCOTTISH ANTIQUES FAIR	
Essen ·	EQUITANA – equestrian sports	86 (biennial)
Frankfurt	INTERNATIONAL TRADE FAIR	
Geneva	AUTO – international automobile show	
Genoa	PRIMAVERA – household, gifts, holidays and leisure fair	
Gothenburg	EXHIBITION OF STORAGE MATERIALS HANDLING TUR	
	AUTO – trade fair for motor, workshop, service station and garage equipment	
Graz	MARKETING IMPULSE CONGRESS	
Grenoble	HOLIDAY AND TRAVEL FAIR	
	SIG – international winter sports equipment trade show	
The Hague	FOVIAM	
Hamburg	INTERNOGRA – restaurants and catering convention	
Hanover	LIGNA – woodworking machines and equipment	
Helsinki	INTERNATIONAL FUR AUCTION	Feb to Mar
Karlsruhe	LEISURE TIME EXHIBITION	
Lausanne	CAMPING + CARAVANING	
	HABITAT + JARDIN – house and garden exhibition	
	INTERNATIONAL HOLIDAY AND TOURISM EXHIBITION	
Leipzig	SPRING FAIR – consumer goods fair where East meets West to talk business	
	BOOK FAIR	
	TECHNICAL FAIR	
	GDR AGRICULTURAL EXHIBITION	
London	INTERNATIONAL FOOD EXHIBITION	Feb to Mar
Luxembourg	EUROPLEINAIR – European leisure and recreation exhibition	
Lyons	INTERNATIONAL SPRING FAIR – consumer goods, the world's largest in terms of exhibition area	
Milan	SICOF – film, photography and lab technology	Mar or Apr
	IPACK-IMA – packaging material and machinery	
	COVERLEX – paper production machinery	
Moscow	TECHNOLOGY – modern technologies in industry and economy	
Nancy	GASTROLOR – trade exhibition for gastronomy (in Metz)	
Naples	NAUTICSUD – international nautical exhibition	
Nice	GRAND INTERNATIONAL FAIR	
Nuremberg	KUNST UND ANTIQUITÄTEN – art and antiques	Mar or Apr
Oslo	THE SEA FOR ALL – international boat and engine show	
Paris	SIF – furs	
	SIA – agriculture and	
	SIMA – agricultural machinery	
	MECANELEM – propelling techniques	
	SIG – winter sports equipment	
Prague	INTERKAMERA – international audio-visual exhibition	
Rotterdam	ANTIKBEURS AHOY – antiques fair	Mar or Apr
	VISMA AHOY – sport fishing fair	
Salzburg	JASPOWA – hunting and sports weapons	
Seville	VIBEXPO – wine and beverage fair	
	MOBILARIA – furniture and machinery	
Stockholm	CAD/CAM – trade fair and conference	
	INTERNATIONAL SHOE TRADE FAIR	
Stuttgart	DIDACTA – school, education and vocational training	
Turin	EXPOVACANZE – vacation, tourism and sports fair	Feb to Mar

Place	Event	Time
Valencia	MAICOP – baking fair	Feb or Mar
Verona	INTERNATIONAL AGRICULTURAL AND ZOO-TECHNICAL FAIR	
Vienna	VIENNA SPRING FAIR – for household goods, music, gardening, agriculture, cooking, machines and tools	
Warsaw	AGPOL – consumer goods exhibition	
Zaragoza	ROBOTICA	
Zurich	MODEXPO – ladies fashion fair	
	SWISSPO – Swiss winter sports goods fair	
	SAFT – syndicate for avant-garde fashion trends	

April

Antwerp	HORECANT – enterprises fair	
Barcelona	EXPOTRONICA – clothing machine exhibition	
	EXPOMOVIL – international automobile exhibition	
Basle	SWISSPACK – packaging industry	
	ART AND ANTIQUES FAIR OF SWITZERLAND	
Belgrade	INTERNATIONAL AUTOMOBILE SALON	
	INTERNATIONAL SPORTS, NAUTICAL AND TOURISM FAIR	
Berne	LOGIC – microcomputer exhibition	Apr or
	BEA – handicraft, agricultural, industrial and commercial exhibition	May
Bilbao	AMBIENTE – international industrial equipment fair	
	PROMA – international environmental protection exhibition	
	ARTEDER – international art fair	
Birmingham	CAD/CAM – computer-aided-design exhibition	
	INTERNEPCON – electronic production conference	
	BREWEX – brewing, bottling and allied trades	
	PAKEX – packaging	
Bologna	COSMOPROF – international perfumes and cosmetic show	
Bremen	AUTOVISION – motor show	Mar or Apr
Brussels	AUTOTECHNICA – automobile accessories	
Budapest	MIPEL – industrial electronics and instrument design	
	AUTOSERVICE – motorcar maintenance and repair	
	CONSTRUMA – construction industry	
	AVIAEXPO – aviation exhibition	
Copenhagen	SCANDEFA – dentistry	
Düsseldorf	IGEDO – fashion fair	
	WIRE – wire and cable trade fair	
Essen	HANDARBEIT – textile design	
	INATEC – food and nutrition	
	OPTICA – optometrics	
Frankfurt	FUR TRADE FAIR	
Geneva	INTERNATIONAL EXHIBITION OF INVENTIONS AND NEW TECHNOLOGIES	
	INDEX – trade fair for the nonwovens and disposables industries	
	NASCON – intern. security conference and exhibition	
	SPEMAC – special technologies	
Gothenburg	KEMI – trade fair for chemistry	
	ISM – industrial trade fair	
Graz	AUSTRIAN IRON FAIR FOR HEAVY INDUSTRY	
Grenoble	DOG SHOW	Apr or
	SAM – mountain and ski resort equipment	May
The Hague	HOVIMEX	
Hamburg	VITALIS – nature and health	

Place	Event	Time
Hanover	ART AND ANTIQUES FAIR	
	WORLD TRADE ARENA (HANNOVER MESSE) – world's largest industrial fair, an orgy for lovers of technology	
Innsbruck	SPRING FAIR – house and garden exhibition	
Istanbul	TOURISMFAIR	
Karlsruhe	FIT UND GESUND – health exhibition	
Lille	LILLE INTERNATIONAL FAIR	
London	›DAILY MIRROR‹ PHOTOWORLD EXHIBITION	
Lucerne	ARTISWISS/ORNARIS – Swiss handicrafts and international boutique articles	Apr or May
Madrid	IBERDISCO – recording industry fair	
Marseilles	PROMO–LOISIRS FAIR	
Milan	INTERNATIONAL DESIGN FAIR	Apr
Moscow	INTERCON – production and treatment in electronics and microelectronics	
Nancy	INTERNATIONAL FORESTRY FAIR	
	ANTIQUES EXHIBITION and FLEA MARKET	
Nantes	INTERNATIONAL GRAND FAIR	
Naples	BI-MI-SUD – biennial machine tool exhibition	Apr or May
	EXPO-SPORT and VACANZA – sports and recreation exhibition	
Nuremberg	KUNST UND ANTIQUITÄTEN – art and antiques	
Oslo	MIKRODATA – microcomputers for home, office and education	biennial
Paris	SICOP–SPECIAL – office machinery	Apr or May
Rheims	INTERNATIONAL PHOTO EXHIBITION	
Rotterdam	VISMA AHOY – sport fishing fair	Mar or Apr
Seville	FERIA DE ANTIQUEDADES – antique fair	
	FERIA DE MUESTRAS IBEROAMERICANA – industrial fair	
Stockholm	NORDIC BUILDIN	
	INTERNATIONAL ANTIQUES FAIR	
	INTERNATIONAL ELECTRONICS PRODUCTION TRADE FAIR	
	KOMMUNAL FRITID – trade fair for suppliers and projectors within sports and recreation areas	
Toulouse	TOULOUSE INTERNATIONAL FAIR	Apr or May
Trieste	INTERNATIONAL FLOWER EXHIBITION	
Valencia	FIAM – jewellery, lamps and metal art	
	CEVIDER – decorative articles	
Verona	VINITALY – wine industry fair	
	REGALIT – food gifts exhibition	
Vienna	SPIEL – Austrian toy fair	
Zaragoza	FIMA – international technical fair for agricultural machinery	
Zurich	ANTIC – international art and antiques fair	

May

Amsterdam	INTERCLEAN – international trade fair of professional maintenance and cleaning	
	REIMATO – cleaning machinery for towns and municipal refuse destruction	
	EUROFINISH – technical and maintenance services	
Antwerp	INTERNATIONAL TRADE FAIR	
Belgrade	INTERNATIONAL TECHNICAL FAIR	
Berlin	FREE BERLIN ART EXHIBITION	
	SHOWTECH – international congress for entertainment technology, in conjunction with VIDEO exhibition	
Berne	BEA – handicraft, agricultural, industrial and commercial exhibition	Apr or May

Place	Event	Time
Bielefeld	NATURA – regional health exhibition	
	URLAUB – tourism and leisure exhibition	
	WISA – regional consumer goods exhibition	
Bilbao	EXPOCONSUMO – consumer goods	
	EXPOVACACIONES – tourism and recreation	
Birmingham	OPTRAFAIR – optics	
	HEVAC – heating, ventilating, air conditioning	
	COMMUNICATIONS – communications equipment and systems	
	ROSPA – safety exhibition	
Bordeaux	INTERNATIONAL FAIR	
Bremen	HAFA – home and family	
Budapest	INTERNATIONAL SPRING FAIR – technology	
Cannes	INTERNATIONAL FILM FESTIVAL – the one and only with a huge film convention	
Copenhagen	SCANDINAVIAN FURNITURE FAIR	
Dublin	SPRING INDUSTRIAL FAIR	
	FOREX – foreign exchange dealers conference	
Düsseldorf	DRUPA – printing and paper fair	
Essen	ENTSORGA – urban sanitation	
Florence	INTERNATIONAL ARTS AND CRAFTS FAIR	May or Jun
	CAMPIONARIA DI FIRENZE – leather goods fair	
Frankfurt	INFOBASE – data processing	
Geneva	SITEV – intern. exhibition for suppliers of the motor vehicle industry	
Genoa	RIABITAT – exhibition of building renovation and maintenance	
Gothenburg	RORO – roll-on/roll-off and ferry transport	
Graz	GRAZ SOUTH-EAST FAIR	1st week-end
Grenoble	SAM – mountain and ski resort equipment	Apr or May
	SPRING FAIR	
Hamburg	PORTEX – harbour convention	
Helsinki	EUCEPA – environmental protection in the 90's	
Karlsruhe	REHAB – international exhibition for technical aids for rehabilitation with workshops	1987, biennial
Lausanne	IFFEX – international frozen food exhibition	May or Jun
	COMPUTER – Swiss computer exhibition	
Lille	TOBACCO FAIR	
	APPLICA – trade fair for practical electronics and information systems	
Lisbon	FIL – international fair	
London	INTERIOR DESIGN INTERNATIONAL	
Lucerne	ARTISWISS/ORNARIS – Swiss handicrafts and international boutique articles	Apr or May
Luxembourg	INTERNATIONAL SPRING FAIR	May or Jun
Mannheim	MAY MARKET – popular industrial exhibition	
Marseilles	SETSO – energy techniques and security exhibition	
Milan	INTEL – electrotechnology and electronics	
Naples	EXPO-SPORT und VACANZA – sports and recreation exhibition	Apr or May
Oslo	ELIADEN – electrotechnical exhibition	biennial
	NOR-SHIPPING – shipping exhibition	biennial
Palermo	INTERNATIONAL MEDITERRANEAN FAIR	
Paris	SICOP–SPECIAL – office machinery	Apr or May
Sofia	GREAT INTERNATIONAL BOOK FAIR	
Stockholm	INTERNATIONAL TRADE FAIR OF CONTROL SYSTEMS IN PULP, PAPER, BOARD, PARTICLE BOARD, FIBREBOARD AND CONVERTING INDUSTRY	
Stuttgart	IWB – weapons fair	
	PRO SANITA – health and nature	
Toulouse	TOULOUSE INTERNATIONAL FAIR	Apr or May
Trieste	TRANSADRIA – international exhibition and conference on sea and roll-on, roll-off transport	

Place	Event	Time
Valencia	FIV – industrial trade fair	
	SALON INTERNATIONAL DE LA MUSICA – musical instruments	
	MUNDO BELLEZA – perfumes, cosmetics and hairdressing articles	
	DROGUEXPO – drugstore articles	
	EXPOFARMACIA – congress and exhibition of pharmaceutical specialities	
Verona	EUROPFREST – forestry fair	biennial
Vienna	IFABO – international trade fiar for office organization	
Warsaw	INTERNATIONAL BOOK FAIR	
Zaragoza	NATIONAL GARDEN AND FLORAL ART COMPETITION	
	EXPOARAGON – regional popularization fair	
	FONM – official and natioanl trade fair	

June

	PARK ILLUMINATION – the park of the spa flooded in light	summer
Baden-Baden	ROSE SHOW – noble flowers nobly presented	
Barcelona	ST. JOHN'S NIGHT – the city celebrates all night long, with dazzling lights fireworks and dancing	23 Jun
Berlin	WORLD CULTURES FESTIVAL – international folklore, singing, dancing and handicrafts	
Berne	INTERNATIONAL THEATRE FESTIVAL	
Bielefeld	BIELEFELDER SOMMERTREFF – jazz, folk, organ concerts and theatre	May to Sep
Bonn	BONN SUMMER – folklore, concerts and street theatre	May to Oct
Brest	JOURNEES VERTES – agricultural fair	
Cologne	INTERNATIONAL COMPUTER EXHIBITION	
Copenhagen	WORLD FISHING	
Düsseldorf	METAV – metalworking industry	
Florence	CAMPIONARIA DI FIRENZE – leather goods fair	May/Jun
Grenoble	SCALE MODEL AND MINIATURE SHOW	
The Hague	BOVAG	
Karlsruhe	FENSTERBAU – international exhibition of the window industry	
	KOMMTECH – German communications fair for microcomputer, videotex and office communications	
Lausanne	COMPUTER – Swiss computer exhibition	
London	GROSVENOR HOUSE ANTIQUES FAIR	
	COMPUTER FAIR	
	INTERNATIONAL CERAMICS FAIR	
Luxembourg	INTERNATIONAL SPRING FAIR	May or Jun
Madrid	FINART – handicrafts fair	
Moscow	ENERGIE – alternative energy resources	
Nancy	NANCY INTERNATIONAL FAIR	
Nuremberg	WILDTIER UND UMWELT – German hunting and fishing exhibition, with international participation	
Oslo	SKOG TRE TEKNIK – wood processing and woodworking	biennial
Paris	TAPIS – rugs and floor coverings	May or Jun
Stuttgart	TELEMATIKA – international telecommunication technics	86 biennial
	WINDOW CONSTRUCTION EXHIBITION	
Toulouse	SALON AERONAUTIQUE ET SPATIAL	
Trieste	INTERNATIONAL SAMPLES FAIR	
Vienna	VONOVA – international wine fair	

Place	Event	Time

July

Bristol	WORLD WINE FAIR	
Cologne	IT'S COLOGNE – international fashion trends	
Deauville	INTERNATIONAL DOG Show	
Düsseldorf	PM – powder metallurgy	
Nantes	WINE FAIR	
Naples	FIERA INTERNAZIONALE DELLA CASA – international house and garden fair	
Rome	ROMA ALTA MODA – fashion fair	

August

Berne	ORNARIS – trade fair of furnishing articles and arts and crafts	
Bordeaux	OYSTER FESTIVAL – in the oyster beds of Arcachon	
Bremen	TIER and NATUR / BIOTA – animals, nature and health	Aug or Sep
Budapest	AGROMASEXPO – agricultural, food machinery and equipment	
	TECHNOLOGY FOR THE PEOPLE	
Cologne	INTERNATIONAL MEN'S FASHION WEEK/ INTERJEANS	
Copenhagen	FUTURE FASHION SCANDINAVIA	
	TEXPO – home and household textiles	
Deauville	AUCTION OF ONE YEAR OLD TOP HORSES	end-month
Düsseldorf	IGEDO JUNIOR – first night collections	
	HIFI – VIDEO	
Frankfurt	INTERNATIONAL TRADE FAIR	
	INTERSTOFF – textiles	
Helsinki	FINNISH FASHION FAIR	
Karlsruhe	PHARMACEUTICAL EXHIBITION	Aug to Sep
Lucerne	SWISS FORESTRY TRADE FAIR	
Oslo	GAVE – EXP / INTEX – Norwegian gift and decoration fair	
Wiesbaden	EDE – German iron merchant congress	

September

Amsterdam	AUTOBUS RAI – international autobus and touring cars exhibition	
	W + G – national trade fair for wine and spirits	
Antwerp	ISOLTIE & ENERGIESPARING – insulation and energy conservation	
	JEDIFA – diamonds and jewellery	
Barcelona	LIBER – international book fair	Sep to Oct
	EXPOHOGAR – house and garden fair	
	SONIMAG – tv, sound and electronics fair	
Basle	VIDEO-EUROPA – Swiss videotext congress and exhibition	
	INTERFEREX – international trade fair for hardware, tools and household goods	
	FABRITEC – trade fair for fabrication installations in electronics	
	SAMA – international exhibition of advanced techniques	

Place	Event	Time
Belgrade	INTERNATIONAL EXHIBITION OF WORKS SECURITY AND ENVIRONMENTAL PROTECTION	
Berlin	OVERSEAS IMPORT FAIR	Sep or Oct
	INTERNATIONAL BROADCASTING EXHIBITION CAMP – computer graphics exhibition	
Berne	BESPO – summer sports and textile fairs	
Birmingham	SURFACE TREATMENT AND FINISHING SHOW	
	METCUT – metal cutting machinery	
	SUBCON – subcontracting industries	
	GLEE – garden and leisure exhibition	
Bologna	MICAM – international shoe fair	quadrennial
	TECHNO TM 4 – quadrennial exhibition of technologies and machinery for the textile, knitting and clothing industry	
Bremen	IMMOBILIA – construction and housing industry fair	Sep or Oct
	BAUEN and WOHNEN – building, living, furnishing	
Brest	FOIRE ST. MICHEL – antiques fair	
Bristol	ELECTRONICS SHOW	
	GIFTWARE AND FASHION ACCESSORIES TRADE SHOW	
	AUTUMN FASHION FAIR	
Budapest	PROTENVITA – ecology and water conservation	
	HOVENTA – restaurants and catering	
Cannes	INTERNATIONAL BOAT WEEK	
Cologne	PHOTOKINA – film, photography, video	
	IFMA – bicycles and motorcycles	
	SPOGA – sports, camping and garden exhibition	
Copenhagen	WORLD CONTRACT MEETING	
Düsseldorf	IGEDO – fashion fair	
	GDS – footwear trade fair	
Essen	SCHWEISSEN UND SCHNEIDEN – international exhibition of welding techniques	
Florence	MOSTRA MERCATO INTERNAZIONAL DELL' ANTIQUARIATO – an orgy for antique lovers	Sep or Oct, biennial
Frankfurt	IAA – international automobile exhibition	biennial
Genoa	SIC – international coffee exhibition	
Gothenburg	LANGEDRAG – floating boat show	
	DAGENS HUSHALL – international consumer goods fair	
The Hague	DAMESBEURS	
Hamburg	NORDBÜRO – office technology	
Hanover	EMO – tool machinery	
Helsinki	FORMA – giftware trade fair	
	FINNISH BOOT AND SHOE FAIR	
Innsbruck	INNSBRUCK FAIR – tourism and alpine agriculture	
Karlsruhe	PHARMACEUTICAL EXHIBITION	Aug or Sep
Lausanne	COMPTOIR SUISSE – national fair	
Lisbon	INTERCASA – electrical appliance exhibition	
Lucerne	BUILDING MODERNIZING FAIR	
Madrid	FIDEC – sporting goods fair	
	INTERMODA – international ready-to-wear fashion fair	
Marseilles	INTERNATIONAL FAIR	
Nancy	EURODESIGN – European fair for industrial innovations	
Nantes	PECHE – international trade fair for fishing and the fishing industry	
Naples	TECNOMESU – trade fair for machinery, equipment and leather for shoe production	
	SUDSPEL – leather goods exhibition	
Nice	SCAME – summer fashion fair	
Nuremberg	NUREMBERG MINERAL AND FOSSIL MARKET – international fair	Sep or Oct
Oslo	MOTEUKEN – fashion week	
Paris	SEHM – men's and boys' fashions	Sep or Oct
Rheims	AUTUMN FAIR with AUTOMOBILE EXHIBITION	

Place	Event	Time
Salzburg	GATEHA – household and garden technologies	
	FASHION MADE IN AUSTRIA – traditional Austrian folk dress and knitted goods	
	ÖSFA – sporting goods exhibition	
	SOUVENIR FAIR	
Southampton	SOUTHAMPTON INTERNATIONAL BOAT SHOW – largest in-water boat show in the United Kingdom	
Stockholm	POSTTEC – international post technics exhibition	
	INTERNATIONAL FASHION TRADE FAIR	
	INTERNATIONAL SHOE TRADE FAIR	
Stuttgart	OFFICE SUPPLIES EXHIBITION	
Toulouse	SALON MEUBLE ET DE LA DECORATION – furniture and interior decorating	
Turin	CARAVAN-EUROPA – mobile homes and accessories	
Vaduz	LIHGA – light industry, commerce and trade exhibition (in the neighbouring town Schaan)	
Valencia	FIM – furniture fair	
Verona	MARMORAC – international fair for the marble, granite, and stone processing industry	
Vienna	HIT – home entertainment electronics and household technology	
	VIENNA AUTUMN FAIR – for construction, agriculture, musical instruments, cooking, machines, tools, and winter articles	
	JUWELIA – jewellery and watches trade fair	
	AGRARIA – agricultural exhibition	
Zaragoza	FORESTAL – national show of forestry industry	biennial
Zurich	ZÜSPA – Zurich autumn show for household, home, sport and fashion	
	FERA – international radio, television and hi-fi exhibition	
	BANQUE – European trade fair for techniques and organization in banking	

October

Amsterdam	EFFIGIENCY BEURS – office machines and equipment	
	SALE – sales promotion trade fair	
	COMDEX EUROPE – Europe international computer trade show	
Antwerp	BENELUX ROBOT AUTOMATION	
Athens	DEFENDORY – army equipment	
Barcelona	SONIMAG – tv, sound and electronics fair	Sep or Oct
Basle	HOLZ – Swiss woodworking trade fair	Oct–Nov
	PRO AQUA – PRO VITA – engineering in environmental protection and ecology	
	BASLE WINE FAIR	
Belgrade	INTERNATIONAL FASHION FAIR	
	INTERNATIONAL BOOK FAIR	
Berlin	BÜRO – DATA BERLIN – office organization exhibition	
Berne	SWISS FURNITURE FAIR	Oct or Nov
	SWISS CARAVAN EXHIBITION	
Bilbao	FERROFORMA – international hardware exhibition	biennial
Bologna	CERSAIE – international exhibition for building industrialization	
	SAIE SITEL – Italian exhibition of technology and organization for local bodies and public services	
Bordeaux	SRIBA – word processing, office equipment and automation exhibition	
	RADIO, TELEVISION, ELECTROACOUSTIC AND AUDIOVISUAL SHOW	
	BATIBOIS – international exhibition for the use of wood in construction	

Place	Event	Time
Bremen	BAUEN and WOHNEN – building, living and furniture	
Bristol	CATERING EXHIBITION	
Bucharest	TIB – international fair	mid-month
Budapest	INTERNATIONAL AUTUMN FAIR	
	INTERNATIONAL DO-IT-YOURSELF AND GARDENING	
	EQUIPINTERPLAYEXPO – toys	
	BUDATRANSPACK – packaging and transport	
	BUSPARTEXPO – bus manufacture	
	INTERPLAY EXPO – toys and games	
	HOBBY AND GARDEN SUPPLIES CONVENTION	
	INTERNATIONAL FALL EXPOSITION-consumer products	
Cannes	IDCOM – video and communication exhibition	
Cologne	ORGATECHNIK – office equipment and systems	
Copenhagen	KONTOR & DATA – business and data	
	AUTOMATIK – industrial automation	
Düsseldorf	INTERKAMA – instrumention and automation	
	IGEDO – fashion fair	
Essen	CARAVAN-SALON – Europe's largest camping fair and exhibition	
Florence	MOSTRA MERCATO INTERNAZIONALE DELL' ANTIQUARIATO – an absolute orgy for antique lovers	Sep to Oct, biennial
Frankfurt	INTERNATIONAL BOOK FAIR	
	PUBLIC DESIGN EXHIBITION	
Genoa	INTERNATIONAL BOAT SHOW	
	INTERNATIONAL EXHIBITION OF UNDERWATER EQUIPMENT	
Gothenburg	DATA INFO – computer and information technology	
	INTERNATIONAL TIMBER, WOOD PRODUCTS AND WOODWORKING MACHINERY INDUSTRY TRADE FAIR	
	INTERFOOD/INTEREST – food products and machinery, restaurant equipment, shop fitting	
Graz	INTERNATIONAL ASTRONAUTICAL FEDERATION MEETING – GRAZ SOUTH-EAST FAIR	
Grenoble	AUTUMN FAIR	
Gütersloh	GÜWA – regional consumer goods	
Hamburg	EMTC – trade convention for the boating industry	
Hanover	INTERRADIO – computer technology and electronics for the home	
Innsbruck	TKS – Tyrolean handicrafts and souvenir exhibition	
Karlsruhe	OFFERTA – consumer goods fair	Oct to Nov
Lausanne	MUSIC FAIR	
Leipzig	FALL INDUSTRIAL FAIR – consumer goods fair	
London	BRITISH DESIGNER SHOW	
	MOTOR FAIR	
Luxembourg	INTERNATIONAL AUTUMN FAIR	
Madrid	LIBER – international book fair	
Nancy	BUROTERT – exhibition for office, information and enterprising services	
	INTERNATIONAL TRADE FAIR (in Metz)	
Nice	MEDAX MEDITERRANEAN – medical profession	
Nuremberg	NUREMBERG MINERAL AND FOSSIL MARKET – international fair	Sep or Oct
Oslo	TRADE FAIR OF THE FURNITURE INDUSTRY	biennial
	BYGG-REIS DEG – Scandinavian building exhibition	
Palermo	MEDI–VINI – international exhibition market for wine advertising	
Paris	SEHM – men's and boys' fashions	Sep or Oct
Rheims	ANTIQUES FAIR	
Rome	EUROPHILA – stamps and telecommunication	

Place	Event	Time
Rotterdam	SKI HAPP – winter sport fair	Oct or Nov
	FEMINA – international consumer goods fair	
	TOTAL ENERGY – energy control, production and insulation	
Salzburg	AUSTRO BÜRO – information and organisation technology	
	AUSTRIAN FURNITURE FAIR	
Seville	AGROMEDITERRANEA – national exhibition and fair for the agricultural industry	
Stockholm	INTERNATIONAL ELECTRICAL TRADE FAIR	
	INTERNATIONAL TECHNICAL TRADE FAIR	
Stuttgart	ELTEFA – electrotechnology	
	HOBBY ELEKTRONIK – microcomputer to model building	
Toulouse	SALON DU TEMPS LIBRE – sports and recreation	biennial
	SITEF – international exhibition of technologies and energy of the future	
Trieste	TRANSADRIA – international exhibition and conference on sea and roll-on, roll-off transport	
Turin	TECNICA – the latest in technology	Oct–Nov
Valencia	IBERFLORA – gardening	
	EUROGARDO – agricultural production	
Verona	EUROCARNE – international exhibition for the meat processing industry	biennial
	INTECSOL – agricultural energy convention	
Vienna	IE – industrial electronics	
Zaragoza	METROMATICA – international show of measurement,	biennial
	testing and control	
Zurich	MODEXPO – ladies fashion fair	biennial
	INTERCOM – trade fair for the communication and information industry	
	Microtechnic – international fair for precision technology	

November

Amsterdam	SPEEL-GOED – international exhibition of toys and hobby articles	
	HOLLAND OFFSHORE – international offshore technology and service exhibition	
Antwerp	KEUKEN EN SANICOMFORT – kitchens and bathrooms	
	VLOEREN, WANDEN, HAARDEN – floors, walls and fireplaces	
Barcelona	EXPOMATEX – textile machinery exhibition	
	TECNOCLINIC – international exhibition of hospital techniques and equipment	
Basle	SNOW – winter sports and recreation show	Oct to Nov
	BASLE WINE FAIR	
Belgrade	INTERN. FURNITURE, FURNISHINGS AND INTERIOR DECORATION EXHIBITION	
Berlin	ANTIQUA	Nov/Dec
Berne	SWISS CARAVAN EXHIBITION	Oct/Nov
Bilbao	SINAVAL – international shipbuilding and harbour industries fair	
	FOSMINER – international exhibition of minerals and fossils	
Birmingham	WOODMEX – woodworking industries	
	I.C.E. – construction equipment	
Bologna	EIMA – international agricultural machinery manufacturers fair	

Place	Event	Time
Bordeaux	CONFOREXPO – interior decorating & furniture exhibition	
	RACING CARS AND RACING MOTORBIKE EXHIBITION	
Bristol	BICYCLE SHOW	
	FOOD, WINE AND KITCHEN EXHIBITION	
Brussels	INTERNATIONAL FURNITURE FAIR	Nov/Dec
	EUREKA – industrial innovations	
Cologne	ART COLOGNE – international art market	
Copenhagen	INDUSTRITRANSPORT – road transport, internal materials, handling and storage systems	
	INTERTOOL – machine tools and tools	
	TRIROBOT – industrial robots and robot technology	
	KEM-TEK – plant and equipment for the chemical processing industries	
Düsseldorf	K – plastics and rubber	
	DISCOTEC – entertainment catering	
	HOGATEC – hotels, gastronomy, catering	
	MEDICA – diagnostica, therapeutica, technica	
	INTERBAD – pools, medical baths, saunas, technical equipment	
Essen	MODE + HEIM + HANDWERKER – fashion home and hobby – consumer fair	Nov/Dec
	MOTOR-SHOW – world's largest racing car exhibition	
Florence	CAMPIONARIA DI FIRENZE – leather goods fair	Oct or Nov
Frankfurt	FBA – office supplies	
	TOURISTICA – tourism	
	DO-IT-YOURSELF – handymen's needs	
	AGRITECHNICA – agricultural technology	
Genoa	TECNHOTEL – international exhibition of hotel equipment	
	BIBE – international beverage exhibition	
	INTERFOOD – international exhibition of food and fast food	
Gothenburg	ELFACK – electrotechnical trade fair – power, production, distribution	
	SCAN AUTOMATIC hydraulics, pneumatics, electronics, transmission equipment, control technology	
Graz	BÜRODATA – office information	
	MEDICAL TRADE FAIR and CONGRESS FOR GENERAL MEDICINE	
Grenoble	ALPEXPO	
	ARTISA – arts and crafts fair	
The Hague	MICRO COMPEX	
Hamburg	NORDPOSTA – a philatelic paradise	
Hanover	PFERD & JAGD – horseback riding and hunting, with an indoor riding tournament	
Helsinki	FINNTEC – technical fair	
Innsbruck	SENIOR AKTUELL – everything for the older generation	
Karlsruhe	OFFERTA – consumer goods fair	Oct to Nov
Lausanne	ANTIQUE DEALERS SHOW	
	AGRAMA – Swiss agricultural machinery fair	
London	CARAVAN CAMPING HOLIDAY SHOW	
Lucerne	ANTIQUES EXCHANGE	
Madrid	EXPO PLASTICA – plastic manufacturers	
	VINTER – international wine fair	
	IBERPIEL – leather goods fair	
	SIMO – international trade fair for office equipment and data processing	
	FERIARTE – Spanish antiques fair	
Marseilles	SANTONS FAIR – clay and carved wood nativity figures on sale for Christmas	
Moscow	UPAKOVKA – packaging techniques	Nov to Dec
Nancy	ANTIQUES FAIR (in Metz)	
Naples	OPTICA – international optics fair	
Nice	OFNUX – international exhibition for doors, windows, locks and accessories	

Place	Event	Time
Nuremberg	CONSUMENTA – consumer goods fair	
	IENA – international exhibition for ›ideas and inventions‹	
	BRAU – brewing and beverages	
	KUNST UND ANTIQUITÄTEN – art and antiques	
Oporto	PORTEX LAR – household textiles fair	
Oslo	HJEM OG HOBBY – consumer goods fair	Oct–Nov, biennial
	AUTOMATICA/ELECTRONICS	
Paris	EQUIP'HOTEL – hotel and catering equipment	
Prague	PRAGOTHERM – international exhibition of heating, air conditioning, ventilation and cooling	
Rotterdam	TOTAL ENERGY – energy control, production and insulation	Oct/Nov
Seville	SANITARIA – hospital and surgical supplies, pharmaceuticals	
	FLORANDALUCIA – measuring and testing systems	
Stockholm	EDUCATION – trade fair for education	
Stuttgart	HAFA – sports for the whole familiy	
Toulouse	REGIONAL ANTIQUES FAIR	
	VILLAGE GOURMANDE SALON	
	SALON DES ARTISANS CREATEURS	
Turin	TECNICA – the latest in technology	Oct to Nov
Valencia	INTERARTE – art fair	
	FIMMA MADERALIA – wood processing machines	
Verona	INTERNATIONAL HORSE AND RIDING ACCESSOIRES SALON	
Warsaw	INTERNATIONAL EXHIBITION FOR BABY GOODS	
	CONTROLA – scientific research materials and equipment	
Zurich	INTERPHEX – international exhibition and conference for the pharmaceutical, cosmetics and toiletry industry	
	EXPOVINA – Zurich wine fair	

December

Amsterdam	ENERGY ECONOMY – energy control and management, equipment and systems	
	TOUR – tourism trade fair	
Antwerp	INTERNATIONAL FOOD AND DOMESTIC COMFORT FAIR	
Belgrade	INTERNATIONAL FOOD FAIR	
Berlin	ANTIQUA – antiques fair	Nov or Dec
Bologna	EXPO HI–FI – hi-fi equipment exposition	
	INTERNATIONAL MOTORING EXHIBITION	
Brussels	EUREKA – industrial innovations	Nov or Dec
Essen	MOTOR SHOW – world's largest racing car exhibition	Nov or
Grenoble	INTERNATIONAL MOTOR SHOW	
Helsinki	INTERNATIONAL FUR AUCTION	
	FINN-CONSUM – consumer goods	
Innsbruck	OFFICE FAIR	
Moscow	UPAKOVKA – packaging techniques	Nov to Dec
Nancy	INTERNATIONAL POULTRY IMPROVEMENT EXHIBITION (in Metz)	
Nuremberg	NUREMBERG BOOK FAIR	
Oporto	PORTEX – autumn & winter ready-to-wear fashion fair	

Place	Event	Time

January

Place	Event	Time
Aachen	CARNIVAL – culminating with the bestowal of the ›Order of Beastly Earnest‹ on politicians, presidents or other public personalities	Jan to Feb
Barcelona	EPIPHANY procession – fabulously colourful	5 Jan
Berlin	BERLIN MUSIC DAYS	
Bologna	OPERA SEASON	Nov to May
Bonn	CARNIVAL	Dec to Mar
Cannes	MIDEM – international record and music publications festival	
Essen	CARNIVAL – non-stop nonsense throughout the city	Jan to Feb
London	CHINESE NEW YEAR – fire-breathing dragons and lots of fireworks	Jan or Feb
Malaga	GREAT RIDERS PARADE – a grand equestrian show	5 Jan
	WINTER FESTIVAL – tennis, golf, riding, rowing and shooting contests	Jan or Feb
Milan	OPERA SEASON at La Scala	
Monte-Carlo	RALLYE MONTE-CARLO – magnificent men in a mad dash to the Principality	
Moscow	RUSSIAN WINTER – theatres, ballets, exhibitions	25 Dec to 5 Jan
Munich	FASCHING – galas, balls and artists' parties	Jan to Feb
Paderborn	PUPPENSPIELWOCHEN	Jan or Feb
Rome	EPIPHANY – huge celebration at the Piazza Navona	5 Jan
Rotterdam	FILM FESTIVAL – featuring both commercial and more serious films	Jan or Feb
Seville	EPIPHANY – grand procession through the city in honour of the Wise Men of the East	
Stuttgart	FASTNACHT – Stuttgart's celebrations	Jan to Mar
Vienna	FASCHING – the carnival celebrations, galas, balls, concerts and parades	Jan to Mar
Zurich	NEW YEARS RUN – New Year's Eve	

February

Place	Event	Time
Basle	FASTNACHT – world famous ›Mummenschanz‹ pantomime with fantastic disguises, flutes and drumrolls	
Berlin	BERLIN FILM FESTIVAL – one of the most respected in the world	
Bologna	OPERA SEASON	Nov to May
Bonn	CARNIVAL – culminating in the days before Ash Wednesday, when the Chancellor turns his office over to a Carnival clown and nobody notices the difference	Dec to Mar
Bremen	SCHAFFERMAHLZEIT – the city of Bremen invites the local élite and their guests to a gala dinner	
Cannes	INTERNATIONAL AMATEUR FILM FESTIVAL	
Deauville	RALLYE DE LA COTE FLEURIE OLDTIMER-RALLYE	mid-month
Düsseldorf	CARNIVAL – the liveliest carnival celebration in Germany culminates in a big parade on the Monday preceding Ash Wednesday	Feb or Mar
Essen	CARNIVAL – non-stop nonsense throughout the city	Jan to Feb
Frankfurt	FASTNACHTSSONNTAG – parading through the streets on the Sunday before Lent	
Karlsruhe	FASTNACHTSUMZUG – carnival procession	Jan or Feb

Place	Event	Time
Lisbon	CARNIVAL – four days of parades and flower fights before Ash Wednesday	
London	CHINESE NEW YEAR – fire-breathing dragons and lots of fireworks	Jan or Feb
Lucerne	FASTNACHT – carnival costumes filled with whistling, drumming and noise-making revellers	Feb or Mar
Madrid	CARNIVAL	
Malaga	GREAT RIDERS PARADE – a grand equestrian show	Jan or Feb
	WINTER FESTIVAL – tennis, golf, riding, rowing and shooting contests	Jan or Feb
Milan	OPERA SEASON at La Scala	
Monte-Carlo	INTERNATIONAL TELEVISION FESTIVAL	
Munich	FASCHING – galas, balls and artists' parties	Jan or Feb
Nice	CARNIVAL – two weeks of celebrations rivalling those in Rio, with processions, flower fights and music in the streets	
Paderborn	PUPPENSPIELWOCHEN	Jan or Feb
Reykjavik	FILM FESTIVAL	
Rotterdam	FILM FESTIVAL – featuring both commercial and more serious films	Jan to Feb
Sofia	NEW BULGARIAN MUSIC – a festival for Bulgarian composers	
Stuttgart	FASTNACHT – Stuttgart carnival celebrations	Jan to Mar
Trieste	CARNIVAL	
Vaduz	FASTNACHT – the final celebrations before Lent	Feb or Mar
Venice	CARNIVAL – classical, mystical; Europe's best masked balls and most élite carnival celebrations	Feb or Mar
Verona	BACCHANAL DE GUOCCHI – the closing festivities of carnival in Verona	
Vienna	FASCHING – the carnival celebrations, galas, balls, concerts and parades	Jan to Mar
Wiesbaden	FASTNACHT – a refined farewell to the pleasures denied during Lent	
Zurich	FASTNACHT – music, parades and masked balls	Shrove Tuesday

March

Basle	FASTNACHT – world famous ›Mummenschanz‹ – pantomime with fantastic disguises, flutes and drum-rolls	Feb or Mar
Belgrade	INTERNATIONAL FILM FESTIVAL	
	INTERNATIONAL FILM FESTIVAL	
Berne	OSTEREIERMARKT	
Bilbao	HOLY WEEK – a week of festivities with processions and masses	Mar or Apr
Bologna	OPERA SEASON	Nov to May
Bonn	CARNIVAL – culminating in the days before Ash Wednesdays, when the Chancellor turns his office over to a Carnival clown and nobody notices the difference	Dec to Mar
Bremen	OSTERWIESE – an Easter celebration of spring, lots of folklore	Mar or Apr
Dublin	ST. PATRICK'S WEEK – celebrations surrounding Ireland's National Holiday, St. Patrick's Day on 17 March, the city goes wild	
Düsseldorf	CARNIVAL – the liveliest carnival celebrations of Germany culminate in a big parade on the Monday preceding Ash Wednesday	Feb or Mar
Frankfurt	DIPPEMESS – ceramics and pottery market	
Hamburg	FRÜHLINGS-DOM – folk festival with rides, games and high-tech joy machines	

Place	Event	Time
Leipzig	INTERNATIONAL BACH FESTIVAL – in honour of the great Johann Sebastian, son of Leipzig	
Lille	INTERNATIONAL FESTIVAL OF SHORT SUBJECT AND DOCUMENTARY FILMS	
Lisbon	HOLY WEEK – processions galore	
Liverpool	GRAND NATIONAL – the world's most famous steeplechase	
London	BOAT RACE along the Thames, between Oxford and Cambridge	
Lucerne	FASTNACHT – carnival costumes filled by whistling, drumming and noise-making revellers	Feb or Mar
Luxembourg	EMAISCHEN – Easter Monday celebrations	
Madrid	MADRID THEATRE AND CINEMA FESTIVAL	Mar or Apr
Malaga	SEMANA SANTA (holy week) – processions, liturgical celebrations and passion plays	Mar or Apr
Manchester	SPEEDWAY & STOCK CAR RACING	Mar to Nov
Milan	OPERA SEASON at La Scala	
Monte-Carlo	BAL DE LA ROSE	
	INTERNATIONAL TENNIS TOURNAMENT – tennis millionaires on the court and in the stands	
	SPRING ARTS FESTIVAL – international ensembles bring the best in opera and drama	
Nantes	FETES DE MI-CAREME – festival of the Fast of Lent	mid-month
Nuremberg	SPRING FESTIVAL	Mar or Apr
Rome	JOSEPH'S DAY – a celebration of spring	19 March
Seville	HOLY WEEK – the last week of Lent is Seville's biggest festival, with magnificent processions and thousands of believers out on the streets	Mar or Apr
Stuttgart	FASTNACHT – Stuttgart's carnival celebrations	Jan to Mar
Vaduz	FASTNACHT – the final celebrations before Lent	Feb or Mar
Valencia	FALLAS – week-long celebration on the coming of spring, with the highpoint on 19 March, when wood and paper mâché effigies of historical or current political figures are set on fire and the entire city is ablaze	
Valletta	HOLY WEEK – festive celebrations, culminating with a grand procession on Good Friday	Mar or Apr
Venice	CARNIVAL – Europe's best masked balls and most élite carnival celebrations	Feb or Mar
Vienna	VIENNALE FILM FESTIVAL	Jan to Mar
	VIENNA SPRING MARATHON – jogging on cobblestones	
	FASCHING – the carnival celebrations, galas, balls, concerts and parades	
Zaragoza	SEMANA SANTA – religious celebrations and bullfights	Mar or Apr

Place	Event	Time
April		

Place	Event	Time
Barcelona	ROSE MARKET – at the Ramblas, on ›Lovers' Day‹	23 Apr
Berlin	ART DAYS – a festival of the fine and the performing arts, throughout the city	
Berne	GRAND PRIX DE BERNE – Epée fencing World Cup	
Bilbao	HOLY WEEK – a week of festivities, with processions and masses	Mar or Apr
Bologna	OPERA SEASON	Nov to May
Bremen	OSTERWIESE – Easter celebration of spring, lots of folklore	Mar or Apr
Bristol	BRISTOL MARATHON – Bristol is on the run	
Cannes	CHURCH HYMN FESTIVAL	
Cologne	OSTERVOLKSFEST – folk festival from Easter Saturday to beginning of May	
Copenhagen	DRONNINGENS FØDSELSDAG – the Queen celebrates her birthday	16 Apr
Dublin	OPERA FESTIVAL – Dublin listens for a change	
Edinburgh	FOLK FESTIVAL – the Scots sing up a storm as only they can	Apr or May
Florence	SCOPPIO DEL CARRO – a wagon loaded with fireworks is lit up and explodes	Easter Sunday
Gothenburg	GOTHENBURG SCANDINAVIAN HORSE SHOW	Apr
	GARDEN PARTY – horticulture show	to Sep
	LISEBERG AMUSEMENT PARK – concerts, entertainment, theatre, dancing	
The Hague	HAAGSE VLOIENMARKT	
Hamburg	FRÜHLINGS-DOM – folk festival, with rides, games and high-tech joy machines	
Hanover	SPRING FESTIVAL – annual fair with booths, amusements and fireworks	
Helsinki	VAPPU NIGHT – a carnival-like celebration of spring	3 Apr
Lisbon	HOLY WEEK – processions galore	
London	MAUNDY THURSDAY – The Queen distributes alms	
	EASTER PARADE	
Luxembourg	EMAISCHEN – Easter Monday celebrations	Mar or Apr
Madrid	MADRID THEATRE AND CINEMA FESTIVAL	
Malaga	SEMANA SANTA (Holy Week) – processions, liturgical celebrations and passion plays	Mar or Apr
Manchester	SPEEDWAY & STOCK CAR RACING	Mar to Nov
Milan	OPERA SEASON at La Scala	
Nancy	UNIVERSITY THEATRE FESTIVAL	
Naples	NAPLES SYMPHONY SEASON	
Nuremberg	SPRING FESTIVAL	Mar or Apr
Paderborn	LUNAPARK	last weekend in Apr
Rome	EASTER – all Rome and especially the Vatican celebrates the resurrection of Christ from Maundy (Holy) Thursday to Easter Sunday – hundreds of thousands of pilgrims from around the globe	Easter
Seville	HOLY WEEK – the last week of Lent is Seville's biggest festival, with magnificent processions and thousands of believers out on the streets	
	FERIA DE ABRIL – partying Seville style – coaches, horsemen, big hats and Amazons	
Toulouse	FETE DE LA VIOLETTE – folkloristic Festival	Easter time
Valletta	HOLY WEEK – festive celebrations, culminating in a grand procession on Good Friday	
Vienna	STADTFEST – dancing in the streets and squares of the inner city	

605

Place	Event	Time
Wiesbaden	CASINO BALL – a party in the grand style for those who love glamour	Spring
Zurich	ZURICH SPRING FESTIVAL ZURICH WEAPON RACE ZURICH MARATHON	

May

Aachen	STUDENTISCHER FRÜHSCHOPPEN – students of Aachen at an early morning gala against the historic backdrop of the marketplace	
Belgrade	YOUTH DAY – with a wide variety of sports events BELGRADE MUSIC CELEBRATIONS	
Berlin (East)	MAYDAY – parades, banners and demonstration of solidarity	1 May
Berne	INTERNATIONAL JAZZ FESTIVAL ERLACHER HOFFEST – classical music GERANIENMARKT – flowers all over the city	
Bielefeld	BIELEFELDER SOMMERTREFF – jazz, folklore, organ concerts and theatre	May to Sep
Birmingham	LORD MAYOR'S PROCESSION – Birmingham pulls out the stops for the new mayor TULIP FESTIVAL	end of month
Bologna	OPERA SEASON	Nov to May
Bonn	BONNER SUMMER – folklore, concerts and street theatre	May to Oct
Bordeaux	MUSICAL MAY, Bordeaux's big music festival	
Bremen	FLEAMARKET	Saturdays
Bristol	NORTH SOMERSET SHOW	
Brussels	QUEEN ELISABETH MUSIC COMPETITION – for violin and piano, every two years 1986: piano	
Copenhagen	WONDERFUL COPENHAGEN MARATHON – jogging Scandinavian style	mid-month
Dublin	›FEIS CEOIL‹ – FOLKLORE FESTIVAL – Dublin sings POLO GAMES at the All-Ireland Polo Club in Phoenix Park	
Edinburgh	FOLK FESTIVAL – the Scots sing up a storm as only they can	Apr or May
Essen	MAITEMBER – five months of fun, from circus to fireworks, jousting knights and Essen's own Hawaiian luau	May to Sep
Florence	CALCIO IN COSTUME – a rugby-like football match with the players in colourful, historic costumes	1st Sunday in May
Frankfurt	WÄLDCHESTAG – the Tuesday after Whitsuntide finds the streets filled with Frankfurters, music and apple wine, a local speciality JAZZ IN THE PALMEN GARTEN	May to Sep bi-weekly
Glasgow	INTERNATIONAL GATHERING SCOTLAND – typical Scotch celebration, with clan meetings, music, theatre and dance	May or Jun
Gothenburg	LISENBERG AMUSEMENT PARK – concerts, entertainment, theatre, dancing	Apr to Sep
Gütersloh	CITY-TREFF PFINGSTKIRMES – folk festival	
The Hague	RESIDENCE ORCHESTRA OF THE HAGUE NETHERLANDS DANCE THEATRE SPORTS DAY	May
Hamburg	HAMBURG BALLET DAYS – the world-renowned Hamburg ballet under the direction of John Neumeier	May to Jan
Karlsruhe	FRÜHJAHRSMARKT	May to Jun
Lausanne	FESTIVAL INTERNATIONAL – world famous dancers and musicians flock to the city and fill its stages	May to Jun
Liverpool	INTERNATIONAL WATERWAYS FESTIVAL – a landed party for seamen from around the world	

Place	Event	Time
London	SUMMER EXHIBITION – what's up in British arts	
	CHELSEA FLOWER SHOW – four days of flower power	
Luxembourg	OCTAVE OF OUR LADY OF LUXEMBOURG – festive religious processions	5th Sunday after Easter
Madrid	FESTIVAL OF THE PATRON SAINT ISIDOR – with bullfights, processions, fireworks, theatre and concerts	8–15 May
	MADRID OPEN TENNIS CHAMPIONSHIP	
Manchester	MANCHESTER AIR SHOW	May or Jun
	SPRING BANK HOLIDAY WEEKEND – public boat trip	
	TEXACO TROPHY INTERNATIONAL MATCH – sponsored cricket international	
Mannheim	AMUSEMENT FAIR – huge festival concurrent with the May Market	till end May
Milan	OPERA SEASON at the Scala	till end May
Monte-Carlo	GRAND PRIX – a day at the race, Monte-Carlo style	
	GRAND GALA – donning Dior the beautiful people dine and dance to help the Red Cross	
Moscow	MOSCOW SPRING – concerts, symphonies and orchestras	
Munich	THEATRE FESTIVAL – international stages giving guest performances	May or Jun
Nancy	WORLD THEATRE FESTIVAL	
Naples	S. GENNARO FESTIVAL	1st Sunday
Nice	GREAT MARKET OF NICE	
	INTERNATIONAL BOOK FAIR	
Nuremberg	SUMMER IN NUREMBERG – cultural programmes	May to Sep
Oslo	17 MAY – national holiday celebrating signing of constitution, parades and partying	
Paderborn	FRÜHLINGSFEST – Spring celebrations	
Paris	INTERNATIONAL TENNIS CHAMPIONSHIPS	May or Jun
Prague	PRAGUE SPRING – music festival in all theatres and concert halls	
Rheims	JOAN OF ARC FESTIVAL	
Salzburg	HELLBRUNN FESTIVAL / MOZARTEUM FOUNDATION CONCERTS / CASTLE CONCERTS AND . . . AND . . .	May to Oct
Seville	ROMERIA DEL ROCIO – pilgrimage to the Guadalquivir	
	MAYO MUSICAL HISPANLENSE – classical music festival	
Sofia	INTERNATIONAL SOFIA MUSIC WEEKS – the biggest musical event in Bulgaria	May or Jun
Stockholm	WALPURGIS NIGHT – bonfires, songs and speeches to welcome the long-awaited advent of spring	beginning of May
Toulouse	GRAND FENETRA – more folkloristic festivities	
	ACADEMIE DES JEUX FLORAUX – poetry competition	1–3 of May
Valletta	CARNIVAL – partying in the streets, pure kodachrome	2nd weekend
Vienna	VIENNA FESTIVAL – music indoors and out, exhibitions, theatre, one of Europe's best festivals	May or Jun
Warsaw	STUDENT THEATRE DRAMA FESTIVAL	
Wiesbaden	CASINO BALL – a party in the grand style for those who love glamour	Spring
Zaragoza	FIESTAS DE PRIMAVERA – spring celebrations with biennial art fair	

Calendar of Events

Place	Event	Time
June		

Place	Event	Time
Amsterdam	HOLLAND FESTIVAL – ballet, street theatre, symphonies and more, a cultural cornucopia	Jun to Jul
Baden-Baden	ROSE SHOW – noble flowers nobly presented	
Barcelona	ST. JOHN'S NIGHT – the city goes crazy all night long, with dazzling lights fireworks and dancing	23 Jun
Berlin	WORLD CULTURES FESTIVAL – international music, folklore and handicrafts	
Berne	INTERNATIONAL THEATRE FESTIVAL	
Bonn	BONN SUMMER – folklore, concerts and street theatre	May to Oct
Bremen	FLEAMARKET	Saturdays
Bristol	LORRY DRIVER OF THE YEAR COMPETITION – looking for the fastest and trickiest jumbo-pilot	
	BRISTOL POWER BOAT GRAND PRIX – on the Bristol waters	
	WEST OF ENGLAND INTERNATIONAL TENNIS TOURNAMENT – Bristol's centre court as centre of West of England	
Cannes	INTERNATIONAL CABARET AND COFFEE-HOUSE THEATRE FESTIVAL	
Cologne	COLOGNE SUMMER – on the Roncalliplatz, Rhine and in the Volksgarten changing cultural activities during 4 months	Jun to Sep
Copenhagen	TIVOLI SEASON – solists and orchestras from around the world play in the Tivoli Gardens	May to Sep
Deauville	INTERNATIONAL TRIATHLON COMPETITION	end of the month
Dublin	ORGAN FESTIVAL	May to Sep
	POLO GAMES at the All-Ireland Polo Club in Phoenix Park	
Essen	MAITEMBER – five months of fun, from circus to fireworks, jousting knights and Essen's own Hawaiia luau	May to Sep
Frankfurt	JAZZ IN THE PALMENGARTEN	May to Sep bi-weekly
Geneva	FOLKLORE FESTIVAL in the Bois de la Bâtie	
Glasgow	INTERNATIONAL GATHERING SCOTLAND – a typical Scotch celebration, with clan meetings, music, theatre and dance	May or Jun
Gothenburg	MIDSUMMER – dancing round the Maypole, games and celebrations	21–23 Jun
Hamburg	GALOPP-DERBY-WOCHE – Ascot in Hamburg	May to Jun
	HAMBURG BALLET DAYS – the world-renowned Hamburg ballet under the direction of John Neumeier	
Hanover	LICHTERFEST – musicians, dancers, choirs, and bands parade ›thousands of lights light up the magnificent fountains, and it's all topped off by a display of fireworks to the accompaniment of Handel's music	
	MARKSMEN'S FESTIVAL – the world's largest shooting spree	
Helsinki	MIDSUMMER NIGHT – the longest day of the year is longer here than in most places and well worth celebrating	21/22 Jun
Istanbul	ISTANBUL FESTIVAL – folk-dancing, concerts at historic sites, ballet, mime, performing arts	20 Jun to 25 Jun
Karlsruhe	FRÜHJAHRSMARKT – Spring market	May to Jun
Lausanne	FESTIVAL INTERNATIONAL – world famous dancers and musicians flock to the city and fill its stages	May to Jun
Liège	ST. PHOLIEN FOLKLORE FESTIVAL	4th Sunday
Lille	GRAND PARADE AND CITY FESTIVAL	mid Jun
Lisbon	ST. ANTHONY'S FESTIVAL and POPULAR SAINTS FESTIVAL – parades in traditional costumes and general gaiety	

Place	Event	Time
Liverpool	MERSEY RIVER FESTIVAL – non-stop action on the water, on land and in the pubs	
London	TROOPING THE COLOUR	Jun or Jul
	WIMBLEDON TENNIS TOURNAMENT	
Luxembourg	MUSICAL SPRING – just what the name implies	May to Jun
Lyons	FLEA MARKET	
Madrid	FOLK FESTIVAL IN HONOUR OF ST. ANTONY	
Manchester	TEXACO TROPHY INTERNATIONAL MATCH – sponsored cricket international	May or Jun
Marseilles	MEDITERRANEAN HORSE SHOW	
Milan	OPERA SEASON at the Scala	
Munich	THEATRE FESTIVAL – international stages giving guest performances	May or Jun
Nancy	FOLKLORE FESTIVAL	last Saturday
Naples	FIRE FESTIVAL – in front of the Church of S. Maria del Carmine	
Nuremberg	OLD CITY FESTIVAL – dancing in the medieval atmosphere	
	SUMMER IN NUREMBERG – cultural programmes	May to Sep
Oporto	SAINTS' FESTIVAL – high life in Oporto	23rd Jun
Oslo	CARNIVAL – Norway says welcome to the summer	
	23 JUNE – midsummer festival, strange things can happen on the longest day of the year	
Paris	INTERNATIONAL TENNIS CHAMPIONSHIPS	May or Jun
Rheims	RHEIMS JAZZ FESTIVAL	
Reykjavik	ARTS FESTIVAL	
Rotterdam	POETRY INTERNATIONAL – the literary meet and compare notes	
	HOLLAND FESTIVAL – concerts and exhibitions throughout the land	
Salzburg	HELLBRUNN FESTIVAL / MOZARTEUM FOUNDATION CONCERTS / CASTLE CONCERTS AND ... AND ...	May to Oct
Seville	CORPUS CHRISTI PROCESSION	Jun or Jul
Sofia	INTERNATIONAL SOFIA MUSIC WEEKS	
Stockholm	MIDSUMMER NIGHT – all Stockholm dances through the shortest night of the year – out in the country, just like in an Ingmar Berman – or Woody Allen – film	21 Jun
Strasbourg	ANNUAL MUSIC FESTIVAL	2nd and 3rd weeks
Toulouse	WEEK OF THE ORGAN MUSIC	Jun to Sep
	MUSIC FESTIVAL – in the Dominican monastery	
Trieste	SOUND AND LIGHT – dramatic tragedies performed daily at the Miramare castle	Jun to Sep
Turin	ST. JOHN'S DAY – ›orge e baccanale‹ in honour of the city's patron saint ...	Jun 24th
Valletta	FESTA – each village on the island(s) celebrates its very own patron saint with processions and fireworks	Summer
Vienna	VIENNA FESTIVAL – music indoors and out, exhibitions, theatre, one of Europe's best festivals	May or Jun
Wiesbaden	INTERNATIONAL RIDING TOURNAMENT – Whitsuntide breeding is everything, for horse, rider and spectator	
	STREET FESTIVAL – high living takes to the streets	
Zurich	INTERNATIONAL FESTIVAL WEEKS in the Zurich Opera House	

Place	Event	Time

July

Place	Event	Time
Amsterdam	HOLLAND FESTIVAL ballet, street theatre, symphonies and more – a cultural cornucopia	Jun to Jul
Baden-Baden	MUSICAL SUMMER – concerts galore for the well-dressed public	Saturdays
Barcelona	FESTIVAL OF THE ›VIRGEN DEL CARMEN‹ – parades, flowers, dancing and fireworks	15 Jul
Berlin	BACH DAYS – fugues for the masses	
Berne	INTERNATIONAL FOLK FESTIVAL on the Gurten	biennial
Bielefeld	BIELEFELDER SOMMERTREFF – jazz, folk, organ concerts and theatre	May to Sep
Bilbao	NUESTRA SENORA DEL CARMEN – festive celebrations in honour of Our Lady	16 Jul
Birmingham	HIGHLAND GATHERING – for Scots feeling homesick	
Bonn	BONN SUMMER – folklore, concerts and dancing	May to Oct
Bremen	FLEAMARKET	Saturdays
Bristol	INTERNATIONAL MUSIC FESTIVAL – music all over the town	
	BRISTOL HORSE SHOW – four-legged power and elegance	
Brussels	OMMEGANG – huge parade of the city's representatives in medieval costumes at the ›Grand‹ Place‹	1st Thursday
Cologne	COLOGNE SUMMER – on the Roncalliplatz, Rhine and in the Volksgarten changing cultural events during 4 summer months	Jun to Sep
Copenhagen	COPENHAGEN SUMMER FESTIVAL – music and dancing	Jul to Aug
Dublin	INTERNATIONAL FOLKLORE FESTIVAL the world comes to Dublin – and sings	May to Sep
	POLO-GAMES at the All-Ireland Polo Club in Phoenix Park	
Düsseldorf	SCHÜTZENFEST – marksmen's festival, with green-clad musicians and a parade on horseback, accompanied by the KIRMES, a huge amusement fair on the Rheinwiesen	
Edinburgh	EDINBURGH CROQUET TOURNAMENT	
Essen	MAITEMBER – five months of fun, from circus to fireworks, jousting knights and Essen's own Hawaiian luau	May to Sep
Frankfurt	JAZZ IN THE PALMENGARTEN	May to Sep biweekly
Gothenburg	LISEBERG AMUSEMENT PARK – concerts, entertainment, theatre, dancing	
Graz	STYRIARTE GRAZ – music festival in the Old City	
Grenoble	FESTIVAL OF FILM SHORTS	
Gütersloh	GÜTERSLOH SUMMER	Jul to Aug
Hanover	MARKSMEN'S FESTIVAL – the world's largest shooting spree, with 2 million spectators	
	SUMMER FESTIVAL – fancy black-and-white-garden-party in the Stadtpark	
	HERRENHAUSER SUMMER – Handel's music out behind the castle	
Innsbruck	MUSIC FESTIVAL – musical treatment of a chosen theme, different each year	
Istanbul	ISTANBUL FESTIVAL folk-dancing, concerts at historic sites, ballet, mime, performing arts	20 Jun to 15 Jul
Karlsruhe	HANDEL FESTIVAL	Jun to Jul
Lausanne	LAUSANNE VOUS OFFRE POUR UN ETE – summer festival of concerts and theatre, free of charge	
Lille	OPEN-AIR CLASSICAL MUSIC FESTIVAL – in the Parc Vauban, near the citadel	Jul to Aug

Place	Event	Time
Liverpool	MERSEY RIVER FESTIVAL – non-stop action on the water, on land and in the pubs	
	LIVERPOOL SUMMER – string quartets in Cavern Walks, seaman's songs on Albert Dock and rock concerts in Senfton Park	
London	SWAN-UPPING – counting of the swans along the Thames	
	WIMBLEDON TENNIS TOURNAMENT	Jun or Jul
Lucerne	SWISS ROWING CHAMPIONSHIP	summer
	SEA NIGHT FESTIVAL – Lucerne's most enchanting night, with a 250-year tradition	
Madrid	FESTIVAL OF THE PATRONESS CARMEN	
Malaga	EVENING PROCESSION IN HONOUR OF THE HOLY VIRGIN – along the coast	16 Jul
Manchester	EUROPEAN MODEL AIRCRAFT CHAMPION-SHIP	Mar to Nov
	SPEEDWAY & STOCK CAR RACING	
Marseilles	INTERNATIONAL FOLKLORE FESTIVAL in the Château Gombert	
Munich	CASTLE CONCERTS in Nymphenburg, Schleißheim und Blutenburg	Jun to Jul
Nancy	SON ET LUMIÈRE DRAMA FESTIVAL	15 Jul–15 Sep
Nantes	INTERNATIONAL FESTIVAL OF ARTS AND POPULAR TRADITIONS	
Nuremberg	SUMMER IN NUREMBERG – cultural programmes	May to Sep
Paderborn	ORGAN SUMMER	Jul to Aug
	MARKSMEN'S FESTIVAL	
	LIBORIFESTIVAL	
Palermo	ST. ROSALIE FESTIVAL – with processions, street parties and fireworks	mid-month
	INTERNATIONAL UNDERWATER MEETING in Ustica	
	OPERA AND BALLET FESTIVAL in the Villa Castelnuovo	Jul or Aug
Paris	SUMMER FESTIVAL OF PARIS – concerts throughout the city	
	TOUR DE FRANCE – the arrival at the Avenue des Champs-Elysées	
Rheims	SUMMER OF CULTURE IN RHEIMS – cultural events and bubbling entertainment	Jul to Aug
Rome	NOIANTRI – the people of Trastevere loudly celebrate in honor of the Madonna del Carmine	15 to 29 Jul
Salzburg	HELLBRUNN FESTIVAL / MOZARTEUM FOUNDATION CONCERTS / CASTLE CONCERTS AND . . . AND . . .	May to Oct
Seville	CORPUS CHRISTI PROCESSION	Jun or Jul
Southampton	SOUTHAMPTON SHOW – on The Common	2nd week
Stockholm	SUMMER EVENING CONCERTS (usually Tuesdays) in the National Museum	Jul to Aug
Toulouse	MUSIC FESTIVAL in the Dominican monastery	Jun to Sep
Trieste	FOLK FESTIVAL – the city celebrates	
	LIGHT AND SOUND – dramatic tragedies performed daily at the Miramare castle	Jun to Sep
Vaduz	INTERNATIONAL MASTER COURSES – musicians from around the world teach and give concerts	
Valencia	FERIA – flower fights, sports events and fireworks; the highpoint comes on 25 July with the corridas of the most celebrated bull-fighters	
Valletta	FESTA – each village on the island(s) celebrates its very own patron saint with processions and fireworks	summer
Venice	FESTA DEL REDENTORE – grand celebration in memory of the plague	3rd Sunday
Verona	OPERA FESTIVAL in the Arena di Verona	
Zurich	ZURICH NIGHT FESTIVAL – every three years at the lake, with a lot of fireworks	mid-month

Place	Event	Time

August

Aachen	SOMMERABEND – folk festival	
Antwerp	FLANDERS FESTIVAL – Europe's musical élite in concerts, operas, ballets and jazz sessions	Aug to Oct
Athens	THEATRE AND MUSIC FESTIVAL – classical drama on modern stages with historic backdrops	Aug to Sep
Baden-Baden	ROSE SHOW – noble flowers nobly presented	late Aug to
	GRAND WEEK OF HORSE RACING – truly grand	early Sep
Barcelona	FIESTA DE GARCIA – dancing, fireworks and flower power	15 Aug
Berne	GURTEN-SCHWINGET – original Swiss sporting event for strong fellows	
Bielefeld	BIELEFELDER SOMMERTREFF – jazz, folk music, organ concerts and theatre	May to Sep
Bilbao	BASQUE DANCE FESTIVAL	Aug or Sep
Birmingham	CHILDREN'S FUNWEEK	
	CITY OF BIRMINGHAM SHOW – living it up out on the streets	
Bologna	INTERNATIONAL ›CINEMA LIBERO‹ FESTIVAL	
Bonn	BONN SUMMER – folklore, concerts and street theatre keep the sleepy town jumping	
Bordeaux	INTERNATIONAL JAZZ FESTIVAL	
Bremen	FLEAMARKET	Saturdays
Bristol	HARBOUR REGATTA – white triangles on blue waters	
	INTERNATIONAL BALLOON FIESTA	
	MARITIME CARNIVAL – high life in the historic harbour	
Brussels	FLANDERS FESTIVAL – international orchestras and conductors	End Aug to Oct
	MEYBOOM – setting up the Maypole, in August for some reason	Aug 9
Cannes	INTERNATIONAL ADVERTISING FILM FESTIVAL	
	BLUES FESTIVAL	
Cologne	COLOGNE SUMMER – on the Roncalliplatz, Rhine and in the Volksgarten changing cultural events during 4 summer months	Jun to Sep
Copenhagen	TIVOLI SEASON – solists and orchestras from around the world play in the Tivoli Gardens	May to Sep
Deauville	INTERNATIONAL BRIDGE FESTIVAL	
Dublin	DUBLIN HORSE SHOW – the country's main equestrian event	
	POLO GAMES at the All-Ireland Polo Club in Phoenix Park	May to Sep
Essen	MAITEMBER – five months of fun, from circus to fireworks, jousting knights and Essen's own Hawaian luau	May to Sep
Frankfurt	MAIN FESTIVAL – fireworks on the banks of the Main	1st Sunday
	FOUNTAIN FESTIVAL – folk festival with a 500-year tradition	mid-month
Geneva	FETES DE GENEVE – the whole city decks itself out in flowers and parties	
	BOL D'OR – Europe's largest and most beautiful lake regatta	
Glasgow	SCOTTISH NATIONAL TENNIS CHAMPIONSHIP	
Gothenburg	LISEBERG AMUSEMENT PARK – concerts, entertainment, theatres and dancing	Apr to Sep
Grenoble	WORLD ASSEMBLY OF DAUPHINOIS KINSMEN	
Gütersloh	GÜTERSLOH SUMMER	Jul to Aug
Hanover	LICHTERFEST – in the grounds of Schloss Herrenhausen – musicians, dancers, choirs and bands parade, thousands of lights light up the magnificent	

Place	Event	Time
	fountains, and it's all topped off by a display of fireworks to the accompaniment of Handel's music SUMMER FESTIVAL	
Helsinki	HELSINKI FESTIVAL – theatre, classical concerts, folklore, ballet and cultural events	Aug or Sep
Innsbruck	OLD MUSIC FESTIVAL WEEK – Tyrolean tunes fill the air	Aug or Sep
Karlsruhe	SCHLOSSFESTSPIELE ETTLINGEN	Jul to Aug
Lausanne	LAUSANNE VOUS OFFRE POUR UN ETE – summer festival of concerts and theatre, free of charge	
Liège	FOLK FESTIVAL in the Ourthe-Meuse Quarter	15. Aug
Lille	OPEN-AIR CLASSICAL MUSIC FESTIVAL – in the Parc Vauban, near the citadel	Jul to Aug
Liverpool	BEATLES CONVENTION – stars, movies, discussions and entertainment in honour of Liverpool's most famous lads	
	LIVERPOOL SUMMER – string quartets in Cavern Walks, seamen's songs on Albert Dock, rock concerts in Sefton Park	
London	NOTTING HILL CARNIVAL – the Caribbean comes to London	
Lucerne	INTERNATIONAL MUSIC FESTIVAL – one of the world's best known musical events	Aug or Sep
Luxembourg	SCHOBERMESSE – amusement fair with open market	last 2 weeks
Malaga	BALLET FESTIVAL – in the cave grottoes of Nerja	
	SUMMER FESTIVAL – with bullfights	
	FESTIVALES DE ESPANA	
Manchester	THE CITY OF MANCHESTER SHOW	
	MORRIS DANCING & RUSHCART FESTIVAL	Mar to
	SPEEDWAY & STOCK CAR RACING	Nov
Munich	OPERA FESTIVAL	Jul to Aug
Nancy	PLUM FESTIVAL – costumes, dancing and singing	mid-month
Nantes	INTERNATIONAL FESTIVAL OF ARTS AND POPULAR TRADITIONS	
Nice	HOLIDAY ON ICE	
Nuremberg	SUMMER IN NUREMBERG – cultural programmes	May to Sep
Oporto	CORTEJO DE PAPEL – High Life in Oporto	24th Aug
Oslo	MARIDAL DRAMA – open-air historical theatre	mid-month
Paderborn	LIBORIFESTIVAL	Jul to Aug
Palermo	OPERA AND BALLET FESTIVAL in the Villa Castelnuovo	Jul or Aug
Rheims	SUMMER OF CULTURE IN RHEIMS – cultural events and bubbling entertainment	Jul to Aug
Salzburg	SALZBURG FESTIVAL – attracts the world's most celebrated classical music superstars and the appropriate people to applaud them	Jul to end of Aug
Seville	FESTIVAL OF THE ›VIRGIN DE LOS REYES‹ – in honour of the city's patron saint	15 Aug
Stuttgart	WINE VILLAGE – street festival with much ›Gemütlichkeit‹ all over the Schillerplatz and Marktplatz	
Toulouse	MUSIC FESTIVAL in the Dominican monastery	Jun to Sep
Trieste	LIGHT AND SOUND – dramatic tragedies performed daily at the Miramar castle	Jun to Sep
Vaduz	NATIONAL HOLIDAY – fireworks in the Alps	15 Aug
Valletta	FESTA – each village of the island(s) celebrates its very own patron saint with processions and fireworks	summer
Venice	VENICE FILM FESTIVAL – one of the most resnected in the world, on the Lido	
	BIENNALE D'ARTE – art exhibition featuring living artists	biennial
Verona	OPERAFESTIVAL in the Arena di Verona	
Vienna	MUSICAL SUMMER concerts everywhere	Aug or Sep
Wiesbaden	RHINE VALLEY WINE FESTIVAL – the jewel of the Rhine Valley celebrates its noble potables in the palace courtyard	
Zurich	INTERNATIONAL LIGHT ATHLETICS MEET – in Letzigrund	

Place	Event	Time

September

Aachen	PARK ILLUMINATION – the park of the spa flooded in light	
	EUROPEAN HANDICRAFT DAY – handmade in Europe	
Amsterdam	KUNSTTIENDAAGSE a ten-day open house in the city's museums, galleries, theatres and opera house – free of charge, with peeks behind the scenes encouraged	end of Sep to Oct
Antwerp	FLANDERS FESTIVAL – Europe's musical élite in concerts, operas, ballets and jazz sessions	Aug to Oct
Athens	THEATRE AND MUSIC FESTIVAL – classical drama on modern stages with historic backdrops	Aug to Sep
Baden-Baden	GRAND WEEK OF HORSE RACING – truly grand	Late Aug – early Sep
Belgrade	INTERNATIONAL BELGRADE THEATRE FESTIVAL – a world renowned gathering of avant-garde theatre groups	
Berlin	BERLIN FESTIVAL – a different theme is chosen each year	
Berlin (East)	BERLIN FESTIVAL – concerts, ballet and folk art	Sep or Oct
Berne	DREHORGELFESTIVAL	biennial
Bielefeld	BIELEFELDER SOMMERTREFF – jazz, folk music, organ concerts and theatre	May to Sep
Bilbao	BASQUE DANCE FESTIVAL	Aug or Sep
Bonn	BONN SUMMER – folklore, concerts and street theatre	May to Oct
Bremen	VEGESACK HARBOUR FESTIVAL – the district of Vegesack throws a party	Aug or Sep Saturdays
Brussels	FLANDERS FESTIVAL – international orchestras and conductors	End Aug to Oct
Bucharest	INTERNATIONAL MUSIC FESTIVAL GEORGE ENESCU' – every three years	
Cologne	COLOGNE SUMMER – on the Roncalliplatz, Rhine and in the Volksgarten changing cultural events during 4 summer months	Jun to Sep
Copenhagen	TIVOLI SEASON – solists and orchestras from around the world play in the Tivoli Gardens	May to 2nd weekend in Sep
Deauville	AMERICAN MOVIE FESTIVAL	mid-month
Dublin	POLO GAMES at the All-Ireland Polo Club in Phoenix Park	May to Sep
Essen	MAITEMBER – five months of fun, from circus to fireworks, jousting knights and Essen's own Hawaiian luau	May to Sep
Frankfurt	JAZZ IN THE PALMENGARTEN	May to Sep bi-weekly
Geneva	GENEVA MUSIC FESTIVAL	
Genoa	THEATRE AND CONCERT SEASON	
Gothenburg	LISEBERG AMUSEMENT PARK – concerts, entertainment, theatre, dancing	Apr to Sep
Graz	JAZZ AND POP FESTIVALS	
	WORLD CHAMPIONSHIPS IN BODYBUILDING	
Gütersloh	PARK ILUMINATION – the park is flooded in light	
The Hague	PRINSJESDAG – the Queen opens the legislature period with a speech	3th Tuesday
Helsinki	HELSINKI FESTIVAL – theatre, classical concerts, folklore, ballet and cultural events	Aug or Sep
Innsbruck	OLD MUSIC FESTIVAL WEEK – Tyrolean tunes fill the air	Aug or Sep
Karlsruhe	KULTURMARKT	
Liège	NIGHTS OF SEPTEMBER – a Walloon (Belgian French) music festival	4th Sunday

Place	Event	Time
Lille	GRANDE BRADERIE – flea, antiques and assorted junk market	1–2 Sep
London	BATTLE OF BRITAIN DAY – fighter plane formations in the sky	15 Sep
Lucerne	INTERNATIONAL MUSIC FESTIVAL – one of the world's best known musical events	Aug or Sep
Lyons	BERLIOZ FESTIVAL – famous and not-so-famous works by Berlioz	
	FILM FESTIVAL – rare films are shown by the Lumière Institute	
	INTERNATIONAL MARIONETTE FESTIVAL	beginning Sep
Madrid	AUTUMN FESTIVAL – ballet, concerts and theatre	Sep or Oct
Manchester	CASTLEFIELD CARNIVAL	Mar to
	SPEEDWAY & STOCK CAR RACING	Nov
Marseilles	CINEMA FESTIVAL	
Milan	BALLET PERFORMANCES at La Scala	
Munich	OKTOBERFEST – largest public festival in the world; beer funfair	end of Sep
Nancy	›SON ET LUMIERE‹-DRAMA FESTIVAL	15 July–15 Sep
Naples	S. GENNARO FESTIVAL	19 Sep
Nuremberg	SUMMER IN NUREMBERG – cultural programmes	May to Sep
Rotterdam	OPEN HAVENDAG – a look behind the scenes on the harbour	
	ROTTERDAM ORGAN MONTH – recitals in the city's churches	
	HEINEKEN JAZZ FESTIVAL – hot jazz and cool beer	
Salzburg	CASTLE CONCERTS / HELLBRUNN FESTIVAL / MOZARTEUM FOUNDATION CONCERTS and . . . and . . .	May to Oct
Seville	BULLFIGHT SEASON	
Stuttgart	CANNSTATTER VOLKSFEST – famous outdoor festival with 4–5 million visitors each year	Sep or Oct
Toulouse	ACADEMIE INTERNATIONALE DE CHANT – international music festival	end of month
	HOLIDAY ON ICE	
Trieste	LIGHT AND SOUND – dramatic tragedies performed daily at the Miramare castle	Jun to Sep
Valletta	LIBERATION DAY – celebrating the end of the occupation in 1565 and 1943, a large regatta sails by	1st weekend
Venice	VENICE FILM FESTIVAL – one of the most respected in the world; on the Lido	Aug or Sep
	BIENNALE D'ARTE – art exhibition featuring living artists	Aug or Sep
Verona	SHAKESPEARE FESTIVAL – in the Roman Theatre	
	SAGRA DEI OSEI – a festival of birds	
Vienna	MUSICAL SUMMER – concerts everywhere	Aug or Sep
Warsaw	WARSAW AUTUMN – international contemporary music festival	
	INTERNATIONAL JAZZ FESTIVAL	
	WARSAW POETRY AUTUMN	every five
	CHOPIN PIANO CONTEST	years
Wiesbaden	VINTNERS' FESTIVAL	autumn

615

Place	Event	Time
October		
Amsterdam	KUNSTTIENDAAGSE – a ten-day open house in the city's house – free of charge, with peeks behind the scenes encouraged	end Aug to Oct
Antwerp	FLANDERS FESTIVAL – Europe's élite in concerts, operas, ballets and jazz sessions	Aug to Oct
Basle	BASLE AUTUMN FAIR – Switzerland's oldest and largest annual fair	Oct to Nov
Belgrade	MUSIC CELEBRATIONS	
Berlin	BERLIN FESTIVAL – a different theme is chosen each year	
Berlin (East)	BERLIN FESTIVAL – concerts, ballet and folk art	Sep or Oct
Berne	KRONENBURG-TROPHY	
Bonn	BONN SUMMER – folklore, concerts and street theatre	May to Oct
Bremen	FLEAMARKET	Saturdays
Brest	INTERNATIONAL BAGPIPE FESTIVAL	
Brussels	FLANDERS FESTIVAL – international orchestras and conductors	end Aug to Oct
Cologne	FLEAMARKET	3rd Saturday
Deauville	PARIS-DEAUVILLE VINTAGE CAR RALLY	
Dublin	DUBLIN CITY MARATHON - Dublin jogs	
Frankfurt	OCTOBER MUSIC AND THEATRE FESTIVAL – music in autumn leaves, from classical to jazz	
Geneva	VINTNER'S FESTIVAL – Switzerland's third largest wine-producing area celebrates the new grape harvest	autumn
Genoa	THEATRE AND CONCERT SEASON	
Graz	JAZZ AND POP FESTIVALS	
	TRIGON – tristate biennial festival	
	STEYRISHER HERBST – autumn cultural festival, widely acclaimed in Europe	
Gütersloh	MICHAELISKIRMES – festival in honour of the patron saint	Sep to Oct
The Hague	HAAGSE VLOIENMARKT	
Hanover	OKTOBERFEST – like the Spring Festival, but a little bigger	
Helsinki	GREAT FISH MARKET	
Leipzig	GEWANDHAUSFESTTAGE – celebration in music, with Leipzig's world famous Gewandhaus Orchestra	
Lille	FESTIVAL DE LILLE – international cultural festival with classical and modern music, dance, theatre and puppet shows	
Madrid	AUTUMN FESTIVAL – ballet, concerts and theatre	Sep or Oct
Manchester	SPEEDWAY & STOCK CAR RACING	Mar to Nov
Milan	OPERA SEASON at La Scala	
Nancy	JAZZ FESTIVAL	
Paderborn	HERBST-LIBORIFEST	
Paris	VINTNERS FESTIVAL – at Montmartre	
	PRIX DE L'ARC DE TRIOMPHE – betting on the Aga Khan's horses	
	INTERNATIONAL DANCE FESTIVAL	Oct or Nov
Rheims	FICTION AND CRIME FILM FESTIVAL	
Salzburg	SALZBURG CULTURE DAYS – opera, concerts and folkore to close the summer season	
Stuttgart	CANNSTATTER VOLKSFEST – famous outdoor festival with 4–5 million visitors each year	Sep or Oct
Vaduz	ANNUAL FAIR – fun and games in Liechtenstein	
Warsaw	GRAPHICS FESTIVAL – graphic arts fair	biennial
Wiesbaden	VINTNERS' FESTIVAL	autumn
Zaragoza	FESTIVAL OF THE PATRON SAINT PILAR – masked processions, flower festivals, bullfights	
Zurich	INTERNATIONAL JAZZ FESTIVAL	

Place   Event   Time

November

Place	Event	Time
Aachen	CHRISTMAS MARKET – magical booths in the snow	22 Nov–22 Dec
Basle	BASLE AUTUMN FAIR – Switzerland's oldest and largest annual fair	Oct to Nov
Belgrade	BELGRADE JAZZ FESTIVAL	
Berlin	BERLIN JAZZ DAYS – singing and playing the blues in Berlin	
Berne	GALA SHOW for handicapped children	
Birmingham	GUY FAWKES – annual fair with mammoth firework display	
Bologna	OPERA SEASON	Nov to May
Bordeaux	SIGMA MEETING – contemporary art festival	
Cologne	KÖLNER PRESSEBALL – Germany's journalists, politician and public people celebrate each other	autumn
Düsseldorf	ST. MARTIN'S DAY – children parade through the streets, singing and bearing lanterns in honour of the saint	10 Nov
Geneva	INTERNATIONAL HORSE SHOW	
Genoa	THEATRE AND OPERA SEASON	
Graz	CHRISTMAS MARKET	
Grenoble	SIX–DAY BICYCLE RACE – Grenoble's world famous spectacle for pedal pushers	
Gütersloh	AMATEURFILMTAGE – Movies of non-professionals	11 Nov.
	ST. MARTINS PROCESSION	
The Hague	THUISKUNSTMARKT	end-Nov
Hamburg	WINTER-DOM – folk festival, with rides, games and high-tech joy machines	
Karlsruhe	AUTUMN FESTIVAL FOLK FESTIVAL	
Leipzig	INTERNATIONAL LEIPZIG DOCUMENTATION AND SHORT MOVIE FESTIVAL – politically engaged festival	
London	GUY FAWKES DAY fireworks for the not forgotten hero	5 Nov
Lyons	MUSIC FESTIVAL in the Old City of Lyons	
Manchester	WHITWORTH YOUNG CONTEMPORARIES	Nov to Dec
Marseilles	SANTON FAIR – clay and carved wood nativity figures on sale for Christmas	
Milan	CONCERT SEASON at La Scala	
Monte-Carlo	NATIONAL HOLIDAY – the 4000 natives and their paying guests celebrate the Prince and each other	
Moscow	ANNIVERSARY OF THE GRAND SOCIALISTIC REVOLUTION	7 Nov
Naples	SAN CARLO THEATRE SEASON	
Nuremberg	CHRISTKINDLESMARKT – Nuremberg's toys in beautiful booths	Nov to Dec
Paris	INTERNATIONAL DANCE FESTIVAL	Oct or Nov
Sofia	BULGARIAN JAZZ AND CONTEMPORARY MUSIC SHOW	
Venice	FESTA DELLA MADONNA DELLA SALUTE – grand celebrations in memory of the Plague	21 Nov
Vienna	SCHUBERT DAYS	

Place	Event	Time

December

Aachen	CHRISTMAS MARKET – magical booths in the snow	23 Nov–22 Dec
Berlin (East)	CHRISTMAS MARKET – a folk festival with booths rides and amusements without brash commercialism, at the Alexanderplatz	
Berne	BERNER BROCANTE – Fleamarket	
Bologna	OPERA SEASON	Nov to May
Bonn	CARNEVAL – begins	Dec to Mar
Bremen	CHRISTMAS MARKET	
Bristol	CHRISTMAS ILLUMINATED WATER CARNIVAL	
Cannes	INTERNATIONAL PUPPET FESTIVAL	
Dublin	INTERNATIONAL OPERA FESTIVAL	
Essen	ESSENER LICHTERWOCHEN – the ›weeks of lights‹; Christmas lights strung in unique shapes to ring in the Christmas spirit	
	ALT ESSEN – international Christmas market offering wares from near and far	
Frankfurt	CHRISTMAS MARKET – seasonal handicrafts and gifts	
Geneva	ESPLANADE – the city celebrates its liberation from the House of Savoy by parading through the streets at night	2nd Sunday
Genoa	THEATRE AND OPERA SEASON	
Gothenburg	ST. LUCIA'S DAY – Lucia procession of the Queen of Light	13 Dec
Graz	CHRISTMAS MARKET	
Gütersloh	KUNSTHANDWERKER MARKT – artists and handicraftsmen show their work	1st week
Hanover	JAZZ DAYS	
	CHRISTMAS MARKET – the aroma of roasted almonds float about as you get into the Christmas spirit	
Karlsruhe	CHRISTKINDLESMARKT	
Liège	LIVING NATIVITY – Christmas plays	25 Dec
Lyons	FESTIVAL OF LIGHTS – getting into the Christmas spirit	
Manchester	WHITWORTH YOUNG CONTEMPORARIES	Nov to Dec
Milan	the OPERA SEASON at La Scala starts	Dec 7 to end of May
Monte-Carlo	INTERNATIONAL CIRCUS FESTIVAL – animals, people, and lots of sawdust	
Moscow	RUSSIAN WINTER – theatre, ballet, exhibitions	25 Dec to 5 Jan
Munich	CHRISTKINDLESMARKT	
Nancy	ST. NICHOLAS CHRISTMAS FESTIVITIES	1st week
Naples	S. GENNARO FESTIVAL	16 Dec
Nice	ITALIAN FILM FESTIVAL	25 Dec
	CHRISTMAS BATHING in the Baie des Anges	
Nuremberg	CHRISTKINDLESMARKT – Nuremberg's toys in beautiful booths	Nov to Dec
Rotterdam	KERSTLAND – a Christmas spectacle	
Stockholm	LUCIA DAY – maidens in white robes end the longest night of the year bringing candelabras and breakfast in bed	13 Dec
Wiesbaden	ANDREAS FESTIVAL AND CHRISTMAS MARKET – ringing in the Christmas holidays	
Zurich	CHRISTMAS MARKET	

Alternative Hotels

Austria

SCHLOSSBERGHOTEL
30 Kaiser-Franz-Josef-Kai
A–8010 **Graz**
Tel. 70 25 57–0

CLIMA-HOTEL BELLE EPOQUE
7 Zeughausgasse
A–6021 **Innsbruck**
Tel. 28 3 61 u. 28 3 62

ÖSTERREICHISCHER HOF
5–7 Schwarzstr.
A–5024 **Salzburg**
Tel. 7 25 41

SACHER
4 Philharmonikerstr.
A–1015 **Vienna**
Tel. 52 55 75 or 5 14 56

BRISTOL
1 Kärntner Ring
A–1015 **Vienna**
Tel. 5 15 16-0

INTERCONTINENTAL
28 Johannesgasse
A–1037 **Vienna**
Tel. 75 05

Belgium

DE KEYSER
66 De Keyserlei
B–2018 **Antwerp**
Tel. 2 34 01 35

HILTON
38 bvd Waterloo
B–1000 **Brussels**
Tel. 5 13 88 77

SHERATON TOWERS
3 Place Rogier
B–1000 **Brussels**
Tel. 2 19 34 00

Czechoslovakia

INTER-CONTINENTAL
Namesti Curievych
11015–**Prague 1**
Tel. 23 11 8 12

Denmark

SAS SCANDINAVIA
70 Amager Boulevard
DK–2300 S **Copenhagen**
Tel. 11 23 24

PLAZA-SHERATON
4 Bernstorffsgade
DK–1577 V **Copenhagen**
Tel. 14 92 62

Finland

KALASTAJATORPPA
1 Kalastajantorpantie
SF–00330 **Helsinki 33**

France

NOVOTEL
Route de Gouesnou
B. P. 349
F–29273 **Brest**
Tel. 98 02 32 83

CARLTON
58 La Croisette
F–06406 **Cannes**
Tel. 93 68 91 68

MAJESTIC
La Croisette
F–06407 **Cannes**
Tel. 93 69 91 00

ROYAL
Boulevard E.-Cornuché
F–14800 **Deauville**
Tel. 31 88 16 41

ANGLETERRE
5 Place Victor-Hugo
F–38000 **Grenoble**
Tel. 76 87 37 21

BELLEVUE
5 Rue J.-Roisin
F–59800 **Lille**
Tel. 20 57 45 86

GRAND HOTEL CONCORDE
11 Rue Grolée
F–69002 **Lyons**
Tel. 78 42 56 21

LE PETIT NICE
Anse de Maldormé
hauteur 160 Corniche Kennedy
F–13007 **Marseilles**
Tel. 91 52 14 39

MÉRIDIEN
1 Promenade des Anglais
F–6000 **Nice**
Tel. 93 82 25 25

PLAZA-ATHÉNÉE
25 Avenue Montaigne
F–75008 **Paris**
Tel. 47 23 78 33

BRISTOL
112 Rue du Faubourg St-Honoré
F–75008 **Paris**
Tel. 42 66 91 45

CRILLON
10 Place Concorde
F–75008 **Paris**
Tel. 42 65 24 24

SOFITEL
Place St-Pierre-le-Jeune
F–67000 **Strasbourg**
Tel. 88 32 99 30

SOFITEL
Rue F. Picaud
Aeroport de Blagnac
F–31700 **Blagnac** (Toulouse)
Tel. 61 71 11 25

East Germany

PALASTHOTEL DE LUXE
Karl-Liebknecht-Strasse
DDR–1020 **Berlin**
Tel. 24 10

Germany

STEIGENBERGER HOTEL BADISCHER HOF
47 Lange Str.
D–7570 **Baden-Baden**
Tel. 2 28 27

STEIGENBERGER HOTEL EUROPÄISCHER HOF
2 Kaiserallee
D–7570 **Baden-Baden**
Tel. 2 35 61

BRISTOL HOTEL KEMPINSKI
27 Kurfürstendamm
D–1000 **Berlin** 15
Tel. 88 10 91

INTERCONTINENTAL
2 Budapester Strasse
D–1000 **Berlin** 30
Tel. 2 60 20

BRISTOL
Poppelsdorfer Allee/Prinz-Albert-Str.
D–5300 **Bonn**
Tel. 2 01 11

CP BREMEN PLAZA
20 Hillmannplatz
D–2800 **Bremen**
Tel. 1 76 70

DOM-HOTEL
2a Domkloster
D–5000 **Cologne** 1
Tel. 23 37 51

INTER-CONTINENTAL
14 Helenenstrasse
D–5000 **Cologne** 1
Tel. 22 80

BREIDENBACHER HOF
36 Heinrich-Heine-Allee
D–4000 **Düsseldorf** 1
Tel. 86 01

NIKKO
41 Immermannstrasse
D–4000 **Düsseldorf** 1
Tel. 86 61

HILTON
20 Georg-Glock-Strasse
D–4000 **Düsseldorf**
Tel. 43 49 63

HANDELSHOF HOTEL MÖVENPICK
2 Am Hauptbahnhof
D–4300 **Essen**
Tel. 1 70 80

HESSISCHER HOF
40 Friedrich-Ebert-Anlage
D–6000 **Frankfurt** 97
Tel. 7 54 00

INTERCONTINENTAL
43 Wilhelm-Leuschner-Strasse
D–6000 **Frankfurt** 1
Tel. 23 05 61

PARKHOTEL
36 Wiesenhüttenplatz
D–6000 **Frankfurt**
Tel. 2 69 70

GRAVENBRUCH-KEMPINSKI
2 Gravenbruch
D–6078 **Neu-Isenburg/Frankfurt**
Tel. (61 02) 50 50

ATLANTIK-HOTEL KEMPINSKI
72 An der Alster
D–2000 **Hamburg** 1
Tel. 24 80 01

INTERCONTINENTAL
10 Fontenay
D–2000 **Hamburg** 36
Tel. 41 41 50

ELYSEE
10 Rothenbaumchaussee
D–2000 **Hamburg**
Tel. 41 41 20

INTER-CONTINENTAL
11 Friedrichswall
D–3000 **Hanover**
Tel. 1 69 11

SCHWEIZERHOF
6 Hinüberstrasse
D–3000 **Hanover**
Tel. 3 49 50

KARSTENS HOTEL LUISENHOF
1 Luisenstrasse
D–3000 **Hanover**
Tel. 1 61 51

PARKHOTEL
23 Ettlinger Strasse
D–7500 **Karlsruhe**
Tel. 6 04 61

MARITIM PARKHOTEL
2 Friedrichsplatz
D–6800 **Mannheim**
Tel. 4 50 71

**STEIGENBERGER HOTEL
MANNHEIMER HOF**
4 Augusta-Anlage
D–6800 **Mannheim**
Tel. 4 50 21

VIER JAHRESZEITEN KEMPINSKI
17 Maximilianstrasse
D–8000 **Munich** 22
Tel. 23 03 90

**BAYERISCHER HOF-PALAIS
MONTGELAS**
6 Promenadeplatz
D–8000 **Munich** 2
Tel. 2 12 00

HILTON
7 Am Tucherpark
D–8000 **Munich** 22
Tel. 3 84 50

GRAND-HOTEL
1 Bahnhofstrasse
D–85000 **Nuremberg**
Tel. 20 36 21

AM SCHLOSSGARTEN
23 Schillerstrasse
D–7000 **Stuttgart**
Tel. 29 99 11

Greece

**ATHENAEUM INTER-
CONTINENTAL**
89–93 Syngru Avenue
GR–117 45 **Athens**
Tel. 9 02 36 66

HILTON
46 Vassilissis Sofias Avenue
GR–612 **Athens**
Tel. 7 22 02 01

Hungary

FORUM
12–14 Apáczai Csere J. u.
H–1368 **Budapest** V
Tel. 17 80 88

ATRIUM HYATT
2 Roosevelt Terrace
H–1051 **Budapest**
Tel. 3 83 00

Ireland

WESTBURY
Grafton Street
IRL– **Dublin**
Tel. 79 11 22

Italy

GRAND HOTEL ELITE
36 Via Aurelio Saffi
I–40131 **Bologna**
Tel. 43 74 17

REGENCY
3 Piazza Massimo d'Azeglio
I–50121 **Florence**
Tel. 24 52 47

VILLA MEDICI
42 Via il Prato
I–50123 **Florence**
Tel. 26 13 31

SAVOIA MAJESTIC
Mauro Placiso
5 Via Arsenale di Terra
I–16126 **Genoa**
Tel. 26 18 41

PALACE
20 Piazza della Repubblica
I–20124 **Milan**
Tel. 63 36

EXCELSIOR HOTEL GALLIA
Piazza Duca d'Aosta 9
I–20124 **Milan**
Tel. 6277

DUCA DI MILANO
Piazza della Repubblica 13
I–20124 **Milan**
Tel. 6284

VESUVIO
45 Via Partenope
I–80121 **Naples**
Tel. 417044

HASSLER
6 Piazza Trinità dei Monti
I–00187 **Rome**
Tel. 6792651

LORD BYRON
5 Via G. de Notaris
I–00197 **Rome**
Tel. 3609541

EXCELSIOR
125 Via Vittorio Veneto
I–00187 **Rome**
Tel. 4708

EDEN
49 Via Ludovisi
I–00187 **Rome**
Tel. 06/4743551

JOLLY PRINCIPI DI PIEMONTE
15 Via Gobetti
I–10123 **Turin**
Tel. 519693

DANIELI
4196 Riva degli Schiavoni
I–30122 **Venice**
Tel. 26480

MONACO E GRAND CANAL
1325 Calle Vallaresso
I–30124 **Venice**
Tel. 700211

Luxembourg

CRAVAT
29 Boulevard Roosevelt
L–2450 **Luxembourg**
Tel. 21975

INTER-CONTINENTAL
Rue Jean-Engling
L–1466 **Luxembourg-Dommeldange**
Tel. 43781

Malta

HILTON
St. Julians
M–**Malta**
Tel. 36201

Monaco

LOEWS
Avenue des Spélugues
MC–**Monte-Carlo**
Tel. 93506500

MIRABEAU
1 Avenue Princesse-Grace
MC–**Monte-Carlo**
Tel. 93254545

Netherlands

AMSTEL
P. J. Vermey
1 Professor Tulpplein
NL–1018 GX **Amsterdam**
Tel. 226060

HILTON
138–140 Apollolaan
NL–1077 BG **Amsterdam**
Tel. 780780

PROMENADE ET REST. CIGOGNE
1 van Stolkweg
NL–2585 JL **The Hague**
Tel. 525161

PARKHOTEL
70 Westersingel
NL–3015 LB **Rotterdam**
Tel. 363611

Norway

CONTINENTAL
24–26 Stortingsgt.
N–0161 **Oslo** 1
Tel. 419060

Poland

NOVOTEL
U. 1–Sierpnia 1
PL–02–134 **Warsaw**
Tel. 812525

Portugal

RITZ
88 Rua Rodrigo da Fonseca
P-1093 **Lisbon**
Tel. 69 20 20

MERIDIEN
Rua Castillo
P-1000 **Lisbon**
Tel. 69 09 00

ALTIS
11 Rua Castilho
P-1200 **Lisbon**
Tel. 56 00 71

MERIDIEN
Avenida da Boavista
P-4000 **Oporto**
Tel. 66 88 63

Romania

ATHÉNÉE PALACE
1–3 Str. Episcopiei
R–**Bucharest**
Tel. 14 08 99

Spain

RITZ
668 Gran Via de les Corts Catalanes
E–08010 **Barcelona**
Tel. 3 18 52 00

AVENIDA PALACE
605 Gran Via
E–08007 **Barcelona**
Tel. 3 01 96 00

GRAND HOTEL ERCILLA
37 Ercilla
E–48011 **Bilbao**
Tel. 4 43 88 00

VILLA MAGNA
22 Paseo de la Castellana
E–28046 **Madrid**
Tel. 2 61 49 00 or 2 75 12 27

PALACE
7 pl. de las Cortes
E–28014 **Madrid**
Tel. 4 29 75 51

Sweden

SCANDINAVIA
10 Kustgatan
S–40000 **Gothenburg**
Tel. 42 70 00

SERGEL PLAZA
9 Brunkebergstorg
S–10327 **Stockholm**
Tel. 22 66 00

STRAND
9 Nybrokajen
S–103 27 **Stockholm**
Tel. 22 29 00

Switzerland

EULER
14 Centralbahnplatz
CH–4051 **Basle**
Tel. 23 45 00

BELLEVUE
3–5 Kochergasse
CH–3001 **Berne**
Tel. 22 45 81

RHONE
Quai Turrettini
CH–1201 **Geneva**
Tel. 31 98 31

BEAU RIVAGE
13 Quai Mont-Blanc
CH–1201 **Geneva**
Tel. 31 02 21

LES BERGUES
33 Quai Bergues
CH–1201 **Geneva**
Tel. 31 50 50

LE BEAU RIVAGE PALACE
Place Général Guisan, Ouchy
CH–100 **Lausanne**
Tel. 26 38 31

SAVOY HOTEL BAUR EN VILLE
12 Poststrasse
CH–8022 **Zurich**
Tel. 2 11 53 60

EDEN AU LAC
45 Utoquai
CH–8023 **Zurich**
Tel. 44 47 94 04

Turkey

HILTON
Cumhuriyet Caddesi Harbiye
TR–**Istanbul**
Tel. 1 46 70 50

United Kingdom

THE ALBANY
Smallbrook Queensway
GB–**Birmingham** B 5 4 EW
Tel. 6 43 81 71

LADBROKE DRAGONARA
Redcliffe Way
GB–**Bristol** B56 6 NJ
Tel. 2 00 44

GEORGE'S HOTEL
19–21 George Street
GB–**Edinburgh** EH 2 2 PB
Tel. 2 25 12 51

BRITANNIA ADELPHI
Ranelagh Place
GB–**Liverpool** L3 5UL
Tel. 7 09 72 00

ST. GEORGE'S
St. John's Precinct
Lime Street
GB–**Liverpool** L1 1NQ
Tel. 7 09 70 90

BERKELEY
Wilton Place
GB–**London** SW 1
Tel. 2 35 60 00

RITZ
Piccadilly
GB–**London** W1V 9DG
Tel. 4 93 81 81

DORCHESTER
Park Lane
GB–**London** W1A 2HJ
Tel. 6 29 88 88

CONNAUGHT
16 Carlos Place
GB–**London** W1Y 6 AL
Tel. 4 99 70 70

CLARIDGE'S
Brook Street
GB–**London** W1A 2JQ
Tel. 6 29 88 60

PICCADILLY
P.O. Box, 107 Piccadilly Plaza
GB–**Manchester,** M60 1QR

POLYGON
Cumberland Place
GB–**Southampton** S09 4GD
Tel. 2 26 40 1

USSR

NATIONAL
Marx-Prospekt 14/1
Moscow 103 009
Tel. 2 03 55 68 or 2 03 66 69